OXFORD EU LAW LIBRARY

General Editors: David Anderson, QC
Barrister at Brick Court Chambers and
Visiting Professor of Law at King's College London.
Piet Eeckhout, Professor of Law at University College London.

EU SECURITIES AND FINANCIAL MARKETS REGULATION

Third Edition

OXFORD EUROPEAN UNION LAW LIBRARY

The aim of this series is to publish important and original studies of the various branches of EC and EU law. Each work provides a clear, concise, and critical exposition of the law in its social, economic, and political context, at a level which will interest the advanced student, the practitioner, the academic, and government and community officials. Formerly the Oxford European Community Law Library.

The General Principles of EU Law
Third edition
Takis Tridimas

EU Anti-Discrimination Law
Second edition
Evelyn Ellis and Philippa Watson

The EU Common Security and Defence Policy
Panos Koutrakos

EU Employment Law
Fourth edition
Catherine Barnard

EU External Relations Law
Second edition
Piet Eeckhout

EU Justice and Home Affairs Law
Third edition
Steve Peers

The EC Common Fisheries Policy
Robin Churchill, Daniel Owen

Goyder's EC Competition Law
Fifth edition
Joanna Goyder and Albertina Albors-Llorens

EU Customs Law
Second edition
Timothy Lyons, QC

The European Union and its Court of Justice
Second edition
Anthony Arnull

Directives in EC Law
Second edition
Sacha Prechal

EC Company Law
Vanessa Edwards

EC Agriculture Law
Second edition
J.A. Usher

The Law of Money and Financial Services in the EU
Second edition
J.A. Usher

Workers, Establishment, and Services in the European Union
Robin C.A. White

EU SECURITIES AND FINANCIAL MARKETS REGULATION

THIRD EDITION

NIAMH MOLONEY

OXFORD

UNIVERSITY PRESS

OXFORD

UNIVERSITY PRESS

Great Clarendon Street, Oxford, OX2 6DP,
United Kingdom

Oxford University Press is a department of the University of Oxford.
It furthers the University's objective of excellence in research, scholarship,
and education by publishing worldwide. Oxford is a registered trade mark of
Oxford University Press in the UK and in certain other countries

Published in the United States of America by Oxford University Press
198 Madison Avenue, New York, NY 10016, United States of America

British Library Cataloguing in Publication Data
Data available

Library of Congress Control Number: 2014940435

ISBN 978-0-19-966434-4

Printed and bound by
CPI Group (UK) Ltd, Croydon, CR0 4YY

1007350995

To my mother, Mary, and in memory
of my father, Noel

SERIES EDITOR'S PREFACE

The third edition of this marvellous analysis of EU securities and financial markets regulation could hardly have come at a better time. True, it is customary for a preface to a further edition of a basic treatise to state that much has happened in the intervening period. How else could a new edition be justified? And it is not unimagineable for such a statement to suffer from some degree of hyperbole—but not this preface. The second edition of this volume was published in 2008, and was written before the financial crisis hit. Little more needs to be said about the welcome timing of this third edition.

Clearly, the crisis has fundamentally altered the EU's role in financial markets regulation (understood in a broad sense), in many different ways. For a start, the crisis has triggered a worldwide reflection on its causes, and a fundamental rethinking of the role played by financial regulation. That reflection has of course affected EU policy. But the particular features of the Eurozone crisis, with its feedback loop between sovereign debt and banking crises, have required an even greater focus on financial markets regulation than in most other jurisdictions. It is true that the banking sector, on which this volume does not focus, has been mainly in the spotlight. However, the securities and financial markets branch (as defined by the author) has also undergone a fundamental transformation. In addition one should add the Lisbon Treaty to the mix, because of the changes it made to the EU's system of administrative lawmaking; as well as the ever increasing role played by EU regulatory agencies.

It is hazardous for this non-expert to attempt a general assessment of the current direction of EU financial markets policy. What perhaps stands out from reading this wonderful treatise, is that the EU's harmonization and regulation effort is grappling with its original market integration focus. The objective of ensuring financial stability, which by the way is insufficiently recognized in the EU's founding treaties, is seen as requiring greater central-ization and stronger regulation, rather than mere liberalization. It is at any rate clear that the EU is becoming an ever more significant actor in financial markets regulation, and that it pursues several, at times competing, objectives.

There could hardly be a better guide to EU securities and financial markets regulation than Niamh Moloney's treatise. Her analysis is clear and lucid throughout the book, and perfectly accessible even on the most technical topics. It is firmly grounded in the law and finance literature and in economic and regulatory theory. It is knowledgeable on the EU institutional context, and contributes to a better understanding of general questions of EU law. This third edition will, in a word, serve its diverse audiences extremely well.

Piet Eeckhout
July 2014

PREFACE

EU Securities and Financial Markets Regulation addresses the harmonized regulatory regime, pan-EU supervisory infrastructure, and EU-level governance arrangements which govern the EU financial market.

The second edition of this book went to press in early autumn 2008 as the EU financial system was about to be gripped by a series of monumental crises. From then to the closing of the crisis-era reform period (which can, roughly, be placed at April 2014) the EU has been engaged in a reform process of titanic and historic proportions which has sought not only to achieve the massive repair required to the financial system but also to stabilize the euro area which came under existential threat as the financial crisis turned into a sovereign debt and euro-area crisis. *EU Securities and Financial Markets Regulation* charts, contextualizes, and reflects on the outcomes of this dramatic period, while retaining the longer historical and wider regulatory perspectives contained in earlier editions.

The scale of the reforms which have followed over 2008–2014 confounds efforts to identify appropriate superlatives. It is not an exaggeration to state that the EU regulatory system for financial markets has been changed out of all recognition. The financial crisis in the EU has led to a reconsideration of the purpose of markets and of regulation, to a radical redesign of regulation, and to a reconfiguring of how supervision should be carried out. Related institutional reform has seen the establishment of the European System of Financial Supervision and the new EU supervisory authority for financial markets, the European Securities and Markets Authority (ESMA). For the first time since the EU's initial foray into this area in 1966 (with the Segré Report), a breach has been made in the single market (the construction of which has long been the governing priority of EU securities and financial markets regulation) with the construction of Banking Union in response to the euro-area fiscal crisis. This period has led to the final dominance of the EU in this area, although this dominance has placed and continues to place significant stress on the foundation constitutional settlement which governs the allocation of power between the EU and its Member States and between EU institutions. The crisis era has also led to EU regulation being shaped by (and shaping) international financial governance to an extent previously unparalleled; the implications for the EU's role in the international financial system may be profound.

While this book is therefore formally a third edition, in practice it is an entirely new work, re-written and re-organized (and longer) in order to reflect the crisis-era reconfiguration of how the EU regulates financial markets and the new balance of power between the EU and its Member States which has followed the crisis. It also addresses the new intellectual architecture for the subject. The first and second editions of this book were written over a time when the prevailing orthodoxy was to challenge the need for financial market regulation given the perceived efficiencies of markets in imposing appropriate discipline and, in the EU context, to question the appropriateness of harmonization given the perceived benefits of regulatory competition and of market discipline. This edition was written over a period when these orthodoxies came under sustained attack. The book accordingly seeks to place the EU regulatory regime within the changed intellectual framework for financial regulation generally and draws on a range of different perspectives, including from political science, law and finance, and regulatory theory.

At the risk of creating a hostage to fortune, with the closing of the crisis-era Commission and European Parliament terms in 2014, the new regulatory regime looks to be, broadly, stable, although it remains to be seen how it will shape the EU financial market over time. Having said that, it is clear that it continues to deepen, evolve, and be refined; the regime is, as discussed throughout the book, dynamic and supported by a distinct institutional apparatus which allows for revision, refreshment, and refinement. The support of newly-appointed Commission President Juncker on 15 July 2014 of a 'Capital Markets Union' suggests that the EU institutions still have ambitions in this area, notably with respect to the deeper embedding of market finance and to the weaning of the EU from its current dependence on bank finance (as discussed in Chapters I and II).

A note on scope is warranted. *EU Securities and Financial Markets Regulation* addresses market-based financial intermediation between suppliers of capital and firms seeking capital. It accordingly considers how the array of market actors engaged (including issuers of securities, investment funds, 'gatekeepers' such as credit rating agencies and investment analysts, intermediating investment firms, and market infrastructures) are regulated and supervised. It does not address the particular rules and supervisory requirements which apply to deposit-taking credit institutions; distinct requirements govern these institutions, reflecting their unique role in the economy and their vulnerability to runs and credit contractions, as the financial crisis exposed to devastating effect. Brief comparative reference is, however, made to key requirements, notably with respect to: capital (in relation to credit risk), liquidity, and leverage requirements (Chapter IV); recovery and resolution (Chapter IV); structural (ring-fencing) requirements (Chapter VI); deposit protection (Chapter IX); and supervisory organization, notably Banking Union (Chapter XI). The market-facing activities of deposit-taking institutions are, however, covered by EU securities and financial markets regulation which applies on a functional basis. The scale of EU securities and financial markets regulation means that cognate spheres of regulation, notably rules governing money-laundering and terrorism financing, rules relating to EU company law generally (including takeover regulation), and the fiscal and monetary rules and institutional arrangements governing Economic and Monetary Union cannot be considered within the scope of this book. Similarly, the book does not cover in detail the related Treaty rules and Court of Justice jurisprudence governing the free movement guarantees (particularly with respect to services, establishment, and capital), which provide background support to the single financial market. The scale of the rulebook means that financial market actors rely on the regulatory regime and its passporting devices, rather than on the free movement guarantees directly, to access cross-border markets, although, as discussed in Chapters I and XI, the scale of the crisis-era reform agenda has led to constitutional challenges, based on the Treaty, to elements of the reform programme.

Much of the book was written over a period of research leave in spring 2013 from the law department of the London School of Economics and Political Science, for which I am very grateful. I continue to learn from my LSE students and from my LSE colleagues; the LSE law department is a most intellectually exciting and supportive place to work. My understanding of this subject and its ever-changing subtleties has been deepened by engagement with a wide range of experts. I would like to record my thanks in particular to Dr Despina Chatzimanoli, Carlo Comporti, Professor Jesper Lau Hansen, Gareth Murphy, Carmine di Noia, Jonathan Overett Somnier, Peter Parker, Professor Jennifer Payne, and Jane Welch. I owe a special debt of gratitude to Professors Pierre-Henri Conac, Guido Ferrarini, and, in particular, Eilís Ferran, with whom I have discussed many of the issues considered in this book. Oxford University Press has been exemplary in guiding the book through to publication. I am very grateful to my commissioning editors, Alex Flach and Natasha Flemming, and I would like to record my particular thanks to my production editor, Briony Ryles. Any errors or material omissions are my responsibility.

My greatest debt of gratitude is—as it always is—to my wonderful husband, Iain. Without his constant patience and support, and unflagging interest and enthusiasm, this book could not have been written.

The book aims to state the law and major policy developments as at 15 April 2014. On this date (rapidly termed 'Super Tuesday'), the European Parliament voted on a final suite of crisis-era reform measures during the last plenary session before its 2009–2014 term completed. It has, however, been possible to squeeze in some later developments in places.

Niamh Moloney
1 August 2014

SUMMARY TABLE OF CONTENTS

DETAILED TABLE OF CONTENTS

TABLE OF CASES

EUROPEAN COURT OF JUSTICE: ALPHABETICAL LIST OF CASES

EUROPEAN COURT OF JUSTICE:
NUMERICAL LIST OF CASES

NATIONAL CASES

TABLE OF LEGISLATION

Commission Recommendations

Charters, Conventions, Agreements

LIST OF ABBREVIATIONS

ABLJ	*American Business Law Journal*
ACER	Agency for the Co-operation of Energy Regulators
ADR	Alternative Dispute Resolution
AG	Advocate General
AIF	Alternative Investment Fund
AIFM	Alternative Investment Fund Manager
AIFMD	2011 Alternative Investment Fund Managers Directive
ALER	*American Law and Economics Review*
Am Econ Rev	*American Economic Review*
Am J Comp L	*American Journal of Comparative Law*
APA	Approved Publication Arrangement
AUM	Assets Under Management
BAC	Banking Advisory Committee
BCD II	1989 Second Banking Co-ordination Directive
BCS	Broker Crossing System
Bell J Econ and Management Sci	*Bell Journal of Economics and Management Science*
BJIBFL	*Butterworths Journal of International Banking and Financial Law*
Brooklyn J Int L	*Brooklyn Journal of International Law*
Brooklyn LR	*Brooklyn Law Review*
BTS	Binding Technical Standard
Cal LR	*California Law Review*
Cardozo LR	*Cardozo Law Review*
CCP	Central Clearing Counterparty
CDO	Collateralized Debt Obligation
CDS	Credit Default Swap
CEBS	Committee of European Banking Supervisors
CEIOPS	Committee of European Insurance and Occupational Pensions Supervisors
CESR	Committee of European Securities Regulators
CfD	Contract for Difference
CFILR	*Company, Financial and Insolvency Law Review*
CIS	Collective Investment Scheme
CJIL	*Chicago Journal of International Law*
CME	Co-ordinated Market Economy
CMLJ	*Capital Markets Law Journal*

CMLR	*Common Market Law Review*
Col J T'nal Law	*Columbia Journal of Transnational Law*
Col LR	*Columbia Law Review*
Cornell LR	*Cornell Law Review*
CRA	Credit Rating Agency
CRD IV	2013 Capital Requirements Directive IV
CRR	2013 Capital Requirements Regulation
Denver J of Int'l L and Policy	*Denver Journal of International Law and Policy*
Duke LJ	*Duke Law Journal*
EBA	European Banking Authority
EBLR	*European Business Law Review*
EBOLR	*European Business Organization Law Review*
ECB	European Central Bank
ECFLR	*European Company and Financial Law Review*
ECMH	Efficient Capital Markets Hypothesis
ECOFIN	Economic and Financial Affairs Council
ECON	Economic and Monetary Affairs Committee
EECS	European Economic and Social Committee
EFAMA	European Fund and Asset Management Association
EFC	Economic and Financial Committee
EFSIR	European Financial Stability and Integration Report
EFSL	*European Financial Services Law*
EIOPA	European Insurance and Occupational Pensions Authority
ELJ	*European Law Journal*
ELR	*European Law Review*
ELTIF	European Long Term Investment Fund
EMIR	2012 European Market Infrastructure Regulation
EMU	Economic and Monetary Union
ERP	European Ratings Platform
ESA	European Supervisory Authority
ESCB	European System of Central Banks
ESFS	European System of Financial Supervision
ESMA	European Securities and Markets Authority
ESME	European Securities Markets Expert Group
ESRB	European Systemic Risk Board
ETF	Exchange Traded Fund
EU	European Union
Euro Rev Contract L	*European Review of Contract Law*
FAQs	Frequently Asked Questions

FCA	UK Financial Conduct Authority
FESCO	Federation of European Securities Commissions
Fordham Int LJ	*Fordham International Law Journal*
FRR	*Financial Regulation Report*
FSA	UK Financial Services Authority
FSAP	Financial Services Action Plan
FSB	Financial Stability Board
FSC	Financial Services Committee
FTT	Financial Transaction Tax
G-SIFI	Global Systemically Important Financial Institution
GDP	Gross Domestic Product
Harv B Rev	*Harvard Business Review*
Harv Int LJ	*Harvard International Law Journal*
Harv LR	*Harvard Law Review*
HFT	High Frequency Trading
Hofstra LR	*Hofstra Law Review*
Houston LR	*Houston Law Review*
IAS	International Accounting Standards
IASB	International Accounting Standards Board
ICCLJ	*International and Comparative Corporate Law Journal*
ICLQ	*International and Comparative Law Quarterly*
ICMA	International Capital Market Association
IDD	1989 Insider Dealing Directive
IFLR	*International Financial Law Review*
IFR	*International Financing Review*
IFRS	International Financial Reporting Standards
IIMG	Inter-institutional Monitoring Group
IMD I	2002 Insurance Mediation Directive
IMF	International Monetary Fund
Ind LJ	*Indiana Law Journal*
Int'l Rev of L and Econ	*International Review of Law and Economics*
IOSCO	International Organization of Securities Commissions
IPO	Initial Public Offering
ISCD	1997 Investor Compensation Schemes Directive
ISD	1993 Investment Services Directive
ISLA	International Securities Lending Association
ITS	Implementing Technical Standard
J	*Journal*
J Comp Bus and Capital Markets L	*Journal of Comparative Business and Capital Markets Law*

J Consumer Res	*Journal of Consumer Research*
J Corp L	*Journal of Corporation Law*
J Fin Intermed	*Journal of Financial Intermediation*
J Fin	*Journal of Finance*
J L and Econ	*Journal of Law and Economics*
J Legal Studies	*Journal of Legal Studies*
J of Accounting Research	*Journal of Accounting Research*
J of Business	*Journal of Business*
J of Econ Lit	*Journal of Economic Literature*
J of Econ Perspectives	*Journal of Economic Perspectives*
J Portfolio Mgmt	*Journal of Portfolio Management*
JACF	*Journal of Applied Corporate Finance*
JBL	*Journal of Business Law*
JCLS	*Journal of Corporate Law Studies*
JCMS	*Journal of Common Market Studies*
JEPP	*Journal of European Public Policy*
JFE	*Journal of Financial Economics*
JFRC	*Journal of Financial Regulation and Compliance*
JIBFL	*Journal of International Banking and Financial Law*
JIBL	*Journal of International Banking Law*
JIEL	*Journal of International Economic Law*
JILB	*Journal of International Law & Business*
JLE	*Journal of Law and Economics*
JLEO	*Journal of Law, Economics & Organization*
JPE	*Journal of Political Economy*
KIID	Key Investor Information Document
L Pol Int Bus	*Law and Policy of International Business*
LFMR	*Law and Financial Markets Review*
LIEI	*Legal Issues of European Integration*
LJ	*Law Journal*
LMCLQ	*Lloyd's Maritime and Commercial Law Quarterly*
LME	Liberal Market Economy
LQ	*Law Quarterly*
LR	*Law Review*
MAR	2014 Market Abuse Regulation
Mich LR	*Michigan Law Review*
MiFID I	2004 Markets in Financial Instruments Directive I
MiFID II	2014 Markets in Financial Instruments Directive II
MiFIR	2014 Markets in Financial Instruments Regulation
MLR	*Modern Law Review*

MMF	Money Market Fund
MoU	Memorandum of Understanding
MTF	Multilateral Trading Facility
NAV	Net Asset Value
NCA	National Competent Authority
NLJ	*New Law Journal*
NorthWestern JILB	*NorthWestern Journal of International Law and Business*
Notre Dame LR	*Notre Dame Law Review*
NYU LRev	*New York University Law Review*
OECD	Organization for Economic Co-operation and Development
OEIC	Open-ended Investment Company
OJLS	*Oxford Journal of Legal Studies*
OTC	Over-the-counter
OTF	Organized Trading Facility
POD	Public Offers Directive
PRIPs	Packaged Retail Investment Products
PRA	UK Prudential Regulation Authority
QJ Econ	*Quarterly Journal of Economics*
QMV	Qualified Majority Vote
REIT	Real Estate Investment Trust
Rev Fin Studies	Review of Financial Studies
RTS	Regulatory Technical Standard
SEC	US Securities and Exchange Commission
SI	Systematic Internalizer
SME	Small and Medium Sized Enterprises
SMS	Standard Market Size
So Cal LR	*Southern California Law Review*
SRM	Single Resolution Mechanism
SSM	Single Supervisory Mechanism
Stanford LR	*Stanford Law Review*
TEU	Treaty on European Union
Texas LR	*Texas Law Review*
TFEU	Treaty on the Functioning of the European Union
TLR	*Tulane Law Review*
TREM	Transaction Reporting Exchange Mechanism
TTIP	Transatlantic Trade and Investment Partnership
UCITS	Undertaking for Collective Investment in Transferable Securities
University of Chicago LR	*University of Chicago Law Review*
University of Colorado LR	*University of Colorado Law Review*

UPaJIEL	*University of Pennsylvania Journal of International Economic Law*
UPaJIL	*University of Pennsylvania Journal of International Law*
UPaLR	*University of Pennsylvania Law Review*
Va LR	*Virginia Law Review*
Vanderbilt J Transn'l L	*Vanderbilt Journal of Transnational Law*
VAR	Value at Risk
Villanova LR	*Villanova Law Review*
VJIL	*Virginia Journal of International Law*
VoC	Varieties of Capitalism
Washington University JLP	*Washington University Journal of Law and Policy*
Yale J Reg	*Yale Journal of Regulation*
Yale LJ	*Yale Law Journal*
YBEL	*Yearbook of European Law*

I

INTRODUCTION

I.1 EU Securities and Markets Regulation

This book addresses EU securities and financial markets regulation (hereafter securities and markets regulation). It considers the harmonized rules which govern financial markets in the EU; it is concerned with market-based financial intermediation between suppliers of capital and firms seeking capital, and with the wide range of relationships and related risks which this form of financial intermediation produces.[1] It does not, accordingly, address the specific rules which apply to deposit-taking institutions.[2] The book examines how the EU regulates the major actors in market-based finance, including issuers of securities, investment firms, investment funds, rating agencies and investment analysts, and market infrastructures, such as trading venues and central clearing counterparties (CCPs). It also examines the process through which the massive EU rulebook has emerged, how supervision in the EU is organized, and the role of the European Securities and Markets Authority (ESMA), established in January 2011 as part of the European System of Financial Supervision (ESFS). This Chapter outlines the main features of EU securities and markets regulation and considers how it has evolved to become the regulatory behemoth which it now is, following the crisis-era reforms.

---

[1] Financial intermediation relates to the process whereby surplus funds are transferred from suppliers (savers) to those in deficit (borrowers).

[2] This book does not address the regulation of bank-based finance (deposit-based and loan-based financial intermediation). It does not, accordingly, address the regulation of deposit-taking and lending and the raft of capital, liquidity, and leverage rules which apply to deposit-taking institutions only, or how the financial crisis has changed the structural regulation of multifunction deposit-taking institutions, including with respect to structural ring-fencing and recovery and resolution requirements.

EU rules targeted solely at deposit-taking institutions (credit institutions, as defined under the EU regime) include, eg, the structural/ring-fencing reforms proposed by the Commission in February 2014 (Ch VI sect 1.1), the institutional reforms which support the Single Supervisory Mechanism and Single Resolution Mechanism for euro-area banks (sect 4.3.1), and the raft of rules which govern the own funds, liquidity, and leverage levels which must be maintained by credit institutions, particularly in respect of credit risk. The book does address the market-based activities of credit institutions and of their banking groups which fall within securities and markets regulation. EU securities and markets regulation applies on a functional basis, applying to credit institutions where they engage in market intermediation activities.

As noted in the Preface, the book does not cover areas associated with EU securities and markets regulation more generally, such as rules relating to financial crime (such as anti money-laundering rules) and the fiscal and monetary rules which govern the euro area.

1

I.2 Securities and Markets Regulation and the Financial Crisis

Securities and markets regulation and supervision addresses the actors which raise capital on, manage risk through, and seek returns from the financial markets, and the related infrastructures and intermediating actors. It is concerned with issuers of securities, the vast array of actors which provide market-based financial intermediation services (such as brokerage, underwriting, and risk management in the form of the issuance of risk-management and risk-transfer products, including derivatives), and the infrastructures (including trading venues) which support trading and risk management.

Financial markets (and the actors therein) accordingly provide a range of functions, including the support of capital-raising and the reduction of related transaction costs, and the facilitation of risk management (including through derivatives and other risk-management products which support market 'completion'[3]).[4] The different bundles of regulation which address the different segments of the financial markets (securities and markets regulation) have discrete (if often closely related) objectives, drivers, and components, as discussed in subsequent Chapters. But, overall, securities and markets regulation has primarily been directed to the support of market efficiency, transparency, and integrity, and with related consumer/investor protection.[5] The traditional neoclassical economics-based analysis of the rationale for regulatory intervention (in financial or other markets) relates the justification for intervention to correction of market failures (failures in a market's self-regulatory mechanism which obstruct the efficient allocation of resources by an otherwise perfect market).[6] In the securities and markets field, the major market failures which arise relate to asymmetric information and to externalities (or wellbeing-influencing consequences which are visited on a third party by the actions of another),[7] such as the instability-generating effects which can be caused when a market participant fails. Two major families of corrective regulation can be identified: conduct regulation, which is associated with client-facing and market-facing conduct; and prudential regulation, which is directed to the stability and soundness of financial market actors and the financial system as a whole and has a particular focus on the management and regulation of risk.

---

[3] A theoretically complete market is one in which individuals can hedge against all contingencies: Spencer, P, *The Structure and Regulation of Financial Markets* (2000) 2–3. A complete market is strongly associated with the availability of risk management products such as derivatives. On the benefits (and risks) of collateralized debt obligations (CDOs), eg in 'completing' fixed income securities markets by providing investment opportunities which would not otherwise be available, see Partnoy, F and Skeel, D, 'The Promise and Perils of Credit Derivatives' (2007) 75 *U of Cincinnati LR* 1019.

[4] Levine, R, 'Financial Development and Economic Growth: Views and Agenda' (1997) 35 *J of Econ Lit* 35 688.

[5] See, eg, Black, B, 'The Legal and Institutional Preconditions for Strong Securities Markets' (2001) 48 *UCLA LR* 781, and, from a policy perspective, International Organization of Securities Commissions (IOSCO), Mitigating Systemic Risk. A Role for Securities Regulators (2011) (2011 IOSCO Systemic Risk Report).

[6] See, eg, Ogus, A, *Regulation, Legal Form and Economic Theory* (1994). Market failures are generally characterized in terms of resulting in risks not being correctly priced in the marketplace.

[7] An externality (and a justification for regulation) arises 'when the well-being of one economic agent (consumer or firm) is directly affected by the actions of another': Kay, J and Vickers, J, 'Regulatory Reform: An Appraisal' in Majone, G (ed), *Deregulation or Re-regulation. Regulatory Reform in Europe and the United States* (1990) 221, 226.

Conduct regulation is, very broadly, associated with disclosure and transparency-related tools, while prudential regulation has traditionally been associated with more intrusive tools, in particular capital rules. The nature and intensity of regulation varies according to the actor in question. Non-financial corporate issuers seeking capital on the markets, for example, do not pose stability risks but are subject to an array of disclosure-related requirements designed to support market efficiency. Investment firms, by contrast, are subject to an array of client-facing conduct rules, as well as to firm-directed prudential rules designed to support firm stability.

The rationale for (and style of) regulation in this area is closely related to the long scholarly and policy association made between strong financial markets and economic growth,[8] although the evidence is not always clear as to the direction of causality and as to which forms of financial market intermediation are most effective and should be supported through regulation.[9] International regulatory policy pre-crisis tended to support complete financial markets by means of, for example, reliance on facilitative 'new governance' regulatory techniques.[10] Some degree of deregulation[11] was generally regarded as beneficial as it was associated with the promotion of strong incentives for market participants, with the completion of markets, and with the intensification of financial market activity (or 'financialization'[12]).[13] Institutional support came internationally from bodies such as the International Monetary Fund (IMF), which assumed that greater financial market intensity would increase allocative efficiency by increasing liquidity, and would increase financial stability by dispersing risk more effectively.[14] The destructive force of poorly regulated and unstable financial markets which the financial crisis exposed has since led to a recalibration of the objectives of securities and markets regulation and of the relationship between regulation and financial markets.

---

[8] See, eg, Khan, M and Senhadji, A, Financial Development and Economic Growth: An Overview, International Monetary Fund (IMF) WP No 00/209 (2000); Levine, R and Zervos, S, 'Stock Markets, Banks and Economic Growth' (1998) 88 *Am Econ Rev* 537; Levine, n 4; Demirgüc-Kunt, A and Maksimovic, V, 'Law, Finance and Firm Growth' (1998) 53 *J Fin* 2107; and King, R and Levine, R, 'Finance and Growth: Schumpeter Might be Right' (1993) 108 *Q J Econ* 717. For a review of the major studies see Arner, D, *Financial Stability, Economic Growth and the Role of Law* (2007), ch 1.

[9] The IMF has argued that evidence from the crisis era suggests that some forms of financial intermediation and particular 'mixes' of intermediation models are likely to be more closely related to positive economic outcomes than others: IMF, Global Financial Stability Report, October 2012, ch 4 (Changing Global Financial Structures: Can they Improve Economic Outcomes) 1.

[10] Ch X sect 1.2.

[11] The pre-crisis regulatory era was not a deregulatory era. But the governing assumption was that in weighing the costs and benefits of intervention and of market discipline, the latter would prove more effective: Langevoort, D, 'Global Securities Regulation after the Financial Crisis' (2011) 13 *JIEL* 799.

[12] Financialization is typically associated with more complete financial markets and a growth in finance. See generally Deakin, S, 'The Rise of Finance: What Is It, What Is Driving It, What Might Stop It?' (2008) 30 *Comparative Labour Law & Policy J* 67. Financialization has been linked to political support for, and belief in, the superior efficiency of allocation through competitive markets rather than through governmental intervention, financial deregulation, financial innovation, and 'financial markets becom[ing] the pace-setters of all markets': Dole, R, *Stock Market Capitalism: Welfare Capitalism. Japan and Germany versus the Anglo-Saxons* (2000) 3–5.

[13] UK Financial Services Authority (FSA) Chairman Adair Turner, Speech on 'How Should the Crisis Affect our Views About Financial Intermediation?', 7 March 2011.

[14] IMF, Global Financial Stability Report, April 2006, ch 1, highlighting the importance of markets in dispersing credit risks away from banks and in increasing the 'shock-absorbing' capacity of the financial system, although noting the related risks.

The main causes of the paradigm-shifting global financial crisis[15] are well known.[16] International macroeconomic policy led to a destabilizing build-up of cheap debt or leverage and a destructive search for yield. Burgeoning financial innovation, particularly in the form of securitization products, facilitated the search for yield by transferring leverage into financial markets which, undermined by an array of regulatory weaknesses, including with respect to the management of pro-cyclical behaviour, proved unable to recycle it efficiently and began to accumulate acute levels of risk which threatened the stability of the financial system. The financial crisis was ultimately a crisis of markets, not institutions:[17] financial markets proved unable to recycle credit risk effectively; complex securitized products were priced incorrectly; the mechanisms of market efficiency, including the risk management functions provided by derivatives and the information intermediary functions provided by rating agencies, failed. Multiple channels for risk transmission quickly amplified the scale of the risks to which the financial system as a whole was exposed.[18]

The crisis also exposed the failure of securities and markets regulators to recognize, monitor, and respond to the market-based, cross-sector,[19] and systemic risks to financial stability[20] which can arise and threaten the financial system.[21] Disclosure and anti-fraud rules, and related supervisory strategies, had long been the stock-in-trade of securities and markets regulation. Heavy reliance on disclosure reflected the prevailing assumption that, as described in the (then) UK Financial Services Authority's (FSA) Turner Review, 'financial markets are capable of being both efficient and rational and that a key goal of financial market regulation is to remove the impediments which might produce inefficient and illiquid markets'.[22] But disclosure failed. Internationally, mandatory disclosures did not extend to the range of markets and instruments implicated in the crisis.[23] Market-driven, contractual/voluntary disclosures, particularly in the securitization market and with respect to complex products, did not support market discipline.[24] The assumptions of market efficiency and rationality which drove the reliance on disclosure were already under siege

---

[15] Described as 'likely to be viewed as a pivotal event in the financial and economic history of the twentieth and twenty-first centuries': HM Treasury, Single Market: Financial Services and the Free Movement of Capital, Call for Evidence (2013) (2013 HM Treasury Call for Evidence) 21.

[16] For a review of the massive literature see Lo, A, 'Reading about the Financial Crisis: A 21 Book Review' (2012) 50 *J of Econ Lit* 151. The major policy assessments in the EU include FSA, The Turner Review. A Regulatory Response to the Global Banking Crisis (2009) (the 2009 Turner Review) and accompanying FSA Discussion Paper No 09/2, and The High Level Group on Financial Supervision in the EU, Report (2009) (the 2009 de Larosière or DLG Report).

[17] FSA Chairman Turner, Speech on 'Reforming Finance: Are We Being Radical Enough?', 1 February 2011.

[18] 2009 Turner Review, n 16, 11–49.

[19] eg Whitehead, C, 'Reframing Financial Regulation' (2010) 90 *Boston University LR* 1 and Kroszner, R, 'Making Markets More Robust' in Kroszner, R and Shiller, R (eds), *Reforming US Financial Markets. Reflections Before and Beyond Dodd-Frank* (2011) 51.

[20] eg 2011 IOSCO Systemic Risk Report, n 5, noting the traditional focus of securities and markets regulators on market efficiency, fairness, and transparency, and their reliance on disclosure-based and conduct-based techniques.

[21] eg Anand, A, 'Is Systemic Risk Relevant to Securities Regulation' (2010) 60 *University of Toronto LJ* 941.

[22] n 16, 39.

[23] eg Fisch, J, 'Top Cop or Regulatory Flop—the SEC at 75' (2009) 96 *Va LR* 785.

[24] Generally, Jackson, H, 'Loan-level Disclosure in Securitization Transactions: A Problem with Three Dimensions' (2010) Harvard Public Law WP No 10–40, available at <http://ssrn.com/abstract=1649657> and Schwarcz, S, 'Protecting Financial Markets: Lessons from the Subprime Mortgage Meltdown' (2008) 93 *Minnesota LR* 373.

from the empirical findings of behavioural finance and cognate disciplines,[25] but the crisis placed further stress on these assumptions.[26] Securities and markets regulation also failed to build on lessons from its previous defining crisis. The Enron era underlined the risks which flawed incentives can pose to market efficiency.[27] But the array of related reforms internationally (and particularly in the EU and US), which addressed, *inter alia*, investment analyst and auditor risk, did not sharpen the focus on incentive risks elsewhere in the financial markets. Regulators also had little experience with the major risks related to procyclicality and system interconnectedness. For example, despite securities and markets regulation's long-standing focus on liquidity, regulators failed to understand how changing risk profiles and systemic risks could lead to a catastrophic drying-up of liquidity, and were unable to ensure that instruments remained tradable.[28]

Hamstrung by a long tradition of disclosure-based intervention and by allowing discrete sectors to operate outside the regulatory net, securities and markets regulators struggled over the financial crisis to contain the build-up of risk. The first major initiative associated with market regulators was the autumn 2008 series of prohibitions on short selling internationally, which have since been associated with the need to be 'seen to act'[29] and, with hindsight, have been of questionable value in supporting market stability.[30] Overall, the traditional suite of tools at the disposal of securities and markets regulators was not designed to address major risks to financial stability; regulators misunderstood risk and the nature of threats to financial stability and did not apply the tools at their disposal to limit undesirable or improperly priced risk-taking.[31]

In response, and as discussed throughout this book, support of financial stability[32] and the management of systemic risk have been injected into securities and markets regulation as governing objectives.[33] Much of the reform agenda is designed to ensure that financial institutions internalize the risks and costs of their activities and that financial stability is

---

[25] See further Ch II sect 2.1.

[26] Avgouleas, E, 'The Global Financial Crisis, Behavioural Finance and Financial Regulation in Search of a New Orthodoxy' (2009) 9 *JCLS* 23.

[27] Coffee, J, 'Understanding Enron: It's the Gatekeepers, Stupid' (2002) 57 *The Business Lawyer* 1403.

[28] McCoy, P, Pavlov, A, and Wachter, S, 'System Risk through Securitization: The Result of Deregulation and Regulatory Failure' (2009) 41 *Connecticut LR* 1327.

[29] Enriques, L, 'Regulators' Response to the Current Crisis and the Upcoming Reregulation of Financial Markets: One Reluctant Regulator's View' (2009) 30 *UPaJIEL* 1147.

[30] See further Ch VI sect 3.

[31] 2011 IOSCO Systemic Risk Report, n 5. ESMA (European Securities and Markets Authority) Chairman Maijoor similarly noted that pre-crisis, securities and markets regulators were focused on transparency and investor protection and that stability was not a 'topical topic': Keynote Address, International Capital Markets Association Conference, 26 May 2011.

[32] The European Central Bank (ECB) has described financial stability as follows: 'Financial stability can be defined as a condition in which the financial system—which comprises financial intermediaries, markets and market infrastructures—is capable of withstanding shocks and the unravelling of financial imbalances. This mitigates the likelihood of disruptions in the financial intermediation process that are severe enough to significantly impair the allocation of savings to profitable investment opportunities': ECB, Financial Stability Review, May 2013, 5.

[33] Well illustrated by IOSCO's new annual Securities Markets Risk Outlook (first issued for 2013–14), which is designed to identify new potential systemic risks. Similarly, ESMA has begun to develop indicators for systemic risk in securities markets, a process which it has found to be challenging: IMF, Financial Sector Assessment Program, European Union. European Securities and Markets Authority. Technical Note. March 2013 (2013 IMF ESMA Report) 19.

thereby promoted. Accordingly, prudential regulation has been significantly strengthened.[34] In addition, client-facing conduct regulation is increasingly becoming associated with the support of financial stability, as are the rules governing market efficiency, transparency, and integrity, traditionally at the core of securities and markets regulation.[35] Oversight of the financial system generally, in the form of 'macroprudential' oversight, is also shaping securities and markets regulation.[36] The reach of regulation is also being extended through the shadow banking regulatory agenda, which seeks to capture the maturity and liquidity transformation functions traditionally associated with credit institutions (banks) and regulated within the banking perimeter but increasingly being carried out by market intermediaries, particularly different types of funds, and through different forms of intermediation, including securities repurchasing and lending activities.[37]

More generally, the financial crisis can be associated with a questioning of the social utility of markets, the extent to which they support economic growth,[38] and the value of untrammeled innovation.[39] The extent to which regulation can or should be used to limit or control levels of financial market development is also being questioned.[40] The Organization for Economic Co-operation and Development (OECD), for example, has drawn a distinction between 'primary instruments' associated with consumption, saving, and fixed capital formation and used to create wealth (loans and equity and debt securities), and 'other instruments' used to hedge risk, arbitrage prices, gamble, and reduce tax and regulatory/agency costs and associated with wealth transfer. It has argued that the market for the former finances productivity and enhances innovation and investment, but the market for the latter could be associated with an increase in systemic risk and with 'less socially useful' activities, including regulatory and tax arbitrage and gambling.[41] An allied concern to support 'fundamental investors', who operate on the basis of the fundamental value of securities rather than on speculative grounds, can also be discerned in the policy

---

[34] IMF, n 9, ch 3 (The Reform Agenda: An Interim Report on Progress towards a Safer Financial System) 2. Examples include the Basel III capital regime which imposes higher capital costs on riskier activities and the new regime governing counterparty margin requirements for transactions in derivatives which are not cleared through central clearing counterparties (CCPs): Basel Committee on Banking Supervision and IOSCO, Margin Requirements for Non-centrally Cleared Derivatives (2013).

[35] 2011 IOSCO Systemic Risk Report, n 5, 42.

[36] In the EU, the European Systemic Risk Board (ESRB) is responsible for the macroprudential oversight of the financial system within the EU, in order to contribute to the prevention or mitigation of systemic risks to the financial stability of the EU that arise from developments within the financial system (defined as all financial institutions, markets, products, and market infrastructures), and taking into account macroeconomic developments, so as to avoid periods of widespread financial distress (ESRB Regulation (EU) No 1092/2010 [2010] OJ L331/1 Art1(1) and Art 2(b)). See further Ch XI sect 6.

[37] See Ch III sect 3.14.

[38] eg querying, in the wake of the crisis, whether excessive financial development can stymie economic growth: Arcand, JL, Berkes, E, and Panizza, U, Too Much Finance? IMF WP No 12/161 (2012) and, similarly, Cecchetti, C and Kharroubi, E, Reassessing the Impact of Finance on Growth, Bank for International Settlements (BIS) WP No 381 (2012).

[39] eg Lerner, J and Tufano, P, The Consequences of Financial Innovation: A Counterfactual Research Agenda, NBER WP 16780 (2011), available at <http://www.nber.org/papers/w16780> and Blair, M, 'Financial Innovation, Leverage, Bubbles and the Distribution of Income' (2010–2011) 30 *Rev of Banking and Finance Law* 225.

[40] eg Arup, C, 'The Global Financial Crisis: Learning from Regulatory and Governance Studies' (2010) 32 *Law & Policy* 363.

[41] OECD, Bank Competition and Financial Stability (2011) 36–9.

debate.[42] The nature of financial innovation has also come under scrutiny. The International Organization of Securities Commissions (IOSCO) has identified a changed approach to financial innovation, with regulators now paying greater attention to risks, and called for securities and markets regulators to find the right balance between unrestrained innovation and over-regulation,[43] while the Financial Stability Board (FSB) is monitoring financial innovation generally.[44] The monitoring of innovation is also appearing in national regulatory mandates; the US Securities and Exchange Commission (SEC), for example, has established a Division for monitoring financial innovation.[45] This trend has taken expression in a raft of crisis-era rules broadly directed to the dampening of speculation and 'excessive' innovation and financial market intensity, which have been a particular feature of the EU reform programme.

Much of the international reform agenda has been driven by the G20 agenda, as initially agreed in the 2008 Washington Action Plan[46] and expanded in subsequent key summits, including the April 2009 London Summit and the September 2009 Pittsburgh Summit.[47] Central steering has come from the FSB, established in April 2009 following a G20 decision and the successor to the earlier Financial Stability Forum, which adopts a range of regulatory and supervisory standards broadly directed towards prudential regulation and the support of global financial stability and monitors progress, including through peer review.[48] The major international standard-setter for financial markets, IOSCO, has also been reinvigorated by the crisis and has produced an array of standards, notably with respect to the over-the-counter (OTC) derivatives markets, money-market funds, and trading practices.[49]

The international crisis-era reform agenda is now, very broadly, complete, although major reforms remain underway, notably with respect to the treatment of shadow banking.[50]

---

[42] IOSCO, Regulatory Issues Raised by the Impact of Technological Changes on Market Integrity and Efficiency, Consultation Report (2011) 12.

[43] n 5.

[44] eg FSB (Financial Stability Board), Progress in the Implementation of the G20 Recommendations for Strengthening Financial Stability (2011) 11–12.

[45] Division of Risk, Strategy and Financial Innovation, established in 2009.

[46] Washington G20 Summit, November 2008, Declaration of the Summit on Financial Markets and the World Economy, Action Plan to Implement Principles for Reform.

[47] London G20 Summit, April 2009, Leaders' Statement on 'Strengthening the Financial System' and Pittsburgh G20 Summit, September 2009, Leaders' Statement on 'Strengthening the International Financial Regulatory System'. The Pittsburgh summit, eg, noted the earlier progress on the regulation and oversight of over-the-counter (OTC) derivative markets, securitizations, rating agencies, and hedge funds, and called for further reforms with respect to building high quality capital and mitigating pro-cyclicality; reforming compensation practices; improving the OTC derivatives markets; cross-border crisis management resolution for systemically important institutions; and the adoption of a single set of high-quality global accounting standards.

[48] See Arner, D and Taylor, M, The Global Financial Crisis and the Financial Stability Board: Hardening the Soft Law of International Financial Regulation (2009), available at <http://ssrn.com/abstract=1427085>.

[49] A burgeoning scholarship addresses international standard-setters and the growth in 'international financial regulation' over the crisis era, eg Verdier, PH, 'The Political Economy of International Financial Regulation' (2013) 88 *Indiana LJ* 14–15; Kelly, C and Cho, S, 'The Promises and Perils of New Global Governance: A Case of the G20' (2012) 12 *CJIL* 491; Helleiner, E and Pagliari, S, 'The End of an Era in International Financial Regulation? A Postcrisis Research Agenda' (2011) 65 *International Organization* 169; and Brummer, C, 'How International Financial Law Works (and How It Doesn't)' (2011) 99 *Georgetown LJ* 257.

[50] As noted, the shadow banking system is the non-bank system of credit intermediation which engages in the maturity and liquidity transformation functions of banks, but which often falls outside banking regulation while being functionally equivalent: Ch III sect 3.14.

Stability is, slowly, returning to the financial system generally and to financial markets in particular.[51] The costs and implications of the massive reform programme are becoming clearer.[52] In the EU, while the crisis-era regulatory programme can be regarded as having closed with the 2014 completion of the crisis-era Commission (2010–14) and European Parliament (2009–14) terms (a final suite of reforms was adopted at the Parliament's last plenary session on 15 April 2014—rapidly dubbed 'Super Tuesday'), and while the EU financial system is slowly stabilizing, it remains fragile,[53] and the costs and implications of the massive regulatory reform programme remain unclear (section 5).

I.3 Securities and Markets Regulation and the EU: Building an Integrated EU Financial Market

I.3.1 The Treaty and the Single Market: the Role of Law

EU securities and markets regulation addresses the preoccupations of securities and markets regulation generally. But it has a distinctive quality. While typically characterized since the crisis in terms of a 'single rulebook', EU securities and markets regulation is, at its bedrock, concerned with the construction and regulation of a single financial market. While the crisis has led the EU to become preoccupied with the pathology of the single market and

---

[51] For one of the first positive reports see IMF, Global Financial Stability Report. Old Risks New Challenges, April 2013, xi and 3–5. The October 2013 Report reported that financial stability risks were in transition; while a normalization of global asset allocation was underway, market and liquidity risks were growing and emerging markets posed concerns: IMF, Global Financial Stability Report, Transition Challenges to Stability October 2013, ch 1 ('Making the Transition to Stability') and ch 2 ('Assessing Policies to Revive Credit Markets').

[52] eg Santos, A and Elliott, D, Estimating the Costs of Financial Regulation, IMF Staff WP (2012). The study suggests that the reforms will lead to a 'modest increase' in bank lending rates (17 basis points in the EU), and that banks have the ability to adapt to the new regulatory regime without taking action which would harm the wider economy. By contrast, the industry-based Institute of International Finance has predicted a reduction of 3.2 per cent of GDP in the US, the euro area, the UK, Switzerland, and Japan between 2011 and 2015: IIF, The Cumulative Impact on the Global Economy of Changes in the Financial Regulatory Framework (2011).

[53] In its October 2013 report, the IMF was broadly positive, noting that the euro area was moving towards a more robust and safer financial sector, but noting the challenges: n 51, ch 1. However, ESMA's second (September 2013) report on Trends, Risks and Vulnerabilities in EU Securities Markets was more pessimistic than its first report (February 2013) and reported on a deterioration in key risk indicators: ESMA, Report on Trends, Risks, and Vulnerabilities. Report No 2 (2013) (ESMA/2013/1138) (ESMA 2013(2) TRV). Its fourth quarterly Risk Dashboard similarly reported that market risk was increasing and risks generally were still at an elevated level: ESMA, Risk Dashboard, No 4 2013 (ESMA/2013/1454). By March 2014, ESMA was more optimistic, noting an improvement in EU securities market conditions and a stabilization of market risk; but it warned of the ongoing fragility of the EU market, given in particular risk transmission from emerging markets: ESMA, Report on Trends, Risks, and Vulnerabilities. Report No 1 (2014) (ESMA/2014/0188) (ESMA 2014 (1) TRV). Similarly in March 2014, the Joint Committee of the European Supervisory Authorities (ESAs) was cautious, noting that the financial system was stabilizing, but warning of risks related to search-for-yield behaviour and from global market conditions, and that 'there is still uncertainty regarding the strength of the financial sector in the EU': ESA Joint Committee, Report on Risks and Vulnerabilities in the EU Financial System (2014) (JC/2014/018) 4. The Commission's April 2014 assessment of 2013 came to similar conclusions, finding a reduction in financial stress and a normalization of markets, but warning that risks to financial stability remained: Commission, European Financial Stability and Integration Report 2014 (2014) (SWD (2014) 170) (2013 EFSIR).The ECB has similarly been cautious (see sect 5.3.2).

destabilizing cross-border risk transmission, EU securities and markets regulation remains fundamentally concerned with market construction and the related regulation of the integrated market.

EU securities and markets regulation is based on the Treaty objective of constructing an internal (single) market (Article 3(3) TEU).[54] The single financial market, the construction of which has generated the rules of EU securities and markets regulation, is part of a wider project to create a single market comprising 'an area without internal frontiers in which the free movement of goods, persons, services and capital is ensured' (Article 26 TFEU).

A single financial market—within which, supported by a harmonized legal infrastructure, market actors can access national markets across the EU—has long been assumed to broaden and deepen pools of capital in the EU. It has also long been assumed that integration should drive a reduction in the cost of capital for firms, promote stronger risk management, and lead to stronger growth and employment.[55] This governing presumption can be traced back to 1966 and the seminal Segré Report.[56] As EU securities and markets regulation has developed, efforts to identify the features of an integrated market and its benefits have become more sophisticated. Empirical support for the first major liberalizing and reform period—the Financial Services Action Plan (FSAP) era of 1999–2004—came from the widely cited 2002 London Economics report for the Commission.[57] It reported that integration of financial markets would generate higher risk-adjusted returns for investors through enhanced opportunities for portfolio diversification and more liquid and competitive capital markets, that the corporate sector would benefit from generally easier access to financing capital, and that competition in the intermediation sector would offer companies a wider range of financial products at attractive prices.[58] It reported that EU-wide gross domestic product (GDP) would increase by 1.1 per cent, that total business investment would increase by 6 per cent, that private consumption would increase by 0.8 per cent, and that total employment would increase by 0.5 per cent.[59] The most pronounced impact was predicted for the primary markets in which issuers raise capital; the headline benefit was a reduction in the cost of equity capital in the order of approximately 40 basis points, and a similar reduction was projected for bond-financing costs.[60] The integration of retail financial services markets was projected to bring GDP increases of

---

[54] References to 'the Treaty' are to the two Treaties which govern the EU: the Treaty on European Union (TEU) and the Treaty on the Functioning of the EU (TFEU).

[55] The ECB has described the benefits of integration as follows: 'The importance of fostering financial integration lies partly in the fact that reducing financial barriers between Member States is expected to create productivity gains which will increase the efficiency and competitiveness of the EU's economy. In addition, financial integration, by opening up new financial opportunities for individuals and businesses (especially small businesses), is, if properly regulated, a potentially powerful tool to attain higher standards of freedom, equity and welfare for society as a whole. In an integrated market, producers and consumers can better tailor their risk and return profiles to their preferences or requirements, and unjustified rents and hidden exploitation opportunities for dominant players are more easily identified and removed. Financial integration promotes cross border contacts between financial institutions, which in turn helps institutions to learn from each other and in this way promotes general welfare.' ECB, Financial Integration in Europe (2012) 33.

[56] Report by a Group of Experts Appointed by the EEC Commission, The Development of a European Capital Market (1966).

[57] London Economics, Quantification of the Macro-Economic Impact of Integration of EU Financial Markets. Final Report to the EU Commission (2002) (2002 London Economics Report).

[58] 2002 London Economics Report (n 57).   [59] 2002 London Economics Report (n 57).

[60] 2002 London Economics Report (n 57), iv.

between 0.5 per cent and 0.7 per cent, lower prices for retail services, and lower interest rates.[61] Since then, the depth of integration has been closely monitored by the Commission and the European Central Bank (ECB) (section 5.3.2).

As discussed throughout the course of this book, single market construction is a complex business. Integration depends on a wide range of variables, including taxation, infrastructure—including trading (trading venues) and post-trade (clearing and settlement platforms) structures, investor demand (and the removal of the investor home bias which privileges domestic investments),[62] the availability of risk management mechanisms, and strong intermediation through investment firms and other intermediating actors. Many of these variables are not immediately susceptible to regulatory intervention, but this is the main mechanism at the EU's disposal. The EU has, accordingly, focused on the removal of regulatory barriers and reduction of the costs which flow from diverging regulatory regimes and, thereby, on creating a regulatory environment supportive of cross-border activity.

At the start of the single financial market programme, considerable variations existed across the EU as to how markets were regulated. Even where these rules were not actively obstructionist and designed to protect national markets from competition, the existence of divergence between rules caused problems for the construction of the single market. Regulatory divergences and the duplication of rules can amount to non-tariff barriers, given that the costs they represent for market participants can obstruct access to other Member States' markets. They can distort competition between market participants and prevent the development of the level playing field on which the single market depends.

The foundation Treaty free movement guarantees, which support the single market generally, go some way to removing regulatory obstacles. The freedom to provide services (Articles 56–62 TFEU) and the freedom to establish (Articles 49–55 TFEU) are the Treaty cornerstones on which the single market is based. They provide the basis for market access by virtue of the prohibition they place on discriminatory and free-movement-restrictive national rules, and have been important in the investment services sphere.[63] They are, however, subject to exceptions which allow Member States to retain free-movement-restricting rules in certain circumstances and, in particular, where the public interest justifies such rules.[64]

---

[61] ZEW/IEP Report on The Benefits of a Working European Retail Market for Financial Services (2002) for the European Financial Services Roundtable.

[62] Investors tend to invest a disproportionately large proportion of their equity portfolios, eg, in geographically proximate stocks. See, eg, Coval, J and Moskowitz, T, 'Home Bias at Home: Local Equity Preference in Domestic Portfolios' (1999) 54 *J Fin* 2045.

[63] eg Case C-101/94 *Commission v Italy* [1996] ECR I-2691, in which the European Court of Justice struck down Italy's 'SIM' law which imposed non-discriminatory but obstructive regulatory requirements on non-Italian EU investment firms.

[64] The Court of Justice's 'general good' jurisprudence allows Member States to retain an obstructive rule where the measure is non-discriminatory, proportionate, necessary to meet the objective in question and serves a legitimate public policy goal (the 'general good' requirement) (eg Case 205/84 *Commission v Germany* [1986] ECR 3755). See, eg, Case C-384/93 *Alpine Investments v Minister van Financiën* [1995] ECR I-1141 in which the Court confirmed the validity of a Dutch prohibition on cold-calling which prevented firms from accessing markets outside the Netherlands but which the Court accepted was necessary to protect the reputation of Dutch financial markets.

Where the single market cannot be achieved by means of the free movement guarantees alone and regulatory barriers remain in place (as is typically the case in the highly regulated financial market sphere, given the strong public interest in retaining national rules), the harmonization process steps in by supporting the adoption of harmonized rules which remove regulatory obstacles to integration by putting common standards in place which replace national measures. As discussed in Chapter X, harmonizing measures must meet the Treaties' competence (in that the measure falls within a competence to act conferred on the EU), proportionality, and subsidiarity (in that, broadly, the outcome sought is best achieved at EU level) requirements (Article 5 TEU).

The procedures governing the adoption of harmonizing measures are considered in Chapter X. In short outline, harmonizing 'legislative' measures in the securities and markets sphere are adopted by the Treaties' law-making institutions.[65] They are enacted under the 'ordinary legislative procedure', under which the Commission adopts a proposal, which is then adopted into law by the Council of Ministers (Council)[66] and the European Parliament (Article 289 and Article 294 TFEU). Legislative measures are accordingly the outcome of often complex and fractious negotiations between these institutions. Legislative measures stand at the top of the rule hierarchy. In addition, extensive technical administrative rules are adopted by the Commission (Article 290 and Article 291 TFEU), with ESMA engaged to different degrees.

Under Article 288 TFEU, binding EU rules (whether legislative or administrative) can take three forms: regulations, directives, and decisions. Regulations are the most intrusive or intensive of EU measures in that they are self-executing: they apply in the Member States once adopted and do not depend on further action at Member State level. Directives are binding as regards the result to be achieved but leave the choice of form and method of implementation to the Member State. They will contain an implementation date, which varies according to the severity of the changes required to existing rules or the new rules demanded and the degree of market upheaval which might be expected, by which the obligations must be implemented by the Member States. Decisions have specific addressees which may include private parties. Until the crisis era, the directive was the dominant type of measure used in EU securities and markets regulation, due to the flexibility it allowed Member States. Directives have, however, led to the EU regime becoming porous in places,

---

[65] The Treaty-based institutions of the EU are the Council of Ministers (representing the Member States at ministerial level), the European Council (composed of the heads of government), the European Parliament (representing the citizenry directly), the Commission (the EU's executive), the ECB, the Court of Auditors, and the Court of Justice (Art 13 TEU). The Treaties also provide for other actors, including advisory committees, two of which are of relevance to securities and markets regulation: the Economic and Financial Committee (EFC) (Art 134 TFEU), which primarily supports the work of the Council, and the European Economic and Social Committee (EESC) (previously ECOSOC) (Art 300 TFEU), which provides opinions on legislative initiatives and represents civil society generally, but which has become less influential on EU securities and markets regulation over time.

[66] The Economic and Financial Affairs (ECOFIN) Council configuration is composed of finance ministers and addresses securities and markets regulation. In adopting securities and markets rules it operates under a qualified majority vote (QMV). This can result in Member States being bound against their will. A QMV is 55 per cent of Council members, comprising at least 15 of them, and representing Member States comprising at least 65 per cent of the EU population. A blocking minority for a measure must include at least four Council members, absent which the QMV is deemed to be attained (Art 16 TEU).

as national regimes can diverge significantly following implementation. The crisis era has seen much greater reliance on regulations.

A vast array of soft law supports the binding EU rulebook, primarily (and somewhat problematically) generated by ESMA. The EU's institutions are also, however, empowered to adopt non-binding recommendations and opinions, and the Commission, in particular, has frequently deployed these measures in the financial markets sphere.

The Court of Justice also shapes the binding EU rulebook through its interpretation of EU law. Prior to the crisis, it had not played a major role in the development of the regime. Its securities and markets jurisprudence was in the main concerned with interpreting the foundation Treaty free movement guarantees,[67] although it had ruled on substantive aspects of the harmonized regime,[68] notably the market abuse regime.[69] The crisis era, however, has seen the Court take a more central role. As tensions have increased between Member States in relation to the intensification of harmonization, litigation has followed. Challenges to the validity of ESMA's powers,[70] to the validity of the major banking measure (the 2013 Capital Requirements Directive IV),[71] and to the validity of the proposed (2013) Financial Transaction Tax being adopted among a group of Member States under the Treaty-based 'enhanced co-operation' mechanism[72] have been brought to the Court,[73] and together represent an unprecedented challenge to the validity of EU intervention in this area.[74] While the substantive questions vary in each case, these challenges all required the Court to rule on how the foundation Treaty settlement as to the organization of power at EU level relates to the location of control over securities and markets regulation and supervision, and are likely to have important implications for the future direction of EU securities and markets regulation.

The EU rulebook is also shaped by international standard-setters, including IOSCO, the Basel Committee on Banking Supervision, and the FSB.[75] While the Basel Committee has long shaped bank capital regulation in the EU, since the outbreak of the financial crisis international standard-setters have come to play a central role in shaping the EU rulebook; so too have the related competitive dynamics associated with the regulation of the international

---

[67] eg *Alpine Investments*, n 64, and Case C-101/94 *Commission v Italy*, n 63. The Commission has also on many occasions taken action against Member States before the Court with respect to their failure to implement elements of EU securities and markets regulation, as it is empowered to do under the Treaty (Art 258 TFEU). For an example see Case C-233/10 *Commission v Netherlands* [2010] ECR I-170.

[68] Including on the pivotal Markets in Financial Instruments Directive (2004 MiFID I) 2004/39/EC [2004] OJ L145/1. See, eg, Case C-604/11 *Genil 48 SL, Comercial Hostelera de Grandes Vinos SL v Bankinter SA, Banca Bilbao Vizcaya Argentaria SA*, 30 May 2013 (not yet reported).

[69] See Ch VIII.

[70] Case C-270/12 *UK v Council and Parliament*, 22 January 2014 (not yet reported).

[71] n 199; Case C-507/13 *UK v Council and Parliament*, pending.

[72] Case C-209/13 *UK v Council*, 30 April 2014 (not yet reported).

[73] In all cases, the actions were brought by the UK, reflecting the increasingly asymmetric impact of the crisis-era rulebook on the wholesale markets in particular. At the time of writing, the UK has also challenged the 'location policy' of the ECB, which requires that CCPs which clear particular proportions of a market in euro-denominated financial products must be located in the euro area: Cases T-93/13, T-45/12, and T-496/11, *United Kingdom v ECB*.

[74] As discussed in Ch X sect 3.1, challenges by Member States to the validity of EU measures have, up until now, been rare.

[75] With respect to respectively (and broadly) securities and markets standards, capital and related rules for banks, and the crisis-era reform programme generally, particularly with respect to financial stability.

market. Subsequent Chapters examine the influence of relevant international standard-setters and of associated international dynamics with respect to discrete elements of the EU rulebook.

I.3.2 Market Finance and Financial Market Integration

The construction of an integrated financial market implies the EU's engagement, to a significant extent, with market-based finance.[76] In very broad terms, in economies based on market finance (or on market-based financial intermediation), banks typically rely heavily on fee-based income sources, trading activities, and non-deposit liabilities; non-bank intermediaries play a significant role in the capital intermediation process; and there is significant reliance on financial products to manage risks (such as securitization products and derivatives). Firms also rely on market-based financing through the issuance of securities. In economies based on bank finance (or on bank-based financial intermediation), banks take deposits and make loans and are the major form of financial intermediation between capital suppliers and providers, relying on net interest income as their main source of income.[77] Market finance can accordingly be associated with higher levels of market intensity and of financialization generally.[78]

Whether or not, and how, bank- or market-finance-based economic systems should be adopted or supported has been the subject of a rich debate which stretches across a range of disciplines, but in particular those of financial economics and political science. It engages discussion of the relative merits of market finance or bank lending, in terms of firm-level and economy-level effects,[79] and of how different economic systems develop and evolve[80] and the related determinative factors, including social and cultural factors[81] and political forces and interest-group dynamics.[82]

Very broadly, market finance (and particularly equity-based finance) is typically associated with more flexible financing techniques for firms, particularly innovative, growth firms.[83]

---

[76] This account of a complex and subtle debate which engages a range of distinct analyses, including from financial economics, comparative political economy, and political science perspectives, is necessarily brief and in outline only.

[77] As recently characterized by the IMF: n 34, 3. Bank and market finance systems are also associated with different forms of firm governance: very broadly, dispersed ownership in the market finance system and block-holder-based, stakeholder governance in the bank finance system.

[78] eg Hardie, I and Howarth, D, What Varieties of Financial Capitalism? The Financial Crisis and the Move to 'Market-Based Banking' in the UK, Germany, and France, Political Studies Association Paper (2010).

[79] See, eg, Goergen, M, 'What Do We Know About Different Systems of Corporate Governance?' (2007) 7 *JCLS* 1 and Black, B and Gilson, R, 'Venture Capital and the Structure of Capital Markets: Banks or Stock Markets' (1998) 47 *JFE* 243. This debate is also associated with the rich scholarship on the evolution of dispersed ownership governance (associated with market finance) and block-holding governance (associated with bank finance). See, eg, Coffee, J, 'The Rise of Dispersed Ownership: The Roles of Law and the State in the Separation of Ownership and Control' (2001) 111 *Yale LJ* 1 and Cheffins, B, 'Does Law Matter? The Separation of Ownership and Control in the United Kingdom' (2001) 30 *J Legal Studies* 459.

[80] The influential Varieties of Capitalism literature will be discussed further on in the Chapter.

[81] See, eg, Guiso, L, Sapienza, P, and Zingales, L, 'The Role of Social Capital in Financial Development' (2004) 94 *Am Econ Rev* 526.

[82] See, eg, Rajan, R and Zingales, L, 'The Great Reversals: the Politics of Financial Development in the Twentieth Century' (2003) 69 *JFE* 5.

[83] Better access to external equity capital and stock markets is associated with higher, long-term rates of R&D development, while credit market development appears to have little impact on R&D: Brown, R, Martinsson, G, and Petersen, B, 'Law, Stock Markets, and Innovation' (2013) 68 *J Fin* 1517.

Banks, by contrast, may have conservative lending policies and may stunt innovative growth strategies. As the financial crisis has shown to devastating effect, bank finance is subject to paralyzing credit squeezes which impact the real economy, while the shocking impact of systemic failures is now clear.[84] The sharp decrease in bank lending to the real economy has led to intensifying reliance on securities markets for corporate funding.[85] The financial crisis has also, however, underlined the stability risks which markets can generate, as well as how intense levels of market intermediation can create destructive levels of risk and lead to a proliferation of risk transmission channels. Nonetheless, market-based intermediation allows funding sources to be diversified[86] and, where credit intermediation is carried out through market channels such as money-market funds or other funds, can diversify and stabilize sources of funding.[87]

Whatever the respective risks and benefits of different intermediation models, the EU's commitment to market finance and to the related benefits of financial market integration has long been a feature, if often an implicit one, of the harmonization programme—but it became express over the FSAP era, which saw the merits of market finance closely linked to the burgeoning integration agenda. In 2000, for example, the Commission[88] asserted that '[t]he assessment that market-based financing heralds substantial benefits for European investors and issuers is not overturned by periodic bouts of volatility or occasional market corrections'.[89] The Commission's 2005 White Paper on Financial Services, which marked the end of the FSAP period, saw the Commission assert that 'financial markets are pivotal for the functioning of modern economies' and that greater integration was associated with more efficient allocation of resources and long-term economic performance.[90] In a similar vein, its subsequent 2007 progress report on the single market in financial services argued that open, competitive, and deep financial markets were key to competitiveness and growth.[91]

But there has long been an asymmetry between the policy aspiration and reality (although market conditions are changing and continue to change—see section 5.3.1). In the EU, as has been extensively examined, market finance lags bank finance.[92] Bank finance has

---

[84] See, eg, Gambetti, L and Musso, L, Loan Supply Shocks and the Business Cycle, ECB WP No 1469 (2012) and Hempell, H and Kok Sørensen, C, The Impact of Supply Constraints on Bank Lending in the Euro Area. Crisis Induced Crunching? ECB WP No 1262 (2010).

[85] IOSCO, Securities Markets Risk Outlook 2013–2014 (2013) 10. IOSCO noted that the $2.2 trillion in bank loan funding raised in the EU and Europe in 2012 was around half the amount raised through equity and bond markets.

[86] For a recent discussion in the context of loan origination by investment funds see Central Bank of Ireland, Loan Origination by Investment Funds, Discussion Paper (2013).

[87] For a crisis-era discussion of the relative merits of bank and market funding see ECB, 'The External Financing of Household and non-Household Corporations: a Comparison of the Euro Area and the United States' *Monthly Bulletin*, April 2009, 69. The IMF has suggested that there is little resounding evidence as to whether the bank- or market-based systems are superior and warned against 'one-size-fits-all' solutions: n 9, 10, and 25.

[88] The ECB also emerged as a strong supporter of integrated and efficient securities markets over the FSAP era given in particular the role of markets in supporting monetary policy goals: ECB, Review of the Application of the Lamfalussy Framework to EU Securities Markets (2005) 2.

[89] Commission, Communication on Upgrading the Investment Services Directive (COM (2000) 729) (2000 ISD Communication).

[90] Commission, White Paper on Financial Services Policy 2005–2010 (2005) (COM (2005) 629) (2005 White Paper) 4.

[91] Commission, Single Market in Financial Services Progress Report 2007 (2007) (SEC (2007) 263) 3.

[92] Recently, eg, 2013 IMF ESMA Report, n 33, 6.

traditionally been associated with the major economies of France and Germany and with continental Europe generally; market finance with the UK and, to differing degrees, the Netherlands and the Nordic Member States.[93] The construction of an integrated financial market and the related adoption of market finance accordingly demands some very heavy lifting by the EU. In particular, while the EU has useful tools at its disposal (primarily the harmonization of regulation—see section 3.3), how it deploys these tools, and the effectiveness of these tools, is dictated by the deeply embedded national interests and related institutional structures which shape Member States' intermediation models and, accordingly, by how Member States interact with the EU's market finance and related financial market integration agenda.

A sharp light has been thrown on the nature of Member State interests with respect to intermediation models, and the related challenges faced by the EU's agenda, by the influential Varieties of Capitalism (VoC) literature.[94] It relates the type of economic model adopted by States (including their intermediation models) to their distinct institutional structures. Famously, it has classified the dominant economy types as the Liberal Market Economy (LME) and the Co-ordinated Market Economy (CME).[95] This broad classification, which probes the underlying political economy of States, has important implications for the EU's financial market integration project. It describes the CME as being, *inter alia*, based on 'patient' (long-term) capital, typically supplied by banks through loan assets, close relationships between banks and firms (including through cross shareholdings), the monitoring of firms (and capital) by networks including of banks, employees, and clients, strong stakeholder relationships (including between firms and employees/clients and based on cross-shareholdings), and as not dependent on publicly available information. The LME, by contrast, is based on market-based funding, a related focus on share price and current earnings and a more short-term orientation, strong market monitoring—including through aggressive takeover activity—and publicly available information. National legal frameworks for contracting and standard-setting tend to reinforce these patterns of economic co-ordination; the LME is typically associated with more facilitative and the CME with more intrusive regulation. The VoC analysis posits that States derive a comparative advantage from these interlinked institutional infrastructures and related economy types, and can be expected to protect those institutions; both models are durable and can be expected to resist convergence.

From the perspective of EU financial market integration and the promotion of market finance, the VoC analysis exposes the scale of the challenge. While it implies that EU law (harmonization), as an aspect of institutional structure, can shape and drive economic

---

[93] An extensive literature documents and critiques this structural feature of Europe's economy. See, eg, from the foundational FSAP era, Van der Elst, C, 'The Equity Markets, Ownership Structures and Control: Towards an International Harmonization' in Hopt, K and Wymeersch, E (eds), *Capital Markets and Company Law* (2003) 3, Barca, F and Becht, M, *The Control of Corporate Europe* (2001), Hertig, G, 'Western Europe's Corporate Governance Dilemma' in Baums, H, Hopt, K, and Horn, N (eds), *Corporations, Capital Markets and Business in the Law* (2000) 265, and Berglöf, E, 'Reforming Corporate Governance: Redirecting the European Agenda' (1997) 24 *Economic Policy* 93.

[94] The foundational work is Hall, P and Soskice, D (eds), *Varieties of Capitalism. The Institutional Foundations of Comparative Advantage* (2001). For a review of the scholarship see Thelen, K, 'Varieties of Capitalism: Trajectories of Liberalization and the New Politics of Social Solidarity' (2012) 15 *Annual Rev Political Science* 137.

[95] Hall, D and Soskice, D, 'Introduction' in *Varieties of Capitalism* (n 94), 1.

models, it also suggests that Member States can be expected to protect their long-standing institutional models, and their related competitive advantages, in single market-related negotiations.[96] In an oversimplification, CME States might be expected to resist moves to a more liberal, market-based system of regulation for the single financial market and to be sceptical of market finance, while LME States might be expected to resist a more intrusive regulatory model for the single financial market and to support market finance.[97]

The VoC analysis has great explanatory power. But the underlying institutional and related economic models of Member States are only one among the many and complex forces which shape not only Member States' negotiating interests but also the dynamics of EU financial market integration and engagement with market finance across the EU more generally,[98] and which are dissipated and/or concentrated across the EU's complex policy-formation and rule-making apparatus.[99] An array of Member State/intergovernmental, supranational, and industry/private forces have shaped the legal infrastructure supporting financial market integration and the extent to which and how financial markets have integrated and market finance has developed in the EU.[100]

Intergovernmental analyses, for example, have long located primary influence over the single market with the Member States and, chiming with the VoC analysis, initially characterized financial market integration as a 'battle of the systems' in which, particularly in the early stages of the single market project, Member States sought to shape financial integration to their own domestic models and to avoid conferring competitive advantage on other States. In these accounts, the legal infrastructure supporting financial market integration has been shaped by negotiations between the Member States representing the major financial systems in the EU—France and Germany on the one hand (broadly CME), and the UK on the other (broadly LME).[101] More recently, intergovernmental interaction has been characterized less in terms of 'bank versus market finance' (or 'CME versus LME') and, reflecting the array of forces which seem to shape Member States' interests, more broadly in terms of the 'market-making' coalition (led by the UK and typically including

---

[96] On the single market context generally see Höpner, M and Schäfer, A, Integration Among Unequals: How the Heterogeneity of European Varieties of Capitalism Shapes the Social and Democratic Potential of the EU, MPIfG DP 12/5 (2012), available at <http://ssrn.com/abstract=2149634> and Snell, J, 'Varieties of Capitalism and the Limits of European Economic Integration' (2010–2011) 13 *Cambridge Yearbook of European Legal Studies* 415.

[97] For a VoC analysis of EU takeover regulation, eg, see Clift, B, 'The Second Time as Farce? The EU Takeover Directive, the Clash of Capitalisms, and the Hamstrung Harmonization of European (and French) Corporate Governance' (2009) 47 *JCMS* 55.

[98] A massive scholarly literature theorizes the nature of EU integration generally and is not referenced here. It can be understood as producing two main explanatory theories: supranational governance, which emphasizes EU-level actors, and liberal intergovernmentalism, which emphasizes the Member States and their preferences.

[99] The rule-making process is discussed in Ch X. Across this process, coalitions form and re-form, and influence strengthens and dissipates. See, eg, Quaglia, L, *Governing Financial Services in the European Union. Banking, Securities, and Post-trading* (2010), noting that while the largest Member States, the Commission, the European Parliament, and some private stakeholders (notably the leading financial trade associations and firms) are more influential than others, this can change depending on the stage of the policy/rule-making process: at 7.

[100] See, eg, Mugge, D, Financial Regulation in the EU: A Research Agenda, Centre for European Studies, Harvard University (2012), available at <http://ssrn.com/abstract=2034916> and Quaglia, L, The 'Old' and 'New' Politics of Financial Services Regulation in the EU, OSE Paper Series No 2/2010 (2010).

[101] Classically, Story, J and Walter, I, *Political Economy of Financial Integration in Europe* (1997).

the Netherlands and the Nordic Member States, and associated with market-led, more liberal regulation) and the 'market-shaping' coalition (led by France and typically including Italy and Spain, and associated with more intrusive regulation).[102] This analysis, which sees Germany shifting between coalitions, has been associated in particular with the pivotal FSAP era.[103] Supranational accounts, by contrast, locate significant power with the Commission and other supranational institutions; influence has also been located within the networks of agencies and committees which have come to shape the EU rulebook for financial markets.[104] Private actors have also become increasingly influential on single market negotiations.[105]

These forces change over time. While the FSAP era can be associated with the 'market-making' coalition of Member States as well as with a dominant Commission[106]—and, overall, with a 'permissive consensus' on the benefits of integration[107]—the crisis era has seen the 'market-shaping' coalition of Member States, and their institutionally shaped economic interests, come to the fore, as a more intrusive approach to regulation and a more sceptical approach to market finance have developed.[108] The crisis has also, however, exposed how coalitions can shift between Member States depending on the particular 'mix' of interests at stake, as well as the changing positions of the supranational institutions, notably the Commission.[109]

The embedding of market finance in the EU and the related achievement of financial market integration is not therefore a straightforward outcome to achieve. This is all the more the case as it is not clear that market finance should be aggressively promoted. The range of institutional factors which shape a particular economy's dominant financing model are so variable and intermeshed, and the path dependencies are so significant, that any attempt to promote a particular model is fraught with danger. Even before the financial crisis underlined the difficulties with both bank and market financing models, it was argued that a combination of both bank- and market-finance techniques was likely to provide the most effective financing model for economic development.[110] The law and finance

---

[102] 'Market-making' coalitions have been analysed as privileging trust in markets, favouring market liberalization, light-touch and competition-friendly regulation, and strong private sector governance; 'market-shaping' coalitions tend to show distrust of markets and favour re-regulation, a prescriptive, rules-based approach to regulation, and strong central steering by public authorities: Quaglia, L, 'Completing the Single Market in Financial Services: the Politics of Competing Advocacy Coalitions' (2010) 17 *JEPP* 1007.

[103] Quaglia, n 99.

[104] Coen, D and Thatcher, M, 'Network Governance and Multilevel Delegation: European Networks of Regulatory Agencies' (2008) 28 *J of Public Policy* 49.

[105] Mugge, D, *Widen the Market, Narrow the Competition. Banker Interests in the Making of a European Capital Market* (2010).

[106] Quaglia, n 99.

[107] Mugge, n 100, 2.

[108] eg Quaglia, L, 'The "Old" and "New" Political Economy of Hedge Fund Regulation in the EU' (2011) 34 *West European Politics* 665.

[109] eg Buckley, J and Howarth, D, 'Internal Market Gesture Politics? Explaining the EU's Response to the Financial Crisis' (2010) *JCMS* 119. For an extensive analysis of the nuanced and shifting nature of intergovernmental and supranational relations over the crisis era see Ferran, E, 'Crisis-driven Regulatory Reform: Where in the World is the EU Going?' in Ferran, E, Moloney, N, Hill, J, and Coffee, C, *The Regulatory Aftermath of the Global Financial Crisis* (2012) 1.

[110] eg Levine, R and Beck, T, New Firm Formation and Industry Growth: Does Having a Market- or Bank-Based System Matter? World Bank Policy Research WP (2000), available at <http://ssrn.com/abstract= 630753>.

scholarship, which probes the relationship between law and financial market development and which has led to a wide-ranging if inconclusive debate on the extent to which law can drive market development and on which legal systems are most supportive of market development,[111] also counsels caution. While it suggests that law may have transformative effects with respect to the development of strong financial markets, the causal relationship between law and strong markets is fiercely contested, with challenges relating to the direction of causation, the institutions which can substitute for laws (such as networks of private capital and trading venues), the particular rules which have transformative effects, and the relative impact of 'law on the books' and 'law in action' (enforcement).[112]

But while it is not clear that the harmonization programme has been determinative,[113] overall it is clear that market finance has taken root in the EU and that significantly more intense market intermediation and financialization has followed, reflecting shifts in Member States' institutional structures (and a related nuancing of CME and LME models)[114] and, in particular, industry developments (section 5.3.1). On the eve of the financial crisis, market-based financing techniques (including the securitization of loan assets) were widely used by banks in France and Germany, while even the German SME (small and medium-sized enterprises) sector, classically dependent on bank patient capital, was beginning to rely on market-based funding.[115] It is also clear that financial market integration has, overall, deepened,[116] even if—as discussed in subsequent Chapters—variable patterns of integration obtain across different market segments. Despite the upheavals wrought by the financial crisis, there appears to be significant political and institutional consensus in support of financial market integration and market finance, at least to some degree (section 5.3.2).

But the location and intensity of financial market intervention remains contested, reflecting the deep fault-lines which continue to rumble underneath the relatively stable single market consensus and which reflect persistent differences across the Member States with respect to economic models and in approaches to regulation. While the regulatory programme is now relatively well settled, new occasions for conflict continue to emerge and to shape EU securities and markets regulation—including with respect to the institutional structure for

---

[111] The research was originally spearheaded by the work of financial economists La Porta, Lopez de Silanes, Shleifer, and Vishny (LLSV)—see, eg, La Porta, R, Lopez de Silanes, F, and Shleifer, A, 'The Economic Consequences of Legal Origins' (2008) 46 *J of Econ Lit* 285 and La Porta, R, Lopez de Silanes, F, Shleifer, A, and Vishny, R, 'Law and Finance' (1998) 106 *JPE* 1113.

[112] See, eg, Armour, J, Law and Financial Development: What We are Learning from Time-Series Evidence, ECGI Law WP No 148/2010 (2010), available at <http://ssrn.com/abstract=1580120>; Siems, M, What Does Not Work in Comparing Securities Laws: A Critique of La Porta et al's Methodology, CPC-RPS No 0009 (2008), available at <http://ssrn.com/abstract=608644>; Armour, J and Lele, P, Law, Finance and Politics: The Case of India, ECGI Law WP No 107/2008 (2008), available at <http://ssrn.com/abstractid=1116608>; Milhaupt, C and Pistor, K, *Law & Capitalism. What Corporate Crises Reveal about Legal Systems and Economic Development Around the World* (2008), Coffee, J, 'Law and the Market. The Impact of Enforcement' (2007) 156 *UPaLR* 229; and Cheffins, n 79.

[113] As discussed in subsequent Chapters.

[114] eg Buckley and Howarth, n 109.

[115] Hardie, I and Howarth, D 'Die Krise but not La Crise? The Financial Crisis and the Transformation of German and French Banking Systems' (2009) 47 *JCMS* 1017.

[116] For an overview see Grossman, E and Leblond, P, 'European Financial Integration: Finally the Great Leap Forward' (2011) 49 *JCMS* 413.

EU securities and markets regulation, discussed in Chapters X and XI, and with respect to the emerging tension between the single market and the euro area (section 5.1).

I.3.3 Harmonization: From Liberalization to Regulation

Financial market integration in the EU is primarily achieved through the harmonization of rules. In principle, harmonization of rules is justified where it is necessary to correct a market failure which extends beyond national boundaries and which cannot be corrected by action by individual States,[117] and where doing so increases welfare, taking into account the costs of harmonization.[118] Typical market failures include protectionist barriers, the regulatory costs and inefficiencies represented by multiple regimes, and the externalities which are generated by effects with an influence on well-being occurring in one State as a result of an activity which is regulated (or not) in another State (classically systemic risks to financial stability).

In the securities and markets regulation sphere, harmonization is typically regarded as justified where markets interact such that intermediaries, investors, and transactions move between them, leading to the potential for cross-border externalities such as fraud[119] and systemic risk,[120] as well as for increased transaction costs.

But while harmonization may support cross-border activity, harmonization of standards requires political agreement and can be a slow process, which may result in the adoption of standards which rapidly become obsolete. Harmonization also has the potential to restrict regulatory innovations which are typically incubated at national level, to limit the extent to which markets can tailor their regimes to reflect different market participant and transaction profiles, and to impose excessive costs. Harmonization—like any form of law-making, but with the additional risk of inflexibility—is vulnerable to regulatory capture. It can also, by standardizing rules and thereby shaping market behaviour, heighten systemic risk by incentivizing similar types of behaviours, whether regionally or internationally.[121] These risks are exacerbated where standards emerge from bodies with insecure governance and accountability foundations and poor technical capacity.[122]

Alternatively, the objectives pursued by harmonization can be achieved through regulatory competition between States,[123] the merits of which have been fiercely debated in the EU

---

[117] Ferrarini, G, 'Securities Regulation and the Rise of Pan-European Securities Markets: An Overview' in Ferrarini, G, Hopt, K, and Wymeersch, E (eds), *Capital Markets in the Age of the Euro: Cross-border Transactions, Listed Companies and Regulation* (2002) 249.

[118] Enriques, L and Gatti, M, 'The Uneasy Case for Top-Down Corporate Law Harmonization in the European Union' (2006) 27 *UPaJIEL* 939.

[119] For an early analysis see Bentson, G, 'Regulation of Stock Trading: Private Exchanges Versus Government Agencies' (1997) 83 *Va LR* 1501.

[120] For an early analysis see Davis, E, 'Problems of Banking Regulation—An EC Perspective' in Goodhart, C (ed), *The Emerging Framework of Financial Regulation* (1998) 533.

[121] Romano, R, For Diversity in the International Regulation of Financial Institutions: Rethinking the Basel Architecture (2013), Yale Law & Economics Research Paper, available at <http://ssrn.com/abstract= 2127749>.

[122] Enriques, L, 'EC Company Law Directives and Regulations: How Trivial Are They?' (2006) 27 *UPaJIEL* 1.

[123] Regulatory competition has been defined as 'the alteration of national regulation in response to the actual or expected impact of internationally mobile goods, services or factors of national economic activity': Sun, J-M and Pelkmans, J, 'Regulatory Competition in the Single Market' (1995) 33 *JCMS* 67, 68.

context[124] and in the US federal context.[125] The regulatory competition model is premised on regulatory arbitrage and on effective discovery of the different features of regulatory regimes. Where regimes differ, the regulatory competition model assumes that consumers will choose products/services which meet their price and quality requirements, but which originate from a State with a regulatory regime that is more efficient and less costly than the domestic regime, over domestic products/services produced under the less efficient domestic regime. Firms may choose to relocate to another regime in response to these signals, while investors may choose to invest their capital in a State in which the regulatory regime reflects, from the investor's perspective, the optimal balance between risk and reward. In the securities and markets sphere, clients should follow intermediating actors located in the most efficient States, and capital should similarly follow the most efficient regulatory systems. Regulatory competition has the twin advantages of easing the informational asymmetry under which regulators labour and improving the quality of intervention by allowing signals to be transmitted from the marketplace to regulators. It can reduce the risk of regulatory capture and potentially deliver regulation which reflects a more diverse range of interests, allows regulatory innovation and the exercise of choice, and checks the expansionist regulatory tendencies of government.[126] Paradoxically, regulatory competition may provide valuable evidence on how harmonization should proceed where clear evidence emerges of market support for particular regulatory choices.[127] In the EU context, it also appeals to the concept of subsidiarity by shifting the location of regulation from the EU to the Member States.

Among the problems generated by regulatory competition in the context of securities and markets regulation are the disadvantages of an uncertain regulatory environment and multiple regulatory regimes, particularly given the benefits of standardization with respect to disclosure, the risk of externalities and prejudice to third parties—including, as the financial crisis made graphically clear, financial stability risks—and the risk that protectionist barriers will remain in place. Difficulties also arise concerning the level to which competition drives regulation: the 'race to the bottom'/'race to the top' debate[128] queries whether market actors' choice of regime is driven by a concern to adopt rules which maximize value and lower the cost of capital or, alternatively, is a function of stakeholder interests—namely management's—and asks how States respond.

---

[124] See, eg, Deakin, S, Legal Diversity and Regulatory Competition: Which Model for Europe?, Centre for Business Research, University of Cambridge, WP No 323 (2006).

[125] An extensive US literature addresses the dynamics of regulatory competition in corporate law (largely a function of the States and the State of Delaware in particular) and with respect to issuer disclosure (a function of the federal government). For a major contribution see Romano, R, *The Genius of American Corporate Law* (1993). With respect to securities and markets regulation, see generally Jackson, H, 'Centralization, Competition and Privatization in Financial Regulation' (2001) 2 *Theoretical Inquiries in Law* 649 and, for contrasting perspectives in the issuer-disclosure debate, see Fox, M, 'Retaining Mandatory Issuer Disclosure: Why Issuer Choice is Not Investor Empowerment' (1999) 85 *Va LR* 1335 and Romano, R, 'Empowering Investors: A Market Approach to Securities Regulation' (1998) 107 *Yale LJ* 2359.

[126] See Bratton, W, McCahery, J, Picciotto, S, and Scott, C, 'Introduction: Regulatory Competition and Institutional Evolution' in Bratton, W, McCahery, J, Picciotto, S, and Scott, C (eds), *International Regulatory Competition and Coordination. Perspectives in Economics Regulation in Europe and the United States* (1996) and Esty, D and Geradin, G (eds), *Regulatory Competition and Economic Integration. Comparative Perspectives* (2001).

[127] Ferran, E, *Building an EU Capital Market* (2004) 54.

[128] Charny, D, 'Competition among Jurisdictions in Formulating Corporate Law Rules: An American Perspective on the "Race to the Bottom" in the European Communities' (1991) 32 *Harv LR* 423.

Effective regulatory competition depends on a number of factors, including the mobility of market participants and their ability to choose regulatory regimes; the related willingness and ability of investors to discount choices of regulation which increase their risks;[129] the extent to which regulators can decipher signals from market participants and are politically inclined to react, given path dependencies; the willingness of States to enter the competition;[130] and the absence of market failures which require intervention in the form of harmonized common standards. In addition, it is unlikely that competition is simply a function of regulation or 'law on the books'; the institutional and market structures, particularly with respect to enforcement and monitoring, which combine to drive market efficiency and investor protection are also likely to play a role in regime choices.[131]

In the EU, harmonization has long been the integration tool of choice.[132] Some element of competition was embedded within the regime during the 'minimum standards' period—broadly, the period related to the Commission's seminal 1985 Internal Market White Paper (1985–late 1990s), see further section 4.1—but this period was followed by the intensive FSAP and crisis eras which, in effect, removed regulatory competition and led to harmonization becoming ever more intensive and interventionist,[133] as discussed in section 4.2.2. The debate on the respective merits of regulatory competition and harmonization had, however, considerable traction over the 1980s and 1990s as EU securities and markets regulation developed.[134] It can now be regarded as somewhat sterile, given the crisis-era move to a 'single rulebook' and the location of regulatory power at EU level. The nature and quality of EU intervention remains contested, however, and has been queried from a range of analytical perspectives, including those of political science[135] and regulatory theory.[136] Rule-making for financial markets is, in principle, prone to risks and failures, given the scale of the information asymmetries between regulators/legislators and the markets, the speed of innovation, and the complexity which regulation must capture; resource constraints; capture risks; political risks; and the behavioural biases and groupthink risks to which rule-makers are vulnerable.[137] The EU's status as the monopoly supplier of securities and markets regulation makes the production of effective regulation all the more difficult; the EU law-making process is complex and multilayered, and often obstructed by intractable political disputes which reflect long-standing institutional differences across the Member States, while the ability of Member States to innovate, experiment, and correct

---

[129] Scott, H, 'Internationalisation of Primary Securities Markets' (2000) 63 *Law and Contemporary Problems* 71.

[130] Enriques, L, 'EC Company Law and the Fears of a European Delaware' (2004) 15 *EBLR* 1259.

[131] See, eg, Black, B, 'The Legal and Institutional Preconditions for Strong Securities Markets' (2001) 48 *UCLA LR* 781.

[132] On the various harmonization methods which have been used in the construction of the single market generally see the analysis in Slot, P, 'Harmonisation' (1996) 21 *ELR* 378, 382–7.

[133] Between 2003 and 2013, eg, there has been (approximately) a tenfold increase in the volume of EU law on financial services generally: 2013 HM Treasury Call for Evidence, n 15, 19.

[134] For two early studies see Wymeersch, E, *Control of Securities Markets in the European Economic Community, Collection Studies. Competition—Approximation of Legislation Series No 31* (1977), and Buxbaum, R and Hopt, K, *Legal Harmonisation and the Business Enterprise* (1988).

[135] eg, Quaglia, L, Eastwood, R, and Holmes, P, 'The Financial Turmoil and EU Policy Co-operation in 2008' (2009) 47 *JCMS* 63.

[136] eg, Black, J, 'Restructuring Global and EU Financial Regulation: Capacities, Coordination and Learning' in Ferrarini, G, Hopt, K, and Wymeersch, E (eds), *Rethinking Financial Regulation and Supervision in Times of Crisis* (2012) 3.

[137] For a reform prescription for rule-making processes see OECD, Recommendations of the Council on Regulatory Policy and Governance (2012).

regulatory errors has been almost entirely removed. As discussed in subsequent Chapters, the new rulebook which has emerged from the crisis era is not without risks. Neither is the fast-evolving and new location for contestation between the Member States and the EU—supervision and enforcement (Chapter XI).

I.4 The Evolution of EU Securities and Markets Regulation

I.4.1 Prior to the FSAP

The early progress of EU securities and markets regulation was less than auspicious and contained few signs of the explosive developments which would follow. The 1966 Segré Report marked the EU's first significant foray into securities and markets regulation and identified many of the market-integration and regulatory themes which continue to preoccupy the regulatory regime some 50 years later. It highlighted the poor condition of the EU financial market[138] and the benefits which could follow from the integration of markets; identified the obstacles to integration, chief among them the imposition by Member States of diverging and duplicative rules on market participants; and proposed remedial measures, notably with respect to the capital-raising process and the harmonization of disclosure standards. Subsequent developments took place on two fronts: the liberalization of capital movements,[139] which was an essential precondition for the establishment of a single financial market, and the harmonization of Member State rules. Although the first proposal was presented in 1972 (for an issuer-disclosure regime),[140] the first tentative steps were taken in 1977 with the Commission's Recommendation for a European Code of Conduct Relating to Transactions in Transferable Securities.[141] This was followed by the first generation of issuer disclosure directives, adopted between 1979 and 1982, which sought to construct a single securities market in which issuers could raise capital and which relied on detailed rule harmonization.

The second phase can be traced to 1985 and the presentation of the Commission's Internal Market White Paper, which set out a programme of measures designed to deliver the single market (generally) by 1992[142] and underlined the Commission's intention to accelerate the harmonization process by means of the mutual recognition/minimum-harmonization/home Member State control device. The White Paper accordingly reflected the earlier, ground-breaking judgment from the Court of Justice in *Cassis de Dijon*,[143] in which the

---

[138] '[Community] savers generally prefer to hold cash or short term assets and it would be difficult to alter that liquidity preference radically in the short term' and '[i]n several Community countries, the equity markets are suffering from a shortage of available capital and from a rather unsatisfactory pattern of business demand for capital . . . business firms often find it hard to obtain risk capital and at the same time the investing public does not always find attractive opportunities on the market': n 56, 17 and 27.

[139] See Usher, J, *The Law of Money and Financial Services in the European Community* (2nd edn, 2000) 7–38 and Barnard, C, *The Substantive Law of the EU: the Four Freedoms* (3rd edn, 2010) ch 15.

[140] [1972] OJ C131/61.

[141] Recommendation 77/534/EEC [1977] OJ L212/37 (1977 Code of Conduct).

[142] Completing the Internal Market (COM (85) 310) (1985 Internal Market White Paper). The Paper set out an agenda of 279 legislative measures to be brought into force by 1992 and proposed the building blocks of the single market as it currently operates.

[143] Case 120/78 *Rewe-Zentral AG v Bundesmonopolverwaltung für Branntwein (Cassis de Dijon)* [1979] ECR 649.

Court stated that products legally in circulation in one Member State were to be admitted to other Member States without being required to meet additional regulatory requirements. Member States were, in other words, subject to a 'mutual recognition' rule, or required to recognize the regulatory regimes of other Member States. Member States could, however, impose those requirements which could be classified as 'mandatory requirements', such as consumer protection rules. Mutual recognition, combined with harmonization of rules at a minimum level and the allocation of primary regulatory control for integrated market activities to the 'home' Member State (very broadly the Member State in which the regulated party was resident or registered), then became the touchstone for the second phase of EU securities and markets regulation, following the White Paper's translation of the Court's ruling into this device for market integration. Mutual recognition was designed to lever open the single market and access to 'host' States, once the regulated actor had complied with the minimum harmonized standards which were imposed by the actor's home Member State; in theory, costly duplications of regulation were avoided. The minimum-harmonization model allowed a degree of regulatory competition as a home Member State could impose additional rules above the minimum level on actors who chose to register in that Member State. It also accommodated some degree of flexibility and innovation in national regimes, as well as sensitivity towards local market features, but placed a limit on prejudicial regulatory competition.

In the securities and markets sphere, the White Paper argued that the 'liberalisation of financial services, linked to capital movements, will represent a major step towards Community financial integration and the widening of the Internal Market'.[144] It broadened the previous focus of the harmonization programme from issuers by including a collective investment schemes regime (to be adopted by 1985, adopted on schedule) and an investment advisers regime (to be adopted by 1989, adopted in 1993). Issuer-facing reforms were also included: a public offer prospectus regime was to be adopted by 1988 (adopted in 1989) and a regime concerning the information to be published on the acquisition of major holdings was to be adopted by 1988 (adopted on schedule).

With the 1985 collective investment regime, the EU gave the regulatory 'passport' device, which has since come to shape all of EU securities and markets regulation, its first airing.[145] The regime was based on authorization of the collective investment scheme by the home Member State in accordance with the regime's common standards and the conferral of a regulatory passport on the authorized scheme to operate across the EU (in 'host' Member States). It was followed by the second generation of issuer-disclosure directives (adopted between 1986 and 1994) which grafted the mutual-recognition concept on to the first generation of issuer-disclosure measures. In 1989, EU securities and markets regulation turned to the pathology of financial markets with the adoption of an insider-dealing regime designed to protect the integrity of and confidence in the new marketplace.

In 1993, after protracted negotiations, EU securities and markets regulation took a major step forward with the adoption of the cornerstone investment-services regime. In 1997 this was bolstered by the adoption of a directive which required that investor compensation schemes be established in all Member States and set out common rules. By 1997, which can

---

[144] 1985 Internal Market White Paper, n 142, 27.
[145] Directive 85/611/EEC [1985] OJ L375/3.

be seen as the approximate end of phase 2, the harmonized structure contained the basic elements of securities and markets regulation such that a common core of basic rules applied in most Member States. A network of national competent authorities (NCAs) had also been established, designed to supervise the harmonized rules and to provide a pan-EU co-operation system, albeit embryonic in form, on which the supervision of the integrated market could be based.

Nonetheless, the regulatory structure supporting the integration process was inadequate. Large areas of regulation were not harmonized. The existing regimes were deficient in a number of respects and did not support mutual recognition effectively. Implementation of directives was inconsistent and often badly delayed. Supervisory co-operation was underdeveloped. All in all, the signs were already there that the regime would be ill equipped to cope with the enormous demands which would be placed on it imminently, notably the arrival of monetary union, the explosion in market and technological innovation, and the upsurge in cross-border activity which followed in the wake of these two developments.

During the first and second phases of EU securities and markets regulation, the preoccupation with integration and the piecemeal development of the regime resulted in a certain bankruptcy concerning the underlying regulatory objectives being pursued by the common standards which underpinned the new market. While EU securities and markets regulation served primarily as a lever to open the marketplace, it also, even at that stage, served as the regulatory basis for many activities on the EU market. But it was not always clear what underlying regulatory objectives were pursued by the harmonized rules. These early reform periods were grounded in pragmatism and shaped by market-access requirements rather than by any particular attachment to the rights and wrongs of market regulation or any particular regulatory philosophy. Even at this early stage, however, the pull exerted by different economic models on Member States' approaches to harmonization and financial market integration was apparent; the negotiations on the 1993 directive on investment services, in particular, saw sharp distinctions between the UK-led 'Alliance' coalition and the France-led 'Club Med' coalition with respect to the extent to which trading on stock exchanges should be liberalized (Chapter V).

I.4.2 The FSAP and Post-FSAP Eras

I.4.2.1 The FSAP, Market Finance, and Integration

The FSAP era which followed (1999–2004) was highly regulatory in orientation, but was predominantly concerned with liberalization and the embedding of market finance.

As phase 2 came to an end—and largely independently of the harmonized regime—market finance began to take root, and integration to develop, at a rate that posed significant challenges for the limited EU regulatory regime. The euro removed currency risk, enhanced price transparency within the euro area, and supported changes in investment patterns as investors began to shift to pan-EU rather than Member State-based investment patterns. New technologies (including online delivery methods) began to increase the ease with which cross-border investment services could be offered and to enhance the dissemination of market information and access to trading, bringing greater numbers of investors to their own national markets and, increasingly, to the integrated marketplace. In a related development, changes to trading venues led to greater competition, reduced transaction costs, and increased cross-border trading. Consolidation in the intermediation industry occurred on an intra- and inter-Member State basis. Demographic developments and changes in how State-supported pensions schemes were funded provoked massive growth in the institutional investment segment and higher levels of retail investor activity. Issuers began to turn to the capital markets for their financing needs to a much greater extent than was previously the case.[146] In response, EU securities and markets policy began to engage seriously with the embedding of market finance and with the development of appropriate legal infrastructures to support financial market integration.

The initial impetus was intergovernmental and came from the European Council. The 1998 Cardiff European Council requested the Commission to prepare a framework for action for financial services which would ensure that the full benefits of the euro were realized with respect to financial services and that the stability and competitiveness of EU financial markets were ensured. The Commission duly issued a Communication later in 1998 on 'Financial Services Building a Framework for Action'[147] which strongly supported market finance and integration. It found that while some progress had been made, financial services markets remained segmented and cross-border provision of financial services, particularly in the retail sector, remained limited. Five areas were identified for reform in order to 'equip the EU with financial markets capable of sustaining competitiveness and weathering financial instability':[148] an overhauling of the legislative apparatus in order to ensure more effective responses to regulatory challenges; a market-driven modernization of wholesale markets in order to remove the remaining barriers to cross-border public offers and investment-related activities; completion on an incremental basis of the single market for retail financial products; review and clarification of the mechanisms for supervisory and regulatory co-operation; and creation of the general conditions for a fully integrated financial market, including construction of an integrated infrastructure with respect to payments, stricter application of the Treaty rules on competition and state aid, and progress on tax harmonization.

Later in 1998, the Vienna European Council called for the translation of these objectives into a specific work programme. Construction of the work programme was undertaken by the newly constituted Financial Services Policy Group, composed of representatives of the Council, the ECB, and the Commission, and it was presented by the Commission in its 1999 Financial Services Action Plan (the FSAP).[149] The FSAP was a programme of 42 measures which would radically change the shape of EU securities and markets regulation. The FSAP's proposals recognized that deficiencies in the harmonized regime were blocking greater integration and were designed to plug the major gaps and thereby support liberalization and integration. A second, more regulatory, theme of the FSAP was the need to protect the marketplace against the risks posed by greater integration, to meet the regulatory challenges posed by market developments, and to ensure the protection of retail investors in the integrated marketplace. The main proposals for financial markets were

---

[146] Subsequent Chapters discuss these developments with respect to particular market segments.
[147] COM (1998) 625 (the 1998 Communication).
[148] 1998 Communication, 1b.
[149] Commission, Communication on Implementing the Framework for Financial Markets Action Plan COM (1999) 232 (FSAP).

grouped into four categories—wholesale markets, retail markets, prudential rules and supervision, and wider conditions for an optimal single financial market.

The FSAP completed more or less on time, with 39 of the 42 measures adopted by the end of 2004. Its success, simply in terms of the formal completion of the programme, reflects the interplay of a series of factors. In particular, the FSAP period saw the holding together of a complex coalition of interests,[150] and was characterized by a strong political,[151] market,[152] and institutional[153] consensus on the benefits of market finance and of financial integration which reflected institutional changes to economic models in some Member States and the coincidence of the FSAP with a period of stock market exuberance (prior to the 2002 dotcom crash). By way of example, the 2000 Lisbon European Council—which took place at the height of wider stock market exuberance and before the bursting of the dotcom bubble, and the conclusions of which were described as bringing about a 'step change' in the movement towards greater integration[154]—provided important support for the FSAP and for the regulatory encouragement of market finance generally.[155] It highlighted the need for action on the wholesale markets, given the contribution these markets could make to economic growth, and identified as priority areas the widest possible access to investment capital on an EU basis, elimination of barriers to investment in pension funds, further integration of sovereign bond markets, an enhancement of comparability of companies' financial statements, and an intensification in co-operation by regulators. Although coalitions shifted as different FSAP measures were negotiated, a broadly pro-market and pro-integration coalition held.

Further impetus for reform came from the Lamfalussy Report of the Committee of Wise Men on the Regulation of European Securities Markets, chaired by Baron Alexandre Lamfalussy and constituted by the Council and which was delivered in February 2001.[156] While it proposed the first major institutional reform to EU securities and markets

---

[150] The Commission reported that the FSAP generated an 'unprecedented degree of co-operation between the institutions': Commission, FSAP Evaluation. Part I Process and Implementation (2005) (2005 FSAP Evaluation Report) 5.

[151] The UK, while often otherwise a robust critic of the FSAP's substantive reforms, supported the FSAP integration agenda in principle on the grounds that it was expected to lower the cost of capital and improve the allocation of capital, give firms increased opportunities to access markets, and give retail consumers access to a wider range of products: HM Treasury and FSA, Strengthening the EU Regulatory and Supervisory Framework: A Practical Approach (2007) 9.

[152] See, eg, the support for the FSAP from the series of industry reports issued towards the end of the FSAP era: the FSAP Expert Group Reports (by the Securities, Banking, Asset Management, and Insurance Expert Groups, all entitled Financial Services Action Plan. Progress and Prospects) were published in May 2004.

[153] See, eg, the support (albeit sometimes qualified) of the European Parliament: European Parliament, Resolution on Financial Services Policy (2005–2010) White Paper, 11 July 2007 (P6_TA(2007)0338) (2007) (Van den Burg II Resolution), based on the Economic and Monetary Affairs Committee (ECON) 2007 Van den Burg Report on Financial Services Policy 2005–2010 (A6-0248/2007). Support also came from the ECB: ECB, Financial Integration in Europe (2007) 4.

[154] Report from the Commission, Progress on Financial Services. Second Report (COM (2000) 336) 2.

[155] The Lisbon agenda was designed to make the EU 'the most competitive and dynamic knowledge-based economy in the world, capable of sustained economic growth with more and better jobs and greater social cohesion': Lisbon Council Conclusions, 23–4 March 2000. The Commission has suggested that the Lisbon agenda was 'one which the world's press, public leaders and private individuals all came to know', and that the linkage between the FSAP and this agenda gave impetus to the FSAP: 2005 FSAP Evaluation Report, n 150, 6.

[156] Final Report of the Committee of Wise Men on the Regulation of European Securities Markets (2001) (2001 Lamfalussy Report).

regulation and ultimately paved the way for ESMA (Chapter X), it also reviewed progress on integration more generally and was strongly supportive of market finance. But its findings were a searing indictment of the inadequacy of the harmonized structure, its inability to cope with market developments and support greater integration, and the failure of EU legislative procedures to deliver regulation quickly and effectively. It warned that unless steps were taken to complete the regulatory structure and open the marketplace and to revise the law-making process, 'economic growth, employment and prosperity will be lower, and competitive advantage will be lost to those outside the European Union. And the opportunity to complement and strengthen the role of the euro and to deepen European integration will be lost'.[157]

I.4.2.2 Harmonization and the FSAP: Liberalization and Re-regulation

The FSAP led to a new EU rulebook for financial markets. Its main elements were the 2002 Distance Marketing of Financial Services Directive, the 2003 Prospectus Directive, the 2004 Transparency Directive, the 2002 International Accounting Standards Regulation, the 2009 'UCITS IV' reforms to the Undertakings for the Collective Investment of Transferable Securities (UCITS) collective investment regime (which were initiated shortly after the close of the FSAP but are associated with the FSAP period), the 2004 Markets in Financial Instruments Directive I (2004 MiFID I) governing investment services and trading venues, and the 2003 Market Abuse Directive (2003 MAD) on insider dealing and market manipulation.[158] Detailed technical administrative rules amplifying these measures were adopted by the Commission, exercising powers delegated from the European Parliament and Council. The FSAP era also led to institutional reform in the form of the establishment of the Committee of European Securities Regulators (CESR), which supported the new 'Lamfalussy process' for the adoption of technical administrative rules by the Commission by providing technical advice to the Commission and, through a range of non-binding 'supervisory convergence' measures (including 'soft' quasi-rule measures), supported co-operation and convergence between NCAs.

With hindsight, it is now clear that the FSAP 'rulebook' was incomplete and, reflecting the wider regulatory zeitgeist, left large segments of the market—particularly in the wholesale sector—largely unregulated. But at the time, it represented a significant expansion of the pre-FSAP regime and largely removed the ability of Member States to engage in regulatory competition.

Under the FSAP, harmonization changed in character. It was no longer simply a functional device for removing obstacles and addressing market failures in the form of regulatory costs. It became the device through which centralized regulation was imposed on the EU marketplace (and on domestic and cross-border actors). This change in tone is well illustrated by the Commission's 2000 Investment Services Directive (ISD) Communication, which laid the foundations for what would become the 2004 MiFID I, in which it argued that the removal of regulatory obstacles to free movement was no longer sufficient

---

[157] 2001 Lamfalussy Report, 7, 8.
[158] Respectively: Directive 2002/65/EC [2002] OJ L271/16; Directive 2003/71/EC [2003] OJ L345/64; Directive 2004/109/EC [2004] OJ L390/38; Regulation (EU) No 1606/2002 [2002] OJ L243/1; Directive 2009/65/EC [2009] OJ L302/32; Directive 2004/39/EC [2004] OJ L145/1; and Directive 2003/6/EC [2003] OJ L96/16.

and that a regulatory framework was needed to secure the benefits of efficient and stable market-based systems.[159] Thus, although the FSAP era generally represented the ascendancy of the (very broadly) liberalization-supporting market-making/LME Member States, it also reflected the regulatory orientation of the market-shaping/CME Member States.[160]

The FSAP did not, however, entirely remove Member State control over financial market rules. The 2003 Prospectus Directive was not expressed as a maximum-harmonization measure (maximum harmonization is typically associated with the removal of the ability of Member States to impose additional or more stringent rules in the area concerned upon domestic actors). Neither was the 2003 MAD I, which was structured as a minimum-standards measure, as was the 2004 Transparency Directive. Notwithstanding the scale of its regulatory ambitions, the 2004 MiFID I did not formally oust the Member States. The 2002 Distance Marketing of Financial Services Directive provides a rare FSAP example of formal maximum harmonization in that it expressly prevents Member States from adopting additional rules.[161] In practice, the raft of technical administrative rules adopted under the major FSAP measures significantly limited Member States' freedom to operate, particularly given market hostility to the 'gold-plating' of rules by Member States (or the adoption of additional requirements for domestic markets). But administrative rules were often based on minimum harmonization and adopted a flexible approach—although maximum harmonization was adopted under the MiFID I administrative regime[162] and regulations were regularly deployed at the administrative level. Overall, however, maximum harmonization was not fully embraced across the FSAP despite its detail.[163]

The appropriate level of harmonization for the financial markets, and by extension the balance of control between the EU and the Member States, generated political debate over the FSAP, however, particularly with respect to whether a directive or regulation should be employed and the degree of Member State flexibility which should be supported. Charges of over-regulation were frequently raised, particularly with respect to the array of technical administrative rules.[164] Market support for the FSAP's more intrusive harmonization was, nonetheless, generally strong; the minimum-harmonization model which, unusually for the FSAP, was expressly adopted by the 2004 Transparency Directive was criticized for allowing divergences to appear and compliance costs to increase.[165] There was some circumspection from the consumer sector, with concern expressed that a maximum harmonization

---

[159] n 89, 5.

[160] One analysis has described the FSAP as favouring the (broadly) continental approach to harmonization as the UK preference was traditionally for minimum harmonization and regulatory diversity: Welch, J, 'Decomposing MiFID' (2006) *Financial World* July/August 46.

[161] The Directive's disclosure requirements are not subject to this requirement: Art 4(2).

[162] Commission MiFID I Directive 2006/73/EC [2006] OJ L241/26. The Art 4 'goldplating prohibition' prevented Member States from applying rules additional to the Directive on their domestic markets unless approval had been obtained from the Commission.

[163] Tison, M, 'Financial Market Integration in the Post FSAP Era. In Search of Overall Conceptual Consistency in the Regulatory Framework' in Ferrarini, G and Wymeersch, E (eds), *Investor Protection in Europe—Corporate Law Making, the MiFID and Beyond* (2006) 443 and Enriques, L and Gatti, M, 'Is there a Uniform EU Securities Law After the Financial Services Action Plan?' (2008) 14 *Stanford J of Law, Business and Finance* 43.

[164] eg Inter-institutional Monitoring Group, Third Interim Report Monitoring the Lamfalussy Process (November 2004) 20 and Inter-institutional Monitoring Group, Final Report Monitoring the Lamfalussy Process (October 2007) 9.

[165] See Ch II sect 5.

approach could threaten national consumer protection regimes.[166] But overall, by the end of the FSAP period and immediately prior to the crisis, a commitment had emerged to limit Member State discretion in order to curb the encrustation of national rules through 'gold-plating' and to support effective implementation.[167] The crisis era would see this translated into the 'single rulebook' agenda.

I.4.2.3 The post-FSAP Era and the Legislative Pause

Phase 4 of EU securities and markets regulation, the post-FSAP and pre-crisis phase, can be traced to the Commission's 2005 White Paper which set out the policy agenda for 2005–10.[168]

Over this period, and in a significant strategic shift, EU regulatory intervention went into abeyance, reflecting both the Commission's support for a 'regulatory pause'[169] and the pre-crisis-era zeitgeist internationally. The 2005 White Paper focused on 'dynamic consolidation' towards an integrated, open, and efficient financial market; removal of the remaining economically significant barriers; implementation, enforcement, and evaluation of existing legislation and rigorous application of the EU's 2002 Better Regulation agenda to new initiatives; and enhancement of supervisory co-operation and convergence and a strengthening of European influence in the global marketplace. Ensuring the effectiveness of the FSAP became the Commission's major priority.

This period also saw the Commission rely more heavily on non-regulatory tools and 'enrol' private sector actors in the standard-setting process,[170] reflecting the wider pre-crisis movement towards facilitative 'new governance' techniques for intervention[171] and a 'decentred' approach to financial market regulation.[172] This was most marked with respect to the reliance on codes of conduct with respect to the credit rating agency and clearing and settlement sectors, but was projected to become a feature of Commission policy more generally.[173]

---

[166] FIN-USE, Financial Services, Consumers and Small Businesses. A User Perspective on the Report on Banking, Asset Management, Securities and Insurance of the Post FSAP Stocktaking Groups (October 2004) 16.

[167] Following the 2007 'Lamfalussy Review' (Ch X sects 2.2 and 2.3), the Council undertook to limit the use of national discretion in future legislative measures: 2836th Council Meeting, 4 December 2007, ECOFIN Press Release No 15698/07, 16. The Commission also committed to a greater use of regulations to support more effective implementation: Commission, Review of the Lamfalussy Process. Strengthening Supervisory Convergence (2007) 5.

[168] n 90.

[169] While a range of factors, not least among them the need for the FSAP reforms to bed in, shaped this period, the withdrawal from regulation is strongly associated with then Internal Market Commissioner McCreevy, who typically favoured market discipline, where possible, and supported a lighter regulatory touch. See, eg, McCreevy, C, Speech on 'Assessment of the Integration of the Single Market for Financial Services by the Commission', CESR Conference, Paris, 6 December 2004.

[170] On enrolment see Black, J, 'Enrolling Actors in Regulatory Systems: Examples from UK Financial Services Regulation' (2003) *Public Law* 63.

[171] See further Ch X sect 1.2.

[172] The decentred characterization of regulation emphasizes the complex, fragmented, multi-actor process through which regulation can emerge where the state relinquishes its monopoly on regulatory intervention and as regulation extends beyond formal legal rules. See Black, J, 'Decentring Regulation: Understanding the Role of Regulation and Self Regulation in a "Post Regulatory World"' (2001) 54 *Current Legal Problems* 103.

[173] Wymeersch, E, Standardization by Law and Markets, Especially in Financial Services, Financial Law Institute WP No 2008-02 (2008), available at <http://ssrn.com/abstract=1089037>.

I.4.3 The Crisis Era

I.4.3.1 The Financial Crisis and the EU

(a) The Financial Crisis

In the EU, the financial crisis rapidly became hydra-headed, spawning interconnected banking, market, and fiscal crises[174] and—leaving economic stimulus and recovery measures aside[175]—leading to a series of interconnected reform programmes, of which the massive reforms to EU securities and markets regulation form only one part.[176]

The catastrophic costs of bank rescue by the Member States, and the destructive feedback loop which emerged between sovereign risk and bank stability, transformed the 'EU financial crisis' into a 'euro-area fiscal crisis' with far-reaching effects.[177] The initial banking crisis and the related bank rescues (from 2008) placed intense pressure on the sovereign debt of several Member States (notably Greece and Ireland). Contagion effects on euro-area sovereign debt generally rapidly intensified (driven by the Greek crisis in particular) from mid-2010, further intensified over 2011, and continued into the first half of 2012, generating an existential threat to the euro.[178] The sovereign debt crisis forced the EU into unprecedented support of a number of Member States through financial assistance programmes, and led to historic liquidity support to banks and to the euro from the ECB and euro-area central banks (the Eurosystem).[179] Far-reaching changes to the institutional settlement governing Economic and Monetary Union (EMU) also followed: new rules governing budgetary co-ordination and discipline were put in place, along with a new

---

[174] The ESRB has described the EU financial crisis as involving overlapping and inter-related crises with destructive feedback loops: ESRB, Annual Report (2012) 7.

[175] The EU's economic recovery plan was originally based on some €200 billion of expenditure, automatic stabilizers (such as social security benefits) to the value of some €200 billion, and sector-specific support, including €7 billion to the car industry. For an early EU agenda see Commission, A European Economic Recovery Plan (2008) (COM (2008) 800).

[176] This short introductory outline can only note the major features of the crisis-era period, and focuses on the securities and markets reform agenda. From the vast literature on this period see for a wide-ranging review Ferran, n 109, and, from an earlier stage of the crisis, the discussions in the (2009) 47 Special Edition of the *JCMS*.

[177] The main transmission channels between sovereign debt risk and bank stability risk were: direct exposures by banks to the home sovereign; the consequential downgrade of bank ratings following a sovereign rating downgrade; a weakening of the implicit funding discount for banks, where the market lost faith in the ability of a sovereign to bailout a bank; and a reduction in the value of sovereign debt as collateral: Commission, Financial Stability and Integration Report 2011 (2012) (SWD (2012) 103) (2011 EFSIR) 12–13.

[178] Concerns over the possibility of a Greek default led to pressure on other euro-area sovereign debt and to related pressure on banks holding sovereign debt.

[179] Liquidity support for banks included unlimited liquidity provision through fixed-rate tenders, the lengthening of refinancing operations, an extension of eligible collateral, and the provision of liquidity in foreign currencies. The ECB also conducted 'Outright Monetary Transactions' in euro-area sovereign debt secondary markets (the OMT programme) where the sovereign was in a financial assistance programme; this controversial programme was launched in August 2012 (following ECB Chairman Draghi's widely reported defence of the euro—n 181) and replaced the previous Securities Market Programme. The ECB and national central banks also engaged in covered bond purchases. The OMT programme was regarded by some as amounting to an ECB monetary bailout, prohibited by the Treaties (Art 123 TFEU). In February 2014, in a landmark and closely followed ruling, the German Constitutional Court ruled that the OMT programme was likely to breach the Treaties (and the German Constitution), and asked for guidance from the Court of Justice.

institutional structure to finance rescue/support programmes for euro-area Member States (the European Stability Mechanism).[180] The sovereign debt crisis was not brought under some degree of control until the massive intervention by the Eurosystem in euro-area sovereign debt markets (from July 2012)[181] and the seismic Banking Union reform (agreed by euro-area Member States in June 2012). The latter, composed of a new euro-area Single Supervisory Mechanism (SSM) and a euro-area Single Resolution Mechanism (SRM)[182] (the mutualized euro-area deposit guarantee scheme, often regarded as the third pillar of Banking Union, remains incomplete), and supported by the dense banking rulebook which applies across the single market (as well as by EU state aid rules), is designed to ensure euro-area banks are appropriately regulated and supervised and can be effectively and safely resolved where they fail, and to protect the euro area from the fiscal costs of bank failure.[183]

Outside the euro area and across the EU generally, the reform of banking regulation has been intense, and has led to the dense banking rulebook (which also supports Banking Union) which includes a new harmonized bank resolution and rescue regime. The securities and markets reforms discussed across this book have similarly led to a far-reaching extension of the perimeter of the regulatory regime and a decisive shift in the location of regulatory control from the Member States to the EU. The regulatory reforms have been underpinned by institutional change in the form of the European System of Financial Supervision (ESFS). The ESFS comprises the NCAs, the three European Supervisory Authorities (ESAs)—ESMA, the European Banking Authority (EBA), and the European Insurance and Occupational Pensions Authority (EIOPA)—and the macro-prudential oversight body, the European Systemic Risk Board (ESRB).

The EU regulatory reform agenda for the EU financial system generally[184] is designed to address the failures which the crisis exposed in financial system regulation internationally, and so follows the related G20 reform agenda. But specific and additional difficulties beset the EU,[185] arising from the mismatch between the pan-EU operations of some major

---

[180] For an outline of the support from the ECB and euro-area central banks and the reforms to economic governance see 2011 EFSIR, n 177, 47–3, and Commission, Financial Integration and Stability Review 2012 (2013) (SWD (2013) 156) (2012 EFSIR) 12–13 and 40–5.

[181] Following the 26 July 2012 announcement by ECB President Draghi that '[w]ithin our mandate, the ECB is ready to do whatever it takes to preserve the euro. And believe me, it will be enough': Speech to Global Investment Conference, London.

[182] The SSM is based on Council Regulation (EU) No 1024/2013 [2013] OJ L287/63 and Regulation (EU) No 1022/2013 [2013] OJ L287/5. The SRM is based on Regulation (EU) No 806/2014 [2014] OJ L225/1 and a related Intergovernmental Agreement. In each case, 'non-participating' (non-euro-area) States can take part, should they wish to.

[183] See further Ch XI sect 7 on Banking Union and the SSM. On the SRM, see in brief outline Ch IV sect 13.

[184] For reviews see, eg, Moloney, N, 'Resetting the Location of Regulatory and Supervisory Control over EU Financial Markets: Lessons from Five Years On' (2013) 62 *ICLQ* 955; Howarth, D and Quaglia, L, 'Banking Union as Holy Grail: Rebuilding the Single Market in Financial Services, Stabilizing Europe's Banks, and "Completing" Economic and Monetary Union' (2013) 51 *JCMS* 103; Moloney, N, 'EU Financial Market Regulation after the Global Financial Crisis: "More Europe" or More Risks?' (2010) 47 *CMLR* 1317; and Mülbert, P and Wilhelm, A, 'Reforms of EU Banking and Securities Regulation after the Financial Crisis' (2010) 26 *Banking and Finance LR* 187.

[185] On the early stages of the crisis in the EU and the initial reform agenda see, eg: Begg, I, 'Regulation and Supervision of Financial Intermediaries in the EU: the Aftermath of the Financial Crisis' (2009) 47 *JCMS* 1106; Dabrowski, M, The Global Financial Crisis: Lessons for European Integration, Case Network Studies and Analysis No 384/2009, available at <http://ssrn.com/abstract=1436432>; and Wouters, J and van

banking groups and nationally based supervision and resolution regimes:[186] the 'global in life, national in death' conundrum.[187] At the core of the original EU banking crisis (which would become a fiscal crisis) was a destructive imbalance in the EU's regulatory and supervisory architecture. The post-FSAP regulatory structure facilitated the cross-border activities of large financial institutions, but it did not adequately address cross-border supervision, co-ordination, crisis resolution, and deposit protection. The early stages of the crisis were characterized by local solutions, including the extension of deposit guarantee schemes, which often paid little heed to pan-EU financial stability consequences.[188] The Fortis group, which came to close to collapse in September 2008, became emblematic of EU supervisory and co-ordination failures. It was initially supported through a co-ordinated injection of €11.2 billion by the governments of Luxembourg, the Netherlands, and Belgium on 28 September 2008. The rescue subsequently fell apart as tensions arose concerning burden-sharing, with the Netherlands nationalizing the Dutch element of Fortis and Belgium and Luxembourg selling the remaining elements to BNP Paribas.[189] The Dexia group fared better, with the cross-border rescue co-ordinated by Luxembourg, France, and Belgium succeeding. Other major cross-border groups, notably RBS and ING, were the subject of home State rescues.[190]

The scale of the damage to the stability of the EU financial system has been recorded in detail by the ECB through its regular financial stability reports. In December 2008, for example, the ECB reported on an uncertain financial stability outlook and on the threats to the funding positions of banks and ongoing liquidity contraction in money markets, on the risks associated with hedge funds' exposures to redemptions, and on the impact of unexpected events on then exceptionally volatile markets of thin liquidity, as well as on the impact of poor macroeconomic conditions.[191] By December 2010, the situation 'was still fraught with risk', given the new instability in the euro-area sovereign debt market.[192] By December 2012, although pressure on the euro had eased, the ECB was concerned about ongoing stress in the euro-area sovereign debt market, the risks of a decrease in bank profitability, and the impaired ability of fragmented markets to support bank funding.[193] Although by May 2013 the ECB could report that stress on the euro area had fallen markedly, it remained concerned about bank profitability, funding sources, and the resilience of the euro-area sovereign debt market, and had become concerned as to the ongoing global reassessment of risk premia for assets, as investors began to move from safe

---

Kerckhoven, S, The EU's Internal and External Regulatory Actions after the Outbreak of the 2008 Financial Crisis, Leuven Centre for Global Governance Studies, WP No 69 (2011).

[186] Ferrarini, G and Chiodini, F, Regulating Multinational Banks in Europe. An Assessment of the new Supervisory Framework, ECGI Law WP No 158/2010 (2010), available via <http://ssrn.com/abstract=1596890>.

[187] Coined by Bank of England Governor Meryvn King: Turner Review, n 16, 36.

[188] Well illustrated by some Member States' (initially Ireland's) unilateral extension of their deposit guarantee schemes in autumn 2008.

[189] eg Cotterli, S and Gualandri, E, Financial Crisis and Supervision of Cross Border Groups in the EU (2009), available via <http://ssrn.com/abstract=1507750> and Fonteyne, W, et al, Crisis Management and Resolution for a European Banking System, IMF Working Paper WP/10/70 (2010), available via <http://www.imf.org/external/pubs/ft/wp/2010/wp1070.pdf>.

[190] Fonteyne, n 189, 13–14.

[191] ECB, Financial Stability Review, December 2008.

[192] ECB, Financial Stability Review, December 2010.

[193] ECB, Financial Stability Review, December 2012.

havens to riskier assets.[194] The 2012 and 2013 ECB reviews also highlighted the risk posed by financial innovation and the shadow banking sector.

The scale of the regulatory and supervisory repair required was massive. The agenda-setting February 2009 de Larosière Group (DLG) Report[195] exposed the regulatory gaps and weaknesses in the post-FSAP banking and securities and markets regulation regimes, many of which the EU had in common with a number of major regulatory systems worldwide. But it also pointed to poor supervisory co-ordination, co-operation, and information-sharing, and the absence of emergency and crisis resolution mechanisms. The EU's Economic and Financial Committee (EFC)[196] similarly found that the distribution of tasks between home and host banking NCAs was not clear, that host NCAs had limited powers and were often unable to challenge home NCAs, that NCAs were not mandated to consider pan-EU financial stability, and that there were significant inconsistencies in Member States' intervention and rescue powers.

The subsequent reform agenda for banking and for securities and markets regulation sought to establish a uniform and enhanced 'single rulebook' for the single market which would reflect the G20 reforms and close the regulatory gaps which had emerged, enhance supervision and supervisory co-ordination, and identify and mitigate the distinct financial stability risks generated within the single market.

The banking reform programme, however, developed a distinct trajectory. The fiscal implications of cross-border supervisory failure had been clear in the early stages of the crisis as home NCAs and tax-payers carried the costs of bank rescue. But they became acute as euro-area sovereign debt came under pressure and the costs of bank rescue became mutualized across the euro area with the establishment of support programmes for the weakest peripheral economies (Greece, Ireland, and Portugal). The later stages of the banking reform programme, accordingly, focused on management of the fiscal risks of bank failure and ultimately led to the radical Banking Union reform for euro-area banks.

(b) The Securities and Markets Reform Agenda

The massive crisis-era reform programme has redrawn EU securities and markets regulation. Large segments of the wider EU reform programme focus on the prudential regulation of deposit-taking banks (notably the bank capital, liquidity, and leverage requirements, the resolution and rescue reforms, and, for the euro area, Banking Union), and are designed to address the acute financial stability and fiscal risks which the crisis generated. But the regulatory and supervisory reforms are also designed to address the regulatory gaps which the financial crisis exposed, and in particular the stability risks which markets can generate, and so have reshaped EU securities and markets regulation.[197]

---

[194] ECB, Financial Stability Review, May 2013. In April 2014, the ECB was similarly cautious, warning that further progress towards financial stability could not be taken for granted: ECB, Financial Integration in Europe (2014) 9.

[195] n 16.

[196] EFC, High Level Working Group on Cross-Border Financial Supervision Arrangements, Lessons from the Crisis for European Financial Stability Arrangements (2009). On the EFC, see n 65.

[197] The new securities and markets regime also, of course, applies to deposit-taking banks in respect of their market-facing activities.

Subsequent Chapters discuss the forces which have shaped the different elements of the new securities and markets regulation regime.[198] Overall, however, the EU's banking-driven euro-area fiscal crisis can be associated with the emergence of a strong anti-speculation agenda and a related suspicion of market intensity, both of which became defining influences on the securities and markets regulation regime. Institutional differences in economic models across the Member States had long led to variations in the extent to which Member States supported intense financial market activity and market finance. These underlying tensions burst out to dramatic effect as the financial crisis deepened, and became explosive as turmoil gripped the EU's sovereign debt markets over 2010 to 2012. Hostility to perceived excessive speculation—and suspicion of market intensity and innovation generally—has shaped, in particular, the new rating agency regime, the new regime governing alternative investment fund managers, and the new trading regime.

I.4.3.2 The Major Securities and Markets Regulation Reforms

Two distinct waves of reform to EU securities and markets regulation over the crisis period can be identified.

The first wave of EU financial system reform generally was closely related to the G20 agenda and was concerned with supporting financial stability and ensuring a secure regulatory perimeter; it was also concerned with the distinct risks to the EU market arising from cross-border risk transmission and, as the sovereign debt crisis took hold, the destructive feedback loop between the fiscal implications of banking failure and the resilience of sovereigns. These reforms focused on strengthening EU banking regulation, most notably through the massive 2013 Capital Requirements Directive IV (CRD IV) and Capital Requirements Regulation (CRR) reforms which implemented the Basel III reforms to bank capital, liquidity, and leverage regulation, and introduced related risk management and governance reforms;[199] these reforms also apply to investment firms within the scope of the CRD IV/CRR regime.

During this phase of stability-orientated reform, securities and markets regulation experienced its first set of major reforms. These reforms are exemplified by two perimeter-changing measures which captured market actors not previously subject to EU regulation. The 2011 Alternative Investment Fund Managers Directive (2011 AIFMD)[200] has extended the asset management regime, which was previously liberalization-driven and focused on the retail-market-orientated 'UCITS' collective investment scheme, to include all non-UCITS fund managers, including private equity, property, and commodity fund managers, although it has become most associated with hedge fund regulation. The 2012 European Market Infrastructure Regulation (2012 EMIR)[201] has brought radical change to the OTC derivatives markets, requiring in-scope derivatives to be cleared through CCPs and, in effect, imposing major reform on a previously lightly regulated segment of the

---

[198] The general positions of the Commission, the Council, and the European Parliament over the crisis are discussed in Ch X sect 3.3.

[199] The banking rulebook is heavily based on the 2013 Capital Requirements Directive IV (which covers governance, sanctions, capital buffers, supervision, and a reduction in reliance on rating agencies) and the Capital Requirements Regulation (which covers capital, liquidity, leverage, and counterparty credit risk)—respectively, Directive 2013/36 [2013] OJ L176/338 and Regulation (EU) No 575/2013 [2013] OJ L176/1.

[200] Directive 2011/61 [2011] OJ L174/1 (2011 AIFMD).

[201] Regulation (EU) No 648/2012 [2012] OJ L201/1 (2012 EMIR).

financial markets. This reform wave also includes the EU's new rating agency regime, composed of Credit Rating Agency (CRA) Regulations I (2009),[202] II (2011),[203] and III (2013)[204] and the 2013 CRA Directive,[205] and the 2012 Short Selling Regulation, which imposes new restrictions on short selling in a range of financial instruments, including sovereign debt.[206]

This first phase can also be associated with the initial institutional reforms to EU financial system governance: the 2011 establishment of the ESFS, composed of NCAs, the ESAs (conferred with a range of quasi-regulatory and supervisory tasks), and the ESRB, charged with macro-prudential system oversight. The second set of institutional reforms relate to Banking Union but may have 'spillover' effects for securities and markets regulation (Chapter XI section 7).

A second wave of securities- and markets-specific reform has followed, and has led to the reform programme extending beyond financial stability and embracing reforms which can be more closely associated with the traditional securities and markets regulation objectives of market efficiency (in particular the effectiveness of markets in supporting long-term savings and growth),[207] transparency, and integrity, and consumer/investor protection. Many of these reforms have their roots in the review obligations which the FSAP imposed on its major measures, but the reviews have been coloured by the financial crisis. For example, the cornerstone of investment firm and trading venue regulation, the 2004 MiFID I, has been radically overhauled by the 2014 Markets in Financial Instruments Directive II (2014 MiFID II) and 2014 Markets in Financial Instruments Regulation (2014 MiFIR) reforms,[208] which have the effect of capturing a very wide range of firms, venues, instruments, and trading practices within the regulatory net. The asset management regime has been expanded by discrete regimes for venture capital funds, social entrepreneurship funds, and long-term investment funds, designed to enhance the ability of markets to raise capital.[209] The retail investor protection regime is undergoing major reforms which include the adoption of a new, cross-sector measure designed to address the disclosure provided in relation to packaged investment products and to close gaps in the current disclosure regime (the Packaged Retail Investment Products, or PRIPs, reform).[210] Long-standing elements of

---

[202] Regulation (EU) No 1060/2009 [2009] OJ L302/1 (2009 CRA I).

[203] Regulation (EU) No 513/2011 [2011] OJ L145/30 (2011 CRA II).

[204] Regulation (EU) No 462/2013 [2013] OJ L146/1 (2013 CRA III).

[205] Directive 2013/14/EU [2013] OJ L145/1.

[206] Regulation (EU) No 236/2012 [2012] OJ L86/1.

[207] Commission, Green Paper. Long-Term Financing of the European Economy (2013) (COM (2013) 150/2) (2013 Long-Term Financing Green Paper).

[208] Markets in Financial Instruments Directive II 2014/65/EU [2014] OJ L173/349 (2014 MiFID II) and Markets in Financial Instruments Regulation EU (No) 600/2014 [2014] OJ L173/84 (2014 MiFIR) (see Ch IV n 28 on the implementation timeline). The MiFID regime provides perimeter control for much of EU securities and markets regulation. Accordingly, the 2014 reforms clarify that all references to the precursor MIFID I Directive (n 68) are to be construed as references to the MiFID II/MiFIR regime (and should be read in conjunction with the correlation tables set out in MiFID II). Similarly, all references to terms defined in or to Arts of MiFID I (or the earlier 1993 Investment Services Directive (Directive 93/22/EC [1993] OJ L141/27)) are to be construed as references to the 2014 MiFID II/MiFIR regime: 2014 MiFID II Art 94. As noted in relevant Chapters, the discussion in this book is based on the 2014 MiFID II/MiFIR regime, although reference is made to MiFID I as appropriate.

[209] Respectively, Regulation (EU) No 345/2013 [2013] OJ L115/1; Regulation (EU) No 346/2013 [2013] OJ L115/18; and COM (2013) 462.

[210] COM (2012) 352. The reforms were agreed in April 2014.

EU securities and markets regulation, including the capital-raising regime,[211] the market abuse regime,[212] and the UCITS regime[213] have also been reformed. An extensive administrative rulebook relating to these legislative measures is under development. The review process is already underway, underlining the state of permanent revolution which EU securities and markets regulation has been in since October 2008. The 2012 Short Selling Regulation, for example, has been reviewed, and the 2013–14 ESFS review is underway.

I.5 EU Securities and Markets Regulation
After the Financial Crisis

I.5.1 The Single Market

The single market has long been a governing priority of EU securities and markets regulation. In the wake of the financial crisis, it remains of central importance, although the single market consensus has come under strain.

In the early stages of the crisis, the single market came under threat, with some support for a 'less Europe' approach (based on limited passporting and on market access being limited to locally capitalized and regulated subsidiaries).[214] As the crisis deepened, Commissioner Barnier highlighted the importance of the single market and warned against protectionism.[215] The reform era has ultimately led to a 'More Europe' approach, in the form of the new rulebook and related institutional reforms. But a related re-conceptualization of the single market has taken place, with the remarkable FSAP consensus on the benefits of a single, deep, and liquid financial market being replaced by a more sober realization of the fiscal risks of integration.

This recognition of the risks of the single market has been accompanied, nonetheless, by continued policy support for the integration project. From an early stage in the crisis, the Commission identified the single market as a 'lever for recovery' and warned against protectionism.[216] The Commission's 2010 European Financial Stability and Integration Report similarly highlighted financial market integration as a 'major policy objective' of the EU, and underlined the benefits in terms of cost reduction, instruments which met investor

---

[211] The cornerstone 2003 Prospectus Directive has been reformed (Directive 2010/73/EU [2010] OJ L327/1), as has the 2004 Transparency Directive, which governs ongoing disclosure (Directive 2013/50/EU [2013] OJ L294/13) and the related accounting regime (Directive 2013/34/EU [2013] OJ L182/19). These reforms are broadly designed to streamline the relevant regulatory regimes, to bring greater efficiencies to the capital-raising process, and to respond to market innovation.

[212] Regulation (EU) No 596/2014 [2014] OJ L173/1 (2014 MAR) and Directive 2014/57/EU OJ [2014] L173/179 (2014 MAD) (on the implementation timeline see Ch VIII nn 3 and 4).

[213] COM (2012) 350 (the 'UCITS V' reforms, which focus in particular on the UCITS depositary): the reforms were agreed by the Council and European Parliament in February 2014 (Council Document 7411/14, 13 March 2014 (not yet published in the OJ)). A wide-ranging UCITS VI reform agenda has also been presented: Commission, UCITS. Product Rules, Liquidity Management, Depositary, Money Market Funds and Long-term investments (2012).

[214] 2009 Turner Review, n 16, 101–2.

[215] Speech by Commissioner Barnier on 'Financial Services in Europe—Where Next?', 31 March 2010.

[216] Commission, Driving European Recovery (2009) (COM (2009) 114) 10–11.

and issuer needs, better risk diversification, and easier access to finance.[217] Its 2011 Report, following unprecedented turmoil in euro-area sovereign debt markets, argued that economic and financial integration was not an obstacle to stability and that 'financial integration delivers huge benefits and has been a key source of economic growth'.[218] In 2012, the ECB likewise strongly supported integration and its benefits for households and firms, and called for continued policy support.[219] The Council adopted a similar approach, suggesting that the 'balanced development' of the EU financial system required regulatory reform but also greater financial integration.[220] This institutional support for the single financial market reflects the EU's wider 2011 'Single Market Act' project,[221] which is designed to combat 'integration fatigue' post-crisis. But amid the seemingly irrepressible dynamism of the single market movement, there is evidence of a more measured approach. The 2010 European Financial Stability and Integration Report also called for integration to deepen at 'more sustainable pace', and related the 'rapid convergence' pre-crisis to the credit boom and misperceptions regarding credit risk.[222]

The financial crisis has accordingly not dealt a fatal blow to the integration project, although integration has become strongly associated with the containment of risk. But while liberalization has taken a back seat to market protection, it remains a feature of the regulatory regime. The new fund vehicles for venture capital, social entrepreneurship, and long-term capital funds, for example, are designed to support market access. The 2012 EMIR, to take another example, seeks to support competition among CCPs in the clearing of derivatives, while the new 2014 MiFID II/MiFIR regime is designed to level the playing field between all types of trading venue.

The financial crisis has, however, exposed new lines of tension with respect to the single market, externally and internally.

First, as discussed throughout this book, there are clear indications of something of a 'fortress Europe' agenda in some regulatory spheres.[223] Across much of the new rulebook, the EU has sought to impose its regulatory policies internationally by linking third country access to the single market to onerous, mandatory 'equivalence' requirements which require, in effect, that third country regulation and supervision reflect EU requirements. As discussed in subsequent Chapters, this development is most marked with respect to new areas for EU intervention, notably the rating agency regime, the 2011 AIFMD, the 2012 EMIR, and the new trading rules which apply to derivatives trading under the 2014 MiFID II/MiFIR. But the equivalence assessment is also extending to more settled areas; the 2014 MiFID II/MiFIR regime, for example, imposes a new equivalence regime on the provision of investment services by third country investment firms in the EU. Although the trade negotiations between the US and the EU on a Transatlantic Trade and Investment

---

[217] Commission, European Financial Stability and Integration Report 2010 (2011) (SEC (2011) 489) (2010 EFSIR) 5.

[218] 2011 EFSIR, n 177, 6 and 13.

[219] ECB, Financial Integration in Europe (2012) 31–48.

[220] 2990th Council Meeting, 19 January 2010, ECOFIN Press Release No 5400/10.

[221] Commission, The Single Market Act—Twelve Steps to Boost Growth and Strengthen Confidence (2011) (COM (2011) 206).

[222] n 217, 8.

[223] On the EU's engagement with global financial system governance and with third countries see, eg, Mügge, D (ed), *Europe and the Governance of Global Finance* (2014).

Partnership (TTIP), launched in summer 2013, suggest the beginnings of a more liberal approach,[224] the equivalence model remains a policy preference. The September 2013 proposal for benchmark regulation, for example, proposes that the use of benchmarks provided by non-EU 'benchmark administrators' be subject to an equivalence assessment. Few countries, however, have addressed benchmark regulation; the equivalence mechanism accordingly allows the EU to shape the international response.[225] As discussed in subsequent Chapters, the political and market consequences of this approach to international engagement can be significant.[226]

Second, new tensions have been exposed within the single market. The wider the regulatory perimeter, the greater the risk that EU rules have asymmetric impact across the Member States, given the tendency for financial market segments to concentrate in particular national markets. This is particularly the case with respect to wholesale market regulation, as these markets are concentrated in particular Member States, most notably the UK.[227] The construction of the single financial market has long been attended by competing national interests and tensions as to the nature of financial market regulation. Prior to the financial crisis, these tensions were, broadly, contained; the regulatory programme was generally facilitative and regulatory costs could be offset by market access benefits. But the crisis-era programme is significantly more regulatory in orientation and reaches deep into the wholesale markets. It can more easily be associated with prejudicial regulatory costs and with the differential imposition of regulatory burdens, and has accordingly placed pressure on the single market consensus.

The highly contested Financial Transaction Tax (FTT) Proposal provides a useful example (Chapter VI section 5). The cacophony of protest which the Commission's 2011 FTT Proposal,[228] widely regarded as an anti-speculation measure, prompted in some markets, and the prospect of a veto from a number of Member States, led to its being recast in 2013

---

[224] The EU's negotiating position on financial services is set out in Commission, EU-US Transatlantic Trade and Investment Partnership, Co-operation on Financial Services Regulation, 27 January 2014. The EU is concerned to press for consistent rule-making, mitigation of the unintended effects of necessary inconsistency, and regulatory co-operation based on: joint work on implementation of international standards; mutual consultation on new measures that may significantly affect the provision of financial services between the EU and US; joint examination of existing rules to ascertain barriers to trade; and a commitment to assessing whether the other jurisdiction's rules are equivalent (outcome-based equivalence is a 'core element' of the EU proposal) (at 3).

[225] COM (2013) 641. See further Ch VIII sect 8.2.3.

[226] As is evident from the careful observation by ESMA Chairman Maijoor (ESMA has been very closely engaged with equivalence assessments) that equivalence assessments should move from being designed as binary equivalent/not equivalent assessments and embrace a more nuanced approach which accommodates partial equivalence: Speech on 'International Co-ordination of the Regulation and Supervision of OTC Derivatives Markets', 17 October 2013 (ESMA/2013/1485).

[227] The crisis-era reform programme, increasing tensions between the euro area and the single market, and the reported isolation of the UK during key negotiations (associated with political tensions linked to, eg, the UK veto of proposed revisions to the Treaties in December 2011 related to euro-area governance) have heightened long-standing concerns in the UK as to the impact of EU regulation on the City (eg Thornhill, J and Jenkins, P, 'Ties that Bind', *Financial Times*, 2 April 2013). In 2012, the UK government launched an extensive assessment of the balance of competences between the EU and UK, including with respect to financial services and markets: the major financial market reviews include HM Government (Department of Business Innovation and Skills), Review of the Balance of Competences between the UK and the EU: the Single Market (2013) and 2013 HM Treasury Call for Evidence, n 15.

[228] COM (2011) 594.

as a measure for a smaller group of Member States under the Treaties' Enhanced Co-operation mechanism.[229] But the spillover effects of the FTT outside the 'FTT zone' and on the single market more generally are potentially considerable and have led to the UK challenging the FTT proposal before the Court of Justice.[230] Tensions within the single market can also be identified in the reforms to the regulation of trading venues under the 2014 MiFID II/MiFIR; the UK successfully negotiated a recital statement that no action taken by an NCA or ESMA in the performance of their duties should directly or indirectly discriminate against any Member State or group of Member States as a venue for the provision of investment services and activities in any currency. Similarly, the UK's 2012 challenge to ESMA's powers to impose controls on short selling in national markets,[231] while based on the Treaty limits imposed on agencies, can be associated with a concern to shield the UK wholesale markets from perceived excessive and costly supervision, and with the likely differential impact of such powers on the UK market given the scale of its wholesale market.

The most serious threat to the single market, however, arises in the cognate banking context, and from the euro-area 19/internal market 28 split associated with Banking Union. The likelihood of the 'euro-area 19' acting as a block when it comes to rule-making for the 'internal market 28' is real and poses a potentially serious challenge to the single market.[232] There are, however, some indications of increasing Commission sensitivity to single market tensions, in the banking sphere at least. Its highly contested 2014 proposal for a bank ring-fencing regime allows Member States the possibility to retain more restrictive national regimes, where applicable, to avoid any costly realignment of national rules.[233] Albeit a very different measure and operating in a different context, this facilitative approach stands in contrast to the maximum harmonization approach adopted to own funds/capital requirements, which has generated hostility on the part of some Member States.[234]

I.5.2 Harmonization and an Ever Expanding Regulatory Perimeter

I.5.2.1 The Location of Control

Over the FSAP era, liberalization-driven regulatory reform in support of cross-border activity saw the location of securities and markets regulation shift to the EU from the Member States. The crisis era has led to the almost complete ascendancy of the EU. This has been driven by a host of factors. The 'single rulebook', initially proposed by the 2009

---

[229] COM (2013) 71. Art 20 TEU and Arts 326–34 TFEU allow Member States to establish 'enhanced co-operation' between themselves within the framework of the EU's non-exclusive competences and to use the EU's institutions and competences to do so, as long as the related Treaty conditions are met.

[230] n 72. The Court of Justice rejected the challenge, primarily on grounds related to the premature nature of the action as an FTT regime had not, at the time of the UK action, been adopted on foot of the Council authorization to engage in enhanced co-operation. A subsequent substantive challenge may, however, follow if/when an FTT regime is adopted.

[231] n 70.

[232] And is reflected in the non-discrimination clause which applies to the SSM: Regulation 1024/2013, n 182, Art 1. See further Ch XI sect 7.

[233] COM (2014) 43.

[234] See Ch IV sect 8.7.

DLG Report, enjoyed early and widespread support from the Member States and the EU institutions. While the EU's supranational actors would always have been expected to support greater uniformity, from an intergovernmental perspective, the rulebook had the potential to act as a hedge against the fiscal risks of cross-border activity and poor supervision; the rulebook consensus might also be associated with a pragmatic transfer by the Member States of the risks associated with financial market regulation at a time of intense crisis. The extensive G20 reform agenda and the EU's related concern to shape the international rulebook also strengthened support for more intensive intervention. The extent to which rule-making power has moved to the EU is well illustrated by the Commission's seizing the initiative when the global interest-rate fixing scandal broke over summer 2012 and producing related proposals for reform.[235]

As discussed throughout this book, the new rulebook is characterized by detailed legislative measures which, more often than not, take the form of a regulation, rather than a directive, in order to avoid implementation risks.[236] This is perhaps best exemplified by the behemoth 2014 MiFID II/MiFIR and 2013 CRD IV/CRR regimes which, together, form the twin pillars of the massive EU regime governing the authorization and prudential and conduct regulation of investment firms and credit institutions. In each case, a directive (albeit of great detail), which accommodates some degree of implementation flexibility, is partnered with a regulation, which applies directly in the Member States and which addresses the matters on which uniformity of application is essential. In addition, extensive delegations to administrative rule-making have been conferred across the new rulebook; a dense administrative rulebook, which dwarfs that constructed over the FSAP era, is under development. The new rulebook is also characterized by extensive reliance on ESMA-produced soft law which is 'hardened' through 'comply or explain' mechanisms. In many respects, ESMA, which is examined across the book, may come to be the defining influence on the future development of EU securities and markets regulation given the very many channels through which it can exert influence.

I.5.2.2 The Breadth of the Rulebook

The preoccupation with financial stability over the financial crisis, and the recharacterization of the single market in terms of risk, has led to the regulatory function of EU securities and markets regulation trumping the liberalization function. A vast new rulebook has followed. The perimeter of EU securities and markets regulation surrounds a much wider set of market participants. An array of asset managers (under the 2011 AIFMD), proprietary traders and dealers (under the 2014 MiFID II/MiFIR), previously unregulated OTC markets (under MiFID II/MIFIR and the 2012 EMIR), and rating agencies (CRA I-III), for example, are now within the EU rulebook. A much wider range of asset classes and a host of trading venues have also been pulled in: the combined effect of MiFID II/MiFIR, the 2012 Short Selling Regulation, and EMIR, for example, is to impose an entirely new and detailed rulebook for derivatives trading in the EU which, for the most part, had largely

---

[235] Commission Proposals COM (2011) 651 and COM (2011) 654 (both bringing benchmark manipulation within the EU's market abuse regime) and COM (2013) 641 (proposing a general benchmark regulation regime). See further Ch VIII sect 8.2.3.

[236] eg, the 2012 EMIR and the 2012 Short Selling Regulation take the form of regulations. Elsewhere, regulations have been deployed where powers have been conferred on ESMA, given the need for uniformity with respect to ESMA's powers (notably under the credit rating agency regime).

been disciplined through market dynamics prior to the crisis. Entities which do not participate in the financial markets professionally but which engage in incidental financial activities are also being pulled into the regulatory net; EMIR and MiFID II/MiFIR, for example, have led to the imposition of rules on non-financial entities which use derivatives as hedging tools for their commercial business. The regulatory agenda in the funds sphere (2009 UCITS Directive/2011 AIFMD) appears unstoppable; the 2014 UCITS V reforms are likely to be followed by a series of reforms addressing issues arising from the shadow banking agenda. The re-emergence of market liberalization as the reform programme began to recede, over 2012–13 in particular, has led to a further suite of actors, notably certain types of fund vehicles, being pulled within the rulebook, albeit on an opt-in basis.

I.5.2.3 Correction and Review

Financial market integration will always be a goal of EU securities and markets regulation, however troublesome the causal relationship between a facilitative EU legal infrastructure and cross-border activity. But, given its ascendancy, the success of EU securities and markets regulation is now largely a function of its ability to meet traditional regulatory goals with respect to the support of financial market stability; market efficiency, transparency, and fairness; and investor protection, both for national markets and in the cross-border context.

The institutions appear relatively sanguine. The ESAs, for example, regard the new regulatory framework as providing a resilient framework for the EU financial sector generally.[237] But regulation of this ambition, range, depth, and intensity places great pressure on the EU rule-making process. Of the very many challenges which arise, two can be highlighted.

Careful calibration is required given the differential impact which rules of this range and intensity can have on market actors, based on their size, complexity, and business model. Second, unintended consequences, which can include a reduction in market efficiency where regulatory costs prejudice risk management and thereby liquidity, can be significant. There is considerable uncertainty as to the cumulative impact of the reform programme generally on the availability, for example, of the high-quality collateral (or assets) now required to secure a range of different transactions.[238]

Review is required. As discussed throughout this book, the complex process through which EU securities and markets regulation emerges makes the already difficult process of rule-making for financial markets all the more challenging.[239] It remains to be seen whether the new rulebook will have prejudicial effects, although some indications augur well.[240] But it

---

[237] ESA Joint Committee, Report on Risks and Vulnerabilities in the Financial Sector (2013) (JC/2013-010) 7.

[238] The cumulative impact of the G20 reform programme on the stock of global high-quality collateral has become a recurring theme of the international policy debate. The Commission has also raised concerns: 2012 EFSIR, n 180, 26.

[239] One analysis has identified the following challenges: the introduction of national interest-driven exemptions; ensuring the proportionality of rules; ensuring appropriate economic analysis; ensuring rules facilitate new technologies and innovation; setting the level of harmonization appropriately; choosing the optimum form of intervention (regulation or directive); assessing the appropriateness of EU intervention; and ensuring the rule-making process is robust: 2013 HM Treasury Call for Evidence, n 15, 19.

[240] ESMA has reported that the 2012 Short Selling Regulation, despite some febrile speculation as to its potentially prejudicial effects, did not have material adverse effects on market liquidity and price discovery (Ch VI sect 3).

seems clear that an effective capacity to correct and calibrate is critical. The extensive review clauses[241] to which all crisis-era measures are subject (and which were initially used over the FSAP period) provide a means for releasing political tensions during the negotiating process. But they also hold the promise of useful *ex-post* review. The Commission has committed to reviewing the new regime,[242] while in 2013 the European Parliament pressed for such review to commence.[243] ESMA has significantly enhanced the EU's technical capacity at the administrative rule-making level, and has demonstrated its ability to corral complex market data, engage with market stakeholders, liaise with international standard-setters, and adopt complex rules. ESMA has also opened a safety valve in that it has shown itself capable of providing temporary 'soft law' mitigations where confusion and the risk of prejudice to market efficiency arise. But correction at the legislative level is likely to remain necessary, given the scale of the crisis-era rulebook—whether or not the law-making process can cope with large-scale refinements and recalibrations remains to be seen.

I.5.3 Market Finance and Market Integration

I.5.3.1 Market Finance

Since the start of the FSAP era, market finance has become embedded within the EU and a related intensification of market-based intermediation and of financial market activity generally has occurred, although the extent to which this is related to the regulatory programme is contested. In 2002, as the FSAP began to unfold, more sophisticated products had developed, securitization activity had increased, the corporate sector was embracing market finance to a greater extent,[244] and the household sector had become more engaged with the financial markets.[245] Nonetheless, bank-based financing remained dominant, with bank lending the chief source of external finance in the EU in 2004.[246]

Subsequently—and as discussed in later Chapters—the asset management sector enjoyed strong growth, trading volumes increased, issuers relied more heavily on market-based

---

[241] Which typically set a date (usually within 2–3 years of the measure coming into force) by which the measure must be reviewed and identify the particular issues which the review must address; these issues usually include contested measures at the time of the original negotiations as well as proposals for future action.

[242] It originally promised a 'fundamental review' of the crisis-era reforms in 2014, although by the end of 2013 a number of key measures had only just been adopted: Commission, Regulating Financial Services for Sustainable Growth, A Progress Report—February 2011 (2011). An initial survey was published in May 2014 (Commission, A Reformed Financial Sector for Europe (2014) (COM (2014) 279) and accompanying Staff Working Document (SWD (2014) 158)). The Commission argued that financial reform inevitably leads to economic costs for financial intermediaries, noted that a significant element of the costs related to transitional adjustment costs, and highlighted the mitigating strategies which had been adopted, including with respect to phase-in periods, exemptions, and review procedures. Given its timing, the survey was broadly qualitative but the Commission committed to ongoing review of the new regime.

[243] European Parliament, Resolution on Financial Services. Lack of Progress in the Council and Commission Delay in the Adoption of Certain Proposals, 13 June 2013 (P7-TA (2010) 0276). It also commissioned an early-stage review of the banking reforms: Directorate General for Internal Policies, Economic and Monetary Affairs Committee, Assessment of the Cumulative Impact of Various Regulatory Initiatives on the European Banking Sector (IP/A/ECON/ST/2010-21) (2011).

[244] 2002 London Economics Report, n 57, 5.

[245] 2002 London Economics Report, n 57, 1.

[246] At 109.6% of EU GDP for the (then) EU-15: Commission, Financial Integration Monitor (2004) (SEC (2004) 559) (2004 FIM).

funding and, overall, intermediation increased and markets became more complete, with an ever-increasing array of risk management products being used to diversify risk;[247] in particular, banks were securitizing their loan portfolios. In 2007, immediately prior to the crisis, the ECB's 2007 Report on Financial Integration reported on a significant increase in market finance opportunities and on the continued development of corporate bond and equity markets.[248] EU stock market capitalization as a proportion of GDP rose over 2004–7,[249] narrowing the still significant gap with the US.[250]

The crisis era provides vivid evidence of the extent to which market intensity has deepened and market-based intermediation has developed. The extensive monitoring since the early days of the crisis of financial stability in the EU[251] paints a clear picture of the extent to which market-based intermediation has become embedded, and, accordingly, of the extent to which financial markets have come to threaten the stability of the wider EU financial system. The ECB's six-monthly Financial Stability Reviews, for example, have, since 2008, highlighted the ongoing fragility of the EU financial market and the risks it poses to overall system stability arising from, for example, sovereign debt markets, shadow banking, financial innovation, and volatility in particular market segments, notably the money-market segment. ESMA's first (February 2013) report on 'Trends, Risks, and Vulnerabilities' similarly underlined the scale of market finance and of related intermediation in the EU.[252] It examined risks to the financial system from markets (including liquidity, contagion, market, and credit risks) and assessed activity in and risks from securities markets (including equity, sovereign bond, corporate bond, money market, and structured retail product markets); commodities markets; derivatives markets; wholesale market investor activity (including by traditional funds, alternative investment funds, exchange-traded funds, and money-market funds); retail investor activity; and market infrastructures, including trading venues and CCPs. Its refined second report (September 2013) extended the examination to include covered bond and securitization markets, and additionally addressed securities lending, short selling, and the risks posed by financial benchmarks.[253] The Joint Committee of the ESAs has highlighted, for example, risks arising from increased reliance on and demand for high-quality collateral (increasingly mandated by measures such as the 2012 EMIR but also increasingly being sought by market actors following a loss of trust in credit ratings) and increased interconnections between markets and institutions as collateral is used and re-used, the need for strong risk disclosures by financial institutions,

---

[247] Firms' recourse to market-based funding, a key indicator of the strength of the market finance model, is considered in Ch II sect 9.

[248] ECB, Financial Integration in Europe (2007) 31.

[249] It grew from 71.4% of EU GDP in 2004 to 73.7%, 91.9%, and 91.9% in 2005, 2006, and 2007 respectively. World Bank Data, available at: <http://data.worldbank.org/indicator/CM.MKT.LCAP.GD.ZS?order=wbapi_data_value_2007+wbapi_data_value+wbapi_data_value-last&sort=asc&page=1>.

[250] In 2004, US stock market capitalization as a percentage of GDP was 138.4%. By 2007 it was 142.9%: World Bank Data, n 249.

[251] The interlinkages between markets and the financial system generally are now regularly monitored by a range of EU actors, including the ECB (through its six-monthly Financial Stability Reviews), the ESAs (including through ESMA's regular Trends, Risks, and Vulnerabilities Reports (TRVs)), and the ESRB.

[252] ESMA, Report on Trends, Risks, and Vulnerabilities. Report No 1 2013 (2013) (ESMA/2013/212) (ESMA 2013(1) TRV).

[253] ESMA 2013(2) TRV, n 53. The third report (ESMA 2014(1) TRV) continued to refine the indicators deployed and examined vulnerabilities arising from, *inter alia*, central securities depositaries.

and the risks posed by misconduct with respect to financial benchmarks.[254] Similarly, the ESRB has warned of risks from CCPs, sovereign debt exposures, money-market funds, and intra-financial sector interconnectedness arising from securities lending and repurchase activities and the shadow banking sector.[255]

In terms of firm funding sources, while EU firms remain dependent on bank finance, the crisis-era contraction in bank lending, investors' search-for-yield efforts, and the low cost of issuing longer-term high-yield bonds can all be associated with the emerging evidence of a stronger EU corporate bond market,[256] which has led the Commission to suggest increased firm reliance (in the financial sector at least) on market-based funding.[257]

The development of market finance and the related impact of the financial crisis has had two effects on EU securities and markets regulation. First, a strong anti-speculation agenda has emerged in some Member States, as has a related concern to dampen levels of intermediation and innovation. Similarly, the Commission has supported something of a 'regulatory rethink'—including with respect to intense financial innovation—and called for a financial sector that supports job creation and sustainable growth,[258] and identified a positive relationship between financial innovation and overall welfare as an indicator of progress on the reform agenda,[259] while the European Parliament has frequently shown itself to be sceptical of intense financial markets, and particularly of derivatives and related financial innovation.[260] The ECB has also repeatedly highlighted the risks of financial innovation and called for strong monitoring,[261] as has the ESRB.[262] While this zeitgeist has shaped regulation in a number of ways, as discussed across the book, it has also led to institutional change: all the ESAs were charged with establishing 'financial innovation committees' which would support a co-ordinated approach to 'new and innovative activities' and advise the EU legislators accordingly.[263]

Second, and while the crisis-era anti-speculation agenda and the ascendancy of a more market-sceptical style of EU regulation might suggest otherwise, policy support for market-based funding of firms remains strong, reflecting the contraction in bank funding and the persistent dominance of bank funding over market funding (some 70 per cent of EU funding is bank-based as compared to 20 per cent in the US). As the crisis reform agenda began to reach its closing stages, the Commission launched a major policy initiative

---

[254] n 237.

[255] ESRB, Annual Report (2012) 15.

[256] eg ECB, Financial Stability Review, May 2013 (2013) 43. See further Ch II sect 9. The rapid growth in bond funding has been described as moving the EU financial system closer to the UK market-based system: Atkins, R and Stothard, M, 'A Change of Gear', *Financial Times*, 1 July 2013, 9.

[257] 2011 EFSIR, n 177, 32 and 2013 ESFIR, n 53, 13 and 24–25.

[258] EU Internal Market Commissioner Barnier, Speech on 'Restoring Trust in the Financial Sector', 26 April 2010.

[259] 2010 EFSIR, n 217, 51.

[260] eg European Parliament, Resolution on Derivatives Markets: Future Policy Actions, 15 June 2010 (P7_TA(2010)0206).

[261] eg ECB, Financial Stability Review, May 2013, 10.

[262] See further Ch XI sect 6.

[263] Early indications suggest the ESAs are taking this mandate seriously. The EBA financial innovation standing committee, eg, produced a report in early 2012 which identified potentially harmful innovations, including collateralized commercial paper and convertible bonds, which were in need of further examination (EBA, Financial Innovation and Consumer Protection (2012)) while ESMA has focused closely on the emerging risks posed by shadow banking, eg, including exchange-traded funds: ESMA 2013(1) TRV (n 252).

designed to strengthen financial markets as a source of long-term funding and to stabilize and diversify sources of funding. The 2013 Long-Term Financing Green Paper[264] queried whether the EU's long-standing and heavy dependence on bank-based intermediation for long-term funding would give way to reliance on more diversified market funding sources (including institutional investors and alternative financial markets), and proposed a range of reforms to support market-based funding.[265] The tentative moves towards supporting alternative market-based funding mechanisms (such as crowdfunding platforms) can also be associated with this agenda, as can the more longstanding but recently refreshed agenda to support market-based SME funding (Chapter II).

I.5.3.2 Financial Market Integration

Financial market integration has also deepened, as discussed in subsequent Chapters. As the FSAP drew to a close, the Commission began to grapple with the complexities of quantifying financial market integration,[266] albeit somewhat belatedly,[267] and has since produced a series of annual reports on integration.[268] They focus in particular on cross-border capital flows, convergence in asset pricing,[269] and the provision of financial services through branches and subsidiaries. Since 2005, the ECB has also produced an annual report on integration in the euro area.[270]

The Commission's first (2004) Financial Integration Monitor reported that while integration was progressing, it varied across market sectors, with the unsecured money market and the market for consumer loans representing the strongest and weakest ends of the spectrum; liquidity was pooling for common tradable assets, bond yields were converging, and equity returns were becoming increasingly sensitive to EU rather than local shocks.[271] Although a home bias persisted, a significant proportion of trading occurred cross-border, with non-residents representing 20 per cent of shares traded in almost all European exchanges.[272] Financial institutions were increasingly becoming organized on an EU basis, while professional investment horizons were becoming increasingly EU in nature.[273] The 2007 report

---

[264] n 207.

[265] The Commission highlighted the need for 'other intermediaries to complement the role of banks by channeling financing to long-term investments in a more productive way': 2013 Long-Term Financing Green Paper, n 207, 7–8. The Green Paper was followed by a March 2014 Commission Communication on Long-Term Financing of the European Economy (COM (2014) 168), which set out a policy agenda for promoting the EU capital market and included measures designed to strengthen the corporate bond and equity markets.

[266] The Commission's 2007 European Financial Integration Report characterized an integrated market in general terms as one in which prices for similar products and services converged across geographical borders and where supply and demand could react immediately to cross-border price differences: Commission, European Financial Integration Report 2007 (2007) (SEC (2007) 1690) (2007 EFIR) 8.

[267] Following a July 2000 Council request that the Commission propose indicators of progress towards an integrated financial services sector.

[268] Which have gone through a number of iterations: Financial Integration Monitors (FIMs), European Financial Integration Reports (EFIRs) and, most recently, European Financial Stability and Integration Reports (EFSIRs).

[269] The extent to which asset prices are based on common factors (and related levels of price dispersion or convergence) is a key variable for quantifying levels of integration and is relied on heavily by the Commission.

[270] The ECB Financial Integration in Europe reports focus in particular on asset price convergence/divergence and quantitative volume indicators (with respect to cross-border activity) in the bond, money market, and equity segments, and on cross-border banking/loan activity.

[271] 2004 FIM, n 246, 4.

[272] 2004 FIM, n 246.

[273] 2004 FIM, n 246, 9.

also reported good progress in integration in the wholesale sector, and noted that financial services providers, large clients, and institutional investors were operating on a pan-European scale. It reported on increasing correlation in equity market returns, continuing convergence in bond yields, and a (limited) weakening of the home bias.[274] But while EU bond markets had deepened, equity market liquidity remained fragmented.[275] Similarly, a 2011 review related to the MiFID I Review reported that between 2006 and 2009, between 30 per cent and 70 per cent of equity investments (managed by institutional investors in major financial centres) were allocated to domestic securities.[276]

The financial crisis led to a material retrenchment and a reappearance of the home bias,[277] with a significant contraction in cross-border activity (in terms of reduced cross-border capital flows and a greater dispersion in asset prices)[278] and a retreat to domestic markets, as reported by the Commission for 2008, 2009, and 2010.[279] The Commission's 2010 review, however, also suggested that the main cross-border channels for integration remained in place (including cross-border subsidiaries and branches and cross-border membership of trading platforms) and predicted a more sustainable pace of integration. But in 2011, with the euro-area sovereign debt crisis intensifying, the Commission reported that the financial integration process had been halted or reversed in some segments;[280] it highlighted, however, that financial firms had largely preserved their cross-border presence and that the integration of market infrastructures was progressing.[281] By the fifth year of the financial crisis (2012), the Commission's review focused mainly on financial stability, but reported on continuing market fragmentation.[282] ECB euro-area assessments have been similar. The ECB's 2011 financial integration report, for example, noted the initial domestic retrenchment over 2007–8 but also an underlying trend towards integration, despite the financial crisis, and suggested that while bond and money-market integration, in

---

[274] 2007 EFIR, n 266, 8–9.

[275] 2007 EFIR, n 266, 31–2.

[276] Oxera, Monitoring Prices, Costs, and Volumes of Trading and Post-Trading Services. Report for the Commission (2011).

[277] The Joint Committee of the ESAs reported in 2013 that the 'process of EU and Euro area financial integration and cross-border banking has stalled': ESA Joint Committee, Report on Risks and Vulnerabilities (2013), n 237, 12.

[278] Although the ESAs have related this to a realignment of risk assessments (particularly with respect to sovereign debt) and suggested that the wider integrity of the single market and its legal and institutional infrastructure has not been impaired: ESA Joint Committee, Report on Risks and Vulnerabilities (2013), n 237, 14. Sovereign debt spreads in particular have moved to reflect Member-State-specific risk rather than, as before the crisis, market determinations of euro-area risk generally: 2011 EFSIR, n 177, 9.

[279] The Commission was relatively sanguine in its review of 2008, noting that while a reversal of integration trends was taking place, it was not likely to be permanent (Commission, European Financial Integration Report 2008 (2009) (SEC (2009) 19) (2008 EFIR)). In its review of 2009, the Commission was generally optimistic, noting an improvement in the main integration indicators, and particularly with respect to pan-EU convergence in the cost of capital (Commission, European Financial Integration Report 2009 (2010) (SEC (2009) 1702) (2009 EFIR)). The Commission's review of 2010, however, reflected the impact of severe turbulence in the sovereign debt markets and related reverses in the sovereign debt, money, and credit markets, and reported that integration of financial markets was 'at a stand still' with respect to cross-border financial flows and convergence in pricing: 2010 EFSIR, n 217, 8.

[280] 2011 EFSIR, n 177, 6 and 45. The Commission reported that since the crisis and over 2011 cross-border capital flows had fallen sharply. It described the 2011 intensification of the sovereign debt crisis as 'putting a halt to and in some cases reversing capital flows and financial integration and threatening the foundations of monetary integration': at 8.

[281] 2011 EFSIR, n 177.

[282] n 180.

particular, were experiencing difficulties, the crisis should not endanger the long-term trend to integrate.[283] The 2012 report noted a 'marked deterioration' in financial integration[284] but reported that the bond markets had suffered most damage, with the impact on equity markets more limited.[285]

Integration remains fragile, although some signs of improvement are emerging. In 2013, the ECB reported on continuing fragmentation in the bond and money markets[286] and on outflows from certain euro-area securities, but in 2014 it saw some signs of improvement.[287] Recent Commission assessments have been similar.[288]

The retrenchment over the financial crisis underscores the array of non-legal factors which drive cross-border integration. But the commitment to financial market integration remains very strong, albeit now typically articulated in terms of financial stability support, rather than liberalization.

---

[283] ECB, Financial Integration in Europe (2011) 7. It reported that equity markets had been less affected by the crisis and that cross-border investment levels remained strong, with almost 40% of equity holdings of euro-area residents issued in other euro-area Member States (22–4).

[284] ECB, Financial Integration in Europe (2012) 8.

[285] ECB, Financial Integration in Europe (2012) 9 and 25–6.

[286] ECB, Financial Integration in Europe (2013) 9–10 and 15–16, noting a home bias and a high level of dispersion in the money markets and varying patterns of bond issuance across the euro-area Member States.

[287] The ECB reported that bond market integration was showing signs of 'slight improvement', that the level of integration in the sovereign debt market was showing a 'clear improvement', and that equity market integration was improving, but that significant financial fragmentation remained: ECB, Financial Integration in Europe (2014) 9.

[288] In April 2014 the Commission found that the European economic and financial area was substantially more segmented on national lines as compared to 2007–8, and an increased home bias and weaker pan-EU diversification, but that improvements were emerging (including with respect to the sovereign debt market): 2013 EFSIR, n 53, 12–53.

II

CAPITAL-RAISING

II.1 Introduction

II.1.1 Introduction

This Chapter addresses the harmonized EU rules which govern capital-raising through the markets by firms (market finance).[1] As EU capital-raising regulation is largely a function of the rules which apply to the disclosures required of firms when they sell securities to the public, it is primarily concerned with disclosure regulation.[2]

The regulation of capital-raising through the markets engages a number of policy objectives (section 2.1). Its primary objective is to ensure the efficiency of the securities markets in allocating capital to firms offering securities (issuers) and to reduce the cost of capital and the related regulatory frictions for such issuers seeking market-based funding through securities issuance.[3] In so doing, regulation typically distinguishes between the public markets, subject to the highest levels of regulation, and the private markets in which issuers raise finance from, usually, sophisticated investors (although the recent development of techniques such as crowdfunding has seen a private retail market emerge), which are less intensively regulated. Within the regulated sphere, disclosure is the dominant regulatory mechanism deployed internationally;[4] capital-raising regulation is largely concerned with 'truth-telling' by issuers and the related removal of 'lemons'—or poorly performing issuers—from the marketplace.[5] Mandatory issuer-disclosure rules typically require issuers to make comprehensive disclosures to the market on the initial raising of funds, on a regular basis thereafter, and at particular points, usually linked to the occurrence of material events.

The nature of disclosure regulation reflects multiple determinative factors. These include the extent to which market finance is embedded within the economy in question, the

---

[1] On the distinction between bank and market finance see Ch I and sect 2.2.2.

[2] This Chapter does not accordingly address the background company law and corporate governance requirements which apply to firms. See further Armour, J and Ringe, WG, 'European Company Law 1999–2010: Renaissance and Crisis' (2011) 48 *CMLR* 125 and Enriques, L and Gatti, M, 'The Uneasy Case for Top-Down Corporate Law Harmonization in the European Union' (2006) 27 *UPaJIEL* 939.

[3] Choi, S, 'Law, Finance and Path Dependence. Developing Strong Securities Markets' (2002) 80 *Texas LR* 1657.

[4] Black, B, 'The Legal and Institutional Preconditions for Strong Securities Markets' (2001) 48 *UCLA LR* 781, relating the 'magical' process whereby intangible securities can be used to raise capital to disclosure and to the different institutions (such as auditors, investment analysts, rating agencies, and trading venues) which support effective disclosure.

[5] Langevoort, D, 'Global Securities Regulation after the Financial Crisis' (2011) 13 *JIEL* 799.

impact of the international market and related competitiveness risks, the relative size and strength of private capital markets, the extent to which recourse by small and medium-sized enterprises (SMEs) to market finance is supported, and the relative importance of the retail investor constituency. In the EU, all of these influences are at play, but the dominant influence on regulatory design is the overarching market-integration imperative.

Regulation in this field also addresses the venues on which securities, once issued in the primary markets, are traded in the secondary markets. In the EU, admission of securities to trading on a 'regulated market' and admission to 'official listing' are subject to requirements designed to support issuer disclosure and to ensure that there is sufficient liquidity in the securities traded.[6]

II.1.2 The EU Regime

The crisis era has left a mark on the regulation of capital-raising in the EU. Nonetheless, regulation remains largely based on the earlier Financial Services Action Plan (FSAP)-era[7] reforms. At the heart of the regime is the foundation 2003 Prospectus Directive,[8] as amended by the 2010 Amending Prospectus Directive,[9] which imposes prospectus requirements on issuers offering securities to the public and on issuers whose securities are or will be admitted to trading on a 'regulated market'. A dense administrative rulebook also applies. The 2003 Prospectus Directive was first amplified by the massive 2004 Commission Prospectus Regulation, which sets out the detail of the issuer-disclosure regime.[10]

The related transparency regime imposes ongoing disclosure obligations on issuers through the 2004 Transparency Directive, as amended by the 2013 Amending Transparency Directive.[11] The 2004 Directive was initially amplified at the administrative level by the 2007 Commission Transparency Requirements Directive[12] and by a 2007 Commission Recommendation on the dissemination of ongoing disclosures.[13] The 2014 Market Abuse Regulation (2014 MAR) imposes *ad hoc* disclosure obligations on issuers related to the disclosure of material information.[14]

---

[6] Reflecting the fact that '[t]he economic function of the trading markets is to create liquidity—a market characteristic that enables investors to dispose of or purchase securities at a price reasonably related to the preceding price'; Poser, N, 'Restructuring the Stock Markets: A Critical Look at the SEC's National Market System' (1981) 56 *NYULR* 884, 886.

[7] Commission Communication on Implementing the Framework for Financial Markets: Action Plan, COM (1999) 232 (the Financial Service Action Plan (FSAP)).

[8] Directive 2003/71/EC [2003] OJ L345/64.

[9] Directive 2010/73/EU [2010] OJ L327/1.

[10] Commission Regulation (EC) No 809/2004 [2004] OJ L149/1 (2004 Commission Prospectus Regulation).

[11] Directive 2004/109/EC [2004] OJ L390/38, as amended by Directive 2013/50/EU [2013] OJ L294/13. Specific corporate-governance-orientated disclosure requirements apply under the shareholders' rights regime (n 521) and under the financial reporting regime.

[12] Commission Directive 2007/14/EC [2007] OJ L69/27.

[13] [2007] OJ L267/16.

[14] The new market abuse regime is set out in Regulation (EU) No 596/2014 [2014] OJ L173/1 (the 2014 MAR) which replaces Directive 2003/6/EC [2003] OJ L96/16 (the 2003 Market Abuse Directive (2003 MAD I). On the 2014 MAR implementation timeline see Chapter VIII n 3.

While the scope of each of the prospectus, transparency, and market abuse regimes is not identical, the regulatory perimeter is, broadly, cast around issuers of equity and debt securities and derivatives who make a public offer of their financial instruments or who seek the admission of their financial instruments to a regulated market in the EU and, thereafter, whose financial instruments trade on a regulated market in the EU.

Financial reporting is governed by the 2002 IAS Regulation,[15] which requires that consolidated accounts for issuers admitted to trading on a regulated market be presented in accordance with International Accounting Standards (IAS)/International Financial Reporting Standards (IFRS).[16]

The admission to trading of securities on a regulated market is governed by the 2014 MiFID II/MiFIR regime.[17] Although the 'admission to official listing' concept has been largely overtaken, a small subset of rules continues to govern 'official listing' under the 2001 Consolidated Admission Requirements Directive 2001.[18]

The prospectus regime is dynamic. At the legislative level, the 2003 Prospectus Directive was first reformed by the 2010 Omnibus I Directive, which revised the original (2003) delegations to administrative rule-making to reflect the establishment of the European Securities and Markets Authority (ESMA) and the Lisbon Treaty settlement on administrative rule-making.[19] More substantive revisions were made under the 2010 Amending Prospectus Directive, while the 2014 Omnibus II Directive provides for additional delegations to administrative rule-making.[20] New administrative rules have also followed under the prospectus regime. The 2004 Commission Regulation was originally revised in 2006 with respect to the disclosure required of particular issuers[21] and in 2007 with respect to the financial reporting regime.[22] A series of new Commission Regulations followed in 2012[23]

---

[15] Regulation (EC) No 1606/2002 [2002] OJ L243/1.

[16] As discussed in sect 6, IAS are being replaced by IFRS (the term IFRS will be used unless the context demands otherwise).

[17] Markets in Financial Instruments Directive 2014/65/EU [2014] OJ L173/349 (2014 MiFID II) and Markets in Financial Instruments Regulation (EU) No 600/2014 OJ [2014] L173/84 (2014 MiFIR) (on the implementation timeline see Ch IV n 28). The discussion of the EU's admission rules in this Chapter is based on the 2014 MiFID II/MiFIR. The MiFID I regime (Directive 2004/39/EC OJ [2004] L145/1), on which the MiFID II/MiFIR regime is based, will be repealed when the MiFID II/MiFIR regime is applied (from 3 January 2017 (MiFID II Art 94 and MiFIR Art 55)). Reference is made to the MiFID I regime as appropriate.

[18] Directive 2001/34/EC [2001] OJ L184/1.

[19] Directive 2010/78/EU [2010] OJ L331/120. The Prospectus Directive was also reformed earlier in 2008 to incorporate earlier changes to the delegations to administrative rule-making (Directive 2008/11/EC [2008] OJ L76/37) but the 2008 changes were overridden by the Lisbon Treaty settlement on administrative rule-making and the establishment of the European Securities and Markets Authority (ESMA). See further Ch X sects 4 and 5 on administrative rule-making.

[20] Directive 2014/51/EU [2014] OJ L153/1. The Directive is primarily concerned with revisions to the 'Solvency II' insurance regime.

[21] Commission Regulation (EC) No 1787/2006 [2006] OJ L337/17 (on the disclosure required of issuers with complex financial histories or significant financial commitments).

[22] Commission Regulation (EC) No 211/2007 [2007] OJ L61/24. The Regulation extended the time period within which third country issuers could rely on third country financial reporting requirements, rather than on IFRS, in preparing financial reports under the Prospectus Directive, pending the adoption of a decision on the equivalence of third country GAAP with IFRS.

[23] Commission Delegated Regulation (EU) No 486/2012 [2012] OJ L150/1 (ESMA Final Advice/2011/323), addressing the format and content of the prospectus, the base prospectus, the summary and final terms; and Commission Delegated Regulation (EU) No 862/2012 [2012] OJ L256/4 (ESMA Final Advice/2012/137),

and 2013,[24] adopted under the standard Commission-driven process for administrative rule-making. The first set of ESMA-proposed Binding Technical Standards (BTSs) were proposed in 2013.[25]

The transparency regime is similarly dynamic. The 2004 Directive was reformed initially by the 2010 Omnibus I Directive (primarily to reflect the establishment of ESMA), and since by first the 2010 Amending Prospectus Directive, which aligned the Transparency and Prospectus Directives following the 2010 reforms to the prospectus regime, and second the 2013 Amending Transparency Directive. The 2003 Market Abuse Directive, which originally governed *ad hoc* disclosure, has since been replaced by the 2014 MAR. The IFRS regime has also experienced frequent reform, albeit that the reform process is driven by the International Accounting Standards Board (IASB) (section 6).

The capital-raising regime also includes the extensive soft law measures which were adopted by the Committee of European Securities Regulators (CESR) and which since 2011 have been adopted by its successor, ESMA, to support national competent authorities (NCAs) in particular. These are examined in the relevant sections later in the Chapter.[26]

II.2 The Capital-raising Process, Regulation, and the EU

II.2.1 Regulating Capital-raising and Issuer Disclosure

II.2.1.1 Regulating Capital-raising: the Regulatory Context

As discussed in Chapter I, the market-finance-based economic model is associated with market-based funding of firms through the issuance of securities. While the financial crisis has led to some questioning of the efficacy and role of the public equity markets, in particular, it has not led to a retreat from policy support of the market finance model as an effective means of financing firm and economic growth generally[27]—notwithstanding concerns as to the threats which potentially excessive intermediation, innovation, and financialization can pose to the efficiency of markets as funding mechanisms.[28]

---

addressing consent to use the prospectus, information on underlying indices, and the report required, where necessary, of an independent accountant.

  [24] Commission Delegated Regulation (EU) No 759/2013 [2013] OJ L213/1 (ESMA Final Advice/2013/864), addressing the disclosure requirements for convertible and exchangeable debt securities.

  [25] ESMA's first proposed BTSs focused on the prospectus supplement (ESMA/2013/1970) and were adopted as Commission Delegated Regulation (EU) No 382/2014 [2014] OJ L111/36.

  [26] The scale of the EU capital-raising regime and the range of issues it raises, both within the EU and for third-country issuers, means that its subtleties cannot all be addressed in a chapter-length treatment. For two extensive and critical book-length treatments see Ferran, E, *Building an EU Securities Market* (2004) and Schammo, P, *EU Prospectus Law. New Perspectives on Regulatory Competition in Securities Markets* (2011).

  [27] For an assessment of the validity of stock market capitalization as an indicator of economic development see Aguilera, R and Williams, C, 'Law and Finance': Inaccurate, Incomplete and Important' (2009) 6 *Brigham Young University LR* 1413.

  [28] For a review of the literature and policy developments see Moloney, N, 'The Legal Effects of the Financial Crisis on Regulatory Design in the EU' in Ferran, E, Moloney, N, Hill, J, and Coffee, J, *The Regulatory Aftermath of the Global Financial Crisis* (2012) 111.

Taking the equity market example, although equity markets experienced significant losses of value over the crisis,[29] they did not experience particular difficulties, global contagion was limited,[30] diversification proved effective,[31] the equity trading market infrastructure proved resilient,[32] and global equity markets began to recover in 2010.[33] The crisis era nonetheless generated a policy focus on how best to support the efficiency of markets in funding capital-raising by issuers,[34] and on how the comparative advantages of the public equity markets, in particular, as a major vehicle for finance-raising, for risk management, and for mobilizing long-term public savings could be strengthened and secured.[35] While this policy focus reflects the previously noted crisis-era concern to support productive markets, and scepticism with respect to 'excessive' levels of intermediation and speculation (Chapter I), it also reflects the growing concern pre-crisis that the public equity markets were being eclipsed, given the increasing scale of private market funding—particularly through private-equity-based mechanisms[36]—and given the ever-widening range of risk management techniques which allowed issuers to diversify risk and to decrease their reliance on the public equity markets.[37]

As part of this re-consideration of the role and efficiency of the public equity markets and of how they can be supported, the ability of public trading venues to support capital-raising, has, for example, been questioned (section 7). In the UK, for example, the 2012 UK Kay Review highlighted that UK firms had significantly reduced their reliance on the public equity trading markets for new investment funding.[38] In the US—where there has been a decline in the number of initial public offers (IPOs) admitted to trading, initially over the reform period associated with the Enron-era failures and the 'dotcom' bubble bursting, but also since—concerns have been raised as to the condition of the public equity and related

---

[29] eg Bartram, S and Bodner, G, 'No Place to Hide: The Global Crisis in Equity Markets' (2009) 28 *J of International Money and Finance* 1246. Similarly, Graham, J and Harvey, C, The Equity Risk Premium amid a Global Financial Crisis (2009), available at <http://ssrn.com/abstract=1405459>.

[30] Bekaert, G, Ehrmann, M, Fratzcher, M, and Mehl, A, Global Crises and Equity Market Contagion (2011), ECB WP No 1381/201, available at <http://ssrn.com/abstract=1856881>.

[31] Vermeulen, R, International Diversification During the Financial Crisis: A Blessing for Equity Investors, De Nederlandsche Bank WP No 234 (2011), available at <http://ssrn.com/abstract=1971686>.

[32] Financial Services Authority (FSA), The FSA's Markets Regulatory Agenda (2010) 4 and 19 and Securities and Exchange Commission (SEC), Release No 34-61358, Concept Release on Equity Market Structure (2010) 64. Similarly, Angel, J, Harris, L, and Spatt, C, Equity Trading in the 21st Century, Marshall School of Business WP No FBE 09-10 (2010), available at <http://ssrn.com/abstract=1584026>.

[33] In 2010, global stock market capitalization amounted to $54 trillion, up from $34 trillion in 2008, although down from $65 trillion in 2007: McKinsey, Mapping Global Financial Markets (2011) 2.

[34] eg, in the UK, the Kay Review of Equity Markets and Long-Term Decision Making, Final Report (2012) (2012 Kay Review).

[35] eg Langevoort, n 5, Zingales, L, 'The Future of Securities Regulation' (2009) 47 *J of Accounting Research* 391, and Thomson, R, 'The SEC after the Financial Meltdown: Social Control over Finance' (2009) 71 *University of Pittsburgh LR* 567.

[36] Roe, M, 'The Eclipse of the Public Corporation' (1989) 67 *Harvard Business Review* 61 and, albeit more sceptically, Cheffins, B and Armour, J, The Eclipse of Private Equity, ECGI Law WP No 82/2007 (2007), available at <http://ssrn.com/abstract=982114>. Similarly, from a policy perspective, FSA, Discussion Paper 06/6, Private Equity: A Discussion of Risk and Regulatory Engagement (2006).

[37] Gilson, R and Whitehead, C, 'Deconstructing Equity: Public Ownership, Agency Costs and Complete Capital Markets' (2008) 108 *Col LR* 231 and, more generally, Henderson, M and Epstein, R, 'The Going Private Phenomenon: Causes and Implications' (2009) 76 *University of Chicago LR* 1.

[38] The Review reported that the UK primary equity market was not working well, and that equity issuance was dropping and generally limited to corporate restructurings: n 34, 22–3.

trading markets.[39] But market conditions differ (and change); global equity markets began to strengthen significantly over 2013 and 2014, while even over the crisis-era equity capital-raising levels increased in Australia, for example,[40] as well as in the massive emerging Chinese market.[41] EU market conditions are discussed in section 9 of this Chapter.

Reform in this sphere is not, however, straightforward. The relationship between strong funding markets and regulation is not clear, as was discussed in Chapter I. It is, however, clear that regulation of the capital-raising process requires multiple design decisions. It demands, for example, decisions as to the appropriate design of the regulatory perimeter and as to how public and private markets are to be differentiated. The 'public offer', however defined, is typically the main perimeter for capital-raising regulation, along with large trading venues which admit securities to trading. Private markets—which can encompass, for example, private placements, private equity transactions, and offers by small issuers (typically SMEs)—typically operate outside the main regulatory perimeter, for a variety of reasons.[42]

This perimeter can be difficult to fix. A shifting public/private perimeter has always been a feature of capital-raising regulation. But a range of factors, including the growing institutionalization of public equity markets,[43] competitive pressures,[44] demands for greater support for SME market finance (section 3.3.2), new financing techniques such as crowdfunding,[45] and allied technological innovation which supports trading by private investors,[46] are increasingly leading to deregulatory pressure on capital-raising

---

[39] eg Weild, D and Kim, E, Market Structure is Causing the IPO Crisis. Grant Thornton Paper (2010); Weild, D and Kim, E, A Wake Up Call for America. Grant Thornton Paper (2009), and, on the US share of the global IPO market, Committee on Capital Markets Regulation, Interim Report (2006) (the 2006 Paulson Report) (and related quarterly surveys). While equity markets strengthened over 2013–14, conditions have yet to improve with respect to the competitive position of the US globally. The Quarter 4 2013 report by the Committee on Capital Markets Regulation reported that the US share of the global IPO market was 7 per cent, the lowest since 2008.

[40] Connal, S and Lawrence M, Equity Capital Raising in Australia During 2008 and 2009 (2010), available at <http://ssrn.com/abstract=1664889>.

[41] Mason, C, Trends in IPO Listings by SMEs in the EU, Paper for City of London Economic Development (2011) (2011 City of London SME Report) 12. The Chinese market has accounted for some 17–25 per cent of global IPO value in recent years (IPO activity was suspended in mainland China over 2013): EY Global IPO Trends, Q4 2013, 2.

[42] See generally Langevoort, D and Thompson, R, 'Publicness in Contemporary Securities Regulation after the JOBS Act' (2013) 101 *Georgetown LJ* 337.

[43] For a US perspective, Langevoort, D, 'The SEC, Retail Investors, and the Institutionalization of the Securities Markets' (2009) 95 *Va LR* 1025 and in the UK context, Kay Review, n 34.

[44] 'Explosive growth' in the use of the US private placement market by foreign issuers has been associated with competitiveness dynamics related to the regulatory costs of the public US equity market: Committee on Market Regulation, Survey on Use by Foreign Issuers of the Private Rule 144a Equity Market (2009).

[45] Crowdfunding is based on the raising of capital, in small increments, from large numbers of investors, usually under the regulatory thresholds for public offers and typically through an online platform, usually in the form of a specialist website, or through social media. Fund raising can be non-financial in nature (in that a donation is made, or the return is in the form of a reward or product; globally, most crowdfunding activity takes this form) or financial (equity or debt). Targets for the funding are usually set, and funds returned if the target is not met. It was initially associated with social and cultural projects but is increasingly being used to finance start-ups. On the structure of crowdfunding transactions see, eg, Kirby, E and Worner, S, Crowdfunding: An Infant Industry Growing Fast, International Organization of Securities Commissions (IOSCO) Staff Working Paper (SWP 3/2014) (2014) and Mollick, E, The Dynamics of Crowdfunding: Determinants of Success and Failure (2013), available at <http://ssrn.com/abstract=2088298>.

[46] Most notably, perhaps, the US Second Market, and SharePost and FirstPEX in Europe, which provide liquidity in privately held shares. Liquidity, while generally limited, can nonetheless be significant, as underlined by the extent of pre-IPO trading in Facebook: Langevoort and Thompson, n 42.

generally[47] but also to calls for a greater focus on the role of private markets.[48] The nature of investor protection in the sale of securities is accordingly being reconsidered, as policymakers craft exemptions designed to promote private markets and their finance-raising capacity, but also to ensure sufficient levels of transparency and protection.[49] This is most marked in the US, where the 2012 JOBS Act represents the most radical deregulation of US disclosure regulation since the 1930s reforms which established the current US disclosure regime.[50] Perimeter design demands, however, careful consideration of the proxies deployed to distinguish public and private markets, if investor protection[51] and market efficiency are to be appropriately supported.[52]

II.2.1.2 The Issuer-disclosure Debate

But while the design challenges change, the imposition of mandatory disclosure requirements on issuers has long been a linch-pin of regulation in this area. Very broadly, two related rationales can be associated with mandatory issuer disclosure. In the primary market, in which the issuer sells securities to investors, issuer disclosure serves to address the information asymmetry between the issuer (and its advisers) and the investor, and thereby to inform the investor, reduce the risk of fraudulent sales of over-valued securities, and support the issuer in signalling its quality.[53] In the secondary markets, where securities subsequently trade between investors, issuer disclosure is primarily associated with the support of efficient pricing mechanisms, although it is also associated with the support of efficient corporate governance and with remedying the agency problems of dispersed (and block-holding) firms.[54]

---

[47] eg Zingales, L, *A Capitalism for the People. Recapturing the Lost Genius of American Prosperity* (2012) 232–4.

[48] eg Pritchard, A, 'Facebook, the JOBS Act and Abolishing IPOs' (2012) 35 *Regulation* 12, calling for different tiers of public and private market through which new issuers can progress.

[49] eg, with respect to the regulation of crowdfunding in the US, Hazen, T, 'Crowdfunding or Fraudfunding? Social Networks and the Securities Laws—Why the Specially Tailored Exemptions Must be Conditioned on Meaningful Disclosure' (2012) 90 *North Carolina LR* 1735, and in the EU, European Crowdfunding Network and Osborne Clarke, Regulation of Crowdfunding in Germany, the UK, Spain and Italy and the Impact of the European Single Market (2013).

[50] The Act is designed to reduce the regulatory costs of emerging growth companies by, eg, facilitating IPOs for companies with under $1 billion in revenue, allowing smaller companies to benefit from lighter regulation for the first five years following their public offering (the 'on ramp' provisions), addressing crowdfunding, and relaxing the rules which apply to the marketing (or 'general solicitation') of offers targeted to institutional investors. See Langevoort and Thompson, n 42.

[51] The sale of securities through crowdfunding techniques, eg, has been associated with default, fraud, illiquidity, dilution, transparency, platform failure, and governance risks: Commission, Consultation on Crowdfunding in the EU—Exploring the Added Value of Potential EU Action (2013) 8 and Kirby and Worner, n 45 (who reported on a 50 per cent default/investment failure risk with equity-based crowdfunding).

[52] eg Langevoort and Thomson, n 42, critiquing (in the context of the JOBS Act) the piecemeal and reactive nature of deregulatory reforms which change the coverage of issuers subject to the obligations of 'publicness', and calling for a more coherent approach to reform—including consideration of the extent of public trading by issuers when setting the public/private perimeter.

[53] Investors in the public primary market do not benefit from the price-setting mechanisms provided by liquid secondary securities markets, as primary-market prices are established by the issuer and the underwriters who sell the securities on the issuer's behalf: Scott, H, 'Internationalization of Primary Public Securities Markets' (2000) 63 *Law and Contemporary Problems* 71.

[54] Mahoney, P, 'Mandatory Disclosure as a Solution to Agency Problems' (1995) 62 *University of Chicago LR* 1047.

Although policymakers and regulators have rarely shown any weakening of their commitment to mandatory issuer disclosure, whether in the primary or secondary markets, a lively debate considers the appropriateness or otherwise of mandatory issuer disclosure.[55] It was initially most strongly associated with the US Securities and Exchange Commission (SEC)'s issuer-disclosure regime, in relation to which the debate—initially framed in terms of the costs which the foundational 1933 Securities Act and 1934 Securities Exchange Act imposed on issuers—first took root over the 1960s and 1970s.[56] Through the 1980s, scholarship engaged with the then-ascendant market efficiency theory and grappled with the question of whether mandatory disclosure supported market efficiency mechanisms and led to stronger resource allocation.[57] The debate still rages, although it has now turned to, *inter alia,* the challenge which behavioural finance poses to market efficiency and mandatory disclosure;[58] the risks associated with the supporting institutional structure for issuer disclosure, including informational intermediaries such as auditors and investment analysts;[59] the application of law and finance models of analysis to the link between enforcement and the effectiveness of disclosure policy;[60] and appropriate perimeter design for the application of disclosure rules.[61] A very brief overview of the debate follows in order to place the EU's disclosure regime in context, although the EU's commitment to mandatory disclosure has always had pragmatic rather than philosophical drivers, and has been heavily shaped by the market-integration imperative.

With respect to the primary markets, while mandatory prospectus requirements for public offers are a long-standing feature of regulation, a lively and extensive scholarship has queried whether disclosure requirements should be mandatory. Securities are intangible assets whose value is contingent on the future performance of the issuer; they are 'credence goods', in that their quality cannot be assessed easily in advance and their *ex-post* effects can take some time to emerge. Information is accordingly essential to an informed decision.[62]

---

[55] This debate is noted only in broad outline here. See Gullifer, L and Payne, J, *Corporate Finance Law. Principles and Policy* (2011) 421–3 and 455–9 and for a re-consideration see Goshen, Z and Parchomovsky, G, 'The Essential Role of Securities Regulation' (2006) 55 *Duke LJ* 711. For a recent wide-ranging analysis of the limitations of disclosure as a regulatory tool generally (across a range of spheres, and beyond issuer disclosure) given, *inter alia*, its costs, the empirical evidence of its failure, and its 'inevitable failure' given the false assumptions disclosure makes as to the decision-making process and the 'large series of unlikely achievements by lawmakers, disclosers and disclosees' which a successful regime would require, see Ben-Shahar, O and Schneider, C, 'The Failure of Mandated Disclosure' (2011) 159 *UPaLR* 647.

[56] For two seminal empirical attacks see Bentson, G, 'Required Disclosure and the Stock Market: An Evaluation of the Securities Exchange Act 1934' (1973) 63 *Amer Econ Rev* 132 and Stigler, G, 'Public Regulation of the Securities Markets' (1964) 37 *J of Business* 117.

[57] For a major contribution over this period in support of mandatory disclosure and based on the link between mandatory disclosure and market-efficiency mechanisms see Coffee, J, 'Market Failure and the Economic Case for a Mandatory Disclosure System' (1984) 70 *Va LR* 717.

[58] From the massive literature see, eg, Gilson, R and Kraakmann, R, 'The Mechanisms of Market Efficiency Twenty Years Later: the Hindsight Bias' (2003) 28 *J Corp L* 715; Stout, L, 'The Mechanisms of Market Efficiency: An Introduction to the new Finance' (2003) 28 *J Corp L* 635; Langevoort, D, 'Taming the Animal Spirits of the Stock Markets: A Behavioural Approach to Securities Regulation' (2002) 97 *North-Western University LR* 135; and Bainbridge, S, 'Mandatory Disclosure: A Behavioural Analysis' (2000) 68 *University of Cincinnati LR* 1023.

[59] eg Goshen and Parchomovsky, n 55.

[60] For leading discussions see La Porta, R, et al, 'What Works in Securities Laws? (2006) 61 *J Fin* 1 and Coffee, J, 'Law and the Market: The Impact of Enforcement' 156 *UPaLR* (2007) 229.

[61] Langevoort and Thomson, n 42.

[62] Ogus, A, *Regulation. Legal Forms and Economic Theory* (1994) 138–41.

But the severe information asymmetry between the issuer (and the underwriter) and the investor exposes the investor to risks of fraud and of a poor resource allocation decision being made.[63] Mandatory disclosure is argued to expose fraud and sharp practices by requiring extensive disclosure of corporate activity; in the absence of mandatory disclosure requirements, issuers (and more specifically their managers) may have incentives to suppress unfavourable information. Mandatory disclosure also supports issuers. In the absence of mandatory disclosure, even where an issuer sells high-quality securities and produces optimal disclosure for investors, it remains exposed to risks, in that rational investors should discount the investment where they cannot clearly identify the issuer as a high-quality issuer; this can arise where the marketplace contains poor-quality issuers, the standard and quality of information is variable, and it is difficult for high-quality issuers to signal their quality.[64] One response to this difficulty is a merit or substantive assessment of the securities by a trusted entity. Merit regulation, however, has never been a mainstream element of capital-raising regulation.[65] The dominant regulatory response internationally has been to impose mandatory issuer-disclosure requirements, in the form of prospectus requirements.

Mandatory disclosure requirements represent, however, a significant transaction cost for issuers accessing the capital markets, and their appropriateness has been the subject of a vigorous scholarship,[66] although in practice the policy commitment to mandatory disclosure has rarely been in doubt. Legally mandated rules run the efficiency, capture, and other risks attendant on law-making generally. Rational investors should discount securities in respect of which less disclosure is available; accordingly, issuers have strong incentives to provide information to reduce their cost of capital.[67] In so doing, issuers are supported by informational intermediaries, such as auditors, analysts, and rating agencies, which can lend their reputational capital to issuers by certifying or branding the issuer's disclosures or securities in different ways.[68] On the other hand, the 'public good' quality of information[69] and strong prejudicial incentive effects within issuers are likely to obstruct information flows, a failure to standardize makes it difficult for high-quality issuers to signal their credibility to investors and thereby to reduce the cost of capital, and the costs and complexities of private enforcement and of contracting for disclosure are significant.

---

[63] In the oft-quoted comment by Brandeis, '[s]unlight is said to be the best of disinfectants': Brandeis, L, *Other People's Money and How the Bankers Use It* (1913) 92.

[64] As predicted by the famous 'lemons' hypothesis: Akerlof, G, 'Market for Lemons: Quantitative Uncertainty and the Market Mechanism' (1970) 222 *Q J Econ* 488.

[65] This form of intervention is found in certain US States. The merit debate also formed part of the discussions which ultimately led to the adoption of the federal Securities Act, 1933. One of the foundation analyses is Douglas, W, 'Protecting the Investor' (1934) 23 *Yale LJ* 521.

[66] eg Ferrell, A, 'The Case for Mandatory Disclosure in Securities Regulation Around the World' (2007) 2 *Brooklyn J of Business Law* 8; Macey, J, 'A Pox on Both Your Houses: Enron, Sarbanes-Oxley and the Debate Concerning the Relative Efficiency of Mandatory Versus Enabling Rules' (2003) 81 *Washington University LQ* 329; Romano, R, 'Empowering Investors: A Market Approach to Securities Regulation' (1998) 107 *Yale LJ* 2359; and Easterbrook, F and Fischel, D, 'Mandatory Disclosure and the Protection of Investors' (1984) 70 *Va LR* 1335.

[67] Romano, n 66, 2373–80.

[68] eg Goshen and Parchomovsky, n 55, 711.

[69] The 'public good' nature of information—the fact that it becomes public once disseminated, that use of information by one person does not lower its value to others, and that suppliers of information cannot easily control free-riding on information or restrict its dissemination to those who will directly or indirectly pay for it—means that suppliers of information are not given adequate incentives to supply it. See Ogus, n 62, 33–5 and 40.

In the secondary markets, the imperative to protect investors against opportunistic issuers (and their management) which drives primary market disclosure also shapes disclosure regulation. But secondary market disclosure is additionally (and strongly) associated with the support of efficient pricing mechanisms and with market efficiency generally. Where the secondary market prices securities efficiently, it should allocate scarce capital efficiently[70] and support investor monitoring through the share price. But efficient securities pricing is dependent on efficient information transmission, in the absence of which high-quality issuers and securities may be unable to signal their value and, ultimately, poor-quality securities and issues may dominate, leading to a flight of capital.[71] Mandatory disclosure supports pricing efficiency by working in tandem with the efficiency dynamics which markets display, as assumed by the Efficient Capital Markets Hypothesis (ECMH).[72] Under the ECMH, markets are assumed to reflect all publicly available information[73] and where irrationalities exist which distort the pricing mechanism, they are assumed to be corrected by arbitrage mechanisms. Mandatory disclosure accordingly economizes the information costs associated with the institutional mechanisms of market efficiency,[74] such as analysis by investment analysts,[75] and supports the flow of public information and, thereby, the pricing mechanism.

The extent to which mandatory disclosure supports market efficiency is, however, heavily contested. The ECMH has come under sustained attack given well-documented evidence of market irrationality, failures in arbitrage mechanisms, and pervasive and systemic biases which distort rational investor decision-making and, accordingly, the price-formation process.[76] These arguments received a considerable fillip in the wake of the Enron collapse and the evidence that disclosures on Enron's impending bankruptcy were publicly available but had not been processed through the mechanisms thought to drive market efficiency,

---

[70] For a criticism of the extent to which markets are allocatively efficient see Stout, L, 'The Unimportance of Being Efficient: An Economic Analysis of Stock Market Pricing and Securities Regulation' (1988) 87 *Mich LR* 613.

[71] As predicted by the 'lemons' hypothesis: n 64.

[72] The seminal discussion is in Fama, E, 'Efficient Capital Markets: A Review of Theory and Empirical Work' (1970) 25 *J Fin* 1575.

[73] Under the ECMH, the market price of securities in active, liquid markets, which are well followed by analysts, should reflect all publicly available information about that security. Investors trade on the basis of publicly available information, signals are sent to other investors, and the price should adjust accordingly. It predicts quick (informationally efficient) and accurate (allocatively efficient) pricing responses to information. The ECMH also suggests that investment strategies based on looking for new information which the market has overlooked are flawed in that if information is publicly available, it will have fed into the share price: 'The power of this statement [Fama's ECMH] is dazzling. . . . In plain English, an average investor cannot hope to consistently beat the market, and the vast resources that such investors dedicate to analysing, picking and trading securities are wasted. Better to passively hold the market portfolio, and to forget active money management altogether. If the EMH holds, the market truly knows best': Shleifer, A, *Inefficient Markets* (2000) 1.

[74] The relationship between disclosure, its processing costs, and market efficiency dynamics was subject to a famous critique in 1984 by Gilson and Kraakmann: Gilson, R and Kraakmann, R, 'The Mechanisms of Market Efficiency' (1984) 70 *Va LR* 549.

[75] Coffee, n 57.

[76] See generally the articles examining the ECMH on the 20th anniversary of Gilson and Kraakman's seminal analysis of the mechanisms of market efficiency in (2003) 28 *J Corp L,* summer issue, and Shleifer, n 73. On investor behaviour, see the references at n 58 and Barr, M, Mullainathan, S, and Shafir, E, 'The Case for Behaviorally Informed Regulation' in Moss, D and Cistrenino, J (eds), *New Perspectives on Regulation* (2009) 25.

particularly information intermediaries such as analysts.[77] By the eve of the financial crisis, the assumptions as to market efficiency and rationality deployed to support mandatory issuer disclosure had long been under empirically driven attack. The financial crisis placed market efficiency and rationality assumptions under greater pressure.[78] The UK's crisis-era Turner Review usefully summarized the prevailing views as suggesting the following: that market efficiency does not imply market rationality; individual rationality does not ensure collective rationality; individual behaviour is not entirely rational; allocative efficiency benefits have limits; and large-scale herd effects and market over-shoots occur.[79] The UK's Kay Review similarly highlighted the persistence of asset mispricing problems over the financial crisis.[80]

Certainly, regulated disclosures—issuer-facing and otherwise—failed to extend to the range of markets and securities implicated in the crisis.[81] Market-driven disclosures did not support market discipline.[82] Pricing mechanisms did not predict the scale of the crisis which was to unfold. Nonetheless, notwithstanding its flaws, the ECMH remains a reasonably robust explanation for pricing dynamics relating to issuer capital-raising and a justifiable support for mandatory disclosure,[83] particularly given empirical evidence supporting a link between mandatory issuer disclosure and lower costs of capital,[84] as long as its limitations are acknowledged.

While mandatory issuer disclosure is generally assumed to be primarily concerned with market efficiency and with addressing information-related market failures, it is also associated, primarily in regulatory and policy discussions, with retail investor protection[85] and with the related promotion of investor confidence;[86] the EU's prospectus regime has long

---

[77] See, eg, Prentice, R, 'Whither Securities Regulation? Some Behavioural Observations Regarding Proposals for the Future' (2002) 51 *Duke LJ* 1397.

[78] Among the major crisis-era reviews see, eg, Hu, H, 'Efficient Markets and the Law: A Predictable Past and an Uncertain Future' (2012) 2 *Ann Rev of Financial Economics* 179; Lo, A, Adaptive Markets and the New World Order (2010), available at <http://ssrn.com/abstract=1977721>; and Avougleas, E, 'The Global Financial Crisis, Behavioural Finance and Financial Regulation in Search of a New Orthodoxy' (2009) 9 *JCLS* 23.

[79] FSA, The Turner Review. A Regulatory Response to the Global Banking Crisis (2009) (2009 Turner Review) 40–1.

[80] 2012 Kay Review, n 34, 34–7.

[81] See, eg, Fisch, J, 'Top Cop or Regulatory Flop—the SEC at 75' (2009) 95 *Va LR* 785.

[82] Generally, Schwarcz, S, 'Protecting Financial Markets: Lessons from the Subprime Mortgage Meltdown' (2008) 93 *Minnesota LR* 373 and Schwarcz, S, 'Regulating Complexity in Financial Markets' (2009) 87 *Washington University LR* 211.

[83] For a recent re-consideration, examining how the ECMH became the victim of a 'bubble' and calling for the ECMH to be given a more modest (but still important) role in policy formation, rooted in informational efficiency (rather than fundamental market efficiency) see Gilson, R and Kraakman, R, Market Efficiency After the Financial Crisis: It's Still a Matter of Information Costs (2014), ECGI Law WP No 242/2014, available at <http://ssrn.com/abstract=2396608>.

[84] eg Hail, L and Leuz, C, 'International Differences in the Cost of Equity Capital: Do Legal Institutions and Securities Regulation Matter?' (2006) 44 *J of Accounting Research* 485.

[85] Famously, Easterbrook and Fischel castigated the notion that securities market rules are necessary to protect investors as unsophisticated as the investors they are supposed to protect (n 66).

[86] The link between investor confidence and the federal US mandatory disclosure system has long reflected a deep-rooted policy concern that small and unsophisticated investors might 'withdraw their capital to the detriment of the markets and the economy as a whole when they fear that they may be exploited by firms or better-informed traders': Easterbrook, F and Fischel, D, *The Economic Structure of Corporate Law* (1991) 296. One commentator has noted that, from the simple premise that investors gain the necessary confidence to invest when protected, the SEC has built a vast regulatory system: Choi, S, 'Regulating Investors not Issuers: A Market-Based Proposal' (2000) 88 *Cal LR* 279, 280.

linked harmonization in this area with retail investor protection and investor confidence.[87] This troublesome rationale for intervention assumes retail investors read and understand mandatory issuer disclosure, although the mandatory disclosure required of issuers is generally accepted to exceed retail investors' well-documented limited capacity to absorb information.[88] Retail market-orientated justifications also carry significant law-making risks as they carry considerable political weight[89] and can generate entrenched and costly assumptions as to the role of mandatory disclosure.[90] This risk became sharply apparent during the development of the 2003 Prospectus Directive regime.

II.2.2 The EU, Market Finance, and the Integration of Capital Markets

II.2.2.1 A Transformative Regime

The EU regime governing capital-raising reflects the major policy objectives and regulatory devices which shape regulatory intervention internationally, although the market-integration imperative which drives the regime has often obscured the extent to which the traditional objectives of disclosure policy are expressly articulated; similarly, the policy objectives and regulatory devices that are common internationally are refracted through an EU lens. In particular, the EU regime has transformative ambitions with respect to the embedding of market finance in the EU and with respect to the construction of an integrated capital market. But while the capital-raising regime may enable issuers to raise capital on a pan-EU basis and facilitate investors in supplying capital to a more diversified range of issuer, it requires considerable faith in the power of regulation to assume that it will, in itself, transform market behaviour. This issue is further explored later in the Chapter.

II.2.2.2 Market Finance

As discussed in Chapter I, finance-raising in the EU is typically associated with bank finance rather than with market finance, and accordingly with, on a macro level and using the influential Varieties of Capitalism (VoC) typology, the Co-ordinated Market Economy (CME) funding model rather than the Liberal Market Economy (LME) funding model. A key tenet of the VoC analysis is that, given the range of institutions which influence whether an economy is LME- or CME-based, legal reforms designed to (or with the potential to) alter the dominant model are likely to face significant resistance, or to be

---

[87] The promotion of investor confidence through disclosure, and the consequent benefits in terms of market integration and investor protection, were key drivers of the Commission's approach to what would become the 2003 Prospectus Directive: Revised 2003 Directive Prospectus Proposal (COM (2003) 460) 6.

[88] From an extensive literature see, eg, Paredes, T, 'Blinded by the Light: Information Overload and its Consequences for Securities Regulation' (2003) 81 *Washington University LQ* 417 and Langevoort, D, 'Towards More Effective Risk Disclosure for Technology-Enhanced Investing' (1997) 75 *Washington University LQ* 753.

[89] See Bradley, C, 'Disorderly Conduct and the Ideology of Fair and Orderly Markets' (2001) 26 *J Corp L* 63 and Langevoort, D, 'Structuring Securities Regulation in the European Union: Lessons from the US Experience' in Ferrarini, G and Wymeersch, E (eds), *Investor Protection in Europe: Corporate Law Making, the MiFID and Beyond* (2006) 485.

[90] eg, Langevoort has argued that the retail investor-protection argument has allowed the SEC to build a regulatory power base founded on limited empirical evidence as to the value of intervention: Langevoort, n 58, 173–5.

ineffective, given the scale of the institutional change required to change these models. The extent to which firms draw on external market finance as opposed to bank-based credit is only one aspect of whether an economy is an LME or CME. But the caution which the theory calls for with respect to reform measures, given the institutional apparatus which supports these economic models, suggests that some care is needed in promoting a particular market- or bank-based finance agenda at EU level and through harmonized capital-raising rules. A similar need for caution can be inferred from the law and finance literature which underlines the complex and dynamic relationship between law and markets.

Nonetheless, the promotion of market-based financing by issuers (and the related integration of capital markets) has been an entrenched element of EU regulatory policy for some time. The seminal 1966 Segré Report[91] found that the financing of economic growth was dependent on the capital markets and reported that the securities markets 'are . . . markets where efficiency can be notably improved by integration'.[92] It found that national debt markets were overextended domestically, but that foreign investors and borrowers were unable to enter due to exchange controls, discriminatory legislative obstacles, and inefficient techniques for placing securities. There was a shortage of equity capital and action was needed to increase investment by institutional investors. Establishing a wider market would, the Report suggested, offer new and varied sources of funding, align the conditions under which finance could be obtained and so remove competitive distortions, and ultimately increase the supply of capital. This theme re-emerged in the soft law 1977 Code of Conduct on Transactions in Transferable Securities.[93] While it has long been overtaken by regulatory reforms, the Code underlines the early commitment to market finance (and integration), stating that the 'harmonious development of economic activities', as required under Article 2 EC at the time, required that sufficient capital be available and that sources of capital were sufficiently diversified to enable investments in the common market to be financed as rationally as possible.[94] Support for market finance—and across multiple dimensions beyond issuer finance-raising—has since remained a tenet of EU policy, as discussed in Chapter I. Although the crisis-era reform programme did not focus closely on issuer funding, the contraction in bank funding and the EU's wider growth agenda led to SME access to market funding appearing on the reform agenda (section 3.3). Towards the end of the crisis era the policy agenda also began to grapple with the wider implications of the contraction in bank-based funding, and with whether EU capital markets are sufficiently resilient and efficient to provide an effective alternative source of funding for long-term funding requirements.[95]

---

[91] Report by a Group of Experts Appointed by the EEC Commission, The Development of a European Capital Market (1966).

[92] Segré Report, n 91, 5.

[93] Commission Recommendation 77/534/EEC concerning a European Code of Conduct relating to transactions in transferable securities [1977] OJ L212/37 (the 1977 Code of Conduct).

[94] 1977 Code of Conduct, n 93, para 1. Advocate General Jacobs read the 1977 Code of Conduct as supporting the construction of a regulatory framework in order to 'encourage investment, and so enable the securities markets to perform their economic function, namely the efficient allocation of resources': Case C–384/93 *Alpine Investments v Minister van Financiën* [1995] ECR I–1141, Opinion of the AG, para 76.

[95] Commission, Green Paper. Long-Term Financing of the European Economy (2013) (COM (2013) 150/2) (2013 Commission Long-Term Financing Green Paper) and Commission, Communication on Long-Term Financing of the European Economy (2014) (COM (2014) 168) (2014 Commission Long-Term Financing Communication). The 2014 Communication highlighted the importance of strong capital markets

In practice, the institutional complexity associated with different varieties of capitalism, and the lessons which the law and finance literature holds as to the limits of law as a transformative agent, cast doubt on the extent to which law can achieve such radical effects. Empirical evidence appears to bear this out. As discussed in section 9, it is not clear that the EU's harmonized capital-raising regime can be associated with growth in firms' reliance on market-based funding. This is not to suggest that the capital-raising regime is a failure: as discussed in the following sections, it promotes and facilitates market finance by means of a harmonized regulatory regime which seeks to support market efficiency in the public and private markets and to deliver high standards of investor protection in the public markets. Accordingly, it forms part of the wider international rulebook which associates strong outcomes for issuers, investors, and markets with the regulation of capital-raising and in particular with mandatory issuer disclosure. It is also the case that the regime is now highly dynamic and capable of self-correction.

II.2.2.3 Market Integration

It is axiomatic that mandatory disclosure imposes costs on issuers. The cost burden intensifies in the cross-border context given the costs of compliance with multiple disclosure regimes (and the related liability costs).[96] Given the benefits of cross-border capital-raising,[97] regulators worldwide have long grappled with the treatment of multi-jurisdictional offers. The techniques[98] range from mutual recognition,[99] to convergence of standards (driven, in particular, by the range of standards which the International Organization of Securities Commissions (IOSCO) has adopted[100]), to 'substitute compliance'.[101] The management of cross-border disclosure, however, reaches its apotheosis in the EU's sophisticated regime.

Market integration remains the touchstone of EU securities and markets regulation, notwithstanding the stresses wrought by the financial crisis. This core priority can, with respect to capital-raising, be traced back to the 1966 Segré Report[102] which set out a proposed model prospectus for both public issues and stock exchange admission and, foreshadowing by some 20 years the mutual-recognition device, suggested that minimum

---

and considered the need for related reforms, including with respect to private placements and the trading of corporate bonds.

[96] See generally Kraakman, R, et al, *The Anatomy of Corporate Law* (2nd edn, 2009) 281–9, 294–300.

[97] A vast literature considers the regulatory treatment of multi-jurisdictional offerings and the value of cross-listings. For a review see Jackson, H, 'Centralization, Competition, and Privatization in Financial Regulation' (2001) 2 *Theoretical Inquiries in Law* 649.

[98] See Scott, H, An Overview of International Finance: Law and Regulation (2005), available via <http://www.ssrn.com/abstract=800627>.

[99] As under the US/Canada Multi-Jurisdictional Disclosure System.

[100] IOSCO, International Disclosure Standards for Cross-Border Offerings and Initial Listings by Foreign Issuers (1998); International Disclosure Principles for Cross-Border Offerings and Listings of Debt Securities by Foreign Issuers (2007); and Principles for Periodic Disclosure by Listed Entities (2010).

[101] Substitute compliance was trialled by the SEC prior to the crisis, and is based on allowing third country actors access following a determination that the third country regulatory, supervisory, and enforcement regime is broadly equivalent in practice: Tafara, E and Peterson, R, 'A Blueprint for Cross-Border Access to U.S. Investors: A New International Framework' (2006) 48 *Harv Int LJ* 31. While a series of related international agreements were entered into by the SEC, it went into abeyance in the early stages of the financial crisis. It has since been reactivated in the context of OTC derivatives market regulation: Ch VI sect 4.2.13.

[102] n 91.

standards be adopted which would allow Member States the freedom to broaden the application of the rules, or enforce different rules, within the limits of the minimum rules.[103]

Initially, change was slow to come. The position in 1977, for example, was that 'there cannot be said to be any wide, unified securities market: lack of transparency, unfamiliarity with other markets or pure absence of interest contribute to this fragmentation'.[104] But in the 1980s a new policy impetus to enhance the interpenetration of national securities markets and deepen the pools of capital available to issuers emerged, reflecting a range of developments (in the EU and globally), including deregulation and regulatory competition between marketplaces, developments in technology which reduced trading costs and facilitated the disclosure of information, the growth of the investment fund industry, privatizations, financing techniques such as the development of depositary receipts which represent an issuer's shares and facilitate foreign offerings, and the dismantling of exchange controls.[105]

Although intuition suggests that deeper markets which pull together fragmented pools of capital should lead to reduced costs of capital for issuers, more efficient allocation of resources, and stronger economic development,[106] empirical support was finally given to the Commission's enthusiasm for market integration (and the market finance model) by the 2002 London Economics Report.[107] Although the report focused in particular on trading market integration and trading costs, it found that debt and equity market integration should result in a 40 basis points decrease in the cost of equity capital and debt financing. This headline reduction in the cost of capital was related to a range of factors, including larger markets for high-risk capital (including venture capital), lower required rates of return (following from increased diversification opportunities), access to a wider pool of investors, and better information flows.[108]

As discussed further on in the Chapter, the EU capital-raising/issuer-disclosure regime relies on harmonization and on a related 'regulatory passport' to remove regulatory obstacles. But barrier removal via regulatory competition remains an alternative method to achieve this.[109] The relative desirability of a market for, or competition between, national regulatory regimes[110] (as compared to harmonization of standards as a mechanism for

---

[103] n 91, 231.

[104] Wymeersch, E, Control of Securities Markets in the European Economic Community. Collection Studies. Competition—Approximation of Legislation Series No 31 (1977) 117.

[105] From among the earlier literature see, eg, Warren, G, 'The Common Market Prospectus' (1989) 26 *CMLR* 687 and Merloe, P, 'Internationalization of Securities Markets: A Critical Survey of US and EEC Disclosure Requirements' (1986) 8 *J Com Bus and Capital Markets L* 249.

[106] Ferran, n 26, 10.

[107] London Economics, Quantification of the Macro-Economic Impact of Integration of EU Financial Markets. Final Report to the EU Commission (2002) (2002 London Economics Report).

[108] 2002 London Economics Report, n 107 9–10.

[109] On the respective benefits and rationales of harmonization and regulatory competition, see Ch I sect 1.3.3.

[110] It may be more accurate to view regulatory competition in this area less in terms of the traditional 'race to the bottom' or 'race to the top' in regulatory standards and more in terms of a process which results in disclosure regimes reflecting certain types of issuer and investor preferences; eg certain regimes may tailor their regimes towards low-disclosure, higher-risk offerings which will be priced accordingly. See Choi, S and Guzman, A, 'Portable Reciprocity: Rethinking the International Reach of Securities Regulation' (1998) 71 *So Cal LR* 903.

managing the costs of diverging sets of rules) has generated a rich scholarship in the issuer-disclosure context.[111] Competition is typically promoted on the ground that it allows regimes to be tailored to particular investor preferences and can correct regulatory errors. But for regulatory competition to be effective, the related information transmission device must be efficient. National regulators must receive signals from the marketplace (ultimately via the discounting of securities prices[112]) and respond to those signals free from constraints such as the risk of regulatory capture. Further, effective regulatory competition is dependent on the absence of other market failures which might otherwise distort the competition,[113] while rule enforcement remains a troublesome variable.

Whatever the benefits of regulatory competition, it is reasonable to suggest, in the context of EU policy support for an integrated capital market, that market failures exist with respect to issuer disclosure—particularly with respect to the risks of protectionism—which justify harmonization.[114] Harmonization, at the least, facilitates cross-border activity by issuers (to the extent that issuers choose to operate cross-border and that market conditions are conducive) by reducing the transaction costs inherent in diverging regimes, and by providing protection against any destabilizing races to the bottom or regulatory arbitrage which may, all indications to the contrary aside,[115] emerge. In practice, and as discussed more generally in Chapter I, the changed EU institutional context following the financial crisis, the recent entrenchment of political and market support for the single rulebook, the institutional technology now available to the EU to ensure the harmonized regime remains dynamic and flexible, and the well-tested channels through which industry interests can raise their concerns all render the regulatory competition option almost redundant in the EU context.

The impact of the issuer-disclosure regime on market integration remains, however, unclear. The scale and intensity of the harmonized regime and the relatively trouble-free passport scheme certainly facilitate pan-EU capital-raising. Whether or not the regime can drive cross-border funding is much less clear, as discussed in section 9 of this Chapter. But at this point in the regime's development, political and market consensus on the appropriateness of the EU governing this field is sufficiently strong as to make any practical disconnection between the regime and levels of cross-border activity largely irrelevant.

---

[111] This scholarship is strongly associated with the dynamics of State and federal regulation in the US. For leading accounts see, eg, Romano, n 66 and Fox, M, 'Securities Disclosure in a Globalizing Market: Who Should Regulate Whom' (1997) 95 *Mich LR* 2498. In the EU context see Schammo, n 26, 309–41.

[112] For a challenge to regulatory competition, based in part on the extent to which securities prices can effectively signal investors' positions on different disclosure standards, see Cox, J, 'Regulatory Duopoly in US Securities Markets' (1999) 99 *Col LR* 1200.

[113] Cox, n 112, 1231–3.

[114] For an early endorsement of the securities directives harmonization project see Buxbaum and Hopt, who found (in 1988) that, by comparison with the company law harmonization programme, 'legal harmonization measures that open up national capital markets or pave the way to a European capital market make a much clearer contribution to European integration': Buxbaum, R and Hopt, K, *Legal Harmonization and the Business Enterprise* (1988) 2.

[115] For an analysis prior to the coming into force of the harmonized prospectus regime see Jackson, H and Pan, E, 'Regulatory Competition in International Securities Markets: Evidence from Europe in 1999—Part I' (2001) 56 *The Business Lawyer* 653.

II.3 The Evolution of the Harmonization Programme

II.3.1 The Initial Approach to Harmonization

Harmonization in the issuer-disclosure sphere has undergone three major phases. In the first phase, detailed harmonization was deployed. In the second phase, mutual-recognition devices were attached to the earlier, detailed disclosure directives. The final phase, which can be strongly associated with the FSAP period (1998–2004) and with the crisis-era reforms (2008–2014 (approximately)) is seeing the removal of Member State regulatory autonomy, detailed harmonization, and support of home Member State control. This phase has been shaped by the regulatory paradigm shift which followed the adoption of the Lamfalussy model and the adoption of the FSAP and, more recently, the decisive shift of regulatory power from the Member States to the EU in the wake of the financial crisis.

By the early 1970s, work had commenced on proposals for directives designed to harmonize admission-to-listing (in effect, admission to a stock exchange) and disclosure requirements for 'officially listed' securities. By the early 1980s, harmonizing directives covered listing requirements (the Consolidated Admissions Requirement Directive),[116] the contents of the 'listing particulars' to be published as a condition of admission to official listing (the 1980 Listing Particulars Directive[117]—since repealed), and the ongoing publication of interim reports by issuers whose shares were admitted to official listing (the 1982 Interim Reports Directive[118]—since repealed).[119] These early directives were designed to set out exhaustively the minutiae applicable in the areas harmonized and to operate as a code, which could be applied by the Member States without significant further elaboration at national level and which would support market integration.[120] But this harmonization model failed to remove the regulatory burdens placed on issuers. Not only did the heavy reliance on directives mean that implementation was left to the discretion of the Member States and accordingly rendered vulnerable to misinterpretations, delays, and wilful misconstructions, but the directives also contained substantial escape opportunities for Member States in the form of a network of exemptions, derogations, and generally worded obligations. Particular problems arose, for example, with respect to the loose definition of a 'public offer' of securities.[121] This problem was implicitly acknowledged in the early directives in that they were all monitored by a Contact Committee, the functions of which included facilitating consultation between Member States on the extent to which additional or more stringent conditions were being imposed. Real harmonization was also hindered by a degree of mutual suspicion between EU NCAs; the paradigm shift in

---

[116] n 18.

[117] Directive 80/390/EEC [1980] OJ L100/1.

[118] Directive 82/121/EEC [1982] OJ L48/26.

[119] The 1977 soft law Code of Conduct (n 93) sat alongside these measures and recommended disclosure requirements for publicly offered and listed securities.

[120] See generally Wymeersch, E, 'The EU Directives on Financial Disclosure' (1996) 3 *EFSL* 34.

[121] See generally the ECOSOC (now the European Economic and Social Committee (EESC)) opinion on the Commission's Communication on European Capital Markets for Small and Medium-Sized Issuers—Prospects and Potential Obstacles to Progress [1998] OJ C235/13 (the ECOSOC SME Opinion) para 3.4.1.2.2.

supervisory dialogue and co-operation which would follow under the Lamfalussy process and with the establishment of CESR, and in the wake of the financial crisis, was some way off. The detailed approach also led to a fossilization of the rule negotiation process because of the level of detail on which agreement was needed.[122]

In 1985, the Commission's White Paper on the Internal Market provided the policy background for the next phase of the harmonization programme.[123] Although its main focus in the financial sphere was on intermediation and financial services, the White Paper highlighted the need to achieve a single securities market, and promoted integration via liberalization and mutual recognition rather than detailed harmonization. The White Paper did not present a significant legislative programme for issuers,[124] but its endorsement of the mutual-recognition device led to the more flexible harmonization technique of mutual recognition and home-country control being applied in this area and to related revisions to the earlier directives. Specifically, once a prospectus or listing particulars were approved in accordance with the relevant directive's requirements by one Member State (the home State), other Member States (host States) were required to accept the document, although they could impose certain additional information and translation requirements. The revisions of the (then) Treaty by the Single European Act also increased the speed at which legislative measures were adopted with its introduction of qualified majority voting. The 1988 Substantial Shareholdings Directive[125] (now repealed) and the 1989 Public Offers Directive[126] (now repealed) were adopted soon after.

But the White-Paper-era articulation of mutual recognition was not a success. Very considerable difficulties arose with the mutual-recognition-of-disclosure regime, largely due to the degree to which Member States could legitimately continue to impose requirements on issuers from other Member States.

II.3.2 The FSAP and Reform

The poor state of integration became a matter of acute concern towards the end of the 1990s. The pre-FSAP 1998 Communication highlighted as an imperative for action the elimination of any remaining fragmentation in the EU capital market and completion of the establishment of 'deep and liquid European capital markets which serve both issuers and investors better'.[127] It found that the adoption of 'a coherent programme of action to smooth out the remaining legislative, administrative and fiscal barriers to cross-border flotations and investment-related activities'[128] was necessary, and expressed concern that the disclosure regime had failed to resolve the problem of national authorities imposing

---

[122] Wymeersch, E, The Harmonisation of Securities Trading in Europe in the New Trading Environment, WP 2000–16, Working Paper Series of the Financial Law Institute, Universiteit Gent, 2.
[123] Completing the Internal Market, COM (85) 310 (the 1985 Internal Market White Paper).
[124] The now repealed Substantial Shareholdings Directive (Directive 88/627/EEC [1988] OJ L348/62) was the only capital market measure proposed by the 1985 Internal Market White Paper.
[125] Directive 88/627/EEC [1988] OJ L348/62.
[126] Directive 89/298/EEC [1989] OJ L124/6.
[127] Commission, Financial Services. Building a Framework for Action (1998) (COM (1998) 625).
[128] n 127, 2.

demanding and frequently different disclosure requirements on issuers and thereby generating significant costs.[129]

In response, the 1999 FSAP contained a proposal to provide for a single prospectus passport for issuers[130] and aimed to improve the financial reporting system and enhance the comparability of accounts. Following the adoption of the FSAP, the 2000 Lisbon European Council highlighted the widest possible access to investment capital on a EU-wide basis, by means of a single passport for issuers, as a matter of critical importance for the completion of the internal market in financial services, while the 2001 Lamfalussy Report identified the adoption of a single-prospectus scheme for issuers, a mandatory shelf-registration system, and reform of the accounting rules as priorities.[131]

Following the FSAP reforms, a radically upgraded disclosure regime—in the form of the 2003 Prospectus Directive, the 2004 Transparency Directive, the 2003 Market Abuse Directive, and the 2002 IAS Regulation—was adopted which, with revisions, continues to govern the disclosure required on a public offer or admission of securities to trading on a regulated market. This period was also strongly characterized by the establishment of CESR and its deepening and intensification of the capital-raising regime, as discussed across this Chapter.

II.3.3 The Crisis Era and the Growth Agenda

II.3.3.1 The Crisis Era and Capital-Raising Reforms

Pre-crisis, little EU policy attention was directed to the relative efficiency of the public funding markets in the EU and their impact on growth. Private equity funding, for example, grew significantly in the lead-up to the financial crisis, raising some concern that the efficiency and transparency of the public equity markets might be compromised. Even allowing for the reality that most private equity funding in the EU was based in the UK,[132] the EU policy response was sanguine,[133] despite considerable opposition to private equity from the Parliament's Socialist grouping.[134] This is not to claim that the growth of the private equity funding model called for EU regulatory intervention, or that the EU public markets (bond and equity) were inefficient, but only to highlight the relative lack of attention given to the efficiency and quality of the public funding markets once the supporting passport regime for pan-EU offers was in place.

---

[129] n 127, 6.

[130] FSAP, n 7, 4.

[131] The initial Lamfalussy Report noted that the cost of raising capital in the EU was higher than in the US, even for blue-chip issuers, as a result of the complexity of cross-border capital-raising and diverging Member State rules which impaired liquidity and efficient pricing. In a worst-case scenario it predicted that business might be driven out of Europe to the US, with potentially damaging long-term consequences for the European economy: Initial Report of the Committee of Wise Men on the Regulation of European Securities Markets (2000) 7. The final 2001 Lamfalussy Report reinforced the importance of reforming the rules governing capital-raising (see n 732).

[132] Ferran, E, Regulation of Private Equity-Backed Leveraged Buyout Activity in Europe, ECGI Law WP No 84/2007 (2007), available at <http://ssrn.com/abstract=989748>.

[133] Then Commissioner McCreevy was reluctant to address the relative efficiencies of the public and private markets: eg Speech on 'Private Equity: Getting it Right', 22 March 2007. On the regulation of private equity see further Ch III sect 4.13.

[134] eg PES, Hedge and Private Equity Funds (2007).

The post-implementation reviews of key measures mandated under the FSAP, combined with the 'second wave' of the crisis-era reform programme (Chapter I), have, however, led to a finessing of the EU capital-raising regime and to the final dominance of the EU in this regulatory space. Harmonization has widened and intensified, with the remaining vestiges of minimum harmonization being largely removed from the regime, the administrative rule-making process intensifying, and ESMA's activities burgeoning. In parallel, harmonization has been required to undertake ever heavier policy lifting as the EU has displaced the Member States as the regulator of the capital-raising process and as the instigator of reforms to issuer-disclosure regulation generally, including with respect to the promotion of growth via market finance. Recent initiatives range from highly detailed finessing of the harmonized regime to reflect the market complexities of, for example, debt issuance programmes and rights issues, to policy-driven and operationally focused revisions designed to lighten the regulatory burden for SMEs and other smaller companies and to enhance retail investor disclosure, to efforts to shape the IFRS system internationally, to ESMA's closer engagement with the related supervisory process, particularly with respect to prospectus approval.

The tentative moves by the Commission to engage with the promotion and regulation of the nascent EU crowdfunding market underline the extent to which policy innovation has moved to EU level, as well as the linkage being made between issuer disclosure policy and growth.[135] Crowdfunding in the EU is still at an early stage[136] and most Member States, thus far, are in the very early stages of developing their regulatory approach;[137] the policy/regulatory space is relatively uncluttered. But while the Commission's initial orientations suggest a light-touch—if facilitative—approach, it is also clear that it regards the crowdfunding regulatory space as one in which the EU should be proactive.[138]

---

[135] In 2013 the Commission hosted a workshop which was followed by a Consultation: Commission, Crowdfunding. Untapping its Potential, Reducing the Risk. Workshop Agenda. 3 June 2013 and 2013 Crowdfunding Consultation (see n 51). The Commission also highlighted the potential of crowdfunding as source of long-term financing in its 2013 LongTerm Financing Green Paper: n 95. A supportive Commission Communication, designed to facilitate crowdfunding by means of a series of soft measures (including investigation of 'labelling' devices, the mapping of regulatory developments, and the raising of awareness), followed in March 2014: Communication on Unleashing the Potential of Crowdfunding in the EU (COM (2014) 172). Similarly, ESMA and the European Banking Authority (EBA) engaged in joint surveys of NCAs on approaches to crowdfunding and in joint analyses of the risks of crowdfunding over 2013–14: eg EBA, EBA Consumer Trends Report 2014 (2014) 14 and 32.

[136] In 2012, financial crowdfunding grew by 65 per cent on 2011, with some €735 million raised through crowdfunding techniques (by comparison, €3 billion was raised through the venture capital market). More than 200 crowdfunding platforms are active in the EU: 2013 Crowdfunding Consultation, n 51, 2 and 3. Funds raised through securities are, however, small, with a crowdfunding offer typically raising in the region of €50,000 (at 5). Globally, the financial crowdfunding market is estimated at $1 billion (Kirby and Worners, n 45).

[137] Regulators across the EU are experimenting with a range of approaches, including case-by-case regulation of online funding platforms, and with restrictive and liberal models: Regulation of Crowdfunding, n 49. In March 2014, eg, the UK Financial Conduct Authority (FCA) presented its regulatory approach for loan-based and investment-based crowdfunding platforms (FCA, Policy Statement 14/4) (based on Consultation Paper 13/3, The FCA's Regulatory Approach to Crowdfunding (and similar activities) (2013)), which is based on restricted marketing in the retail segment of investment-based platforms (given in particular the liquidity risks faced by retail investors).

[138] The Commission's 2013 Consultation, eg, considered 'how to unleash' the potential of crowdfunding, including through awareness-raising, and queried whether the rules applied by Member States to crowdfunding-type offers (which typically fall outside the Prospectus Directive) were appropriate and whether the rules governing trading venues supported crowdfunding platforms. The 2014 Communication was similarly facilitative and supportive in tone, if short on specific measures.

The EU capital-raising regime has also been drawn into the crisis-era trading venue reform agenda (Chapter V). The suspicion of speculation and of financial market intensity associated with the crisis-era reforms to trading practices, while not impacting directly on the regulation of issuer access to market finance, has led to a concern to ensure markets/trading venues serve a productive function, including with respect to capital allocation, and to a privileging in EU regulatory policy development of 'patient capital allocation' over speculation. The Commission's 2013 Green Paper on Long-Term Financing, for example, related the swathe of trading venue reforms to the enhancement of market structure generally, and highlighted that the effectiveness of these reforms in ensuring that capital markets channel long-term financing as effectively as possible would be monitored.[139] Related regulatory reforms have not been consistent, however. For example, while the exclusion of primary market issuance from the proposed Financial Transaction Tax (FTT) is designed to protect issuance activity, and thereby acknowledges and responds to some of the risks the FTT poses to funding, industry evidence has suggested that the tax will, more generally, create strong incentives to shift capital allocation from securities to deposits.[140]

There are, however, some indications that the Commission has come to acknowledge that its regulatory tools for promoting strong funding markets may be limited; it has come to recognize, for example, that trading venues may not be primarily allocative in nature with respect to capital formation, instead serving liquidity-related functions.[141] Nonetheless, supporting the efficiency with which firms raise funds through the markets remains a central policy tenet, with some indications that additional reforms designed to promote market finance may follow from the long-term financing agenda in particular.[142]

II.3.3.2 The SME Agenda

In the EU, the capital market dimension of SME[143] finance has long been a policy concern of the Commission.[144] The financial crisis has significantly sharpened the focus on the SME

---

[139] 2013 Long-Term Financing Green Paper, n 95, 11.

[140] See Ch VI sect 5.

[141] Commission, Staff Working Document Accompanying the Long-Term Financing Green Paper (SWD (2013) 78) 22–3.

[142] The Commission's Green Paper queried, eg, whether reforms could be adopted to promote the efficiency of bond markets in channeling long-term funds and to address the slowdown in the EU IPO market and the related 'equity gap': n 95, 11–12.

[143] SMEs in the EU are subject to a range of different definitions. In the policy debate, they are often defined by reference to Commission Recommendation 2003/361/EC concerning the definition of micro, small and medium-sized enterprises [2003] OJ L124/36. This defines the 'micro' and SME sector as covering enterprises which employ fewer than 250 persons, have an annual turnover not exceeding €50 million, and/or have an annual balance sheet not exceeding €43 million. This definition is also deployed in the Prospectus Directive (sect 4.4.3). Within this category, 'small' enterprises employ fewer than 50 persons and their annual turnover/balance sheet total does not exceed €10 million. A 'micro' enterprise is one which employs fewer than ten persons and whose annual turnover/balance sheet total does not exceed €2 million: Annex, Art 2. Distinct definitions apply for the purposes of the financial reporting regime and are set out in the 2013 Accounting Directive, which adopts new definitions designed to expand the category of SMEs benefiting from calibrated treatment.

[144] The initial policy agenda was set out in Commission, Risk Capital: A Key to Job Creation in the EU (1998) (SEC (1998) 552).

sector, internationally[145] and domestically.[146] In the EU, and reflecting wider political, market, and policy concern,[147] the support of efficient SME access to finance has become a central pillar of crisis-era economic policy and of the current 'Europe 2020' economic strategy.[148] Access-to-finance difficulties have long troubled the SME sector. In particular, bank lending has been dominant,[149] given the information asymmetry, signalling, and relating discounting risks that SMEs face in the capital markets, which are exacerbated by the difficulties SMEs face in ensuring coverage by market gatekeepers/information intermediaries, notably investment analysts.

Access-to-finance difficulties for SMEs accordingly became acute over the period of the crisis and in the time since, given the contraction in bank funding.[150] The proportion of small bank loans as a proportion of total EU lending has dropped, reflecting de-leveraging pressures, reduced bank risk appetite,[151] and regulatory effects relating to increased capital charges.[152] In the wake of the financial crisis venture capital funding also fell, in part as a result of the contraction in equity IPO markets and so in exit opportunities for venture capital funds; funding dropped from €6–7 billion annually pre-crisis to €3–4 billion in 2009 and 2010,[153] and continues to fall.[154] Market finance has not provided a reliable substitute. While SMEs do not typically raise equity on the major public markets, from those SME issuers who do there is evidence of SMEs delisting from major public equity markets,[155] of a reduction in the

---

[145] Seoul G20 Summit, November 2010, Leaders' Declaration, para 9. For an early review of international efforts on SME financing see OECD, Impact of the Global Crisis on SME and Entrepreneurship Financing and Policy Measures (2009).

[146] For a review of the swathe of UK government measures see Thompson, B, Can New Forms of Finance Provide Support for the Real Economy. Clifford Chance Paper (2012).

[147] eg the own initiative report by ESMA's Securities and Markets Stakeholder Group: Reporting on Helping Small and Medium Sized Companies Access Funding (2012) (ESMA/2012/SSMG/59) and Demarigny, F, An EU-Listing Small Business Act, European Capital Markets Institute Paper (2010).

[148] The 'Europe 2020' Strategy replaced the earlier Lisbon Strategy for economic growth. Of its seven 'flagship initiatives' two address SME finance: the Innovation Union Initiative (which focuses in particular on venture capital) (COM (2010) 546); and the Industrial Policy for the Globalization Era Initiative (COM (2010) 614) (which addresses SME access-to-finance difficulties).

[149] Generally, bank loans accounted for 85 per cent of non-financial corporate debt in the euro area and the UK in 2011: Commission, European Financial Stability and Integration Report 2012 (2013) (SWD (2013) 156) (2012 EFSIR) 125.

[150] eg ECB, Financial Stability Review June 2012 (2012) 33–4, Ernst & Young, Funding the Future (2012), 2012 EFSIR, n 149, 29, and Commission, European Financial Stability and Integration Report 2011 (2012) (SWD (2012) 103) (2011 EFSIR) 34. The series of SME Access to Finance Surveys regularly carried by the ECB repeatedly report on industry lack of confidence in the availability of funding.

[151] SME credit risk arises from a combination of factors, including the generally more limited information available, the perceived risk of higher possibility of failure, lack of track record, and, as most SMEs do not issue publicly traded securities, the absence of a mechanism for continuously updating information, all of which increases the costs of setting a risk premium and monitoring the loan asset: ECB, Financial Stability Review June 2012, 134.

[152] In 2012, eg, credit standards tightened for SMEs in the second half of 2012, although they remained stable for big enterprises; the overall rejection rate for SME loans over January-April 2012 was 15 per cent, as compared to 5 per cent for large firms: 2012 EFSIR, n 149, 29.

[153] British Venture Capital Association (BVCA), Private Equity and Venture Capital Report on Investment Activity (2010) and BVCA, 2011 Global Trends in Venture Capital (2011).

[154] In 2012, venture capital funding to SMEs fell by 14 per cent on the previous year: 2013 Crowdfunding Consultation, n 51, 7.

[155] European Securities Committee (on the role of the Committee in administrative rule-making see Ch X sect 4) Minutes, 12 April 2010.

number of SME IPOs generally,[156] and of concern that the regulatory costs of regulated market admission (including with respect to prospectus publication) do not generate the traditional associated benefits, such as visibility and analyst coverage, for SMEs.[157]

The related SME access-to-finance agenda[158] is extensive and multilayered. It includes state aid, specific EU financing instruments for SMEs, bankruptcy reform, and late payments reform.[159] The Commission's important 2013 Green Paper on Long-Term Financing and related 2014 Communication also highlighted a range of reforms, including with respect to SME markets and networks, securitization networks, tailored 'scoring' measures for SMEs (designed to address the difficulties SMEs face in ensuring the availability of verifiable public disclosures on their performance),[160] and non-traditional funding methods,[161] notably crowdfunding.[162]

The access-to-finance agenda also includes the calibration and, in places, deregulation of key regulatory measures to support easier access to finance.[163] The issuer-disclosure aspects of the related reforms, which seek to reduce the costs of the issuer-disclosure regime for smaller issuers,[164] are considered in section 4.4.3 and 5.5 of this Chapter, the relating accounting reforms are discussed in section 6, and the 2014 MiFID II/MiFIR reforms related to access to appropriate trading venues are addressed in section 7.1.2. The reform programme also extends to the investment management sphere[165] and the assessment of the impact of the Solvency II and CRD IV capital reforms on SME lending.

---

[156] 2011 City of London SME Report, n 41.

[157] Commission, 2011 MiFID II/MiFIR Proposals Impact Assessment (SEC (2011) 1226), charting the thin liquidity in SME stocks and the relative costs for SMEs of admission to regulated markets as compared to the low amounts of capital raised: at 97.

[158] eg, Commission, Driving European Recovery (2009) (COM (2009) 114) 10–12 and Commission, Regulating Financial Services for Economic Growth (2010) (COM (2010) 301) 2.

[159] The access-to-finance element of SME policy has been developed across the three main strands of the Commission's wider SME agenda. The 2011 and 2012 Single Market Acts I and II include SME access-to-finance initiatives: Commission Communication on a Single Market Act (2011) (COM (2011) 206) and Commission Communication on a Single Market Act II (2012) (COM (2012) 573). The 2008 Small Business Act strand contains a number of reforms related to the business environment generally and on access-to-finance specifically: Communication on 'Think Small First' a 'Small Business Act' for Europe (COM (2008) 394) and Communication on Review of the 'Small Business Act' (COM (2011) 78). Finally, the Commission adopted a specific policy strand in relation to access to finance which put forward policy initiatives in relation to, eg, taxation, state aid, payments, EU financing instruments, and business angels: Communication on an Action Plan to Improve Access to Finance for SMEs (2011) (COM (2011) 870).

[160] Visibility-enhancing scoring mechanisms were addressed in some detail in the Commission's 2012 EFSIR: n 149, 125–42.

[161] n 95, 15–16.

[162] See n 138.

[163] eg, Single Market Act I Communication, n 159, highlighting venture capital fund reform and reforms to the market abuse, transparency, and prospectus regimes (at 6). More generally, the Industrial Policy for the Globalization Era Initiative called for all future proposals for legislation in the financial sector to assess the impact on SME access to finance: n 148, 8.

[164] On the costs of disclosure for SMEs see Ferrarini, G and Ottolia, A, 'Corporate Disclosure as a Transaction Cost: The Case of SMEs' (2013) 9 *Eur Rev of Contract L* 363.

[165] The main initiatives relate to venture capital funds, social entrepreneurship funds, and long-term investment funds: Ch III sect 5.

II.4 The Prospectus Directive

II.4.1 The Evolution of the Prospectus Directive Regime

II.4.1.1 Initial Efforts

As one of the pillars of EU securities and markets regulation, the long evolution of the Prospectus Directive warrants some attention.

At the time of the Commission's first major legislative initiative in the capital-raising area in 1972 (the proposal for what would become the 1980 Listing Particulars Directive), disclosure standards varied widely,[166] resulting in patchy standards of investor protection and high transaction costs for issuers engaging in multiple issues and/or listings.[167] The listing particulars proposal languished for some time and was overtaken by the 1977 Code of Conduct.[168] The Explanatory Memorandum to the Code of Conduct pointed out that 'the lack of full information on the securities themselves and ignorance or misunderstanding of the rules governing the various markets have certainly helped to confine the investment of a great majority of savers to the markets of the countries in which they live or to a few well-known major international securities' (paragraph 1). Accordingly, Principle 2 provided that '[i]nformation should be available to the public which is fair, accurate, clear, adequate and which is given in good time' and went on to require that 'the information should be provided in such a way that its significance and intent can be easily understood'.

Mandatory EU disclosure requirements were first imposed on issuers in 1979, by the now repealed Admission Directive. Its main concern was to facilitate access to official listing (in effect, admission to a stock exchange) by harmonizing the conditions applicable to admission to official listing, but it also addressed the ongoing disclosure obligations of officially listed issuers. The now repealed Listing Particulars Directive followed in 1980 and harmonized the disclosure requirements for the document required on admission to listing (the listing particulars). In 1989 the gap in the disclosure regime was somewhat haphazardly filled when, after a tortured genesis (its negotiation took more than eight years), the now repealed Public Offers Directive (the POD) introduced a prospectus regime governing offers of securities to the public generally.

This basic disclosure framework was subsequently subject to a complex and fragmented system of mutual recognition designed to allow issuers to prepare a single disclosure document which, once approved by the relevant Member State's NCA, could be used for admission applications and public offers across the EU without the need for further modification or approval, bar the inclusion of certain local market-specific information

---

[166] Despite the existence of disclosure regimes (of varying degrees of sophistication) in most of the Member States in the early 1970s, in establishing a disclosure regime the EU had to combat an anti-disclosure bias (in continental Europe at least) in European corporate culture: Buxbaum and Hopt, n 114, 169.

[167] eg, Suckow, S, 'The European Prospectus' (1975) 23 *A J Comp L* 50, 52–4.

[168] The EU was not the first international body to acknowledge the importance of adequate disclosure. In 1974, in its Recommendation concerning Disclosure Requirements and Procedures to be Applicable to all Publicly Offered Securities, the OECD recognized the principle that the investor is entitled to the highest practical degree of protection in respect of standards of securities and that the ultimate responsibility in this area lies with government.

and subject to translation requirements. Mutual recognition was initially addressed for listing particulars (1987) and then for public offer prospectuses (1990). The Eurolist Directive, which followed in 1994, attempted to remove the need for mutual recognition by giving Member States the option to exempt issuers from the listing particulars requirements where they sought admission to official listing on an exchange but their securities had been officially listed in another Member State exchange for at least three years.

This unwieldy system failed to support mutual recognition and facilitate capital-raising; fewer than two or three issuers a year attempted to use the complex regime,[169] with the implications most pronounced for public offers.[170] The open-textured nature of the disclosure regime and its multitude of exemptions, derogations, and options resulted in widely varying interpretations of its requirements across the Member States. The insistence of many NCAs on full translation of the entire approved prospectus or listing particulars was particularly burdensome and restricted the mutual-recognition regime in practice to only the largest of issuers, while the requirement to include local information with respect to taxation, paying agents, and notification procedures also represented a significant obstacle. The brunt of these difficulties fell on smaller issuers, who were often forced for cost reasons to limit their offers to one Member State.[171] In practice, most cross-border offers were carried out through private placements.[172] But even here difficulties could arise from the failure to harmonize the pivotal definition of 'public offer'. The same offering could be treated as a private placement and so as exempt from the requirement to produce a prospectus in one Member State, and as a public offer subject to prospectus requirements in another, thereby increasing issuer costs and investor protection risks.[173] The basis of the disclosure regime in 'official listing' under the Listing Particulars Directive also became outdated, with capital-raising occurring outside 'official' stock exchange segments, and with high-tech and innovative-growth companies being traded on second-tier or non-official trading markets. The regulatory regime more generally also began to address trading on 'regulated markets' rather than trading on stock exchanges and official lists.

It also became apparent that the disclosure provided under the regime was inadequate as compared to international best practice.[174] The event-specific nature of the disclosure

---

[169] See, eg, Gros, D and Lannoo, K, *The Euro Capital Market* (2000) 129–30 and Jackson and Pan, n 115.

[170] The 1999 and 2000 Deutsche Telekom pan-EU public offering therefore represented the exception rather than the rule, and even this offering faced considerable difficulties from the multiple translation requirements: Pietrancosta, A, 'The "Public Offering of Securities" Concept in the New Prospectus Directive' in Ferrarini and Wymeersch, n 89, 339, 341–2. See also HM Treasury, Public Offers of Securities. A Consultation Document Proposing Amendments to United Kingdom Legislation on the Public Offers of Securities and Seeking Views on Reforming Public Offers of Securities within the European Union (1998) (1998 Treasury Public Offers Consultation), which pointed to the very low incidence of 'regular pan-European offers of securities': 1 and 18.

[171] The 1998 Treasury Public Offers Consultation reported trenchantly that 'the transaction costs of using the mutual-recognition procedure are an expensive and cumbersome hurdle which very few offerors of securities find worth surmounting... Given the largely fixed nature of these transaction costs in relation to the size of the offer, these costs are felt disproportionately by small and medium-sized enterprises': n 170, 18.

[172] The cross-border wholesale market was described as 'relatively straightforward and seamless': Burn, L and Wells, B, 'The Pan-European Retail Market—Are We There Yet?' (2007) 2 *CMLJ* 263.

[173] eg FESCO, A 'European Passport' for Issuers, A Report for the EU Commission (2000) (2000 FESCO Issuer Passport Commission Paper) (FESCO/00/138b).

[174] Becht, M, 'European Disclosure for the New Millennium' in Hopt, K and Wymeersch, E (eds), *Capital Markets and Company Law* (2003) 87.

regime also caused difficulties as it involved the preparation and approval of lengthy disclosure documents upon an application for admission to official listing or when a public offer was made. It was slow and cumbersome and not sensitive to the requirements of issuers who made repeated calls on the capital markets. Disclosure documents also varied in format, making comparability difficult (a problem exacerbated by variations in accounting standards: section 6).

Technical weaknesses in the directives were not the only drivers of limited use of the initial mutual-recognition regime.[175] The home bias of investors, particularly retail investors, meant that there was little demand for cross-border investments. Institutional investors who had such an investment appetite were able to access cross-border securities through private placements, but uncertainties persisted as to when an offer could be constructed through a private placement.

II.4.1.2 The FSAP and the Lamfalussy Report

The pre-FSAP 1998 Commission Communication highlighted as an imperative for action the elimination of any remaining fragmentation in the EU capital market and the completion of the establishment of 'deep and liquid European capital markets which serve both issuers and investors better'.[176] It expressed concern that NCAs were imposing demanding and differing disclosure requirements on issuers, which were ultimately discouraging issuers from engaging in cross-border issues, to the detriment of both capital formation and investor choice.[177] In response, the 1999 FSAP contained proposals to provide for a single passport for issuers and to facilitate repeat access by issuers to the markets via a shelf-registration mechanism based on the issuer's annual reports.[178]

The 2000 Lisbon European Council prioritized the disclosure reforms and highlighted the widest possible access to investment capital on an EU-wide basis by means of a single passport for issuers as a matter of critical importance for the completion of the internal market in financial services. This political imprimatur was reflected in the 2000 Second FSAP Progress Report, in which particular attention was paid to reform of the mutual-recognition regime.[179] The Commission reported that the disclosure directives had not worked, citing as obstacles the tendency of NCAs to limit the scope of mutual recognition to narrowly defined classes of securities, frequent demands for additional information, concerns that minimum-disclosure requirements were insufficient, the unsuitability of traditional systems for listings and public offers of securities for issuers wishing to raise successive instalments of capital, and the failure of the disclosure regime to deal with investor needs for regular updating of market information. The unsatisfactory state of the prospectus regime was also given prominence in the Initial Lamfalussy Report, which identified as a priority the adoption of a single-prospectus system for issuers and of a mandatory shelf-registration system.[180]

[175] Ferran, E, 'Cross-border Offers of Securities in the EU: The *Standard Life Flotation*' (2007) 4 *ECFLR* 462.
[176] n 127, 1.
[177] n 127, 6.
[178] n 7, 4.
[179] Report from the Commission, Progress on Financial Services. Second Report (2000) (COM (2000) 336).
[180] 2000 Initial Lamfalussy Report, n 131, 16.

The momentum for reform was sustained by the activities of the Federation of European Securities Commissions (FESCO, which would subsequently become CESR), which placed the weight of the NCA community behind the prospectus reform process.[181]

II.4.1.3 The 2003 Prospectus Directive Negotiations

Notwithstanding the consensus from the market and the supervisory community that reform was required, the genesis of the 2003 Prospectus Directive[182] was troublesome. The rather economically reasoned 2001 Proposal called for an issuer-disclosure passport and was designed to overhaul the pre-FSAP prospectus disclosure regime completely in order to facilitate the widest possible access to investment capital for all issuers, including SMEs. In the absence of reform, the Commission warned that the European financial market would remain fragmented and that 'cross border capital-raising will remain the exception, rather than the rule—the antithesis of the logic of the single currency'.[183]

The Commission was largely the architect of its own misfortunes in the subsequent troubled negotiations, as it did not follow the consultation principles associated with the then novel Lamfalussy process. The Commission did not engage in any public consultations prior to the publication of the proposal and adopted a rather naïve, retail investor-based model, based on extensive prospectus publication requirements; this threatened to disrupt the long-established wholesale bond market which had previously operated free of retail-standard prospectus requirements. This approach, the removal of issuer choice of NCA for all offerings, and the initially limited scope of the exemption regime—all of which exposed the wholesale bond markets to significant regulatory costs—generated a deluge of adverse comment, as well as criticism of the Commission's failure to consult adequately.[184] The Commission proved open to revising its original model and, unusually, presented a revised Proposal in 2003, following the extensive revisions tabled by the European Parliament and concern expressed in the Council's Prospectus working

---

[181] FESCO, A European Passport for Issuers (2000) (FESCO/99–098e) and 2000 FESCO Issuer Passport Commission Paper, n 173.

[182] Directive 2003/71/EC [2003] OJ L345/64, as amended by Directive 2010/73/EU [2010] OJ L327/1. References to the Prospectus Directive or the 2003 Directive are to the Directive as amended, unless the context requires otherwise.

The main elements of the legislative history are as follows: Original Commission Proposal at COM (2001) 280 (also at [2001] OJ C272/240); ECOSOC's opinion at [2002] OJ C80/52; ECB opinion at [2001] OJ C344/4; first Parliament reading at T5–0114/2003 (and [2003] OJ C47/417) (the report by the Economic and Monetary Affairs Committee (ECON) is at A5–0072/2002 (First ECON Report)); Revised Commission Proposal at COM (2003) 460 (and [2003] OJ C20/122); Council's Common Position at [2003] OJ C125/21; and second Parliament reading at T5–0311/2003 [2004] OJ C74/98 (the report by ECON is at A5–0218/2003 (Second ECON Report)). On the legislative history of the 2010 Amending Prospectus Directive see n 191.

[183] 2001 Original Prospectus Directive Proposal, n 182, 1.

[184] Boland, V, 'Battle Looms over Brussels Plan for Capital Markets Regulation', *Financial Times*, 11 June 2001. Although the Commission was initially robust in defending the adequacy of the consultation, pointing to the discussions with FESCO, the need to demonstrate the Lamfalussy process as soon as possible, and the urgency with which reform was required (Original 2001 Prospectus Directive Proposal, n 182, 2), by the end of the FSAP it acknowledged that it had made a 'serious error' in not formally consulting the public and industry participants: Commission, FSAP Evaluation. Part I: Process and Implementation (2005) 12–13.

group. As the revised proposal reflected most of the Parliament's revisions,[185] adoption followed reasonably quickly in November 2003; the Directive came into force in July 2005.[186]

The consultation process also saw some nervousness as to the nature of the delegations to administrative rule-making, as the 2003 Prospectus Directive, together with the 2003 Market Abuse Directive, provided the first test-case for the new administrative law-making process adopted under the Lamfalussy model (Chapter X sections 4 and 5). Although the institutions generally expressed support for the adoption of detailed administrative disclosure requirements, the Parliament was particularly concerned to ensure the scope of the delegations was carefully defined.[187]

The 2003 Directive, which remains at the core of the prospectus regime, represented a sea-change from the earlier regime and illustrates the more sophisticated approach to securities and markets regulation which emerged over the FSAP. The regime grappled with, for example, shelf registration, incorporation by reference, dissemination, and the challenges represented by retail market disclosure. It was also the first FSAP measure to adopt a quasi-maximum harmonization/home Member State control model, which limited the host State to, largely, precautionary intervention.

II.4.1.4 The 2010 Reforms and the Crisis

The establishment of ESMA led to a series of reforms to the 2003 Prospectus Directive under the 2010 Omnibus I Directive,[188] which had two broad functions. First, they empowered ESMA to propose, and the Commission to adopt, a series of Regulatory Technical Standards (RTSs) and Implementing Technical Standards (ITSs) under the 2003 Directive. As discussed further in section 4.2, these delegations will thicken the prospectus rulebook but they are, broadly, directed to templates, common procedures, and notifications, rather than to substantive rule-making. Second, they conferred a series of quasi-supervisory and operational powers and privileges on ESMA, designed to support supervisory convergence (section 4.10.3).[189]

More substantive reforms were adopted under the 2010 Amending Prospectus Directive.[190] The 2003 Prospectus Directive was to be reviewed by the Commission by the end of 2008 (Article 31); the 2010 Amending Prospectus Directive followed this review.[191] In what was

---

[185] Although not all. The Commission retained restrictions on issuer choice of NCA which generated an immediate backlash from the investment banking community (and the European Banking Federation in particular), which criticized the Commission for not opening the revised proposal to consultation: Evans, M, 'Bankers Dismayed by Prospectus Directive Overhaul' (2002) 21 *IFLR* 3.

[186] Implementation was supported by the Commission's Prospectus Transposition meetings which were designed to allow Member States to raise questions on the interpretation of the Directive and which the Commission also used to highlight the importance of timely transposition: see, eg, Prospectus Transposition Meeting, 8 March 2005.

[187] First ECON Report, n 182, Amendments 23 and 39. The Commission was sensitive to this concern in its Revised Proposal and significantly clarified the administrative delegations.

[188] n 19.

[189] The 2014 Omnibus II regime has a similar effect (n 20).

[190] n 9.

[191] The main publicly available elements of the legislative history are: Commission Proposal COM (2009) 491 (the 2009 Amending Prospectus Directive Proposal), Impact Assessment (SEC (2009) 1223); report by the ECON Committee, 27 March 2010 (A7-010/2010) (the 2010 ECON Report), on which the Parliament's Negotiating Position was based; and Council General Approach, 17 December 2009 (Council Document 17541/09).

a new departure for EU securities and markets regulation at the time but has since become standard practice, the Commission's review was empirically informed by a number of studies. These included those by the European Securities Market Expert Group (ESME),[192] CESR,[193] and the Centre for Strategy & Evaluation Services (CSES).[194] The large-scale 2009 study for the Commission on the impact of the FSAP generally also considered the prospectus regime.[195] CESR (and, since, ESMA) also provided an important institutional forum for collating experience with the Directive generally, including by means of the CESR/ESMA Prospectus Q&A.

The first public offerings subject to the 2003 Directive had produced a generally positive assessment.[196] But difficulties subsequently emerged in the Directive's application and were documented by the studies on the 2003 Directive.[197] ESME, for example, described the Directive as a milestone in the construction of a single European securities market, praising the shelf-registration system, the notification regime, the harmonized disclosure rules, and the language regime. But it also identified a wide range of problems, including with respect to definitions, the length of prospectuses, the treatment of particular offers (including 'retail cascades', rights issues, and employee share offerings), the base prospectus and final terms, and prospectus validity, and called for legislative reform. CESR's 2007 review, based on consultations with market participants, revealed that most market participants were satisfied with the Directive and considered the new regime a step in the right direction to achieve a single market. The passport mechanism was found to be considerably more effective than the earlier mutual-recognition mechanism, with the related language regime a particularly important reform. But CESR's review also highlighted practical difficulties in the operation of the Directive, for the most part arising from diverging supervisory practices, including with respect to the passport approval process and co-ordination between NCAs—although concerns were also raised with respect to core elements of the Directive, including in relation to divergences in the interpretation of a 'public offer' and in relation to the burdensome nature of prospectus disclosure. The 2008 CSES Report, based on market consultations, was broadly positive, but while it found that 58 per cent of respondents felt the Directive had a positive impact, it raised specific difficulties with the

---

[192] European Securities and Markets Expert Group (ESME), Report on Directive 2003/71/EC (2007) (2007 ESME Report). ESME also produced a related report on alignment between the Directive's and MiFID I's treatment of professional investors: Differences between the Definition of Qualified Investor in the Prospectus Directive and Professional Client and Eligible Counterparty in MiFID. Is Alignment Needed? (2008) (2008 ESME Professional Investor Report).

[193] CESR, CESR's Report on the Supervisory Functioning of the Prospectus Directive and Regulation (2007) (CESR/07-225) (2007 CESR Prospectus Report) and An Evaluation of Equivalence of Supervisory Powers in the EU under the Market Abuse Directive and the Prospectus Directive. A Report to the Financial Services Committee (2007) (CESR/07-334) (2007 CESR Supervisory Convergence Report).

[194] Centre for Strategy & Evaluation Services, Study on the Impact of the Prospectus Regime on EU Financial Markets. Final Report (2008) (2008 CSES Report).

[195] CRA, Evaluation of the Economic Impact of the FSAP (2009) (2009 CRA Report) ch 5.

[196] The first two UK IPOs under the Prospectus Directive proved easy to manage under the new regime: Rice, J, 'Equity Markets Take Prospectus Directive in their Stride' (2005) 24 (August) *IFLR* 6. For an analysis of the 2006 Standard Life equity offering which included cross-border offers in Ireland, Germany, and Austria and a considerable retail segment, and which concluded that the prospectus regime came through the major test represented by the flotation well, see Ferran, n 175.

[197] See, eg, Revell, S and Cole, E, 'Practical Issues Arising from the Implementation of the Prospectus Directive—What Are the Equity Capital Markets Worrying About?' (2006) 1 *CMLJ* 77 and Craven, K, Assessing the Impact of the Prospectus Directive, ICMA Regulatory Policy Newsletters No 5, April 2007, 1.

operation of the passport which reflected the CESR and ESME Reports. Overall, however, the Commission concluded that the market was broadly happy with the regime and that it had made it easier to offer securities and admit securities to trading.[198]

The Commission's initial consultation on reform of the Directive was published in January 2009.[199] The main driver of the review was, reflecting the wider pre-crisis regulatory zeitgeist, to simplify the Directive, enhance administrative efficiency, and reduce inefficiencies in fund-raising.[200] The pre-crisis regulatory mood was also apparent in the Commission's determination to adopt revisions only where necessary and to be cost-sensitive. The consultation was accordingly broadly deregulatory in nature, suggesting reform of the rules governing the 'qualified investor' exemption, retail cascades, employee share offerings, SME issuers, and rights issues. The September 2009 Proposal followed this approach, highlighting the administrative cost reductions that would follow,[201] albeit that it also proposed significant reforms to the retail market summary prospectus. But it also located the reforms in the need to respond effectively to the financial crisis and investor protection risks.[202] The 2010 Directive was adopted under the 'fast-track' single reading procedure which became the norm over the financial crisis. During the negotiations, the European Parliament adopted a more ambitious agenda than the Commission's, introducing, for example, revisions to support SME financing,[203] which were largely accepted by the Council. The 2010 Amending Prospectus Directive was adopted in October 2010 and was to be implemented by July 2012.

The range of issues addressed by the 2010 Amending Prospectus Directive reflects the increasing technical sophistication of the EU prospectus regime. The main reforms address the following: the bond markets, in particular the disclosure provided in 'base prospectuses' and related 'final term' documents; the retail markets, in particular a new short-form key information document to replace the discredited summary prospectus, and the mechanism for distribution of bonds through 'retail cascades'; and SME financing and the adoption of a proportionate disclosure regime. The 2010 Amending Directive and its related three sets of administrative rules[204] has also, and by contrast with the crisis-era reform programme generally, a deregulatory quality, although this also reflects the crisis-era concern to promote growth and the efficiency of market funding mechanisms. The scope of the exemptions available for private placements, for example, has been extended, while extensive calibrations have been made to the disclosure required of in-scope offerings, including with respect to rights issues and offers by SMEs. Elsewhere, however, the scope of the

---

[198] Commission, Background Document. Review of Directive 2003/71 (2009) 2–3.

[199] n 198.

[200] n 198, 1. This approach reflected the 2007 European Council commitment to reducing administrative burdens on companies by 25 per cent by 2012: 2010 Prospectus Amending Directive recs 1–3. The prospectus reform also formed part of the Commission's Simplification Rolling Programme.

[201] The Proposal noted, eg, the annual savings of €173 million projected for companies with a reduced market capitalization and annual savings of €30 million relating to the new employee share scheme regime: n 191, 4.

[202] 2009 Amending Prospectus Directive Proposal Impact Assessment, n 191, 3.

[203] Including raising the exemption thresholds for small offers and adding companies with a reduced market capitalization as beneficiaries of a proportionate disclosure regime: ECON Report, n 191, Amendments 19 and 24. It also proposed that offers to 250 persons be exempted from the Directive, but this amendment did not survive the negotiations (Amendment 25).

[204] nn 23 and 24.

Directive has tightened, most notably with respect to bond offerings, where the threshold for the exemption for bond offerings with a denomination or individual consideration of €50,000 has been increased to €100,000.

The prospectus regime is now dynamic. As discussed later in this Chapter, ESMA's supervisory convergence activities continue to thicken and deepen the prospectus regime. But the legislative and administrative regimes are also likely to change. The 2010 Amending Prospectus Directive's review clause requires the Commission to review the Directive by 1 January 2016, and identifies the liability implications, the summary prospectus, the employee share-offering exemption regime, the proportionate disclosure regime, online prospectus publication, and the application of issuer choice in the small-denomination bond markets as particular targets for the review; a review, in order to enhance the effectiveness of EU capital-raising markets, is also envisaged by the Commission's 2014 Long-Term Financing Communication. Reforms can certainly be expected to the Directive's sanctioning and supervision regime, given the strengthening of supervision and enforcement which has followed in other measures over the crisis era (Chapter XI).

II.4.2 The Prospectus Regime, Harmonization, and ESMA

The Prospectus Directive is not formally based on maximum harmonization. It acknowledges, for example, that Member States remain free to impose corporate governance disclosure requirements through the process of admission to trading on a regulated market (recital 15), and permits NCAs to require the inclusion of supplementary information on investor protection grounds (Article 21(3)(a)). But overall the level of regulatory convergence achieved is extensive,[205] with prospectus rules now clearly a function of the EU process.[206]

The prospectus regime is dense and multilayered, composed of three elements: first, legislative acts—the foundation 2003 Prospectus Directive, as amended; second, administrative acts—the current suite of Commission Regulations and the emerging BTS rulebook; and, finally, supervisory convergence measures, including the major legacies from CESR— the Prospectus Recommendation[207] and the Prospectus Q&A[208]—and, potentially, new ESMA initiatives. Commission interpretations of the regime[209] also fit, if somewhat uneasily, with this framework.

---

[205] CESR took the view that the Directive adopts a maximum harmonization model (2007 CESR Prospectus Report, n 193, 5) as did ESME: 2008 ESME Report, n 192, 6.

[206] The regime has been described as marking a peak in the EU's regulation of mandatory disclosure: Enriques, L and Tröger, T, 'Issuer Choice in Europe' (2008) 67 *Cambridge LJ* 521, 525. Similarly, see Schammo, n 26, describing the regime as regulating disclosure exhaustively (at 69–73).

[207] Recommendation for the Consistent Implementation of the 2004 Regulation. Initially adopted by CESR in 2005 (CESR/05-054b), but revised and updated by ESMA in 2011 (ESMA/2011/81) and subsequently (ESMA/2013/319), particularly with respect to mineral company disclosures.

[208] The Prospectus Q&A was initially adopted by CESR in 2006 and has been subject to 20 updates since then. This discussion refers to the 21st version (ESMA/2014/35, adopted in January 2014) (Prospectus Q&A).

[209] These include bilateral advice (see, eg, Letter from the Financial Markets Law Committee to the Commission, 25 September 2007, seeking an interpretation on aspects of the definition of offer to the public (available at <http://www.fmlc.org>) (2007 FMLC Letter)) and interpretations from the Commission's initial transposition meetings.

It is through the administrative rule-making process that the prospectus regime has expanded most dramatically. The massive administrative 2004 Commission Prospectus Regulation,[210] which derives from the original 2003 Prospectus Directive, vividly illustrates how the administrative rule-making process allowed the EU to write a prospectus rulebook. The 2010 Amending Prospectus Directive subsequently significantly expanded the scope for the expansion of the prospectus regime by nuancing the Commission's original 2003 powers to adopt administrative rules, in order to reflect the Lisbon settlement and the new regime for adopting administrative rules.[211] But it also thereby reactivated, finessed, and extended the original delegations to administrative rule-making and conferred new delegations. The new delegations cover, for example, rules adjusting the thresholds applicable to different exemptions,[212] a more nuanced delegation for the key Article 2 definitions,[213] a new delegation to update the thresholds for the Article 3 prospectus exemptions,[214] a delegation for the new equivalence regime for third country firms issuing employee share programmes,[215] a new delegation for the base prospectus/final terms and prospectus summary,[216] and a more extensive third country equivalence delegation.[217] The 2010 Omnibus I Directive similarly expanded the 2003 Directive by setting out delegations for ESMA-proposed ITSs and RTSs to be adopted by the Commission. Some RTS/ITS delegations are highly technical, such as the ITS delegations relating to the NCA delegation procedure, prospectus notification, and co-operation and information exchange.[218] Other ITS delegations are, notwithstanding their generally operational nature, more substantive and relate to the summary prospectus template and to ensuring the uniform application of the administrative rules governing disclosure.[219] The RTS delegations, which have a quasi-rule-making quality, relate to further specification of the Article 4 exemption regime, of when a prospectus supplement is required, and of which information must be exchanged between NCAs.[220] The 2014 Omnibus II Directive regime adds to these delegations, but it has a stronger quasi-regulatory quality, being concerned with RTS delegations.[221]

The process for adopting administrative rules in this sphere seems effective, auguring well for the future development of the prospectus regime but also reflecting the generally non-contentious nature of the prospectus regime. Initial evidence from the ESMA era suggests

---

[210] n 10.

[211] Under Art 24a the delegations are valid until 31 December 2014 and will be automatically extended unless revoked by the European Parliament or Council under the Art 24b procedure. The procedure under which the Parliament and Council may object to (veto) delegated acts (within three months of their notification by the Commission) is set out in Art 24c. The post-Lisbon Treaty procedure for adopting administrative measures is considered in Ch X sect 4.

[212] Relating to the exclusion of offers under €5 million and small debt offerings by credit institutions: Art 1(4).

[213] Requiring the Commission to consider the situation in different national markets and the approaches adopted by regulated markets: Art 2(4).

[214] Art 3(4), and reflecting the need to take into account developments in financial markets, including inflation.

[215] Art 4(1)(e).

[216] Art 5(5).

[217] Art 20(2), empowering the Commission to establish general equivalence criteria.

[218] Arts 13(5), 18(3), and 22(4).

[219] Arts 5(2) and 7(4).

[220] Arts 4(3), 16(3), and 22(4).

[221] The 2014 Omnibus II regime (n 20) confers on ESMA the power to propose RTSs in relation to the information which can be incorporated by reference, the procedures for prospectus approval, the publication of prospectuses, and the dissemination of advertisements related to prospectuses (Art 1).

that the positive dynamic originally established between the Commission and CESR with respect to the administrative prospectus regime is unlikely to change, notwithstanding the relatively much stronger institutional position of ESMA and the related potential for institutional tensions (Chapter XI section 5).

With respect to administrative rules adopted under the standard Article 290/291 TFEU process in which ESMA provides the Commission with 'technical advice',[222] ESMA's technical advice to the Commission on the two 2012 Commission Regulations,[223] which was detailed and reflected extensive market consultation,[224] was in large part accepted. The Commission's failure to follow ESMA's technical advice with respect to the proportionate regime for SME issuers,[225] however, represents an unusual and unwelcome departure given the unanimous and strongly expressed ESMA position and the poorly reasoned Commission response.[226] Relations with the European Parliament and Council have similarly been smooth, with none of the ESMA-era administrative Commission Regulations being subject to veto. Initial evidence also suggests that ESMA is sensitive to market concerns and costs in preparing its technical advice. It revised its initial advice on Commission Delegated Regulation 486/2012 to, for example, provide greater flexibility in the preparation of the prospectus summary and avoid overly lengthy documents.[227] But it has also proved to be robust in pursuing its aims, rejecting, for example, industry calls for a more flexible approach to the inclusion of disclosures in the non-NCA-scrutinized 'final terms' to a base prospectus, acknowledging the costs of its proposed requirements, but warning that the new regime was designed—particularly given the growing importance of structured securities sold through base prospectus/final terms structures—to prevent 'further excesses'.[228]

The administrative BTS regime, by contrast, has been slow in developing, reflecting the pressure which the major stability-orientated crisis-era measures placed on ESMA's resources. In 2013, however, the first set of BTSs were developed by ESMA in relation to the prospectus supplement.[229]

Outside the formal administrative rule-making process, ESMA's ability to shape and thicken the prospectus regime is considerable. The Q&A device, which is also employed under the Transparency Directive regime, has emerged as an effective and flexible technique for identifying, addressing, and placing on the reform agenda difficulties which emerge in practice with the prospectus regime. It was initially adopted by CESR, and ESMA has committed to playing an active role in its development. Its purpose is to promote common supervisory approaches and practices and to respond to queries raised on the operation of the regime.[230] Although it might be regarded as a rather workaday

---

[222] See further Ch X sect 4.

[223] n 23.

[224] Although an impact assessment was not carried out, given the tight time frame for the adoption of the rules, ESMA's advice reflected a public consultation and the input of three working groups set up under its Corporate Finance Standing Committee, its Consultative Working Group (external experts), and its Securities and Markets Stakeholder Group.

[225] The proportionate regime is covered in Commission Delegated Regulation 486/2012, n 23.

[226] See further sect 4.4.3.

[227] ESMA Feedback Statement/Final Advice/2011/323.

[228] n 227.

[229] n 25.

[230] Prospectus Q&A, n 208, 7.

device, in practice it delivers practical and timely guidance to the market on the operation of the regime and is regarded as a considerable success.[231] Running now to over 80 questions, and regularly updated, it addresses questions of significant practical importance, with the incorporation by reference mechanism, pricing supplements, and the powers of host Member States among the topics receiving close attention. While the Commission might have been expected to look askance at the Q&A, given its quasi-rule quality, it has been supportive of its role in clarifying the rulebook.[232] The Q&A has also provided an important mechanism for remedying, in the short term, deficiencies with the Directive. Most notably, following a Commission request, and reflecting very significant market concern, the Q&A provided guidance on short-form disclosure for employee share-offer programmes, given the difficulties caused by the application of the 2003 prospectus regime to these programmes. The Q&A also provided guidance on prospectus requirements for 'retail cascades'. In both cases, legislative change followed under the 2010 Amending Prospectus Directive, reflecting Commission concern that a supervisory-convergence-based response was not sufficiently robust,[233] but the Q&A provided an important short-term response as well as a template for legislative change. The Q&A is not binding and is not subject to consultation or impact assessment. Neither does it take the form of ESMA Regulation Article 16 Guidelines, in relation to which NCAs are subject to a 'comply-or-explain' requirement (Chapter X section 5.6). Its unsteady status is clear from ESMA's highlighting that only the Court of Justice can provide legally binding interpretations of EU law, as well as from evidence of the care taken by ESMA to consult the Commission in more contentious areas. But it provides comfort to market participants and promotes supervisory convergence; the strengthening peer-pressure dynamics within ESMA suggest that an NCA would, in practice, be reluctant to diverge from the Q&A, absent exceptional circumstances.

The ESMA Recommendation, originally developed at the Commission's request, is a more static document, but it provides important guidance and has been subject to material updating, notably with respect to mineral company disclosures. Although ESMA adopted the Recommendation under ESMA Regulation Article 16 when re-adopting the original CESR Recommendation, it did not subject it to the Article 16 NCA 'comply-or-explain' mechanism, reflecting the sensitivities associated with applying this ESMA-era quasi-enforcement mechanism to CESR-era measures.

ESMA has also deployed its power to adopt Opinions in support of supervisory convergence (ESMA Regulation Article 29(1)(a)) in relation to the equivalence of third country prospectuses;[234] in a reflection of the sensitivities associated with international engagement by ESMA generally (Chapter X section 5.9), its recommendations were adopted as an ESMA Opinion, rather than in the form of Article 16 'comply-or-explain' Guidelines.

---

[231] It is regarded by the markets as a quick, flexible, and efficient means of reducing diverging practices across the Member States: 2007 CESR Prospectus Report, n 193, 8 and 42. See also Franx, J-P, 'Disclosure Practices under the EU Prospectus Directive and the Role of CESR' (2007) 2 *CMLJ* 295, 305.

[232] The 2009 Amending Directive Proposal Impact Assessment, eg, highlighted ESMA's role in providing guidance, although it noted this would not be sufficient where legislative change was necessary: n 191, 6.

[233] eg Commission Background Document, n 198, 7, expressing support for CESR's solution but arguing that a legislative solution was needed.

[234] ESMA Opinion. Framework for the Assessment of Third Country Prospectuses under Article 20 of the Prospectus Directive. 20 March 2013 (ESMA/2013/317).

In a similarly sensitive context, ESMA has deployed an Opinion to highlight the correct application of the base prospectus regime and to signal the prospect of ESMA enforcement action under ESMA Regulation Article 17 if NCA non-compliance was to continue.[235]

Overall, recent experience suggests that, while the prospectus regime is continually intensifying, it is also dynamic and has some capacity to self-correct, whether through supervisory convergence strategies such as the Q&A, reliance on the extensive delegations to administrative rule-making, or the regular revisions of the legislative regime which the different review clauses imply. It also suggests that ESMA is in a pivotal position to shape and deepen the regime.

II.4.3 Setting the Perimeter: Public and Private Markets

II.4.3.1 The Core Prospectus Publication Obligation

Article 1 describes the purpose of the Directive as the harmonization of requirements for the drawing up, approval, and distribution of the prospectus to be published when securities are offered to the public or admitted to trading on a regulated market situated or operating within a Member State. The issuer who is the subject of the regime is defined as a legal entity which issues or proposes to issue securities, while the 'person making the offer' (also the subject of the Directive) is defined as a legal entity or individual which offers securities to the public (Articles 2(1)(h) and (i)).

Article 3(1) establishes the regime's regulatory perimeter. It provides that Member States shall not allow any offer of securities to be made to the public within their territories without prior publication of a prospectus. This obligation is extended to the admission of securities to trading on a regulated market by Article 3(3), which provides that Member States shall ensure that any admission of securities to trading on a regulated market situated or operating within their territories is subject to the publication of a prospectus.

Where a prospectus is not required, an equality-of-access principle is applied to any information supplied. Any material information provided by the issuer or an offeror and addressed to qualified investors or special categories of investors (including information disclosed in the context of a meeting relating to offers of securities) must be disclosed to all qualified investors or special categories of investors to whom the offer is exclusively addressed.[236]

The Directive contains a number of devices to set the regulatory perimeter which are noted in the following sections. The net effect of these is, first, to direct the Prospectus Directive towards the public markets and give it a strongly retail flavour and, second, to create a regime within which the private markets can operate with legal certainty. The 2010 deregulatory reforms reinforce the importance of the perimeter-control aspect of the Directive and its role in protecting private markets from excessive regulation.

---

[235] ESMA Opinion on the Base Prospectus Format 2013. 18 December 2013 (ESMA/2013/1944).

[236] Where a prospectus is required, information of this nature must be included in the prospectus or in a prospectus supplement.

II.4.3.2 Public Offers

The reach of the Directive is governed in large part by whether the securities are offered to the public (Article 1). Unlike the earlier regime,[237] and in what was at the time of its adoption in 2003 a major innovation,[238] the Prospectus Directive attempts to clarify the scope of 'offer to the public' under Article 2(1)(d). Article 2(1)(d) defines an offer of securities to the public as a communication to persons, in any form and by any means, which presents 'sufficient information'[239] on the terms of the offer and the securities to be offered so as to enable an investor to decide to purchase or subscribe[240] to the securities in question. Uniformity in the application of this key concept is central to achievement of the Directive's objectives, although its interpretation is a matter for national systems. Although the open-textured nature of the definition carries risks, and while some difficulties emerged in its application,[241] including with respect to market practice concerning pre-offer communications,[242] it was not subject to major revision under the 2010 reforms. The Commission acknowledged some difficulties with the implementation of the definition, but highlighted the dangers in changing the definition, given its benchmark effects.[243] The lack of enthusiasm for reform also perhaps reflects the significant degree of comfort which market participants can draw from the range of exemptions which are available from the Directive's application. The 2010 Amending Prospectus Directive called, however, for an enhanced definition of 'public offer' and included review of this key definition in the issues to be discussed in the review of the Directive which must be completed by January 2016.

II.4.3.3 Regulated Markets

The 'regulated market' perimeter for the prospectus regime reflects the heavy reliance across EU securities and markets regulation—prior to the financial crisis, at least—on the regulated market as a form of perimeter control which sets the boundary between the regulated public markets and the often lightly regulated private markets. The Prospectus Directive uses the regulated market as a convenient proxy for the large, public, liquid trading venues which, in part because of the branding associated with these venues, should attract the highest levels of regulation—whether with respect to issuers, intermediaries, or the venues themselves.

As discussed further in section 7, the regulated market perimeter in the issuer-disclosure context also reflects the central role played by trading venues and admission-to-trading rules

---

[237] The forlorn admission in the Public Offers Directive that 'so far, it has proved impossible to furnish a common definition of the term "public offer"' highlighted a glaring weakness in the regime.

[238] 2003 Revised Prospectus Directive Proposal, n 182, 12.

[239] The Commission stated at an early stage that it would take a broad view of this key requirement, but that it was ultimately to be determined by the Member States: Prospectus Transposition Meeting Minutes 26 January 2005.

[240] Free offers (such as options provided to employees without consideration) are therefore not subject to the prospectus requirement, as has been highlighted by the Q&A: n 208, Q6.

[241] Some market concerns were expressed as to the consistent application of this definition in CESR's 2007 Prospectus Report, n 193, 19. The CSES and ESME Reports also pointed to difficulties in implementation.

[242] Some concern was expressed at an early stage that the 'offer to the public' definition does not catch pre-sales communications (which provide supplementary investment information or research) to intermediaries who may be potential subscribers to an offer: 2007 FMLC Letter, n 209, 2.

[243] The Commission underlined that it would continue to use its enforcement tools to address implementation difficulties, and suggested that guidance would be the most appropriate tool for addressing remaining legal certainty issues: Background Document, n 198, 15.

in the capital-raising process, and the dynamics of competition and differentiation between venues. Specifically, in the prospectus context, the regulated market perimeter allows EU trading venues choosing to operate as regulated markets to brand themselves as high-quality venues, thereby facilitating the Prospectus Directive's objectives with respect to market finance promotion and, potentially, market integration, as well as investor protection.

II.4.3.4 Securities

The securities subject to the Article 3(1) and (3) prospectus publication requirements are defined as 'transferable securities', broadly defined under the 2014 MiFID II/MiFIR regime,[244] but with the exception of money-market instruments having a maturity of less than 12 months (Article 2(1)(a)). Although EU securities and markets regulation generally had a close focus on the equity markets pre-financial crisis, since its 2003 adoption the Directive has applied well beyond the equity markets, although its disclosure requirements are calibrated to reflect the particular class of security engaged.

Equity and non-equity securities are further defined, given their differential treatment with respect to certain aspects of the regime. Equity securities (Article 2(1)(b)) are defined as shares and other transferable securities equivalent to shares in companies, as well as any other type of transferable securities giving the right to acquire any of these securities as a consequence of their being converted or the rights conferred on them being exercised. Convertible securities must, however, be issued by the issuer of the underlying shares or by an entity belonging to the issuer's group. Non-equity securities are simply defined under Article 2(1)(c) as all securities that are not equity securities.[245]

Article 1(2) sets out a number of classes of securities which are excluded from the Directive. Under Article 1(2)(a), units issued by collective investment undertakings other than the closed-end type[246] are excluded, as particular disclosure requirements typically apply to these open-ended funds. Open-ended funds in the form of a 'UCITS' are subject to the extensive UCITS regime discussed in Chapter III.

Government debt and other quasi-sovereign securities are also exempt. Non-equity securities issued by a Member State or by one of a Member State's regional or local authorities, by public international bodies of which one or more Member States are members, by the European Central Bank (ECB), or by the central banks of the Member States are excluded (Article 1(2)(b)). So too are shares in the capital of central banks of the Member States (Article 1(2)(c)). Article 1(2)(d) exempts securities unconditionally and irrevocably guaranteed by a Member State or by one of a Member State's regional or local authorities. Notwithstanding support in some quarters, as the EU sovereign debt crisis deepened over

---

[244] See Ch V sect 4.3 for this definition.

[245] Although some clarification is given in that rec 12 provides that depositary receipts and convertible notes are non-equity securities. This approach runs the risk of considerable divergences in the treatment of complex securities and hybrid instruments (Revell and Cole, n 197, 87), although NCAs appear to be co-operating on the treatment of such securities.

[246] The object of these entities is the collective investment of capital provided by the public. They operate on the principle of risk-spreading and their defining feature is that units are, at the holder's request, repurchased or redeemed, directly or indirectly, out of the undertaking's assets (Art 1(2)(o)). A 'unit' in a collective-investment undertaking covers securities issued by a collective-investment undertaking as representing the rights of the participants in such an undertaking over its assets (Art 2(1)(p)).

the crisis era, for more extensive disclosure with respect to the risks which sovereign debt carries, there has been little enthusiasm for reform in this area, reflecting the extensive disclosure already available with respect to sovereign issuers. A similar policy is evident in the removal by the 2010 Amending Prospectus Directive of disclosure requirements relating to a Member State guarantor.

Securities which are issued by associations with legal status or by non-profit-making bodies, are recognized by a Member State, and are issued in order to allow the bodies in question to achieve their non-profit-making objectives are also excluded (Article 1(2)(e)).

II.4.3.5 Private Markets and Placements

While the Prospectus Directive is strongly associated with the prospectus requirement for public offers, perhaps its most significant achievement is its delineation of the perimeter between the notionally 'public' markets which are subject to the Directive and the notionally 'private' markets within which capital can be raised by issuers without being subject to the Directive. Appropriate perimeter control is a key element of capital-raising regulation internationally, and has long been a feature of the EU regime. The current regime, reflecting the 2010 reforms, provides a significant space within which 'private' markets can operate outside the Prospectus Directive. Although these exemptions reflect long-established policy rationales for disapplying public market disclosure standards, they are increasingly being used to support novel forms of financing, such as crowdfunding, which raise small amounts of capital from a wide range of investors and which operate outside the Prospectus Directive. The Directive provides for two major classes of private market exemption: exemptions for finance-raising by SMEs and similar companies (section 4.4.3) and exemptions for wholesale-market-orientated private placements.

The private placement regime (which can also be used for finance-raising by SMEs) represented in 2003 a significant advance on earlier attempts to address prospectus disclosure. The 1989 Public Offers Directive, for example, contained a complex network of exemptions which was based on the premise that professional investors did not need the protection of a mandatory prospectus requirement. Among the most notorious of the exemptions was that for Euro-securities[247] which were not the subject of 'a generalised campaign of advertising or canvassing'. The failure to define what was meant by 'a generalised campaign of advertising or canvassing' allowed Member States to set the parameters of this important exemption in different ways, and meant that it was not widely used in practice. The clarity which the 2003 Directive brought to private placements was widely welcomed at the time of the Directive's adoption;[248] further enhancements have followed with the 2010 Amending Prospectus Directive.

Under Article 3(2)(a) a key private-placement-orientated exemption applies to public offers of securities addressed solely to 'qualified investors' (but only as long as the securities are not also admitted to trading on a regulated market—a prospectus must be published where the

---

[247] Defined as transferable securities which were to be underwritten and distributed by a syndicate, at least two of the members of which had their registered offices in different States, which were offered on a significant scale in one or more States other than that of the issuer's registered office, and which could be subscribed for or initially acquired only through a credit institution.

[248] eg Ferran, n 26, 200–1.

admission of securities to trading on a regulated market is sought (Article 3(3)[249]). Following the 2010 reforms, and reflecting significant market concern on this issue,[250] the definition of a 'qualified investor' was aligned to the 2004 MiFID I definition, in the first instance (it is now aligned to the 2014 MiFID II definition),[251] of a 'professional investor'.[252] Accordingly, the following four classes of entity are deemed to be qualified investors: entities required to be authorized or regulated to operate in the financial markets (including credit institutions, investment firms, insurance companies, collective investment schemes, pension funds and other institutional investors); large undertakings;[253] national and regional governments and similar public bodies, including international and supra-national organizations; and other institutional investors whose main activity is to invest in financial instruments. A second category of investors can be deemed to be qualified upon request and provided they meet two of the following criteria: the investor has carried out transactions, in significant size, on the relevant market at an average frequency of ten per quarter over the previous four quarters; the investor's financial instrument portfolio must exceed €500,000; or the investor must have worked in the financial sector for at least one year in a professional position. This 'opt-in' process is subject to a range of procedural requirements.[254] The earlier 2003 Directive definition of a qualified investor, while similar to the 2004 MiFID I regime and, later, the 2014 MiFID II regime, differed in a number of key respects, notably its reliance on a self-certification system for qualified investors; MiFID I originally and MiFID II now are based on assessment by the relevant investment firm, typically advisers and underwriters. The MiFID II-aligned regime accordingly brings cost reductions to private placements as it allows advisers and underwriters (subject to MiFID II) to rely on their client-base classifications when they design private placements, and abolishes the need for investment firms to maintain complex lists of different categories of professional or qualified investors. Under the 2003 regime, a related registration system was established for SMEs and natural persons classed as qualified investors, to facilitate capital-raising by issuers through private placements. This requirement, which proved cumbersome and ineffective in practice,[255] has now been abolished.[256]

---

[249] A prospectus is not, however, required where shares representing (over a 12-month period) less than 10 per cent of the shares of the same class already admitted to trading on the same regulated market are admitted: Art 4(2)(a).

[250] Reflected in the 2008 ESME Professional Investor Report, n 192.

[251] While broadly similar, the 2003 Prospectus Directive and 2004 MiFID I concepts differed in various ways, reflecting the product-driven orientation of the prospectus regime and the service-driven orientation of MiFID I: 2008 ESME Professional Investor Report, n 192, 5. The 2004 MiFID I definition has since been refined by the 2014 MiFID II/MiFIR reforms, which also govern 'qualified investors' under the prospectus regime: Ch IV sect 5.2.

[252] The Prospectus Directive definition of a 'qualified investor', via MiFID II, encompasses two classes of professional investor: those considered to be professional and those who may be treated as professional on request, subject to their meeting the relevant criteria.

[253] Firms must meet two of the following criteria: balance sheet of €20 million or more, or net turnover of €40 million or more or own funds of €2 million or more.

[254] See further Ch V sect 5.2.

[255] 2009 Amending Prospectus Directive Proposal Impact Assessment, n 191, 26, and 2008 ESME Professional Investor Report, n 192 (reporting on the different national registers and finding little evidence of their use—only four investors were noted on the German BaFIN's register by end-2007).

[256] During the original negotiations on the 2003 Directive, the European Parliament presciently argued that this requirement was costly, cumbersome, and likely to dissuade natural persons from otherwise available investments: Second ECON Report, n 182, Amendment 12.

A specific exemption regime, which also supports private placements, applies for wholesale debt market securities; offers designed in practice to be sold to sophisticated investors are excluded, in that offers addressed to investors who acquire securities for a total consideration of at least €100,000 per investor for each separate offer are exempted (Article 3(2)(c)).[257] In a related exemption, so too are offers whose denomination per unit amounts to at least €100,000 (Article 3(2)(d)). These exemptions were originally placed at a €50,000 threshold by the 2003 Directive; market practice suggested that this level was not sufficiently high to ensure a predominantly wholesale market, given evidence that retail investors were purchasing investments of that denomination.[258]

The private placement regime extends to offerings according to their size, including small offerings reflecting SME financing needs (section 4.4.3) as well as those designed for sophisticated investors. Offers of securities addressed to fewer than 150 natural or legal persons per Member State (other than qualified investors) are excluded (Article 3(2)(b)). So too are offers with a total consideration in the EU[259] of less than €100,000 (calculated over a 12-month period) (Article 3(2)(e)).

II.4.3.6 Exempted Transactions, including Employee Share Offerings

An additional series of exemptions, which broadly addresses particular funding and share-capital transactions where disclosure is generally already available, applies under Article 4. The restricted nature of these exemptions (and particularly those for rights issues and employee share offerings) under the 2003 Directive was criticized for imposing restrictions on the ability of companies to raise equity finance,[260] and a series of reforms followed under the 2010 Amending Prospectus Directive.

Article 4(1) provides an exemption from the obligation to publish a prospectus for certain types of public offer. The obligation does not apply to shares issued in substitution for shares of the same class already issued, where the issuing of the new shares does not involve any increase in the issued share capital (Article 4(1)(a)). Securities offered in connection with a takeover by means of an exchange offer are also exempt, as long as a document is available which contains disclosure regarded as equivalent to the prospectus disclosure required by the NCA (Article 4(1)(b)). An exemption applies to securities offered, allotted, or to be allotted in connection with a merger or division as long as, again, an equivalent document is made available (Article 4(1)(c)). The exemption for rights issues provides that dividends paid out to existing shareholders in the form of shares of the same class as the shares in respect of which such dividends are paid are exempted, provided a document is available setting out information on the number and nature of the shares, and the reasons for and details of the offer (Article 4(1)(d)).

---

[257] Across the Directive, where the denomination is non-euro, the rules apply to values equivalent to the euro value at the date of issue.

[258] 2010 Amending Prospectus Directive rec 9 (introduced by the Parliament, which was concerned as to evidence in some Member States of the threshold being used to evade prospectus requirements and of related investor detriment: ECON Report, n 191, Amendment 30).

[259] The 2003 Directive did not specify whether the offer amount was to be calculated on a Member State or pan-EU basis, leading to the 2010 clarification.

[260] ESME warned that the exemptions were internally inconsistent, delayed the raising of capital, and imposed the full prospectus obligation on too many transactions: 2007 ESME Report, n 192, 16.

An exemption is also available for occupational share schemes. The 2003 Directive contained an exemption for director and employee share schemes. Its very limited scope (it applied only where the company had securities admitted to trading on a EU regulated market, and did not support smaller issuers admitted to other trading venues or multi-national issuers operating within the EU but admitted to trading elsewhere) led to significant market concern, given the resultant poorer access to share schemes by employees of firms outside the exemption (evidence emerged of some global and EU firms cancelling their share schemes).[261] A significantly revised regime was adopted under the 2010 Amending Prospectus Directive. It provides an exemption for securities offered, allotted, or to be allotted to existing or former directors or employees by their employer or an affiliated undertaking, provided the company has its head or registered office in the EU, and as long as a document is made available concerning the number and nature of the securities and the reasons for and details of the offer (Article 4(1)(e)). The exemption also applies to non-EU companies whose securities are admitted to trading on an EU regulated market or on a third country regulated market. Where the securities are admitted to a non-EU regulated market, the company must provide the Article 4(1)(e) document in a language customary in the sphere of international finance and the regulated market in question must have been the subject of an equivalence decision by the Commission. As noted in Chapter I, the EU is increasingly relying on equivalence techniques to extend the reach of EU securities and markets regulation; this equivalence regime, which reflects the approach to equivalence adopted with respect to, for example, rating agencies,[262] provides a practical example of its reach in a relatively uncontroversial area.

A similar series of exemptions applies under Article 4(2) to the obligation to publish a prospectus where the securities are admitted to trading on a regulated market. The Article 4(1) exemptions with respect to takeovers, mergers and divisions, and rights issues apply.[263] An exemption also applies where the shares represent, over a period of 12 months, less than 10 per cent of the number of shares of the same class already admitted to trading on the same regulated market, and where the shares are issued in substitution for shares of the same class already admitted to trading on the same regulated market (as long as the issuing of the shares does not involve any increase in the issued share capital). Convertible issues are also covered, with the prospectus obligation disapplied from shares which result from the conversion or exchange of other securities, or from the exercise of the rights conferred by other securities, as long as the shares are of the same class as the shares already admitted to trading on the same regulated market. Reflecting the Directive's passport structure, the prospectus obligation is also lifted where the securities are already admitted to trading on another regulated market.

---

[261] 2008 CSES Report, n 194, 41–2. Similarly, 2007 CESR Prospectus Report, n 193, 23.

[262] In essence, the Art 4(1)(e) equivalence regime requires that the third country ensures that the regulated market complies with requirements equivalent to the market abuse, transparency, and MiFID regimes, and that the third country legal and supervisory framework ensures that markets are subject to authorization and effective supervision and enforcement, that markets have clear and transparent rules governing the admission of securities to trading, that issuers are subject to periodic and ongoing disclosure requirements, and that market transparency and integrity are ensured by the prevention of market abuse.

[263] With respect to offers and allotments free of charge to shareholders, the shares offered/allotted (and dividends in the form of shares) must be of the same class as the shares already admitted to trading. The same requirement applies to shares which are offered/allotted to directors/employees.

II.4.4 Calibration and Differentiation

II.4.4.1 Calibration and Differentiation

The risks of regulatory error and blunt application generated by the extensive harmonization achieved by the prospectus regime are significantly mitigated by the extensive calibration and differentiation within the regime. The clearest manifestation of this is in the disclosure regime which, as required by Article 7, reflects different issuers, securities, and types of offers. Recent reforms have finessed this differentiation. The 2010 reforms, for example, introduce a differentiated, proportionate disclosure regime for rights issues (where the relevant class of shares is admitted to trading on a regulated market or a multilateral trading facility (MTF))[264] to support easier capital-raising,[265] and also focus closely on the mechanics of the base prospectus and final terms used in debt offering programmes, reflecting the particular dynamics and risks of these programmes (section 4.5.2). The differentiation is marked, however, with respect to the wholesale debt markets, SME finance, and the retail markets, as discussed further in this section.

II.4.4.2 The Wholesale Debt Markets

The EU corporate bond market, while still lagging some way behind the massive US market, has recently achieved significant growth (section 9). The bond markets generally receive differentiated treatment across the Prospectus Directive, including with respect to the choice of home Member State (section 4.7.1), the particular disclosures required (section 4.6), and, as noted in section 4.5.2, with respect to particular offering structures (notably base programmes and retail cascades).

Calibrated treatment of offerings of bonds (debt securities) in the wholesale markets in particular is, however, a defining feature of the Prospectus Directive and reflects the dominance in those markets of sophisticated investors who do not require the detailed disclosure provided in the retail-orientated prospectus, as well as the influence of a well-organized lobby during the original 2003 Directive negotiations. It also reflects the wider concern in EU securities and markets regulation to ensure the efficiency of the cross-border private placement market, which is seen as a critical support to pan-EU capital-raising. This concern is now all the stronger given growth in the EU corporate bond market in the wake of the financial crisis.

The Commission's original retail market approach to the 2003 Prospectus Directive Proposal resulted in a 'one-size-fits-all' model which severely limited the exemptions available for wholesale market debt issuance, removed issuer choice from the wholesale debt markets, and threatened to disrupt the operation of the eurobond market in particular by moving prospectus approval from the London and Luxembourg marketplaces where it

---

[264] An MTF is a form of regulated trading venue: Ch V sect 6.3. This form of perimeter control represents an exception for the Directive, which typically addresses securities admitted to regulated markets only. It led ESMA to consider whether two proportionate disclosure regimes should be adopted, but to opt finally for a single approach: ESMA Consultation Paper/2011/141, 52 and 2004 Commission Regulation Art 26a(2) (revised by 2012 Commission Delegated Regulation 486/2012).

[265] Prospectus Directive Art 7(2)(g) and 2004 Commission Regulation Art 2, point 13 (revised by the 2012 Commission Delegated Regulation 486/2012).

had concentrated.[266] An effective lobbying effort,[267] combined with strikingly cohesive institutional support,[268] led to a considerably altered regime which applies to 'non-equity securities' generally and supports the wholesale bond market. Although the 2010 reforms have scaled back the extent to which wholesale market bond offerings benefit from special treatment, overall the wholesale bond markets continue to benefit from highly calibrated treatment.

The application of the Directive to the wholesale bond markets is tailored across three dimensions: exemptions from the obligation to publish a prospectus, issuer choice of NCA, and disclosure.

A range of offerings, including offerings of 'securities' with a denomination of at least €100,000 and subscription requirements of at least €100,000 (originally €50,000 under the 2003 Directive), is exempt from the requirement to produce a prospectus; a prospectus is, however, required for admission to trading on a regulated market, and preparation of a prospectus also affords such issuers the opportunity to benefit from a passport with respect to multiple admissions, to the extent that they occur (Article 3(2)).

Issuers of non-equity securities with a denomination of at least €1,000 may choose the home Member State NCA responsible for the approval of the prospectus (Article 2(1)(m)(ii)).

Non-exempt offers of non-equity securities with a denomination per unit of €100,000 (€50,000 under the 2003 Directive) benefit from a series of calibrations to the disclosure regime, including that prospectus requirements must be calibrated (Article 7(2)(b)) and the disapplication of the requirement for a retail summary (Article 5(2)), unless one is requested by the host NCA (Article 19(4)). These issuers are also subject to a discrete translation regime (Article 19(4)).

II.4.4.3 SME Finance and the Prospectus Regime

The calibration of prospectus requirements to ease burdens on the SME segment, and the related deregulation of SME access to the public markets, is not a straightforward exercise.[269] In its favour, the costs represented by prospectus (and other) disclosures[270] can

---

[266] eg, Preston, A, 'Home Country Rule Threat to Eurobond Market', *Euromoney*, July 2001, 33. The strength of the opposition can be tracked through the *Financial Times'* discussion of the 2001 Original Prospectus Directive Proposal: see, eg, Guerrera, F and Dickson, M, 'Passport to Discord', *Financial Times*, 22 November 2001; Norman, P and Boland, V, 'LSE Demands Brussels Listens to City Concerns', *Financial Times*, 16 November 2001; and Letters, *Financial Times*, 16 November 2001 (a letter from a group of 56 chairmen, chief executives, and directors of smaller UK companies).

[267] The bond markets have long been adept in lobbying on key measures. The exemption for euro-securities in the precursor 1989 Public Offers Directive followed strong representations from the UK, Luxembourg, France, Germany, and the International Primary Market Association (IPMA).

[268] The European Economic and Social Committee (then ECOSOC), the European Parliament, and the Council all supported a calibrated regime for the wholesale bond markets. ECOSOC, eg, criticized the original regime as disproportionate and threatening the private placement market and called for a lighter regime which would 'display greater recognition of the needs of the professional debt markets, while protecting the legitimate interests of retail investors': ECOSOC Opinion, n 182, para 13.4.

[269] Well illustrated by the reported SEC uneasiness with respect to the deregulatory 2012 JOBS Act, and by the different positions adopted by the Commission and ESMA with respect to the deregulation of SME issuer disclosure (noted in this section ahead).

[270] Prospectus preparation costs have been estimated as in the region of €200,000–€300,000: 2008 CSES Report, n 194, 49.

be significant. But any segmentation between large and smaller issuers on EU regulated markets (subject to the prospectus regime) with respect to prospectus (and other) obligations could generate investor confusion and damage to the regulated market 'brand'. In addition, SME investment poses risks, particularly from a liquidity perspective; while a very small subset of the SME segment, and while distinct, the risks inherent in crowdfunding underline the difficulties in deregulating public markets on the basis of issuer size.[271] Given the dominance of bank finance, it is also unlikely that large segments of the SME sector will raise significant funding through the major public regulated markets, while admission to second-tier markets remains the preserve of only the largest firms in the SME sector.[272] Deregulation may accordingly have limited benefits. On the other hand, admission to major trading venues (such as regulated markets) serves a visibility function for SMEs, which deregulation can support.

From the outset, the Prospectus Directive attempted to deal with the regulatory costs faced by smaller issuers. Although not expressly targeted to SME issuers, two exemptions from the Directive apply to smaller offers. Under Article 1(2)(h), the Directive does not apply to securities included in an offer where the initial consideration for the offer in the EU is less than €5 million (calculated over a period of 12 months), whether the offer takes the form of a public offer or admission to trading on a regulated market. Article 3(2)(e) further provides that an offer of securities with a total consideration in the EU of less than €100,000 (calculated over a period of 12 months) is not subject to the prospectus obligation,[273] although this exclusion from scope lifts on admission to trading on a regulated market. In effect, Member States retain the option to impose prospectus requirements (governed by national law) on offers of less than €5 million, but may not impose national requirements on offers with a total consideration of less than €100,000.[274] While these are long-standing exemptions, the 2010 Amending Prospectus Directive's increase of the original Article 1(2)(h) threshold from €2.5 million to €5 million reflects an intensifying EU policy concern, driven by the financial crisis, to ease the regulatory burden on smaller issuers.[275] The 2010 revisions to the employee and director share-offer regime were also designed in part to support SME issuers.[276]

In addition, debt securities issued by deposit-taking credit institutions benefit from two exemptions which are designed to support the easy issuance of bonds by smaller credit institutions, given that credit institutions are subject to solvency supervision and that

---

[271] The risks posed by crowdfunding, which operates outside the public perimeter for capital-raising regulation, have been extensively examined in the US, where the 2012 JOBS Act reforms have expanded the (lightly-regulated) space within which crowdfunding can occur. See, eg, Verstein, A, 'The Misregulation of Person-to-Person Lending' (2011) 47 *UC Davis LR* 447. While in the EU the Prospectus Directive limits the amount of capital that can be raised in this way, the UK FCA has highlighted the risks in terms of returns, liquidity, and fraud: FCA, Crowdfunding: Is Your Investment Protected (2012).

[272] Only 6,000 or so of the 23 million SMEs in the EU are admitted to trading on a regulated market or other venue: SMSG Report, n 147, 4.

[273] Both calculations are to be made on a pan-EU basis.

[274] While both exemptions are similar, the second has the effect of disapplying the Directive completely: issuers cannot accordingly opt-in.

[275] Reflecting the deregulatory potential of these measures, the UK opted to implement them ahead of the implementation deadline: HM Treasury and FSA, Consultation Paper 11/28, UK Implementation of the Amending Directive 2010/73 (2011).

[276] 2010 Amending Directive rec 14.

facilitating bond issuance ultimately supports bank financing for SMEs. Article 1(2)(f) excludes non-equity securities which are issued by credit institutions in a continuous or repeated manner, as long as they are not subordinated, convertible, or exchangeable, they do not give a right to subscribe or acquire other types of securities and are not linked to a derivative instrument, they do not materialize the reception of repayable deposits, and they are covered by the EU's deposit-guarantee scheme. A less onerous exemption applies for another category of non-equity securities issued in a continuous or repeated manner by credit institutions, as long as the total consideration for the offer is less than €50 million (calculated over a 12-month period); the conditions in this case are limited to the securities not being subordinated, convertible, or exchangeable, not giving a right to subscribe to or acquire other types of securities, and not being linked to a derivative instrument (Article 1(2)(j)).

For larger offers within the scope of the Directive, the disclosure regime is calibrated to reflect the costs incurred by smaller issuers. Generally, Prospectus Directive disclosures are subject to a materiality principle (Article 5(1)), which allows smaller issuers to calibrate the required disclosures, and a materiality test is built into many of the detailed 2004 Commission Prospectus Regulation requirements.[277] The incorporation by reference mechanism (available for all issuers) also supports cost-reduction.

In addition, more targeted calibrations apply. The Prospectus Directive originally required, and continues to require, that its administrative disclosure rules take into account the various activities and sizes of issuers, in particular SMEs, defined as companies which, according to their last annual or consolidated accounts, meet at least two of three criteria: an average number of employees during the financial year of less than 250; total balance sheet not in excess of €43 million; and annual net turnover not in excess of €50 million[278]) (Article 7(2)(e)). This injunction was not followed under the 2004 Commission Prospectus Regulation. The omission relates in part to lack of support for the key distinguishing requirement that two, rather than three, years' financial information be required for smaller issuers.[279] Change has since followed. The 2010 Amending Prospectus Directive added a new classification of firms to benefit from such proportionate disclosure rules: companies with a 'reduced market capitalization', defined as companies listed on a regulated market with an average market capitalization of less than €100 million, on the basis of end-year quotes from the previous three calendar years (Article 7(2)(e)). It also added credit institutions which choose to issue a prospectus although benefiting from the Article 1(2)(j) exemption for bond issuance.[280] The Commission additionally activated the related delegation for proportionate disclosure (including the original delegation in relation to SMEs), requesting technical advice from ESMA in 2011 and adopting related administrative rules in the 2012 Commission Delegated Regulation 486/2012, which amends the 2004 Commission Prospectus Regulation. The reforms apply when securities issued by SMEs or companies with a reduced market capitalization are offered to the public or admitted to trading on a

---

[277] Including, eg, with respect to the issuer's principal investments, activities, and markets, and material contracts.

[278] Art 2(1)(f).

[279] Ferran, n 26, 181.

[280] The reforms do not, however, reflect the call from ESME for small and medium-sized credit institutions to be permitted to place 'plain vanilla' debt securities with their own clients without a prospectus and without any threshold on the total consideration for the securities offered: 2007 ESME Report, n 192, 9.

regulated market.[281] The key reform is to allow such companies to disclose two, rather than three, years of audited historical financial information.[282]

But the new proportionate disclosure regime is not problem-free.[283] Injecting a lighter sub-regime for smaller issuers within a prospectus regime which applies to all securities admitted to regulated markets confuses the scope of the Directive by applying rules of varying intensity within the regulated market perimeter. It may accordingly, as discussed in section 7, damage the regulatory branding effects associated with regulated markets. The related benefits may be limited. Even with respect to the small subset of SME firms which are likely to undertake a public offering and admit their securities to a regulated market, and thereby to come within the new, calibrated prospectus regime, significant difficulties arise with respect to pricing, market sentiment and liquidity, a lack of venture capital support, and an increasing tendency for venture capitalists to exit through trade sales rather than public offerings.[284]

The new proportionate SME/companies with reduced market capitalization regime provides early evidence, however, that ESMA may—where it is followed—act as a counterforce to potential regulatory error. During the development of the 2012 Commission Delegated Regulation 486/2012, which contains the new proportionate disclosure regime, ESMA advised against a differentiated prospectus regime for smaller issuers, given the risks to investor protection and to regulatory consistency, and advised, were the regime to be pursued, that any such differentiation not apply to IPOs or to first admissions to trading on a regulated market.[285] In a poorly reasoned response,[286] the Commission acknowledged the 'de facto reduction in disclosure'[287] and the particular risks generated by IPOs and initial admissions to trading, given lower levels of visibility and credibility.[288] But it simply argued that calibration of the regime would reduce administrative burdens for SMEs and noted industry support, deciding that a calibrated regime generally would make a 'real difference' in terms of market access.[289]

II.4.4.4 The Retail Markets

(a) Retail Investor Protection

The Prospectus Directive was the first FSAP measure to engage closely with the retail markets and with retail investor protection[290] as is clear from the strongly retail

---

[281] 2004 Commission Prospectus Regulation Art 26b (inserted by 2012 Commission Delegated Regulation 486/2012). A new administrative proportionate disclosure regime also applies to credit institutions issuing non-equity securities under the Art 1(2)(j) exemption, where issuers opt-in to the prospectus regime, and to rights issues.

[282] The detail of the new regime, which extends beyond financial reporting, is set out in, eg, a new Proportionate Schedule for the Share Registration Document for SMEs and Companies with Reduced Market Capitalization: 2004 Commission Prospectus Regulation, Annex XXV. The refinements address, eg, disclosure concerning capital resources, borrowing requirements, and funding structure.

[283] Such as shortening the prospectus approval period for SMEs given the short window they typically have in which to raise funds, and delegation of home NCA prospectus approval to the NCA of the relevant second tier or other specialized market on which the securities are to be admitted: SMSG Report, n 147, 17.

[284] 2011 City of London SME Report, n 41, 20–2.

[285] ESMA, Prospectus Directive Consultation Paper (ESMA/2011/141) and ESMA, Final Advice (ESMA 2011/323).

[286] Commission Prospectus Regulation 486/2012 Proposal Impact Assessment (SWD (2012) 77) 22–9.

[287] n 286, 19.

[288] n 286, 22.

[289] n 286, 28–9.

[290] For a characterization of the Directive as a retail-market measure see Morris, T and Machin, J, 'The pan-European Capital Market—is the Prospectus Directive a Success or Failure?' (2006) 1 *CMLJ* 205.

orientation of the original Commission Proposal which threatened to derail the negotiations. The Directive is, for example, couched in the language of investor protection.[291] It also assumes that issuer disclosure is not only a device for supporting market efficiency but is read by individual retail investors, notwithstanding the very significant doubt as to whether retail investors read or understand prospectus disclosure.[292] Disclosure must, for example, be presented in an 'easily analysable and comprehensible form' and a prospectus summary, setting out key investor information, is required (Article 5). The website publication requirements (Article 14), to take another example, are in part designed to support easy access by retail investors. More generally, the Directive is careful to segment the public debt and equity markets from the wholesale debt markets through significant exemptions. The Directive accordingly reflects a long-standing association internationally between prospectus regulation and retail market protection, as well as the equally long-standing disconnection between this association and the realities of retail market behaviour.[293] But in one respect the Directive is novel. The important 2010 reforms to the prospectus summary, discussed in section 4.5.1, represent a striking enhancement of the disclosure regime from a retail investor perspective and an overdue recognition of the need to tailor disclosure for the retail markets.

There are, however, persistent weaknesses in the Directive's retail investor protection scheme. The ability of issuers to choose to prepare the full prospectus in a language 'customary in the sphere of international finance' (section 4.7.5) means that in practice retail investors may be faced with a prospectus they cannot read, although the summary will be translated into the official language of the retail investor's Member State.[294] The risks and costs to investors are exacerbated by Article 5(2)(c) which provides that where a claim relating to the information in a prospectus is litigated, the investor might, depending on the national rules applicable, have to bear the costs of translating the full prospectus before legal proceedings are initiated (disclosure to this effect must be made in the prospectus summary).[295] Advertising (section 4.9) is subject to only minimum harmonized rules. It might be argued that advertising regulation is best a function of host Member State rules. But there is nonetheless a disconnect, from a retail investor protection perspective, between the high level of harmonization which applies to the prospectus, which is probably rarely read by retail investors, and the minimal harmonization of rules governing advertisements, on which retail investors are very likely to rely. Dissemination also remains unsatisfactory, with the prospectus regime lagging behind the transparency regime in terms of the

---

[291] eg recs 10, 12, 16 (which provides that one of the objectives of the Directive is to protect investors), 18, 19, 20, 21, 27, and 30.

[292] eg Baums, T, Changing Patterns of Corporate Disclosure in Continental Europe: the Example of Germany, ECGI WP No 4/2002 (2002), available at <http://ssrn.com/abstract=345020>, and Paredes, n 88.

[293] eg Langevoort, D, 'Theories, Assumptions, and Securities Regulation: Market Efficiency Revisited' (1992) 140 *UPaLR* 851, 911–2.

[294] See Mattil, P and Möslein, M, 'The Language of the Prospectus: Europeanisation of Prospectus Law and Consumer Protection' (2007) 18 *Zeitschrift für Wirtschafts und Bankrecht* 819 (also published in (2008) 1 *JIBFL* 27).

[295] Mattil and Möslein draw on the real example of a German retail offering by a French issuer of bonds with a €1,000 denomination by means of a prospectus of approximately 220 pages in English and French, and a 15-page German-language prospectus summary, which summary pointed to the risk that translation of the prospectus could be required and stated that French law governed the prospectus: n 294.

centralization of electronic disclosure storage, which is of critical importance in supporting easy retail investor access to disclosure.

(b) Market Integration and Promoting Household Savings

The Directive can also be associated with the promotion of cross-border investment by retail investors and stronger household engagement with market-based saving generally. The 2010 reforms, for example, are designed to promote greater share ownership among employees[296] and to encourage retail investors to compare securities offerings, aided by the new summary prospectus. But given the now very substantial evidence concerning weaknesses in EU retail investor decision-making, any regulatory strategy based on the promotion of retail engagement with the markets poses risks in the absence of significantly more aggressive regulatory strategies, including with respect to downstream distribution and upstream literacy initiatives (Chapter IX). In the massive US retail equity market, the 'signalling' effects of mandatory issuer disclosure have been criticized for implicitly encouraging retail investors into the market and for imbuing them with a false sense of security (leading them to believe they can generate equal returns to market professionals) by emphasizing the benefits of disclosure without highlighting the impact of trading costs and diversification.[297] While the EU retail equity market is some long distance behind the US market, similar risks can arise. The prospectus approval process, for example, which is directed towards the completeness of prospectus disclosure rather than towards its quality, might present risks to those uninformed retail investors who assume a quality assessment is carried out;[298] the current move towards more robust product intervention (Chapter IX section 7) may lead, however, to a more merit-style review of securities as part of the prospectus approval process, particularly with respect to complex structured securities.

In practice, however, the Directive has not proved to have strong transformative effects with respect to retail investor behaviour; retail investors continue to rely heavily on intermediation and to purchase packaged investment products and there is limited appetite for direct purchases of firms' securities (Chapter IX section 1.2.1). There is also little evidence that a pan-EU retail market for primary market offers has developed, or of the Directive breaking down the dominant home bias (section 4.12).

In one respect, however, the Directive has had a transformative effect—but this effect has been prejudicial; a contraction has occurred in the retail bond market. Two features of the Directive can be associated with this contraction.

The first relates to the distribution of securities by means of a 'retail cascade.' Exemptions designed for wholesale market participants carry the risk that sales will subsequently 'leak' to the retail sector. Accordingly, the Article 3(1) exemptions from prospectus publication do not apply to subsequent resales of exempted offers (Article 3(2)). Under the 2003

---

[296] 2010 Amending Prospectus Directive rec 14.

[297] See, eg, Jackson, H, 'To What Extent Should Individual Investors Rely on the Mechanisms of Market Efficiency? A Preliminary Investigation of Dispersion in Investor Returns' (2003) 28 *J Corp L* 671; Hu, T, 'Faith and Magic: Investor Beliefs and Government Neutrality' (2000) 78 *Texas LR* 777; Stout, L, 'Technology, Transaction Costs, and Investor Welfare: Is a Motley Fool Born Every Minute?' (1997) 75 *Washington University LQ* 791; and Stout, L, 'Are Stock Markets Costly Casinos: Disagreement, Market Failure, and Securities Regulation' (1995) 81 *Va LR* 611.

[298] Schammo, P, 'The Prospectus Approval System' (2006) 7 *EBLR* 501, 513, and 517–21.

Directive formulation, any subsequent resale of securities which were previously the subject of one or more of the exemptions was to be regarded as a separate offer, and the Article 2(1)(d) definition of a public offer applied to the determination of whether the resale was an offer of securities to the public which required an approved prospectus. In a similar vein, the placement of securities through financial intermediaries was subject to the obligation to publish a prospectus where the final placement did not meet the exemption conditions set out in Article 3(2). This regime generated particular difficulties for retail cascades, under which issuers sell bonds to the underwriters, who sell them on to retail distributors, who subsequently sell the securities at different prices, depending on market conditions, to retail investors, over a period which can extend to several months. Although this distribution method is long established in the retail bond markets, the Directive threatened to disrupt it and to obstruct access to investments by retail investors, given the costs associated with distributors being potentially required to publish a prospectus at different points across the distribution chain and given a lack of clarity generally with respect to the responsibility for prospectus publication.[299] While in practice the difficulty affected issuers in only a small number of Member States, reform of the retail cascade problem became an early priority for the Commission.[300] The revised Article 3(2), following the 2010 Amending Prospectus Directive reforms, now provides additionally that Member States must not require another prospectus in any such subsequent resale or final placement of securities through financial intermediaries, as long as a valid prospectus is available and the issuer or person responsible for the prospectus consents to its use under a written agreement.[301]

The other driver of contraction is the Directive's privileging of large-denomination bond issues (initially of a denomination of €50,000 and now of €100,000, following the 2010 reforms) by means of a range of exemptions and calibrations. This has had the effect of significantly reducing the small-denomination bond market in the EU.[302] Retail investor access to bond investments, and to related diversification opportunities, has therefore contracted. Accordingly, while seeking, if somewhat problematically, to promote retail market investment, the Directive has at the same time limited the ability of retail investors to diversify their portfolios.

II.4.5 The Prospectus: Structure and Validity

II.4.5.1 Structure: Short-form Disclosure and the Retail Markets—the Summary

The retail market orientation of prospectus disclosure under the Directive is reflected in the core requirement that disclosures must be presented in an 'easily analysable and

---

[299] UK Listing Authority, List!, Issue No 16 (2007).

[300] Commission Background Document, n 198, 6. CESR attempted to clarify when a prospectus was needed through the Prospectus Q&A but legislative action was deemed necessary.

[301] The nature of the written agreement is addressed in the 2004 Commission Prospectus Regulation, as amended by the 2012 Commission Delegated Regulation 862/2012.

[302] The 2008 CSES Report suggested that the calibrations and exemptions had led to a reduction in the retail bond market from €147.4 billion (2003) to €97.6 billion (2007), and to significant effects in the traditionally large retail bond markets in France, Italy, and Germany (Daimler Chrysler stopped issuing bonds below €50,000): n 194, 55–6, 59, and 62. ESME earlier reported that while only 8 per cent of bonds listed in Stuttgart (a major debt venue) had a denomination of €50,000 in 2005, this had risen to 42 per cent in 2006: 2007 ESME Report, n 192, 14.

comprehensible form' (Article 5(1)). But there is ample evidence that the prospectus has failed as a retail market document.[303] Prospectuses are typically dense and technical,[304] reflecting in part the litigation risk which can re-characterize prospectuses as liability shields,[305] but also the information demands of the wholesale market. One leading French review suggested that retail investors find prospectus disclosures overly lengthy, difficult to read, technical and inaccessible, often alarmist, and insufficiently prioritized.[306] Retail investors also tend to use prospectuses as *ex-post* legal documents rather than as *ex-ante* information sources,[307] and often rely instead on shorter marketing materials for disclosure.[308]

The failure of the prospectus as a retail market document and with respect to the 'processability' of information is not surprising. Despite the Directive's retail market orientation, the content of the prospectus disclosure regime reflects institutional and political consensus on the need for a harmonized regime to support the issuer passport, and its disclosure requirements are based on market expectations and regulatory practice. The 'processability' of prospectus disclosure[309] was not accordingly road-tested on retail investors in the EU—reflecting international practice, including in the US, the traditional 'home' of prospectus disclosure.[310]

In mitigation, and in one of the clearest examples of the Directive's retail orientation, Article 5(2) requires that the prospectus include a prospectus summary.[311] The summary regime has been significantly enhanced by the 2010 reforms, reflecting very serious difficulties with the original 2003 model, as well as a belated policy recognition of the need for major enhancements to retail-orientated short-form disclosure generally across EU securities and markets regulation (Chapter IX section 6).

The original 2003 Directive short-form regime required issuers to produce a prospectus summary which, in a brief manner (a recital directed that the summary not exceed 2,500 words) and in non-technical language, conveyed the essential characteristics and risks associated with the issuer, any guarantor, and the securities, in the language in which

---

[303] CESR reported that the prospectus was a burdensome document to produce and very difficult to read: 2007 CESR Prospectus Report, n 193, 16. Similarly, the 2008 CSES Report found that retail investors, on average, do not use prospectus disclosures: n 194, 51.

[304] ESME reported that the average length of a prospectus exceeds 300 pages and, somewhat alarmingly, that the typical 'registration document' (a form of prospectus—discussed later in the Chapter) can weigh in at almost 4 kilos: n 192, 10–11.

[305] The 2008 CSES Report found that many market participants regarded prospectuses primarily as liability shields: n 194, 51.

[306] TNS-Sofres, Report for the AMF, Investigation of Investment Information and Management Processes and Analysis of Disclosure Documents for Retail Investors (2006) 28.

[307] 2008 CSES Report, n 194, 54.

[308] 2007 ESME Report, n 192, 10. ESME highlighted that the average prospectus length (from a two-Member State sample) between January and June 2007 was in excess of 300 pages.

[309] The 'processability' of retail market-focused disclosure is a key indicator of its effectiveness: eg Cox, J and Payne, J, 'Mutual Fund Expense Disclosures: A Behavioural Perspective' (2005) 83 *Washington University LQ* 907.

[310] The SEC's failure to test issuer disclosures has long been a cause of concern in US scholarship (eg Langevoort, n 293). As required under the 2010 Dodd-Frank Act, however, it is now focusing more closely on how disclosures are designed and on related literacy strategies: SEC, Study Regarding Financial Literacy Among Investors (2012).

[311] The summary requirement does not apply where the prospectus relates to the admission to trading on a regulated market of non-equity securities with a denomination of at least €100,000. Member States may, however, require that a summary is prepared (Art 19(4)).

the prospectus was originally drawn up. In terms of content, and by sharp contrast with the degree of harmonization elsewhere in the 2004 Commission Prospectus Regulation, Article 24 of the Regulation originally provided that the issuer determine on its own the content of the summary. Annex I to the 2003 Directive suggested, however, that the summary include the most important information in the prospectus, and provided an indicative and extensive list of disclosure items.

The summary prospectus failed as a retail document. Chief among the reasons for this was the failure to design a regime which reflected evidenced retail investor needs and competences, to develop and test an appropriate template, and to impose a minimum degree of standardization. Summaries were often simply a 'cut-and-paste' version of the prospectus; prospectus disclosures were, typically, not simplified or recast to aid retail investor understanding. Over-zealous application by NCAs of the informal 2,500-word limit generated the danger that key information was not appropriately presented to investors, and that over-simplification obscured the risks of the offer.[312] The requirement to produce a Directive-compliant summary also led to the abolition of some well-established and generally effective local retail-orientated/short-form disclosures.[313]

The 2010 reforms brought major change to the 2003 regime with the requirement for a 'short, simple, clear, and easy . . . to understand' document.[314] Under Article 5(2) the summary, which must be written in a concise manner and in non-technical language, must provide 'key information' in the language in which the prospectus is drawn up (host States can require translation). The format and content of the summary must provide, together with the prospectus, 'appropriate information' about 'essential elements' of the securities concerned, in order to aid investors when considering whether to invest in the securities (Article 5(2)). 'Key information' is defined as essential and appropriately structured information which is to be provided to investors with a view to enabling them to understand the nature and risks of the issuer, guarantor, and securities in question and to decide which offers of securities to consider further (Article 2(1)(s)). Specifically, key information must include: a short description of the risks associated with and essential characteristics of the issuer (and guarantor), including assets, liabilities, and financial position, and of the securities, including any rights attaching to the securities; the general terms of the offer, including estimated expenses charged to the investor; details of the admission to trading; and reasons for the offer and use of proceeds (Article 2(1)(s)).

In a major departure from the 2003 model, the Directive addresses format, and requires that the summary be drawn up in a common format to facilitate comparability. It also contains extensive delegations to administrative rule-making, which have led to a standardized template for the summary being adopted under the related 2012 revisions to the

---

[312] CESR, however, suggested that NCAs could allow for some leeway. It noted in its Supervisory Convergence Report that the recital's word limit was not a binding provision: n 193, 24–5.

[313] The UK FSA was required to remove its earlier 'mini prospectus' and 'summary particulars' requirements. Although the FSA argued that the summary prospectus would make it easier to understand core prospectus provisions, consultations on the implementation of the prospectus regime revealed concern that the summary was inadequate: FSA, Policy Statement No 05/7, The Listing Review and Implementation of the Prospectus Directive (2005) 5.

[314] 2010 Amending Prospectus Directive rec 15.

2004 Commission Prospectus Regulation.[315] The 2004 Regulation as revised sets out detailed content requirements and a mandatory order for the summary and also addresses length—the problem which bedeviled the 2003 version. While it acknowledges that less complex offerings may require shorter disclosures by noting that summaries should take into account the complexity of the issuer and the securities, the 2004 Regulation imposes a length limit of 7 per cent of the prospectus, or 15 pages, whichever is the shorter.[316] The detailed 2004 Regulation (Annex XXII) requirements are, closely reflecting ESMA's technical advice, based on a modular approach: the content of the summary is drawn from five tables,[317] the application of which will differ depending on the issuer, the securities, and the type of offer. The table order in which information is presented is mandatory; 'other information' (that is, information other than that required by the Regulation) cannot be presented, in order to ensure comparability;[318] cross-references are prohibited; and descriptions must be brief.[319] A discrete regime governs the summary where a base prospectus is used (section 4.5.2 on the base prospectus). Further harmonization will follow with the adoption of ESMA-proposed ITSs on the summary template, as required under the 2010 Omnibus I Directive revisions to the Prospectus Directive (Article 5(2)).

The new commitment to short-form prospectus disclosure[320] suggests a more nuanced approach to how the prospectus regime applies in the retail markets and may have wider ramifications—ESMA's first statement on the equivalence of third country prospectus regimes illustrates the extent to which the enhanced summary may become influential internationally.[321] The reforms are, however, unlikely to lead to major enhancements to the processability of disclosure. The summary remains based on line-item presentation of issuer- and securities-focused information.[322] In sharp contrast with the new suite of packaged product disclosure reforms (Chapter IX section 6), the summary was not tested on retail investors, does not address presentation in any detail, does not contain risk indicators of any kind, does not require generic warnings as to the risks posed by investment generally, and does not require disclosure of the type of investor the investment is designed for. On the other hand, prospectus disclosure (save with respect to structured securities, as discussed later in this section) is different to packaged product disclosure. In particular, the corporate issuer does not, unlike the packaged product developer, issue securities with the express purpose of selling the securities as a product to the retail sector; the wide range of

---

[315] 2004 Commission Prospectus Regulation Art 24 and Annex XXII, as revised by Commission Delegated Regulation 486/2012.

[316] ESMA's approach (on which this requirement is based) was based on providing issuers with flexibility, but setting an upper limit for more complex prospectuses and securities: ESMA Final Advice/2011/323, 61.

[317] The tables cover introduction and warnings, issuer and guarantor, securities, risks, and offering, and set out the particular disclosure items, and the order in which they should be presented, for each table and with respect to the type of issuer, security, and offering.

[318] ESMA Consultation Paper/2011/411, 25.

[319] 2004 Commission Prospectus Regulation Annex XXII, 1–6.

[320] Clear, eg, from the Commission's robust dismissal of a market call to remove the translation requirement for summaries as being 'seriously detrimental to investor protection': 2009 Amending Prospectus Directive Proposal, n 191, 5.

[321] The EU 'wrap' which Israeli prospectuses must provide to be deemed equivalent (see sect 4.11) must include the new prospectus summary: ESMA/2011/37.

[322] ESMA developed the modular system by examining the prospectus disclosure regime, drawing out 'key information', and presenting this in the form of points: ESMA Consolation Paper/2011/141, 25.

motivations associated with public offers and admissions to trading governs the issue decision, not the sale of a product to the retail sector. Nonetheless, as long as a summary is provided, and given that retail investors in the EU do, if not in numbers, invest directly in corporate securities, further enhancements are needed. At the least, ESMA could support stronger NCA enforcement of the Prospectus Directive Article 5 requirement that disclosure be presented in an easily analysable and comprehensible form. ESMA's appetite for improving prospectus disclosure appears to be strong; its 2012 peer review report on prospectus approval practices, for example, addressed the comprehensibility of prospectus disclosures[323] and augurs well for future reforms.

Beyond content and format, other difficulties arise with the summary. As under the 2003 regime, the civil liability regime for summaries is limited (Article 5(2)(d)). Civil liability attaches to those persons who have 'tabled' the summary (and any translation) and applied for its cross-border notification, but liability attaches only where the summary is misleading, inaccurate, or inconsistent when read together with the other parts of the prospectus, or when it does not provide, when read together with the other parts of the prospectus, key information in order to aid investors when considering whether to invest in such securities (Article 6(2)). A warning to this effect must be given in the summary. Issuers also face risks from the summary's liability regime. Under the Directive's language regime, the host NCA can require that the summary is translated. But the limited nature of the disclosure thereby provided to retail investors in the host Member State has raised concerns that, where it can be reasonably concluded that retail investors were not in a position to read the full foreign-language prospectus, issuers may be liable where material information has not been provided to investors as a result, particularly where more general consumer protection laws may require fuller disclosure. Additional disclosure, however, runs the risks of being classed as a non-approved prospectus, leaving the issuer exposed to liability.

There is, however, progress on one front, where the issuer is, in practice, a product provider. Structured securities (which provide a return linked to a basket of assets), often developed and issued by intermediaries as products for retail market sale,[324] are subject to the issuer-disclosure rules of the Prospectus Directive, including with respect to the summary. But although discrete disclosure rules apply, under the prospectus regime, to different types of securities,[325] the regime does not contain specific disclosure rules governing the particular risks posed by complex retail investment products such as structured securities,[326] including with respect to risk/reward profile, liquidity risks, redemption and costs: CESR's 2009 review of Lehman structured securities underlined these difficulties.[327] NCAs have limited room to tailor domestic prospectus regimes to reflect the risks posed by structured securities,

---

[323] n 404.

[324] See further Ch IX sect 2.3.

[325] Specific requirements apply, eg, to derivatives and asset-based securities: 2004 Commission Prospectus Regulation Annexes VII, VIII, and XII.

[326] FIN-USE, a forum for consumer interests established by the Commission and since replaced by the Financial Services User Group, eg, criticized the Commission's decision to exclude disclosure concerning retail structured securities from the reform of the 2003 Directive: FIN-USE, Response to Review of Directive 2003/71 (2009) 3.

[327] CESR, The Lehman Brothers Default: An assessment of the Market Impact (2009) (CESR/09-255) 3. CESR's assessment included that disclosures were not always meeting the Art 5 requirement that disclosure be provided in an easily analysable and comprehensible form.

although Article 3 of the 2004 Commission Prospectus Regulation allows home NCAs to require the addition of prospectus disclosures in the summary on a case-by-case basis. The Dutch regulator, for example, relied on industry initiatives to enhance the Directive's requirements for structured securities, but progress was slow.[328] Arbitrage risks also arise. Issuers of structured securities are subject to a lighter summary disclosure regime than are managers of mutual funds (who are subject to the sophisticated UCITS Key Investor Information Document requirement), although both investments are often substitutable in the retail market. The ongoing reforms to packaged product short-form disclosure will address this gap, however (Chapter IX section 6).

II.4.5.2 Structure: Shelf Registration and Base Prospectuses

The shelf-registration process, and the related registration document/securities note structure for the prospectus, attempts to streamline and reduce the costs of prospectus disclosure. The preparation and approval of a lengthy disclosure document each time an issuer makes an offer of securities to the public, or applies for admission of its securities to trading, can represent a major burden for issuers that repeatedly access the capital markets.[329] In order to ease this burden and facilitate the speed with which issuers can access the capital markets and the extent to which they can exploit market conditions, shelf registration has become a standard feature of prospectus regimes internationally. Shelf-registration schemes typically require that an initial disclosure document/registration document is filed/approved and that supplements are produced each time securities are offered.

One of the 2003 Directive's most successful innovations, which reflected demand from international issuers, was the introduction of a shelf-registration regime.[330] Under Article 5(4), the issuer, offeror, or person asking for the admission to trading on a regulated market may draw up the prospectus as a single document or, where shelf registration is used, as separate documents; the choice as to whether or not to adopt a shelf-registration model remains with the issuer or other person.[331] Where the shelf-registration route is used, the prospectus is drawn up in the form of a registration document, a securities note, and the short-form summary note (summary prospectus). The initial registration document contains the prospectus disclosure required under the Directive concerning the issuer. This is supplemented by the securities note(s) which contain(s) the required disclosure concerning the securities for the first and each subsequent offer/admission of securities. Where a registration document has been approved by the NCA, the issuer is required to draw up the securities note and the summary note only when the securities are subsequently offered to the public or admitted to trading on a regulated market (Article 12(1)). The securities note must, however, contain the information that would normally be provided in the registration document if there has been a material change or recent development which

---

[328] Commission, Record of the Open Hearing on July 15 2008 on Retail Investment Products (2008) 16–17.

[329] IOSCO, Adapting IOSCO International Disclosure Standards for Shelf Registration Systems (2001).

[330] ESME reported that by the end of July 2007, one Member State had seen 200,000 issues of securities carried out under a shelf-registration-based 'base prospectus' which would not have been possible under a traditional single prospectus: n 192, 18.

[331] In another example of the blunt approach taken by the Commission in its Original Proposal, it made the shelf-registration structure mandatory for all issuers seeking admission to trading on a regulated market and imposed an annual updating obligation, notwithstanding the costs this structure imposed, and its limited use for smaller issuers unlikely to make repeated calls on the market.

could affect the investors' assessment since the last updated registration document or any supplement (Article 12(2)). Both the securities note and the summary must be separately approved by the NCA.

Particular attention is given to the dynamics of bond market fund-raising by the 'base prospectus' regime, which addresses a form of shelf registration of particular importance for the issuance of structured securities. A 'base prospectus' mechanism can be employed at the choice of the issuer (Article 5(4)). A base prospectus is one which contains all the prospectus information (Articles 5 and 7) required concerning the issuer and the securities to be offered to the public or admitted to trading, and, at the choice of the issuer, the final terms of the offering (Article 2(1)(r)). The base prospectus must be supplemented where necessary, in accordance with Article 16 (which addresses prospectus supplements), with updated information on the issuer and on the securities; accordingly, it cannot take the form of a tripartite prospectus and use a securities note.[332] Where the final terms of the offer are not included in either the base prospectus or (in accordance with Article 16) in a related supplement, they must (following refinements made under the 2014 Omnibus II Directive) be made available to investors, filed with the home NCA, and communicated by the home NCA to the host NCA as soon as practicable on the making of a public offer and, where possible, before the beginning of the public offer or admission to trading (the home NCA must also communicate the final terms to ESMA);[333] a 'final terms' document, which must contain only information which is related to the securities note disclosure required in the context of tripartite formats, and which cannot be used to supplement the base prospectus, is used to achieve this (Article 5(4)). This mechanism is available for two types of securities. A base prospectus can be prepared for non-equity securities, including warrants in any form, which are issued under an 'offering programme'.[334] It can also be prepared for non-equity securities issued in a 'continuous or repeated manner'[335] by credit institutions.

The review of the 2003 Directive revealed difficulties with the base prospectus regime. From an early stage, CESR had expressed concerns that issuers were using the final terms document (which is not subject to NCA oversight) to update the base prospectus rather than an Article 16 prospectus supplement (which is reviewed by the NCA) and thereby eluding supervisory review, and that NCAs' supervisory practices differed.[336] Market practice also varied significantly on the treatment of base prospectuses and final terms, increasing legal and investor uncertainty. The 2010 reforms, accordingly, are designed to clarify the type of information which must be included in the base prospectus (and in related supplements, if necessary), and to minimize the disclosures contained in the final terms document.[337] The 2010 Amending Prospectus Directive and the related 2012

---

[332] ESMA Opinion/2013/1944.

[333] The base prospectus must cover the criteria and/or the conditions in accordance with which the final terms are determined.

[334] Defined as a plan which permits the issuance of non-equity securities (including warrants in any form), having a similar type and/or class, in a continuous or repeated manner during a specified issuing period (Art 2(1)(k)).

[335] Defined as issues on tap or at least two separate issues of securities of a similar type and/or class over a 12-month period (Art 2(1)(l)).

[336] Also discussed in Commission Prospectus Regulation 486/2012 Proposal Impact Assessment, n 286, 9.

[337] The final terms should be limited to, eg, last-minute, issue-specific information such as the issue price, date of maturity, any coupon (interest rate), the exercise price, and the redemption price (2010 Amending Directive rec 17).

Commission Delegated Regulation 486/2012 reforms to the 2004 Commission Prospectus Regulation have clarified how information is allocated between both documents and confirm that final terms must not amend or replace disclosures contained in the base prospectus which may affect the investor's assessment of the issuer and of the securities, and which should be covered in a prospectus supplement.[338] They also make a series of technical reforms to clarify the regime and limit reliance on the final terms document.

While a largely technical reform, the new base prospectus regime illustrates the EU's appetite and capability for highly technical reforms and its capacity to address emerging weaknesses relatively quickly. It also provides a revealing case study on ESMA's approach to prospectus regulation. Originally, the 2003 Directive did not address the nature of the split between the base prospectus and final terms, while the 2004 Commission Prospectus Regulation adopted a flexible approach. CESR's concern in its 2007 Prospectus Report led it to address the split in its Q&A in 2007; CESR sought to maintain issuer flexibility while guarding against abuses. This softer approach hardened with the 2010 reforms to the Directive and ESMA's technical advice that a detailed category-based approach be adopted in the related administrative rules. This advice, acknowledged by ESMA as being 'more restrictive',[339] was accepted by the Commission in the 2012 Commission Delegated Regulation 486/2012, which amends the 2004 Commission Prospectus Regulation. ESMA adopted a nuanced approach, however, and did not, for example, recommend a particular format for final terms disclosure (as requested by the Commission mandate for advice), noting the very wide range of complex structured securities issued under base programmes and the potential risks to innovation from any harmonization of formats.[340]

The base prospectus saga is also revealing as to ESMA's approach to disclosure review and the potentially thin borderline between substantive merit review of securities and supervisory review of the accuracy, comprehensiveness, and completeness of disclosures. ESMA called, for example, for complex payment formulae to be disclosed in the base prospectus and to be subject to supervisory review as regards completeness and comprehensibility,[341] although such a review may bring an NCA very close to an examination of the substantive merit of a key product feature. ESMA also called for disclosures concerning redemption procedures and settlement procedures for derivative securities to be disclosed in the base prospectus, in order to allow for supervisory review, although it acknowledged that the Prospectus Directive does not empower NCAs to 'make an economic assessment' of a

---

[338] 2004 Commission Prospectus Regulation, as amended by 2012 Commission Delegated Regulation 486/2012 Art 2a. The new administrative regime is based on a categorization of required disclosures as 'A', 'B', or 'C' and, accordingly, a determination as to whether the information must be disclosed in the base prospectus or in the final terms. In a rare 2014 ruling on the Prospectus Directive, the facts of which pre-date these 2012 reforms but in which the Court of Justice reflected the objective of the reforms, the Court highlighted that final terms documents must not contain information extraneous to that required by the prospectus regime, and that any supplement to the base prospectus must only relate to a significant new factor, material mistake, or inaccuracy, in accordance with Art 16 of the Prospectus Directive: Case C-359/12 *Michael Timmel v Aviso Zeta AG*, 15 May 2014, not yet reported.

[339] ESMA Consultation Paper/2011/141, 8. Market opinion is similar: see Clifford Chance, Briefing Note, April 2012, noting that the reforms severely limit the final terms document and will likely lead to a more restricted range of securities being offered under debt issuance programmes or much greater precision in the base programme disclosures.

[340] ESMA Consultation Paper/2011/141, 9.

[341] n 340, 17. This approach was adopted in the 2012 Commission Delegated Regulation 486/2012.

product. It highlighted, however, that structured securities disclosure must be examined for comprehensibility, consistency, and completeness. Disclosure review could therefore drift very close to the product intervention borderline under the new base prospectus regime.

II.4.5.3 Structure: Prospectus Supplements

Article 16 imposes updating requirements on prospectus disclosure, whether in the form of the traditional unitary prospectus or otherwise. Under Article 16(1), every significant new factor, material mistake, or inaccuracy relating to the information included in the prospectus which is capable of affecting the assessment of the securities, and which arises or is noted between the time the prospectus is approved and the final closing of the offer to the public or the time when trading on a regulated market begins—whichever occurs later[342]—must be mentioned in a supplement to the prospectus.[343] The supplement must be approved in the same way (but in a maximum of seven working days) and published in accordance with at least the same arrangements as were applied when the original prospectus was published. The prospectus summary (and any translations) must also be supplemented where this is necessary to take into account the new information included in the summary.

The publication of a prospectus supplement triggers withdrawal rights. Where the prospectus relates to an offer to the public, investors who have already agreed to purchase or subscribe for the securities before the supplement is published have the right, exercisable within two working days after the publication of the supplement, to withdraw their acceptance, as long as the factor requiring the supplement publication arose before the final closing date of the offer and the delivery of the securities (Article 16(3)).[344] This time limit may be extended by the issuer/offeror, but the final date for withdrawal must be stated in the supplement. The risk of abuse of the withdrawal regime, particularly with respect to speculative investments, and legal certainty issues relating to the exact scope of the supplement obligation, prompted early clarification of the regime by CESR[345] and ultimately led to the 2010 refinements.[346] The regime will be further refined by RTSs currently under development by ESMA, which will specify the situations in which a prospectus supplement obligation arises.[347]

---

[342] The priority rule was added by the 2010 Directive to address market uncertainty as to when the supplement obligation arose, given in particular the implications for withdrawal rights: 2010 Directive rec 23.

[343] Where information arises which does not meet the Art 16 requirement but would be useful for investors, issuers should make an announcement to this effect (as prospectuses cannot under Art 14(6) be modified except by the prospectus supplement): Prospectus Q&A, n 208, Q23.

[344] Reflecting market uncertainty as to when withdrawal rights arose, the 2010 Amending Directive introduced the two-working-day limit (previously, the limit could not be shorter than two days), and made clear that withdrawal rights depended on the supplement trigger having occurred before the final closing date and delivery of the securities.

[345] Including with respect to the need for supplements with respect to profit forecasts and interim financial information, and the need to disclose the length of the withdrawal period in the supplement: Prospectus Q&A, n 208: Qs19–22.

[346] n 344.

[347] The proposed RTSs identified ten situations which should be considered as a significant new factor or a material mistake or inaccuracy and which required a prospectus supplement, and included the publication of new annual, audited financial statements and the publication of profit forecasts for equity securities and depositary receipts. ESMA underlined that relevant triggering factors could be positive as well as negative: RTS Consultation Paper, n 25, 8. The RTSs were adopted in 2014 (n 25).

II.4.5.4 Validity

A prospectus is valid for 12 months after its approval for offers to the public or admission to trading on a regulated market, as long as it is completed by any supplements required under Article 16 (Article 9(1)).[348] A registration document, previously filed and approved, is also valid for up to 12 months, as long as it has been updated as necessary by the securities note or a prospectus supplement (Article 9(4)). Article 9(4) also clarifies that the registration document, accompanied by the securities note (updated where applicable) and the summary note, is considered, as a whole, to constitute a valid prospectus. The base prospectus of an offering programme is also valid for 12 months (Article 9(2)). The prospectus issued in support of non-equity securities issued by credit institutions in accordance with Article 5(4)(b) is valid until no more of the securities are issued in a continuous or repeated manner (Article 9(3)).

II.4.6 The Prospectus: Disclosure

II.4.6.1 The Core Obligation

The horizontal disclosure obligation and materiality test—which governs the content of all prospectuses, regardless of the issuer or the nature of the offering—is set out in Article 5. It provides that the prospectus must contain all information which, according to the particular nature of the issuer and of the securities offered to the public or admitted to trading on a regulated market, is necessary to enable investors to make an informed assessment of the assets and liabilities, financial position, profit and losses, and prospects of the issuer (and of any guarantor) and of the rights attaching to the securities (Article 5(1)). This provision also serves a deterrent function, providing the NCA with grounds for *ex-post* enforcement. The retail orientation of the Directive is underlined by the requirement that the information be presented in an 'easily analysable and comprehensible form'. Article 5(2) specifies that the prospectus must contain information concerning the issuer and the securities to be offered to the public or to be admitted to trading on a regulated market, and include a summary.

II.4.6.2 The Annexes: An Upgraded Disclosure Regime

The Annexes to the Directive set out the categories of information required in the different prospectus documents, and served as a guide to the initial development of what has since become an extensive administrative regime.[349] During the development of the 2003 Directive and the 2004 Commission Prospectus Regulation, the Annexes also provided the basis for the upgrading of the previous disclosure regime in accordance with international best practice, as codified in IOSCO's disclosure standards. Adoption of IOSCO's approach (through the Annexes) not only provided a convenient template for the EU but also facilitated EU issuers seeking capital internationally, particularly in the US, given that the US regime for third country issuers closely reflects IOSCO prospectus standards. Key Annex-based reforms to reflect IOSCO's approach included the introduction of disclosure requirements governing risk factors, related party transactions and corporate governance,

---

[348] The validity provision reflects a minor revision made by the 2010 Amending Directive to clarify that validity runs from approval, a point in time which can be easily verified.

[349] The Annexes are indicative only and do not impose binding obligations: Prospectus Transposition Meeting Minutes, 8 March 2005.

and, in line with international trends at the time,[350] an operating and financial review/management discussion and analysis of performance. The Annexes have since been overtaken by the extensive administrative regime.

II.4.6.3 A Calibrated Regime: Administrative Rules and the Building Blocks

Since the Directive's adoption, the detail of the disclosure regime has been covered at the administrative level by the massive 2004 Commission Prospectus Regulation. The Regulation has been revised by, to date, five amending Regulations,[351] which evidence the flexibility of the administrative rule-making process in updating the complex and detailed disclosure regime.

The 2004 Commission Prospectus Regulation, as revised, is based on a schedule and building-block model. The schedules and building blocks are to be combined by issuers as necessary, depending on the nature of the issuer and of the securities. The Regulation also requires that financial information be presented in the form of IAS/IFRS (section 7).[352] The Regulation supports comparability by specifying the format of the prospectus, which must be organized as follows: table of contents, summary, risk factors, and the detailed information required under the relevant schedules and building blocks.[353] Separate requirements apply to shares, debt securities, and derivative securities with a denomination of less than €100,000, and to debt and derivative securities with a denomination of at least €100,000. Discrete disclosure requirements apply to guarantees, asset-backed securities, and depositary receipts, while particular issuers (banks, sovereign issuers, and closed-end collective investment schemes) receive differentiated treatment. This regime is further amplified by the ESMA Recommendation.[354]

The regime has been repeatedly reformed by administrative rules. The first revision, by 2006 Commission Regulation 1787/2006, related to financial disclosures and the postponement of the Commission's decision on the equivalence of third country reporting regimes. In 2007, Commission Regulation 211/2007 revised the 2004 Regulation to address the disclosures required of issuers with complex financial histories (or with significant financial commitments). The 2012 Commission Delegated Regulation 486/2012 addresses the format and content of the prospectus, particularly with respect to the base prospectus, final terms, the summary document, and proportionate disclosure, and has made extensive amendments to the schedules and building blocks. The 2012 Commission Delegated Regulation 862/2012 addresses the written agreement required before intermediaries use a prospectus in a retail cascade. It also addresses disclosure in relation to structured securities, finessing the rules which apply to disclosures with respect to the indices which can underpin structured securities to ensure that disclosure obligations are not evaded and are not unduly burdensome. Commission Delegated Regulation 862/2012 also nuances the obligation on independent auditors and accountants to produce a report,

---

[350] Karmel, R, 'Reform of Public Company Disclosure in Europe' (2005) 26 *University of Pennsylvania JIEL* 379, 391–2.

[351] See sect 4.2.

[352] The 2004 Regulation requires, eg, that the registration document for shares contain historical financial information for the last three years, and the audit report, prepared in accordance with IAS/IFRS: Regulation Annex I, para 20.1.

[353] Regulation Arts 25 and 26.

[354] Initially adopted by CESR (CESR/05–054b).

particularly when a complete set of financial statements is not available. The 2013 Commission Delegated Regulation 759/2013 clarifies the disclosure regime for convertible/exchangeable debt securities, including with respect to the disclosure required on underlying shares, and also addresses the applicability of the proportionate disclosure regime for rights issues and offerings by SMEs and companies with a reduced market capitalization.

Notwithstanding the weight of the administrative regime, it is not, and cannot be, exhaustive, particularly given the speed with which the market develops new products. In places, the regime is deliberately flexible, to accommodate innovation and complexity. The regime for issuers with complex financial histories, for example, is expressly designed not to provide line-item disclosure requirements but to be flexible, given the complexities of the situations addressed.[355] To the extent that material gaps emerge in the regime with respect to particular transactions, they are typically addressed initially through supervisory dialogue[356] and communicated to the market under the frequently revised Q&A.

II.4.6.4 Omission of Information

Article 8 sets out the limited conditions under which information can be omitted from the prospectus. Article 8(1) addresses the final offer price and amount and requires that where this disclosure cannot be included in the prospectus, the criteria and/or the conditions in accordance with which they will be determined (or the maximum price, with respect to price) are either disclosed in the prospectus or, alternatively, the acceptances of the purchases or subscription of the securities may be withdrawn for not less than two working days after the final offer price and amount of securities have been filed. The final price and amount of securities offered must be filed with the home NCA.

More generally, the home NCA may authorize the omission of required information from the prospectus where the stringent conditions set out in Article 8(2) are met. The first condition addresses unusual situations and provides that information may be omitted where it is contrary to the public interest. The second condition permits the omission of information where disclosure would be seriously detrimental to the issuer, but only where the omission would not be likely to mislead the public with regard to facts and circumstances essential for an informed assessment of the issuer, the offer, the guarantor (where relevant), and the rights attached to the securities in question. The third condition relates to immaterial omissions and permits omission where the information is of minor importance only, for a specific offer or admission to trading on a regulated market, and is not such as will influence the assessment of the financial position and prospects of the issuer, offeror, or guarantor.

The omission regime also provides for the omission of information required under the administrative regime where, exceptionally, that requirement is inappropriate to the issuer's sphere of activity or to the legal form of the issuer or to the securities to which the

---

[355] Commission Regulation 211/2007 recs 8 and 9.

[356] Rec 32 to the 2004 Commission Prospectus Regulation provides that, with respect to completely new securities, NCAs are to try to find similarities with the disclosures required under the Regulation. The evidence suggests that initial supervisory convergence through CESR did result in co-operation between NCAs with respect to offers of new securities: 2007 CESR Supervisory Convergence Report, n 193, 14.

prospectus relates (Article 8(3)). In such cases, the issuer must provide equivalent information, where possible.

II.4.6.5 Incorporation by Reference

As disclosure concerning an issuer may be available from a number of public sources, integration of the disclosure, so that the issuer is not required to repeat disclosure already in the public domain, can generate cost savings. If, for example, an annual report has been published, market efficiency mechanisms should ensure that securities prices reflect that disclosure. In the US, for example, where the integration of disclosure in order to simplify the complex and onerous disclosure regime and reduce the burden on issuers represents a major component of the SEC's disclosure policy, ongoing disclosure reports can be integrated into the disclosure required on a subsequent offer of securities.[357]

The EU prospectus regime similarly provides for 'incorporation by reference'. Article 11(1) requires Member States to allow information to be incorporated in the prospectus by reference to one or more previously or simultaneously published documents that have been approved by the home Member State NCA or filed in accordance with the Prospectus Directive or the Transparency Directive.[358] Previously, the regime incorporated information published under the now removed Article 10 requirement that issuers admitted to trading on a regulated market provide a document containing all regulated information made available to the public in the previous 12 months; this requirement, obsolete since the adoption of the 2004 Transparency Directive, was removed by the 2010 Amending Directive. The information incorporated must be the latest available to the issuer. Information which is incorporated by reference must be identified by means of a cross-referenced list to enable investors to easily identify specific items of information (Article 11(2)). Reflecting its focus on disclosing key information, the summary may not incorporate disclosure by reference.

II.4.7 Market Integration: Prospectus Approval and the Passport Mechanism

II.4.7.1 Approving the Prospectus: Home Member State Control

In one of the most fiercely contested of the Directive's original provisions, the prospectus regime is anchored to the home Member State NCA; Article 13 provides that no prospectus may be published until it has been approved by the NCA of the 'home Member State'. Accordingly, issuer choice and regulatory or—more accurately, given the Directive's intensive harmonization—supervisory competition with respect to the approval process is

---

[357] Explaining the rationale for its integrated disclosure system, the SEC stated that it 'recognizes that, for companies in the top tier, there is a steady stream of high quality corporate information continually furnished to the market and broadly digested, synthesized and disseminated . . . the widespread market following of such companies and the due diligence procedures being developed serve to address the concerns about the adequacy of disclosure and due diligence and, thus, ensure the protection of investors': SEC Release No 33–6499 (1983) para I.

[358] Art 28 of the 2004 Commission Prospectus Regulation lists the types of documents which may be incorporated by reference. A delegation (under the 2014 Omnibus II regime) empowers ESMA to propose RTSs in relation to the information which can be incorporated by reference.

considerably restricted. As discussed in section 4.10.3, the extent to which supervisory competition is possible in the new institutional landscape, given ESMA's powers and influence, is debatable. Nonetheless, the removal of issuer choice of NCA remains an important feature of the Directive.

Issuer choice is removed for securities offerings under the default regime which applies under Article 2(1)(m)(i). It defines the home Member State for all EU issuers of securities which are not covered by Article 2(1)(m)(ii) as the Member State where the issuer has its registered office: in effect, the registered office State anchors equity issues and issues of debt with a denomination of less than €1,000.

This removal of issuer choice was subject to widespread criticism from the outset, particularly with respect to bond issues. It was thinly justified in terms of the regime thereby allocating supervisory jurisdiction to the NCA best placed to supervise the issuer for the purposes of the Directive (recital 14). The governing assumption is, reflecting the Directive's retail market orientation, that the NCA in which the issuer has its registered office is best placed to supervise prospectus disclosure. The removal of issuer choice raises, however, the risk that the potentially corrective effects of competition are removed, and that the danger of monopoly supervisors making little effort to deliver efficiency benefits and innovation is increased. It also assumes that NCAs have sufficient incentives to supervise the prospectus appropriately where the offer takes place in another Member State. Practical difficulties arise from the language regime, as issuers who seek to make an offer in a deep capital market outside the home Member State have the option of providing the prospectus in a language customary in the sphere of international finance, which may well not be the official language of the home Member State responsible for prospectus approval (Article 19(2)). Although delegation of prospectus approval is a possibility under Article 13(5), delegation is a cumbersome and risky tool for NCAs (although it is being enhanced: Chapter XI section 4.2.3).

On the other hand—and although there is some evidence that some NCAs are more flexible than others with respect to cross-border issuers,[359] as well as of supervisory competition and specialization, particularly with respect to employee share offerings[360]— the supervisory competition argument can be overplayed, particularly with respect to equity offerings which tend to have a primary listing/offer in the home Member State in any event. The establishment of ESMA was designed to drive strong supervisory convergence and remove supervisory competition—now typically termed supervisory arbitrage. As discussed in section 4.10, evidence is emerging of stronger co-operation between NCAs, and of efforts by ESMA to shape best practice with respect to prospectus approval.

In one of the Directive's many calibrations to the bond markets, issuer choice is maintained for certain bond market offerings. EU bond markets are mainly concentrated in London

---

[359] The 2008 CSES Report found a perception that NCAs in Luxembourg and Ireland were more flexible and open to cross-border transactions, than, eg, the French NCA: n 194, 20.

[360] The 2008 CSES Report noted the practice of issuers bringing new issues to jurisdictions where the NCAs looked favourably on the type of issue, and of a related move to NCA specialization, particularly with respect to employee share offerings for third country firms who have some freedom to choose the home NCA. France, in particular, was regarded as successful in attracting third country firms, given its flexible approach to employee share schemes: n 194, 42.

and Luxembourg, which have developed extensive supervisory expertise. The Commission's original 2001 proposal that the Member State of issuer registration govern all offers prompted widespread hostility from the bond industry on the grounds that a successful market segment would be subject to supervision by inexperienced NCAs.[361] The proposal was also severely criticized during the institutional negotiations, with the arguments against the removal of issuer choice ranging from the risks of monopoly supervision to the strains this model would place on inexperienced supervisors.[362] Issuer choice was accordingly maintained for certain bond market offerings.

But the execution of the bond market exemption has been problematic. Under the Article 2(1)(m)(ii) compromise for bond markets, the home Member State is the Member State where the issuer has its registered office, or where the securities were or are to be admitted to trading on a regulated market, or where the securities are offered to the public, chosen by the issuer or the offeror of securities, as the case may be. This regime applies to issues of non-equity securities whose denomination per unit amounts to at least €1,000.[363] It also applies to issues of convertible non-equity securities which give the right to acquire any transferable securities or to receive a cash amount as a consequence of their being converted or the rights conferred on them being exercised, but the issuer of the convertible securities may not be the issuer of the underlying securities or an entity belonging to the issuer's group.

There is little justification for the denomination-based difference in treatment between bond issues. The investor protection argument is troublesome as small investors invest in denominations of €1,000 and above, the risks of bond investment are not related to the denomination, and the threshold has led a contraction in the retail bond market. Issuers face significant practical difficulties, including that issuers' bond issues can become subject to two NCAs—often Luxembourg and the home NCA.[364] The review of the 2003 Directive accordingly led to renewed calls for issuer choice to be allowed for all non-equity offerings.[365] Although the Commission proposed removal of the €1,000 threshold,[366] the

---

[361] The London Stock Exchange, eg, raised concerns with respect to the implications for NCA resources and expertise, monopoly risks, the lack of incentive for NCAs to provide more efficient services, and the costs imposed on intermediaries: London Stock Exchange, Comments on the Proposed Prospectus Directive, August 2001, paras 4.4–4.5. Its solution to the arbitrage problem was harmonization of standards and a new requirement that issuers disclose the reason for avoiding the home NCA: London Stock Exchange, Comments, paras 4.6–4.7.

[362] ECOSOC argued that the Commission's model would prejudice the centralization of expertise in major market centres and a 'relatively efficient working system for the euromarket and eliminate competition as a driver of more efficient services': n 182, para 4.3.3.4. The European Parliament raised similar concerns with respect to monopoly risks and a loss of concentrated expertise: First ECON Report, n 182, Amendments 2 and 16.

[363] The 2008 CSES Report found that market participants regarded this threshold as not making any sense: n 194, 20. Consistency with the original wholesale bond market regime might have suggested a €50,000 threshold. The Commission proposed a €50,000 threshold in its revised 2003 Proposal, on the grounds that this would distinguish retail and professional markets. The Council adopted a rather arbitrary €5,000 threshold (n 182, 50). The Parliament called for a €1,000 threshold on the grounds that investment funds frequently invested in small-denomination bonds for ease of handling and diversification and (presciently) that a higher threshold would limit cross-border access by retail investors to bond investments: Second ECON Report, n 182, Amendment 10.

[364] 2008 CSES Report, n 194, 38.

[365] 2008 CSES Report, n 194, 20 and 38.

[366] The Commission noted the practical difficulties faced by issuers as well as the absence of 'concrete risks' to investor protection: 2009 Amending Prospectus Directive Proposal, n 191, 6.

European Parliament favoured its retention on investor protection and regulatory arbitrage risk grounds.[367] NCAs similarly had divergent views as to the removal of the threshold.[368] The final compromise was to direct the Commission to review the €1,000 limit and to consider whether it should be removed.[369]

II.4.7.2 Prospectus Approval

The Directive's investor protection and passport mechanisms are based on the prospectus being approved;[370] publication cannot take place until the prospectus has been approved (Article 13). Approval assumes supervisory review of the prospectus, but not of the securities; the latter would suggest the merit model of review, although, as noted above, ESMA increasingly seems comfortable with intensive review of prospectus disclosure relating to complex securities, which may lead indirectly to a substantive review. Approval is defined as 'the positive act' which follows supervisory scrutiny of the 'completeness' of the prospectus, including the 'consistency' of the information given and its 'comprehensibility' (Article 2(1)(q)); the review must, therefore, extend beyond a mechanical review of line-item inclusions, although the review is not designed to assess the veracity of the disclosure or the quality of the disclosure.

Supervisory consistency and best practice in the approval process is now largely a function of ESMA's supervisory convergence activities.[371] The Directive imposes some minimum standards and time limits, however (Article 13). The NCA must notify the issuer (or the offeror or person asking for admission to trading on a regulated market) of its decision regarding prospectus approval within ten working days of the submission of the draft prospectus. This limit may be extended to 20 working days where the offer involves a first-time issuer (Article 13(3)), where closer scrutiny is required. In addition, where the NCA finds, on reasonable grounds, that the documents submitted to it are incomplete or that supplemental information is needed, the time limits apply only from the day on which the information in question is provided (Article 13(4)). But where the NCA fails to give a decision within the time limits, this is not deemed to constitute approval of the prospectus (Article 13(2)). Reflecting the Directive's light-touch approach to liability generally, the NCA's liability with respect to prospectus approval is not affected by the Directive and remains governed solely by national law (Article 13(6)). The 2010 Omnibus I Directive reforms tie ESMA into the approval process, with ESMA being notified of the approval of the prospectus (and any supplement), and receiving copies of the prospectus and supplements (Article 13(2)).

As discussed in section 4.10.3, supervisory convergence was, initially, limited but more recently greater progress has been made, and more can be expected as ESMA's reach extends.

II.4.7.3 The Passport and Mutual Recognition

The Directive's extensive harmonization of disclosure supports the ousting of host NCAs. Under Article 17, where an offer to the public or admission to trading on a regulated

---

[367] ECON Report, n 191, Amendment 3.

[368] Schammo, n 26, 27 (noting the difficulties CESR faced in presenting a common position in response to the Commission's consultation on what would become the 2010 reforms).

[369] 2010 Amending Prospectus Directive rec 8.

[370] For an extensive discussion of the Directive's approach to prospectus approval see Schammo, n 26.

[371] The 2014 Omnibus II regime empowers ESMA to propose RTSs in relation to the approval process.

market is carried out in one or more Member States, or in a Member State other than the home Member State, the prospectus approved by the home NCA (and any supplements thereto) is valid for the public offer or the admission to trading in any number of host Member States.[372] In particular, host NCAs may not undertake any approval or administrative procedure relating to prospectuses. This remains the case even where there are flaws in the prospectus; the home NCA remains in control of the prospectus. Article 17(2) provides that where significant new factors, material mistakes, or inaccuracies have arisen since the original approval of the prospectus, the home NCA must require that a prospectus supplement be approved. The host NCA and ESMA may, however, draw the attention of the home NCA to the need for new information.

The review of the 2003 Directive suggested that the passport mechanism was regarded as working well but, as noted in section 4.10.3, a number of supervisory inefficiencies across NCAs have emerged, which have typically drawn a robust response—from CESR initially, and subsequently from ESMA.

II.4.7.4 Notification

As is typical across EU securities and markets regulation generally, mutual recognition and supervisory co-operation under the prospectus regime are based on notification (Article 18)), which is carried out on an NCA–NCA basis. The home NCA must, at the request of the issuer (or the person responsible for drawing up the prospectus), provide the host NCA with a certificate of approval (a template has been developed by CESR/ESMA), which attests that the prospectus has been drawn up in accordance with the Directive and which identifies any omission of information under Article 8(2) and (3) and explains the reasons for the omission. The host NCA must also be provided with a copy of the prospectus. Where applicable, the notification must be accompanied by a translation of the summary. The 2010 Amending Prospectus Directive added the requirement that the issuer (or other responsible person) be notified of the certificate of approval at the same time as the host NCA. Time limits apply to the notification process to facilitate mutual recognition. The documents must be notified by the home NCA within three working days of the issuer's request (or within one working day after the approval of the prospectus where the request was submitted along with the draft prospectus). This procedure, the operational details of which may be subject to amplification through ITSs (Article 18(4)), must also be followed for any prospectus supplements. ESMA must also be notified of the certificate of approval and, along with the host NCA, must publish a list of certificates of approval for prospectuses and any supplements, together with a link to these documents on the home NCA site, where relevant (Article 18(3)).

II.4.7.5 The Language Regime

Translation burdens were strongly associated with the failure of the pre-FSAP prospectus/listing particulars regime. It was not uncommon for passporting issuers to be required to translate the entire prospectus.[373] In support of mutual recognition, the Directive introduced a new translation regime (Article 19) which is, for the most part, governed by issuer

---

[372] Defined as the State where an offer to the public is made or admission to trading is sought where that State is different from the home Member State (Art 2(1)(n)).
[373] This was the case in Germany: eg Mattil and Möslein, n 294, 2.

choice and which is generally regarded as successful in reducing the costs of translation and in supporting the prospectus passport;[374] it was not affected by the 2010 reforms. Some difficulties remain, however, in that where an issuer chooses to prepare a prospectus in a language customary in the sphere of international finance, and where the prospectus is required for an offering/admission in the home Member State and one or more host Member States, the prospectus may be subject to a translation requirement; the home NCA responsible for approving the prospectus may require that the prospectus is drawn up in a language accepted by the authority (Article 19(3)).

Where an offer to the public is made or admission to trading on a regulated market is sought only in the home Member State, the prospectus must be drawn up in a language accepted by the home NCA (Article 19(1)).

Where the offer to the public is made or the admission to trading is sought in one or more Member States but not in the home Member State, the prospectus must be drawn up either in a language accepted by the NCAs of those Member States or in a 'language customary in the sphere of international finance' (Article 19(2)). In practice, this formula typically leads to use of the English language.[375] The choice of language is for the issuer, offeror, or person seeking admission. Host NCAs may, however, require that the prospectus summary is translated into their official languages. Host NCAs are prevented from assessing the quality of the translation.[376] Although the prospectus must be approved by the home NCA, whose official language may be different from either of the languages chosen, issuer choice still governs the language regime. But for the purposes of scrutiny by the home NCA, the prospectus must be drawn up either in a language accepted by the home NCA or in a 'language customary in the sphere of international finance'. Again, this is at the choice of the issuer, offeror, or person asking for admission.

Where the offer to the public is made or the admission to trading is sought in one or more Member States including the home Member State, a third regime applies (Article 19(3)). The prospectus must be drawn up in a language accepted by the home NCA, but it must also be made available either in a language accepted by the NCAs of each host Member State or in a 'language customary in the sphere of international finance'—at the choice of the issuer, offeror, or person asking for admission. As with host-State-only offers, the host NCAs can require only that the summary is translated into their official languages.

A discrete regime applies to the admission to trading on a regulated market of non-equity securities whose denomination per unit amounts to at least €100,000 and where admission is sought in one or more Member States. The prospectus must be drawn up either in a language accepted by the home and host NCAs or in a 'language customary in the sphere of international finance'—at the choice of the issuer, offeror, or person asking for admission to

---

[374] It has been described by ESME as 'one of the core success factors' of the Directive: n 192, 22.

[375] Although the Commission at an early stage emphasized that other languages can be used as long as they are customary in the sphere of international finance: Prospectus Transposition Meeting Minutes 26 January 2005.

[376] Prospectus Q&A, n 208, Q33. ESMA has published an 'information note' which sets out the languages accepted (in each Member State) for the purposes of prospectus scrutiny, and summary translation requirements (for each Member State) (ESMA/2014/342).

trading. Member States may also require that a summary be drawn up in their official languages.[377]

II.4.7.6 Home Member State Control and the Transfer of Approval

The anchoring of equity and small-denomination debt offers to the issuer's Member State of registration raises potential—at least—risks with respect to NCA expertise and incentives, particularly where the offer has large cross-border elements. Article 13(5) represents a partial response to these risks by providing for the delegation of functions from NCAs.

The home NCA may, on its own initiative, transfer the approval of the prospectus to the NCA of another Member State, subject to the agreement of that NCA and prior notification to ESMA. The transfer must be notified to the issuer (or the offeror or the person seeking admission to trading on a regulated market) within three working days of the decision by the home NCA. There has, however, been only limited reliance on the delegation power, with just a few instances occurring prior to the crisis era.[378] In each case the delegation was initiated at the request of the issuer, suggesting there is still some (limited) room for issuer choice within the supervisory regime. ESMA's enhanced powers in this area (Chapter XI section 4.2.3), and its specific powers under the Directive to adopt ITSs governing related forms and procedures, may, however, lead to greater reliance on delegation, particularly given the ongoing strengthening of supervisory convergence.

II.4.7.7 Precautionary Powers

As is typical for EU securities and markets regulation generally, the home Member State/NCA-control principle is dominant across the Directive, but provision is made for exceptional powers to be exercised by the host NCA under the Directive's precautionary regime (Article 23). Where the host NCA finds that irregularities have been committed by the issuer (or by the financial institutions in charge of the public offer), or that breaches have been committed with respect to the admission of securities to trading on a regulated market,[379] it must refer these findings to the home NCA and to ESMA. The host Member State may act only where, despite measures taken by the home NCA or because those measures are inadequate, the issuer (or the financial institution) persists in breaching the relevant legal or regulatory provisions. In these circumstances, the host NCA may, but only after informing the home NCA, take 'all appropriate measures' to protect investors. In a provision designed to deter abuse of this power, the Commission and ESMA must be informed at the earliest opportunity.

II.4.8 Publication and Dissemination

Article 14 addresses the prospectus publication process.[380] Once approved, the prospectus must be filed with the home NCA and made accessible to ESMA. It must also be made

---

[377] Offers of this nature are not subject to the prospectus summary requirement unless required by the Member States under their national law.

[378] 2007 CESR Prospectus Report, n 193, 13.

[379] 'Breaches and irregularities' relates to the harmonized rules adopted under the prospectus regime and not to other host Member State rules.

[380] The 2014 Omnibus II regime empowers ESMA to propose RTSs in relation to prospectus publication.

'available to the public' by the issuer, offeror, or person asking for admission to trading on a regulated market 'as soon as practicable' and, in any case, 'at a reasonable time in advance of' (and at the latest at the beginning of) the offer to the public or the admission to trading (Article 14(1)). Where the offer concerns an initial public offer of a class of shares not already admitted to trading on a regulated market and to be admitted to trading for the first time, the prospectus must be available at least six working days before the end of the offer.

A prospectus is deemed to be 'available to the public' when it is published through one of the different distribution channels specified in Article 14(2)). Home Member States may accordingly require publication of a notice stating how the prospectus has been made available and where it can be obtained by the public (Article 14(3)). Host Member States may not impose publication requirements; the adequacy of pan-EU publication is the responsibility of the home Member State.[381] Under Article 14(2), the prospectus can be made available to the public through insertion in one or more newspapers circulated throughout, or widely circulated in, the Member States in which the offer to the public is made or the admission to trading is sought, although this mode of publication is now outmoded.[382] It can also be published in printed form and made available (free of charge) to the public at the offices of the market on which the securities are being admitted to trading or at the registered office of the issuer and at the offices of the financial intermediaries placing or selling the securities.

Online publication is a particular concern of Article 14, which was updated by the 2010 Amending Prospectus Directive. The prospectus is deemed available to the public where it is published on one of a number of websites: the issuer's website[383] (or, if applicable, the website of the intermediaries placing or selling the securities); the website of the regulated market where the admission to trading is sought; and the website of the home NCA (where the NCA offers this service).[384] Since the 2010 reforms, Member States must also require issuers or responsible persons who publish the prospectus in a printed form to publish the prospectus online.

The home NCA must also publish on its website over a period of 12 months, and at its choice, either all the prospectuses approved or a list of prospectuses approved, including a link to the prospectuses published on the issuers' or regulated markets' websites (Article 14(4)). ESMA must also publish on its website a list of approved prospectuses with a link to the NCA site for the prospectus, as appropriate. While this enhances the availability of prospectuses, the regime does not provide for centralized access to all approved prospectuses.

Article 14(5) addresses publication where the prospectus is composed of a number of constituent elements and/or incorporates information by reference. The documents and information making up the prospectus may be published and circulated separately as long as the documents are made available free of charge to the public in accordance with Article 14(2).

---

[381] This point is highlighted in the Q&A: n 208, Q3.

[382] Newspaper publication is addressed by Art 30 of the 2004 Commission Prospectus Regulation.

[383] Art 29 of the 2004 Commission Prospectus Regulation imposes standards on website publication, including that the prospectus is easily accessible and downloadable and cannot be modified.

[384] Where the prospectus is published in electronic form, a paper copy must be delivered to the investor (on request and free of charge) (Art 14(7)).

II.4.9 Advertising

A limited regime applies to the advertising of public offers or admissions to trading under Article 15. It provides that the home NCA is empowered to exercise control over the compliance of advertising[385] with Article 15. The Directive does not, however, grant a passport to advertising communications, and host Member States remain empowered to impose requirements concerning advertising.[386] Basic standards are imposed (Article 15(2)–(5)). These include that advertisements must state that a prospectus has been or will be published and must indicate where investors are or will be able to obtain it. Advertisements must also be clearly recognizable as such, and the information must not be inaccurate or misleading and must be consistent with the information contained in the prospectus, where the prospectus is published, or with the information required to be in the prospectus, where the prospectus is subsequently published. More generally, all information concerning the offer to the public or the admission to trading (whether disclosed in oral or written form and whether or not for advertising) must be consistent with the information contained in the prospectus. This limited regime is bolstered by the extensive marketing communications rules which apply under the EU investment product distribution regime (Chapter IX).[387]

II.4.10 Supervision and Enforcement

II.4.10.1 NCAs

The Prospectus Directive, when originally adopted, marked a break with pre-FSAP securities and markets regulation by rationalizing and reinforcing the institutional structure for prospectus approval and supervision. In particular, it addressed the controversies then swirling around the extent to which commercially driven, demutualized stock exchanges should be responsible for the review of issuer disclosure. The Directive introduced an independence requirement (still in force) which, in effect, removed prospectus approval from stock exchanges.[388] Under Article 21(1), each Member State is to designate a central competent administrative authority[389] responsible for carrying out the obligations imposed by the Directive and for ensuring that the Directive is applied.[390] These authorities must be 'completely independent' of all market participants (Article 21(1)), such that their

---

[385] The scope of the communications which come within Art 15 has been amplified in the 2004 Commission Prospectus Regulation.

[386] The risk therefore arises that host NCAs could block the prospectus passport in practice by imposing more onerous requirements, including approval requirements, on ancillary advertising communications.

[387] In addition, the 2014 Omnibus II regime confers on ESMA the power to propose RTSs in relation to the dissemination of advertisements.

[388] In 2007 CESR reported that, compared with the situation obtaining in 2004 (prior to the implementation of the Directive), supervisory powers had moved from regulated markets to independent administrative authorities: 2007 CESR Supervisory Convergence Report, n 193, 2.

[389] This requirement was designed to eliminate the practice of multiple authorities within a Member State having different powers over the approval of prospectuses/listing particulars: Prospectus Directive rec 37.

[390] Member States may, where required by national law, designate other administrative authorities to apply the prospectus approval, publication, and advertisements regime. But where the offer or admission to trading is sought in a Member State other than the home State, only the central competent authority designated in the home State is entitled to approve the prospectus.

independence from economic actors is guaranteed and conflicts of interest avoided (recital 37). Delegation (including to stock exchanges and regulated markets) was, however, permitted for an interim period, which closed on 31 December 2011, and was subject to a range of conditions designed to address conflict-of-interest risks.

Although the Prospectus Directive was, in 2003, at the vanguard of the movement to enhance the supervisory powers of NCAs, since the crisis-era reforms it has slipped back. The raft of 'second wave' crisis-era securities and markets regulation reforms (Chapter I section 4.3), which strengthened the supervisory and enforcement powers of NCAs across a range of measures, came after the 2010 Amending Prospectus Directive. The Directive's approach is not, accordingly, aligned with the related market abuse and transparency regimes, which were revised under the crisis-era reform programme, particularly with respect to enforcement and sanctioning.

The Directive confers a range of powers on NCAs with respect to prospectus approval and advertising, reflected in the requirement that decisions taken in accordance with the Directive must be subject to the right to appeal to the courts (Article 26). The Directive specifies in some detail the powers which must be conferred on NCAs with respect to the approval of prospectuses (Article 21(3)). These range from information-gathering powers to more interventionist powers concerning the suspension of trading. The information-gathering powers[391] include the power to require issuers, offerors, and persons asking for admission to trading on regulated markets to include supplementary information in the prospectus, where this is necessary for investor protection; to require those persons and the persons that control them (or are controlled by them) to provide information and documents; and to require auditors and managers of those persons, as well as financial intermediaries commissioned to carry out the offer or ask for admission, to provide information. The suspension powers include the power to suspend a public offer or admission to trading (for a maximum of ten consecutive working days on a single occasion) where the NCA has reasonable grounds for suspecting an infringement of the Directive, prohibit a public offer where the NCA finds that the Directive has been infringed (or has reasonable grounds for suspecting an infringement), suspend (or ask the relevant regulated market to suspend) trading on a regulated market (for a maximum of ten consecutive working days on a single occasion) where the NCA has reasonable grounds for believing the Directive has been infringed, and prohibit trading on a regulated market where the NCA finds that the Directive has been infringed. More generally, the NCA must also be empowered to make public that an issuer has failed to comply with its obligations.

Additional powers apply once the securities have been admitted to trading on a regulated market (Article 21(4)). NCAs must be empowered to require the issuer to disclose all material information which may have an effect on the assessment of the securities admitted to trading on regulated markets, in order to ensure investor protection or the smooth operation of the market. They must also be empowered to suspend (or ask the regulated market to suspend) the securities from trading where, in the opinion of the NCA, the issuer's situation is such that trading would be detrimental to investors' interests.[392] The

---

[391] Professional secrecy obligations apply under Art 22(1) and (3).

[392] NCAs are also empowered to consult with operators of regulated markets as necessary and, in particular, when deciding to suspend or prohibit trading (Art 22(2)).

NCA must also be empowered to carry out on-site inspections in its territory to verify compliance with the Directive.

II.4.10.2 Supervisory Co-operation

The prospectus regime is anchored to the home Member State and home NCA. Efficient supervisory co-operation is therefore essential, particularly where offers and admissions to trading occur outside the home Member State, and is supported by the formal co-operation obligations set out in Article 22(2). ESMA, as discussed in section 4.10.3, has brought a new dynamic to the co-operation process, strengthening the supervisory convergence process initiated by CESR.

The core obligation imposed on NCAs, in a formula familiar across EU securities and markets regulation, is to co-operate with each other whenever necessary for the purpose of carrying out their duties and making use of their powers. The 2010 Omnibus I Directive reforms added the requirement that all NCAs must also co-operate with ESMA (Article 21(1a)) and provide ESMA, without delay, with all necessary information to carry out its duties (Article 21(1b)). They must also render assistance to NCAs of other Member States (Article 22(2)). Information exchange is supported by Article 22(3), which provides that the professional secrecy obligation does not prevent NCAs from exchanging confidential information or from transmitting such information to ESMA or the European Systemic Risk Board (ESRB).[393] More specific co-operation and assistance obligations, particular to the prospectus and trading context, are imposed under Article 22(2). NCAs must exchange information and co-operate where an issuer has more than one home NCA because of its various classes of securities (for example, equity securities and debt securities with a denomination of at least €1,000) or where the approval of a prospectus has been transferred to the NCA of another Member State. NCAs must also co-operate closely when requiring the suspension or prohibition of trading in securities in other Member States, in order to ensure a level playing field between trading venues and the protection of investors. Host NCAs may request the assistance of the home NCA, particularly with respect to a new type or rare form of securities. Similarly, the home NCA may seek information from the host NCA with respect to items specific to the relevant market.

The co-operation regime has been strengthened to reflect ESMA's establishment by the requirement that ESMA be entitled to participate in on-site inspections where these are carried out jointly by two or more NCAs (Article 21(4)), and by the conferral on ESMA of powers to propose RTSs governing the type of information to be exchanged and ITSs governing related procedural processes and templates (Article 22(4)). In addition, the general enabling clause for ESMA to engage in binding mediation between NCAs (2010 ESMA Regulation Article 19) is activated by Article 22(2), which empowers ESMA to mediate where a request for co-operation has been rejected (see Chapter XI section 5.3.1 on ESMA/NCA mediation).

---

[393] Subject to the rules which govern information exchange with ESMA and the ERSB under their founding Regulations. Information exchanged between authorities or with ESMA and the ESRB is also subject to the general obligation of professional secrecy.

II.4.10.3 Supervisory Convergence and ESMA

The Prospectus Directive achieves a very high degree of regulatory convergence. Supervisory convergence, and strong supervisory co-operation, in a network-based supervision system anchored to the home NCA, was always a more difficult challenge.

The evidence suggests, however, that supervisory arbitrage risks, and related weaknesses in supervision to the detriment of investor protection and market efficiency, have not been realized. NCAs tend to enjoy similar powers,[394] although the intensity of supervision can vary, with some NCAs taking a proactive approach and monitoring markets regularly and others adopting a more risk-based approach.[395]

Levels of supervisory co-operation have tended to be strong; from an early stage, NCAs co-ordinated through CESR, particularly with respect to the treatment of new securities, complex products, multiple offerings, and requests for the suspension or prohibition of trading in securities in different markets across the Member States.[396] NCAs also agreed a communication procedure and a standardized certificate of approval for the passporting process. This has continued over the ESMA era. ESMA's suite of powers in support of co-operation, including with respect to support of delegation, mediation, and participation in home/host on-site inspections, are designed to enhance co-operation.

Poor convergence in operational supervisory practices, however, has bedeviled the prospectus regime and represents the major supervisory challenge. The review of the 2003 Directive revealed often significantly different practices in supervising and interpreting the regime.[397] These ranged from the imposition by host NCAs of translation requirements (in breach of the Directive), to additional filing requirements (typically of documents incorporated by reference), to additional publication requirements (including requirements to publish a notice of publication of a prospectus).[398] Other difficulties have related to time limits for prospectus approval being breached.[399] These divergences have obstructed the passport mechanism and led to significant issuer costs and inefficiencies.[400]

Lacking formal legal powers and a sound institutional basis, although enjoying Commission support,[401] CESR nonetheless developed techniques for promoting greater convergence, including the Q&A and good practices for prospectus approval.[402] ESMA, by

---

[394] 2007 CESR Supervisory Convergence Report, n 193, 3.
[395] 2007 CESR Supervisory Convergence Report, n 193, 5.
[396] 2007 CESR Supervisory Convergence Report, n 193, 14.
[397] 2007 ESME Report, n 192, 5.
[398] 2007 CESR Prospectus Report, n 193, 39–40.
[399] 2008 CSES Report, n 194, 36.
[400] ESME warned that 'in all cases, the effect is to increase the complexity, risk and cost of cross-border offers and admission to trading which is detrimental to issuers and investors and frustrates the objectives of the passporting regime': n 192, 6.
[401] The Commission noted that CESR was the appropriate forum for addressing incorrect transposition and encouraged CESR to carry on this work with its support: 2010 Commission Background Note, n 198, 4.
[402] Principles for good practices were agreed in November 2010 and cover: consistency in reviewing prospectuses; the application of a 'four-eyes principle'; review of financial information; prospectus consistency; comprehensibility; and prospectus structure. The consistency principle, eg, suggests that NCAs maintain a database of precedents or some form of internal working instruction, while the prospectus consistency principle suggests that NCAs examine, eg, reliance on incorporation by reference and consistent treatment of risk factors. CESR members were given six months to comply and a peer review subsequently took place under ESMA: ESMA/2012/300.

contrast, has been formally placed within the prospectus approval and passporting process. It must, for example, host links to prospectuses, supplements, and certificates of approval. It must be notified in advance of delegation arrangements, and before and after host NCAs exercise precautionary powers. It is empowered to take part in joint home/host NCA inspections and to mediate in cases of supervisory disagreement. Through the third country equivalence process (section 4.11), it assesses third country regimes. It holds and publishes data on prospectus notifications. All of this, in combination with the new hierarchical dimension which ESMA has brought to supervision (Chapter XI), is likely to have the effect of increasing its capacity to influence NCAs.

Its formal powers to promote convergence are considerable and range from enforcement-type powers under ESMA Regulation Articles 17–19 (Chapter XI section 5.3.1), to the issuing of guidelines subject to NCA 'comply-or-explain' disciplines (ESMA Regulation Article 16) (Chapter X section 5.6), to peer review powers (Chapter XI section 5.6.4), to the issuing of Opinions which may signal enforcement action (section 4.2). The peer review example is instructive. CESR's early attempts at peer review under the prospectus regime did not drill into NCAs' supervisory practices, and were directed to simply mapping the supervisory environment.[403] A more intrusive approach, based on ESMA's enhanced peer review powers under ESMA Regulation Article 30 and ESMA's Review Panel Methodology, has been followed in the ESMA era. The 2012 prospectus peer review, which followed a self-assessment by ESMA members, is notable for its focus on operational reality and on the particular practices which NCAs use in reviewing prospectuses.[404] Suggesting that ESMA's capacity to drive convergence is real, the peer review found full application of the relevant good practice principles in 25 Member States.

In what direction might supervision move in the prospectus sphere? Indications from early in the CESR era suggested some CESR appetite for prospectus approval.[405] As discussed in Chapter XI, the institutional structure for supervision in the EU is nothing if not dynamic and the implications of Banking Union and in particular the Single Supervisory Mechanism for ESMA's operational supervisory powers remain unclear. The 2013 review of the European System of Financial Supervision saw some stakeholder support for prospectus approval to be moved to ESMA (Chapter XI section 5.10). But there are few compelling reasons to locate prospectus approval within ESMA. Its ever intensifying and increasingly sophisticated convergence activities should drive best practice across the EU, and limit the costs to the market of supervisory divergences. By contrast with the supervision of rating agencies and trade repositories—both subject to ESMA supervision, but both also concerned with relatively small and discrete sectors and with new regulatory territory for the Member States—very significant volumes of prospectuses are approved annually, prospectus approval is well-embedded within NCAs, and the incentives for strong local supervision, given in particular the risks to investor protection in domestic markets, are significant.

---

[403] CESR/07-383.

[404] ESMA/2012/300. This peer review process dates back to 2009 and the adoption in 2010 of principles of good practice in prospectus approval (n 402).

[405] CESR, Preliminary Progress Report, Which Supervisory Tools for the EU Securities Markets? An Analytical Paper by CESR (2004) (CESR/04–333f) 17. Rec 47 of the 2003 Directive also contains the now obsolete but then intriguing possibility of consideration being given to the establishment of a 'European Securities Unit' for prospectus approval.

While there may be marginal benefits from centralized approval of prospectuses relating to offers which take place outside the home State, supervisory convergence, combined with delegation, is likely to be more effective in supporting supervision.

II.4.10.4 Enforcement, Sanctions, and Civil Liability

EU securities and markets regulation is, by necessity, based on a public-enforcement model, although some tentative moves to address civil liability are underway (Chapter XI section 4.1.3). The Prospectus Directive follows this model, being based on *ex-ante* supervision through NCA prospectus approval and *ex-post* NCA enforcement (Article 25).

Under Article 25, Member States must ensure (without prejudice to their right to impose criminal sanctions and their civil liability regimes) that appropriate administrative measures (which are quicker and easier to impose than criminal sanctions) can be taken, or administrative sanctions imposed against the persons responsible, where the Directive is breached. These measures must be effective, proportionate, and dissuasive. NCAs must be empowered to disclose to the public any measures and sanctions imposed, unless disclosure would seriously jeopardize the financial markets or cause disproportionate damage to the parties involved.

In practice, and in common with EU securities and markets regulation generally, convergence in sanctioning powers has been weak, with the same infraction subject to different types of administrative measures or sanctions across the Member States,[406] although efforts are being made to promote convergence through the ESMA Prospectus Group. Elsewhere, the crisis-era reform programme has led to the major FSAP directives being revised to significantly enhance the sanctions regime, both with respect to the type of sanctions imposed and with respect to how sanctions are applied (Chapter XI section 4.1.2). Although the Prospectus Directive has not been reformed in this regard, reforms are likely to follow.

The pre-2003 regime did not address civil liability, but the Prospectus Directive introduced in 2003 a limited and tentative civil liability regime, which has been enhanced by the 2010 reforms.[407] Article 6(1) addresses responsibility statements and requires Member States to ensure that responsibility for the information given in a prospectus attaches, at least, to the issuer (or its administrative, management, or supervisory bodies), the offeror, the person asking for the admission to trading on a regulated market, or the guarantor. These persons must be clearly identified in the prospectus by their names and functions (or registered offices). The prospectus must also include declarations by these persons that, to the best of their knowledge, the information contained in the prospectus is in accordance with the facts and that the prospectus makes no omission likely to affect its import. Article 6(2) does not address how Member States approach civil liability, but simply provides that their laws, regulation, and administrative provisions on civil liability apply to those persons responsible for the information given in a prospectus. Member States must also ensure that civil liability

---

[406] 2007 CESR Supervisory Convergence Report, n 193, 13.

[407] Which was originally inserted following representations by the German government: Hopt, K, 'Modern Company and Capital Market Problems: Improving European Corporate Governance After Enron' in Armour, J and McCahery, J (eds), *After Enron. Improving Corporate Law and Modernising Securities Regulation in the EU and the US* (2004) 445, 475.

does not attach to any person solely on the basis of the summary (including any transla-tions), unless it is misleading, inaccurate, or inconsistent when read together with other parts of the prospectus.

Approaches to civil liability regimes vary considerably across the EU in terms of, *inter alia*, the basis for liability (fraud or negligence), causation, the statutory or common-law nature of the remedy, and those persons able to take a cause of action.[408] This diversity represents a significant risk to pan-EU issuers (not least given the reputational risk posed by potential litigation[409] and the related resource implications for issuers[410]) and injects significant possi-bility for legal arbitrage, in terms of forum shopping, in an otherwise harmonized regime.[411]

The review of the 2003 Directive led to a closer stakeholder focus on the liability regime, with ESME, for example, calling, ambitiously, for harmonization of liability standards.[412] But in practice, private liability suits, whether based on statutory causes of action or otherwise, remain rare (although they are common in particular Member States, notably Austria and Italy). This reflects in part the absence of class-action mechanisms and in part the absence of a strong EU equity culture which could drive a more aggressive litigation culture. The Commission's appetite for further reform seems limited,[413] but, reflecting the European Parliament's addition to the 2010 Amending Prospectus Directive of a require-ment for a review of civil liability regimes and the wider crisis-era focus on stronger enforcement and deterrent mechanisms, the Commission's 2011 mandate to ESMA for advice on administrative rules under the Prospectus Directive included a request for ESMA to develop a comparative table recording Member States' liability regimes.[414] ESMA's related 2013 report does not contain recommendations as to future action but underlines the wide variety of approaches taken to civil liability across the Member States.[415]

II.4.11 Third Country Issuers

The dynamics of international competition can significantly shape disclosure regimes globally, particularly with respect to third country actor access. In the period prior to the financial crisis, international capital-raising regulation was preoccupied by the dynamics of competition and with how regulation should respond—best exemplified by the initial 2006 report by the Committee on Capital Market Competitiveness (the Paulson Report) on

---

[408] For a review of the different approaches to prospectus liability which obtain across the EU, see ESMA, Comparison of Liability Regimes in Member States in Relation to the Prospectus Directive (2013) (ESMA/2013/619).

[409] Burn and Wells, n 172, 275.

[410] Ferran has distinguished between liability risk, which can be managed by complete and candid disclosure, and litigation risk, which is much less easy to manage and dependent in part on the robustness of courts in dismissing hopeless actions: n 175, 21.

[411] Enriques and Tröger, n 206, 526 and Ferran, E and Chan Ho, L, *Principles of Corporate Finance Law* (2nd edn, 2014) 435–7.

[412] 2007 ESME Report, n 192, 19.

[413] Over the prospectus regime review, it argued that the increasing number of passports under the regime suggested that the liability system was not hindering the Directive and highlighted the complexities of harmonization, given the deep embedding of civil liability rules within national regimes: Background Document, n 198, 15.

[414] Commission Mandate Letter to ESMA, 14 November 2011.

[415] n 408.

a perceived weakening in the competitive position of the US capital market from the early 2000s,[416] the causes of which, while contested, were associated with the impact of the 2002 Sarbanes-Oxley Act.[417] While the financial crisis prompted an initial retrenchment to local markets,[418] capital-raising, and related issuer regulation, operates in a global context. Although the public equity markets in the EU have recently been sluggish (although strengthening since 2013; section 9), there is strong evidence that the EU generally, and the UK in particular, have been able to attract public offers and admissions to trading from the US and internationally.[419] While this drift is largely a function of local Member State market dynamics and how they attract third country issuers,[420] the EU prospectus regime is engaged. But by contrast with the related financial reporting system (section 6), the prospectus regime has not focused closely on international engagement. The 2010 reforms, however, suggest some sensitivity to the international market, with international competitiveness noted as a driver for the reform process[421] and the new employee share-offering regime designed, in part, to support third country firms.

The prospectus regime does, however, address the treatment of third country issuers.[422] The home NCA of issuers having a registered office in a third country[423] may approve a prospectus for an offer to the public or for an admission to trading on a regulated market where that prospectus is drawn up in accordance with the legislation of a third country. The prospectus must be drawn up in accordance with international standards set by international securities commissions, including the IOSCO Standards, and the information requirements must be 'equivalent' to the Directive (Article 20). The mutual-recognition regime then applies to offers to the public or admissions to trading on a regulated market in a Member State other than the home Member State (Article 20(2)).[424]

---

[416] n 39. The Committee has continued to raise concern as to the relative competitiveness of the US public equity market (on a quarterly basis) (as noted in n 39).

[417] eg Litvak, K, 'Sarbanes-Oxley and the Cross-Listing Premium' (2007) 105 *Michigan LR* 1857; Coffee, J, 'Law and the Market. The Impact of Enforcement' (2007) 156 *UPaLR* 229; and Zingales, L, Is the US Capital Market Losing its Competitive Edge? ECGI Finance WP No 192/2007 (2007), available at <http://ssrn.com/abstract=1028701>.

[418] Ferran, E, 'Capital Market Openness after the Financial Turmoil' in Koutrakos, P and Evans, M, *Beyond the Established Orders* (2010) and Ferran, E, 'Financial Supervision' in Mügge, D, *Europe and the Governance of Global Finance* (2014).

[419] eg 2011 City of London SME Report, n 41, 12. This trend persisted in the early stages of the financial crisis: CESR, Annual Report (2009) 7–8, noting that IPO activity in the EU was mainly by third country issuers. This trend has been pronounced with respect to London Stock Exchange listings: 2012 Kay Review, n 34, 23.

[420] Such as the efforts to attract listings to the UK market, including through the UK Listing Authority's review of the listing regime, and the effort in France to attract admissions by means of a more flexible employee share-offering regime.

[421] 2009 Amending Prospectus Directive Proposal, n 191, 2.

[422] For further discussion see Schammo, n 26, 142–90.

[423] The home country regime was revised by the 2013 Amending Transparency Directive. Art 2(1)(m)(iii) as revised provides that the home Member State for third-country issuers (which do not come within the debt-securities exemption) is the Member State where the securities are intended to be offered to the public for the first time after the entry into force of the Directive or where the first application for admission to trading on a regulated market is made, at the choice of the issuer, the offeror, or the person asking for admission. A subsequent election may be made by the issuer where the home Member State was not determined by their choice or where the securities are no longer admitted to trading on a regulated market in that State.

[424] A full discussion of the third country regime cannot be presented here. See sect 6 for a brief discussion of the equivalence regime concerning IAS/IFRS reporting, which is at the heart of the equivalence regime, given the necessity for the financial statements which are required in the prospectus to be reported under IAS/IFRS (2004 Commission Prospectus Regulation rec 28 and Art 35).

By contrast with the Commission-led equivalence regime which governs prospectus exemptions for third country firms' employee share schemes, and by contrast with the more robust and centralized approach to equivalence adopted generally over the crisis era, a formal equivalence procedure does not apply to third countries' prospectus disclosures regimes; this is despite the original Article 20(3) delegation to the Commission to adopt an equivalence framework.[425] But in a clear example of ESMA's potential to expand the prospectus regime, it has adopted an equivalence framework, following third country market requests for prospectus approvals and a Commission request for (what was then) CESR to adopt a common approach.[426] The equivalence framework, which takes the form of an ESMA Opinion, is based on third country issuers providing a 'wrap' for prospectuses which sets out the additional information required of third country issuers where the third country regime is deemed not to be completely equivalent to the EU regime.[427] ESMA has provided a checklist of the disclosure items which must be provided in a wrap when not required under the third country regime, and of those items which, although not required under the third country regime, are deemed to be provided in an equivalent form.[428] Based on this framework, ESMA will assess the equivalence of particular third country regimes,[429] following which assessment NCAs can scrutinize the prospectus for approval. This regime differs from the approach adopted to equivalence across the major crisis-era measures by reposing control in ESMA (although NCAs ultimately exercise the decision to approve the prospectus); typically, equivalence regimes are based on Commission rules.

II.4.12 Impact

The Prospectus Directive regime is now regarded as a cornerstone of EU securities and markets regulation.[430] The ambitious claims made for the Directive in terms of market integration, investor protection, and wider economic development were initially asserted rather than reasoned. Empirical analysis and cost–benefit assessment were limited.[431] The EU can, however, be forgiven its assumption that harmonized mandatory disclosure would deliver enhanced investor protection and stronger markets generally.[432] Evidence from the

---

[425] A more extensive delegation was conferred under the 2010 Amending Prospectus Directive Art 20(2), empowering the Commission to establish general equivalence criteria.

[426] CESR Statement of 17 December 2008 (CESR/08-972), noting the Commission's desire for CESR to adopt an equivalence framework.

[427] ESMA Legal Opinion ESMA/2013/317. The equivalence framework was originally adopted as a Public Statement (ESMA/2011/36).

[428] ESMA will not require a wrap for certain classes of disclosure where, although the disclosures are provided in a different form, it is reasonable to assume that investors would be able to make an informed assessment.

[429] An assessment has been made of the Israeli regime, which sets out the wrap requirements which, if met, allow NCAs to consider the regime to be equivalent and to proceed to scrutinize the prospectus: ESMA/2011/37.

[430] 2007 ESME Report, n 192, 2.

[431] The impact assessment for the original 2001 Prospectus Directive Proposal simply stated that the reforms would have positive effects on job creation by facilitating capital-raising and lowering the cost of capital, but did not provide empirical support.

[432] In support of disclosure driving strong markets see Coffee, J, 'Privatization and Corporate Governance: The Lessons from Securities Market Failure' (1999) 25 *J Corp L* 1. See also Black, n 4, which identifies disclosure (to minority shareholders) as an essential prerequisite for strong public securities markets.

law and finance school suggests that under-disclosure by issuers can be systemic[433] and that mandatory issuer disclosure can lead to a stronger market where it is coupled with strong enforcement.[434] But in its impact assessment for the 2010 reforms, the Commission suggested that, in the context of the financial crisis, the prospectus regime had provided a sound framework for investor protection and disclosure, met its objectives with respect to market efficiency and investor protection, boosted competition among issuers, generated a wider variety of products, played an important role in developing the single securities market, and had a positive impact on the quality and appropriateness of information.[435] While the 2010 Directive reform process suggests broad market satisfaction, the Commission's bold claims warrant closer inspection, particularly with respect to the more quantifiable impacts on market development and market integration.

The development of market finance in the EU generally is considered at the end of this Chapter (section 9). With specific reference to the Prospectus Directive, the Directive has had a number of demonstrable market impacts, not always positive, but overall it is difficult to assess the extent to which it directly changed market behaviour in the public markets.

It seems reasonably clear that the Directive has played some role in the development of private markets by delineating the scope of the private markets within which the prospectus requirement does not apply. At one end of the private markets spectrum, the Directive facilitates the wholesale funding market through its different exemptions and private placement mechanisms; at the other end, the crowdfunding and related funding techniques which are increasingly drawing in retail capital across EU also benefit from exemptions from the Directive. But an array of other factors also drive funding in these markets.

The evidence that the Directive can be directly associated with an increase in cross-border capital-raising activity in the public markets is unclear.[436] Initial evidence suggested that the regime enjoyed early success in facilitating issuers in offering and admitting securities to trading cross-border. A marked increase occurred in the number of prospectus passports sent from home NCAs, from 206 in 2004–5 (prior to the application of the Directive) to 1,150 in the first year of the Directive's application (2005–6).[437] A similar dynamic can be seen in the number of prospectus passports received—up from 81 in 2004–5 to 2,837 in 2005–6. The number of passports does not, however, indicate that pan-EU offerings are on the increase.[438] Although the wide-ranging 2009 review of the FSAP generally noted the

---

[433] In the sovereign bond markets (which fall outside the prospectus regime), one study has shown that issuers have tended not to disclose significant changes in the contractual terms which underpin bond issues, and tend to use boiler-plate disclosures: Mitu Gulati, G and Choi, S, An Empirical Study of Securities Disclosure Practices, Duke Law School Legal Studies Paper No 97 (2006), available at <http://ssrn.com/abstract=876652>.

[434] One frequently cited study suggests that mandatory disclosure rules combined with strong private enforcement (including the ease with which the liability of issuers, distributors, and accountants can be established in terms of burden of proof) appear to be correlated with larger stock markets (including ratio of stock market capitalization to GDP, number of domestic publicly traded firms, and value of IPOs relative to GDP): La Porta et al, n 60 (2006).

[435] 2009 Amending Prospectus Directive Proposal Impact Assessment, n 191, 3–4.

[436] Although market participants associate it with an increase in the number of cross-border transactions: 2008 CSES Report, n 194, 19.

[437] 2007 CESR Prospectus Report, n 193, 11.

[438] CESR noted that the effective functioning of the passport does not necessarily mean an increase in pan-European offers, as issuers can request passporting in circumstances where no offer in the host Member State subsequently occurs: n 193, 10.

increase in the number of prospectuses passporting, it also pointed to the range of potential determinative factors, including taxation and the impact of 'round-tripping', where a bond prospectus is approved in a Member State known to be efficient in dealing with prospectus but the securities are sold in the home Member State.[439] The 2008 CSES Report similarly reported that while CESR (and, since, ESMA) data on prospectuses approved (and passported) suggested high reliance by issuers on the regime[440] and an increase in passporting activity,[441] there was significant room for the expansion of passporting activity,[442] particularly in the equity markets.[443] It also revealed the impact of specialization in the bond market, with Luxembourg and Ireland approving and 'exporting' significantly more passports than they received,[444] reflecting their accommodation of, and experience with, specialist offers. While it concluded that the Directive had succeeded in opening EU capital markets to a wider range of Member State issuers, it was sceptical as to the extent to which real change was taking place in the public cross-border market. Overall, crisis-era data from CESR and, since, ESMA suggests that prospectus and passporting activity has become broadly stable, with similar numbers of prospectuses approved and sent over 2009–12, although the data on prospectuses received suggests some significant volatility.[445]

It is also the case that pan-EU visibility no longer requires multiple cross-border offerings. The liberalization of share order execution means that equity issuers no longer need to engage in multiple admissions to trading to ensure sufficient visibility and liquidity for their securities: public capital-raising can be limited to the home Member State, with additional funds being raised through private placements, and visibility can be ensured through a domestic admission to trading which exposes issuers to pan-EU trading.[446] In practice, cross-border admissions to trading continue to fall, and are often carried out for non-funding reasons, including the need to demonstrate a commitment to a particular market in the wake of a merger or acquisition, for example.[447] One change seems relatively clear. The Prospectus Directive, along with the issuer-disclosure regime more generally, can be associated with a shift towards admission on non-regulated markets, which operate outside the EU's issuer-disclosure regime—the implications of which are discussed in section 7.

---

[439] 2009 CRA Report, n 195, 169–70.

[440] 2008 CSES Report, n 194, 8.

[441] By June 2007, 1 in 5 prospectuses was passported: n 194, 10.

[442] It found that in most Member States, more than 90 per cent of passports were not passported. Passporting activity was concentrated in Germany (more than half being used to access other markets), the UK and Luxembourg (around 25 per cent), the Netherlands (18 per cent), and France (10 per cent).

[443] Passports were often used to access large retail bond markets, such as the German market: 2008 CSES Report, n 194, 12. The Report also noted market perception that the passporting regime, including the base prospectus structure, worked more effectively for bonds than for equity: at 17.

[444] n 194, 15.

[445] In total, 4,113, 4,453, 4,788, and 4,902 prospectuses were approved across the EU in 2012, 2011, 2010, and 2009 respectively; 967, 1,151, 979, and 1,330 prospectuses were sent from home NCAs, respectively. While 3,316 and 3,671 prospectuses were received in 2009 and 2010 respectively, 2011 saw a significant uptick to 6,316; this dropped back to 3,139 in 2012. Data for the first half of 2013 showed a slight drop on activity from the same period in 2012, with the number of prospectuses approved down to 1,931 from 2,320, the number of prospectuses sent down to 538 from 722, and the number of prospectuses received down to 1,788 from 2,463. See CESR/ESMA, Data on Prospectuses Approved and Passported, updated bi-annually.

[446] eg 2008 CSES Report, n 194, 18.

[447] 2009 CRA Report, n 195, 180–1.

In the retail markets, the positive impact of the Directive has been limited and it has had some prejudicial effects. As previously discussed in section 4.4.4, the Directive can be associated with a contraction in the retail bond market and a consequent diminution in retail access to the diversification and other benefits of bond market investments. It is also clear that the Directive has not led to a cross-border retail market for equity offers[448] and that there is limited market appetite for such offers,[449] particularly given the attractions of private placements and the liability risks associated with retail offers. One major pan-EU offering, the Standard Life offering, was based on the geographical organization of the issuer rather than on a pan-EU offering structure per se, with the cross-border element reflecting the Member States in which the insurer had significant business activities.[450] While alone the Directive's impact on portfolio diversification was always likely to be limited, particularly given the importance of advised sales and intermediation in the EU, nonetheless the Directive's impact on portfolio diversification has not been significant.[451]

II.5 Ongoing and Periodic Disclosure: The Transparency Directive and the Market Abuse Regime

II.5.1 Transparency Directive: Evolution

II.5.1.1 Initial Efforts: Limited and Fragmented Transparency

The Transparency Directive and its supporting administrative rules, and as amended by the 2013 Amending Transparency Directive,[452] is at the heart of the EU's regulatory framework governing the publication of ongoing issuer disclosure. In addition to addressing substantive disclosure requirements, it governs the dissemination of disclosure. Unlike the prospectus regime, the transparency regime is not event-specific; it addresses ongoing disclosure for issuers within the perimeter of the transparency regime. It is, accordingly, of central importance to the price-formation process for traded securities and for market-based monitoring of issuers. Although the Transparency Directive is less dense than the prospectus regime, it sits at the centre of a network of related measures, chief among them the IFRS financial reporting standards (section 6).

The evolution of the Transparency Directive has followed a different path to the evolution of the Prospectus Directive. The Transparency Directive has, for example, been more closely shaped by the different approaches to market finance across the EU. At an early stage of the regime's evolution, for example, attempts to introduce share ownership reporting rules led to opposition in Germany arising from concern that such rules favoured the speculative investor and engendered uncertainty,[453] which slowed implementation of the

---

[448] eg, 2009 CRA Report, n 195, 171 and 2008 CSES Report, n 194, 17.

[449] eg Ondrej, P, 'ICMA's Response to CESR on the Prospectus Directive and the Regulation', ICMA Regulatory Policy Newsletters No 5, April 2007, 2.

[450] Ferran, n 175.

[451] 2008 CSES Report, n 194, 52.

[452] Directive 2004/109/EC [2004] OJ L390/38, as amended by Directive 2013/50/EU [2013] OJ L294/13. References to the Transparency Directive are to the 2004 Directive as amended by the 2013 reforms.

[453] The German stock exchange was 'adamantly opposed': Committee on the European Communities, Report on the Disclosure of Significant Shareholders, HL (1985–86), 16th Report, para 27.

regime.[454] More recently, concerns as to speculation and innovation in financial markets have been reflected in the inclusion of Contracts for Differences (CfDs) within the Transparency Directive's ownership reporting regime. By contrast with the Prospectus Directive, the regime has also long been based on a minimum-harmonization model, which, with some modifications, remains in place—although detailed harmonization applies in practice through the related IFRS financial reporting system and through related 'soft' CESR/ESMA measures. Also unlike the Prospectus Directive, operational initiatives to address the dissemination of issuer disclosure have been a recurring feature of the regime's evolution.

Prior to the adoption of the 2004 Transparency Directive,[455] ongoing issuer disclosure was addressed through a patchwork regime which was limited in scope and did not support mutual recognition. The 1979 Admission Directive introduced the principle of ongoing disclosure for issuers whose securities were admitted to 'official listing' (including with respect to annual reports), and put in place a framework for *ad hoc* (material events) disclosure, including a requirement that issuers were required to report to the public on any major new developments not public knowledge and likely to affect the issuer's ability to meet its commitments (in the case of debt securities) or lead to substantial price movements (in the case of shares). The general annual reporting regime for all companies, contained in the (now repealed) Fourth and Seventh Company Law Directives,[456] imposed annual reporting obligations on all companies, private and public, with some exceptions for smaller companies.

This regime was first supplemented by the 1982 Interim Reports Directive, which imposed a very limited half-yearly reporting obligation[457] (based on minimal financial information and an explanatory statement on company activities in the relevant period) on issuers of shares admitted to official listing.[458] Publication was required in the Member State(s) in which the shares were admitted to official listing. Member States were empowered to subject issuers to obligations additional to or more stringent than those set out in the Directive and host control was not restricted; the prospect therefore arose of divergent reporting obligations for companies with multiple listings.

The 1988 Substantial Shareholdings Directive addressed changes in the capital structure of issuers and built on the very limited requirements imposed by the 1979 Admission Directive in order to address the significant divergences in this area.[459] The large-shareholdings disclosure obligation had two strands: (1) notification of the company concerned by holders

---

[454] Gros and Lannoo, n 169, 127.

[455] The main legislative history of the 2004 Directive is as follows: Commission Proposal at COM (2003) 138; ECOSOC's Report at [2004] OJ C80/128; ECB Opinion at [2003] OJ C242/6; and First (and final) Parliament reading at T5–0220/2004 (the First (and final) ECON Report at A5–0079/2004). The legislative history of the 2013 Amending Transparency Directive is at n 472.

[456] Fourth Council Directive 78/660/EEC on the annual accounts of certain types of companies [1978] OJ L222/11 and Seventh Council Directive 83/349/EEC on consolidated accounts [1983] OJ L193/1. See further sect 6 on the accounting regime.

[457] The scaleback followed difficult negotiations concerning the more onerous disclosure regime initially proposed by the Commission, and concerns as to the liability of NCAs where issuers failed to comply.

[458] Debt securities were excluded on the assumption that holders were protected by the rights bestowed by the securities.

[459] The Commission's Explanatory Memorandum noted that there were 'very marked discrepancies in this area' (COM (85) 791, 3).

of voting rights in a company whose shares were officially listed when a disposition or acquisition of voting rights (detailed rules applied to the attribution of voting rights) by such holders resulted in their holdings of voting rights achieving, exceeding, or falling below certain thresholds (10 per cent, 20 per cent, 33.3 per cent, 50 per cent, or 66.6 per cent),[460] and (2) the onward dissemination of this information to the public by the company. The regime was, however, more a creature of company law than of capital market transparency. Although reporting obligations of this nature form a central element of ongoing issuer-disclosure regulation (section 5.7), the relevant thresholds were a function of company law thresholds and did not fully capture the nature of control and influence in an issuer (the first threshold started at 10 per cent and then jumped to 20 per cent). The regime was accordingly limited as a capital-markets-transparency mechanism. Implementation of the Directive was also slow, which further impeded its effectiveness.

II.5.1.2 The FSAP

The ongoing issuer-disclosure regime came under scrutiny as part of the FSAP's drive to promote integration and more efficient capital formation through an upgraded disclosure regime, and following concerns as to the inadequacy of the regime (and potential prejudice to the reputation of the EU market internationally), notably by comparison with the US regime which, in practice, produced more ongoing disclosure regarding EU issuers than the EU regime.[461] In response, the FSAP period led to a re-orientation of the regime, from one largely based in the requirements of company law to a capital markets, transparency-directed regime.

The reforms were given a political imprimatur by the 2000 Lisbon 'dotcom' Council, which highlighted the enhancement under the FSAP of the quality and comparability of financial statements as central to the achievement of an integrated securities market, and by the 2001 and 2002 Stockholm and Barcelona Councils. The ongoing disclosure regime also became subsumed within, and benefited from, the political priority afforded to the wider 'disclosure and transparency' agenda for all securities admitted to trading on a regulated market. This agenda included the Commission's 2000 programme for reform of the accounting and financial reporting regime[462] (which would ultimately lead to the adoption of the 2002 IAS Regulation (section 6)), the 2003 Market Abuse Directive, and the 2003 Prospectus Directive.

II.5.1.3 The 2004 Directive Negotiations

The 2004 adoption of the Transparency Directive benefited from the commitment under the Lamfalussy process to extensive consultation[463] and from the lessons learned from the

---

[460] Limited policy discussion informed the choice of thresholds and the linkage of the regime to company law, rather than the transparency requirements of the capital markets, is clear. The Commission argued that 'the choice of thresholds which trigger compulsory notification are necessarily somewhat arbitrary' and chose the thresholds to ensure consistency with other harmonized company law measures: n 459, 6–7.

[461] 2000 Initial Lamfalussy Report, n 131, 6.

[462] Commission, Communication on the EU Financial Reporting Strategy: the Way Forward (2000) (COM (2000) 359) (2000 Financial Reporting Strategy).

[463] Extensive consultation took place in July 2001 (Commission, Towards an EU Regime on Transparency Obligations of Issuers Whose Securities are Admitted to Trading on a Regulated Market (July 2001)) and December 2001 (Commission, Towards an EU Regime on Transparency Obligations of Issuers Whose Securities are Admitted to Trading on a Regulated Market, Second Consultation by the Services of the Internal Market Directorate General of the European Commission (December 2001)). The Proposal followed in March 2003.

Commission's earlier failure to consult on the prospectus regime. Its progress was relatively smooth, reflecting widespread agreement on the limitations of the ongoing disclosure regime.[464] But its development suffered from the Commission's initial inclusion of a quarterly reporting requirement, which was not subject to rigorous impact assessment and which generated significant market hostility, leading to its removal in the Commission's formal proposal.

In its March 2003 Proposal, adopted after extensive discussions on quarterly reporting, the Commission argued that transparency was 'essential for the functioning of capital markets, enhancing their overall efficiency and liquidity', but also made the traditional connection between harmonization and market integration.[465] Four major reforms to the pre-FSAP transparency regime were proposed: the improvement of annual financial reporting by the imposition of a deadline for publication; the enhancement of periodic disclosure through enhanced half-yearly disclosure and a compromise interim management-reporting requirement; the extension of half-yearly reporting to issuers of only debt securities; and an upgrading of the ownership notification regime to change its orientation from company law to capital markets.

The final adoption of the Directive in December 2004 occurred under conditions of considerable time pressure, as the 2005 deadline approached for the end of the then Commission's term and the Parliamentary elections. But—and very unusually for the FSAP period, although now standard since the crisis-era reform period—the Directive was adopted under the 'fast-track' legislative procedure (Chapter X section 3). The Transparency Directive came into force on 20 January 2007.

II.5.1.4 Crisis-era Reform and the 2011 Proposal

In common with FSAP measures generally, the Directive was subject to a review requirement.[466] The review process, like the Prospectus Directive review, was informed by a number of reports, chief among them the 2009 Mazars Review,[467] the 2007 ESME Review,[468] and CESR's reports.[469] While these reports typically found broad satisfaction with the Directive and with the quality of issuer disclosures,[470] a number of themes recurred, including the costs to the market of the minimum-harmonization model, high

---

[464] In its initial Consultation, the Commission found that the interim reporting regime, eg, had become outdated following the evolution of markets and accounting requirements, did not adequately assist investors to make an informed judgement of an issuer's development and activities, contained only basic financial information, and was published on an infrequent cycle: July 2011 Consultation, n 463, 10.

[465] It argued that the Proposal would 'help further integrate Europe's securities markets by reducing or eliminating information asymmetries, which may hamper comparability and market liquidity, by enhancing investor confidence in the financial position of issuers, and by reducing the cost of accessing capital': n 455, 2.

[466] The Commission was to report on the operation of the Directive to the European Parliament and the Council by June 2009 (Art 33).

[467] Mazars, Transparency Directive Assessment Report (2009) (2009 Mazars Report).

[468] ESME, First Report of ESME on the Transparency Directive (2007) (2007 ESME Report).

[469] CESR's 2010 review of whether the ownership notification regime should be extended to interests economically equivalent to shares (CESR/09-1215b) (2010 CESR Major Shareholdings Report), CESR's mapping exercise of supervisory powers under the Transparency Directive (CESR/09-058) (2009 CESR Supervisory Powers Review), and CESR's mapping exercise on the Directive's implementation (CESR/08-514b) (2008 CESR Mapping Review).

[470] The 2009 Mazars Report, eg, found that 82 per cent of stakeholders canvassed found the disclosures useful: n 467, xiii.

SME issuers' costs, the difficulties represented by diverging approaches to the ownership notification regime and its failure to address market innovation, notably with respect to CfDs, and weaknesses in the disclosure dissemination system.[471]

The Commission's subsequent 2011 Proposal[472] suggested that while the Directive was widely regarded as being useful for the proper and effective functioning of the market, a series of clarifications and enhancements were required. Like the 2010 prospectus regime reforms, the 2013 revisions as finally adopted are broadly concerned with deregulating the regime in order in particular to respond to the SME cost burden. The revisions are also designed to reflect market changes, particularly with respect to the inclusion of a wider range of equity-like instruments within the ownership notification regime. The revisions additionally align the Transparency Directive's administrative sanctions regime with the new and more intrusive approach to sanctions adopted across the crisis-era reform programme generally. The crisis-era preoccupation with financial stability is another theme of the reforms, particularly with respect to the ownership notification regime and the inclusion of CfDs.[473] Negotiations were relatively uncontroversial;[474] agreement on what would become the 2013 Amending Transparency Directive was reached by the European Parliament and Council in May 2013.

II.5.2 Transparency Directive: Harmonization and ESMA

The Transparency Directive was originally based on minimum harmonization, unlike the Prospectus Directive.[475] Key provisions were cast in broad terms which invited diverging implementation,[476] and Member States enjoyed significant discretion to 'goldplate' the regime (or adopt super-equivalent provisions).[477] The home Member State was expressly permitted to subject an issuer to super-equivalent requirements more stringent than those laid down in the Directive, and empowered to subject shareholders and other relevant

---

[471] Which were highlighted in the Commission's formal response to the review of the Directive: Report to the Council, European Parliament, ECOSOC, and Committee of the Regions on the Operation of the Transparency Directive (COM (2010) 243) (2010 Commission Report).

[472] The main publicly available elements of the legislative history of the 2013 Amending Transparency Directive are: Commission Proposal COM (2011) 683 and Impact Assessment COM (2011) 683; the European Parliament's Negotiating Position, which followed the report adopted by the ECON Committee (27 September 2012, A7-0292/2012); and the Council General Approach, 29 May 2012, Council Document 10384/12.

[473] 2011 Amending Transparency Directive Proposal, n 472, 3.

[474] The most significant change to the Commission's Proposal concerned the Commission's original proposal that the interim management statement requirement be removed, and for a related prohibition on Member States adopting additional national requirements. The Council and European Parliament, however, supported Member State discretion. The text as adopted provides for Member State discretion, subject to constraints. The new ownership notification regime for financial instruments of similar economic effect to shares also changed over the negotiations, although in its essentials, as adopted it is similar to the Commission's proposal.

[475] Ferran has argued that the difference in approach was more a function of a pragmatic response to widely diverging approaches to periodic disclosure across the Member States than of a policy commitment to minimum harmonization: n 26, 145.

[476] eg 2009 Mazars Report, n 467, 37 and 2008 CESR Mapping Review, n 469, generally.

[477] The extent to which the regime has been goldplated is evident in ESMA's 2011 report on the Transparency Directive: Mapping the Transparency Directive—Options, Discretions, and Goldplating (ESMA/2011/194) (2011 ESMA Mapping Report).

persons to more stringent obligations than those that applied under the ownership notification regime (Article 3(1)).

This model has been reshaped somewhat by the 2013 Amending Transparency Directive, reflecting widespread market concern as to the costs of divergence (particularly with respect to the ownership notification regime) and support for greater harmonization.[478] Following the 2013 Directive reforms, the home Member State is still permitted to make an issuer subject to requirements more stringent than those laid down in the Directive. But it cannot adopt more stringent requirements with respect to requiring issuers to publish periodic financial information on a more frequent basis than annual financial reports (covered by Article 4) and half-yearly financial reports (covered by Article 4 (Article 3(1)). By way of derogation to Article 1, Member States may, however, require more frequent reports outside the annual and half-yearly cycle, but only where the relevant conditions are met (Article 3(1a)) (section 5.6.3). The 2013 Directive also reduces Member State discretion by prohibiting Member States from applying more stringent requirements under the ownership notification regime, unless the related conditions are met (Article 3(1a)) (section 5.7).

Nonetheless, the Transparency Directive does not harmonize to the same extent as the Prospectus Directive. Similarly, the administrative rulebook adopted under the Transparency Directive is less dense than that which has been adopted under the Prospectus Directive. The 2004 Directive was initially amplified by the 2007 Commission Transparency Requirements Directive,[479] which, *inter alia*, amplifies the specific disclosures required—including with respect to the half-yearly report and ownership notifications—and contains detailed technical specifications on the ownership notification regime. Much of the supporting disclosure requirements were, however, already in place under the financial reporting regime, obviating the need for extensive administrative rules; the IFRS reporting system now carries much of the regulatory weight with respect to ongoing reporting for issuers subject to IFRS.

The administrative regime is, however, becoming denser. The 2010 Omnibus I Directive provides for the adoption of ITSs by the Commission following an ESMA proposal. These include ITSs governing the standard forms, templates, and procedures to be used for ownership notifications and issuer-disclosure filings. The 2013 Amending Transparency Directive confers additional delegations to administrative rule-making on the Commission, including for ESMA-proposed BTSs. These focus in particular on the new ownership notification system, with ESMA enjoined to propose a series of RTSs in this regard and the Commission's pre-existing delegations in this area enhanced (section 5.7). The new disclosure dissemination system (section 8) will also be developed through Commission administrative rules, including ESMA-proposed RTSs.[480]

Related supervisory convergence measures, initially adopted by CESR and since by ESMA, have a strong regulatory dimension through the Transparency Directive Q&A.[481] The

---

[478] 2009 Mazars Report, n 467, xi–xii.
[479] Directive 2007/14/EC [2007] OJ L69/27.
[480] Arts 4(7a), 21(4), and 22.
[481] At the time of writing, the Q&A has been updated twice, and runs to some 18 questions, many of which focus on the interim management statement obligation (which was removed by the 2013 Amending Transparency Directive): ESMA/2012/98.

different CESR/ESMA convergence initiatives have also, however, a strong operational dimension and relate, for example, to the building of an electronic network for the storage and dissemination of regulated issuer disclosures. In addition, CESR, in conjunction with the Commission, earlier developed a series of standard forms to be used in making the ownership notifications required under the Directive[482] which, while non-binding, attempted to address the significant costs of the notification regime (section 5.7).

II.5.3 Transparency Directive: An Integrated Regime?

Alignment with the 2003 Prospectus Directive was a key theme of the institutional negotiations on the 2004 Transparency Directive; this concern was also reflected in the 2010 Amending Prospectus Directive, which accordingly made aligning reforms to the 2004 Transparency Directive. The Transparency Directive therefore adopts the market integration and perimeter-control devices originally agreed under the prospectus regime (including with respect to the determination of the home Member State, the treatment of the wholesale debt market, and the language regime) and as recently revised under the 2010 Amending Prospectus Directive. But while internally consistent in many respects, the two measures do not form a fully integrated issuer-disclosure regime, particularly as the transparency regime does not map on to the operating and financial review disclosures required under the Prospectus Directive. Accordingly, the benefits of the Prospectus Directive's incorporation by reference regime are limited, certainly as compared to the US integrated-disclosure regime which allows repeat issuers to produce short prospectuses.[483] The SEC's integrated-disclosure regime is, however, based on an issuer rather than an offering-based model; radical overhaul would have been needed to achieve the same result under the Transparency Directive.

II.5.4 Transparency Directive: Scope

Perimeter control under the Transparency Directive is broadly similar to perimeter control under the Prospectus Directive. The regime applies to issuers whose securities (both concepts are broadly the same as under the Prospectus Directive)[484] are already admitted to trading on a regulated market[485] situated or operating within a Member State. It does not

---

[482] Letter from Commissioner McCreevy to CESR Chairman Wymeersch, March 2007, attaching forms TR-1 and TR-2, and CESR 2004/109/EC.

[483] Karmel, n 350, 393–4.

[484] The definition of 'issuer', however, is more nuanced than that under the Prospectus Directive and refers to a natural legal entity, governed by private or public law, including a State, whose securities are admitted to trading on a regulated market. The definition also specifies that the issuer in the case of depositary receipts representing securities is the issuer of the securities represented by the depositary receipts: Art 2(1)(d). The 2013 Amending Transparency Directive nuances the definition to include natural persons and to clarify that, in the case of depositary receipts (admitted to trading on a regulated market), the issuer means the issuer of the securities represented, whether or not those securities are admitted to trading on a regulated market. Reflecting the Prospectus Directive, 'securities' covers transferable securities within the scope of the MiFID (now MiFID II) regime, with the exception of money-market instruments with a maturity of less than 12 months: Art 2(1)(a). Units issued by collective investment undertakings other than the closed-end type are also excluded from the Transparency Directive (Art 1(2)).

[485] See sect 7.

133

apply to securities listed on other trading venues, notably MTFs; as with the prospectus regime, the regulated market is a proxy for perimeter control.[486]

II.5.5 Transparency Directive: Differentiation, Exemptions, and SMEs

Reflecting the Prospectus Directive regime, the Transparency Directive regime is differentiated to reflect different issuers. In particular, sovereign and public debt issuers[487] are exempt from the annual and half-yearly reporting obligations (Article 8(1)(a)). The half-yearly reporting requirement may also, at the discretion of the home Member State, be disapplied for credit institutions whose shares are not admitted to trading on a regulated market and which have, in a continuous or repeated manner, issued only debt securities (Article 8(2)).[488]

Like the Prospectus Directive, the regime is calibrated to the wholesale bond market. An exemption from the annual and half-yearly reporting obligations is available for issuers exclusively of debt securities admitted to trading on a regulated market, with a denomination per unit of at least €100,000[489] (Article 8(1)(b)).[490] The exemption also applies where the denomination is of at least €50,000 (reflecting the regime prior to the 2010 Amending Prospectus Directive alignment), as long as the securities were admitted to trading before 31 December 2010.[491]

By contrast with the 2003 Prospectus Directive, SME issuers were not originally directly addressed by the 2004 Directive, although the calibrations which apply in the related annual reporting and IFRS regime applied. SME interests were, however, to the fore in the review of the Transparency Directive,[492] with concerns repeatedly raised as to the costs of the transparency regime, the visibility and 'bottleneck' problems faced by SME issuers (when the market is processing extensive disclosures and focused on the largest issuers as a result, particularly between annual and half-year reports), a related reduction in the value of regulated markets to SME issuers, and the disproportionate impact on the SME segment of the absence of a consolidated regime for pan-EU disclosure dissemination.[493] The Commission's 2011 Proposal related the reform process to the wider SME and growth

---

[486] Although ten Member States extended the application of the regime to MTF-admitted issuers: 2011 ESMA Mapping Report, n 477, 8.

[487] A State, a regional or local authority of a State, a public international body of which at least one Member State is a member, the ECB, and the European Stability Mechanism or similar mechanism.

[488] This exemption is available only where the total nominal amount of debt securities issued remains below €100 million and as long as a prospectus has not been published. An exemption is also available for issuers already existing at the time of the coming into force of the Transparency Directive which exclusively issue debt securities which are unconditionally and irrevocably guaranteed by the home Member State or by one of its regional or local authorities.

[489] As under the Prospectus Directive, where the denomination is non-euro, the rules apply to values equivalent to the euro value at the date of issue.

[490] Reflecting aligning reforms by the 2010 Amending Prospectus Directive and the 2013 Amending Transparency Directive.

[491] Art 8(4), as amended by the 2010 Amending Prospectus Directive and the 2013 Amending Transparency Directive.

[492] 2011 Amending Transparency Directive Proposal Impact Assessment, n 472, 9–10.

[493] eg 2009 Mazars Report, n 467, xi and xiii–xiv, and 44 and 57 and 2011 Amending Transparency Directive Proposal Impact Assessment, n 472, 11–12, 16–17, and 22–4.

agenda,[494] and focused closely on enhancing regulated market venues for SME issuers and on reducing the cost of capital for SMEs.

The major SME-related reform under the 2013 Amending Transparency Directive[495] relates to the interim reporting regime; while general in application it has been driven by SME sector concerns. Similarly, the general reforms to the dissemination regime are designed to support SME issuers.[496] The Directive also extends the period within which the half-yearly report must be published, in an attempt to address SME bottleneck problems.

II.5.6 Transparency Directive: the Issuer-disclosure Regime

II.5.6.1 Periodic Annual Financial Reports

Prior to the adoption of the Directive in 2004, annual reporting obligations applied to issuers under the pre-existing company law financial reporting regime. The Transparency Directive clarified the contents of the annual report, with reference in particular to the IFRS reporting regime, and thereby orientated the company-law-based reporting regime to the disclosure and comparability requirements of capital market disclosure.

An issuer must make public its annual financial report at the latest four months[497] after the end of the financial year, and ensure that it remains publicly available for at least ten years[498] (Article 4(1)). As the heavy lifting on annual report disclosure is carried by the financial reporting regime, the Transparency Directive simply specifies the content of the annual report as including (i) the audited financial statements, (ii) the management report, and (iii) responsibility statements.

Where the issuer is required to prepare consolidated accounts, the financial statements must include the consolidated accounts (drawn up in accordance with IFRS) as well as the annual accounts of the parent company (drawn up in accordance with the national law of the Member State in which the parent company is incorporated). Where consolidated accounts are not required, the audited financial statements must comprise the individual accounts prepared in accordance with the national law of the Member State in which the company is incorporated.[499] The financial statements must be audited in accordance with the requirements of the 2013 Accounting Directive, and the audit report must be disclosed in full to the public, along with the annual financial report. The management report must also be drawn up in accordance with the 2013 Accounting Directive. The responsibility statements are designed to align responsibility with the 'true and fair view' model which governs the

---

[494] Transparency Directive reform was a specific reform commitment in the Single Market Act (n 159).

[495] Which repeatedly highlights the need to address SME costs: eg 2013 Amending Transparency Directive, recs 3 and 4.

[496] 2011 Amending Transparency Directive Proposal, n 472, 3.

[497] This deadline caused considerable difficulties during the 2004 Directive negotiations. The Commission initially proposed a 60-day deadline, but revised this to three months following market concerns. The four-month deadline was introduced during the institutional negotiations.

[498] Reports were originally to be available for five years, but this was extended to ten under the 2013 Amending Transparency Directive.

[499] The requirement to produce individual accounts was added by the Council as being 'prudent in light of the Parmalat scandal': ECON Report, n 455, Amendment 52.

2013 Accounting Directive and the IFRS reporting regime. Statements must accordingly be made by the persons responsible within the issuer (whose names and functions are clearly indicated) to the effect that, to the best of their knowledge, the financial statements prepared in accordance with the applicable set of accounting standards give a true and fair view of the assets, liabilities, financial position, and profits or loss of the issuer and the undertakings included in the consolidation taken as a whole. The statements must also refer to the management report and state that the report includes a fair review of the development and performance of the business and position of the issuer and the undertakings included in the consolidation taken as a whole.

The 2013 Amending Transparency Directive has added a requirement, in order to support electronic dissemination, that all annual financial reports be subject to a requirement (from January 2020) to follow a new 'single electronic reporting format'; the new format will only be imposed where ESMA has conducted a related positive cost-benefit assessment, and will be governed by RTSs (Article 4(7)).

II.5.6.2 Periodic Half-yearly Financial Reports

Half-yearly reporting requirements are imposed under Article 5. They apply to issuers of shares and to issuers who only issue debt securities; other securities, such as covered warrants, do not trigger the reporting obligation. Price-formation mechanisms in the debt markets are less dependent on issuer disclosure,[500] but the regime has an investor protection dimension in that it is designed to ensure sufficient disclosure is available on the insolvency risk posed by debt securities, and reflects a policy concern to ensure consistent levels of transparency across debt and equity asset classes.[501]

Issuers within the scope of Article 5 must make public a half-yearly financial report which covers the first six months of the financial year, as soon as possible after the end of the relevant period but at the latest three months thereafter;[502] like the annual report, the six-monthly report must remain available to the public for at least ten years. It must include the condensed set of financial statements, the interim management report, and responsibility statements (reflecting those required for the annual report).

Where the issuer is not required to prepare consolidated accounts under the 2013 Accounting Directive, the condensed set of financial statements must include a condensed balance sheet, a condensed profit-and-loss account, and explanatory notes.[503] Where the condensed accounts must be consolidated, the issuer must follow the IFRS regime applicable to interim financial reporting in producing the condensed accounts.

---

[500] See further Ch V on the debt markets.

[501] The Commission argued that action was needed to protect those investing in debt securities from insolvency risk and to maintain a level playing field between share issuers and debt-securities issuers: 2011 Amending Transparency Directive Proposal, n 472, 17.

[502] The 2013 Amending Transparency Directive extended the deadline from two to three months to ease bottleneck problems for SMEs with respect to analyst coverage in particular: 2013 Amending Transparency Directive, rec 6.

[503] The issuer must follow the same recognition and measurement principles as apply when preparing the annual financial report. Non-consolidated half-yearly financial statements are governed by the 2007 Commission Directive: Art 3.

The interim management report must include at least an indication of important events that have occurred during the first six months of the financial year and of their impact on the condensed financial statements. It must also include a description of the principal risks and uncertainties for the remaining six months of the financial year. Issuers of shares must also report on major related party transactions.[504]

The Directive does not require that the half-yearly report is audited,[505] but where it has been the subject of an auditor's review, the report must be reproduced in full. Where the report has not been audited or reviewed by auditors, a statement to that effect must be made in the report.

II.5.6.3 Quarterly Reporting and the Interim Management Statement

Quarterly reporting by issuers has long attracted controversy in the EU. While it increases the volume of issuer disclosures, it has been associated with promoting short-termism and with associated risks in terms of earnings management and market volatility. These concerns have recurred, being associated with the Enron-era equity market crisis[506] as well as with the crisis-era debate on the efficiency of public equity markets.[507] Quarterly reporting is also associated with the difficulties faced by SME issuers. The problems which bottlenecks of issuer disclosure can generate for SME issuers, as investment analysts and other informational intermediaries focus on disclosures from the largest issuers, reflect the processing demands which quarterly disclosures pose for the market. The necessity for quarterly reporting has also been queried, given the requirement for *ad hoc* disclosure by issuers of material events.[508]

Prior to the 2004 adoption of the Transparency Directive, quarterly reporting was not required by all EU Member States or by major trading venues—although it was (and is) in the US, which difference in treatment quickly became part of the original reform discussions. The Commission's two 2001 consultations on reform proposed that a new quarterly obligation be adopted. Lacking cost-benefit analysis, thinly argued,[509] and heavily based on aligning the harmonized regime with international practice and that of several Member States, the proposal met with significant hostility from issuers, albeit that it was supported by NCAs, a number of trading venues, and consumer associations.

The Commission remained supportive of quarterly reporting in some form through the negotiations on the 2004 Transparency Directive,[510] although its position softened

---

[504] This related party disclosure requirement has been amplified by the 2007 Commission Directive.

[505] A delegation empowers the Commission to clarify the nature of the auditor's review, but this has not yet been acted on.

[506] eg: '"[Quarterly reporting] leads to the unintended consequences of destroying long-term value, decreasing market efficiency, reducing investment returns, and impeding efforts to strengthen corporate governance". None of these consequences is good': Editorial, 'Misguided Guidance', *Financial Times*, 25 July 2006 (citing the Business Roundtable Institute for Corporate Ethics and the CFA Institute).

[507] eg 2012 Kay Review, n 34.

[508] In the context of the original 2004 Transparency Directive reforms, eg, the London Stock Exchange supported ongoing *ad hoc* disclosure of material events rather than quarterly reporting (London Stock Exchange, News Dissemination and the EU Transparency Directive (2003)).

[509] Lannoo, K and Casey, J-P, EU Financial Regulation and Supervision Beyond 2005, CEPS Task Force Report No 54 (2005) 10–11.

[510] In an unusually extensive defence of its position, in the 2003 Transparency Directive Proposal the Commission pointed to the trend towards quarterly reporting, as evidenced by the decision by eight Member States to require such reporting and the provision of quarterly reporting by 1,100 of 6,000 European publicly

between the initial consultations and the Proposal in terms of the disclosures required. Over difficult institutional negotiations, the European Parliament's strong stance against quarterly reporting,[511] which was driven in particular by concerns as to the prejudicial impact on SME issuers,[512] ultimately prevailed. Under the original compromise solution, the 2004 Directive did not impose a quarterly reporting obligation or require the quarterly disclosure of key financial data. A narrative-based, attenuated, and historically orientated management statement requirement was imposed instead under Article 6. This obligation applied only to issuers of shares admitted to trading on a regulated market. These issuers were to make public two statements by management, one during the first six-month period of the financial year and one during the second six-month period of the financial year. Issuers were to provide (i) an explanation of material events and transactions that had taken place during the relevant period and their impact on the financial position of the issuer (and its controlled undertakings), and (ii) a general description of the financial position and performance of the issuer (and its controlled undertakings) during the relevant period. The historic orientation, and the absence of trend disclosure, reflected concern as to volatility risk, which emerged repeatedly during the Commission consultations, and, in particular, the risk of earnings management by issuers.[513] These rather economical provisions were, for the most part, 'copied out' in national regimes, leaving issuers with only limited guidance as to the content of the statement.[514] The minimum-harmonization model adopted also allowed trading venues to incorporate different approaches to quarterly/interim reporting in their admission products and to differentiate market segments accordingly.

Reflecting widespread concern with the interim statement requirement,[515] the 2011 Proposal proposed that the interim regime be abolished and Member States prevented from adopting any such requirement for domestic issuers. The 2013 Amending Transparency Directive differs from the 2011 Proposal by abolishing the harmonized interim statement regime but allowing Member States flexibility in adopting additional reporting

---

traded companies. It accepted, in principle, that market incentives to reduce the cost of capital could prompt issuers to provide more extensive disclosure, but related mandatory quarterly reporting to better investor protection, increased market efficiency, and improved capital allocation (albeit without evidence). *Ad hoc* disclosure was rejected as an alternative technique, with the Commission arguing that it was discretionary and did not provide standardized and comparable information.

[511] The ECON Report rejected the Commission's model in its entirety, arguing that quarterly reporting could generate incentives to withhold bad news to the next reporting cycle and encourage a focus on short-term earnings performance at the expense of long-term strategy: ECON Report, n 455, Amendment 68.

[512] The ECON Report argued that the SMEs did not have the resources to manage a quarterly reporting obligation: n 455, Explanatory Statement. It also argued (unsuccessfully) for an exemption for SMEs from the half-yearly reporting requirement.

[513] The Commission noted in its Proposal that 'there is no public interest in promoting a kind of "earnings guidance" leading to short-termism and undue pressure by analysts and fund managers': n 455, 16.

[514] Fischer-Appelt, D, 'Implementation of the Transparency Directive—Room for Variations Across the EEA' (2007) 2 *CMLJ* 133, 142. The UK Listing Authority, however, provided 'negative guidance' and on what was not required: UK Listing Authority, List!, Issue 14, December 2006.

[515] Despite some evidence of support (2009 Mazars Report, n 467, xiv and 89 and 2011 Amending Transparency Directive Proposal Impact Assessment, n 472, 29–30), concerns were widespread as to the lack of standardization and auditing which reduced the comparability benefits of the statements, and their costs and relevance, given the availability of other periodic and *ad hoc* material disclosures: 2011 Amending Transparency Directive Proposal Impact Assessment, n 472, 11 and 13.

requirements. The Transparency Directive accordingly, at the instigation of the European Parliament and Council, now permits home Member States to require issuers to publish additional periodic financial information on a more frequent basis than the annual and half-yearly reports (Article 3(1a)). But two conditions apply: the additional reporting requirement must not constitute a disproportionate financial burden in the Member State concerned, in particular for SMEs, and the content of the additional reporting requirement must be proportionate to what contributes to investment decisions by investors in the Member State concerned. Member States are also to assess whether the additional requirement may lead to an excessive focus on short-term results and performance and impact negatively on SME access to regulated markets. Issuers are also free to make discretionary quarterly or other disclosures; the ability of the market to drive the appropriate level of interim disclosure is assumed by the reform.[516]

The reform is designed to reduce prejudicial short-termism, reflecting wider crisis-era concerns as to excessive market volatility.[517] It also responds to concerns as to the regulatory costs faced by regulated-market-admitted SMEs and as to the visibility problems for SMEs which arise from bottlenecks of regulated disclosures. But by contrast with the SME-orientated reforms under the 2010 Amending Prospectus Directive, the 2013 Amending Transparency Directive adopts a nuanced approach. The interim management statement requirement is removed for all issuers; accordingly, it does not lead to uneven levels of investor protection in SME investments trading on regulated markets. Also by contrast with the 2010 Amending Prospectus Directive reforms, the regulated market brand is not disturbed by this reform as it applies to all issuers; the Commission expressly noted the dangers, which were also widely acknowledged during the review process,[518] were different rules to apply to issuers admitted to regulated markets according to their size.[519]

II.5.6.4 Ongoing Disclosure on Rights Attached to Securities

Issuers of shares admitted to trading on a regulated market must also make public without delay any change in the rights attaching to various classes of shares, including changes in the rights attaching to derivative securities issued by the issuer which give access to the shares of the issuer (Article 16(1)). Issuers of securities other than shares admitted to trading on a regulated market must make public without delay any changes in the rights of holders of such securities, including changes in the terms and conditions of these securities which could indirectly affect those rights (particularly changes with respect to loan terms or interest rates) (Article 16(2)).[520]

---

[516] 2011 Amending Transparency Directive Proposal Impact Assessment, n 472, 29–30.

[517] 2011 Amending Transparency Directive Proposal Impact Assessment, n 472, 14–16, and 2011 Amending Transparency Directive Proposal, n 472, 5 and 7.

[518] In its 2010 pathfinder Consultation, the Commission queried whether a differentiated ongoing disclosure regime for 'small listed companies' on regulated markets would ease regulatory burdens. Stakeholder reaction was hostile, with concern raised that the regulated market brand could be damaged by such a change to the scope of the Directive: Commission, Feedback Statement to Transparency Directive Proposal (2010).

[519] 2011 Amending Transparency Directive Proposal, n 472, 5.

[520] The 2013 Amending Transparency Directive reforms remove the earlier Art 16(3) requirement for issuers to disclose new loan issues and related guarantees and security.

II.5.6.5 Access to Information for Holders of Securities Admitted to Trading on a Regulated Market

The Transparency Directive additionally imposes requirements with respect to shareholder communications generally,[521] and particularly with respect to shareholder meetings,[522] following the governing principle that equal treatment must be ensured by the issuer for all holders of shares who are in the same position (Article 17(1)). In support of this principle, the issuer must ensure that all the facilities and information necessary to enable holders of shares to exercise their rights are available in the home Member State, and that the integrity of data is preserved (Article 17(2)). A similar regime applies to debt securities (Article 18).

II.5.6.6 Payments to Governments

A new set of disclosures relating to payments to governments in extractive industries (oil, gas, and mining) have been introduced by the 2013 Amending Transparency Directive (Article 6). Fitting somewhat awkwardly in the Directive, they are designed to drive greater accountability by governments and to inform civil society; they also respond to the parallel reforms under the 2010 US Dodd-Frank Act and related G8 commitments.[523]

II.5.7 Transparency Directive: Ongoing Disclosure on Major Holdings

II.5.7.1 The Notification Regime

Reporting obligations relating to ownership levels in publicly traded firms are common internationally, reflecting the importance of this disclosure to firm monitoring. These disclosures are particularly associated with the monitoring dynamics of the market for corporate control,[524] as they shed light on potential takeover activity as well as on the structure of corporate control generally.[525] Notwithstanding that ownership notifications are in large part a creature of takeover regulation—which has had a very troubled history in the EU, reflecting significantly divergent Member State positions on the role of the market

---

[521] In this regard, the Transparency Directive forms part of the wider corporate governance regime which addresses shareholders' rights. See, eg, Directive 2007/36/EC [2007] OJ L184/17 on cross-border voting rights. In April 2014, the Commission presented a proposal to reform the 2007 Directive by means of enhanced corporate governance requirements, including a requirement for additional disclosures on executive remuneration (and a related shareholder vote) and in relation to proxy advisers (COM (2014) 213).

[522] The rules address the use of proxies and reliance on electronic means of communications.

[523] 2011 Amending Transparency Directive Proposal, n 472, 8. The reforms also relate to sector-specific EU initiatives, including with respect to payments in the timber industry and the import of illegal wood into the EU.

[524] While the market-for-corporate-control debate is outside the scope of this discussion, see, eg, Jarrell, G and Bradley, M, 'The Economic Effects of Federal and State Regulations of Cash Tender Offers' (1980) 23 *J L and Econ* 371 and Davies, P, 'The Take-over Bidder Exemption and the Policy of Disclosure' in Hopt, K and Wymeersch, E (eds), *European Insider Dealing* (1991) 243, 256. The US provides the classic example of the large-shareholding reporting obligation as an instrument of takeover regulation. Under s 13(d) of the Securities Exchange Act, 1934 any person or group that becomes the owner of more than 5 per cent of any class of securities listed on a national exchange must file related disclosures with both the issuer of the securities and the SEC within ten days of the acquisition.

[525] See generally Brav, A, Jiang, W, Partnoy, F and Thomas, R, 'Hedge Fund Activism, Corporate Governance, and Firm Performance' (2007) 63 *J Fin* 1729.

for corporate control[526]—notification requirements have long been a feature of EU securities and markets regulation, initially under the 1988 Substantial Shareholders Directive and subsequently under the Transparency Directive. The original 2004 Transparency Directive regime was largely concerned, reflecting market conditions at the time, with upgrading and re-orienting the 1988 regime from its company law-driven model to a more extensive capital market-orientated model. In particular, the reporting thresholds, which previously were a function of company law voting thresholds, were re-adjusted and reduced, reflecting market demand for more effective disclosure on the nature of control, and in order to ensure that disclosure was made to the market concerning the structure of influence in an issuer.[527]

The effectiveness of these disclosures came under scrutiny following the increasing reliance on cash-settled equity derivatives (typically CfDs),[528] which do not carry rights to the underlying shares but which can be used to acquire economic exposure to the shares without the acquisition of voting rights, as an instrument for exerting control. In particular, long CfD positions, where the CfD counterparty acquires the related shares as a hedge, can potentially allow the CfD holder to exercise significant influence without disclosure to the market of stake-building. Transparency risks to efficient price formation accordingly arise, as do market abuse risks.[529] The governance risks engaged by the potential these instruments hold for 'empty voting' are also considerable, given the possibility for influence without the financial risks of share ownership, and the resulting disconnect between influence and consequences.[530] Reflecting widespread market concern[531] and a series of high-profile control acquisitions through cash-settled derivatives,[532] the 2013 Amending Transparency Directive accordingly extends the ownership notification obligation.[533]

---

[526] eg Clift, B, 'The Second Time as Farce? The EU Takeover Directive, the Clash of Capitalisms and the Hamstrung Harmonization of European (and French) Corporate Governance' (2009) 27 *JCMS* 55.

[527] The capital-market orientation was clear from the decision not to exclude investment companies from the notification process, although there were some calls for this. The Commission argued that the 'overall goal of moving towards more capital-market orientated thinking would be undermined by exceptions for investment companies. Companies have a strong interest to know which investment companies invest in them and what their position is' (2003 Transparency Directive Proposal, n 455, 19).

[528] 2011 Amending Transparency Directive Proposal Impact Assessment, n 472, 18.

[529] As noted by the Commission: 2011 Amending Transparency Directive Proposal Impact Assessment, n 472, 18–19.

[530] Hu, T and Black, B, 'Hedge Funds, Insiders and the Decoupling of Economic and Voting Ownership: Empty Voting and Hidden (Morphable) Ownership' (2007) 13 *J of Corporate Finance* 343. In the EU context, see Schouten, M, 'The Case for Mandatory Ownership Disclosure' (2009) 15 *Stanford J of Law, Business & Finance* 127 and Conac, P-H, 'Cash Settled Derivatives as a Takeover Instrument and the Reform of the EU Transparency Directive' in Birkmose, H, Neville, M, and Sorensen, K (eds), *The European Financial Market in Transition* (2012) 49.

[531] eg ESME, Views on the Issue of Transparency of Holdings of Cash Settled Derivatives (2009), 2009 Mazars Report, n 467, xviii, and 2011 Amending Transparency Directive Proposal Impact Assessment, n 472, 33.

[532] Including the high-profile 2008 72 per cent position built by Porsche in Volkswagen through cash-settled derivatives (representing around 30 per cent of the position) which led to significant volatility in the Volkswagen share price once the position was suddenly disclosed in October 2008, revealing that the Volkswagen free float was potentially reduced to only 6 per cent: (2010 CESR Major Shareholdings Report n 469, 7). On recent reliance on CfDs in the market for corporate control see Conac, n 530, 52–5.

[533] CESR, and lately ESMA, were in the vanguard of these developments at EU level. CESR was an early supporter of extended reporting requirements, proposing a principles-based regime in 2010 (2010 CESR Major Shareholdings Report, n 469), while ESMA considered the empty voting question more generally (ESMA/2011/288).

The original Transparency Directive ownership reporting regime also became a casualty of the Directive's minimum-harmonization approach, with divergent approaches widely reported.[534] Significant divergences relating to the thresholds which governed notification, the identification of holdings, and the mechanics of notification all imposed significant costs on investors.[535] In response, the 2013 Amending Transparency Directive reshapes the notification regime as a maximum harmonization obligation, prohibiting Member States from imposing more stringent notification requirements (Article 3(1a));[536] lower notification thresholds can be set, however, in order to allow Member States to reflect distinctive market conditions.[537]

The core obligation is set out in Article 9(1), which imposes a notification obligation on shareholders.[538] The home Member State must ensure that where a shareholder acquires or disposes of shares of an issuer whose shares[539] are admitted to trading on a regulated market (and to which voting rights are attached), the shareholder notifies the issuer of the proportion of voting rights[540] in the issuer held by the shareholder as a result of the acquisition or disposal where the proportion reaches, exceeds, or falls below the following thresholds: 5 per cent, 10 per cent, 15 per cent, 20 per cent, 25 per cent, 30 per cent,[541] 50 per cent, and 75 per cent.[542] The notification system is therefore relatively sensitive to the nature of corporate influence, as it starts at the lower threshold of 5 per cent[543] and proceeds in 5 per cent increments until 30 per cent. The Directive expressly permits Member States to retain lower reporting thresholds, although they may not otherwise impose more stringent requirements (Article 3(1a)). Passive crossing of the relevant thresholds is also covered. Notification must be made where the proportion of voting rights reaches, exceeds, or falls below the thresholds as a result of events which change the

---

[534] ESMA's 2011 review identified a series of material divergences across the Member States, and noted 'significant divergences in the trigger levels, deadlines, and procedures for the reporting requirements of major shareholdings', as compared to the new short selling regime: 2011 ESMA Mapping Report, n 477, 12–15. Similarly, 2009 Mazars Report, n 467, xii and xv–xix, finding that the notification regime was 'the most problematic' element of the 2004 Directive.

[535] eg, 2011 Amending Transparency Directive Proposal Impact Assessment, n 472, 20; 2009 Mazars Report, n 467, xii and xv–xix, finding that the notification regime was 'the most problematic' element of the Directive; and 2007 ESME report, n 468.

[536] This reshaping, reflecting strong market demand, is designed, ambitiously, to create a uniform approach, reduce legal uncertainty, enhance transparency, simplify cross-border investments, and reduce costs: 2011 Amending Transparency Directive Proposal, n 472, 6.

[537] Particularly in those Member States where widely dispersed share ownership is common.

[538] Defined as any natural person or legal entity governed by private or public law who holds, directly or indirectly, shares of the issuer in its own name and on its own account, shares of the issuer in its own name but on behalf of another natural person or legal entity, and depository receipts, in which case the holder of the depository receipts is considered to be the holder of the underlying shares represented by the depository receipts: Art 2(1)(e).

[539] The notification obligation does not apply to shares acquired for the sole purpose of clearing and settling within the usual short settlement cycle or to custodians holding shares in their custodian capacity, as long as such custodians can exercise the voting rights attached to such shares only under instructions given in writing or by electronic means: Art 9(4).

[540] Voting rights are calculated on the basis of all the shares to which voting rights are attached, even if their exercise is suspended.

[541] Member States have the option of applying a one-third threshold.

[542] Member States have the option of applying a two-thirds threshold.

[543] Member States have tended to converge towards a 5 per cent threshold, although Member States with significant financial markets have adopted 3 per cent thresholds, leading ESME to suggest that a uniform 3 per cent threshold be adopted to ease administrative burdens: 2007 ESME Report, n 468, 5.

breakdown of voting rights, and on the basis of the information which must be disclosed by the issuer concerning its share capital under Article 15 (Article 9(2)). Article 15 requires the issuer to disclose to the public the total number of voting rights and capital at the end of each calendar month during which an increase or decrease occurs.

Notification obligations of this nature represent a considerable burden for dealers in securities who hold proprietary positions, and are of doubtful value where they do not shed light on those who control the issuer. An exemption is accordingly available for market-makers.[544] A market-maker is not subject to the notification requirements where holdings reach or cross the 5 per cent threshold, as long as the market-maker is authorized by its home NCA under the 2014 MiFID II/MiFIR and does not intervene in the management of the issuer concerned or exert any influence on the issuer to buy the shares or back the share price.[545] A similar exemption is available for voting rights held in the 'trading book' (an own funds/capital concept which covers short-term investments—see Chapter IV section 8) of credit institutions and investment firms (Article 9(6)),[546] for voting rights attached to shares acquired for stabilization purposes (see Chapter VIII section 8.3.2) (Article 9(6a)),[547] and for shares provided to or by members of the European System of Central Banks in carrying out their monetary functions (Article 11).

Issuers are also subject to the notification obligations in that an issuer must, where it acquires or disposes of its own shares (either itself or through a person acting on its behalf), make public the proportion of shares (as soon as possible but not later than four trading days following the acquisition or disposal) where the proportion reaches, exceeds, or falls below 5 per cent or 10 per cent of the voting rights (Article 14).

The 2013 Amending Transparency Directive reforms focus in particular on the expansion of the notification regime to address cash-settled instruments (such as CfDs). While the 2004 Directive applied the reporting requirement to 'financial instruments' it, in effect, only applied where the instruments required settlement through share delivery. The logic for addressing additionally cash-settled instruments in the Transparency Directive and through a maximum harmonization model is not entirely compelling. These disclosures support the market for corporate control, but the Directive is not primarily a takeover market measure, and takeover regulation in the EU is highly contested and operates under minimum-harmonization disciplines.[548] The reforms are, however, pragmatic in that they respond to widespread market concern as to the costs of divergence in this area, and bring greater coherence to the notification regime. They also support the price-formation

---

[544] A market-maker is defined as a person who holds himself out on the financial markets on a continuous basis as being willing to deal on own account by buying and selling financial instruments against his proprietary capital at prices defined by him: Art 2(1)(n).

[545] The 2007 Commission Transparency Requirements Directive requires that the market-maker notify the home NCA that it conducts (or intends to conduct) market-making activities in a particular issuer (Art 6). Art 6 also envisages that the market-maker be required to identify the shares held for market-making purposes, but be allowed to make the identification by any verifiable means (in particular, the market-maker may only be required to hold the securities in a separate account where it is not able to identify them).

[546] Conditions apply under Art 9(6). A new delegation has been conferred under the 2013 Amending Transparency Directive for RTSs to amplify aspects of the market-making and trading-book exemptions.

[547] This exemption was added by the 2013 Amending Transparency Directive.

[548] Conac, n 530, 61–2, but arguing against the formalistic division of EU measures and noting the efficiency gains from extending the regime to include these instruments.

efficiencies which are at the heart of the Directive's objectives by ensuring more accurate information is conveyed to the market, particularly with respect to an issuer's free float.

Under the 2013 Amending Transparency Directive, the Article 13(1) notification regime for 'share-like' 'financial instruments' has been revised to apply more generally to financial instruments[549] that, on maturity, give the holder, under a formal agreement, either the unconditional right to acquire, or the discretion as to his right to acquire, shares to which voting rights are attached, already issued, of an issuer whose shares are admitted to trading on a regulated market (Article 13(1)(a)). In addition, financial instruments which do not come within this classification, but which are referenced to shares and which have 'economic effects similar to' these instruments, whether or not they give a right to physical share settlement, are covered (Article 13(1)(b)). The related notification must include a breakdown by type of the financial instruments held under each classification, distinguishing between instruments which give right to a physical settlement, and those which give right to a cash settlement.

Capturing CfDs and related interests is a complex exercise, particularly with respect to how these interests are identified and calculated, and how exemptions apply, given the multiplicity of instruments engaged, and the different structures possible (including, for example, instruments referenced to a basket of shares or index). A number of Member States have recently addressed these notifications, with particular reference to CfDs,[550] and adopted a range of different approaches, experimenting with, for example, 'aggregated' regimes and regimes based on a 'delta-adjusted' analysis,[551] typically reflecting (certainly in the case of the UK regulator[552]) extensive consultations and impact assessments, as well as relevant local market conditions.[553] The new regime engages with some of the related complexities, clarifying, for example, how voting rights are to be calculated[554] and aggregated.[555] The substantive, operational requirements are, however, generally delegated to administrative rules, underlining the pivotal role ESMA now plays in the elaboration of complex rules, whether by proposing BTSs or providing technical advice to the Commission. The reforms provide for the adoption of RTSs with respect to the calculation of voting rights in relation

---

[549] Defined as transferable securities, options, futures, swaps, forward rate agreements, CfDs, and other contracts or agreements with similar economic effects which can be settled physically or in cash: Art 13(1b). ESMA is to establish and update an indicative list of financial instruments subject to the Art 13 notification requirement.

[550] The UK, France, Germany, and Italy all adopted new regimes between 2007 and 2011.

[551] Regimes can, eg, be based on aggregating CfD disclosure with share ownership disclosure, and can also be calibrated (or delta-adjusted) to reflect the exact relationship between the CfD and the related share.

[552] eg FSA, Consultation Paper 07/20, Disclosure of Contracts for Difference (2007).

[553] The UK approach, eg, reflects a number of UK-specific influences, including the very large volumes of trading in CfDs given the stamp duty tax which applies to equity trades. The 2007 FSA Consultation revealed that some 30 per cent of trades in equities took place through CfDs: n 552.

[554] Art 13(1a). Voting rights are to be calculated by reference to the full notional amount of shares underlying the instrument, except where the instrument provides exclusively for cash settlement, in which case a delta-adjusted basis is required. All financial instruments relating to the same issuer are to be aggregated and notified, but only long positions are to be taken into account (long positions are not to be netted with short positions related to the same issuer). RTSs will amplify the voting rights regime.

[555] Art 13a. The new aggregation regime adopts a 'share basket' approach and is designed to require a new notification where the holder of financial instruments exercises an entitlement to acquire shares, and the total holding of physical shares exceeds the notification threshold, but does not affect the overall percentage of the previous notification.

to financial instruments where instruments are referenced to a basket or index, the delta-adjusted calculation method for voting rights, and the application of the Article 9 exemptions for share ownership notifications (these exemptions apply also to Article 13 financial instrument notifications),[556] while a delegation for Commission rule-making generally applies with respect to the contents of the Article 13 financial instrument notification.[557]

II.5.7.2 Attribution of Voting Rights to other Natural Persons and Legal Entities

The objective of enhancing market transparency on the nature of corporate control requires that the scope of the share notification obligation extend considerably beyond shareholders to cover a wide range of indirect control relationships. Article 10 provides that the Article 9 notification requirements are applied to a natural person or legal entity to the extent that it is entitled to acquire, dispose of, or exercise voting rights in the circumstances identified in Article 10 (or in any combination of these circumstances).

Article 10 covers voting rights held by a third party with whom that person or entity has concluded an agreement, which obliges them to adopt, by concerted exercise of the voting rights they hold, a lasting common policy towards the management of the issuer in question (10(a)). It also covers voting rights held by a third party under an agreement concluded with that person or entity which provides for the temporary transfer for consideration of the voting rights (10(b)). Voting rights attached to shares which are lodged as collateral with that person or entity are covered (as long as the person controls the voting rights and declares an intention to exercise them) (10(c)), as are voting rights attaching to shares in which the person or entity has a life interest (10(d)). Where voting rights held in the situations covered in (a)–(d) are held by an undertaking controlled by the person or entity, they also are treated as voting rights held by the person or entity. Article 10(f) covers voting rights attaching to shares deposited with the person or entity, but where the person or entity can exercise the voting rights at its discretion (in the absence of specific instructions from the shareholders). Article 10(g) covers voting rights held by a third party in its own name but on behalf of the person or entity, while Article 10(h) covers voting rights which the person or entity can exercise as a proxy (but only where the voting rights can be exercised at the discretion of the person or entity in the absence of instructions from the shareholders). Although some market concern as to the clarity of this regime was raised during the review process,[558] it has not been addressed by the 2013 reforms.

II.5.7.3 The Notification Procedure

Article 12 addresses the notification procedure. The notification must cover the resulting situation in terms of voting rights, the chain of controlled shareholdings through which voting rights are held (where relevant), the date on which the threshold was reached or crossed, and the identity of the shareholder (even where the shareholder is not entitled to exercise voting rights under the conditions set out in Article 10) and of the natural person or legal entity entitled to exercise voting rights on behalf of the shareholder. A distinct regime

---

[556] Art 13(4).

[557] Art 13(2).

[558] 2009 Mazars Report, n 467, xvi (noting concern as to the application of the 'acting in concert' requirement, particularly with respect to the line between co-ordinated shareholder activism generally, and acting in concert).

applies to Article 13 financial instrument notifications.[559] The notification burden is eased somewhat in that shareholders (and relevant natural persons or legal entities) may notify the information in a language customary in the sphere of finance (Article 20(5)).

The notification to the issuer must be made as soon as possible, but not later than four trading days after the date on which the shareholder (or the natural person or legal entity subject to Article 10) learns of the acquisition, disposal, or possibility of exercising voting rights (or on which, having regard to the circumstances, should have learned of it (regardless of when the event took effect)) or is informed about the events which changed the breakdown of voting rights for the purposes of the Article 9(2) notification obligation (Article 12(2)).

The amplification of the regime under the 2007 Commission Transparency Requirements Directive has a distinctly practical orientation. The regime governs whether the shareholder or natural person or legal entity should make the notification (and addresses the treatment of proxies)[560] as well as the circumstances under which the notifying person should have learned of the acquisition, disposal, or possibility of exercising voting rights.[561]

A series of exemptions applies, particularly in the context of asset management where an aggregation of holdings could create the misleading impression that a stake was being built in an issuer.

Following the notification, the issuer must make public all the information contained in the notification no later than three days after receipt.[562] A home Member State may exempt issuers from this requirement where the information in question is made public by its NCA either on receipt of the information or no later than three trading days thereafter.

II.5.8 Transparency Directive: Market Integration and Home Member State Control

II.5.8.1 Home Member State Control

The Transparency Directive does not apply an NCA approval requirement to ongoing issuer disclosures, reflecting long-standing practice and the central role played by informational intermediaries (notably auditors) in policing these disclosures. The Directive does not, therefore, require an anchor Member State/NCA for the purposes of supervision. It is, however, necessary to provide an anchor Member State/NCA with respect to the substantive content of the disclosure rules which apply and with respect to related disclosure filing rules. The adoption of a home Member State control model was, accordingly a key objective of the Transparency Directive. The home Member State therefore anchors the regime and, although to a more limited extent now in the wake of the 2013 Amending

---

[559] Administrative rules will govern the regime: Art 13(2).

[560] 2007 Commission Transparency Requirements Directive Art 8.

[561] Knowledge is deemed to exist no later than two trading days following the transaction (Art 9), given that it is reasonable to assume that natural persons or legal entities exercise a high duty of care when acquiring or disposing of major holdings and will very quickly become aware of the implications (rec 11).

[562] Where the notification has been made in a language customary in the sphere of finance, Member States may not require the issuer to translate it into a language accepted by the NCAs.

Transparency Directive reforms which have diluted the original minimum-harmonization approach, shapes how the different obligations are applied. Host Member State control is largely eliminated from the regime, easing the burden faced by issuers, although a precautionary powers regime, which tracks the equivalent regime in the Prospectus Directive, applies.

The powers of the host Member State (the Member State in which securities are admitted to trading on a regulated market where this State is different from the home Member State) are confined by Article 3(2).[563] The host State may not impose disclosure requirements on the admission of securities to trading on a regulated market in its territory which are more stringent than those set out in the Directive or under the market abuse regime (section 5.12) or impose more stringent requirements concerning notification of major holdings on shareholders and other relevant persons. The precautionary principle applies, however, to the jurisdiction of the host Member State and, reflecting the Prospectus Directive, allows the host NCA to intervene in exceptional circumstances to protect investors once the home NCA's response has proved inadequate (Article 26).

As under the Prospectus Directive, the home Member State definition is segmented to reflect the different needs of issuers and investors in the retail and wholesale markets. Accordingly, issuer choice does not govern the identification of the home Member State in the case of issuers of shares and of debt securities with a denomination per unit of less than €1,000. The home Member State for these issuers is, reflecting the Prospectus Directive, where the issuer is incorporated in the EU, the Member State in which it has its registered office (Article 2(1)(i)).[564] For other issuers, the home Member State is chosen by the issuer from among the issuer's State of registration and those Member States in which its securities are admitted to trading on a regulated market (Article 2(1)(ii)).[565]

II.5.8.2 Language Regime

A language regime (Article 20) applies in support of the notional 'passport' extended to ongoing disclosure. It is closely based on the Prospectus Directive's language regime, although with some variations, and supports issuer choice of publication in a 'language customary in the sphere of international finance'.

As under the Prospectus Directive, where securities are admitted to trading on a regulated market in the home Member State only, 'regulated information' (which includes Transparency

---

[563] The Commission described this approach as a balance between investor interests, which called for full harmonization, and issuer/market interests, which called for Member State discretion: 2011 Amending Transparency Directive Proposal, n 472, 9.

[564] Following the 2013 Amending Transparency Directive revisions, where the issuer is incorporated in a third country, the home Member State is chosen by the issuer from among the Member States where its securities are admitted to trading on a regulated market; this choice remains valid unless the issuer chooses a new home Member State following its securities not being admitted to trading on a regulated market in the first home State, in accordance with Art 2(1)(i)(iii): Art 2(1)(i)(i).

[565] The issuer may choose only one Member State, and the choice remains valid for three years, unless its securities are no longer admitted to trading on a regulated market in that State, in which case the Art 2(1)(i)(iii) regime applies. The 2013 Amending Transparency Directive revises the 2004 Directive to refine this regime, and provides that where an issuer's securities are no longer admitted to trading on a regulated market in its home State (identified under Art 2(1)(i)(i) or (ii)) but are admitted to trading on a regulated market elsewhere, it may choose a new home State from the States on which it is admitted to trading on a regulated market or its State of registration: Art 2(1)(i)(iii).

Directive requirements—see section 8) must be disclosed in a language accepted by the home NCA.[566] But unlike the regime which applies under the Prospectus Directive, where securities are admitted to trading on a regulated market both in the home Member State and in one or more host States, information must be disclosed in a language accepted by the home NCA and, at the issuer's choice, either in a language accepted by the host NCA or a 'language customary in the sphere of international finance'. Translation requirements may, therefore, be imposed where the language required by the home NCA differs from the issuer's choice. Where the securities are not admitted to trading on a regulated market in the home Member State but are admitted in one or more host-State-regulated markets, the issuer may choose either a language accepted by the host NCA or a 'language customary in the sphere of international finance'. The home NCA may also require that the disclosure is, depending on the choice by the issuer, made in a language which it accepts or is 'customary in the sphere of international finance'.

A discrete regime applies to wholesale offers (or securities with a denomination of at least €100,000); issuers may choose either a language accepted by the home and host NCAs or one customary in the sphere of international finance.

II.5.9 Transparency Directive: Supervision and Enforcement

II.5.9.1 Supervision: NCAs, Co-operation, and Convergence

The supervisory regime is closely based on the Prospectus Directive. Article 24 requires Member States to designate the central authority required under the Prospectus Directive as the central competent administrative authority responsible for carrying out the Transparency Directive's obligations, and inform the Commission and ESMA accordingly.[567]

The powers which must be conferred on NCAs are broadly similar to those required under the prospectus regime, but are calibrated to relate to the ongoing disclosure context (Article 24(4)). The NCA must be empowered to: require auditors, issuers, holders of securities, those required to provide major holdings notifications, and relevant controlling or controlled persons to provide information and documents; require the issuer to disclose information to the public (an NCA may publish the information on its own initiative where the issuer fails to do so); require notifications to be made; suspend (or request the relevant regulated market to suspend) trading in securities (for a maximum of ten days at a time) where it has reasonable grounds for suspecting that the provisions of the Directive have been breached by the issuer; prohibit trading on a regulated market; monitor that the issuer discloses timely information with the objective of ensuring effective and equal access to the public in all Member States where the securities are traded and take appropriate action where this is not the case; make public any failures to comply with the major holdings notification regime; examine whether information is drawn up in accordance with the relevant reporting framework; and carry out on-site inspections. Following the 2013

---

[566] Where the securities are admitted to trading on a regulated market without the issuer's consent, the language-regime obligations fall to the person who has requested the admission: Art 20(4).

[567] Supervision of compliance with the financial reporting regime can be allocated to a separate competent authority (rec 28).

Amending Transparency Directive reforms, NCAs are also to be given all investigative powers necessary for the exercise of their functions (Article 24(4a)).

Co-operation obligations are also imposed between NCAs (Article 25(2)) and, following the 2010 Omnibus I Directive reforms, between NCAs and ESMA (Article 25(2b)), and reflect those applicable under the Prospectus Directive in that NCAs must co-operate with each other, whenever necessary, for the purpose of carrying out their duties and making use of their powers. Professional secrecy obligations apply under Article 25(1) but they must not prevent the exchange of confidential information between NCAs; ESMA has been added as an actor with which confidential information can be exchanged (Article 25(3)). NCAs must also provide ESMA without delay with all information necessary to carry out its duties under the ESMA Regulation (Article 25(2c)). They must also render assistance to NCAs of other Member States. ESMA is empowered to mediate between NCAs where co-operation requests have been rejected or not acted on within a reasonable time (Article 25(2a)).

By contrast with the Prospectus Directive, significant difficulties do not appear to have arisen with respect to supervisory convergence under the Directive. The 2009 CESR report on the Directive[568] did not, unlike the 2010 CESR peer review of NCA prospectus approval practices, drill into operational supervisory practices. But at a formal level it found that, in general, most NCAs enjoyed the necessary powers under the Directive—although it also found evidence of significant divergences in discrete areas, including with respect to powers over periodic disclosure and in particular with respect to sanctioning. More generally, the Transparency Directive review process did not suggest significant difficulties with divergent supervisory practices and approaches under the Directive.[569] This reflects in part the lack of close market engagement with NCAs, as approval and passporting mechanisms do not apply under the Directive. Supervisory convergence activities under the Directive are, accordingly, less intense than those under the prospectus regime, but include the transparency regime Q&A and the standard forms for ownership notifications.

II.5.9.2 Liability and Sanctions

(a) Civil Liability

Reflecting the approach pioneered under the Prospectus Directive, but also the post-Enron reform movement,[570] responsibility for the annual and six-monthly reports must lie at least with the issuer or its administrative, management, or supervisory bodies. Member States must also ensure that their liability rules apply to issuers, their administrative, management, or supervisory bodies, or the persons responsible within the issuer (Article 7).

Under this non-harmonized regime, the possibility of multiple actions across the Member States arises, along with the attendant costs.[571] The Article 7 regime, however, arguably

---

[568] n 469.

[569] eg 2009 Mazars Report, n 467, xxi.

[570] The Commission related the liability regime to the post-Enron certification requirements introduced by the US SEC and which require directors and financial officers to certify quarterly and annual reports. The Commission argued that these measures 'set a pace against which Community legislation must find a proper response for promoting European capital markets at an international level': 2003 Transparency Directive Proposal, n 455, 8–9.

[571] Attempts were made over the course of the development of the 2004 Transparency Directive to dilute the risks of liability across different legal regimes by anchoring liability to the home Member State of the issuer, but this requirement was not adopted in the Directive.

heightened (initially) the potential litigation risks and costs as some Member States interpreted Article 7 as a requirement to enhance or adopt new liability regimes.[572] The Commission stated, however, that the Directive did not have the aim of extending the scope of existing liability regimes, did not take a position on the scope of Member States' regimes or prescribe who should benefit, and was not designed to provide incentives for Member States to introduce more extensive regimes.[573]

(b) Sanctions

By contrast with the prospectus regime, the administrative sanctions regime (which operates without prejudice to the right of Member States to provide criminal sanctions) has been revised (by the 2013 Amending Transparency Directive) in order to align the Transparency Directive with the new approach to administrative sanctions adopted over the crisis era. Accordingly, Member States must lay down rules on administrative sanctions and take all necessary measures to ensure they are implemented; these sanctions must be effective, proportionate, and dissuasive (Article 28(1)). The sanctions must apply to members of the administrative, management, or supervisory boards and any other person responsible under national law for a breach (Article 28(2)). The new regime also specifies the particular breaches to which sanctions must apply (Article 28a), the minimum suite of administrative sanctions which must be available (Article 28b),[574] and the framework governing how sanctions should be applied (Article 28c).[575] NCAs are also required to publish every decision on sanctions without undue delay (including information on the type and nature of breach and the identity of the person); publication may be delayed or on an anonymous basis in certain situations (Article 29).[576] Sanctioning powers may be exercised directly, in collaboration with other authorities, by delegation to other authorities, and by application to the competent judicial authorities (Article 24(4b)). Cross-border co-operation with respect to sanctions is expressly addressed: NCAs must co-operate to ensure that sanctions (or other measures) produce the desired results and co-ordinate their action when dealing with cross-border cases (Article 25(2)).

II.5.10 Transparency Directive: Third Country Regime and Equivalence

An equivalence regime applies to third country issuers otherwise within the scope of the regime by virtue of their securities being admitted to trading on a regulated

---

[572] The UK interpreted Art 7 as requiring the adoption of a new statutory liability regime. For discussion see Burn, L, 'Only Connect—the Importance of Considering Disclosure Requirements in the Light of their Legal Consequences' (2007) 2 *CMLJ* 41.

[573] Letter from Director General Schaub to the Financial Markets Law Committee, 3 May 2006. The letter was in response to concerns expressed in the UK that Art 7 could increase the risk of multi-jurisdiction liabilities (Letter from Lord Woolf, Financial Markets Law Committee, to Director General Schaub, 23 March 2006).

[574] Public statements, injunctions, suspension of voting rights, and pecuniary sanctions (the higher of up to €10 million or up to 5 per cent of total annual turnover in the preceding year for legal persons and €2 million for natural persons, or, in each case, of up to twice the amount of the profits gained or losses avoided because of the breach, where those can be determined).

[575] The regime requires NCAs, in assessing the type and level of sanction, to take into account: the gravity and duration of the breach; the degree of responsibility of the responsible person; the financial strength of the responsible person; the importance of the profits gained or losses avoided; the losses to third parties; the level of co-operation provided by the responsible person; and previous breaches by the responsible person.

[576] Where, in the case of natural persons, publication would be disproportionate, would seriously jeopardize the stability of the financial system or an ongoing official investigation, or would cause disproportionate and serious damage to the institutions or natural persons involved.

market.[577] Home NCAs may exempt third country issuers from disclosure requirements where 'equivalent' obligations are imposed in the third country (Article 23(1)). The nature of equivalence, which is governed by administrative rules, has been amplified in some detail;[578] a discrete equivalence regime applies to the related financial reporting system (section 6).

II.5.11 Transparency Directive: Impact

Particularly because it is not event-driven like the prospectus regime, it is very difficult to disentangle the impact of the Transparency Directive from that of the issuer-disclosure regime as a whole, although there is some evidence to suggest that it can be associated with a deepening of liquidity.[579] The extent to which the Directive has had a direct impact on issuance and offering activity seems to be limited,[580] while the related IFRS regime has been identified as the major driver of enhanced comparability.[581]

II.5.12 *Ad Hoc* Disclosure and the Market Abuse Regime

The market abuse regime, by addressing the disclosure of material, price-sensitive events which arise outside the periodic reporting cycle, represents a key component of the EU's issuer-disclosure matrix. As the regime is deeply embedded in the concepts deployed by the market abuse regime, it is discussed in Chapter VIII section 7.

II.6 Financial Reporting and International Financial Reporting Standards

II.6.1 The EU Financial Reporting Framework: Main Features

The EU's issuer-disclosure requirements are supported by the parallel financial reporting system.[582] This system is based on (i) the general reporting rules originally contained in the (now repealed) Fourth and Seventh Company Law Directives and which are now consolidated within and reformed by the 2013 Accounting Directive, which addresses the

---

[577] The regime was revised by the 2010 Omnibus I Directive, which, in particular, clarified the Commission's role in establishing an equivalence mechanism and ESMA's supporting role.

[578] Art 13 of the 2007 Commission Transparency Requirements Directive, eg, sets out the equivalence requirements for the annual management report required in the annual financial report, while Art 14 sets out the equivalence requirements for the half-yearly financial report.

[579] Christensen, H, Hail, L, and Leuz, C, Capital-Market Effects of Securities Regulation: Prior Conditions, Implementation and Enforcement, ECGI Finance WP No 407/2014 and Chicago Booth Research Paper No 12-04 (2013), available at <http://ssrn.com/abstract=1745105>.

[580] 2009 Mazars Report, n 467, xii and 42–3, reporting that 50 per cent of stakeholders canvassed were of the view that the regime had no effect on the IPO market or primary market issuance generally.

[581] 2009 Mazars Report, n 467, xiv.

[582] For FSAP-era discussions of the reporting regime see Schön, W, 'Corporate Disclosure in a Competitive Environment—the Quest for a European Framework on Mandatory Disclosure' (2006) 6 *JCLS* 259 and Van Hulle, K, 'Financial Disclosure and Accounting' in Hopt, K and Wymeersch, E (eds), *Capital Markets and Company Law* (2003) 153.

presentation of annual accounts and consolidated accounts and which applies regardless of whether a firm is publicly traded;[583] and (ii) the IFRS adopted by the IASB which apply to issuers admitted to trading on a regulated market.[584] Harmonized rules[585] also address the related statutory audit.

From a financial markets perspective, the IFRS regime stands at the heart of the EU's financial reporting system. Under the 2002 IAS Regulation, all EU issuers admitted to trading on a regulated market must prepare their consolidated accounts in accordance with IFRS adopted by the IASB. Prospectus disclosures must be prepared in accordance with the IAS Regulation,[586] while the annual and half-yearly reports required of in-scope issuers under the Transparency Directive must also follow IFRS.[587] IFRS are now established as the dominant global financial reporting standard;[588] their importance is underlined by convergence between IFRS and US GAAP (Generally Accepted Accounting Principles) forming part of the G20's recommendations for financial market reform over the crisis.[589] The EU experience with IFRS has been broadly positive, with issuers generally rewarded for providing the perceived investor benefits of IFRS application in terms of quality of disclosures and convergence.[590] But by adopting IFRS as the major EU financial reporting standard, the EU has largely ceded control over the financial reporting regime to the IASB.[591] Accordingly, the allocation of standard-setting power for the EU market to the IASB, and the related dependence by the EU on the quality of the reporting standards produced by IASB,[592] has led to the complex dynamics of the IASB/EU relationship becoming the defining influence on the shape of the EU financial reporting regime.

---

[583] Additional reporting rules apply to banks and insurance companies.

[584] Directive 2013/34/EU [2013] OJ L182/19; IFRS apply by virtue of the 2002 IAS Regulation (Regulation (EC) No 1606/2002 [2002] OJ L243/1).

[585] These were originally contained in Directive 2006/43/EC [2006] OJ L157/87 (see Anand, A and Moloney, N, 'Reform of the Audit Process and the Role of Shareholder Voice' (2004) 5 *EBOLR* 223).

Reflecting an EU crisis-era policy concern as to the quality of audits, the regime has been reformed by two audit proposals designed to strengthen the quality of audits of 'public interest entities' (the PIE concept is designed to capture large firms and was established by the original 2006 Directive) and of statutory audits more generally and to facilitate a wider choice of audit provider (Proposals at COM (2011) 779 and COM (2011) 778).

The new regime, which was adopted by the Council and European Parliament in April 2014, is designed to strengthen the audit process by, eg, prohibiting (in relation to PIEs) the provision of certain non-audit services to audited firms and capping non-audit fees, and imposing a ten-year rotation period on PIE audits. The regime is also designed to enhance the quality of all audit reports and to provide a passport for audit firms.

[586] 2004 Commission Prospectus Regulation Art 35, and, eg, Annex I para 20 (share registration document requirements).

[587] Transparency Directive Arts 4(3) and 5(3).

[588] Some 128 jurisdictions either permit or require IFRS for their domestic issuers: Deloitte, IAS Plus, Use of IFRS by Jurisdictions (as at March 2014).

[589] The G20 called for a single set of global accounting standards and for completion of convergence between IFRS and US GAAP (the major global accounting regime which does not follow IFRS). For a summary of the G20 recommendations and a progress report on their implementation see IASB, Response to the G20 Conclusions (2011).

[590] Armstrong, C, Barth, M, Jagolinzer, A, and Riedl, E, Market Reaction to the Adoption of IFRS in Europe (2009), available at <http://ssrn.com/abstract=903429>, examining stock market reaction to the adoption of IFRS by EU issuers.

[591] The IASB has been described as providing highly technical regulation in a regulatory space ceded by national regulators: Pan, E, 'The Challenge of International Cooperation and Institutional Design in Financial Supervision: Beyond Transgovernmental Networks' (2010) 11 *CJIL* 243.

[592] The SEC has reported that IFRS 'are generally perceived to be of high quality by the global financial reporting community', albeit as also having some underdeveloped areas: SEC, Work Plan for the

Overall, the financial reporting regime is highly dynamic, reflecting not only ongoing changes to the IFRS regime—which have intensified in the wake of the financial crisis—but also repeated amendments, over time, to the framework accounting regime: most recently, the 2013 Accounting Directive has replaced the earlier 4th and 7th Company Law Directives with a single, consolidated reporting regime, which contains a subset of rules designed to lessen the reporting burden for smaller firms[593] and which clarifies the reporting regime more generally. Financial reporting is also supported by ESMA's extensive activities, which are primarily directed to the enforcement and clarification of IFRS.

II.6.2 IFRS and the IAS Regulation

II.6.2.1 The Road to the 2002 IAS Regulation

Prior to the adoption of the IFRS regime, large divergences existed across the Member States with respect to how the financial information required in prospectuses and ongoing issuer disclosures was presented. Significant risks to comparability and to the costs of capital were generated by the open-textured nature of the original accounting directives, particularly with respect to local tax and legal requirements. Member States also remained (and remain, outside the scope of the 2002 IAS Regulation) free to adopt their own accounting standards in applying the directives. These accounting standards could, variously, be in the form of the standards adopted by the IASB (then the International Accounting Standards Committee) in the form of IAS (now IFRS),[594] US GAAP, or domestic GAAP. These variations in reporting standards, which reflected long-standing path dependencies relating to institutional structures, financing models, and cultural influences,[595] exacerbated the risks to comparability already generated by the options, derogations, and exemptions contained in the framework accounting directives.

Fragmentation in accounting standards can prejudice transparency and comparability and increase the cost of capital where investors struggle with non-comparable disclosures.[596]

Consideration of Incorporating IFRS into the Financial Reporting System for US Issuers. Final Staff Report (2012) (2012 SEC Report) 3. The quality of reporting standards is, however, difficult to assess, given the range of factors, including firm incentives and the wider economic environment, which shape how firms report their performance. See, eg, Barth, M, Landsman, W, and Lang, M, International Accounting Standards and Accounting Quality, Stanford University Graduate School of Business Research Paper No 1976 (2007), available at <http://ssrn.com/abstract=688041>.

[593] The 2013 reforms are designed to ease the administrative burden on smaller companies, including by means of a 'mini-regime' which allows 'small' companies to prepare a simpler profit and loss account, balance sheet, and a limited number of accompanying notes; removal of the audit requirement for small companies; the introduction of a more graduated reporting system generally, calibrated to the different sizes of firm; and an increase in the thresholds for determining whether firms are small or medium-sized for the purposes of the financial reporting regime. The reporting regime can be disapplied by Member States in respect of the smallest of companies ('micro' companies), following the earlier 2012 accounting reforms (which are incorporated within the 2013 Directive): Directive 2012/6/EU [2012] OJ L81/3.

[594] IAS are gradually being replaced by IFRS. This discussion will refer to IFRS unless IAS is more appropriate in the context.

[595] Generally, Leuz, C, 'Different Approaches to Corporate Reporting Regulation: How Jurisdictions Differ and Why' (2010) 40 *Accounting and Business Research* 229. The US SEC has similarly noted the fundamental differences between US GAAP and IFRS which relate in part to the impact of different market and regulatory structures: 2012 SEC Report, n 592, 14.

[596] See, eg, Cunningham, L, 'The SEC's Global Vision: A Realistic Appraisal of a Quixotic Quest' (2008) 87 *North Carolina LR* 1.

In the EU, the difficulties were compounded as large firms began to use US GAAP or (then) IAS to fulfil US stock exchange listing requirements. But the difference between US GAAP and domestic EU standards led to very different financial statements being produced in respect of the same set of issuer financial information, creating the potential for investor confusion and a lack of transparency. Additionally, some Member States allowed companies to report domestically on the basis of US GAAP (as long as the accounting directives' requirements were met), others required that reports based on national reporting standards be adopted in parallel, while still others permitted companies to report under IAS, which was popular with issuers whose securities were traded in the institutional markets.

As the EU's efforts to develop and integrate its capital markets intensified, and as the financial reporting regime became more strongly associated with the support of market finance, rather than with the reporting requirements of company law, resolution of the difficulties represented by the fragmented financial reporting regime became a central element of the FSAP suite of reforms.[597] The 2000 Lisbon European Council, for example, called for greater comparability across the financial statements of issuers listed on regulated markets. In response, the Commission produced its important 2000 Communication on an EU Financial Reporting Strategy, which asserted a link between reporting standards harmonization and the depth and efficiency of the EU capital market.[598] At the heart of the strategy was the then radical proposal that all listed companies prepare their consolidated accounts in accordance with IFRS by 2005.

The choice by the EU of IFRS as its reporting standard reflected a multiplicity of influences, extending from international regulatory relations (particularly with the US) to market preferences.[599] From 1995, it was clear that the (then) IAS regime was the preferred policy option.[600] In its 2000 Communication on a Financial Reporting Strategy, the Commission confirmed its preference for the adoption of IAS, highlighting, *inter alia*, the international perspective of IAS and the inability of the EU to exert any influence over the development of the US GAAP regime. The availability of IAS as a set of internationally accepted standards, supported by an institutional structure, also made it the most practical option from the outset, even if the initial development of the IAS/IFRS regime was not auspicious. During the 1980s, what was then the International Accounting Standards Committee (IASC) produced a number of standards (IAS) which were rather loose in texture and gave reporting companies a series of options. By the 1990s, the IASC had tightened its standards by removing options and thereby supporting greater comparability between IAS-prepared accounts. In 1995 the IASC entered into an agreement with IOSCO to develop a set of IAS by the mid-1990s, which, if acceptable, would be adopted by IOSCO as the recommended reporting standard for cross-border capital-raising. Resistance by the US SEC limited the worldwide adoption of IAS as an international reporting

---

[597] 2000 Financial Reporting Strategy, n 462, arguing that the fragmentation was an obstacle to the development of a deep and liquid EU securities market and its global competitiveness: at 3 and 5.

[598] 2000 Financial Reporting Strategy, n 462.

[599] See Ferran, n 418, 28–31 and Karmel, R, 'The EU Challenge to the SEC' (2007) 31 *Fordham International LJ* 1692.

[600] Commission Communication on Accounting Harmonisation: A New Strategy vis-à-vis International Harmonisation (1995) (COM (95) 508).

standard, but, following the May 2000 recommendation by IOSCO that its membership permit the use of IAS in preparing financial statements, a significant step forward was taken in their acceptance. A major structural overhaul of the IASC was undertaken in 2001, leading to the establishment of what is now the IASB and its oversight bodies, in order to enhance the adoption of IAS internationally. In that restructuring, the decision was also taken to rename future standards as IFRS.

II.6.2.2 The IAS Regulation

The 2002 IAS Regulation, which, reflecting strong political support,[601] was adopted under the fast-track legislative procedure, was designed to provide the EU with a 'comprehensive and conceptually robust set of standards specifically intended to serve the needs of the international business community'.[602] The Regulation's objective is the adoption and use of 'international accounting standards' (defined as including IAS, IFRS, their related interpretive documents and subsequent revisions, and future standards (Article 2)) in the EU, with a view to harmonizing the financial information presented by the companies covered and in order to ensure a high degree of transparency and comparability of financial statements and the efficient functioning of the Community capital market and the internal market (Article 1).

For each financial year starting on or after 1 January 2005, companies governed by the law of a Member State must prepare their consolidated accounts in conformity with international accounting standards if, at the balance sheet date, their securities are admitted to trading on a regulated market (Article 4). Under Article 5, Member States have the option of extending the reporting regime to (i) listed companies in respect of their annual accounts (not just the consolidated accounts) (Article 5(a)), and (ii) other companies with respect to their consolidated and/or their annual accounts (Article 5(b)). Where Member States exercise this (these) option(s), they must immediately communicate this to the Commission and other Member States (Article 8).

II.6.3 Incorporating IFRS in the EU: Risks and Challenges

II.6.3.1 The Endorsement Mechanism

Reliance on IFRS as the EU reporting standard raises a number of constitutional and institutional challenges. The EU cannot devolve standard-setting to a private third party and so some form of internal review and adoption is required. More operationally, it must be procedurally possible to accommodate revisions to IFRS without full-scale revision of the relevant EU rules each time a standard is revised by the IASB; the crisis era, for example, has generated significant reforms to the IFRS regime based on G20 recommendations.[603] The solution adopted by the EU was to deploy an 'endorsement mechanism' (for IFRS and IAS, amendments and revisions thereto, and interpretive documents (and revisions thereto)

---

[601] Commission, FSAP Evaluation. Part I: Process and Implementation (2005) 22.

[602] Proposal ([2001] OJ C154/285) 3.

[603] A series of G20 summits called for enhancements, particularly with respect to the treatment of provisioning and financial instruments. For the IASB response see IASB, Response to G20 Conclusions (2011).

(2002 IAS Regulation Article 2)), which is designed to incorporate IFRS effectively and speedily, while respecting the EU's constitutional imperatives.[604]

The Commission adopts IAS/IFRS in the form of Commission regulations, supervised by the Accounting Regulatory Committee (ARC) which represents Member State interests and oversees the delegation of the IAS/IFRS endorsement (law-making) power to the Commission from the Council and European Parliament. The endorsement process is driven by the Commission:[605] under Article 3 of the 2002 IAS Regulation, the Commission decides on the applicability within the EU of international accounting standards. A technical advisory group, the European Financial Reporting Advisory Group (EFRAG), provides expert advice to the Commission and to the ARC on the endorsement of standards. While superficial parallels could be made with CESR/ESMA, EFRAG is a much less institutionally sophisticated actor. EFRAG is an independent, private sector body which represents accounting and standard-setting expertise.[606] It carries out the initial technical review of the proposed standard(s) and ensures that the wider constituency of interest groups affected is consulted during the endorsement process. Significant difficulties have, however, emerged with EFRAG as the location of technical expertise: its resources are limited; it is not formally a public interest body; tensions have arisen between EFRAG and national accounting standard-setters; its focus on technical issues and its exclusion of the economic and political implications of particular standards has been criticized; difficulties have arisen with respect to its independence and the extent to which it is representative; and communication lines to the IASB have become blurred as national standard-setters also communicate directly with the IASB.[607] Further complicating the institutional structure, technical capacity is also provided by ESMA, which plays an active role in advising EFRAG (and the IASB).

Two principles apply to the endorsement of IFRS under the 2002 IAS Regulation (Article 3(2)). The first reflects a core underpinning principle of the EU's accounting regime (now set out in the 2013 Accounting Directive): standards may be adopted only if they are not contrary to the 'true and fair view' principle. It is clear, however, that this does not require that standards are tested against the rules of the EU accounting regime (recital 9). Standards must also be conducive to the rather nebulous European 'public good'. The second principle requires that the standards meet the criteria of understandability, relevance, reliability, and comparability required of the financial information needed for making economic decisions and for assessing the stewardship of management. Investor, creditor, and shareholder perspectives are therefore included.

---

[604] In this respect the EU, despite its distinct constitutional environment, reflects practice in a number of jurisdictions internationally in incorporating IFRS: 2012 SEC Report, n 592, 3.

[605] Although proposed Commission regulations endorsing IFRS can be vetoed by the European Parliament and Council within three months of their original adoption by the Commission.

[606] It is funded by its member organizations and the EU. EFRAG is overseen by its Supervisory Board and in practice operates through two key committees, the Technical Expert Group (independent experts) and the Planning and Resources Committee (national accounting standard bodies). The Standards Advice Review Group, established by the Commission and composed of independent experts, assesses EFRAG reports for objectivity and balance.

[607] Maystadt, P, Should IFRS Standards be More European? Mission to Reinforce the EU's Contribution to the Development of International Accounting Standards Report for the Commission (2013) (2013 Maystadt Report) 10–12.

The combined effect of the adoption of the IFRS regime as the EU financial reporting standard and of the filtering of IFRS through the Commission endorsement process, while a practical and constitutional necessity, is to demand a delicate balancing act of the Commission. The acceptance of IFRS as the EU financial reporting standard implies acceptance of the integrity and robustness of the IFRS adoption process. The endorsement mechanism should accordingly be sensitive to the risk that the integrity of IFRS as a global standard could be prejudiced, with related risks and costs to EU issuers operating internationally, were the Commission to adapt IFRS to the EU. But difficulties remain relating to the appropriateness of IFRS as the EU standard, particularly in crisis conditions for the EU, or where EU-specific competitiveness risks arise from IFRS application. The importance of effective IASB liaison is formalized under Article 7 of the 2002 IAS Regulation, which provides that the Commission is to liaise on a regular basis with the IASB on active projects in order to co-ordinate positions and facilitate discussions. The endorsement process has generally proven to be smooth,[608] but two major exceptions, relating to accounting for financial instruments and noted in the following sections, underline the complexities of the relationship between the EU and the IASB and the related risks to the integrity of IFRS as well as to the competitiveness of EU issuers.

II.6.3.2 EU/IASB Relations and IFRS

The effectiveness of the endorsement mechanism depends in large part on the quality of EU/IASB relations. These have proved tense on occasion. The IASB's interests as a private standard-setting body, with a global agenda and open to an array of influences,[609] have at times conflicted with the particular interests pursued by the EU, leading to tensions with respect to IASB governance and operation generally, as well as with respect to particular standards. From the outset the EU was a major critic of IASB governance, particularly with respect to its dependence on private sector funding and to the resilience of its accountability to major stakeholders, such as the EU,[610] albeit that the EU has also provided practical support to the IASB.[611] Recent major reforms have strengthened the IASB's financing model,[612] as well as its related governance and accountability structures.[613] Nonetheless, difficulties arising from the EU's status as,

---

[608] The ever-lengthening list of Commission Regulations endorsing particular IAS and IFRS standards and related interpretations by the IASB is available online at <http://ec.europa.eu/internal_market/accounting/legal_framework/regulations_adopting_ias/index_en.htm>.

[609] Fleckner, A, 'FASB and IASB: Dependence despite Independence' (2008) 3 *Virginia Law & Business Rev* 2008.

[610] The Commission, eg, produced a series of reports on IASB governance between January 2007 and March 2008, and was an active participant in the 2008–2010 IASB constitution review. The Commission also joined forces with leading regulators worldwide to support the IASB reform process: Combined Statement of the European Commission, Financial Services Agency of Japan, IOSCO, and the SEC Proposing Changes to Strengthen the Institutional Framework of the IASCF and Encourage the Foundation's Related Activities, While Emphasizing the Continued Importance of an Independent Standard-Setting Process, 7 November 2007 (MEMO/07/451).

[611] Decision 716/2009/EC [2009] OJ L253/8 allows the EU to provide financial support to the IASB.

[612] The organization is seeking to move away from private sector funding and towards a public sponsorship, intermediated funding model.

[613] Following major reforms, including the 2008–2010 constitution review, the IASB sits within the IFRS Foundation, which has the objective of developing a single set of high-quality, understandable, enforceable, and globally accepted financial reporting standards. Standard-setting is undertaken by the IASB (composed of technical experts), which is overseen by the IFRS Foundation Trustees. The Trustees (six from Europe, six from North America, one from South America, one from Africa, and two from the rest of the world) are overseen by a Monitoring Board composed of representatives of capital market regulators (IOSCO, the SEC,

ultimately, a consumer (albeit a major consumer) of IFRS, the limitations on its formal representation at the IASB,[614] and the IASB's determination to maintain its independence and reflect the views and interests of its varied stakeholders have yet to be resolved.

The difficulties which the endorsement mechanism poses where EU and IASB interests diverge, and the related risks to IFRS as an international standard, were clear before the crisis. Strong EU market and regulatory interests led to the Commission adopting in 2004 two 'carve-outs' to IAS 39 on the reporting of financial derivatives and on hedging techniques.[615] Although a degree of resolution was subsequently achieved,[616] the related furore[617] underlines the instability which the endorsement mechanism can generate. The financial crisis led to a deepening of this instability, as noted in the following section. While major change to the endorsement mechanism is unlikely, institutional reforms designed to streamline the currently complex institutional relationship between the EU and the IASB—which is currently managed across a range of bodies, including EFRAG, ESMA, the Commission and national accounting standard-setting bodies—are likely.[618]

II.6.3.3 IFRS in Practice in the EU: the Mark-to-Market Problem

(a) The Transition

The initial transition to IFRS was an operationally complex exercise. It was all the more so given the related move to 'mark-to-market' or fair value accounting under IFRS, which had the effect of changing the character of financial positions and of increasing notional losses as assets were revalued. Non-cash items (such as stock options, pension-fund deficits, and financial instruments, particularly derivatives) were brought on to the accounts and valued at market value—frequently damaging, at least in accounting terms, a company's overall earnings and profit, given volatility risks.[619] The impact of the standards on profits became increasingly controversial, with companies expressing concern that profit lines in the accounts did not accurately reflect cashflow and underlying performance, given the injection of volatility into the profit-and-loss account.[620] More generally, the costs and

---

the Japanese FSA, and the EU Commission). The US SEC has recently described the governance structure as providing a reasonable balance between IASB oversight and independence: 2012 SEC Report, n 592, 5.

[614] Although the EU is a member of the Monitoring Board and the EU accounts for six of the IFRS Foundation Trustees.

[615] The carve-out related to the fair value option and hedge accounting. See generally Whittington, G, 'The Adoption of International Financial Reporting Standards in the European Union' (2005) 14 *European Accounting Rev* 127. The Commission stressed that the carve-out was 'exceptional and temporary' and 'not the preferred solution...the Commission prefers full endorsement of any international accounting standard': Commission, IAS 39 Financial Instruments: Recognition and Measurement—Frequently Asked Questions (19 November 2004) MEMO/04/265.

[616] Resolution was achieved on the fair value option in 2005; the hedge accounting carve-out remains under negotiation.

[617] The acknowledgement in the IASC Annual Report that it 'has, of course, been disappointing that the European Union has carved out of our main financial instruments standards' (International Accounting Standards Committee Foundation, Annual Report (2004) 12) hid a frequently ill-tempered debate. See Fleckner, n 609, 298–300.

[618] The 2013 Maystadt Report (n 607) made a series of recommendations designed to enhance EU liaison with the IASB and strengthen EU influence, following a 2012 direction from Council Meeting 13 November 2012, ECOFIN Press Release No 16051/13. See further sect 6.4.

[619] Particular concerns arose as to the impact on dividends and share options: Jopson, B, 'Accounting Rules Hit Share Option Schemes', *Financial Times*, 11 August 2005, 21.

[620] Jopson, B, 'Enthusiasm for Reporting Standards Cools', *Financial Times*, 25 August 2005, 3.

complexities of the new regime were considerable and were exacerbated by a perceived lack of clarity and stability in the IFRS regime.[621]

By 2007, however, CESR was reporting that although the transition to IFRS had represented a major challenge, there was no evidence of a loss of confidence and the quality of financial reporting had improved due to increased transparency of financial information and greater comparability.[622] The crisis period generated specific compliance and application difficulties,[623]—particularly within financial institutions[624]—related in part to rapid changes to IFRS over this period,[625] and led to increased enforcement action by NCAs over this period.[626] But overall, the regular CESR and, since, ESMA reports on IFRS application suggest that the application of IFRS has strengthened and improved.[627] By 2011, ESMA was able to report that the overall quality of IFRS financial statements was improving every year,[628] although persistent weaknesses in financial instrument reporting remain an enforcement priority.[629]

(b) The Financial Crisis

The crisis era placed IFRS, and in particular the fair value model, under significant stress with respect to financial reporting by financial institutions. The volatility and related liquidity risks of the fair value model, which requires mark-to-market valuation, have been associated with pro-cyclicality and with the development of the financial crisis.[630] A major reform effort by the IASB is now underway.[631] But the initial stages of the crisis saw the fair value problem intensify tensions between the EU and the IASB.

---

[621] Hoogendoorn, M, 'International Accounting Regulation and IFRS Implementation in Europe and Beyond—Experiences with First Time Adoption in Europe' (2006) 3 *Accounting in Europe* 23.

[622] CESR, Review of the Implementation and Enforcement of IFRS in the EU (2007) (CESR/07–352). A similar view was taken by the Commission in its April 2008 report, which also noted that the endorsement process was proving a success, as well as on preliminary findings that the new regime had reduced the cost of capital: Report on the IAS Regulation (COM (2008) 215).

[623] CESR, Activity Report on IFRS Enforcement (2009) (CESR/10-917), noting difficulties with, eg, the valuation of financial instruments, the reporting of deferred taxes, and aspects of impairment reporting; ESMA, Activity Report on IFRS Enforcement in 2010 (2011) (ESMA/2011/355), noting difficulties with, eg, financial instrument reporting (impairment, fair value assessments, and risk disclosures), impairment of non-financial assets, and share-based payments; and ESMA, Activity Report on IFRS Enforcement in 2011 (2012) (ESMA/2012/412), noting difficulties with reporting on sovereign debt holdings.

[624] CESR, eg, reported on poor compliance with IFRS financial instrument requirements for financial year 2008 across the EU's largest banks and insurers: CESR, Statement on the Application of Disclosure Requirements Related to Financial Instruments in 2008 (CESR/09-821).

[625] CESR 2009 IFRS Enforcement Report, n 623, 11.

[626] As was noted in CESR's 2009 IFRS Enforcement Report, which noted the increase in enforcement activity in response to the heightened risk to, and concerns of, the investment community. As the crisis receded, and reflecting in part co-ordinated review of IFRS application by CESR and ESMA (sect 6.4), enforcement actions dropped from 900 enforcement actions in 2009, to 700 in 2010, and to 600 in 2011.

[627] eg ESMA 2010 IFRS Enforcement Report, n 623, noting a 'year on year' improvement since 2005 (at 11), as well as specific improvements relating, to, eg, valuation techniques and credit risk reporting.

[628] ESMA 2011 IFRS Enforcement Report, n 623, 3.

[629] ESMA Enforcement Priorities for 2012 Financial Statements (ESMA/2012/730).

[630] For a review see Strampelli, G, 'The IAS/IFRS After the Crisis: Limiting the Impact of Fair Value Accounting on Company Capital' (2011) 1 *ECFLR* 1, Ojo, M, 'The Role of the IASB and Auditing Standards in the Aftermath of the 2008/2009 Financial Crisis' (2010) 16 *ELJ* 604, and Laux, C and Leuz, C, 'Did Fair-Value Accounting Contribute to the Financial Crisis?' (2010) 24 *J of Economic Perspectives* 93.

[631] The reforms relate to IAS 39/IFRS 9 governing financial instruments, and address the classification and measurement of financial instruments, impairment methodology, and hedge accounting.

In October 2008 the IASB made an urgent reform to the core accounting standard IAS 39/ IFRS 9 (on the measurement of financial instruments), to reflect the severe market volatility and illiquidity which was causing difficulties for mark-to-market valuations.[632] The reform reflected very significant EU pressure[633] which led to a heightening of tensions between the EU and the IASB,[634] and which has been associated with an undermining of the IASB's ability to project itself as a global standard-setter.[635] Further difficulties arose at CESR level, following CESR's strenuous efforts over 2008–9 to shape the debate on reform of the fair value standard, particularly with respect to its application in illiquid markets.[636] These led to some industry concern that CESR was usurping the IASB's function[637] and to CESR ultimately affirming the IASB's authority as standard-setter and interpreter of those standards, albeit also at the same time underlining its role in supporting the consistent application and enforcement of IFRS[638]—thereby establishing a very permeable line between IASB 'interpretation' and CESR 'support of application'. Subsequently the de Larosière Report underlined the extent of the tensions, calling for the IASB to review the fair value principle but in so doing to 'open itself up more to the views of the regulatory, supervisory and business communities'.[639]

The tensions, which have been reflected in the G20 recommendation that stakeholder involvement in standard-setting be improved,[640] have since subsided, reflecting the ongoing

---

[632] The reforms allowed entities to reclassify certain non-derivative financial assets and to change their accounting treatment accordingly (in effect, disapplying fair value). Financial institutions in particular could reclassify assets from trading assets to 'held to maturity', thereby shielding the assets from the prevailing volatility in markets. The classification had positive effects on the profit and loss account: CESR, Statement on the Application of and Disclosures Related to the Reclassification of Financial Instruments (2009) (CESR/09-575).

[633] Reflecting in particular concern to ensure a level playing field between the EU and US, particularly with respect to the treatment of illiquid assets, following US FASB (Financial Accounting Standards Board) clarifications on fair value accounting under US GAAP in late September and October 2008, and which were highlighted by the ECOFIN Council of 7 October 2008. The subsequent revision to IAS 39 adopted by the IASB in October 2008 makes clear that the revision was designed to address divergences between US GAAP and IAS 39.

[634] A subsequent exchange of letters between the Commission and the IASB on further fair value reforms later in October and November 2008 underline the Commission's concern for urgent reforms to be adopted and the IASB's countervailing concern to respond to all stakeholders, not just the EU: letters available at <http://ec.europa.eu/internal_market/accounting/ias/revision/index_en.htm>.

[635] House of Commons Treasury Select Committee, 9th Report 2008–2009, The Banking Crisis, Reforming Corporate Governance and Pay in the City (2009), paras 258–67. IASB Chairman Sir David Tweedie reported to the Committee that the IASB was subject to a 'blunt threat to blow [the IASB] away'. On the machinations, and the EU threat of an IAS carve-out, see Ferran, n 418.

[636] CESR's intensive activities on fair value reform (summarized in CESR's Annual Report for 2008 at 40–2 and for 2009 at 41–2) included a consultation and statement on fair value measurement of financial instrument in illiquid markets (CESR/08-437 and CESR/08-713b) and a review of the IASB's October 2008 reclassification reforms (CESR/09-575). CESR, CEBS (the Committee of European Banking Supervisors), and CEIOPS (the Committee of European Insurance and Occupational Pension Supervisors) also issued a joint statement in October 2008 supporting the reclassification reforms and calling for further international convergence on fair value reform (CESR/08-839).

[637] CESR Feedback Statement on Fair Value Measurement in Illiquid Markets (2008) (CESR/08-712) 5–6, noting market concern that CESR should not issue interpretive guidance but instead provide input to the IASB, as well as concern as to a lack of institutional and international co-ordination.

[638] CESR acknowledged that competence relating to the setting and interpretation of standards lay with the IASB and that its work did not constitute formal IASB guidance: n 637, 3–4.

[639] The High-Level Group on Financial Supervision in the EU, Report (2009), 21.

[640] IASB, n 603.

IASB governance review process as well as the strenuous IASB fair value reform process, in which the Commission and CESR/ESMA have been actively engaged. Difficulties remain, however, with ESMA's role in the application of IFRS and with respect to IASB liaison (section 6.4).

II.6.3.4 IFRS in Practice in the EU: SMEs

As under the issuer-disclosure regime, the costs of the financial reporting regime for SMEs have led to a number of reviews and calibrations.

A new regime for 'micro' companies was adopted in 2012 and allows Member States to exempt micro entities from report and account publication obligations.[641] From the market finance perspective, however, reforms of this nature address very small firms which do not interact with the capital markets.[642] The most significant reforms have been wrought by the 2013 Accounting Directive which seeks to reduce the costs of reporting for small companies.[643]

The IFRS regime is directed to large issuers admitted to trading on regulated markets and, accordingly, has little traction with SMEs not admitted to trading on these markets. While a specific IFRS standard is available for SMEs, the EU has not applied this standard to EU SMEs, given a lack of stakeholder support and the generally increased costs it would bring.[644] Member States can apply IFRS to SMEs outside the scope of the 2002 IAS Regulation but must reflect the related calibrations and exemptions for SMEs in the 2013 Accounting Directive.

II.6.4 CESR/ESMA and the Financial Reporting Regime

The adoption of the IFRS regime in itself does not assure the consistency and integrity of reporting standards across IFRS-scope issuers in the EU's major public trading markets. The enforcement of IFRS, and related decisions as to the compliance of issuers with the IFRS regime, remains a national competence. The Transparency Directive requires the NCAs appointed under that Directive to police compliance with the reporting regime.[645] But different supervisory/institutional structures and reporting cultures impact on the enforcement process. Particular difficulties arise where authorities provide different interpretations on IFRS application and take different decisions on the enforcement of what are interpreted as breaches of the reporting regime. Diverging institutional structures and

---

[641] Directive 2012/6/EU [2012] OJ L81/3. The reforms permit Member States to require instead the filing of balance sheet information.

[642] Micro firms are those which meet two of the following: balance sheet not in excess of €350,000; net turnover not in excess of €700,000; and average number of employees during the financial year not in excess of ten. This definition represents a finessing of the definition of a micro enterprise under the 2003 Commission SME Definition Recommendation (n 143), and a reduction in the balance sheet total/annual turnover threshold of €2 million under the Recommendation.

[643] n 593.

[644] 2011 Accounting Directive Proposal Impact Assessment (SEC (2011) 1289), 27–8, noting the lack of evidence as to its benefits, and strong divergences across stakeholders. Similarly, CSES, Report for the Commission on the 4th Company Law Directive and IFRS for SMEs (2010).

[645] Art 24(4)(h) requires that NCAs have the powers to examine whether the disclosure required under the Directive is drawn up in accordance with the relevant reporting framework.

national approaches have the potential to destabilize IFRS internally in the EU and, internationally, to threaten the coherence of the IFRS regime.[646]

An effective institutional framework for delivering IFRS consistency in the EU presents something of a conundrum, however, given the need to maintain the integrity of the IFRS regime and to reflect the primacy of the IASB as the interpreter of the system. From the outset CESR provided an institutional capacity to support consistency in IFRS application and enforcement. Its activities included advising the Commission on the equivalence of third country reporting regimes (section 6.5), co-ordination with the US SEC on IFRS/US GAAP interpretation and application, monitoring the IFRS endorsement process, advising on the application of IFRS,[647] supporting the introduction of the IFRS regime,[648] liaising with the IASB, and engaging with the statutory audit regime[649] and, in particular, the supervision of auditors.[650] Chief among its activities, however, was its co-ordination of the enforcement of IFRS application,[651] which had two strands: the adoption of non-binding standards for the enforcement of IFRS at national level, and the support of co-ordinated enforcement by means of a CESR forum for dialogue and co-operation. In 2003, it recommended basic principles for the robust and consistent enforcement of IFRS by the Member States (Enforcement Standards on Financial Information in Europe).[652] These were followed in 2004 by a standard on co-ordination of national approaches to enforcement (Co-ordination of Enforcement Activities),[653] which also established the European Enforcers Co-ordination Sessions (the EECS). The EECS (originally based within CESR and now ESMA) is designed to support convergence on enforcement decisions and on emerging issues,[654] and played a key role in monitoring enforcement over the crisis era. CESR also provided the EU with an enhanced capacity for assessing IFRS and engaging with the IASB, particularly over the crisis era.[655] But, as noted previously, CESR's activities in support of the application of IFRS with respect to the fair value assessment pushed it dangerously close to interpreting IFRS and generated market confusion as to the scope of IFRS standards, leading to significant market concern.

---

[646] Schipper, K, 'The Introduction of International Accounting Standards in Europe: Implications for International Convergence' (2005) 14 *European Accounting Rev* 101. Institutional risks have featured recently in relation to the risks which a lack of consistency in application and in enforcement pose to the integrity of the IFRS regime and, accordingly, to its adoption by the US: 2012 SEC Report, n 592, 29, noting that different enforcement structures can 'greatly impact' comparability.

[647] See, eg, CESR's recommendations on the adoption of Alternative Performance Measures (CESR/05–178b) and its exhortation that issuers provide clear disclosure on their use of options in the reporting regime (CESR/05-758).

[648] CESR produced a roadmap for the transition: CESR, Recommendations for Additional Guidance Regarding the Transition to IFRS (2003) (CESR/03–323e).

[649] CESR asserted that it had a 'strong interest' in being associated with the Audit Regulatory Committee and European Group of Auditors Oversight Bodies (which supported administrative rule-making in the audit sphere) and with the International Forum of Independent Audit Regulators: CESR, Annual Report (2006) 35. Similarly, CESR, Annual Report (2009) 43 and (2010) 63.

[650] It, eg, reviewed the powers exercisable by audit supervisors: CESR/06-260.

[651] CESR identified reinforcement of the co-operation between national enforcers as its major challenge in the financial reporting sphere: CESR, Annual Report (2006) 35.

[652] Enforcement Standard No 1: CESR/03-073.

[653] Enforcement Standard No 2: CESR/03-317c.

[654] For a description see CESR, 2007 Interim Report on the Activities of CESR (2008) (CESR/07-671) 13.

[655] CESR regularly provided comments to EFRAG and the IASB on the development of IFRS: eg, CESR, Annual Report (2009) 42–3 and Annual Report (2010) 62–3.

The potential for tension has become all the greater since the establishment of ESMA. Enjoying a significantly enhanced suite of powers (particularly with respect to the adoption of guidance and opinions), specifically enjoined to address financial reporting,[656] and committed to enhancing convergence,[657] ESMA's activities[658] span two main areas—the consistent application of IFRS and the enforcement of IFRS—although these overlap.

First, with respect to IFRS application,[659] ESMA, which has focused in particular on the quality of financial reporting over the crisis,[660] has produced a series of consultations and statements on IFRS since 2011, related to crisis-era credit risk and instrument risk difficulties in particular, and reflecting ESMA's concern to ensure that IFRS principles are met by clear and firm-specific disclosures.[661] They cover, *inter alia*, materiality,[662] the impairment of goodwill,[663] the treatment of (highly sensitive) loan forbearance practices,[664] and the treatment of (highly sensitive) sovereign debt disclosures.[665] While in all cases ESMA has been careful to underline that it does not interpret or provide recommendations on IFRS, it typically also stresses that national authorities should reflect its approach in their enforcement activities, and that auditors and firms should consider its findings.[666] As ESMA's statements are often associated with a related intensification of national fact-finding and/or enforcement action co-ordinated through the EECS,[667] and given the wider 'hardening' of ESMA's quasi-regulatory initiatives (Chapter X section 4), they have quasi-binding force. Accordingly, and, as some market concern as to the scope of its activities underlines,[668] the potential for tension with the IASB and with the market may be growing. The legitimacy of ESMA's activities in this sphere is somewhat doubtful;

---

[656] ESMA Regulation Art 29(1)(c) requires ESMA to develop high-quality and uniform supervisory standards, including reporting standards, and international accounting standards.

[657] ESMA Chairman Maijoor has highlighted that pan-EU co-ordination of IFRS is one of ESMA's primary objectives: Speech on 'Developments in European Financial Reporting', 12 November 2012.

[658] Which closely reflect CESR's, including with respect to the audit process, the development of IFRS, and equivalence determinations: eg, ESMA, Annual Report (2011) 68–70. ESMA is likely to acquire additional powers relating to the audit process following the current reform process: n 585.

[659] Beyond IFRS application, ESMA has also sought to shape the financial reporting regime more generally through, eg, its development of guidelines on the 'Alternative Performance Measures' which can be used by issuers to provide other information on the business more generally or to amplify financial information: Consultation Paper on ESMA Guidelines on Alternative Performance Measures (ESMA/2014/1751).

[660] ESMA, Annual Report (2011) 65.

[661] Maijoor, n 657.

[662] ESMA/2011/373.

[663] ESMA/2013/2 (a review by the EECS on the treatment of goodwill impairment, and assessing the appropriateness of related disclosures in the 2011 financial statements of a sample of issuers).

[664] ESMA/2012/853 (public statement on the appropriate treatment of forbearance practices in IFRS financial statements, setting out ESMA's opinion on how IFRS apply to forbearance practices).

[665] ESMA/2011/226 (public statement on the appropriate treatment of sovereign debt in IFRS financial statements, setting out ESMA's opinion on how IFRS apply to these instruments, stressing the need for transparency, and encouraging firms to provide any additional information which would be relevant to investors' understanding) and ESMA/2011/397 (public statement, highlighting issues to be considered in the treatment of sovereign debt and including an ESMA Opinion on Exposure to Greek Sovereign Debt, examining the outcomes of a fact-find from the 2011 interim reporting season).

[666] eg the 2012 public statement on forbearance calls for financial institutions and auditors to take the statement into due consideration when preparing 2012 financial statements: at 3.

[667] As was the case with respect to sovereign debt reporting and the treatment of forbearance.

[668] Respondents to ESMA's materiality consultation, eg, called for this issue to be addressed through the IASB: ESMA Feedback Statement/2013/218.

lacking the power to interpret and enforce IFRS, ESMA's statements in this sphere exist in the rather grey zone of 'public statements' and similarly opaque measures,[669] and outside the formal rulebook. ESMA has also shown an appetite for sensitive areas, notably with respect to its 2012 public statement on forbearance practices.

Second, the co-ordination of enforcement activity through ESMA and the EECS,[670] which now operates formally under the oversight of ESMA under the revised and updated CESR enforcement standards,[671] has intensified. ESMA is increasingly reviewing the enforcement of particular and controversial reporting issues through the EECS, particularly financial reporting by financial institutions[672] (including with respect to sovereign debt reporting[673] and forbearance practices), as well as pan-EU enforcement practices generally. The regular enforcement reports from the EECS point to an appetite for addressing emerging issues as well as increasing levels of convergence on the issues addressed by EECS members.

Overall, the current EU institutional settlement with respect to IFRS, and in particular ESMA's role, is problematic. Endorsement is, in principle, a risky process, given the tensions between the EU and the IASB to which it may lead. More specifically, the IASB has noted that it is difficult for the EU to present a consistent position, given the different national bodies and EU-level bodies (chief among them the Commission, EFRAG, and ESMA) which engage with the IASB. But, conversely, the intensification and concentration of EU-level IFRS co-ordination/application through ESMA may deepen tensions with the IASB, while ESMA's statements on the application of IFRS have insecure foundations.

Reflecting the political and institutional complexities and sensitivities, the 2013 Maystadt Report did not recommend major change. With respect to IFRS endorsement generally, it recommended that great caution be exercised before a more flexible approach to endorsement, which would accommodate the EU adaptation of IFRS, be pursued, and called instead for a clarification of the IFRS adoption criteria.[674] It did not support radical institutional change (in the form of, for example, concentrating IFRS endorsement advice within ESMA and thereby aligning the endorsement process with the administrative

---

[669] ESMA's 2013 review of financial institutions' accounting practices with respect to financial instrument disclosures in particular (IFRS 7), eg, takes the form of a 'report' which 'provides an overview' but includes 'recommendations' to financial institutions and, variously, notes that ESMA 'expects'/'urges' financial institutions to follow the practices recommended: ESMA, Review of Accounting Practices. Comparability of IFRS Financial Statements of Financial Institutions in Europe (2013) (ESMA/2013/1664) (2013 ESMA Financial Institutions Review) 4–7.

[670] Now composed of some 37 enforcement authorities from across the EEA: n 669, 6.

[671] A consultation on review of the CESR standards and their transformation into ESMA guidelines (subject to a 'comply or explain' mechanism) was launched in 2013: ESMA/2013/1013.

[672] Its review of accounting practices by selected financial institutions with respect to compliance with IFRS 7 (financial instrument disclosure) in the 2012 financial statements called for improved and more detailed disclosures in a number of sensitive and controversial areas, including credit risk disclosures and forbearance practices: 2013 ESMA Financial Institutions Review, n 669.

[673] ESMA's review of 2011 financial statements found that issuers generally fell short of meeting IFRS requirements in a number of key areas: ESMA/2012/482.

[674] Including by means of requiring that IFRS not endanger financial stability and not hinder the economic development of the EU.

rule adoption process more generally). It proposed instead that EFRAG's governance be strengthened and did not recommend that the current contested private sector representation on EFRAG be removed.[675] While the Report also canvassed (and supported) a more radical institutional reform based on integrating EFRAG within ESMA, it did not pursue this option, given the extent of stakeholder resistance to any strengthening of ESMA's powers over reporting standards.[676] Major reforms are unlikely in the short term, although ESMA (and the other European Supervisory Authorities, or ESAs) have expressed strong opposition to the persistence of private sector involvement in EFRAG and to formal engagement by the private sector in the adoption of endorsement advice to the Commission, a role which ESMA regards as properly the preserve of public interest bodies.[677]

II.6.5 Third Country Issuers and Equivalence

II.6.5.1 Equivalence

Notwithstanding the IASB/EU tensions, the EU has emerged as a major influence on the global uptake of IFRS through its adoption of IFRS—which strengthened IFRS' credibility[678]—and its deployment of related third country equivalence mechanisms. Under the Prospectus Directive and the 2004 Commission Prospectus Regulation, third country issuers are required to publish a prospectus which includes financial statements (based on IFRS) when they publicly offer securities or seek to admit securities to trading on a regulated market in the EU.[679] Ongoing IFRS-based financial reporting requirements for these issuers also apply under the Transparency Directive.[680] The IFRS reporting requirement does not apply, however, where the third country disclosure regime (including financial reporting requirements) is deemed 'equivalent' to the EU regime.[681] If the regime is not equivalent, the financial information must be restated—a costly and complex process

---

[675] Including by means of funding reforms, composition reforms (including an enhanced role for ESMA), a new board structure, and impact assessment requirements: n 607, 16–17.

[676] The Report noted 'massive opposition from stakeholders', reflecting a range of factors, including concern that ESMA's approach to accounting standards was overly restrictive and investor-protection-focused, resistance from certain Member States to empowering ESMA further, and fears that ESMA could become an SEC-style 'stock market watchdog': n 607, 18.

[677] The ESAs objected strongly to the Report's recommendations, raising 'serious concerns' as to whether the proposed reforms would allow the accurate reflection of their views as the concerned public interest bodies and as to the role of the private sector in EFRAG, and in particular as to the absence of a mechanism to allow the ESAs to offer a dissenting view and to veto EFRAG advice which they deemed to run counter to the public interest. Their position was that, within EFRAG, only the ESAs should decide on endorsement advice. Accordingly, they refrained from accepting membership in the newly constituted EFRAG and requested, instead, observer status: ESA-2014-001.

[678] Ferran, n 418, 29–30, noting the 'sheer weight' of numbers associated with the EU's adoption in terms of firms reporting under IFRS.

[679] Prospectus Directive Art 20(b) requires that information of a financial nature be equivalent to the requirements of the Directive. The disclosure regime set out in the Annexes to the related Commission Prospectus Regulation requires that financial information is presented under the IFRS regime: 2004 Prospectus Regulation Art 35 and, eg, Annex I, para 20.1 (share registration document).

[680] Transparency Directive Art 23 (the core Arts 4 and 5 annual and half-yearly reporting requirements are based on IFRS reporting (for consolidated accounts)).

[681] 2004 Commission Prospectus Regulation Art 35 and Transparency Directive, Art 23.

for the third country issuers who access the EU capital market.[682] The transparency and prospectus regimes both originally required financial statements to be either reported in accordance with IFRS, reported in an equivalent form, or restated from 1 January 2007.

The equivalence project for financial reporting has been a multilayered and politically sensitive process. Although it has been led by the Commission, Council engagement has been significant—particularly with respect to US relations—as has European Parliament oversight,[683] and CESR and, since, ESMA have provided technical support. Following a series of preparatory measures[684] and a 2006 extension of the original 1 January 2007 deadline for IFRS application or an equivalence determination to 1 January 2009,[685] which was designed to encourage IFRS convergence[686] as well as to build support for lifting reconciliation requirements for EU issuers,[687] the Commission adopted a framework equivalence mechanism in 2007.[688] As a hedge against any loss of momentum in the IFRS convergence movement and to encourage IFRS take-up, it also laid down the conditions under which third country GAAPs would be accepted, on a temporary basis, until 31 December 2011.[689]

---

[682] A 2007 study reported that 5.8 per cent of issuers admitted to trading on a regulated market within the EU were third-country issuers reporting under third-country GAAP (594 issuers in total). Of these, by far the biggest group was those issuers reporting under US GAAP (233), followed by those reporting under Japanese GAAP (84): Commission, First Report to the European Securities Committee and the European Parliament on Convergence between IFRS and Third Country GAAP (2007) (COM (2007) 405) 3.

[683] Particularly with respect to the progress towards convergence of third countries who have committed to adopt IFRS but who have benefited from an extension of the equivalence deadline from the Commission. The 2007 equivalence mechanism (n 688) requires the Commission to report to the Parliament on progress, which it carries out through its regular reports on the 'State of Play on Convergence between IFRS and Third Country GAAP'.

[684] CESR's 2005 Concept Paper on Equivalence (CESR/04-509c) suggested that the equivalence decision should be based on whether investors could make similar (not identical) investment decisions under the third-country reporting regime as they would under IAS/IFRS, and suggested a three-pronged approach based on: (i) review of the general principles in the relevant reporting regime; (ii) technical assessment of significant differences with IFRS; and (iii) adoption of additional requirements to meet investors' needs, such as additional disclosures, supplementary statements, and early warning mechanisms.

[685] Commission Regulation (EC) No 1787/2006 [2006] OJ L337/17 (amending the Prospectus Regulation) and Commission Decision 2006/891/EC [2006] OJ L343/96 (amending the Transparency Directive). The extension permitted third country issuers to report under IFRS, Canadian, Japanese, or US GAAP, or third country GAAP where the country was in an IFRS convergence programme.

[686] The postponement was also (see also n 687) motivated by the Commission's concern to ensure good relations with the US and the SEC during the parallel negotiations on the removal of the US GAAP/IFRS reconciliation requirement: European Securities Committee Minutes, 30 January 2006.

[687] See, eg, Commission Press Release, 6 December 2006 (IP/06/691), quoting Commissioner McCreevy, who described the delay as giving the EU 'more leverage' in its efforts to obtain the removal of reconciliation requirements for EU issuers.

[688] Commission Regulation (EC) No 1569/2007 [2007] OJ L340/66. Reflecting CESR's approach, Art 2 defines equivalence as arising where an investor can make a 'similar assessment' of the assets and liabilities, financial position, profits and losses, and prospects of the issuer as it would under IFRS, with the result that the investor is likely to make the same decision about the acquisition, retention, or disposal of the securities of an issuer. The equivalence decision is made by the Commission but follows an application by a Member State NCA or the third country authority; the Commission may also act on its own initiative (Art 3). The equivalence decision is also dependent on EU issuers not being subject to reconciliation requirements in the third country (rec 3): it is no coincidence that the Regulation followed soon after the SEC's decision to remove the reconciliation requirement for IFRS (see sect 6.5.2).

[689] The conditions broadly related to the third country being in an IFRS convergence programme.

The first equivalence decisions followed at the end of 2008, with the Commission, based on CESR's technical assessments,[690] declaring US and Japanese GAAP to be equivalent to IFRS.[691] The Commission also identified Chinese, Canadian, Korean, and Indian GAAP as being in convergence programmes and progressing towards IFRS adoption, and confirmed that third country issuers could, on a temporary basis, report under these regimes for financial years starting before 1 January 2012.[692] The Commission has continued to monitor progress towards IFRS convergence by these countries (and others),[693] deciding in 2011 that Chinese, Canadian, and Korean GAAP were equivalent to IFRS.[694] In 2011 it extended the 31 December 2011 deadline for Indian GAAP to 31 December 2014.[695]

II.6.5.2 US GAAP and IFRS

The requirement imposed on EU issuers to reconcile their accounts to US GAAP when listed on a US stock exchange or with a certain minimum number of US shareholders was long a source of tension between the US and the EU. In April 2005, the Commission succeeded in brokering a commitment from the US SEC to take the necessary steps by 2009, based on convergence arising between US GAAP and IFRS, to remove the requirement for EU issuers reporting under IFRS to reconcile their accounts to US GAAP.[696] But major progress would not be made until the February 2006 Memorandum of Understanding between the US Financial Accounting Standards Board (FASB) (which oversees US GAAP) and the IASB, which set out a work programme on IFRS/US GAAP convergence.[697] While 2006 also saw CESR become closely involved with the negotiations and enter into a joint work programme,[698] intense political

---

[690] In June 2005 CESR found US, Japanese, and Canadian GAAP to be equivalent to IAS/IFRS, but specified the 'remedies' required before financial statements prepared under these reporting regimes could be determined as equivalent (CESR 05–230b). In 2008, it found that the environment for accounting standard convergence in the US had 'radically altered', with the IASB/FASB convergence programme and agreement by the SEC to accept IFRS-stated accounts from third country issuers (sect 6.5.2). Accordingly, CESR advised that the remaining divergences between US GAAP and IFRS were being addressed and that both regimes would be 'effectively equivalent'. Similarly with respect to Japanese GAAP, it found that the differences identified in 2005 were being addressed through IASB/Accounting Standards Board of Japan discussions, and advised that it could be considered equivalent: CESR/08-179.

[691] Commission Decision 2008/961/EC [2008] OJ L340/112. Commission Regulation (EC) No 1289/2008 amended the 2004 Commission Prospectus Regulation to include US and Japanese GAAPs among the permitted accounting regimes.

[692] Based on the significant progress shown by these regimes as well as the Commission's concern to encourage the global adoption of IFRS.

[693] See, eg, the 2010 and 2011 IFRS Convergence Reports (SEC (2010) 681 and SEC (2011) 991).

[694] Commission Delegated Regulation (EU) No 311/2012 [2012] OJ L103/13, amending the 2004 Commission Prospectus Regulation, and Commission Implementing Decision of 11 April 2012 [2012] OJ L103/49, amending the original 2008 Equivalence Decision (n 691).

[695] Commission Delegated Regulation (EU) No 310/2012 [2012] OJ L103/11. The extension reflected slippage in the Indian convergence timetable.

[696] Press Release IP/05/469 April 2005.

[697] The FASB/IASB convergence project initially generated some market concern that convergence would lead to more prescriptive rules and a more rules-based regime than the principles-based IFRS system, and to some calls for the IASB to focus instead on the improvement of its own standards: Jopson, B, 'PWC Opposes IASB Proposals', *Financial Times*, 2 May 2006, 19, reporting on a draft position paper by accounting firm PricewaterhouseCoopers which raised concerns as to the convergence project.

[698] CESR/06–434. The work programme was established to promote the development of high-quality accounting standards, the high-quality and consistent application of IFRS worldwide, consideration of international counterparts' positions regarding application and enforcement, and the avoidance of conflicting regulatory decisions on the application of IFRS and US GAAP.

negotiations[699] ultimately led to the SEC's November 2007 agreement to removal of the US GAAP reconciliation requirement for foreign issuers reporting under IFRS as adopted by the IASB.[700] While a range of factors shaped the SEC's decision, the convergence programme between the IASB and the FASB was a major factor in securing the lifting of the reconciliation requirement, underlining the dependence of the EU on the IASB.

The US remains outside the IFRS regime. The financial crisis, however, led to a global concern (articulated through the G20) as to the quality of accounting standards, particularly with respect to the fair value assessment, and to related close contacts between FASB and the IASB on the reform process. Convergence remains an international priority, reflected in the G20's support over the financial crisis of a single set of global accounting standards and for US GAAP and IFRS convergence.[701] But the initial US enthusiasm for adoption of IFRS as the US standard[702] has now waned significantly[703]—reflecting the complex factors implicated in this decision,[704] including the political climate,[705] the ability of the US to influence the IASB, and the priority being given to crisis-era regulatory reforms over IFRS/US GAAP convergence.[706]

From an EU perspective, this development may lead to a further destabilization of relations between the EU and the IASB. The Commission position that the representation of 'non-implementing' countries on the IASB threatens IASB governance, its concern that failure by the US to adopt IFRS threatens the credibility of IFRS,[707] and frustration at the lack of progress, despite concessions on IFRS by the IASB's EU constituents designed to accommodate the US,[708] do not augur well.

---

[699] IFRS/US GAAP reconciliation was catapulted to the highest political level. It appeared on the agenda of the April 2007 EU/US summit, which included among the conclusions a commitment by the Presidents of the US, the Commission, and the Council that reconciliation requirements be removed by 2009: Framework for Advancing Transatlantic Economic Integration between the EU and the US. Annex 2, Lighthouse Priority Projects.

[700] SEC Press Release 2007–235, SEC Takes Action to Improve the Consistency of Disclosure to US Investors in Foreign Companies, 15 November 2007 (the reconciliation requirement was removed from March 2008: SEC Release Nos 33-8879 and 34-57026). Accordingly, carve-outs from IFRS do not benefit from the reconciliation exemption, although a two-year transitional period (until November 2009) originally applied to the EU hedge accounting carve-out.

[701] The G20 recommendations and related progress are discussed in IASB, n 603.

[702] In October 2008, the SEC issued a roadmap for transitioning to IFRS: SEC, Roadmap for the Potential Use of Financial Statements Prepared in Accordance with IFRS by US Issuers (Release Nos 33-8982 and 34-58960).

[703] 2012 SEC Report, n 592. The Report provides a final assessment of the work undertaken under the SEC's 2010 work programme in relation to IFRS adoption, and reports on the extensive challenges, but does not contain a final recommendation or timetable for action.

[704] See Hail, L, Leuz, C, and Wysocki, P, 'Global Accounting Convergence and the Potential Adoption of IFRS by the U.S. (Part I): Conceptual Underpinnings and Economic Analysis' (2010) 24 *Accounting Horizons* 355 and Hail, L, Leuz, C, and Wysocki, P, 'Global Accounting Convergence and the Potential Adoption of IFRS by the U.S. (Part II): Political Factors and Future Scenarios for U.S. Accounting Standards' (2010) 24 *Accounting Horizons* 567.

[705] Ferran, n 418, 27–8.

[706] As noted by the Commission in its 2010 IFRS Convergence Report.

[707] n 706, 4.

[708] Maijoor, n 657.

II.7 Admission to Trading and to Official Listing

II.7.1 Regulated Markets and Capital-raising

II.7.1.1 The Regulated Market and Perimeter Control

(a) Trading Venues and Perimeter Control

Trading venues,[709] and related admission-to-trading rules, play a central role in the capital-raising process by providing issuers with a means for signalling their credibility to investors and by providing a mechanism for supporting secondary market liquidity.[710]

The initial admission-to-trading process provides a quality 'filter' mechanism, by means of which issuers can signal their quality. Admission to trading typically also imposes on issuers a series of ongoing requirements, including with respect to ongoing disclosure, the size of the 'free float' (or shares in public issue),[711] and corporate governance.[712] Issuers can use their compliance with these requirements (or 'bond' with the venue in question) to continue to signal their quality and thereby reduce the cost of capital.[713] The admission of securities also supports the trading of securities on a trading venue which can provide liquidity and an efficient price-formation process, supported in part through issuer-disclosure rules but also through trading transparency rules (discussed in Chapter V). Admission thereby facilitates the realization of capital gains and so can reduce the issuer's cost of capital by providing major investors (such as venture capitalists) with an exit.

The admission-to-trading process also supports capital-raising by serving as an instrument of trading venue competition and differentiation. Trading venues often operate a range of different market segments which reflect different issuer and investor requirements.

---

[709] Trading venue regulation is considered in Ch V and is addressed here only with respect to issuers and admission to trading. This section uses the term 'venue' given the array of trading platforms beyond traditional stock exchanges on which organized trading can take place and which can come within the regulatory net: Macey, J and O'Hara, M, 'From Markets to Venues: Securities Regulation in an Evolving World' (2005) 58 *Stanford LR* 563.

[710] An extensive literature assesses the signalling/bonding dynamic in the context of cross-listings and competition for listings/admissions to trading. See, eg, Hail and Leuz, n 84 and Coffee, J, 'Racing Towards the Top? The Impact of Cross-Listings and Stock Market Competition on International Corporate Governance' (2002) 102 *Col LR* 1757. On the role of trading venues in supporting issuers through liquidity provision see, eg, Poser, N, 'Restructuring the Stock Markets: A Critical Look at the SEC's National Market System' (1981) 56 *NYULR* 884 and on the role of liquidity in supporting the economy generally, Naes, R, Skjeltorp, J, and Ødegaard, B, 'Stock Market Liquidity and the Business Cycle' (2011) 66 *J Fin* 139.

[711] eg the 2012 proposals by the UK Listing Authority to consider, in accordance with the EU's 'official listing' regime (sect 7.2.2), exemptions to the current minimum requirement that 25 per cent of shares be in public distribution (a 25 per cent free float) where sufficient liquidity is available (Consultation Paper No 12/25, Enhancing the Effectiveness of the Listing Regime and Feedback on CP 12/2 (2012)) attracted some market hostility given the potential risk to minority shareholders: Sullivan, R, '"Watered Down" Free Float Rules Cause Concern', *Financial Times, Fund Management Supplement*, 15 October 2012.

[712] The quality of the corporate governance rules which apply to third country, blockholder-dominated issuers, particularly with respect to minority shareholder protection, eg, has been raised as a risk to the international reputation of the UK market: FSA, Consultation Paper No 12/2, Amendments to the Listing, Disclosure, Transparency, and Prospectus Rules (2012) 9.

[713] From the extensive literature see: Cheffins, B, 'The Undermining of UK Corporate Governance (?)' (2013) 33 *OJLS* 503; Kraakman et al, n 96, 275–6 and 289–94; and Levine, R, 'Financial Development and Economic Growth: Views and Agenda' (1997) 35 *J of Econ Lit* 688.

Admission to the 'main' segment typically implies that the securities have been issued by a well-established issuer which meets certain size and trading-record requirements. 'Second'- and 'lower'-tier segments (or venues) typically admit securities to trading on the basis of less onerous and more flexible requirements, particularly with respect to size and trading record. Trading venues can accordingly compete with respect to their admission products and the degree of protection/cost burden represented by their admission and trading rules.[714]

The admission-to-trading process has, accordingly, long been a concern of regulators. Regulatory attention has focused on the large public (primarily equity) trading venues, which have long been regarded as a key element of the institutional structure supporting capital allocation, and to which retail investors are most likely to be exposed.[715] The main public trading venues accordingly typically act as a proxy for regulatory perimeter control with respect to issuer disclosure, and are additionally often subject to other mandatory admission standards.

The policy link between the perimeter of mandatory issuer disclosure, the regulation of the admission process, and the major public trading venues remains strong. But the central position and treatment of public trading venues in regulation and policy is being questioned. The current concerns as to the health of the public equity market generally[716] have been shaped in part by the global downturn in admissions to public equity trading venues which has occurred in recent years (although market conditions are improving),[717] and related concerns as to the effectiveness of the major public trading venues have also been expressed.[718] Difficulties relating to admission (or listing) costs and regulatory costs[719] and poor-quality listings, for example, have been highlighted. So have wider market structure changes, particularly with respect to the emergence of high frequency trading (HFT)[720] and the associated withdrawal of long-term investors.[721] Similarly, doubts have been cast on

---

[714] Macey, J and O'Hara, M, 'The Economics of Stock Exchange Listing Fees and Listing Requirements' (2002) 11 *J of Fin Intermed* 297.

[715] See sect 2.1.1.

[716] Sects 2.1.1 and 9.

[717] One US report referred to the 'Great Depressions in Listings' and the related 'precipitous decline' in the number of publicly listed companies in the US: Weild and Kim (2009) n 39, 1 and 4. It found that since 1991, the number of US exchange-listed companies had dropped by more than 22 per cent (53 per cent when adjusted for inflation). Similarly, Burgess, K, Grant, J, and Demos, T, 'A Market Less Efficient', *Financial Times,* 14 November 2011, 11 reporting on market concern at the sharp drop in listings on stock exchanges over the previous five years. In 2013–14, however, there were improvements globally, in part related to pent-up demand for exit by private equity and venture capital investors, reflecting the debt-related contraction in the market for trade buyers and a related demand for equity market exit.

[718] See generally 2012 Kay Review, n 34, the surveys on US capital market competitiveness (n 39), and Weild and Kim (2009) and (2010), n 39. The trend reached its apotheosis, perhaps, with the news in early 2013 that NASDAQ-OMX had been in talks with private equity funders about a going-private route: Reuters, February 11, 2013.

[719] Particularly in the US, and driven by the 2002 Sarbanes-Oxley Act requirements for issuers (n 39).

[720] Leading to a major UK government review of the impact of HFT on market quality. One strand of the review, however, suggested that market quality, in terms of trade volume and liquidity, had not changed materially over the past ten years or so: Linton, O, What has happened to UK Equity Market Quality in the Last Decade? An Analysis of the Daily Data (2011). A Report for the UK Government Foresight Project on the Future of Computer Trading in Financial Markets. See further Ch VI sect 2.3 on high frequency trading.

[721] Recent moves by major trading venues to reduce trading costs, and to support, *inter alia*, high frequency traders, have been associated with the removal of economic support for the value components needed to support strong long-term markets (such as research, sales, and capital commitment): Weild and Kim (2010), n 39.

whether admission to trading on a public equity market is primarily capital-raising in nature.[722] The public equity markets are increasingly being characterized less as capital-raising mechanisms and more as mechanisms for ensuring good stewardship in firms, for pooling liquidity and supporting efficient secondary market trading, and for supporting strong returns to savers—albeit that excessive intermediation and speculation has been charged with damaging these functions.[723] In the EU, the Commission has acknowledged that major equity trading venues may act as providers of liquidity rather than as sources of issuer capital, and highlighted the decrease in the number of listed companies in the EU.[724]

But, whatever the doubts as to the extent to which public equity trading venues support capital-raising, the EU regulatory programme remains committed to supporting the efficiency of major public trading venues in order to support capital-raising;[725] the issuer-disclosure regime, and a small array of mandatory minimum admission requirements, are accordingly designed to apply to the large public trading venues.

(b) Regulated Markets and Official Listing

The 'regulated market' concept acts as a proxy for large public trading venues in EU securities and markets regulation, and is accordingly one of the key perimeter controls on the EU issuer-disclosure regime; it also sets the perimeter for the EU's admission-to-trading rules. 'Regulated markets' are those trading venues governed by the 2014 MiFID II/MiFIR requirements for regulated markets, which include authorization, membership, access, and operating requirements, and which are subject to the highest level of regulation (Chapter V section 7). Regulated markets are distinguished from other trading venues by the admission standards which apply to issuers—regulated markets are subject to the most onerous standards with respect to issuer admission.[726] Trading venues accordingly 'opt in' to regulated market status where they seek the branding effects associated with this status.[727]

The EU's reliance on the 'regulated market' as a form of perimeter control for issuer disclosure and admission to trading regulation is rooted in pragmatism; the adoption of the regulated market proxy is not based on a nuanced policy view of which venues should be subject to issuer disclosure and other admission requirements, or of the common features of

---

[722] eg, Mitchell, L, Towards a New Law and Economics: the Case of the Stock Market, GWU Legal Studies Research Paper No 495 (2010), available at <http://ssrn.com/abstract=1557730>, suggesting that the US public equity markets no longer support the formation of productive capital, albeit that they provide an important exit route for venture capitalists.

[723] In the UK, the 2012 Kay Review (n 34) has suggested that UK public equity markets are no longer a significant source of funding for new investment for issuers (with internal cash flow the major source), with share issues and admissions to trading often designed to provide liquidity for early stage investors. The principal role of equity trading markets, the report concluded, is oversight of capital allocation by companies: at 10 and 14.

[724] Commission Staff Working Document Accompanying the Green Paper on Long-Term Financing of the European Economy (2013) (SWD (2013) 76) 22–3.

[725] As is clear from the Commission's 2013 Green Paper on Long-Term Financing: n 95, 12–13.

[726] A 'regulated market' is a multilateral system which is operated and/or managed by a market operator, and which brings together, or facilitates the bringing together, of multiple third party buying-and-selling interests in financial instruments (in the system and in accordance with its non-discretionary rules) in a way that results in a contract, in respect of the financial instruments admitted to trade under its rules and/or systems, and which is authorized and functions regularly in accordance with the 2014 MiFID II/MiFIR rules for regulated markets (2014 MiFID II Art 4(1)(21)).

[727] Regulated markets are typically the largest and most liquid public trading venues in the EU. See further Ch V.

the issuers admitted to such venues, including with respect to size and 'societal foot-print'.[728] Its roots are in the EU's repeated attempts to grapple with the regulatory treatment of trading venues generally, which led to the regulated market concept; this concept has since been deployed to set the perimeter for a wide range of regulatory requirements, including—but not only—with respect to capital-raising.

Pre-FSAP, the EU's regulation of capital-raising was based on the now outmoded concept of 'official listing'. In particular, the 1979 Admission Directive imposed harmonized admission requirements in respect of the admission of securities to 'official listing' on stock exchanges. Although this Directive regime did not define 'official listing', the regime was designed to cover that segment of an exchange's market which offered the maximum guarantees for investors and in respect of which access was the most difficult (or the 'official' segment of the national stock exchange). By imposing controls on the official listing process, the Admission Directive relied on a perception of the trading venue as a monopoly provider of admission or 'listing' services, which would, in the absence of controls, abuse its monopolistic position by, for example, discriminating against certain issuers in the application of admission rules.[729] This model rapidly became outmoded as venues became demutualized and subject to competitive pressures,[730] developed multiple trading segments, and competed in different listing products, and as increasingly large segments of major trading venues accordingly operated outside the 'official listing' perimeter.[731] The limitations of the official listing concept were a recurring theme of the subsequent FSAP[732] and led to the adoption of the 'regulated market' model, based on the MiFID I regulated market definition, although the 'official list' concept still persists with respect to a subset of admission rules (section 7.2.2). But while the MiFID I (now the 2014 MiFID II) definition of a 'regulated market' reflects a policy concern to capture the 'publicness'[733] of certain issuers and securities,[734] it is also deeply rooted in the fiercely contested negotiations on the liberalization of share trading in the EU and the regulatory regime applicable to different classes of equity trading venue, which shaped the regulated market concept (Chapter V). It does not, therefore, represent a clear policy position on which trading venues should be subject to issuer-disclosure and admission rules.

---

[728] As has been noted in the context of the US regime, which similarly ties ongoing issuer disclosure to listing on certain markets: Langevoort and Thompson, n 42.

[729] For this analysis see Ferrarini, G, 'The European Regulation of Stock Exchanges: New Perspectives' (1999) 36 *CMLR* 569, 573–8, and Ferrarini, G, 'Securities Regulation and the Rise of Pan-European Securities Markets: An Overview' in Ferrarini, G, Hopt, K, and Wymeersch, E (eds), *Capital Markets in the Age of the Euro* (2002) 272.

[730] Self-regulation by exchanges and the impact of demutualization are briefly canvassed in the context of the trading venue regime in Ch V.

[731] Ferrarini, G, 'Pan-European Securities Markets: Policy Issues and Regulatory Responses' (2002) 3 *EBOLR* 249.

[732] The 2001 Lamfalussy Report, eg, expressed concern at the failure of EU securities regulation to distinguish between admission to trading and admission to official listing: Final Report of the Committee of Wise Men on the Regulation of European Securities Markets (2001) (2001 Lamfalussy Report) 13.

[733] Langevoort and Thompson, n 42.

[734] During the MiFID I adoption process, the Commission argued that the distinguishing feature of a regulated market as compared with other markets was 'the operation of strict controls regarding the "quality" of the instruments admitted to trading so as to render them freely negotiable on the basis of all information which may have an incidence on its fair valuation': Overview of Proposed Adjustments to the Investment Services Directive, Working Document of Services of DG Internal Market, Document 1 (2001) (2001 ISD Working Paper) 28.

II.7.1.2 Regulated Markets, Exchange-regulated Markets, and SME Funding

As the regulated market system is an 'opt-in' regime, the regulated market concept (and related regulation) potentially embraces second- and lower-tier venues. But the regulatory implications of designation as a regulated market mean that these venues, where they operate as regulated markets, carry potentially heavy disclosure and other admission costs for smaller issuers.

Although second-tier venues had been developing strongly since the mid-1990s in particular,[735] the adoption of the FSAP issuer-disclosure regime and the related application of the regulated market perimeter generated speculation that some venues would avoid regulated market status (operating as 'exchange-regulated markets'[736]), and the consequent application of the extensive issuer-disclosure regime.[737]

This projected change to market structure has been realized, with very strong growth in the 'second-tier' exchange-regulated market segment shortly after the FSAP closed.[738] This has been associated with the 2003 Prospectus Directive, but most strongly with the 2004 Transparency Directive's ongoing obligations and IFRS reporting requirements for regulated markets.[739] Leading examples include the London Stock Exchange's Alternative Investment Market (AIM),[740] Euronext-NYSE's Alternext, Deutsche Börse's Entry Standard, and the Warsaw Stock Exchange's New Connect Market, but in all some 20 trading venues operate second-tier exchange-regulated market segments which do not take the form of regulated markets and are not subject to the prospectus and transparency regimes.[741] The shift occurred with respect to a range of securities, not just equity.[742] Reflecting

---

[735] 1995 saw the establishment of the London Stock Exchange's Alternative Investment Market. Over 1996–9 the Nouveau Marché (Paris), Neuer Markt (Frankfurt), and Nouvo Mercato (Milan) were established and offered a combination of stringent disclosure requirements and lighter admission standards (with respect to age, size, and minimum profitability in particular). See further Goergen, M, Khurshed, A, McCahery, J, and Renneboog, L, The Rise and Fall of the European New Markets: On the Short and Long-Term Performance of High Tech Initial Public Offerings, ECGI Finance WP No 27/2003 (2003), available at <http://ssrn.com/abstract=443861>, and for an examination of the role of second-tier markets in raising finance for smaller issuers (in the pre-MiFID I context) see Röell, A, 'Competition among European Exchanges' in Ferrarini, G (ed), *European Securities Markets. The Investment Services Directive and Beyond* (1998) 220–2.

[736] Formally, exchange-regulated markets are venues in the form of 'multilateral trading facilities' (MTFs) under the original MiFID I (now MiFID II/MiFIR classification). In practice, MTFs (non-regulated markets) are typically termed exchange-regulated markets where they admit issuers and are not simply trading platforms. The exchange-regulated market concept is associated in particular with the major second-tier trading venues in the EU.

[737] Ferran, n 26, 187–8.

[738] See, eg, Arcot, S, Black, J and Owen, G, From Local to Global. The Rise of AIM as a Stock Market for Growing Companies (2007). In 2006, eg, there was an increase in the number and volume of IPOs on exchange-regulated markets from 369 and €6.9 billion in 2005 to 402 and €8.2 billion in 2006: PriceWaterhouseCoopers, IPO Watch Europe. A Survey (2006) 8–9.

[739] 2008 CSES Report, n 194, 32. Although respondents to the CSES study associated the shift to exchange-regulated market admission with the Prospectus Directive, they placed more emphasis on the transparency regime.

[740] The decision not to treat AIM as a regulated market was motivated by a concern to avoid the full impact of the Prospectus Directive: Blackwell, D, 'AIM Faces Rule Changes over Prospectus Directive', *Financial Times*, 31 January 2005, 22.

[741] Commission, 2011 MiFID II/MiFIR Proposals Impact Assessment (SEC (2011) 1226) 98.

[742] The shift of bonds from regulated markets to the Luxembourg-based EuroMTF, which specializes in bonds and warrants (it was established in 2005 and designed to take advantage of the lighter regime applicable to exchange-regulated markets), was particularly striking, with 981 securities moving between 2005 and 2008: 2008 CSES Report, n 194, 33.

international developments,[743] this trend has continued. Some 60 per cent of IPOs took place outside regulated markets in 2010, for example.[744] Similarly, the London Stock Exchange's AIM hosted the majority of the listings in London over the 2000s,[745] while the Warsaw Stock Exchange's New Connect Market has experienced very strong growth since 2008.[746]

The exchange-regulated market segment is, however, coming under increased scrutiny. Notwithstanding that only a small subset of the SME issuer segment is likely to access the public equity markets, recent regulatory reforms have focused on the role of trading venues, including 'second-tier'/'exchange-regulated' segments, in supporting SME finance (as well as high-growth issuers more generally), and on enhancing trading venues as vehicles for venture capital exit from SMEs.[747] The support of specialized segments through tailored regulatory regimes is a key theme of the reform movement,[748] which includes the joint effort by the London Stock Exchange and the UK regulatory authorities to develop a new IPO/admission-to-trading route for high-growth companies which sits alongside the current AIM (exchange-regulated market) and Main Market (regulated market) routes.[749]

As noted in sections 4.4.3 and 5.5, the related EU initiatives (albeit directed to regulated markets) include the adoption of a proportionate disclosure regime, designed to lessen the burdens represented by regulated market admission. In addition, the 2014 MiFID II/MiFIR reforms provide for a specialist 'SME Growth Market', as a subset of the exchange-regulated market/MTF classification and on an opt-in basis[750] (MiFID II Article 33); Member States must provide that the operator of an MTF can apply to its home NCA to have the MTF registered as an SME Growth Market (Article 33(1)). The admission of securities to exchange-regulated markets/MTFs is not subject to extensive regulation under MiFID II/MiFIR (see further Chapter V section 8); registration of such a trading venue as an SME Growth Market, however, requires that the exchange-regulated market/MTF comply with a range of additional criteria.[751] The venue must be primarily designed to

---

[743] New public trading venues dedicated to SME trading have opened in 14 of the G20 members in recent years: Ernst & Young, n 41.

[744] 2011 City of London SME Report, n 41.

[745] 2011 City of London SME Report, n 41, 17. Similarly, FSA, Discussion Paper 08/1, A Review of the Listing Regime (2008) 16–17, noting the 'sharp rise' in companies seeking admission to AIM.

[746] 2011 City of London Economic SME Report, n 41, 17.

[747] The 2012 UK Kay Review reported that the admission process had become burdensome and expensive, with venture capitalists increasing seeking exit through trade sales and other non-public mechanisms: n 34, 26.

[748] eg Schwartz, J, 'The Twilight of Equity Liquidity' (2012) 34 *Cardozo LR* 531 and Högborn, C and Wagenius, H, 'Growing Necessity for Innovative SME Exchanges in Europe' (2011) 226 *World Federation of Exchanges Focus* 7.

[749] In February 2013, the London Stock Exchange announced the establishment of a new 'High Growth Segment' on its Main Market, within the regulated market classification, but with a lighter regulatory regime. The new Segment is based on issuers not being required to comply with the 'Official Listing' regime which the UK Listing Authority applies to 'listed securities' and which applies to Main Market issuers more generally, given the Main Market's status as a 'listed' market. The new Segment is designed to form a platform for issuers to progress to full Official Listing/Main Market admission: Press Release, 12 February 2013.

[750] Exchange-regulated markets which have traditionally been orientated to the SME sector would not be required to register as SME Growth Markets, while SME issuers would not be required to admit their securities to such markets: MiFID II rec 134.

[751] Which are to be amplified by administrative rules under a Commission delegation.

support 'SME'[752] trading, in that at least 50 per cent of the issuers admitted to trading are SMEs at the time the venue is registered as an SME Growth Market and in any calendar year thereafter. Appropriate criteria must be set for initial and ongoing admission to trading of issuers. The quality of disclosure is also addressed: on initial admission to trading, there must be sufficient information published to enable investors to make an informed judgement about investing in the instruments (either an 'appropriate admission document' or a prospectus under the Prospectus Directive). 'Appropriate ongoing periodic financial reporting' is also required (for example, annual audited financial reports). The venue must have in place systems and procedures for the storage and public dissemination of regulatory information relating to issuers. Market abuse controls also apply: issuers on the market and persons discharging managerial responsibilities (and persons closely associated with them) must comply with the market abuse regime, and effective controls and systems aimed at preventing market abuse must be in place. The new market abuse regime dovetails with this regime, providing that a lighter *ad hoc* issuer-disclosure regime apply to SME Growth Market issuers.[753] A venue may be de-registered as an SME Growth Market where it no longer complies with these conditions.

The new regime, which was broadly uncontroversial over the MiFID II/MiFIR negotiations,[754] is designed to address the visibility and branding difficulties which exchange-regulated markets/MTF venues can pose for SMEs, as well as related liquidity difficulties and issuer costs.[755] It is designed to accommodate the currently wide range of exchange-regulated markets, and to balance between the need to ensure high levels of investor protection to strengthen confidence in SME investments and the countervailing need to reduce the regulatory burdens faced by SME issuers.[756]

But providing a regulatory brand for less heavily regulated 'second-tier' venues which admit higher-risk securities can generate investor protection risks. The collapse of the Neuer Markt in 2002 serves as a reminder of the risks of weak venue enforcement,[757] and of the risks to investor protection which can follow where lighter regimes apply to particular classes of security. The SME Growth Market reforms may also threaten the distinction between regulated markets and exchange-regulated markets/MTFs with respect to mandatory issuer disclosure and admission requirements. Exchange-regulated markets/MTFs operate outside the regulated market perimeter (and the related issuer disclosure and admission rules) and so can offer distinct admission products which signal to investors that they provide a platform for higher-risk securities which are subject to a lower level of

---

[752] A distinct definition applies to SMEs for the purposes of the SME Growth Market regime: they are defined as companies that have an average market capitalization of less than €200 million on the basis of end-year quotes for the previous three calendar years: 2014 MiFID II Art 4(1)(13).

[753] See further Ch VIII sect 7.1.4.

[754] The Council was broadly supportive of the Commission's proposal (Cyprus Presidency Progress Report on MiFID II/MiFIR, 13 December 2012, Council Document 16523/12, 8). The Commission earlier reported that the Member States with the most active SME markets (Germany, France, and the UK) were supportive, and that a lack of support from some stakeholders could be related to the Commission's failure to clarify that the new regime was designed to operate as an opt-in 'quality label' and not to restrict the current range of SME exchange-regulated markets: 2011 MiFID II/MiFIR Proposal Impact Assessment, n 741, 36–7.

[755] 2011 MiFID II/MiFIR Proposal Impact Assessment, n 741, 11 and 34.

[756] 2014 MiFID II rec 133.

[757] The Neuer Markt was closed in 2002 following a series of insider dealing and market manipulation scandals. See, eg, Goergen et al, n 735, 8–9.

regulation than applies on regulated markets. This distinction may become blurred. It is also difficult to see how this new regulated segment will enhance the current flexible, second-tier, exchange-regulated market/MTF-based regime, which has experienced significant growth. It may, for example, increase costs by imposing regulatory determinations as to how second-tier markets should work. After some initial difficulties, associated with the enforcement of market abuse prohibitions and in particular with Germany's Neuer Markt, market-based discipline appears to be operating well in the EU's second-tier markets.[758] A new SME-focused regime, within the exchange-regulated market/MTF segment, may bring uncertainties and costs, and will atomize the regulatory regime still further. Investor confusion may be considerable, particularly as the new regime is discretionary.

II.7.2 The Admission of Securities to Trading

II.7.2.1 Regulated Markets

(a) Admission to Trading

The 2014 MiFID II regime imposes minimum standards on securities admitted to trading on a regulated market in order to support efficient price formation, transparency, liquidity, and transferability.[759] The admission to trading regime (MiFID II Articles 51–2[760]) applies without prejudice to the other admission requirements of the parallel 'official listing' regime—although the distinction between admission to trading and official listing remains unclear, as discussed in section 7.7.2.

The admission-to-trading regime for regulated markets operates in tandem with the issuer-disclosure rules which apply to securities admitted to trading on a regulated market under the 2003 Prospectus and 2004 Transparency Directives. The issuer-disclosure regime is incorporated within the admission-to-trading framework in that regulated markets must, under Article 51(3), establish and maintain effective arrangements to verify that issuers of transferable securities admitted to trading comply with their disclosure obligations under EU law in relation to initial, ongoing, or *ad hoc* disclosure obligations. The regulated market must also establish arrangements which facilitate its members or participants in obtaining access to information which has been made public under EU law.

The admission regime otherwise focuses on negotiability and on fair and orderly trading. Under Article 51(1), regulated markets must have clear and transparent rules governing the admission of financial instruments to trading which ensure that any financial instruments admitted to trading in a regulated market are capable of being traded in a fair, orderly, and efficient manner, and, in the case of transferable securities, are freely negotiable. The rules must also ensure that the design of derivatives allows for orderly pricing and effective settlement (Article 51(2)). Compliance with these rules must be regularly monitored (Article 51(4)).

---

[758] FSA Discussion Paper 08/1, n 745, 16.

[759] An extensive literature addresses admission to trading rules and their type and function, particularly as monitoring mechanisms for firm governance. Full discussion is outside the scope of this Chapter. See, eg, Fleckner, A, 'Stock Exchanges at the Crossroads' (2006) *Fordham LR* 2541.

[760] The 2014 MiFID II regime is closely based on the 2004 MiFID I approach.

Article 51(5) clarifies that where a transferable security has been admitted to trading on a regulated market, it can be subsequently admitted to other regulated markets, even without the consent of the issuer (who must, however, be informed by the regulated market where its securities are admitted).[761]

The specific conditions governing the admission of instruments are the subject of a delegation to RTSs (Article 51(6)). The delegation is similar in character to the MiFID I delegation[762] and can be expected to generate rules similar to those adopted under the administrative 2006 Commission MiFID I Regulation,[763] which covered transferable securities, units in collective investment schemes, and derivatives. A principles-based approach was adopted by the 2006 Commission MiFID I Regulation, which was designed to allow regulated markets flexibility in designing admission requirements. Article 35 of the Regulation set out the conditions which transferable securities were to meet to be freely negotiable (Article 35(1)–(3))[764] and which governed whether the securities were capable of being traded in a fair, orderly, and efficient manner.[765] In addition, in exercising its discretion as to whether shares should be admitted to trading (and, in particular, whether the shares were capable of being traded in a fair, orderly, and efficient manner), the regulated market was to consider the distribution of the shares to the public (although minimum distribution requirements were not imposed) and the historical financial information and disclosure available concerning the issuer and its business (in overview) which was required under the Prospectus Directive or was (or would be) otherwise publicly accessible (Article 35(4)). The Regulation did not, therefore, dictate particular conditions, such as the minimum free float necessary, or specify minimum trading record/financial history requirements (by contrast with the official listing regime).

Article 36 addressed units in collective investment schemes and required that the regulated market satisfy itself that the scheme (whether in UCITS form or not) complied with the relevant registration, notification, or other procedures which were a condition of the

---

[761] The issuer is not subject to any related disclosure obligations where it has not consented to the admission of the securities.

[762] It covers: the characteristics of the different classes of instrument to be taken into account by the regulated market when assessing whether an instrument is issued in a manner consistent with the conditions imposed under Art 51(1); the arrangements the regulated market must implement to verify that the issuer complies with disclosure obligations; and the arrangements the regulated market must establish to facilitate the access of its members or participants to issuer disclosure.

[763] Commission Regulation (EC) No 1287/2006 [2006] OJ L241/1.

[764] The securities were freely negotiable where they were capable of being traded between the parties to a transaction and subsequently transferred without restriction, and where all securities of the same class were fungible. Transferable securities that were not fully paid could be considered as freely negotiable where arrangements had been made to ensure that negotiability was not restricted and adequate disclosure concerning their partly paid status and the implications was publicly available. Art 18 also acknowledged that restrictions on transfer would not prevent shares from being freely negotiable where the restriction was not likely to disturb the market (given that some Member States allow certain types of issuer to approve a transfer of securities).

[765] Admission depended on the following criteria being satisfied: the terms of the security were clear and unambiguous (and allowed for a correlation between the security's price and the price of any underlying measure); the price was reliable and publicly available; there was sufficient information publicly available of the kind needed to value the security; settlement arrangements ensured that the settlement price properly reflected the price (or value) of the security; and, where settlement required/provided for the possibility of delivery of an asset rather than cash settlement, there were adequate settlement and delivery procedures for the underlying and adequate arrangements to obtain relevant information about the underlying: Art 35(6).

scheme being marketed in the jurisdiction of the regulated market (although Member States could lift this requirement). Article 36 also set out the conditions which governed assessment of whether the units in open-ended collective investment undertakings were capable of being traded in a fair, orderly, and efficient manner, which included the distribution of the units to the public, whether there were appropriate market-making arrangements (or whether the scheme's management company provided alternative redemption arrangements), and whether the value of the units was sufficiently transparent to investors by means of the periodic publication of net asset value. Units in closed-end schemes were subject to a similar regime—with the exclusion, of course, of the market-making/redemption requirement—and transparency could be additionally supported by disclosure on the fund's investment strategy.

Derivatives were addressed under Article 37 which covered the terms of the contract establishing the derivative, the reliability and availability of the price of the underlying, the availability of the information required to value the derivative, and the settlement of the derivative.

(b) Suspension and Removal

The procedures governing the suspension and removal of instruments have become significantly more sophisticated under the 2014 MiFID II regime, which seeks to enhance communication between NCAs of regulated markets[766] and pan-EU monitoring of trading on different regulated markets; it accordingly requires co-ordinated removal and suspension of instruments across the range of venues on which they may be traded, in order in particular to address risks from market abuse or disorderly trading.[767]

The market operator of a regulated market may suspend or remove from trading a financial instrument which no longer complies with the rules of the regulated market, unless this would be likely to cause significant damage to investors' interests or the orderly functioning of the market.[768] This is without prejudice to the power of the NCA to demand the suspension or removal of an instrument from trading under MiFID II Article 69 (Article 52(1)). The market operator must also suspend or remove MiFID II-scope derivatives that are related to the instrument in question (where this is necessary to support the objectives of the suspension or removal of the underlying instrument), and make its decision public and communicate it to its NCA (including any decision relating to derivatives) (Article 52(2)).

Where the suspension or removal is due to suspected market abuse, a takeover bid, or non-disclosure of inside information about the issuer or financial instrument in breach of the market abuse regime, distinct procedures apply, designed to protect the efficiency and integrity of pan-EU trading in the instrument. The NCA in whose jurisdiction the suspension or removal originated must require other regulated markets and trading venues within the 2014 MiFID II/MiFIR regime which fall under its jurisdiction and which trade the relevant instrument and derivatives to suspend or remove the instrument in question, unless such suspension or removal could cause significant damage to investors' interests or

---

[766] On the supervision of trading venues, see Ch V sect 12.

[767] Commission, Public Consultation. Review of the Markets in Financial Instruments Directive (2010) 19.

[768] The nature of these conditions is to be amplified by the Commission through administrative rules: Art 52(4).

the orderly functioning of the market (Article 52(2)). Each NCA must also make public and communicate to ESMA and the NCAs of other Member States this decision (including an explanation if the decision was not to suspend or remove), and the notified NCAs must require that other regulated markets and MiFID II/MiFIR trading venues within their jurisdiction suspend or remove the instrument in question, except where to do so would cause significant damage to investors' interests or the orderly functioning of the market; each notified NCA must communicate its decision to ESMA and other NCAs and include an explanation where it decides not to suspend or remove the instrument in question (Article 52(2)).[769] RTSs will be adopted governing situations in which there is a connection between a financial instrument and a derivative, such that the derivative should also be suspended or removed, in order to ensure this requirement applies proportionately (Article 52(2)).

II.7.2.2 Official Listing

The requirements for admission to 'official listing', originally established under the 1979 Admission Directive, remain, somewhat unhappily, in force under the 2001 Consolidated Admission Requirements Directive (CARD),[770] most of which has long since been repealed by the Prospectus Directive and the Transparency Directive.[771] The requirements sit uneasily with the acceptance by MiFID I originally and, since, by MiFID II that admission to trading should primarily be a function of trading venue expertise and of commercial dynamics, and are increasingly anachronistic.

The persistence of an official listing concept in parallel with the regime governing admission to trading on a regulated market carries with it the assumption that officially listed securities are of a higher quality than those simply admitted to trading on a regulated market. The MiFID II admission regime, however, is designed to support trading, primarily by ensuring orderly and liquid trading in the admitted securities and the negotiability of those securities, and by supporting price formation. It is not clear what official listing is, additionally, designed to achieve.[772] The very limited harmonization achieved under the harmonized official listing regime means that in practice the official listing rules are less rigorous than those applied to the admission process by most regulated markets.[773] While the oversight of 'official listing' by a public authority rather than a regulated market might provide grounds for a clearer distinction between both concepts, the official listing regime does not require

---

[769] The same procedure applies with respect to the lifting of suspension decisions, and where an NCA (rather than the market operator) suspends or removes the instrument from trading.

[770] n 18.

[771] The admission to official listing regime is covered in Arts 1 (definitions), 2 (scope), 5–7 (general admission conditions), 8–9 (ability of Member States to impose more stringent conditions and derogation regime), 11–15 (powers of the NCA relating to official listing), 16 (information requirements), 17–19 (action where an issuer fails to comply with official listing conditions), 42–64 (the core of the regime: specific obligations in respect of particular securities, including shares, debt securities, and sovereign debt securities), 64 (treatment of newly issued shares of the same class as those officially listed), and 105–7 (general rules applicable to NCAs).

[772] The UK Official Listing regime, eg, is designed to support an appropriate level of investor protection, facilitate market access, and maintain the integrity and international competitiveness of the UK market: FSA Discussion Paper 08/1, n 745, 27–30.

[773] A point made by ESME: ESME, Report on MiFID and the Admission of Securities to Official Stock Exchange Listing (2007) 7–8. 'Premium Listing' under the UK official listing regime, eg, demands significantly higher standards than those which apply under the 2001 CARD.

that official listing is supervised by a public authority. The 2001 CARD imposes harmonized requirements on the official listing process in part to support multiple listings, but this objective has become something of an anachronism. It was also designed to control monopolistic exchanges' abuse of their position—an objective which has had a similar fate. Official listing might be characterized as an additional marketing/branding device (additional to regulated market admission) on which issuers can rely,[774] but this characterization has weaknesses, given the limited nature of the regime.

Given its minimum standards nature, it might be best characterized as a device for allowing Member States to compete on the quality of their 'official listing process'; the UK authorities regard the 2001 CARD regime as allowing them to continue to operate the long-standing UK Official List, operated by the UK Listing Authority, in parallel with the admission-to-trading regime which applies to UK regulated markets,[775] and to rely accordingly on this vehicle for promoting the UK market to issuers and investors.

'Official listing' is not common across the EU; the main regulated markets typically operate the admission process, thereby 'listing' (or admitting) securities to their markets, and are subject to the MiFID II regime.[776] The 'official listing' concept operates in the UK, however, through the Official List maintained by the UK Listing Authority. It stands independently of, albeit closely connected to, the regime which UK regulated markets apply to the admission of securities under MiFID II.[777] It is, however, significantly more articulated and sophisticated than the 2001 CARD official listing regime[778] and, while it has an investor protection function, it is strongly associated with the global branding of the UK market generally. It can be associated with the long history of official listing in the UK, as well as with the size and importance of the UK fund-raising market.[779] The connection between the CARD regime and the UK regime is now limited, however, with even the basic harmonized CARD rules proving problematic, reflecting market changes (the UK Listing Authority has faced difficulties with certain of the CARD minimum rules[780]), further shedding doubt on the utility of the CARD regime.

The harmonized CARD official listing regime applies to securities which are 'admitted to official listing or are the subject of an application for admission to official listing on a stock exchange situated or operating within a Member State' (CARD Article 2(1)). The Directive

---

[774] ESME has suggested that it is designed to 'add quality not only to the financial instrument but also to the issuer': n 773, 12.

[775] FSA Discussion Paper 08/1, n 745, 28.

[776] 'Admission to listing' has become synonymous with 'admission to trading': n 745, 4.

[777] Securities admitted to the London Stock Exchange's Main Market (a regulated market) must, eg, be admitted to the Official List (and vice versa), as well as comply with the admission rules which apply to the regulated market generally.

[778] The official listing regime includes, eg, general listing principles, the 'sponsor' regime, which is designed to support the issuer through the listing process and provide a quality control process, and rules governing pre-emption rights, corporate governance, directors' dealings, significant transactions, related parties, repurchases of securities, and circulars to shareholders.

[779] FSA Discussion Paper No 08/1, n 745, ch 3.

[780] Notably the CARD's 'free float' rules, which are designed to support liquidity, but which, because of the generous minimum 25 per cent free float requirement for equity issues, have been associated with allowing foreign companies with block-holding structures in particular to list in the UK, and enjoy related branding effects without providing sufficient protection to minority shareholders. Reforms are in train to support minority shareholders: Consultation Papers 12/25 and 12/2, nn 711 and 712 and FCA, Consultation Paper No CP 13/15 (2013).

does not define 'official listing' or 'stock exchange'. The standards are pegged at a minimum level. Member States enjoy a general power to adopt additional and more stringent conditions (Articles 8(1) and (2)), subject to a non-discrimination principle—thereby allowing for a degree of competition, although regulatory policy was not framed in these terms in the 1970s when the regime was originally adopted. Article 12 also allows Member States, 'solely in the interests of protecting the investors', to permit NCAs to subject the listing of a security to such 'special conditions' as they deem appropriate and which have been notified to the applicant issuer. The Directive is also shot through with derogations. Member States may authorize derogations from any additional or more stringent obligations which they impose, although only where they 'apply generally for all issuers where the conditions justifying them are similar' (Article 8(3)). Similarly, the Directive's admission conditions are subject to derogations, as long as the non-discrimination principle is met.

The admission conditions for shares and debt securities are set out in Article 6(1), Articles 42–51 (shares), and Articles 52–63 (debt securities). The conditions include minimum capitalization requirements,[781] operating history requirements (shares only),[782] free transferability and negotiability requirements,[783] and minimum distribution or 'free float' requirements.[784] The disclosure requirements for officially listed securities are now subsumed within the Prospectus Directive and Transparency Directive regime for admission to trading on a regulated market.

Oversight of the official listing regime is carried out by NCAs (Article 11). Reflecting the dominance of exchange self-regulation at that time, the Directive does not stipulate that the NCA take a particular legal form or be a public authority. The official listing function can therefore be carried out by trading venues. The Directive simply requires that the designated NCA has such powers as may be necessary to carry out its tasks (Article 105(2)). Article 19(1), however, provides that Member States must ensure that decisions by the NCA refusing or discontinuing a listing be subject to a right to apply to the courts.[785] Issuers must also provide NCAs with all the information considered appropriate by the authority to protect investors or ensure the smooth operation of the market (Article 16(1)).

---

[781] A €1 million requirement is imposed for shares, although derogation is permitted where an 'adequate market' will be created in the shares (Art 43). A €200,000 requirement is imposed on debt securities (Art 58).

[782] A total of three years of financial accounts are required for shares although, again, derogation is permitted where investors have the information necessary to make an informed judgement on the issuer and the shares (Art 44).

[783] Art 46 (shares) and Art 54 (debt securities).

[784] The distribution requirement is met for shares when the shares in respect of which the application is made are in the hands of the public to the extent of at least 25 per cent of the subscribed capital represented by the class of shares concerned. A lower percentage will fulfil the sufficiency requirement when, in view of the large number of shares of the same class and the extent of their distribution to the public, the market will operate properly with a lower percentage: Art 48(5).

[785] Challenges under Art 19 can raise difficulties for NCAs operating in a time-sensitive market environment. In the UK, in *R v International Stock Exchange, ex parte Else* [1993] QB 534, however, it was found that the primary purpose of the Directive was to co-ordinate the listing practices of NCAs in Member States, and not the provision of additional protection for investors. The Court also found that the Directive was concerned with relations between NCAs and issuers and not with relations between NCAs and investors. As a result, the Directive did not confer enforceable rights on investors. The Court also paid particular attention to the position of the NCA, finding at 550 that the rights claimed by the applicant investors would 'gravely restrict the discretion of the competent authorities … Recent history in more than one field emphasises the need for regulatory authorities to take quick and decisive action where the situation requires it. The Directive, in my view, recognizes that need and gives effect to it. The applicants' argument subverts that intention'.

The MiFID I Review period saw some appetite for a review of the harmonized official listing regime,[786] although it was not ultimately addressed. But its removal may be hazardous in the absence of careful analysis: ESME has pointed to the entrenching of the concept in the asset-management industry and to the difficulties removal may generate in terms of large-scale revision of investment policies.[787] Official listing also remains a key concept in some Member States, although it is marginal in most.[788] The difficulty may ultimately, however, be more a matter of conceptual untidiness than of substantive difficulty. Regulated markets retain wide discretion under MiFID II to operate distinct market segments, the official listing regime itself does not specify when its rules apply, and the distinct harmonized requirements of the official listing regime are now minimal.

II.8 Filing and Dissemination of Issuer Disclosures

II.8.1 Substantive and Operational Harmonization

The efficient filing and dissemination of mandated issuer disclosures has long been the Achilles heel of the EU issuer-disclosure regime; the intensity of substantive harmonization has not been matched by related operational dissemination initiatives. The fragmentation of issuer disclosure across different dissemination channels and different legal regimes has the potential, however, to weaken the effectiveness of the disclosure regime and to threaten investor protection and efficient price formation. The EU has long been hamstrung by its lack of operational capacity in its attempts to develop a dissemination network. The two recent cycles of institutional reform, however, have seen significant development of the still embryonic dissemination regime, with CESR supporting the initial attempts at dissemination under the 2004 Transparency Directive[789] and ESMA at the heart of the current efforts to build an operational platform for pan-EU dissemination of issuer disclosures under the reforms introduced by the 2013 Amending Transparency Directive.

The Prospectus Directive established a basic framework for the publication of prospectuses. The prospectus 'filing' regime is, following the 2010 Omnibus I Directive and 2010 Amending Prospectus Directive reforms, based on prospectus filing with the home NCA, but also on ESMA acting as a central repository for information on prospectuses. Dissemination of prospectuses pan-EU is supported by the publication regime, which has been refined under the 2010 Amending Prospectus Directive to include online publication and to insert ESMA in the publication process.

Ongoing regulated disclosures represent a significantly greater challenge, given the weight and range of this material, its multiple dissemination channels, and its central importance

---

[786] The relationship between MiFID I's admission-to-trading rules and the official listing regime formed part of CESR's MiFID Level 3 Work Programme (CESR/07–704c, 8), while ESME was commissioned to examine the official listing concept: n 773.

[787] n 773, 9.

[788] n 773, 11.

[789] The Commission described CESR as pivotal to the initial development of a pan-EU network under the related 2007 Commission Recommendation (n 791): European Securities Committee Minutes, 13 September 2007.

to price formation. Benefiting from an operational capacity through CESR, the 2004 Transparency Directive was designed to enhance public access to and pan-EU dissemination of ongoing issuer disclosures. But while the Transparency Directive established a basic framework for dissemination, and applied minimum standards to national filing and access systems, it was not successful in building a system for distributing disclosures. The 2013 Amending Transparency Directive, however, envisages a step-change, with ESMA set to play a central role in this new operational phase of EU issuer-disclosure regulation.

II.8.2 Filing Issuer Disclosures

A framework filing and dissemination regime applies to 'regulated information' under the Transparency Directive. This concept covers the ongoing disclosure required of issuers under the Transparency Directive, the *ad hoc* disclosures required under the market abuse regime, and any super-equivalent disclosure required by Member States where they exercise the power to impose additional rules to the Transparency Directive under Article 3(1).[790]

All regulated information must be 'filed' in the issuer's home Member State. Article 19(1) provides that whenever an issuer discloses regulated information to the market it must, at the same time, file that information with the home NCA (Article 19(1)); that NCA may decide to publish the filed information on its website. The filing obligation extends to the information notified to the issuer under the ownership notification regime (Article 19(3)). The filing of regulated information is not characterized as the distribution of disclosures, but simply as the deposit of information with the NCA; dissemination to the public is a distinct function and is based on the Officially Appointed Mechanism system, as discussed in section 8.3.

II.8.3 Dissemination of Disclosure

Under the Transparency Directive, the home Member State must ensure that the issuer (or the person who has applied for admission to trading on a regulated market without the issuer's consent) discloses regulated information in a manner which ensures fast access to such information on a non-discriminatory basis (Article 21(1)). The home Member State must require the issuer to use such media as may reasonably be relied on for the effective dissemination of information to the public throughout the EU, but may not require that issuers only use media whose operators are established on its territory. Although this regime is governed by the home Member State, an exception applies where the securities are admitted to trading on a regulated market in only one Member State where this is not the home State; in this case that State is responsible for ensuring dissemination in accordance with Article 21. The administrative 2007 Commission Transparency Directive imposes minimum standards on the dissemination of information (Article 12). The regime is based on the principle that mere availability of information, which means that it must be actively sought out by investors, is not sufficient for the purposes of Article 21 and that dissemination should involve the active distribution of information from issuers, to the media, and with a view to reaching investors (recital 15).

---

[790] Art 2(1)(k). A number of Member States include prospectuses within the definition of regulated information, aligning the dissemination regimes: 2011 ESMA Mapping Report, n 477, 9.

Regulated information must also be made available to (and stored in) an 'officially appointed mechanism' (Article 21(2), discussed later in this section). The home Member State must ensure that there is at least one 'officially appointed mechanism' (OAM) for the central storage of information which must meet minimum quality standards as to security, certainty as to information source, time recording, and easy access by end-users (Article 21(2)). A delegation to administrative rule-making was granted under the 2004 Transparency Directive to provide for minimum standards for OAMs;[791] the delegation has since been revised by the 2013 Amending Transparency Directive to provide for rules ensuring the interoperability of OAMs and the proposed new EU 'Access Point', noted further in this section (Article 21(4)).

National dissemination and filing has not proved problematic. The national OAMs were, however, designed to support the construction of, first, national electronic networks (between, *inter alia*, NCAs, company registries, and regulated market operators), but also, second, the subsequent development of a pan-EU single electronic disclosure network or a platform of related networks.[792] But progress was slow. The Transparency Directive review process underlined the costs and difficulties associated with information being filed in (then) 27 different national data systems with a poor level of interconnection,[793] and the related visibility difficulties for SMEs in particular.[794] Although all Member States have OAMs in place, which are often closely integrated with local trading venues and regulated information services, dissemination across the EU occurs through multiple channels and integration levels are poor.[795] The establishment of ESMA, however, has significantly enhanced the EU's operational capacity in this field, while related developments in the company law sphere have also facilitated a more ambitious approach.[796]

A new model has accordingly been adopted by the 2013 Amending Transparency Directive. It provides that a web portal serving as a 'European electronic access point' is to be established by January 2018, and to be established and operated by ESMA; the Access Point is to link together the central storage mechanisms (OAMs) of Member States and provide a platform for access to all regulated issuer disclosures (Article 21a). In support of the construction of this new platform, ESMA is to adopt a series of RTSs governing, *inter alia*, the communication technology used by OAMs, the technical operation of the Access Point, the unique identifiers to be used by each issuer which will support the new platform, the common format in which OAMs are to deliver regulated disclosures, and the common classification of regulated information by OAMs and the common list of types of regulated information (Article 22).

---

[791] The delegation was not acted upon and the Commission proceeded instead by means of a Recommendation: Commission Recommendation 2007/657/EC on the electronic network of officially appointed mechanisms for the central storage of information referred to in the Transparency Directive [2007] OJ L267/16.

[792] The 2007 Commission Recommendation established operating standards for OAMs and was designed to encourage Member States to create a pan-EU electronic network of OAMs.

[793] Actica, Feasibility Study for a pan-EU storage system for information disclosed by issuers of securities (2011).

[794] 2009 Mazars Report, n 467, xix.

[795] 2011 Actica Report, n 793.

[796] In 2012, a new regime governing an electronic network of company law registers was adopted: Directive 2012/17/EU [2012] OJ L156/1.

II.9 Market Impact of the Issuer-disclosure Regime

II.9.1 Issuers and Market Finance

The EU's faith in the power of regulation (harmonized rules) to drive market outcomes with respect to capital-raising may not be misplaced. The extensive law and finance scholarship[797] suggests that there is a link of some kind between law and strong securities markets.[798] Concerns pre-crisis, and since the crisis, as to the weakening of the competitive position of the US also suggest, at the least, that the potential for a negative impact from over-regulation on finance-raising through the markets by issuers cannot be easily dismissed[799]—although it is not easy to make the correlation that appropriate regulation drives strong outcomes.

The evidence suggests that, pre-crisis, while bank finance remained dominant, recourse to market finance by issuers[800] was increasing across the EU, with the decade prior to the crisis witnessing particularly strong growth,[801] and with relative levels of debt and equity issuance activity in the EU over this period outstripping US issuance activity.[802] This represented a marked change from the early years of the legislative programme. Prior to the major FSAP reforms, the bank finance model prevailed across the EU.[803] Germany provided the paradigm of a bank-finance-based economy,[804] with financing dominated by universal banks; trading venues remained on the fringes of the funding process.[805] With specific reference to the EU's public equity markets, in 1998, at the outset of the FSAP reforms,

---

[797] Noted in Ch I.

[798] In the EU context, Rajan and Zingales have related the growth in market finance in the EU to the impact of law and, in particular, to stronger disclosure and insider trading rules: Zingales, L and Rajan, R, Banks and Markets—the Changing Character of European Finance, CRSP WP No 546 (2003), available at <http://ssrn.com/abstract=389100>.

[799] See references at n 39.

[800] On general trends with respect to market finance and related market intensity see Ch 1.

[801] Between 1996 and 2006, bond issuance doubled and equity market capitalization tripled. Growth in bank assets was also overtaken by growth in bond assets: Casey, J-P and Lannoo, K, The MiFID Revolution, ECMI Policy Brief No 3 (2006) 3.

[802] n 801. The relative performance of US and EU markets, and concern as to the impact of presumed over-regulation on the competitive position of the US, led to a high-profile political and academic debate in the US, particularly with respect to the impact of regulation and enforcement on cross-listing, which was triggered by the Paulson Report (n 39) and the subsequent Bloomberg/Schummer Report (Bloomberg, M and Schummer, C, Sustaining New York's and the US's Global Financial Leadership (2007)).

[803] In its 1998 pre-FSAP Communication, the Commission reported that dependence on debt as a source of corporate finance varied, at the time, from 50 per cent in the Netherlands to over 70 per cent in France, Germany, and Italy and 80 per cent in Spain, as compared with 20 per cent in the US: n 127, 1. The Initial Lamfalussy Report similarly noted that at the start of the 1980s, over 80 per cent of the external financing of continental European firms was provided by credit institutions: n 131, 9.

[804] The 2002 London Economics Report (using Commission and OECD data) reported that equity, bond, and bank financing represented, respectively, 32.3 per cent, 1.2 per cent, and 66.5 per cent in Germany and 54.8 per cent, 2.0 per cent per cent, and 43.2 per cent in the UK: n 107, 120.

[805] See further Pagano, M and Steil, B, 'Equity Trading I: The Evolution of European Trading Systems' in Steil, B (ed), *The European Equity Markets: The State of the Union and the Agenda for the Millennium* (1996) 1, 16, and Moran, M, 'Regulation Change in German Financial Markets' in Dyson, K (ed), *The Politics of German Regulation* (1992) 137, 145–9.

total EU stock market capitalization (a useful, if limited, proxy for issuance activity) as a percentage of GDP was 80 per cent, as compared with 145 per cent in the US.[806]

Recourse to market finance increased in the wake of the establishment of monetary union and the arrival of the euro.[807] Bond (both sovereign and corporate) markets began to develop strongly,[808] while the stock market capitalizations of Member States began to show signs of growth.[809] Although bank finance continued to dominate,[810] by late 2000, and before the major FSAP reforms were in place, the Commission suggested that 'market-based financing is beginning to overturn the traditional predominance of bank-based lending in most EU Member States',[811] while in early 2001 the Lamfalussy Report pointed to record levels of turnover on EU stock exchanges as 'further evidence of an emerging European equity culture'.[812] These trends continued, with the 2002 London Economics Report commenting on growth in the bond market (as well as growth in equity issues).[813] By mid-2002, the euro-denominated bond market was in excess of $8,000 billion, although only 6.4 per cent represented corporate debt[814] and the EU corporate bond market still remained small compared with the US market.[815] Progress was not linear, however; the IPO market, for example, experienced significant reverses between 2000 and 2003.[816]

In the years between the conclusion of the FSAP and the onset of the financial crisis, reliance on market-based funding continued to increase. Numbers and values of IPOs, for

---

[806] Gros and Lannoo, n 169, 166, Table A1.2. In its 1998 pre-FSAP Communication the Commission reported that stock market capitalization in the EU, excluding the UK and Netherlands, amounted to only 32 per cent of GDP: n 127, 6.

[807] Gros and Lannoo predicted that with the establishment of EMU the dominance of universal banks as finance providers would be lessened in favour of market-based disintermediated finance: n 169, xiii.

[808] The 2000 Second Progress Report on the FSAP noted that in early 1999 the market value of listed private-sector bond issues represented more than 110 per cent of GDP in Denmark, almost 70 per cent in Germany, and over 40 per cent in the Netherlands: n 179, 4. The Lamfalussy Report also noted the strong growth in bond markets, although it pointed to the considerable gap between the euro corporate-bond market and its dollar equivalent: n 732, 10. See further Gros and Lannoo, n 169, 83–93.

[809] While the stock market capitalization of Member States remained low compared with the US, in 1999 newly admitted companies raised over €130 billion in European markets, more than double the amount raised in 1998: Second FSAP Progress Report, n 179, 4.

[810] The Commission reported in 2000 that while financial markets were becoming a more popular way of raising finance, as evidenced by the decline in debt-to-equity ratios in EU firms and the large increases in stock market capitalizations in all Member States (with the exception of Austria and Luxembourg), banks still accounted for the larger part of corporate financing, with bank assets in 1999 in the euro-area Member States amounting to 212 per cent of GDP, as compared with 47.9 per cent for equities. In the US the inverse was true, with equities, at the time of the Commission's report, amounting to 160 per cent of GDP and bank assets amounting to 62.5 per cent: Second FSAP Progress Report, n 179 5.

[811] Commission's 2000 Communication on Upgrading the Investment Services Directive (93/22/EEC) (1993) (COM (2000) 729) 6.

[812] n 732, 10.

[813] n 107, 5.

[814] Although the 2002 London Economics Report noted that this represented a 'sharp upward trend' from recent years: n 107, 57.

[815] The share of debt securities as a percentage of total liabilities of non-financial issuers was 2.4 per cent in the euro area, as compared with 10.6 per cent in the US, while loans represented 23.3 per cent of total liabilities, as compared with 5.4 per cent in the US: n 107, 66.

[816] 2011 City of London Economic Development SME Report, n 41, 8 (but including third country IPOs).

example, increased strongly between 2004 and 2007.[817] The Commission's 2004 Financial Integration Monitor reported that the European financial landscape had changed significantly and that market finance had gained in importance, fuelled by demand for market-based investments and the emergence of a population of institutional investors. It also acknowledged, however, that bank financing, equity financing, and bond financing played different roles in the different Member States and that, overall, bank lending (at 109.6 per cent of GDP) remained the predominant source of financing in the (then) EU-15 Member States.[818] Bank financing remained particularly prevalent in the new Member States.[819]

By 2007, immediately prior to the crisis, the ECB's 2007 Report on Financial Integration reported a significant increase in market finance opportunities and the continued development of corporate bond and equity markets.[820] The Commission's 2007 Financial Integration Report agreed, reporting strong growth in bond and equity capital markets—with the value of the EU bond market as a proportion of GDP, for example, increasing from 183 per cent in 2004 to 198 per cent.[821] IPO growth generally remained strong, with an increase in new admissions to regulated markets and, in particular, exchange-regulated markets over 2004–7.[822] EU stock market capitalization as a proportion of GDP rose over 2004–7,[823] narrowing the still significant gap with the US.[824] Growth was not uniform across the EU, however. More general concerns as to the health of public equity markets internationally were reflected in sluggish issuance activity in the UK market in particular. The number of firms with equities listed on the London Stock Exchange's Main Market, for example, began to decline from 2001,[825] while UK stock market growth as a proportion of GDP was generally static over this period, although other Member States experienced very significant growth.[826] But overall, while EU securities markets grew at a rate of 9 per cent in the period prior to the financial crisis[827] the EU financial system remained strongly bank-based.[828]

---

[817] n 41, 8 and 10–11 (but including third country IPOs).

[818] Unquoted shares and other equity represented 31 per cent of total corporate financing: Commission, Financial Integration Monitor 2004 (2004) (SEC (2004) 559) 3.

[819] The Commission reported in 2005 that 'all new Member States have predominantly bank-based financial systems', with the banking sector representing 80 per cent of total financial assets: Commission, Financial Integration Monitor 2005 (2005) (SEC (2005) 927) 1.

[820] ECB, Report on Financial Integration (2007) 31.

[821] Commission, European Financial Integration Monitor 2007 (2007) (SEC (2007) 1696) (2007 EFIR) 34.

[822] 2009 CRA Report, n 195, 177 (albeit that both market segments experienced a slowdown in 2007).

[823] It grew from 71.4 per cent of EU GDP in 2004, to 73.7 per cent, 91.9 per cent, and 91.9 per cent in 2005, 2006, and 2007 respectively: World Bank Data, available through <http://data.worldbank.org/indicator/CM.MKT.LCAP.GD.ZS>.

[824] In 2004, US stock market capitalization as a percentage of GDP was 138.4 per cent. By 2007 it was 142.9 per cent: n 823.

[825] FSA Discussion Paper 08/1, n 745, 16, noting a steady decline between 2001 and 2007.

[826] Between 2003 and 2007, UK stock market capitalization grew from 132.6 per cent to 136.6 per cent. Growth elsewhere in the EU was significantly greater, across new and more established markets, eg Poland (17.1 per cent to 48.7 per cent), Czech Republic (18.5 per cent to 40.7 per cent), Croatia (17.9 to 111.2 per cent), Germany (44.5 per cent to 63.3 per cent), France (75.7 per cent to 107.3 per cent), Denmark (57.2 per cent to 89.2 per cent), Belgium (55.7 per cent to 84.1 per cent), and Luxembourg (123.1 per cent to 323.7 per cent): World Bank Data, n 823. For an analysis of the market capitalization of different regulated markets and exchange-regulated markets over this period see 2008 CSES Report, n 194, 25–7.

[827] ECB, Financial Integration in Europe (2011) 7 and 13, noting that the EU capital market grew at a rate of 9 per cent between 2000–4 and 2005–9.

[828] 2007 EFIR, n 821, 33–4 and, for the euro area, ECB, 'The external financing of household and non-household corporations: a comparison of the euro area and the United States' *Monthly Bulletin*, April 2009, 69, reporting that in 2007 euro-area capital markets generally represented 311 per cent of GDP, as compared

Over and since the financial crisis, conditions have changed again. In the equity markets, the crisis took a severe toll, although by 2014 markets were recovering strongly. While it is not a reliable indicator of corporate funding behaviour, given the range of factors which shape the volume of secondary market trading, EU stock market capitalization provides at least an indication as to the strength of equity markets generally. Between 2008 and 2011 it experienced steep falls, dropping to pre-2003 levels,[829] although the degree of contraction varied across the Member States.[830] While a similarly limited proxy, the numbers of prospectuses approved in the EU fell by 50 per cent between 2006 and 2012.[831]

Nonetheless, recourse to a broader range of market finance instruments has been a feature of the crisis era, reflecting the contraction in bank lending.[832] Equities remained an importance source of non-bank external funding for non-financial firms in the euro area over the worst of the crisis, although the volume of issuance decreased[833] and remained well below the 2007 peak.[834] There was a sharp drop in IPO activity in 2008 and 2009,[835] although IPO activity recovered in 2010.[836] Overall, the IPO market remained volatile over the crisis era.[837] The Commission's review of financial markets in 2011, for example, found that high volatility in secondary market trading[838] had spilled into the primary markets and reported on a general decline in IPO issuance since the start of the financial crisis, concluding that the capacity of EU equity markets to fund the real economy was subdued.[839] While some signs of revival were noted in 2011,[840] overall the EU IPO market performed poorly in 2012.[841] Although the later stages of 2013 saw a recovery,[842] overall

---

to 375 per cent in the US, and that euro-area bank lending represented 145 per cent of GDP, as compared to 63 per cent in the US.

[829] A steep fall took place in 2008 to 41.5 per cent of GDP (from 91.9 per cent in 2007). It stabilized somewhat in 2009 and 2010 (to 60.2 per cent and 64.9 per cent, respectively) but fell again in 2011 (52.7 per cent): n 823.

[830] Between 2007 and 2011, dramatic falls were recorded in, eg, the Czech Republic (40.7 per cent to 17.7 per cent) and Slovenia (61.2 per cent to 12.8 per cent) as well as in more established markets, eg, Germany (63.3 per cent to 32.9 per cent) and Italy (51.7 per cent to 19.7 per cent): n 823.

[831] ESMA, Data on Prospectuses Approved and Passported. January 2012–December 2012 (2013) (ESMA/2013/741), reporting on a drop from 8,481 in 2006 to 4,113 in 2012 (Table V).

[832] ECB, Financial Stability Review, December 2012 (2012) 35 and Financial Stability Review, June 2012 (2012) 33.

[833] ECB, Financial Stability Review, December 2012 (2012) 35 and 2012 EFSIR, n 149, 31 (reporting on 'subdued' levels of net issuance of shares by euro-area non-financial corporations, albeit that issuance levels were marginally higher than in 2011).

[834] 2012 EFSIR, n 149, 31.

[835] CESR, Annual Report (2009) 7 and Annual Report (2008) 9.

[836] CESR, Annual Report (2010) 10–11.

[837] 2011 City of London Economic Development SME Report, n 41, 8 and 10–11 (including third country IPOs).

[838] Which has been a strong feature of the crisis era. The significant and repeated contractions and recoveries are charted in the ECB's six-monthly Financial Stability Reviews.

[839] 2011 EFSIR, n 150, 32.

[840] ESMA, Annual Report (2011) 17, noting an increase in numbers and value of IPOs between the first half of 2010 and the first half of 2011.

[841] 2012 saw a 59 per cent decrease in the value of IPOs in Europe on 2011: PWC, IPO Watch Europe Survey (2012).

[842] By Q3 2013, more funding had been raised through IPOs than in 2012: PWC, IPO Watch Europe Survey, Q3 2013 (2013). Similarly, EY Global IPO Trends, Q4 (2013). The UK market in particular strengthened over 2013, with the value of UK-issued IPOs estimated at eight times the value at the previous point in 2012: Bolger, A and Bounds, A, 'IPOs Head for Best Year Since Crisis', *Financial Times,* 23 September 2013, 1. ESMA similarly reported on an increase in the number and value of IPOs in the second

the EU primary issuance and IPO market remained sluggish throughout much of 2013.[843] Early 2014, however, saw the IPO market recover strongly, with a 'queue' of IPOs developing, reflecting in part pent-up demand for exit by venture capitalists and private equity funders.[844]

While 2014 accordingly started well, concerns had earlier been expressed on the conditions for equity issuance in the UK, in particular, given the overall drop in the number of admissions to trading (and even allowing for growth in the second-tier segment).[845] One key review (the 2012 Kay Review) suggested that admission to trading was often regarded as a 'last resort' to support venture capital exit[846] and reliance by UK firms on the UK equity market as a source of funding was becoming increasingly limited, with the IPO no longer an aspiration for firms.[847] More generally, the number of listed companies has also decreased across the EU as a whole, and the Commission has warned that equity funding markets remain sluggish and cannot close the funding gap left by the contraction in bank loans.[848]

The bond markets, by contrast, performed more strongly, reflecting international trends.[849] While EU firms remain, overall, dependent on bank finance,[850] the crisis-era contraction in bank lending, investors' search-for-yield efforts, and the low cost of issuing longer-term high-yield bonds can all be associated with the emergence of a significantly stronger EU corporate bond market,[851] although issuance levels have varied.[852] Bond issuance by financial institutions still dominates in the EU bond market, but greater recourse to

---

half of 2013: ESMA, Report on Trends, Risks, and Vulnerabilities. Report No 1 (2014) (ESMA/2014/0188) (ESMA 2014(1) TRV).

[843] ESMA, Report on Trends, Risks, and Vulnerabilities. Report No 1 2013 (2013) (ESMA 2013(1) TRV) 10. ESMA's second TRV similarly reported that the value of IPOs had increased significantly in the first half of 2013 relative to the first half of 2012, but that the number of deals remained weak at around 61 a quarter, down from a quarterly average of 107 on 2011: ESMA, Report on Trends, Risks, and Vulnerabilities. Report No 2 2013 (2013) (ESMA/2013/1138) (ESMA 2013(2) TRV) 9.

[844] This development was widely reported: eg, Chassany, A-S and Wigglesworth, R, 'Listings Worth $8 billion Lined Up in IPO Flurry', *Financial Times,* 19 February 2014 (reporting on the busiest start to the year since 2007) and Bolger, A and Chassany, A-S, 'Europe Primed for IPO Wave', *Financial Times,* 24 January 2014, 2.

[845] Kay Review of UK Equity Markets and Long-Term Decision Making, Interim Report (2012) (2012 Interim Kay Review) 26.

[846] 2012 Kay Review, n 34, 26.

[847] 2012 Kay Review, n 34, 88.

[848] Commission, European Financial Stability and Integration Report 2013 (2014) (SWD (2014) 170) (2013 EFSIR) 28-29. The number of listed companies decreased by 27 per cent between 2007 and 2011, while the level of capital raised fell by 65 per cent: Commission Long-Term Financing Staff Working Document, n 723, 22–3.

[849] eg, 2011 McKinsey Report, n 33, 20, noting the global increase in corporate bond issuance by non-financial firms, which initially doubled in 2009 from 2008.

[850] Non-financial corporate bonds in the EU account for only 15 per cent of corporate debt generally: 2013 Long-Term Financing Green Paper, n 95, 11.

[851] ECB, Financial Stability Review, May 2013 (2013) 43; Financial Stability Review, December 2012 (2012) 50; Financial Stability Review, June 2012 (2012) 33–5; Financial Stability Review, June 2011 (2011) 77; 2011 EFSIR, n 150, 32; and 2013 ESFIR, n 848, 24–25.

[852] eg ECB, Financial Stability Review, December 2010 (2010) 70, noting the drop in issuance levels between 2010 and 2009, and Financial Stability Review, December 2009 (2009) 70, noting record levels of debt issuance in the euro area in the first half of 2009 as many large firms replaced bank credit with market-based instruments.

bond financing is occurring on the part of non-financial companies,[853] reflecting the contraction in bank funding and the longer maturities and lower interest rates available from bond financing. Large, liquid corporate bond markets remain concentrated in only a few Member States, however.[854] Bond market issuance is also typically only engaged in by large firms; the SME sector in particular finds it difficult to access bond financing, although Germany has become the exception to the rule, with the crisis era seeing the development of a vibrant corporate bond market among smaller companies[855] and the related development of trading facilities for these bonds.[856] Allied to this is the developing market for retail bonds, particularly in the UK, where household investors have not traditionally invested in bonds.[857] The marked rate of growth led the Commission to suggest that—while this development might be temporary[858]—bond issuance had become a viable alternative source of funds for larger, non-financial firms, and to suggest reforms to ease the bond market for SMEs.[859] The Commission has also associated the corporate bond markets with its long-term financing agenda.[860]

The outlook generally is relatively strong, with the ECB suggesting that the crisis should not endanger the long-term trend towards financial market development.[861]

With respect to the EU's regulatory programme, the extent to which the development and contraction of market-based funding by firms can be directly related to regulatory intervention is not clear, given the multiplicity of drivers, including the differential fiscal treatment of debt and equity finance, which shape the extent to which issuers access the bond and equity markets. Certainly, the pre-FSAP evidence underlines that recourse by firms to market finance was intensifying (particularly in the private markets) in the absence of intensive regulation,[862] while the 2009 CRA Report on the impact of the FSAP found that the issuer-disclosure measures had a 'mixed impact', enhancing the quality of disclosure in some cases, bringing costs in others, and not having a clear effect on issuance or

---

[853] Non-financial firm bond-raising represented 34 per cent of EU bond issuance in 2012, up from 20 per cent in 2011: ESMA 2013(1) TRV, n 843, 12. The Commission similarly reported that the total amount outstanding of debt securities issued by non-financial firms reached a historical high of €978 billion at the end of 2012 (2012 EFSIR, n 149, 32), representing a sharp rise from €652 billion at the start of 2008 (Commission Long-Term Financing Staff Working Document, n 724, 20). Similarly, in December 2012, the ECB reported strong issuance of debt securities since early 2012—by contrast with a deceleration in bank lending—with firms diversifying their sources of funding in response to risks relating to the availability of bank credit: ECB, Financial Stability Review, December 2012 (2012) 34.

[854] Particularly Germany, France, Italy, the Netherlands, and Belgium: ECB, Financial Stability Review, June 2012 (2012) 34.

[855] The family-run but large companies (which would typically be listed in market-finance-based economies) which dominate the 'Mittelstand' have increasingly resorted to bond finance following the contraction in bank lending: Commission Long-Term Financing Staff Working Document n 724, 21.

[856] 2011 EFSIR, n 150, 34. Between 2011 and 2013, four of the eight German exchanges began trading 'Mittelstand' bonds: Commission Long-Term Financing Staff Working Document, n 724, 21.

[857] The London Stock Exchange Group launched a new electronic order book for retail bonds (the ORB) which saw early growth: London Stock Exchange Press Release, 31 July 2012 (reporting on retail bond issuances by three issuers in July 2012).

[858] In September 2013, ESMA reported on subdued issuance levels, albeit particularly in the banking sector: ESMA 2013(2) TRV, n 843, 11.

[859] 2011 EFSIR, n 150, 33 and Commission Long-Term Financing Staff Working Document, n 724, 22.

[860] eg 2013 Green Paper on Long-Term Financing, n 95, 12.

[861] ECB, Financial Integration in Europe (2011) 12.

[862] Ferran, n 26, 30–8.

admission to trading activity.[863] The multiplicity of determinative factors associated with the pre-crisis intensification of recourse by issuers to the markets in the EU[864] include growth in the institutional investor community, the impact of the euro,[865] innovation in financing techniques (including securitization),[866] a massive pre-crisis increase in financialization generally,[867] the initial wave of establishment of new trading venues (particularly the second-tier venues which support venture capital), technological innovation supporting stronger price formation, and favourable global macroeconomic conditions.[868] Conversely, the persistent dominance of bank lending as the dominant form of funding, notwithstanding these influences, can be related to a swathe of non-legal factors,[869] including, in the pre-crisis period, the financialization of banks in the form of their significantly greater engagement in trading and in securitization activities, which facilitated lending (as well as the embedding of market finance).[870]

Non-legal factors continue to shape funding behaviour. For example, a range of non-legal difficulties came to be associated with sluggish primary equity markets in the EU generally over the crisis era,[871] and in the UK in particular. Listing costs, for example, were implicated in the contraction in the UK public equity markets.[872] The drop in UK equity market activity was also associated with a range of other factors, including concerns as to the over-pricing of IPOs,[873] the impact of HFT on trading venue quality, the cost of intermediation more generally, persistent tax discrimination between debt and equity funding, greater reliance on private equity funding, and less demand, generally, for physical capital.[874] The dramatic change in macroeconomic and financial system conditions over the crisis era, and the related impact on the price of credit and on bond issuance, further underlines the impact of non-legal factors on the development of funding models. Overall, perhaps the upsurge in IPO activity in early 2014, as economic conditions strengthened, underlines the facilitative rather than determinative role of law.

The VoC scholarship certainly cautions as to the limited role of law in shaping different varieties of finance.[875] More specifically—and allowing, as seems reasonable, some role for

---

[863] The Report found it difficult to disentangle the impacts of the regime, given in particular the cyclical nature of admission to trading: 2009 CRA Report, n 195, 169–83.

[864] The Commission's 2004 Financial Integration Monitor, eg, pointed to the growth of institutional investors (and particularly investment funds), globalization, advances in technology, conglomeration, and new financing techniques as driving greater recourse to market finance: n 818, 3.

[865] Casey and Lannoo, n 169, 4.

[866] ECB, 2009 *Monthly Bulletin*, n 828, 71, noting the impact of the rapid growth in securitization pre crisis on the development of a 'stronger market orientation'. Similarly, Hardie, I and Howarth, D, 'Die Krise but not La Crise? The Financial Crisis and the Transformation of German and French Banking Systems' (2009) 47 *JCMS* 1017.

[867] Illustrated, eg, by the very significant increase in turnover in the EU's leading trading venues over the 2003–7 period: 2008 CSES Report, n 194, 28.

[868] eg Rajan and Zingales, n 798, 5–10 and 45–8 and ECB, Financial Integration in Europe (2007) 31.

[869] See further Ch I.

[870] Hardie, I and Howarth, D, What Varieties of Financial Capitalism? The Financial Crisis and the Move to 'Market-based Banking' in the UK, Germany, and France, Political Studies Association Paper (2010).

[871] Johnson, S, 'Facebook Flop Stirs Anger over IPOs', *Financial Times, Fund Management Supplement*, 21 January 2013, 1, reporting on the 'stuttering market for new issues'.

[872] 2012 Interim Kay Review, n 845, 26.

[873] Which was repeatedly raised by leading fund managers in the UK, particularly over 2012–13: eg, Gray, A and Stothard, M, 'Investors Warn Esure Against IPO Overpricing', *Financial Times,* 27 February 2013, 1.

[874] Interim Kay Review, n 845, 26–7 and Kay Review, n 34, 25 and 84–7.

[875] See Ch 1.

regulation—the range of critiques of the law and finance scholarship[876] suggest that complex and inter-related forces shape the relationship between law and strong markets. But while it is difficult to establish a transformative relationship between levels of market finance in the EU and the now vast regulatory programme, it is equally difficult to assume that law has no impact. Ultimately, whatever its market impact, the EU's regulation of issuer disclosure is now an embedded element of EU securities and markets regulation, reflecting systems of financial market regulation internationally. It is also a necessary condition supporting pan-EU capital-raising, the status of which is discussed in the next and final section of this Chapter.

II.9.2 Integration Trends

Over the FSAP period, evidence of integration began to emerge in the primary markets, in the form of, on the supply side, pan-EU capital-raising by issuers and, on the demand side, stronger portfolio diversification and a loosening of the 'home bias'. Evidence of integration also began to emerge in the secondary markets, in the form of the narrowing of price dispersion in asset classes[877] which began to take place.[878] The debt markets quickly became associated with a high degree of integration.[879] Even as the financial crisis began to take root, the Commission could report on the 'remarkable' degree of integration in EU wholesale bond markets, as well as good, if less intense, levels of integration in the equity markets.[880]

Over the financial crisis, significant retrenchment took place, with the ECB reporting on a 'slow erosion' of progress towards integration, including in previously highly integrated segments, notably the bond markets;[881] some improvements were, however, reported as the crisis receded, particularly over 2013.[882] The equity markets appear to have been less heavily impacted after the initial phase of the crisis,[883] displaying lower levels of cross-border price differentiation (albeit from a lower base)[884] and significant levels of cross-border investment by euro-area investors.[885] The equity markets remain vulnerable,

---

[876] See Ch I.

[877] This variable for integration, which assesses the extent to which common factors impact on the price of assets, is used to quantify financial market integration levels in the ECB's Financial Integration Reports and by the Commission in its original series of Financial Integration Monitors and, more recently, its Financial Stability and Integration Reports.

[878] eg Financial Integration Monitor 2004, n 818, 7–8.

[879] London Economics, n 107, 54–64. The Report noted, however, that the market was cross-border in character before the introduction of the euro (which drove further integration), as the small size of national markets compelled corporate bond issuers to tap other markets: 54 and 63.

[880] Commission, European Financial Integration Report (2009) (SEC (2009) 19) (2009 EFIR) 7.

[881] ECB, Financial Integration in Europe (2012) 9 and 24–5 and ECB, Financial Integration in Europe (2013) 10.

[882] ECB, Financial Integration in Europe (2014) 24, noting 'slightly receding' fragmentation in corporate bond markets in 2013.

[883] In 2009, the Commission reported a significant rise in cross-country dispersion in equity prices, which it related to a sharper investor focus on domestic markets, and to information asymmetries with respect to cross-border information: 2009 EFIR, n 880, 9.

[884] ECB, Financial Integration in Europe (2012) 25 and ECB Financial Integration in Europe (2013) 10.

[885] At one point over the crisis, 40 per cent of equity holdings of euro-area residents were issued in other euro-area Member States: ECB, Financial Integration in Europe (2011) 22.

however, to domestic retrenchment and to related pricing differentiation.[886] But this has been associated with better risk differentiation by investors, rather than with structural problems with integration.[887] Pan-EU public offers remain rare, however, and public offerings can often be limited to the minimum necessary to meet listing requirements.

The extent to which the harmonized issuer-disclosure regime, its related delineation of the scope of private markets, and its associated passporting mechanisms have driven higher levels of cross-border capital-raising is unclear, given the range of factors which drive funding decisions and the structure of offerings. Standardization through the issuer disclosure and financial reporting regimes facilitates cross-border funding, but it is only one of a range of determinative factors. Funding drivers aside, general corporate law, consumer protection requirements, taxation, and legal liability risks all impact on cross-border funding decisions.[888] It is also likely that the radical restructuring of order execution under MiFID I has had a significant effect, by ensuring that that multi-Member State offerings and admissions to trading are no longer necessary to ensure pan-EU investor access to and the visibility of an issuer's securities (Chapter V).

---

[886] ESMA 2013(1) TRV, n 843, 10, reporting on increasing differentiation across EU equity markets. Similarly, the ECB's 2014 report on 2013 was broadly positive if cautious, reporting in particular on a reduction in the degree of cross-country heterogeneity in stock market returns, although noting the continued risk of fragmentation: ECB, Financial Integration in Europe (2014) 24–5.

[887] ESMA, EBA, EIOPA, Joint Committee Report on Risks and Vulnerabilities in the EU Financial Sector, March 2013, 14–15.

[888] 2008 CSES Report, n 194, 20.

III

ASSET MANAGEMENT

III.1 Introduction

III.1.1 Collective and Discretionary Asset Management in the EU

III.1.1.1 A Fragmented Regime

This Chapter addresses the harmonized EU regime which applies to asset (or investment) management.

Asset management can take two broad forms: discretionary (or individual) asset management, involving the management of a client's portfolio (whether retail or professional), on an individual basis and in accordance with the mandate agreed between the asset manager and the client (section 2); and collective asset management, involving the management of a fund of pooled assets in accordance with specified risk levels and asset-allocation parameters (typically associated with investment fund or collective investment scheme (CIS) structures) (sections 3–5 below). The EU asset management market, which by and large has recovered well from the financial crisis, although it remains volatile,[1] is the second largest asset management market globally (after the US),[2] with some €13.8 trillion assets under management (AUM),[3] and is of central importance to the EU capital market.[4] AUM in the EU are split broadly evenly between assets managed collectively and assets managed under discretionary mandates.[5]

Asset management was first addressed by the 1985 UCITS Directive (now the 2009 UCITS IV Directive, as amended),[6] which addressed collective asset management only,

---

[1] European Fund and Asset Management Association (EFAMA), Asset Management in Europe. 5th Annual Review (2012) (2012 EFAMA Asset Management Report) 2 (reporting on 2010) and European Securities and Markets Authority (ESMA), Report on Trends, Risks, and Vulnerabilities. Report No 1 (2013) (ESMA/2013/212) (ESMA 2013(1) TRV) 17 (reporting on 2012). In its 2013 report, EFAMA reported that the asset management industry had recorded a modest decline after two years of growth: Asset Management Report in Europe. 6th Annual Review (2013) (2013 EFAMA Asset Management Report) 7.

[2] It represents 31 per cent of global AUM: 2013 EFAMA Asset Management Report, n 1, 2.

[3] 2013 EFAMA Asset Management Report, n 1, 2.

[4] It accounts for some 31 per cent, eg, of shares and 21 per cent of debt issued by euro-area firms: 2013 EFAMA Asset Management Report, n 1, 35.

[5] AUM subject to discretionary mandates represented 52.8 per cent (€7,275 billion) of total EU AUM at the end of 2011, while AUM subject to collective asset management represented 47.2 per cent (€6,515 billion): 2013 EFAMA Asset Management Report n 1, 15.

[6] Directive 85/611/EC [1985] OJ L375/3 (since repealed). Following a series of reforms, now Directive 2009/65/EU [2009] OJ L302/32, as amended since by the 2014 UCITS V reforms (Council Document

and in relation to a particular form of retail-market-orientated CIS, the Undertaking for Collective Investment in Transferable Securities (UCITS).[7] From then until the financial crisis and the adoption of the 2011 Alternative Investment Fund Managers Directive (2011 AIFMD),[8] the UCITS regulatory regime acted as a proxy for EU collective asset management regulation and policy generally. Although the major pre-crisis review of asset management—the UCITS Review (2004–9)—engaged with wider aspects of collective asset management policy, particularly with respect to alternative (non-UCITS) CISs,[9] the subsequent reform programme focused on the UCITS regime.

The EU's regulation of discretionary asset management has developed separately and as an offshoot of the wider harmonized investment services regulation regime. It was not addressed until some years after the 1985 UCITS Directive, under the 1993 Investment Services Directive.[10] EU regulation of discretionary asset management remains part of the investment services regime generally, under the 2014 Markets in Financial Instruments Directive II (MiFID II)/Markets in Financial Instruments Regulation (MiFIR) regime.[11]

Appropriate calibration and differentiation is essential to good regulatory design in the asset management sphere, given the different risks which different types of asset managers can generate and the very wide variety of asset management business models across the EU industry.[12] But so too is the avoidance of arbitrage and level playing field risks, where rules are calibrated and differentiated but are insufficiently sensitive to functionally similar activities and business models. As this Chapter outlines, the EU has made some progress in this regard. But the incremental and silo-based development of the regime has led to inconsistencies, level playing field difficulties, and an ever more fragmented regime. Even allowing for the functional differences between the different types of asset manager, UCITS collective asset managers, non-UCITS collective asset managers, and discretionary asset managers have been subject to very different regulatory regimes at various stages since 1985. Some degree of convergence has been taking place recently: the regulation of asset managers under the 2011 AIFMD, for example, has been closely based on the related UCITS and investment services/discretionary asset management regimes. But silo-based regulation, and related arbitrage and level playing field risks, remain features of the regime, and in some

---

7411/14, 13 March 2014 (not yet published in the OJ)). The 2014 Directive comes into force in 2016. References to the 2009 UCITS Directive or the UCITS Directive are to the 2009 Directive as amended.

[7] UCITS AUM represent some 70 per cent of EU AUM: ESMA, Report on Trends, Risks and Vulnerabilities. Report No 2 (2013) (ESMA/2013/1138) (ESMA 2013(2) TRV) 49.

[8] Directive 2011/61/EU [2011] OJ L174/1 (the 2011 AIFMD).

[9] The Review culminated in the 2006 Investment Funds White Paper: Commission, White Paper on Enhancing the Single Market Framework for Investment Funds (2006) (COM (2006) 686).

[10] Directive 93/22/EC [2003] OJ L141/27.

[11] Markets in Financial Instruments Directive II 2014/65/EU OJ [2014] L173/349 (2014 MiFID II) and 2014 Markets in Financial Instruments Regulation (EU) No 600/2014 [2014] OJ L173/84 (2014 MiFIR) (on the implementation timeline see Ch IV n 28). The discussion in this Chapter is based on the 2014 MiFID II/MiFIR. The MiFID I regime (n 23), on which the MiFID II/MiFIR regime is based, will be repealed when the MiFID II/MiFIR regime is applied (from 3 January 2017 (MiFID II Art 94 and MiFIR Art 55)). Reference is made to the MiFID I regime as appropriate.

[12] These range from the banking group model, which dominates in most Member States, to the specialist, standalone asset manager model, which is common in the UK and in France: 2013 EFAMA Asset Management Report, n 1, 13. Some 3,100 asset management companies operate across the EU: ECMI and CEPS, Rethinking Asset Management. From Financial Stability to Investor Protection and Economic Growth (2012) (2012 ECMI/CEPS Report) 10–11 and 13.

respects are increasing. The ever-intensifying UCITS regime, for example, threatens to generate arbitrage risks in relation to functionally equivalent non-UCITS CISs subject to lighter regulation.

III.1.1.2 An Intensifying Regime

Prior to the financial crisis, market integration and the effectiveness of the UCITS CIS passport were the main drivers of regulatory intervention in this area, even if the allied rules designed to support the resilience of the UCITS passport (particularly with respect to risk management, and the UCITS manager and depositary) became increasingly dense over the pre-crisis period. The crisis era has seen the UCITS regime expand significantly, with ever more specific rules now applying to a range of different UCITS CISs. The diffuse and far-reaching 2012 UCITS VI reform agenda (sections 3.3.4 and 3.8.7) suggests that the UCITS regime has become something of a laboratory for permanent reform and experimentation, while the enthusiasm of the European Securities and Markets Authority (ESMA) for ever more detailed UCITS risk regulation seems unquenchable. But the crisis-era volume of UCITS regulation sits uneasily with the relative stability of the UCITS sector over the crisis and the very strong industry incentives to protect the UCITS brand.

The crisis era also led to a radical extension of the non-UCITS collective investment regime through the 2011 AIFMD, which addresses all EU (and in certain circumstances non-EU) managers of CISs, unless they come within the UCITS regime, and which has produced a regulatory regime of great depth and breadth. The AIFMD has also, indirectly, led to the adoption of a number of additional and discrete reforms designed to provide regulatory passports for managers of smaller CIS portfolios who come within the scope of the AIFMD but are subject to a lighter regime and do not qualify for the AIFMD passport (section 5).

There is little sign of the reforms abating. The collective asset management regime has been drawn into the Europe 2020 growth agenda and to related reforms (section 3.3.4); the global 'shadow banking' reform agenda is likely to lead to further reforms (section 3.14); and discretionary and collective asset management is likely to become subject to new rules under the EU's wider corporate governance reform agenda.[13]

III.1.2 The Regulation of Collective Asset Management

Collective asset management concerns the management of CISs. A CIS is a form of investment vehicle which pools investors' funds and which delivers returns related to

---

[13] In the closing stages of the Commission and European Parliament crisis-era terms, the Commission presented a proposal for a range of reforms relating to the encouragement of long-term shareholder engagement, including proposed requirements that MiFID, UCITS and AIFMD asset managers be required to adopt 'shareholder engagement policies' governing their voting and oversight responsibilities in relation to investee companies, and to disclose their 'equity investment strategies' and how these strategies contribute to medium/long-term asset performance (COM (2014) 213).

For a regulator's perspective on the ever-intensifying UCITS regime post-crisis, and on the related need to ensure that the execution of the reform programme is effective, see Speech by Gareth Murphy (Head of Markets, Central Bank of Ireland) to the Alternative Investment Management Association Global Policy and Regulatory Forum, 20 March 2013.

pre-set asset-selection and risk-management criteria.[14] While CISs can take myriad forms, three predominant types can be identified. Scheme assets can be owned by a company in which investors are given a share representing their investment. Scheme assets can also be held within a structure without separate legal personality and held by a trustee on behalf of investors.[15] Contractual schemes represent a third form of CIS. They are closely related to the trust structure, in that an independent legal personality is not created on establishment of the scheme. Whatever the structure adopted, risk and asset management by the CIS manager will be separate from the safe-keeping (custody) of the assets by the CIS depositary which will also monitor the manager. The CIS share or unit gives the investor the right to participate in the profits or income which arise from the CIS' investment activities and which form the return on the CIS.

As is discussed further in sections 3 and 4, collective asset management regulation serves a number of objectives, primarily in relation to investor protection and, reflecting the scale of CIS-related trading activity and the related credit and market risks which can be generated, financial stability. In the retail market context, it can additionally be associated with investor engagement and the support of long-term savings.

With respect to regulatory tools, while disclosure is strongly associated with CIS regulation, so too is portfolio regulation, which is akin to product regulation and which addresses asset allocation (including related fund leverage and liquidity levels) by CIS managers. CIS regulation also typically governs the CIS manager and depositary and so includes authorization, conduct, and, increasingly, prudential and related risk-management rules.

The management of CISs in the EU is governed by the 2011 AIFMD. It addresses asset management for all CISs, apart from those authorized under the UCITS Directive; as the UCITS Directive is an opt-in regime, in that CISs and their managers choose to adopt a CIS fund design model which brings them within the UCITS regime, the AIFMD accordingly provides the default regime for collective asset management in the EU. The AIFMD does not, apart from indirectly, regulate CISs; it addresses the manager and the depositary of in-scope CISs. The AIFMD has been amplified by three administrative measures, chief among them the 2013 Commission AIFMD Regulation,[16] and by extensive ESMA supervisory convergence measures (section 4.5). The UCITS Directive, by contrast, focuses closely on the design of the UCITS CIS, although it also regulates the UCITS manager and the UCITS depositary. The UCITS Directive has been amplified by five sets of administrative rules: the 2007 Commission Eligible Assets Directive;[17] the 2010

---

[14] By contrast, packaged investment products, which often act as functional substitutes for retail market-orientated CIS investments, deliver a return related to the structure of the product.

[15] For an examination of the features of a unit trust in the UK industry see Franks, J and Mayer, C, *Risk, Regulation and Investor Protection* (1989) 23–4 and Gray, J, 'Personal Finance and Corporate Governance: The Missing Link: Product Regulation and Policy Conflict' (2004) 4 *JCLS* 187, 201.

[16] Commission Delegated Regulation (EU) No 231/2013 [2013] OJ L83/1 (which amplifies the AIFMD with respect to the operating conditions of in-scope asset managers) (2013 Commission Delegated AIFMD Regulation). The other measures relate to discrete issues: Commission Implementing Regulation (EU) No 448/2013 [2013] OJ L132/3 (aspects of the third country access regime); Commission Implementing Regulation (EU) No 447/2013 [2013] OJ L132/1 (the procedures for managers wishing to 'opt in' to the AIFMD); and Commission Delegated Regulation on Types of AIF (C(2013) 9098).

[17] Commission Directive 2007/16/EC [2007] OJ L79/11. This administrative Directive remains in force although the legislative measure on which it is based, the 1985 UCITS Directive, has been repealed. Provision was made for it to remain in force through a legislative measure.

Commission Management Company Directive;[18] the 2010 Commission Mergers and Master-Feeder Directive;[19] the 2010 Commission Key Investor Information Document (KIID) Regulation;[20] and the 2010 Commission Notification and Information Exchange Regulation.[21] An extensive range of Committee of European Securities Regulators (CESR)/ESMA supervisory convergence measures also apply (section 3.4).

Although this classification is inevitably somewhat blunt, the UCITS regime can be strongly associated with retail market collective asset management and risks; accordingly, it engages closely with the design of the UCITS, and thereby confers a form of regulatory 'label' on the UCITS fund. The AIFMD regime is more closely associated with the professional collective asset management market, alternative investments and, in particular, with financial stability risks—although UCITS regulation has increasingly come to focus on stability risks. As a professional-market-orientated measure, the main concern of the AIFMD is with the management of in-scope schemes, and not with the particular design which these schemes adopt.

III.1.3 The Regulation of Discretionary Asset Management

Discretionary asset management involves the agency management by the asset manager, and in accordance with a discretionary investment mandate, of an individual client's funds and assets (retail and (more typically) institutional[22]); client assets are segregated from those of other clients. Discretionary asset management regulation serves a number of objectives, but is strongly associated with investor protection. The crisis-era focus on the financial stability risks which particular trading practices (whether proprietary or agency in nature) can generate has, however, led to tighter controls on trading generally, including by asset managers.

As an in-scope 'investment service' governed by the 2014 MiFID II, discretionary asset management is governed by the 2014 MiFID II/MiFIR regime. The reach of the EU over the discretionary asset management sphere has been extended to a striking extent since the first suite of rules were adopted in 1993 under the Investment Services Directive, extended under MiFID I,[23] and further refined by the MiFID II/MiFIR reforms.

III.2 Discretionary Asset Management: The 2014 MiFID II Regime

Discretionary asset management is an 'investment service' under the 2014 MiFID II/MiFIR regime and is governed by the extensive 2014 MiFID II requirements for

---

[18] Commission Directive 2010/43/EU [2010] OJ L176/42.
[19] Commission Directive 2010/42/EU [2010] OJ L176/28.
[20] Commission Regulation (EU) No 583/2010 [2010] OJ L176/1.
[21] Commission Regulation (EU) No 584/2010 [2010] OJ L176/16.
[22] 2013 EFAMA Asset Management Report, n 1, 15.
[23] Directive 2004/39/EC [2004] OJ L145/1.

investment services discussed in Chapters IV, VI, and IX.[24] Accordingly, the rules which govern the provision of investment services generally, and in relation to authorization and operating requirements (including conduct rules and prudential rules governing organization, operation, and capital requirements), apply.

Where discretionary asset management services (and identified 'non-core' investment services, including investment advice) are provided by UCITS or AIFMD collective asset managers along with collective asset management services, the 2014 MiFID II regime applies in respect of those services. Both the 2009 UCITS and 2011 AIFMD regimes provide that identified investment services can be provided by the collective asset managers within the scope of each measure, and that the MiFID II regime applies to these services (for example, 2011 AIFMD Article 6(4) and 7(6), and 2009 UCITS Directive Article 6). Revisions to the AIFMD by MiFID II have clarified that where an authorized alternative investment fund manager under the AIFMD (managing EU funds) provides qualifying MiFID II services in another Member State (such as discretionary asset management and/or investment advice), a passport is available. Once the cross-border activity has been appropriately notified, no further host State measures can be imposed (2014 MiFID II Article 92, revising 2011 AIFMD Article 33). These revisions follow some doubt as to the availability of the AIFMD passport, and instances of Member States imposing restrictions, such as requirements for establishment through a separate legal entity.

The 2014 MiFID II regime is designed as a generic investment services regime and does not, for the most part, impose specific requirements on discretionary asset managers. But the risks which investment services pose can become acute in the asset management context, even allowing for the monitoring capacities of the institutional clients which dominate in this segment. Agency costs, arising in particular from conflict-of-interest risk and competence failures,[25] can be significant where an agency mandate is given over discretionary client assets; good client outcomes are accordingly in part dependent on the resilience of MiFID II's generic conduct, asset protection, order handling, best execution, and conflict-of-interest management requirements. The risks are all the more acute for the small segment of (typically high net worth) retail clients who rely on discretionary asset management.[26]

The 2014 MiFID II, like MiFID I, recognizes the scale of the agency risks by imposing suitability requirements on discretionary asset management services (MiFID II Article 25(2)). But otherwise, it contains few requirements specifically targeted to asset management risks.[27] The particular vulnerability of clients to conflict-of-interest risk was,

---

[24] Generally on the harmonized regime which applies to discretionary asset management and the related liability consequences (and on the different national regimes) see Busch, D and De Mott, D (eds), *Liability of Asset Managers* (2012).

[25] Busch, D and de Mott, D, 'Introduction' in Busch and de Mott, n 24, 3, 6, describing the investment management relationship as a 'prototypical principal-agent relationship'.

[26] Research by the UK authorities has not been encouraging and has repeatedly found serious failures in the asset management segment: eg, FSA (Financial Services Authority), Letter to CEOs. Wealth Management Review (2011), reporting on the poor findings of a wealth management review, which included that 79 per cent of files reviewed had a high risk of unsuitability.

[27] Targeted reporting requirements applied under the MiFID I administrative regime, however, and can be expected to be reflected in the new MiFID II administrative regime. A discrete best execution regime is also likely to govern the best execution requirement for asset managers (Ch VI sect 2.2.2).

however, recognized under the MiFID I Review, which led to the (heavily resisted[28]) MiFID II prohibition on discretionary asset managers accepting and retaining fees, commissions, or any monetary or non-monetary benefits paid or provided by a third party in relation to the provision of services to clients (MiFID II Article 24(8)).[29] Whether or not this provision will address the particular conflict of interests which arise in the context of 'softing' and 'bundling' arrangements remains to be seen.[30] The MiFID I Review contained some indications that a more tailored regime for asset management services, focused in particular on appropriate compliance with and senior management oversight of investment mandates, would follow;[31] legislative reforms were not made, however, although the MiFID II administrative rulebook is likely to contain tailored discretionary asset management rules.

III.3 Collective Asset Management: the UCITS Regime

III.3.1 Introduction

Collective asset management regulation in the EU operates under two distinct regimes. This section is concerned with the UCITS regime which, very broadly, is concerned with retail market CISs and their management.[32] The UCITS regime addresses the UCITS CIS as well as the UCITS collective asset manager and depositary.[33] Non-UCITS collective asset management is governed by the 2011 AIFMD, which focuses on the asset manager and the depositary (section 4).

The UCITS regime is based on the 2009 UCITS IV Directive (or UCITS Directive), which Directive consolidates a series of earlier reforms while also imposing new requirements; it has recently been revised by the 2014 UCITS V reforms.[34] The roots of the

---

[28] eg EFAMA Annual Report (2011) 18, warning of the related increase in asset management fees were a prohibition to apply.

[29] A *de minimis* exception applies in that minor non-monetary benefits that are capable of enhancing the quality of the service provided to the client, and which are of a scale and nature that they could not be judged to impair compliance with the investment firm's duty to act in the best interest of the client, should be clearly disclosed but are not subject to the prohibition.

[30] Services provided to the asset manager by brokers may be 'bundled' together in a single fee, usually in the form of a dealing commission which is passed on to the client (services are 'softed' where they are provided through a contractual arrangement between the broker and a third party—which may be an independent research house). Arrangements of this nature can create an artificial bias for asset managers to acquire additional services, which are paid for through opaque dealing commissions which do not make transparent to clients the additional services for which they have paid, and for channelling trading business to particular brokers (thereby threatening best execution). Softing and bundling arrangements can accordingly generate conflicts of interests within the asset manager and raise the costs of fund management for investors. Hitherto, regulation in this sphere has been the preserve of the Member States. Commissions were the subject of major reforms in the UK, eg, which were initiated by the Myners Review: Institutional Investment in the UK: A Review. HM Treasury (2001).

[31] Commission, Consultation on the MiFID I Review (2010) 69.

[32] As noted below, the investor base of the UCITS CIS is broadly retail. Retail market exposure to UCITS investment is, however, often intermediated through institutional investment in UCITSs.

[33] For more extensive treatment of UCITS regulation see further Moloney, N, *How to Protect Investors. Lessons from the EC and the UK* (2010) 152–79.

[34] n 6.

UCITS IV regime lie in the original 1985 UCITS Directive[35] which was repeatedly revised, most significantly by the two 2003 'UCITS III' reforms.[36] As noted in section 1.2, the UCITS Directive has been amplified by five sets of administrative rules.[37] It has also been revised by the 2010 Omnibus I Directive[38] (to reflect the establishment of ESMA[39] and the Lisbon Treaty settlement relating to administrative rule-making[40]). The crisis-era reform programme led to two further reform streams—the UCITS V reforms (now adopted) and the UCITS VI reforms (section 3.8.7).

III.3.2 Rationale for and Forms of Retail Market CIS Regulation

III.3.2.1 The Rationale for Regulating Retail Market CISs and CIS Management

The regulation of retail market CISs has a strong investor protection orientation, reflecting the still burgeoning scale of the CIS industry[41] and the related central role CISs have played in intermediating household funds and in thereby institutionalizing the retail/household investment market.[42] Retail market CISs, such as UCITSs, offer a number of advantages to retail investors. CIS investment can address the behavioural weaknesses from which retail investors suffer (see Chapter IX) as it involves the delegation of decision-making to the CIS manager.[43] CIS trading costs, particularly for passive schemes, are lower than direct trading costs.[44] Schemes can support diversification,[45] particularly where they offer international portfolios, and can facilitate retail investor access to higher-risk/higher-return schemes.

---

[35] n 6.

[36] Directive 2001/107/EC [2002] OJ L41/20 and Directive 2001/108/EC [2002] OJ L141/35.

[37] Each as noted in nn 17–21.

[38] Directive 2010/78/EU [2010] OJ L331/120.

[39] The reforms confer a range of delegations for administrative rule-making on the Commission which also empower ESMA to propose related RTSs and ITSs, primarily with respect to the content of different notifications and with respect to information exchange, but also with respect to specifying the conditions of application of the administrative rules to be adopted by the Commission under the extensive 2009 UCITS IV Directive delegations. The reforms also require national competent authorities (NCAs) to co-operate with ESMA (and impose related ESMA notification obligations on NCAs) and apply ESMA's binding mediation powers (Ch XI sect 5.3.1) to failures by NCAs to co-operate.

[40] See Ch X sect 4.

[41] For pre-crisis analysis see Choi, S and Kahan, M, 'The Market Penalty for Mutual Fund Scandals' (2007) 87 *Boston University LR* 1021, Khorana, A, Servaes, H, and Tufano, P, Explaining the Size of the Mutual Fund Industry Around the World, Harvard NOM WP No 03-23 (2004), available at <http://ssrn/abstract=573503> and, in the US context, Mahoney, P, 'Manager Investor Conflicts in Mutual Funds' (2004) 18 *J of Econ Perspectives* 161 (the latter pointing to the dramatic increase in mutual fund investment between World War II ($1.2 billion) and 2002 ($6 trillion)). For a crisis-era analysis of the scale of fund intermediation, see Zingales, L, 'The Future of Securities Regulation' (2009) 47 *J of Accounting Research* 391.

[42] Langevoort, D, 'The SEC, Retail Investors, and the Institutionalization of the Securities Markets' (2009) 95 *Va LR* 1025, eg, and Deaves, R, Dine, C, and Horton, W, How Are Investment Decisions Made, Research Report prepared for the Task Force to Modernize Securities Legislation in Canada. Evolving Investor Protection (2006) (2006 Deaves Report).

[43] eg Barber, B, Lee, Y-T, Liu, Y-J, and Odean, T, 'Just How Much Do Individual Investors Lose by Trading' (2009) 22 *Rev of Financial Studies* 609 and Choi, S and Pritchard, A, 'Behavioural Economics and the SEC' (2003) 56 *Stanford LR* 1.

[44] French, K, 'Presidential Address: The Cost of Active Investing' (2008) 63 *J Fin* 1537.

[45] eg Jackson, H, 'To what Extent Should Individual Investors Rely on the Mechanisms of Market Efficiency: A Preliminary Investigation of Dispersion in Investor Returns' (2003) 28 *J Corp Law* 671 and Freeman, J and Brown, S, 'Mutual Fund Advisory Fees: The Costs of Conflicts of Interests' (2001) 26 *J Corp Law* 609.

Intermediation through a CIS can also mitigate the risks of counterparty failure, particularly with respect to bond investments. Retail investors can also benefit from the liquidity advantages of CIS and related easy redemption, particularly through investing in open-ended CISs which allow redemption on request by investors at a price related to the scheme's net asset value (NAV).[46]

CIS regulation has accordingly typically reflected two rationales. The first is reactive in nature, and relates to the distinct investor protection risks generated by intermediation through CISs and by the related agency costs.[47] These risks relate to, *inter alia*, the potential for the extraction of benefits by CIS managers (by means of, for example, excessive costs and abusive trading practices),[48] incompetence in asset management, and fraudulent diversion of assets from the CIS.[49] In addition, retail investors can face liquidity and redemption risks in realizing their investments and can struggle to decode often complex CIS disclosures (section 3.11). The risks also extend down the CIS distribution chain and include related conflict-of-interest and competence risks in CIS sales and advice.

CIS regulation accordingly typically deploys asset-allocation rules (or portfolio-shaping rules) which, by addressing risk management and diversification, attempt to address the agency risks which cannot be efficiently addressed through disclosure or by private contracting.[50] Asset-allocation rules also, in the case of open-ended funds,[51] support CIS liquidity and the related ability of the scheme to meet redemptions by investors. CIS regulation similarly typically addresses the valuation and redemption of CIS assets. The structure of the CIS and, in particular, the separation of fund management and custody are also typically subject to regulation, while prudential and conduct-of-business regulation of the fund manager and of the custodian/depositary, as well as disclosure rules, are common.

Second, CIS regulation has also, reflecting the extent to which household investment internationally has become institutionalized through CIS investments, become associated with the increasingly proactive regulatory efforts to promote long-term market-based saving by households. A recurring feature of the policy debate on household investment is the extent to which retail investors should (or should be encouraged or even compelled to)[52] access the markets through lower-cost, diversified, and passive (index-tracking) CISs.[53]

---

[46] Current net asset value is the current market value of the scheme's portfolio divided by the number of units outstanding.

[47] eg Frankel, T and Cunningham, L, 'The Mysterious Ways of Mutual Funds: Market Timing' (2006) 25 *Annual Rev of Banking and Financial L* 235 and Mahoney n 41. From earlier discussions see Jackson, H, 'Regulation in a Multi-sectored Financial Services Industry: an Exploration Essay' (1999) 77 *Washington University LQ* 319, Clark, R, 'The Four Stages of Capitalism' (1981) 94 *Harv LR* 561 and Clark, R, 'The Soundness of Financial Intermediaries' (1976) 86 *Yale LJ* 1.

[48] See generally Frankel and Cunningham, n 47 and McCallum, J, 'Mutual Fund Market Timing: A Tale of Systemic Abuse and Executive Malfeasance' (2004) 12 *JFRC* 170.

[49] eg Gray, n 15.

[50] Jackson, n 47 and Palmiter, A, 'The Mutual Fund Board: A Failed Experiment in Regulatory Outsourcing' (2006) *Brooklyn J of Corporate, Financial, and Commercial L* 165.

[51] On open-ended funds see sect 3.5.2.

[52] One analysis has suggested that retail investors be corralled into tracker schemes: Choi, S, 'Regulating Investors not Issuers: A Market-Based Proposal' (2000) 88 *California LR* 279. Less radically, it has been suggested that the benefits of CIS investment are such that broker/investor contracts for direct investment should contain a risk warning as to the risks of direct investment: Zingales, n 41.

[53] From an extensive and primarily US scholarship see, eg, Roiter, E, 'Delivering Fiduciary Services to Middle and Working Class Investors' (2004) 23 *Annual Rev of Banking and Financial Law* 851, Jackson, n 45,

Similarly, the asset-allocation/portfolio regulation element of CIS regulation affords the regulator the opportunity to steer retail investors towards asset allocations which hedge against market risk.[54]

The financial stability implications of CISs and CIS management have come to the fore over the crisis era. This is most marked with respect to alternative investment CISs and their management (section 4) but has also had implications for retail-focused CISs, particularly exchange traded funds (ETFs) (section 3.14.2).

III.3.2.2 The EU and Retail Market CIS Regulation

The EU's regulation of the UCITS CIS reflects these rationales, but, as with EU securities and markets regulation generally, must also be placed in the context of the driving market integration imperative.

Although the investor base of the EU asset management industry generally is largely institutional,[55] the UCITS CIS is strongly associated with retail investment.[56] Some 10 per cent of EU households hold UCITS investments, and some 90 per cent of the UCITS investor base, directly and indirectly (through, for example, pension funds and life insurance policies), is estimated to be constituted by households.[57]

But although the EU regards the UCITS as a retail market product, it has only recently engaged closely with investor protection in its regulation of the UCITS market; market integration has long been the driving concern. The 1985 UCITS regime was designed as a supply-side measure and to support cross-border UCITS marketing; it was crafted long before the retail market had impinged seriously on EU policy and regulation, as is clear from the regime's very limited approach to retail market disclosure (section 3.11). The drive to support long-term savings and private pension provision through CIS/UCITS investment is also relatively new, being associated with the Financial Services Action Plan (FSAP) era in particular.[58]

Ribstein, L, 'Bubble Laws' (2003) 40 *Houston LR* 77, and Langevoort, D, 'Selling Hope. Selling Risk. Some Lessons from Behavioural Economics about Stockbrokers and Sophisticated Investors' (1996) 84 *California LR* 627.

[54] Hu, H, 'Illiteracy and Intervention: Wholesale Derivatives, Retail Mutual Funds, and the Matter of Asset Class' (1996) 84 *Georgetown LJ* 2319, 2378.

[55] With institutional investors accounting for 75 per cent of total AUM: 2013 EFAMA Asset Management Report, n 1, 3.

[56] Although not to the same extent as in the US, where the first-time equity investors—'the ones on training wheels and especially deserving of regulatory attention'—are far more likely to invest in equity mutual funds than in individual shares: Hu, H, 'The New Portfolio Society, SEC Mutual Fund Disclosure and the Public Corporation Model' (2005) 60 *Business Lawyer* 1303, 1307.

[57] Commission, 2012 UCITS V Proposal Impact Assessment (SWD (2012) 185) 21 and 37 and ESMA 2013(2) TRV, n 7, 49. The popularity of UCITSs as household investments varies significantly across the Member States, however. Some 6 per cent of UK households, eg, hold UCITSs as investments, as compared to 16 per cent in Germany (2012 UCITS V Proposal Impact Assessment, Annex, 3).

[58] eg, Interim Report of the Financial Services Committee Subgroup on the Implications of Ageing Populations for Financial Markets, FSC 4180/06 (October 2006). Similarly, the 2005 Investment Funds Green Paper argued that an integrated and efficient EU CIS market could contribute significantly to retirement provisioning: Commission, Green Paper on the Enhancement of the EU Framework for Investment Funds (2005) (COM (2005) 314) 3 and 16. The 2006 Investment Funds White Paper built on this theme, and argued that European investors needed a capable and well-regulated asset management industry to meet the long-term financing needs of an ageing population: n 9, 2.

The extent to which market integration has long been the dominant concern of the regime is well illustrated by the 2001 UCITS III extensions to the previously restrictive UCITS asset-allocation regime, which were designed to allow the UCITS industry to expand, but which brought investor protection risks (section 3.8). Similarly, although the 2009 UCITS IV reforms introduced a raft of significant investor protection measures, chief among them the retail-orientated KIID, they also sought to support pan-EU UCITS industry organization and related economies of scale. More generally, and reflecting the link between the depth of CIS/institutional investor (including UCITS) activity and the health of market finance in the EU,[59] the promotion of a vibrant cross-border UCITS market has long been closely associated with the promotion of market finance and with the related development of a deep and liquid EU capital market.[60]

III.3.3 The Evolution of the UCITS Regime

III.3.3.1 Early Developments

The potential of CISs as agents to stimulate and integrate the European capital market was noted by the Segré Report in 1966. Identifying a shortage of capital and, in particular, 'the inadequate supplies of capital from private investors', the Report recognized that 'institutional investors are best suited to manage the savings of a large section of the public with no practical experience of direct and judicious investment in securities', but reported that these institutional investors were hindered in attracting public funds by regulation and needed to be stimulated if the equity markets, in particular, were to attract the savings of the public at large.[61] Disclosure was a key component of the nascent regulatory agenda.[62]

By 1976, CISs with a corporate structure were operating in Denmark, France, Luxembourg, and the Netherlands. Of these Member States, only France applied discrete regulation; other Member States simply relied on general company law. CISs without a corporate structure operated in most of the Member States. These CIS vehicles typically consisted of a management company, a depositary which acted as custodian of the scheme assets, and a fund which collected the funds invested by unit-holders. They were subject to specific regulation in Germany, Belgium, France, and the United Kingdom.[63]

---

[59] eg, Levine, R, 'Financial Development and Economic Growth: Views and Agenda' (1997) 35 *J of Econ Lit* 688, 699. Similarly, Black, B, 'The Legal and Institutional Preconditions for Strong Securities Markets' (2001) 48 *University of California LR* 781, 801. CISs have also been associated with the development of emerging market economies and, in particular, have been used as the vehicle for delivering privatization programmes. See, generally, International Organization of Securities Commissions (IOSCO), Collective Investment Schemes in Emerging Markets (2006).

[60] See, eg, the analysis in the Initial Report of the Committee of Wise Men on the Regulation of European Securities Markets (2000) (the Initial Lamfalussy Report) 5. Subsequently, the 2006 Financial Integration Monitor pointed to a positive correlation between the development of equity funds and equity markets across the EU: Commission, Financial Integration Monitor (2006) (SEC (2006) 1057) 19–21.

[61] Report by a Group of Experts Appointed by the EEC Commission, The Development of a European Capital Market (1966).

[62] n 61, 207–8.

[63] See further Scott Quinn, B, 'EC Securities Markets Regulation' in Steil, B (ed), *International Financial Market Regulation* (1994) 121, 148.

The Commission first presented a proposal for the harmonization of CIS regulation in 1976.[64] While the Proposal is now of historical interest only, its approach to market integration remains striking. Member States could not apply 'any provisions whatsoever' to CISs situated in another Member State. In a very early example of mutual recognition, Member States were required to permit schemes authorized in another Member State in accordance with the proposal's requirements to operate within their territory without further regulation, except for local marketing rules. Although there was some institutional support,[65] the proposal languished for some time while the measures which formed the foundations of the prospectus regime (Chapter II) slowly came into force.

By 1985, however, the single market programme had intervened. The 1985 Internal Market White Paper[66] observed that, with respect to 'participation in collective investment schemes', along with other 'financial products' such as mortgages and insurance policies, 'it should be possible to facilitate the exchange of such "financial products" at Community level, using a minimal co-ordination of rules (especially on such matters as authorization, financial supervision and reorganization, winding up, etc) as the basis for mutual recognition by Member States of what each does to safeguard the interests of the public'.[67] The first UCITS Directive was finally adopted in December 1985 and was to be implemented by the Member States by October 1989.

III.3.3.2 The FSAP and the UCITS III Reforms

Notwithstanding the 1985 introduction of the UCITS passport, integration of the UCITS market was slow.[68] This was partly due to diverging practices in the European fund industry, which still persist. To take one example, different investment policies were pursued by UCITSs across the various national lines. In the UK, for example, CISs tended to invest more heavily in equities, in Germany fixed-interest securities were the dominant form of investment, while in France money-market funds were dominant.[69] The varying structures which could (and can) be adopted by UCITSs also slowed the process of integration, as investors tended to be suspicious of unfamiliar structures. Dissatisfaction also arose with the UCITS Directive as an integration vehicle. The investment restrictions placed on UCITSs (which limited investment opportunities to investments in transferable securities) prevented the CIS industry and investors from fully exploiting the benefits of the

---

[64] [1976] OJ C171/1, Explanatory Memorandum at COM (76) 152. The proposal was lightly amended by COM (77) 277. CISs were not covered in the foundation Commission Recommendation 77/534/EEC concerning a European Code of Conduct relating to transactions in transferable securities [1977] OJ L212/37.

[65] [1977] OJ C57/31 (European Parliament) and [1977] OJ C75/10 (Economic and Social Committee (ECOSOC) (now EESC)), although neither institution gave the proposal a ringing endorsement and both were concerned as to the thin level of harmonization.

[66] Completing the Internal Market (COM (85) 310) (the 1985 Internal Market White Paper).

[67] n 66, para 102.

[68] Although the adoption of the UCITS Directive had significantly raised expectations. On the passing of the implementation deadline in October 1989, it was heralded as 'the first tangible indication of a single European market in retail financial services': Poser, N, *International Securities Regulation. London's Big Bang and the European Securities Markets* (1991) 364.

[69] Overall, across the EU CISs investing in debt securities formed the largest group: Gros, D and Lannoo, K, *The Euro Capital Market* (2000) 67.

UCITS passport and of CISs as investment vehicles. Variations in the implementation of the Directive also emerged, increasing industry costs.[70]

In 1993 the Commission presented a proposal to extend the scope of the 1985 UCITS Directive.[71] After widespread industry consultation, the Commission issued a revised proposal to amend the Directive in 1994.[72] The main concern of the revisions was asset allocation by UCITSs, and the extension of the previously restrictive asset-allocation regime to allow UCITSs to invest in, *inter alia*, deposits with credit institutions up to 25 per cent of the value of scheme assets. In addition, three new categories of UCITS were added. These were: cash funds, investing solely in deposits with credit institutions; funds of funds, investing solely in units of other UCITSs; and master-feeder funds, investing solely in the units of a single UCITS. Little progress was made in the Council where the provisions on feeder funds and cash funds proved controversial, and the proposal ultimately foundered.

The adequacy of the 1985 Directive's supervision of the management companies entrusted with UCITS asset management but subject only to minimal regulation under the 1985 Directive also came under scrutiny. With the adoption of the Investment Services Directive (ISD) in 1993, and the introduction of an embryonic discretionary asset management regime, it became obvious that the regulation of UCITS collective asset managers, particularly with respect to authorization and operating standards, was out of kilter with the regulation of investment firms generally. Market integration and level playing field risks were also generated, as UCITS management companies were ineligible for the ISD passport (as collective asset managers) and were not conferred with a passport under the 1985 UCITS regime.

Progress on a proposal to amend the 1985 Directive remained stalled for some time, until 1998, when the Commission presented two proposals—one focusing on the UCITS scheme and extending the range of funds which could benefit from the UCITS passport through more liberal asset-allocation rules, the other addressing the UCITS manager as well as the UCITS prospectus and short-form disclosure. In the 1999 FSAP, the Commission highlighted progress on the UCITS reforms as an urgent political priority in the interests of maximizing the ability of investors to exploit the benefits of the single market.[73] Both related Directives (together, the 'UCITS III' reforms)[74] were finally adopted in 2003.

III.3.3.3 Post-FSAP and the UCITS Review

The UCITS sphere is notable as the only major sector which experienced reform and review over the otherwise quiet post-FSAP and pre-crisis period. As the FSAP era drew to a close, the UCITS regime was very broadly regarded as successful.[75] The UCITS industry enjoyed

---

[70] Although not all commentators agreed. It was observed that, by contrast with the admission to official listing/public offer regime, 'the harmonised legal regime has worked for unit trusts': n 69, 34.

[71] COM (93) 37.

[72] COM (94) 329.

[73] Commission, Financial Services: Implementing the Framework for Financial Markets: Action Plan (1999) (COM (1999) 232) 3.

[74] n 36.

[75] It was described, at the time, as a 'recognized global label of quality and investor protection': Asset Management Expert Group Report, Financial Services Action Plan: Progress and Prospects (2004) 8.

a strong reputation: '[f]rom an investor protection perspective, there have not been notable financial scandals involving UCITS. UCITS has provided a solid underpinning for a well-regulated and generally well-managed fund industry.'[76]

But a series of risks were emerging which were reflected in the post-FSAP review of the UCITS regime. The 2009 UCITS IV Directive emerged from an extensive review process which, at the time, represented a landmark in EU regulatory reform due to its sophistication. Starting in 2004 with the report of the Asset Management Expert Group,[77] the review process included extensive discussion of the UCITS regime in the European Securities Committee[78] and in the Parliament,[79] reports from specialist working groups,[80] a number of studies to examine trends in the asset management industry generally and to quantify potential cost savings,[81] as well as a specialist series of workshops on reform of UCITS disclosure. A 2005 Commission Green Paper[82] led to further extensive consultation[83] and to the Commission's agenda-setting 2006 Investment Funds White Paper.[84] The White Paper was followed by a suite of 'Initial Orientations' designed to serve as the basis for public consultation on how specific White Paper reforms might proceed, and which included impact assessments, discussion of rationales, and draft legislative proposals.[85]

The UCITS Review revealed a series of difficulties with the UCITS regime, particularly on the supply side. Scale efficiencies and cost reductions were prejudiced by a proliferation of small funds and obstacles to funds merging. The requirement under the UCITS Directive that the depositary be located in the same Member State as the UCITS fund, and restrictions on the cross-border activities of management companies, obstructed the construction of efficient pan-EU organizational structures. Significant delays and obstructions in the notification procedure (a precondition for cross-border marketing) for authorized UCITSs handicapped the UCITS in competing with other investment products. The 2006 CRA study on cost savings pointed to consequent poor exploitation of economies of scale,

---

[76] 2005 Investment Funds Green Paper, n 58, 3. In response, the leading consumer stakeholder FIN-USE noted that this could not be taken as a guarantee for the future, given the increased complexity of the UCITS industry: FIN-USE, Opinion on the European Commission Green Paper (2005) 5.

[77] n 75.

[78] eg, the European Securities Committee Minutes of 3 March 2005 contain an extensive report on trends and risks in the UCITS industry and on UCITS review. The Committee advises the Commission on administrative rule-making (see Chapter X sect 4).

[79] eg, European Parliament, Klinz I Report on Asset Management to the Committee on Economic and Monetary Affairs, 26 April 2006 (A6-0106/2006).

[80] Including: Asset Management Expert Group Report, n 75, Report of the Expert Group on Investment Fund Market Efficiency (2006); Report of the Alternative Investment Expert Group Report, Managing, Servicing, and Marketing Hedge Funds in Europe (2006), and Report of the Alternative Investment Expert Group, Developing Private Equity (2006).

[81] The study on industry trends had two elements: (i) Oxera, Current Trends in Asset Management (2006) and (ii) ZEW/OEE, Current Trends in the European Asset Management Industry (2006). A second study was commissioned on costs: CRA International, Potential Cost Savings in a Fully Integrated European Investment Fund Industry (2006).

[82] n 58.

[83] The results are summarized in the Commission's February 2006 Feedback Statement. Enhancing the European Framework for Investment Funds (2006), which regarded the high level of market engagement as impressive.

[84] n 9. It was accompanied by a detailed Impact Assessment (COM (2006) 686).

[85] Commission, Initial Orientations of Possible Adjustments to the UCITS Directive (March 2007). They reflected the White Paper's priorities and covered the UCITS notification procedure, the management company passport, asset pooling, the simplified prospectus, and supervision.

and highlighted fund distribution as the industry segment most lacking in competitive efficiencies.[86] The 2006 Oxera study similarly pointed to the costs imposed on the industry by regulatory requirements, chief among them the notification process.[87] The 2004 Asset Management Group Report,[88] which also highlighted the inefficiencies deriving from the regulatory framework, called for a range of related reforms, including simplified UCITS registration, facilitation of cross-border fund mergers, recognition of asset-pooling techniques and structures, an effective management company passport, greater freedom of choice for depositaries, facilitation of fund operation and administration, the removal of tax discrimination, and careful implementation of the generic MiFID I investment advice/distribution regime to support efficient and competitive UCITS distribution to investors. The 2006 Investment Funds White Paper, which enjoyed widespread market support,[89] similarly acknowledged that core elements of the UCITS regime were not functioning effectively, compliance costs were too high, the regulatory structure was inflexible, and the resulting inefficiencies were increasing costs and reducing returns.[90]

While industry inefficiencies were increasing the costs to investors, investor protection risks were also intensifying. As discussed in section 3.8, the UCITS III reforms had loosened the original asset-allocation restrictions, generating related risks to investor protection. Arbitrage risks also began to emerge as product providers sought to take advantage of the EU's silo-based product regime, which imposed the highest level of regulation on the UCITS CIS 'product' but lower levels of regulation on functionally similar investment products, such as unit-linked life insurance contracts, investment certificates, and structured products. Serious difficulties also emerged with the inefficient and inappropriate summary retail market prospectus (section 3.11).

Ultimately, the Commission's multifaceted review process yielded dividends, with the Commission reporting on a 'broad base of support' for its reforms across industry, investors, and regulators.[91] A reforming Proposal was presented in 2008[92] which was designed to deliver efficiencies in UCITS structures and in pan-EU distribution[93] by means of a new merger process, and by permitting asset pooling by funds through UCITS 'master-feeder' structures. It also proposed that the cumbersome UCITS notification process be revised and that the UCITS supervision framework, by now badly outdated in comparison with key FSAP measures, be updated. The Proposal also provided for a new

---

[86] n 81, 13.

[87] 2006 Oxera Report, n 81, Executive Summary, iii.

[88] n 75.

[89] Laitner, S and Burgess, K, 'New Rules to Update Europe's Asset Fund Market', *Financial Times*, 17 November 2006, 8.

[90] 2006 Investment Funds White Paper, n 9, 3.

[91] Commission, Preparation of Amendments to the UCITS Directive. Summary of Stakeholder Responses to Commission Exposure Draft (September 2007) 1. However, only 9 per cent of the responses came from investors' associations, compared with 61 per cent from industry sources.

[92] The main publicly available elements of the UCITS IV legislative history are: Commission Proposal, COM (2008) 458/3 (the 2008 UCITS IV Proposal), Impact Assessment at SEC (2008) 264; report by the Economic and Monetary Affairs (ECON) Committee, 2 December 2008 (A6-0479/2008) (2008 ECON Report), on which the Parliament's negotiating position was based; and First/Single Reading and Parliament Position, 13 January 2009 (T6-0012/2009).

[93] The Proposal noted that the Directive was excessively constraining and prevented UCITS managers from fully exploiting development opportunities and that 'estimated potential annual savings amount to several billion euros': 2008 UCITS IV Proposal, n 92, 2.

short-form disclosure document for the retail market—the KIID. The complexities associated with the new management company passport, however, led to it being excluded from the Proposal (section 3.7). Following a relatively smooth legislative process,[94] the end of which coincided with the start of the financial crisis, the 2009 UCITS IV Directive was adopted in January 2009. It was to be adopted by July 2011.

The UCITS IV reforms are strongly supply-side in orientation, being designed to facilitate cross-border UCITS activity by means of more efficient cross-border notification procedures, making asset pooling available through a scheme merger process, supporting a more effective UCITS business chain (in particular through a passport for management companies), and enhancing supervision. They are also designed to support investor choice: the rationalization of schemes through the new mergers process, for example, is designed to make investor choice easier and to reduce confusion.[95] In this enlarged UCITS market, investor protection has also been enhanced through the new KIID short-form disclosure document, designed for retail investors, as well as by the extensive new conduct and prudential rulebook which now applies to UCITS management companies. The reforms have not, however, been entirely successful, with administrative barriers and structural obstacles still a feature of the UCITS market,[96] and further UCITS VI reforms likely.

III.3.3.4 Post UCITS IV and the Crisis Era: the Financial Stability Agenda and the Growth Agenda

The crisis era has led to further radical change to the UCITS regime and to a state of almost permanent regulatory revolution.

The Commission had faced diametrically opposed policy options over the UCITS Review: (i) to engage in a radical overhaul of the UCITS regime which would dismantle the UCITS-based strategy and introduce a general risk-based regime for all CIS investment, or (ii) to engage in incremental and targeted reform of specific supply and demand-side inefficiencies in the UCITS regime.[97] It became clear early on that the Commission did not have the appetite for a radical overhaul of the regime.[98] While it is difficult to unpick the rationale for the Commission's approach—and whether to characterize it as an example of regulatory restraint or a failure of nerve—it certainly reflects a degree of pragmatism, as a major overhaul would have taken considerable time and political effort at a time of post-FSAP strain.[99] The UCITS Review did, however, see some discussion of CIS regulation more generally, particularly with respect to the treatment of non-UCITS alternative investment funds. But it would take the financial crisis for the CIS agenda to be re-opened and more radical reform considered. As discussed in section 4, an entirely new regulatory regime now

---

[94] The revisions and amendments were largely concerned with clarifying and simplifying the Commission's proposals for fund mergers and master/feeder structures. The most significant revisions related to the late introduction of the management company passport during trilogue negotiations (sect 3.7).

[95] 2008 UCITS IV Proposal Impact Assessment, n 92, 32.

[96] KPMG, The Perfect UCITS (2012) 20–3.

[97] Industry views were also divided: Norman, P, 'Tweak the Old Banger or Overhaul the Lot', *Financial Times, Fund Management Supplement*, 14 February 2004, 7.

[98] 2005 Investment Funds Green Paper, n 58, 4. The Commission reported to the European Securities Committee that there were not sufficient compelling reasons to rewrite the UCITS Directive but that targeted adjustments were needed urgently: European Securities Committee Minutes, 14 March 2007.

[99] This was also the view of the European Parliament's Klinz I Report (n 79), which supported targeted legislative reform.

applies to the management of non-UCITS CIS. But the crisis also led to sweeping reforms to the UCITS regime.

The UCITS industry performed relatively well over the crisis,[100] despite the exposure of some UCITSs to money-market instruments, collateralized debt obligations, and derivatives, and the outflow of funds from the CIS segment to the discretionary asset management segment.[101] Scheme losses and outflows were, however, significant from the outset of the financial crisis,[102] retail investors sustained heavy losses, and the money-market funds which represent 15 per cent of UCITS assets were, like their US counterparts, heavily affected[103] (see further section 3.14.1 on money-market funds). Although AUM are recovering towards 2007 levels, confidence has been slow to return to the sector.[104] But very few EU schemes closed (four),[105] only a few suspended redemption (12, of which four re-opened) and the investors affected were predominantly institutions and high net worth individuals.[106] The financial crisis also saw schemes raise liquidity levels, focus on counterparty risk and on operational resilience, particularly with respect to depositary functions, and shift to less risky assets in certain cases.[107] Internationally and in the EU, the regulatory reform programme has acknowledged that the CIS industry generally (and in the EU, the UCITS segment specifically) was not excessively leveraged and did not play a major role in the financial crisis.[108]

UCITS reform has nonetheless been swift and wide-ranging, and so underlines the momentum of the crisis-era reform period. The 2014 UCITS V reforms to the 2009 UCITS IV Directive[109] can be strongly associated with the financial crisis in two respects.

---

[100] ESMA 2013(2) TRV, n 7, 50, describing the UCITS segment as being resilient over the crisis, and noting the return of most of the industry to positive returns. Earlier, the Commission suggested that the UCITS regulatory framework had 'proved very resilient' and reported that no more than a handful of UCITS schemes closed or suspended trading: Commission, Press Release 26 January 2009 (IP/09/126). Similarly, bar those few UCITSs associated with the Madoff fraud, 'the UCITS structure has proved scandal-free during the severe ructions of the past 18 months': Johnson, S and Aboulian, B, 'Convergence Strategy Under Threat', *Financial Times, Fund Management Supplement*, 16 March 2009, 1. The German NCA (BaFIN) also noted the limited impact of the crisis on retail UCITS schemes (BaFIN, Annual Report 2007–2008, 164), although the French NCA (the AMF) focused on risk controls and the quality of disclosure (Annual Report 2007, 3).

[101] Associated with the generally more risk-averse approach taken under discretionary asset management mandates: 2013 EFAMA Asset Management Report, n 1, 15.

[102] By the third quarter of 2007, net outflows represented one third of total sales from the beginning of the year, with bond schemes most heavily affected: CESR, Annual Report (2007) 19.

[103] EFAMA, Annual Report (2007–2008) 12.

[104] n 1.

[105] Johnson, S, 'UCITS Outflows Soar in Q3', *Financial Times, Fund Management Supplement*, 1 December 2008, 2, reporting on some rationalization and cost-cutting, but that the industry remained broadly robust.

[106] EFAMA, Annual Report (2007–2008) 9.

[107] n 106, at 10 and 11.

[108] eg, 2012 ECMI/CEPS Report, n 12, 29, noting IMF and World Bank data on the moderate levels of leverage across the asset management sector generally, and the significantly lower level of leverage in the sector as compared to the banking sector. The de Larosière Report's recommendations in relation to CISs, eg, were largely limited to a tightening of the asset-allocation rules applicable to money-market funds to protect against liquidity, credit, and market risks, and to addressing the Madoff-related depositary and custodian problems: The High Level Group on Financial Supervision in the EU, Report (2009) (the DLG Report).

[109] The UCITS V reform (n 6) was agreed, following trilogue discussions, in February 2014. The main publicly available elements of the legislative history are: Commission Proposal COM (2012) 350/2, Impact Assessment, n 57, 5; European Parliament Negotiating Position, 3 July 2013 (T7-0309/2013), and Council General Approach, 2 December 2013 (Council Document 17095/13).

First, they address the specific risks which arose with respect to the crisis-era Madoff failure and in relation to depositary liability (section 3.10). Second, the stability-related, crisis-era 2011 AIFMD reforms for non-UCITS collective asset management were influential on the UCITS V reforms. Developed under very different conditions, and with very different drivers from the largely retail-focused UCITS regime, the AIFMD has put in place a sophisticated suite of rules addressing, for the most part, the management of higher-risk CISs designed for the professional market, and directed to the support of financial stability. But it thereby exposed some gaps in the parallel UCITS regime. The UCITS V reforms are accordingly designed to align the UCITS regime with the AIFMD regime in some respects, notably in relation to the detailed depositary rules adopted under the AIFMD (albeit with calibrations to reflect the retail investor base of UCITS schemes); the depositary alignment also reflects the Madoff scandal. Similarly, the AIFMD executive remuneration regime, designed to control the risks to financial stability arising from excessive risk-taking in AIFMD-scope schemes, is being applied to UCITS schemes. The remuneration alignment reform also reflects the G20 commitment to link executive remuneration with effective risk management, which has been implemented through the 2013 Capital Requirements Directive IV (CRD IV)/Capital Requirements Regulation (CRR) and the 2011 AIFMD reforms in the EU.[110] But while UCITS III schemes, in particular, can be very similar in practice to AIFMD-scope schemes, many UCITS schemes are conservative and focused on traditional asset classes, and have much less potential for excessive risk-taking—and detailed risk-management rules apply to the more complex UCITS funds. The extent to which alignment was required is not accordingly clear, particularly with respect to the contested remuneration rules. The regulatory arbitrage possibilities became significant, however, once the 2011 AIFMD regime was in place. The UCITS V reforms also provided EU legislators with the opportunity to align the UCITS sanctioning and enforcement regime with the new approach to sanctioning which was adopted over the crisis (section 3.13.4).

The UCITS VI reform process (section 3.8.7), launched in July 2012,[111] may lead to further stability-related reforms. It is closely associated with the wider international regulatory agenda on shadow banking and on the treatment of securities repurchasing (repo) transactions and money-market funds. But it also addresses asset allocation and risk management more generally, particularly in relation to derivatives. The current dominance of the crisis-era financial stability agenda is perhaps best exemplified by the consideration being given under the UCITS VI agenda to allowing exceptions to the fundamental UCITS 'redemption on demand' right (which is central to UCITS design) where liquidity and stability pressures arise.

In parallel with the financial stability reform strand, the crisis era has also seen UCITS policy (and CIS policy generally) form part of the EU's wider growth agenda,[112] particularly

---

[110] 2012 UCITS V Proposal Impact Assessment, n 57, 7–8. See further sect 4.9 on the AIFMD remuneration regime and Ch IV sect 8.6 on the CRD IV/CRR remuneration requirements for investment firms.

[111] Commission, UCITS. Product Rules, Liquidity Management, Depositary, Money Market Funds and Long-term Investments (2012) (the 2012 UCITS VI Consultation).

[112] The Europe 2020 Growth Strategy has a number of elements. The Innovation Union strand, eg, identifies the CIS industry, and particularly the venture capital segment, as a means of supporting access to finance for innovative firms.

with respect to the funding of small and medium-sized enterprises (SMEs).[113] Given the impairment of banks' ability to provide long-term funding, market-intermediation channels, including institutional investors (such as UCITS CISs), have been identified as providing a functional substitute for bank financing, and as potentially contributing to a more stable and diversified funding base.[114] In addition, while the retail investors associated with the UCITS regime have long been characterized as capital suppliers, this trend is becoming more pronounced. As discussed in section 5, discrete pan-EU CIS institutional investment vehicles for Social Entrepreneurship Funds and for Venture Capital Funds have been established. But similar reforms are taking place in the retail segment: the proposed retail-orientated long-term investment vehicle is designed to provide retail investors with exposure to long-term investment assets, such as infrastructure projects, and to deepen the pool of capital available for such projects.

Overall, therefore, it may be some time before the UCITS regime stabilizes, although it is always likely to be dynamic. Whether or not the now behemoth regulatory regime will prove effective in delivering financial stability, investor protection, and market efficiency remains to be seen. Regulatory error at the legislative level has been a persistent feature of the regime's development; the legacy effects of the UCITS III programme remain in place, while the speed at which reforms have been proposed to the 2009 UCITV IV Directive (particularly under the UCITS VI process)[115] does not instil confidence as to the efficiency of the legislative process or as to the Commission's restraint.[116] A 'legislative pause' seems apposite for the UCITS regime so that outstanding difficulties can be addressed.

III.3.4 Harmonization and ESMA

The UCITS regime has evolved very significantly since its initial adoption in 1985. Perhaps more than all other areas of EU securities and markets regulation (at least, prior to the crisis-era reforms), and despite the centrality of privately contracted fund rules/instruments of incorporation to UCITS regulation, this area is characterized by detailed harmonization and amplification by legislative and administrative measures, and has generated a vast array of supervisory convergence measures. Its scale reflects the technical complexity of the regulatory issues (particularly with respect to portfolio regulation given the impact of financial innovation), the multilayered nature of UCITS regulation (which includes the conduct and prudential regulation of management companies and depositaries), the challenges posed by retail investor protection in this area, and the operational and co-ordination risks which cross-border activity by UCITSs and their depositaries and management companies pose to pan-EU supervision.

---

[113] See further Ch II on SME funding.

[114] Commission, Green Paper. Long-Term Financing of the European Economy (2013) (COM (2013) 150/2) 2.

[115] The Commission has suggested technical enhancements to the master-feeder, merger, and notification reforms introduced by the UCITS IV reforms: 2012 UCITS VI Consultation, n 111, para 9.

[116] Some industry concern has been reported as to the necessity for further tinkering with the UCITS IV regime: Aboulian, B, 'Brussels May Curb Use of Derivatives', *Financial Times, Fund Management Supplement,* 30 July 2012, 13 and KMPG, n 96, 5.

At the legislative level, the 2009 UCITS IV Directive provides that a Member State may adopt additional or stricter requirements for UCITSs established within its territory, as long as these requirements are of general application and do not conflict with the Directive (Article 1(7)). This provision was of some significance at the outset, when the UCITS Directive imposed only minimum rules; the multifaceted nature of collective investment regulation and the range of rules it potentially encompasses, including with respect to UCITS design and governance, the management company and depositary, and distribution and disclosure protections for investors, meant that UCITS regulation, in practice, was only partly harmonized. Over time, the harmonized regime has been filled in to the extent that, following the 2009 UCITS IV Directive and its extensive suite of administrative rules, the only real gap relates to marketing by the UCITS, which, falling outside MiFID II and subject only to a general obligation under Article 77 of the 2009 Directive, remains subject to host regulation.

Although the 2009 Directive is a detailed measure, it has been amplified by a suite of administrative measures. The UCITS regime was a latecomer to administrative rule-making as the 1985 Directive, as amended by the UCITS III reforms, was not an FSAP/Lamfalussy Directive, and thus provided limited opportunities for delegations to administrative rule-making. Revisions to the Directive in 2005,[117] however, allowed the Commission to adopt administrative rules and led to the pivotal 2007 Commission Eligible Assets Directive. Under the 2009 UCITS IV reforms, a new set of delegations was conferred on the Commission. Accordingly, five detailed sets of administrative rules now apply under the UCITS regime: the 2007 Commission Eligible Assets Directive; the 2010 Commission Management Company Directive; the 2010 Commission Mergers and Master-Feeder Directive; the 2010 Commission KIID Regulation; and the 2010 Commission Notification and Information Exchange Regulation.[118] With the exception of the latter Regulation, these measures take an exhaustive and often highly operational approach to harmonization and together form an administrative rulebook of formidable breadth and depth. The 2010 Omnibus I Directive reforms to the 2009 UCITS IV Directive aligned the process for adopting administrative rules to the Lisbon Treaty settlement. But they also conferred multiple new delegations on the Commission to adopt Regulatory Technical Standards (RTSs) and Implementing Technical Standards (ITSs) proposed by ESMA, which have yet to be adopted. While many of the ITSs relate to technical amplification of areas already subject to administrative rules, many of the RTS delegations will lead to new administrative rules, including with respect to the information to be provided in UCITS, management company, and investment company authorization applications, the information to be provided by a management company in the cross-border notification, the content and format of the UCITS prospectus, annual report and half-yearly report, the UCITS borrowing regime, and the suspension of unit redemption.[119]

---

[117] Directive 2005/1/EC [2005] OJ L79/9.
[118] See nn 17–21.
[119] Respectively, Arts 5(8), 7(6), and 29(5); Arts 17(10) and 18(5); Art 69(5); Art 83(3); and Art 84(4) (each as revised by the 2010 Omnibus I Directive).

It is at the supervisory convergence level, however, that the most extensive intensification of the regime has taken place. CESR's legacy in the UCITS sphere was significant.[120] In the risk-management and asset-allocation sphere, for example, it includes the 2007 eligible assets guidelines,[121] the 2009 risk-management guidelines for UCITSs,[122] and the pivotal 2010 sets of guidelines on risk measurement and the calculation of global exposure and counterparty risk for UCITSs[123] and on money-market funds.[124] ESMA has quickened the pace of intervention, adopting an array of detailed measures. These include opinions on the UCITS regime[125] and regular updates of the important 2010 Risk Measurement and Global Exposure Guidelines through the well-established 'Q&A' mechanism[126] and through tailored applications of the Guidelines to particular UCITSs.[127] It has also adopted new guidelines in response to the stresses exposed by the financial crisis, including with respect to the use by UCITSs of repurchase and reverse repurchase arrangements,[128] on the risk disclosures to be provided by particular types of UCITSs in relation to their asset-allocation and investment policies, and on the operational requirements to be followed by particular UCITSs, including UCITSs in the form of ETFs, and in relation to specific investments, including financial indices.[129] The KIID regime has also generated a thicket of supervisory convergence measures relating to the format and presentation of the KIID and the methodologies used in producing KIID disclosures (section 3.11).

The UCITS regime underlines the technical capacity which CESR could and ESMA can bring to harmonization. It also illustrates the extent to which supervisory convergence can be used to provide necessary calibrations to the legislative/administrative rulebook as market practices evolve; ESMA's extensive measures related to structured UCITSs are a

---

[120] CESR also—and presciently, given the product intervention powers conferred on ESMA under the 2014 MiFID II reforms (Ch IX sect 7)—suggested a possible role for itself with respect to innovative UCITSs and considered whether 'significant innovations [should] be subject to a pan-EC assessment at an early stage without impairing market developments.... [and whether a Member State] would [through CESR] seek the opinion of colleagues before deciding to allow the performance of a new service or the offering of a new financial instrument that could have a significant impact on other market places': CESR, Preliminary Progress Report, Which Supervisory Tools for the EU Securities Market? An Analytical Paper by CESR (CESR Ref: 04–333f) (October 2004) 13 and 15.

[121] CESR/07-044 and CESR/07-044b (CESR 2007 Eligible Assets Guidelines).

[122] CESR, Risk Management Principles for UCITS (2009) (CESR/09-178) (CESR 2009 Risk Management Guidelines).

[123] CESR, Guidelines on Risk Measurement and the Calculation of Global Exposure and Counterparty Risk (2010) (CESR/10-788) (CESR 2010 Risk Measurement and Global Exposure Guidelines).

[124] CESR, Guidelines on a Common Definition of European Money Market Funds (CESR/10-049) (CESR 2010 MMF Guidelines).

[125] ESMA Opinion/2012/721 (see n 213).

[126] eg ESMA Q&A on the 2010 Guidelines, addressing their treatment of hedging strategies and leverage (ESMA/2012/429).

[127] ESMA Guidelines on Risk Management and Calculation of Global Exposures for Certain Types of Structured UCITS (2012) (ESMA/2012/197) (ESMA 2012 Structured UCITSs Guidelines). It sets out an optional calculation regime for structured UCITSs.

[128] Guidance on Repurchase and Reverse Repurchase Agreements (2012) (ESMA/2012/722) (ESMA 2012 Repo Guidelines).

[129] Guidelines on ETFs and other UCITS Issues (2012) (ESMA/2012/832) (ESMA 2012 ETF and UCITS Guidelines). The Q&A mechanism is being used to amplify further and clarify these Guidelines: eg, Q&A on ESMA's Guidelines on ETFs and other UCITS Issues (2013) (ESMA/2013/314) and (2014) (ESMA/2014/295).

case in point.[130] The crisis era has also thrown into sharp relief ESMA's potential for addressing emerging regulatory issues which fall outside the legislative/administrative rule-book and its capacity and appetite for so doing, particularly with respect to money-market funds and ETFs (sections 3.14.1 and 3.14.2).

But the scale of ESMA's activities in this sphere raises the risk of regulatory overreach; the UCITS rulebook (including softer supervisory convergence measures) is now immense and shows little sign of stabilizing. Given the challenges which the UCITS sector is facing (section 3.15), the point of diminishing returns may be in sight, particularly given the relative stability of the UCITS sector and the very strong branding and related incentive dynamics associated with the UCITS product.

III.3.5 Setting the Perimeter: Scope of the UCITS Regime

III.3.5.1 Defining Features

Under Article 1(1), the Directive applies to UCITSs. UCITSs are further defined as undertakings the sole object of which is the collective investment in transferrable secur-ities[131] and/or in other 'liquid financial assets' (listed in Article 50(1)) of capital raised from the public, and which operate on the principle of risk-spreading;[132] diversification is therefore built into the UCITS structure.

In addition, the units of the UCITS must, at the request of the unit-holder, be capable of repurchase or redemption, directly or indirectly, from the UCITS's assets.[133] This feature, which governs the extensive asset-allocation regime, is at the heart of the UCITS regulatory and investor protection regime and is reflected in Article 84(1), which provides that a UCITS must repurchase or redeem its units at the request of any unit-holder. Redemption on demand protects retail investors against liquidity risks; it allowed retail investors to move in large numbers to deposits over the worst period of the 2008 market turbulence. The UCITS Directive leaves the management of related valuation and redemption risk to the scheme and/or the Member States (Article 85).

Article 1(3) provides that a UCITS may be constituted according to the law of contract (as common funds without a separate legal personality and managed by management com-panies),[134] according to trust law (as unit trusts), or under statute (as investment compan-ies).[135] Under Article 1(5), Member States must prohibit UCITSs which are subject to the

---

[130] These include guidance on risk management and global exposure calculations (ESMA/2012/197) (n 127) as well as guidance on the KIID performance scenarios disclosure for structured UCITSs (CESR/ 10-1318).

[131] Defined as shares in companies and other equivalent securities; bonds and other forms of securitized debt; and any other negotiable securities which carry the right to acquire any such transferable securities by subscription or exchange: Art 2(1)(n).

[132] A scheme which does not operate on the principle of risk-spreading is one which, eg, seeks to exercise control over the undertakings in which it invests.

[133] For clarification, Art 1(2) of the Directive also provides that any action taken by a UCITS to ensure that the stock exchange value of its units does not vary significantly from their NAV is regarded as equivalent to repurchase or redemption.

[134] eg French *fonds commun de placement*.

[135] eg French SICAVs and, in the UK, OEICs or open-ended investment companies. OEICs have an overt EU focus in that they were set up as a response to the difficulties faced by the UK fund-management industry

Directive's provisions from transforming themselves into CISs which fall outside the Directive's scope.

A further distinction relates to UCITSs in the form of investment companies and UCITSs with a separate management company. The latter form of UCITS (termed a 'common fund' in the Directive) consists of three separate entities: the capital raised from unit-holders; the management company[136] which manages the assets and markets the UCITS; and the depositary which has custody of the assets.[137] In an investment company (the former type of UCITS), the UCITS takes the form of an investment company (in which the UCITS investor holds shares) which is also the management company (or it may designate a separate management company), but the assets are held by a depositary. Crucially, in the common fund form of UCITS, unit-holders do not have direct control over the management company as they hold units in the UCITS, not shares in the management company; by contrast, shareholders in an investment company UCITS, as shareholders, exercise control over the investment company and its directors.[138] Investment companies, management companies, and depositaries are all regulated by the Directive, albeit with varying degrees of intensity.

III.3.5.2 Open and Closed-end CIS

Article 3(1) sets out the exclusions from the Directive's scope. One of the most significant exclusions, which follows from the Directive's definition of a UCITS as a scheme in which units can be redeemed or repurchased, relates to UCITSs 'of the closed-end type' (Article 3(a)). CISs can be broadly divided into the closed-end type and the open-ended type. In a closed-end scheme, restrictions apply to the redemption of the units representing the capital of the scheme: in effect, the investor buys a share in a company the main activity of which is investment[139] and holds the usual equity risk held by shareholders (as well as the well-known risk that investment companies of this type typically trade at a discount to their net assets).[140] Liquidity is provided by open market sales.[141]

By contrast, in an open-ended scheme of whatever form, units are issued continuously, or at short intervals, at a price related to current NAV and may be redeemed by unit-holders on

---

in fully exploiting the UCITS passport, as continental investors were wary of the trust form of collective-investment scheme, being more familiar with corporate or contractual schemes.

[136] Defined as a company the regular business of which is the collective portfolio management of UCITS: Art 2(1)(b).

[137] The depositary is the institution entrusted with the depositary's duties as set out under the Directive: Art 2(1)(a).

[138] For ease of reference, holders of units in UCITSs, whether in the form of an investment company UCITS or other UCITS, will be collectively referred to as unit-holders, unless the distinction is material.

[139] These typically take the form of fixed-capital funds, an example of which is the French *société d'investissement à capital fixé*. The misleadingly named UK 'investment trusts' (they are companies, not trusts) are also closed-end in that the manager of the scheme is not obliged to buy back the original investment by the subscriber (who holds a share in the company which owns the fund assets). Investment trusts have a long lineage—the Foreign and Colonial Investment Trust, eg, dates back to 1868.

[140] 'Few problems in finance are as perplexing as the closed-end fund puzzle': Shleifer, A, *Inefficient Markets. An Introduction to Behavioural Finance* (2000) 53. The discount is often linked to liquidity risks attached to the portfolio, agency costs, and tax liabilities: at 53–88.

[141] Investment trusts represent a significant proportion of the London Stock Exchange and the UK Official List, eg (although open-ended OEICs are also listed). Although they are subject to discrete admission and disclosure requirements they are, for the most, part governed by company law and related prospectus rules.

request, again at current net asset value, or a price related to it. Liquidity support is therefore built into the scheme's structure. The Directive's restriction to open-ended schemes reflects the popularity of open-ended schemes at the time of the Directive's adoption. In addition, as open-ended schemes often lie outside the safeguards of company law, and are subject to the defining redemption obligation which demands careful asset-selection and portfolio management, they were seen as more susceptible to failure unless specific rules were applied. The distinction underlines, however, the risks of segmentation and arbitrage which are closely associated with the UCITS regime.

The other exclusions from the scope of the Directive are UCITSs which raise capital without promoting the sale of their units to the public within the EU, or any part of it, UCITSs whose units may be sold only to the public in third countries, and categories of UCITSs which must be prescribed by the Member States and in respect of which the Directive's investment and borrowing rules are inappropriate.

III.3.6 Differentiation and Calibration

By contrast with, for example, the capital-raising regime (Chapter II), differentiation and calibration is not a strong feature of the UCITS regime, although the administrative rulebook typically, and increasingly, distinguishes between different types of UCITS, notably structured and other UCITSs. Calibration and differentiation is, however, a function of the recent development of the 2011 AIFMD and its relationship with the UCITS regime. The extensive conduct and prudential rulebook developed for UCITS CISs provided a convenient template for the AIFMD administrative rulebook; a major theme of the reform process, however, was that appropriate distinction was made between UCITS schemes, which have a strong retail orientation, and the alternative investment funds within the scope of the AIFMD (section 4.4).

III.3.7 Market Integration: the Passport and UCITS Mergers

III.3.7.1 Authorization: the UCITS

Authorization of the UCITS by the UCITS home Member State[142] supports the UCITS passport—it is, in effect, a marketing passport. Authorization of the management company (where a separate management company forms part of the structure) supports the management company passport. The depositary is not subject to an authorization regime and, accordingly, does not benefit from a passport.[143] As the management company's home Member State may be a different State to the UCITS home State, UCITS and management company authorization and supervision can be split across two jurisdictions, which is reflected in the distinct supervisory co-operation regime which applies under the Directive (sections 3.7.3 and 3.13.2). In practice, the management company in the case of a

---

[142] Defined as the Member State in which the UCITS is authorized (Art 2(1)(e)), thereby allowing significant regulatory competition, albeit within the limitations imposed by the detailed UCITS rulebook. Ireland and Luxembourg are the dominant home Member States for UCITSs.

[143] Although a depositary passport may be developed, in light of the UCITS V depositary reforms: 2012 UCITS VI Consultation, n 111, para 6.

'common fund', or the investment company where the UCITS is self-managed, runs the UCITS authorization process.[144]

Article 5 provides that no UCITS can pursue activities as such unless it has been authorized in accordance with the Directive. Once authorized, a regulatory passport is conferred in that the UCITS authorization is valid for all Member States. The nature of UCITS authorization depends on its structure. In the case of a common fund, authorization is conditional on the national competent authority (NCA) of the home Member State of the UCITS having approved the application of the management company to manage the UCITS (Article 5(2)). Management company authorization, however, is the responsibility of the management company's home Member State NCA (Article 6(1)). UCITS authorization reflects this split in that it is conditional on the management company being authorized to manage UCITSs in its home Member State (Article 5(4)(b)). Similarly, authorization of a UCITS in the form of a common fund requires that the UCITS home Member State NCA approve the choice of depositary. Finally, the UCITS home Member State NCA must also approve the fund's rules.

Where the UCITS takes the form of an investment company, the home Member State NCA must approve the instruments of incorporation and the choice of depositary. Where the investment company appoints a separate manager, the home NCA must approve the application of the relevant management company (Article 5(2)). UCITS authorization is also subject to the investment company meeting the authorization and operating requirements imposed under Articles 27–31.

For both common fund and investment company UCITS, the UCITS may not be authorized by its home Member State NCA if the directors of the depositary are not of sufficiently good repute or are not sufficiently experienced in relation to the type of UCITS to be managed (Article 5(4)). Neither the management company nor the depositary can be replaced, nor the fund rules/instruments of incorporation amended, without the approval of the UCITS home NCA (Article 5(6)).

Given the potential split in UCITS supervision between the UCITS and the management company (which, in effect, takes all key decisions), a number of mechanisms specific to the UCITS field are relied on to support effective supervision and to provide strong supervisory incentives. The UCITS home NCA may not grant authorization where the UCITS is legally prevented from marketing its units in the home Member State (Article 5(5)), thereby ensuring the home NCA has an incentive to monitor the UCITS. Additionally, where the UCITS home Member State is different to that of the management company, a tailored co-operation regime applies to the relationship between the two home States involved with respect to the management company (Article 5(3)—see sections 3.7.3 and 3.13.2).

III.3.7.2 Authorization: the Management Company

Prior to the 2009 UCITS IV reforms, significant difficulties attended the UCITS management company passport. Although the UCITS III reforms attempted to liberalize the

---

[144] And must be informed as to the success of the UCITS authorization application within two months: Art 5(4).

management company industry and support cross-border management activity, diverging interpretations across the Member States and weaknesses in the Directive[145] limited the extent to which companies could engage in the management of UCITSs cross-border.[146] In practice, most Member States required that the management company be established in the Member State where the UCITS was registered.[147] As a result, the potential for more effective risk management across funds, economies of scale, and cost reduction[148] through the centralization of management functions was severely constrained.

The symbiosis between the management company and the UCITS, however, raises delicate questions of supervisory co-ordination where supervisory jurisdiction is split. The adoption of a management company passport in the 2009 UCITS IV regime accordingly proved challenging. Despite some initial nervousness in the 2005 Investment Funds Green Paper concerning supervision risks where UCITS and manager supervision was potentially split between two jurisdictions,[149] the 2006 Investment Funds White Paper contained a commitment to extending the management company passport to include the management of UCITS funds in other Member States. The scale of the operational and legal difficulties became clear as the 2008 UCITS IV Proposal developed[150] and led the Commission to exclude the management company regime from the Proposal, given, in particular, the significant difficulties related to: distinguishing the business functions and related rules which should be attached to the UCITS' Member State and the management company's Member State; the allocation of supervisory responsibilities and related compliance costs and accountability risks; and effective enforcement where supervisory responsibilities across the UCITS/management company chain were split across jurisdictions. Instead, CESR was charged with delivering technical advice on this issue.[151] Although the scale of the difficulties is well illustrated by the failure of CESR to reach a unanimous position,[152] its final technical advice[153] ultimately formed the basis of the complex regime adopted in the 2009 UCITS IV Directive,[154] which sets out in detail the arrangements for supervisory

---

[145] The 2006 Investment Fund Market Efficiency Group noted that while some jurisdictions allowed corporate funds to be managed by cross-border companies, they changed their position when it became clear that Member States taking a restrictive approach would not support mutual recognition: n 80, 23.

[146] See, eg, 2004 Asset Management Expert Group Report, n 75, 18.

[147] The Investment Fund Market Efficiency Group reported that it was not aware of any UCITS managed by a foreign management company and that management companies remained landlocked within their own Member States: n 80, 22. Similarly, 2008 UCITS IV Proposal Impact Assessment, n 92, 16.

[148] It cost from €500,000 to €1 million to establish a management company for a 'foreign' UCITS: n 92.

[149] 2005 Investment Fund Green Paper, n 58, 5.

[150] The 2008 UCITS IV Proposal Impact Assessment proposed that the status quo be maintained, given the significant operational and legal difficulties associated with remote supervision of management companies: n 92, 28–30.

[151] Commission Letter to CESR on a Request for Assistance on the UCITS Management Company Passport, 16 July 2008.

[152] The advice was adopted by a qualified majority of CESR's members: five members (including the NCAs of the major fund domiciles of Luxembourg and Ireland) voted against and published their dissenting arguments. CESR Advice on the Management Company Passport (2008) (CESR/08-867) 3. Luxembourg and Ireland were concerned as to the potential risks to investor protection were supervision to be split between management company and UCITS NCAs in different Member States.

[153] n 152.

[154] The management company regime was added during the trilogue negotiations between the European Parliament, Commission, and the Council on the 2008 Proposal: Summary Document. Text Adopted by Parliament. 1st/Single Reading, 13 January 2009. Both institutions were supportive of CESR's approach, with the Parliament in particular supportive of the management company passport; the ECON Report had earlier

co-operation and the allocation of regulatory obligations to the UCITS and the management company. A centralization of management company functions across the industry was expected to follow,[155] and the related degree of reliance on the management company is likely to test the resilience of the new prudential and supervisory co-ordination rules.

The 2009 management company passport is supported by an authorization requirement. The management company must be authorized by the NCA of its home Member State (Article 6(1));[156] once granted, the authorization supports the management company passport, being valid for all Member States (Article 6(1)). Prudential supervision is the responsibility of the NCA of the management company's home Member State, whether or not the management company passports into another Member State (Article 10(2)). As under the MiFID II model for discretionary asset management, conduct regulation with respect to branches is the responsibility of the host Member State (Article 17(4) and (5)).[157] In order to support the management company passport, the related UCITS authorization regime provides that UCITS authorization cannot be conditional on the UCITS being managed by a management company with its registered office in the UCITS home Member State, or conditional on the management company pursuing or delegating any activities in the UCITS home Member State (Article 5(3)).[158]

The authorization regime is closely related to the MiFID II regime for investment services (which includes discretionary asset management). Authorization by the management company's home Member State NCA is conditional on the management company only engaging in collective UCITS management (Article 6(2)).[159] A number of exceptions apply, however. Management companies may engage in collective portfolio management for non-UCITS schemes, as long as the management company is subject to related prudential supervision and the units cannot be marketed in other Member States (Article 6(2)). Management companies are also permitted to engage in discretionary asset management, including for pension funds, where the portfolio includes one or more MiFID II-scope instruments and, as non-core services[160] only, to provide investment advice in relation to MiFID II-scope instruments and safekeeping and administration in relation to CIS units (Article 6(3)).[161] The authorization process for management companies is broadly similar to, if lighter than, the MiFID II model,[162] incorporating capital,[163] 'fit and proper'

---

adopted a 'political decision' to introduce a passport, in advance of the trilogue negotiations: 2008 ECON Report, n 92, Explanatory Statement.

[155] 2012 EFAMA Asset Management Report, n 1, 12.

[156] The Member State within which it has its registered office (Art 2(1)(c)).

[157] The home NCA remains responsible for conduct regulation carried out on a cross-border services basis: Art 18(3).

[158] Similarly, the ongoing organizational and other prudential rules which apply to the management company, and which are supervised by the home NCA (Art 10(2) and 19(1)), can be no stricter than those which apply where the management company conducts activities only within the home Member State: Art 19(1). In addition, the Directive clarifies that management companies may not be subject to additional requirements in the UCITS home Member State, save as specified in the Directive (typically with respect to marketing): Art 19(8).

[159] The scope of which is set out in Annex II to the Directive.

[160] Management companies cannot, accordingly, be authorized to provide only these services.

[161] MiFID II's operational regime applies to Art 6(3) services.

[162] See Ch IV sect 6.

[163] The capital regime is calibrated to the particular risks posed by collective investment, focuses on operational risk, and is related to the value of the assets under management: Art 7(a).

management, business plan, 'close links,' and qualifying shareholder requirements, as well as a requirement for the head office and registered office to be in the same Member State (Articles 7 and 8).

A broadly similar but somewhat lighter authorization regime (Articles 27–9)[164] applies to investment companies which do not appoint a separate management company, reflecting the single focus of these companies as well as the monitoring provided by shareholders.

III.3.7.3 The Passport and Notification

(a) The UCITS

UCITS authorization is valid for every Member State (Article 5(1)) and Member States may not apply any other provisions in the field covered by the Directive to authorized UCITSs established in another Member State, or to the units issued by such UCITSs, where those UCITSs market their units within the territory of that Member State (Article 1(6)). Similarly, UCITS host Member States[165] are prohibited from imposing any additional requirements or administrative procedures on UCITSs in the field governed by the Directive (Article 91(2)). Where host State rules outside the scope of the Directive apply, and particularly with respect to UCITS marketing, these rules must be easily accessible, including by electronic means, and available in a language customary in the field of international finance (Article 91(3)).[166]

The operation of the UCITS passport is governed by Articles 91–6. Passporting is subject to notification requirements which—in order to streamline the regime and remove the disadvantages UCITSs faced from the earlier cumbersome and costly notification procedures (which could take up to eight or nine months and often involved a reassessment of compliance with the UCITS Directive),[167] and which placed UCITSs at a disadvantage to functionally similar retail investment products[168]—were introduced by the 2009 Directive.[169] Once these requirements are met, the host Member State must ensure that the UCITS can market its units within the host Member State (Article 91(1)).[170] Notification is made by the UCITS to its home NCA,[171] which verifies whether the documentation is complete and then transmits it to the host NCA, together with an attestation that the

---

[164] Authorization is the responsibility of the investment company's home NCA. Where a company appoints a separate management company, the authorization conditions are limited and apply only to restricting the scope of business to collective investment management and the capital required.

[165] The Member State, other than the home Member State, in which the UCITS units are marketed: Art 2(1)(f).

[166] Administrative rules govern the information on host rules which must be made available to the UCITS: 2010 Commission Merger and Master-Feeder Directive.

[167] The 2006 Investment Fund Market Efficiency Group Report noted that notification had almost become a second authorization process: n 80, 7.

[168] 2008 UCITS IV Proposal, n 92, 10.

[169] Previously, the regime was based on UCITS-host NCA notification. It was aligned by the Directive to the NCA-NCA notification model followed by the major Financial Services Action Plan (FSAP) measures, including MiFID I.

[170] Host NCAs may not ask for documents or disclosures additional to those specified for the notification: Art 93(6).

[171] The notification must include the arrangements relating to how the units are to be marketed (the host NCA must be updated by the UCITS if these arrangements change (Art 93(8)), the fund rules or instruments of incorporation, the UCITS prospectus, latest annual report and, where appropriate half-yearly report, and the UCITS KIID (Art 93(1) and (2)).

UCITS fulfils the conditions imposed by the Directive.[172] Once this notification has been made by the home NCA and the UCITS informed, the UCITS can access the market of the host Member State. By contrast with the management company notification regime the UCITS home NCA's powers to block cross-border notification are limited, and relate only to UCITS compliance with the Directive. The UCITS must, however, ensure that payment and related subscription and redemption facilities are available in the host State (Article 92). Administrative rules govern the technical operation of the notification regime and are designed to ensure that the notification regime is streamlined and subject to detailed harmonization to facilitate cross-border marketing.[173]

(b) The Management Company

The management company passport is similar to the MiFID II investment services passport, being based on similar notification procedures[174] with respect to the provision of management company services by way of the freedom to provide services and by way of the freedom to establish,[175] although, reflecting Article 91(3) and the exclusion of marketing rules from the Directive, host State marketing rules may apply (Article 16(1)).[176]

In order to address the potential split of supervision between the UCITS home NCA and the management company home NCA, and the related risks generated by remote supervision by the home NCA of the management company in the host State, a jurisdiction-sharing regime applies. Where a management company provides collective portfolio management services on a cross-border basis, it must comply with the home country regime with respect to organizational matters.[177] The management company must, however, comply with the rules of the UCITS home Member State with respect to UCITS-related matters, which are supervised by the UCITS home NCA.[178] To support the UCITS home NCA under this split model, the management company's home NCA is responsible

---

[172] The notification must be made in a language customary in the sphere of international finance, unless the two NCAs agree to it being in one of their official languages: Art 93 (4).

[173] 2010 Commission Notification and Exchange of Information Regulation Arts 1–5. The administrative regime provides a standard template for the notification letter.

[174] Arts 17 (branches) and 18 (services).

[175] Management companies may pursue authorized activities in another Member State through the freedom to provide services, or the freedom to establish (Art 16(1)), and the host Member State may not make these activities subject to any authorization requirement, any additional capital requirements, or any other measure having equivalent effect (Art 16(2)). The notification system for branches (Art 17) and services (Art 18) is based on the investment-services model and gives the home NCA the ability to block the establishment of a branch cross-border where it doubts the adequacy of the administrative structure or the financial situation of the management company (Art 17(3)); the services notification process is largely automatic. The notification process is adjusted to the particular supervisory and substantive risks posed by collective investment management in that it focuses in particular on risk management and the notification must include information on the nature of the collective investment management services which the management company can engage in and on any restrictions as to the type of UCITSs which the company can manage.

[176] More generally, limited precautionary powers can also be exercised by host NCAs over passporting management companies (Art 21).

[177] Including delegation arrangements, risk management, prudential rules and procedures, and reporting requirements: Art 19(1) (reflecting Art 10(2), which confers prudential supervision responsibility on the home Member State). This regime is supervised by the home NCA (Art 19(2)).

[178] Including UCITS authorization, issuance, and redemption of units, investment policies and limits, restrictions on borrowing, asset valuation, income distribution, UCITS disclosure and reporting requirements, the merging and restructuring of UCITS, and UCITS winding up and liquidation: Art 19(3). Supervision of these rules is the responsibility of the UCITS home NCA (Art 19(5)).

for supervising the adequacy of the management company's arrangements and organization, such that the company is in a position to comply with the UCITS-related rules (Article 19(7)). The UCITS authorization process also reflects the risk of split supervision. Where the UCITS is established in a different State to the management company, the UCITS authorization process must include the provision by the management company of information on delegation arrangements and on the agreements between the depositary and the management company[179] (Article 20(1)). Additionally, the UCITS home NCA may ask the management company's home NCA for clarification regarding the management company's authorization documentation and regarding the compliance of the UCITS for which authorization is sought with the scope of the management company's authorization (Article 20(2)). The UCITS home NCA may only refuse the management company's application to manage the UCITS in question where it does not comply with the home NCA's UCITS-related rules, the company is not authorized in relation to the UCITS in question, or the Article 20(1) documentation has not been provided (Article 20(3)). This regime is supported by distinct supervisory co-operation obligations (Articles 107–10, section 3.13.2).

III.3.7.4 Mergers of UCITSs

The 2009 UCITS IV Directive introduced a regime for UCITS mergers, in order to bring efficiencies to the UCITS market by making it easier for UCITSs to pool their assets and to generate pan-EU efficiencies (particularly with respect to cross-border mergers). The UCITS Review had earlier highlighted the small size of the average UCITS fund[180] and the legal difficulties associated with constructing fund mergers, which had resulted in a proliferation of funds. The industry was dominated by funds of sub-optimal size[181] and fund managers and administrators were accordingly limited in their ability to exploit scale economies of an order, potentially, of €2–6 billion.[182] Although mergers between UCITSs were not prohibited under the UCITS Directive, they faced considerable problems given operational costs, national legal barriers, and tax disadvantages.[183] The 10th Company Law Directive on Cross Border Mergers was of limited value as it only applies to corporate structures and does not reflect the particular risks and issues raised by fund merger.[184] Reflecting strong industry support (albeit that other sectors were less supportive),[185] the

---

[179] See sect 3.10 on the depositary.

[180] See generally 2006 Investment Fund Market Efficiency Group Report, n 80, 10–16.

[181] n 80, 13 and 2006 Investment Funds White Paper, n 9, 6 (reporting that 54 per cent of UCITS funds had less than €50 million AUM). Similarly, it was reported in 2004 that the EU had three times as many funds as the US, but funds were on average six times smaller, sharply reducing scale efficiencies: 2004 Asset Management Expert Group, n 75, 9. More recently, it has been reported that there are some 54,000 open-ended CISs in the EU (67 per cent of which are structured as UCITSs), as compared to 7,000–8,000 mutual funds in the US: 2012 ECMI/CEPS Report, n 12, 13.

[182] Invesco, Building an Integrated European Fund Management: Cross Border Merger of Funds, a Quick Win? (2005).

[183] The 2006 Investment Fund Market Efficiency Group Report pointed to the discrepancy between domestic and cross-border mergers, noting that in France while very few cross-border mergers had taken place, there had been more than 600 domestic mergers since 2003: n 80, 11.

[184] Directive 2005/56/EC [2005] OJ L310/1.

[185] There was some political concern that any attempts to ease fund mergers could result in a migration of funds to low-tax jurisdictions, particularly Luxembourg, and a concentration of expertise in particular centres: Davis, P, 'Pan-European Fund Mergers "Blocked by Red Tape"', *Financial Times, Fund Management Supplement*, 2 October 2006, 2.

2006 Investment Funds White Paper argued that fund mergers were complex, time-consuming, and expensive, and committed to the development of a new merger regime,[186] while the subsequent 2008 UCITS IV Proposal linked the new merger regime to greater economies of scale in the UCITS industry.[187]

Under the new regime, mergers between UCITSs, whether domestic or cross-border, are subject to an approval process and the production of a related 'terms of merger' document (Articles 39–40); monitoring by the depositaries[188] (and auditors) involved (Articles 41–2); disclosure to unit-holders of the merging and the receiving UCITS (Article 43); rules governing approval by unit-holders (Article 44);[189] a range of unit-holder rights, including with respect to the redemption of their units or the conversion of their units into units of other UCITSs (Article 45); rules governing the costs of the operation (Article 46); rules governing when the merger comes into force (Article 47); and rules governing the consequences of the merger in terms of the asset and liabilities of the UCITSs concerned, and the status of unit-holders (Article 48). The framework regime established under the Directive is amplified by the 2010 Commission Mergers and Master-Feeder Directive.[190]

III.3.8 Asset Allocation and Investment Limits

III.3.8.1 An Evolving Regime

Asset-allocation and diversification rules, designed to ensure that a UCITS can meet its core Article 84 investor protection obligation and redeem units on request, are at the heart of the Directive's regulatory design. The original 1985 UCITS regime was restrictive and was replaced by the UCITS III regime, since consolidated within (and refined by) the 2009 UCITS IV Directive. Assets eligible for UCITS investment were originally limited to 'transferable securities' (undefined) and excluded a range of instruments, including financial derivatives and money-market instruments.[191] UCITSs were also prohibited from investing in other CISs unless they took the form of a UCITS. Restrictive diversification rules, designed to ensure appropriate risk-spreading across the asset portfolio, also applied. Only limited exemptions were available from the core requirement that a UCITS could not invest more than 5 per cent of its assets in transferable securities issued by the same issuer (or UCITS).

The 2001 UCITS III Product Directive[192] was designed to extend the UCITS passport to CISs investing in financial assets other than transferable securities, to offer more

---

[186] Costs were projected to reduce by €5–6 billion if related economies of scale were realized: 2006 Investment Funds White Paper, n 9, 6.

[187] 2008 UCITS IV Proposal, n 92, 7.

[188] Including with respect to whether the draft terms of merger conform with the Directive and the fund rules of instruments of incorporation.

[189] The Directive does not require unit-holder approval, but where approval is required under the relevant national law, it must not require more than 75 per cent of the votes actually cast by unit-holders at the general meeting.

[190] Arts 3–7, governing the disclosure required and how it must be provided.

[191] The original proposal was less strict and, presciently given the 2001 reforms, limited UCITSs to investing 'mainly in transferable securities and *liquid assets*' [emphasis added]. 'Mainly' was further defined as at least 80 per cent of the UCITS' assets.

[192] Directive 2001/108/EC [2002] OJ L41/35.

opportunities to the collective investment industry, and to provide greater choice for investors. It widened the investment objectives of UCITSs in order to permit them to invest in financial instruments, other than transferable securities, which were sufficiently liquid. Related disclosure and transparency requirements were introduced with respect to the new range of investments, as were risk-management and diversification rules. The 2009 UCITS IV reforms have further refined the asset-allocation regime by addressing master-feeder funds.

The regime was also significantly extended and amplified by administrative rules under the 2007 Commission Eligible Assets Directive. The 2007 reforms were a response to growing uncertainty as to which instruments were 'eligible assets' as firms pushed at the boundaries of the 2001 UCITS III regime. NCAs began to take different approaches, ranging from risk-averse to allowing great flexibility, which led to confusion as to how UCITS funds could be designed. Particular difficulties arose with respect to the treatment of structured products, closed-end funds (units which can be akin to transferable securities), money-market instruments, and financial derivatives, particularly those based on indices. CESR took the initiative at an early stage, adopting a related own-initiative mandate in June 2004.[193] A formal Commission mandate for CESR technical advice on the 'eligible assets' for UCITS investment followed in October 2004. Following a lengthy and somewhat fraught market consultation process which included two consultation papers,[194] CESR's advice was presented in January 2006.[195] Lengthy European Securities Committee discussions followed[196] and opinions were received from the European Parliament and the European Central Bank (ECB).[197] The extensive 2007 Commission Directive was finally adopted in March 2007.[198] Related CESR guidelines were also adopted.[199]

III.3.8.2 Strand (1): Eligible Assets

(a) Transferable Securities and Money-market Instruments

The asset-allocation regime is based on the assumption that it is for each UCITS to choose its own investment profile and its degree of specialization in particular securities, economic sectors, or geographic areas. Accordingly, the scope of UCITS investment is widely defined and covers collective investment in 'transferable securities', and other 'liquid financial instruments' set out in Article 50 ('financial instruments' are defined by reference to the 2014 MiFID II/MiFIR regime (see Chapter IV section 4.3)).

Accordingly, an extensive range of 'eligible assets' can be invested in by UCITSs, extending from 'plain vanilla' securities admitted to trading on regulated markets to complex financial derivatives.

---

[193] CESR/04–160.
[194] CESR/05–064b and CESR/05–490b.
[195] CESR/06–2005; Feedback Statement at CESR/06-013.
[196] Although the Committee was broadly supportive of CESR's approach (Minutes, 29–30 March 2006). For an example of the detailed discussion see Minutes, 26–27 April 2006.
[197] European Securities Committee Minutes, 17 January 2007: both institutions were praised for their 'co-operative spirit'.
[198] n 17.
[199] CESR 2007 Eligible Assets Guidelines, n 121.

Article 50 eligible assets cover 'transferable securities' and money-market instruments[200] admitted to or dealt in on a MiFID II regulated market,[201] as well as these instruments when dealt in on 'another' regulated market in a Member State which operates regularly and is recognized and open to the public and when admitted to official listing on a stock exchange or dealt in on another regulated market in a non-Member State (which operates regularly and is recognized and open to the public), as long as the choice of stock exchange or regulated market has been approved by the NCAs or is provided for in law, the fund rules, or the instruments of incorporation (Article 50(1) (a)–(c)). Article 50 also extends to recently issued transferable securities (Article 50(1)(d)), subject to a series of restrictions with respect to the issue's admission to trading.

The foundation definition of 'transferable securities' (Article 2(1)(n)) is based on legal characteristics and is widely cast. The elastic nature of the 'transferable securities' definition means that it encompasses a potentially wide range of instruments which, while legally constituted as shares or bonds, have different features and, in particular, different liquidity levels. Many of these instruments are inappropriate for a retail investment vehicle and to the particular liquidity and risk-diversification requirements of the UCITS structure. Article 2(1) of the 2007 Commission Eligible Assets Directive accordingly employs a range of criteria (chief among them liquidity, valuation, information, and transferability criteria) linked to the underlying objectives of the UCITS regime and against which instruments can be assessed as to whether they can be characterized as 'transferable securities'. For example, the potential loss to the UCITS with respect to the instrument must be limited to the amount paid, and the instrument's liquidity must not compromise Article 84 (compliance is assumed for instruments traded on a regulated market). Reliable valuation must also be available, as must 'appropriate information' (either in the form of regular, accurate, and comprehensive information to the market, for instruments traded on a regulated market, or regular and accurate information to the UCITS, for other instruments). The instrument must also be negotiable (assumed for instruments traded on a regulated market), its risk must be adequately captured by the UCITS' risk-management process, and its acquisition must be consistent with the investment objectives of the

---

[200] The original inclusion of money-market instruments represented at the time a significant extension of the eligible assets regime. Money-market instruments are defined under Art 2(1)(o) as instruments normally dealt in on the money market which are liquid and which have a value that can be accurately determined at any time.

[201] Under Art 50(1)(h) OTC money-market instruments (such as treasury and local authority bills, certificates of deposit, commercial paper, and bankers' acceptances) are permitted as investments, but only if they meet certain liquidity and valuation standards. The issue or issuer of the instruments must be regulated for the purpose of protecting investors and savings, and only certain issuers' instruments will be eligible. The eligible issuers are eligible institutions who issue or guarantee the instruments (the list includes central, regional, and local authorities; central banks of Member States; the ECB; the EU; the European Investment Bank; non-Member States; and public international bodies to which one or more Member States belong); undertakings any securities of which are dealt in on the regulated markets covered by Art 50(1)(a), (b), and (c); establishments who issue or guarantee the instruments and are subject to prudential supervision in accordance with criteria defined by EU law or subject to and complying with prudential rules considered by the NCAs to be at least as stringent as those laid down by EU law; and other bodies belonging to the categories approved by the UCITS' NCAs. This last case is designed to catch particularly specialized issuers (such as group financing vehicles and securitization vehicles) and is subject to a number of qualifications which include that the issuer's capital and reserves amount to at least €10 million and that the issuer is an entity which, within a group of companies which includes one or several listed companies, is dedicated to the financing of securitization vehicles which benefit from a banking liquidity line.

UCITS' investment policy. The related CESR 2007 Eligible Assets Guidelines additionally cover how, for example, liquidity risk should be assessed.[202]

Although a UCITS may not take the form of a closed-end fund, many non-UCITS closed-end funds are admitted to trading on regulated markets, and their units are akin to transferable securities, particularly shares. Units in such funds can provide exposure to riskier investments, such as hedge fund and private equity investments. The approach taken by the administrative regime is to bring investments in such closed-end funds within the scope of 'transferable securities' (and within the range of UCITS eligible assets) where they are akin to shares in companies and, specifically, where the vehicle is subject to the corporate governance requirements (or equivalent) applied to companies (2007 Commission Eligible Assets Directive Article 2(2)). The intention with this approach was to expand the range of investments possible while limiting riskier investments.[203]

Structured products (which pay a return linked to the performance of assets which may not constitute 'eligible assets') are addressed in Articles 2(2)(c), 2(3), and 10 of the 2007 Commission Eligible Assets Directive.[204] Liquidity tests and restrictions on the investment exposing the UCITS to additional liabilities govern their eligibility as 'transferable securities'. But, reflecting considerable market concern on this issue at the time, the UCITS is not required to 'look through' the product to the embedded asset[205]—which, particularly in the case of embedded commodities, may not be within the scope of the UCITS regime.

A detailed administrative regime also applies to regulated-market-traded and over-the-counter (OTC) money-market instruments (Articles 3–7). Key criteria include maturity tests (Article 3), risk profile requirements (Article 3), and liquidity and valuation requirements (Article 4—these are considerably expanded through supervisory convergence guidance).

(b) CISs

The asset-allocation regime recognizes that investments in other CISs can provide liquid investments and reduce transaction costs, in particular by facilitating diversification. Under Article 50(1)(e), a UCITS may invest in the units of a UCITS authorized under the Directive and/or other CISs within the meaning of Article 1(2)[206] (whether or not they are situated in a Member State), as long as these other CISs meet the eligibility conditions of Article 50(1)(e). These conditions are based on equivalence, and are designed to ensure that investor protection is not prejudiced.

(c) Deposits

Under the original 1985 regime, cash could only be held by a UCITS as an ancillary liquid asset. Article 50(1)(f) provides that investments in deposits with credit institutions which are (in order to ensure adequate liquidity) repayable on demand, or which have the right to

---

[202] CESR 2007 Eligible Assets Guidelines, n 121, 6.

[203] CESR noted that the regime would make real-estate fund (REIT) and private-equity fund investments possible but, given the information requirements which apply for closed-end fund units to qualify as transferable securities, would exclude hedge-fund vehicles. 2006 CESR Eligible Assets Technical Advice, n 195, 13.

[204] The aim of the regime is to ensure that embedded derivatives are brought within the UCITS regime where appropriate, that the UCITS Directive's risk-management and asset-allocation regimes apply, and that products are not developed in order to bypass the UCITS regime for derivatives.

[205] An asset will be embedded only where the specific requirements of Art 10 are met.

[206] See sect 3.5.

be withdrawn and mature in no more than 12 months, are permissible. The credit institution with which the deposit is made must, however, have its registered office in a Member State or, where the registered office is in a non-Member State, must alternatively be subject to prudential rules considered by the investing UCITS' NCA to be equivalent to those applicable under EU law.

(d) Financial Derivatives

In a significant revision, the UCITS III reforms brought financial derivative instruments within the asset-allocation regime; previously financial derivatives could only be used for portfolio management purposes, such as risk reduction and cost reduction. Article 50(1)(g) provides that investments may be made in financial derivative instruments, including equivalent cash-settled instruments, dealt in on a regulated market and/or financial derivative instruments dealt on OTC derivatives markets.[207] Derivatives can, accordingly, be used by a UCITS manager to hedge risks but also to gain or reduce exposure to assets (and to generate cost savings relative to the costs of direct investment) and, within the Directive's limits, to generate leverage.[208]

Foreshadowing the crisis-era reforms relating to the OTC derivatives markets (Chapter VI section 4), the UCITS III reforms subjected financial derivatives to a number of prudential conditions designed to address the liquidity and valuation difficulties and counterparty risk problems which investing in OTC derivatives may generate, and to provide investors with a level of protection close to that applicable to investments in derivatives which are dealt in on regulated markets. For both types of derivative instrument (regulated-market-traded and OTC), the underlying asset must consist of instruments covered by Article 50(1), financial indices, interest rates, foreign exchange rates, or currencies, in which the UCITS may invest according to its investment objectives as stated in its fund rules or instruments of incorporation. Additionally, counterparties to OTC derivatives transactions must be institutions subject to prudential supervision and must belong to the categories approved by the investing UCITS' NCAs. OTC derivatives must also be subject to reliable and verifiable valuation on a daily basis and must be capable of being sold, liquidated, or closed by an offsetting transaction at any time at their fair value at the UCITS' initiative.

Detailed administrative rules apply to financial derivatives under the 2007 Commission Eligible Assets Directive. Article 8(1) addresses OTC and regulated-market-traded financial derivatives and sets out the criteria for assessing whether, reflecting the UCITS Directive's core requirement, a financial derivative is a 'liquid financial asset' (as required by Article 50(1)). This regime is based on identifying the derivative's eligible underlyings, which must consist of other assets listed in Article 50(1), interest rates, foreign exchange rates

---

[207] In an augury of the debates on OTC derivative regulation which would follow over the financial crisis, in the original UCITS III proposal the Commission restricted investments in derivative instruments to standardized derivatives traded on regulated markets, and excluded OTC instruments on prudential grounds. This exclusion was strongly criticized by ECOSOC (which raised the problem of the restrictions which would be placed on UCITSs operating in countries with underdeveloped derivatives exchanges), the European Parliament, and the ECB. All the institutions accepted that prudential controls over the use of OTC derivatives were desirable, but felt that prudential regulation was a more measured response to investments in OTC derivatives than a blanket prohibition. The Council Working Group also favoured the inclusion of OTC derivatives.

[208] 2012 CEPS/ECMI Report, n 12, 61–3.

or currencies, or financial indices. OTC financial derivatives are regarded as liquid where they meet the underlying, counterparty, and valuation requirements of Article 50(1)(g).

Under Article 8(2) of the 2007 Commission Directive, credit derivatives are included as eligible financial derivatives and meet the Article 50(1) 'liquid financial asset' requirement where they allow the transfer of credit risk of eligible underlyings (independently of the other risks associated with the asset), they do not result in the delivery or transfer of assets other than those covered by the UCITS Directive, they comply with the Article 50(1)(g) criteria for OTC derivatives as well as those set out in the 2007 Commission Eligible Assets Directive, and their risks are adequately captured by the UCITS' risk-management process and its internal control mechanisms. In an attempt to capture the information risks posed by credit derivatives, risk-management procedures must be able to manage the risks which arise where an information-asymmetry risk arises between the UCITS and the derivative counterparty, reflecting the potential access of the counterparty to non-public information on firms the assets of which are used as underlyings by credit derivatives.

Detailed rules govern financial indices, which have been associated with the adoption by UCITS III funds of hedge-fund-like strategies[209] and are designed to balance the risk-diversification benefits of derivatives on financial indices with the danger that retail investors are unable to assess their impact on the risk profile of a UCITS. Under Article 9 of the 2007 Commission Eligible Assets Directive, a financial index must be sufficiently diversified, represent an adequate benchmark for the market, and be published in an appropriate manner. Hedge fund indices generated particular difficulties, reflecting wide-spread concern at the time as to the risks of retail investment in hedge-fund-like products. Over the development of the 2007 Commission Directive, CESR raised a number of concerns with respect to hedge fund indices, including survivor bias (underperforming hedge funds are not included in indices as they usually close down) and selection bias, and initially decided to exclude hedge fund indices from its advice but to revisit the issue after gaining sufficient experience. In 2007, however, CESR re-opened the issue and agreed to limited UCITS investment in particular hedge fund indices, although this decision remains a function of supervisory convergence and not of EU regulation.[210]

(e) Investment in securitization positions

The 2011 AIFMD imposes restrictions on these investments (section 4.9). In order to ensure cross-sector consistency, the AIFMD amends the UCITS Directive to provide for similar administrative rules for the UCITS sector.[211]

III.3.8.3 Strand (2): Investment Limits—Risk-spreading Rules

Investment limits, designed to avoid excessive concentrations of risk, are imposed under Article 50(2).[212] A UCITS may invest no more than 10 per cent of its assets in transferable

---

[209] 2012 CEPS/ECMI Report, n 12, 55.

[210] CESR Level 3 Guidelines on Classification of Hedge Fund Indices as Financial Indices (2007) (CESR/07–434).

[211] Art 63 of the AIFMD adds a new Art 50a, containing the new delegation, to the UCITS Directive.

[212] The investment policy rules do not apply where a UCITS is exercising subscription rights attaching to transferable securities or money-market instruments in accordance with Art 57.

securities and money-market instruments other than those covered in Article 50(1),[213] and may not acquire precious metals (or related certificates). Restrictions are also placed on property investments: an investment company may acquire moveable and immoveable property, but only where it is essential for the direct pursuit of its business (Article 50(3)). Pre-crisis moves to develop a passportable retail market property fund,[214] reflecting the popularity of real estate investment trusts (REITs), were abandoned; such funds now come within the 2011 AIFMD. UCITS are also permitted to hold ancillary liquid assets (Article 50(2)), chiefly bank deposits, in order to cover, for example, exceptional payment obligations.[215]

Article 52(1) is the core investment limits provision. It provides that a UCITS may invest no more than 5 per cent of its assets in transferable securities or money-market instruments issued by the same body; it may not invest more than 20 per cent of its assets in deposits with the same body. Article 52(1) also provides that the UCITS risk exposure to a counterparty of the UCITS in an OTC derivative transaction may not exceed 10 per cent of its assets when the counterparty is a credit institution (as referred to in Article 50(1)(f)) or, in all other cases, 5 per cent of its assets. A UCITS may not, overall, have exposure to a single body of more than 20 per cent of its assets (Article 52(2)).

For transferable securities and money-market instruments, the 5 per cent limit may, under Article 52(2), be raised to 10 per cent, but in this case the total value of these instruments held by the UCITS in the issuing bodies in each of which it invests more than 5 per cent of its assets, must not then exceed 40 per cent of the value of its assets (this limit does not apply to deposits and OTC derivative transactions made with financial institutions subject to prudential supervision). The basic 5 per cent limitation can be raised by the Member States to 35 per cent for transferable securities and money-market instruments issued or guaranteed by public authorities (Member States, local authorities, non-Member States, or public international bodies to which one or more Member States belong) and to 25 per cent for bonds issued by credit institutions where, in each case, certain conditions are met (Article 52(3) and (4)).

The Article 52(1)–(4) limits may not be combined: as a result, investments in transferable securities or money-market instruments issued by the same body or in deposits or derivative instruments made with this body in accordance with Article 52(1)–(4) may not, in any circumstances, exceed in total 35 per cent of the assets of the UCITS (Article 52(5)). The Directive also provides that the transferable securities and money-market instruments referred to in Article 52(3) and (4) are not to be taken into account for the purposes of applying the Article 52(2) 40 per cent limit (Article 52(5)).[216]

---

[213] Following some market confusion on this issue, ESMA has confirmed that this relaxation does not apply to CISs, whose eligibility as investment assets remains governed by Art 50(1)(e): ESMA Opinion/2012/721.

[214] For discussion see Moloney, n 33, 475–6.

[215] 2009 UCITS IV Directive rec 41. Liquid financial assets may also be held where, eg, because of unfavourable market conditions, investments by the UCITS are suspended.

[216] The overall limit of 35 per cent was a matter of some controversy when the UCITS III reforms were adopted. The ECB noted in its Opinion on the UCITS III Product Proposal that 'it seems questionable whether the investment of up to 35 per cent of the assets of a fund in instruments of one issuer can be reconciled with the principle of risk spreading': [1999] OJ L285/9 para I, 4.

Article 52(5) addresses groups. It provides that companies included in the same group for the purposes of consolidation are to be regarded as a single body for the purpose of the investment limits. Member States may allow cumulative investment in transferable securities and money-market instruments within the same group up to a limit of 20 per cent.

Article 54 addresses investment in securities issued by public authorities. By way of derogation, Member States may authorize UCITSs to invest (in accordance with the principle of risk-spreading) up to 100 per cent of their assets in different transferable securities and money-market instruments issued or guaranteed by any Member State, its local authorities, any non-Member State, or public international bodies of which one or more Member States are members (Article 54(1)). The securities must, however, be from at least six different issues, securities from any single issue must not account for more than 30 per cent of the UCITS' total assets, and the NCA may only grant the derogation to a particular UCITS where it is satisfied that unit-holders have protection equivalent to those unit-holders in UCITSs which comply with the investment limits set out in Article 52.

Further protection is given to unit-holders by a disclosure requirement. The UCITS must make express mention in either the fund rules or the instruments of incorporation (which must be approved by the NCA) of any permitted entity in which it intends to invest more than 35 per cent of its assets, and include a 'prominent statement' referring to this authorization and the entities concerned in its prospectus and any promotional literature (Article 54(2) and (3)).

Finally, in order to encourage appropriate risk-spreading and to prevent a UCITS from pursuing control over the issuers in which it invests,[217] which activity is outside the function of a UCITS, restrictions are placed by Article 56 on the voting rights and management control which a UCITS may acquire through its investment activities. The central requirement is that the investment company or the management company (acting in connection with all of the common funds which it manages and which fall within the scope of the Directive) may not acquire any shares carrying voting rights which would enable it to exercise significant influence over the management of an issuing body (Article 56(1)).[218]

III.3.8.4 Strand (2): Investment Limits–Particular Investment Policies and UCITS Structures

(a) Tracker Funds

Article 53 is designed to reflect the popularity of tracker funds and to encourage greater investment in equities. It permits Member States to adopt a limit of up to 20 per cent of assets for investments in shares or debt securities issued by the same body when, according to the fund rules or instruments of incorporation, the aim of the UCITS' investment policy is to 'replicate' (or track) the composition of a certain stock or debt securities index which is recognized by the NCAs according to the criteria set out in Article 53. These criteria, which are designed to ensure that the replication technique is not abused, require that the index is sufficiently diversified, that it represents an adequate benchmark for the market to which it

---

[217] The UCITS regime therefore falls outside the debate as to the influence exerted by large funds, particularly hedge funds and private equity funds, on issuers. See, eg, Brav, A, Jiang, W, Partnoy, F, and Thomas, R, 'Hedge Fund Activism, Corporate Governance and Firm Performance' (2008) 63 *J Fin* 1729.
[218] The regime is amplified in Arts 56(2) and (3).

refers, and that it is published in an appropriate manner. The 20 per cent limit may, under Article 53(2), be raised to 35 per cent where this is justified by 'exceptional market conditions in particular in regulated markets where certain transferable securities or money-market instruments are highly dominant'. This extension is permitted only for a single issuer.

(b) Funds of Funds

With respect to CIS investments, a limit of 10 per cent of total assets applies to investments in a CIS, which Member States may raise to 20 per cent (Article 55) (see below on the related master-feeder fund regime). Investments made in units of CISs other than UCITSs may not exceed, in aggregate, 30 per cent of the assets of the UCITS; a UCITS may, however, invest 100 per cent of its funds in units of other UCITSs.

Article 50(1)(e) is designed to protect investors against cascades of investments in CISs which may result in opaque cross-investments in other CISs. It provides that a UCITS may not invest in units of another UCITS or CIS which invests itself more than 10 per cent of its assets in units of other UCITSs and/or CISs.

Finally, Article 55(3) addresses the conflicts of interest which arise where the UCITS invests in a UCITS or other CIS which is managed by the same management company (or by any other company with which the management company is linked by common management or control or by a substantial direct or indirect holding). That management company or other company may not charge subscription or redemption fees on account of the UCITS' investment in the units of such other UCITS and/or CIS. Article 55(3) also provides that a UCITS that invests a 'substantial proportion' (undefined) of its assets in other UCITSs and/or CISs must disclose in its prospectus and annual report the maximum level of the management fees that may be charged to both the UCITS itself and the other UCITSs or CISs in which it intends to invest.

(c) Master-feeder Funds

The UCITS III regime prohibited UCITSs from taking the form of feeder funds which invest all their assets exclusively in the units of one UCITS (the master fund). Scale efficiencies can, however, be generated by asset-pooling techniques through which assets of different funds are aggregated and managed as a single pool.[219] The 2006 Investment Funds White Paper acknowledged the scale, liquidity, and trading benefits which can flow from pooling techniques, and committed to revising the diversification regime to permit asset pooling in the form of 'master-feeder' fund structures.[220] The 2009 UCITS IV Directive accordingly introduced a new regime for master-feeder UCITSs, reflecting market practice with respect to CISs in many Member States[221] and strong industry demand for easier cross-border access by these structures.

---

[219] Asset pooling allows assets to be combined into a common account for the purposes of investment management and custody. 'Virtual-pooling' techniques combine the assets in a single account but preserve the separate legal entity of the funds in question. 'Entity pooling' involves the assets being combined in a separate legal vehicle. For an extensive discussion see 2006 Investment Fund Market Efficiency Expert Group Report, n 80, 16–21.

[220] The 2008 UCITS IV Proposal similarly acknowledged that master-feeder structures would allow UCITS funds to increase the efficiency of their investment policy: n 92, 8.

[221] 2009 UCITS IV Directive rec 50.

A feeder UCITS is a UCITS (or an investment compartment thereof) which has acquired specific approval to invest at least 85 per cent of its assets in the units of another UCITS (or an investment compartment of that UCITS) (the 'master UCITS') (Article 58); the regime is accordingly limited to structures involving one 'master' for each 'feeder' UCITS.[222] This regime represents a significant departure from the investment limit rules and has the potential to carry significant risks for investors, given the scale of the exposure to another UCITS, although these risks are mitigated by the panoply of UCITS rules which apply to the master UCITS. Accordingly, there is a discrete and detailed regime designed to ensure initial supervisory oversight of the decision by the UCITS to invest in the master UCITS and, thereafter, to ensure that the feeder UCITS can appropriately act in the best interests of its unit-holders. It covers the approval of these UCITSs (Article 59);[223] the required agreements between the master and feeder funds (Article 60);[224] asset allocation (with respect to the remaining 15 per cent) (Article 58); co-ordination between the different master and feeder depositaries and auditors (Articles 61–2); the feeder UCITS prospectus, annual report, and half-yearly report (Article 63);[225] the procedure for the conversion of existing UCITSs into master-feeder structures (Article 64); and the specific monitoring obligations imposed on the feeder UCITS in relation to the master UCITS, the general obligations of the master in relation to the feeder,[226] and NCA obligations relating to notifications[227] (Articles 65–66). A highly detailed administrative regime amplifies the requirements which apply to master-feeder structures.[228]

III.3.8.5 Strand (2): Investment Limits–Disclosure of Investment Policies

Risk assessment by investors forms part of the asset-allocation regime. Under Article 70(1), the UCITS prospectus must indicate in which categories of assets a UCITS is authorized to invest. If it is authorized to engage in transactions in financial derivatives, it must include a 'prominent statement' indicating whether these transactions may be carried out for the purposes of hedging or with the aim of meeting investment goals, and the possible outcome of the use of financial derivatives instruments on the UCITS' risk profile. Under Article 70(2), when a UCITS invests principally in assets other than transferable securities and money-market instruments or when it replicates an index, its prospectus and, where necessary, any other marketing literature must include a prominent statement drawing attention to this investment policy. Similarly, when the NAV of a UCITS is likely to have high volatility due to its portfolio composition or the portfolio management techniques that may be used, its prospectus/marketing literature must include a prominent statement

---

[222] This restriction is designed to support supervision, but also to facilitate investor understanding of these structures: rec 51.

[223] The approval process applies to the initial decision of the feeder UCITS to invest in the master UCITS.

[224] This agreement is central to the support of communication between the feeder and master structures and must cover, eg, the supply of documents from the master to the feeder structure, NAV calculation timings, the suspension of redemptions, and liquidation of each structure.

[225] The prospectus, eg, must include specific disclosures on the feeder structure, including on the alignment (or otherwise) of the master and feeder structures' investment objectives, on the master structure, and on the master and feeder agreements.

[226] Chief among these is the prohibition on the imposition of fees by the master structure on the feeder structure with respect to UCITS subscription and redemption: Art 66.

[227] Including notification of the feeder UCITS of decisions taken in relation to the master UCITS: Art 67.

[228] 2010 Commission Mergers and Master-Feeder Directive Arts 8–28, covering, *inter alia*, the master-feeder agreement, the conduct rules governing the master-feeder relationship, including with respect to dealing and conflicts of interests, liquidations, merger, and division procedures, and monitoring by the auditor and depositary.

drawing attention to this fact (Article 70(3)). Finally, under Article 70(4), on the request of an investor, the management company must provide supplementary information relating to the quantitative limits which apply to the risk management of the UCITS, to the methods chosen to this end, and to the recent evolution of the risks and yields of the main instrument categories.

III.3.8.6 Strand (3): Efficient Portfolio Management Techniques, Managing Derivatives Exposure, and Risk Management

Under the original 1985 UCITS Directive, Member States could authorize a UCITS to employ 'techniques and instruments relating to transferable securities' under the conditions and within the limits which they laid down, provided that such techniques and instruments were used for the purpose of efficient portfolio management.[229]

With the introduction of the use of financial derivatives as investments and not simply as general hedging or portfolio management devices, the UCITS risk-management regime was recast by the UCITS III reforms, and is now set out in Article 51 of the 2009 UCITS IV Directive; the legislative regime has been subject to detailed amplification by the 2010 Commission Management Company Directive. While of central importance to UCITS risk management, the regime has wider importance as the first major attempt by the EU to address risk management in relation to derivatives. In order to ensure that the risks and commitments arising from derivative transactions are contained, Article 51(1) requires that the management or investment company must have a risk-management process in place which enables it, at any time, to monitor and measure the risk of the positions held and their contribution to the overall risk profile of the portfolio. A process for the accurate and independent assessment of the value of OTC derivative instruments must also be in place. With respect to each UCITS, the NCAs (and ESMA) must be informed regularly, and in accordance with rules set by the NCAs, of the types of derivative instruments involved, the underlying risks, the quantitative limits, and the methods chosen to estimate risk.

In a throwback to the earlier position, Article 51(2), which has been amplified by administrative rules, provides that Member States may authorize UCITSs to 'employ techniques and instruments relating to transferable securities and money-market instruments' (such as the repo transactions currently under review internationally—section 3.14.4) under the conditions and limits they lay down for the purposes of efficient portfolio management but, where derivatives are involved, the conditions and limits must conform with the Directive: 'under no circumstances shall these operations cause the UCITS to diverge from its investment objective' (Article 52(2)). The administrative regime (under the 2007 Commission Eligible Assets Directive) has amplified this somewhat Delphic provision. Article 13 of the 2007 Directive is designed to accommodate the rapid development of portfolio management techniques[230] and sets out general criteria for establishing the scope

---

[229] Art 21(1). This convoluted provision was designed to cover the use by UCITSs of derivative instruments such as futures and options. Considerable difficulties arose in the course of the original UCITS Directive negotiations over the treatment of options traded on a regulated option market (the main ones at the time were in London and the Netherlands) and whether they would be treated as transferable securities. The unhappy solution was Art 21(1).

[230] As was clear during the negotiations on the 2007 Commission Eligible Assets Directive (ESC/44/2006 Rev 2, 10). Market participants were concerned to ensure that techniques should not be restricted to low-risk techniques. 2006 CESR Eligible Assets Technical Advice, n 195, 37.

of Article 52 (2) 'techniques', including that they are economically appropriate (realized in a cost-effective way); are entered into for the purpose of risk reduction, cost reduction, or the generation of additional capital or income for the UCITS consistent with the UCITS' risk profile; and their risks are adequately captured by the UCITS' risk-management process.

Exposure and leverage are addressed by Article 51(3), which requires that a UCITS must ensure that its global exposure relating to derivative instruments (the calculation of which must be carried out in accordance with the Directive's general guidelines[231]) does not exceed the total net value of its portfolio. Exposure to the underlying assets must also be considered. Under Article 51(3), UCITS exposure to underlying assets through derivative investments must not exceed in aggregate the Article 52 investment limits. The limits are relaxed for index-based derivatives. Where a UCITS invests in index-based financial derivative instruments, these investments do not have to be combined to the limits laid down in Article 52. At all times, where a transferable security or money-market instrument embeds a derivative, the derivative must be taken into account when complying with Article 51(3). Member States are required under Article 51(4) to provide the Commission with full information concerning the specific methods used to calculate risk exposures and of any changes.

The basic legislative framework has been subject to a series of refinements and amplifications.

The first attempt to amplify the risk-management regime came in the form of the 2004 Commission Recommendation[232] which adopted common basic principles for risk-management. It established a number of key risk-management principles which were subsequently implemented 'at a reasonably good level' across the Member States.[233] The Recommendation covers risk-management systems, limitations on the overall risk exposure of a UCITS, the measurement of market, counterparty, and issuer risk, and rules for listed and OTC financial derivatives. Recommendation 2 is at the heart of the regime and limits global exposure to financial derivative instruments to 100 per cent of the UCITS' NAV and UCITS overall risk exposure to 200 per cent of NAV.[234] Considerably high levels of gearing or borrowing are therefore tolerated, increasing the risk profile of a UCITS. Other key recommendations include that Member States ensure that fund managers employ tailored risk-management systems which are adapted to the particular risk profile of the UCITS (Recommendation 1). Many of the procedural risk-management recommendations were, however, overtaken by the 2010 Commission Management Company Directive, adopted under the 2009 UCITS IV Directive. This puts in place a detailed rulebook governing the measurement of risk and addressing: risk-management policies and their review (Articles 38–9); measuring and managing risk, including through stress tests (Article 40); the

---

[231] The exposure must be calculated taking into account the current value of the underlying assets, the counterparty risk, future market movements, and the time available to liquidate the positions.

[232] Commission Recommendation on the use of financial derivative instruments for undertakings for collective investment in transferable securities (2004/383/EC) [2004] OJ L144/33 (the 2004 Commission Risk Management Recommendation).

[233] CESR, Implementation of the European Commission's Recommendations on UCITS. Report of the Review conducted by CESR (2005) (CESR/05–302b) 5.

[234] The Recommendation also provides that the overall risk exposure may not be increased by more than 10 per cent by means of temporary borrowing, so that the overall risk exposure may not exceed 210 per cent in any circumstances.

calculation of 'global exposure' (Article 41);[235] the commitment approach for calculating global exposure (Article 42); counterparty risk and issuer concentration (Article 43); valuing OTC derivatives (Article 44); and reporting on derivatives (Article 45).

The extent to which the risk-management regime has been further refined and operationalized through detailed supervisory convergence measures vividly illustrates how CESR initially and since ESMA can thicken the legislative/administrative rulebook by addressing detailed operational questions. The burgeoning 'soft' risk measurement and management regime can be traced to the 2009 CESR Risk Management Guidelines which were adopted (as an interim measure pending the 2010 Commission Management Company Directive) in the teeth of the financial crisis and in order to ensure a comprehensive approach pan-EU to UCITS risk management.[236] Although the 2009 Guidelines have, in many respects, been overtaken by the 2010 Commission Management Company Directive, the 2010 CESR Guidelines on Risk Measurement and Global Exposure, which provide detailed operational guidance on the 2010 Commission Management Company Directive,[237] remain of central importance. They have been updated by ESMA on a regular basis,[238] and have also been refined by tailored ESMA guidelines for particular types of UCITS.[239] Additional guidelines have been adopted with respect to discrete elements of the asset allocation and related risk management, particularly with respect to Article 51 efficient portfolio management techniques and with respect to repo arrangements (section 3.14.4).[240]

III.3.8.7 Asset Allocation and UCITS VI

Further refinement to the asset-allocation regime is likely to follow from the UCITS VI process. The 2012 UCITS VI Consultation suggests a Commission concern to restrict the scope of eligible assets and the extent to which UCITSs can be exposed to non-eligible assets (including through indices),[241] to impose additional restrictions on the current range of eligible assets, particularly derivatives, and, reflecting the international reform agenda

---

[235] The calculation, which must be carried out daily, can be made by reference to either (i) the incremental exposure and leverage generated by the UCITS from financial derivatives and which may not exceed total UCITS NAV; or (ii) the market risk of the UCITS' portfolio. The calculation can be made under the commitment approach, the Value at Risk (VAR) approach, or under any other advanced risk-management technique, as appropriate. In this regard, the Directive reflects in part the earlier 2004 Commission Risk Management Recommendation, although it recommended that the commitment approach apply to 'simple' UCITS, and that the VAR method be used for more advanced UCITS.

[236] CESR/09-178.

[237] n 123. The Guidelines were developed in tandem with CESR's technical advice on the 2010 Directive, and as accompanying guidance. They cover, in great operational detail, the detailed methodologies to be used for calculating global exposure and counterparty risk, and include detailed guidance on the commitment and VAR methods for calculation, and on the assets which can be regarded as collateral.

[238] eg ESMA Q&A on the 2010 Guidelines, addressing their treatment of hedging strategies and leverage (ESMA/2012/429).

[239] ESMA 2012 Structured UCITS Guidelines, n 127. The extensive guidance addresses, in relation to complex and structured funds, the use of Art 51 efficient portfolio management techniques (including with respect to repos), investments in financial derivatives, and the management of collateral for efficient portfolio management techniques and in relation to OTC financial derivative transactions.

[240] ESMA 2012 Repo Guidelines, n 128.

[241] Although the Consultation also queries whether UCITSs should invest in low-liquidity long-term assets, such as real estate investment: n 111, para 8.

relating to securities lending and repurchasing, to impose restrictions on the types of efficient portfolio management techniques which can be used.[242]

III.3.8.8 The Risks Associated with Asset-allocation Regulation

The UCITS asset-allocation regime is highly detailed but facilitative, and is supported by extensive and operationally focused risk-management rules which look set to expand under UCITS VI. It has also had significant transformative effects. In the immediate wake of the UCITS III reforms, structured financial instruments, non-UCITS CISs, and financial derivatives, including those based on hedge fund indices, all became eligible for UCITS investment.[243] From the outset, the new 'UCITS III' structures began to adopt more sophisticated derivatives-based investment techniques.[244]

Two risks in particular are associated with the facilitative UCITS asset-allocation regime. The first relates to the heavy lifting which risk-management rules and internal procedures must carry out. Here, the risks have not yet been realized, or at least not to a significant degree;[245] the intense policy attention focused on UCITS risk management may not accordingly be warranted. Prior to the massive expansion in the risk-management regime over 2010, the UCITS III legislative regime, in combination with the 2004 Commission Recommendation and along with market discipline dynamics, seems to have delivered relatively strong risk management prior to the crisis.[246] The financial crisis did not reveal significant weaknesses in risk management, with the UCITS industry performing reasonably well under significant strain.

The more significant risk lies with the retail market. The relatively crude UCITS diversification rules only limit exposure to single issuers; they are not linked to factors more likely to impact on diversification and returns, such as the degree of concentration in particular industry sectors or in particular asset classes. The UCITS investment limits did not protect investors from market risk related to over-exposure to particular asset classes as the financial crisis deepened;[247] for example, the retail sector experienced proportionately heavier losses than the institutional sector over the financial crisis, given the predominance of equity

---

[242] n 111, paras 2 (eligible assets), 3 (efficient portfolio management), and 4 (OTC derivatives).

[243] By 2007, the industry was preparing a range of sophisticated alternative investment funds for mass-market investors, based on hedge-fund strategies but using the UCITS III vehicle: Johnson, S, 'Sophistication Goes Mass Market', *Financial Times, Fund Management Supplement*, 5 November 2007, 1.

[244] While the market took some time to use the full range of UCITS III investment strategies, 2007 saw the emergence of more radical derivatives-based funds such as ABN Amro's first pure derivatives, UCITS III fund in March 2007: Johnson, S, 'New Products Make Use of UCITS Power', *Financial Times, Fund Management Supplement*, 12 March 2007, 3.

[245] Although the 2012 CEPS/ECMI Report warned that the risk-management rules relating to derivatives were vulnerable to arbitrage risks: n 12, 72.

[246] A 2008 PriceWaterhouseCoopers Report found that while reliance on derivatives had increased, UCITS III investment powers were being used effectively and market risk levels were not significantly higher as compared to those of other CISs: PriceWaterhouseCoopers, Investment Funds in the European Union: Comparative Analysis of Use of Investment Powers, Investment Outcomes and Related Risk Features in Both UCITS and Non-Harmonised Markets (2008).

[247] In 2013, ESMA reported that some 42 per cent of UCITS funds take the form of equity funds, 28 per cent bond funds, and 20 per cent mixed asset funds.

investments in retail AUM.[248] Neither do asset-allocation rules protect investors from the herding risks associated with the fund industry generally.[249]

More seriously in terms of retail market risk, the asset-allocation regime is highly facilitative and supports very complex UCITSs.[250] While, in practice, UCITS III products are typically used as investment vehicles by sophisticated investors, UCITS III schemes can be marketed to the public and related 'retailization' can occur, with attendant investor confusion and mis-selling risks. The international distribution of UCITSs faced some related early difficulties following the stretching of the asset-allocation regime under UCITS III.[251] But over the crisis era, the risk of detriment to the retail sector, following the stretching of the UCITS brand to include funds with complex and high-risk portfolio management techniques—in particular hedge fund-like products[252]—and the use by banks of complex UCITS products to generate balance sheet-repairing revenues,[253] came into sharp policy focus.

At the heart of the difficulty is the success of the generic UCITS 'label' and of the related regulatory regime in 'branding' the UCITS as a relatively conservative, mass-market savings product.[254] But the issues raised by any reforming change to the UCITS label (by means of, for example, the identification and differential regulation of different types of UCITS) are many and complex. The exclusion of 'structured UCITSs' from the 2014 MiFID II execution-only regime, for example, proved controversial, as noted in Chapter IX section 5.2.6. Industry opposition was considerable, given the potential damage to the wider UCITS brand globally and potential damage to the integrity of the UCITS regulatory regime.[255] The wider consequential impact on UCITS regulation generally, which assumes

---

[248] Retail investor AUM lost 22 per cent in value in 2008, as compared to a loss of 7 per cent in the institutional segment: 2012 EFAMA Asset Management Report, n 1, 28.

[249] US mutual funds were among the main purchasers of asset backed securities, leading to significant litigation in the US: Ferrell, A, Bethel, J, and Hu, G, Legal and Economic Issues in Litigation after the 2007–2008 Credit Crisis, Harvard Law and Economics Discussion Paper No 612 (2008), available at <http://ssrn/abstract=1096582>.

[250] One report has suggested that with UCITS III, UCITS funds evolved from deploying traditional asset management strategies to deploying a full set of alternative strategies: 2012 KPMG Report, n 96, 6.

[251] Johnson, S, 'How UCITS Became a Runaway Success', *Financial Times, Fund Management Supplement,* 27 November 2006, 3. UCITS funds came under much closer scrutiny in Hong Kong and Singapore, eg, where before they had enjoyed a relatively straightforward authorization process.

[252] This development was extensively reported, following the move by hedge funds into UCITS III structures in early 2009, driven by investor demand for higher standards of investor protection, liquidity, and transparency: eg, Kelleher, E, 'Listed Funds of Hedge Funds Lose Out to UCITS III', *Financial Times, Fund Management Supplement,* 18 April 2011, 8. The leverage capacity of one UCITS fund, which holds a total return swap on a proprietary index that can be leveraged up to 35 times, while permissible, was described by some industry figures as 'horrid' and 'extraordinary': Johnson, S, 'Swaps Tactic Threatens UCITS Brand', *Financial Times, Fund Supplement,* 14 November 2011, 1.

[253] Skypala, P, 'What will the banks think of next?', *Financial Times, Fund Management Supplement,* 14 November 2011, 6.

[254] eg Deutsche Bank Research, EU Asset Management, EU Monitor No 37 (2006) 6, describing the UCITS as an investment with a degree of risk and complexity that ordinary investors can be expected to bear. Similarly, EFAMA expressed concern that the Madoff scandal might damage the UCITS brand and the high levels of investor protection associated with the brand: EFAMA, Press Release, 15 January 2009.

[255] eg, in the context of the execution-only reforms, the responses by the Association of British Insurers and EFAMA to the MiFID I Review (available online at <http://ec.europa.eu/internal_market/consultations/2010/mifid_en.htm>) and the 2012 KPMG Report, n 96, 11. But while industry opposition was intense (19 of 23 fund managers in one survey opposed the reform: Cookson, R, 'Few Votes for Complex UCITS',

that the UCITS product is a 'gold-standard' retail market product, is also considerable, as reflected in CESR's considerable nervousness in addressing this question.[256]

III.3.9 The Management Company: Ongoing Regulation

Management companies are subject to detailed harmonized operating rules (conduct and prudential in nature) which respond to the agency risks in the UCITS/investor relationship and support the passport.

The operational regime reflects the major principles which govern the investment services regime generally (Chapter IV), but it is tailored to the particular risks posed by collective asset management. Management companies must comply with the authorization conditions (Article 10(1)) and a qualifying shareholders regime (Article 11), and follow the prudential requirements, specific to collective investment management, set out in Article 12.[257] The Article 12 conflict-of-interest regime is directed to ensuring that the management company is structured and organized in such a way as to minimize the risk of clients' or UCITSs' interests being prejudiced by conflicts of interest.[258] The conflicts regime applies particular requirements where the management company engages in discretionary asset management: the management company cannot invest all or part of the investor's portfolio in units of a CIS it manages without prior general approval from the client (Article 12(2)). A discrete regime applies to delegation by management companies (which can include asset management functions, but which must not be of such an extent that the management company becomes a 'letter box') (Article 13(1) and (2)).[259] Of central operational importance is the requirement that the liability of the management company (and of the depositary) cannot be affected by delegation of any functions to third parties (Article 13(2)).

Conduct rules also apply to management companies, which are similar to the investment services conduct regime (Article 14).[260] Management companies are also required to have in place appropriate investor complaints' systems (Article 15).

Financial Times, Fund Management Supplement, 17 September 2012, 2), it was not monolithic: Grene, S, 'Industry Call for Simplified UCITS', *Financial Times*, 8 February 2010, 4.

[256] eg CESR, Advice on the MiFID I Review (2010) (CESR/10-859), declining to give the Commission technical advice on this question given the complexities involved.

[257] These relate to administrative and accounting procedures, internal control mechanisms (including personal transactions by employees), compliance, and record-keeping (in order, in particular, to ensure that UCITSs' transactions can be reconstructed, where necessary): Art 12(1)(a).

[258] Including conflicts between two UCITSs managed by the management company: Art 12(1)(b).

[259] The regime is designed to ensure that supervision is not prejudiced, that the entity to which functions are delegated is appropriately regulated and supervised, and that the management company monitors the entity. In order to protect the independence of the depositary and avoid serious related conflict of interest risk, core investment management functions must not be delegated to the depositary or to any undertaking whose interests may conflict with those of the management company or unit-holders.

[260] The principles with which Member States' conduct rules must comply include that the management company: act honestly and fairly in the best interests of the UCITSs under management and the integrity of the market; act with due care, skill, and diligence; has and employs effectively the resources and procedures necessary for the proper performance of its business; tries to avoid conflicts of interest and, where they are unavoidable, ensures the UCITSs it manages are fairly treated; and complies with all regulatory requirements.

A highly detailed prudential and conduct administrative rulebook for management companies is now in place under the 2010 Commission Management Company Directive. It sets out in considerable detail a suite of rules applicable to prudential and organizational matters,[261] although the rules are tailored to the nature, scale, and complexity of the management company's business. Detailed administrative conduct rules also apply under the 2010 Directive to the particular conduct risks generated by collective investment management, and in particular by trading practices.[262]

The adoption of the 2010 Commission Management Company Directive markedly increased the intensity of the EU's regulation of collective investment management. The administrative rulebook is notable for its breadth and for its detail, even by comparison with the earlier MiFID I prudential and conduct administrative rulebook governing discretionary asset management (Chapter IV). Accordingly, the 2010 Commission Directive provided a useful template for the 2011 AIFMD administrative prudential and conduct regime.

A broadly similar operating regime (Article 30–1) applies under the UCITS Directive to investment companies which do not appoint a separate management company,[263] although the regime is significantly more attenuated in places,[264] reflecting the reduced agency risks in these structures.

The 2014 UCITS V reforms to the 2009 Directive[265] further intensify these operating requirements and align them with the 2011 AIFMD by addressing the remuneration policies and practices of management companies (Articles 14a and 14b). In a striking example of how reforms leaked across regulated sectors over the crisis era, the 2012 UCITS V Proposal (which was broadly reflected in the final UCITS V text) applied the detailed AIFMD remuneration regime to UCITS management companies, in order to promote effective risk management. Under the UCITS V reforms, management companies are required to establish and apply remuneration policies and practices consistent with, and that promote, sound and effective risk management; remuneration policies and practices must not encourage risk-taking inconsistent with the risk profiles, rules, or instruments of incorporation of the UCITSs managed, and must not impair compliance with the

---

[261] The Directive covers: organizational procedures, including accounting systems and business continuity (Art 4); resources (Art 5); complaints handling (Art 6); data processing (Art 7); accounting procedures (Art 8); senior management controls and functions (Art 9); the permanent compliance, audit, and risk management functions (Arts 10–12); personal transactions (Art 13); recording of portfolio transactions (Art 14); recording of subscription and redemption orders (Art 15); record-keeping (Art 16); and conflict of interest management, including identification, conflict of interest policy, management, and related voting right strategies (Arts 17–21).

[262] The conduct regime addresses: the obligation to act in the best interests of the UCITS (Art 22); due diligence and related risk management (Art 23); reporting on execution of subscription and redemption orders (Art 24); best execution (Art 25); order handling and trading processes (Arts 26–28); and safeguarding the UCITS' best interests (Art 29).

[263] Where an investment company appoints a separate management company, the operating regime for management companies supplants that applicable to investment companies, although the basic authorization conditions for investment companies apply.

[264] Although the same delegation and conduct rules (including the administrative regime) apply (Art 30), the prudential regime has not been amplified through administrative rules and remains governed by general principles (save with respect to risk management—Commission 2010 Management Company Directive Art 12): Art 31.

[265] See n 109 for the legislative history.

management company's duty to act in the best interests of the UCITSs managed (Article 14a(1)). Remuneration policies and procedures must include fixed and variable components of salaries, as well as discretionary pension benefits (Article 14a(2)). These policies and procedures must apply to those categories of staff (including senior management, risk-takers, control functions, and any employee receiving total remuneration that falls within the remuneration bracket of senior management and risk-takers) whose professional activities have a material impact on the risk profiles of the management company or of the UCITSs managed (Article 14a(3)). The new regime includes detailed remuneration principles, based on the 2011 AIFMD regime and to be amplified by ESMA guidance (under Article 14a(4) ESMA is to adopt guidelines on remuneration, in co-operation with EBA, which take into account, *inter alia*, the size of the management company and UCITSs managed, as well as the nature, scope, and complexity of activities) governing remuneration policies, and which must be complied with by management companies in a way and to an extent appropriate to their size, internal organization, and the nature, scope, and complexity of their activities (Article 14b(1)).[266] Management companies which are significant in terms of size (or the size of UCITSs they manage), their internal organization, and the nature, scope, and complexity of their activities (ESMA guidelines will govern this assessment) must establish a remuneration committee, responsible for remuneration; unusually, the committee is to take into account the long-term interests of investors and other stakeholders, as well as the public interest (Article 14b(3)). Remuneration must also be reported on in the UCITS prospectus and annual report (Article 69(1) and (3)). In addition, information on remuneration policies may be requested from NCAs by ESMA (Article 14b(2)). Efforts by the European Parliament to introduce a bonus cap similar to the highly contested cap which applies under the 2013 CRD IV/CRR regime failed, following intensive lobbying by the fund management industry.[267]

The UCITS V regime also reinforces the 2009 UCITS IV Directive Article 14 conduct regime by means of a new, overarching legislative requirement that the management

---

[266] Some 18 principles govern remuneration. These range from the general (eg aligning remuneration with sound and effective risk management and with the business strategy, objectives, and values of the management company and UCITSs managed; and the assessment of performance within a multiyear framework appropriate to the holding period recommended to the investors in the UCITSs managed) to the specific (eg guaranteed variable remuneration must be exceptional and limited to employees in their first year; 40 per cent of variable remuneration must be deferred (over a period which is appropriate in view of the holding period recommended to the investors in the UCITSs concerned, but at least three years)—where the variable component of remuneration is 'of a particularly high amount' at least 60 per cent must be deferred; and 50 per cent of variable remuneration must consist of units in the UCITS concerned (or equivalent ownership interests) or of share-linked instruments or equivalent non-cash instruments with 'equally effective incentives'—the 50 per cent rule does not apply where the management of UCITSs accounts for less than 50 per cent of the total portfolio managed by the management company). See further sect 4.9 on the parallel 2011 AIFMD remuneration regime.

[267] Barber, B and Marriage, M, 'Fund Managers Thank Stalinists for Bonus Vote', *Financial Times*, 3 July 2013, 3. The 2013 CRD IV/CRR regime (discussed in Ch IV sect 8.6) applies, however, to bank-owned asset managers, which led to concerns that they would be placed at a significant disadvantage to independent asset managers: Marriage, M, 'EU Bonus Cap Hits Bank-owned Asset Managers', *Financial Times Fund, Management Supplement*, 8 July 2013, 1. Difficulties also arose with respect to the application of the regime to third country managers of UCITS funds (to whom asset management is delegated), particularly with respect to the requirement of payment in UCITS units, but these were resolved at the last minute by means of a proportionality device (contained in rec 2 to the 2014 Directive): Mariage, M, 'EU Pay Rules Softened for US Fund Companies', *Financial Times, Fund Management Supplement*, 17 March 2014, 2.

company act honest, fairly, professionally, independently, and in the interests of the UCITS and the investors of the UCITS (Article 25(2)).

III.3.10 The Depositary

III.3.10.1 The Depositary and the 2009 Regime

The depositary, to which scheme assets must be entrusted[268] and which is subject to detailed regulation following the 2014 UCITS V reforms,[269] is central to the Directive's investor protection scheme.[270] It acts as the custodian of UCITS assets and is responsible for essential technical procedures relating to asset administration.[271]

Under the pre-UCITS V 2009 regime, the depositary was not subject to extensive authorization requirements, reflecting in part that depositaries were (and still are) often regulated credit institutions, but some restrictions were placed on the types of entity which could act as a depositary. The directors were required to be of sufficiently good repute and sufficiently experienced in relation to the type of UCITS to be managed,[272] and the depositary was to take the form of an institution subject to prudential regulation and ongoing supervision[273] and to furnish sufficient financial and professional guarantees that it could effectively pursue its business and meet its commitments.[274] The choice of depositary was also restricted by the requirement that it have its registered office or be established in the UCITS home Member State, so as to ensure the UCITS NCA could easily engage with

---

[268] Under Art 22(1) an investment company and, for each of the common funds it manages, a management company, must ensure that a single depositary is appointed (under the pre-UCITS V regime, a distinct regime applied to 'common funds' and 'investment companies', but a single regime now applies to management companies and investment companies).

[269] Sect 3.10.3.

[270] The home Member State of the investment company could lift the depositary requirement where the investment company marketed at least 80 per cent of its units through one or more stock exchanges (designated in the UCITS' instrument of incorporation), as long as the UCITS was admitted to 'official listing' on the exchanges in question (see Ch II sect 7.2.2 on 'official listing') and transactions with the UCITS outside the relevant exchanges were carried out at stock exchange prices only. The complex exemption included requirements relating to the calculation of prices for ex-stock-exchange transactions and rules relating to the maintenance and calculation of NAV: Art 32(5). This provision was removed under the UCITS V reforms.

[271] Under Art 22(3) the depositary is to ensure that the sale, issue, repurchase, redemption, and cancellation of units are carried out in accordance with applicable national law and fund rules/instruments of incorporation and that the value of units is calculated in accordance with applicable national law and fund rules/instruments of incorporation; carry out the instructions of the management company/investment company, unless they conflict with applicable national law or fund rules/instruments of incorporation; ensure that any consideration due is remitted within the usual time limits; and ensure that the scheme's income is applied in accordance with national law and the fund rules/instruments of incorporation (these requirements were not changed by the UCITS V reforms).

[272] Art 5(4). This requirement is still in force, following the UCITS V reforms.

[273] Member States were to determine which institutions were eligible to act as depositaries: Art 23(3) (common funds) and Art 33(2) (investment companies). This regime has been abolished by the UCITS V reforms and replaced by a harmonized set of conditions governing those institutions which can act as depositaries (see sect 3.10.3).

[274] Under Art 23(2) (common funds). A similar regime applied under Art 32(2) to investment companies—the requirement for guarantees did not apply. These requirements have been replaced by the UCITS V reforms (see sect 3.10.3).

the depositary (this requirement continues to apply).[275] The passporting regime did not accordingly (and does not under the UCITS V reforms) apply to depositaries. Independence was supported by the requirement that a single company could not act as both a management company and a depositary;[276] this requirement remains in force under the UCITS V reforms (Article 25(1)—which also applies to investment companies).

These restrictions on depositary choice aside, the depositary was not subject to ongoing regulation to any meaningful extent under the 2009 UCITS IV Directive, given that the banking regime, in practice, provided a regulatory proxy. The depositary was, however, to enable the UCITS home NCA to obtain, on request, all information that the depositary had obtained while discharging its duties and that was necessary for the NCA to supervise UCITS compliance; a similar requirement applies under the 2014 UCITS V reforms.[277] Similarly, underlining the monitoring role of the depositary, where the management company's home Member State was different to the UCITS home Member State the depositary was to sign a written agreement with the management company which regulated the flow of information deemed necessary to allow the depositary to fulfil its tasks; written agreement requirements also apply under the 2014 UCITS V reforms.[278] A detailed set of administrative rules governed the coverage of this agreement.[279]

The centrality of the depositary to investor protection was underlined by the specific liability regime which applied. The depositary, in accordance with the national law of the UCITS home Member State, was liable to the management company and to the unit-holders for any loss suffered by them as a result of its 'unjustifiable failure' to perform its obligations, or its improper performance of them; liability to unit-holders could be invoked directly or indirectly through the management company, depending on the legal nature of the relationship between the depositary, the management company, and unit-holders. This liability was not affected by the fact that the depositary had entrusted all or some of the assets to a third party.[280] The Madoff scandal, however, exposed the weaknesses of this regime,[281] and the 2014 UCITS V reforms have brought major change.

III.3.10.2 Madoff and Depositary Liability

While enhancements to the depositary regime had been under discussion since the start of the UCITS Review in 2004,[282] the regime has now undergone a significant reform, driven

---

[275] Under Art 23(1) (common funds) (Art 33(1) (investment companies)). This requirement is still in force for depositaries under the UCITS V reforms (Art 23(1)).

[276] Arts 25 (common funds) and 35 (investment companies).

[277] Arts 23(4) (common funds) and 33(4) (investment companies). Similar requirements apply under the UCITS V reforms. Art 26a requires that the depositary make available to its NCA on request all information which it has obtained while performing its duties and that may be necessary for its NCA or for the UCITS or management company NCAs. Where the UCITS or management company NCAs are different to that of the depositary, the depositary NCA must share the information received without delay.

[278] Arts 23(5) (common funds) and 33(5) (investment companies). The UCITS V reforms similarly require that the appointment of a depositary be evidenced by a written contract which, *inter alia*, must regulate the flow of information deemed necessary to allow the depositary to perform its functions for the UCITSs in question (Art 22(2)).

[279] 2010 Commission Management Company Directive Arts 30–37.

[280] These provisions have been reformed (sect 3.10.3).

[281] Sect 3.10.2.

[282] For a review of the different policy communications, see 2012 UCITS V Proposal Impact Assessment, n 57, 51–9.

by the financial crisis but also by the particular risks which the Madoff scandal[283] exposed. In the EU, only a very small number of UCITSs were affected by the scandal.[284] But the scandal exposed weaknesses in the Directive's depositary arrangements, as well as the risks attached to cross-border supervision and the associated risks related to splitting UCITS, depositary, and management company supervision, and led to the 2014 UCITS V reforms (section 3.10.3).

As the Madoff scandal unfolded over 2009, and shortly after the adoption of the 2009 UCITS IV reforms, concerns arose that Luxembourg and Ireland, the two centres with UCITSs exposed to the Madoff fraud, had not imposed sufficiently rigorous controls on UCITSs' depositaries who had outsourced custodian functions to Madoff affiliates and had not confirmed the existence of the underlying assets.[285] The financial crisis further underlined the risks associated with delegation by the depositary,[286] given the heightened need for careful asset recording and robust custody arrangements in times of acute market volatility.[287] Pressure for reform was increased by legal uncertainty as to the requirements of the 2009 UCITS IV Directive with respect to depositary liability in relation to failures by sub-custodians;[288] this uncertainty led to political tensions,[289] industry concern as to damage to the UCITS brand were assets to be perceived as being under threat,[290] and industry fears as to potentially massive liability costs were a liberal interpretation, attaching strict liability to depositaries for sub-custody failures, to be required.[291] In this febrile environment, reaction from the Commission was swift. Following a speedy review of depositary regulation across

---

[283] In the region of $50 billion of losses were sustained following the exposure of the Madoff funds as forming part of a Ponzi scheme which dissipated client assets.

[284] 4 UCITS funds entrusted assets to Madoff affiliates: Commission, Press Release 29 January 2009 (IP/09/126). One UCITS fund, however, lost in the region of $1.4 billion in acting as a feeder fund to a Madoff fund. Its authorization was withdrawn and it was placed in liquidation: 2012 UCITS V Proposal Impact Assessment, n 57, 6 and 22.

[285] eg Grene, S, 'Luxembourg Called On to "Brush Up" Governance', *Financial Times, Fund Management Supplement,* 26 January 2009, 3, highlighting the risks to the UCITS brand as over 30 per cent of UCITS funds were domiciled in Luxembourg, and Skypala, P, 'UCITS Victory Soured by Madoff Scandal', *Financial Times, Fund Management Supplement,* 19 January 2009, 6.

[286] eg, the 2009 DLG Report called for tighter harmonized regulation of delegation, and warned that the separation between asset management and custody, required by the UCITS regime, should be respected whatever delegation model was used: n 108, 26.

[287] FSA, Financial Risk Outlook (2009) 66.

[288] Under Arts 24 and 34 of the Directive, a depositary was liable for any loss suffered as a result of its 'unjustifiable' failure to perform its obligations, or its 'improper' performance of them, and liability was not affected by entrusting all or some of the assets in its safe-keeping to a third party. The depositary regime did not, however, expressly address the nature of delegation and the sub-custody relationship, or the interpretation of 'unjustifiable failure', leading to significant litigation in some Member States from Madoff failures.

[289] France, whose investors were significantly exposed to Madoff failures, claimed that its rules relating to depositary liability were of a higher standard than those of other Member States, and implicitly criticized the Luxembourg regime, triggering a hostile response from the Luxembourg authorities: Hollinger, P, Hall, B, and Tait, N, 'Grand Duchy Hits Back at Madoff', *Financial Times,* 14 January 2009, 23. French Finance Minister Lagarde wrote to the Commission and Luxembourg, warning of the risk which the Madoff scandal posed to the EU fund industry, given different interpretations of the UCITS Directive: Hollinger, P and Chung, J, 'Madoff Affair Sparks Demand for Revamp of Investment Fund Rules', *Financial Times,* 13 January 2009, 15.

[290] Grene, S, 'Luxembourg Called On to "Brush Up" Governance', *Financial Times, Fund Management Supplement,* 26 January 2009, 3, reporting on industry calls for Luxembourg to ensure its depositary regulation did not damage the UCITS brand.

[291] Skypala, n 285.

the EU, led by CESR[292]—which revealed significant divergences across the Member States[293]—and two Commission Consultations,[294] the Commission presented its Proposal for the UCITS V reform.[295] The 2012 UCITS V Proposal (on which institutional agreement was reached in February 2014), which was heavily based on the 2011 AIFMD template for depositary regulation, addressed the delegation and liability issues associated with the Madoff scandal and the significant divergences across the Member States in relation to depositary regulation. But it was also concerned more generally with the heightened custody risks which arise with more sophisticated UCITS funds, whose complex investments may be issued and held in third countries and across chains of custodians,[296] and with the updating of the regime to engage with electronic custody of dematerialized securities.[297]

III.3.10.3 The UCITS V Reforms and the Depositary

The new UCITS V regime imposes an enhanced depositary regime, closely based on the 2011 AIFMD model, on UCITSs.

Under a new Article 22, and as under the 2009 Directive, a single depositary must be appointed for each UCITS and a written contract must govern the flow of information necessary for the depositary to carry out its functions. The depositary's monitoring functions generally have not been reviewed and follow the 2009 regime (Article 22(3)), but a specific new monitoring obligation applies in relation to cash accounts and to cash flows, designed to ensure a Madoff-style fraudulent diversion of funds could not occur (Article 22(4)).[298] The regime also imposes new custody obligations and sets out the particular custody methods to be used for financial instruments which may be held in custody, and the ownership verification and record-keeping obligations for complex OTC assets which cannot be held in custody (Article 22(5)).[299] A depositary must provide the management company (or investment company) with a comprehensive inventory of all UCITS' assets on a regular basis (Article 22(6)). A prohibition applies to the re-use by the depositary of assets held in custody (including their transfer, pledge, sale, or lending) (Article 22(7)); re-use is permitted only where the re-use is executed for the account of the UCITS, the depositary is carrying out the instructions of the management company on behalf of the UCITS, the re-use is for the benefit of the UCITS and in the interests of unit-holders, and the transaction is covered by high-quality and liquid collateral.

---

[292] CESR seized the initiative at an early stage, co-ordinating the initial efforts to establish the scale of investor losses and the response by local NCAs: CESR Public Statement, 4 February 2009.

[293] Including with respect to liability and delegation: CESR, Mapping of Duties and Liabilities of UCITS Depositaries (2009) (CESR/09-175).

[294] July 2009 and December 2010.

[295] n 109.

[296] 2012 UCITS V Proposal, n 109, 3 and 5.

[297] 2012 UCITS V Proposal Impact Assessment, n 57, 7.

[298] The regime is designed to ensure that no cash account associated with the UCITS' transactions can be opened without the depositary's knowledge. Under Art 22(4), the depositary must, *inter alia*, ensure that the cash flows of the UCITS are properly monitored and that all UCITS' cash is booked in cash accounts that meet the Art 22(4) requirements (including that the account be in the name of the UCITS, management company, or depositary, and be opened in an eligible institutions (essentially, a central bank or EU/third country authorized deposit-taking credit institution)).

[299] This distinction is drawn from the 2011 AIFMD custody regime.

A new delegation regime now applies, modelled on the 2011 AIFMD regime (Article 22a). Depositaries are not permitted to delegate their Article 22(3) and (4) monitoring functions and can only delegate custody and verification/record-keeping obligations (Article 22(5)) where a series of conditions are met, including that the delegation is not designed to avoid the Directive, there is an objective reason for it, and the depositary has exercised all due skill care and diligence in the selection, appointment, and monitoring of the third party delegate (Article 22a(2)). Conditions apply to the third party delegate (Article 22a(3)).[300]

The new regime also limits the entities which can act as depositaries to national central banks, EU-authorized credit institutions, or 'other legal entities' authorized by an NCA to carry out depositary functions and which are subject to capital adequacy requirements and prudential requirements in accordance with the minimum standards applicable, which address, *inter alia*, infrastructure, compliance, management, internal controls, conflicts of interest, record-keeping, and business continuity (Article 23(2)); this regime (which was heavily negotiated in the final Commission/Council/European Parliament trilogue negoti-ations) reflects in particular the varying approaches across the Member States to those institutions eligible to act as depositaries, particularly with respect to capital requirements for depositary functions.[301]

The 2014 UCITS V regime has also replaced the depositary liability regime with stricter and more articulated rules. The depositary will be liable to the UCITS and its unit-holders for loss by the depositary (or a third party to whom custody is delegated); where loss occurs, the depositary will be required to return a financial instrument of identical type and corresponding amount to the UCITS (or management company) without delay. The depositary will not be liable if it can prove that the loss has arisen as a result of an external event beyond its reasonable control, the consequences of which would have been unavoid-able despite all reasonable efforts to the contrary (Article 24(1)).[302] This liability will not be affected by any delegation and, by contrast with the 2011 AIFMD regime but reflecting the retail orientation of the UCITS regime, cannot be excluded by agreement (Article 24(2), (3) and (4)). UCITS unit-holders have a direct right of redress against the depositary and are not required to proceed through the management company (or investment company), as long as this does not lead to a duplication of redress or to the unequal treatment of unit-holders.

Depositaries also become subject to a new and overarching obligation to act honestly, fairly, professionally, independently, and solely in the interest of the UCITS and UCITS investors (Article 25(2)). The depositary is also subject to a new conflict-of-interest rule requiring that it not carry out activities regarding the UCITS or management company that may create conflicts of interest, unless the depositary has functionally and hierarchically

---

[300] These include that the delegate has structures and expertise adequate and proportionate to the nature and complexity of the assets (or the management company), is subject to effective prudential regulation (including minimum capital requirements), its custody tasks are subject to external periodic audit, depositary assets are segregated, and complies with the Art 22(5) and (7) custody and asset re-use requirements.

[301] The Commission noted, eg, that of the 17 Member States that require depositaries to be credit institutions, 12 impose specific capital requirements in relation to custody functions: 2012 UCITS V Proposal, n 109, 4.

[302] The depositary is also liable for all other losses suffered because of the depositary's negligent or intentional failure to properly fulfill its obligations under the Directive.

separated the performance of its depositary tasks from other potentially conflicting tasks, and the potential conflicts are properly identified, managed, monitored, and disclosed to the UCITS' investors (Article 25(2)).

A new supervisory co-operation obligation also applies (similar to the 2009 Directive obligation); a depositary will be required to make available to its NCA, and the NCA of the management company home State and of the UCITS home State, all information obtained while performing its duties and which may be necessary for the NCA to carry out its functions (Article 26a). The new regime is accompanied by an extensive delegation to the Commission for administrative amplification of the rules (Article 26b).

Retail investors may be additionally protected through the proposed reforms to the 1997 Investor Compensation Schemes Directive, which will likely make compensation available where units or funds are lost as a result of depositary or sub-custodian failure.[303]

Although the UCITS V reform was relatively uncontroversial,[304] further reform may follow from the UCITS VI process which has considered whether, given the UCITS V reforms, a depositary passport should be introduced.[305]

III.3.11 UCITS Disclosure

III.3.11.1 Prospectus and Ongoing Disclosure

Notwithstanding the depth and range of the UCITS rulebook, disclosure remains a central element of the regulatory scheme. An investment company or management company must publish a prospectus (which must be kept up to date),[306] an audited annual report (within four months of the end of the financial year), and a half-yearly report, covering the first six months of the financial year (within two months of the end of the six-month period) (Articles 68 and 73).

The Directive adopts a framework approach to the UCITS prospectus (which is not subject to NCA approval). The catch-all material disclosure obligation requires that the prospectus include the information necessary for the investor to be able to make an informed judgement on the investment and of its risks (Article 69(1)). The legislative regime also requires that the UCITS prospectus contain a clear and easily understandable explanation of the scheme's risk profile (Article 69(1)). The substantive content is not harmonized, although the Directive contains a basic schedule of the information which must be disclosed, unless it is otherwise disclosed in the fund rules or instruments of incorporation,

---

[303] Ch IX sect 8.

[304] The Council UCITS V General Approach was broadly similar to the Commission's Proposal. It adopted a more flexible approach, however, to those entities which could act as depositaries, opening up depositary functions additionally to 'authorized legal entities' (which approach was ultimately adopted; the Commission's approach was more restrictive). The Council tightened the Proposal, however, by introducing the prohibition on the re-use by the depositary (or its delegate) of assets held in custody, unless conditions were met. The European Parliament's approach was also similar to the Commission's, although it also supported a prohibition on re-use of assets held in custody and imposed further reporting requirements.

[305] 2012 UCITS VI Consultation, n 111, para 6. The Commission suggested that the passport could represent a 'capstone' of the harmonization achieved. The AIFMD (rec 36) also trails this possibility.

[306] The nature of the review or review cycle is not specified: Art 72.

which form an integral part of the prospectus and must be annexed to it (Article 71(1)[307]).[308]

Unlike the Prospectus Directive, the Directive does not impose any minimum requirements concerning sanctions or remedies in respect of false or misleading disclosure. Although the audit requirement imposes an external control on the quality of the information contained in the annual report, the harmonized rules do not protect investors against incomplete, misleading, or false disclosure. In particular, a responsibility statement in respect of the prospectus disclosure is not required.

III.3.11.2 Disclosure Distribution and Passporting

The prospectus (and any related amendments) and annual and half-yearly reports must be sent to the UCITS home NCA; these documents must also be provided to the management company's home NCA on request, an obligation which forms part of the Directive's scheme for supporting remote supervision of the management company where jurisdiction is split between the UCITS and management company NCAs (Article 74). The prospectus and most recent financial reports must also be provided on request to investors; the prospectus must be provided in a durable medium or by means of a website (Article 75).[309] The UCITS must also make public the issue, sale, repurchase, or redemption price of its units each time it issues, sells, or repurchases them, and at least twice a month (Article 76(1)).[310]

The notification required of a UCITS before marketing its units outside the home Member State must include the prospectus, financial reports, KIID, and the fund rules or instruments of incorporation (Article 93(2)). The UCITS must also provide investors in the UCITS' host State with all documents provided to investors in the UCITS' home Member State (Article 94(1)). Only the KIID must be translated into the official language of the UCITS' host State (or other language approved by the NCA) (Article 94(1)(b)); all other documents, reflecting the Prospectus Directive translation regime, are to be translated into either the official language(s) of the UCITS' host State, a language approved by the host

---

[307] The requirement to annex these documents is lifted where the investor is informed that the documents will be sent on request, or informed of where the document may be consulted in each Member State in which UCITS units are marketed: Art 71(2).

[308] Annex I, Sch A. The requirements range from basic requirements such as name and address, management information, and particulars concerning the auditor to detailed requirements concerning the units, such as their tax treatment; their characteristics; issue, sale, repurchase, and redemption procedures; and the rules for determining and applying income, to descriptions of the common fund's or investment company's investment objectives. Information must also be provided on how UCITS assets are valued and how the sale, issue, redemption, and repurchase prices of units are determined. Information requirements also apply to the depositary, including disclosure of the depositary's identity, a description of its duties and of any safe-keeping functions delegated by the depositary, the identification of the delegate, and any conflicts of interest which may arise from the delegation (as amended by the 2014 UCITS V reforms). Disclosure is also required concerning any advisory firms or external investment advisers who give advice under a contract which is paid for out of the assets of the UCITS. The Directive also addresses the content of the required financial report: Art 69(3) and (4) and Annex I, Sch B.

[309] Administrative rules govern prospectus publication through a durable medium under the 2010 Commission KIID Regulation. The financial reports are to be provided in accordance with the distribution mechanism which the UCITS specifies in the prospectus or KIID.

[310] The frequency can be reduced where the NCA is satisfied that a derogation does not prejudice unit-holders' interests: Art 76(2).

NCA, or a language customary in the sphere of international finance, at the choice of the UCITS (Article 94(1)(c)).

III.3.11.3 Short-Form Disclosure, the Retail Markets, and the KIID

Disclosure is strongly associated with investor protection in the CIS sphere.[311] Where it improves decision-making, disclosure can support optimal CIS selection, enhance CIS quality, and lead to downward pressure on CIS costs.[312] But designing effective disclosure for CISs is complex given the weight of evidence that retail investors do not read CIS disclosures, find them complex, and favour short-form disclosures.[313] Past performance information, strongly associated with CISs, is often poorly understood and vulnerable to over-reaction.[314] Retail investors struggle in comparing risk profiles and risk-return models. While standardized or synthetic risk indicators can support investor understanding and comparability,[315] they raise complex issues for regulatory design, as they must engage with poor retail investor understanding of risk and be based on appropriate risk proxies. Costs disclosure is particularly troublesome,[316] given the range of costs which can be incurred directly and indirectly,[317] and as costs are a key determinant of returns.[318] Costs are also the most important way in which managers can extract value to the detriment of investors.[319] The difficulties are all the greater as cost disclosure in isolation is of limited use without comparability.[320] More generally, a convincing argument can be made that typical CIS disclosures, which traditionally focus on the scheme's investment management mandate and objectives, do not appropriately capture retail investor risks, as returns are largely dependent on the scheme's choice of asset class, and regulatory disclosures should

---

[311] Zingales, n 41. An extensive scholarship and policy literature address CIS disclosure. For a review see Moloney, n 33, 288–312.

[312] Cox, J and Payne, J, 'Mutual Fund Expense Disclosures: A Behavioural Perspective' (2005) 83 *Washington University LQ* 907.

[313] One US industry study (Investment Company Institute, Understanding Investor Preferences for Mutual Fund Disclosure (2006)) found that only one third of investors surveyed read fund prospectuses, 60 per cent found them difficult to read, and 90 per cent preferred short-form disclosure: at 4–5 and 8–9. The similar and extensive UK evidence includes FSA, Consumer Research Paper No 5, which reported that investors were 'simply not reading' product disclosures (at 22–3) and FSA, Consumer Research Paper No 41, Key Facts Quick Guide. Research Findings (2005).

[314] eg Hu, H, 'The New Portfolio Society, SEC Mutual Fund Disclosure, and the Public Corporation Model' (2005) 60 *Business Lawyer* 1303. Similarly, FSA, Standardization of Past Performance Information (2003), Report of the Task Force on Past Performance Information (2001) and Past Imperfect. The Performance of UK Equity Managed Funds (2000).

[315] eg Optem, Pre-contractual Information for Financial Services. Qualitative Study in the 27 Member States (2008) 109.

[316] An extensive policy and scholarly literature addresses the difficulties posed by cost disclosure: eg CRA International, Benefits of Regulation: Effect of Charges Table and Reduction in Yield (2008), Bogle, J, 'Reformulating the Mutual Fund Industry: The Alpha and Omega' (2004) 45 *Boston College Law LR* 391, and Ramsay, I, Disclosure of Fees and Charges in Managed Funds (2002).

[317] Including direct exit and entry costs; indirect costs charged to the scheme, including marketing and distribution costs, management and administration costs, and portfolio transaction costs (or the brokerage costs of executing fund transactions); performance fees; and fee-sharing arrangements and soft commissions.

[318] Oxera, Towards Evaluating Consumer Outcomes in the Retail Investment Products Markets: A Methodology. Prepared for the Financial Services Authority (2008).

[319] eg Coates, J and Hubbard, R, 'Competition in the Mutual Fund Industry: Evidence and Implications for Policy' (2007) 33 *J Corp L* 151.

[320] Payne and Cox, n 312, 935–6.

accordingly focus on the relative risks and performance of different asset classes.[321] The design challenges are therefore formidable.

The EU's new short-form disclosure document for UCITS disclosure (the KIID) reflects a wider international movement,[322] but emerged from a pathbreaking development process in the EU, notable for the extent to which it relied on testing and empirical assessment, managed through CESR.[323] Short-form UCITS disclosure in the EU has had a long and troublesome history. A 'simplified prospectus' requirement was initially introduced with the UCITS III reforms,[324] supported by a partner 2004 Commission Recommendation on the content of the simplified prospectus.[325] The simplified prospectus was to provide a 'clear and easily understandable' explanation of the UCITS risk profile, introduced the elusive notion of the 'average investor' able to understand the summary prospectus easily, and required a discussion of the profile of the 'typical investor' for whom the UCITS was designed. But the simplified prospectus was adopted without *ex-ante* testing and only shortened the lengthy prospectus disclosures. It did not engage with presentation or format. The related 2004 Recommendation was equally traditional, containing, for example, a risk disclosure regime of such detail as would represent a challenge to the most diligent of retail investors.[326] The significant weaknesses of the simplified prospectus, and the industry costs, led to it becoming a major feature of the UCITS Review.[327] By 2006, the Commission's dismal finding was that the summary prospectus had 'manifestly failed . . . [it was] too long . . . not understood by its intended readers', and had generated a 'massive paper chase of limited value to investors and a considerable overhead for the fund industry'.[328]

The process through which the KIID emerged warrants brief consideration as a landmark in the development of EU retail market disclosure. The initial 2006 Commission prospectus workshops in which a wide range of stakeholders participated saw the policy debate engage, for the first time, with a range of practical design issues, including how to differentiate the KIID from a marketing document, structure, cost disclosures, risk disclosure and synthetic risk indicators, and past performance, and, overall, adopted a practical approach, addressing the question 'what does the investor need to know'? The subsequent Commission 'Initial Orientations' document set out a framework for possible reforms and was followed by a detailed request to CESR for advice. CESR's extensive initial consultations included three calls for evidence (one on the content of the prospectus, one on distribution, and one targeted to the retail sector[329]) in April 2007, a subsequent October

---

[321] Hu, n 314.

[322] Reflected in the US SEC's mutual fund 'profile', the UK 'Key Features Document', and the Dutch 'Financial Leaflet'. See further Moloney, n 33, 308–10.

[323] For a detailed account see Moloney, n 33, 312–22.

[324] Directive 2001/107/EEC [2002] OJ L41/20.

[325] Commission Recommendation 2004/384/EC [2004] OJ L199/30.

[326] More innovative reforms under the Recommendation included the suggestion that Member States develop a quantitative synthetic risk indicator to represent a UCITS' volatility and adopt a 'Total Expense Ratio' for cost disclosure.

[327] Major concerns included inconsistent implementation of the Recommendation, leading to increased complexity and poor comparability; overly long and complex simplified prospectuses which varied in length from 2–4 pages (UK), to eight (France), to 11 (Italy); and its non-binding nature: Commission Feedback Statement to the Green Paper on Enhancing the European Framework for Investment Funds (2006) 8.

[328] 2006 Investment Funds White Paper, n 9, 10.

[329] CESR/07-241, CESR/07-214, and CESR/07-205.

2007 consultation paper[330] (including a summary retail market version[331]), and concluded with its February 2008 technical advice to the Commission on the KIID.[332] CESR's advice was followed by the 2008 UCITS IV Proposal and subsequent 2009 UCITS IV Directive, strenuous testing efforts,[333] further CESR consultation reflecting the testing,[334] and a mandate from the Commission to CESR for technical advice on related administrative KIID rules.[335]

The KIID regime is set out in the 2009 UCITS IV Directive Articles 78–81, and is amplified by the 2010 Commission KIID Regulation, which sets out in detail the format and content of the KIID.[336] The KIID regime is also supported by a detailed and extensive suite of CESR/ESMA supervisory convergence measures, which address, *inter alia*, the transition from the simplified prospectus to the KIID,[337] the use of 'clear language' and layout in the KIID,[338] and the template for KIID design.[339] These measures also cover the particular methodologies to be used to produce the mandated disclosures, including with respect to performance scenarios for structured UCITSs,[340] the synthetic risk indicator,[341] and ongoing charges disclosure.[342] ESMA continues to refine the regime by means of its Q&A device,[343] while an ITS delegation has been conferred in relation to the KIID.[344] The level of harmonization achieved with respect to the KIID, in terms of content, format, and the methodologies used to produce the required disclosures, is without precedent across the EU's retail disclosure regime for financial markets. So too is the extensive testing and empirical assessment which the regime experienced.

The 2009 UCITS IV Directive replaces the simplified prospectus requirement with the obligation that each investment company or management company draw up a 'short document' containing 'key information' for investors (the KIID) (Article 78(1)) and which includes appropriate information about the essential characteristics of the UCITS, which is to be provided to investors so that they are reasonably able to understand the nature and risks of the investment product being offered to them and, consequently, to take investment decisions on an informed basis (Article 78(2)). The KIID is not approved by an NCA but, supporting *ex-post* supervision of compliance, it must be sent to the home NCA (Article 82(1)). The KIID, which is designed as a regulated, pre-contractual disclosure

---

[330] CESR/07-669.

[331] CESR/07-753.

[332] CESR/08-087.

[333] The initial test results and the testing process are outlined in Commission, Workshop on KII 20 October 2008 and, in outline, in CESR, Consultation Paper on Technical Issues related to KII Disclosures for UCITS (2008) (CESR/09-047).

[334] CESR/09-047.

[335] Commission, Provisional Request to CESR for Technical Advice on Possible Implementing Measures Concerning the Future UCITS Directive (2009).

[336] n 21.

[337] CESR/10-1319.

[338] CESR/10-1320.

[339] CESR/10-1321.

[340] CESR/10-1318.

[341] CESR/10-673.

[342] CESR/10-674.

[343] Questions and Answers. Key Investor Information Document (KIID) for UCITS (2012) (ESMA/ 2012/592).

[344] Art 78(8), added by the 2010 Omnibus I Directive.

document and not as a marketing document,[345] must be written in a concise manner and in non-technical language; it must also be drawn up in a common format which allows for comparability, and presented in a way likely to be understood by retail investors (Article 73(5)). The legislative underpinning for the detailed administrative regime governing content is provided by Article 78(3), which identifies KIID disclosures as relating to: identification of the UCITS; a short description of its investment policy; past performance information or, where relevant, performance scenarios; costs and associated charges; and the investment's risk/reward profile. The KIID is designed to operate as a stand-alone document; its essential elements must be comprehensible without reference to any other documents (Article 78(3)), although the KIID must also specify where additional information (including the prospectus and annual report) can be obtained (Article 78(4)). The KIID regime provides some protection against 'tick-the box' compliance in that the disclosure must be 'fair, clear and not misleading', as well as consistent with relevant parts of the prospectus (Article 79(1)).

The KIID also addresses distribution risks through a direct/indirect sales model (Article 80) which requires, with respect to direct sales, that the investment company or management company which sells UCITS units directly or through a tied agent provide investors with the KIID in good time before their proposed subscription of units. For indirect sales (such as those by investment advisers), and in a significant innovation, the investment company or management company must provide the KIID to product manufacturers and intermediaries who sell and advise investors on potential UCITS investments or, importantly, on products which offer exposure to such UCITSs (such as wrapped products). The KIID is to be provided in a durable medium or by means of a website (Article 81(1)).[346]

The KIID liability regime reflects that applicable to the Prospectus Directive summary and provides that Member States must ensure that a person does not incur civil liability on the basis of the KIID (or any translation of the KIID) unless it is misleading, inaccurate, or inconsistent with the relevant parts of the UCITS prospectus, and the KIID must contain a clear warning in this respect (Article 79(2)).

From the passporting perspective, the KIID is to be used without alteration or supplements, except translation, in all Member States where the UCITS is notified to market its units (Article 78(6)). It must, however, as befits a retail document, be translated into the official language or one of the official languages of the host Member States or into a language approved by the host NCA(s) (Article 94(1)(b)).

The extensive administrative delegation, which provides for 'detailed and exhaustive' rules on the format and content of the KIID, as well as for tailored rules for a range of different schemes,[347] has led to the 2010 Commission KIID Regulation, which specifies in an 'exhaustive manner' the form and content of the KIID (Article 1(1)). The Regulation

---

[345] The KIID must contain a legend to this effect: Commission 2010 KII Regulation Art 4(3).

[346] The 2010 Commission KIID Regulation addresses the nature of durable medium distribution.

[347] Including UCITSs with different investment compartments, UCITSs with different share classes, fund-of-fund UCITSs, master-feeder UCITSs, and structured, capital-protected, and similar UCITS: Art 78(7).

covers the title and content of the KIID, including the order of information (Article 4), presentation and language (Article 5),[348] length—the KIID must not exceed two A4 pages (Article 6), description of objectives of investment policy (Article 7), the presentation of risks and reward, including the synthetic risk indicator, which is based on a numerical (1–7) scale[349] (Articles 8 and 9), charges disclosure (Articles 10–13), and past performance disclosure (Articles 15–19). The KIID regime is also calibrated to particular types of UCITSs, including UCITSs with different investment compartments (Articles 25–27), funds of funds (Articles 28–30), feeder UCITSs (Articles 31–5), and structured UCITSs (Articles 36–7). The Regulation also requires that the KIID is reviewed every year (Article 22).[350]

The KIID is a landmark reform, in terms of substantive reform (particularly with respect to the synthetic risk indicator), the process through which it emerged, and the level of standardization. As discussed in Chapter IX section 6, the KIID has also acted as the template for retail investment product disclosure more generally under the PRIPs (packaged retail investment products) initiative. But while it represents a significant step forward, more radical solutions could have been canvassed. The persistence of past performance disclosure remains problematic, particularly given the pro-cyclicality risks exposed by the financial crisis and dotcom eras. The KIID also sits uneasily with the evidence that retail investors have poor understanding of different asset classes and of diversification—some room might have been made to mandate the inclusion of signposts to standardized investor education materials. Little attention has been paid to whether the KIID is likely to support specific decision-making outcomes; testing has focused on clarity. Difficulties have also emerged in practice, particularly with respect to the synthetic risk indicator and the related risks of funds 'herding' to a similar indicator,[351] as well as to investor over-reliance, particularly where the risk indicator is not sufficiently calibrated. Cost disclosure is not comprehensive, particularly with respect to distribution costs.[352] Until the KIID model is rolled out to other retail investment products under the PRIPs reforms, regulatory arbitrage risks remain strong, given that the KIID requirement applies only to the UCITS sector. Nonetheless, KIID standardization has been associated with stronger investor understanding,[353] and investors have expressed support for the indicator as well as for the new charges disclosure.[354]

---

[348] It specifies, eg, that characters of readable size must be used, that jargon must be avoided, and that colours must not diminish comprehensibility: Art 5(1)(a)–(c).

[349] The indicator requirements are amplified by Annex I to the 2010 Commission Regulation and by CESR/ESMA guidance. It captures the fund's historic volatility, based on five years of data.

[350] Interim updates are required where, eg, the synthetic risk indicator changes over a four-month rolling basis, due to market performance or volatility, or where changes occur to, eg, the fund's name, investment objectives, or charges.

[351] EFAMA and PriceWaterhouseCoopers, UCITS IV. Time for Change. The Asset Management Industry's Views on the Key Information Document (2010).

[352] 2012 KPMG Report, n 96, 12.

[353] Study for the Commission, Consumer Decision Making in Retail Investment Services. A Behavioural Perspective. Coordinated by Decision Technology (2010).

[354] UCITS Disclosure Testing Research Report. Prepared by IFF Research and YouGov for the Commission (2009).

III.3.11.4 Beyond Disclosure and the Retail Market

While the KIID represents a landmark in EU retail market policy, disclosure is a limited tool for delivering investor protection and supporting strong investor outcomes,[355] and in itself it is unlikely to address persistent weaknesses in the UCITS market from the retail demand-side perspective.

UCITS design remains troublesome from the retail market perspective. The facilitative asset-allocation regime poses few restrictions on UCITS development. While an extensive conduct and prudential rulebook now applies to management companies, the product governance rules which are increasingly becoming associated with EU retail market policy do not apply; UCITS designers are not subject to an obligation to stress-test the asset-allocation strategy or to engage in market identification/market testing prior to launch. Given the proliferation of UCITS funds, investor confusion risks can be generated.[356] Funds also run the risk of not responding to evidenced investor needs. The risks are all the greater as 'shopping around' is limited,[357] and as retail investors have very limited ability to extend downward pressure on costs[358] or to drive particular fund designs. The recent embrace of product governance rules by EU retail market policy may, however, lead to related reforms in the UCITS sector (Chapter IX section 7).

The sale of UCITSs, and the nature of the UCITS distribution chain, also raises investor protection risks. Difficulties can arise with respect to the distribution of the prospectus, for example, given the different distribution chains through which sales occur. Direct UCITS sales may occur through direct UCITS marketing and execution-only channels. Sales may also occur through entities associated with the UCITS (including associated life insurance companies or cross-border distribution agents). Finally, sales can occur through third parties, with no contractual connection to the UCITS, under advised sales through investment advisers or execution-only sales through brokers, or through open-architecture distribution networks which carry a range of different investment products. UCITSs may also be wrapped within insurance and tax products, in which case a prospectus may not be supplied to the investor and it may not be clear that a UCITS III scheme with a potentially aggressive risk profile is being sold. The KIID reforms have, however, led to significant improvement by requiring that the KIID is provided regardless of the distribution chain.

Difficulties also arise in relation to the intersection between the UCITS regime and the investment services regime with respect to the point of sale or advice. The harmonized investment services regime (particularly the 2014 MiFID II investment advice, marketing, disclosure, and conflict-of-interest rules) governs the distribution of UCITS units through firms within the scope of MiFID II; this regime does not apply to marketing by the UCITS.[359] The extensive MiFID point-of-sale advice protections accordingly do not extend to direct sales by the UCITS (see further Chapter IX on these protections).

---

[355] See further Ch IX sect 6.

[356] 2006 Investment Fund Market Efficiency Group Report, n 80, 10.

[357] 2006 Oxera Report, n 81, v.

[358] One study has warned that, in part because of product complexity and poor financial capability, cost savings would be only slowly passed on to consumers: 2006 CRA International Report, n 81, 4.

[359] On the interaction between the investment services (pre MiFID II) and UCITS regimes see Janin, S, 'MiFID Impact on Investment Managers' (2007) 15 *JFRC* 90.

More generally, investors carry the costs of segmented distribution systems. National distribution systems tend to dominate in the UCITS market. These are typically in the form of local large bancassurance/financial supermarket institutions which are often closed to cross-border UCITS products developed by third party providers or which extract very high fees for access, which are passed on to investors.[360] Competition is therefore limited, with distribution charges significantly higher in the EU than in the US.[361] Strong national preferences in asset allocation also provide incentives for segmented distribution. The industry is, however, moving towards a more competitive 'open or guided architecture' model under which local channels are opened up to third party funds;[362] some degree of convergence towards more open distribution structures has been observed, driven by the development of large pan-EU distribution networks, although distribution remains largely organized through closed local networks in a number of Member States.[363] The Commission has been somewhat sanguine as to the efficiency risks raised by UCITS distribution and has generally relied on market forces to drive innovation.

The marketing of UCITSs cross-border remains largely the preserve of host Member State rules, as is clear from the 2009 UCITS IV Directive passporting regime, which specifies the rules which a host Member State may impose; the extensive 2014 MiFID II investment services marketing regime does not apply to CIS managers or UCITSs. The 2009 Directive introduced, however, a principles-based marketing requirement which requires that all marketing communications to investors must be clearly identified as such, and be fair, clear, and not misleading (Article 77).[364] Retail market protection in the marketing conduct is therefore primarily a function of local rules, which may be more attuned to local risks than harmonized rules. But from the supply-side perspective, the costs of diverging marketing rules can be significant.[365]

III.3.12 General Obligations

III.3.12.1 Redemption

Article 84 is at the heart of the 2009 UCITS IV Directive and shapes the asset-allocation regime which is, at bedrock, designed to ensure that the UCITS is sufficiently liquid to meet its redemption obligations. Article 84(1) requires that a UCITS must repurchase or redeem its units at the request of any unit-holder. Two derogations apply to this rule. First, a UCITS may temporarily suspend the repurchase or redemption of units in the cases and

---

[360] Commission, Financial Integration Monitor 2004 (2004) (SEC (2004) 559) 17 and 2005 Investment Fund Green Paper, n 58, 5.

[361] 2006 Financial Integration Monitor, n 60, 22.

[362] Under open-architecture distribution models, networks carry a range of products. Under guided-architecture models, distributors select only a limited number of additional products. For a discussion, see the 2006 Oxera Report, n 81, 7.

[363] Grene, S, 'EU Distribution Channels Converge', *Financial Times, Fund Management Supplement*, 4 March 2012, 2.

[364] Marketing communications which contain an invitation to purchase UCITS units must not contradict or diminish the significance of information in the prospectus or KIID, must indicate that a prospectus exists and that a KIID is available, and must specify how these documents can be obtained.

[365] 2012 KPMG Report, n 96, 17.

according to the procedures set out by law, the fund rules, or the investment company's instruments of incorporation (Article 84(2)(a)). Suspension may be provided for only in exceptional cases and must be justified having regard to the interests of unit-holders or the public. Second, Member States may allow NCAs to require the suspension of repurchases or redemptions in the interests of unit-holders or the public (Article 84(2)(b)).

While some 'liquidity bottlenecks' arose from the Article 84 obligation over the financial crisis, they were rare. But, and notwithstanding its centrality to the UCITS' investor protection model, the crisis-era preoccupation with financial stability appears to be placing Article 84 under pressure, given the liquidity pressures and stability risk which it can, in theory, generate. In addition, concerns are growing as to whether the contraction in the ability of banks to provide liquidity to funds is placing liquidity under pressure, and with respect to the extent to which fund assets generally can be illiquid (particularly where funds invest in 'small cap' equities).[366] The money-market fund reform agenda, in particular, has prompted discussion of how liquidity pressures can be reduced where redemption is under strain and whether redemption restrictions should be adopted (section 3.14.1 below), while more generally consideration is being given to amplifying the emergency conditions which can justify redemption restrictions.[367]

III.3.12.2 Borrowing and Loans

A series of prudentially orientated measures apply to fund leverage. Investment companies, management companies, and depositaries are prohibited from borrowing under Article 83, which accordingly restricts the degree of leverage a UCITS can sustain.[368] Member States may derogate from this rule by authorizing a UCITS to borrow up to 10 per cent of its assets (in the case of an investment company) or 10 per cent of the value of the UCITS (in the case of a common fund), but the borrowing may only be on a temporary basis. A Member State may, additionally, authorize an investment company to borrow up to 10 per cent of its assets where the borrowing is for the acquisition of immovable property essential for the direct pursuit of its business. Where any such borrowing is authorized, it may not exceed in total 15 per cent of the investment company's assets/UCITS fund value (Article 83(2)). Very considerable leverage can be sustained by the UCITS, however, through financial derivatives; a UCITS can be leveraged through financial derivatives up to 100 per cent of its NAV (section 3.8.6). In addition, neither an investment company, nor a management company, nor a depositary may grant loans or guarantees.[369] Finally, the investment company, and the management company or depositary acting on behalf of a common fund, are prohibited from carrying out uncovered sales of transferable securities, money-market instruments, or the CIS, financial derivative, and OTC money-market instruments listed in Article 50 as eligible assets (Article 89).

---

[366] Marriage, M, 'Liquidity Fears Put Regulators on the Offensive', *Financial Times, Fund Management Supplement*, 18 November 2013, 1.

[367] 2012 UCITS VI Consultation, n 111, para 5.

[368] ESMA is empowered to propose RTSs specifying the Art 83 borrowing regime: Art 83(3).

[369] Art 88, although this prohibition does not prohibit the acquisition of transferable securities, money-market instruments, or the CIS, financial derivative, and OTC market instruments listed in Art 50 as eligible assets, and which are not fully paid.

III.3.12.3 Conflicts of Interest and Remuneration

Article 90 requires that the UCITS home Member State law or the fund rules must prescribe the remuneration and the expenditure which a management company may charge to the UCITS and the way in which such remuneration is to be calculated, and provides that the law or an investment company's instruments of incorporation prescribe the nature of the costs to be borne by the company.

III.3.13 Supervision and Enforcement

III.3.13.1 NCAs

Prior to the 2009 UCITS IV reforms, the UCITS supervisory regime was outdated, certainly by comparison with the MiFID I regime governing discretionary asset management. Co-operation obligations were limited and supervisory powers were not harmonized. The 2009 UCITS IV Directive updated the UCITS regime to reflect the model previously adopted across the FSAP;[370] further revisions were introduced by the 2010 Omnibus I Directive to reflect the establishment of ESMA and minor changes have since been made under the UCITS V reforms.

Accordingly, the Directive addresses the form and organization of NCAs under the Directive (they must take the form of public authorities (Article 97)), and prescribes the minimum powers which NCAs must have at their disposal (Article 98).[371] Supervision is reinforced by the requirement imposed on auditors to report to the relevant NCAs with respect to identified matters, including breaches of the UCITS Directive (Article 106).

III.3.13.2 Supervisory Co-operation

The 2009 UCITS IV Directive follows the co-operation scheme deployed across much of EU securities and markets regulation. NCAs are subject to a general co-operation obligation, as well as obligations in relation to information exchange, on-the-spot verifications, and investigations, and with respect to notifying NCAs where one NCA suspects acts contrary to the Directive are being carried out in another Member State (Article 101).[372] A related information exchange regime applies to protect the confidentiality of information and impose professional secrecy obligations, and to clarify the NCAs with which information can be exchanged (Articles 102–4). The 2010 Omnibus I Directive revised the regime

---

[370] 2008 UCITS IV Proposal, n 92, 11.

[371] These are similar to the powers which must be available to NCAs under the investment services regime (albeit prior to the MiFID II reforms), and include the power to access documents, carry out on-site inspections, impose injunctions, require the freezing of assets, temporarily prohibit professional activities, and, more specifically, require the suspension of the issue, repurchase, or redemption of UCITS units in the interests of unit-holders or of the public, withdraw UCITS authorization, and adopt any type of measure to ensure that investment companies, management companies, and depositaries comply with the Directive: Art 98(2). The UCITS V reforms have refined this regime to empower NCAs to acquire data traffic records from a telecommunications operator where there is a reasonable suspicion of a breach, and where such records are relevant to an investigation, and to require existing recordings of telephone calls or electronic communications or other data traffic records held by UCITSs, management companies, investment companies, depositaries, or any other entities regulated by the Directive.

[372] Administrative rules govern information exchange and verifications/inspections: 2010 Commission Notifications and Information Exchange Regulation.

to extend the co-operation obligation to co-operation with ESMA and to insert ESMA's binding mediation powers into the management of disputes between NCAs, particularly in relation to on-the-spot investigations and verifications. Since then, the UCITS V reforms have clarified the limited conditions under which an NCA may refuse to act on a request for information or to co-operate with an investigation, thereby aligning the regime with securities and markets regulation generally (Article 99(3)).

Reflecting the UCITS passport, the UCITS home NCA is allocated the power to take action where the UCITS infringes the UCITS regime or any of its fund rules or instruments of incorporation;[373] UCITS host NCAs retain jurisdiction with respect to rules which fall outside the UCITS Directive (Article 108(1)). As is the case across EU securities and markets regulation generally, the host NCA also retains exceptional precautionary powers (Article 108(4) and (5)).

A discrete co-operation regime applies where the management company of a UCITS is established in a different Member State, which is designed to support the co-operation and jurisdiction allocation regime that applies in relation to UCITS and management company authorization and passporting (section 3.7.3). Article 108(3) clarifies that the management company home NCA or the UCITS home NCA are to take action against the management company where the company infringes rules under their respective responsibility (Article 108(3)). The home NCA of the UCITS must inform the NCA of the management company's home State where it has taken serious measures against the UCITS.[374] In addition, the home NCA of the management company must notify the UCITS home NCA of any problems which may materially affect the ability of the management company to perform its duties with respect to the UCITS, or of any breach of the Directive's management company rules; conversely, the UCITS home NCA must notify the management company home NCA of similar problems at the level of the UCITS (Article 109(3) and (4)).

With respect to host NCA obligations, where a management company operates in one or more host Member States, all the NCAs of the Member States concerned must collaborate closely, including with respect to information exchange likely to facilitate the monitoring of the company (Article 109(1)). The management company host NCA(s) must also inform the management company home NCA of any precautionary measures taken against the management company under Article 21(5) (Article 109(2)). Host NCAs of a management company are also required, where the management company pursues activities in the Member State through a branch, to ensure that the home NCA, having informed the host NCA, can carry out (on its own or through an intermediary) an on-the-spot verification of information likely to facilitate the monitoring of the management company (Article 110(1)).

---

[373] The home NCA must notify the host NCA where it has withdrawn the UCITS' authorization, suspended the issue, repurchase, or redemption of its units, or taken other serious measures against the UCITS: Art 108(2).

[374] Including the withdrawal of authorization and the suspension of the issue, repurchase, or redemption of units: Art 108(2).

III.3.13.3 Supervisory Convergence and ESMA

CESR and, since, ESMA's supervisory convergence activities have been significant under the UCITS regime, although they have been targeted in the main to quasi-regulatory convergence. The troublesome original UCITS notification regime, since replaced by a new regime under the 2009 UCITS IV Directive, however, was addressed by guidance designed to ease the process and drive greater convergence across NCAs.[375] Over the financial crisis, CESR co-ordinated the response by NCAs to the Madoff scandal and provided advice to investors in this regard.[376] CESR also engaged in peer review of the UCITS regime, particularly with respect to the technical operation of the UCITS passporting regime,[377] albeit with mixed results. The 2009 UCITS peer review, for example, revealed low levels of compliance with the earlier CESR guidelines on UCITS notification, with only five Member States in full application of the guidelines and 20 Member States not applying at least one. With the establishment of ESMA, and with the dense rulebook which now applies to almost all aspects of the UCITS fund, stronger convergence in operational practices can be expected.

III.3.13.4 Sanctions and Enforcement

The limited sanctions regime in place prior to the 2014 UCITS V reforms required Member States to have appropriate (and effective, proportionate, and dissuasive) administrative measures or penalties available, and specified that effective, proportionate, and dissuasive sanctions be in place concerning the duty to present the KIID in a way likely to be understood by retail investors in accordance with Article 78(5) (Article 99(1) and (2)). Member States were also to allow NCAs to disclose any sanctions imposed (Article 99(3)).

The 2014 UCITS V reforms are designed to align the UCITS sanctioning regime with the new approach to sanctioning adopted in crisis-era securities and markets regulation (Articles 99 and Articles 99a–e) (Chapter XI section 4.1.2). Accordingly, the 2009 UCITS IV Directive, as amended, requires that effective, proportionate, and dissuasive administrative sanctions must be available (Article 99(1)) (criminal sanctions may be deployed in substitution for administrative sanctions, but these must be notified to the Commission and appropriate measures must be in place such that NCAs have all necessary powers to liaise with the judicial authorities to receive information and to transmit it as required to other NCAs and ESMA); specifies the particular breaches of the Directive which must be subject to administrative sanctions or measures (Article 99a); specifies the minimum suite of administrative sanctions and measures which must be available (Article 99(5));[378] details

---

[375] CESR/06-120b. The 2009 UCITS IV Directive notification regime has also been the subject of guidance through the UCITS Q&A: ESMA/2012/428.

[376] CESR Public Statement, 4 February 2009.

[377] Most recently, CESR/09-1034.

[378] The suite of measures, which follows the crisis-era sanctioning reforms to, eg, the 2014 market abuse regime, the 2014 MiFID II/MiFIR, and the 2013 transparency regime, include public statements, injunctions, withdrawals of authorization, temporary and permanent bans on exercising management functions, and pecuniary sanctions (up to (as a minimum) 10 per cent of annual turnover of a legal person or €5 million, and up to €5 million in the case of a natural person), including pecuniary sanctions of up to twice the amount of the profits gained or losses avoided (even where that exceeds the aforenoted thresholds).

how sanctions are to be applied (Article 99c);[379] addresses whistle-blowing (Article 99d); and provides for mandatory NCA public reporting of administrative sanctions and measures (and the conditions under which the public reporting requirement can be lifted) (Article 99b) and for NCA reporting to ESMA on sanctioning (Article 99e).

Member States must also ensure that efficient and effective complaints and redress procedures are in place for out-of-court settlement of consumer disputes relating to UCITS activity (Article 100).

III.3.14 The Crisis-era Financial Stability Agenda, Shadow Banking, and UCITS Regulation

III.3.14.1 The Shadow Banking Agenda and Money-market Funds

The influence of the crisis-era reform programme on the UCITS sector can be seen most clearly in the money-market fund (MMF) reform. This reform has drawn the UCITS sector into the shadow banking reform agenda which came to dominate the later stages of the international reform cycle and of the EU's reform programme.[380]

Although the 'shadow banking' risks generated by entities performing functionally similar roles to banks were identified at an early stage of the crisis,[381] it was not until 2012 and the

---

[379] Including, as across the crisis-era reforms to sanctioning generally, with reference to the gravity and duration of the breach, the degree of responsibility of the person responsible and that person's financial strength, the importance of profits gained or losses avoided, the degree of co-operation by the person concerned, and previous breaches by that person. In addition, the assessment must take into account the damage to other persons and, where applicable, the damage to the functioning of markets or the wider economy.

[380] The massive reform agenda associated with shadow banking is noted here in outline only and to provide context for the EU's CIS-specific MMF reforms. The wide-ranging and still fluid EU shadow banking agenda is concerned with an array of banking and more generally-applicable stability-related reforms, including in relation to: prudential/stability regulation under the CRD IV/CRR and Solvency II suite of reforms, which are designed to prevent the use of shadow banking structures to circumvent regulation, particularly with respect to securitization activities; trading-related reforms, including ring-fencing proposals (for deposit-taking credit institutions only) (Ch VI sect 1); the 2011 AIFMD reforms, particularly with respect to fund liquidity and leverage (sect 4); the new rating agency regime (Ch VII); and securities financing transactions (sect 3.14.4). For an outline see Commission, Green Paper on Shadow Banking (2012) (COM (2012) 102) (2012 Shadow Banking Green Paper), Commission, Communication on Shadow Banking—Addressing New Sources of Risk in the Financial Sector (COM (2013) 614/3) (2013), and Commission, European Financial Stability and Integration Report 2013 (2014) (SWD (2014) 170) 94-126.

The EU agenda is being developed across a range of EU institutions, including the ECB, the European Systemic Risk Board (ESRB), and the European Supervisory Authorities (ESAs). The European Parliament has also adopted a number of key reports, including the October 2012 ECON Report on Shadow Banking (A7-0354/2012) (2012 ECON Shadow Banking Report).

For discussion of the substantive reforms and the risks of the extensive international regulatory programme see, eg: Gerding, E, The Shadow Banking System and its Legal Origins (2012), available at <http://ssrn.com/abstract=1990816>; Bakk-Simon, K, Borgiolo, S, Giron, C, Hempell, H, Maddaloni, A, Recine, F, and Rosati, S, Shadow Banking in the Euro Area. An Overview. ECB Occasional Paper No 133/2012; Gorton, G and Metrick, A, Regulating the Shadow Banking Sector (2010), available at <http://ssrn.com/abstract=1676947>; and Ricks, M, Shadow Banking and Financial Regulation, Columbia Law and Economics WP No 370 (2010), available at <http://ssrn.com/abstract=1571290>.

[381] eg, FSA, The Turner Review. A Regulatory Response to the Global Banking Crisis (2009) (the Turner Review) 21 and DLG Report, n 108, 25–6.

important series of assessments by the Financial Stability Board[382] that a degree of consensus as to the nature of the fluid and elusive 'shadow banking' concept,[383] and as to the related risks to be captured by regulation from this segment of the financial system,[384] emerged. The related shadow banking reforms are designed to capture the risks associated with maturity and liquidity transformation.[385] Maturity and related liquidity transformation is the central function of the banking sector: banks hold longer-term (loan) assets than (deposit) liabilities and are exposed to maturity mismatch risk accordingly where short-term liquid liabilities (deposits) are withdrawn in a 'run'. As has been extensively documented, banking regulation, including liquidity, capital, and lender-of-last resort regulation, has evolved to address this risk (and, of course, has increased exponentially in sophistication over the crisis). But the crisis revealed that an array of institutions and practices were achieving maturity and related liquidity transformation effects outside the banking regulatory perimeter and, while providing an important alternative funding source, generating significant systemic risks.[386] In particular, the importance of securitization and of securities repurchase ('repo') and lending agreements in allowing market actors to fund long-term assets with short-term liabilities, and of the securitization vehicles and conduits and Special Investment Vehicles which perform these activities, became clear.[387]

In the CIS segment, MMFs have emerged as a key component of the shadow banking market.[388] MMF units are regarded as a functional substitute for deposits. They are short-term liquid assets which provide a market-based yield and a high degree of principal protection, and are heavily relied on for cash management by a wide range of household and institutional investors, including corporates,[389] pension funds, and insurance companies. MMFs also provide an important funding channel for issuers of the short-term money-market instruments in which MMFs invest, and so fund an array of actors, including

---

[382] The Financial Stability Board (FSB) shadow banking project has five streams: a Basel Committee stream on the interaction between banks and shadow banking; an IOSCO stream on MMFs; an IOSCO stream on securitization; an FSB stream on other shadow banking entities; and an FSB stream on securities lending and repos. The work-streams followed the earlier Seoul G20 invitation to the FSB to address shadow banking risk: FSB, Reforming Oversight and Regulation of Shadow Banking. An Overview of Policy Recommendations (2013).

[383] In the early stages of the crisis shadow banking was often associated with the ability of market actors to pose similar systemic risks to banks: eg DLG Report, n 108, 25–6.

[384] The shadow banking segment is estimated at some $67 trillion, representing half the size of global banking assets and around 25 per cent of total financial intermediation and financial system assets: FSB, Global Shadow Banking Monitoring Report (2012) 3 and 19. Euro-area shadow banking activities are estimated at $22 trillion, as compared to $23 trillion in the US and $9 trillion in the UK (at 4).

[385] The FSB regards shadow banking as the system of credit intermediation that involves entities and activities outside the regular banking system. Shadow banking entities can accept funding with deposit-like functions, perform maturity and/or liquidity transformation, undergo credit risk transfer, and use direct or indirect financial leverage. They also can act as an important source of non-bank funding.

[386] Including in relation to runs on deposit-like funding structures, the build-up of hidden leverage, regulatory arbitrage risks, and disorderly failures: 2012 Shadow Banking Green Paper, n 380, 5–6.

[387] eg Dive, M, Hodge, R, and Jones, C, 'Developments in the Global Securities Lending Market' (2011) *Bank of England Quarterly Bulletin*, Quarter 2 2011, 224.

[388] The MMF and repo/securities lending markets have been identified as those most acutely in need in intervention: Clifford Chance, Into the Light: A Response to the EU Commission Green Paper on Shadow Banking (2012) 3.

[389] Many firms invest in MMFs to manage excess cash holdings in advance of a major expenditure, such as a payroll run: Commission 2013 MMF Proposal (COM (2013) 615/2) (2013 MMF Proposal).

sovereigns, banks, and firms.[390] Trading by MMFs is a key driver of liquidity in the commercial paper, short-term bank debt, and sovereign debt markets.[391]

But maturity transformation risk is significant given the mismatch between longer-term MMF credit assets and short-term MMF unit liabilities; while MMF credit assets are short-term, they are more long-term than MMF liabilities, in that MMF investors can withdraw on demand and with a relatively stable principal value. Where the NAV of the fund is constant (CNAV funds),[392] heightening the similarity of the fund unit to a bank deposit,[393] very significant liquidity and redemption risks can arise.[394] Market volatility and liquidity squeezes can lead to pressure on the CNAV of an MMF, particularly where the MMF has invested in illiquid assets and struggles to meet redemption requests, and to the risk that it 'breaks the buck' (or that its capital value falls such that redemption at the initial investment par value cannot occur). This can generate a run (MMF investors, typically highly risk-averse, have strong incentives to redeem first, thereby creating further downward pressure on the NAV),[395] which can lead to systemic liquidity pressure and instability as contagion spreads across the MMF market, as occurred in the US over the financial crisis.[396] In addition, MMFs can be supported by 'sponsor' banks or asset managers, which may also come under funding pressure and through which risk can be transmitted.[397] Overall, the structural mismatch between MMF assets and liabilities, and the functional substitute for deposits which MMF units provide, make all MMFs vulnerable to runs, as the EU experience highlights.[398] Accordingly, and although MMFs did not cause the financial crisis, the crisis underlined that, in conditions of market turbulence, an MMF can come under pressure and amplify systemic risks.[399]

---

[390] 2013 MMF Proposal, n 389, 2.

[391] 2012 UCITS VI Consultation, n 111, 12.

[392] As is the case with US MMFs which maintain a CNAV of $1.00 per unit. Variable NAV (VNAV) funds do not face the same liquidity constraints and 'run' risks.

[393] In that an expectation is generated that the investor will redeem at par. Investor expectations can be heightened by ratings, often triple-A.

[394] IOSCO, Consultation on Money Market Funds (2012) 11.

[395] n 394, 5–7. This risk relates to the 'first mover advantage' associated with MMFs.

[396] On 18 September 2008 the Reserve Primary Fund 'broke the buck' having written down Lehman assets, leading to a run on MMFs generally and some $300 billion of withdrawals across the MMF sector. The US Treasury was required to temporarily guarantee investments in MMFs, while the US Federal Reserve provided exceptional liquidity support. Over 2011, a 'quiet' or 'slow' run on MMFs took place, reflecting market concerns as to the exposure of US MMFs to EU sovereign debt risk: IOSCO, n 394, 6.

[397] Major EU banks are assumed to have experienced major losses arising from MMF support over the crisis: 2013 MMF Proposal Impact Assessment (SWD (2013) 315) 14.

[398] In 2007, several EU MMFs experienced difficulties arising from investment in securitized assets exposed to the US sub-prime market: n 397, 9. EU MMFs came under redemption pressure more generally in 2008, reflecting unease in the money markets after the Lehman collapse, increased demand for cash by investors, poor liquidity in the related money-market instrument market, and outflows from MMFs to bank deposits, given the enhancements to bank deposit protection over the crisis. The MMF industry sought support from the ECB and national monetary authorities to support liquidity in the money markets and prevent a run on MMFs: ESMA, Response to the Commission Shadow Banking Green Paper (2012) (ESMA/2012/476) (2012 ESMA Shadow Banking Paper Response) 8. The ECB did not support MMFs directly, but eased liquidity pressure by lowering interest rate and broadening the scope of eligible collateral for ECB credit: n 397, 17.

[399] ESRB Recommendation on Money Market Funds (2012) (ESRB/2012/01) rec 5.

While MMF reform in the US market has been beset by difficulties,[400] the international MMF reform agenda is hardening.[401] But whether, and if so the extent to which, the EU should intervene is contested. Most (some 60 per cent) EU MMFs take the form of UCITSs[402] and are accordingly subject to intensive risk-management regulation. The managers of MMFs which do not take the form of a UCITS are subject to the 2011 AIFMD.[403] Investment firms which deposit client funds with MMFs are also subject to regulation.[404] The majority of EU MMFs take the form of variable VNAV funds,[405] which do not act as substitutes for deposits in the same way as CNAV funds and so are not subject to the same liquidity pressures, and which have a predominantly institutional investor base.[406]

Nonetheless, and reflecting the international reform movement, MMFs were placed on the reform agenda by the DLG Report in February 2009.[407] A 2009 Commission consultation on reform of the Investor Compensation Schemes Directive queried whether compensation should be available in relation to investment losses on MMFs (given that investment firms could place client funds on deposits with MMFs); while this proposal did not acquire traction, it underlines the prominence which reform quickly acquired.[408] The first formal response came through CESR. CESR had strong incentives to bolster its institutional position over the crisis by addressing perceived regulatory gaps, but in this case it provided a useful channel for action by corralling industry intelligence and regulatory experience outside the legislative process which, at that stage, was experiencing somewhat febrile

---

[400] Following the dissent of three Commissioners, the US SEC failed to adopt reforms (including a requirement for MMFs to move to a floating or variable NAV or apply enhanced capital requirements) in August 2010 (Statement by SEC Chairman Schapiro (SEC Press Release 2012-166)), leading to the US dissenting from the 2012 IOSCO Recommendations (n 401). A reform proposal was finally unanimously adopted in 2013 which was based on requiring certain MMFs to either adopt a floating NAV or, where a constant NAV was maintained, to use liquidity fees and redemption gates in times of stress to protect MMF liquidity: SEC Press Release 5 June 2013 (Press Release 2013-101).

[401] The IOSCO-led MMF stream of FSB shadow banking work has recommended liquidity management policies, valuation rules, and disclosure to investors, and addressed reliance on ratings and on repos, as well as issues related to the stable/constant NAV: IOSCO, Policy Recommendations for Money Market Funds (2012). Reflecting in particular risks in the US market, it has recommended that stable (constant) NAV MMFs be converted into floating (variable) NAV funds where possible and, where not possible, that additional safeguards, functionally equivalent to the capital, liquidity, and prudential requirements which are designed to prevent bank runs, apply to stable NAV funds. This approach has been endorsed by the FSB.

[402] 2013 MMF Proposal, n 389, 2. The AUM of a UCITS MMF is typically significantly larger than a UCITS; an MMF can reach €50 billion AUM.

[403] ESMA's response to the Commission Shadow Banking Green Paper highlighted the strict UCITS (and AIFMD) regulatory framework which captures many of the shadow banking-related risks associated with CISs, and called for appropriately tailored intervention accordingly: 2012 ESMA Shadow Banking Paper Response, n 398, 5–6.

[404] See, eg, 2006 Commission MiFID I Directive (Directive 2006/73/EC [2006] OJ L241/26) Art 18(2), which governed the entities with which client funds can be placed and placed conditions on the MMFs which can be used, and which is likely to be a feature of the new administrative rulebook under MiFID II.

[405] CNAV funds were first marketed in the 1980s and, often denominated in dollars, were designed to serve US investors: 2012 CEPS/ECMI Report, n 12, 44.

[406] Bakk-Simon et al, n 380, 15. In all, 40 per cent of EU MMFs are CNAV funds and 60 per cent take the form of VNAV funds: 2012 UCITS VI Consultation, n 111, 13. By contrast, US MMFs seek to maintain a $1.00 constant NAV per unit and have a wide institutional but also retail investor base (being used as substitutes for current accounts and as cash management vehicles).

[407] It highlighted that consideration should be given to adoption of a common definition for MMFs and to clarification of eligible MMF investment assets, given the related credit, liquidity, and market risks: n 108, 21.

[408] Commission, Directive 1997/9/EC on Investor Compensation Schemes. Call for Evidence (2009) 8.

conditions. The outcome was the 2010 CESR MMF Guidelines, which are designed to address UCITS and non-UCITS MMFs. The Guidelines[409] apply criteria to any fund which markets itself as a MMF; they address, *inter alia*, credit quality, maturity of underlying investments, and prospectus/KIID transparency, and are designed to ensure that the capital value of MMF investments is maintained and that daily redemption is supported.[410] Their quasi-binding status is underlined by the 2013 ESMA peer review of their application (one of the first examples of an ESMA peer review), which found that NCA compliance with the non-binding Guidelines has been strong (albeit not uniform),[411] including with respect to compliance with the pivotal requirements which apply to potentially unstable CNAV MMFs. Notably, the major jurisdictions in which MMFs are based have all followed the Guidelines.[412] The Guidelines also enjoy institutional backing (they have been recognized by the Commission as forming part of the wider framework on shadow banking[413] and incorporated into the ECB's legal regime[414]) and command industry support.[415]

Pressure for legislative action came, however, from a number of sources. A more robust approach than CESR's was adopted by the European Systemic Risk Board (ESRB) in its 2012 MMF Recommendation.[416] The ESRB recommended that the CNAV MMF be prohibited, made a series of recommendations relating to liquidity requirements, public disclosure, regulatory reporting, and information sharing, and called for a related legislative response. Action on MMFs was also supported by the European Parliament[417] and, eventually, by the Commission. In its 2012 Green Paper on shadow banking,[418] it highlighted the liquidity risks posed by MMFs and proposed reform. The 2012 UCITS VI Consultation accordingly consulted on the main features of a potential reform, including CNAV fund risk management (including capital requirements for CNAV MMFs and CNAV valuation methods[419]), stability and liquidity support measures, and the quality of MMF investments, particularly money-market instruments.[420]

---

[409] n 124. The Guidelines are supported by an ESMA Q&A (ESMA/2013/113).

[410] The Guidelines set out two categories of MMF—Short Term Money Market Funds and Money Market Funds. Short Term MMFs must maintain the principal value of the investment and the relevant return in line with money-market rates. Fund assets must take the form of UCITS Directive-compliant money-market instruments and deposits, and meet, *inter alia*, credit quality, liquidity profile, and external rating requirements. MMFs are subject to a similar regime, but can also invest in sovereign debt.

[411] Reflecting the centrality of MMF reform to its asset management agenda, ESMA prioritized peer review of the 2010 Guidelines. The results showed that 17 of the 27 NCAs had implemented the Guidelines through binding measures, and six had used non-binding measures but had used different 'hooks' to achieve industry compliance. In all, ten NCAs had not implemented the Guidelines by the review period, although four had done so after the review period: ESMA, Money Market Fund Guidelines Peer Review (2013) (ESMA/2013/476) 6–7.

[412] Including France, Luxembourg, Ireland, and Spain: n 411, 14.

[413] 2012 UCITS VI Consultation, n 111, 12.

[414] The ECB uses the Guidelines as a classification mechanism for different operational purposes.

[415] The guidance has been supported by EFAMA: EFAMA Annual Report (2011) 22.

[416] n 399.

[417] 2012 ECON Shadow Banking Report, n 380, para 31.

[418] n 380, 12.

[419] CNAV MMFs typically use the 'amortized cost valuation', which allows them to disregard any gap between the real and book value of MMF assets.

[420] The Consultation addressed whether the UCITS Directive definition of 'money-market instruments' was sufficiently robust, considered the risks arising from the investment criteria which MMF managers follow

In September 2013, the Commission presented a Proposal for a new MMF Regulation, which would apply exhaustively to all MMFs within its scope, ousting national rules, and impose authorization and discrete regulatory requirements on MMFs.[421] The influence of the ESRB on the Proposal is clear, although the Proposal does not ban CNAV funds, as called for by the ESRB.[422] The proposed regime[423] would apply to UCITSs and to non-UCITS Alternative Investment Funds (AIFs) under the 2011 AIFMD, which invest in short-term assets, and which have as distinct or cumulative objectives the offering of returns in line with money-market rates or the preservation of the value of the investment. The proposed MMF regime is designed to operate as a UCITS-like 'product' regime[424] and to sit within the wider UCITS or AIFMD frameworks which would govern the MMF manager. MMFs would require authorization, either under the UCITS Directive or, for non-UCITS AIFs, under the new authorization process proposed; the designation 'money-market fund' or MMF would be limited to such funds (Proposal Articles 3–5).

The proposed MMF product rules, which are all broadly concerned with supporting liquidity and MMF stability, include rules governing MMF investment policies[425] and investment diversification[426] which are, in effect, specialized applications of the UCITS regime. MMFs would also be required to comply with 'weighted average maturity' and 'weighted average life' portfolio requirements and with requirements governing holdings of daily and weekly maturing assets,[427] designed to support the MMF's ability to meet

---

and from manager over-reliance on external ratings, and reviewed the appropriate features of MMF asset selection policies: n 111, 15.

[421] n 389.

[422] The Commission suggested that the ESRB had 'provided a sound analysis of the system risks inherent in the operation of MMFs' and highlighted that the ESRB recommendations had been 'largely reflected' in the Proposal: n 389, 2.

[423] Which is designed to prevent the risk of contagion to the real economy, to prevent the risk of contagion to the sponsor, and to reduce the risks faced by late redeemers: n 389, 5.

[424] For MMFs in the form of a UCITS, the regime is supplementary to the UCITS product regime: n 389, 6. A number of the UCITS regime rules (relating to investment policies) would be disapplied, reflecting the limited range of MMF eligible assets and the discrete MMF investment policy requirements under the Proposal.

[425] MMFs would be limited to investing only in money-market instruments, deposits with credit institutions, financial derivative instruments, and reverse repurchase agreements (each in accordance with the eligibility conditions set out in the proposed Regulation), and prohibited from investing in other assets, short-selling money-market instruments, taking direct or indirect exposure to equity or commodities, entering into securities lending agreements, securities borrowing arrangements, and repurchase agreements, or any other agreement that would encumber the MMF's assets, and from borrowing and lending cash: Arts 8–13. The Proposal also suggests credit quality requirements for money-market instruments.

[426] Including with respect to limits on exposures to single issuers and exposures to single counterparties. MMFs would, eg, be prevented from investing more than 5 per cent of assets in money-market instruments issued by the same body and in deposits made with the same credit institution; the aggregate risk exposure to the same counterparty from OTC derivative transactions would not be permitted to exceed 20 per cent; and the aggregate amount of cash provided to the same counterparty of an MMF in a reverse repurchase agreement would not be permitted to exceed 20 per cent of assets: Art 14.

[427] These rules (Art 21) are designed to support liquidity by requiring a minimum level of daily and weekly liquid assets. 'Weighted average maturity' (WAM) relates to the average length of time to the legal maturity (or next interest rate reset to a money-market rate, if shorter) of all the underlying assets in the fund reflecting the relative holdings in each asset. Weighted average life (WAL) refers to the average length of time to the legal maturity of all the underlying assets in the fund reflecting the relative holdings in each asset (Art 2). Short-term MMF (which invest in short-term money-market instruments—ie, of legal maturity of less than 397 days) portfolios would be required to have a WAM of no more than 60 days, and a WAL of no more than 120 days; at least 10 per cent of AUM would be required to be composed of daily maturing assets and 20 per cent of

redemptions. The proposed regime would also impose rules governing valuation, stress testing, 'know your client' obligations, transparency requirements (public and supervisory reporting), and, reflecting the crisis-era concern to reduce reliance on ratings, would prohibit MMFs from soliciting or financing an external credit rating. The most contested element of the Proposal is the requirement for CNAV MMFs to maintain a 3 per cent of AUM NAV cash 'buffer';[428] this reform represents the Commission's attempt to address the stability risks posed by CNAV MMFs. CNAV MMFs would also be prevented from receiving other external forms of support.[429]

An earlier leaked version of the Commission's Proposal generated a hostile industry response, particularly in relation to the cash buffer requirement, which was widely regarded as damaging to the industry.[430] The fate of the Proposal remains to be seen.[431] The adoption of a legislative measure for MMFs might, however—given the specificities of the EU MMF market and the matrix of rules and soft measures already in place—suggest a potentially prejudicial momentum for constant reform.

III.3.14.2 Exchange Traded Funds

The shadow banking agenda has also engaged with ETFs. But this reform agenda has a wider reach than the MMF agenda and also engages with retail market issues and risks.

When they were originally designed in the 1990s, ETFs followed a relatively simple structure and were designed to track equity and bond indices. The ETF sector has since experienced very strong growth globally and has become considerably more complex.[432] ETFs now address a wide range of sectors and assets, use physical or synthetic (derivative-based) techniques[433] to replicate indices, can rely heavily on leverage, and are increasingly engaging in securities lending activities. Accordingly, they are being drawn into the shadow banking reform programme; the Financial Stability Board and the International Monetary Fund (IMF) have highlighted the potential stability risks arising from ETF exposure to counterparty risk and from market illiquidity and called for careful monitoring.[434] Retail

---

weekly maturing assets. Other MMF portfolios would be required to have a WAM of no more than six months, a WAL of not more than 12 months, at least 10 per cent of AUM in the form of daily maturing assets, and at least 20 per cent of AUM in the form of weekly maturing assets.

[428] The buffer is designed to absorb market fluctuations and support MMF liquidity.

[429] This proposal is designed to ensure that sponsor support is delivered through the transparent CNAV fund NAV buffer. Sponsor support for other MMFs would be required only where the proposed Regulation's conditions (which in effect require NCA approval, that exceptional circumstances exist, and the support is limited in amount and duration) were met.

[430] Johnson, S, 'Brussels Plan will "Kill Off" Money Funds', *Financial Times, Fund Management Supplement*, 29 April 2013, 1. The September 2013 Proposal had a similar reception: Johnson, S, 'EU Tightens the Noose on Money Funds', *Financial Times, Fund Management Supplement*, 2 September 2013, 1.

[431] Failure to reach agreement on the Proposal by the closing of the Commission and Parliamentary terms in 2014 meant that it was pushed back to the following parliamentary session. Particular difficulties arose in relation to the CNAV cash buffer, with the European Parliament's ECON committee split on its desirability (earlier, a supportive report had been adopted by the ECON Rapporteur in November 2013, which called for more intensive rules, including a 3 per cent capital buffer for CNAV funds and a requirement for all CNAV funds to covert into VNAV funds by end 2019 (PE523.111v01-00)): Johnson, S, 'EU Abandons Reform of Money Market Funds', *Financial Times, Fund Management Supplement*, 10 March 2014, 2.

[432] IMF, Global Financial Stability Report, April 2011 (2011) 68.

[433] FSB, Potential Financial Stability Issues Arising from Recent Trends in ETFs (2011) 2.

[434] n 433 and IMF, n 432, 68–72.

market risks have also emerged. At Member State level in the EU, the UK authorities and the French authorities, for example, have highlighted the increased 'retailization' of these complex products,[435] while the trading of UCITS ETF units has led ESMA to highlight the risks arising from the absence of a direct redemption right against the UCITS and the potential for disclosures not to be delivered directly to investors.[436]

The reform initiative in this area was taken by ESMA.[437] It adopted Guidelines on UCITS ETFs (and other UCITS issues) in 2012[438] which address prospectus, financial report, and KIID disclosure by ETF UCITSs; highlight the applicability of the 2009 UCITS IV Directive Article 51(3) exposure rules (given the significant exposure to derivatives of some of these funds) and of the 2010 CESR Risk Measurement and Global Exposure Guidelines; and address the use by UCITS ETFs of a 'UCITS ETF' identifier and the treatment of secondary market investors in UCITS ETFs.[439] By contrast with the MMF Guidelines, the ETF Guidelines are based on a disclosure model, although they also contain more interventionist guidelines with respect to the ability of investors to redeem their investments in an ETF. While the EU's legislative agenda is likely to address ETFs,[440] ESMA's willingness to engage early and with a supervisory convergence measure underlines its potential to shape the EU's CIS regulatory agenda.

III.3.14.3 Structured UCITSs

Complex and structured UCITSs which rely heavily on financial derivatives[441] are increasingly becoming subject to tailored regulation. The UCITS KIID regime imposes specific disclosure requirements for structured UCITS.[442] Tailored risk-management rules apply under the 2012 ESMA ETF and UCITS Guidelines and the 2012 ESMA Structured UCITS Guidelines.[443] The potential risks to retail investors from these complex products also drove the Commission's proposal that structured UCITSs be excluded from the new MiFID II execution-only regime.

---

[435] FSA, Retail Conduct Risk Outlook 2011, 69–71 and AFM, 2011 Risk and Trend Mapping for Financial Markets and Savings (2011) 6.

[436] 2012 ESMA Shadow Banking Paper Response, n 398, 9–10.

[437] EBA has also produced supervisory guidance in relation to risk management practices for credit institutions which engage in ETF business, whether as counterparties, market-makers, or investors: EBA, Opinion on Good Practices for ETF Risk Management (2013) (EBA-Op-2013-01). The guidance is designed to assist NCAs in gaining an accurate picture of risks to credit institutions from ETF business.

[438] n 129.

[439] UCITS ETF units traded on secondary markets cannot usually be sold back to the ETF directly; the Guidelines address the disclosures and risk warnings which should accordingly be given to investors.

[440] The 2012 Green Paper on Shadow Banking highlighted the potential liquidity disruptions which ETFs can cause: n 380, 12.

[441] Structured UCITSs are defined under the UCITS regime as UCITSs which provide investors, at certain predetermined dates, with algorithmic-based payoffs that are linked to the performance, or to the realization of price changes or other conditions, of financial assets, indices, or reference portfolios, or UCITSs with similar features: 2010 Commission KIID Regulation Art 36. The related KIID must include explanations of the pay-out formula and of the different performance scenarios.

[442] 2010 Commission KIID Regulation Art 36.

[443] n 127 and n 129.

III.3.14.4 Securities Lending, Repos, and Collateral Management: UCITS Risk Management

The international response to the shadow banking risks posed by securities lending, repos, and collateral management more generally is crystallizing.[444] These reforms have a wide reach and extend significantly beyond the CISs who, as major investors, rely heavily on these transactions. While the reforms are likely to have implications for UCITSs, and form part of the Commission's agenda,[445] the UCITS regime has already addressed repo risk and collateral management.[446]

III.3.15 Impact

While the pace of reform might suggest otherwise, the UCITS regulatory regime is generally regarded as a success.[447] From the supply-side perspective, it seems clear that the UCITS regime has facilitated the rapid development of the UCITS market. UCITS AUM have grown from €3,403 billion in 2001 (prior to the UCITS III reforms) to €6, 298 billion at the end of 2011.[448] UCITS are domiciled, for the most part, in only four Member States, underlining the scale of cross-border marketing activity.[449] The extent to which the regulatory framework has driven growth in the UCITS industry is unclear,[450] however—given in particular the stark evidence from the financial crisis of the impact of turbulence and market sentiment on UCITS sector growth[451]—although the Commission has found

---

[444] eg FSB, A Policy Framework for Addressing Shadow Banking Risks in Securities Lending and Repos (2013). The report sets out 13 recommendations relating to, eg, reporting and market transparency (including requirements for reporting to a trade repository, enhanced corporate reporting, regulatory reporting, and reporting by fund managers to investors), haircut and collateral requirements, valuation practices, central clearing, and bankruptcy law treatment.

[445] 2012 Shadow Banking Green Paper, n 380, 12 and 2013 Shadow Banking Communication, n 380. In January 2014 the Commission presented a proposal for a regulation addressing, *inter alia,* the reporting of securities financing transactions by in-scope (financial and non-financial) counterparties to trade repositories and the reporting by UCITS and AIFMD asset managers to investors on their use of such transactions (COM (2014) 40).

[446] Repos, eg, are addressed by the 2009 UCITS IV Directive Art 51(2) efficient portfolio management rules, the related administrative 2007 Commission Eligible Assets Directive, the 2007 CESR Eligible Assets Guidance, the 2012 ESMA Repo Guidelines, and the 2012 ESMA ETF and UCITS Guidelines. Collateral management, with respect to efficient portfolio management techniques as well as OTC derivative transactions, is addressed by the 2012 ESMA ETF and UCITS Guidelines, as well as by the foundation CESR 2010 Guidelines on Risk Measurement and Global Exposure.

[447] Pre-crisis, one commentator observed that 'almost by accident, Brussels appeared to have engineered a rip-roaring success in the world of investment funds': Johnson, S, 'How UCITS Became a Runaway Success', *Financial Times, Fund Management Supplement,* 27 November 2006, 3. The 2004 Report of the Expert Group on Asset Management similarly noted that the UCITS brand was a recognized global label of quality and investor protection: n 75, 8.

[448] 2012 UCITS V Proposal Impact Assessment, n 57, 10 and EFAMA Annual Report (2012) 60.

[449] Luxembourg (32.4 per cent of UCITSs), France (20.6 per cent), Ireland (14.4 per cent), and the UK (11.5 per cent): 2012 UCITS V Proposal Impact Assessment, n 57, 11.

[450] See, eg, 2006 Oxera Report n 81, v, noting that while the UCITS III reforms appeared to have had a positive impact, the evidence was not uniform.

[451] UCITS AUM fell from €6,126 billion in 2007 to €4,525 billion in 2008: EFAMA Annual Report (2011) 48.

cause and effect.[452] But the UCITS brand has certainly been a success; internationally, the UCITS regulatory framework has conferred a global reputation on the UCITS.[453]

The UCITS regime has nonetheless struggled in delivering structural reforms. Although it has not long been in force, the 2009 UCITS IV Directive has yet to deliver the efficiency and consolidation gains it sought,[454] and further enhancements seem likely under the UCITS VI reform process. Difficulties persist with respect to the retail market. The dense and ever-intensifying UCITS rulebook also generates significant regulatory arbitrage risks with respect to the management and distribution of functionally similar products. On the '25th birthday' of the first UCITS product in April 2013, the UCITS industry identified regulatory arbitrage risk as among the greatest of the challenges facing the sector.[455]

III.4 Collective Asset Management: the 2011 AIFMD

III.4.1 Introduction

The regulation by the EU of the disparate alternative investment (non-UCITS) collective asset management sector is a recent, crisis-era phenomenon. But it is also a legacy product of the EU's long-standing focus on the retail market UCITS in developing collective asset management policy. The framing of collective asset management regulation in terms of the UCITS CIS has led to a determinative, if not particularly scientific, UCITS/non-UCITS distinction in EU collective asset management regulation.

The 2011 AIFMD[456] addresses the collective asset management of the universe of non-UCITS alternative investment funds (AIFs) by AIF managers (AIFMs); as discussed in sections 4.6 and 4.7, it accordingly captures a vast array of different funds and their managers. The tortured genesis of the AIFMD and the febrile political context in which it was negotiated makes it difficult to pull out distinct objectives for regulating the collective asset management of such a disparate group of CISs, but two broad themes can be identified. First, these CISs, albeit to very different degrees, can generate financial stability risks. Second, and despite the largely professional base of these funds (the AIFMD does not provide a passport for the marketing of in-scope AIFs to retail investors), particular investor protection risks arise from the foundational agency risks, notably in relation to CIS liquidity and redemption, opaque disclosures, and fair treatment.

---

[452] See, eg, 2012 UCITV V Proposal Impact Assessment, n 57, 5 and 11.

[453] eg 70 per cent of all funds authorized for distribution in Hong Kong are UCITS funds: 2012 KPMG Report, n 96, 2. UCITS investments are also popular elsewhere in Asia, the Middle East, and Latin America; some 25 per cent of UCITS AUM are sourced outside the EU: 2012 ECMI/CEPS Report, n 12, 12 and 25.

[454] There are some 54,000 open-ended CIS in the EU (the majority of which are UCITS funds), as compared to 7–8,000 in the US: 2012 ECMI/CEPS Report, n 12, 15. Similarly, 2012 KPMG Report, n 96, 20–2.

[455] Johnson, S, 'UCITS Fund Celebrates 25th Birthday', *Financial Times*, 15 April 2013, 2.

[456] n 8. The main publicly available elements of the legislative history are: Commission Proposal COM (2009) 207 (2009 AIFMD Proposal), Impact Assessment (SEC (2009) 576); report by the ECON Committee, 11 June 2010 (A7-0171/2010) (2010 ECON Report), on which the European Parliament's Negotiating Position was based; and Council General Approach, 18 May 2010 (Council Document 7377/10).

Regulation of the collective asset management of non-UCITS CISs is now governed by the 2011 AIFMD and a series of administrative measures, chief among them the 2013 Commission Delegated AIFMD Regulation,[457] and related and extensive ESMA supervisory convergence measures.

III.4.2 The Rationale for Regulating CIS Management in the Alternative Investment Segment

The AIF sector is typically associated with a great variety of schemes which are primarily, although by no means always, designed for institutional investment. While it includes property funds, commodity funds, and infrastructure funds, it is strongly associated with the hedge fund and private equity/venture capital sectors. Prior to the crisis, most regulatory discussion was framed in relation to one or the other of these two sectors.

Hedge funds, as has been widely recognized, can defy categorization.[458] They are typically characterized as actively managed funds which use a diverse range of investment strategies, and in particular leverage (debt- and derivative-based), arbitrage, and short selling, to generate high absolute returns.[459] The fund, often based offshore, will typically be managed by the fund manager and draw credit, broking, research, marketing, and other facilities from an investment bank or 'prime broker'. Independent fund administrators provide independent fund valuations to investors and prime brokers. Hedge fund managers typically enjoy great management freedom and are incentivized to generate high performance fees based on fund profitability. Investors (typically institutional or high net worth and sophisticated) usually access funds through private placements, are provided with limited information, given the proprietary nature of hedge fund strategies and the need for management flexibility, and, given the illiquid nature of hedge fund assets, are subject to redemption restrictions.

Hedge funds are widely acknowledged to support market efficiency by providing liquidity; supporting price efficiency, risk distribution, and diversification; and delivering strong returns.[460] But they are also vulnerable to a range of risks which have been extensively discussed in both the pre-crisis and crisis-era contexts.[461] Four families of risk are typically

---

[457] n 16.

[458] As was acknowledged by IOSCO in the development of its crisis-era response to hedge fund risk: IOSCO, Hedge Funds Oversight. Consultation Report (2009) paras 8–9. Pre-crisis, the US SEC had struggled with the design of a new hedge fund regime and the related classification difficulties: Paredes, T, 'On the Decision to Regulate Hedge Funds: The SEC's Regulatory Philosophy, Style, and Mission' (2006) *University of Illinois LR* 975.

[459] eg FSA, Discussion Paper No 05/3, Wider Range Retail Investment Products. Consumer protection in a rapidly changing world (2005) 5. Similarly, SEC, Staff Report to the United States Securities and Exchange Commission, Implications of the Growth of Hedge Funds (2003) 3–4.

[460] eg FSA, Discussion Paper No 05/4, Hedge Funds. A Discussion of Risks and Regulatory Engagement (2005) 14. One recent study has reported that hedge funds outperformed shares, bonds, and commodities over 1994–2011: Hedge Fund Research Centre Imperial College London, The Value of the Hedge Fund Industry to Investors, Markets and the Broader Economy (2012).

[461] From the pre-crisis legal literature see, eg, McVea, H, 'Hedge Funds and the New Regulatory Agenda' (2007) 27 *Legal Studies* 709 and Karmel, R, 'Mutual Funds, Pension Funds, Hedge Funds and Stock Market Volatility: What Regulatory Action by the Securities and Exchange Commission is Appropriate' (2005) 80 *Notre Dame LR* 909. For a crisis-era perspective see Awrey, D, 'The Limits of EU Hedge Fund Regulation' (2011) 5 *LFMR* 119.

identified.[462] First, systemic risks, which are magnified by leverage levels, can be significant.[463] These can be generated through the credit risk transmission channel, given the extent to which hedge funds can represent counterparty risks to entities providing hedge funds with leverage; classically, this form of systemic risk is associated in particular with the provision of leverage by prime brokers. Systemic risks can also be generated through the market risk transmission channel, given the scale of trading by hedge funds.[464] Second, microprudential risks, which can lead to fund failure and investor losses, can be generated from the extent to which the hedge fund is exposed to market, credit, settlement, liquidity, and operational risks. Third, investor protection risks arise from the illiquid nature of hedge fund assets, redemption and liquidity restrictions, and the opacity which typically attends hedge fund investments. Investor protection risks can also be generated by conflicts of interest and governance failures. Finally, hedge funds have been associated with risks to market efficiency and transparency. Financial market risks aside, the aggressive activism often associated with hedge fund shareholders has led to extensive discussion of whether they bring efficiencies to firms or generate prejudicial short-termism.[465]

Hedge funds came under close scrutiny from the mid-2000s as their AUM grew very significantly both in the EU and globally,[466] as new classes of investors became exposed to hedge fund risk (particularly pension funds and, through funds-of-hedge-funds, retail investors), and as the scale of hedge fund trading activity began to generate market volatility and stability concerns.[467] International dialogue on hedge funds had been taking place since the 1998 Long-Term Capital Management fund crisis, which led to the 2000 recommendations of the (then) Financial Stability Forum (now the FSB), which were updated in 2007.[468] The International Organization of Securities Commissions (IOSCO) produced two key reports,[469] and recommended standards in relation to valuation and funds-of-hedge-funds.[470] In the US, ill-fated attempts at reform were made over

---

[462] See generally Athanassiou, P, 'The Conceptual Underpinnings of Onshore Hedge Fund Regulation: A Global and European Perspective' (2008) 8 *JCLS* 251.

[463] For a crisis-era discussion see Lo, A, Hedge Funds, Systemic Risk and the Financial Crisis of 2007–2008. Written Testimony for the House Oversight Committee Hearing on Hedge Funds (2009), available at <http://ssrn.com/abstract=1301217>.

[464] See, eg, Garbaravicius, T and Dierick, F, Hedge Funds and their Implications for Financial Stability, ECB Occasional Paper 24 (2007), available via <http://ssrn.com/abstract=752094> and ESMA 2013(1) TRV, n 1, 35–8 (reviewing the financial economics literature).

[465] Particularly with respect to the extent to which, through derivative-based strategies, they exert corporate influence without carrying equivalent risks (the 'empty voting' problem): eg Hu, T and Black, B, 'Hedge Funds, Insiders and the Decoupling of Economic and Voting Ownership: Empty Voting and Hidden (Morphable) Ownership' (2007) 13 *J Corp Fin* 343. For a recent analysis see, eg, Cheffins, B, Hedge Fund Activism Canadian Style, ECGI Law WP No 202 (2013), available at <http://ssrn.com/abstract=2204294>.

[466] FSA, Discussion Paper 05/4, n 460, 11–12.

[467] Moloney, N, 'The EC and the Hedge Fund Challenge: A Test Case for EC Securities Policy after the Financial Services Action Plan' (2006) 6 *JCLS* 1.

[468] The recommendations included: a strengthening of counterparty risk assessment; enhanced oversight of prime brokers; stronger risk management by hedge funds and managers; enhanced disclosure by hedge funds to investors, counterparties, and the market generally; and improvement of market practices, including documentation and valuation practices.

[469] Regulatory and Investor Protection Issues Arising from Participation by Retail Investors in (Funds of) Hedge Funds (2003) and The Regulatory Environment for Hedge Funds. A Survey and Comparison (2006).

[470] Principles for Valuation of Hedge Fund Portfolios (2007) and Funds of Hedge Funds (2008). See McVea, H, 'Hedge Fund Asset Valuations and the Work of the International Organisation of Securities Commissions (IOSCO)' (2008) 57 *ICLQ* 1.

2004–7,[471] while the UK regulator produced two major reports on hedge fund risk and on the retailization of hedge funds through funds-of-hedge-funds.[472] While the general tenor of this reform movement was to call for greater industry transparency, the implicit threat of intervention and general support for industry-led initiatives led to pre-emptive action by the hedge fund industry and the adoption of a series of standards.[473]

The financial crisis re-ordered the broadly facilitative policy environment,[474] notwithstanding the widespread agreement that hedge funds were not closely implicated in the financial crisis.[475] Although hedge fund failure was associated with the early stages of the crisis in summer/autumn 2007,[476] hedge fund leverage was well below that of the banking sector in the run-up to the crisis—and was declining;[477] hedge funds provided liquidity over the crisis;[478] and, while hedge fund AUM plummeted[479] and a number of major hedge funds failed, the failures did not have systemic consequences. But the massive and destabilizing market volatility over 2007–8 was widely associated with major hedge funds deleveraging and unwinding positions in response to tightened credit conditions,[480] with investor redemption demands, and with the generation thereby of powerful pro-cyclical effects.[481] Additionally, the general opacity and complexity associated with the hedge fund sector,[482] and the widespread use by hedge funds of short-selling strategies, made them a politically attractive target for the nascent reform movement.

The first signs of potentially radical change[483] came with the initial Washington November 2008 G20 Summit commitment to ensure that all markets, products, and participants were

---

[471] On the SEC's failed attempts to regulated hedge fund managers see Paredes, n 458.

[472] nn 459 and 460.

[473] The major standards include those originally issued by The Hedge Funds Standards Board in 2008 and since regularly updated (the HFSB Standards), which cover disclosure, valuation, risk management, fund governance, and shareholder conduct. Work on the HFSB Standards commenced in 2007 as an effort by leading European hedge funds to develop a code of conduct in an attempt to head off political pressure for regulation: Mackintosh, J, 'Big Hedge Funds Look at a Code of Practice', *Financial Times*, 19 June 2007, 1. Other major standards include those issued by the Managed Funds Association and the Association of Alternative Investment Managers.

[474] For a detailed analysis of how the international reform developed see Ferran, E, 'After the Crisis: The Regulation of Hedge Funds and Private Equity in the EU' (2011) 12 *EBOLR* 379.

[475] eg DLG Report (n 108, 24) and IOSCO's 2009 review (n 458, paras 44–46).

[476] Two major Bear Sterns hedge funds failed over summer/autumn 2007, triggering liquidity contractions and a wider loss of confidence.

[477] Turner Review, n 381, 72 and Ang, A, Gorovyy, S, and van Inwegen, G, 'Hedge Fund Leverage' (2011) 102 *J Fin* 102.

[478] Aragon, C and Strahan, P, Hedge Funds as Liquidity Providers. Evidence from the Lehman Bankruptcy (2009), available at <http://ssrn.com/abstract=1462315>.

[479] Hedge fund assets fell by 22 per cent over 2007–2008: ESMA 2013(1) TRV, n 1, 20.

[480] The hedge fund/prime broker chain led to funding pressures on hedge funds, as funds typically obtain cash leverage from prime brokers and provide collateral which is often in the form of illiquid assets.

[481] eg, 2009 Turner Review, n 381, 72.

[482] Gerding, E, 'Code, Crash and Open Source: the Outsourcing of Financial Regulation to Risk Models and the Global Financial Crisis' (2009) 84 *Washington LR* 127, suggesting that the SEC's initial failed attempts to regulate hedge funds reflected the extent to which regulators had become 'daunted by complexity' (at 134).

[483] Hedge funds were not a major concern of the Financial Stability Forum's (now the FSB) Report on Enhancing Market and Institutional Resilience (2008), one of the first major crisis-era reviews.

regulated to an appropriate degree,[484] which took tentative steps towards more interventionist regulation of AIFs, including hedge funds.[485] Subsequently, the London April 2009 G20 Summit reached political agreement[486] on hedge funds being subject to regulation, while the 2010 Joint Forum Report on the Scope of Financial Regulation, which responded to the Washington November 2008 G20 Summit, recommended a series of regulatory reforms.[487] Although the hedge fund sector would contract significantly over the crisis period and develop resiliency strategies,[488] the stage was nonetheless set for the EU's wide-ranging intervention.

Although private equity funds share some points of commonality with hedge funds, the private equity sector posed significantly less risk to financial markets and received materially less attention prior to the crisis.[489] The private equity funding model is based on the pooling of capital from (typically) institutional investors and its investment by private equity fund(s) in private firms (portfolio companies) over medium-term horizons. As in the hedge fund sector, leverage is closely associated with private equity investments, but leverage applies at the level of the portfolio company. Private equity funding is based on extracting efficiencies through debt financing.[490] Debt finance is raised through the portfolio company and funded through revenue flows from the portfolio company, which undergoes radical efficiency-driven reorganization to deliver the value which the private equity fund has identified. Prior to the financial crisis, explosive growth in the private equity sector, and a number of controversial and highly publicized 'going private'

---

[484] The related Action Plan contained a commitment to reviewing the scope of financial regulation to ensure that all systemically significant institutions were appropriately regulated: Washington November 2008 G20 Summit, Declaration on Financial Markets and the World Economy, para 9 and Action Plan.

[485] The Action Plan called on private sector bodies that had already developed best practices for private pools of capital and/or hedge funds to bring forward proposals for a set of unified best practices, and called on Finance Ministers to assess the adequacy of these proposals.

[486] Negotiations were eased by IOSCO's adoption of six recommendations for the regulation of hedge funds and hedge fund managers, which included the recommendation that the hedge fund and/or manager be registered and that the manager be subject to appropriate ongoing regulation and supervision, including in relation to organizational and operational standards, conflicts of interest and conduct of business, investor disclosure, prudential valuation, and regulatory risk reporting. The recommendations were provided to the G20 for the April 2009 Summit: IOSCO, Hedge Funds Oversight (2009) paras 3–4. A change in the US position, which had previously favoured indirect regulation of hedge funds, also facilitated the April 2009 agreement: Ferran, n 474.

[487] Joint Forum (IOSCO, the Basel Committee, and the International Association of Insurance Supervisors), Review of the Differentiated Nature and Scope of Financial Regulation. Key Issues and Recommendations (2010) 53–67.

[488] In 2012, the UK FSA's regular review of hedge fund systemic risk reported that the aggregate 'footprint' of hedge funds remained modest in most markets, that leverage was relatively low, that there was no evidence of liquidity pressure on hedge funds, and that hedge funds' resiliency strategies included increased margin requirements: FSA, Assessing the Possible Sources of Systemic Risk from Hedge Funds (2012). Similarly, ESMA reported on generally stable leverage in the AIF sector generally in 2012, and that leverage levels across the AIF sector were still below those in December 2008: ESMA 2013(1) TRV, n 1, 20.

[489] On the evolving regulatory approach to private equity pre-crisis see Payne, J, 'Private Equity and its Regulation in Europe' (2011) 12 *EBOLR* 559, MacNeil, I, 'Private Equity: the UK Regulatory Response' (2007) *CMLJ* 18, and Ferran, E, Regulation of Private Equity-Backed Leveraged Buyout Activity in Europe, ECGI Law WP No 84/2007 (2007), available at <http://ssrn.com/abstract=989748>.

[490] See further Cheffins, B and Armour, J, The Eclipse of Private Equity, ECGI Law WP No 82/2007 (2007), available at <http://ssrn.com/abstract=982114>.

transactions which led to major public companies going into private equity ownership,[491] led to close political and policy scrutiny. From a financial markets perspective, private equity funds have some limited capacity for generating systemic risk in that highly leveraged portfolio companies are more at risk of failure and of defaulting on debt, with consequent risk to counterparties holding the debt.[492] In their heyday, they were also associated with potential damage to market efficiency were 'going private' transactions to become of such a scale as to threaten price formation and efficiency in the public markets.[493] Most attention focused, however, on corporate-governance-related risks and, in particular, on the potential for detriment to stakeholders from the aggressive debt-based funding model, particularly employees.[494] As with the hedge fund sector, the industry fought a rearguard action as the threat of intervention was raised.[495]

Although private equity received some crisis-era attention from IOSCO,[496] it was not associated with the financial crisis reform movement to any significant degree, and became rolled up within the wider movement to bring AIFs generally within the reform net.[497] Its inclusion in the EU response is a function of the particular political conditions which prevailed in the EU and the significant hostility in some quarters to the aggressive form of capitalism associated with private equity, as well as of the decision to address the AIF sector generally.

III.4.3 The EU and the AIF Sector: the Evolution of the AIFMD

III.4.3.1 The Pre-crisis Position

The EU AIFM/AIF sector was not unregulated prior to the crisis.[498] EU-registered AIFMs were subject to conduct and prudential requirements under MiFID I, for example,[499] and to market abuse prohibitions under the market abuse regime. Disclosure and transparency requirements applied to AIFs admitted to trading on regulated markets.[500] Some 80 per

---

[491] 2007 saw the announcement of the largest ever leveraged buy-out transactions in the US (the TXU utility group and KKR/Texas Pacific Group deal ($44.5 billion)) and in the UK (the KKR-led bid for Alliance Boots (£11.1 billion)).

[492] Although the ECB was sanguine, and reported that the exposure of EU banks to leveraged buy outs was not large relative to banks' capital buffers: ECB, Large Banks and Private-Equity-Sponsored Leveraged Buyouts in the EU (2007).

[493] On the financial market risks see FSA, Discussion Paper No 06/6, Private Equity: A Discussion of Risk and Regulatory Engagement (2006).

[494] The impact of the private equity funding model on firm efficiency and on employees received close political attention in the UK, driven in part by the publicity given to the very large returns to the private equity sector immediately prior to the crisis: eg, House of Commons Treasury Committee, Private Equity (Tenth Report of Session 2006–07).

[495] This was particularly the case in the UK, which was the centre of pan-EU private equity funding, and where the private equity industry signed up to the transparency-focused Walker Guidelines (Guidelines for Transparency and Disclosure in Private Equity, initially published in 2007).

[496] eg IOSCO, Private Equity (2008) and Private Equity Conflicts of Interest (2010).

[497] Ferran, n 474.

[498] See generally Wymeersch, E, The Regulation of Private Equity, Hedge Funds and State Funds, Financial Law Institute WP No 2010-06 (2010), available at <http://ssrn.com/abstract=1685202>.

[499] As was widely acknowledged during the crisis-era reform discussions and in relation to hedge fund managers in particular: eg, DLG Report, n 108, 24.

[500] On the pre-crisis regulatory position see, eg, Moloney n 467 and Athanassiou, P, *Hedge Fund Regulation in the EU. Current Trends and Future Prospects* (2009).

cent of hedge fund managers and 60 per cent of private equity fund managers in the EU were authorized and supervised by the (then) UK Financial Services Authority (FSA).[501] Industry self-regulation efforts were also intensifying prior to the crisis.

Before the crisis broke out, EU policy engagement with the AIF/AIFM sector generally took the form of a frequently highly politicized debate on hedge fund regulation and, to a lesser extent, on the private equity sector; the very different nature of these funds meant, however, that the policy debate was neither coherent nor holistic. It was not until late 2008/early 2009, with the crisis-driven G20 commitment to extending regulation to all major markets, products, and participants, that the AIFM/AIF sector as a whole became the target for intervention.

The Commission was initially reluctant to intervene.[502] A low-key, facilitative approach to the AIF sector emerged from the 2006 Investment Funds White Paper, reflecting, by and large, the industry position as articulated in two key 2006 reports from the hedge fund expert group and the private equity expert group.[503] In the 2006 White Paper, the Commission focused on supporting cross-border transactions in these funds, removing obstructive rules where appropriate, and supporting efforts to build a common consensus as to the definition of a 'private placement', which would facilitate the cross-border operation of hedge and private equity funds in the institutional sector. Although the Council took a similar and relatively sanguine approach to the alternative investment market in 2007,[504] a more hostile position was adopted in some Member States, notably France and Germany.[505] The European Parliament and the ECB were also more sceptical, auguring the ways in which institutional positions would change in 2008. The ECB had repeatedly highlighted the potential systemic stability risks posed by hedge funds, in particular, prior to the financial crisis.[506] The Parliament's position, while cognizant of the potential systemic and stability risks of hedge funds, was driven by concerns as to 'aggressive'

---

[501] Speech by Dan Waters (FSA) on 'Evaluating the Prospects for the UK and European Market under the AIFMD', 25 February 2010. The UK MiFID I-based regime for hedge fund AIFMs included, eg, authorization requirements (fit and proper requirements), light-touch ongoing controls (organizational requirements concerning manager competence to manage the assets in line with the investment mandate, adequate interfaces with the administrator and prime broker, appropriate information feeds for market information, adequate internal reporting systems, and compliance systems), and dealing requirements concerning trade allocation and best execution.

[502] Commissioner McCreevy repeatedly argued that hedge funds and private equity funds were good for the market, supported liquidity, drove innovation, and increased shareholder value: eg, Buck, T, 'Hedge Funds and Private Equity "Are Good for the Market"', *Financial Times*, 9 February 2007, 6.

[503] n 80.

[504] The May 2007 ECOFIN Council adopted a resolution on hedge funds which acknowledged their role in supporting market efficiency, stressed the potential risks they posed, noted indirect supervision through monitoring of the exposure of credit institutions (prime brokers) to hedge funds, and supported the Commission's study of whether retail access should be supported: 2798th Council Meeting, ECOFIN Council Conclusions on Hedge Funds, 8 May 2007.

[505] Political criticism was particularly strong in France and Germany, with then presidential candidate Sarkozy calling for a tax on speculative capital movements: Arnold, M, 'Sarkozy Aims to Push for European Tax on Hedge Funds', *Financial Times*, 14 February 2007, 8. In Germany, hedge funds came in for significant opprobrium (a widely reported remark by the Minister for Labour in 2005 likened hedge funds to locusts), related in part to the success of the highly activist The Children's Fund in scuppering Deutsche Börse's bid for the London Stock Exchange. Germany's calls for code-of-conduct and transparency standards for the hedge fund industry failed at the May 2007 G8 meeting following US and UK opposition.

[506] eg ECB, Financial Stability Review (2006).

speculation and shareholder capitalism more generally, and by concerns as to the impact of private equity funds on employees in particular. Between 2004 and 2007, however, it adopted a largely facilitative approach, typically recommending that the Commission monitor the alternative investment sector.[507]

In parallel with the stability-focused discussions, the pre-crisis policy debate, in sharp contrast to the crisis-era debate, also addressed retail access to alternative investments.[508] The UCITS Review saw extensive discussion on whether a new regulatory regime should be developed to accommodate easier retail access to alternative investments, reflecting the increasingly febrile discussion at the time on retail investor exposure to hedge fund risk,[509] through funds-of-hedge-funds in particular.[510] Caution was, however, a watchword of the discussions, and the Commission's 2006 Investment Funds White Paper took a restrained approach, committing only to studying retail access to alternative investments.[511] While this initiative would not survive the financial crisis, it underscores the broadly facilitative approach taken to alternative investments immediately prior to the crisis.

III.4.3.2 The Crisis and the AIFMD Negotiations

The deepening of the financial crisis and the initial stages of the EU's response to reform of the AIF sector over autumn/winter 2008 and spring 2009 can be associated with two antithetical developments: consensus that the AIF sector and in particular hedge funds had not played a major role in the crisis, and agreement that legislative reform in the AIF sector, and not only in relation to hedge funds and private equity funds, was needed.

Over 2008, institutional positions in the EU shifted rapidly, reflecting the changed political environment and the international reform agenda (as expressed in particular by the November 2008 Washington G20 commitment to ensuring that all financial markets, products, and participants were subject to appropriate regulation). Driven by political dynamics within the European Parliament[512] and by the deepening crisis, the Parliament's position hardened over autumn 2008; a Parliament resolution called for the Commission to present legislative proposals for the regulation of hedge funds and private equity,[513] while

---

[507] Purvis Report (ECON Committee) on the Future of Hedge Funds and Derivatives, 17 December 2003 (A5–0476/2003); European Parliament Klinz II Resolution on Asset Management, 13 December 2007 (P6_TA(2007)0627); and European Parliament Van den Burg II Resolution on Financial Services Policy 2005–2010, 11 July 2007 (P6_TA-(2007)0338).

[508] For a more extensive discussion of the implications of the retailization of alternative investments in the period preceding the crisis see Moloney, n 33, 168–76.

[509] The febrile debate drove the Expert Group on Alternative Investments to call for a 'rational and dispassionate debate on the conditions under which retail access to hedge-fund-based investments could be contemplated': n 80, 6. The leading consumer stakeholder FIN-USE, by contrast, was 'alarmed' by the Expert Group's view that the provision of investment services in respect of the full range of hedge funds and related products by MiFID-authorized firms be allowed without further restrictions at the level of the fund, its managers, or elsewhere in the value chain: FIN-USE, Response to the Report of the Alternative Investment Expert Group—Managing, Servicing and Marketing Hedge Funds in Europe (2006) 1.

[510] See IOSCO, Consultation Report—The Regulatory Environment for Hedge Funds. A Survey and Comparison (2006).

[511] n 9, 12. A major study on retailization in the non-UCITS sector was published in 2008 but action was suspended with the advent of the crisis: PriceWaterhouseCoopers, The Retailization of non-Harmonized Investment Funds in the European Union. Prepared for the European Commission (2008).

[512] eg, Socialist Group, Hedge Funds and Private Equity—A Critical Analysis (2007).

[513] Resolution with Recommendations to the Commission on Hedge Funds and Private Equity, 23 September 2008 (P6_TA-PROV(2008)0425) (based on the earlier Rasmussen Report (for the ECON

the Parliament's Lehne Report called on the Commission to adopt proposals on the transparency of hedge funds and private equity.[514]

The Commission initially refused to accede to the Parliament's requests for legislative proposals.[515] In December 2008, in response to the changed EU and international climate, the Commission, in something of a rearguard action, issued a consultation which was limited to hedge fund regulation.[516] The consultation related the Commission's change in position to the November 2008 Washington G20 commitment to ensure that all financial market products and participants were regulated or subject to oversight, as appropriate to their circumstances, as well as to the risks posed by the 'comparatively limited extent' to which hedge funds and their managers were subject to macroprudential oversight and the limited transparency on their activities.[517] While the consultation noted that hedge funds had not traditionally been considered of systemic relevance, it highlighted the prime broker lending transmission channel as generating systemic risk, as well as the stability risks arising from pro-cyclical volatility effects flowing from the scale of their trading activities. Overall, however, the consultation did not commit to extensive regulation of the AIF sector.[518]

The narrowly focused consultation was followed by the February 2009 DLG Report. The Report did not address the AIF sector specifically, although it called for the EU to extend appropriate regulation, in a proportionate manner, to all firms and entities conducting financial activities of a potentially systemic nature.[519] It highlighted, however, hedge fund risk (acknowledging that while the hedge fund sector not been strongly associated with the financial crisis, it had transmitted risk through its trading activities), and recommended that a registration- and disclosure-based regime be introduced.[520] The momentum for reform continued to build in spring 2009,[521] but by now reform was being cast in terms of AIF/AIFM regulation generally to reflect the November 2008 Washington G20 commitment to address unregulated sectors. In a major political landmark, the Economic and

---

Committee) with Recommendations to the Commission on Hedge Funds and Private Equity, 22 September 2008 (A6-0338/2008)). The wide-ranging Resolution, which addressed the regulation of the financial sector generally, called on the Commission to bring forward legislative proposals covering, *inter alia*, the transparency of prime brokerage services, a harmonized EU framework for venture capital and private equity, a harmonized EU framework for private placements, including placements of AIFs (and including investment strategy, leverage, risk management and valuation rules), leverage use, and asset stripping by private equity funds.

[514] Lehne Report (for the Committee on Legal Affairs) with Recommendations to the Commission on Transparency of Institutional Investors, 22 September 2008 (A6-0296/2008).

[515] The refusal led to tensions between Commissioner McCreevy and the European Parliament, evident in Commissioner McCreevy's December 2008 speech to the Parliament on the Commission's subsequent change of approach, in which he challenged his characterization as 'the ultimate market liberal who would like to deregulate the world': Commissioner McCreevy, Speech to the ECON Committee, 1 December 2008 (Speech/08/665).

[516] Commission, Consultation Paper on Hedge Funds (2008).

[517] n 516, 2–3.

[518] Commissioner McCreevy remained sceptical as to the benefits of hedge fund regulation into 2009: Speech to EC Conference on Private Equity and Hedge Funds, 26 February 2009 (Speech/09/80), warning that hedge funds and private equity funds had become the 'poster boys' of the financial crisis, and calling for a proportionate response.

[519] 2009 DLG Report, n 108, 25.

[520] 2009 DLG Report, n 108, 24.

[521] The March 2009 Turner Review provided another important staging point by supporting greater transparency on hedge fund activities and 'the power to apply appropriate prudential regulation': n 381, 73.

Financial Affairs (ECOFIN) Council's support for regulation to be extended to hedge funds but also other AIFs[522] was endorsed by the Spring 2009 European Council;[523] the common EU position also shaped the April 2009 London G20 commitment to subject hedge funds to registration and disclosure requirements. Following internal political machinations,[524] the Commission's Proposal for the AIFMD was adopted in April 2009[525] and marked the start of protracted and bruising political negotiations in the European Parliament and Council, as well as between the Commission, Parliament, and Council in the subsequent trilogue negotiations;[526] these negotiations have been strongly associated with the 'clash of capitalisms' engaged by the different varieties of capitalism across the EU.[527] They completed on 11 November 2010 with the adoption by the Parliament of the agreed text which had been finalized by the institutions on 27 October 2010.

The Proposal was designed to extend (in response to the November 2008 Washington G20 Summit commitment) appropriate regulation and oversight to all actors and activities that generate significant risks, but also had an eye to shaping the emerging international response.[528] Although the Commission noted that AIFMs generally had not caused the crisis, it highlighted the range of systemic, microprudential, investor protection, market efficiency, and integrity risks which could arise.[529] It suggested these risks had crystallized in the case of hedge funds, which had contributed to market volatility by unwinding large, leveraged positions in response to tightening credit conditions, and thereby magnifying pro-cyclicality effects and damaging market liquidity.[530] Although the Commission was more sanguine in relation to private equity funds and acknowledged they did not contribute to systemic risks, it highlighted the wider economic impact of the contraction in private equity funding on the highly leveraged companies (portfolio companies) in which private equity funds invest.[531] The risks posed by AIFMs such as hedge fund and private equity fund managers were addressed by a patchwork of different national rules and industry standards which did not effectively address cross-border oversight of systemically significant

---

[522] ECOFIN, Key Issues Document for the Spring 2009 European Council, 5 March 2009 (Council Document 6784/1/093).

[523] European Council Conclusions, 19–20 March 2009 (7880/1/09 Rev 1).

[524] The *Financial Times* reported that the Proposal was 'forged in a backroom deal between socialist groups in the European Parliament and [Commission President] Barosso': Editorial, *Financial Times*, 15 April 2010, 10.

[525] The main elements of the publicly available legislative history are noted at n 456.

[526] During the 'trilogue' stage of negotiations, the Commission, European Parliament, and Council seek to reach a final text on the basis of the agreed Parliament and Council texts. See further Ch X sect 3.2.

[527] The 2011 AIFMD negotiations have been subject to extensive review and will not be considered here in detail. See, eg, Woll, C, 'Lobbying under Pressure: the Effect of Salience on EU Hedge Fund Regulation' (2012) 51 *JCMS* 55, Ferran, n 474, and Quaglia, L, 'The "Old" and "New" Political Economy of Hedge Fund Regulation in the EU' (2011) 34 *West European Politics* 665. For a policy and politically orientated review see House of Lords, EU Committee, Directive on Alternative Investment Fund Managers. 3rd Report of Session 2009–2010. Vol 1 (2010) (2010 HL AIFMD Report).

[528] The Commission hoped that the Proposal would make an important contribution to the debate on the global approach to the supervision of the AIFM/AIF industry (n 456, 4), while the accompanying Press Release trumpeted the Proposal as the 'first attempt in any jurisdiction to create a comprehensive framework for the direct regulation and supervision of the alternative fund industry': Commission Press Release, 29 April 2009 (IP/09/669).

[529] 2009 AIFMD Proposal, n 456, 2–3.

[530] 2009 AIFMD Proposal, n 456, 3.

[531] 2009 AIFMD Proposal, n 456, 3.

AIFMs and AIFs; a harmonized regime was therefore required. Side-stepping the severe definitional difficulties posed by the legislative capture of hedge funds and private equity funds, the Commission proposed that the regime apply to 'non-UCITS' funds generally in order to avoid the significant regulatory arbitrage risks which would otherwise be generated, but called for calibration to avoid 'one-size-fits-all' risks.[532]

At this point of the crisis, there was industry-wide and political agreement (following the November 2008 Washington and April 2009 London G20 Summits) on the need to bring AIFMs in general and hedge fund managers in particular within the regulatory net.[533] The Commission's Proposal broke new ground, however, by presenting a detailed template for regulation which was based on the earlier UCITS and MiFID I collective and discretionary asset management frameworks, but designed to reflect AIF industry risk. This template extended far beyond transparency requirements, and engaged with operational, organizational, liquidity, leverage, and asset custody regulation. Designed to establish a harmonized EU framework for monitoring and supervising AIFMs and to provide a related passport, the proposed regime changed very significantly over the negotiations, although the basic elements of the 2009 Commission Proposal remained in place.[534] While regarded as not sufficiently ambitious in some quarters[535] and enjoying NCA support for some, at least, of its provisions,[536] it generated widespread political and industry hostility, and quickly became regarded as an overly blunt measure which threatened to seriously disrupt the EU's alternative investment market.[537] The weaknesses in the Proposal remain surprising, given the detailed and road-tested UCITS and MiFID I templates which were available.[538] But the febrile political, market, and institutional environment, the tangle of objectives and rationales related to the measure, and the late change of heart by the Commission were not conducive to effective rule-making—which was all the more difficult given the elusive quality of the AIF and AIFM sector, and the technical challenges posed by leverage, liquidity, and depositary regulation in particular.

The main concerns related to: the Proposal's wide scope and failure to acknowledge the massive diversity within the AIFM/AIF population and the need for proportionality to

---

[532] 2009 AIFMD Proposal, n 456, 4.

[533] IOSCO's 2009 standards for hedge fund regulation, prepared for the April 2009 G20 London Summit, acknowledged that while they were addressed to hedge funds they could be applied to other market participants who held or controlled large pools of capital: n 486, para 4.

[534] Including in relation to authorization, capital requirements, disclosure, operational and organizational requirements, leverage controls, valuation, the depositary, and passporting.

[535] The Parliament's European Socialist Party, eg, called for a more ambitious measure—2010 HL AIFMD Report, n 527, 9—as did the French government. Finance Minister Lagarde regarded the Proposal as 'way below the demands that Europeans should have. It is regulation at its minimum. We need to have a maximalist position at the start': reported in Barber, T, Tait, N, and Arnold, M, 'Paris Pushes EU to Impose Tighter Regulation on Hedge Funds', *Financial Times*, 6 May 2009, 7.

[536] The (then) UK FSA, which supervised the EU's largest centre for hedge fund management, supported the creation of a harmonized set of 'sensible regulatory standards', although it expressed concern across the AIFMD negotiations as to the implications of the restrictive approach to third countries: Waters, n 501.

[537] eg Masters, B, Arnold, M, and Tait, N, 'EU Plans for Hedge Fund Rules Under Fire', *Financial Times*, 30 April 2009, 1. The *Financial Times* reported on the 'accusations of protectionism, anti-Anglo-Saxon bias and unnecessary meddling' and on the proposal being regarded as motivated by 'deep seated envy in continental Europe of London's success': Woolfe, J, 'Brussels Official Faces Up to Sharp Criticism of "Ogres"', *Financial Times, Fund Management Supplement*, 27 July 2009, 8.

[538] Commissioner Barnier was subsequently reported as conceding that the Proposal had been rushed and badly drafted: Parker, G and Tait, N, 'City Purrs After Charm Offensive,' *Financial Times*, 3 March 2010.

avoid prejudicial restructuring of the industry; the risk of a reduction in investor choice and returns; the proposal that the Commission be empowered to adopt leverage limits for AIFMs; the depositary regime (particularly with respect to liability and the delegation of custody functions); the requirement for an independent valuer; the restrictive approach to third country access to the EU market, given the tough equivalence regime implied in the Proposal; and the empirical basis for the measure, given the evidence that AIFMs were not strongly associated with the financial crisis.[539]

As the negotiations developed, different and parallel Council and European Parliament[540] drafts introduced further difficulties as well as enhancements;[541] the leverage, delegation, depositary, disclosure, and third country rules, in particular, were subject to repeated and often conflicting revisions across the different texts as institutions liberalized or tightened the rules. The Parliament's initial November 2009 ECON Report introduced significant technical nuance to the Commission's Proposal,[542] but it fuelled controversy by, for example, proposing 'naked short-selling' restrictions[543] and remuneration require-ments.[544] A record number of amendments were subsequently tabled over the Parliament process.[545] Overall, the Parliament has been credited with improving the Proposal, par-ticularly with respect to refining the Proposal's application to the specificities of particular AIFMs, calibrating the depositary liability regime to the institutional context of AIF investment, supporting the use of non-EU depositaries, and pressing for a more facilitative third country regime.[546]

Council negotiations proved extremely difficult (although alliances shifted depending on the issues at hand, the UK—the centre of the EU's hedge fund industry—generally led the efforts to dilute the Proposal, while France and Germany were most strongly associated with toughening the Proposal)[547] and stretched across three Council Presidencies. Early predictions that the Swedish Presidency (July–December 2009) text (which had secured agreement on a number of issues, introduced technical nuance, injected more

---

[539] An analysis of the Commission's Impact Assessment for the Parliament concluded that the Commis-sion's analysis was 'vague, sweeping, and inadequate as a basis for justifying regulation': Report for the ECON Committee, Analysis of the Commission's Impact Assessments of the proposed AIFM (2009) (IP/A/ECON/ 2009-3) 1.

[540] The ECB's opinion was broadly supportive of the Proposal, although it suggested detailed revisions, including with respect to the Commission's approach to leverage: [2009] OJ C272/1.

[541] A comparative table of the main points of difference between the final Commission, Parliament, and Council texts is contained in ECON Committee, Background Note on the AIFMD 7–9 (AIFMD Compara-tive Table).

[542] Including with respect to the initial capital regime, the valuation regime, the depositary regime, and the leverage rules (in respect of which it suggested a disclosure-based regime and limited the scope of the Commission's leverage-limit-setting powers under the Proposal).

[543] On naked short selling see Ch VI sect 3.

[544] PE430.709v02 (the Gauzès Report).

[545] The revised and final Gauzès Report was subsequently tabled to the Parliament's plenary session in June 2010. Some 1,700 amendments were tabled by MEPs.

[546] eg Ferran, n 474. ECON Rapporteur Gauzès was generally praised for his flexible approach: Woolfe, J, 'Big Issues to Resolve to Wrap up the Directive', *Financial Times, Fund Management Supplement,* 18 January 2010, 8.

[547] The UK's final agreement was reported as being linked in part to a decision not to deploy any further political capital on a measure which was strongly supported by France and Germany, in light of the need to keep capital for the parallel negotiations on the European Supervisory Authorities: Parker, G, Tait, B, and Jones, S, 'Osborne Bows to EU Hedge Fund Rules', *Financial Times,* 19 May 2010, 1.

proportionality, and removed many of the onerous equivalence conditions attached to the third country access regime)[548] would lead to a final compromise proved overly optimistic. The following Spanish Presidency (January–June 2010) led to a re-opening of a number of issues and pressure for a more restrictive third country regime, particularly from France.[549]

During trilogue discussions, negotiations remained difficult, with the European Parliament concerned in particular to strengthen the depositary regime and the private equity fund requirements (notably the asset stripping rules),[550] and Council difficulties with respect to the third country regime.[551] Agreement was finally formalized with the Parliament's adoption of the agreed text on 11 November 2010.[552]

It remains to be seen whether the AIFMD will navigate successfully between the Scylla and Charybdis of financial stability and industry efficiency. The stakes are high, given the potential impact on investor choice and returns and the novelty of the Directive, as has been acknowledged in the AIFMD text.[553] Structural industry change, particularly with respect to depositaries and custodians, is following. But the pre-crisis status quo became untenable once the crisis broke out; the changed political conditions, the G20 commitment to closing regulatory loopholes, widespread consensus on the lack of transparency in the AIF sector, and the pre-crisis momentum for reform in parts of the EU's legislative apparatus meant that some form of intervention was always likely. Not all the empirical evidence on the new regime was damning,[554] and the AIFMD does have some de-regulatory effects in respect to AIF/AIFM passporting and third country AIF/AIFM access. While the often histrionic industry response[555] may have unhelpfully intensified the will to intervene, it is also clear that the AIFMD has emerged from a process through which the bulk of its most initially troubling features were removed and nuance was introduced. Some of the more apocalyptic industry criticisms of the regime (particularly the depositary

---

[548] The Swedish Presidency was associated with achieving agreement on close to 80 per cent of the issues: Woolfe, n 546.

[549] See further Ferran, n 474.

[550] Parliament Summary on the Adoption of the Text at 1st/Single Reading, 11 November 2010.

[551] The last minute sticking-points in the trilogue negotiations in October 2010 included the asset stripping regime for private equity funds: Tait, N and Arnold, M, 'Brussels Agrees Hedge Fund Rules', *Financial Times*, 27 October 2010, 2.

[552] The Directive and its administrative rules were to be implemented by 22 July 2013. It applied to all new AIFMs and AIFs as at that date, but existing AIFMs did not become subject to the rules until 22 July 2014.

[553] In the context of third country access, the AIFMD notes that 'as the practical consequences and possible difficulties resulting from a harmonized regulatory framework' and from the passport are 'uncertain and difficult to predict', a review mechanism was needed: rec 4. It also acknowledges a more general need for review to assess whether the 'harmonized approach has caused any ongoing major market disruption': rec 5.

[554] The CRA study for the UK FSA, eg, found little evidence to suggest that the Proposal would lead to a reduction in private equity funding and that, after the initial compliance costs, ongoing costs to hedge funds would be modest: CRA, Impact of the Proposed AIFM Directive Across Europe (2009) 4 and 6.

[555] The exodus of the hedge fund industry from the EU was a recurring theme of the industry response. eg, Johnson, S, 'Law Firm Warns of Hedge Fund Exodus', *Financial Times, Fund Management Supplement*, 14 December 2010, 1 (in relation to the remuneration rules), Jones, S, 'EU Rules would see Hedge Funds go Overseas', *Financial Times*, 21 September 2010 (reporting on an industry survey and in relation to the Proposal's 'unworkable and heavy-handed' structure), and Mackintosh, J, Parker, G, and Tait, N, 'Hedge Funds Threaten to Quit UK over Draft EU Investment Law', *Financial Times*, 4 June 2009, 1 (reporting on the intensifying hedge fund campaign against the Proposal). Private equity opposition to the Proposal was similarly ferocious. See, eg, BVCA Response to House of Lords Enquiry on the AIFMD Proposal, Minutes of Evidence Taken Before the House of Lords Sub-Committee on the European Union, 7 July 2009.

liability regime, which remains a feature of the regime as adopted) can be related to its novelty and to its extension of regulation to a sector which, by and large, had not been subject to intensive or targeted regulation. Certainly, the AIFMD has created a regulatory regime of significant breadth and depth, and extends significantly beyond the registration- and disclosure-based regime which enjoyed support across the AIF industry.[556] But it is no more intrusive, in many respects, than the risk-management aspects of the UCITS regime and the newer elements of EU securities and markets regulation generally post-crisis. It has benefited from the regulatory templates with the UCITS and MiFID I regimes provided, as well as from ESMA's technical capacity and ESMA's extensive consultation with the industry in relation to the detailed administrative regime through which much of the AIFMD becomes operational (section 4.5). Perhaps the only safe conclusion that can be drawn, at this stage, is that the legislative process proved equal to the task of delivering a workable compromise[557] and the hostility to the AIFMD has softened somewhat.[558]

III.4.3.3 The Directive

The overarching objective of the 2011 AIFMD is the establishment of common require-ments governing the authorization and supervision of AIFMs in order to provide a coherent approach to the related risks[559] and their impact on investors and markets in the EU.[560] In order to achieve that objective, it seeks to ensure that AIFMs are subject to supervision, to improve the monitoring of systemic risk generated in the AIF sector, to enhance risk management, to ensure a common approach to investor protection (through disclosure, conduct, and fair treatment rules), and, specifically with respect to private equity funds, to bring greater public accountability to bear on funds in relation to investments in firms.[561] It addresses AIFMs, but also prime brokers, depositaries, providers of AIF valuation services, AIF administrators, and, in the case of private equity funds, the boards of directors of portfolio companies. Unsurprisingly, given its troubled genesis, its reach, and the new ground which it broke, the AIFMD is to be reviewed by the Commission by 2017.

---

[556] eg Deutsche Bank and State Street Presentations to ECON 10 November 2009, Hearing on the AIFMD.

[557] eg Herbert Smith, The AIFMD. Case Studies and Reference Manual (2011) 3, noting the 'long, difficult, but ultimately largely successful battle to remedy the Directive's most worrying shortcomings' and suggesting that major industry restructuring would not be required.

[558] eg Slaughter and May, The Alternative Investment Fund Manager Directive: A Tolerable Comprom-ise? (2012), suggesting that while the AIFMD would curtail operational freedom and bring costs, it was 'not all bad news' and should improve ease of access to EU investors: at 1. Similarly the UK FSA noted that the Directive could lead to business opportunities given its deregulatory passporting effects: FSA, Discussion Paper No 12/1, Implementation of the AIFMD (2012) 7 and 9. The AIF industry was also reported to regard the text as adopted as an improvement on the Proposal and as representing a viable way forward: Sullivan, R, 'Industry Mulls over Alternatives Directive', *Financial Times, Fund Management Supplement*, 22 November 2010, 3.

[559] The Directive encapsulates the rationale for intervention as follows: 'AIFMs...can exercise an important influence on markets and companies in which they invest. The impact of AIFMs...is largely beneficial but recent financial difficulties have underlined how the activities of AIFMs may also serve to spread or amplify risks through the financial system': recs 1 and 2.

[560] AIFMD rec 2.

[561] As summarized by the Commission in the 2012 Commission Delegated AIFMD Regulation Proposal Impact Assessment (SWD (2012) 386) 14.

III.4.4 The UCITS Directive and the AIFMD

The 2011 AIFMD is now the default regime for collective asset management in the EU. Paradoxically, although the AUM within the scope of the UCITS Directive are three times larger than those within the scope of the AIFM, the UCITS regime is voluntary. A CIS 'opts in' to the UCITS regime by choosing to be designed as a UCITS fund. A conservative, retail-facing fund would, for example, come within the AIFMD where the fund did not follow the UCITS asset-allocation rules by investing in, for example, real estate assets.

Accordingly, together the UCITS Directive (on an 'opt-in' basis) and the AIFMD (on a default basis) cover all CISs (and their managers) in the EU. In many respects, and particularly with respect to organizational, conduct, and risk-management regulation (and notably with respect to the central position of the depositary in the regulatory scheme), the two regimes are similar; in particular, the UCITS IV advances with respect to UCITS risk-management regulation meant that it provided a convenient template for the AIFMD. AIF and UCITS III fund investment strategies are also increasingly converging, as evidenced in particular by the pre-AIFMD move by hedge funds into UCITS III structures in order to strengthen investor protection for institutional investors.[562]

Nonetheless, important differences remain across the regimes, at legislative and administrative levels. This reflects the very different genesis and objectives of both regimes and the 'labelling' dynamics associated with the UCITS regime, for institutional as well as retail investors.[563] The UCITS regime has evolved over time and is at bedrock concerned with retail market investor protection and passporting, although it has increasingly become engaged with financial stability risks. The AIFMD is a creature of the financial crisis and is primarily concerned with financial stability. While it addresses investor protection, the predominantly institutional base of AIFMD-scope funds means that traditional retail market risks are not the Directive's concern; the marketing of retail AIFs is left to the discretion of the Member States. Similarly, the AIFMD, unlike the UCITS Directive, is not a product-related measure; it does not regulate the AIF through portfolio-shaping rules or confer a regulatory label on AIFs. AIFs are, however, indirectly drawn into the regulatory net, including by means of the AIFMD's liquidity and leverage requirements. Accordingly, while the quasi-product-focus of the UCITS Directive renders it vulnerable to regulatory arbitrage in the retail markets, given the range of retail investment products which can provide a functional substitution for the UCITS fund—the AIFMD regime, given its different scope and focus, is not similarly vulnerable.

Both regimes are also structurally different. CESR and, since, ESMA have played a determinative role with respect to the development of the UCITS regime through a plethora of guidance, particularly with respect to risk management; the AIFMD regime is likely to follow a similar path, but is at an earlier stage.

---

[562] Sect 3.8.8

[563] The extent to which institutional investors will preference UCITS III investments over AIF investments has been associated with their relative efficiency in terms of regulatory capital: 2012 ECMI/CEPS Report, n 12, 54.

The regimes are, however, increasingly coming to shape each other, particularly with respect to risk management. The UCITS V reforms are designed to align the UCITS regime to the AIFMD regime with respect to the remuneration and depositary rules which the latter developed. Conversely, the AIFMD administrative regime has drawn extensively on the UCITS administrative regime for management company and risk-management regulation. Further convergence with respect to financial stability and risk management can be expected, not least given the industry synergies, although the retail focus of the UCITS regime demands that both regimes will remain distinct in key respects.

III.4.5 Harmonization and ESMA

The 2011 AIFMD is not formally a maximum harmonization measure.[564] Any such ambition would be impractical given the multiplicity of AIFs and AIFMs which it covers. The Directive accordingly expressly refers to Member State rules in places, including with respect to the *de minimis* regime (Article 3), reporting to NCAs (Article 24(5)), and valuation (Article 19). The Directive is also calibrated in that NCAs are to apply some of its requirements subject to a proportionality principle, notably with respect to risk management. Nonetheless, it achieves a very high level of harmonization and is, for a legislative measure, highly detailed.[565]

It has also been amplified to a very significant extent; some 50 of the AIFMD's Articles are subject to amplification by administrative rules.[566] The 2013 Commission Delegated AIFMD Regulation[567] is at the centre of the administrative regime[568] and significantly intensifies the single rulebook for AIFMs, although it is designed to apply flexibly. Running to more than 100 Articles, it addresses a host of key operational areas, including the key calculation of AUM, which drives the AIFMD's exemption regime; the method and calculation of leverage; the initial own funds regime; operating conditions for AIFMs; investment in securitized positions; organizational requirements; valuation; delegation; the depositary; transparency requirements; third country rules; and information exchange between NCAs.

---

[564] The Commission has described it as a minimum standards measure: 2012 Commission Delegated AIFMD Regulation Proposal (C(2012) 8370) 2.

[565] Leading the Commission to highlight that its discretion in adopting the administrative regime was limited as a result: 2012 Commission Delegated AIFMD Regulation Proposal Impact Assessment, n 561, 62. Similarly, the UK FSA described it as having maximum harmonization effects: Discussion Paper No 12/1, n 558, 7.

[566] In total, some 99 delegated rules, technical standards, and guidelines are provided for: Speech by Nicoll, S (FSA), on 'The AIFMD – The Road Ahead', 17 March 2011.

[567] A regulation was employed in order to reduce the costs of cross-border activity, ensure uniform requirements applied given the systemic risks posed by some fund managers, and given the detailed operational calculations and methodologies which govern many of the administrative regime's requirement, particularly with respect to leverage and reporting: 2012 Commission Delegated AIFMD Regulation Proposal, n 564, 4.

[568] Additional administrative rules have been and are in the process of being adopted and relate to specialist aspects of the AIFMD. The three measures adopted thus far relate to the AIFMD's 'opt-in' procedure (Commission Implementing Regulation 448/2013/EU [2013] OJ L132/3), the third country access regime (Commission Implementing Regulation 447/2013/EU [2013] OJ L132/1), and types of AIF (Commission Delegated Regulation C(2013) 9098).

The genesis of the 2013 Commission Delegated AIFMD Regulation was, however, troubled,[569] and had the potential to generate significant institutional tensions between ESMA and the Commission. For the first time since the establishment of ESMA, the Commission diverged significantly from ESMA's technical advice in developing the Delegated Regulation.[570] Given the extent of the related ESMA consultations,[571] as well as ESMA's more facilitative approach in a number of key areas,[572] industry reaction to the leaked April 2012 Commission draft of the Regulation was hostile,[573] leading to concerns that the febrile environment was not conducive to the adoption of an administrative regime of such fundamental importance.[574] Despite (or perhaps because of) intense industry lobbying,[575] the formal proposal finally issued by the Commission in December 2012 and the final rules as adopted in 2013 did not vary to any material extent from the contested April 2012 draft,[576] and enjoyed institutional support from the European Parliament and Council.[577] The major areas of difference between ESMA and the Commission related to the initial capital requirements regime (the Commission did not follow ESMA's advice that AIFMs be allowed to combine professional indemnity insurance with capital to meet the professional liability capital requirement); the calculation of leverage (the Commission did not follow ESMA's advice that firms be allowed to employ the 'advanced' approach for calculating leverage); delegation (the Commission added stricter quantitative conditions to the assessment of when an AIFM had 'excessively' delegated its functions in breach of the

---

[569] One senior UK regulator noted that it developed in a 'highly charged political environment': Speech by Nicoll, S (UK FSA) on 'Update on EU Fund Management Regulatory Developments', 1 November 2011.

[570] ESMA, Technical Advice to the European Commission on Possible Implementing Measures of the AIFMD, Final Report (2011) (ESMA/2011/379) (2011 ESMA Technical Advice).

[571] The Advice followed a CESR Call for Evidence (CESR/10-1459), two consultation papers (ESMA/2011/209 and ESMA/2011/270), and three open hearings.

[572] ESMA sought to draw from the UCITS and MiFID I operating rules for collective and discretionary asset management, as appropriate, and to calibrate them to the institutional sector, to take into account the wide diversity of AIFs and assets in which they invest, to apply rules proportionately in view of the nature, scale, and complexity of the AIFM's business and the nature and range of its activities, and to draw on industry guidance and good practice standards as appropriate: 2011 ESMA Technical Advice, n 570, 7–14. The industry was broadly supportive of ESMA's approach: Davis, P, 'ESMA Helps Alternatives Storm Clouds Blow Over', *Financial Times, Fund Management Supplement,* 5 December 2011, 19.

[573] Masters, B and Barber, A, 'EU Warned on New Fund Rules', *Financial Times,* 12 July 2012, 17, reporting on industry concerns that the rules unravelled the legislative compromise and could, particularly with respect to delegation, damage the EU fund market. The Alternative Investment Management Association (AIMA) produced a comparative table outlining the major differences between the Commission's and ESMA's approaches and warned that the Commission text 'could be disruptive to the asset management industry in the EU and globally, potentially undermining some of the stated policy goals of investor protection and financial stability': AIMA, Analysis of Divergences between the EU Commission's Draft Regulation implementing the AIFMD and the ESMA Advice (2012) 1. The April 2012 draft was also associated with increasing political tensions between the Commission and the UK: Speech by MEP Skinner on the AIFMD, 24 April 2012.

[574] Deloitte, Regulatory News Alert. AIFMD: Where Are We in the Process? (2012) 1.

[575] ECON MEP Gauzès was widely reported as having warned the hedge fund lobby that their efforts risked having counter-productive effects: Aboulian, B, 'MEP Bites Back at Hedge Fund Lobby', *Financial Times, Fund Management Supplement,* 23 April 2012.

[576] Clifford Chance. Briefing Note. AIFMD Level 2 Regulation Final Text Released: an Early Christmas Present? (2012) 1.

[577] Which had been extensively consulted by the Commission: Deloitte, Regulatory News Alert. AIFMD: the Level 2 Regulation for Christmas (2012) 2. The Commission also engaged in a series of industry consultations: 2012 Commission Delegated AIFMD Regulation Proposal, n 564, 3.

Directive); and the depositary regime (the Commission did not follow ESMA's advice that assets subject to collateral requirements be excluded from the custody obligation).[578]

The fracas[579] underlines the hierarchical relationship between ESMA and the Commission with respect to rule-making (see further Chapter X sections 4 and 5). The pre-eminence of the Commission has been further underlined by the subsequent outbreak of further hostilities between the Commission and ESMA on the first AIFMD Binding Technical Standards (BTSs) proposed by ESMA, as noted later in this section. Overall, however, and particularly in light of the scale of the AIFMD administrative regime, a generally effective working relationship seems to have developed between ESMA and the Commission.[580]

ESMA's ability to shape the regime as it develops further is considerable. The administrative rulebook also includes the significant number of BTSs which ESMA is either required or empowered to propose for Commission endorsement. The BTS process got underway after the completion of the 2013 Commission Delegated AIFMD Regulation and will further thicken the AIFMD rulebook. The AIFMD delegations to BTSs are concerned, for the most part, with the technical operation of the third country regime and related supervisory co-operation arrangements, as well as with supervisory co-operation between NCAs. But a number of BTSs have a more substantive colour and relate to, for example, the types of AIFs which should be taken account of in the application of the Directive[581] and the information required in an authorization application.[582]

The first BTS to be proposed (an RTS on types of AIF) was, however, rejected by the Commission. Although ESMA ultimately revised the BTS to accord with the Commission's views, it was robust in defending its position.[583] The episode accordingly underlines the potential for the BTS process to heighten institutional tensions between the Commission and ESMA, particularly given the greater degree of procedural protection afforded to ESMA with respect to its BTS proposals, as compared to that which is afforded to its technical advice.[584]

---

[578] The specific difficulties are noted in relevant sections later in the Chapter.

[579] The Commission's 2013 consultation on the European System of Financial Supervision Review saw some market participants raise related concerns as to the Commission's ability to override technical advice from ESMA (responses available at: <http://ec.europa.eu/internal_market/consultations/2013/esfs/contributions_en.htm>).

[580] ESMA's publicly recorded reaction to the Commission's rejection of parts of its technical advice was sanguine, acknowledging that divergences were likely to arise: Board of Supervisors Meeting, 17 April 2012 (ESMA/2012/BS/66).

[581] Art 4(4).

[582] Art 7(6).

[583] In July 2013, towards the very end of the RTS adoption process, the Commission rejected a key element of ESMA's proposed RTS (April 2013, ESMA/2013/413; ESMA Consultation Paper/2012/844) with respect to the classification of open-ended and closed-ended AIFs. The Commission argued that ESMA's approach did not conform to the AIFMD legislative text (Commission Letter to ESMA, 4 July 2013 (Ref.Ares (2013)2569526)). The Commission found that ESMA's proposal that an open-ended fund redeem at least annually and that a closed-end fund be one that redeemed on a less than annual frequency imposed frequency-related conditions which were not in accordance with the AIFMD. ESMA broadly followed the Commission's position in its subsequent Opinion (ESMA/2013/1119), but was robust in defending its approach and in underlining the difficulties caused by the Commission's delay in responding. The RTS was adopted by the Commission shortly after (n 568).

[584] See Ch X sect 5.4 and 5.5.

As required under AIFMD Article 13, ESMA has also produced guidelines on the Directive's remuneration requirements[585] and, as required under a series of AIFMD provisions, produced guidelines on the supervisory arrangements to be adopted between NCAs and third country authorities in the form of a Model Memorandum of Understanding (MoU).[586] ESMA has also shown itself to have an appetite for own-initiative efforts in this area, as evidenced by its supervisory convergence guidance efforts in relation to 'key concepts' under the AIFMD[587] and AIFMD reporting,[588] and its adoption of an AIFMD Q&A.[589]

III.4.6 Calibration and Differentiation

The scope of the 2011 AIFMD is vast; it captures massive hedge funds with the potential for generating significant systemic disruptions, as well as the smallest property funds which have little market impact. The scale of the regime has led to significant difficulties in assessing the size of the in-scope population.[590]

Accordingly, and notwithstanding its scale, the AIFMD regime is designed as a framework regime. It does not generally prescribe tailored rules for particular AIFMs or AIFs. Certain rules are, however, calibrated to different types of AIF and AIFM. The valuation regime, for example, tailors the rules applicable according to whether an AIF is open- or closed-end (Article 19(3)). Similarly, the liquidity management rules apply only to AIFs other than unleveraged closed-end funds (Article 16(1)). The Directive also provides for an RTS to set out types of AIFM, where relevant to the application of the Directive (Article 4(4)).[591]

More generally, the regime acknowledges the need for proportionality in application, given the universe of AIFMs and AIFs within its scope. The *de minimis* exemption (section 4.7) is designed to remove managers of smaller funds with low potential for systemic risk from the

---

[585] ESMA, Guidelines on Sound Remuneration Principles under the AIFMD (2013) (ESMA/2013/201) (2013 ESMA Remuneration Guidelines).

[586] ESMA, Guidelines on the Model MoU for International Co-operation (2013) (ESMA/2013/998). See further sect 4.16 on international co-operation.

[587] ESMA Guidelines on Key Concepts of the AIFMD (ESMA/2013/600). The Guidelines were adopted under ESMA Regulation Art 16; NCAs are accordingly subject to a 'comply-or-explain' obligation. The 'key concepts' initiative arose from the Art 4(4) RTS delegation and ESMA's determination, arising from earlier consultations, that certain of the issues amenable to the adoption of a common approach were not suitable for inclusion in an RTS but could lead to guidance or to a Q&A. The Guidelines address concepts relevant to the definition of an AIF (see n 598).

[588] ESMA has produced guidelines covering the reporting obligations which the AIFMD imposes on AIFMs with respect to their AIF portfolios: ESMA, Guidelines on Reporting Obligations under AIFMD Articles 3(3)(d) and 24(1), (2), and (4) (2013) (ESMA/2013/1339). It has also produced a series of related templates and operational guidance, and an opinion, directed to NCAs, on the information required for effective monitoring of systemic risk (ESMA/2013/1340) and designed to support cross-NCA consistency where NCAs request, as they are empowered to under the AIFMD, additional information in relation to monitoring systemic risks (ESMA/2013/1340).

[589] Originally adopted as ESMA/2014/163 and since updated. The Commission also maintains a regularly updated AIFMD Q&A.

[590] FSA Discussion Paper No 12/1, noting the difficulties in assessing the number of actors subject to the AIFMD, and estimating that some 1,000 AIFMs and AIFs came within its scope in the UK: n 558, 10. ESMA has estimated that between 25,650 and 28,975 AIFs come within its scope: 2013 ESMA Guidelines on Key Concepts of the AIFMD, n 587, Annex I Impact Assessment, 24.

[591] See n 583 on the RTS on open-ended and closed-ended funds.

AIFMD's scope. The application of some provisions, particularly with respect to risk management, is calibrated to the size and organization of the AIFM and the nature, scale, and complexity of the AIFs under management.[592] NCAs have been charged with supervising the manner in which the regime is applied by AIFMs in particular market sectors.[593]

Private equity funds, however, have been subject to discrete regulation (section 4.13). While for the most part this has led to the imposition of additional requirement on the AIFMs of these funds, the Directive also makes (limited) concessions to market practice and industry structure in the private equity segment.[594]

More generally, calibration to the distinct risks of the AIFM/AIF sector has been a recurring theme of the development of the regime. Both the UCITS and MiFID I regimes, particularly at the administrative level, provided templates for the operational regulation of AIFMs and facilitated related cost synergies for AIFMs.[595] ESMA repeatedly, however, highlighted the need to tailor both regimes to the particularities of the AIF/AIFM sector and the dominance of institutional investors.[596]

III.4.7 Setting the Perimeter: Scope

Setting the regulatory perimeter for the 2011 AIFMD proved to be among the greatest of the many challenges posed by the new regime. Under Article 1, the Directive lays down rules governing the authorization, ongoing operation, and transparency of the managers of alternative investment funds (AIFMs) which manage and/or market AIFs in the EU. AIFs are very widely defined as collective investment undertakings[597] which raise capital from a number of investors, with a view to investing it in accordance with a defined investment policy for the benefit of those investors, and which do not require authorization under the UCITS Directive (Article 4(1)(a)).[598] AIFMs are defined as legal persons whose regular business is the managing of one or more AIFs (Article 4(1)(b)). This 'non-UCITS'

---

[592] The risk-management and compliance requirements, in particular, can be adjusted for smaller AIFMs, as long as conflict of interest risks are appropriately managed: 2013 Commission Delegated AIFMD Regulation Arts 42–43 and 45 (risk management) and 61 (compliance function). The remuneration regime is also designed to reflect the different features of AIFMs and the AIFs they manage (AIFMD rec 24). ESMA's extensive and detailed Remuneration Guidelines are designed to apply proportionately and to reflect the nature of the AIFM in question; the proportionality assessment by the AIFMD may lead to certain guidelines being disapplied: n 585, 10–12.

[593] 2012 Commission Delegated AIFMD Regulation Proposal, n 564, 4.

[594] Particularly with respect to the appointment of depositaries: n 662.

[595] AIFMs which are also UCITS management companies also benefit from a number of calibrations to the authorization process to avoid duplicating requirements.

[596] 2011 ESMA Technical Advice, n 570.

[597] As under the UCITS regime, including investment compartments thereof.

[598] The AIF's structure (closed- or open-ended), form (whether based on the law of contract, trust law, corporate law, or otherwise), and legal structure do not have a bearing on whether such a fund comes within the scope of the Directive (Art 2(2)). The application of the regime is calibrated in certain respects where a fund is closed- or open-ended, and an RTS has been adopted defining the nature of closed- and open-ended funds. ESMA has also adopted Guidelines on key concepts related to the definition of AIF, including on 'defined investment policy', 'number of investors', 'raising capital', and 'collective investment undertaking' (n 587).

definition[599] is pragmatic and avoids the contortions which would have been entailed by capturing the nature of, in particular, hedge funds with sufficient certainty for the purposes of regulation. But it has powerful centrifugal effects, pulling in a multiplicity of very different funds, including funds which invest in less liquid assets (such as hedge funds, property funds, infrastructure funds, commodity funds, and private equity funds) and more traditional funds—including equity funds, which, because of their design, fall outside the UCITS regime. The range of assets, investment strategies, and risk profiles engaged by the AIFMD is immense.[600]

'Managing of AIFs' is defined in terms of the AIFM performing at least portfolio management or risk-management services for one or more AIFs.[601] 'Marketing', which is relevant in particular for the EU AIFM passport and for how the AIFMD applies to non-EU AIFMs, is defined in terms of a direct or indirect offering or placement at the initiative of the AIFM, or on behalf of the AIFM, of units or shares in an AIF which it manages, to or with investors domiciled or with a registered office in the EU.[602]

Unlike the retail-orientated UCITS regime, the AIFMD does not address the AIF itself directly or confer any form of regulatory brand on the AIF,[603] but regulates the fund manager. That the manager anchors the Directive is clear from Article 5(1), which provides that each AIF managed within the scope of the Directive must have a single AIFM responsible for compliance with the Directive. The AIFM can either take the form of an external manager appointed by the AIF or on its behalf, or, where the legal form of the AIF permits internal management, the AIF itself, which must accordingly be authorized as an AIFM (Article 5(1)).[604] The manager orientation of the AIFMD creates, however, a potential regulatory loophole, where the structure of a particular AIF means that certain decisions and operations, regulated by the Directive, are carried out by the AIF;[605] the Directive closes this gap by providing that where the AIFM cannot ensure compliance, it must resign, failing which the AIFM's authorization must be revoked (Articles 5(2) and (3)).

Only limited exemptions from the Directive's scope are available.[606] The Directive reflects, however, the Commission's original proposal for a *de minimis* regime; the European Parliament, by contrast, had called for the Directive's scope to be controlled by the

---

[599] Formally justified as necessary to establish a framework capable of addressing the risks that many AIFM strategies can generate, taking into account the diverse range of investment strategies and techniques employed by AIFMs: rec 3.

[600] The Commission has suggested it covers 'all possible investment strategies and legal forms': 2012 Delegated AIFMD Regulation Proposal Impact Assessment, n 561, 4.

[601] Art 4(1)(w).

[602] Art 4(1)(x). The scope of the marketing definition (and the related application of the AIFMD) is of material significance for the industry as certain marketing-related activities may fall outside the scope of the Directive, depending on how the definition is applied in practice: Slaughter and May, n 558, 6.

[603] AIF-related regulation remains a national competence: rec 10.

[604] Where the external AIFM is unable to ensure compliance, it must immediately inform the relevant NCAs and, ultimately, must resign (Art 5(2) and (3)).

[605] In some structures, eg, the AIF appoints the depositary.

[606] Including for holding companies; occupational retirement schemes; employee participation schemes or employee saving schemes; public authorities such as the ECB and national central banks; national, regional and local governments; and securitization special purpose entities: Art 2(3). The AIFMD is also disapplied from intra-group activities where the AIFM manages only AIFs whose only investors are the AIFM, its parent companies, its subsidiaries, or subsidiaries of the parent: Art 3(1).

application of different levels of regulation according to the type of AIF engaged.[607] A discrete and light-touch *de minimis* regime accordingly applies to two types of AIFM (Article 3(2)): AIFMs managing portfolios of AIFs[608] whose AUM,[609] including assets acquired through the use of leverage, do not exceed €100 million; and AIFMs managing portfolios of AIFs whose AUM do not exceed €500 million, where the AIFs are unleveraged and have no redemption rights exercisable within five years of the initial investment in each AIF. These *de minimis* thresholds are designed to take smaller funds with less potential for systemic risk outside the scope of the Directive. Where the AIFM falls into these categories, a light-touch, registration-based regime applies. The limited exemptions available from the AIFMD, and the extent of the Directive's obligations, led to significant market pressure for calibration of its rules to the size and complexity of AIFMs. The 2013 Commission Delegated AIFMD Regulation makes some concessions to the vast range of AIFMs within the Directive's scope, but not many.

The jurisdictional scope of the Directive is equally wide, and generated significant difficulties with respect to third country AIFs and AIFMs (section 4.16). The Directive applies to EU AIFMs[610] which manage one or more AIFs, irrespective of whether such AIFs are EU or non-EU AIFs. But it also applies to non-EU AIFMs which manage one or more EU AIFs or which market one or more AIFs in the EU, irrespective of whether the AIFs are EU or non-EU (Article 2(1)); only non-EU AIFMs of non-EU AIFs which are not marketed in the EU escape the reach of the Directive.

III.4.8 Authorization and the AIFM Passport

III.4.8.1 AIFM Authorization and the Home Member State

At the heart of the Directive is the obligation on Member States to ensure that no AIFMs manage AIFs unless they are authorized (Article 6(1)); non-AIFM investment firms and credit institutions are not required to secure special AIFMD authorization to provide services such as discretionary asset management services to AIFs (MiFID II governs these services), but units of AIFs may not be offered to or placed with investors unless the AIF is marketed by the AIFM in accordance with the Directive (Article 6(8)). A central register of all authorized AIFMs is maintained by ESMA (Article 7(5)).

As across EU securities and markets regulation, authorization is the responsibility of the AIFM's home Member State (Article 7(1)), defined as the AIFM's Member State of registration;[611] AIFMs must comply with the authorization conditions at all times and provide home NCAs with the information required to monitor compliance with the authorization conditions (Article 6(1) and (7)). The authorization process is broadly similar

---

[607] AIFMD Comparative Table, n 541.

[608] The *de minimis* regime applies in relation to AIFs which are either directly or indirectly, through a company with which the AIFM is linked by common management or control, or by a substantive direct or indirect holding, managed by the AIFM.

[609] The calculation of AUM is addressed by the 2013 Commission Delegated AIFMD Regulation Arts 2–5. Reflecting the importance of this calculation for the scope of the Directive, AUM must be constantly monitored.

[610] Defined as an AIFM which has a registered office in the EU: Art 4(1)(l).

[611] A distinct regime applies to third country AIFMs (sect 4.16).

to that which applies to discretionary asset managers under MiFID II and UCITS collective investment managers under the 2009 UCITS IV Directive, albeit calibrated to the particular risks posed by alternative asset management. The authorization application, for example, must include information on remuneration policies and practices, as well as on delegation arrangements, along with the information typically required across EU securities and markets regulation in relation to management, qualifying shareholders, and programme of activities, including compliance arrangements (Article 7(2)). Additionally, AIFMs must provide extensive information on the AIFs managed, including with respect to: investment strategies, use of leverage, risk profiles, and the Member States or third countries in which the AIFs are established; master-feeder AIFs; the rules and instruments of incorporation of the AIFs; and depositary monitoring arrangements (Article 7(3)).[612] Similar to the UCITS regime, the authorization process is subject to amplification through RTSs and ITSs (Article 7(6) and (7) and Article 8(6)).

The authorization conditions also share many of the features of the UCITS regime for UCITS collective asset managers and the MiFID II regime for discretionary asset managers. AIFMs are, for example, limited in the range of activities they can carry out. To promote strong incentive alignment, internal and external AIFMs can only carry out the asset management activities listed in AIFMD Annex I (external AIFMs can also carry out UCITS management activities).[613] Reflecting the structure of the asset management industry, external AIFMs can additionally engage in discretionary asset management, including for institutional clients, and in the identified 'non-core' services of investment advice, safekeeping and administration of shares and CIS units, and brokerage (Article 6(4)), subject to a series of restrictions[614] designed to support strong incentives for robust risk management.[615] As under the UCITS and MiFID II regimes, AIFMs are subject to requirements relating to 'fit and proper' managers, qualifying shareholders, alignment of head office and registered office, and the necessity for any close links between the AIFM and other persons not to prejudice supervision (Article 8(1) and 8(3)). A distinct initial capital regime applies (Article 9);[616] internal AIFMs must have initial capital[617] of €300,000 and external AIFMs of €125,000. An additional capital charge related to the value of AUM applies,[618] as does a specific capital charge related to potential professional

---

[612] Where a UCITS Directive-authorized management company applies to be authorized as an AIFM, it is not required to provide any still current information already provided in the context of its prior authorization: Art 7(4).

[613] Art 6(2) and (3). The Annex I activities include portfolio and risk management, as well as AIF administration, marketing, and activities relating to the assets of AIFs and necessary to meet the fiduciary duties of the AIFM, and including real estate administration and advice to undertakings on capital structure.

[614] And compliance with the related MiFID II rules governing these services: Art 6(6).

[615] AIFMs cannot be authorized to provide only Art 6(4) services, may not be authorized to carry out non-core services unless they also carry out discretionary asset management services, and may not be authorized to carry out only the administration, marketing, and other AIFM services under Annex I, or to provide AIFM portfolio management services, without risk-management services, and vice versa: Art 6(5). As noted in section 2 of this Chapter, a passport is available in respect of these services, following clarification by the 2014 MiFID II.

[616] AIFMs which are also management companies are not required to meet the capital requirements, save with respect to professional liability risks: Art 9(10).

[617] Defined by reference to the own funds identified in the CRR/CRD IV regime.

[618] Where the value of the portfolio of AIFs (including AIFs for which the AIFM retains delegated responsibility, but not including those in relation to which it is acting under a delegation) exceed €250 million, an additional own funds requirement, equal to 0.02 per cent of the amount by which the portfolio

liability risks,[619] which has been controversially amplified by the 2013 Commission Delegated AIFMD Regulation.[620]

As under the MiFID II and UCITS regimes, consultation obligations are imposed on the home NCA in relation to interested NCAs where the AIFM is, for example, a subsidiary of an AIFM authorized in another Member State (Article 8(2)), deadlines for the authorization process (Article 8(5)) apply, and the withdrawal of authorization is required in identified circumstances (Article 11). Home NCAs may also impose restrictions on the investment strategies of the AIFM's AIFs (Article 8(4)).

III.4.8.2 *De Minimis* AIFMs

Where the AIFM falls into a *de minimis* category, a light-touch, registration-based regime applies (Article 3(3)) as a safeguard against the risks which these funds may pose in aggregate. The AIFM must register with its home NCA, identify itself and the AIFs under management, provide the NCA with information on its investment strategies at the time of registration, and thereafter provide the NCA with information on the main instruments in which it trades and on the principal exposures and most important concentrations of the AIFs managed, to enable the NCA to monitor systemic risk. It must also inform the NCA where it no longer meets the *de minimis* conditions. Member States may apply additional rules to these AIFMs. Article 3(2) *de minimis* AIFMs do not enjoy passport rights under the Directive but may opt-in to the Directive,[621] thereby triggering passport rights as well as the full range of obligations which apply under the Directive (Article 3(4)).

III.4.8.3 The Passport and EU AIFMs

Once granted, AIFM authorization is valid for all the Member States (Article 8(1)). The AIFMD contains a related passport regime for EU AIFMs[622] and with respect to the marketing of EU AIFs[623] (Articles 31 and 32) and the management of EU AIFs (Article 33); a distinct regime applies in relation to non-EU AIFs (section 4.16). The definition of the EU AIFM host Member State is accordingly broad.[624] The AIFMD has significant

---

exceeds €250 million, applies. This amount is capped at €10 million (Art 9(3)) and AIFMs may benefit from a 50 per cent reduction in these additional capital charges where an equivalent guarantee is provided by an EU-registered (or equivalent third country) credit institution or insurance company.

[619] AIFMs must either have additional own funds to cover professional liability risks, or hold professional indemnity insurance: Art 9(7).

[620] The 2013 Commission Delegated AIFMD Regulation (Arts 12–15) sets out the conditions applicable to indemnity insurance (including that insurance cover 0.7 per cent of AUM per individual claim) and to additional own funds (which must, *inter alia*, represent 0.01 per cent of the value of AUM). ESMA's advice had suggested that AIFMs be permitted to combine liability insurance and capital. This was not followed by the Commission, leading to significant industry concern.

[621] This procedure is governed by administrative rules.

[622] Defined as an AIFM which has its registered office in a Member State: Art 4(1)(l).

[623] Defined widely as an AIF which is authorized or registered in a Member State under the applicable national law, or an AIF which is not authorized or registered in a Member State but which has its registered office or head office in a Member State: Art 4(1)(k).

[624] The host Member State of an EU AIFM is one of the following: a Member State, other than the home Member State, in which an EU AIFM manages EU AIFs; a Member State, other than the home Member State, in which an EU AIFM markets an EU AIF; or a Member State, other than the home Member State, in which an EU AIFM markets a non-EU AIF: Art 4(1)(r).

deregulatory effects, allowing AIFMs to operate across the EU on the basis of a single authorization for the first time.

The EU AIFM marketing passport for EU AIFs has two elements: marketing of EU AIFs in the AIFM home Member State (Article 31); and marketing of EU AIFs in other Member States (Article 32).

Under Article 31, Member States must ensure that EU AIFMs can market EU AIFs[625] which they manage to professional investors in the AIFM home Member State. Notification requirements apply (to the AIFM home NCA)[626]—which will be amplified by ITSs— and marketing can only be prevented by the AIFM's home NCA where the AIFM's management of the AIF, and the AIFM generally, does not or will not comply with the Directive. The AIFM is required to notify its home NCA of any changes to the disclosures originally provided with the notification.

The Article 32 passport for marketing of EU AIFs in other Member States (the AIFM host Member State[627]) is conditional on the AIFM notifying its home NCA and providing the related notification,[628] and on the home NCA's transmission of the notification to the authorities of the Member States in which it is intended the AIF is marketed (the notification must be in a language common in the sphere of international finance), once the home NCA is satisfied that the AIFM's management of the AIF, and the AIFM generally, complies with the Directive.[629] Marketing rules relating to the marketing of AIFs to retail investors are the responsibility of the AIFM host Member State; the passport applies only to marketing to professional investors.[630]

The EU AIFM management passport is addressed by Article 33. The passport applies in relation to the management of EU AIFs which are established outside the AIFM home Member State (whether management services are provided directly by the AIFM by means of a cross-border services or through a branch).[631] The notification system follows the system deployed across EU securities and markets regulation. Management on a services basis requires notification to the home NCA, as does branch-based management, but more detailed information is required of branch-based activity.[632] The home NCA must transmit

---

[625] The passport rules apply to 'units of shares of any EU AIF'.

[626] The content of the notification required of the AIFM is set out in Annex III to the Directive and includes, *inter alia*, the programme of operations identifying the AIF to be marketed; the AIF rules; identification of the depositary; a description of, or information on, the information available to AIF investors; and the mechanisms which will be used to prevent marketing to retail investors, as appropriate. The AIFM home NCA must also notify the AIF's NCA where it has granted permission to market the AIF.

[627] Art 32(4).

[628] The Art 32 notification is similar (and subject to ITS amplification) but also requires identification of the Member States in which the AIF will be marketed: Annex IV.

[629] The home NCA must also include a statement that the AIFM is authorized to manage AIFs with a particular investment strategy.

[630] Art 32(5) and (9).

[631] A branch is defined as a place of business which is part of an AIFM but has no legal personality, and which provides services for which the AIFM has been authorized; all places of business established in the same Member State by an AIFM acting on a cross-border basis are regarded as a single branch (thereby facilitating exercise of the host NCA's supervisory powers of branches): Art 4(1)(c).

[632] Services-related management requires disclosure of the Member State in which the management services will be carried out and the programme of operations to be carried out (including an identification of the AIFs). Branch-related management requires additional disclosures related to the branch's organizational

the notification to the AIFM host Member State for management activities where the management by the AIFM of the AIF(s), and the AIFM generally, complies with the Directive.[633] The passport is then available and, accordingly, the host AIFM authority may not impose any additional requirements, within the scope of the AIFMD, on the AIFM.

As across EU securities and markets regulation, the AIFM allocates supervisory obligations between the different NCAs engaged (Article 45). In principle, the prudential supervision of the AIFM is the responsibility of the AIFM home Member State, whether or not the AIFM manages or markets AIFs in another Member State. As also is standard across EU securities and markets regulation, particular responsibilities are allocated to branch NCAs: the general operating requirements applicable under Article 12 and the Article 14 conflicts of interest regime are the responsibility of the AIFM host NCA where the AIFM manages or markets AIFs through a branch in that Member State. Host AIFM NCAs are empowered to require AIFMs managing or marketing AIFs in their territory to provide the information necessary for the supervision of the AIFM's compliance with the rules for which the authority is responsible.[634] A host NCA precautionary powers regime, based on the model which applies across EU securities and markets regulation, also applies. Where the AIFM breaches rules under the responsibility of the host NCA or refuses to provide information required by the host NCA, and the action taken by the home NCA (following a request by the host NCA) is inadequate, the host NCA can take action in respect of the breach, once notification requirements are met.[635] Where the rules in question are not the responsibility of the host State but a breach has taken place, the host NCA can still take action (absent an adequate response by the home NCA and subject to notification obligations), but only where the AIFM continues to act in a manner clearly prejudicial to the interests of investors in the AIF(s) or to financial stability and the integrity of the market in the host State.[636] ESMA is empowered to mediate between NCAs where disagreements arise related to the Article 45 distribution of NCA power.

III.4.9 Operational and Organizational Requirements

An intensive operational and organizational regime, which serves investor protection and financial stability objectives, applies under the 2011 AIFMD and the 2013 Commission Delegated AIFMD Regulation and draws heavily from the UCITS management company regime and from the MiFID I discretionary asset management regime, albeit with significant calibrations.[637] The AIFMD regime is significantly more intrusive than the UCITS

---

structure, the address in the AIF's home Member State from which documents may be obtained, and the names and contact details of those responsible for the branch: Art 33(2) and (3). ITSs and RTSs will govern the detailed content and format of the notification.

[633] The AIFM home NCA must also provide a statement to the host authority that it has authorized the AIFM.

[634] Including, eg, retail marketing requirements. Any related information requirements imposed cannot be more stringent than those which the host NCA imposes on its domestic AIFMs.

[635] The host NCA may take appropriate action (including administrative measures and penalties) to prevent or penalize further irregularities and, so far as necessary, to prevent the AIFM from initiating further transactions in the host State. The host NCA may also prevent an AIFM from managing AIFs.

[636] The host NCA may take all appropriate measures needed to protect the investors in the relevant AIF and the financial stability and integrity of the host State market, including a prohibition on AIF marketing.

[637] 2011 ESMA Technical Advice, n 570, 7–8.

regime with respect to leverage, for example. The scale of the regime and its application to the universe of non-UCITS AIFMs, from managers of the largest hedge funds to managers of the smallest real estate and private equity funds, led to very significant industry concern over the development of the AIFMD and of the accompanying Commission Delegated Regulation.

A series of general principles apply under AIFMD Article 12[638]—including an AIF investor fair treatment obligation[639]—which reflect the MiFID I and UCITS asset management regimes but are calibrated to the AIF context.[640]

Reflecting the crisis-era focus on the link between remuneration and risk management, which was initially addressed in the EU under the Capital Requirements Directive III reforms,[641] the AIFMD, at the initiative of the Parliament,[642] imposes detailed and controversial[643] remuneration policy requirements on AIFMs (Article 13). AIFMs must apply remuneration policies and practices which are consistent with and promote sound risk management and which reflect the detailed AIFMD Annex II remuneration requirements[644] to identified staff.[645] In addition to the Annex II requirements, ESMA has adopted extensive remuneration guidelines, as required under Article 13. Designed to support cross-sectoral alignment of remuneration provisions as well as to reflect the specificities of the AIFM sector,[646] the regime is highly detailed, but its application is

---

[638] Including that the AIFM act honestly and with due care, skill, and diligence, act in the best interests of the AIF or AIF investors and the integrity of the market, have and employ the necessary resources and procedures, avoid or identify, manage, monitor, and disclose conflicts of interest, and comply with all regulatory requirements: Art 12(1).

[639] AIFMs must treat all AIF investors fairly and no AIF investor should obtain preferential treatment unless this is disclosed in the AIF rules or instruments of incorporation: Art 12(1).

[640] Art 12 is amplified in detail by the 2013 Commission Delegated AIFMD Regulation Arts 16–29, which include rules governing due diligence when investing in assets of limited liquidity and in selecting counterparties and prime brokers, inducements, and order handling.

[641] See Ch IV sect 8.6.

[642] AIFMD Comparative Table, n 541. The addition was designed to apply to AIFMs the remuneration principles initially developed by the FSB in 2009 and endorsed by the 2009 G20 Pittsburgh Summit and which were also reflected (in a revised form) in the CRD III.

[643] Given the restrictions placed as a result on long-established pay practices in the AIF industry. The new clawback and deferral requirements proved particularly controversial: Barker, A and Jones, S, 'EU Hedge Funds Face Pay Threat', *Financial Times,* 13 August 2012, 17.

[644] The detailed Annex II reflects the approach adopted under CRD III (now contained within the CRD IV/CRR regime—see Ch IV sect 8.6) and addresses remuneration governance, alignment with risk-taking, and the design of remuneration, including with respect to the treatment of fixed and variable remuneration (eg each component must be appropriately balanced, at least 50 per cent of variable remuneration must consist of units or shares in the AIF concerned, and guaranteed variable remuneration must be exceptional and only apply in the context of the first year of remuneration for new staff).

[645] The remuneration regime must apply to those categories of staff (including senior management, risktakers, and control functions) whose professional activities have a material impact on the risk profiles of the AIFM or its AIFs.

[646] 2013 ESMA Remuneration Guidelines (n 585), Annex II. Like Art 13, the ESMA Guidelines proved controversial, with different AIFM industry segments underlining the particular and different dynamics of remuneration across the sector, notably where remuneration takes the form of distributions to AIFM owners. The treatment of remuneration of private equity managers proved particularly controversial given the importance of 'carried interest' to the remuneration of private equity managers. Carried interest represents a share by the manager in the profits relating to the underlying portfolio company investments (it is defined under the AIFMD as a share in the profits of the AIF accrued to the AIFM as compensation for the management of the AIF, and excluding any share in the profits of the AIF accrued to the AIFM as a return on any investment by the AIFM into the AIF: Art 4(1)(d)). Its appropriate treatment under the ESMA

subject to a proportionality principle designed to calibrate the regime to the multiplicity of remuneration structures across the AIF industry.[647] The annual report now required of AIFs must also include disclosure on remuneration (Article 22(2)).

Conflict-of-interest management receives close attention. Conflict-of-interest avoidance and management is one of the AIFMD Article 12(1) general principles. As under the UCITS regime, the increased conflict-of-interest risk which arises where AIFMs provide discretionary asset management services is addressed by a prohibition on the AIFM investing all or part of a client's portfolio in AIFs under management, absent prior approval from the client (Article 12(2)). Article 14 sets out the specific and wide-ranging conflict-of-interest management rules which require AIFMs to maintain and operate effective organizational and administrative arrangements with a view to taking all reasonable steps designed to identify, prevent, manage and monitor conflicts of interest, and to disclose those conflicts where it cannot be ensured with reasonable confidence that damage to investor interests will be prevented. The particular conflicts of interest inherent in the prime broker/fund relationship are expressly addressed by Article 14(3), which requires the AIFM to exercise due care, skill, and diligence in the selection of the prime broker[648] and to ensure all terms are set out in a written contract, including the possibility of any transfer and re-use of AIF assets by the prime broker.[649]

Risk-management requirements apply under Article 15, which requires AIFMs to implement adequate risk-management systems to identify, measure, manage, and monitor all relevant risks.[650] AIFMs must also functionally and hierarchically separate risk-management functions from operational units. This separation is subject to a proportionality principle, as long as the AIFM can demonstrate that the risk-management function is independent.[651]

Guidelines (carried interest is included within the AIFMD remuneration regime under AIFMD, Annex II, sect 2) generated significant comment from the industry: 2013 ESMA Remuneration Guidelines, n 585, 10–11.

[647] The appropriate application of the proportionality principle is addressed at length by the Guidelines which contain very detailed recommendations relating to, *inter alia*: the definition of in-scope remuneration; the identification of 'identified staff' subject to the regime; application in a group context; remuneration governance; risk alignment arrangements (including in relation to any personal hedging arrangements, discretionary pensions, and severance pay); variable remuneration; performance assessment and risk management; *ex-post* risk adjustment; retention policy; and disclosure.

[648] Defined as a regulated institution which provides services to professional investors primarily to finance or execute transactions in financial instruments as counterparty, and which may also provide other services, such as clearing and settlement of trades, custodial services, securities lending, customized technology, and operational facilities: Art 4(1)(af).

[649] The detailed administrative regime amplifies the nature of potential conflict of interest risk, the conflict of interest policy, the particular procedures and measures for preventing, managing, and monitoring conflict of interest risk, and the management of conflict of interest risk in relation to the exercise of voting rights: 2013 Commission Delegated AIFMD Regulation Arts 30–37.

[650] AIFMs must at least implement a due diligence process for AIF investments, ensure that risks are appropriately identified, measured, managed, and monitored, including through stress testing, and ensure that AIFs' risk profiles correspond to their size, portfolio, investment strategies, and objectives: Art 15(3). Leverage risk-management requirements also apply: sect 4.11.

[651] The 2013 Commission Delegated AIFMD Regulation addresses, *inter alia*, the functions of the permanent risk-management function, the risk-management policy, review of risk-management systems, the separation requirement, and risk limits: Arts 38–45.

Liquidity management is governed by Article 16, which requires AIFMs to apply appropriate liquidity risk-management procedures, including stress tests and testing of alignment between redemption, investment, and liquidity risk-management policies, to leveraged funds.[652]

Tracking the 2013 CRD IV/CRR approach, administrative rules apply (through Article 17) to investments by AIFMs in securitization positions in order to ensure equivalence across the EU rulebook applicable to securitization.[653]

Extensive organizational requirements also apply to the AIFM, including in relation to general organizational principles and the deployment of appropriate resources to the management of AIFs (Article 18),[654] valuation (Article 19—valuation may be carried out by an external valuer or, where conditions are met, and following compromises made as the AIFMD negotiations progressed, an internal valuer),[655] and delegation (Article 20).

As under the UCITS regime, a series of restrictions apply to the delegation of functions[656] which are designed to reinforce the ultimate responsibility of the AIFM and to support effective supervision. The delegation regime,[657] which has significant operational significance for the AIFM industry, is based on the following: the delegation being subject to notification to the home NCA; a series of conditions applying to the delegation;[658] restrictions on further sub-delegations by the delegate; a prohibition on the delegation of portfolio or risk-management functions to the depositary or to entities whose interests may conflict with those of the AIFM or AIF investors; the AIFM's liability not being affected by

---

[652] The 2013 Commission Delegated AIFMD Regulation addresses, *inter alia*, the functions to be carried out by the liquidity management system, and liquidity limits and stress tests: Arts 46–49.

[653] 2013 Commission Delegated AIFMD Regulation Arts 50–56. The rules are designed to ensure that any securitization investments in which the AIF invests meet the requirement that the originator, sponsor, or original lender has disclosed to the AIFM that it has retained a material net economic interest of not less than 5 per cent. The AIFM must also ensure that the sponsor and originator meet certain conditions (in relation to credit risk management), and additionally the AIFM must meet qualitative requirements relating to its understanding of the risks of the securitization in question, stress testing, and risk management.

[654] Amplified by the 2013 Commission Delegated AIFMD Regulation Arts 57–66 (including in relation to data processing, accounting, senior management control, the permanent compliance function, the permanent audit function, personal transactions, recording of portfolio transactions, and record-keeping).

[655] Valuation is governed by national rules, but the AIFMD imposes a series of requirements, including: that AIFMs have in place appropriate and consistent procedures to support proper and independent valuation and that the valuation be performed impartially and with all due skill, care, and diligence; that valuation be carried out by an external valuer (appointment conditions apply) or, as long as independence requirements are met, internally by the AIFM (a depositary may not act as a valuer, unless it has functionally and hierarchically separated this function from its other tasks and managed the related conflicts of interest); and that NAV calculations take place at least once a year and, for open-ended AIFs, at intervals appropriate to its issuance and redemption frequency, and, for closed-end AIFs, whenever the fund's capital is increased or decreased: Art 19. The 2013 Commission Delegated AIFMD Regulation (Arts 67–74) amplifies this regime and addresses, *inter alia*, valuation policies and procedures, the use of models, consistent application and periodic review of policies and procedures, review of individual asset values, and the calculation of NAV.

[656] The delegation regime applies to the core portfolio and risk management and administration functions set out in AIFMD, Annex I.

[657] Which has been significantly amplified by the 2013 Commission Delegated AIFMD Regulation Arts 75–82.

[658] Including that the delegation must be justifiable by objective reasons; that where the delegation relates to portfolio or risk management, the delegate is authorized or registered for that purpose and, where the delegate is a third country undertaking, supervisory co-operation is ensured; and that the AIFM can demonstrate that the delegate is qualified and capable of undertaking the functions in question: Art 20(1).

any delegation or sub-delegation; and a prohibition on the AIFM delegating activities to the extent that it can no longer be considered to be the AIF's manager and has become a 'letter box' entity.[659]

III.4.10 The Depositary

The depositary is central to the AIFM's investor protection scheme; by acting as a monitor of the AIFM's activities, it also forms part of the AIFMD's supervisory infrastructure. The regime was highly contested at legislative and administrative levels given the costs of the new regime and the restrictions it placed on operational flexibility, which arise in particular from stricter custody and liability rules and related extensive due diligence requirements and from restrictions on the extent to which depositary functions can be delegated. The regime is likely to be extended further given some institutional appetite for a depositary passport.[660]

An extensive regime applies to the AIFM depositary, which has since been applied to the UCITS funds by the UCITS V reforms.[661] Article 21 specifies and restricts the types of entity which may act as a depositary, essentially restricting depositary activities to EU-registered financial institutions,[662] although a third country regime applies (at the Parliament's instigation[663]).[664] It also prohibits AIFMs from acting as depositaries (Article 21(3) and (4)). Prime brokers too may not act as depositaries unless, and in response to the widespread industry practice whereby prime brokers provide depositary services, they have functionally and hierarchically separated depositary functions from prime brokerage

---

[659] A series of requirements apply in this respect, including that the AIFM must engage in either risk management or portfolio management. In the most contested element of delegation regime, the 2013 Regulation provides that where the AIFM delegates the performance of asset management functions to an extent that exceeds by a 'substantial margin' the asset management functions performed by the AIFM, it must be deemed a letter-box entity. In making this quantitative assessment, the NCA must also take into account a range of qualitative criteria, including in relation to the importance of the assets delegated: Art 82. ESMA, by contrast, did not adopt a quantitative approach in its related technical advice on the 2013 Regulation. The softening of the Commission's original quantitative approach by the introduction of some qualitative factors which allow NCAs more discretion in examining delegation structures was widely welcomed by the industry, which had regarded the earlier quantitative approach as not reflecting industry practice.

[660] AIFMD rec 36, inviting the Commission to examine the possibility of a horizontal depositary regime which governs the cross-border access rights of depositaries.

[661] The legislative regime has been subject to very detailed amplification by the 2013 Commission Delegated AIFMD Regulation Arts 83–102.

[662] Essentially, EU-authorized credit institutions and investment firms, and UCITS Directive-scope depositaries: Art 21(3). In an exemption primarily designed to ease the costs of the depositary regime for private equity, venture capital, and real estate funds which typically do not have investments in the types of assets which must be placed in custody (rec 34), where the AIF has a five-year lock-up on redemption, does not generally invest in assets which must be held in custody, and generally invests in order to acquire control, the depositary may be another entity which carries out depositary functions as part of its professional or business activities.

[663] The European Parliament called for the possibility for depositaries to be located outside the EU, subject to conditions; the Commission and Council positions required the depositary to be located in the EU: Comparative Table, n 541. The Parliament's more facilitative approach to the entities qualified to act as depositaries reflected concerns that restricting the pool of available depositaries could increase systemic risk: Woolfe, J, 'Big Issues to Resolve to Wrap Up the Directive', *Financial Times, Fund Management Supplement*, 18 January 2010, 8.

[664] See sect 4.16.

functions and managed the related conflicts of interest arising from their acting as counterparty to the AIF (Article 21(4)). For EU AIFs, depositaries must also be established in the home Member State of the AIF.[665] A single depositary must be appointed to each AIF (Article 21(1)) and is responsible for asset custody and verification (Article 21(8)), for monitoring AIF cash flows (Article 21(7)),[666] for overseeing transactions in AIF assets more generally (Article 21(9)),[667] and for making available to the NCA all information necessary (Article 21(16)). Information flows between the depositary and the AIFM and AIF are supported by the mandatory written agreement which must evidence the appointment of the depositary and regulate the required flows of information (Article 21(2)); reporting obligations to the depositary also apply in relation to the prime broker where one has been appointed.[668] In performing their respective duties, the depositary and the AIFM must act honestly, fairly, professionally, independently, and in the interests of the AIF and its investors; the depositary is also subject to a specific conflict-of-interest avoidance obligation (Article 21(10)).

Given the complex AIF assets in which AIFMs often invest and industry practices under which AIF assets were typically subject to collateral and similar arrangements (typically involving the prime broker in the case of hedge funds), and thus not regarded as being in formal custody by the depositary, considerable controversy attended the nature of the depositary's custody obligations. Under the compromise adopted by the Directive, two forms of custodial obligation apply. Where financial instruments can be held in custody,[669] the Directive specifies the required custody and segregation arrangements (Article 21(8)(a)).[670] For all other instruments, the depositary is to verify the ownership of the AIF or AIFM of the assets and to maintain an up-to-date record of these assets.[671]

---

[665] Art 21(5). A discrete regime applies to the depositaries of third country AIFs: sect 4.16.

[666] The operational requirements for cash monitoring are set out in the 2013 Commission Delegated AIFMD Regulation Arts 85–86. The regime is designed to ensure the depositary has a clear overview of all AIF cash flows, controls the accounts to which cash payments are made, and monitors cash flows and undertakes related reconciliations (including on a daily basis for significant cash flows).

[667] Including ensuring that the sale, issue, repurchase, redemption, and cancellation of AIF units, valuation, and the application of AIF income are all carried out in accordance with the applicable rules.

[668] Under 2013 Commission Delegated AIFMD Regulation Art 91 and in relation to assets held in custody, as well as in relation to loans, trading-related information (including in relation to short sales by the prime broker on behalf of the AIF), and cash margins held by the prime broker in respect of open futures contracts.

[669] The custody obligation applies to all financial instruments which can be physically delivered to the depositary and to those which can be registered in a financial instrument account—essentially transferable securities (including those which embed derivatives), money-market instruments, and units in CISs: Art 21(8)(a) and 2013 Commission Delegated AIFMD Regulation Art 88.

[670] The nature of these arrangements is further amplified by the 2013 Commission Delegated AIFMD Regulation Art 89 which addresses, *inter alia*, record-keeping and segregation, reconciliation, the assessment of custody risks, the care obligation ('due care' must be exercised in order ensure a high standard of investor protection), organizational arrangements, and the verification of ownership rights. The reach of the custody obligation is underlined by the liability regime (noted later in this section). Art 89 also specifies the particular obligations the depositary remains subject to where custody is delegated, and provides that the custody obligations apply on a 'look-through' basis, to underlying assets held by the AIF or AIFM through legal and financial structures under their direct or indirect control.

[671] The verification is to be based on information or documents provided by the AIF or AIFM or on external evidence, where available. The nature of this Art 21(8)(b) obligation is specified in detail by Art 90 of the 2013 Commission Delegated AIFMD Regulation which addresses, *inter alia*, information requirements, record-keeping, verification procedures, the detection of anomalies, and a look-through obligation in similar terms to Art 89.

Despite significant industry opposition, assets may not be excluded from the scope of the custody obligation because they are subject to particular business transactions, such as collateral arrangements.[672]

The restrictions placed on the entities which can act as a depositary, combined with long-standing industry practices concerning the use of third country custodial structures, led to difficult negotiations, at legislative and administrative levels, on the depositary delegation regime. As with the AIFM delegation regime generally, extensive conditions and restrictions are imposed on the extent to which depositaries can delegate functions, including with respect to the objective necessity of the delegation, the diligence of the depositary in selecting the sub-depositary, the ability of the sub-depositary to carry out the delegated functions (including with respect to asset segregation),[673] and the effective regulation and supervision of the sub-depositary in the relevant jurisdiction[674] (Article 21(11)). Particular conditions apply where the assets must be held in custody by a third country depositary, and where that depositary does not meet the Article 21(11) requirements.[675]

The depositary liability regime, which proved one of the most insuperable obstacles over the negotiations given the costs to the industry,[676] was a stumbling block from the outset of the negotiation process, although the Commission and Council took a more facilitative approach than the European Parliament by supporting transfers of liability.[677] The final version broadly follows the Parliament's strict liability approach, but it permits a transfer of liability to sub-depositaries in limited circumstances and so responds to strongly voiced industry concern, as well as the institutional investor base of AIFs. The depositary is liable to the AIF (or AIF investors)[678] for loss by the depositary or a third party to whom custody has been delegated of financial instruments held in custody under Article 21(8)(a); the depositary must return a financial instrument of identical type (or the corresponding amount) without undue delay (Article 21(12)). The depositary is not liable where it can prove that the loss has arisen as a result of an 'external event' beyond its 'reasonable control', the consequences of which would have been unavoidable despite all reasonable efforts to the contrary (Article 21(12)).[679] The depositary is also liable for all other losses suffered by the

---

[672] 2013 Commission Delegated AIFMD Regulation rec 100, which responded to the very significant industry opposition to this extension to the scope of the custody obligation, and which was not contained in ESMA's technical advice. The rec also specifies the types of custody arrangements which are to be used in relation to assets subject to collateral and similar arrangements. In practice, prime brokers who hold AIF assets as collateral will be required to act as delegates of the depositary and become subject to the delegation rules applicable to depositary functions.

[673] The delegation must not be designed to avoid the Directive; there must be demonstrable objective necessity; and the depositary must exercise due care, skill, and diligence in selecting and monitoring the delegate and ensure the delegate has appropriate structures and expertise. The delegate must also comply with the general Art 21(8) and (10) custody and conduct obligations: Art 21(11).

[674] The delegate must be subject to effective prudential regulation (including minimum capital requirements) and supervision in the relevant jurisdiction and be subject to external periodic audit to ensure the financial instruments are in its possession: Art 21(11).

[675] Including that AIF investors are accordingly informed.

[676] FSA Discussion Paper No 12/1, n 558, 70.

[677] Comparative Table, n 541.

[678] Liability to the investors of the AIF may be invoked directly or indirectly through the AIFM: Art 21(15).

[679] Although the Commission has acknowledged that the European Court of Justice is the final arbiter of this contested formula (2012 Commission Delegated AIFMD Regulation Proposal Impact Assessment, n 561, 36), Art 101 of the 2013 Commission Delegated AIFMD Regulation clarifies in detail the strict conditions

AIF or AIF investors as a result of negligent or intentional failure by the depositary to fulfil its obligations. The depositary's liability is not affected by delegation, although it can discharge itself of liability under the Directive and in accordance with the Directive's strict conditions (Article 21(13)).[680] Discharge is also possible where the assets were required to be held in a third country depositary and where the related conditions are met (Article 21(14)).

III.4.11 Leverage

One of the Directive's main objectives is to improve information flows on levels of leverage held by AIFs and to ensure leverage levels are subject to appropriate risk management. While leverage has long been a feature of banking regulation, it is new to asset management regulation; in this respect the 2011 AIFMD represents a major change to EU securities and markets regulation and underlines the impact of the financial stability agenda on fund regulation. Leverage has the capacity to magnify the risks which the AIF sector generates, across the different market and credit channels through which risks can be generated and in relation to financial stability, market efficiency, and investor protection risks. In order to support the range of obligations which apply, and given the myriad ways in which the AIF sector calculates leverage, the calculation of AIF leverage—which is defined as any method by which the AIFM increases the exposure of an AIF it manages, whether through borrowing of cash or securities, or leverage embedded in derivative positions or by another means (Article 4(1)(v))—is subject to detailed (and contested) operational rules under the 2013 Commission Delegated AIFMD Regulation.[681]

---

which govern when liability is not triggered (in relation to the depositary (or delegate where liability has been transferred in accordance with the Directive)) as: (a) that the event which led to the loss was not the result of any act or omission of the depositary or its delegate; (b) that the depositary could not reasonably have prevented the occurrence of the event which led to the loss, despite adopting all precautions incumbent on a diligent depositary as reflected in common industry practice; and (c) that, despite rigorous and comprehensive due diligence, the depositary could not have prevented the loss (the conditions under which the due diligence standard is met are specified). The Art further specifies that (a) and (b) are deemed to be fulfilled in relation to (i) natural events beyond human control or influence; (ii) the adoption of any law or decree by government (including the courts) which impacts on the financial instruments held in custody; and (iii) war, riots, or other major upheavals.

[680] Liability may be discharged where the requirements for delegation have been met, a written agreement between the depositary and delegate expressly transfers liability and makes it possible for the AIF to claim against the delegate, and a written contract between the depositary and the AIF or AIFM expressly permits the discharge and establishes an 'objective reason' for it: Art 21(13). Given that Art 101 of the 2013 Commission Delegated AIFMD Regulation clarifies that the conditions for depositary liability discharge generally (n 679) are not deemed to be met where the loss involves accounting error, operational failure, fraud, or failure to apply segregation, whether at the depository or delegate level (Art 101(3)), the nature of the 'objective reasons' which can be accepted for liability transfers are amplified in the Regulation (Art 102).

[681] Arts 6–11. The Regulation requires AIFMs to use the 'gross' and the 'commitment' levels (reflecting experience with the commitment method under UCITS regime, as well as the benefits of the gross method for monitoring macro-prudential risks). Despite significant industry agitation, as these methods may lead to higher levels of leverage being reported, the Commission did not follow ESMA's technical advice that AIFMs be allowed, additionally, to use the 'advanced' regime, although the Commission left open the possibility for additional administrative rules to this effect: 2012 Commission Delegated AIFMD Regulation Proposal, n 564, 6. The Commission's decision to reject ESMA's technical advice was based on its concern that the advanced method, which affords AIFMs considerable discretion, might lead to an under-reporting of leverage levels: 2012 Commission Delegated AIFMD Regulation Proposal Impact Assessment, n 561, 25.

The leverage regime has two dimensions: disclosure to investors and disclosure to and supervisory control by NCAs. Information on leverage must be disclosed to investors in the initial AIF disclosure document (Article 23(1)) and periodically (in relation to the total amount of leverage employed by the AIF and changes to the maximum level of leverage which the AIFM may employ (Article 23(5)). Leverage disclosure also forms part of the AIFM authorization process (Article 7(3)(a)) and is subject to a discrete ongoing reporting regime. AIFMs employing leverage on a 'substantial basis'[682] must report to the home NCA on the overall level of leverage employed by each AIF under management, on the breakdown between leverage arising from borrowing and from derivatives, and on the extent to which the AIF's assets have been re-used under leverage arrangements; the five largest sources of borrowed cash or securities for each AIF, and the amount of leverage from each, must also be disclosed (Article 24(4)). These disclosures are to be used by the home NCA to assess the extent to which reliance on leverage contributes to the build-up of systemic risk, risks of disorderly markets, or risks to long-term economic growth, and must be shared with the other NCAs, ESMA, and the ESRB (Article 25(1) and (2)).

More intrusive leverage limit regulation was a feature of the regime from the outset, with the Commission's Proposal containing the ill-fated proposal that the Commission be empowered to impose leverage levels. This element of the Directive changed significantly over the negotiations. The European Parliament's position (that AIFMs be required to set leverage limits) ultimately prevailed over the Commission's more interventionist approach and over the Council's rejection of any form of leverage limit regulation.[683] The AIFMD nonetheless has the potential to allow material NCA interference with AIF leverage levels. The AIFM must set a maximum level of leverage which it may employ for each AIF it manages (Article 15(4)), and must demonstrate that the leverage limits for each AIF are reasonable and that it complies with the limits (Article 25(3)). In a significant change for most NCAs,[684] the AIFM NCA must assess the risks posed by the use of leverage and, where necessary to support the stability and integrity of the financial system, impose limits on the level of leverage which an AIFM can employ, or other restrictions (Article 25(3)). Given the seriousness of this form of intervention, ESMA, the ESRB, and the NCA of the AIF must all be notified in advance and ESMA must issue advice to the relevant NCA about the leverage measure in question and as to whether the Article 25(3) conditions are met, whether the measure is appropriate, and the duration of the intervention (Article 25(3)–(6)). ESMA is additionally conferred with a general facilitation and co-ordination role (Article 25(5)), and is also empowered to intervene more radically and to issue advice to NCAs specifying remedial action (including leverage limits) where it determines that the leverage employed by an AIFM (or group of AIFMs) poses a substantial risk to the stability and integrity of the financial system. Where an NCA does not follow this advice (or ESMA's advice in relation to national intervention on leverage), it must notify ESMA accordingly and ESMA can choose to make public disclosures to this effect (Article 25(7)–(8)).

---

[682] Leverage is employed on a 'substantial basis' where the exposure of the AIF, calculated under the commitment method, exceeds its NAV by a factor of 3: 2013 Commission Delegated AIFMD Regulation Art 111.

[683] AIFMD Comparative Table, n 541.

[684] FSA Discussion Paper No 12/1, n 558, 17.

As discussed in Chapter XI section 5.3.2, this power is one of a series of powers across EU securities and markets regulation which allow ESMA to shape NCA decision-making in potentially sensitive areas.

III.4.12 Disclosure and Transparency

As can be expected of a Directive which was, from early in its evolution, designed to shed light on hedge fund risk in particular, detailed disclosure and transparency obligations are imposed on the AIFM with respect to initial and ongoing disclosure to investors and with respect to NCA reporting.[685]

The relevance of the mandatory investor-facing disclosures is doubtful, given the strong market discipline which investors can exert on AIFs and AIFMs in relation to the disclosures required. Nonetheless, the AIFM must produce, for each EU AIF it either manages or markets, an annual report containing the disclosures set out in the Directive (Article 22) and amplified in the 2013 Commission Delegated AIFMD Regulation.[686] It must also provide the required initial (prospectus) disclosures relating to the AIFs,[687] as well as the required periodic disclosures.[688]

The extensive NCA reporting obligations are likely to have more traction. The AIFM must report to its home NCA, in relation to each of the AIFs it manages or markets in the EU, on a wide range of matters;[689] the frequency of the reports depends on the size and complexity of the AIFs under management.[690] In exceptional circumstances, ESMA may request home NCAs to impose additional reporting requirements (Article 24(5)).

---

[685] The 2011 AIFMD obligations have been extensively amplified by the 2013 Commission Delegated AIFMD Regulation (Arts 103–110).

[686] Including: balance sheet or statement of assets and liabilities; income and expenditure account; report on activities; and total amount of remuneration paid (split into fixed and variable components). Where the AIF already provides an annual report under the Transparency Directive (Ch II sect 5) only those requirements additional from the AIFMD must be provided. The 2013 Commission Delegated AIFMD Regulation amplifies the content of these disclosure items in great detail (Arts 103–107).

[687] Art 23(1) and (2). The detailed list of legislative requirements includes disclosure relating to investment strategies and objectives and to leverage and how it is employed, as well as disclosures relating to delegation, valuation, liquidity risk management and redemption, the fair treatment obligation and any preferential treatment of investors, the latest NAV, the identity of the prime broker, and any discharges of depositary liability.

[688] Art 23(4) and (5) and 2013 Commission Delegated AIFMD Regulation Arts 108–109. The legislative requirements include disclosure relating to new liquidity arrangements, the current risk profile of the AIF, changes to the maximum leverage level which the AIFM may employ, and the total amount of leverage employed. The administrative regime amplifies the disclosures related to liquidity arrangements and leverage changes.

[689] Set out in Art 24 and 2013 Commission Delegated AIFMD Regulation Art 110. The reporting requirements relate to, *inter alia*, the AIFs' risk profiles, liquidity arrangements, the assets in which the AIFs are invested, and the principal markets and instruments in which the AIFM trades. Particular requirements apply to leverage levels.

[690] 2013 Commission Delegated AIFMD Regulation Art 110. The most frequent reporting cycle (quarterly) applies to AIFMs who manage portfolios of AIFs in excess of €1 billion.

III.4.13 Private Equity Funds

Private equity funds are subject to calibrated regulation in places across the AIFMD regime. But they are also subject to additional rules, primarily reflecting the European Parliament's hostility to the private equity industry, although private equity was addressed in the Commission's 2009 Proposal.[691] The rules (Articles 26–30) apply to AIFMs managing one or more AIFs which acquire control (more than 50 per cent of the voting rights) of a non-listed company,[692] and AIFMs co-operating with one or more other AIFMs on the basis of an agreement under which the AIFs managed by those AIFMs jointly acquire such control (Article 26(1) and (5)). Reflecting the current concern to promote SME investment across EU securities and markets regulation, the regime does not apply where the non-listed company is an SME.[693]

These AIFMs[694] must make ownership notifications similar to those required in respect of ownership in regulated-market-admitted companies under the Transparency Directive, although the reporting requirements are significantly less fine-grained as the companies are not publicly traded and the related market efficiency and pricing risks do not arise (Article 27).[695] Notification and disclosure requirements (to the company, its shareholders, and the AIFM home NCA) apply on an acquisition of control and relate to, *inter alia*, the voting rights held by the AIF, the conditions subject to which control was acquired, the identity of the AIFM which manages the AIF, the policy for preventing and managing conflicts of interest between the AIFM, the AIF, and the company, and the policy for communications regarding employees (Articles 27 and 28). The AIFM must also, on a change in control, disclose (to the company, its shareholders, and the AIFM home NCA) its intentions regarding the future business of the company and the likely repercussions on employment and employment conditions, although these disclosures are typically regarded as commercially sensitive (Article 28(4)).[696] Particular requirements also apply to the notification of and disclosure to employees.[697] The AIFM must also report to the AIF's

---

[691] The Commission's more limited regime was based on requiring enhanced disclosures to shareholders and to employees of portfolio companies.

[692] Either individually or jointly on the basis of an agreement aimed at acquiring control.

[693] Art 26(2)(a). The definition of SME is linked to that used in the Commission's 2003 Recommendation on micro, small and medium-sized enterprises (Recommendation 2003/362/EC). The exemption also applies to special purpose vehicles for purchasing, holding, or administering real estate. The Council has related this exemption to the concern to avoid hampering start-up or venture capital: Council Press Release on Adoption of the AIFMD: 27 May 2011 (Council Document 10791/11).

[694] Which may include AIFs other than private equity funds where the relevant thresholds are passed.

[695] The AIFM must notify its home NCA where the AIF's holding in the non-listed company reaches, exceeds, or falls below 10, 20, 30, 50, and 75 per cent.

[696] Rec 58 acknowledges, however, that the regime is not aimed at making public proprietary information which would put the AIFM at a disadvantage to potential competitors, and that confidentiality obligations apply.

[697] The board of directors of the company in question must inform the employee representatives (or the employees) of the acquisition of control, and ensure that they receive the related disclosures specified in the Directive (Arts 27(4) and 28(3)). Where the AIFM meets the Directive's annual reporting disclosure obligations by providing the relevant disclosures in the annual report, the AIFM must request and 'use best efforts' to ensure the annual report is made available by the company's board of directors to employees: Art 29(1). The 'best efforts' formula reflects the legal reality that the AIFM is a distinct entity from the portfolio company and cannot direct the legally distinct AIF shareholder in the relevant portfolio company, as well as the reality that portfolio company shareholders do not have a legal relationship with employees.

investors and its home NCA on the financing of the transaction—disclosures hitherto also typically regarded as commercially sensitive (Article 28(5)).

In addition to specific annual disclosure requirements,[698] private equity fund managers are also, under a provision added at the instigation of the European Parliament,[699] subject to an asset stripping prohibition.[700]

As the AIFMD is primarily concerned with financial stability risk, its capturing of private equity funds was a source of significant controversy, and of trenchant opposition from the private equity and venture capital industry, from the outset.[701] But aside from the general *de minimis* exemption, these funds benefit from relatively few specific exemptions.[702] Accordingly, although the AIFMD capital requirements, for example, are in practice relatively limited, they will impose additional costs but without immediately apparent benefits, as private equity funds do not engage in significant risk-taking necessitating a capital charge. Similarly, the different NCA reporting obligations have little relevance for private equity funds, which typically do not generate liquidity or leverage risk, but will generate compliance costs. The disclosure requirements are somewhat otiose in so far as they relate to portfolio company shareholders, given the sophisticated disclosure arrangements which apply in relation to portfolio companies and their private equity owners and funders under private contracting arrangements; by contrast, the employee disclosure requirements—the main novelty—are limited. Although an important concession applies in relation to the range of actors which can act as private equity fund depositaries,[703] the limited nature of private equity funds' investments, their long-term nature, and the disclosures which apply to private equity investments reduce the risks which depositary rules are designed to address. Most seriously, the asset stripping prohibition may disrupt the private equity funding model, which is based on distributions from the portfolio company to the private equity fund, and thereby limit its ability to provide finance.[704] The AIFMD private equity regime accordingly sits uneasily with the current policy concern to support market-based funding as an alternative to bank funding.[705]

---

[698] Either the relevant AIF annual report or portfolio company annual report must contain the required disclosures, including disclosures relating to a fair review of the development of the company's business, the company's likely future development, and disclosures related to acquisition by the company of its own shares (Art 29).

[699] AIFMD Comparative Table, n 541.

[700] For a period of 24 months from the acquisition of control, the AIFM may not facilitate, support, or instruct or vote in support of any distribution, capital reduction, share redemption and/or acquisition of own shares by the company. It must also 'use its best efforts' to prevent such transactions: Art 30(1).

[701] The industry's opposition was based in particular on the inappropriate alignment by the Proposal of hedge fund and private equity risk, the non-systemic impact of private equity funds, and the damage the Proposal could have wreaked on the industry's potential to support economic recovery in the EU.

[702] The major concessions which impact on the private equity sector include the wide range of institutions which can act as a depositary (Art 21(3)(c), n 662) and the application of a proportionality requirement to the risk-management regime.

[703] n 702.

[704] For a detailed analysis see Payne, n 489.

[705] 2013 Long-Term Financing Green Paper, n 114.

III.4.14 The Retail Markets

Notwithstanding the pre-crisis discussion on facilitating retail investor exposure to alternative investments, the 2011 AIFMD does not confer a passport in relation to the retail markets. Member States may permit AIFMs to market units or shares of the AIFs they manage to retail investors in their territory irrespective of whether the AIFs are marketed on a domestic or cross-border basis, or whether they are EU or non-EU AIFs (Article 45). The local sensitivities associated with retail access to alternative investments are underlined by the confirmation that Member States may impose stricter requirements on the AIFM or the AIF than those applicable in relation to AIFs marketed to professional investors in the territory in accordance with the Directive.[706]

III.4.15 Supervision and Enforcement

The 2011 AIFMD follows the supervisory and enforcement framework which applies across EU securities and markets regulation, but is not aligned to the new crisis-era approach to administrative sanctions.

Accordingly, it requires Member States to designate NCAs (in the form of public authorities) for the purposes of the Directive (Article 44), identifies the powers which they must have (Article 46),[707] and imposes co-operation obligations between NCAs and between NCAs and ESMA (Article 50) in relation to information exchange and on-the-spot verifications (Articles 50 and 54) and with respect to informing the relevant NCAs of AIFMD breaches (Article 50). ESMA's ability to resolve disputes between NCAs is also specified (Article 55). The standard professional secrecy and related information exchange rules, including with respect to third countries, apply.[708]

With respect to supervisory convergence, ESMA is specifically (if somewhat redundantly, given the powers conferred under the ESMA Regulation) conferred with the power to adopt guidance in relation to the authorization process and NCA reporting obligations (Article 47(1)). A specific set of obligations applies in relation to the obligation to exchange information relevant to monitoring the potential systemic consequences of AIFM activity (Article 53).[709] By contrast with the UCITS regime, ESMA is also conferred with interventionist powers, chiefly with respect to the level of leverage deployed (section 4.11) and in relation to the third country regime (section 4.16). Thus far, ESMA's primary influence on the AIFMD has been through its extensive quasi-rule-making activities, although it can be expected to shape supervisory practices more generally.

The sanctioning regime is not aligned to the new approach to sanctioning which was adopted in the later series of crisis-era measures, and accordingly is based on the Member State ensuring (without prejudice to Member States' rights to impose criminal penalties)

---

[706] Member States may not, however, discriminate by imposing stricter or additional conditions on EU AIFs established in another Member State and marketed on a cross-border basis.

[707] These powers are similar to those which are required under the UCITS regime: sect 3.13.1.

[708] Arts 47(2) and (3), 51, and 52.

[709] Art 116 of the 2013 Commission Delegated AIFMD Regulation identifies the information to be exchanged.

that appropriate administrative penalties are available which are effective, proportionate, and dissuasive (Article 48(1)). Member States have the option of requiring NCAs to make their sanctioning decisions public (Article 48(2)) and ESMA is to report annually on the application of administrative measures and penalties (Article 48(3)).

III.4.16 The Third Country Regime

The 2011 AIFMD has significant extraterritorial effects. It exports the EU approach to AIFM regulation through a number of channels and has been associated with a tightening of AIFM regulation outside the EU, given the need for third countries to conform to the EU regime if their AIFs and AIFMs seek access to the EU.[710]

The AIFMD's delegation regime, for example, has the effect of imposing equivalence-like conditions on non-EU entities to whom risk-management and portfolio management services are delegated.[711] Similarly, although the AIFMD permits non-EU entities to act as depositaries,[712] stringent conditions apply, and the concessions available apply only to non-EU AIFs.[713]

Most controversy attended the third country access regime.[714] Paradoxically, the AIFMD is more liberal than the UCITS Directive in that it supports EU access by non-EU AIFMs and AIFs; the UCITS Directive does not. The third country access regime evolved very significantly over the negotiations to its current complex form. Earlier Commission and Council texts—in particular by their reliance on stringent equivalence requirements—threatened to close off third country AIF and AIFM access to the EU market which, given the scale of the global AIF industry,[715] generated intense opposition,[716] particularly in the

---

[710] Most notably in Switzerland, which previously adopted a relatively light-touch approach to AIFMs, but post-AIFMD tightened its rules significantly (and to a higher level than the AIFMD): Jones, S, 'Tangled Up Anew', *Financial Times*, 30 May 2012, 13.

[711] AIFMD Art 20(1)(c) and (d) and 2013 Commission Delegated AIFMD Regulation Art 78.

[712] The depositary of a non-EU AIF can be established in the third country where the AIF is established, in the home Member State of the AIFM, or in the 'Member State of reference' where the AIFM is non-EU: Art 21(5).

[713] AIFMD Art 21(3) and (6). The regime requires that the host State in which the non-EU AIF is marketed and the relevant AIFM home NCA enter into co-operation arrangements with the competent authority of the depositary; the depositary must be subject to effective prudential regulation, including minimum capital requirements, and supervision which has the same effect as Union law and is effectively enforced; the third country where the depositary is established must not be listed as non-co-operative by the Financial Action Task Force (on money-laundering and related terrorism financing); and the relevant EU host and home Member States must have entered into taxation information exchange agreements with the third country where the depositary is established, in accordance with the OECD Model Tax Convention on Income and on Capital. The depositary must also be liable to the AIF or its investors in accordance with the AIFMD. The nature of the equivalence obligation is set out in the 2013 Commission Delegated AIFMD Regulation Art 84.

[714] Well illustrated by the plea made by US Treasury Secretary Geithner for the EU not to discriminate against US fund managers: Politi, J, 'Geithner Urges EU Fund Rules Rethink', *Financial Times*, 7 April 2010, 12.

[715] Some 94 per cent of global AUM of hedge funds were domiciled outside the EU at the time of the Directive's negotiation: 2009 CRA Report, n 554, 4.

[716] The impact assessment prepared for the European Parliament, eg, warned that the equivalence model adopted in the Commission's proposal was protectionist and could lead to retaliation: n 539, 1. Similarly, 2010 HL AIFMD Report, n 527, 6.

UK.[717] While a significant improvement on the some of the earlier negotiating texts, the AIFMD in effect requires the global AIF/AIFM industry to comply, for the most part, with EU rules, particularly with respect to cross-border activities in the EU;[718] access to the pan-EU market has not come cheap.

The complex (and contingent) third country access regime,[719] which has been amplified by administrative rules,[720] is based on current national private placement regimes applying on a transitional basis, and on full passporting being available (the related legal regimes are set out in the Directive) following an ESMA assessment and the adoption of a related Commission administrative act.

With respect to an EU AIFM marketing non-EU AIFs which are managed by the AIFM (Articles 35–6),[721] very broadly, national private placement regimes (through which Member States can impose additional rules) will continue to apply, on a transitional basis (Article 36). The EU AIFM must comply with the Directive (apart from the depositary requirements[722]), and minimum harmonized requirements relating to the third country apply.[723] Two years on from the coming into force of the Directive, ESMA is charged with providing the Commission with opinions on the operation of the EU AIFM/EU AIF managing/marketing passport (already operative under Articles 32–3), on the operation of the Article 36 private placement regime,[724] and on whether the full passport for EU AIFMs[725] should accordingly be activated (Article 67(1)). On receipt of positive advice

---

[717] UK government minister Mark Hoban warned that without third country access 'it would have meant an iron curtain not so much falling across Europe, as encircling it': Speech to TheCityUK Conference, 29 March 2011.
[718] Ferran has warned that non-EU AIFMs may simply decide to let EU investors come to them: Ferran, n 474.
[719] Which is considered here in outline only. For a detailed and lucid analysis, with helpful tables, see Ferran, n 474.
[720] Which address the supervisory co-operation arrangements between EU NCAs and the relevant third country supervisors which are required across the AIFMD third country regime: 2013 Commission Delegated AIFMD Regulation Arts 113–115.
[721] The management by EU AIFMs of non-EU AIFs is addressed by Art 34 which provides that EU AIFMs may manage such funds in the EU, as long as the AIFM complies with the Directive (the depositary and annual report requirements do not apply), and appropriate co-operation arrangements are in place between the AIFM home NCA and the supervisory authority of the AIF third country.
[722] Although an entity must be appointed to fulfill the Art 21(7)–(9) cash monitoring, custody, and oversight requirements, and the AIFM cannot perform these functions: Art 36(1).
[723] Art 36. Essentially, co-operation arrangements must be in place between the AIFM home NCA and the AIF third country authority, and the third country must not be non-co-operative under the Financial Action Task Force regime (on money-laundering and terrorist financing).
[724] Art 67(2) sets out the issues which ESMA is to consider and focuses in particular on problems experienced and the effectiveness of co-operation arrangements with third countries and between EU authorities. With an eye to reciprocity, it also includes an assessment of any difficulties EU AIFMs encountered in establishing themselves or in marketing AIFs in third countries.
[725] The passport regime is set out in Art 35. It is notification-based (the AIFM must provide a notification (which covers the AIFMD Annex III disclosures) to the AIFM home NCA) and is largely the same as the EU AIFM/EU AIF passport. Additional co-operation obligations relating to the non-EU AIF's supervisory authority apply, as do requirements relating to the third country not being a non-co-operative State under the FATF regime and entering into information exchange arrangement with the AIFM home and host States in accordance with the OECD Model Tax Convention on Income and Capital.

from ESMA,[726] the Commission is to adopt an administrative act specifying when the full passport will become available (Article 67(6)).[727] The full passport is, depending on ESMA and Commission decision-making, envisaged to be in operation by 2015, but national private placement regimes are envisaged to operate in tandem until 2018, when a Commission administrative act is expected to terminate the parallel national regime.[728] The activation of the full passport regime for EU AIFM marketing of non-EU AIFs, and the de-activation of the related national private placements, is accordingly dependent on a supportive ESMA opinion and on a Commission administrative act which specifies the relevant dates; the review process implied by the Directive is intensive. Political and market conditions may have a significant determinative impact on whether the hard-fought decision in principle to support pan-EU access by non-EU AIFs is ever implemented.

The management of EU AIFs and/or the marketing of AIFs by non-EU AIFMs is subject to a similar regime, based initially on national private placement regimes (Article 42)[729] and subsequently on the ultimate application of a full passport[730] after a transitional period.[731] At the heart of the non-EU AIFM regime is the requirement that the AIFM is authorized in accordance with the Directive before it can carry out marketing or management activities in the EU.[732] Authorization is carried out by the 'Member State of reference', which is determined according to a detailed and highly complex formula.[733] Authorization is subject to the same conditions as apply to EU AIFMs under the Directive, but additional requirements apply, including with respect to the requirement for a legal representative, responsible for compliance, to be established in the Member State of reference; co-operation arrangements with the AIFM's home third country supervisor;[734] the effective exercise by the relevant EU authorities of their supervisory functions not being prevented by the legal or supervisory regime of the third country

---

[726] ESMA may adopt a positive opinion only where it considers there are no significant obstacles regarding investor protection, market disruption, competition, and the monitoring of systemic risk impeding the application of the passport: Art 67(4).

[727] The Commission in so doing is to take into account the criteria which the ESMA opinion must consider and the objectives of the AIFMD, including in relation to the internal market, investor protection, and the effective monitoring of systemic risk.

[728] Art 68; a similar decision path applies, involving a positive opinion from ESMA and consideration of a range of factors relating to, *inter alia*, problems experienced with cross-border activity, the effectiveness of third country co-operation arrangements and between EU authorities, and the impact on investor protection, systemic risk monitoring, market disruption, and competition.

[729] The private placement regime for marketing by non-EU AIFMs requires additionally that the non-EU AIFM complies with the Directive's disclosure and reporting regime (Arts 22–24), as well as with the specific requirements which apply to funds which take 50 per cent control stakes (Arts 26–30).

[730] Art 39 (marketing passport for marketing EU AIFs, modelled on the notification-based Art 32 EU AIFM marketing passport for EU AIFs); Art 40 (marketing passport for marketing non-EU AIFs, modelled on the notification- and third country requirements-based Art 35 EU AIFM passport for non-EU AIFs); and Art 41 (management passport for EU AIFs cross-border, based on the Art 33 EU AIFM management passport).

[731] Arts 67 and 68.

[732] Arts 37(1) and 41(1).

[733] Set out in the lengthy Art 37. The determination is a function of the extent to which the AIFM manages and/or markets AIFs on a cross-border basis in the EU. Detailed rules govern the regime, and cover, *inter alia*, disputes between Member State NCAs as to the determination and related mediation by ESMA. An RTS has also been adopted: n 568.

[734] The FATF and OECD Model Tax Convention on Income and Capital requirements also apply.

governing the AIFM; and additional information requirements.[735] Authorized non-EU AIFMs accordingly become subject to the Directive,[736] although an exemption is available where legal conflicts arise between the Directive and the law to which the non-EU AIFM (and/or the non-EU AIF marketed in the EU) is subject, as long as equivalent rules apply under the relevant law.[737]

The third country access regime is buttressed by a discrete supervisory co-operation framework[738] in which ESMA plays a central role. Earlier versions of the third country regime were significantly simpler, but simplicity came at the cost of transferring the third country authorization decision to ESMA; many Member States were not prepared to accept this transfer of authority, however, and this model foundered.[739] ESMA's operational powers over the regime are, however, significant. It is empowered to carry out a peer review of authorization and supervision in the EU of non-EU AIFMs (Article 38).[740] ESMA has also been conferred with specific powers in relation to the third country aspects of the AIFMD and is empowered to request EU NCAs to take three forms of action: ESMA can request NCAs to prohibit the marketing of AIFs managed by non-EU AIFMs and of non-EU AIFs by EU AIFMs where the passporting requirements have not been met; to impose restrictions on non-EU AIFMs relating to the management of an AIF in the case of an excessive concentration of risk in a specific market on a cross-border basis; and to impose restrictions on non-EU AIFMs relating to the management of an AIF where its activities potentially constitute an important source of counterparty risk to a credit institution or other systemically relevant institution (Article 47(4)). While ESMA can only request this action, requests of this type are clearly of very considerable sensitivity[741] and have the potential to cast doubt on the resilience of the relevant NCA's supervision. ESMA can only make such a request, therefore, when a series of conditions are met: consultation requirements must be followed;[742] a substantial threat (originating from or aggravated by the activities of AIFMs) to the orderly functioning and integrity of the financial markets or the stability of the whole or part of the financial system in the EU must exist and there must be cross-border implications; and the relevant NCAs must not have taken measures to address the threat or the measures must not have sufficiently addressed the threat (Article 47(5)). The AIFMD does not envisage the NCA not complying with the ESMA

---

[735] Art 37 (3), (7), and (8). The additional information requirements focus in particular on the AIFMD rules with which the AIFM cannot, because of legal conflicts, comply, and on the related equivalent rules (n 737).

[736] In relation to the AIFM's management and marketing of EU AIFs and the marketing of non-EU AIFs. The Directive specifies that the leverage reporting obligations, eg, do not apply in relation to AIFs not marketed in the EU: Art 25(4).

[737] Art 37(2). Detailed rules apply to this determination; ESMA, eg, is required to make a determination that equivalent rules apply.

[738] Otherwise, the standard co-operation requirements apply. The Directive provides that the precautionary powers which host NCAs can exercise in relation to activity which does not otherwise come within their jurisdiction apply (Art 45(9)).

[739] De Manuel Aramendía, M, Third Country Rules for Alternative Investments: Passport Flexibility Comes at a Price. ECMI Commentary No 27/16, December 2010.

[740] NCAs must also notify ESMA where they are of the belief that an authorized non-EU AIFM is in breach of its obligations under the Directive: Art 46(3).

[741] As reflected in the ability of the NCA of the Member State of reference to challenge the ESMA request: Art 47(10).

[742] ESMA is to consult, where appropriate, the ESRB and other relevant authorities: Art 47(7).

request[743]—although elsewhere under the AIFMD, NCAs must notify ESMA and provide reasons where they do not follow its advice in relation to the imposition of leverage limits, and ESMA may disclose the non-compliance and related reasons (Article 25(7) and (8)). Where an ESMA request is made, notification requirements also apply[744] and ESMA must review the related measures taken by the NCAs at least on a quarterly basis (Article 47(9)).

In a major exercise, ESMA co-ordinated the negotiation of the required co-operation agreements with third countries (which also cover the co-operation required with respect to the cross-border supervision of AIFM delegates and depositaries),[745] although they were executed bilaterally by the relevant NCA and the third country authority.[746]

III.5 Venture Capital Funds, Social Entrepreneurship Funds, and Long-term Investments

III.5.1 Venture Capital Funds and Social Entrepreneurship Funds

The regulation of collective asset management is becoming increasingly atomized, particularly under the UCITS regime. This trend has been intensified with recent initiatives to develop discrete passporting regimes for particular CIS vehicles which are designed to support the EU's growth agenda.[747]

The first strand relates to the wider EU programme to promote SME finance[748] and has developed in response to the restrictions imposed by the AIFMD. The AIFMD regulates all collective investment/fund management in the EU and provides a related passport for fund managers. Its wide scope is reflected in the *de minimis* exemption from its scope. But while the *de minimis* exemption protects the managers of non-systemic AIFs from overly burdensome regulation, it also withholds the pan-EU passport from a large population of AIFs and their managers. Two passporting regimes have accordingly been developed for venture capital funds and for social entrepreneurship funds, the managers of which typically fall far below the AIFMD's AUM thresholds, in order to promote access to finance, particularly for smaller and growth firms. These initiatives are strongly associated with the EU's SME agenda, but also with the EU's growth agenda more generally.

---

[743] Art 47(6) details the conditions with which the NCA action must comply in relation to effectively addressing the threat, not creating a risk of regulatory arbitrage, and not having a detrimental effect on market efficiency and liquidity.

[744] To the NCA of the Member State of reference of the AIFM and the non-EU AIFM's host Member State NCAs (where marketing and/or management is carried out).

[745] See n 713.

[746] ESMA negotiated co-operation arrangements (which came into effect from July 2013) on behalf of the EU NCAs (as well as on behalf of Croatia, Iceland, Liechtenstein, and Norway) and with 34 of their global counterparts: ESMA Press Release 30 March 2013 (ESMA/2013/629). The co-operation arrangements adopted follow the MoU agreed by the Board of Supervisors and adopted as ESMA Guidelines (n 586).

[747] Set out in, eg, the EU's Europe 2020 Strategy (2010) and the related Innovation Union Strategy (COM (2010) 546). Similarly, the Commission's highly contested 2014 proposal to prohibit proprietary trading within large banks, which includes a prohibition on investment in hedge funds, expressly excludes bank investment in private equity, venture capital, and social entrepreneurship funds, given their role in funding the real economy (Ch VI sect 1).

[748] See further Ch II sect 3.3.2.

The venture capital segment in the EU has long been a source of policy concern,[749] but it has recently received close attention as part of the crisis-era SME agenda.[750] The venture capital segment is small[751] and has contracted in the wake of the financial crisis.[752] Venture capital funds are typically of a small size, certainly in relation to the related private equity sector generally,[753] and economies of scale are limited.[754] Funds seeking to expand their investor base cross-border face a series of restrictions.[755] In response, the 2013 European Venture Capital Funds Regulation[756] provides an 'opt-in' regime for AIFMs registered under the AIFMD. It makes available a marketing passport designed, like the AIFMD passport, for the pan-EU institutional market, and the designation 'EuVECA' for AIFs whose managers meet the requirements set out in the Directive (Article 1); ESMA maintains a central database of all in-scope AIFMs and EuVECAs (Article 17). The regime applies to EU-established AIFMs registered under the AIFMD who fall below the AIFMD's €500 million threshold for total AUM[757] (98 per cent of EU venture capital funds fall below the threshold[758]) and who manage portfolios of 'qualifying venture capital funds' (Article 2). A qualifying venture capital fund must invest at least 70 per cent of its

---

[749] Venture capital funds, and the benefits of a related harmonized regime, were a feature of the 2004–2006 UCITS Review and the related 2005 Green and 2006 White Investment Fund Papers. Early initiatives included the 1998 Risk Capital Action Plan (SEC (1998) 552), a series of taxation and state-aid related initiatives, and the Commission's 2007 Communication on Venture Capital (COM (2007) 853). The Commission has also engaged in a number of fact-finds, including its 2009 Report on Cross-border Venture Capital in the EU. The European Parliament's Resolution on Hedge Funds and Private Equity (n 513) also supported a harmonized EU regime for venture capital funds.

[750] Venture capital fund market reform has been a recurring theme of the three main strands of the Commission's SME policy agenda, and has been referenced in the 2011 and 2012 Single Market Acts I and II, which are designed to support the single market (Commission Communication on a Single Market Act (COM (2011) 206) and Commission Communication on a Single Market Act II (COM (2012) 573)); in the Small Business Act strand (Communication on 'Think Small First', a 'Small Business Act' for Europe (COM (2008) 394) and Communication on Review of the 'Small Business Act' (COM (2011) 78)); and in the Communication on an Action Plan to Improve Access to Finance for SMEs (COM (2011) 870).

[751] Representing some €50 billion AUM: 2011 EuVECA Regulation Proposal Impact Assessment (SEC (2011) 1516) 13.

[752] Funding levels fell from €17 billion to 7,500 firms in 2009, to €3 billion to 2,800 firms in 2010: 2011 EuVECA Regulation Proposal Impact Assessment, n 751, 10.

[753] EFAMA, Annual Report (2011) 99.

[754] The average venture capital fund in the EU has €60 million AUM, as compared to €130 million in the US: 2011 EuVECA Regulation Proposal Impact Assessment, n 751, 26.

[755] Including in relation to regulatory fragmentation and duplication, procedural costs and complexities relating to private placement mechanisms, local distribution and registration requirements, and investor bias against riskier venture capital investments: 2011 EuVECA Regulation Proposal Impact Assessment, n 751, 16–30.

[756] Regulation (EU) No 345/2013 [2013] OJ L115/1; Commission Proposal (COM (2011) 860), Impact Assessment, n 751); European Parliament Negotiating Position, 13 September 2012 (T7-0346/2012); Council General Approach, 26 June 2012 (Council Document 11761/12). The Regulation is supported by an ESMA Q&A (ESMA/2014/311) and ITSs are in preparation.

[757] Where the AUM subsequently exceeds the €500 million threshold and the AIFM becomes subject to AIFMD authorization, the AIFM may continue to use the 'EuVECA' label in order to market qualifying AIFs in the EU, as long as the manager complies with the AIFMD, meets the portfolio composition requirements for EuVECAs under the Regulation, and provides the disclosures to investors specified for EuVECA AIFs (Art 2(2)).

[758] 2011 EuVECA Regulation Proposal Impact Assessment, n 751, 7.

capital in 'qualifying investments', or in equity/quasi-equity,[759] securities, and/or loans issued or granted by a 'qualifying portfolio undertaking' (Article 3(b) and (e)). These 'qualifying portfolio undertakings' define the scope of the EuVECA vehicle and cover undertakings which are not (at the time of the investment) admitted to trading on a regulated market or multilateral trading facility (MTF), which employ fewer than 250 persons, and which have an annual turnover not exceeding €50 million or an annual balance sheet total not exceeding €43 million (Article 3(d)).[760] Use of the EuVECA designation for EU marketing is contingent on compliance with a series of requirements, including in relation to portfolio allocation, leverage (Article 5),[761] marketing (the fund can only be marketed to professional investors (Article 6)[762]), and attenuated organizational and operational requirements which, very broadly, reflect—albeit in significantly less detail— the main principles underlying the UCITS and AIFMD regimes;[763] a limited number of delegations to administrative rule-making apply in relation to the regime.[764] In-scope AIFMs managing EuVECAs are also subject to registration by the home NCA (Article 14).[765] A passport follows the notification process for cross-border marketing (Articles 15–16), which allows the AIFM to use the EuVECA designation across the EU (Article 15).

---

[759] Defined as a financing instrument which is a combination of equity and debt, where the return on the instrument is linked to the profit or loss of the undertaking and where the repayment of the instrument in the event of default is not fully secured: Art 3(h).

[760] A qualifying portfolio undertaking must also not be an identified financial institution (essentially banks, investment firms, CISs, and insurance companies) and must be established in the EU. Non-EU undertakings can qualify as investments but only where (as under the AIFMD third country regime) the third country is not listed as non-co-operative under the FATF regime, and has entered into an agreement with the AIFM's home NCA and with the NCAs of the host Member States in which the EuVECA is to be marketed, and it complies with the OECD Model Tax Convention on Income and on Capital on the exchange of taxation-related information (Art 3(d)(iv)).

[761] The AIFM may not employ at the level of the EuVECA any method by which the exposure of the fund is increased beyond the level of its committed capital (or the commitment under which an investor is obliged to acquire an interest in, or to make capital contribution to, the fund), whether through cash or securities borrowing, through derivatives, or through other means. Borrowing is only permitted where it is covered by uncalled commitments: Art 5(2).

[762] Defined in accordance with MiFID II. The fund may also be marketed to investors who commit to a minimum investment of €100,000 and state in writing that they are aware of the risks associated with the investment (Art 6(1)). This restriction does not apply to the executives, directors, or employees of portfolio undertakings.

[763] Principles-based requirements apply with respect to conduct of business (Art 7), delegation (Art 8), conflicts of interest management (Art 9), own funds (AIFMs must ensure the fund has 'sufficient own funds': Art 10), valuation (valuation rules must be set out in the fund's rules and ensure a sound and transparent valuation process: Art 11); annual NCA reporting (the report, which is to be produced in accordance with existing reporting standards and the terms agreed between the AIFM and the investors, must cover the composition of the EuVCA's portfolio, the previous year's activities, the profits earned by the fund on dissolution and any distributions made over its life, and the fund's audited financial statements: Art 12— the fund must be audited annually); and disclosure to investors (including in relation to the fund's manager, investment strategy, amount of own funds available, risk profile, valuation procedures, manager remuneration, costs, historical financial performance, where relevant, and procedures for changing the fund's investment strategy: Art 13). The Art 12 annual report must also be made available to investors on request.

[764] Art 9 (conflict-of-interest management).

[765] The home Member State is the State within which the AIFM is established and registered in accordance with the AIFMD: Art 3(k).

The 2013 European Social Entrepreneurship Funds (EuSEF) Regulation[766] is also associated with supporting AIFs which do not benefit from the AIFMD passport in order to support growth. But while its legal model is the same as that which applies to EuVECAs under the 2013 European Venture Capital Funds Regulation, its objectives and the regulatory challenges which it addresses are subtly different. Social Entrepreneurship Funds (SEFs) invest in what can be broadly be described as firms which seek to achieve social goals through the use of business techniques and which have a strong focus on sustainable or inclusive development and on addressing social challenges.[767] As the 'social business' sector has grown, investor interest in 'social returns'[768] has led to the development of a small but growing SEF segment in the AIF market which focuses on social businesses.[769] SEFs have, however, struggled to draw in capital across the EU because of regulatory barriers, poorly tailored rules, size constraints, weak branding dynamics which make it difficult for SEFs to identify themselves to potential investors, and investor wariness.[770] The embryonic SEF sector has also been hampered by the diffuse nature of 'social business' and the related difficulties in quantifying 'social impact' and 'social returns'.

Accordingly, and by contrast with the 2013 European Venture Capital Funds Regulation which responds to long-standing difficulties in the venture capital market, the EuSEF Regulation is designed to promote an emerging investment class and to establish key metrics, particularly with respect to the measurement of social impact; the Commission has highlighted that the Regulation is designed to promote a nascent sector and to provide it with a distinct profile, and to establish the major regulatory parameters before differences in regulatory culture take hold.[771] It is therefore reminiscent of the original 1985 UCITS Directive and underlines the EU's ambitions with respect to the EU collective investment industry and the delivery of post-crisis growth.

The EuSEF Regulation[772] follows the 2013 European Venture Capital Funds Regulation's model (including in relation to the 70 per cent minimum qualifying investments requirement) and provides an 'EuSEF' label and related marketing passport (to professional investors). It is, however, tailored to the distinct challenges posed by the emerging SEF asset class. It therefore establishes a definition for qualifying EuSEF investments,[773] imposes

---

[766] Regulation (EU) No 346/2013 [2013] OJ L115/18; Commission Proposal COM (2011) 862; Impact Assessment, SEC (2011) 1512/2; European Parliament Negotiating Position, 13 September 2012 (T7-0345/2012); Council General Approach, 26 June 2012 (Council Document 11762/12).

[767] 2011 EuSEF Regulation Proposal Impact Assessment, n 766, 5.

[768] Particularly in the high net worth/philanthropic sector: 2011 EuSEF Regulation Proposal Impact Assessment, n 766, 12 and 14.

[769] Given the diffuse nature of social businesses, there is disagreement on the number of SEFs and the size of the market. The Commission has adopted one industry estimate of 50–200 SEFs, with on average €10–20 million AUM, and a total market of between €500–4,000 million: 2011 EuSEF Regulation Proposal Impact Assessment, n 766, 13.

[770] 2011 EuSEF Regulation Proposal Impact Assessment, n 766, 19–26.

[771] 2011 EuSEF Regulation Proposal Impact Assessment, n 766, 31–3.

[772] Which forms part of the EU 2020 Growth Strategy, but which also forms part of the Commission's wider social business (Commission, Social Business Communication (COM (2011) 682)) and SME finance initiatives.

[773] A qualifying investment relates to an undertaking which, in addition to not being admitted to trading on a regulated market or MTF at the time of the investment, has the achievement of measurable, positive social impacts as its primary objective; provides services or goods to vulnerable, marginalized, disadvantaged, or excluded persons; employs a method of production of goods or services that embodies its social objectives; or

discrete requirements in relation to the measurement of the achievement of 'positive social impact' by the undertakings which qualify as investments,[774] addresses the particular valuation challenges posed by 'social returns',[775] and imposes specific investor disclosure requirements.[776]

III.5.2 Long-term Investment Vehicles

The second strand relates to unlocking investor capital, and particularly household capital, for long-term investments such as infrastructure-related projects, and is designed to respond to the projected high level of demand for infrastructure funding,[777] banks' impaired ability to engage in long-term financing,[778] and the related funding gap which is emerging.[779]

The Commission's 2013 Proposal for a European Long-Term Investment Fund vehicle (the ELTIF Proposal)[780] is designed to increase the pool of 'long-term' capital available for long-term and often large-scale infrastructure projects by means of specialist vehicles which take a long-term investment horizon and which 'lock up' the pooled capital accordingly;[781] the investment restrictions and redemption requirements which apply to UCITS funds render them inappropriate for long-term, infrastructure-orientated investments. The Proposal is designed to address the current barriers to long-term funding vehicles, which include under-developed legal structures at Member State level and divergences across the Member States in how such funds are treated which make pan-EU capital-raising through such vehicles difficult, minimize the potential for economies of scale, and hamper the development of appropriate expertise.[782] The new vehicle is designed to capture

---

provides financial support exclusively to undertakings of this nature. The undertaking must also use its profits primarily to achieve its primary social objectives and employ predefined processes and rules which determine the circumstances in which profits are distributed to owners and shareholders to ensure that distributions do not undermine its primary objectives. The undertaking must also be managed in an accountable and transparent way, in particular by involving workers, customers, and stakeholders affected by its business activities: Art 3(1)(d).

[774] Art 10 requires the AIFM to have procedures in place to measure the extent to which the relevant undertaking achieves the positive social impact to which it is committed. The indicators can include impacts in relation to, *inter alia*, employment and labour markets, social inclusion, equal treatment, social protection, and public health and education.

[775] The same valuation regime as applies to EuVECAs applies here, with the addition of an obligation on ESMA to develop guidance which sets out common principles on the treatment of investments in the related undertakings, taking into account the primary objective of the undertakings of achieving a measurable positive social impact and the use of profits first and foremost for the achievement of that impact.

[776] Art 13 specifies the content of the annual report which is to be provided on request to investors in greater detail than the parallel provision in the 2013 Venture Capital Regulation, while Art 14 requires tailored disclosures to investors, including in relation to the positive social impact being sought by the EuSEF's investment policy.

[777] Some €1,500–2,000 billion in infrastructure funding has been estimated as required within the EU by 2020: Commission, ELTIF—Frequently Asked Questions, 26 June 2013 (MEMO/13/611).

[778] This strand accordingly also forms part of the Commission's wider examination of the efficiency of long-term financing mechanisms in the EU economy, and of the relative efficiency of bank and capital market-based intermediation in this area: 2013 Long-Term Financing Green Paper, n 114.

[779] The Commission reported that many infrastructure projects have not been able to raise financing suited to their time horizon and that there was a need to replace bank-based funding with capital market funding: Commission, European Long-Term Investment Fund Proposal Impact Assessment (SWD (2013) 230) 18.

[780] COM (2013) 462.

[781] The Proposal envisages that it will increase the capital available for energy, transport and communication infrastructures, industrial and service facilities, and education and research and development: n 780, 2.

[782] n 780, 3.

demand from the institutional segment but also, and more problematically, to stimulate retail market demand by providing a 'second retail passport,' additional to the UCITS passport.[783]

The 'ELTIF' Proposal,[784] which, like the EuVECA and EuSEF regimes, takes the form of a Regulation,[785] proposes uniform rules on the authorization, investment policies, and operating conditions of EU AIFs that are marketed as European long-term investment funds (ELTIFs);[786] under the Proposal, a long-term investment AIF can choose to remain outside the restrictions imposed by the new regime, but cannot use the ELTIF designation and will not benefit from the related marketing passport. The ELTIF Proposal is a product-orientated measure. But in addition, as they take the form of AIFs, ELTIFs also sit within the 2011 AIFMD regime which provides the governing regulatory regime for ELTIF managers (AIFMs). Co-ordination mechanisms between the AIFM NCA and the ELTIF NCA accordingly apply.[787] While the ELTIF is designed to attract institutional investment, the ELTIF is also designed as a retail investment product, and accordingly the Proposal contains a number of protections designed to address the liquidity risks in particular which flow from ELTIFs.

Under the Proposal, the authorization process has two strands: the ELTIF must apply for authorization to its NCA (the NCA of the home Member State of the EU AIF seeking authorization as an ELTIF); and the related EU AIFM must apply to the NCA of the ELTIF for approval to manage the ELTIF (Article 4). The ELTIF application process is based on the submission of identified information to the relevant NCA.[788] Given the potentially split supervision between the ELTIF and AIFM NCAs, the Proposal empowers the ELTIF NCA to request additional information and clarifications from the AIFM's NCA. Under the Proposal, once an ELTIF is authorized[789] it is conferred with a regulatory passport (in effect, a marketing passport), the mechanics of which are governed by the AIFMD.

The Proposal follows the 'tried and tested'[790] UCITS model for retail market fund regulation and so is primarily concerned with asset-allocation rules. An ELTIF may only invest in 'eligible investment assets' and in eligible assets under the UCITS regime; at least 70 per cent of its assets, however, must be invested in 'eligible investment assets' (Article 8(1) and 12(1)). The 30 per cent UCITS assets tranche is designed to operate as

---

[783] 2013 ELTIF Proposal Impact Assessment, n 779, 2–3 and 4.

[784] Given the very early stage of the Proposal (which was not adopted by the closing of the crisis-era Commission/Parliament session in 2014), its main features are noted here in outline only.

[785] The Proposal provides that Member States may not add any additional requirements in the field covered by the Regulation (Art 1).

[786] The ELTIF vehicle is only available to EU AIFs (Art 2).

[787] The framework for supervision, eg, which is based on the AIFMD, allocates tasks between the ELTIF NCA and the AIFMD NCA and provides for co-ordination as necessary.

[788] In the case of the ELTIF, the fund rules/instruments of incorporation, information on the identity of the manager and depositary, a description of the information to be made available to investors, and any other information required by the NCA to verify compliance with the ELTIF regime. In the case of the AIFM, the written agreement with the depositary, information on delegation arrangements relating to asset administration and information about the investment strategies, risk profile, and other characteristics of the AIFs which the AIFM is authorized to manage.

[789] ESMA must maintain a register of all authorized ELTIFs and their managers and NCAs.

[790] 2013 ELTIF Proposal, n 780, 4.

a liquidity buffer for ELTIFs to manage cash flow requirements as assets are constituted and/or replaced.[791] Eligible investment assets are very broadly defined as equity[792] and debt in 'qualifying portfolio undertakings' or loans to qualifying portfolio undertakings, as well as units in other ELTIFs, EuVECAs, and EuSEFs,[793] and direct holdings of individual 'real assets' that require upfront capital expenditure of at least €10 million (Article 9).[794] A qualifying portfolio undertaking is one which is not a CIS, not a financial undertaking,[795] not admitted to trading on a MiFID II/MiFIR trading venue,[796] and which is established in a Member State or a third country jurisdiction which meets the regime's requirements.[797] The main qualifying condition for an eligible long-term investment, accordingly, is that the underlying non-financial undertaking is not listed on a trading venue; the Proposal envisages that this flexible qualifying regime will capture SME investments, infrastructure projects, and investments in real estate generally.[798] All investments are subject to a conflict-of-interest management requirement: an ELTIF may not invest in an eligible investment asset in which the AIFM has a direct or indirect interest, other than by holding units or shares through the ELTIF (Article 11).

The retail orientation of the regime is clear in the series of restrictions which apply under the Proposal to the investment activities in which the ELTIF can engage. It is prohibited from engaging in short selling; taking direct or indirect exposures to commodities, including through derivatives; entering into securities lending and borrowing agreements and repurchase agreements and other agreements that would encumber the ELTIF's assets; and, in a significant contrast to the UCITS regime, from using financial derivatives (unless the derivatives are used solely for hedging the ELTIF's duration and exchange risks) (Article 8(2)); borrowing limits requirements also apply (Article 14).[799]

The risk-spreading rules are broadly similar in design to those which apply under the UCITS regime and are designed to limit concentration risk. The ELTIF cannot invest more than 10 per cent of its capital in assets issued by a single qualifying portfolio undertaking and in an individual real asset;[800] more than 10 per cent of its capital in units or shares of any single ELTIF, EuVEC, or EuSEF;[801] or more than 5 per cent of its assets in UCITS

---

[791] 2013 ELTIF Proposal, n 780, 4.

[792] Including equity (shares or other form of direct participation in the capital of the undertaking) and quasi-equity (any type of financing instrument where the return on the instrument is linked to the profit or loss of the undertaking and where the repayment of the instrument is not fully secured): Art 2(2) and (3).

[793] As long as these other CISs do not have investments of more than 20 per cent of their capital in ELTIFs.

[794] Real assets are likely to include real estate, ships, and aircraft: 2013 ELTIF Proposal, n 780, 10.

[795] Essentially, credit institutions, investment firms, insurance undertakings, and related holding companies regulated under the EU regime: Art 2(4).

[796] Regulated markets, MTFs, and organized trading facilities (see Ch V).

[797] As is common with determinations of equivalence, the jurisdiction must not be high-risk and non-co-operative under the FATF (anti money-laundering and anti terrorism financing) regime and must comply with the OECD Model Tax Convention with respect to information exchange.

[798] 2013 ELTIF Proposal, n 780, 4.

[799] In essence, ELTIF borrowing may not represent more than 30 per cent of its capital, must serve the purpose of acquiring a participation in eligible investment assets, and must not encumber the ELTIF's assets or hinder their realization.

[800] The ELTIF may raise this limit to 20 per cent, as long as the aggregate value of the assets held in which it invests more than 10 per cent of its capital does not exceed 40 per cent of its capital.

[801] Additionally, the aggregate value of units or shares of ELTIFs, EuVECAs, and EuSEFs may not exceed 20 per cent of the ELTIF's capital and the ELTIF may not acquire more than 25 per cent of the units or shares of a single one of these entities: Art 12(3) and 13(1).

eligible assets issued by a single body.[802] The risk-spreading rules which govern UCITS eligible assets also apply (Article 13). The ELTIF has up to five years to ensure compliance with the risk-spreading limits in order to allow the AIFM sufficient time to construct the fund's portfolio of assets (Article 15).

ELTIFs will not be liquid investments, reflecting the long-term nature of the underlying investments and the related illiquidity premium associated with such investments.[803] The proposed regulatory regime for ELTIFs is accordingly designed to ensure that AIFMs have sufficient flexibility to design the ELTIF such that the risk/return profile of the underlying assets is reflected in the investment holding period and in the ELTIF's life, and to prohibit early redemption rights which could disturb the ELTIF's structure. Accordingly, the decision as to the lifetime of the ELTIF is reserved to the AIFM,[804] and investors may not ask for redemption of their investment before the end of the ELTIF's life[805] (which must be clearly indicated in the fund's rules and disclosed to investors). The Proposal does not place parameters on the ELTIF life-cycle, save to require that it must be sufficient in length to cover the life-cycle of the individual assets held by the ELTIF, measured according to the illiquidity profile and economic life-cycle of the assets and the ELTIF's investment objective (Article 16).[806]

Investors are not, however, without an exit mechanism: the Proposal envisages that the ELTIF shares or units can be admitted to trading on a MiFID II/MiFIR trading venue (Article 17). An ELTIF may offer new shares or units in accordance with its rules, but where these are offered below NAV, there must also be a prior offering of these shares or units at that price to existing investors. Investors are also protected against redemption risks through rules governing the end-of-life disposal of ELTIF assets and the distribution of income throughout the life of the ELTIF (Articles 19 and 20).

As under the UCITS and AIFMD regimes, transparency requirements apply, but they are tailored to the particular risks posed by ELTIFs (Articles 21–2). A prospectus[807] containing the information necessary for investors to be able to make an informed judgement regarding the investment and the risks attached must be published prior to the marketing of the ELTIF, as must a Key Information Document (KID), prepared in accordance with the PRIPs disclosure regime (Chapter IX section 6), where the ELTIF is marketed to retail investors. The illiquid nature of the ELTIF must be highlighted in the prospectus, KID,

---

[802] Additionally, the aggregate risk exposure to an ELTIF counterparty arising from eligible OTC derivative transactions or from reverse repurchase agreements cannot exceed 5 per cent of its capital.

[803] An illiquidity premium is typically contingent on an investment being held for 10–20 years.

[804] The Proposal argues that it is not prudent to determine minimum holding periods as each investment decision by the AIFM will be different and the AIFM is best placed to determine the appropriate holding period to maximize the return to investors: n 780, at 4.

[805] To avoid the danger of 'fire sales' of assets originally acquired to be held for longer periods, and related prejudice to the returns of investors remaining in the fund.

[806] The Proposal suggests that RTSs specify the circumstances in which the life of the ELTIF is sufficient in length to cover the life-cycle of each individual asset.

[807] The prospectus must contain a statement on how the ELTIF's investment objectives and strategy qualify it as a long-term fund; the requirements of the prospectus regime for closed-end funds (see Ch II on the prospectus regime); the AIFMD disclosure requirements for investors; a prominent indication of the categories of assets in which the AIFM is authorized to invest; and any other information requested by the NCA as relevant.

and any other marketing documents;[808] discrete cost-disclosure requirements also apply, including for the KID. The retail-directed protections contained in the KID disclosures are reflected in the retail-market-specific marketing obligations which require that the ELTIF's rules must provide that all investors benefit from equal treatment and that no preferential treatment or specific economic benefits are granted to individual investors or groups of investors, that the ELTIF is not structured as a partnership, and that retail investors have a two-week 'cooling-off' period after investing in an ELTIF.

The ELTIF, like the EuSEF and the EuVECA, is designed to shape market behaviour by providing a vehicle which may unlock new sources of capital, and so represents a muscular application of EU CIS policy. It has been associated with significant growth in the institutional fund sector.[809] But its likely impact on the retail market, with which it was strongly associated from the outset,[810] is uncertain. The ELTIF marks a significant development in EU retail market policy by supporting, for the first time, a harmonized, retail-orientated AIF vehicle.[811] While, in practice, UCITSs (particularly UCITS III funds) can provide exposure to alternative investment strategies, the UCITS fund is not designed as an alternative investment vehicle. The ELTIF contains a number of protections which reflect its retail orientation, including with respect to risk-spreading, marketing requirements, and transparency; the enhanced MiFID II/MiFIR rules which now govern distribution provide an additional hedge against mis-selling. It is also the case that long-term investments may offer more stable returns[812] and that more innovation is needed in the retail markets, particularly with respect to longer-term products which match the long-term liabilities (such as tertiary-level education fees and mortgage expenses) which households may face and which offer enhanced opportunities for diversification. But it remains to be seen whether the long-standing resistance of retail investors to illiquid investments can be overcome, and whether the ELTIF's supporting regulatory scheme is sufficiently resilient to protect retail investors against the illiquidity and redemption risks which these investments represent. Certainly, the ELTIF Proposal characterizes retail investors as competent capital suppliers rather than as vulnerable consumers, and adopts a more robust approach to the retail investor than that adopted elsewhere in current retail market policy.

---

[808] These documents must specify clearly the long-term nature of the ELTIF's investments, the end-of-life date of the ELTIF, that redemption will not take place until after the ELTIF's life, and the frequency and timing of any income payments during the ELTIF's life and whether it is intended to be marketed to retail investors.

[809] Industry sources have estimated that it could double the size of the real estate investment trust market and expand the venture capital market by 8 per cent: Marriage, M, 'Europe Courts Long Term Investment', *Financial Times, Fund Management Supplement*, 1 July 2013, 9.

[810] The earlier UCITS VI consultation associated the development of a pan-EU long-term investment vehicle, designed for retail investors, with significant benefits, including in relation to growth and job creation, the promotion of financial stability given the long-term horizon of these funds, and wider investment opportunities for households, but it acknowledged that the design complexities, given the need to achieve UCITS-level protections, were considerable: 2012 UCITS VI Consultation, n 111, 15–17.

[811] Earlier efforts under the UCITS Review to develop a pan-EU real estate vehicle foundered: Expert Group Report, Open Ended Real Estate Funds (2008).

[812] US data suggests, eg, that long-term assets have lower volatility than equity (the annualized deviation in asset values for real estate between 1990–2004 was 12.74 per cent, as compared to 14.65 per cent for the S & P 500): 2013 ELTIF Proposal Impact Assessment, n 780, 21.

IV

INVESTMENT FIRMS AND INVESTMENT SERVICES

IV.1 Intermediaries, Regulation, and the EU

IV.1.1 The Regulation of Intermediaries

The intermediation function of financial markets—in particular, the intermediation function (or investment services) provided by investment intermediaries—has long been recognized as an important means for addressing the 'frictions' which information and transaction costs generate for efficient capital allocation.[1] Similarly, the financial innovation associated with intermediation has been characterized as a catalyst for welfare-enhancing growth in the financial system.[2]

Intermediation plays a critical role in the financial markets by providing market-access channels for capital providers and for capital seekers.[3] By providing services such as investment advice, discretionary asset management, and brokerage services, and by acting as distribution channels for investment products, investment intermediaries act as a bridge between capital providers and the financial markets. Through activities such as underwriting and own-account dealing/market-making, and by supporting the development of strong secondary trading markets, they facilitate market access for firms seeking capital. Investment intermediaries also generate and promote innovation in financial markets and thereby drive the production of risk-management techniques and products (in particular derivatives) which allow risks to be hedged, diversified, and traded,[4] markets to be 'completed',[5] and resources to be productively allocated. Financial innovation, in combination with intermediation, has been linked to the lowering of transaction costs and the reduction of agency costs, and with driving the financial system to greater economic

---

[1] eg Levine, R, 'Financial Development and Economic Growth: Views and Agenda' (1997) 35 *J of Econ Lit* 688.

[2] For a review of the literature see Awrey, D, 'Complexity, Innovation and the Regulation of Modern Financial Markets' (2012) 2 *Harvard Business LR* 401.

[3] On the rise of market intermediaries as a dominant economic influence see Clark, R, 'The Four Stages of Capitalism' (1981) 94 *Harv LR* 561.

[4] Merton, R, 'A Functional Perspective of Financial Intermediation' (1995) 24 *Financial Management* 23 and Silber, W, 'The Process of Financial Innovation' (1983) 73 *Amer Econ Rev* 89.

[5] A theoretically complete market is one in which actors can hedge against all contingencies: Spencer, P, *The Structure and Regulation of Financial Markets* (2000) 2–3. A complete market is strongly associated with the availability of risk management products such as derivatives.

efficiency.[6] A strong intermediary sector has accordingly long been associated with financial development and economic growth.[7]

The investment intermediary sector engages in a vast array of activities and services which are continually expanding and which range from the traditional suite of advice, asset management, brokerage, dealing/market-making, and underwriting activities[8] to trading venue operation, data reporting, and benchmark construction services. It is populated by a multitude of actors, ranging from multifunction credit institutions which provide investment services and multi- and single-function investment firms, to commercial firms which engage in investment services incidentally to hedge commercial risks, and to specialist algorithmic dealers.

It is accordingly a challenge to capture the risks of investment intermediation which require regulation and to protect productive intermediation and innovation from undue regulatory burdens. Broadly, intermediary regulation has traditionally been concerned with the correction of market failures related to asymmetric information and to externalities, notably systemic risk. These failures fall into two broad categories.

First, agency costs arise between the client and the intermediating firm where the interests of the principal client and agent firm diverge, and where monitoring is difficult, typically because of information asymmetries.[9] Costs can become significant where conflicts of interests, driven by firm incentive structures which promote mis-aligned incentives, are strong. In the retail markets, agency costs and risks are acute, given the poor monitoring ability of retail clients and the very strong incentives for mis-selling which remuneration structures and product complexity generate. But agency costs arise across the intermediation chain. Asset management, for example, generates the risk that rents are extracted from clients through portfolio churning and through over-payment for brokerage services, the costs of which are passed on to clients; agency costs can also take the form of simple incompetence or, at the other end of the spectrum, fraud and loss of assets. The regulatory response to client-facing agency costs has typically been some combination of authorization (designed to filter out incompetent, fraudulent, or otherwise unsound firms), conduct regulation (including default and standardized conduct standards governing disclosure, fair treatment, quality of advice, and order handling rules), and operational regulation (including conflict of interest, internal controls, and asset protection requirements).[10] Regulation of this type is not only client-facing, however; it also supports intermediaries in signalling their credibility to clients and can therefore prevent suboptimal intermediaries (or 'lemons') from dominating, and consequent poor resource allocation.[11]

---

[6] Merton, n 4.

[7] eg Levine, R, 'Law, Finance, and Economic Growth' (1999) 8 *J Fin Intermed* 8.

[8] And including also investment analysis and rating services.

[9] See generally Mahoney, P, 'Manager-Investor Conflicts in Mutual Funds' (2004) 18 *J of Econ Perspectives* 161.

[10] See generally Page, A and Ferguson, R, *Investor Protection* (1992) 59–77 and Choi, S, 'A Framework for the Regulation of Securities Market Intermediaries' (2004) 1 *Berkeley Business LJ* 45.

[11] Akerlof, G, 'Market for Lemons: Quantitative Uncertainty and the Market Mechanism' (1970) 222 *Q J Econ* 488.

The second broad category of market failure relates to the externalities which can prejudice the stability of the financial market.[12] These externalities are associated in particular with the liquidity and solvency risks which can arise from large-scale dealing activities and related market-making activities; since the financial crisis, these activities have come to be linked with excessive risk-taking and with mis-aligned incentives. Where incentives for prudent risk-taking and careful monitoring of risk are weak, and incentives for aggressive risk-taking and for related highly engineered financial innovation are strong, the risks to financial stability can become acute, given the interconnections between investment intermediaries.[13] For example, highly complex and poorly understood instruments can be issued by investment intermediaries and traded along chains of intermediaries and, where liquidity in the instrument thins and values drop, lead to solvency and liquidity problems along the chain and to systemic risks where counterparties fail or are at risk of failure. Similarly, where a complex and high-volume trading strategy is incorrectly executed by a major dealer, the relevant trading venue can be severely disrupted. The regulatory response to financial stability risks has typically taken the form of prudential requirements. Prudential rules address the solvency of intermediaries and financial stability generally. They are designed to reduce, but not eliminate, the risk of intermediary failure by managing the level of risk which intermediaries assume and by containing the risks of intermediary failure.[14] While mainly concerned with financial stability, they also serve a client-facing function by bolstering the soundness and solvency of firms and, thereby, protecting client assets.[15] Authorization is a form of prudential regulation[16] in that it should prevent riskily structured, ill-equipped, and undercapitalized firms from entering the market; authorization can also limit insolvencies by protecting incumbent firms from competition, although the extent to which competition should or can be deployed in intermediary regulation remains contested.[17] Ongoing prudential requirements typically include operational requirements, including internal controls and risk-management requirements, incentive management

---

[12] Long before the financial crisis, the systemic risks posed by major intermediaries had been recognized: Organization for Economic Co-operation and Development (OECD), Report on Systemic Risks in Securities Markets (1991).

[13] In the period leading to the financial crisis, a series of destabilizing factors, including, eg, the large-scale searching for yield in a low interest-rate environment, financial innovation which led to the disintermediation of risk through complex securitized products, and poor governance (including remuneration structures), all combined to create strong incentives for levels of risk-taking which proved to be excessive, and for poor monitoring of risks: eg, UK Financial Services Authority (FSA), The Turner Review. A Regulatory Response to the Global Banking Crisis (2009) (2009 Turner Review) and Schwarcz, S, 'Systemic Risk' (2008) 97 *Georgetown LJ* 193.

[14] The primary objective of the UK Prudential Regulation Authority (PRA), eg, is promoting the stability and soundness of PRA-authorized persons. It is to advance this objective primarily by seeking to ensure that the business of PRA-authorized persons is carried on in a way that avoids any adverse effect on the stability of the UK financial system and by seeking to minimize the adverse effect that the failure of such persons could be expected to have on the stability of the UK financial system: 2012 Financial Services Acts 2B(2) and (3).

[15] For an early analysis of the dual system-facing and client-facing function of prudential rules see Goodhart, C, 'Some Regulatory Concerns' in Goodhart, C (ed), *The Emerging Framework of Financial Regulation* (1998) 213.

[16] See generally on prudential tools Jackson, H, 'Regulation in a Multi-sectored Financial Services Industry: An Exploration Essay' (1997) 77 *Washington University LQ* 319.

[17] Given the need to balance efficient outcomes with the potential stability risks arising from pressure to increase market share. See, eg, Moloney, N, 'The Legacy Effects of the Financial Crisis on Regulatory Design in the EU' in Ferran, E, Moloney, N, Hill, J, and Coffee, J, *The Regulatory Aftermath of the Global Financial Crisis* (2012) 111.

rules (including with respect to governance and remuneration), and capital requirements, which are designed to absorb losses which an intermediary does not expect to make in the ordinary course of business, to impose costs on the carrying of risks by intermediaries, and to support orderly winding up in an insolvency.

The extent to which a particular activity generates risks has tended to dictate the nature of the regulatory response. Retail investment advice and the distribution of investment products, for example, are prone to agency costs given of sharp conflict-of-interest risks, but do not carry material risks to financial stability. Own-account dealing in complex financial instruments and market-making, by contrast, can generate significant systemic risks, particularly where a dealer withdraws from market-making in volatile market conditions. The particular actor's organization and business model can also dictate the nature of the regulatory response. Multifunction investment intermediaries, for example, are significantly more prone to conflict-of-interest failures than single-function proprietary dealers. Similarly, where regulation attaches to non-financial counterparties who engage only sporadically in activities such as proprietary dealing (typically to hedge commercial risks), the costs and inefficiencies can be significant and calibration is typical. Calibration to the client also matters; traditionally, professional clients have been treated as more informed and better equipped to monitor agency costs than retail clients, and the client/firm relationship has been less heavily regulated. The type of financial instrument engaged also impacts on the risks generated: as the financial crisis illustrated, trading in poorly understood and complex derivative products can lead to major liquidity and solvency problems. But while calibration matters to effective regulatory design, regulatory arbitrage can be a significant risk where functionally similar actors and activities are not subject to the same rules. Given the pace at which intermediation develops, and the arbitrage risks which follow regulatory classifications and segmentation, obsolescence is a similarly acute risk to effective regulation.

By contrast with the relatively stable suite of regulatory tools deployed in the capital-raising sphere (Chapter II), the tools deployed by investment intermediary regulation have undergone repeated cycles of reform as securities and markets regulation has moved from reliance on market discipline to deploying more intensive regulation, and as particular tools, whether conduct or prudential, have been refined. Most recently, the financial crisis has led to the regulatory perimeter being cast around a significantly wider set of investment services and financial instruments, and to a material intensification in the nature of intervention; the space within which investment intermediaries can operate under market discipline rather than under regulatory fiat has shrunk dramatically. Overall, financial stability-related regulation has become a significantly greater component of intermediary regulation.[18]

The intensification of investment intermediary regulation since the financial crisis is primarily related to the raft of new prudentially orientated measures which are designed to promote more prudent risk-taking and to provide stronger incentives (regulatory and

---

[18] The International Organization of Securities Commissions (IOSCO) has, eg, re-characterized conduct rules, which have typically been associated with investor protection, as important tools for mitigating systemic risk by promoting better interest alignment between intermediaries and their principal clients: IOSCO, Mitigating Systemic Risk. A Role for Securities Regulators (2011) 42.

otherwise) for firms to monitor risks. This intensification has been driven in particular by the need, which the crisis exposed, to promote prudent risk-taking in multifunction, deposit-taking banks which also engage in trading and market-orientated activities, given the extent of the interconnections between banks and other intermediating entities and the related potential for destructive risk transmission and for the consequent damage to the wider economy which is associated with bank failure. Governance controls (including remuneration requirements), stronger internal risk-management requirements, capital, liquidity, and leverage requirements, and *ex-post* resolution mechanisms have all been deployed to support the stability of institutions engaging in intermediation in the financial markets. The distinct international agenda for Global Systemically Important Financial Institutions (G-SIFIs) underlines the extent to which the prudential regulation of inter-mediaries has become a central pillar of the international crisis-era reform programme,[19] as does the related raft of measures designed to address the 'too big to fail' problem generated by large banking groups and their engaging in riskier intermediation-related activities along with deposit-taking and lending. These include, in the EU, the Commission's 2014 proposals for a ring-fencing regime for the EU's largest banks.[20]

The shift towards more intrusive prudential regulation also reflects something of a policy suspicion of 'excessive' levels of intermediation and of related innovation. The social utility of intermediation has come under scrutiny,[21] as has the extent to which regulation can be used to limit or control levels of market and intermediary development.[22] This movement reflects the increased attention given over the crisis era to the deep-seated behavioural dynamics of the financial markets[23]—dynamics which can generate stability risks and entrench agency costs, and which are very difficult to address through regula-tion.[24] Close attention is also focusing on the nature of the financial innovation produced by intermediaries[25] and on the ability of intermediaries to manage innovation

---

[19] The G-SIFI agenda is spearheaded by the Financial Stability Board (FSB). It is based on applying common resolution standards, higher loss absorbency capacity requirements (through higher capital require-ments under the Basel III agreement), and more intensive supervisory oversight to institutions of such size, market importance, and global interconnectedness that distress or failure would cause significant dislocation in the global financial system and adverse economic consequences across a range of countries: FSB, Reducing the Moral Hazard Posed by Systemically Important Financial Institutions (2010) and FSB, Policy Measures to Address Systemically Important Financial Institutions (2011). Initial efforts have focused on banks. To date, 29 global banking groups have been identified by the FSB as G-SIFIs: FSB, 2013 Update of Group of Global Systemically Important Banks (2013).

[20] See Ch VI sect 1. For a wide-ranging review of how and why the prudential regulation of intermediaries changed over the crisis see Avgouleas, E, *Governance of Global Financial Markets: The Law, the Economics, the Politics* (2012).

[21] eg Whitehead, C, 'Reframing Financial Regulation' (2010) 90 *Boston University LR* 1, suggesting that while intermediation can smooth the allocation of capital, the related agency costs can be significant.

[22] eg Arup, C, 'The Global Financial Crisis: Learning from Regulatory and Governance Studies' (2010) 32 *Law & Policy* 363.

[23] Which have long been under scrutiny. See, eg, Barr, M, Mullainathan, S, and Shafir, E, 'The Case for Behaviorally Informed Regulation' in Moss, D and Cistrenino, J (eds), *New Perspectives on Regulation* (2009) 25 and Barr, M, Mullainathan, S, and Shafir, E, 'Behaviourally Informed Regulation' in Shafir, E (ed), *Behavioural Foundations of Public Policy* (2012) 440.

[24] eg Langevoort, D, 'Chasing the Greased Pig Down Wall Street: A Gatekeeper's Guide to the Psych-ology, Culture and Ethics of Financial Risk' (2008) 96 *Cornell LR* 1209.

[25] eg Lerner, J and Tufano, P, The Consequences of Financial Innovation: A Counterfactual Research Agenda, NBER WP No 16780 (2011).

productively.[26] Among the major policy contributions to this debate was the UK Financial Services Authority's 2009 Turner Review, which suggested that 'beyond a certain degree of liquidity and market completion, the additional allocative efficiency benefits of further liquidity and market completion' might be relatively slight and outweighed by additional instability risks.[27]

A group of Chapters examine intermediary regulation from different perspectives. This Chapter considers the framework regime which applies to the provision of investment services generally, Chapter VI considers the particular issues raised by the trading process, and Chapter IX considers the distinct regulatory issues which arise in the retail markets and in relation to retail investment services. The gatekeeping functions provided by rating agencies and investment analysts, which raise distinct regulatory issues, are addressed in Chapter VII. Trading venues, a specialist form of intermediation, are considered in Chapter V.

IV.1.2 Intermediary Regulation and the EU

The regulation of investment services in the EU is primarily a function of the behemoth 2014 Markets in Financial Instruments Directive II (MiFID II)/Markets in Financial Instruments Regulation (MiFIR) regime,[28] which replaces the precursor 2004 MiFID I.[29] MiFID II/MiFIR will be amplified by a detailed administrative rulebook.[30]

---

[26] eg Blair, M, 'Financial Innovation, Leverage, Bubbles and the Distribution of Income' (2010–2011) 30 *Rev of Banking and Finance Law* 225 and Gennaioli, N, Shliefer, A, and Vishny, R, Neglected Risks, Financial Innovation and Financial Fragility, NBER WP No 16008 (2010).

[27] 2009 Turner Review, n 13, 16–18 and 41–2. Then FSA Chairman Turner similarly queried the value of financial intermediation and asked 'how much' financial intermediation is optimal: Speech on 'How should the Crisis Affect our Views about Financial Intermediation', March 7 2011 and Speech on 'The Future of Finance', 14 July 2010.

[28] Markets in Financial Instruments Directive II 2014/65/EU [2014] OJ L173/349 (2014 MiFID II) and Markets in Financial Instruments Regulation EU (No) 600/2014 [2014] OJ L173/84 (2014 MiFIR). MiFID II is to be implemented by the Member States by 3 July 2016 and is to be applied by the Member States from 3 January 2017 (MiFID II Art 93). MiFIR, which, as a regulation, is directly applicable, applies from 3 January 2017 (MiFIR Art 55). The application of MiFIR has been tied to the application of MiFID II to ensure the regime operates as a 'regulatory package'; accordingly, the delegations within MiFIR for administrative rule-making (like the MiFID II delegations) apply from June 2014 (to allow for the EU rule-making process to take place). There are transitional arrangements for particular aspects of the regime, including with respect to the third-country access rules relating to investment-services provision (sect 10), the trading venue/CCP (central clearing counterparty) access regime (Ch V sect 13), and the regime governing exchange-traded derivatives (Ch VI sect 4.3).

The discussion in this Chapter is based on the 2014 MiFIR II/MiFIR regime (the 2004 MiFID I regime (n 29) will be repealed from 3 January 2017). Reference is made to the MiFID I regime as appropriate.

The main elements of the publicly available legislative history of the 2014 MiFID II/MiFIR are: MiFID II Commission Proposal (COM (2011) 656/4), MiFIR Commission Proposal (COM (2011) 652/4), and MIFID II/MiFIR Proposals Impact Assessment (2011 SEC (2011) 1226); MiFID II Council General Approach, 18 June 2013 (Council Document 11006/13) and MiFIR Council General Approach 18 June 2013 (Council Document 11007/13); and European Parliament Resolution adopting a Negotiating Position on MiFID II, 26 October 2012 (P7_TA(2012)0406) and on MiFIR, 26 October 2012 (P7_TA(2012)0407).

[29] Directive 2004/39/EC [2004] OJ L145/1. In its early days, MiFID I was described as a 'sprawling directive with far-reaching implications for any firm involved in buying and selling securities in Europe': Editorial, *Financial Times*, 23 August 2005, 14. But it has since been dwarfed by MiFID II/MiFIR.

[30] The precursor MiFID I regime was amplified extensively by two measures. The 2006 Commission MiFID I Directive (2006/73/EC [2006] OJ L241/26) addressed organizational and operational matters and covered the nature of investment advice, prudential organizational requirements, conduct-of-business regulation, best execution, order handling, and the eligible counterparty concept. The 2006 Commission MiFID

The 2014 MiFID II/MiFIR regime addresses a wide range of investment services, including brokerage, dealing, investment advice, underwriting, asset management, and the operation of trading venues.[31] MiFID II applies to investment firms, market operators (considered in Chapter V as part of the trading venue regime), data-reporting service providers (considered in Chapter V as part of the trading venue regime), and third country firms providing investment services or performing investment activities through the establishment of a branch in the EU (MiFID II Article 1(1)). Accordingly, it governs the authorization and operating conditions for investment firms; the provision of investment services or activities by third country firms through the establishment of a branch; the authorization and operation of regulated markets; the authorization and operation of data-reporting service providers; and supervision, co-operation, and enforcement by national competent authorities (NCAs) (MiFID II Article 1(2)).

The 2014 MiFIR governs the disclosure of trade data to the public; the reporting of transactions to NCAs; the trading of derivatives on organized venues; non-discriminatory access to clearing and non-discriminatory access to trading in benchmarks; the product intervention powers of NCAs and the European Securities and Markets Authority (ESMA), and NCAs' and ESMA's position-management and position-limit powers; and the provision of investment services or activities by third country firms (following an applicable equivalence decision by the Commission) with or without a branch (MiFIR Article 1(1)).[32]

The 2014 MiFID II is the main source of intermediary regulation in the EU, but operates in parallel with the massive 2013 Capital Requirements Directive (CRD IV)/Capital Requirements Regulation (CRR) prudential regime[33] which governs credit institutions and investment firms, and which imposes detailed prudential requirements, including capital rules, as well as a distinct supervisory framework, on the supply of investment services by in-scope firms.

The regulation of investment services is, however, fractured across a number of other measures, reflecting the scale of the post-crisis EU rulebook as well as the distinct regulatory issues which arise in different segments of intermediary activity. The provision of investment services in the retail markets is primarily governed by the 2014 MiFID II/MiFIR, but a number of other measures also apply (Chapter IX). The MiFID II requirements relating to investment services discussed in this Chapter apply to discretionary asset management, including where discretionary asset management is provided by collective asset managers, but collective asset managers are otherwise governed by the 2009 Undertakings for Collective Investment in Transferable Securities (UCITS) and 2011 Alternative Investment

---

I Regulation (Commission Regulation (EC) No 1287/2006 [2006] OJ L241/1) addressed the regulation of trading and trading venues and covered pre- and post-trade transparency, admission to trading, and transaction reporting requirements. While these measures (which will be repealed when MiFID II/MiFIR is applied) will be reflected in the new MiFID II/MiFIR administrative regime, MiFID II/MiFIR contains a great many more delegations to administrative rule-making which will significantly expand and refine the administrative rulebook.

[31] Trading venue regulation is considered in Ch V.
[32] MiFIR is largely concerned with trading venue regulation (Ch V). Product intervention powers are considered in Ch IX 7.1.
[33] Directive 2013/36/EU [2013] OJ L176/338 (Capital Requirements Directive (CRD IV)) and Regulation (EU) No 575/2013 [2013] OJ L176/1 (Capital Requirements Regulation (CRR)).

Fund Managers Directive (AIFMD) collective asset management regimes (Chapter III).[34] The trading process, and in particular dealing and brokerage, is subject to a discrete set of rules (Chapter VI): MiFID II/MiFIR provides the core regulatory framework, but distinct rules apply under the 2012 Short Selling Regulation[35] and with respect to the organization of the over-the-counter (OTC) derivatives market under the 2012 European Market Infrastructure Regulation (2012 EMIR).[36]

IV.2 The Evolution of the EU Regime

IV.2.1 Initial Developments and the 1993 Investment Services Directive

IV.2.1.1 Early Developments

The roots of EU investment firm regulation are in market integration. The seminal 1966 Segré Report focused primarily on the integration of securities markets and the capital-formation process. But it also found that while the participation of market intermediaries was critical to the creation of a European capital market, they were hampered by varying rules and supervisory practices, and so called for harmonization.[37] The first step was taken in 1977 with the adoption of the non-binding Code of Conduct.[38] Very little progress would be made thereafter until the early 1990s. Accordingly, prior to the launch of the investment services harmonization programme in 1993, Member States regulated investment firms to widely varying degrees and in very different ways. Regulation varied according to whether the intermediary was a credit institution, a dealer registered with a stock exchange, or an intermediary operating outside the structure of a stock exchange and engaged in investment services, such as investment advice or asset management.[39] While the regulatory requirements of certain Member States hindered the ability of undertakings from other Member States to offer investment services,[40] conversely the lack of any substantial regulation in certain Member States[41] impeded the development of an

---

[34] Directive 2011/61/EU [2011] OJ L174/1 (the 2011 Alternative Investment Fund Managers Directive (2011 AIFMD)) and Directive 2009/65/EC [2009] OJ L302/32 (the 2009 Undertakings for Collective Investment in Transferable Securities IV Directive (2009 UCITS IV)).

[35] Regulation (EU) No 236/2012 [2012] OJ L86/1.

[36] Regulation (EU) No 648/2012 [2012] OJ L201/1.

[37] Report by a Group of Experts Appointed by the EEC Commission, The Development of a European Capital Market (the Segré Report) (1966) 32 and 267–71.

[38] Commission Recommendation 77/534/EEC concerning a European Code of Conduct Relating to Transactions in Transferable Securities [1977] OJ L212/37. It contained very general high-level principles relating to the regulation of investment firms.

[39] Wymeersch, E, *Control of Securities Markets in the European Economic Community. Collection Studies. Competition—Approximation of Legislation Series No 3* (1977).

[40] In Germany, eg, investment services could be carried out only through a credit institution incorporated in Germany.

[41] The description in the 1977 Wymeersch study of the regulatory landscape is illuminating: '[t]he present approach as regards regulation differs fairly considerably. In France, the passing-on of stock exchange orders, as well as portfolio management, is subject to some measures of investor protection. In the United Kingdom, some investment consultants and intermediate brokers could come within the scope of the Prevention of Fraud (Investments) Act . . . there are many exceptions to this rule . . . In Belgium and the Netherlands only securities brokerage is reserved to the recognized securities business: investment advisory services or portfolio management are offered absolutely freely . . . In Luxembourg the question is solved by the application of the

integrated market. Market structures also varied considerably, reflecting the varying degrees to which market finance formed a central element of national economies. The dominance of large universal banks in some continental markets, particularly Germany, made market penetration by specialist investment services providers difficult.[42]

The integration problems caused by variations in regulation[43] became acute during the late 1980s and early 1990s, when changes to market conditions and an explosion of regulatory activity took place[44] which led to many new national regulatory regimes.[45] In some cases, the new regimes shielded domestic market participants from outside competition. In 1991 Italy adopted a securities law (the SIM law) which introduced licensing requirements for securities firms which, controversially, included an establishment requirement. Overall, the Commission expressed its general concern with respect to the impact of such abruptly introduced rules, particularly given their adoption after the EU's liberalization of capital movements.[46]

IV.2.1.2 The 1985 White Paper and the Single European Act

The mutual recognition/minimum-harmonization model for EU intervention has long since been superseded by a mutual recognition/intensive harmonization model in the financial markets sphere. But this model provided the initial impetus for the investment services programme. In its 1985 White Paper on 'Completing the Internal Market', the Commission noted that 'experience has shown that the alternative of relying on a strategy based totally on harmonization would be over-regulatory, would take a long time to implement, would be inflexible and could stifle innovation'.[47] Accordingly, it proposed that each Member State retain its own system of regulation and that the internal market be supported through mutual recognition of the regulation carried out by each Member State, as well as that cross-border activity be anchored to the regulatory and supervisory regime of the home Member State (essentially, the State of the relevant market actor's registration). In the financial services sphere generally, in respect of which the Commission noted that 'liberalisation of financial services, linked to that of capital movements, will represent a major step towards Community financial integration and the widening of the Internal Market', the Commission proposed that financial services be supervised by the home

---

Order controlling the opening of new business, while in Germany problems have arisen both with portfolio managers or consultants and with sellers of securities from their own portfolios. In Italy there is complete freedom': n 39, 60–1.

[42] eg Farmery, P, 'Looking Towards a European Internal Market in Financial Services: Some Paradoxes and Paradigms: A Survey of Current Problems and Issues' (1992) 3 *EBLR* 94.

[43] For an early examination of the barriers to integration, see Commission, *Research on the 'Cost of Non-Europe', Basic Findings*, vol 9, 'The Cost of Non-Europe in Financial Services' (1988) 62.

[44] In his Opinion in *Commission v Italy*, Lenz AG noted at para 40 that '[i]n a period of less than 10 years the legislatures of the Member States of the European Communities evidently recognized a need for regulation': Case C-101/94 *Commission v Italy* [1996] ECR I-2691.

[45] The UK, eg, in 1986 introduced the Financial Services Act which changed the regulation of investment services from a self-regulatory regime to a statutory system, while in 1988 France introduced a major reform of the regulation of stockbrokers. Also in 1988, Spain adopted a Securities Markets Act which radically restructured its securities markets. Earlier, in 1985, the Netherlands introduced a general licensing requirement, which was brought in following problems with the trading practices of firms which were not part of an exchange and so not subject to any authorization requirements or supervision. See Poser, N, *International Securities Regulation. London's 'Big Bang' and the European Securities Markets* (1991) 379–441.

[46] n 44, Opinion of the AG, para 38, highlighting the Commission's position.

[47] COM (85) 310 (the 1985 Internal Market White Paper) para 64.

authority, in accordance with minimum harmonized rules.[48] Member States would remain free to impose regulation beyond the minimum on institutions for which they were the home State. In parallel, the Treaty reforms delivered by the 1987 Single European Act acted as a spur to action as they facilitated the adoption of legislation by introducing qualified majority voting in the Council.

Although new legislative and policy technology was therefore available, the first step towards an investment services regime was a sideways one in the form of the (now repealed) 1989 Second Banking Co-ordination Directive (BCD II).[49] The BCD II followed the White Paper's model and granted a 'passport' to deposit-taking 'credit institutions' in respect of the activities set out in the BCD II—which, critically, included the provision of investment services by credit institutions—and adopted a related set of harmonized rules.[50] The gap in the regime was addressed in 1993 with the Investment Services Directive (ISD),[51] which applied the BCD II model to non-bank investment firms. It granted a regulatory passport to investment firms within its scope, and imposed related minimum authorization and operating requirements. The parallel 1993 Capital Adequacy Directive[52] was a key ancillary measure to the ISD and set out the harmonized capital requirements applicable to investment firms and credit institutions in respect of their investment services activities.

IV.2.2 The Financial Services Action Plan and MiFID I

IV.2.2.1 The Financial Services Action Plan and the Lamfalussy Reforms

The strains in the 1993 ISD's regulatory model quickly became apparent. The scope of the ISD was linked to the traditional broker-dealer model of investment services and it was accordingly soon outpaced by industry developments; the ISD's scope was also linked to a limited range of financial instruments, with the effect that large swathes of transactions, particularly with respect to derivatives, fell outside the ISD. The ISD's minimum-harmonization model also came under strain. Authorization and prudential requirements (including organizational requirements and capital requirements) were harmonized in order to support the ISD passport and home Member State control of prudential regulation, but only to a limited extent; marketing and conduct-of-business rules were not harmonized and, accordingly, were subject to host State control. ISD Article 11, which addressed

---

[48] 1985 Internal Market White Paper, n 47, paras 101 and 103. The adoption by the Commission of the mutual-recognition technique for financial-services harmonization built on the ground-breaking Court ruling in Case 120/78 *Rewe-Zentral AG v Bundesmonopolverwaltung für Branntwein* (the Cassis de Dijon ruling) [1979] ECR 649, which applied mutual recognition to the free movement of goods. The Internal Market White Paper also included in its annexed Timetable For Completing the Internal Market by 1992 the intriguingly entitled 'Proposal for a Directive concerning investment advisors', which was to be presented in 1989 and adopted in 1989 (para 1.3). In the event, investment advice would not come within the Community regime until the adoption of MiFID I in 2004.

[49] Directive 89/646/EC [1989] OJ L386/1.

[50] The initial focus on credit institutions reflects the dominance of bank finance among most major European economies (see further Ch I).

[51] Directive 93/22/EC [1993] OJ L141/27.

[52] Directive 93/6/EC [1993] OJ L141/1.

conduct-of-business regulation, was particularly problematic.[53] It did not harmonize conduct-of-business regulation but merely established the principles to be followed by Member States. As a result, Member States adopted widely varying conduct regimes.[54] Scope problems,[55] the compliance costs of multiple rulebooks, difficulties in ascertaining what the applicable rules were where the relevant Member State did not specify which rules applied to passporting firms, translation burdens, and variations in the ways in which conduct rules could be enforced against investment firms by investors all obstructed market integration and led the Commission to report that Article 11 was a 'main stumbling block' to the ISD passport.[56] Further difficulties were caused by the ability of host Member States to impose national rules generally in the 'general good' (which was a consequence of the limited degree of harmonization) and by technical difficulties with the passport-notification system.[57]

By the end of the 1990s, it was clear that the investment services regulatory framework was neither keeping pace with market developments nor delivering an integrated investment services market, with its assumed associated benefits of a reduction in the costs of capital raising, stimulation of investment and employment, and other economy-wide advantages. The unsatisfactory state of integration was a central preoccupation of the Commission's 1998 pre-Financial Services Action Plan (FSAP) Communication on 'Financial Services: Building a Framework for Action',[58] which found that the benefits of the single market in investment services had not been fully realized. Further progress was reported as being necessary in order that full advantage could be taken of the euro and of the ongoing market-driven modernization of the investment services marketplace.[59] The 1998 Communication was followed by the 1999 FSAP, which set out the key measures which were required to achieve a single market in financial services, and which identified ISD reform as a central element.[60] In parallel, the regulatory framework for the single market in investment services was subject to scathing criticism in the Lamfalussy Report.[61] While the wider regime for integrating and regulating the financial system generally was condemned as being 'too rigid, complex and ill-adapted to the pace of global financial market change',[62] specific reference

---

[53] An extensive literature addresses the difficulties posed by Art 11. See, eg, Tison, M, 'Conduct of Business Rules and Their Implementation in the EU Member States' in Ferrarini, G, Hopt, K, and Wymeersch, E (eds), *Capital Markets in the Age of the Euro* (2002) 65.

[54] Commission, Communication on Article 11 (2000) (COM (2000) 722).

[55] Jurisdiction under Art 11 was linked to the Member State 'within which the service [was] provided'. This Delphic formula generated widespread confusion as to when a Member State's conduct regime was engaged, including with respect to the degree of connection required to the Member State, whether a physical presence was required, and whether distance or unsolicited services triggered Art 11.

[56] n 54.

[57] For a critical review of the ISD see Lambrecht, P and Haljan, D, 'Investor Protection and the European Directives Concerning Securities' in van Houtte, H (ed), *The Law of Cross-Border Securities Transactions* (1999) 257, 265.

[58] COM (1998) 625 (the 1998 Communication).

[59] The Commission warned that '[t]he delayed implementation of the Investment Services Directive has caused market rigidities as a result of lack of competition and difficult market access. Market innovation has been stifled whilst investment firms are less than optimally prepared for the readjustment and enhanced competition that the euro will bring': n 58, 4.

[60] Commission, Communication on Implementing the Framework for Financial Markets Action Plan COM (1999) 232 (FSAP).

[61] Final Report of the Committee of Wise Men on the Regulation of European Securities Markets (2001) (2001 Lamfalussy Report) 8.

[62] n 61, 7.

was made to numerous weaknesses in the ISD and to the inadequate articulation of the home-country control principle.

IV.2.2.2 MiFID I: Negotiation Process

The 2000 ISD Communication[63] launched the ISD review process which would lead to the 2004 MiFID I and argued that '[u]pdating of the ISD can facilitate European progress towards enhanced liquidity, efficiency and stability. Inaction risks undervaluing the positive externalities and public goods that efficient securities markets, characterized by transparency and integrity, embody for the overall economic system'.[64] It acknowledged that the ISD had eliminated only the 'first set of legal obstacles' to the single market and that a 'wide-ranging overhaul of the ISD' was required.[65]

Reflecting the enhanced consultation process which applied to FSAP-era measures,[66] two further public consultations followed the 2000 ISD Communication before the publication of the 2002 MiFID I Proposal (the July 2001 Preliminary Orientations[67] and the March 2002 Revised Orientations[68]). The European Parliament also engaged in the consultations.[69] But while the consultation process was significantly enhanced from the pre-FSAP era,[70] cost and impact analysis remained very limited. The empirical analysis in the Impact Assessment annexed to the MiFID I Proposal was confined to reiterating the main findings of the London Economics study into the integration of securities markets generally,[71] while the analysis overall was sketchy.[72]

The subsequent 2002 MiFID I Proposal[73] relied heavily on the importance of market finance to the economic health of the EU and on the link between regulation, investor confidence, and efficient markets as justifications for action. Referring to the support of the 2000 Lisbon and 2001 Stockholm Councils for competitive and flexible market-based financing,[74] the Commission argued that financial markets acted as a motor for wealth creation, notwithstanding the then-recent reverses suffered by the equity markets in the wake of the dotcom crash, and asserted a need for a robust harmonized framework to support investor confidence and liquidity. The 1993 ISD was no longer an effective framework for undertaking business on a cross-border basis, the level of harmonization

---

[63] Commission, Communication on Upgrading the Investment Services Directive (93/22/EEC) (1993) (2000) (COM (2000) 729).

[64] n 63, 19.

[65] n 63, 1 and 9, respectively.

[66] See further Ch X sect 2.3.4.

[67] Commission, Overview of Proposed Adjustments to the Investment Services Directive. Working Document of Services of DG Internal Market. Document 1, July 2001.

[68] Commission, Revision of the ISD. Second Consultation, Overview Paper (2002).

[69] A5-0106/2001 (the Katiforis Report on ISD reform generally) and A5-0105/2001 (the Kauppi Report on the reforms to conduct-of-business regulation).

[70] Extensive consultations also took place during the subsequent administrative rule-making process. In all, the Commission estimated that more than 15 formal public consultations took place during the MiFID I legislative and administrative processes: Commission, Background Note to Draft Commission Regulation Implementing Directive 2004/39/EC (February 2006) 1.

[71] London Economics, Quantification of the Macro-Economic Impact of Integration of EU Financial Markets. Final Report to the EU Commission (2002).

[72] eg the discussion of what would be required of businesses to comply with the new regime did not capture the scale of the necessary changes or quantify the costs.

[73] COM (2002) 625.

[74] See further Ch I.

was not sufficient to support mutual recognition, and a combination of overly generic principles and 'general good' jurisdiction had limited the scope of the passport and home Member State control. In response, the MiFID I Proposal proposed an extension of the range of investment services within the scope of the investment firm passport, an enhanced authorization and operational regulation regime which included new harmonized prudential and conduct rules, a streamlining of the investment services passport by means of a new notification process, and a significant reduction of the host State's ability to intervene in the regulation and supervision of cross-border investment services.

During the institutional negotiations,[75] the investment firm elements of MiFID I proved, for the most part, uncontroversial; institutional relations were generally good and the negotiations for the most part refined the proposed regime. In particular, the European Parliament's amendments, steered by the influential Economic and Monetary Affairs Committee (ECON), brought more nuance, greater sensitivity to market interests and conditions, and a concern to reduce costs and support investor autonomy and choice to the negotiations. The order execution/trading venue aspects of MiFID I, by contrast, were fraught, as discussed in Chapter V. MiFID I was adopted in April 2004, some 18 months after the presentation of the Proposal: by contrast with the legislative process over the pre-FSAP era, this was a relatively quick process.

The scale and complexity of MiFID I[76] is well illustrated by the unusual extension of its original implementation deadline. The original implementation timetable was extended in 2006,[77] following market and political demands which reflected the difficulties caused by the extensive administrative rule adoption process. The legislative and administrative processes were designed to be simultaneous, but the administrative rules were not adopted until September 2006. Although opening MiFID I up to revision was not without risk or controversy,[78] the 2006 MiFID I Amending Directive amended MiFID I without substantive change and simply extended the Member State implementation deadline from 30 April 2006 to 31 January 2007. It also provided that MiFID I was to be applied from 1 November 2007. The time-lag between implementation and application was designed to allow market participants additional time in which to make the large-scale systems changes required. Late October 2007 saw a cascade of initiatives to mark the imminent application of MiFID I, including measures adopted by the Committee of European Securities Regulators (CESR) on the MiFID I passport and on transitional

---

[75] The legislative history is as follows: Commission Proposal (n 73); ECOSOC Opinion [2003] OJ C220/1; European Central Bank Opinion [2003] OJ C144/6; First Reading by the European Parliament [2004] OJ C77/264 (ECON report at A5-0287/2003 (First ECON Report)); Council's Common Position [2004] OJ C60/1; and Second Reading by the European Parliament [2004] OJ C102/33 (the report by ECON is at A5-0114/2004 (Second ECON Report)).

[76] Its scale did not go unnoticed by the US Securities and Exchange Commission (SEC): 'The unprecedented scope of harmonization and resulting open architecture—particularly in trade execution and reporting—will cause profound changes in existing market structures.' SEC Commissioner Campos, Speech on 'The Challenge of MiFID in the United States', 10 May 2007.

[77] By Directive 2006/31/EC [2006] OJ L114/60 (2006 MiFID I Amending Directive).

[78] The Commission was careful during the amendment process to emphasize that the revision was driven by *force majeure* given industry concerns, highlighted that amendments would be technical, and insisted that it would not 'allow any debates to be re-opened or any deals to re-negotiated'. There was also some concern among the Member States that the revision process would slow down the completion of the FSAP: European Securities Committee (on the Committee's role in rule-making see Ch X sect 4) Minutes, 23 February 2005.

arrangements.[79] The MiFID I application deadline of 1 November 2007 passed with considerable fanfare[80] but without full Member State implementation (required from the previous January),[81] although the Commission reported that it expected full implementation across all Member States by 2008.[82] Application in the markets also proved to be slow in some Member States.[83]

IV.2.2.3 2004 MiFID I: Key Features

The 2004 MiFID I, together with its administrative rules, led to the establishment of a comprehensive EU regulatory framework for the provision of investment services in financial instruments by banks and investment firms. The Commission has since described it as being predicated on a series of key principles: cross-border competition between firms (and venues) on a level playing field; market transparency; non-discriminatory and equal treatment of market participants; diligent corporate governance and avoidance of conflicts of interest by intermediaries; and suitable as well as effective protection of investors.[84] MiFID I brought a wide range of investment services (including investment advice) and an extensive array of financial instruments (including commodity derivatives) within its scope. It imposed a new rulebook on investment firms which addressed authorization, prudential regulation (including systems and controls, asset protection, and conflict-of-interest management requirements), and conduct regulation (including disclosure and quality of advice rules). MiFID I removed, for the most part, the host Member State from the regulation and supervision of cross-border activity and thereby addressed a major weakness of the 1993 ISD. It empowered, however, the branch Member State to impose branch State rules on, and supervise, passporting branches. MiFID I also introduced a streamlined notification system for cross-border passporting and enhanced the NCA co-operation and co-ordination regime supporting cross-border passporting.

From the harmonization perspective, MiFID I can be strongly associated with the decisive shift to regulation over the FSAP era. Although MiFID I was at heart a market integration measure, and its extensive harmonization was designed to support cross-border passporting

---

[79] eg CESR's 22 October 2007 Press Release which announced its 'final steps before MiFID goes live' (CESR/07-726).

[80] The *Financial Times*, which had, at times, been hostile to MiFID I, marked the occasion by opining that ('notwithstanding MiFID's appalling press during its progression'): 'MiFID is a substantial and potentially sweeping piece of EU law-making. Its objectives of creating efficient conditions for trading securities and other financial instruments, promoting competition and providing EU-wide standards for investor protection serve the laudable goal of fostering economic growth in Europe through the creation of deep, liquid, and well-regulated markets of a continental scale' (Editorial, 'Day of the MiFID', *Financial Times*, 1 November 2007, 14).

[81] As at 15 October 2007, the Czech Republic, Cyprus, Estonia, Finland, Greece, Hungary, the Netherlands, Poland, Portugal, Spain, and Slovenia had all failed to notify implementation of MiFID I. By 15 November 2007, however, only the Czech Republic, Spain, and Poland had failed to notify any implementation, although the extent of full implementation across the Member States was not clear. In January 2008, the Commission launched enforcement proceedings against these three Member States: Commission Press Release IP/08/126. Delayed implementation caused one commentator to describe MiFID I as 'creeping into effect': Norman, P, 'Revolution in EU Securities Kicks Off', *Financial Times*, 29 October 2007, 24.

[82] The Commission also suggested that, in addition to pursuing enforcement action, it would provide tacit support to any financial institutions that wished to sue defaulting Member States: Tett, G and Barber, T, 'Brussels Threatens Action Against Countries over MiFID Breaches', *Financial Times*, 2 November 2007, 1.

[83] Hughes, J, 'EU Finance Directive Expected to Cause Confusion for the Unprepared', *Financial Times*, 29 October 2007, 1.

[84] 2011 MiFID II/MiFIR Proposals Impact Assessment, n 28, 5.

and the home Member State control principle,[85] it adopted a regulatory orientation previously unknown to EU securities and markets law. While not formally expressed as a 'maximum harmonization' measure,[86] it was widely regarded as such.[87] This was in large part a function of the heavy reliance on administrative rule-making under MiFID I. MiFID I contained a great number of delegations to administrative rule-making; the investment firm authorization and operating regime, for example, was extensively amplified by the 2006 Commission MiFID I Directive. Any residual Member State discretion in relation to these rules was formally ousted by the then-controversial 'Article 4 prohibition' or 'gold-plating prohibition' which applied to the 2006 Commission MiFID I Directive (and accordingly applied to the administrative operating rules applicable to investment firms). This gold-plating prohibition prevented Member States from adopting rules additional to the 2006 Commission MiFID I Directive:[88] under Article 4 of the 2006 Directive, Member States could do so only where the rules in question were objectively justified and proportionate and addressed specific risks to investor protection or market integrity which were not adequately addressed by the Directive. The additional rules were also required to address a specific risk of particular importance given the Member State's market structure or to address risks or issues that emerged or became evident after the coming into force of MiFID I. By contrast, CESR had advised a minimum-harmonization approach be taken to many of the MiFID I administrative rules, and particularly with respect to the MiFID I conduct regime.[89] The Commission, nonetheless, proposed the Article 4 gold-plating prohibition, which, while ultimately adopted, was very heavily negotiated during the administrative rule-making process, with clear divisions between those Member States demanding a high level of harmonization and those Member States arguing for flexibility and expressing concern that Article 4 went too far.[90] Under the 2014 MiFID II, while a variant of the gold-plating prohibition applies, it is now regarded as a useful concession to the Member States which supports local rule-making in exceptional circumstances and not as an exceptional intrusion into Member State sovereignty, and so underlines the extent to which the single rulebook has become embedded (section 3).

Similarly, the MiFID I era also saw CESR emerge as a pivotal influence on the investment firm regime, particularly through its supervisory convergence measures, which quickly began to form a 'soft rulebook'. CESR issued guidelines on the MiFID I passport,[91] on inducements under MiFID,[92] on best execution,[93] and on the MiFID I record-keeping

---

[85] The Commission argued that the ISD did not establish the 'bedrock of harmonized investor protection obligations' needed to support mutual recognition of authorization and operational requirements. The high level of investor protection adopted by the new regime was designed to ensure that investment firms could operate cross-border under home Member State supervision: 2000 MiFID I Proposal, n 73, 80.

[86] See further Ch I.

[87] Welch, J, 'Decomposing MiFID', *Financial World,* July/August 2006, 46.

[88] Lodge, O and Flight, H, 'Latest MiFiD Offering Tries to Clear the Fog', *Financial Times, Fund Management Supplement,* 21 August 2006, 8, describing Art 4 as requiring 'regulators to go cap in hand to Brussels to seek leave to apply an existing rule or two'.

[89] CESR, Technical Advice on Possible Implementing Measures of Directive 2004/39 on Markets in Financial Instruments. 1st Set of Mandates (2005) (CESR/05-024c).

[90] European Securities Committee Minutes, 22–3 February 2006, 29–30 March 2006, and 26–7 April 2006. Discussions continued until just before the final vote in June 2006. Considerable attention focused on the Article's specification that additional requirements be retained only in 'exceptional' circumstances.

[91] CESR/07-337 and CESR/07/337b.

[92] CESR/07-228b.

[93] CESR/07-320.

regime,[94] and produced a MiFID Q&A. It also adopted Protocols on the passport-notification system and on the supervision of branches.[95]

IV.2.3 The Crisis Era and the MiFID I Review

IV.2.3.1 The 2004 MiFID I Experience

The 2004 MiFID I was amended a number of times prior to the major 2014 MiFID II/MiFIR reforms. It was revised in 2007 to reform the rules applicable to the supervisory review of acquisitions by investment firms,[96] in 2008 to reflect revisions to the process for adopting administrative rules,[97] and in 2010 to reflect the establishment of the ESMA.[98] The MiFID I Review and the consequent 2014 MiFID II/MiFIR reforms, however, have led to large-scale reform.

Most empirical analysis of the impact of MiFID I has focused on its radical market-shaping reforms to order execution and to trading venues, in relation to which the effects of MiFID I have been most easily quantifiable;[99] the two major MiFID I assessments commissioned by the Commission, for example, focused for the most part on trading venue data.[100] But overall, the MiFID I investment firm regime does not appear to have generated excessive costs or inefficiencies. The UK Financial Services Authority's (FSA's) examination of the likely impact of MiFID I (generally and including the trading venue reforms), for example,[101] was more positive than some of the more apocalyptic industry surveys.[102] It predicted one-off costs to the UK investment services industry in the order of £877 million–£1.17 billion and ongoing costs at £80 million.[103] But it suggested that the quantifiable benefits of MiFID I could represent up to £200 million annually with respect to 'first-round' benefits, which related, for example, to a reduction in authorization, compliance, operating, market access, and maintaining market reputation costs.[104] It also predicted gains of up to £240 million with respect to 'second-order' benefits related to the construction of deeper and liquid markets,[105] and, although these were in the realm of speculation, 'third-order' benefits in terms of an increase in the UK's long-term sustainable growth rate.[106] On the other hand, the FSA warned that its benefits would not be spread

---

[94] CESR/06-552c.

[95] CESR/07-317 and CESR/07-672.

[96] Directive 2007/44/EC [2007] OJ L247/1.

[97] Directive 2008/10/EC [2008] OJ L76/33. See further Ch X sect 4.

[98] Directive 2010/78/EU [2010] OJ L331/120 (2010 Omnibus I Directive).

[99] Discussed in Ch V.

[100] Europe Economics, MiFID I Review—Data Gathering and Cost Benefit Analysis (2011) and PriceWaterhouseCoopers, Data Gathering and Analysis in the Context of the MiFID I Review. Final Report (2010).

[101] FSA, The Overall Impact of MiFID (2006) (the analysis was based on Europe Economics, The Benefits of MiFID—A Report for the FSA (2006) (2006 FSA MiFID Impact Report)).

[102] A JP Morgan report, eg, predicted that €19 billion could be removed from the market capitalization of eight leading wholesale banks, given the combination of increased competition and the costs of implementing MiFID I: JP Morgan, MiFID Report II. Earnings at Risk Analysis: the Threat to the Integrated Business Model (2006).

[103] 2006 FSA MiFID Impact Report, n 101, 3.

[104] 2006 FSA MiFID Impact Report, n 101, 11.

[105] 2006 FSA MiFID Impact Report, n 101, 12.

[106] 2006 FSA MiFID Impact Report, n 101, 12–13.

evenly and would mainly accrue to firms operating cross-border.[107] Overall, the message was mixed, with the FSA noting that non-MiFID I effects (competition, innovation, consolidation, taxation, and those relating to clearing and settlement) were more likely to impact on the cost of capital, and that investment firms were generally sceptical as to the benefits of MiFID I.[108] The subsequent 2009 Europe Economics study for the Commission on the costs of key FSAP measures reflected the FSA's predictions, noting that MiFID I had been a major driver of increased costs for banks, investment firms, and asset managers, and that the costs had fallen more heavily on smaller firms; it highlighted, however, that most costs were carried up front, and that firms accepted the value of MiFID I compliance functions in managing reputational risk and acknowledged the business advantages of a tougher regulatory regime.[109] The 2009 CRA International review of the FSAP for the Commission was largely concerned with the impact of MiFID I on trading, but it also reported that an increase in firm passporting activity had occurred and was expected to increase.[110] The Report was, however, somewhat sceptical as to whether (outside the trading venue context where MiFID I had market-shaping effects) MiFID I could actively promote cross-border activity by investment firms and strengthen investor confidence, given the determinative role of market events.

Overall, however, and from the investment firm perspective, it is not unreasonable to at least associate MiFID I with facilitating cross-border activity, even if its quantifiable impact is not clear.[111]

IV.2.3.2 The MiFID I Review and the Financial Crisis

The origins of the MiFID I Review are in the review obligations imposed by 2004 MiFID I Article 65, which required the Commission to review a range of different MiFID I provisions, generally within one to three years of the Directive coming into force in 2007 (over 2008--10). The Review was accordingly undertaken over the financial crisis and was shaped by it, although from the outset the Commission was of the view that MiFID I had stood up relatively well to the onslaught of the financial crisis with respect to the firms and activities within its scope;[112] the most radical reforms to investment firm regulation were introduced under the 2013 CRD IV/CRR and relate to prudential supervision.

---

[107] 2006 FSA MiFID Impact Report n 101, 3.

[108] 2006 FSA MiFID Impact Report n 101, 12 and 20.

[109] Europe Economics, Survey on the Cost of Compliance with Selected FSAP Measures. Final Report by Europe Economics (2009). The survey related the heaviest costs to the initial costs associated with compliance with the MiFID I conduct and prudential requirements, notably the new client classification, disclosure, conflict of interest, and best execution rules, and related internal IT infrastructure, firm process, and firm culture reforms.

[110] CRA International, Evaluation of the Economic Impact of the FSAP (2009) 188–90.

[111] The Commission's 2010 consultation on the MiFID I Review suggested that market participants were broadly satisfied with the investment firm regime: eg British Bankers' Association, Response to the Commission 2010 MiFID I Review Consultation, 2 February 2011, reporting that MiFID I had worked well to open the single market and had provided consistent authorization, conduct, and market rules.

[112] The Commission suggested that MiFID I had provided firms with the freedom to provide investment services across the EU and that higher and more comprehensive investor protection requirements had followed (Commission, Public Consultation on Review of the Markets in Financial Instruments Directive (2010 MiFID I Review Consultation) 5), while the 2011 MiFID II Proposal suggested that MiFID I had been 'largely vindicated amid the experience of the financial crisis': 2011 MiFID II Proposal, n 28, 2.

An extensive fact-finding process preceded the 2011 MiFID II/MiFIR Proposals,[113] and in the early stages of the MiFID I Review the Commission also harnessed CESR's expertise,[114] requesting advice on a range of matters largely concerned with the trading venue and retail market elements of MiFID I.[115] The Commission also requested advice, and evidence of supervisory experience, in relation to the MiFID I client classification system, given crisis-era concerns as to whether professional clients were appropriately protected from mis-selling, in relation to the tied agents regime, and in relation to the scope of MiFID I, including whether it appropriately addressed the underwriting process.[116]

The subsequent December 2010 Commission Consultation on the MiFID I Review[117] was largely concerned with revising the trading venue elements of MiFID I in light of market developments and in light of the G20 commitment to strengthen oversight of the OTC derivatives markets. But more generally, the Commission related the MiFID I Review to the need to ensure 'a safer, sounder, more transparent and more responsible financial system'.[118] While the Commission was relatively sanguine as to the resilience of MiFID I with respect to investment firm regulation, it suggested that it was necessary to strengthen the MiFID I investor protection regime and to reduce Member State optionality and discretion in order to realize the crisis-era 'single rulebook' objective. A series of potential reforms were identified in relation to the scope of MiFID I, including with respect to commodity firms in relation to their (exempted) proprietary dealing activities in commodity derivatives (reflecting concerns as to potential investor protection risks were these exempted firms to engage in investment services more generally); emission allowances (reflecting concerns over the regulation of carbon trading) and structured deposits (reflecting concerns as to the exclusion from MiFID I of deposit-based investments, although they were functionally similar to other MiFID I financial instruments); and the MiFID I exemption for small investment firms which do not hold client assets (reflecting concerns as to potential investor protection risks). The Consultation also proposed a series of enhancements to MiFID I with respect to client classification (designed to enhance the protections for professional investors); firm governance and the 'fit and proper' assessment (designed to clarify senior management roles, strengthen the 'fit and proper' assessment, and improve incentives for sound risk-taking); asset management (designed to enhance organizational and disclosure requirements); asset protection (particularly with respect to title transfer collateral arrangements); underwriting (designed to apply tailored regulatory requirements); tied agents (designed to restrict national discretion in this area); and call recording (designed to introduce a common mandatory regime). Reflecting the crisis-era reform agenda generally, the Consultation also engaged with third country

---

[113] 2011 MiFID II Proposal, n 28 and 2011 MiFIR Proposal, n 28.

[114] From an early stage, CESR's supervisory convergence agenda for MiFID I had focused on the Commission's review obligations (see, eg, CESR, MiFID Level 3 Expert Group—2006–2007 Work Programme (CESR/06-550b) (2006) 5–6 and CESR, MiFID Level 3 Expert Group—Public Consultation on the Draft Workplan for Q4 2007–2008 (CESR/07-704) (2007) 2) and had prioritized the preparatory reviews which the Commission required CESR to undertake—see, eg, its advice on the report required of the Commission with respect to commodity and exotic derivatives (CESR/07-673).

[115] Commission, Request for Additional Information from CESR in relation to the review of MiFID (MARKT G3/SH/cr ARES (2009)).

[116] CESR's advice on the investment firm aspects of the MiFID I Review was contained in CESR/10-1040 (client categorization) and CESR/10-1254 (investor protection and intermediaries) (the relevant Commission mandates are included).

[117] 2010 MiFID I Review Consultation, n 112.

[118] 2010 MiFID I Review Consultation, n 112., 6.

access and proposed a new Commission-led regime governing access by third country firms. Also in common with the wider crisis-era reform agenda, the Consultation addressed supervision and enforcement, suggesting that the MiFID I Review address investment firm liability and the harmonization of sanctions. The October 2011 MiFID II Proposal,[119] which contained the proposed investment firm authorization and operating regime, followed the MiFID I Review Consultation in most respects.

IV.2.3.3 The MiFID II Negotiations

The Commission's view of the MiFID I Review was that the 2004 MiFID I did not require the 'wholesale repairs' required in other segments of the financial system, and that 'a comprehensive review of the underlying precepts and building blocks of MiFID [I]' was neither necessary nor appropriate; rather, an approach targeted at 'fixing visible flaws' was best.[120] Nonetheless, the 2011 MiFID II Proposal would change substantially over the course of the institutional negotiations and become encrusted with regulatory detail and calibrations. Negotiations proved slow, the pace being set by discussions on the highly contested trading venue aspects of the reform.

Council discussions spanned the Polish, Danish, Cypriot, and Irish presidencies (autumn 2011 to June 2013) and focused primarily on the trading venue requirements.[121] But the investment firm authorization and operating conditions also proved contentious. The Council struggled to reach a position on, for example, the exemptions required for energy market undertakings, consequent on the inclusion of emission allowances within MiFID II, the reach of MiFID II with respect to firms selling structured deposits, the new telephone call recording requirement, and the Commission's proposal that it adopt equivalence decisions in relation to third country firm access; by contrast, consensus was more easily achieved with respect to the proposed new firm governance requirements.[122] While the Council's final June 2013 General Approach[123] retained the main elements of the Commission's MiFID II Proposal with respect to investment firm regulation, it adopted a more flexible approach and also reduced the Commission's influence, notably by converting direct delegations to Commission administrative rule-making to indirect Commission delegations based on ESMA-proposed Binding Technical Standards (BTSs).

The European Parliament reached a negotiating position earlier in October 2012,[124] after the ECON Committee's September 2012 agreement on the over 1,300 amendments

---

[119] n 112.

[120] 2011 MiFID II/MiFIR Proposals Impact Assessment, n 28, 6.

[121] An April 2013 progress report from the Irish Presidency reported that the necessary minimum of a qualified majority vote (QMV) on MiFID II/MiFIR was dependent on agreement on the MiFIR provisions related to access to trading venues: Irish Presidency Progress Report on MiFID II/MiFIR, 15 April 2013 (Council Document 8322/13).

[122] The MiFID II/MiFIR negotiations are notable for the extensive numbers of Presidency Compromise drafts circulated over the negotiation period. The first Presidency Compromise was issued in June 2012 by the Danish Presidency, and was followed by repeated compromise drafts, which increased significantly in number over the final stages of the Irish Presidency. Summaries of the status of the negotiations from which the major themes can be drawn were issued at the end of the Cyprus Presidency (Cyprus Presidency Progress Report on MiFID II/MiFIR, 13 December 2012 (Council Document 16523/12)) and the Danish Presidency (Danish Presidency Progress Report on MiFID II/MiFIR, 20 June 2012 (Council Document 11536/12)).

[123] n 28.

[124] n 28.

proposed to its original March 2012 Ferber Report on the MiFID II Proposal.[125] The Parliament's position differed from the Council's in a number of respects, notably with respect to the more stringent conditions it imposed on firm governance (which included industry-specific restrictions on cross-directorships and discrete rules for non-executive directors), more stringent organizational requirements (notably with respect to product development), and the Parliament's support for the Commission making equivalence determinations with respect to third country firm access.

During the final Commission/Council/European Parliament trilogue negotiations, most attention focused on the retail-market-related and trading venue/trading-process-related reforms (Chapters IX, V, and VI). The core investment firm regime was not heavily contested, although some flashpoints emerged, notably with respect to scope and the treatment of insurance-related investment products, the governance requirements applicable to firms, and the treatment of third country actors. Trilogue negotiations were conducted under some time pressure, given the imminent 2014 closure of the Commission and European Parliament terms. Agreement was finally reached on the massive text in February 2014.

While it is less radical than other elements of the EU's crisis-era reform programme, the new regime for investment firm regulation is a creature of the financial crisis. The extension of the regulatory perimeter, the enhancement of conduct protections for professional investors, the focus on firm governance and incentives for prudent risk-taking, and the engagement with third country firm access can all be related to the crisis-era reform agenda. As one of the final elements of the crisis-era reform agenda, the 2014 MiFID II/MiFIR reforms to investment firm regulation have also been influenced by reforms from earlier in the crisis era, particularly with respect to governance, where the reforms can be related to the earlier rating agency,[126] 2012 EMIR, and 2013 CRD IV/CRR reforms. Overall, however, the core MiFID II legislative rulebook for investment firms discussed in this Chapter is not radically different from the earlier MiFID I rulebook, although the nature and scale of the administrative rulebook remains to be seen.

IV.3 Harmonization and ESMA

The 2014 MiFID II regime for investment firms can be regarded as a single rulebook governing the authorization and operation of investment firms. While the authorization and operating regime does not take the form of a regulation,[127] the legislative MiFID II regime is massive in scale and extensive delegations have been conferred on the Commission to adopt administrative rules, including BTSs.[128] The precursor 2004 MiFID I

---

[125] ECON, Draft Report on the MiFID II Proposal (A7-0306/2012) (Ferber Report).

[126] Particularly CRA Regulation I, which established the governance regime for rating agencies: Regulation (EU) No 1060/2009 [2009] OJ L302/1.

[127] Although some definitions are set out in the 2014 MiFIR.

[128] As the MiFID II negotiations began to enter the final stages, the European Securities and Markets Authority (ESMA) highlighted that the new regime would contain an ambitious set of new rules and extensive related delegations, and that, as the deadlines for technical advice to the Commission and for the BTS production process were likely to be challenging, it was committing significant resources to advance preparations: ESMA, Annual Report (2012) 43.

administrative rulebook (2006 Commission MiFID I Directive[129]) suggests that the MiFID II administrative rulebook will be of considerable depth and breadth, and will in practice remove Member State discretion to adopt rules in this field. ESMA has also been charged with adopting guidelines in a number of areas.

The *de facto* maximum harmonization deployed by MiFID II is underlined by the express concessions to the Member States to adopt rules additional to those set out in MiFID II with respect to asset protection (MiFID II Article 16) and to conduct regulation (in relation to conduct-of-business requirements, including conflict-of-interest rules) (MiFID II Article 24). Both concessions are designed to allow Member States to retain more restrictive rules, and reflect the negotiating stances of certain Member States, notably the UK.[130] In these two areas, Member States may, in exceptional cases, impose additional requirements on investment firms, but these requirements must be objectively justified and proportionate so as to address specific risks to investor protection or to market integrity which are of particular importance in the circumstances of the market structure of the Member State in question. Member States must notify the Commission, without undue delay, of any additional rules at least two months before they are due to come into force, and provide a justification (and any such rules must not restrict or otherwise affect the passporting rights of investment firms under MiFID II Articles 34 and 35). While the Commission cannot block the application of the rules, it is empowered to provide an opinion on the proportionality of and justification for the additional rules, which it is to communicate to the Member States and to make public (Article 16(11) and Article 24(12)).

ESMA's influence on the 2014 MiFID II regime will be significant. It has already thickened the MiFID I regime through a raft of soft law measures.[131] The scale of the delegations to administrative rule-making under MiFID II will allow it to shape the new regime through technical advice to the Commission and through the proposal of BTSs. Its influence will be all the greater given its significantly strengthened quasi-rule-making capacity, following its baptism of fire with the behemoth 2012 EMIR and 2011 AIFMD administrative rule-making processes and the related experience it has gained in regulatory design and the management of a complex matrix of stakeholders, both market and institutional.[132] It might be expected to adopt an ambitious approach, given the centrality of investment firm regulation to its core mission.

IV.4 Setting the Perimeter: Scope

IV.4.1 A Functional Approach

The 2014 MiFID II applies to investment firms, market operators, data-reporting services providers, and third country investment firms providing investment services and/or

---

[129] The Directive will be repealed when MiFID II comes into force. Its main features are noted throughout this Chapter where relevant.

[130] On the Art 24 concession with respect to conduct regulation see Ch IX sect 5.2.

[131] These include: a MiFID Q&A (ESMA/2012/382—updating the CESR Q&A); supervisory briefings (suitability (ESMA/2012/850) and appropriateness/execution-only (ESMA/2012/851)); and guidelines (remuneration (ESMA/2013/606), suitability (ESMA/2012/387), and compliance (ESMA/2012/388)).

[132] On ESMA and rule-making see Ch X sect 5.

performing investment activities through the establishment of a branch in the EU (Article 1(1)). It establishes requirements in relation to the authorization and operating conditions for investment firms; the provision of investment services or activities by third country firms through the establishment of a branch; the authorization and operation of regulated markets; the authorization and operation of data-reporting service providers; and supervision, co-operation, and enforcement by NCAs (Article 1(2)). For the purposes of this Chapter's discussion of investment firm authorization and regulation, it applies to investment firms and third country investment firm branches, and addresses the authorization and operating conditions for investment firms and NCA supervision, co-operation, and enforcement. MiFID II also, in many respects, acts as a form of regulatory perimeter control for EU securities and markets generally, as the pivotal MiFID II definitions of 'investment services' and 'financial instruments' often act to define the scope of other measures.

The scope of the 2014 MiFID II is organized on a functional basis. It applies to the provision of 'investment services and activities', and is not dependent on the organizational or legal status of the provider. The application of MiFID II does not depend on whether the provider is, for example, a credit institution, a multifunction investment firm, an asset manager, or a specialist investment firm. This approach dovetails with the structure of the EU investment services industry and has long been a feature of the EU regulation—since the 1993 ISD[133]—but it also dovetails with the crisis-era concern to deploy functional regulation which insures against regulatory gaps.

The 2014 MiFID II does not capture all investment services activity, however, and has been shaped by the silos which still, albeit to a lesser extent following the crisis-era reform programme, segment EU banking, insurance, and investment regulation. Its scope is a function of whether the actor provides 'investment services and activities' in relation to in-scope 'financial instruments'. The exclusion of insurance-related investment products from MiFID II (as under MiFID I) has led to the exclusion of insurance undertakings and insurance intermediaries, although they engage in sales and advisory activities in relation to insurance-related investment products. These activities are governed by the 2002 Insurance Mediation Directive I (IMD I) regime,[134] but, as discussed in Chapter IX on the retail markets, regulatory arbitrage risks had arisen as the MiFID I regime was significantly more detailed with respect to distribution regulation (as is MiFID II). In a compromise solution,[135] MiFID II amends IMD I to impose more intensive rules on the distribution of insurance-related investment products (Chapter IX section 5.3).

---

[133] Ferrarini, G, 'Towards a European Law of Investment Services and Institutions' (1994) 21 *CML Rev* 1283, 1284.

[134] Directive 2002/92/EC [2003] OJ L9/3.

[135] The European Parliament proposed the inclusion of insurance firms in relation to sales and advice with respect to insurance-related investments during the MiFID II negotiations: Parliament Negotiating Position, n 28, Art 3a. Some Council support was also noted: Danish Presidency Progress Report, n 122, 4. The Commission considered more generally whether MiFID II should include insurance undertakings and intermediaries, but rejected this option given the heavy compliance costs it would carry and the fragmentation it would bring to the regulation of the insurance sector, as much of the MiFID II rulebook would not be relevant for many insurance products. The reforms to the IMD I distribution regime with respect to insurance-related investment products made by MiFID II were the compromise solution (Chapter IX sect 5.3).

The 2014 MiFID II captures credit institutions, however, with respect to the regulation of their investment services-related and, particularly, conduct-orientated activities (which are not governed by the 2013 CRD IV/CRR prudential regime for credit institutions and investment firms).[136] Under MiFID II's functional model, credit institutions[137] are not subject to authorization under MiFID II, as they are authorized under the CRD IV/CRR regime,[138] but benefit from the MiFID II passport and are subject to MiFID II rules when they provide one or more MiFID II investment services and/or perform investment activities (Article 1(3)). A subset of MiFID II rules, broadly, the operational rules (particularly with respect to trading activities) and conduct rules, as well as the MiFID II supervisory and enforcement regime, apply to credit institutions; this tailored application of MiFID II is designed to fill the gaps in the CRD IV/CRR regime with respect to the regulation of market conduct.[139]

A distinct regime applies to credit institutions and investment firms (acting as intermediaries for the issuing credit institution) when they sell, or advise clients in relation to, structured deposits[140] issued by deposit-taking credit institutions. This extension of MiFID I reflects the current concern in EU retail market policy to address the regulatory arbitrage risks which arise from silo-based regulation. As deposit-based products, structured deposits were not included within the scope of MiFID I. This led to regulatory arbitrage risks in the retail sector, given the functional similarity of these products to other packaged investment products which were within the scope of MiFID I and subject to MiFID I's array of distribution and quality of advice rules. Under MiFID II, credit institutions and investment firms selling or advising clients in relation to structured deposits are subject to a tailored set of MiFID II rules designed to capture the specific risks to investors from such activity, particularly with respect to the quality of advice (Article 1(4)).[141]

---

[136] Conversely, the 2013 CRD IV/CRR regime applies to the prudential regulation of MiFID II investment firms.

[137] Defined as undertakings whose business is to receive deposits or other repayable funds from the public and to grant credits for their own account: 2013 CRR Art 4(1)(i).

[138] 2014 MiFID II rec 38 and Art 1(3).

[139] Given the extensive 2013 CRD IV/CRR authorization and prudential regime for credit institutions, credit institutions are only subject to: an attenuated firm governance regime (only the rules which apply to the governance arrangements which the management body must oversee under Art 9(3) apply); the investor compensation scheme requirement; and the operational and conduct regime (some exceptions apply with respect to tied agents of credit institutions). They also benefit from passporting rights, but are not subject to the MiFID II notification and related requirements, given the CRD IV passporting regime for credit institutions. MiFID II's supervisory and enforcement regime applies in relation to MiFID II activities.

[140] Defined as a deposit in accordance with the Deposit Guarantee Directive (Directive 2014/49/EU OJ L173/149) that is fully repayable at maturity on terms under which any interest or premium will be paid (or is at risk) according to a formula involving factors such as: (i) an index or combination of indices, excluding variable rate deposits whose return is directly linked to an interest rate index such as Euribor or Libor; (ii) a MiFID II financial instrument or combination of such financial instruments; (iii) a commodity or combination of commodities (or other physical or non-physical fungible assets); or (iv) a foreign exchange rate or combination of foreign exchange rates: 2014 MiFID II Art 4(1)(43). This definition is designed to exclude deposits which cannot be characterized as investment products.

[141] The MiFID II rules in relation to management body oversight of firm governance (Art 9(3)); investor compensation schemes (Art 14); organizational requirements (Art 16(2) (compliance), 16(3) (conflict of interest management), and 16(6) (record keeping)); relevant elements of the conduct regime (Arts 23–6, 28, and 29), and supervision and enforcement apply.

IV.4.2 Investment Services and Activities

The 2014 MiFID II applies to investment firms. As defined under MiFID II (Article 4(1)(1)), an investment firm is any legal person whose regular occupation or business is the provision of one or more 'investment services' to third parties and/or the performance of one or more 'investment activities' on a professional basis. Member States may choose to include investment firms which are not legal persons within the scope of MiFID II/MiFIR, but their inclusion is subject to their meeting certain eligibility conditions (MiFID II Article 4(1)(1)). In particular, their legal status must ensure a level of protection for third parties' interests equivalent to that afforded by legal persons, and they must be subject to equivalent prudential supervision which is appropriate to their legal form. Additional conditions, which are designed to protect client assets and funds on an insolvency or the death of a sole proprietor, apply to natural persons where they provide services involving the holding of third parties' funds or transferable securities. In such cases, they may be considered as investment firms only if, without prejudice to the other requirements of MiFID II/MiFIR and the 2013 CRD IV/CRR, the following conditions are complied with: the ownership rights of third parties in instruments and funds belonging to them are safeguarded, especially in the event of the insolvency of the firm or of its proprietors, seizure, set-off, or any other action by creditors of the firm or of its proprietors; the firm is subject to rules designed to monitor the firm's solvency and that of its proprietors; the annual accounts of the firm must be audited by one or more persons empowered under national law to audit accounts; and, where the firm has only one proprietor, that person is required to make provision for the protection of investors in the event of the firm's cessation of business following his death, his incapacity, or any other such event.

The determinative 'investment services and activities' are defined by reference to Section A of Annex I to MiFID II, and in relation to the instruments listed in Section C of Annex I ('financial instruments') (MiFID II Article 4(1)(2)) and Article 4(1)(15)).

Section A to Annex I sets out an extensive list of investment services and activities. It reflects MiFID I by including the reception and transmission of orders in relation to one or more financial instruments; the execution of orders on behalf of clients;[142] dealing on own account (defined as trading against proprietary capital resulting in the conclusion of transactions in one or more financial instruments (Article 4(1)(6)); portfolio management (defined as managing portfolios in accordance with mandates given by clients on a discretionary client-by-client basis where such portfolios include one or more financial instruments (Article 4(1)(8)); investment advice;[143] underwriting of financial instruments and/or placing of financial instruments on a firm commitment basis; placing of financial instruments without a firm commitment basis; and the operation of order execution trading venues.[144] The classic broking, dealing, underwriting, asset management, and advice functions associated with investment firms all accordingly come within the scope of MiFID II.

---

[142] A client is defined as any natural or legal person to whom an investment firm provides investment or ancillary services: Art 4(1)(9).

[143] See further Ch IX sect 5.2 on the definition of investment advice.

[144] See further Ch V on trading venues.

As under MiFID I, the 2014 MiFID II contains a second tier of ancillary services which are listed in Section B of Annex I. Although authorization may be granted to investment firms which, in addition to Section A activities, cover one or more of these ancillary activities, authorization may not be granted to investment firms which provide only ancillary services (Article 6(1)).[145]

MiFID II has, however, introduced refinements. The main revision relates to the extent of 'execution of orders' activity. Some confusion had arisen under MiFID I as to whether the sale by firms of proprietary products issued by them came within the scope of MiFID I where investment advice was not provided.[146] The scale of issuance by financial institutions,[147] as well as major mis-selling scandals related to mis-sales of proprietary bank securities, notably in Spain,[148] exacerbated concern that such sales did not come within MiFID I and were not subject to the MiFID I conduct-of-business regime. In order to eliminate uncertainty and strengthen investor protection in primary market sales of products (MiFID II recital 45), the definition of order execution has accordingly been extended from acting to conclude agreements to buy or sell one or more financial instruments on behalf of clients, to include the conclusion of agreements to sell financial instruments issued by a credit institution or an investment firm at the moment of their issuance (MiFID II Article 4(1)(5)). The definition of custody services, an ancillary service under Annex I, Section B, has also been nuanced to refer to the new regime governing central securities depositaries (noted in Chapter V Section 13).

IV.4.3 Financial Instruments

The 'financial instruments' which govern the scope of the 2014 MiFID II (and many other measures) are set out in MiFID II Annex I, Section C. This reflects MiFID I by covering an extensive range of broadly defined securities and financial derivatives.[149] The list includes (numbering follows Section C): (1) transferable securities;[150] (2) money-market

---

[145] These non-core activities are: (i) safekeeping and administration of financial instruments for the account of clients, including custodianship and related services such as cash/collateral management and excluding the maintenance of securities accounts (which are governed by the new regime for central securities depositaries; (ii) granting credits or loans to an investor to allow that investor to carry out a transaction in one or more financial instruments, where the firm granting the loan is involved in the transaction (margin-trading services); (iii) advice to undertakings on capital structure, industrial strategy, and related matters, and advice and services relating to mergers and the purchase of undertakings; (iv) foreign-exchange services where these are connected to the provision of investment services; (v) investment research and financial analysis or other forms of general recommendation relating to transactions in financial instruments; (vi) services relating to underwriting; and (vii) investment services and activities (as well as ancillary services) relating to the underlying of commodity derivatives (and derivatives covered by Section C (10)—see ahead).

[146] The Commission noted the concern of NCAs as to whether MiFID I applied to the issuance and sale by credit institutions and investment firms of proprietary products: n 112, 53.

[147] Some 40 per cent of equity-offering issuance in 2009 was by financial services firms: 2011 Europe Economics Report, n 101, xxvii.

[148] See Ch IX sect 2.3.

[149] The European Court of Justice confirmed that interest rate swaps were within the scope of MiFID I: Case C-604/11 *Genil 48 SL, Comercial Hostelera de Grandes Vinos SL v Bankinter SA, Banca Bilbao Vizcaya Argentaria* SA, 30 May 2013 (not yet reported).

[150] Defined in Art 4(1)(44) as those classes of securities which are negotiable on the capital markets, with the exception of instruments of payment. Three examples are given by the Art: (a) shares in companies and other securities equivalent to shares in companies, partnerships or other entities, and depositary receipts in

instruments,[151] (3) units in collective investment undertakings, (4) derivatives in the form of options, futures, swaps, forward rate agreements and any other derivative contracts relating to securities, currencies, interest rates or yields, emission allowances or other derivative instruments, financial indices or financial measures which may be settled physically or in cash; (8) credit derivatives; (9) financial contracts for differences; and (10) cash-settled 'exotic' derivatives relating to a range of underlyings, including climatic variables, freight rates, or inflation rates (or other official economic statistics) which must be settled in cash or which may be settled in cash at the option of one or more of the parties (other than by reason of default or other termination event), as well as any other derivatives not mentioned in Section C which have the characteristics of other financial derivatives, having regard to whether, *inter alia*, they are traded on a regulated trading venue.

In addition to these financial derivatives of various types, MiFID II (reflecting MiFID I[152]) also covers commodity derivatives (Section C provisions (5)–(7)).[153] But only commodity derivatives which are akin to financial derivative instruments are designed to fall within MiFID II. The related definitions are therefore based on qualifications designed to distinguish between commodity derivatives for investment purposes and those for commercial purposes.[154] MiFID II contains a new delegation for the Commission to adopt

---

respect of shares; (b) bonds and other forms of securitized debt, including depositary receipts in respect of such securities; and (c) any other securities giving the right to acquire or sell any such transferable securities or giving rise to a cash settlement determined by reference to transferable securities, currencies, interest rates or yields, commodities or other indices or measures. Depositary receipts are defined as securities which are negotiable on the capital market and which represent ownership of the securities of a non-domiciled issuer while being able to be admitted to trading on a regulated market and traded independently of the securities of the non-domiciled issuer: Art 4(1)(45).

[151] Defined as those classes of instruments which are normally dealt in on the money market, such as treasury bills, certificates of deposit, and commercial paper, but excluding instruments of payment: 2014 MiFID II Art 4(1)(17).

[152] The inclusion of commodity derivatives dates to the initial 2000 ISD Communication (n 63), which proposed that the ISD's approach to 'financial instruments' be revised to include instruments whose current status was unclear and to include commodity derivatives. In its MiFID I Proposal, the Commission argued that the exclusion of commodity derivatives under the ISD regime prevented investment firms from benefiting from the passport with respect to commodity-dealing business and disrupted the application of orderly market and market abuse prevention rules, and that the absence of a single-market framework was anachronistic given in particular the liberalization of underlying commodity and energy markets: 2002 MiFID I Proposal, n 73, 71.

[153] Provision (5) covers cash commodity derivatives or options, futures, swaps, forwards, and any other derivative contracts relating to commodities that must be settled in cash or may be settled in cash at the option of one of the parties (the option is designed to ensure that industry-wide, netting master agreements to manage credit risks can be used). Provision (6) covers commodity derivatives which can be physically settled, as long as they are traded on a MiFID II/MiFIR trading venue, except for certain wholesale energy products traded on an 'organized trading facility' (a form of MiFID II/MiFIR trading venue) that must be physically settled. Provision (7) covers a residual category of commodity derivatives which may be physically settled and which are not covered by (6) and which are not for commercial purposes, but which have the characteristics of other derivative financial instruments. The 'must be physically settled' requirement was a source of some concern over the negotiations, given the danger that this requirement could be deployed to avoid MiFID II/ MiFIR and generate arbitrage risks. Accordingly, the Commission delegation to adopt clarifying administrative rules (Art 4(1)(2)) specifies that the nature of the physical settlement requirement be specified.

[154] See Herbst, J, 'Revision of the Investment Services Directive' (2003) 11 *JFRC* 211, 214. This approach reflects the concern during the MiFID I negotiations to limit the scope of MiFID I to instruments which gave rise to regulatory issues comparable to traditional financial instruments: 2002 MiFID I Proposal, n 73, 72.

administrative rules specifying the commodity derivative contracts included under (6) and (7) and which have the characteristics of other financial derivatives, and under (10).[155]

Difficulties have, however, emerged with the derivatives regime, related to the interaction between the 2012 EMIR and MiFID II (and MiFID I before MiFID II is applied)—the EMIR definition of a derivative (which is pivotal, as EMIR is the major measure governing the OTC derivatives market in particular) is based on the MiFID I/MiFID II regime (reflecting the extent to which MiFID I originally and now MiFID II provides perimeter control for other key measures). In February 2014, prior to the coming into force of the MiFID II regime, ESMA warned the Commission that inconsistencies in how MiFID I Annex C (4)–(10) was implemented across the Member States meant that there was no convergent definition of a derivative or derivative contract, and that the inconsistencies were creating serious difficulties with respect to the application of EMIR;[156] while some of the inconsistencies would be addressed by MiFID II, not all (particularly with respect to foreign exchange derivatives and physically settled commodity forwards) would be.[157] It accordingly called on the Commission, as a matter of urgency, to adopt administrative rules clarifying the nature of derivative contracts under MiFID I.[158]

MiFID II has further extended the regulatory perimeter over financial instruments by including emission allowances created under the EU Emission Trading Scheme (Section C provision (11)).[159] The classification of emission allowances as MiFID II financial instruments has potentially major implications for the commercial actors in the EU's carbon market, which include large and sophisticated industrial organizations, but also small buyers. Following extensive and specialist consultations, emission allowances were included within MiFID II given concerns that the secondary trading of spot emission allowances[160] was largely unregulated and that leaving the regulation of this emerging market to potentially diverging national regimes would be detrimental to the market's development.[161] The effect of the inclusion of emission allowances is that the MiFID II/MiFIR rulebook applies to all trading venues and intermediaries operating in the secondary spot trading market for emission allowances.

---

[155] Art 4(1)(2). The new delegation is designed in part to take account of the 2012 EMIR (n 36) and the impact of the new clearing and margin requirements as well as particular concerns related to commodity derivatives (n 1534).

[156] ESMA Letter 2014/184, 14 February 2014.

[157] ESMA also warned of the time delay given the immediacy of the problem and the delay in the application of the MiFID I regime until 2017.

[158] Particularly with respect to currency derivatives and the related 'frontier between spot and forward contracts' in the foreign exchange markets, and the definition of commodity forwards that can be physically settled. As noted in Ch X n 402, ESMA initially sought to adopt remedial guidance in the form of an opinion, but faced resistance from the Commission which regarded definitional matters as its prerogative. In response, the Commission committed to 'urgently assess' the options for action, and highlighted that it would likely call on ESMA for technical advice (Letter, Jonathan Faull, Markt/G3/PO/or(2014) s.510569).

[159] Directive 2003/87/EC [2003] OJ L275/32 establishes the scheme.

[160] In a 'spot' trade, the asset is delivered immediately (by comparison with derivative trades); the term is associated with the underlying commodity/asset, in this case the emission allowance (rather than derivatives based on such allowances).

[161] 2010 MiFID I Review Consultation, n 112, 43. The Commission's Impact Assessment highlighted that the derivatives market for emissions was regulated (under MiFID I, which covered such derivatives under MiFID I Annex I, section C (10)), that the regulatory regime for the primary market in spot emission allowances was under development, but that secondary spot trading was not regulated, leaving a significant gap in the regulatory treatment of emission allowances: n 28, 14.

The inclusion of a wide range of financial instruments demands parallel calibration of the regulatory regime to reflect the particular risks of these instruments, and also to avoid the disproportionate imposition of regulation on, in particular, non-financial counterparties who use MiFID II instruments, particularly derivatives and commodity derivatives, for hedging in their commercial activities. As is the case under the 2012 EMIR with respect to the treatment of non-financial counterparties who come within its provisions, MiFID II accordingly contains a series of calibrations designed to protect non-financial counterparties from the full rigours of the regulatory regime where their activities are limited to hedging in support of commercial activities. Typically, transactions in derivatives are excluded from regulation or subject to a calibrated regime where the transactions are 'objectively measurable as reducing risks directly related' to commercial activities and/or treasury financing activity.[162]

IV.5 Calibration and Differentiation

IV.5.1 Exemptions

A series of exemptions apply under the 2014 MiFID II. They respond to a range of different drivers, ranging from the effects of the long-standing silo structure of EU financial regulation, to the exemption of actors whose MiFID II activities are incidental and of a small scale and who are accordingly exempted from the reach of MiFID II's often complex and costly rules, to the need to calibrate the regime as it expands to encompass a wider array of financial instruments in order to avoid the imposition of disproportionate regulatory burdens, particularly on non-financial counterparties—a concern to protect legitimate hedging and risk-management techniques from excessive regulation can be discerned across the MiFID II exemption regime, reflecting similar objectives under the 2012 EMIR. Nonetheless, MiFID II has also led to a general tightening of the earlier MiFID I exemption regime, reflecting the single rulebook objective as well as the crisis-era concern to close regulatory loopholes.

MiFID II does not apply to undertakings regulated under discrete EU regulatory regimes. Insurance undertakings or undertakings carrying on reinsurance and retrocession activities governed by the EU insurance regime are excluded from the scope of MiFID II (Article 2(1)(a)), as are collective investment undertakings and pension funds—whether co-ordinated at EU level or not—and the depositaries and managers of such undertakings (Article 2(1)(i)).[163] The expanding reach of crisis-era capital markets regulation is reflected in the exclusion of central securities depositaries, which are being made subject to a new regime (Article 2(1)(o)). As is the case across EU securities and markets regulation, the members of the European System of Central Banks and other national bodies performing similar functions in the EU; other public bodies charged with or intervening in the management of public debt in the EU; and international financial institutions, established by two or more Member

---

[162] This is the case with respect to, eg, the position management regime (Ch VI sect 2.5) and the exemption regime (sect 5.1).

[163] Where UCITS managers and the managers within the scope of the AIFMD engage in discretionary asset management, the MiFID II regime applies.

States, which have the purpose of mobilizing funding and providing financial assistance to the benefit of their members that are experiencing or threatened by severe financial difficulties are also excluded (Article 2(1)(h)).[164]

A major group of exclusions apply to firms providing investment services in particular circumstances, notably where the services are not provided to a third party. Persons which provide investment services exclusively for their parent undertakings, for their subsidiaries, or for other subsidiaries of their parent are excluded under Article 2(1)(b), as are persons that provide investment services consisting exclusively in the administration of employee-participation schemes (Article 2(1)(f)). Article 2(1)(c) excludes persons providing an investment service where that service is provided in an incidental manner in the course of a professional activity, and where that activity is regulated by legal or regulatory provisions or a code of ethics governing the profession which do not exclude the provision of that service.[165] Article 2(1)(k) excludes another category of incidental advice by excluding persons who provide investment advice in the course of providing another professional activity not covered by MiFID II, as long as the advice is not specifically remunerated.

Two exclusions relate to Member State-specific situations. Under Article 2(1)(1), associations set up by Danish and Finnish pension funds with the sole aim of managing the assets of the pension funds which are members of such associations are excluded, as are, under Article 2(1)(m), Italian *agenti di cambio*, regulated under the relevant Italian laws.

As discussed further in Chapter VI, brokerage and own-account dealing in financial instruments are now subject to an intensive regulatory regime of wide scope. In principle, proprietary dealing in financial instruments comes within MiFID II. MiFID II could therefore catch within its scope a vast array of non-financial actors who engage in dealing activities, whether for commercial hedging purposes or otherwise, including persons who trade solely to administer their own assets and on a small scale, and who do not pose the risks which MiFID II seeks to mitigate. A discrete but limited exemption accordingly applies to proprietary dealing activities to avoid disproportionate application of the regime (Article 2(1)(d)). The exemption reflects the earlier MiFID I exemption, but has become more restrictive given the crisis-era focus on prudent risk management and on dampening perceived excessive speculation and financial market intensity, as well as the Council's concern that all MiFID II exemptions be clear and narrowly framed and avoid unintended consequences and loopholes.[166] Persons who deal on own account in financial instruments (other than commodity derivatives or emission allowances or derivatives thereof) and who do not provide any other investment advice and/or perform any other investment activities in financial instruments (other than commodity derivatives or emission allowances or related derivatives) are exempted from MiFID II. The exemption does not apply, however,

---

[164] Similarly, the rights conferred by MiFID II do not extend to the provision of services as counterparty in transactions carried out by public bodies dealing with public debt or by members of the ESCB performing their tasks as provided for by the Treaty and the Statute of the ECB and ESCB, or performing equivalent functions under national provisions: Art 2(2).

[165] A delegation has been conferred on the Commission to adopt administrative rules governing when an activity is provided in an incidental manner.

[166] The exemptions for dealers in financial instruments and in commodity derivatives/emission allowances became more restricted over the Council negotiations, which saw significant Member State concern as to the market efficiency and investor protection risks were the exemptions to allow trading activity to leak outside the regulated sphere.

where the person in question is a market-maker;[167] is a member of or participant in a regulated market or multilateral trading facility (MTF) or has 'direct electronic access' to a trading venue;[168] applies a high frequency algorithmic trading technique,[169] or deals on own account by executing client orders.[170] The exemption[171] is accordingly removed where the dealer's activities may impact on market stability, liquidity, and efficiency, and where investor protection risks (including conflict-of-interest risks) arise where the dealer executes a client order against its proprietary trading book.[172]

A similar exemption applies to dealers in commodity derivatives, emission allowances, and related derivatives (Article 2(1)(j)), albeit that this exemption is primarily designed to avoid pulling the non-financial counterparties who use these derivatives for commercial purposes into the regulatory net, given that these activities should not generate systemic risks, and as the commercial users and producers of commodities addressed by the exemption do not interact with investors. Unlike the Article 2(1)(d) exemption, however, it is available for market-makers, reflecting the particular dynamics of the market in these instruments. Nonetheless, while reflecting the precursor MiFID I exemption for dealing in commodity derivatives, the exemption has become more restrictive.[173] The MiFID II revisions are designed to restrict the commercial firms which benefit from this exemption from engaging in ancillary investment services relating to commodity derivatives[174] while supporting their ability to provide hedging tools for clients.[175] Persons who deal on own account in commodity derivatives, emission allowances, and related derivatives (including market-makers, but excluding persons who deal on own account by executing client orders), or persons who provide investment services (other than dealing on own account) in these instruments to the customers or suppliers of their main business, are exempted from MiFID II. The exemption requires that for each of these two cases, individually and on

---

[167] Defined as a person who holds himself out on the financial markets on a continuous basis as being willing to deal on own account by buying and selling financial instruments against his proprietary capital at prices defined by him: Art 4(1)(7). See further Ch VI sect 2.4.

[168] On the different forms of 2014 MiFID II/MiFIR trading venue (including MTFs) see Ch V. Direct electronic access relates to high frequency trading practices (see Ch VI sect 2.3).

[169] On the MiFID II regime governing algorithmic trading and high frequency algorithmic trading see Ch VI sect 2.3.

[170] Including order execution in the form of 'matched principal trades' (where different client orders are matched).

[171] Art 2(1)(d) clarifies that persons who qualify for exemption as insurance undertakings and as CISs, and for the exemption relating to dealing in commodity derivatives and emission allowances, are not required to meet these conditions.

[172] As discussed in Ch V, where orders are executed against the dealer's proprietary trading book in a systematic manner and on a large scale, the 2014 MiFID II/MiFIR regime for 'systematic internalizers' applies.

[173] Reflecting earlier CESR/CEBS advice to this effect: CESR/CEBS, Technical Advice on the Review of Commodities Business (2008) (CESR/08-752). The additional MiFID I (Art 2(1)(k)) exemption for persons whose main business consists of dealing on own account in commodities and/or commodity derivatives has been removed, reflecting the change of regulatory approach towards commodity and commodity derivatives markets (see further Ch VI sect 2.5 on the commodity markets).

[174] Council discussions in particular focused on how to restrict these exemptions to avoid misuse: Danish Presidency Progress Report, n 122, 3.

[175] Particular difficulties emerged in the oil market, where concerns arose that financially unsophisticated clients were being provided with advice on complex derivatives without MiFID I protections: 2010 MiFID I Review Consultation, n 112, 40. The Commission's Impact Assessment noted that it was necessary to restrict this exemption, as the size of exempted commodity firms had increased and the assumption that their activities had limited effect on the market or on levels of systemic risk might not be as valid as before: n 28, 14.

aggregate basis, the exempted activity is ancillary to the exempted person's main business when considered on a group basis, and that the main business is not the provision of investment services or banking services or acting as a market-maker in relation to commodity derivatives, and that the exempted person does not apply a high frequency algorithmic trading technique. Exempted persons must also notify the relevant NCA annually of their use of the exemption and (on request) report to the NCA the basis on which they consider the relevant activities ancillary to their main business. An extensive delegation for the adoption of RTSs, employing quantitative criteria and designed to ensure the exemption is restricted, requires that RTSs be adopted governing the criteria for establishing when an activity is to be considered as ancillary to the main business on a group level.[176] Similarly, the inclusion of emission allowances has required the addition of an exemption designed to exempt participants in the EU's energy markets, including 'transmission system operators' operating under the EU's energy market regime (Article 2(1)(n)).[177] The exemptions are designed to apply cumulatively, in that a person exempted to deal in commodity derivatives (Article 2(1)(j)) can also be exempted to engage in related commercial treasury risk-management activities in order to manage risk, such as dealing in exchange rate derivatives (Article 2(1)(d)).[178] The derivatives-related exemptions are designed to work in parallel with the 2012 EMIR regime.[179]

A series of optional exemptions (which may be used by the Member States) for identified persons are provided in Article 3, as long as the activities of those exempted persons are authorized and regulated at national level.

The exemptions are (broadly) designed to exempt investment firms which, for the most part, do not operate cross-border, pose little or no systemic risk, and do not hold investor assets, as long as broadly equivalent requirements apply at national level; these firms do not benefit from the MiFID II passport. They also address the particular features of the commodity derivatives and emission allowances market.

Under Article 3(1) Member States may choose not to apply MiFID II to persons for which they are the home Member State and which are not allowed to hold client funds or securities, can only receive and transmit client orders in relation to transferable securities

---

[176] The delegation became more detailed over the negotiations, with the Council in particular concerned that the RTS delegation be more detailed with respect to capturing the nature of the ancillary business permitted: Danish Presidency Progress Report, n 122, 3. With an eye to ensuring consistency across the new regulatory scheme for trading in derivatives, the delegation underlines that transactions in commodity derivatives and emission allowances entered into to fulfil liquidity obligations mandated by law are excluded from the consideration of when activities are 'ancillary' to the main business of the group. See further Ch VI on the regulation of derivatives trading.

[177] These operators are subject to discrete regulation under the energy market regime. Similarly, a specific exemption governs trading in the greenhouse gas emission allowances market under Art 2(1)(e) (which applies to operators with compliance obligations under the related EU regime), as long as the persons in question do not execute client orders, do not provide any investment services or perform investment activities other than dealing on own account, and do not apply a high frequency algorithmic trading technique.

[178] As clarified by rec 22. The rec also underlines that those persons who do not qualify for the Art 2(1)(d) exemption but may benefit from Art 2(1)(j) come within MiFID II in relation to activities outside the scope of the Art 2(1)(j) exemption.

[179] The treatment of intragroup transactions and of transactions in derivatives which are 'objectively measurable as reducing risks directly related to the commercial activity or treasury financing activity' of the exempted person (both of which are relevant to the Art 2(1)(j) exemption), eg, is to be considered in a manner consistent with the 2012 EMIR (rec 21).

and collective investment scheme (CIS) units and/or provide related investment advice, and are allowed to transmit such orders to identified firms (Article 3(1)(a)–(c)).[180]

In an addition to MiFID I that reflects the wider scope of the new regime with respect to derivatives activities, an optional exemption is also available[181] for persons providing investment services exclusively in commodities, emission allowances, and/or related derivatives, for the sole purpose of hedging their clients' commercial risks,[182] where those clients are exclusively local electricity undertakings and natural gas undertakings (Article 3(1)(d)).[183] A similar optional exemption is available in relation to the EU's greenhouse gas emission allowances trading regime (Article 3(1)(e)).

By contrast with the precursor MiFID I exemption, which simply required that exempted persons be regulated, such exempted persons must be subject to 'analogous' authorization, regulatory, and supervisory requirements at national level[184] and with respect to the MiFID II authorization requirements, certain of the organizational/prudential requirements,[185] and the investor protection/quality of advice regime (Article 3(2)).[186] Exempted persons must also be covered by an investor compensation scheme recognized under the 1997 Investor Compensation Schemes Directive[187] or, reflecting some Member State concern that this requirement was disproportionate,[188] by professional indemnity insurance which, taking into account the size, risk profile, and legal nature of the person, provides equivalent cover.[189] The tightening of the original Article 3 regime is designed to ensure a minimum

---

[180] Investment firms, credit institutions, branches of investment firms or credit institutions authorized in a third country and subject to rules equivalent to the MiFID II regime and the EU banking regime, collective investment schemes (CISs) authorized under the law of a Member State to market units to the public and the managers of such undertakings, and investment companies with fixed capital.

[181] The exemption was originally mandatory and placed in Art 2, but during the trilogue negotiations it became optional for the Member States and subject to an obligation to apply analogous rules.

[182] The exemption is designed to respond to the bundling and outsourcing by energy undertakings of trading activities for hedging and commercial risks to non-consolidated subsidiaries in the form of joint ventures: 2014 MiFID II rec 29.

[183] Each as defined by the rules of the EU's energy market regime. These clients must also jointly hold 100 per cent of the capital or voting rights of the exempted person, exercise joint control, and qualify for the Art 2(1)(j) exemption should they carry out these investment services themselves. Earlier drafts of MiFID II (in which the exemption was mandatory for Member States under Art 2) imposed a series of organizational requirements (relating to the establishment of a supervisory committee to oversee trading activity; a requirement for trading rules and a risk management handbook; and a requirement for a profit and loss transfer agreement between the exempted person and the clients), but this model was changed in favour of the optional Art 3 approach, which requires, however, that analogous requirements to MiFID II apply.

[184] The reliance on 'analogous' rather than the more usual 'equivalence' requirement reflects the concern to ensure that the regime remained flexible and that partial market exit did not occur, which risk had been identified by the 2011 Europe Economics Report: n 100, xvii.

[185] With respect to conflict-of-interest management, record-keeping, and call recording.

[186] Where a Member State exercises an optional exemption under Art 3, it must inform the Commission and ESMA, ensure it complies with Art 3, and communicate to ESMA the provisions of national law which are analogous to MiFID II.

[187] Directive 97/9/EC [1997] OJ L84/22. See Ch IX sect 8.

[188] Danish Presidency Progress Report, n 122, 4.

[189] The European Parliament had placed conditions on when indemnity insurance could substitute for compensation scheme membership (Negotiating Position, n 28, Art 3(1b)) but this approach was not followed. Member States may derogate from this requirement where the exempted persons provide order reception and transmission/advice services in relation to CIS units and act as an intermediary for a UCITS management company, and are jointly and severally liable with the management company for any damage incurred by the client.

suite of standards applies to all investment firms on a pan-EU basis. But it also reflects the wider lack of tolerance for allowing discrete market segments to fall outside the EU rulebook,[190] as well as the concern to ensure derivatives transactions are appropriately regulated, even where optional calibrations are appropriate at Member State level, given the particular commercial context.[191]

IV.5.2 Client Classification

As discussed further in Chapter IX on the retail markets, MiFID I relied on a client classification scheme to calibrate the application of the conduct-of-business regime; the application of authorization and operational/prudential rules, however, was not sensitive to client type. This form of regulatory segmentation is designed to ensure that regulation, and particularly regulation designed to protect unsophisticated investors, is appropriately tailored. The MiFID I classification regime was based on three categories of client: eligible counterparties (in effect, financial institutions); professional clients; and retail clients. The MiFID I conduct-of-business regime was dis-applied from order execution (but not other investment services) between eligible counterparties.[192] The conduct-of-business regime was applied to services provided to professional investors, but many of the detailed administrative rules under the 2006 MiFID I Directive were dis-applied.[193] Services provided to retail clients were subject to the full range of conduct-of-business requirements, many of which, particularly with respect to disclosure, the suitability assessment, and best execution, were expressly targeted to retail clients only. Client categorization procedures applied, as did requirements governing the movement of clients between classes.

Although the effectiveness of the classification system came under scrutiny at an early stage of the MiFID I Review,[194] CESR's advice to the Commission on the client classification regime underlined that the new classification system had worked well, that the ability of clients to move 'up' to higher levels of protection provided an important safety valve, and that any revisions to the regime should be limited and carefully designed, given the substantial costs which firms had incurred in implementing the classification regime.[195] The reforms have accordingly not disturbed the MiFID I classification system materially.[196] They reflect two developments. The MiFID I Review exposed the challenges which effective segmentation generates, and the pressure which can be placed on proxies for

---

[190] The Commission argued that disparity between Member States rules 'was no longer tenable in view of the lessons of the financial crisis, the complexity of financial markets and products and the need for investors to be able to rely on similar levels of protection irrespective of the location or the nature of the service provider': 2011 MiFID II Proposal, n 28, 6.

[191] The new regime is designed in particular to ensure that entities covered by Art 3(1)(d) are subject to an analogous authorization process (particularly with respect to the assessment of shareholders) and ongoing supervision, particularly with respect to conduct of business.

[192] 2004 MiFID I Art 24.

[193] In particular, the extensive disclosures required to be provided to retail clients were dis-applied, while firms could assume, for the purposes of the investment advice/discretionary asset management suitability assessment, that the client had the necessary level of experience and knowledge.

[194] n 116.

[195] n 116.

[196] The Commission described the classification system as providing an adequate and satisfactory degree of flexibility: 2010 MiFID I Review Consultation, n 112, 61.

investor/client vulnerability. In particular, list-based classification regimes of the MiFID I type (the professional client category was based on a list of qualifying client types) run the risk of being over- and under-inclusive, of becoming obsolete, and of requiring continual revision in light of market practice. Over the financial crisis, a range of non-retail clients—chief among them municipal and local public authorities—in relation to which there was some uncertainty as to their appropriate classification, sustained heavy losses in relation to sales and advice related to complex financial instruments[197] and came to be regarded as requiring additional protections.[198] More generally, and reflecting the wider change to the previously somewhat laissez-faire approach to the wholesale markets and the related scepticism as to the resilience of market-based monitoring, a consensus emerged over the MiFID I Review that core conduct obligations (including that investment firms act honestly, fairly, and professionally, that disclosures be comprehensive and fair, clear and not misleading, and that independent advice be subject to controls to minimize conflict-of-interest risks) should apply to all classes of client. Accordingly, under the new classification regime, regulatory oversight has been further extended over the professional markets.

Under the 2014 MiFID II, with respect to eligible counterparties,[199] much of the conduct regime remains dis-applied from transactions between these actors—although eligible counterparties may request (generally or on a trade-by-trade basis) treatment as clients whose business is subject to the full range of conduct rules (Article 30(2))—but the regime has been tightened. Under Article 30(1), investment firms authorized to execute orders on behalf of clients and/or to deal on own account and/or to receive and transmit orders, may bring about or enter into transactions with eligible counterparties without being obliged to comply with: the Article 24 requirements (general conduct principles) (but with the exception of the Article 24(3) information requirements); the Article 25 (suitability) requirements (but with the exception of the rules governing independent advice); and the Article 27 (best execution) and Article 28(1) (order handling) requirements. In their relationships with eligible counterparties, investment firms must also act honestly, fairly, and professionally and communicate in a way which is fair, clear, and not misleading, taking into account the nature of the eligible counterparty and of its business.

Professional clients are defined under MiFID II Annex II as clients who possess the experience, knowledge, and expertise to make their own investment decisions and to properly assess the risks they incur. Professional clients are further segmented into two categories: those considered to be professional,[200] and those who are classed as

---

[197] 2010 PWC Report, n 100, 374–9.

[198] 2010 MiFID I Review Consultation, n 112, 61–2.

[199] Defined as investment firms, credit institutions, insurance companies, UCITSs and their management companies, pension funds and their management companies, other financial institutions authorized or regulated under EU law or national law, national governments, and their corresponding offices (including public offices that deal with public debt at national level), central banks, and supranational organizations: Art 30(2). Member States may also recognize as eligible counterparties undertakings meeting pre-determined and proportionate requirements, including quantitative thresholds, and third country entities equivalent to these and Art 30(2) entities (Art 30(3)). A new delegation, replacing the MiFID I delegation, empowers the Commission to adopt administrative rules amplifying the Art 30 regime.

[200] This category includes: entities required to be authorized or regulated in the financial markets (credit institutions; investment firms; other authorized or regulated financial institutions; insurance companies; CISs and their management companies; pension funds and their management companies; commodity and commodity derivatives dealers; and other institutional investors); large undertakings (meeting two of three

non-professional but who may be treated as professional on request. A filtering process applies to non-professional clients who may be treated as professional; the default status for these clients is treatment as retail clients (as discussed further in this section). Conversely, clients considered to be professional can, however, request a higher, non-professional level of protection.[201] The calibration of conduct regulation to professional clients does not apply at the legislative level: the MiFID II conduct-of-business regime applies to all professional clients. But the new administrative rulebook is likely to contain rules which are expressly orientated to retail clients and which do not apply to professional clients.[202]

The non-exhaustive list of non-professional (in effect, retail) clients designed to be subject to the most extensive conduct regulation has been extended from the MiFID I class of public sector bodies, smaller companies, and private individual investors to include local public authorities and municipalities, reflecting the losses which this sector sustained over the financial crisis.[203] Where these clients seek professional treatment, the investment firm is placed under a series of procedural obligations which are designed to make any waiver of professional treatment conditional on the firm's 'adequate assessment of the expertise, experience, and knowledge of the client', this assessment giving the firm a 'reasonable assurance' that, in light of the transactions or services envisaged, the client is capable of making his own investment decisions and of understanding the risks involved.[204] In no case can these clients be presumed to possess market knowledge and experience comparable to that of clients considered to be professional. Professional treatment is also conditional on the person meeting asset and experience requirements.[205] While this re-classification regime for non-professional clients reflects the MiFID I procedure, MiFID II additionally provides that Member States may adopt specific criteria for assessment of the expertise and knowledge of municipalities and local public authorities which request professional treatment.

---

requirements: total balance sheet of €20 million; net turnover of €40 million; and own funds of €20 million); national and regional governments, including public bodies that manage public debt at a national or regional level, central banks, and international and supranational organizations such as the World Bank, the IMF, the ECB, the EIB, and similar institutions; and other institutional investors whose main activity is to invest in financial instruments, including entities dedicated to the securitization of assets or other financing transactions.

[201] Requests to be treated as non-professional are subject to the Annex II, sect I(4) procedure, which provides, *inter alia*, that it is the responsibility of a client which is deemed to be professional to ask for a higher level of protection where it deems it is unable to properly assess or manage the risks involved, and requires that a written agreement be entered into between the professional client and the firm which specifies the range of transactions and services to which the new classification applies.

[202] The 2006 Commission MiFID I Directive applied more intensive rules to, *inter alia*, investment firm disclosures in the retail market, and imposed a retail price benchmark for best execution.

[203] Annex II sect II (1).

[204] Annex II sect II(1)–(2).

[205] The assessment includes the requirement that two of three conditions be met: the client has carried out transactions, in a significant size, on the relevant market at an average frequency of ten per quarter over the previous four quarters; the client's financial instrument portfolio (including cash deposits and financial instruments) exceeds €500,000; and the client works or has worked in the financial sector for at least one year in a professional position, which requires knowledge of the transactions or services envisaged.

IV.6 The Authorization Process

IV.6.1 Jurisdiction to Authorize and the Home Member State

The authorization process anchors the 2014 MiFID II regime to the home Member State. Although the European Financial System of Supervision (ESFS) (Chapter XI) provides a significantly strengthened institutional framework within which cross-border supervision can be co-ordinated, the resilience of the home Member State authorization process remains of key importance to the safety and stability of the pan-EU investment services market. The MiFID II authorization regime has not been heavily revised from MiFID I, save with respect to the new (Article 9) requirements which apply to investment firm governance and management.

Article 5(1) provides that each Member State is to require that the provision of investment services and/or the performance of investment activities as a regular occupation or business on a professional basis must be subject to prior authorization in accordance with MiFID II's requirements. Authorization may not be granted unless and until such time as the NCA is fully satisfied that the applicant complies with all of the MiFID II requirements (Article 7(1)). The investment firm must provide all information (including a programme of operations) necessary to enable the NCA to satisfy itself that the investment firm has established, at the time of initial authorization, all the necessary arrangements to meet its obligations with respect to authorization (Article 7(2)). The authorization obligation is ongoing for the NCA: Member States are to require that investment firms authorized in their territory comply at all times with the conditions for initial authorization (Article 21).[206] Member States must also establish a publicly accessible and regularly updated register of all authorized investment firms (Article 5(3)).[207]

The authorization responsibility imposed on the Member State (and its NCA) applies only to investment firms for which it is the 'home State' (Article 5(1)). Three tests apply to determine whether the Member State is an investment firm's home State (Article 4(1)(55)) and, by extension, whether an NCA is a home NCA. Where the investment firm is a natural person, the Member State in which the head office is situated is the home Member State. Where the investment firm is a legal person, the home Member State is the State in which the registered office is situated. Where the investment firm has, under its national law, no registered office, the home Member State is the State where the head office is situated.

The original allocation of the authorization process to the home Member State under the 1993 ISD opened up the possibility of regulatory arbitrage, as it was a minimum standards directive. This possibility is much weaker under MiFID II given the decisive crisis-era move to a single rulebook, as well as the establishment of the ESFS through which supervisory convergence and co-operation is co-ordinated. Nonetheless, MiFID II incorporates the

---

[206] To that end, NCAs must establish appropriate monitoring methods, and investment firms must notify the NCAs of any material changes to the conditions for initial authorization (Art 21(2)).

[207] Each authorization must also be notified to ESMA; ESMA is required to maintain on its website a list of all investment firms in the EU (Art 5(3)).

checks which originally provided a defence to forum-shopping by ISD firms. In an attempt to prevent investment firms from opening up 'letter box' registered offices or head offices in order to evade stricter authorization standards in force in another Member State where the firm in practice carries on all or the greater part of its activities, Article 5(4) requires that an investment firm which is a legal person must have its head office in the same Member State as its registered office, and that an investment firm which is not a legal person, and an investment firm without a registered office, must have its head office in the Member State in which it actually carries on business. While the risks of regulatory and supervisory arbitrage might not be great, this requirement ensures that the home NCA, as lead pan-EU supervisor, can make contact easily with the firm's top management, which will be involved in key decision-making and in setting firm policy, and dovetails with the MiFID II focus on firm governance (Article 9). Although it is a critical term for the purposes of identifying the home Member State and central to the letter box avoidance system, 'head office' is not defined. Arguably, the term implies that a significant amount of firm management (such as personnel functions and risk management), as well as a considerable degree of high-level, central decision-making, occurs in the Member State in which the 'head office' is situated.

MiFID II recital 46 reinforces the importance of effective home NCA supervision. It provides that the principles of mutual recognition and of home Member State supervision require that authorization should not be granted (or should be withdrawn) where factors such as the content of the programme of operations, the geographical distribution, or the activities actually carried on indicate clearly that an investment firm is choosing the legal system of one Member State in order to evade the standards imposed by the Member State in which it intends to carry on or does carry on the greater part of its activities.[208]

IV.6.2 Scope of Authorization and the Regulatory Passport

Authorization supports and determines the extent of the MiFID II passport. Under Article 6(3) the authorization is valid for the entire EU and allows an investment firm to provide the services or perform the activities for which it has been authorized throughout the EU, through either the right of establishment, including through a branch, or the free provision of services. The authorization must therefore specify the investment services or activities which the firm is authorized to provide (Article 6(1)). While it may cover ancillary services (Annex I Section B), in no case can authorization be granted solely for the provision of ancillary services (Article 6(1)). An extension of authorization must be applied for where an investment firm seeks to extend its business to additional investments or activities (or ancillary services) not foreseen at the time of the initial authorization (Article 6(2)).

---

[208] In practice, there may well be occasions where a home NCA would choose not to authorize a firm where a large number of activities are carried on elsewhere, given the significant responsibilities imposed on the home NCA and the fiscal consequences of failure. Under the ESFS, delegation is available as a means of addressing this risk (see Ch XI sect 4.2.3).

IV.6.3 Authorization Conditions: Minimum Initial Capital

Under Article 15 authorization may not be granted unless the investment firm has sufficient initial capital in accordance with the requirements of the 2013 CRD IV/CRR regime (section 8.4).

IV.6.4 Authorization Conditions: Governance Requirements

Among the many new or re-tooled regulatory devices which the financial crisis produced is regulatory oversight of internal firm governance,[209] and the related imposition of requirements relating to governance structures, the fitness and probity of management, and the allocation of responsibility to directors and senior management.[210] Governance requirements have been used to enhance risk management and to provide related incentives (including through the application of civil liability and other enforcement devices) for directors and senior management to engage in prudent risk management.[211] Governance requirements have traditionally been deployed to improve interest alignment between shareholders and management in the public company; the financial crisis has led to them being re-deployed to respond to the systemic risks posed by financial institutions and, accordingly, to align the interests of a wider set of stakeholders with those of management.[212]

The roots of the 2014 MiFID II governance reform are in the reforms made to governance in the banking sector. Governance controls have been deployed internationally to respond to an array of governance failures associated with the financial crisis and bank failure, including poor risk management at board level, unclear allocation of responsibility among senior management, competence and experience weaknesses, and perverse incentives (primarily in the form of remuneration incentives which did not appropriately address prudent risk-taking).[213] The significantly expanded MiFID II governance regime also forms part of the EU's widely cast crisis-era agenda relating to the governance of financial institutions generally, which was initially set out in the Commission's 2010 Green Paper

---

[209] Governance requirements are not new to EU law, but hitherto have primarily been a function of the EU's corporate governance regime for listed companies. See, eg, Moloney, N, Ferrarini, G, and Ungureanu, MC, 'Executive Remuneration in Crisis' (2010) 10 *JCLS* 73.

[210] The UK PRA, eg, has highlighted the role of firm management in supporting prudential soundness: Bank of England and PRA, Our Approach to Banking Supervision (2011) 11.

[211] In the UK, the design of financial-institution-specific governance requirements and of civil liability regimes and sanctions for bank directors and senior management who engage in excessive risk-taking has been extensively debated. See, eg, from the earlier stages of the crisis era, The Walker Review, A Review of Corporate Governance in UK Banks and other Financial Industry Entities (2009) and, in its latter stages, Parliamentary Commission on Banking, Changing Banking for Good (2013).

[212] In effect, 'debt governance', associated with banking in particular, has come to the fore; equity governance is associated with public companies. Debt governance is associated with aligning management interests with those of, eg, bond holders and depositors, and with a lower tolerance for risk.

[213] eg Basel Committee on Banking Supervision. Principles for Enhancing Corporate Governance (2010). On reform of bank governance see Cheffins, B, The Corporate Governance Movement, Banks, and the Financial Crisis, ECGI Law WP No 232/2013 (2013), available at <http://ssrn.com/abstract=2365738> and Hopt, K, 'Better Governance of Financial Institutions' in Ferrarini, G, Hopt, K, and Wymeersch, E, *Financial Regulation and Supervision. A Post-Crisis Analysis* (2013) 337.

on the governance of financial institutions,[214] and which agenda includes the governance requirements which now apply to rating agencies under the rating agency regime, managers of alternative investment funds under the 2011 AIFMD, central clearing counterparties (CCPs) under the 2012 EMIR, and credit institutions and investment firms under the 2013 CRD IV/CRR. The MiFID II regime accordingly operates in parallel with the governance regime which applies to credit institutions but also investment firms under the 2013 CRD IV/CRR (elements of which are additionally directly incorporated into MiFID II); in practice, the CRD IV/CRR regime carries out most of the regulatory 'heavy lifting' and covers management body composition and function requirements, as well as the highly contested remuneration controls (section 8.6).

From a market-facing perspective, the strengthened MiFID II governance regime accordingly seeks to strengthen senior management oversight of risk management in particular, but additionally, and from a client-facing perspective, it seeks to provide regulatory incentives for senior management to ensure firm activities reflect client interests, and so forms a key element of the strengthened MiFID II regulatory regime governing the client/firm relationship—particularly in the retail markets (see in particular Chapter IX section 5.2).

The 2014 MiFID II governance regime (particularly in combination with the 2013 CRD IV/CRR regime) represents a striking departure from the MiFID I regime. MiFID I simply required that the persons who 'effectively direct the business' of the investment firm be of sufficiently good repute and sufficiently experienced so as to ensure the sound and prudent management of the investment firm[215] (the administrative rules which amplified MiFID I required the clear allocation of responsibility across senior management—defined as those subject to the initial authorization review—and imposed responsibility for compliance on senior management, but did not expand on board-level responsibilities[216]). But despite the scale of the MiFID II reforms, the new governance regime was not heavily contested during the institutional negotiations.[217] The Council and European Parliament articulations of how governance requirements should be designed were, however, somewhat different. While the Council's approach was largely based on the Commission's governance proposals, it was more flexible;[218] the Parliament's model, by contrast, was significantly more detailed and specified the particular duties of non-executive directors, placed additional restrictions on the types of directorships which management body members could hold, particularly in financial institutions, and addressed civil and criminal liability for management board members.[219] During the trilogue, the Council's model ultimately prevailed,

---

[214] Commission, Green Paper on Corporate Governance in Financial Institutions (2010) (COM (2010) 284).

[215] It also required that the investment firm notify the NCA of any changes to its management, along with all information needed to assess whether the new staff met the reputation and experience requirements. Authorization was to be refused where the NCA was not satisfied that this requirement was met or if there were objective and demonstrable grounds for believing that proposed changes to the management of the firm posed a threat to its sound and prudent management.

[216] 2006 Commission MiFID I Directive Arts 5 and 9.

[217] The 2013 CRD IV/CRR regime, however, had earlier provided the institutions with the opportunity to address governance-related issues (particularly with respect to remuneration, limitations on the number of directorships held by management body members, and board diversity).

[218] In particular, the Council removed the Commission's proposal that RTSs be developed with respect to the composition of and obligations imposed on the management board.

[219] European Parliament Negotiating Position, n 28, Art 9.

although the governance regime reflects the Parliament's concern that the management body should oversee the firm's employee remuneration policy, with particular reference to ensuring the fair treatment of clients.

Experience in the corporate governance field suggests that mandatory governance requirements, and particularly harmonized requirements, should be deployed with a light touch, and allow firms' flexibility to adapt governance structures to their business models and operating environment.[220] This is all the more the case in the investment services field, given the relative novelty of governance requirements in this field, the more limited likelihood of systemic risk (as compared to the banking sector),[221] and the very large and diverse population of investment firms, which calls for proportionality and flexibility. The new MiFID II regime (Article 9) is, however, designed to be flexible (the related 2013 CRD IV/CRR regime is similarly designed to be flexible).

It is addressed to the 'management body' of the investment firm,[222] defined as the body or bodies appointed in accordance with national law which is or are empowered to set the firm's strategy, objectives, and overall direction, and which oversees and monitors management decision-making and includes persons who effectively direct the business of the entity (in effect, the board of directors) (Article 4(1)(36)). The regime is designed to capture all forms of board structure.[223]

Under Article 9(1), NCAs granting authorization under Article 5 must ensure that investment firms and their management bodies comply with the Articles 88 and 91 2013 CRD IV governance regime[224]—which addresses in particular the composition of the management body and its duties, and the related nomination committee (section 8.6)— with the calibration that the restrictions therein which apply to the number of non-executive directorships which a management body member can hold, on the approval of the NCA, be increased by one (Article 9(2)).[225] In addition, the management of the firm must be undertaken by at least two persons meeting these requirements (the 'four eyes' principle) (Article 9(6)).[226]

---

[220] See, eg, Enriques, L and Volpin, P, 'Corporate Governance Reforms in Continental Europe' (2007) 21 *J of Econ Perspectives* 117 and Hertig, G, 'Ongoing Board Reforms: One Size Fits All and Regulatory Capture' (2005) 21 *Oxford Rev of Economic Policy* 269.

[221] On the 'specialness' of bank governance structures given systemic risk see, eg, Hopt, n 213 and Macey, J and O Hara, M, 'The Corporate Governance of Banks' April (2013) *Federal Reserve Bank of New York Economic Policy Rev* 91.

[222] The definition includes the management bodies of market operators and data-reporting services providers (considered in Ch V).

[223] 2014 MiFID II rec 55 acknowledges the different governance structures in use across the Member States, and underlines that the regime is designed to embrace all existing structures, 'without advocating any particular structure'.

[224] Accordingly, the very limited types of investment firm which fall outside the scope of the 2013 CRD IV/CRR regime are caught (see sect 8.3 on CRD IV/CRR scope).

[225] The 2013 CRD IV/CRR regime is also calibrated to engage ESMA (EBA is otherwise engaged); the related required guidelines in relation to board composition and functioning are to be adopted by ESMA and EBA jointly, and the collection of the information required in relation to additional non-executive directorships is to be co-ordinated by ESMA and EBA.

[226] The requirement applies to those who 'effectively direct the business of the applicant investment firm'. A derogation is available for firms that are natural persons or legal persons managed by a single person as long as alternative arrangements are in place: Art 9(6).

MiFID II also specifies the nature of the oversight to be carried out by the management body and its responsibilities, additional to the more general oversight requirements imposed under CRD IV Article 88 (Article 9(3)); very broadly, these additional requirements reflect the client-facing dimension of investment firm business, and, in particular, the concern of MiFID II to strengthen the firm's overarching obligation to act in the best interests of clients (discussed further in Chapter IX sections 5.2 and 7.1); senior management is accordingly required to take responsibility for client interests, and for related firm policies (such as those governing remuneration and product design).

The management body of an investment firm must define, oversee, and be accountable for the implementation of governance arrangements that ensure effective and prudent management, including the segregation of duties and the prevention of conflicts of interests, in a manner that promotes the integrity of the market and the interests of clients.[227] Without prejudice to the parallel 2013 CRD IV regime, the management body must also define, approve, and oversee the organization of the firm for the provision of investment services and activities and ancillary services, including the skills, knowledge, and expertise required by personnel, resources, the procedures and the arrangements for the provision of services and activities, taking into account the nature, scale, and complexity of its business. It must in addition define, approve, and oversee a policy relating to the services, activities, products, and operations offered or provided by the firm, in accordance with the firm's risk tolerance and the characteristics and needs of its clients, which includes stress testing where appropriate.[228] Reflecting a European Parliament amendment and the concern under MiFID II to address remuneration-related risks, particularly in distribution (Chapter IX section 5.2), it must also design, approve, and oversee a remuneration policy (in relation to persons involved in the provision of services to clients) aimed at encouraging responsible business conduct and fair treatment of clients, as well as avoiding conflicts of interest in relationships with clients.[229] Finally, the management body must monitor and periodically assess the adequacy and implementation of the firm's strategic objectives in the provision of investment services and activities and ancillary services, the effectiveness of the firm's governance arrangement, and the adequacy of its policies related to the provision of services to clients, and take appropriate remedial steps.[230] In order to fulfil their functions, management body members must have adequate access to the information and documents needed to oversee and monitor management decision-making.

The extent to which weaknesses in governance structures contributed to the financial crisis remains contested, as does the ability of governance requirements to support better risk management.[231] But it seems clear that the effectiveness of this new regulatory tool depends

---

[227] This provision is similar to CRD IV Art 88(1), but with the additional reference to market integrity and client interests.

[228] This obligation forms part of the new product intervention regime, which is of particular importance for the retail markets. See further Ch IX sect 7.1.

[229] This obligation accordingly strengthens the conflict of interest management regime, which applies to the sale of and advice on retail investment products. See further Ch IX sect 5.2.

[230] A similar requirement applies under CRD IV Art 88(1).

[231] eg, Muelbert, P and Citlau, R, 'The Uncertain Role of Banks' Corporate Governance in Systemic Risk Regulation', ECGI Law WP No 179/2011 (2011), available at <http://ssrn.com/abstract=1885866>. In particular, the extent to which governance structures, typically designed to align shareholder interests with management's (and, increasingly, to align debt-holder interests) can engage with wider financial stability

heavily on the quality of related supervision and enforcement. Article 9(4) specifies that the NCA must refuse authorization where it is not satisfied that the members of the management body are of sufficiently good repute, possess sufficient knowledge, skills, and experience, and commit sufficient time to perform their functions, or if there are objective and demonstrable grounds for believing that the management body may pose a threat to its effective, sound, and prudent management and to the adequate consideration of the interests of its clients and the integrity of the market.[232] But on an ongoing basis, the strength of management incentives to deliver effective oversight will depend in part on the robustness with which the new regime is supervised; ESMA has, accordingly, a key role to play in support of supervisory convergence.[233] The effectiveness of the new regime will also depend on enforcement and on whether liability can be attached to senior management and directors. While NCAs must be empowered to require the removal of a natural person from the management board (Article 69), liability for management board members and senior management remains a function of national legal regimes. Nonetheless, and reflecting the new concern with firm governance, sanctions and measures must be applicable to management body members (and any other natural persons responsible for breach), albeit subject to the conditions laid down in national law in areas not harmonized by the Directive (Article 70(2)).

IV.6.5 Authorization Conditions: Organizational Structure and Shareholders

The 2014 MiFID II assessment of the firm also encompasses its organizational structure. Article 7(2) provides that a programme of operations which details the organizational structure of the investment firm and the type of business to be undertaken must be provided prior to authorization.

Authorization procedures typically extend beyond a review of the investment firm itself and its management to an assessment of those who can exercise control over or materially influence the investment firm. The MiFID II authorization procedure applies this wider review to an assessment of significant shareholders (Article 10). Before an NCA grants an authorization it must be informed of the identities of the shareholders or members, whether direct or indirect,[234] and whether natural or legal persons, that have qualifying holdings[235] and of the amount of those holdings (Article 10(1)). Authorization must be refused if, taking into account the need to ensure the sound and prudent management of an

---

interests has been challenged: eg Van der Elst, C, The Risks of Corporate Legal Principles of Risk Management, ECGI Law WP No 160 (2010), available at <http://ssrn.com/abstract=1623526>.

[232] The investment firm must notify the NCA of all members of its management body and of any membership changes, along with all information necessary to ensure compliance with Art 9.

[233] In the banking sphere, EBA has adopted Guidelines on the Assessment of the Suitability of Members of the Management Body and Key Function Holders (2012) (EBA/GL/2012/06).

[234] NCAs are accordingly required to look through the direct shareholder to the ultimate beneficial holder.

[235] Qualifying holdings are any direct or indirect holding in an investment firm which represents 10 per cent or more of the capital or voting rights, each as defined under the Transparency Directive (see Ch II sect 5) and taking into account the conditions regarding the aggregation of holdings set out in that Directive (or which make it possible to exercise a significant influence over the management of the investment firm in which the holding subsists): Art 4(1)(31).

investment firm, the NCA is not satisfied about the suitability of the qualifying shareholders.

Where the influence of persons with qualifying shareholdings is likely to be prejudicial to the sound and prudent management of an investment firm, the NCA is additionally required to take appropriate measures to put an end to that situation. Relevant measures are identified as including applications for judicial orders or the imposition of sanctions against directors and those responsible for management, or suspension of voting rights (Article 10(3))

Article 10(1) also requires that where 'close links' exist between the investment firm and other natural or legal persons, the NCA can grant authorization only where those links do not prevent the effective exercise of the supervisory functions of the NCA. NCAs must also refuse authorization if the laws, regulations, or administrative provisions of a third country governing one or more natural or legal persons with which the undertaking has close links, or difficulties involved in their enforcement, prevent the effective exercise of their supervisory function. These provisions are designed to ensure that the group structure within which the investment firm operates is sufficiently transparent such that the firm can be effectively supervised. 'Close links' are defined as links where two or more natural or legal persons are linked by 'participation'[236] or 'control'.[237]

IV.6.6 Authorization: Notification of Proposed Acquisitions

Although they are in practice a function of ongoing supervision, the 2014 MiFID II authorization requirements include an oversight regime for acquisitions of qualifying holdings in investment firms (Articles 11–13), in order to prevent any evasion of the qualifying holding requirements. This regime is designed to set out the criteria for the NCA's prudential assessment of qualifying holdings to support legal certainty, clarity, and predictability, and to ensure that the assessment is only made on prudential grounds (given the political and commercial risks). The regime is also designed to minimize the risk of disruption to takeover activity and the securities markets generally, and is therefore subject to clear time limits.

Under Article 11, Member States must require any natural or legal person or such persons acting in concert (the proposed acquirer) who have taken a decision either to acquire, directly or indirectly, a qualifying holding in an investment firm, or to further increase, directly or indirectly, such a qualifying holding, as a result of which the proportion of the voting rights or of the capital held would reach or exceed 20 per cent, 30 per cent, or 50 per cent, or so that the investment firm would become the proposed acquirer's subsidiary, to notify in writing the NCA of the investment firm in which they are seeking to acquire or

---

[236] Participation is defined under Art 4(1)(35) in terms of the ownership, direct or by way of control, of 20 per cent or more of the voting rights or capital of the undertaking.

[237] Control (Art 4(1)(35)) is defined in terms of the relationship between a parent undertaking and a subsidiary, as described in the 2013 Accounting Directive (Directive 2013/34/EU [2013] OJ L182/19), and similar relationships between any natural or legal person and an undertaking. The effect of this definition is to ensure that a control relationship exists whenever a Member State's legal regime requires the preparation of consolidated accounts. Close links also exist where two or more natural or legal persons are permanently linked to one and the same person by a control relationship.

increase the qualifying holding. The notification must include the size of the holding and the information which the Member State requires such that the NCA can make an assessment of the holding.[238] Conversely, a decision to dispose of a qualifying holding, or a disposition which reduces the qualifying holding below the thresholds or following which the investment firm ceases to be a subsidiary, must also be notified.

The assessment process is subject to a series of requirements designed to ensure that the assessment is carried out within a transparent procedural framework and that the assessment focuses on prudential matters. The relevant NCAs must work in 'full consultation' with each other in carrying out the assessment in the particular circumstances listed in Article 11(2), which relate to situations where the proposed acquirer is also a regulated entity (or the parent or controller of such an entity) and is authorized in a Member State other than that in which the acquisition is proposed (the entities include credit institutions, investment firms, and UCITS management companies). In these circumstances the NCAs must, without undue delay, provide each other with any information which is 'essential or relevant' for the assessment. In addition, the decision by the NCA that has authorized the investment firm in which the acquisition is proposed must indicate any views or reservations expressed by the NCA responsible for the proposed acquirer.

Article 13(1) requires the NCA to assess the acquisition in order to ensure the sound and prudent management of the investment firm in which the acquisition is proposed and, having regard to the likely influence of the proposed acquirer on the investment firm, to appraise the suitability of the proposed acquirer and the financial soundness of the proposed acquisition. The assessment must be made against all of the following criteria (Article 13(1)(a)–(e)): the reputation of the proposed acquirer; the reputation and experience of any person who will direct the business of the investment firm as a result of the proposed acquisition; the financial soundness of the proposed acquirer (in particular in relation to the type of business pursued and envisaged in the investment firm in which the acquisition is proposed); whether the investment firm will be able to comply with prudential requirements and, in particular, whether the group of which it has become a part has a structure that makes it possible to exercise effective supervision, effectively exchange information among NCAs, and determine the allocation of responsibilities among NCAs; and whether there are reasonable grounds for suspecting money-laundering or terrorist financing in connection with the proposed acquisition.[239] Following this assessment, the NCA may 'oppose' the proposed acquisition, but only if there are 'reasonable grounds' for doing so on the basis of the criteria or if the information provided by the proposed acquirer is incomplete (Article 13(2)). Where the NCA decides to oppose the proposed acquisition, it must inform the proposed acquirer in writing and provide the reasons for the decision within two working days (and not exceeding the assessment time period) (Article 12(4)). Subject to national law, an appropriate statement of the reasons may be made accessible to the public at the request of the proposed acquirer.

---

[238] In order to support efficient securities markets and acquisition activity, this information must be proportionate and adapted to the nature of the proposed acquirer and the proposed transaction: Art 13(4). ESMA is empowered to propose RTSs which specify (exhaustively) the information which Member States are to require: Art 12(8).

[239] A delegation empowers the Commission to adjust the money-laundering/terrorist financing criteria: Art 13(1)(e).

Where the NCA does not oppose the acquisition in writing within the assessment period, the acquisition is deemed to be approved (Article 12(5)). The NCA may fix a maximum period for concluding the proposed acquisition and extend this period where appropriate (Article 12(6)).

The potential political sensitivities of acquisitions in financial institutions, and the risk of national champions being protected through the regulatory system, are addressed by Articles 13(3) and (5). They provide, respectively, that Member States may not impose prior conditions on the level of holding that must be acquired and must not allow their NCAs to examine proposed acquisitions in terms of the economic needs of the market, and that where two or more proposals to acquire or increase qualifying holdings have been received, they must be treated in a non-discriminatory manner. Member States are also prohibited from imposing requirements for the notification to and approval by NCAs of direct and indirect acquisitions of voting rights or capital that are more stringent than those set out in the Directive (Article 12(7)). Commercial risks and sensitivities are also addressed by Article 12, which covers the assessment period and imposes a 60-day time limit for the assessment. It also empowers the NCAs to ask for additional information during this period and provides for the assessment period to be interrupted (for up to 20 working days) while the acquirer responds to the request.

The notification obligations are not restricted to those making the regulated disposals or acquisitions. Article 11(3) places an obligation on investment firms, 'on becoming aware' of the relevant disposals or acquisitions, to inform the NCA to that effect. In addition, at least once a year investment firms are to inform their NCAs of the names of the shareholders and members who possess qualifying holdings, and the sizes of such holdings.

Where persons fail to notify the NCA, the NCA must adopt measures similar to the Article 10(3) sanctions which apply with respect to qualifying shareholders; in addition, where a qualifying holding is acquired despite the opposition of the NCA, the Member States must, regardless of any other sanctions which are adopted, provide either for the exercise of relevant voting right to be suspended, for the nullity of votes cast, or for the possibility of their annulment (Article 11(4)).

IV.6.7 Authorization: Investor Compensation Schemes

The 2014 MiFID II Article 14 requires that any entity seeking authorization as an investment firm meet its obligations under the Investor Compensation Schemes Directive at the time of authorization.[240] Given the cross-over of compensation schemes with respect to structured deposits, the compensation scheme requirement is met where the credit institution issuing the products (and thereby subject to MiFID II as execution of orders includes such sales) is a member of a deposit guarantee scheme recognized under the EU's deposit guarantee scheme regime.

---

[240] See further Ch IX sect 8.

IV.6.8 Authorization: Organizational Requirements

Under Article 16 of the 2014 MiFID II, the home Member State must require that investment firms comply with the Article's organizational/operational requirements, discussed in section 7.2. These extensive prudentially orientated requirements address the compliance function, conflict-of-interest management, product governance, the continuity and regularity of services, internal controls and outsourcing, record-keeping, and client-asset protection. The organizational requirements imposed on investment firms also include the rules relating to the trading process, which are considered in Chapters V and VI, and the 2013 CRD IV/CRR prudential regime (section 8).

IV.6.9 Authorization: Process and Protections

In certain circumstances, NCAs are required to consult the NCAs of other Member States before granting an authorization. Under Article 84(1) of the 2014 MiFID II such consultation is required where the applicant is a subsidiary of an investment firm or credit institution authorized in another Member State, a subsidiary of a parent undertaking of an investment firm or credit institution authorized in another Member State, or controlled by the same natural or legal person as controls an investment firm or credit institution authorized in another Member State. Under Article 84(2), the NCA of the Member State responsible for the supervision of credit institutions or insurance undertakings must be also consulted before the granting of an authorization to an investment firm which is a subsidiary of a credit institution or insurance undertaking authorized in the EU, a subsidiary of the parent undertaking of such a credit institution or insurance undertaking, or controlled by the same natural or legal person who controls a credit institution or insurance undertaking authorized in the EU. The consultations should address in particular the suitability of shareholders and members and the reputation and experience of those directing the business who are involved in the management of another entity of the same group, and NCAs should exchange all relevant information in this regard (and with respect to ongoing assessment of compliance with the MiFID II operating conditions) (Article 84(3)). This consultation requirement (which dates from the ISD/MiFID I eras) is designed to provide a bulwark against the regulatory arbitrage (albeit now, most likely, supervisory arbitrage, given the scale of harmonization) which could occur by an investment firm transferring the business of a parent in one Member State to a subsidiary in another Member State, and thereby achieving the same result as would arise from a transfer of its registered office. The NCA of the parent may not veto the establishment of the subsidiary, although the Member State charged with the subsidiary's authorization would be required to take into account the Preamble's injunction on firms avoiding the stricter rules of a Member State which would normally apply.

The authorization rules extend beyond setting minimum conditions for the grant of authorization and include procedural protections for applicants. Under Article 7(3), an applicant for authorization under MiFID II must be informed within six months of the submission of a complete application whether or not authorization has been granted. Under Article 74, Member States are required to ensure that decisions taken in respect of investment firms under the national measures adopted in accordance with MiFID II, including, accordingly, authorization decisions, are subject to the right to apply to the courts. NCAs are also prevented from arbitrarily withdrawing authorization. Article 8 sets out the circumstances in which authorization may be withdrawn. Withdrawal may take place where the investment firm in question does not make use of the authorization within 12 months, expressly renounces the authorization, or has provided no investment services or performed no investment activity for the preceding six months, unless the Member State concerned has provided for authorization to lapse in such cases (Article 8(a)). Withdrawal is also possible under Article 8(b) where the authorization has been obtained by means of false statements or by any other irregular means. Withdrawal is, of course, permitted as a disciplinary measure. Article 8(c) provides for withdrawal in respect of failure to fulfil the conditions under which authorization was granted, including failure to comply with the capital requirements. Article 8(d) provides for withdrawal where the firm has seriously and systematically infringed the MiFID II rules governing the operating conditions for investment firms. Finally, authorization may be withdrawn in any of the cases where national law (in respect of matters outside the scope of MiFID II) provides for withdrawal (Article 8(e)).

IV.6.10 ESMA and the Authorization Process

Given the fundamental importance of an effective and resilient authorization process to the stability and efficiency of the pan-EU market, it is unsurprising that ESMA has been conferred with a series of powers designed to support consistency in the authorization process, and that it serves as an information hub in relation to authorization. ESMA must be notified by the Member States of all authorizations and withdrawals of authorization (Articles 5(3) and 8) and must publish on its website a list of all investment firms authorized in the EU (Article 5(3)).

An extensive series of delegations to BTSs apply to the authorization process, which allow ESMA to shape the operation of the authorization process pan-EU. These include RTSs relating to the information required of firms for authorization, the requirements applicable to qualifying shareholders, and the nature of the obstacles which may prevent effective exercise of NCAs' supervisory functions (Article 7(4)), as well as RTSs on the information to be provided by acquirers with respect to proposed acquisitions which are subject to assessment under MiFID II (Article 12(8)). ESMA is also charged with developing ITSs on the standard forms, templates, and procedures to be used for the notification of information over the authorization process and in relation to management (Article 7(5)), and to support consultation between NCAs in different Member States where required during the authorization process (Article 84(4)). It can also adopt guidelines relating to the ongoing monitoring of authorization conditions (Article 21(2)).

IV.7 Operating Conditions: 2014 MiFID II Prudential and Conduct Requirements

IV.7.1 Operating Conditions: A Multilayered Regime

A multilayered regime governs the operating conditions of investment firms under the 2014 MiFID II, reflecting the universe of services and activities engaged. It is based on a number of elements. MiFID II requires ongoing compliance with authorization requirements

(Article 21) and imposes the following: prudentially orientated organizational/risk-management requirements (Article 16); prudentially orientated rules governing the operation by investment firms of trading venues, market-making, and algorithmic trading (Articles 17–20 and 31–5);[241] conduct rules (including with respect to conflict-of-interest management (Articles 16(3) and 23), client fair treatment, disclosure, marketing, quality of advice, and execution-only services (Articles 24 and 25));[242] client order handling and best execution requirements (Articles 27–8);[243] and specific rules relating to tied agents (Article 29). The precursors to these legislative rules under MiFID I were amplified extensively under the 2006 Commission MiFID I Directive; new delegations relating to the MiFID II regime have been conferred and can be expected to lead to a similar if enhanced administrative regime. The regime also includes ESMA's extensive supervisory convergence measures in this area, which include guidelines on the compliance function and on the suitability regime.[244]

The MiFID I Review did not deliver extensive reforms to the MiFID I operational regime; the most significant enhancements relate to trading practices and the operation of trading venues and to the conduct-of-business regime, particularly with respect to independent advice. Overall, the operational rules are designed to apply flexibly to the range of activities in which firms engage and the related risks generated, and to apply proportionately to the myriad types of investment firm. Under MiFID I, the 2006 MiFID I Directive, which contained the related administrative rules, followed a principles-based approach, which required investment firms to ensure the relevant firm procedures reflected the particular risk profile, size, and complexity of the firm in question; a similar approach can be expected to continue under the new MiFID II administrative rulebook, particularly as a more granular approach would generate severe risks with respect to regulatory error and arbitrage. The effectiveness of the operational regime accordingly depends in large part on whether regulatory and other incentives are sufficiently strong to ensure compliance, on the strength of the foundational firm governance requirements, and on supervision and enforcement.

In parallel with the MiFID II operational regime, the 2013 CRD IV/CRR regime addresses prudential regulation and supervision for credit institutions and investment firms, and is the main source of prudential regulation for in-scope investment firms. The CRD IV/CRR regime is primarily concerned with capital, liquidity, and leverage requirements—in particular with respect to credit institutions, given its focus on credit risk, but also with respect to investment firms. It also covers a range of related prudential requirements, including risk management and firm governance requirements, and imposes a discrete supervisory review system for prudential requirements (section 8 below).

IV.7.2 Organizational Requirements

IV.7.2.1 The Legislative Regime

Article 16 sets out the high-level legislative rules which govern investment firm organization and which are designed to address risk management and, in particular, operational risk. It is

---

[241] These rules are considered in Ch VI (trading activities) and Ch V (operating trading venues).
[242] These rules are considered in Ch IX on the retail markets.
[243] These rules are considered in Ch VI (trading activities).
[244] n 131.

closely based on the precursor MiFID I Article 10, save for the inclusion of a new requirement that firms record telephone calls and product governance requirements.

Under the cornerstone compliance requirement, firms must establish adequate policies and procedures sufficient to ensure compliance of the firm, including its managers, employees, and tied agents, with obligations under the 2014 MiFID II, and establish appropriate rules governing personal transactions by these persons (Article 16(2)). Conflicts of interest are expressly addressed as an organizational risk: firms must maintain and operate effective organizational and administrative arrangements with a view to taking 'all reasonable steps' designed to prevent conflicts of interest (as defined under Article 23: see section 7.3) (Article 16(3)). A new product governance requirement applies under Article 16(3).[245] Business continuity risk is addressed by the requirement that the firm must take reasonable steps to ensure continuity and regularity in the performance of investment services and activities—appropriate and proportionate systems, procedures, and resources must be deployed to this end (Article 16(4)). Outsourcing risk is addressed by the requirement that the firm, when relying on a third party for the performance of operational functions 'which are critical for the provision of continuous and satisfactory service to clients and the performance of investment activities on a continuous and satisfactory basis', takes reasonable steps to avoid undue operational risk; outsourcing of important operational functions may not be undertaken in such a way as to impair materially the quality of the firm's internal controls and the ability of the NCA to monitor the firm's compliance with all its obligations (Article 16(5)). More generally, the firm must have in place sound administrative and accounting procedures, internal control mechanisms, effective procedures for risk assessment, and effective control and safeguard arrangements for information processing systems (Article 16(5)).[246]

An extensive record-keeping regime applies under Article 16(6)–(7). Article 16(6) is based on the precursor MiFID I obligation and requires the investment firm to arrange for records to be kept of all services, activities, and transactions it undertakes, which must be sufficient to enable the NCA to fulfil its supervisory tasks and perform its enforcement functions under MiFID II, MiFIR, and the market abuse regime, as well as to ascertain that the firm has complied with its obligations, including client-facing obligations and those relating to market integrity. In the most material change from MiFID I, a telephone call recording requirement applies under Article 16(7) which is designed to bring consistency, given the very different approaches adopted by Member States, and to support stronger enforcement.[247] The new regime, which was heavily revised from the Commission's MiFID II Proposal over the institutional negotiations—reflecting the Council's concern that the regime be more clearly designed[248]—requires that firm record-keeping include the

---

[245] As this requirement is of particular importance to the retail markets, it is discussed in Ch IX sect 7.1. It applies generally, however, to the product design process, and catches products designed for professional clients and the wholesale market.

[246] Including the requirement introduced by the Council that investment firms have sound security mechanisms in place to guarantee the security and authentication of the means of transfer of information, minimize the risk of data corruption and of unauthorized access, and prevent information leakage and maintain the confidentiality of data at all times.

[247] 2011 MiFID II/MiFIR Proposals Impact Assessment, n 28, 18.

[248] One Member State, however, was opposed to a recording obligation, and called for an alternative approach based on written documentation: Danish Presidency Progress Report, n 122, 9.

recording of telephone conversations or electronic communications related to, at least, transactions concluded when dealing on own account and the provision of client order services that relate to order execution (in effect, trading-related services). These records must be kept for five years (the period can be extended to a maximum of seven where the NCA so requires). Article 16(7) specifies that the requirements apply in relation to equipment which has been provided by or has had its use sanctioned by the firm, and that notification obligations apply in relation to clients (in the absence of which the trading service in question cannot be provided).

Asset protection rules apply under Article 16(8)–(10).[249] In relation to a client's financial instruments, the firm must make adequate arrangements to safeguard the client's ownership rights (especially in the event of insolvency) and to prevent the use of a client's instruments on own account, except with the client's express consent (Article 16(8)). In relation to client funds, the firm must similarly make adequate arrangements to safeguard the client's rights and, except in the case of credit institutions, prevent the use of client funds for own account. In an addition to MiFID I, but reflecting incidences of asset loss and disputes over firm practices and firm liability over the financial crisis,[250] firms must not conclude title transfer collateral arrangements (related to securities financing transactions) with retail clients for the purpose of securing or covering these clients' present or future, actual or contingent or prospective obligations (Article 16(10)).

IV.7.2.2 The Administrative Regime

Article 16 is subject to a delegation to the Commission to adopt rules to specify the 'concrete organizational requirements' to be imposed on investment firms performing different investment services and/or activities and ancillary services, or combinations thereof (Article 16(12)).

Some indications as to the nature of the 2014 MiFID II administrative rulebook can be gleaned from the MiFID I Review, during which the Commission suggested the MiFID I administrative rules could be enhanced generally, including by specifying that the different internal compliance, risk management, and audit functions report to the management body of the firm. The Commission also suggested that the new administrative regime contain specific rules addressing the organizational risks posed by asset management, including with respect to record-keeping, compliance with investment mandates, and senior management oversight.[251] The new administrative rulebook is also likely to retain much of the MiFID I rulebook, the main features of which are considered in outline in this section, and to reflect the refinements to organizational regulation which have been deployed under the 2011 AIFMD and 2009 UCITS IV regimes, notably with respect to outsourcing and asset custody.

The administrative rulebook which amplified the precursor MiFID I organizational regime (MiFID I Article 13) was wide in reach but flexible in design, and followed a

---

[249] As noted in sect 3, Member States may apply additional national rules with respect to asset protection, as long as the Art 16(11) conditions are met.

[250] 2010 MiFID I Review Consultation, n 112, 70.

[251] 2010 MiFID I Review Consultation, n 112, 67 and 69. The Commission also noted that Member States had recorded numerous complaints relating to compliance with asset management mandates: 2011 MiFID II/MiFIR Proposals Impact Assessment, n 28, 18.

principles-based model:[252] the requirements were designed to be 'sufficiently supple' to allow firms to craft the most appropriate mechanisms for meeting the requirements.[253] Firms were to apply the requirements proportionately and taking into account 'the nature, scale, and complexity of the business of the firm, and the nature and range of investment services and activities undertaken in the course of that business'. More onerous requirements, particularly with respect to discrete and independent risk management and internal-audit functions, were imposed where the complexity of a firm's business implied that generic internal control measures were inadequate. Broadly, the administrative regime amplified Article 13 through a series of rules which addressed organization, compliance, internal audit, risk management, outsourcing, asset protection, conflicts of interest, personal transactions, and record-keeping (2006 Commission MiFID I Directive Articles 5–9, 11–12, 21–3, 26, and 51).

With respect to organizational requirements, for example, Articles 5–9 set out the organizational requirements to be met by all firms, and addressed the 'fundamental organizational elements that should be established by all investment firms to ensure their proper functioning'.[254] Although these requirements were designed to act as a 'common organizational denominator',[255] investment firms were to take into account the nature, scale, and complexity of their business. In essence, firms were required to establish a clearly documented, robust organizational structure, which supported the clear allocation of responsibility, robust risk management, and transparency. General organizational requirements, including with respect to decision-making and the allocation of responsibilities, internal risk-management policies, business continuity policies, and accounting policies, applied, as did a requirement that senior management[256] be responsible for compliance (Articles 5 and 9). The Directive also required the establishment of compliance, risk management, and audit functions (Articles 6–9), although these functions were designed to be embedded in firms in different ways, depending on the firm's organization and business and risk profile. The compliance regime, for example, cascaded from a general obligation to have effective compliance systems in place to the obligation to establish a permanent, effective, and independent compliance function, but tailored the obligation to smaller firms by disapplying the more onerous independence-related requirements where the firm could demonstrate that, in view of the nature, scale, and complexity of its business and the nature and range of its investment services and activities, these requirements were not proportionate. The extensive asset protection regime (Articles 16–20), to take another example, was based on record-keeping and identification rules and requirements governing the selection of third party custodians and depositaries, as well as on retail-client-focused disclosure obligations. It imposed requirements related to asset record-keeping, identification, and segregation; annual audit; the holding of funds and instruments by third party custodians and depositaries (including restrictions on the entities with which client funds

---

[252] The Commission's Background Note to what would become the 2006 Commission MiFID I Directive stated that the regime was principles-based and designed to establish clear standards and objectives that investment firms need to attain rather than to prescribe specific and detailed rules: Commission, Background Note to Draft Commission Directive Implementing MiFID (February 2006) (2006 Commission MiFID I Background Note) 5.

[253] 2006 Commission MiFID I Background Note, n 252, 8.

[254] 2006 Commission MiFID I Background Note, n 252, 7.

[255] 2006 Commission MiFID I Background Note, n 252.

[256] Defined as the persons who effectively directed the business of the firm and were reviewed during the firm authorization process.

could be deposited[257]); stock lending activities (client consent was required); and related disclosure to retail clients.[258]

IV.7.3 Conflict-of-interest Management

IV.7.3.1 The Legislative Regime

Enhancement of the MiFID I conflict-of-interest regime quickly emerged as one of the major themes of the MiFID I Review, albeit in the specific context of the impact of inducements on retail market sales and advice (Chapter IX section 5.2). But in addition to the new quality-of-advice-related inducement/independent advice requirements, the 2014 MiFID II also contains a series of interlocking requirements designed to protect clients and the market generally against conflict-of-interest risk and related prejudicial incentives. The cornerstone measures are the organizational and disclosure requirements (MiFID II Articles 16(3) and 23) discussed in this section. But conflict-of-interest management is also delivered through the best execution and order-handling requirements which apply to the trading process (Chapter VI section 2.2), through the organizational and other requirements which apply to firms which operate trading venues (Chapter V generally), and through the fair treatment and quality of advice conduct requirements which apply to the firm/client relationship (Chapter IX section 5.2). Conflict-of-interest management has also been embedded into firm governance, with the management body enjoined to take responsibility for governance arrangements and policies governing conflicts of interest (Article 9(3)) (section 6.4).

Conflict-of-interest management within the multiservice firm has been a priority preoccupation of regulators internationally for some time, reflecting the changing nature of intermediation and investment services. The ever-increasing range of activities undertaken as investment firms move beyond their traditional corporate finance and securities underwriting roles and, in particular, engage in large-scale proprietary trading and securities issuance/securitization heightens conflict-of-interest risk,[259] even if efficiency gains also follow from which clients benefit.[260]

Investment research, for example, became the poster-child for poor conflict-of-interest management in the multiservice firm over the Enron era.[261] Other occasions for the generation of conflict-of-interest risks include the combination of corporate finance

---

[257] Essentially, central banks, credit institutions, and money-market funds.

[258] The MiFID I Review suggested possible enhancements, including applying diversification requirements to the placement of client funds to avoid concentration risks where client money is placed in group entities: 2010 MiFID I Review Consultation, n 112, 70–1.

[259] See, eg, Kumpans, C and Leyens, P, 'Conflicts of Interest of Financial Intermediaries—Towards a Global Common Core in Conflict of Interest Regulation' (2008) 4 *ECFLR* 72; Mehran, H and Stulz, R, The Economics of Conflicts of Interest in Financial Institutions, NBER WP No W12695 (2007) 5–10; and Band, C, 'Conflicts of Interests in Financial Services and Markets' (2006) 21 *JIBLR* 677.

[260] Full coverage of the range of risks generated by the multiservice investment firm is outside the scope of this Chapter. For an extensive pre-crisis review of the nature of conflict-of-interest risk in the multiservice firm see Tuch, A, 'Investment Banking: Immediate Challenges and Future Directions' (2006) 20 *Commercial LQ* 37.

[261] See further Ch VII.

business (particularly mergers and acquisition advice[262]) and proprietary trading.[263] The combination of corporate finance/securities underwriting and brokerage, to take another example, can generate risks where poor-quality securities are offloaded to the retail sector (in particular). Similarly, the allocation of securities offerings can generate significant conflict risks where favoured clients are offered securities in over-subscribed offerings. Asset-management services generate particularly acute conflicts of interest (for retail clients in particular) with respect to the 'churning' of portfolios to generate fees, the front-running of information as to client orders, the allocation of more resources and expertise to more sophisticated clients, and the use of firm products and of securities which are held on own account in asset allocation.

The Enron-era equity market crisis exposed the extent to which conflicts of interest and incentive risks could disable markets. But conflicts of interest have since been strongly associated with the global financial crisis generally, and have been implicated in, for example, poor internal governance within financial institutions (including the consequent generation of perverse remuneration-related incentives to take excessive risks), excessive rating agency reliance on securitization fees, and the mis-selling of complex products.[264] The multifaceted reform agenda internationally which has followed has also included the conflicts of interest which can arise in the underwriting of securities.[265]

The regulation of internal conflict-of-interest management, which typically requires that conflicts be identified[266] and that they be managed or disclosed, is only one response to the incentive risks which can lead to investor/client costs, poor risk management, and, ultimately, the generation of risks to financial stability. But the regulation of internal conflict-of-interest management has long been a prominent component of the regulatory toolbox. Accordingly, it is not surprising that internal conflict-of-interest management became a major theme of the MiFID I Review. The Review did not, however, disturb the

---

[262] eg Tuch, A, 'Contemporary Challenges in Takeovers: Avoiding Conflicts, Preserving Confidence and Taming the Commercial Imperative' (2006) 24 *Company and Securities LJ* 107 and Hopt, K, 'Takeovers, Secrecy, and Conflicts of Interest: Problems for Boards and Banks' in Payne, J (ed), *Takeovers in English and German Law* (2002) 33.

[263] Pre-crisis, the ill-fated and closely followed action by the Australian regulator (ASIC) against Citigroup (*ASIC v Citigroup Global Markets Australia* [2007] FCA 963) was widely regarded as an attack on proprietary dealing and a statement that conflicts of interest between advisory business and proprietary dealing could not be resolved. The Court's ruling, however, confirmed that Chinese walls could be used to allow a firm to engage in both businesses: Lumsden, A, and Bridgen, V, Chinese Walls—Lessons from the Citigroup Case (2007), available at <http://ssrn.com/abstract=1019176>.

[264] On flawed incentives and conflict-of-interest risks related to the asset securitization bubble, see Joint Forum (IOSCO, Basel Committee, and IAS), Report on Asset Securitization Incentives (2011). Enforcement action, litigation, and settlements have followed. These include the high-profile November 2013 $13 billion in penalties imposed on JP Morgan Chase in settlement of the civil investigation by US authorities into sales by JP Morgan Chase of securitized mortgages, and the SEC's high-profile 2010 enforcement action against Goldman Sachs in relation to the allegations that the firm's broker-dealer subsidiary had conflicts of interest in selling a collateralized debt obligation (CDO) (albeit to an arm's-length professional client) due to undisclosed transactions from which it would profit were certain securities contained in the portfolio of assets on which the CDO was based to fall in value. For discussion see Tuch, A, Conflicted Gate-keepers. The Volcker Rule and Goldman Sachs. Washington University of St Louis Legal Studies Research Paper No 12-12-1 (2011), available at <http://ssrn.com/abstract=1809271>.

[265] The 'Volcker Rule' element of the 2010 Dodd-Frank Act, eg, prohibits any material conflict of interest between the underwriter and buyer of asset-backed securities.

[266] The existence of a conflict usually demands some form of fiduciary relationship, albeit not always, as conflict-of-interest requirements can apply (as under the MiFID II regime) to arm's-length contracting.

foundational conflict-of-interest identification, management, and disclosure obligation which applied under MiFID I, although it has led to a raft of new, targeted obligations—in the trading and retail market context in particular. Overall, the conflict-of-interest management obligation remains broadly generic in design. For example, and by contrast with the US reforms, although underwriting reform appeared in the early days of the MiFID I Review, it has not been expressly addressed under the 2014 MiFID II/MiFIR reforms.[267]

The legislative conflict-of-interest management regime (Articles 16(3) and 23) applies regardless of whether the client is a retail client, a professional client, or a counterparty engaged in, for example, arm's-length, own-account trading with the firm. It does not prohibit conflicts of interest. The conflict-of-interest regime is designed to operate *ex-ante* and to contain damaging conflicts of interests through identification and management techniques.

Under Article 23, investment firms must take 'all appropriate steps' to identify, and to prevent or manage, conflicts of interest that arise in the course of providing investment services (Article 23(1)). These are broadly defined as conflicts arising between themselves (including their managers, employees, and tied agents, or any person directly or indirectly linked to them by control) and their clients, or between one client and another. Reflecting the MiFID II focus on remuneration-related risks (Chapter IX section 5.2), and in a European Parliament addition, conflicts of interest caused by the receipt of remuneration from third parties, or by the firm's own remuneration and other incentive structures, are expressly identified. The conflict-of-interest regime is not therefore dependent on a fiduciary obligation existing.

The Article 23 MiFID II standard is higher than the MiFID I standard which required that firms take all 'reasonable steps', a standard which arguably is more vulnerable to investment firms claiming that their practices were reasonable in light of prevailing practices; 'appropriate' might be associated with an objective assessment.

Article 23 is supported by an organizational requirement. Under Article 16(3), all firms must maintain and operate effective organizational and administrative arrangements with a view to taking all reasonable steps designed to prevent conflicts of interest (as defined in Article 23) from adversely affecting the interests of their clients.

These two obligations are linked by a default disclosure requirement. Under Article 23(2), where the organizational and administrative arrangements adopted by the firm under Article 16(3) to prevent conflicts of interest from adversely affecting the interests of its clients are not sufficient to ensure 'with reasonable confidence' that risk of damage to client interests will be prevented, the firm must clearly disclose to the client the general nature and/or the sources of the conflicts of interest and the steps taken to mitigate those risks, before undertaking business on its behalf. MiFID II has specified in more detail the nature of this disclosure, providing, *inter alia*, that it must include sufficient detail,

---

[267] The Commission queried whether firms should be required to establish specific organizational requirements with respect to underwriting, whether rules governing allotment should be adopted, and whether specific conflict-of-interest requirements should be adopted: 2010 MiFID I Review Consultation, n 112, 72–3.

taking into account the nature of the client, to enable the client to take an informed decision with respect to the service in question: boilerplate disclosure of generic conflicts will not therefore be sufficient.

This approach to conflicts of interest is based on the management of conflicts of interest (rather than their elimination) through widely cast *ex-ante* organizational requirements, which are designed to be tailored by firms to address their particular conflict-of-interest risk profiles. It is generic and does not address the particular conflicts of interest generated by, for example, underwriting and asset management. Much depends on the extent to which these requirements provide strong internal incentives to manage conflicts of interest appropriately; in this respect, the regulatory incentives provided by the new Article 9 firm governance regime should bolster the conflict-of-interest regime. But much also depends on the quality of supervision and the effectiveness of enforcement, whether through the Article 16(3)/Article 23 channel or indirectly through the Article 24 fair treatment channel (section 7.6), and, accordingly, on ESMA's use of its supervisory convergence and co-ordination powers.

IV.7.3.2 The Administrative Regime

A delegation empowers the Commission to adopt administrative rules under Article 23 governing the steps firms might reasonably be expected to take to identify, prevent, manage, and disclose conflicts of interest, and setting out the appropriate criteria for determining the types of conflict of interest whose existence could damage the interests of clients or potential clients (Article 23(4)). As the 2014 MiFID II regime has not changed materially from MiFID I, the new administrative rulebook can be expected to follow the 2006 regime.

The administrative conflict-of-interest regime (2006 Commission MiFID I Directive Articles 11–12 and 21–3) was designed to be principles-based. Its objective was to 'ensure that investment firms take a holistic approach to conflicts management, regularly reviewing their business lines to ensure that at all times their policies reflect the full scope of their activities and the possible conflicts that may emerge'.[268] It reflected a concern to ensure that conflict rules were sufficiently flexible to reflect changing business activities and structures, and attempted to bring about cultural change rather than a box-ticking culture.

The administrative regime reflected the MiFID I legislative framework by favouring *ex-ante* procedural controls over disclosure and thereby placing responsibility on firms to address conflicts—a responsibility which disclosure can reduce or disable altogether.[269] The regime accordingly addressed conflicts identification, providing a set of non-exhaustive circumstances against which the assessment as to the existence of a conflict of interest could be made (Article 21). It also required that firms establish, implement, and maintain an effective, written conflict-of-interest policy (Article 22). Reflecting the emphasis on calibration and self-assessment, the policy was to be appropriate 'to the size and organization of the firm and the nature, scale and complexity of its business'. The policy was to identify, with reference to the specific investment services and activities carried out by or on behalf of

---

[268] 2006 Commission MiFID I Background Note, n 252, 13.

[269] Cain, D, Loewenstein, G, and Moore, D, 'The Dirt on Coming Clean: Perverse Effects of Disclosing Conflicts of Interest' (2005) 34 *J of Legal Studies* 1.

the firm, the circumstances which constituted, or could give rise to, a conflict of interest entailing a material risk of damage to the interests of one or more clients. Although the policy requirement was generic, firms were to pay 'special attention' to the activities of investment research and advice, proprietary trading, portfolio management, and corporate finance. The administrative regime did not specify the particular procedural requirements necessary, but identified procedures which might be 'necessary and appropriate' to ensure the requisite degree of independence, including 'Chinese walls' (which are used to restrict the flow of confidential information and prevent its attribution across different business units); separate supervision of relevant persons where conflict-of-interest risks arose; remuneration-related controls; measures to prevent the exercise of inappropriate influence; and measures to prevent or control the simultaneous or sequential involvement of a relevant person in separate investment services where such involvement could impair the proper management of conflicts of interest.

IV.7.4 Transaction Reporting

Under Article 24 of the 2014 MiFIR, NCAs are charged with monitoring the activities of investment firms to ensure that they act honestly, fairly, and professionally, and in a manner which promotes the integrity of the market. In order to support this requirement, extensive record-keeping and transaction reporting requirements apply under MiFIR Article 25. As these requirements are primarily focused on trading activities, they are considered in Chapter V Section 12.1.

IV.7.5 Trading Rules and Trading Venues

The most striking extension of MiFID I by the 2014 MiFID II/MiFIR regime relates to the new rulebook which applies to trading by investment firms and to the operation by firms of trading venues, and which is examined in Chapters V and VI.

IV.7.6 Conduct Regulation

Client-facing conduct-of-business rules which are designed to support investor protection form a major component of the 2014 MiFID II operating regime.[270]

Article 24 is at the heart of the conduct regime. As under MiFID I, investment firms are subject to an overarching fair treatment obligation in that, when providing investment services (or ancillary services) to clients, they must act honestly, fairly, and professionally, in accordance with the best interests of the client, and comply with the specific Article 24 conduct principles and the related quality of advice rules which apply under Article 25 (Article 24(1)); an overarching product governance/product distribution requirement also applies[271] (Article 24(2)).

---

[270] These rules are addressed in Ch. IX sect 5.2 and noted only in outline here.
[271] Ch IX sect 7.1.

Under Article 24, firms are subject to an overarching disclosure requirement (which also applied under MiFID I): all information—including marketing communications—addressed by the investment firm to clients or potential clients must be fair, clear, and not misleading, and marketing communications must be identified as such (Article 24(3)). Article 24(4) specifies the minimum disclosures which must be provided to clients with respect to the firm and its services, including with respect to the following: the nature of the investment advice provided and whether it is 'independent' within the terms of MiFID II; financial instruments and proposed investment strategies (including risk warnings); and all costs and associated charges (including the cost of advice). This information must be provided in a comprehensible form (it may be in a standardized format), in such a manner that the client or potential client is reasonably able to understand the nature and risks of the investment service and the specific type of financial instrument offered and, consequently, to take investment decisions on an informed basis (Article 24(5)).

The MiFID I conduct/conflict-of-interest regime governing investment advice and sales has been significantly enhanced across a number of dimensions. New restrictions apply to 'independent investment advice', most notably a prohibition on inducements and a requirement that independent investment advice be based on an assessment of a sufficiently diverse range of financial instruments (with regard to type and issuers or product providers) and not be limited to proprietary products (Article 24(7)). A prohibition on inducements also applies to portfolio/asset management (Article 24(8)). More generally, an investment firm must ensure that it does not remunerate or assess the performance of its staff in a way that conflicts with its duty to act in the best interests of the client; in particular, it should not make any arrangement by way of remuneration or otherwise that could incentivize its staff to recommend a particular financial instrument to a retail client when the firm could offer a different financial instrument that would better meet the client's needs (Article 24 (10)). Restrictions also apply to inducements (Article 24(9)). Product bundling and tying has also been addressed: where an investment service is offered together with another service or product as part of a package or as a condition for the same agreement or package, the firm must inform the client whether it is possible to buy the different components separately and provide the costs of these components (Article 24(11)).

Suitability/'know your client' rules apply to investment advice and asset management under Article 25, which requires investment firms to obtain the necessary information regarding the client's knowledge and experience in the investment field relevant to the type of product or service engaged, the client's financial situation (including ability to bear losses), and the client's investment objectives (including risk tolerance) so as to enable the firm to recommend the services and instruments which are suitable for the client and, in particular, are in accordance with the client's risk tolerance and ability to bear losses (Article 25(2)). A written statement (the suitability letter) must be provided to the retail client which specifies the advice and how the advice meets the preferences, objectives, and other characteristics of the client (Article 25(6)). A lighter 'appropriateness' assessment, which imposes significantly less responsibility on the firm, applies to all other investment services. In practice, this category typically relates to execution-only sales of complex products which do not qualify for non-advised execution-only sales (Article 25(3)); the firm in this case is required only to ask the client for information (not obtain information) regarding the client's knowledge and experience relevant to the type of product or service engaged, so as to enable the firm to assess whether the service or product is appropriate for the client.

Where the firm deems the product inappropriate, a warning must be given to the client but the transaction may proceed; similarly, where the client does not provide the required information or provides insufficient information, the firm may proceed, but must warn the client that it is not in a position to determine whether the service or product is appropriate. Article 25(4) governs the execution-only regime and identifies the 'non-complex' instruments which may be sold without a suitability or appropriateness test; margin/loan services to the client cannot be provided in conjunction with execution-only services of this type. Article 25(4) also requires that such services are provided at the initiative of the client, that risk warnings are provided to the effect that an appropriateness assessment is not made, and that the Article 23 conflict-of-interest requirements are met.

More generally, investment firms are required to provide the client with adequate reports on the service provided, including periodic communications (Article 25(6)).

The Article 24/25 regime is subject to extensive delegations (Articles 24(13) and 25(8)); the related administrative rulebook is likely to reflect the extensive administrative rules adopted under the 2006 Commission MiFID I Directive, which specified the particular disclosures required; the nature of the ongoing reporting requirement; the nature of the 'non-complex' financial instruments which qualified for the execution-only regime; and the nature of, and the information required in relation to, the suitability and appropriateness assessments.

The Article 24/25 conduct regime is primarily associated with retail client protection and is strongly concerned with the quality of advice and product sales, and so is examined in Chapter IX. It applies, however, to professional clients. While the MiFID II administrative rulebook is likely to differentiate between professional and retail clients, particularly with respect to the specification of disclosure requirements, the legislative regime (with some minor exceptions, including the suitability letter requirement which applies to retail clients) applies to professional clients. The conduct regime does not, for the most part, apply in relation to order execution services provided to eligible counterparties, reflecting the arm's-length dynamic which characterizes these wholesale market transactions (Article 30). But— as noted in section 5.2, and reflecting the widespread failure of market monitoring by and discipline in the wholesale market over the financial crisis, particularly with respect to the distribution of risk through securitization products—MiFID II has imposed minimum standards on these transactions, primarily with respect to information requirements. While these requirements can be associated with investor protection, they also have a financial stability dimension, by injecting regulatory compliance incentives and incentives relating to the risks of *ex-post* private/public enforcement into wholesale market relationships.

IV.7.7 Tied Agents

A discrete if light-touch registration regime applies to investment firms' tied agents (Article 29).[272] Member States are empowered to adopt additional rules with respect to tied agents registered in their territories (Article 29(6)). The defining characteristic of a tied agent under MiFID II is that the agent operates under the sole responsibility of the appointing investment firm, which remains responsible for MiFID II compliance in

---

[272] CESR amplified the MiFID I regime in its Passport Guidelines (CESR/07-337 and CESR/07-337b).

relation to the agent's activities. A tied agent is defined under Article 4(1)(29) as a natural or legal person who, under the full and unconditional responsibility of only one investment firm (on whose behalf it acts), provides investment and/or ancillary services to clients or prospective clients, receives and transmits instructions or orders from the client in respect of investment services or financial instruments, places financial instruments, and/or provides advice to clients or prospective clients in respect of those financial instruments or services.

The MiFID I regime allowed Member States discretion as to whether to permit the appointment of tied agents, given the very different degree to which these agents were relied on across the Member States (most Member States exercised this option). In the only major change from MiFID I, the MiFID II tied agents regime is prescriptive in this regard, and requires Member States to allow investment firms to appoint tied agents for the purposes of promoting the services of the firm, soliciting business or receiving orders from clients or prospective clients and transmitting those orders, placing financial instruments, and providing advice in respect of such financial instruments and services offered by the investment firm (Article 29(1)).[273] The regime is discretionary with respect to the scope of tied agents' activities, however. Most risks to investor protection in the tied agent context arise with respect to asset protection. The Member State accordingly may, but is not required to, allow tied agents registered in its territory to hold clients' money and instruments (on behalf of and under the full responsibility of the investment firm principal), subject to the MiFID II asset protection regime; the Member State of registration may also allow tied agents to hold client assets in the territory of a Member State which allows tied agents to hold client assets.[274]

The tied agents regulatory regime is generally light-touch, reflecting the responsibility placed on the investment firm principal. Article 29(2) addresses the relationship between the firm and agent and provides that the firm must remain fully and unconditionally responsible for any action or omission on the part of the tied agent when acting for the firm. The investment firm must also ensure that the tied agent discloses the capacity in which it is acting, and the firm which it is representing, before contacting or dealing with any client (Article 29(2)).

Tied agents must be registered in a public register in the Member State in which they are established: ESMA is required to provide links to these registers (Article 29(3)). Tied agents may only be admitted to the register where they are of sufficiently good repute and possess the appropriate general, commercial, and professional knowledge and competence so as to be able to deliver the investment service or ancillary service and to communicate accurately all relevant information concerning the proposed service to the client. Member States may, at their discretion, and subject to appropriate controls, allow investment firms to verify whether their tied agents are of sufficiently good repute and possess the required knowledge (Article 29(3)). An investment firm is required to monitor the activities of its tied agents to ensure the firm complies with MiFID II when acting through tied agents (Article 29(2)).

---

[273] The Commission reported that the MiFID I tied agents regime was regarded as working well by CESR and that only minor adjustments were required; the removal of optionality reflects the wider agenda to remove optionality within the EU rulebook under the crisis agenda: 2010 MiFID I Review Consultation, n 112, 73.

[274] This discretion was added by the Council; the 2011 MiFID II Proposal did not permit tied agents to hold client assets.

An investment firm appointing tied agents must also take adequate measures in order to avoid any 'negative impact' that the activities of the agent not covered by MiFID II could have on the activities carried out by the tied agent on behalf of the investment firm (Article 29(4)).

IV.8 Operating Conditions: the 2013 CRD IV/CRR Prudential Regime

IV.8.1 Capital, Investment Firms, and Basel III

Prior to the crisis era, the prudential supervision of investment firms in the EU was primarily associated with own funds/capital requirements, although MiFID I imposed a range of prudentially orientated authorization and operational requirements. The capital regime was set out in the 2006 Capital Requirements Directive (2006 CRD),[275] which applied to credit institutions[276] and investment firms, and which implemented the 2004 Basel II Capital Accord[277] (which was primarily concerned with credit risk) and, with respect to market risk/'trading book'[278] activity, the Basel Trading Book Review.[279]

From the investment firm perspective, the capital regime was based on the assumption that the major solvency risk faced by investment firms related to the market risk which trading activities can pose and which relates to the exposure of an investment firm to losses which may be sustained from open positions in price-sensitive financial instruments. Market risk involves a number of elements, including the risk of the market moving against a particular instrument, risks inherent in the instrument itself, and general market movement risk (for example, interest rate movement risk) which could affect the security in question. Investment firms are, however, exposed to other significant risks in the trading book, including counterparty risk, the extent of which the financial crisis would make clear. The 2006 CRD regime was based on the 'Value at Risk' (VAR) capital assessment, which linked capital requirements to the probability of losses incurred before positions could be closed, and which was based on firms' internal modelling of risk.

As has been extensively documented, the financial crisis exposed significant weaknesses in the Basel capital regime generally, including with respect to poor-quality capital which was not sufficiently loss-absorbing and with respect to the pro-cyclical nature of capital requirements. From an investment firm perspective, the inadequacy of capital levels held

---

[275] Composed of Directive 2006/48/EC [2006] OJ L177/1 and Directive 2006/49/EC [2006] OJ L177/201.

[276] The 2006 CRD also provided the authorization and operational regulation framework for credit institutions.

[277] The Basel Accords are produced by the Basel Committee on Banking Supervision and set international minimum standards on bank capital adequacy and related prudential requirements. The Commission and ECB are observers at the Basel Committee.

[278] The 'trading book' concept is used to capture the risks associated with market/trading activities (as distinct from credit risk). See further n 341 and sect 8.7.2.

[279] In particular, Basel Committee on Banking Supervision, The Application of Basel II to Trading Activities and the Treatment of Double Default Effects (2005) and Amendments to the Capital Accord to Incorporate Market Risks (1996).

against market risk (against the 'trading book'), which quickly became clear, became associated with excessive levels of leverage in the financial system and implicated in the deepening of the crisis.[280] The financial crisis also exposed the destructive consequences of poor liquidity risk management;[281] the 'drying up' of liquidity, rather than capital-related solvency problems, was—at least in the early stages of the financial crisis—the greatest threat to global financial stability. Accordingly, at an early stage, the G20 called for reform of the capital regime generally (including through additional capital requirements, enhanced quality of capital requirements, and the mitigation of pro-cyclicality risks), but also for the introduction of new liquidity and leverage requirements and an enhancement of the prudential framework more generally through stronger governance and risk-management requirements, particularly with respect to remuneration.[282] The related Basel III reforms were adopted over 2010–14.[283] The main features of the reforms are a strengthened capital regime (which includes new counterparty credit risk requirements, a tougher definition of capital, and higher capital requirements generally), new capital buffers, a liquidity ratio, and a leverage ratio.

While strongly associated with credit risk and with bank liquidity and leverage, the reform programme has also engaged closely with the market risks with which investment services and activities are most closely implicated. The financial crisis revealed that firms were only thinly capitalized against trading losses as a consequence of the pre-crisis assumption that trading book assets were generally liquid and that positions could quickly be unwound. The weaknesses of the prevailing risk assessment model also became clear; the VAR model for assessing trading book capital requirements became associated with pro-cyclicality risks and with poor quantification of the risks arising from the illiquid assets which became prevalent in trading books prior to the financial crisis.[284] It did not, for example, properly capture the risks of securitized assets, as it was based on relatively short periods of historical observation, did not capture systemic risk effectively, and, being based on normal distribution of returns, did not capture extreme loss scenarios ('fat tail' risks).[285] Accordingly, the new Basel regime includes a number of major revisions to the calculation of trading book risk (noted further on in this

---

[280] eg 2009 Turner Review, n 13, 53.

[281] From the initial analyses see, eg, Turner Review, n 13, 51–70, and Brunnermeier, M, Crocket, C, Goodhart, C, Persaud, A, and Shin, H, The Fundamental Principles of Financial Regulation. Geneva Reports on the World Economy 11 (2009) 29–40.

[282] The G20 London Summit, eg, called for a strengthening of prudential regulatory standards, including through new capital buffers, quality of capital enhancements, and the mitigation of pro-cyclicality risk in capital assessments; a 'simple, transparent, non-risk-based measure' to contain the build-up of leverage; a global framework for promoting stronger liquidity buffers; and a remuneration framework which would lead to better alignment between remuneration and strong risk management practices: London G20 Summit, April 2009, Declaration on Strengthening the Financial System.

[283] The bulk of the Basel III reforms to capital were adopted in 2010: A Global Regulatory Framework for More Resilient Banks and Banking Systems (2010). Enhancements to the counterparty credit risk assessment were adopted in 2011. An initial liquidity ratio was adopted in 2010 and a revised version in 2013: The Liquidity Coverage Ratio and Liquidity Risk Monitoring Tools. The leverage regime was adopted in early 2014: Basel III Leverage Ratio Framework and Disclosure Requirements (2014).

[284] 2009 Turner Review, n 13, 58.

[285] 2009 Turner Review, n 13, 22–3, 44, and 58. Similarly, Haldane, A and Nelson, B (Bank of England), Tails of the Unexpected, Bank of England Paper (2012).

section 8);[286] further revisions to the trading book are expected, as the Basel Committee's 'fundamental review' of the trading book is not complete.[287]

IV.8.2 2013 CRD IV/CRR

From an early stage of the financial crisis, reform of prudential regulation was a preoccupation of the EU reform programme. Major reforms were made to the 2006 CRD by the CRD II (2009) and CRD III (2010) reforms, which reflected ongoing work by the Basel Committee as well as EU-specific preoccupations (notably with respect to executive remuneration and the supervision of cross-border banking groups).[288] The 2006 CRD, and the CRD II and CRD II reforms, have now been consolidated within and refined by the massive 2013 CRD IV/CRR legislative regime,[289] which implements the Basel III reforms as well as related earlier reforms,[290] and also introduces EU-specific reforms.[291] The latter include the extensive executive remuneration regime (and in particular the controversial bonus cap), the new firm governance rules and related diversity requirements, a number of transparency requirements, and the three additional capital buffers which the EU has adopted (the systemic risk buffer, the global systemic institutions buffer, and the 'other systemic institutions' buffer).

CRD IV/CRR (and its accompanying, massive administrative rulebook[292]) is a central pillar of the EU's crisis-era reform agenda being primarily concerned with supporting bank solvency and with strengthening bank capital rules and introducing new leverage and liquidity requirements; it is the leviathan of the EU's crisis-era reform programme. Much of the regime is specific to credit institutions and implements the Basel III agreement; it is, accordingly, closely concerned with bank credit risk, liquidity, and leverage. But the CRD

---

[286] Set out in Basel Committee on Banking Supervision, Revisions to the Basel II Market Risk Framework (2010).

[287] Basel Committee on Banking Supervision, Fundamental Review of the Trading Book (2012) (the 2012 Trading Book Review) and Fundamental Review of the Trading Book: A Revised Market Risk Framework (2013) (the 2013 Trading Book Review).

[288] CRD II (2009) (Directive 2009/111/EC [2009] OJ L302/97) addressed, *inter alia*, securitizations and cross-border supervision. CRD III (2010) addressed, *inter alia*, re-securitizations, trading book capital and executive pay and risk-taking (Directive 2010/76/EU [2010] OJ L329/3).

[289] The Commission's Proposals were presented in July 2011 (COM (2011) 453—CRD IV and COM (2011) 452—CRR); the Parliament reached negotiating positions in May 2012 (A7-0170/2012—CRD IV and A7-0171-2012—CRR), and the Council adopted General Approaches in March 2013, following which trilogue negotiations concluded in April 2013. The main points of contention included the single rulebook model adopted and the related prohibition on Member States imposing higher capital requirements, the extent and scale of the capital buffers (which extended beyond the Basel III requirements), and the remuneration regime.

The behemoth CRR contains 521 articles and three annexes. The lighter CRD IV is composed of 165 articles and one annex. Both regimes provide for extensive delegations to administrative rule-making and additionally provide for an array of supervisory convergence measures (mainly guidelines), in both cases to be advised on, proposed by, or adopted by, for the most part, EBA (albeit in places in co-ordination with ESMA where investment firms are closely engaged).

[290] The 2010 market risk reforms (n 287), eg, have been termed Basel 2.5.

[291] The regime as a whole is to be implemented by 1 January 2019, although earlier implementation dates apply to many of its requirements.

[292] At the time of writing, the vast delegated rulebook was under development. EBA had, eg, proposed a swathe of BTSs to the Commission in December 2013 and earlier over 2013. In March 2014, the Commission adopted nine related RTSs.

IV/CRR regime also forms a key element of investment firm regulation and supervision as it is addressed to the prudential regulation of credit institutions and investment firms, even if in practice many of its rules, particularly with respect to credit risk and leverage, are primarily concerned with supporting the solvency and liquidity of credit institutions. As was the case with the Basel II agreement, the Basel III regime has been applied by the EU to all credit institutions and investment firms, given the competitive distortions and arbitrage risks which could arise were it not so applied, particularly as EU regulation of credit institutions and investment firms applies on a functional basis and is not institution-based. The CRD IV/CRR regime is, accordingly, calibrated in places to reflect the wide array of institutions subject to the Basel III agreement in the EU.

The 2013 CRD IV lays down rules concerning access to the activity of credit institutions and investment firms (access to the activity of investment firms is primarily governed by MiFID II; CRD IV contains the parallel authorization and passporting provisions, calibrated to the banking sector, for credit institutions); the supervisory powers and tools for the prudential supervision of credit institutions and investment firms by NCAs; the prudential supervision of credit institutions and investment firms in a manner consistent with the CRR; and the publication requirements for NCAs in the field of prudential regulation and supervision (CRD IV Article 1). From an investment firm perspective, the CRD IV regime is broadly concerned with initial capital, firm governance (including remuneration), risk management, the capital buffers element of the own funds (capital) regime, and the nature of supervisory review by NCAs of prudential requirements.

The 2013 CRR addresses own funds (capital) requirements relating to credit risk, market risk, operational risk, and settlement risk; large exposure reporting and capital requirements; liquidity requirements; leverage reporting; and public disclosure requirements (CRR Article 1). From an investment firm perspective, the main features of the CRR relate to capital requirements relating to risks other than core credit risk (and in particular counterparty credit, market, settlement, and operational risk), the constituents of the own funds which can be used to meet the capital requirements, and the significantly enhanced reporting regime.

From a credit institution perspective, the CRD IV/CRR regime provides a comprehensive 'banking rulebook' governing credit institution authorization, cross-border passporting, and operating conditions, including the behemoth capital, liquidity, and leverage regime; credit institutions which provide investment services are additionally subject to the investment services-specific conduct and operational/prudential rules which apply under MiFID II/MiFIR.[293] From an investment firm perspective, the CRD IV/CRR regime sits alongside the 2014 MiFID II/MiFIR regime and is concerned with particular prudential aspects of investment firm regulation, including with respect to initial capital, firm governance, risk management, and own funds/capital, liquidity, and leverage. CRD IV/CRR does not apply to access to the activity of investment firms insofar as it is regulated by MiFID II/MiFIR (CRD IV Article 2(5)(1)).

Reflecting the very strong association between CRD IV/CRR and banking regulation, the European Banking Authority (EBA) is charged with developing BTSs and supervisory

---

[293] See sect 4.1.

convergence measures (mainly guidelines) under CRD IV/CRR, and has become the *de facto* custodian of the vast CRD IV/CRR 'single rulebook'; the EBA-led single rulebook has come to be widely regarded as a key device for ensuring the pan-EU integrity of the regulatory scheme for the single market in banking, given the potentially de-stabilizing impact of euro-area dominance under Banking Union (Chapter XI section 7). ESMA, however, has been charged with specific responsibilities, where the need for calibration to the investment services context is particularly acute.

The 2013 CRD IV/CRR regime (with its accompanying administrative rules) is typically termed the 'banking rulebook' or 'single rulebook' because of its very high degree of prescription. The 2013 CRR is in the form of a regulation and accordingly does not allow Member States flexibility in implementation; the capital, liquidity, and leverage regimes are all set at EU level. This adoption of a prescriptive model, particularly with respect to capital levels, seems counterintuitive as it prevents Member States from adopting higher standards. But it reflects a number of factors, including the wider political commitment to a single rulebook, the typically granular nature of prudential regulation and the intensity of the Basel III reforms, the crisis-era experience with the more open-textured 2006 CRD regime,[294] and concerns to avoid regulatory arbitrage risks were some Member States to increase capital levels and others not. The latter factor had a strong political dimension, given the concern of some Member States to maintain capital levels at a lower harmonized level (reflecting in some cases weaker capital levels in the domestic banking industry) and to protect their markets from competition. The prohibition on Member States from adopting additional capital requirements was highly contested over the negotiations, however, with some Member States, notably the UK and Sweden, concerned to retain the flexibility to impose additional capital requirements where necessary given local market conditions.[295] Ultimately, while the CRD IV/CRR capital requirements cannot be increased by the Member States, some flexibility is built into the regime. Additional capital (and leverage and liquidity requirements) can be imposed under the 2013 CRD IV supervisory review process and in relation to particular institutions (CRD IV Article 104).[296] Member States are additionally empowered to increase the capital requirements which apply in relation to real estate loan assets, in order to manage local property bubbles (CRR Article 124). The capital buffer regime is also designed to allow Member States some flexibility, particularly with respect to the counter-cyclical buffer which Member States are to adjust to reflect local economic and structural conditions. By contrast, CRD IV, which covers non-capital operational requirements, takes the form of a directive, given the need for flexibility, particularly with respect to the supervisory review process, firm governance, and the capital buffer regime.

Supervision of the CRD IV/CRR regime is subject to a distinct supervisory regime based on intense supervisory review of institutions' compliance and on NCAs adopting specific risk

---

[294] In particular, a number of Member States did not apply (as was permitted under a transitional opt-out) certain 2006 CRD rules which might have reduced the risks of securitization, significant divergences appeared with respect to Member States' requirements for the 'Internal Ratings Based' risk models on which the Basel II capital regime heavily depended (see n 324), and Member States took widely varying approaches to the pivotal definition of the 'own funds' which qualified to meet the CRD's capital requirements: Commission, CRD IV/CRR FAQ, July 2013.

[295] eg ICFR, Basel III: Progress on Implementation. Regulatory Briefing. September 2012.

[296] See further sect 12.

mitigation measures calibrated to particular institutions' risk profiles, including, where appropriate, additional capital and liquidity requirements (section 12).

Given the vast scale of the Basel III/CRD IV/CRR regime and its primary focus on the solvency and liquidity of credit institutions, the main features of the related prudential regime which applies to investment services and activities are considered in this section in outline only.[297]

IV.8.3 2013 CRD IV/CRR: Scope

The 2013 CRD IV and the CRR apply to 'institutions', defined under the CRR as credit institutions[298] and MiFID II/MiFIR investment firms[299] (CRR Article 1 and CRD IV Article 2).

The regime is calibrated to the different range of services provided by investment firms and the different extent to which prudential risks accordingly apply. Chief among the calibrations is the exclusion from the scope of CRD IV/CRR of firms which are not authorized to provide custody-related ancillary services, and which only engage in the reception and transmission of orders, the execution of orders, portfolio management, and investment advice, given the significantly lower prudential risks these firms pose (CRR Article 4(1)(2)(c)).

IV.8.4 2013 CRD IV/CRR: Initial Capital

Minimum initial capital requirements are designed to ensure that investment firms enter the financial system with sufficient financial resources. Initial capital requirements should not, however, be so stringent as to deter competition and stultify the market by imposing unnecessary barriers to the entry of new firms. The 2013 CRD IV regime (reflecting the precursor 2006 CRD regime) mediates between these concerns in Articles 28–32, which set out the minimum initial capital levels for investment firms. The level applicable is a function of the activities which the investment firm undertakes and reflects the range of activities which an investment firm may be authorized to carry out, some of which do not require that the firm be subject to onerous capital requirements, given reduced counterparty and market risk.

---

[297] The Basel III and CRD IV/CRR single rulebook raises myriad issues, including with respect to its costs and impact on credit supply, the effectiveness of its regulatory design, the complexity which it has brought to prudential regulation (particularly given the greater dependence on internal risk modelling by in-scope institutions which has followed), the validity of the assumptions on which it is based, the regulatory arbitrage and competition risks which it may generate, and the resilience of the rulebook in the face of potential euro-area (Banking Union) and single market tensions. See, from an extensive scholarly and policy literature, eg Carmassi, J and Micossi, S, Time to Set Banking Regulation Right, CEPS Paper (2012); Angelini, B, et al, Basel III: Long-Term Impact on Economic Performance and Fluctuation, Bank of Italy Occasional Paper No 87 (2011), available at <http://ssrn.com/abstract=1849866>; Schwerter, S, 'Basel III's Ability to Mitigate Systemic Risk' (2011) 19 *JFRC* 337; and Blundell-Wignall, A and Atkinson, P, 'Thinking Beyond Basel III: Necessary Solutions for Capital and Liquidity' (2010) 1 *Financial Market Trends* 1.

[298] A credit institution is defined as an undertaking the business of which is to take deposits or other repayable funds from the public and to grant credits for its own account: 2013 CRR Art 4(1)(1).

[299] 2013 CRR Art 4(1)(3).

Unless a firm is subject to tailored requirements, the initial capital requirement is €750,000 (Article 28).[300] Where a firm does not deal in financial instruments on own account or underwrite issues of financial instruments on a firm commitment basis, but holds client assets and offers one or more of either order reception and transmission, order execution, and portfolio management services, the initial capital requirement is reduced to €125,000 (Article 29).[301] Where a firm is not authorized to hold client assets (primarily investment advisers),[302] the initial capital requirement takes the form of either: €50,000; professional indemnity insurance covering the whole of the Union or other comparable guarantee against liabilities arising from professional negligence, representing at least €1 million applying to each claim and in aggregate €1.5 million per annum for all claims; or a combination of initial capital and professional indemnity insurance which is equivalent to the latter two requirements (Article 31).[303] The low capital charge reflects the limited risk of investment advisers generating counterparty risk. But it also reflects the structure of the investment advice market, which is dominated by small firms which could face very high barriers to entry were high capital requirements imposed.[304]

IV.8.5 2013 CRD IV/CRR: Risk Management and Systems

The 2013 CRD IV/CRR regime contains extensive requirements related to internal risk-management systems and procedures. In particular (and in addition to the detailed CRR-specific procedures which relate to the capital assessment process), under the CRD IV framework for 'review processes', investment firms must have in place sound, effective, and comprehensive strategies and processes to maintain, on an ongoing basis, the amounts, types, and distribution of internal capital that they consider adequate to cover the nature and level of the risks to which they are or might be exposed (Article 73). More generally, an overarching requirement (which operates in parallel with the lighter and more widely cast 2014 MiFID II Articles 9 (firm governance) and 16 (organizational requirements) regime) prescribes that firms have robust governance arrangements (which include a clear organizational structure with well-defined, transparent, and consistent lines of responsibility); effective processes to manage, monitor, and report the risks they are or might be exposed to; adequate internal control mechanisms (including sound administration and accounting

---

[300] The qualifying own-funds components of the capital requirement are governed by 2013 CRR Art 26(1)(a)–(e).

[301] Where a firm executes investor orders for financial instruments and holds such instruments for own account, the lighter capital regime may be applied by the NCA, as long as the conditions specified are met (these conditions relate to the volume of such positions, as well as to the firm's compliance with the CRR requirements which govern the holding of initial capital on an ongoing basis and apply to large exposures).

[302] Although these firms are otherwise exempted from the scope of CRD IV/CRR, the Art 31 initial capital requirement applies: Art 2(3).

[303] A lower capital requirement applies where the firm is also registered under the EU's insurance mediation regime.

[304] The equivalent MiFID I indemnity regime was examined in Commission, Final Report on the Continued Appropriateness of the Requirements for Professional Indemnity Insurance Imposed on Intermediaries under Community Law (2007) (COM (2007) 178). The Report found that the policy justification for insurance-based regulation remained sound, and that the insurance option was a useful regulatory tool which complemented capital requirements and compensation schemes and provided incentives for firms to improve their own risk assessments and control activities and, accordingly, to reduce their insurance premiums.

procedures); and remuneration policies and practices that are consistent with and promote sound and effective risk management (Article 74(1)). As under the MiFID II regime, these systems must be comprehensive and proportionate to the nature, scale, and complexity of the risks inherent in the firm's business model and activities. Specific requirements apply with respect to recovery and resolution plans (Article 74(4)).[305]

A wide range of risk-management requirements apply under Articles 76–87. Overarching governance requirements apply with respect to the internal organization of risk governance under Article 76. The management body must approve and periodically review the firm's strategies and policies for taking up, managing, monitoring, and mitigating the risks the institution is or might be exposed to, including those posed by the macroeconomic environment in which it operates; it must also devote sufficient time to the consideration of risk issues, and be actively involved in and ensure adequate resources are allocated to the management of all material risks as well in the valuation of assets, the use of external credit ratings, and internal risk models relating to those risks. A risk committee is required for firms which are significant in terms of size and internal organization and the nature, scope and complexity of their activities.[306] Article 76 also requires that an independent risk-management function is established;[307] this requirement is without prejudice to the parallel MiFID II risk-management requirements.

An array of requirements governs specific internal risk-management procedures and systems (Articles 77–87); the requirements range from rules addressing the calculation of required own funds to rules governing specific forms of risk assessment. Some of these requirements are particularly targeted to credit institutions and the assessment of credit risk.[308] The risk-management requirements of more direct relevance to investment services and activities include the requirements relating to the implementation of policies and processes for the identification, measurement, and management of concentration risk from counterparty exposures (Article 81), market risk (Article 83), operational risk (Article 85), liquidity risk (Article 86), and excessive leverage (Article 87).

IV.8.6 2013 CRD IV/CRR: Firm Governance and Remuneration

IV.8.6.1 The Management Body

The 2013 CRD IV firm governance regime (Articles 88 and 91) addresses management body composition and functioning, and is designed to support strong oversight of risk management and to reduce the incidence of excessive risk-taking. For in-scope investment firms, it operates in parallel with the 2014 MiFID II Article 9 governance regime (section 6.4)

---

[305] See sect 13 on investment firm resolution.

[306] The risk committee's structure and functions are prescribed by Arts 76(3)–(4).

[307] The risk management function must ensure that all material risks are identified, measured, and reported. It must be actively involved in elaborating the institution's risk strategy and in all material risk management decisions, and deliver a complete view of the whole range of risks of the institution.

[308] In particular, Art 77(1) requires NCAs to encourage institutions that are significant in terms of their size and internal organization, and the nature, scale, and complexity of their activities, to develop an internal credit risk assessment capacity and to increase use of the CRR's Internal Ratings Based Approach (n 324) for calculating own-funds requirements for credit risk, where their exposures are material in absolute terms and where they have, at the same time, a large amount of material counterparties. Extensive requirements apply under CRD IV/CRR with respect to supervisory review of the Internal Ratings Based Approach.

which, although very similar in places with respect to the functions of the management body, applies in addition to the CRD IV regime; Articles 88 and 91 are directly incorporated into MiFID II Article 9, thereby catching non-CRD IV/CRR-scope investment firms.

Under Article 88(1), the management body must define, oversee, and be accountable for the implementation of governance arrangements that ensure the effective and prudent management of an institution, including the segregation of duties in the organization and the prevention of conflicts of interest. These arrangements must comply with a number of principles: the management body must have overall responsibility for the institution, and approve and oversee the implementation of the institution's strategic objectives, risk strategy, and internal governance; it must ensure the integrity of accounting and financial reporting systems (including financial and operational controls and compliance with the law and relevant standards); it must oversee the process of disclosure and communications; and it must be responsible for providing effective oversight of senior management. The management body must monitor and periodically assess the effectiveness of the institution's governance arrangements, and take appropriate remedial steps. In addition, the chairman of the management body (in its supervisory function, where the function of the body is split, as under the two-tier board system) must not exercise simultaneously the functions of chief executive officer within the same institution (unless justified by the institution and authorized by the NCA).

A nomination committee is, in addition, required for institutions which are significant in terms of size, internal organization, and the nature, scope, and complexity of their activities (Article 88(2)).[309]

Article 91 addresses the composition of the management body. Members must at all times be of sufficiently good repute, and have sufficient knowledge, skills, and experience to perform their duties; the overall composition of the body must reflect an adequately broad range of experiences (Article 91(1)). In addition, capacity-related conditions apply. All members must commit sufficient time to perform their functions (Article 91(2)). Specifically, the number of directorships which may be held by a member of the management body at the same time must take into account individual circumstances and the nature, scale, and complexity of the institution's activities. In particular, unless the member is representing a Member State, members of the management body of an institution that is significant in terms of size, internal organization, and the nature, scope, and complexity of activities must not hold more than one of the following combinations of directorships at the same time: one executive directorship with two non-executive directorships; or four non-executive directorships.[310] An additional non-executive

---

[309] The functions of the nomination committee are specified in some detail under Art 88(2), which requires the nomination committee to identify and recommend candidates, but also periodically (and at least annually) to assess the structure, size, composition, and performance of the management body and to make recommendations for any changes to the management body, as well as to assess the knowledge, skills, and experience of individual board members and of the management body collectively.

[310] These restrictions do not apply to directorships in organizations which do not pursue predominantly commercial objectives. Art 91 also clarifies the nature of a single directorship, including that executive and non-executive directorships within the same group count as one directorship, as do such appointments in an undertaking (including non-financial entities) in which the institution holds a qualifying holding.

directorship can be approved by an NCA for MiFID II investment firms (MiFID II Article 9(2)).[311]

More generally, the management body must possess adequate collective knowledge, skills, and experience to be able to understand the institution's activities (including the main risks), and each member of the management body must act with honesty, integrity, and independence of mind to successfully assess and challenge the decisions of senior management where necessary and to effectively oversee and monitor management decision-making (Article 91(7) and (8)).[312]

The Article 91 regime also addresses board diversity.[313] Institutions and their respective nomination committees must engage a broad set of qualities and competences when recruiting members of the management body, and must put in place a related diversity policy; EBA is charged with benchmarking diversity practices and (in co-operation with ESMA in relation to investment firms) with adopting guidelines on the nature of diversity for the purposes of management body composition (Article 91(11) and (12)). The nomination committee regime (Article 88(2)) additionally requires that the nomination committee decide on a target for the representation of the under-represented gender in the management body, and prepare a related policy on how this target is to be met. Article 88(2) also requires that the nomination committee, to the extent possible and on an ongoing basis, takes account of the need to ensure that the management body's decision-making is not dominated by any one individual or small group of individuals in a manner detrimental to the interests of the institution as a whole.

IV.8.6.2 Remuneration

As has been extensively examined, the regulation of executive remuneration was, from an early stage of the international crisis-era reform programme, identified as a means for embedding stronger risk-management practices within investment firms and credit institutions,[314] although the extent to which disclosure, governance, and substantive remuneration design requirements should be deployed has been highly contested.[315]

---

[311] In parallel, under Art 91(6), NCAs may authorize management body members to hold one additional non-executive directorship; NCAs must inform EBA of such authorizations, and under 2014 MiFID II Art 9(2), EBA and ESMA must co-ordinate on the collection of such information in relation to investment firms.

[312] Institutions must devote adequate human and financial resources to the induction and training of members of the management body (Art 91(9)).

[313] This agenda, which was supported by the European Parliament in particular, is designed in part to avoid group-think and to facilitate critical challenge on the management body, as was highlighted by 2014 MiFID II rec 53.

[314] Internationally co-ordinated reform of remuneration practices was identified as a priority by the London April 2009 G20 Summit and has been driven internationally by means of the FSB (then FSF) Principles for Sound Compensation Practices (2009) and FSB, Principles for Sound Compensation Practices. Implementation Standards (2009), which were endorsed by the Pittsburgh September 2009 G20 Summit, and which have been the subject to FSB peer review (eg FSB, Thematic Review on Compensation (2010) and (2011)) and to implementation oversight (eg FSA, Implementing the FSB Principles for Sound Compensation Practices and their Implementation Standards. Second Progress Report (2013)).

[315] The role of remuneration regulation in supporting bank and systemic stability has been extensively examined in the crisis-era literature. See, eg: Ferran, E, 'New Regulation of Remuneration in the Financial Sector in the EU' (2012) 9 *ECFLR* 1, Ferrarini, G and Ungureanu, MC, 'Economics, Politics, and the International Principles for Sound Compensation Practices' (2011) 64 *Vanderbilt LR* 431, and Bebchuk, L and Spamann, H, 'Regulating Bankers' Pay' (2010) 98 *Georgetown LJ* 247.

Among the most fiercely negotiated and controversial of the 2013 CRD IV's prudential requirements are the remuneration rules (CRD IV Articles 92–6). They reflect the concern across the crisis-era reform programme to promote stronger risk-management practices and more effective risk-management incentives. But they also reflect the febrile debate on perceived excesses in 'bankers' pay' during the CRD IV/CRR negotiations, and the strong concern of the European Parliament to impose limits on variable pay. The new regime is based on the extensive 2010 CRD III reforms which applied a series of principles to the design of executive remuneration; the CRD IV negotiations led to this regime being extended, notably by the highly contested 'bonus cap' and by the similarly contested disclosures required relating to employees earning in excess of €1 million.

The extensive and prescriptive new remuneration regime, which has disclosure, governance, design, and supervisory review elements, applies to credit institutions and investment firms at group, parent company, and subsidiary level, and—generating great industry hostility and concerns as to the competitive position of the EU—to these entities when established in offshore financial centres (Article 92(1)). At the core of the regime is the requirement that firms comply (in a manner and to the extent appropriate to their size, internal organization, and the nature, scope, and complexity of their activities) with the principles set out when establishing and applying the total remuneration policies (inclusive of salaries and discretionary pension benefits) for particular categories of staff, including senior management, 'risk-takers',[316] staff engaged in control functions, and any employee receiving total remuneration that takes that employee into the same remuneration bracket as senior management and risk-takers, whose professional activities have a material impact on the firm's risk profile. The seven principles (Article 92(a)–(g)) require that: the remuneration policy is consistent with and promotes sound and effective risk-management and does not encourage risk-taking that exceeds the level of tolerated risk of the institution; the policy is in line with the firm's business strategy, objectives, values, and long-term interests, and incorporates measures to avoid conflicts of interests; the management body adopts and periodically reviews the general principles of the remuneration policy and is responsible for overseeing its implementation; the implementation of the policy is subject to central and independent internal review; staff engaged in control functions are independent from the business units they oversee, have appropriate authority, and are remunerated in accordance with achievement of the objectives linked to their functions, independent of the performance of the business areas they control; the remuneration of the senior officers in the risk-management and compliance function is overseen by the remuneration committee (or the management body where a committee is not established); and the remuneration policy, taking into account national criteria on wage setting, makes a clear distinction between criteria for fixing basic remuneration (which should primarily reflect relevant professional expertise and organizational responsibility) and variable

---

[316] The identification of 'risk-takers' has proved controversial given EBA's wide approach, which has been associated with significantly extending the population of staff subject to remuneration restrictions (EBA, Consultation on Technical Standards for the Definition of Material Risk Takers for Remuneration Purposes (EBA/CP/2013/11) (2013)). The proposed RTS was presented in December 2013 (EBA/RTS/2013/11) and adopted an approach based on quantitative (including staff earning in excess of €500,000 or in the top 0.3 per cent in terms of level of remuneration) and qualitative measures (relating to seniority and role in decision-making), and the availability of conditions which can be used to rebut the presumption that an individual is a material risk-taker. The Commission adopted the RTS in March 2014 (C(2014) 1332).

remuneration (which should reflect a sustainable and risk-adjusted performance, as well as performance in excess of that required to fulfil the employee's job description). Additional principles apply where the institution is in receipt of exceptional government intervention, which are designed to limit variable pay (Article 93). Remuneration governance is also addressed: where a firm is significant in terms of its size and internal organization, and the nature, scope and complexity of its activities, it must establish a remuneration committee responsible for remuneration decisions (Article 95). Detailed and restrictive requirements apply to the variable elements of remuneration (Article 94). These include: the requirement that performance-related remuneration be based on a combined assessment of the performance of the individual, the business unit, and the firm; the requirement that performance assessment be set in a multi-year framework; the highly contested ratio rule (bonus cap),[317] which requires that the variable component of remuneration cannot exceed 100 per cent of the fixed component of total remuneration for each individual;[318] the requirement that at least 50 per cent of variable remuneration take the form of shares or equivalent ownership interests;[319] the requirement that a substantial portion and at least 40 per cent of variable pay is deferred for not less than three to five years; the direction that all variable remuneration be subject to claw-backs;[320] and the requirement that variable remuneration (including deferred remuneration) vest only if it is sustainable according to the financial situation of the institution as a whole. EBA is charged with developing guidelines on the remuneration regime and with proposing technical standards,[321] but ESMA is to develop guidelines (in co-operation with EBA) on remuneration policies for categories of staff which engage in investment services and activities (Article 75(2)).

Specific supervisory obligations apply in relation to remuneration, which include the benchmarking by NCAs of remuneration trends and practices and the collection by NCAs of data on the number of natural persons per institution that are remunerated by €1 million or more per financial year (Article 75(3)), as well as related aggregated reporting by EBA.[322]

---

[317] Prominent critics include Bank of England Governor Carney, who criticized the cap as adopting the wrong approach to the support of financial stability: Pickard, J, Goff, S, and Fleming, S, 'BoE Chief Deals Blow to Miliband on Bonuses', *Financial Times*, 16 January 2014, 1.

[318] The cap can be raised to 200 per cent, but a series of conditions apply, including with respect to NCA notification and shareholder approval: Art 94(1)(g). The cap, introduced by the European Parliament, was heavily resisted by the UK, which was reported to be in a minority of one in the final Council negotiations: Barber, A, Fontanella-Khan, J, and Parker, G, 'Brussels Deals Rare Blow to City on Bonuses', *Financial Times*, 28 March 2013, 3. In 2013, the UK launched a challenge to the cap before the European Court of Justice (Case C-507/13 *UK v Parliament and Council*). The cap was predicted to lead to a significant increase in cash salaries (Jenkins, P and Oakley D, 'Banks Rush to Redraft Executive Pay Deals', *Financial Times*, 11 March 2013, 1), but the first widely reported consequence (in spring 2014) appeared to be major banks' payment to in-scope managers of additional monthly or quarterly 'allowances', designed to fall outside the CRD IV regime.

[319] Including instruments which can be fully converted into Common Equity Tier I instruments (see sect 8.7): Art 94(1)(l).

[320] The criteria for 'claw-back' must include where the staff member participated in or was responsible for conduct which resulted in significant losses to the institution or failed to meet appropriate standards of fitness and propriety: Art 94(1)(n).

[321] EBA is charged with issuing guidelines on sound remuneration policies which comply with Arts 92–95 (Art 75(2)) and with proposing BTSs. BTSs, eg, have been developed in relation to the identification of risk-takers (n 316) and the classes of instrument which can be used for variable remuneration (eg EBA/CP/2013/32).

[322] Based on the required NCA reports, EBA publishes aggregate data on 'high earners' (over €1 million) on a pan-EU basis (eg EBA, EBA Report. High Earners. 2012 Data (2013)). The data for 2012 showed that the highest values were reported for the UK (2,714 high earners), Germany (212), France (177), Italy (109), and Spain (100).

IV.8.6.3 Governance Reporting

The 2013 CRD IV/CRR regime imposes a very wide range of public and supervisory reporting obligations (section 8.8). The public disclosure obligations extend to firm governance and include the requirement for investment firms to provide disclosures on the risk-management function, the number of directorships held by management body members, the management body recruitment policy, the management body diversity policy, the existence of a risk committee and the frequency of its meetings, and a description of the information flow on risk to the management body (CRR Article 435). Firms must also report on the firm's remuneration policy and practices in relation to those categories of staff whose professional activities have a material impact on its risk profile (CRR Article 450).[323]

IV.8.7 2013 CRD IV/CRR: Own Funds, Liquidity, and Leverage

IV.8.7.1 The Basel III Reforms and CRD IV/CRR

Prior to the crisis-era reforms, the own funds (capital) framework for credit institutions and investment firms was set out in the 2006 CRD, which implemented the Basel II Accord and, for investment firms in particular, the Basel Trading Book Review. Similarly, the Basel III reforms are at the heart of the new CRD IV/CRR regime. The Basel III reforms require additional and better quality capital, impose a new liquidity ratio, and envisage a new leverage ratio. The major reform relates to the new liquidity ratio, which represents a major change for large banks in particular.

The capital assessment required of institutions under Basel III is broadly similar to the risk-weighting-based assessment which applied under Basel II,[324] which has generated some criticism, particularly given the advanced modelling capacity now required of institutions.[325] But the related supervisory review of internal models for assessing capital—particularly the models used for the centrally important risk-weighting of assets (or RWA process)—has become more intensive and intrusive. Additional capital requirements have

---

[323] Including information on: the decision-making process; the link between pay and performance; the ratios between fixed and variable pay; performance criteria; aggregate quantitative information on remuneration (broken down by senior management and members of staff whose actions have a material impact on the firm's risk profile), including amounts of remuneration (split into fixed and variable elements) and amounts and form of variable remuneration; and disclosure relating to the number of individuals being remunerated €1 million or more per financial year.

[324] The capital assessment for credit risk, eg, remains based on the three Basel II Standardized, Internal Ratings Based, and Advanced Internal Ratings Based approaches for assessing the risk weightings of assets (the 'RWA') against which the capital assessment is made. The Standardized model is based on the identification of large buckets of assets to which risk weightings are assigned under the Basel III model; generally, only small banks with under-developed risk-modelling capacities adopt the Standardized model, which adopts a blunt approach to the risk assessment of assets, being based on broad risk buckets. The Internal Ratings Based model, used by most banks bar the most complex and sophisticated, is based on banks using internal models (based on the 'Probability of Default') to determine the risk weighting to be attached to different asset classes, and allows a more calibrated approach (which may be less costly in capital terms) to be adopted. The Advanced Internal Ratings Based Model is more sophisticated again and, in particular, allows banks to calculate credit risk based additionally on an assessment of 'Loss given Default'—eg, it allows a bank to further calibrate the capital required by assessing the exact loss which arises once a loan has defaulted (it may not be 100 per cent, depending on the features of the loan).

[325] Leading to concerns that the regime has become overly complex.

also been imposed, primarily through the new capital buffers which are designed to mitigate pro-cyclicality risks; higher capital requirements have also been imposed with respect to certain assets.[326] In addition, a more prescriptive approach has been adopted towards the constituents of capital, which is designed to increase the quality and loss-absorption capacity of capital. These reforms respond to the weaknesses in the Basel II framework which were revealed by the financial crisis, and which included the consequential prevalence of poor-quality capital (which was not sufficiently loss-absorbing) and of insufficient levels of capital.

From the investment firm perspective, while the new capital, liquidity, and leverage reforms all apply, their impact is most pronounced for banks; the liquidity and leverage requirements, in particular, are primarily directed to banks. With respect to capital and investment firm dealing activities (the most capital-intensive activity), the most significant reforms relate to the material increases in the levels of trading book (market risk) capital required and the new requirements relating to the capital assessment for related counterparty credit risk. These reforms are broadly designed to reduce risk-taking with respect to proprietary dealing.

With respect to counterparty credit risk, the new Basel III regime (which includes a requirement for assessing counterparty credit risk for stressed conditions, and for stronger collateral management and initial margining) is designed to capture 'credit valuation adjustment risk', or the risk associated with a deterioration in the creditworthiness of a counterparty, which can have material systemic implications when related ratings downgrades and capital adjustments occur.[327] As the financial crisis revealed, this risk is particularly acute with respect to OTC derivatives and with respect to repurchases and securities financing activities. The new credit valuation adjustment risk regime applies a capital charge to these instruments and activities. It is designed to capture the mark-to-market losses associated with a deterioration in the creditworthiness of a counterparty, and also to provide incentives to reduce counterparty credit risks by clearing OTC derivatives through CCPs (although capital charges also apply with respect to CCP exposure[328]). [329]

The new trading book/market risk regime includes, for example, a requirement for 'stressed VAR' calculations (designed to ensure higher levels of capital apply to the trading book and to reduce pro-cyclicality risks[330]), an incremental capital charge to cover default risk and

---

[326] Notably investments in hedge funds, real estate, venture capital, and private equity.

[327] The new counterparty credit risk requirements represent a central element of the crisis-era reforms. Although counterparty credit risk was covered under Basel II, it did not address mark-to-market losses arising from readjustments of the credit valuation of assets. Over the financial crisis, over two-thirds of losses attributed to counterparty credit risk arose from credit valuation adjustments and only one third to actual defaults: Basel Committee, A Global Regulatory Framework for More Resilient Banks and Banking System, June 2011 (addressing counterparty credit risk).

[328] The regime governing capital charges for CCP exposure is under development: Basel Committee, Capitalization of Bank Exposures to Central Counterparties (2012) and Capital Treatment of Bank Exposures to Central Counterparties (2013). The proposed regime is, broadly, calibrated to the type of exposure to the CCP and to the extent to which the institution is exposed to mutualized losses from other participants in the CCP. Reflecting the G20 OTC derivatives markets agenda (Ch VI sect 4), it is designed to ensure there are strong incentives for clearing transactions through CCPs, and that the related capital charge is neither too low nor higher than that which applies to bilateral transactions.

[329] Commission, 2011 CRD IV/CRR Proposal Impact Assessment (SEC (2011) 949) paras 3.4 and 5.3.

[330] Basel Committee, Revisions to the Basel II Market Risk Framework (2010) 1.

credit risk migration (for example, the impact of ratings downgrades), and additional capital requirements for securitized products in the trading book. Further and more fundamental reforms to the capital assessment of trading book assets are expected.[331]

In the EU, the Basel III and related reforms to capital are addressed by the CRR, which lays down uniform rules governing own funds (capital) requirements relating to 'entirely quantifiable, uniform and standardized elements' of credit risk, market risk, operational risk, and settlement risk. The CRR also imposes requirements limiting large exposures and sets out the new liquidity and leverage ratios (CRR Article 1). The own funds regime is supplemented by the CRD IV requirements governing additional capital buffers (Articles 128–42).

IV.8.7.2 Own Funds

The behemoth CRR own funds (capital) regime is based on the foundational own funds requirement set out for credit institutions and investment firms in CRR Article 92. It requires that institutions (including in-scope investment firms) satisfy three own funds requirements: a Common Equity Tier 1 capital ratio of 4.5 per cent; a Tier 1 capital ratio of 6 per cent; and a total capital ratio of 8 per cent. In each case, the capital ratio is a percentage of the 'total risk exposure amount' (Article 92(2)). This formula reflects the earlier Basel II capital requirement (which also required an 8 per cent total capital ratio), but demands higher quality capital by specifying the required levels of Common Equity Tier I capital and Tier 1 capital. The 8 per cent capital ratio is, however, supplemented by the new capital buffers. The capital buffers are addressed by CRD IV (Articles 128–42), which provide for the Basel III-required buffers as well as the EU-specific buffers: the capital conservation buffer (Basel III);[332] the counter-cyclical buffer (Basel III);[333] the global systemic institutions risk buffer (EU);[334] the other systemic institutions buffer (EU);[335] and the systemic risk buffer (EU).[336] Additional capital requirements can be imposed on specific institutions under the supervisory review process (section 12).

---

[331] The Basel Committee review of the trading book, which commenced in 2012, is likely to lead to reforms relating to: the identification of trading book assets and the boundary with the banking book (the reforms are likely to make the boundary less permeable—given the large differences in the capital assessments for the risks of banking and trading book assets, the arbitrage incentives are very strong); evidence from firms as to how assets are allocated; a presumption that certain instruments are included in the trading book; a more intensive supervisory review of firms' assessment of the components of the trading book; a new regime for credit-related products in the trading book which takes the capital requirements closer to those applicable to the banking book; a more nuanced approach to risk assessment generally, in the form of requirements for stressed calibration and a move away from the VAR model to an 'expected shortfall' model; more comprehensive incorporation of market illiquidity risks; hedging and diversification requirements; and measures to address the Committee's view that there is excessive reliance on internal models to assess trading book risk: 2012 Trading Book Review, n 287, 1–5 and 2013 Trading Book Review, n 287, 1–6.

[332] This buffer (2.5 per cent of total exposures and composed of Common Equity Tier I capital components) sits above Common Equity Tier 1 capital and is designed to conserve capital; where an institution breaches the buffer (in that the total ratio of Common Equity Tier 1 falls below 7 per cent (4.5 per cent and 2.5 per cent)), progressively tougher restrictions are imposed on the institution in order to ensure capital is conserved.

[333] This buffer is designed to counteract the effects of the economic cycle by requiring banks to hold an additional capital amount (composed of Common Equity Tier 1 capital components) in good economic conditions; this buffer can be released where economic activity slows down or contracts.

[334] Inserted by the European Parliament and designed to apply a capital surcharge to globally systemically important financial institutions (G-SIFIs) (as identified by the FSB).

[335] Designed to apply a surcharge to domestically important institutions as well as EU institutions.

[336] Member States may apply this buffer to the financial sector or one or more subsets of the financial sector.

The 'total risk exposure' amount against which the different capital ratios are set is the sum of the outcome of a series of risk assessments (mainly directed to asset risk), which are governed by the CRR: the risk-weighted exposure amounts (the RWA assessment) for credit risk and dilution risk in respect of all the business activities of an institution, excluding risk-weighted exposure amounts from the trading book of the institution (this credit-risk-related assessment is the central assessment for credit institutions, but is less important for investment firms); the own funds requirements for the trading book of an institution for position risk and for large exposures which exceed the limits set by the CRR; the own funds requirements for foreign exchange risk, settlement risk, and commodities risk; the own funds requirements for the credit valuation adjustment risk of OTC derivatives, other than credit derivatives recognized to reduce risk-weighted exposure amounts for credit risk; and the risk-weighted exposure amounts for counterparty risk arising from the trading book business of the institution for identified derivatives, including credit derivatives, repurchase transactions, securities or commodities lending or borrowing transactions based on securities or commodities, margin lending transactions based on securities or commodities, and long settlement transactions (Article 92(3)).[337] Additionally, the own funds of an institution may not fall below the amount of initial capital required at the time of authorization. A series of calibrations and derogations apply to the calculation of the own funds requirement for investment firms (Articles 94–7), which include a calibrated regime for investment firms with limited authorization (firms not authorized to engage in dealing or underwriting on a firm commitment basis).

The modalities for these different assessments are set out in detail under the CRR; in general, the risk assessment is usually a function of internal ratings models which are subject to supervisory review and approval. The CRD IV/CRR regime seeks greater risk sensitivity and so encourages the use of internal ratings models for calculating own funds requirements (CRD IV Article 77(1))[338] and, like EU securities and markets regulation generally,[339] seeks to reduce mechanistic reliance on external ratings (CRD IV Article 77(2)). But while more intense supervisory review now applies to internal model use, the persistence of internal models in the CRD IV/CRR regime has led to concern, given the weaknesses which the financial crisis exposed in the ability of models to reliably capture risk.[340]

These risk assessment modalities include the determination of the composition of the trading book, which is pivotal to the capital assessment for investment firms; the trading book is defined as all positions in financial instruments and commodities held by an institution, either with 'trading intent' or in order to hedge positions held with trading intent (CRR Article 4(1)(86)); detailed rules govern the identification of trading book assets.[341]

---

[337] The own-funds requirements of Art 92(3)(b)–(e) are additionally to be multiplied by 12.5: 2013 CRR Art 92(4).

[338] See n 324.

[339] See Ch VII sect 2.8.1.

[340] eg Tucker, P (Deputy Governor, Bank of England), Speech on 'Competition, the Pressure for Returns and Stability', 17 October 2012. Similarly, Haldane, A (Bank of England), The Dog and the Frisbee (2012), warning that Basel III has 'spawned startling degrees of complexity and an over-reliance on probably unreliable models'.

[341] The trading book concept is amplified by 2013 CRR Arts 102–106 which set out the core qualifying requirements which apply to trading book assets, the related procedures governing trading and position

They also include the different permitted components of capital, including Common Equity Tier 1 capital and Tier 1 capital (CRR Articles 25–88).[342] Common Equity Tier 1 capital is the highest quality capital and at the core of the regime, and is subject to strict conditions (CRR Article 28).[343]

IV.8.7.3 Liquidity and Leverage

The Basel III reforms are most closely associated with the new liquidity and leverage ratios.

The liquidity ratio (CRR Articles 411–28) was heavily contested over the Basel III negotiations and has not received global support; in the EU, it will be phased in following market observation and subsequent amplification and refinement by the Basel Committee. The ratio is designed to ensure institutions manage their cash flows and liquidity more effectively and can better predict liquidity requirements and respond to liquidity strains; it is particularly concerned with banks' ability to manage deposit outflows in a stressed environment, and to match assets with long-term and more stable liabilities. It is composed of two elements: a Liquidity Coverage Requirement (LCR) (designed to support short-term (30-day) liquidity resilience);[344] and a Net Stable Funding Requirement (NSFR) (designed to ensure an institution has an acceptable amount of stable funding over a one-year period[345]).[346]

The leverage ratio, which has implications for global investment banks in particular, is designed to restrict the build-up of excessive leverage and to provide a backstop against failure of the risk models on which credit risk assessments are made, as well as against related gaming by institutions. As a new prudential tool, it is still at an early stage of development;[347] the CRR regime (Articles 429–30) accordingly is based on data collection (related to institutions' internal leverage ratios) and assessment, and a binding proposal is expected by the end of 2016.

---

management strategies and the inclusion of assets in the trading book, the 'prudent valuation' standard which applies to the valuation of trading book positions, and the treatment of permissible internal hedges within the trading book. These rules are under review (n 331).

[342] Tier 1 capital (the 'purest' form of which is Common Equity Tier 1 capital) is regarded as allowing an institution to continue its activities, and protects the institution against insolvency ('going concern capital'); it is particularly associated with allowing banks to absorb losses and to continue to engage in lending to the wider economy. Tier 2 capital, by contrast, is designed to ensure that depositors and creditors can be repaid on insolvency ('gone concern capital'): 2009 Turner Review, n 13, 53.

[343] It is composed, in effect, of equity capital and retained earnings.

[344] The LCR is designed to test a firm's ability to withstand a severe liquidity freeze that lasts 30 days.

[345] The NSFR addresses risks arising from major maturity mismatches between assets and liabilities.

[346] The original LCR, proposed in 2010, was revised by the Basel Committee in 2013, following concerns that it was overly restrictive and would impede the credit supply. The LCR is accordingly being subject to a review and observation period until final calibration by the Basel Committee (in 2015—the NSFR is to be finalized in 2018). The current regime is based on general requirements (designed to ensure that an institution holds liquid assets to cover its net cash outflows in stressed conditions over a 30-day period) and not on detailed prescription.

[347] The Basel Committee finally reached agreement in January 2014 and the ratio will not apply until 2018. The agreement is regarded as reflecting concerns from the investment banking industry that the earlier approach consulted on would have led to very high capital costs: Fleming, S and Chon, G, 'Banks Win Basel Leverage Concessions', *Financial Times,* 13 January 2014.

IV.8.8 2013 CRD IV/CRR: Public Disclosure and Supervisory Reporting

An extensive public disclosure regime applies to investment firms under the 2013 CRR (Articles 435–51); the disclosures are to be made at least annually and in conjunction with the annual financial statements (Article 433). The extensive disclosures required, which are designed to support market discipline (often termed 'Pillar 3' of the Basel regime), include disclosures relating to risk-management objectives and policies, own funds and capital requirements, exposure to counterparty credit risk, capital buffers, indicators of global systemic importance, credit risk adjustments, unencumbered assets, use of credit rating agencies, exposure to market risk and securitization risk, operational risk, leverage, and remuneration policy. Additional disclosure requirements apply where the firm has been permitted to deploy particular methodologies under CRD IV/CRR, including the Internal Ratings Based approach and internal market risk models (Articles 452–5). More generally, investment firms are required to disclose annually (in the annual financial statements), and by reference to the Member State(s) and third country(ies) in which they have an establishment, a range of information, including with respect to turnover, number of employees, profit or loss before tax, tax on profit or loss, and public subsidies received (CRD Article 89(1)); investment firms are also required to disclose their return on assets (CRD IV Article 90).[348]

However extensive the public reporting regime, it is dwarfed by the massive supervisory reporting regime, which is embedded across the CRD IV/CRR regime and which relates in particular to supervisory review of the internal risk models used by institutions.

IV.9 The Passport

IV.9.1 Passport Rights

IV.9.1.1 The Investment Firm

Home NCA authorization supports mutual recognition by the host NCA[349] and the 2014 MiFID II passport. MiFID II Articles 34 and 35 set out the passport rights which MiFID II-scope investment firms enjoy on authorization.

Article 34 addresses cross-border activity through services provision. It provides that Member States must ensure that any investment firms authorized and supervised by the NCA of another Member State in accordance with MiFID II (and credit institutions authorized under the 2013 CRD IV/CRR banking regime) may freely perform investment services and/or activities, as well as ancillary services, within their territories, as long as such services and activities are covered by the authorization (Article 34(1)). Reflecting Article 6(1), Article 34(1) also provides that ancillary services may only be provided together with a core

---

[348] This somewhat politically driven requirement, added at the Parliament's instigation, is designed to support the re-establishment of trust in the financial sector: CRD IV/CRR FAQ, n 294.

[349] Defined as the Member State, other than the home Member State, in which an investment firm has a branch or performs services and/or activities: Art 4(1)(56).

activity or service. Mutual recognition and home Member State control is at the heart of Article 34(1), which also provides that Member States may not impose any additional requirements on such investment firms or credit institutions in respect of the matters covered by MiFID II.

Article 35 governs the right of establishment, whether through a branch[350] or a tied agent. While very similar to the services passport, the establishment passport is more restrictive as it provides that the branch Member State may not impose any additional requirements save those allowed under Article 35(8) on the organization and operation of the branch. Certain key conduct requirements are devolved away from the home Member State/NCA to the branch Member State/NCA.

Home State control is reinforced by Article 21, which requires that Member States must require that investment firms authorized in their territory comply at all times with the authorization requirements, including the Article 16 organizational requirements: Article 16 expressly reserves compliance with its requirements to the home Member State. The jurisdiction-allocation clause for MiFID II's other operating requirements is not made similarly express,[351] but home Member State control is implicit in Articles 34 and 35. The position with respect to conduct-of-business regulation is different, however. It stays with the home Member State for services, but moves to the branch Member State for branches. But although branch control suggests host State control, the extent of the harmonization of conduct regulation means that differences between the home and host regime are likely to arise only with respect to supervisory techniques and enforcement strategies, and even here the ESFS institutional structure and, in particular, ESMA's supervisory convergence powers are likely to minimize material divergences.

Notwithstanding the centrality of home Member State control to the MiFID II market integration mechanism, there are some restrictions on its operation and some difficulties concerning its scope, particularly with respect to the branch Member State's powers.

IV.9.1.2 Restrictions on the Passport: General Restrictions

The mutual-recognition principle applicable under Articles 34 and 35 is restricted to services covered by an authorization from the home NCA. Investment firms whose activities in the host Member State fall outside the scope of the home NCA authorization, or whose home NCA authorization covers activities which do not come within the scope of authorization under MiFID II, will not benefit from the authorization passport in respect of those activities. Such firms will benefit from the independent Treaty guarantees concerning the freedom to establish and the freedom to provide services.[352]

---

[350] Defined in 2014 MiFID II Art 4(1)(30) as a place of business other than the head office which is a part of an investment firm, which has no legal personality, and which provides investment services and/or activities (it may also perform ancillary services for which the firm has been authorized). Notably, all places of business set up in the same Member State by an investment firm with headquarters in another Member State are regarded as forming a single branch.

[351] Art 22 more generally requires Member States to ensure that the NCAs monitor the activities of investment firms so as to assess compliance with MiFID II's operating conditions.

[352] Host Member States will be constrained by the Court of Justice's 'general-good rule' (which allows Member States to retain certain types of restrictive national rule where the rule is, *inter alia*, proportionate, non-discriminatory, and in the public interest/general good (see Ch I)) in applying rules which restrict the freedom to provide services and to establish. In particular, account must be taken of any authorization

The benefit of the passport and mutual recognition of authorization is limited to where the firm is either establishing a branch or providing services on a cross-border basis. Where an investment firm provides services which come within the scope of MiFID II in another Member State, but uses a subsidiary to do so, it will not benefit from mutual recognition of authorization, and will be subject to the authorization (and other) rules of the Member State in which the subsidiary is established, although that State is required to consult with the NCAs of the parent undertaking's home Member State under Article 84 and MiFID II generally applies.

MiFID II, like MiFID I, is designed to eliminate host Member State control to the greatest extent possible. Nonetheless, important precautionary and other powers remain with the host NCA. Under Article 85 host NCAs may, but only for statistical purposes, require all investment firms with branches in their territories to report to them periodically on the activities of those branches (Article 85(1)). Host NCAs may also require branches of investment firms to provide the information necessary for the monitoring of their compliance with the standards set by the host Member States and which apply to the branch under Article 35(8) (Article 85(2)). Important residual precautionary powers are set out in Article 86(1), which is designed to support dialogue between NCAs and to support host NCA action in respect of serious breaches, but only where the home NCA does not act. Although it confers wide-ranging precautionary powers on host NCAs, it also delineates the grounds on which these powers can be used. Under Article 86(1), where an NCA has 'clear and demonstrable' grounds for believing that an investment firm, acting in its territory under the freedom to provide services, is in breach of MiFID II obligations, or that a firm with a branch in its territory is in breach of MiFID II obligations which do not confer power on the host NCA, it must refer those findings to the home NCA. If, despite the measures taken by the home NCA (or where such measures prove inadequate), the firm persists in acting in a manner that is clearly prejudicial to the interests of host Member State investors or to the orderly functioning of markets, the host NCA may, after informing the home NCA, 'take all appropriate measures' (which can include preventing the firm from initiating any further transactions within the host State's territory) in order to protect investors and the proper functioning of the markets. These measures, in an indication of the risk these powers pose to home Member State control, must be notified to the Commission and ESMA without undue delay; ESMA can also exercise its mediation powers (Chapter XI section 5.3.1) where the host authority refers the issue in question to binding mediation.

IV.9.1.3 Restrictions on the Passport: Branch Member State Control

MiFID I marked a significant break with the ISD by incorporating the branch Member State into the passport mechanism; host NCA control over branches remains a central element of the 2014 MiFID II regime under Article 35(8).

Under Article 35(8), the NCA of the Member State in which the branch is located assumes responsibility for ensuring that all services provided by the branch within its territory

---

procedures or prudential rules to which the firm has been subject in its home State. Where national requirements track those set out in MiFID II, it is unlikely that the general-good justification would be available, as its harmonization represents a codification of the general good. See generally Tison, M, 'The General Good Exception: The Case of Financial Services' in Andenas, M and Roth, W-H (eds), *Services and Free Movement in EU Law* (2002) 350.

comply with the MiFID II Article 24 and 25 conduct rules and Article 27 and 28 order handling/best execution rules (as well as with the rules which apply under the 2014 MiFIR with respect to transaction reporting by investment firms and with respect to the trade transparency requirements imposed on investment firms in the form of 'systematic internalizers' and investment firms generally), and the measures adopted in relation to these provisions by the host State. The branch NCA also enjoys the right to examine branch arrangements and to request such changes as are 'strictly needed' to enforce these obligations with respect to the services and/or activities provided by the branch within its territory (Article 35(8)). The home NCA must, however, be permitted to carry out on-site inspections in the branch (in the exercise of its responsibilities and after informing the host NCA) (Article 35(9)). Although organizational requirements are reserved to the home Member State/NCA (Article 16(1)), the branch NCA is also empowered to enforce the Article 16 record-keeping obligation with respect to transactions undertaken by the branch, without prejudice to the possibility of the home NCA having direct access to those records (Article 16(11)).

Article 86(2) deals with enforcement with respect to branches and provides for gradually increasing intervention by the host NCA. Where the host NCA finds that a firm with a branch in its territory is in breach of the host State's rules adopted under MiFID II and which it may apply to branches, the NCA must require the firm to 'put an end to its irregular situation'. If the firm fails to take the necessary steps, the host NCA must take all 'appropriate measures' to ensure this ends and communicate those measures to the home NCA. But if, despite those measures, the firm persists in its breach, the host NCA may, after informing the Commission and ESMA (without undue delay), take all the appropriate measures needed in order to protect investors and the proper functioning of the markets. The host NCA may also refer the matter to ESMA for binding mediation.

Under the MiFID I regime, the exact scope of the branch NCA's jurisdiction proved troublesome, particularly with respect to whether the branch NCA had oversight of activity which takes place from, but outside, the branch Member State (although the Council's Common Position on MiFID I stated that services provided by a branch outside the Member State in which the branch was located remained the responsibility of the home State[353]). Even before MiFID I came into force, tensions arose between those Member States which took a liberal approach and those which took a restrictive approach on the grounds that the Council's aim was to limit the competence of the host Member State.[354] Following a CESR request (reflecting significant market concern), lengthy European Securities Committee negotiations,[355] and Member State consultation, the Commission finally adopted its guidance on the interpretation of (then) Article 32(7) in a June 2007 Communication.[356] The Commission emphasized that authorization was given to the investment firm as a whole and not to a branch, and that cross-border activities under that authorization were carried out by the investment firm, not by the branch. The

---

[353] MiFID I Common Position, n 75, 51. This position was not given more formal status, however, by, eg, inclusion in a recital.

[354] European Securities Committee Minutes, 17 January 2007.

[355] European Securities Committee Minutes, 17 January 2007, 14 February 2007, 14 March 2007, and 22 May 2007.

[356] Commission, Supervision of Branches under MiFID (2007).

Communication also noted the limited exceptions to home Member State control under MiFID I and argued that the allocation of responsibilities between home and host NCAs was, to a large extent, irrelevant for the wholesale markets, given that conduct rules were generally dis-applied between eligible counterparties. The Commission did, however, isolate three principles governing the allocation of NCA responsibility. First, where both the branch through which the service was provided and the client were in the host Member State, supervisory responsibility was to be allocated to the host/branch NCA. Second, where the client was in the home Member State, the home NCA was to be allocated supervisory responsibility. Finally, the Commission noted a 'grey area' between these areas where responsibility had to be decided on a case-by-case basis, where, for example, the client was not in either the host or home Member State, or where parts of a service were carried out across different Member States (through outsourcing mechanisms, for example, or via electronic means). Here the Commission suggested that the NCAs negotiate as to which NCA was responsible and use the CESR mediation mechanism in the case of disagreement. In practice, the scope of branch supervision has been governed by the CESR Branch Protocol,[357] which establishes a co-operation framework which supports close co-ordination between NCAs[358] and which has brought operational clarity; it can be expected to be enhanced and refined by ESMA.

IV.9.2 The Notification Process

The passport-notification process (which was initially significantly revised by the 2004 MiFID I; the original 1993 ISD notification regime was designed in part to notify the passporting firm of the plethora of host rules which could apply under the ISD regime) supports home NCA supervision of passporting firms by informing the home NCA of the nature of the activities carried out by the investment firm. It also supports the host NCA's precautionary powers.

Notification[359] is controlled by the home NCA, which, in the case of branch establishment, can block the exercise of passport rights. The host NCA cannot block access by the investment firm and is not an operative part of the notification process. The notification regime therefore dovetails with the pre-eminent position of the home Member State/NCA throughout the MiFID II authorization, operational, and supervisory framework.

Where an investment firm wishes to provide services or activities within a Member State for the first time (or wishes to change the range of services or activities provided), it must communicate the following to its home NCA: the Member State in which it intends to operate; a programme of operations which sets out the investment services (and ancillary services) which the firm intends to perform; and whether it intends to provide services through tied agents which are established in the home State (Article 34(2)).[360] With respect

---

[357] CESR, Protocol on the Supervision of Branches under MiFID (2007) (CESR/07/672).

[358] It is based on two models of co-operation which can be agreed by two or more NCAs: joint supervision conducted through common oversight programmes, and standing requests for assistance. NCAs are either to use these two options or other effective models or tools for co-operation.

[359] CESR adopted practical guidelines on the notification process: CESR, Protocol on MiFID Passport Notifications (CESR/07-317) (2007).

[360] Where the firm intends to use tied agents, the investment firm must communicate the identity of the tied agents to the home NCA.

to cross-border service provision through home-State-established tied agents, the home NCA must, within one month of receipt of the required firm information[361] (including the identity of the tied agent(s)), communicate to the host NCA the identity of the tied agents that the investment firm intends to use in the host State. The host NCA must publish this information. ESMA may also request access to this information.

The home NCA must, within one month of receiving the required Article 34(2) information, forward it to the host NCA; the investment firm is then free to provide the investment service(s) in the host Member State (Article 34(3)).

The services passport for credit institutions which provide investment services is governed by the 2013 CRD IV/CRR notification regime. This regime does not, however, provide for cross-border services provision through tied agents; Article 34(5) accordingly applies the MiFID II notification regime to reliance by credit institutions on tied agents to carry out MiFID II services activities on a cross-border services basis.

The provision of cross-border services is not accordingly automatic; it depends on the notification being transmitted to the home NCA. CESR recommended that once the notification was dispatched by the home NCA to a recognized point of contact in the host NCA, the firm could commence cross-border services from that date. But if the home NCA, as a result of exceptional circumstances, does not forward the information within a month of receipt, it cannot be deemed that the firm may commence business after that month;[362] in adopting this recommendation, CESR faced down vocal market calls for an automatic right to commence cross-border services. CESR argued that an automatic right to provide services was not acceptable as the home NCA, responsible for supervising services, needed to prepare for cross-border supervision. CESR also noted that it was important that the host NCA be 'put on notice' as to the firm's activities and 'ha[ve] the comfort that the home Member State knows that this is the case'.[363]

All information exchange takes place on an NCA–NCA basis. Where there is a change in the original particulars, the firm must give written notice of the change to the home NCA at least one month before implementing the change. The home NCA then informs the host NCA (Article 34(4)).

Similar but more intensive procedures apply to the cross-border establishment of a branch. Here the notification serves two purposes, given the split of responsibility between the host and home NCAs with respect to branches: it alerts the host NCA to the activities of the branch and the application of the relevant MiFID II rules (particularly conduct-of-business requirements) and supports the home NCA in supervising the application of home rules.

Where an investment firm wishes to establish a branch in a host State, or to use tied agents established in another Member State in which it has not established a branch, it must notify the home NCA and provide it with more extensive information than is required in relation to services provision (Article 35(2)). The firm must identify the host State(s) in which it

---

[361] A delegation is conferred on ESMA with respect to the development of RTSs governing the information to be notified and ITSs governing related standard forms, templates, and procedures: Art 34(8) and (9).
[362] CESR MiFID Passport Guidance (CESR/07-337), 5.
[363] Feedback Statement CESR MiFID Passport Guidance (CESR/07-318).

plans to establish a branch or the host State(s) in which it has not established a branch but plans to use tied agents established there. Tied agents in the same Member State as a firm branch are affiliated to the branch and subject to the branch regime (Article 35(2)). The required programme of operations must explain the organizational structure of the branch and indicate whether the branch intends to use tied agents and, if so, the identity of the tied agents. Where tied agents are used in a Member State in which the firm has not established a branch, a description must be provided of the intended use of the tied agents, as well as an organizational structure, including reporting lines, indicating how the agents fit into the corporate structure of the firm.[364] CESR's Notification Protocol originally expanded the notification requirement considerably, particularly with respect to the programme of operations;[365] the Protocol can be expected to be overtaken by the RTSs (governing the information requirements) and the ITSs (governing the related standard forms, templates, and protocols for the transmission of information) which ESMA is required to develop (Article 35(11) and (12)).

The home NCA has control over whether or not cross-border operation through branches will be approved. Accordingly, review by the home NCA is more intensive and more time is made available. Unless the home NCA has reason to doubt the adequacy of the administrative structure or the financial situation of an investment firm (taking into account the activities envisaged) it must, within three months of receiving the information, communicate the information to the host NCA (Article 35(3)). Where there is a change in the original particulars, the firm must give written notice of the change to the home NCA at least one month before implementing the change and the home NCA must notify the host NCA (Article 35(10)). The home NCA must also communicate details of the compensation scheme of which the firm is a member to the host NCA (Article 35(4)). The branch may be established and commence business on receipt of a communication from the host NCA or, failing such communication, at the latest two months after the date of the transmission of the communication by the home NCA to the host NCA (Article 35(6)).

These procedures clearly envisage the possibility that the home NCA may raise concerns as to the establishment, and not forward the information to the host NCA (this action blocks the establishment, as establishment is contingent on the firm receiving a communication from the host NCA or transmission of the notification). Article 35(5) deals with refusals to communicate information and requires the authority to give reasons for its refusal to the investment firm within three months of receiving all the information.

As is the case with tied agents under the services regime, the branch notification regime is applied to credit institutions wishing to use a tied agent established in a Member State outside its home Member State to provide investment services and/or activities as well as ancillary services, as the 2013 CRD IV/CRR regime which otherwise governs the establishment of branches by credit institution in relation to MiFID II activities does not cover tied agents (Article 35(7)).

---

[364] The firm must also provide a host State address from which documents may be obtained and the names of those responsible for the branch or of the tied agent.
[365] CESR Passport Notification Protocol, n 359, 7–9.

IV.10 Third Countries

The 2014 MiFID II/MiFIR regime has brought radical change to the regime governing third country access to the EU, primarily by centralizing the access process at EU level to a significantly greater extent than under MiFID I. Under the precursor 2004 MiFID I regime, access by third country firms to the EU market was primarily a function of national law.

In principle, an EU subsidiary of a third country investment firm is formed in accordance with the law of the relevant Member State and has its registered offices in a Member State. Accordingly, like any other Member State firm, it benefits from the Treaty freedoms to provide services and to establish, and is subject to MiFID II/MiFIR.

Under MiFID I, third country access through branches and cross-border services was also the responsibility of the relevant Member State in which access was sought, but in this case, passporting rights did not apply; separate access authorizations were required for each Member State in which the firm operated. In making access decisions in relation to branches and services, Member States were not subject to discrete EU rules, reflecting the limited engagement under MiFID I with third country access. Although MiFID I Article 15 addressed third country access in that it provided an institutional framework within which relationships with third countries were to be assessed, it was outward-facing and designed to ensure that EU firms were afforded reciprocal treatment in third countries.[366]

Over the crisis era, the management of third country actor access to the EU market has increasingly become a function of EU law and of ESMA and Commission decision-making, including under the 2012 EMIR (Chapter VI section 4.2.13), the rating agency regime (Chapter VII section 2.11), and the 2011 AIFMD (Chapter III section 4.16). These new access regimes, which vary in their design, relate, however, to the access, regulation, and supervision of actors which (with the exception of the AIFMD) were generally new to regulation for many Member States, and which represent discrete market segments. The regulatory/supervisory territory at stake under MiFID II was considerably larger, given the scale of the investment services industry and the less-than-compelling logic for centralized management of access, particularly given the sharp implications for local retail markets of access decisions.

The MiFID II third country access regime, following difficult negotiations and sharply diverging institutional positions on the appropriate allocation of responsibility between the Commission/ESMA and the Member States, adopts a twin-track approach which divides responsibility between the Member States and the Commission/ESMA according to

---

[366] Art 15 required Member States to inform the Commission of any difficulties which their investment firms encountered in accessing third countries, and provided a procedural framework which empowered the Commission to negotiate with the relevant third country on the basis of a Council mandate and to require Member States to suspend or limit access decisions in relation to investment firms from the third country in question (but only with respect to the establishment of branches and the provision of cross-border services; the establishment of subsidiaries was not subject to this limitation).

whether the third country firm operates through services or a branch and whether or not services are provided to (broadly) retail clients.

The Commission originally proposed a twin-track (services/branch) model based on a harmonized third country access regime. Access in the form of cross-border provision of services would be limited to the provision of services to eligible counterparties, and be dependent on a Commission equivalence decision and ESMA registration of the firm.[367] Access in the form of a branch[368] (which was mandatory for the provision of services to retail clients) was similarly based on a Commission equivalence decision (which drilled in to the quality of third country regulation and supervision), but the required branch authorization remained at Member State level, albeit subject to new harmonized conditions (including with respect to compliance with international money-laundering and tax co-operation rules, co-operation arrangements, sufficient initial capital, compliance with the MiFID II firm governance regime, and membership of an EU investor compensation scheme). The branch was also required to comply with the MiFID II operating regime. The Commission also proposed that the branch be granted a passport with respect to the cross-border provision of services.

While the European Parliament supported this model, the Council's position (reflecting significant industry hostility to the Commission's model given the risk that many third countries would not meet the equivalence conditions[369]) was sharply different. Several Member States had 'serious concerns' and 'strong reservations' regarding the proposed third country regime, which they regarded as disproportionate and unnecessary.[370] The Council's General Approach removed the harmonized third country services regime and very significantly revised the branch regime (although it retained the requirement that a branch be established for the provision of services to retail clients), removing the Commission equivalence decision, applying only a limited range of harmonized requirements to the Member State's decision to authorize a branch, and removing passport rights for branches.[371] In trilogue discussions, a compromise position was ultimately adopted under which the Commission's harmonized, EU-led model for services was (broadly) retained alongside the Council's light-touch Member-State-led model for branches, although both the Commission and Council models were revised in each case.

The third country branch regime is addressed by MiFID II Articles 39–43. A Member State may (on a discretionary basis) require a third country firm—that is, a firm that would be a credit institution engaging in investment services/activities or an investment firm if its head office or registered office were in the EU (Article 4(1)(57))—intending to provide investment services or to perform investment activities (with or without ancillary services) to retail clients, or to professional clients who are so treated as they 'opt in' to professional

---

[367] 2011 MiFIR Proposal, n 28, Art 36.

[368] 2011 MiFID II Proposal, n 28, Arts 41–46.

[369] The view was repeatedly expressed that access to the EU market could become highly restrictive and cumbersome, and that the Commission's approach was disproportionate: eg House of Lords European Union Committee, Second Report, MiFID II: Getting it Right for the City and EU Financial Services (2012) paras 53–60.

[370] eg Danish Presidency Progress Report, n 122, 13.

[371] Council General Approach, n 28, Arts 41–45.

status,[372] in the Member State's territory to establish a branch in that Member State (Article 39(1)). Where this requirement is imposed, the branch must acquire prior authorization from the Member State NCA (Article 39(2)).[373] Authorization by the home NCA is subject to a limited number of harmonized conditions (which in part reflect those deployed under the 2012 EMIR, the 2011 AIMFD, and the rating agency regime), designed in part to ensure that third country branches are not treated more favourably than EU firms, but is not contingent on a Commission equivalence decision: the services for which the firm requests authorization must be subject to authorization and supervision in the third country where the firm is established and properly authorized, paying due regard to any Financial Action Task Force recommendations in the context of anti-money-laundering and terrorist financing; co-operation arrangements (which include provisions regulating the exchange of information for the purpose of preserving the integrity of the market and protecting investors) must be in place between the relevant NCA where the branch is to be established and the third country authorities; sufficient initial capital must be at the free disposal of the branch; one or more persons must be appointed to be responsible for the management of the branch, and all must comply with the MiFID II firm governance regime (Article 9(1)); the third country must have entered into a tax co-operation agreement with the relevant Member State in which the branch is to be established which complies with the OECD Model Tax Convention on Income and Capital (Article 26 of the Convention) and which ensures an effective exchange of information on tax matters; and the firm must belong to an EU investor compensation scheme (Article 39).

The branch authorization application is accordingly managed at Member State level (Article 39(3)). The firm must provide the Member State in question with the information specified in Article 40 and relating to, *inter alia*, the third country supervisor, the firm's programme of operations, its management, and the branch's initial capital. Authorization by the Member State can only be granted where the Article 39 conditions are met and, in addition, where the NCA is satisfied that the branch can comply with the operating requirements which apply to third country branches under MiFID II (Article 41).[374] The withdrawal conditions which apply to EU firms also apply in relation to branch authorizations (Article 43). No passport is available to such entities.

In order to protect the position of third country firms, where a retail client or relevant professional client initiates at its own exclusive initiative the provision of an investment service or activity by a third country firm, the Article 39 branch authorization requirement (where applicable) may not be applied by the Member State in question (Article 42).[375]

---

[372] This classification of 'client' captures those clients which are more vulnerable than those assumed to be professional, and covers public sector bodies, local public authorities, municipalities, and private individual investors, as long as the relevant qualifying criteria are met (Annex II sect 2) (sect 5.2).

[373] As noted in this section, the 2014 MiFID II specifies that authorization is not required where a person established or situated in the EU initiates 'at its own exclusive initiative' the provision of services or an activity by a third country firm: Art 42.

[374] In essence, the 2014 MiFID II conduct and operational/prudential regime (including as applied to trading activities) applies to branches, as does the MiFIR trading transparency regime. Member States may not impose additional requirements on branches and are also prohibited from affording third country branches more favourable treatment than EU firms: Art 41(2).

[375] Such a client initiative does not entitle the firm to market otherwise than through the branch (where one is required under national law) new categories of investment product or investment service to the client.

There is, accordingly, only minimal harmonization; no provision is made for ESMA registration or for further specification in the form of ESMA-proposed BTSs, and the Commission plays no role in the determination of whether the authorization should be provided.[376] Market access is limited to the Member State in question.

The harmonized services regime, by contrast, is a function of EU decision-making and is passport-based. It is governed by MiFIR. A third country firm may choose to operate in the EU without a branch where it provides investment services for, or performs investment activities with, eligible counterparties and clients which are assumed to be professional (section 5.2); in this case, the firm must be registered by ESMA (MiFIR Article 46(1)).[377] A pan-EU services passport is then available to the firm. A series of conditions apply to the registration process, however (Article 46(2)). Chief among them is the requirement for the Commission to have adopted an equivalence decision in relation to the third country. In addition, the firm must be authorized in the jurisdiction where its head office is established to provide the investment services/activities in question, and be subject to effective supervision and enforcement ensuring full compliance with the applicable third country requirements. Co-operation arrangements must also have been established; ESMA is to establish these arrangements with third countries whose regimes are considered to be effectively equivalent under the equivalence assessment (Article 47(2)). Under Article 46 (6), third country firms are also to offer to submit any disputes to the jurisdiction of a court or arbitral tribunal in a Member State.

The pivotal Commission equivalence decision (which has the effect of 'exporting' much of MiFID II) is governed by MiFIR Article 47; the equivalence assessment is directed towards an assessment that the legal and supervisory arrangements of the third country in question ensure that firms authorized in the third country comply with legally binding prudential and business conduct requirements which have 'equivalent effect' to MiFID II/MiFIR and CRD IV/CRR, and that the third country provides for an effective equivalent system for the recognition of investment firms authorized under third country legal regimes (a reciprocity requirement).[378]

Once the firm is registered with ESMA (the registration process will be governed by BTSs), the passport becomes available (MiFIR Article 47(3))[379] and Member States may not impose additional requirements in respect of the 2014 MiFID II/MiFIR regime and should not treat the firm more favourably than EU firms (Article 46(3)). Where the third country firm has established a branch in a Member State, the NCA of the branch remains responsible for branch supervision, but the host NCA in which services are provided by the third country firm must co-operate with the branch NCA with respect to oversight of

---

[376] Earlier versions provided for such firms to be noted on an ESMA register, and for ESMA to propose BTSs relating to the minimum content of the required co-operation arrangements and the information to be provided by the third country firm and governing the standard forms, templates, and procedures for the provision of information, and for the Commission to adopt administrative rules defining the conditions for the assessment of whether the branch had sufficient free initial capital at its free disposal.

[377] As under the branch regime, the ESMA registration requirement does not apply where the EU counterparty or client initiates the service or activity as its own exclusive initiative (Art 46(5)).

[378] The equivalent assessment will examine authorization, supervision and enforcement; capital; governance; organizational requirements; conduct-of-business requirements; and market transparency and integrity requirements (Art 47(1)).

[379] The Art 34 notification procedures governing cross-border services apply.

the branch (Article 47(3)). Third country firms must inform clients[380] that they can provides services only to eligible counterparties and qualifying professional clients, and that they are not supervised in the EU (Article 46(4)). The conditions governing withdrawal of registration by ESMA (Article 49) broadly relate to ESMA having 'well-founded reasons based on documented evidence' that the firm, in relation to its EU activities, is acting in a manner clearly prejudicial to the interests of investors or the orderly functioning of markets, or that the firm has seriously infringed provisions applicable to it in the third country, and on the basis of which the equivalence decision was made.

In the event that an equivalence decision is not made (or is no longer in effect), Member States may permit third country firms to provide services/activities in their territories and in accordance with their national regimes, but the passport does not apply (MiFIR Article 46 (3) and 47(4)). A transitional regime applies: third country firms may continue to provide services in accordance with national regimes for three years after the adoption of the equivalence decision (MiFIR Article 54).

IV.11 Supervision and Enforcement in the Investment Services Market: 2014 MiFID II

IV.11.1 2014 MiFID II and 2013 CRD IV/CRR

Two parallel but closely inter-related supervisory regimes apply to the supervision of investment firms. The 2014 MiFID II regulatory regime is supervised under the MiFID II framework, which governs the designation and the investigatory and supervisory powers of NCAs, and the organization and co-ordination of cross-border supervision. In parallel with the MiFID II regime, the supervision and enforcement of the prudential rules which apply to investment firms under the 2013 CRD IV/CRR is governed by the CRD IV/CRR regime.[381] In many respects, both regimes are very similar. The CRD IV/CRR regime, however, is significantly more sophisticated and articulated with respect to cross-border supervision and group-wide consolidated supervision, and it imposes a range of specialist 'supervisory review' requirements and powers on NCAs with respect to the prudential regime. The discussion focuses on the MiFID II regime; the CRD IV/CRR enhancements for prudential supervision are considered in section 12.

IV.11.2 The 2014 MiFID II Supervisory Framework

As discussed in Chapter XI, supervision of the EU financial market within the ESFS is based on local supervision by NCAs (typically the home NCA), and on co-ordination and

---

[380] In writing and in a prominent manner.

[381] The split regime, while in part a reflection of how EU securities and markets regulation has evolved, can also be associated with the move to organize supervision in terms of conduct and prudential supervision under the 'twin peaks' model (a variant of which applies in the UK through the split of conduct supervision (Financial Conduct Authority) and prudential supervision (Prudential Regulation Authority)). Similarly in France, supervision is split between the conduct supervisor (the Autorité des Marchés Financier) and the prudential supervisor (Autorité de Contrôle Prudentiel).

oversight through ESMA. The 2014 MiFID II supervisory structure sits within this model, being based on networked supervision which is anchored to the home NCA and supported by ESMA's array of supervisory co-ordination and convergence powers. Networked home NCA/host NCA supervision has been strengthened by MiFID II's material enhancement of the powers of NCAs, notably with respect to enforcement. Although this strengthening is primarily a function of the crisis-era drive to enhance supervision generally, it also reflects specific concerns as to weaknesses in the MiFID I supervisory framework which emerged long before the crisis. CESR's important 2004 'Himalaya Report' had raised a series of concerns as to the particular risks generated by MiFID I's home/host supervisory structure for investment firms.[382] It noted that increased cross-border activity generated more supervisory challenges, particularly with respect to supporting trust between supervisors, given differences in supervisory powers and resources. It was particularly concerned by the ability of MiFID I's networked supervision structure to cope with the challenges of 'trans-European investment firms', were such firms to emerge post-MiFID I. It acknowledged that while MiFID I's framework was 'satisfactory' where the main business was carried out in the home Member State and pan-EU business was carried out through distance services or through subsidiaries, difficulties could arise where major business units (branches) were located in host Member States and firms were organized in a transnational manner which fitted uneasily into home/host structure.[383]

The MiFID II supervisory framework[384] is based on a number of elements: the designation of NCAs in each Member State responsible for supervision; the identification of NCA powers (including enforcement and sanctioning powers); and co-ordination and co-operation requirements which reflect ESMA's centrally important role in supporting supervisory convergence and co-ordination.

IV.11.3 NCAs

IV.11.3.1 Designation and Delegation

Article 67 of the 2014 MiFID II addresses the designation of NCAs and is designed to support co-operation by providing clarity with respect to which authorities are responsible for MiFID II obligations, given the possibility that multiple authorities could be engaged in supervising MiFID II's complex and wide-ranging requirements. Article 67(1) provides that each Member State must designate the NCAs which are to carry out the duties provided for under MiFID II and MiFIR. The Commission, ESMA, and the NCAs of other Member States must be informed of the identity of the NCAs, and of any division of duties.[385] Where a Member State designates more than one NCA, their respective roles must be clearly defined and they must co-operate closely (Article 68(1)). Similarly, each

---

[382] CESR, Which Supervisory Tools for the EU Securities Markets? An Analytical Paper by CESR (2004) (CESR/04-333f).

[383] Such firms were generally dealt with through *ad hoc* supervisory arrangements involving several NCAs or colleges of NCAs.

[384] The MiFID II supervisory framework governs MiFID II and MiFIR; while most of the MiFID II provisions are common to the supervision and enforcement of the rules governing investment services and trading, a number of specific supervisory powers and co-operation requirements apply in relation to trading practices and trading venues and are considered in Chs V and VI.

[385] ESMA maintains a list of MiFID II NCAs: Art 67(3).

Member State must require that co-operation take place between the authorities responsible for MiFID II and those responsible in the Member State for the supervision of credit and other financial institutions, pension funds, UCITSs, insurance and reinsurance intermediaries, and insurance undertakings, and that those authorities exchange any information essential or relevant to the exercise of their functions and duties (Article 68(1)).

MiFID II specifies that NCAs must take the form of 'public authorities' (Article 67(2)). It does not address resourcing; ESMA is likely to provide an important channel for supporting NCA resourcing, although it may also lead to tensions where limited NCA resources are channelled to ESMA. NCAs may, however, delegate tasks to other entities where this is provided for in MiFID II, for the most part with respect to tied agents (Article 29(4)). Delegation within the domestic supervisory framework is subject to a number of restrictions by Article 67(2). Delegation to non-public authorities may not involve the exercise of public authority or the use of discretionary judgment. NCAs must take all reasonable steps to ensure that the entity acting under a delegation has the capacity and resources to effectively execute all tasks. The delegation must also take place in a clearly defined and documented framework for the exercise of delegated tasks, which must include a requirement that the delegated entity act and be organized in such a manner as to avoid conflicts of interest, and that any information obtained in the course of the delegated task is not used unfairly or to prevent competition. Member States must inform the Commission, ESMA, and the NCAs of other Member States of any delegation arrangements and the related conditions. Final responsibility for supervising compliance with MiFID II and its implementing measures remains with the NCAs.

NCAs, all persons who work or who have worked for them or entities to whom tasks are delegated, and auditors and experts instructed by NCAs, are all subject to professional secrecy obligations which are outlined in Article 76. The obligations extend to information received, exchanged, or transmitted under MiFID II, but do not prevent NCAs from sharing confidential information under MiFID II or other EU securities and markets regulation measures (Article 76(4)). The regime also provides for the disclosure of confidential information in civil or commercial proceedings concerning bankruptcy (Article 76(2)).

IV.11.3.2 NCA Supervisory and Investigatory Powers

The 2014 MiFID II regime is significantly more granular than MiFID I in specifying the supervisory and enforcement powers which must be conferred on NCAs, reflecting the crisis-era commitment to enhancing the EU supervisory regime.

Under Article 69, NCAs must be given all supervisory powers (including investigatory powers and powers to impose remedies) necessary to fulfil their duties under MiFID II and MIFiR. These powers are to be exercised either directly, in collaboration with other authorities, by delegation in accordance with Article 67(2), or by application to the competent judicial authorities (Article 72).

These powers must include, at least, the right/power to: have access to documents or other data which the NCA considers could be relevant for the performance of its duties; demand information from any person and, if necessary, summon and question persons; carry out on-site inspections; require existing recordings of telephone and electronic communications held by an investment firm, credit institution, or other entity regulated under MiFID II/ MiFIR; require the freezing or sequestration of assets; request temporary prohibition of professional activity; require authorized investment firms' auditors to provide information; refer matters for criminal prosecution; allow auditors or experts to carry out verifications or investigations; require or demand information including all relevant documentation from any person regarding the size and purpose of a position or exposure entered into via a commodity derivative, and any assets or liabilities in the underlying market;[386] require the temporary or permanent cessation of any practice or conduct the NCA considers contrary to MiFIR/MiFID II and prevent repetition of that practice; adopt any type of measure to ensure that investment firms (and regulated markets and other persons to whom MiFID II/MiFIR applies) continue to comply with legal requirements; require the suspension of trading in a financial instrument; require the removal of a financial instrument from trading, whether on a regulated market or under other trading arrangements; request any person to take steps to reduce the size of a position or exposure; limit the ability of any person to enter into a commodity derivative (including through position limits);[387] issue public notices; require, in so far as permitted by national law, existing data traffic records held by a telecommunication operator, where there is a reasonable suspicion of breach and where such records may be relevant; suspend the marketing or sale of financial instruments or structured deposits where NCA product intervention powers activate or where there is a breach of the Article 16(3) product governance regime;[388] and require the removal of a natural person from the management body.

Supervision, investigation, and enforcement are also supported by the Article 77 rules concerning 'whistle-blowing' by auditors. Under Article 77(1), statutory auditors must 'report promptly' to the NCAs any fact or decision concerning the investment firm of which they have become aware and which is liable to constitute a material breach of the rules governing authorization or of the rules which specifically govern the activities of investment firms, affect the continuous functioning of the investment firm, or lead to either a refusal to certify or a reservation concerning the accounts.[389] As a result of their special access to financial information, statutory auditors are thus brought into the supervisory and enforcement framework as supplementary watchdogs. Statutory auditors who make this disclosure in good faith are protected from liability by Article 77(2).

While auditor whistle-blowing was introduced under MiFID I, MiFID II requires that Member States establish more general whistle-blowing regimes; this obligation has been imposed across a number of crisis-era measures, including the market abuse regime (Chapter VIII section 9.2.4). Under Article 73, Member States must ensure that NCAs establish effective mechanisms to encourage reporting of actual or potential breaches of MiFID II/MiFIR. These mechanisms must include, at least, procedures for the receipt of reports on breaches and their follow-up; appropriate protection for the employees of financial institutions who report breaches committed within the financial institutions against retaliation, discrimination, or other type of unfair treatment; and protection of the identity of the person who reports the breach and of the natural person allegedly responsible for the breach. Member States must also require financial institutions to have in

---

[386] See further Ch VI sect 2.5 on position management.
[387] See further Ch VI sect 2.5 on position management.
[388] See further Ch VI sect 7.1.
[389] This whistle-blowing duty extends to similar facts or decisions in respect of an undertaking having 'close links' with the investment firm.

place appropriate procedures for their employees to report breaches internally through a specific, independent, and autonomous channel.

IV.11.4 Supervisory Co-operation

The pivotal NCA co-operation obligation, at the core of the network mechanism, is set out in the 2014 MiFID II Article 79. NCAs of different Member States must co-operate with each other 'whenever necessary' for the purpose of carrying out their duties under the Directive, making use of their powers, whether set out in MiFID II/MiFIR or in national law (Article 79(1)). In particular, they must exchange information and co-operate in any investigatory or supervisory activities. Member States must also take the necessary administrative and organizational measures to facilitate co-operation (Article 79(3)). Member States must also designate one single NCA as the contact point for the purposes of MiFID II (Article 79(1));[390] the contact points anchor the information exchange regime set out in Article 81. Article 79(3) also makes clear that NCAs may use their powers for the purpose of co-operation, even where the conduct under investigation does not constitute an infringement of any regulation in force in their Member State. Distinct co-operation obligations are imposed with respect to ESMA (Article 87); NCAs must co-operate with ESMA for the purposes of MiFID II and must, without undue delay, provide ESMA with all information necessary to carry out its duties under MiFID and the 2010 ESMA Regulation.

Although supervisory powers are specifically allocated to either the home, the branch, or, in exceptional cases, the host NCA, Article 79(4) reinforces the importance of ongoing co-operation and supervisory dialogue generally, by requiring NCAs to be on the alert for infringements by passporting firms. It provides that where an NCA has good reasons to suspect that acts in breach of MiFID II have been carried out in the territory of another Member State by an entity which is not under its supervision, it must notify the NCA of that other Member State in as specific a manner as possible. The notified NCA must take appropriate action and inform the notifying NCA of the outcome of the action and any interim developments.

More specific obligations are imposed under Article 80, particularly with respect to investigations. An NCA may request the co-operation of the NCA of another Member State in a 'supervisory activity' or for an on-the-spot verification, or in an investigation. Where an NCA receives a request concerning a verification or investigation it must, within the framework of its powers, either carry out the verification or investigation itself, allow the requesting authority to carry out the verification or investigation, or allow auditors or experts to carry out the verification or investigation. ESMA is empowered to participate in such investigations where colleges of supervisors are engaged; it can participate in the activities of colleges of supervisors, including on-site verifications or investigations carried out jointly by two or more NCAs.[391] ESMA is also empowered to propose RTSs governing

---

[390] The authorities designed to receive information exchange or co-operation requests must be notified to the Commission and ESMA.

[391] See further Ch XI sect 5.5.1 on ESMA's powers in relation to colleges of supervisors.

the information to be exchanged between NCAs when co-operating in supervisory activities, on-the-spot verifications and investigations, and ITSs governing the related standard forms, templates, and procedures.

Information exchange is governed by the specific requirements which apply under Article 81. NCAs must immediately supply one another with the information required for the purposes of carrying out the duties of the NCAs (through the contact point system). The NCAs may, however, indicate, at the time the information is communicated, that it must not be disclosed without their express agreement. NCAs in receipt of such information may pass it on through a subsequent 'information gateway', in that they can pass it on to other competent authorities within the Member State—but the receiving authorities may not transmit the information to other bodies or natural or legal persons without the express agreement of the authorities which disclosed it, and then only for the purposes for which the authorities gave their agreement, except in duly justified circumstances. Article 81(3) provides that those in receipt of exchanged information can use it only in the course of their duties. In particular, exchanged information can be used in a number of ways: to check that the conditions governing the taking up of business by an investment firm are met and to facilitate the monitoring (on a consolidated or non-consolidated basis) of the conduct of that business, particularly with respect to the CRD IV/CRR capital adequacy requirements, administrative procedures, and internal control mechanisms; to monitor the proper functioning of trading venues; to impose sanctions; in administrative appeals against decisions by NCAs; in court proceedings against NCA decisions; or in the extra-judicial mechanism for investors' complaints. Additionally, an NCA is not prevented from transmitting confidential information intended for the purpose of its tasks to ESMA, the European Systemic Risk Board (ESRB), central banks, the European System of Central Banks (ESCB), and the European Central Bank (ECB)—the latter in their capacity as monetary authorities—and, where appropriate, to other public authorities responsible for overseeing payment and settlement systems; similarly, these bodies are not prevented from communicating to the NCAs such information as they may need for performing their functions under MiFID II. The operational regime for information exchange is the subject of a delegation for ITSs governing the standard forms, templates, and procedures for the exchange of information.

Refusals to co-operate are addressed by Article 83, which restricts the circumstances in which an NCA can withhold co-operation. An NCA may refuse to act on a request for co-operation in carrying out an investigation, on-the-spot investigation, or authorization of an investment firm which forms part of a pan-EU group, or on a request for information, in only two very limited circumstances: judicial proceedings have already been initiated in respect of the same actions and the same persons before the authorities of the Member States addressed; or final judgment has already been delivered in the Member State addressed in respect of the same persons and the same actions. The refusing NCA must, however, notify the requesting NCA accordingly, and provide as much detailed information as possible. ESMA's binding meditation powers can also be deployed to address co-operation failures. Article 82 specifies that NCAs may refer to ESMA for binding mediation where a request (relating to information exchange, the carrying out of a supervisory activity, on-the-spot verification, or an investigation) has been rejected or has not been acted on within a reasonable time. Ultimately, ESMA can use its powers to take action against an NCA for breach of EU law.[392]

Information exchange with third countries is governed by Article 88. Member States and ESMA may conclude co-operation agreements providing for the exchange of information with third country competent authorities only if the information disclosed is subject to guarantees of professional secrecy equivalent to those required under MiFID II.

IV.11.5 Supervisory Convergence and ESMA

In addition to the array of supervisory powers it can deploy under the 2010 ESMA Regulation (Chapter XI section 5), ESMA is injected into the 2014 MiFID II supervisory process across a number of dimensions—notably as the recipient of NCA notifications related to a range of supervisory issues, including with respect to firm authorization and the exercise of host NCA precautionary powers, and with respect to the exercise of its binding mediation powers where NCAs disagree. As discussed in Chapters IX (section 7.1) and VI (section 2.5), it has also been conferred with direct supervisory powers with respect to product prohibition and position management.

Its more general supervisory convergence activities have been relatively limited, reflecting the intense pressure imposed by the development of the crisis-era rulebook. ESMA has largely been concerned with the adoption of guidelines, including the operationally significant guidelines adopted with respect to remuneration practices, suitability assessments, and compliance procedures under MiFID I, the MiFID I Q&A, and supervisory briefings designed to support NCAs.[393] The extensive array of administrative rules, including BTSs, required under MiFID II may stymie more robust supervisory convergence activities, notably peer review of MiFID II supervision. ESMA remains, however, a key actor in driving strong supervisory practices, particularly with respect to the more intractable difficulties which NCAs face in supervising the MiFID II regime, including with regard to the management of conflicts of interest.

IV.11.6 Enforcement and Sanctions

IV.11.6.1 Sanctions

The most radical 2014 MiFID II supervisory reforms relate to sanctioning. The MiFID I regime was limited and based on the minimum requirement that Member States had in place administrative sanctions which were effective, proportionate, and dissuasive. The crisis-era reform programme has led to significantly greater specification of the sanctions which must be applied and of how those sanctions are determined (Chapter XI section 4.1.2).

Accordingly, MiFID II requires that (without prejudice to NCAs' supervisory powers, including investigatory powers and powers to impose remedies under Article 69, and the

---

[392] See further Ch XI sect 5.3.1 on ESMA's mediation powers and its powers in relation to NCA breach of EU law.

[393] n 131.

right of Member States to provide for and impose criminal sanctions), Member States must lay down rules on and ensure their NCAs can impose administrative sanctions and measures, which must be effective, proportionate, and dissuasive, and apply to breaches even where such breaches are not specifically referenced in MiFID II as requiring an administrative sanction or measure (Article 70(1)). Criminal sanctions may be deployed in substitution for administrative sanctions, but these must be notified to the Commission, and appropriate measures must be in place such that NCAs have all necessary powers to liaise with the judicial authorities to receive information and to transmit it as required to other NCAs and ESMA (Article 70(1) and 79(1)). In common with other crisis-era measures, MiFID II specifies the particular breaches of the Directive which must be subject to administrative sanctions or measures (Article 70(3)); specifies the minimum suite of administrative sanctions and measures which must be available (Article 70(6));[394] details how sanctions are to be applied (Article 72);[395] and provides for mandatory NCA public reporting of administrative sanctions and measures (and the conditions under which the public reporting requirement can be lifted), as well as for NCA reporting to ESMA on sanctioning (Article 71). Reflecting the new concern with firm governance, sanctions and measures must be applicable to management body members (and any other natural persons responsible for breach), albeit subject to the conditions laid down in national law in areas not harmonized by the Directive (Article 70(2)). The new regime also specifies that NCAs must co-operate with each other with respect to facilitating the recovery of pecuniary sanctions (Article 79(1)).

IV.11.6.2 Civil Liability

As discussed in Chapter XI, private causes of action are rarely deployed across EU securities and markets regulation as a disciplining mechanism, and have not been relied in the investment services area. At an early stage of the MiFID I Review, however, the Commission proposed that a harmonized liability regime apply in relation to breaches by investment firms and be designed to support retail clients by providing a harmonized regime governing damages claims in relation to breaches of the disclosure, quality of advice, client reporting, best execution, and order handling rules.[396] The European Parliament similarly proposed that where a member of a firm's management board breached MiFID II/MiFIR, Member States' legal regimes should provide for criminal or civil proceedings.[397] The proposed liability regime did not, however, acquire any traction—reflecting significant, if predictable, industry hostility, but also the wider complexities associated with pan-EU civil liability regimes. MiFID II provides, however, that Member States must ensure that

---

[394] The suite of measures, which reflects the crisis-era sanctioning reforms to, eg, the 2014 market abuse regime, the 2014 UCITS V regime, and the 2013 transparency regime, with calibrations for investment services and activities, includes: public statements; injunctions; withdrawals/suspensions of authorization; temporary and (for frequent, serious breaches) permanent bans on exercising management functions; temporary bans on being a member of a trading venue; pecuniary sanctions (up to (as a minimum) 10 per cent of annual turnover of the legal person or €5 million, and up to €5 million in the case of a natural person), including pecuniary sanctions of up to twice the amount of the profits gained or losses avoided (even where that exceeds the aforenoted thresholds). Additional sanctions and measures can be provided at national level.

[395] Including with reference to the gravity and duration of the breach, the degree of responsibility of the person responsible and that person's financial strength, the importance of profits gained or losses avoided, the degree of co-operation by the person concerned, and previous breaches by that person.

[396] 2010 MiFID I Review Consultation, n 112, 63.

[397] European Parliament Negotiating Position, n 28, Art 9(8a).

mechanisms are in place to ensure that compensation may be paid or other remedial action taken in accordance with national law for any financial loss or damage suffered as a result of breach of MiFID II/MiFIR (Article 69).

Effective retail investor redress is a concern of EU securities and markets policy, given the very considerable difficulties retail investors face in achieving redress (Chapter XI sections 2.2.2 and 4.1.3). The policy agenda has focused primarily on alternative dispute resolution (ADR), which is promoted through MiFID II. Article 75 provides that Member States must ensure the setting up of efficient and effective complaints and redress procedures for the out-of-court settlement of consumer disputes concerning the provision of investment and ancillary services by investment services, using existing bodies where appropriate; these bodies must be notified to ESMA. Member States must also ensure that all investment firms adhere to one or more such bodies. These bodies must actively co-operate with their counterparts in other Member States in the resolution of cross-border disputes.

IV.12 Supervision and Enforcement in the Investment Services Market: 2013 CRD IV/CRR

IV.12.1 NCAs and the ESFS

The supervisory framework which governs the prudential supervision of investment firms under the 2013 CRD IV/CRR (and which is set out in CRD IV) is broadly similar to the 2014 MiFID II framework (including with respect to sanctions), but it is significantly more robust and articulated, and engages to a greater extent with operational supervisory practices (notably the required annual 'supervisory review') than the MiFID II regime, reflecting the greater risk which weaknesses in prudential supervision pose to the EU market and the roots of CRD IV/CRR in the regulation and supervision of banks.

The regime governing NCAs is accordingly more detailed. Unlike the MiFID II regime, which does not address the operational capacity of NCAs in detail, NCAs must have the expertise, resources, operational capacity, powers, and independence necessary to carry out their functions in relation to prudential supervision and related investigatory and enforcement activities (CRD IV Article 4(4)). The CRD IV/CRR regime is also more prescriptive with respect to NCA form, given that prudential supervisors may sit within institutional structures which engage in related activities, including with respect to resolution. CRD IV Article 4(7) accordingly provides that supervision under CRD IV/CRR (and any other functions of CRD IV/CRR NCAs) must be separate and independent from functions relating to resolution; resolution authorities must, however, co-operate closely and consult with the NCAs with respect to resolution plans (which are required for investment firms under CRD Article 74(4)).[398] CRD IV also specifies that where the prudential supervision of the institutions subject to the CRD IV/CRR regime is split across different domestic authorities, all requisite measures must be taken to ensure co-ordination (Article 5).

---

[398] See sect 13 on resolution.

The CRD IV NCA regime is also more robust with respect to information flows and compliance. Appropriate measures must be in place to enable NCAs to obtain the information needed to assess the compliance of investment firms and to investigate breaches, investment firms must provide their home NCAs with all the information necessary for NCAs to assess compliance, and their internal control mechanisms and administrative and accounting procedures must permit the checking of compliance at all times (CRD IV Article 4(3) and (5)). Investment firms must also register all their transactions and document systems and processes in such a manner that NCAs are able to check compliance (CRD IV Article 4(5)).

The most striking difference between the MiFID II regime and the CRD IV/CRR regime relates to the distinct 'supervisory review' process which, reflecting the Basel III agreement (and the earlier Basel II approach), NCAs must engage in to review the arrangements, strategies, processes, and mechanisms implemented by firms to comply with CRD IV/CRR (CRD IV Articles 97–110). Supervisory review (often termed 'Pillar 2') is in part designed to ensure that institution-specific prudential measures (such as additional capital or liquidity requirements) are imposed on institutions where necessary, given the particular risks posed by institutions, and is, accordingly, an important safety valve for NCAs, given the otherwise prescriptive harmonization under the capital regime in particular. Supervisory review, which must take place on at least an annual basis[399] is designed to evaluate the risks to which the institution is or might be exposed, the systemic risks which the institution may pose, and the risks revealed by stress testing, and to cover all CRD IV/CRR requirements; on the basis of the review, the NCA is to determine whether the arrangements, strategies, processes, and mechanisms implemented by firms, and their own funds and liquidity, ensure a sound management and coverage of risks (Article 97). Where appropriate, supervisory review can result in enhanced supervision, including an increase in the number of inspections, a permanent presence by the NCA in the institutions, additional or more frequent reporting by the institutions, additional or more frequent review of the operational, strategic, or business plans of the institutions, and thematic examination of specific risks. Supervisory stress tests must be carried out in support of supervisory review as appropriate, but at least annually (Article 100). The technical criteria for supervisory review are specified in some detail by Article 98, which requires, *inter alia*, that the results of stress tests are considered, that exposure to and management of identified risks are examined, and that governance arrangements, corporate culture and values, and the ability of management body members to perform their duties are examined. NCAs must adopt a related supervisory examination programme for the institutions they supervise[400] which specifies how supervisory tasks will be allocated and resourced, identifies the institutions to be subject to enhanced supervision, and provides a plan for branch and subsidiary inspections (Article 99). Additionally, where an institution has been authorized to use internal approaches and models to calculate own funds requirements, these must be reviewed by NCAs on a

---

[399] NCAs are to establish the frequency and terms of the review, having regard to the size, systemic importance, nature, scale, and complexity of the activities of the institution concerned, and taking into account the principle of proportionality.

[400] Covering at least those institutions for which the results of stress tests or the outcomes of supervisory review indicate significant risks to their financial soundness or breaches of CRD IV/CRR; institutions that pose systemic risk to the financial system; and any other institutions for which the NCAs deem it to be necessary.

regular basis, and at least every three years (Article 101). The supervisory review process is designed to be proactive and precautionary; Article 102, for example, requires NCAs to require an institution to take the necessary measures at an early stage to address relevant problems where the institution does not comply with CRD IV/CRR or is likely to breach CRD IV/CRR within the following 12 months. The swingeing supervisory powers which NCAs must be able to wield for the purposes of the supervisory review process are set out in Article 104, and include powers to: require institutions to hold additional own funds;[401] reinforce internal capital and governance systems; apply specific provisioning policies; require divestment of excessively risky activities; limit variable remuneration where it is inconsistent with the maintenance of a sound capital base; restrict or prohibit distributions or interest payments; require more frequent reporting; and impose specific liquidity requirements.[402] The supervisory review process, while subject to relatively detailed pre-scription under CRD IV, is also subject to review by EBA; NCAs are to report to EBA on their supervisory review processes and supervisory decisions made in order to allow EBA to support the development of consistency in the supervisory review and evaluation process (Article 107).[403]

IV.12.2 Supervisory Co-operation

Although based on the same principles and mechanisms (including the exercise of precau-tionary powers), the 2013 CRD IV/CRR regime is significantly more articulated with respect to cross-border supervision than the 2014 MiFID II regime. The enhancements reflect the heavier reliance on subsidiaries to engage in cross-border activity in the banking sector and the related need to enhance oversight of pan-EU groups, the significant systemic risks which banks can pose, and the weaknesses which the financial crisis exposed in relation to pan-EU co-ordination of bank supervision and resolution/rescue. Nonetheless, the enhanced CRD IV/CRR regime also applies to investment firms in relation to prudential supervision.

One set of enhancements relates to the relationship between NCAs, the ESRB, and EBA; by contrast, the MiFID II regime does not address the NCA/ESMA/ESRB relationship in detail. CRD IV Article 6 specifies that in the exercise of their duties, NCAs must take into account the convergence in respect to supervisory tools and practices achieved under CRD IV/CRR. In particular, NCAs, as parties to the ESFS, must co-operate with trust and full mutual respect, in particular when ensuring the flow of appropriate and reliable informa-tion between them and other parties to the ESFS, in accordance with the Treaty principle of sincere co-operation (Article 4(3) TEU). They must also participate in the activities of EBA and, as appropriate, in colleges of supervisors; make every effort to comply with EBA guidelines and recommendations (adopted under the 2010 EBA Regulation Article 16 and so subject to 'comply or explain' requirements) and to respond to ESRB warnings and recommendations; and co-operate closely with the ESRB; additionally, their national mandates must not inhibit the performance of their duties as members of EBA or of the

---

[401] Conditions apply to how NCAs can deploy this power: Art 104(2) and (3).

[402] The process through which these are determined by the NCA is set out in Art 105.

[403] EBA is also charged with conducting peer reviews on supervisory review and with reporting to the European Parliament and Council on the degree of convergence achieved.

ESRB. More generally, NCAs must, in the exercise of their general duties, consider the potential impact of their decisions on the stability of the financial system in the other Member States concerned and, in particular, in emergency situations, based on the information available at the relevant time.

Outside the group context and in the traditional investment services context of home/host supervision, the co-ordination obligations imposed on the home NCA responsible for prudential supervision (CRD IV Article 49(1)) and the host NCA, and in particular the host NCAs of branches, are set out in more detail than under MiFID II (CRD IV Articles 50–2). The foundational co-operation obligation is imposed under Article 50, which requires NCAs to collaborate closely in order to supervise the activities of investment firms operating, in particular through a branch, in one or more Member States, and to exchange all information (including with respect to firm management and ownership, liquidity, solvency, large exposures, other factors likely to influence the systemic risk posed by the firm, administrative and accounting procedures, and internal control mechanisms) which is likely to facilitate their supervision (Article 50(1)). Specific co-ordination require-ments are imposed in relation to home NCA liquidity assessments (Article 50(2) and (3)). Home NCA and branch NCA co-operation is subject to a distinct co-operation regime with respect to branch on-the-spot checking and inspection of branches, which, *inter alia*, empowers the host (branch) NCA to engage in checks and inspections where it considers them relevant on grounds of host State financial stability; the home NCA, as the prudential supervisor, is also empowered to carry out such checks and inspections in the host State, having informed the host NCA (Article 52). A distinct co-ordination regime applies to 'significant branches' under CRD IV/CRR, which is designed to strengthen cross-border co-ordination in relation to such branches (Article 51). The NCA of a host Member State may apply to the consolidating supervisor of a group (or to the home Member State where consolidated/group supervision does not apply) for a branch to be considered significant; the assessment of significance is based on, with respect to investment services/activities, the likely impact of a suspension or close of the firm on systemic liquidity and on payment, clearing, and settlement systems in the host State, and on the size and importance of the branch in terms of number of clients within the context of the host State financial system. Where a branch is deemed to be significant,[404] the branch State participates in the relevant college of supervisors and enhanced consultation and information exchange obligations are imposed on the home NCA, including with respect to emergency situations, risk assess-ments, and liquidity risks. More generally, the CRD IV/CRR regime sets out in more detail the range of authorities with which information can be exchanged, including macro-prudential authorities, reorganization bodies, liquidation and bankruptcy bodies, govern-ment departments, and committees of enquiry, as well as the relevant conditions which apply (Articles 56–61).

The most significant difference from the MiFID II regime relates to the extension of the cross-border co-ordination regime from the traditional home/host setting to a home/home setting, which reflects the dominance of subsidiaries as cross-border vehicles in the banking sector and the related need for group-wide co-ordination of prudential supervision through

---

[404] 2013 CRD IV Art 51 governs the decision-making process in relation to the determination of significance.

college-of-supervisors structures. The consolidated supervision regime (Articles 111–27) sets out the modalities governing consolidated, group-wide supervision (including the entities to be included in consolidated supervision), identifies the 'consolidating supervisor' as the lead supervisor and the tasks which the consolidating supervisor is charged with in the group oversight context, requires that colleges of supervisors are established (by the consolidating supervisor), and identifies the powers and duties of colleges, including with respect to joint decision-making, information exchange in emergency institutions, and co-ordination and co-operation. College decision-making is supported by EBA's binding mediation powers under EBA Regulation Article 19.

IV.13 Resolution and Recovery

The poor ability of the EU and its Member States to address bank failure and to resolve banks in an orderly manner,[405] which was exposed to devastating effect by the financial crisis, has led to major reforms designed to establish a stable framework for the recovery and resolution of banks. The reforms respond to the disorderly EU efforts to resolve banks over the financial crisis and to the related euro-area sovereign debt crisis, which crisis was partially driven by market scepticism as to the ability of Member States to resolve their banks. The reforms also, however, respond to the G20 reform agenda, which called for a review of resolution regimes and implementation of the Financial Stability Board (FSB) principles on the resolution of financial institutions.[406] A resolution/recovery-specific reform programme has followed with intertwined internal market and euro-area (Banking Union) elements.

In 2012,[407] the Commission presented a proposal for a harmonized recovery and resolution regime. While there was strong political and institutional consensus on the need for the regime, the many contested technical elements of the proposed regime, and in particular the controversial 'bail-in' tool (which determines the allocation of losses across shareholders and creditors), led to intense negotiations. Agreement on a 'single recovery and resolution rulebook' for Member States to apply to all EU banks and to deal with cross-border recovery and resolution was finally reached in December 2013 (the 2014 Bank Recovery and Resolution Directive (BRRD)).[408]

---

[405] The objective of resolution has been described as 'to make feasible the resolution of financial institutions without severe systemic disruption and without exposing tax-payers to loss, while protecting vital economic functions through mechanisms which make it possible for shareholders and unsecured and uninsured creditors to absorb losses in a manner that respects the hierarchy of claims in liquidation': FSB, Key Attributes of Effective Resolution Regimes for Financial Institutions (2011) 3.

[406] London G20 Summit, April 2009, Declaration on Strengthening the Financial System and Cannes G20 Summit, November 2011, para 28.

[407] Earlier in 2010 the Commission issued a Communication on crisis management in the financial sector (COM (2010) 579).

[408] Directive 2014/59/EU [2014] OJ L173/190 (the 2014 BRRD). The Commission Proposal is at COM (2012) 280/3 (Impact Assessment at SWD (2012) 166). The Council reached a General Approach on 27 June 2013 (Council Document 11148/1/13REV1). The European Parliament's ECON Committee report (on which the Parliament's negotiating position was based) was adopted in October 2012 (A7-0196/2013). Final agreement was reached in December 2013 and the new regime is to be applied in the Member States from 1 January 2015 (the bail-in regime is to be applied at the latest by January 2016).

As noted briefly below, the BRRD provides for a network of NCAs and national resolution authorities (and funds) charged with applying the new rulebook and resolving banks. A key part of the Banking Union architecture, however, is that these executive functions, and the related application of the BRRD, for euro-area banks, are centralized, and the related resolution funding support mutualized, through a Single Resolution Mechanism (SRM). In 2013, the Commission's proposal for the SRM, which forms the third pillar of the Banking Union architecture along with the Single Supervisory Mechanism (SSM) (Chapter XI section 7) and the (still incomplete) related deposit guarantee regime, followed. After very difficult negotiations, reflecting, *inter alia*, the considerable fiscal and legal complexities associated with the mutualization of bank losses and with the construction of related support structures, agreement was finally reached in March 2014 (the 2014 SRM Regulation).[409]

The Commission's 2014 proposal for a regulation on the ring-fencing of certain trading and other activities within the EU's largest banks also forms of the EU's resolution/recovery strategy.[410]

The SRM is designed to provide an integrated decision-making structure for euro-area banks in distress which is aligned with the supervision of such banks under the SSM and which thereby ensures consistency of approach in dealing with euro-area banks and signals the resilience of the EU's ability to deal with bank failure. The SRM has two elements. First, the executive session of the Single Resolution Board (SRB) (composed of a Chair, Vice Chair, four permanent members, the relevant national resolution authorities (of the institution in distress), observer representatives from the ECB (which makes the initial determination as to whether an institution is failing or likely to), and the Commission) is responsible for directly overseeing the resolution plans of, and resolving, cross-border banks and banks directly supervised by the ECB/SSM (the larger plenary session of the SRB exercises specified powers). In taking resolution decisions, the SRB applies the BRRD rulebook (thereby mirroring national resolution authorities in Member States not participating in Banking Union). Reflecting the allocation of tasks under the SSM, the SRB is responsible for the resolution of banks directly supervised by the ECB (and cross-border groups), while national resolution authorities are responsible for all other banks (unless

---

[409] Regulation (EU) No 806/2014 [2014] OJ L225/1. The original proposal is at COM (2013) 520.

Negotiations proved to be immensely difficult, not least given significant doubts as to whether the SRM as proposed was compatible with the Treaties—the Council's Legal Service, eg, delivered an opinion in October 2013 which cast doubt on the compliance of the proposed SRM with the Treaty restrictions on delegations of discretionary power from the institutions, as interpreted by the *Meroni* ruling (see Chs X sect 5.5.1 and XI sect 5.8.2 on *Meroni*).

The multiple negotiating difficulties included: the governance of the SRM and the role of institutions such as the Council and Commission; how to achieve a compromise between Member State and institutional sensitivities related to representation on the SRM and SRM operational effectiveness; the legal basis of the SRM and the related Single Resolution Fund (SRF); and the extent to which the SRF should or could be mutualized (rather than split into different national compartments).The Council reached a General Approach, however, in December 2013 (Council Document 18070/13), and the European Parliament reached a negotiating position in February 2014 (T7-0095/2014).

Trilogue negotiations over early 2014 proved very difficult, particularly with respect to SRM decision-making processes and with respect to the construction of the SRF (related to, *inter alia*, its basis in an Intergovernmental Agreement and the extent to which it should be composed of 'national compartments', given legacy debt issues).

[410] COM (2014) 43. See Ch VI sect 1.

resolution requires recourse to the SRM's Single Resolution Fund (SRF)); the SRB has a range of oversight powers over national authorities, however, and may choose to exercise resolution powers over all banks. Second, the SRF, which has a target funding level of 1 per cent of the covered deposits of all Banking Union banks and which is based on bank contributions, will provide fiscal support, mirroring the national resolution funds in Member States not participating in Banking Union. The constitution and operation of the SRF are regulated in part by the SRM Regulation and in part by an Intergovernmental Agreement (the latter addresses, *inter alia*, the transfer of contributions from national resolution authorities to, initially, national compartments within the SRF, the gradual mutualization of contributions (over eight years), and the order in which funds are allocated to cover resolution costs (the 'waterfall'). The SRM is an outcome of the intense political and institutional efforts to preserve the euro area as it threatened to buckle under the fiscal/ sovereign debt crisis and is directed towards deposit-taking institutions; accordingly, its complex features and governance are not outlined in this Chapter.[411]

Outside the Banking Union context, the new harmonized recovery and resolution regime (the 2014 BRRD) is primarily directed to bank recovery and resolution (for all EU banks), given the systemic implications of bank failure and the central role of banks in the economic system. But, given the systemic implications of failure by certain types of investment firm, it also covers investment firms which engage in proprietary dealing and in firm commitment underwriting, and which accordingly can threaten financial stability, in particular through interconnections with other financial institutions.[412] Its main features are outlined briefly in what follows.

The 2014 BRRD addresses prevention and early intervention measures and resolution.[413] Institutionally, the Directive provides for the establishment of resolution authorities in every Member State (in the form of public administrative authorities) to

---

[411] For further discussion see, eg, Ferran, E, European Banking Union: Imperfect, But It Can Work (2014), University of Cambridge Faculty of Law Research Paper No 30/2014, available at <http://ssrn.com/ abstract=2426247>.

[412] Arts 1(1), 2(1)(3), and 2(1)(23). The regime applies to in-scope 'institutions'—essentially credit institutions and specified investment firms—and, in effect, tracks the scope of 2013 CRD IV/ CRR. A separate initiative is underway with respect to other financial institutions (including financial market infrastructures, including CCPs and CSDs, and insurance firms), but is at a much earlier stage: Commission, Consultation on a Possible Recovery and Resolution Framework for Financial Institutions other than Banks (2012).

[413] Given the wide range of complex issues engaged (ranging from the impact on private law rights, to the appropriate design of, eg, the contested 'bail-in' tool, which requires creditors to carry losses, to the related role of creditor monitoring and risk pricing in supporting bank stability), the new regime is noted only in very short and broad outline in this section. For further discussion see, eg, Armour, J, Making Bank Resolution Credible, ECGI Law WP No 244/2014, available at <http://ssrn.com/abstract=2393998>; Avgouleas, E, Goodhart, C, and Schoenmaker, D, 'Bank Resolution Plans as a Catalyst for Global Financial Reform' (2013) 9 *J of Financial Stability* 210; Schoenmaker, D, 'Banking Supervision and Resolution: the European Dimension' (2012) 6 *LFMR* 52; Babis, V, EU Recovery and Resolution Framework: Financial Assistance Between Banking Groups, University of Cambridge Faculty of Law Research Paper No 15/2012, available at <http://ssrn.com/abstract=2091194>; Schillig, M, Bank Resolution Regimes in Europe I—Recovery and Resolution Planning, Early Intervention (2012), available at <http://ssrn.com/abstract=2136101>; Schillig, M, Bank Resolution Regimes in Europe II—Resolution Tools and Powers (2012), available at <http://ssrn. com/abstract=2136084>; Attinger, BJ, Crisis Management and Bank Resolution: Quo Vadis Europe? ECB Legal WP No 13 (2011), available at <http://ssrn.com/abstract=1972326>; and Alexander, K, 'Bank Reso-lution Regimes: Balancing Prudential Regulation and Shareholder Rights' (2009) 9 *JCLS* 61.

oversee the new regime[414] and requires that national resolution funds are established to support resolution.

The prevention regime is based on the financial institution being required to draw up a recovery plan (at group and individual institution levels), to be assessed and approved by the NCA (with resolution authority oversight), which sets out the measures and arrangements to be taken to restore it to viability in the event of a material deterioration of its financial position. The resolution authority is to prepare the institution's related resolution plan (in co-operation with the relevant NCA), which sets out the options for resolving the institution, in a range of scenarios, including systemic crisis conditions. Based on the resolution plan, the resolution authority can require the financial institution to take remedial action where the authority identifies impediments to resolvability.[415] Assessment of the resolvability of pan-EU groups is to be co-ordinated by the group's different resolution authorities, the relevant NCAs, and EBA, through resolution colleges. The 2014 Directive also provides for access to intra-group financial support by providing that financial institutions within a group be able to enter into agreements for financial support.

Where difficulties arise after the prevention phase, resolution under the BRRD provides an alternative to normal insolvency proceedings and supports the orderly restructuring or winding down of a financial institution. It is designed to shore up financial stability and, by allocating losses between shareholders and creditors, to protect tax-payers from the fiscal costs of bailouts. Prior to this stage, however, the related early intervention regime empowers NCAs to intervene at an earlier stage where the financial situation or solvency of an institution is deteriorating.[416] In severe circumstances, the NCA would be empowered to appoint a 'temporary administrator'.[417]

Where these measures fail to stabilize the institution, the resolution regime activates.[418] It empowers resolution authorities to deploy four types of resolution tool under the conditions set out in the BRRD.[419] The sale-of-business tool empowers the resolution authority to sell the institution (or the whole or part of its business) on commercial terms, and without requiring the consent of shareholders. The bridge institution tool, which is a temporary tool, empowers the authority to transfer all or part of the institution's business to a publicly controlled entity with the aim of selling the business when market conditions are

---

[414] Resolution authorities can take the form of, eg, bank regulators (as long as conflict-of-interest management arrangements are in place), central banks, finance ministries, or special authorities (Art 3).

[415] Such action might include reducing complexity through changes to legal or operational structures, limiting exposures, imposing reporting requirements, or restricting new business lines or products.

[416] The powers activate where the financial institution does not meet or is likely to breach the requirements of the 2013 CRD IV/CRR, and include powers to require implementation of the recovery plan, request management to convene, and request the institution to draw up plans for debt restructuring: Art 27.

[417] Where replacement of the senior management body (allowed under Art 28) is deemed insufficient (Art 29).

[418] The resolution process triggers where the resolution authority determines that the institution is failing or likely to fail; having regard to timing and other relevant circumstances, there is no reasonable prospect that any alternative private sector or supervisory action, other than a resolution action, would prevent the failure of the institution within a reasonable time-frame; and resolution action is necessary in the public interest (Art 32).

[419] Minimum harmonization applies in that other resolution tools could be deployed by Member States, although national resolution authorities will only be able to use such tools where none of the EU tools (singly or in conjunction) allows them to take effective resolution action.

appropriate. The asset separation tool enables the authority to transfer impaired assets to an asset-management vehicle, in order to allow them to be managed and sold over time.[420]

The highly contested and controversial 'bail-in' tool allows the resolution authority to write down the claims of unsecured creditors and to convert debt into equity. The bail-in tool is designed to be used to recapitalize an institution (through write-downs of liabilities) to the extent necessary to restore its ability to comply with its authorization conditions and meet the conditions of the 2013 CRD IV/CRR regime, or to convert to equity or reduce the principal amount of claims or debt instruments transferred to a bridge institution, in order to provide capital for the bridge institution. It may only be deployed where there is a realistic prospect of restoring the institution to financial soundness and long-term viability. All liabilities of an institution are subject to bail-in, save those liabilities identified as being excluded from bail-in. The regime is very broadly designed to impose losses on shareholders and bondholders; financial institutions are required to have sufficient 'bail-in-able' debt available.[421] The excluded liabilities cover deposits guaranteed under the Deposit Guarantee Scheme Directive, secured liabilities, client assets or funds, certain liabilities with a maturity of less than seven days (in effect, short-term inter-bank lending and claims of clearing houses and payment and settlement systems), and liabilities to employees, commercial or trade creditors, and tax and social security authorities (as long as these authorities are preferred creditors under national law).[422] In exceptional circumstances, the resolution authority may exclude or partially exclude certain liabilities, subject to the BRRD conditions. The order of the write-down follows the usual allocation of losses in an insolvency, with equity absorbing losses first, followed by subordinated debt and senior debt; deposits of natural persons and SMEs in excess of €100,000 (not covered by the Deposit Guarantee Directive) rank ahead of senior debt. The bail-in tool is designed to apply to up to 8 per cent of a bank's liabilities, after which access to resolution funding may become available; the 8 per cent limit accordingly shapes the institution's decision as to the amount of 'bail-in-able' debt which must be issued.

Once the 8 per cent threshold has been reached with the bail-in tool, the regime provides for potential access to dedicated resolution funding (to a maximum of 5 per cent of bank liabilities, although an exemption is available for extraordinary circumstances) in the form of national resolution funds, funded by *ex-ante* and, where necessary and in extraordinary circumstances, *ex-post* contributions from financial institutions and from borrowing facilities from financial institutions and central banks; the target funding level (by 2025) is 1 per cent of guaranteed deposits in the Member State. Borrowing between national resolution funds is also provided for where the amounts raised are not sufficient to cover expenses incurred. National resolution funds are to be mutualized in the case of a pan-EU group resolution, based on a pre-agreed financial plan adopted by the relevant resolution authorities.

The regime acknowledges that, in exceptional circumstances, public support may be required, but the scope for intervention is circumscribed: in particular, 'government

---

[420] This tool can only be used in conjunction with another resolution tool to minimize competitive distortions and moral hazard risk.

[421] The amount is to be set by the national resolution authority.

[422] Art 44.

stabilization tools' can only be deployed after 8 per cent of a bank's liabilities have been bailed in and EU state aid requirements must be complied with.

Pan-EU co-ordination is to be achieved through resolution colleges, which will be supported by the BRRD rulebook and related BTSs to be adopted by EBA. EBA is also conferred with a co-ordination role to support colleges in taking action.

The BRRD is primarily directed to bank resolution and to protecting the tax-payer from the costs of bank resolution. Nonetheless, it shapes the wider supervisory environment for in-scope investment firms, including with respect to the remedial action which resolution authorities can require *ex-ante* with respect to resolvability.

V

TRADING VENUES

V.1 Trading Venues and Regulation

V.1.1 Introduction

This Chapter addresses the regulation of trading venues by the EU. Trading venue regulation is governed by the behemoth 2014 MiFID II/MiFIR regime, which is composed of two legislative measures, the 2014 MiFID II Directive and the 2014 MiFIR Regulation;[1] the legislative regime will be amplified by a dense administrative rulebook. The MiFID II/MiFIR regime is based on the venue classification and regulatory principles established by the pivotal and much-examined 2004 MiFID I trading venue regime.[2] Similarly, the new administrative rulebook will likely be based, at least to some extent, on the extensive administrative rules which applied under the 2006 Commission MiFID I Regulation.[3] The MiFID II/MiFIR reforms have, however, radically reshaped the MiFID I regime, and materially expanded and intensified EU intervention over trading venues.

Until the crisis era, trading venue regulation was the most sharply contested and ambitious element of EU securities and markets regulation. Over the crisis era, as the protracted 2014 MiFID II/MiFIR negotiations underline, it remained highly contested. It has, with the MiFID II/MiFIR reforms, become ever more ambitious. Given the pivotal importance of EU trading venue regulation, and the extent to which the evolution of the regime has exposed deep rifts between the Member States as to the purpose of venue regulation and the desirability of liberalization, the two epochal development periods—related to the 2004 MiFID I and the 2014 MiFID II/MiFIR—are considered in some detail in this Chapter (sections 2 and 3).

---

[1] Markets in Financial Instruments Directive 2014/65/EU [2014] OJ L173/349 (2014 MiFID II) and Markets in Financial Instruments Regulation EU (No) 600/2014 [2014] OJ L173/84 (2014 MiFIR). MiFID II is to be implemented by the Member States by 3 July 2016 and is to be applied by the Member States from 3 January 2017 (MiFID II Art 93). MiFIR, which, as a regulation, is directly applicable, applies from 3 January 2017 (MiFIR Art 55). The application of MiFIR has been tied to the application of MiFID II to ensure the regime operates as a 'regulatory package'; accordingly, the delegations within MiFIR for administrative rule-making (like the MiFID II delegations) apply from June 2014 (to allow for the EU rule-making process to take place). There are transitional arrangements for particular aspects of the trading venue/trading regime, including with respect to the trading venue/CCP (central clearing counterparty) access regime (sect 13) and the regime governing exchange-traded derivatives (Ch VI sect 4.3).
The discussion in this Chapter is based on the 2014 MiFIR II/MiFIR regime (the 2004 MiFID I regime (n 2) will be repealed from 3 January 2017). Reference is made to the MiFID I regime as appropriate.

[2] Directive 2004/39/EC [2004] OJ L145/1.

[3] Commission Regulation (EC) No 1287/2006 [2006] OJ L241/1.

425

V.1.2 Regulating Trading Venues

V.1.2.1 Trading Venues and the Financial System

Trading venues[4] are a critical component of financial market infrastructure. To different degrees, depending on the nature of the venue and of the instruments traded, trading venues pool liquidity in the instruments traded; facilitate trading and risk management; provide monitoring services (particularly over the stewardship of publicly traded firms and through share price movements); and, overall, allocate resources and mobilize savings.[5] While venues provide different services, trading (execution) services and related liquidity provision services are at the core of the trading venue business model.[6] Cash (equity and bond) venues typically facilitate the raising of capital by capital-seekers and the generation of returns for capital-providers by providing an infrastructure for the trading, hedging, and diversification of securities (and for the related monitoring of publicly traded firms).[7] Venues for derivative instruments typically facilitate the management and pricing of risks by supporting trading in standardized risk-transfer and risk-management instruments, including by making available liquidity providers for the instruments traded; the process of financial innovation is strongly associated with the transformation of bespoke, bilaterally negotiated risk management products into standardized products which are traded on organized venues and which allow markets to become ever more complete.[8]

Order execution can take place on different types of trading venue. Technological developments, the greater standardization of risk-management products, the 'unbundling' of the primary market 'admission to listing' functions associated with cash markets[9] from their secondary market trading functions, the demutualization of incumbent stock exchanges (over the early 1990s–mid-2000s in particular),[10] the arrival of competition in the order execution market generally, and an array of other factors have created the conditions in which a great variety of different venues, which can operate under different trading

---

[4] This Chapter uses the term 'venue' given the array of formal and informal systems, bilateral and multilateral, on which trading can be organized and which can come within the purview of venue regulation: Macey, J and O'Hara, M, 'From Markets to Venues: Securities Regulation in an Evolving World' 58 (2005) *Stanford LR* 563.

[5] For an early assessment see Levine, R, 'Financial Development and Economic Growth: Views and Agenda' (1997) 35 *J of Econ Lit* 685.

[6] For an early review see Fischel, D, 'Organized Exchanges and the Regulation of Dual Class Common Stock' (1987) 54 *University of Chicago LR* 119.

[7] An extensive literature addresses the role of equity trading venues in supporting capital-raising in the primary markets by providing secondary markets in which reliable prices are formed, liquidity is pooled (providing investors with an exit), and exchange is supported through standardized rules: eg Mahoney, P, 'The Exchange as Regulator' (1997) 83 *Va LR* 1453. The extent to which trading venues support capital-raising is, however, increasingly contested. See further Ch II sect 7.

[8] Merton, R, 'A Functional Perspective of Financial Intermediation' (1995) 24 *Financial Management* 23 and Gilson, R and Whitehead, C, 'Deconstructing Equity: Public Ownership, Agency Costs and Complete Capital Markets' (2009) 108 *Col LR* 231. The credit explosion prior to the financial crisis provides a paradigmatic example of this process as loan credit risk was transferred into traded securitization products on a systemic scale: Gubler, Z, 'The Financial Innovation Process: Theory and Application' (2011) 36 *Delaware J of Corporate Law* 55.

[9] On the listing function, see Ch II sect 7.

[10] Between 1993 and 2005, 40 per cent of the membership of the World Federation of Exchanges demutualized. On the progress of demutualization see, eg, International Organization of Securities Commissions (IOSCO), Exchange Demutualization in Emerging Markets (2005).

functionalities (often reflecting the instruments traded) and provide different services, have developed.[11] A very broad distinction can, however, be made between two venue types: (i) formal/organized, multilateral (in that the venue acts as a platform which brings together multiple third party orders and does not itself execute orders); non-discretionary (in that trades are executed according to the venue's pre-set rules or parameters and the venue does not intervene in the trade), and 'lit' (in that trading orders/interest are disclosed to the market at large); and (ii) informal, bilateral (trading is between the venue and the originator of the order), discretionary (in that trading is at the venue's discretion), and 'dark' (trading orders/interest are not publicly disclosed).[12]

The first venue type can be associated with the major public trading venues, including the long-established stock exchanges but also newer multilateral platforms, and particularly with the major public cash equity trading venues. While these venues support some dark trading, they are predominantly associated with lit trading, and accordingly with price formation. These venues are also typically liquidity-providing in nature. They tend to operate through multilateral, non-discretionary, public 'central order books' in which orders interact;[13] liquidity is pooled on the order book and prices are set by the interaction of orders. Dealer-based trading models can also be deployed within this venue type. In dealer-based venues, the market is quote- (not order) driven and liquidity is provided by quote-supplying dealers, connected through electronic networks, acting as market-makers, and providing competing bid and offer (buy and sell) quotes.[14] Many venues incorporate elements of both quote and order trading methodologies.[15] Central order books are most strongly associated with high volumes of trading in highly liquid instruments.[16] Less liquid instruments, in which trading is thinner, are typically traded through dealer-based platforms on which liquidity is provided by dealers. Dealer markets also support specialist trading as they allow traders to execute complex orders (such as large, price-moving orders), supported by bespoke execution services. Overall, venues of this first type have a strong public quality, which is reflected in how they are regulated.[17]

The second venue type embraces a very wide range of trading venues. It can be regarded in terms of a spectrum along which trading is organized to greater or lesser extents—with

---

[11] A vast literature examines the early development of venues for the trading of financial instruments outside traditional stock exchanges (initially these venues were often termed 'Alternative Trading Systems', following the term adopted by the US Securities and Exchange Commission (US SEC)). See, eg, Fleckner, A, 'Stock Exchanges at the Crossroads' (2006) 74 *Fordham LR* 2541, Macey and O'Hara, n 4, and Lee, R, *What is an Exchange? The Automation, Management and Regulation of Financial Markets* (1998).

[12] This analysis of venue type is based in part on Ferrarini, G and Moloney, N, 'Reshaping Order Execution in the EU and the Role of Interest Groups: From MiFID I to MiFID II' (2012) 13 *EBOLR* 557.

[13] A range of orders can be fed into the order book, including 'limit orders' (which specify price and size) and 'at-best orders' and 'market orders', which are executed at the best price available. Central limit order books are a key source of liquidity in the EU cash equity trading market.

[14] On order and dealer trading models see IOSCO, Supervisory Framework for Markets Report (1999).

[15] The London Stock Exchange, eg, operates a number of platforms, including the SETS electronic order book for equities (which includes a quote functionality for market-makers) and the SEAQ dealer/quote platform for bonds and for securities admitted to its Alternative Investment Market.

[16] Liquidity is also provided through market-makers active on the order book. High frequency traders can act as quasi-market-makers where they continuously provide 'two-sided' (buy and sell) liquidity to the order book.

[17] Ferrarini, G and Saguoto, P, 'Reforming Securities and Derivatives Trading in the EU: From EMIR to MIFIR' (2013) 13 *JCLS* 319.

entirely bilateral 'over-the-counter' (OTC) (not organized) trading at one end, and some degree of organization of trading, albeit attached to an essentially bilateral trading model, at the other.[18] This second type of venue is associated with the exercise, to greater and lesser degrees, of venue discretion, whether with respect to venue membership, instruments traded, or order execution,[19] and with dark trading. In the cash equity markets, for example, this form of venue type is associated with investment firms (brokers) providing bilateral, discretionary execution services OTC to their clients. Orders from clients might, for example, be executed bilaterally by brokers against their proprietary order books or 'crossed' internally against other client orders, rather than routed by brokers to an organized trading venue. OTC trading of this type has long been a feature of the cash equity markets in the EU and internationally.[20] But technological developments have led to the development of automated broker execution services (in particular Broker Crossing Systems (BCSs), which support the crossing of client orders) within the OTC space, and to a related blurring of the distinction between formal/informal and multilateral/bilateral venues. Nonetheless, important differences of characterization remain. While broker execution can be delivered through formal, organized systems in the OTC space, it is typically regarded, nonetheless, as a discretionary, client-facing service which arises from the traditional fiduciary duties imposed on investment firms with respect to their clients and from the related best execution obligation. It is therefore functionally different to non-discretionary multilateral venue trading and is generally regulated through firm-facing conduct and prudential requirements.

Overall, liquidity tends to determine the type of venue model deployed. Highly standardized instruments (such as cash equities) are usually traded on organized, multilateral, non-discretionary order books. Venues typically become more bilateral and discretionary in nature as the instruments traded become more complex and bespoke, as trading moves from the secondary to the primary markets, and as liquidity accordingly thins.[21] Similarly, organized, multilateral, non-discretionary venues, and in particular central order books, are often associated with high-volume, highly liquid retail and institutional trading, while other venues are typically associated with lower levels of participation, trading, and liquidity and with institutional investor trading. In general, the more informal and discretionary venues usually support trading in bonds and derivatives and typically deploy quote/dealer-based trading models.[22] Trading in these instruments typically involves counterparty-to-counterparty trading and is largely bilateral, although counterparties may be linked through different types of systems which can display varying degrees of organization; some bond and derivatives systems are highly organized.[23]

---

[18] For an analysis of the two major venue types in terms of public venues and private venues see Ferrarini and Saguoto, n 17.

[19] For an analysis of the major venue types in terms of the degree of discretion deployed see Valiente, D, Setting the Institutional and Regulatory Framework for Trading Platforms: Does the MiFID Definition of OTF Make Sense? ECMI Research Report 8/2012 (2012).

[20] eg IOSCO, Principles for Dark Liquidity. Report of the Technical Committee of IOSCO (2011) 4.

[21] See further Valiente, n 19.

[22] Including voice and electronic dealer-based systems.

[23] In the cash bond segment, eg, the MTS cash platform is a leading dealer-based electronic market for EU sovereign bonds, while Tradeweb is a leading provider of platforms in the bond and derivative segments. In the derivatives segment, the LSE, eg, provides an electronic order book for securitized derivatives.

V.1.2.2 Regulation of Trading Venues

The regulation of trading venues is primarily directed to ensuring market integrity, efficiency, and stability; in support of these aims, it has long been associated with protecting liquidity.[24]

Traditionally, venue regulation has been directed to the major public cash equity venues (organized, multilateral, and non-discretionary). But the major stock exchanges were initially afforded significant discretion and flexibility in running their trading activities; regulators, in effect, outsourced regulation to the exchanges. The grip of regulation tightened following the demutualization movement and the arrival of competition between stock exchanges and other execution venues[25] and subsequent industry consolidation,[26] and the related risk of incentive mis-alignment between venue interests and public interests.[27] As it has evolved, venue regulation in the cash equity segment has typically sought to ensure that venues efficiently support capital-raising, the monitoring of good stewardship in firms, and the generation of strong returns for savers.[28] Extensive transparency rules, or rules which require the disclosure of pre-trade bid (buy)/offer (sell) prices and of post-trade price, volume, and time information, have accordingly applied in support of price formation. These venues have also, as systemically significant venues, typically been subject to authorization, operational, capital, and access requirements.[29]

Venue regulation more generally experienced its first major reform period following the rapid development, noted in section 1.2.1, of new venues, operating in parallel with the traditional stock exchanges but typically providing more limited services (classically secondary market trading services and not primary market listing services, and in particular asset classes, classically bonds and derivatives), from the early 1990s on. These reforms attempted to grapple with the appropriate characterization and regulation of the array of new trading venues and to address the risks they posed. In particular, it became clear that the fragmentation of liquidity across multiple venues could compromise liquidity and damage efficient price formation, and that price formation could be prejudiced where venues were not subject to full transparency requirements. Trading activity on some venues could be subject to lower levels of supervision, making it more difficult to control market manipulation. Venue operators might not impose or enforce adequate admission standards

---

[24] eg Levine, n 5 and Amihud, Y and Mendelson, H, 'Asset Pricing and the Bid Ask Spread' (1986) 17 *JFE* 223.

[25] eg Ferran, E, *Building an EU Securities Market* (2004) 239–54.

[26] Best exemplified by successive waves of international consolidation, including the merger of the New York Stock Exchange and Euronext in 2007 to form NYSE Euronext, whose different trading venues now represent one third of global equities trading.

[27] eg Brummer, C, 'Stock Exchanges and the New Markets for Securities Law' (2008) 75 *University of Chicago LR* 1435; Jackson, H and Gadinis, S, 'Markets as Regulators. A Survey' (2007) 80 *Southern California LR* 1239; Aggarwal, R, Ferrell, A, and Katz, J, US Securities Regulation in a World of Global Exchanges, ECGI Finance WP No 146/2007 (2006), available at <http://ssrn.com/abstract=950530>; Fleckner, n 11; and Mahoney, n 7.

[28] eg Mitchell, L, Towards a New Law and Economics: the Case of the Stock Market, GWU Legal Research Paper No 495 (2010), available at <http://ssrn.com/abstract=1557730> and the (UK) Kay Review of Equity Markets and Long-Term Decision Making, Final Report (2012).

[29] The 2010 IOSCO Objectives and Principles of Securities Regulation recommend that the regulation of trading markets address market authorization, oversight, and ongoing supervision; trading transparency; the detection and prevention of market manipulation and unfair trading practices; the proper management of large exposures; and market disruption: IOSCO, Objectives and Principles of Securities Regulation (2010) para I.

for instruments and participants, or be sufficiently concerned with ensuring that trading was carried out in a fair and orderly fashion. Venues might raise systemic risks where they, or their participants, did not have sufficient financial resources or where their trading mechanisms were not adequately bolstered against counterparty risk; this was particularly the case with respect to derivative exposures. Poor liquidity management controls might lead to a drying up of liquidity in stressed market conditions. Investor protection risks might also arise. Best execution, for example, might become more difficult to achieve where trading fragmented across multiple venues. Conflicts of interest might arise where an investment firm executed a client order by 'internalization' (or by executing the order bilaterally through an internal system). Regulatory arbitrage risks also arose, given a lack of clarity as to whether these new venues were simply a form of execution service provided by investment firms or multilateral trading venues akin to stock exchanges. Regulation accordingly sought to address these risks through classification techniques designed to isolate the trading functionalities which required targeted regulation.

The second major reform period took place over the financial crisis and, as noted in section 1.2.4, can be associated with financial-stability-driven reform and with an expansion of the regulated trading venue space. Prior to the financial crisis, the regulation of trading venues for bonds and derivatives trading (in the EU at least) lagged the regulation of cash equity trading venues. This reflected in part the dominance of professional clients/counterparties in the non-equity markets, but it also reflected the close focus of securities market regulators, prior to the financial crisis, on capital-raising and on related disclosure tools.[30] The crisis era, however, has led to more interventionist stability-driven venue regulation, and to bond and derivatives trading venues, whether organized/multilateral or bilateral/ OTC, being pulled within the regulatory net.

Common to both reform periods, however, are efforts to capture the diverse functionalities which different trading venues (organized/multilateral and informal/bilateral) represent, and to identify which venues should be within the regulatory perimeter.[31] Transparency regulation poses particular challenges in this regard, as discussed in the following section.

V.1.2.3 Venue Regulation and Transparency

Transparency rules (which govern the trading data published by trading venues) are the mainstay of venue regulation, given their role in supporting price formation and in deepening liquidity.[32] The effectiveness of a venue's price-formation process and the depth of its liquidity depends on a number of interacting factors, including the market structure adopted and the trading practices permitted on the market. But the publication of trade transparency data plays a major role in ensuring that prices reflect supply and demand and that a trading venue is liquid and efficient.

---

[30] See further Moloney, N, 'The Legacy Effects of the Global Financial Crisis on Regulatory Design in the EU' in Ferran, E, Moloney, N, Hill, J, and Coffee, J, *The Regulatory Aftermath of the Global Financial Crisis* (2012) 111; Langevoort, D, 'Global Securities Regulation After the Financial Crisis' (2010) 13 *JIEL* 799; and Anand, A, 'Is Systemic Risk Relevant to Securities Regulation?' (2010) 60 *U of Toronto LJ* 941.

[31] See, eg, Lee, n 11, and Lee, R, *Running the World's Markets. The Governance of Financial Infrastructure* (2011).

[32] One analysis has linked the public quality of a venue (and the related intensity of its regulation) to the extent to which transparency requirements are imposed: Ferrarini and Saguoto, n 17.

Trade transparency regulation relates to the mandated disclosure of the price, volume, and transaction information which is produced by a trading venue, and to its availability to the market on a real-time basis. These disclosures support price formation and liquidity, but they also serve related functions. In a transparent marketplace, investors can see all the orders entering the market and the transactions already completed, and can accordingly monitor the execution process.[33] Transparency rules can address fragmentation risk (which arises where trading in an instrument splits across multiple venues) as they tie together execution data from different venues and thereby support price formation, the pooling of liquidity, and the achievement of best execution. Transparency requirements also allow supervisors to monitor the nature of trading and to detect emerging risks, including with respect to market abuse and, as they allow supervisors to monitor liquidity levels, market stability.[34]

But there is a trade-off between transparency and liquidity, as transparency requirements are acutely sensitive to different trading functionalities and can prejudice liquidity in some circumstances. In particular, in quote-driven or dealer trading venues, in which dealers take on principal risk, trading reacts to action by dealers. The publication of trading information accordingly generates liquidity risks for dealers, as the disclosure of an open position can lead to strategic behaviour by other traders and expose the dealer.

The liquidity risks can be acute with pre-trade transparency disclosures. In principle, 'lighting' pre-trade orders carries risks. From the trader perspective, pre-trade transparency rules carry market impact risks, particularly for large orders, as the market may move against the order as it is executed (a large sell order may drive the market down). From the venue perspective, multilateral trading venues do not carry direct risk from pre-trade transparency, as these platforms facilitate the interaction of different orders and do not trade directly or put their capital at risk. They would, however, face the risk of losing business were they not able to provide some degree of dark trading to meet traders' needs, particularly with respect to large orders, but multilateral venues typically benefit from regulatory waivers to transparency rules and can offer dark trading. Dealer-based and bilateral venues, however, face sharper risks. Where dealers execute orders against their proprietary instruments or capital and thereby take on principal risk, they become subject to market impact risk (as their trading position is exposed to the market and their capital is at risk). Dealers' positions could be systematically undermined and it could become uneconomic for them to offer execution services. Liquidity could accordingly suffer were dealers to become less willing to take large positions.

Transparency requirements are also sensitive to the type of instrument traded. The equity markets are associated with order-book trading, with high levels of trading activity and liquidity, and accordingly with significantly lower risks in terms of pre-trade transparency. Bond markets, however, operate with different transparency and price-formation dynamics.[35] Bond markets are considerably less liquid than the equity markets and experience

---

[33] Lee, n 11, 256.

[34] IOSCO, Mitigating Systemic Risk. A Role for Securities Regulation. Discussion Paper (2011) 19 and 41.

[35] eg Centre for Economic Policy Research (Dunne, P, Moore, M, and Portes, R), European Government Bond Markets: Transparency, Liquidity and Efficiency (2006), CESR (Committee of European Securities Regulators), Response to the Commission on Non-Equities Transparency (2007) (CESR/07-284b) 4–5, and

much thinner trading patterns. Trading is typically concentrated at the time of issue and over the months immediately following as the issue is re-distributed; trading typically then thins very significantly until the period shortly before the issue matures, when taxation and other drivers prompt stronger trading. Dealer trading models tend to dominate, although electronic multi-dealer platforms have developed, particularly in the sovereign and corporate bond markets.[36] Investors are typically professional. Pricing is affected by a range of factors beyond trading information, including macroeconomic conditions (particularly for government bonds) and credit risk. Transparency is not a guarantee of liquidity; price transparency does not always indicate the availability of counterparties available to trade at the indicated price. Transplantation of the equity market transparency model can therefore generate liquidity risks, given the potential risks to dealers.[37] But liquidity risks are not distinct to the bond markets; trading in some equities can also be highly illiquid, particularly with respect to SME (small and medium-sized enterprise) shares and the shares of small capitalization ('small cap') issuers.

It is accordingly not easy to design a rulebook which is appropriately calibrated to the wide range of trading functionalities on which different asset classes trade, but which also supports an optimal level of transparency (and of venue regulation generally). Bright-line distinctions between predominantly lit, multilateral, non-discretionary trading venues and predominantly dark, dealer-based/bilateral, discretionary OTC trading venues, as well as between different equity and non-equity asset classes, are not easily made. The troublesome gestation of the EU's new 'organized trading facility' (OTF) classification, which is restricted to non-equity asset classes but which was originally (and problematically) designed to additionally cover equity trading, is instructive in this regard (section 6.4). Ultimately, transparency is a public good and is accordingly exposed to free-riding risks; as one market participant has noted, 'everyone likes transparent markets but nobody likes to contribute'.[38]

V.1.2.4 Trading Venue Regulation and the Financial Crisis

Trading venue regulation was not, in the early stages of the financial crisis, a major feature of the international reform agenda.[39] Trading venues performed reasonably well,[40]

London Economics, Quantification of the Macro-Economic Impact of Integration of EU Financial Markets. Final Report to the EU Commission (2002) 54–6.

[36] In the EU sovereign bond market, eg, institutional platforms include MTS, Brokertec, Tradeweb, Bloomberg, and Bondvision; EuroTLX supports retail trades. See also n 23.

[37] The UK Financial Services Authority (FSA) (now Financial Conduct Authority) has warned that the imposition of transparency requirements on the trading of non-equity asset classes requires careful calibration if adverse impacts on liquidity are to be avoided: FSA, The FSA's Markets Regulatory Agenda (2010) 33–4.

[38] European Parliament, ECON (Economic and Monetary Affairs) Committee, Trading in Financial Instruments—Dark Pools. Workshop Summary. (2010) (2010 ECON Dark Pool Workshop), Deutsche Börse presentation.

[39] eg MacNeil, I 'The Trajectory of Regulatory Reform in the UK in the Wake of the Financial Crisis' (2010) 11 *EBOLR* 483.

[40] eg Angel, J, Harris, L, and Spatt, C, Equity Trading in the 21st Century, Marshall School of Business WP No FBE 09-10 (2010), available at <http://ssrn.com/abstract=1584026> (on equity markets) and FSA, n 37, 19–20. The European Securities and Markets Authority's (ESMA) Board of Supervisors reported that trading market infrastructures held up well over the serious market volatility in the euro-area sovereign debt markets over summer 2011: Board of Supervisors Meeting, 20 September 2011 (2011/BS/209).

although some difficulties with bond market transparency were experienced in the EU.[41] But trading venues were eventually pulled into the reform agenda through a number of channels.

The G20 commitment to closing regulatory gaps and to increasing transparency[42] can be associated with the EU's concern (under the 2014 MiFID II/MiFIR) to bring all organized trading venues within the regulatory net and to extend transparency requirements from equity trading venues to trading venues for bonds and derivatives. Venue regulation in the EU and internationally is also increasingly being directed towards stability and resilience;[43] this can be seen in particular through the new generation of algorithmic trading controls, position management requirements, and liquidity/market-maker requirements.[44]

Organized trading venues have also been deployed as devices for managing the gaps which arise when financial innovation moves ahead of market infrastructure.[45] In particular, the liquidity-supporting benefits of organized venues have been associated with stronger risk management in derivatives trading.[46] The G20 commitment to repatriate the trading of standardized derivatives from the OTC space to organized trading venues (implemented in the EU under the 2014 MiFIR II/MiFIR)[47] is designed to strengthen the resilience and transparency of derivatives trading through the interposition of trading infrastructures, and the related enhancement of transparency, regulatory monitoring, operational and risk management, and liquidity.[48]

In addition, the crisis-era transparency agenda has been a factor in dark/undisclosed equity trading coming under particular scrutiny.[49] Dark trading in the equity markets is not troublesome in itself. The benefits to investors include liquidity provision, price impact protection, and lower execution costs.[50] The difficulties arise where dark equity trading is of a similar functionality to lit equity trading (subject to transparency requirements), and where regulatory objectives are accordingly defeated (price formation and liquidity may be threatened, for example) and arbitrage and competition risks arise. Dark equity trading came to attract close international attention over the crisis era from, *inter alia*, the US Securities and Exchange Commission (US SEC), the Australian Securities and Investments Commission (ASIC), and the Canadian securities industry.[51] Dark trading was also

---

[41] Sect 3.1.

[42] Washington G20 Summit, November 2009, Declaration of the Summit on Financial Markets and the World Economy, Action Plan to Implement Principles for Reform.

[43] FSA, n 37, 4 and Hu, H, 'Efficient Markets and the Law: A Predictable Past and an Uncertain Future' (2012) 4 *Annual Rev of Financial Economics* 179, suggesting that the US SEC has increasingly come to subordinate its traditional market efficiency priority to short-term financial stability concerns.

[44] See Ch VI sects 2.3 and 2.5 and sect 7.3 of this Chapter.

[45] See Merton, n 8 on the relationship between financial innovation and market infrastructures.

[46] McCoy, P, Pavlov, A, and Wachter, S, 'Systemic Risk through Securitization: The Result of Deregulation and Regulatory Failure' (2009) 41 *Connecticut LR* 1327.

[47] Pittsburgh G20 Summit, September 2009, Leaders' Statement.

[48] Financial Stability Board (FSB), Implementing OTC Derivatives Market Reforms (2010) 39–43. See further Ch VI sect 4.3.

[49] IOSCO, eg, has highlighted increasing fragmentation across equity trading venues and the increase in dark trading: IOSCO, Securities Markets Risk Outlook 2013–2014 (2013) 11.

[50] IOSCO, n 20, 11–12.

[51] US SEC Release No 34-60997, Regulation of Non-Public Trading Interests (2010), US SEC Release No 34-61358, Concept Release on Equity Market Structure (2010), ASIC Consultation Paper 145, Australian Equity Market Structure: Proposals (2010), and CSA/IIROC, Joint Position Paper 23-405, Dark

considered by the International Organization of Securities Commissions (IOSCO) in 2011.[52] The EU has followed suit; a major plank of the 2014 MiFID II/MiFIR reforms concerns the restriction of dark equity market trading.

V.1.3 Regulating Trading Venues and the EU

As discussed throughout this Chapter, the regulation of trading venues in the EU has grappled with the major policy issues which trading venue regulation raises generally.

But trading venue regulation in the EU has two distinct features. First, it has long been orientated towards internal market construction. The pivotal 2004 MiFID I regime, which first established a harmonized regulatory framework for venue regulation in the EU, was designed to liberalize order execution in shares and to promote competition between the incumbent stock exchange sector and the emergent OTC/brokerage sector. MiFID I abolished the 'concentration' requirement then in place in some Member States, which required all share orders to be centralized on the main stock exchange in that Member State. It relied on a venue classification and regulation regime, calibrated to different venue functionalities, to support a level playing field between competing share-trading venues, address the stability and transparency of the competitive market, and ensure investor protection. With the 2014 MiFID II/MiFIR reforms, the regime has become more regulatory than liberalizing in orientation. MiFID II/MiFIR is primarily concerned with ensuring that trading takes place on organized and transparent trading venues. It also, unlike the MiFID I regime, acts as a vehicle for the achievement of financial stability objectives, notably by pulling non-equity trading venues within the regulatory net and by tightening the regulation of venues generally. Nonetheless, like MiFID I, MiFID II/MiFIR aims to shape the market, but, by contrast with MiFID I, it seeks to be prescriptive rather than facilitative: MiFID II/MiFIR is designed to repatriate trading on to organized trading venues and away from the OTC markets.

Second, as the fraught MiFID I negotiations underline (section 2), venue regulation has long been highly politicized in the EU, reflecting the competitive territory at stake and the concentration of different types of trading and of trading venue in certain Member States.[53] Member States have accordingly held sharply different positions on, for example, whether equity trading should be moved from the OTC 'space' to organized 'lit' venues, and, more generally, on the extent to which different trading venues should compete with respect to 'dark' and 'lit' trading. Initial efforts through the Committee of European Securities Regulators (CESR) to establish consensus positions on the granting of MiFID I pre-trade transparency waivers (to support dark equity trading on organized trading venues), for

---

Liquidity in the Canadian Market (2010). Attesting to the international reform agenda, the US SEC and the UK FSA hosted an international roundtable on dark trading in October 2011 (SEC Press Release 2011-209).

[52] IOSCO, n 20.

[53] eg over the MiFID I Review preparatory process, CESR reported that 75 per cent of dark pre-trade trading taking place on regulated markets and MTFs under the 'large in scale' MiFID I waiver took place in one jurisdiction: CESR, Technical Advice to the Commission in the Context of the MiFID I Review—Equity Markets. Consultation Paper (2010) (CESR/10-394) (2010 CESR Equity Market Consultation) 8.

example, struggled, with a qualified majority vote (QMV) rather than the usual consensus-based decision being required in some cases.[54]

France and the UK, in particular, have long adopted different approaches to equity trading. Over the crisis era, France pursued a transparency agenda[55] and used its 2011 Presidency of the G20 to promote the movement of equity trading from OTC venues to the organized trading space.[56] This agenda reflects France's long-standing suspicion of pan-EU competition between equity order execution venues, which pre-dates the highly contested MiFID I negotiations and can be traced back to earlier battles over the 1993 Investment Services Directive (1993 ISD)[57] and to France's attempts to prevent trading of French shares on SEAQ-International in London (section 2.1). Conversely, the UK, the location of most OTC trading in the EU, has found the facilitative 2004 MiFID I framework to be 'generally satisfactory' and, over the MiFID I Review, was concerned to prevent any moves to protect 'national champions'.[58] Over the MiFID II/MiFIR negotiations, these long-standing tensions would re-emerge.

Accordingly, while the law-making complexities which trading venue regulation generates are considerable, given the technological challenges and the empirical subtleties,[59] they are all the greater in the EU, where the intense politicization of venue regulation can place considerable pressure on the quality of regulation. For example, MiFID I relied on regulatory venue classification techniques as a means of achieving liberalization and of securing compromises between different Member State interests, but one of the lessons of MiFID I has been that fine distinctions between, for example, 'discretionary' and 'non-discretionary' trading, and between 'bilateral' and 'multilateral' trading, can drive arbitrage and lead to unexpected outcomes. The challenges have not abated under the complex and technical 2014 MiFID II/MiFIR regime.

V.2 The Evolution of the EU's Trading Venue Regime

V.2.1 From Concentration to Competition: 2004 MiFID I

The regulation of trading venues was not comprehensively addressed by the EU until the adoption of the 2004 MiFID I.[60] MiFID I was a transformative measure.[61] It abolished the

---

[54] See further sect 11 on the waiver regime.
[55] French Autorité des Marchés Financiers (AMF), What Are the Priorities for Financial Markets (2011).
[56] G20, Paris Communiqué (2011).
[57] Directive 93/22/EC [1993] OJ L141/27.
[58] FSA, n 37, 23.
[59] The US SEC, in its 2010 Equity Market Report, noted that 'market structure issues are complex and require a broad understanding of statutory requirements, economic principles and practical trading considerations': n 51, 8.
[60] From a massive literature, see generally Gomber, P and Chlistalla, M, MiFID—Catalyst for a New Trading Landscape in Europe? (2007), available at <http://ssrn.com/abstract=1134763>; Davies, R, Dufour, A, and Scott-Quinn, B, 'The MiFID: Competition in a New European Equity Market Regulatory Structure' in Ferrarini, G and Wymeersch E (eds), *Investor Protection in Europe. Corporate Law Making, the MiFID and Beyond* (2006) 163; Alemanni, B, Lusignani, G, and Onado, M, 'The European Securities Industry: Further Evidence on the Roadmap to Integration', in Ferrarini and Wymeersch, 199; and Ferrarini, G and Recine, F, 'The MiFID and Internalisation', in Ferrarini and Wymeersch, 235.
[61] eg Lannoo, K and Casey, JP, The MiFID Revolution. European Capital Markets Institute Policy Brief (2006).

'concentration' rule which, under the 1993 ISD,[62] allowed Member States to require that equity orders were routed to national stock exchanges,[63] and thereby entrenched the centralization of equity trading on the incumbent stock exchanges across the EU.[64] MiFID I accordingly used harmonization to impose competitive discipline on the EU's incumbent stock exchanges and to harness industry innovation.[65] This reform was the most ambitious and most market-shaping (as compared to market-facilitating)[66] of the Financial Services Action Plan (FSAP) period, and generated intense interest internationally.[67]

Prior to MiFID I, the major EU stock exchanges held a monopoly in share trading. From the mid-1980s, competitive pressures from a number of sources jolted exchanges from their isolationist positions, increased competition for trading business,[68] and produced a number of consolidation initiatives.[69] Chief among these competitive pressures were the market changes wrought by the euro, technological developments, the emergence of an equity culture and the strengthening of market finance, and demutualization. Notable developments included the 2000 launch of Euronext (now NYSE Euronext) and the failed 2000 discussions between the London Stock Exchange and Deutsche Börse (the ill-fated iX project). New trading venues with pan-EU functionality (such as virt-X) appeared and, in some cases, disappeared (Nasdaq Europe). But the consolidation process did not break down the market power of the major exchanges, particularly given the vertical integration of trading and post-trading structures in some Member States. In addition, the degree to which different Member States allowed for on- and off-exchange competition in trading services varied, with Member States tending to adopt either a 'competitive market' or (through the concentration rule) a 'central market' approach.[70]

---

[62] n 57. The ISD was the EU's first attempt at venue regulation. It imposed a very limited regime which was largely concerned with investment firm access to major stock exchanges. It introduced the concept of a 'regulated market', conferred a passport on investment firms to access regulated markets across the EU, and empowered regulated markets to maintain remote screens (in effect, a form of passport) in host Member States.

[63] It was most associated with France, Germany, and Italy.

[64] The rule was the outcome of a polarized and highly politicized negotiation which saw the 'Alliance' group of Member States (the UK, Germany, Ireland, Luxembourg, and the Netherlands) support free competition and raise concerns as to the damage which the concentration rule could wreak on OTC markets, and the 'Club Med' group (France, Spain, Portugal, Greece, Italy, and Belgium) demand the centralization of all transactions on a regulated market in order to support the liquidity of that market and ensure a high level of investor protection. The UK was particularly concerned to defeat a mandatory concentration rule given the scale of UK OTC trading. Protectionist undercurrents were strong with certain Member States concerned to protect their markets from the then dominant London Stock Exchange; France, in particular, was concerned to repatriate French share trading, a significant proportion of which took place in London. A compromise position was finally adopted which made the concentration rule optional and imposed conditions on its use.

[65] The US at this time also supported competitive order execution through 'Regulation NMS', which came into force in March 2007.

[66] On market-shaping and market-facilitating interests in the EU, see further Ch I.

[67] US SEC Commissioner Campos stated that 'it is not an overstatement to say that [MiFID] will markedly change the regulatory landscape in Europe and globally. It will be a new global frontier': Speech on 'The Challenge of MiFID in the United States', Amsterdam, 10 May 2007.

[68] See Pagano, M and Steil, B, 'Equity Trading I: The Evolution of European Trading Systems' in Steil, B (ed), *The European Equity Markets: The State of the Union and an Agenda for the Millennium* (1996) 1.

[69] Pagano, M and Padilla, A, LECG Consulting Report on Efficiency Gains from the Integration of Exchanges: Lessons from the Euronext 'Natural Experiment' (2005).

[70] For a review of different trading practices and the competitive/central market dynamic see Davies et al n 60.

While other organized trading venues began to develop over this period, their impact was primarily felt in bond trading (the MTS electronic trading platform for euro-denominated sovereign debt, for example, centralized trading in the sovereign debt market), and they were not notably successful in attracting equity trading.[71] Equity trades remained the almost exclusive preserve of the major stock exchanges, with liquidity remaining 'sticky' and pooling at the major exchanges.[72] The ill-fated Jiway platform, for example, a joint venture between Morgan Stanley and OM, was established as a pan-EU platform for retail trades in European shares, but closed in early 2003.[73] But pressure for reform began to build as greater trading volumes, driven by hedge fund and proprietary trading, increased profit margins at the major exchanges, which drew fire from major investment banks.[74]

MiFID I was accordingly designed to promote competition between different share-trading venues in the interests of innovation, price competition, and investor choice, and to support the transparency and efficiency of the new, competitive trading marketplace; it was also designed to support a related market in the consolidation and supply of transparency data.

But once order execution moves away from the main exchanges and disperses across different venues, a series of risks arise, as noted in section 1.2 above.[75] Chief among them are a fragmentation of liquidity into different pools, and a consequent diminution of the efficiency of the price-formation process (as all orders do not interact[76])—particularly in the equity markets—and of the ability of brokers to deliver best execution,[77] and conflict-of-interest risk for clients, where client orders are executed OTC by a broker and not routed to a non-discretionary multilateral platform.[78] Supervisory risks are also generated, particularly with respect to the monitoring of market abuse and of risks to financial stability arising from liquidity pressures. These risks are typically addressed through transparency rules, which tie together different liquidity pools and, to different degrees, expose trading interests and activity on competing venues, and best execution rules, which require brokers to discover, and direct orders to, the liquidity pool which delivers the 'best' result for the client. But in choosing remedial rules, careful determinations must be made as to the particular functionality of the order execution venue in question, and the intensity and nature of the risks it poses.

---

[71] Webb, S, 'Exchanges, MTFs, Systematic Internalisers, and Data Providers—Winners and Losers in a Post-MiFID World' in Skinner, C (ed), *The Future of Investing in Europe's Markets After MiFID* (2007) 151, 157.

[72] The Commission reported in 2002 that Alternative Trading Systems accounted for only 1 per cent of equity trading volumes in the Community: 2002 MiFID I Proposal (COM (2002) 625) 8.

[73] Its failure was associated with high clearing and settlement costs, the 'stickiness' of liquidity, which remained pooled at the major exchanges, and limited demand from retail investors: JP Morgan, MiFID Report II. Earnings At Risk Analysis—The Threat to the Integrated Banking Model (2006) 33–4.

[74] Davis, P, 'The Grey Areas of Project Turquoise', *Financial World*, July/August 2007 29.

[75] eg Macey and O'Hara, n 4.

[76] Price formation risks can become acute where informative 'limit orders,' which specify a quantity and price, are not channeled through to the central order books of major public venues. Risks also arise where off-exchange trading leads to the 'hiding' of large trading interests.

[77] Costs may increase and spreads widen as a result.

[78] See generally Gadinis, S, 'Market Structure for Institutional Investors: Comparing the US and EU Regimes' (2008) 3 *Virginia Law & Business Rev* 311, 323–31.

The 2004 MiFID I negotiations, however, were fraught. MiFID I sought to re-allocate the benefits of share trading.[79] The negotiations were accordingly the most bitter and complex to have taken place in EU securities and markets regulation pre-crisis, and witnessed fierce clashes between the incumbent stock exchange sector and the emergent brokerage/OTC sector.[80] The former sought to protect its position from competition and to concentrate share orders on exchanges or, failing that, to impose similar rules on off-exchange trading venues. The brokerage/OTC sector argued that its execution functionality was different to that of exchanges, and that the imposition of similar rules, and in particular transparency rules, would generate risks and costs of such magnitude that this business would become unsustainable,[81] with consequent damage to innovation and investor choice.[82] The entrenched negotiating positions of the exchange and brokerage/OTC sectors were reflected in the sharply opposing positions taken by the Member States and the institutions, and shaped the very difficult Council and European Parliament negotiations.[83]

V.2.2 2004 MiFID I's Regulatory Model

The 2004 MiFID I's regulatory model for trading venue regulation was a compromise which reflected the difficult political and institutional negotiations.[84] The four-level MiFID I classification regime (which still forms the basis of the 2014 MiFID II/MiFIR regime) therefore reflected a fraught negotiation process, rather than a coherent expression of order execution regulation.

First, the highest level of regulation applied to multilateral, non-discretionary trading venues (for MiFID I financial instruments) which brought together multiple third party buying and selling interests in accordance with non-discretionary rules, and which took the form of 'regulated markets'. In practice, this classification captured the incumbent stock exchanges. Regulated markets were subject to authorization requirements, including initial

---

[79] The liberalization of share trading was achieved by means of the abolition of the concentration rule and the new transparency regime.

[80] From an extensive literature, see the previous edition of this work at 769–78, and Ferrarini and Recine, n 60.

[81] 'Internalizing' OTC firms (which executed client orders against their proprietary order books) argued that pre-trade transparency (which requires firms, in effect, to act as liquidity providers, commit capital, and stand ready to buy and sell at the disclosed prices, even though investment firms do not carry the liquidity and trading capacity of exchanges) would increase costs, severely prejudice internalization business, remove liquidity from the market, and dilute the benefits of competitive order execution. They argued that investor protection was more appropriately delivered through a matrix of conflict-of-interest rules, best execution requirements, and post-trade transparency requirements.

[82] OTC equity trading was argued to have a range of benefits derived from a breaking-down of the quasi-monopoly control by exchanges. One influential position paper on the MiFID I debate by a group of UK trade associations argued that while the centralized limit order book operated by many exchanges was appropriate for orders of a similar size, where buyers and sellers were equally matched, and where there was no particular demand for immediate execution and investors could wait for their orders to be matched, it suffered from limitations, particularly for large, bespoke trades: APCIMS, FOA, IPMA, ISMA, ISDA, LIBA, and TBMA, Innovation, Competition, Diversity, Choice. A European Capital Market for the 21st Century (2002).

[83] Ferrarini and Recine, n 60.

[84] '[T]he drafters of the Directive...seem to have chosen to compromise with special interest group demands from the investment industry on the one hand and the operators of securities markets on the others': Köndgen, J, and Theissen, E, 'Internalization under the MiFID: Regulatory Overreaching or Landmark in Investor Protection' in Ferrarini and Wymeersch, n 60, 271, 284.

and ongoing 'fit and proper' rules imposed on management and also applicable to the assessment of the regulated market's owners. Organizational rules applied, including with respect to conflicts of interest management, risk management, the adoption of trading rules, and financial resources, as did obligations with respect to market monitoring. Regulated markets were also subject to detailed pre-trade and post-trade trading transparency rules with respect to shares admitted to trading on a regulated market, although Member States could apply waivers which supported dark trading on regulated markets.

The regulated market classification (which remains in place under the 2014 MiFID II/MiFIR) was something of a muddle, in that it blurred the secondary market trading functionality of regulated markets with regulated markets' primary market 'admission to trading' and other issuer-facing functionalities. This blurring arose as regulated markets were distinguished from other multilateral, non-discretionary trading platforms by the distinct regime which applied to the admission of securities to trading on a regulated market and by the extensive issuer-disclosure obligations which followed. The regulated market classification, accordingly, was discretionary. Venues could 'opt in' to the regulated market regime if they wished to be subject to the suite of rules which applied to regulated market admission to trading, and to benefit, accordingly, from the relating branding and other dynamics which followed for venues, issuers, and investors. The regulated market designation thus represented an unhappy combination of two functionalities: secondary market multilateral trading and primary market issuer-facing admission of securities to trading. This mattered (and continues to be somewhat problematic) because there was no real difference between the trading functionalities provided by regulated markets and the second class of venue (multilateral trading facilities), although the regulatory regime governing trading on these venues was not entirely uniform.

Second, multilateral platforms (for MiFID I financial instruments), which brought together multiple third party buying and selling interests in accordance with non-discretionary rules but which did not opt for regulated market status, were designated as multilateral trading facilities (MTFs). The MTF classification was thus MiFID I's attempt to capture the distinct trading functionality which distinguishes organized venues from the OTC markets. An MTF 'investment service' could be provided by a market operator (in effect, a regulated market operator) or by an investment firm. Where provided by a firm, the provision of the MTF service was subject to the MiFID I investment firm regime, albeit with calibrations reflecting the multilateral trading functionality. Thus, the operation of an MTF by an investment firm required that the firm be authorized under MiFID I. The range of MiFID I authorization, organizational, and prudential rules governing investment services applied, although conduct-of-business rules were specifically excluded with respect to the operation of the MTF, given the professional nature of MTF members or participants. Market operators were also permitted to operate MTFs, subject to verification of their compliance with MiFID I's conditions for investment firm authorization. MTF operators, whether investment firms or market operators, were also subject to discrete rules governing the MTF trading process and the monitoring of compliance with the MTF's rules. The same pre- and post-trade transparency rules as applied to regulated markets applied to MTFs with respect to shares admitted to trading on a regulated market.

The OTC space was the default 'venue' for all other forms of execution. MiFID I did not, however, address OTC venues directly. A recital (recital 53) broadly described the characteristics of OTC trades as trades which were *ad hoc* and irregular and carried out with wholesale counterparties; which were part of a business relationship characterized by dealings above the 'standard market size' (SMS)—the 'SMS' list for shares was maintained by CESR/European Securities and Markets Authority (ESMA); and which were carried out outside the systems usually used by the firms concerned for 'systematic internalization' execution business (discussed further on in this section). Investment firms engaging in this trading activity (unless benefiting from one of the proprietary dealing exemptions[85]) were regulated under the MiFID I investment-services regime, including its order execution rules. Pre-trade transparency rules did not apply and so the OTC markets were dark pre-trade. Significantly, however, MiFID I established, for the first time in some Member States, that post-trade transparency disclosures be made for all trades by investment firms with respect to regulated-market-admitted shares.

MiFID I imposed a specific regime on a subset of the OTC sector. The regime for 'Systematic Internalizers' (SIs) applied to investment firms which executed client orders OTC against their proprietary order books, but on a systematic basis. An SI was a firm which, on an 'organized, frequent, and systematic basis', dealt on own account by executing client orders outside a regulated market or MTF. SIs were treated as investment firms providing discretionary execution services, and so, unlike regulated markets/MTFs, were subject to a range of conduct-of-business rules governing the decision to internalize a client order. But, like regulated markets/MTFs, they were additionally subject to a transparency regime governing shares admitted to a regulated market, although this regime was highly complex and calibrated, reflecting difficult negotiations and the concern of the OTC sector that pre-trade transparency would expose internalizing firms to significant position risk; by contrast with MTFs and regulated markets which provide a platform where orders interact, internalizing firms trade against their proprietary capital, and the positions they take as a result are exposed to strategic behaviour by other traders. Like all investment firms and MTFs/regulated markets, SIs were also subject to post-trade transparency requirements covering regulated-market-admitted shares.

This classification and share execution transparency regime was supported by a data publication[86] and data consolidation[87] regime. It was also supported by the best execution obligation imposed on investment firms executing client orders, which was designed to tie execution venues together as well as to protect investors against conflict-of-interest risk where orders were internalized by SIs. The best execution regime (Chapter VI section 2.2.2) took a flexible, process-based approach, designed to support competition between trading venues.[88]

---

[85] See further Ch VI sect 2.1.

[86] Regulated markets and MTFs were to make their transparency data public on reasonable commercial terms and on a continuous basis during normal trading hours (pre-trade) and as close to real time as possible (post-trade). SIs were required to make their pre-trade quotes available to the public in a manner which was easily accessible to other market participants on a reasonable commercial basis, and all investment firms were required to make their post-trade transparency data available to the public as close to real time as possible, on a reasonable commercial basis, and in a manner easily accessible to other market participants.

[87] CESR adopted guidance on the publication and consolidation of MiFID transparency disclosures (CESR/07-043).

[88] Ferrarini, G, 'Best Execution and Competition Between Trading Venues: MiFID's Likely Impact' (2009) 2 *CMLJ* 404.

The essentials of this regime (which was supported by extensive administrative rules under the 2006 Commission MiFID I Regulation), including the regulated market, MTF, and SI classifications, remain in place under the 2014 MiFID II/MiFIR, although the regime has become much broader in scope and more nuanced in application.

V.2.3 The Impact of 2004 MiFID I

Given its market-shaping ambitions, its costs, and the radical operational changes it required of the order execution industry,[89] the impact of the 2004 MiFID I[90] warrants some attention, particularly as the MiFID I experience has shaped the 2014 MiFID II/MiFIR reforms.[91]

It is difficult to disaggregate the impact of MiFID I from the impact of changes in the execution environment generally (these include the MiFID I-era explosion in algorithmic trading,[92] which has been associated with greater demand for dark trading venues—dark venues protect positions from arbitrage strategies executed by algorithmic traders).[93] But the MiFID I abolition of the share-trading concentration rule certainly created a regulatory environment within which multiple competing trading venues could develop.[94] It also

---

[89] Notwithstanding the scale of the MiFID I reforms, the Commission did not engage in *ex-ante* cost-benefit analysis, which generated great industry criticism (the *Financial Times* noted on the day that MiFID was applied on the markets that this failure meant that the Commission played into the hands of its critics: Editorial, 'Day of the MiFID', *Financial Times*, 1 November 2007, 14). Although the 2002 London Economics report (n 35) examined the benefits of financial market integration, it did not address the specific design issues raised by competitive order execution.

One leading study, however, quantified the first-order benefits of MiFID I generally (and including the investment firm provisions) in terms of £200 million annually in direct benefits, second-round economy-wide benefits of £240 million (arising from deeper and more liquid capital markets), and unquantified third-order benefits (related to the potential increase in the long-term sustained growth rate for the UK). It estimated the one-off costs in the region of £877 million to £1.71 billion, and ongoing costs in the region of £88 to £117 million: FSA, The Overall Impact of MiFID (2006).

[90] The market-shaping effects of the 2004 MiFID I have been extensively analysed. See, eg, Assi, B and Valiante, D, MiFID Implementation in the Midst of the Financial Crisis, ECMI Research Report No 6 (2011); Soltani, B, Minh Mai, H and Jerbi, M, Transparency and Market Quality: An Analysis of the Effect of MiFID on Euronext (2011), available at <http://ssrn.com/abstract=1833605>; Lazzari, V (ed), *Trends in the European Securities Industry* (2011); Gresse, C, Multi-Market Trading and Market Quality (2010), available at <http://basepub.dauphine.fr/bitstream/handle/123456789/3148/multimarkettrading_marketquality.pdf?s.>; Petrella, G, 'MiFID, Reg NMS and Competition Across Trading Venues in Europe and the USA' (2010) 18 *JFRC* 257; and Lannoo, K and Valiante, D, The MiFID Metamorphosis, ECMI Policy Brief No 16 (2010). From the array of empirical studies see, eg, CFA Institute, The Structure, Regulation and Transparency of European Equity Markets under MiFID (2011) (2011 CFA Report); MiFID: Spirit and Reality of a European Financial Markets Directive (2010), a report by Gomber, P (Goethe University) and Pierron, A (Celent) (2010 Celent Report); and London Economics, Understanding the Impact of MiFID in the Context of Global and National Regulatory Innovation (2010) and (2011), each for the City of London Corporation (London Economics (2010) and (2011)).

[91] For a more detailed account see Ferrarini and Moloney, n 12.

[92] See further Ch VI sect 2.3.

[93] As was acknowledged by the Commission, which queried whether the growth in OTC dark trading was driven by financial-crisis-engendered uncertainty, the availability of dark OTC systems, MiFID I-driven fragmentation, or overly restrictive MiFID I transparency waivers for organized venues: 2011 MiFID II/MiFIR Proposals Impact Assessment (SEC (2011) 1226) 5.

[94] eg 2010 Celent Report, n 90.

seems clear that MiFID I created the conditions for trading venues to adapt their business models in order to compete for lucrative dark trading.[95]

Over the MiFID I-era, equity trading fragmented across a range of venues—formal/organized and OTC, and dark and lit.[96] The Commission's 2011 MiFID II/MiFIR Impact Assessment identified 231 organized trading venues in the EU, including 139 MTFs and 92 regulated markets—of which 45 regulated markets and 50 MTFs traded equities—and 12 SIs.[97] As the MiFID I Review got underway in 2010, in Germany some 25 per cent of trading in DAX 30 stocks was taking place outside Deutsche Börse, in France some 30 per cent of trading in CAC 40 stocks was taking place outside NYSE Euronext (the dominant regulated market in France),[98] and in the UK equity trading was taking place on a number of organized venues (both regulated markets and MTFs).[99] Most equity trading in the EU was taking place on regulated markets and MTFs, which together accounted for some 60–70 per cent of equity trading as the MiFID I Review progressed. Although regulated markets were dominant in the formal/organized venue space, reflecting their incumbency advantages with respect to liquidity, MTF market share—reflecting developments early in the MiFID I era[100]—significantly increased.[101]

Nonetheless, over the MiFID I Review, a significant minority of trading—some 30–40 per cent—remained OTC,[102] and a significant proportion of dark trades in the OTC space were small.[103]

Although the SI regime had dominated MiFID I discussions, the technology demands, the required risk appetite for managing trading risk, the capital needed, and the necessary trading expertise had made it likely that only a limited number of firms would adopt the SI business model, and that others would either limit their internalization activities or operate

---

[95] eg European Investors Working Group, Restoring Investor Confidence in European Capital Markets (2010).

[96] eg Grob, S, 'The Fragmentation of European Equity Markets', in Lazzari, n 90, 127.

[97] 2011 MiFID II/MiFIR Proposals Impact Assessment, n 93, 88.

[98] FSA, n 37, 15.

[99] In 2010, the FSA reported that equity trading was taking place on 7 organized venues (MTFs or regulated markets) and that the monopoly of the London Stock Exchange in FTSE 100 share trading had been broken, with less than 60% of such trading taking place on the Exchange: FSA, n 37, 5.

[100] November 2006 saw the dramatic announcement of 'Project Turquoise', under which a group of the world's largest investment banks announced plans to build a securities trading platform (under the MiFID I regime) to challenge the major exchanges on share trading. It attracted 0.93 per cent of activity in its first month of operation (August 2008) (Commission, Emerging Trends in the European Equity Market (2008) 2) and is now partly owned by the London Stock Exchange and a group of investment banks.

[101] The largest MTFs accounted for 23 per cent of organized equity trading at January 2011, while MTFs generally accounted for 25–30 per cent of trading activity in the main listed equities: 2011 MiFID II/MiFIR Proposal Impact Assessment, n 93, 88.

[102] The scale of OTC equity trading was heavily contested by the industry (which argued that not all OTC trading represented 'executable liquidity' which could be transferred to organized venues). But over the MiFID I Review, the 30–40 per cent figure was supported by CESR (2010 CESR Equity Market Consultation, n 53), the Commission (2011 MiFID II/MiFIR Proposals Impact Assessment, n 93, 12 and 88 (estimating the OTC market at 37–8 per cent of total trading)), and the European Parliament (Resolution on the Regulation of Trading in Financial Instruments, 14 December 2010 (A7-0326/2010) para H). The leading studies supporting the 30–40 per cent finding include the 2010 Celent Report (n 90).

[103] 2010 Celent Report, n 90. The Report found that some 48 per cent of OTC trades in liquid shares were below 'standard market size': at 18 and 23.

as MTFs instead.[104] In practice, SIs, over the MiFID I era, did not capture large volumes of OTC share trading and accounted for only some 2 per cent of total trading.[105] The unattractiveness of the SI business model was clear from the start, with only 11 firms initially registered as SIs.[106] SIs did prompt market change, however, in that incumbent regulated markets hedged against the threat of growth in the SI sector by providing competing execution products for brokers.[107]

A significant proportion of equity trading (some 45 per cent or so) was dark at the time of the MiFID I Review, reflecting the scale of OTC trading.[108] While dark trading could take place on regulated market/MTF venues (in 'dark pools' supported by transparency waivers), trading on these venues was predominantly (90 per cent) lit; most dark trading was taking place in the OTC space.[109] The number of dark pools operated by regulated markets/MTFs increased, however, following the adoption of MiFID I.[110]

In terms of market quality, some difficulties had emerged by the time of the MiFID I Review. Pre-trade transparency had improved.[111] On the other hand, fragmentation, in combination with the rise of algorithmic trading, had become associated with a reduction in order size[112] and with a related limiting of the capacity of institutional investors to manage large equity trades.[113] Although greater connectivity in data retrieval and a large and competitive market in data had been predicted to follow from MiFID I,[114] poor data

---

[104] Europe Economics, The Benefits of MiFID. A Report for the Financial Services Authority (2006) 32–4. JP Morgan similarly predicted that only firms with strong retail brokerage business were likely to become SIs, given that designation as such was 'not worth the effort' for firms with a primarily institutional business: JP Morgan, MiFID Report II. Earnings At Risk Analysis—The Threat to the Integrated Banking Model (2006) 29.

[105] Federation of European Securities Exchanges (FESE), presentation to September 2010 Commission Public Hearing on the MiFID I Review. Similarly, Grob, n 96, 143.

[106] CESR, Report. Impact of MiFID on Equity Secondary Market Functioning (2009) (CESR/09-355) (2009 CESR Equity Market Report) 15–16. Six were registered with the UK authorities. SIs were also registered in Denmark and France.

[107] eg the London Stock Exchange built a new trading functionality, with reduced tariffs, designed to make it more attractive for major investment firms to pass on orders rather than to internalize them: Cohen, N, 'A Clash of the Titans: Why Big Banks are Wading into the Stock Exchange Fray', *Financial Times*, 24 November 2006, 13.

[108] FESE suggested that 43.4 per cent of total trading was dark and that most dark trading occurred in the OTC sector (37.8 per cent of total trading): FESE, Statement on the CESR Consultation Paper on Equity Markets, 12 May 2010. The Commission identified 45 per cent of trading as dark, with 38 per cent of dark trading in the OTC space: 2011 MiFID II/MiFIR Proposals Impact Assessment, n 93, 12.

[109] Gomber, P and Gsell, M, 'The Emerging Landscape in European Securities Trading', in Lazzari, n 90, 89.

[110] Grob referred to an 'exponential increase' since 2008: n 96, 158.

[111] eg London Economics (2010) and (2011) (n 90). Similarly, Bundesverband Deutscher Banker (German Banking Association) Response to CESR/2010-394 and AFME/BBA Response to CESR/10-394. The industry responses to the CESR/10-394 Consultation Paper (2010 CESR Equity Market Consultation, n 53) referenced are available at <http://www.esma.europa.eu>.

[112] Between 2006 and 2009 the average trade size of a transaction in shares fell from approximately €25,000 to €10,000: Oxera, Monitoring Prices, Costs and Volumes of Trading and Post-Trading Services. Report for the European Commission (2011).

[113] FSA, n 37, 17.

[114] eg Casey and Lannoo, n 61, 9 and McKee, M and Aubry, N, 'MiFID: Where Did It All Come From and Where Is It Taking Us' (2007) 22 *J of International Banking Law and Regulation* 177.

quality was a concern[115] (particularly with respect to OTC post-trade transparency data streams, given the extent to which post-trade OTC reporting was taking place through proprietary OTC channels[116]), as was the limited progress with respect to the consolidation of transparency data.[117] With respect to trading costs, while they had reduced initially,[118] they subsequently increased (reflecting market volatility and reduced trading levels),[119] although the Commission highlighted some material reductions in trading costs.[120] Overall, significant cost reductions took place,[121] but these reductions were asymmetrically allocated; liquidity providers benefited but other traders often did not see a real reduction in trading costs.[122]

The impact on liquidity, at the time of the MiFID I Review, was unclear, with some concern as to a thinning of liquidity[123] and as to MTFs pulling liquidity away from regulated markets rather than creating new liquidity,[124] but with countering evidence that MTFs had attracted new liquidity from the OTC sector.[125] Similarly, little consensus had emerged on the extent to which liquidity fragmentation across different venues had damaged price formation and/or influenced spreads.[126]

---

[115] eg 2009 CESR Equity Market Report, n 106, 26–7.

[116] The Italian Banking Association (IBA), eg, reported that a significant number of intermediaries reported through their own websites: IBA Response to CESR/10-394.

[117] eg European Securities and Markets Expert Group, Fact Finding Regarding the Availability of Post-trade Data in Equities in the EU (2009).

[118] The London Stock Exchange, eg, cut its trading fees by 10 per cent in early 2007 to encourage more trading through its SETS platform, which was interpreted as a challenge to (then) Project Turquoise: Cohen, N, 'LSE Cuts Tariffs Ahead of NASDAQ defence', *Financial Times*, 18 January 2007, 18. By the time of MiFID I's application on the markets in November 2007 it was reported that both the London Stock Exchange and Deutsche Börse (neither of which had been protected by concentration rules pre-MiFID I) had introduced new pricing structures for high-speed, heavy-volume electronic trading to protect their order flow: Cohen, N, 'Seeking to End a Share Trading Monopoly', *Financial Times*, 30 October 2007, 21.

[119] London Economics (2010), reporting a drop in trading costs between 2000–1 and 2006–7 but an increase over 2009: n 90, 7.

[120] It highlighted that the average bid-ask spread on the London Stock Exchange's Alternative Investment Market had become 16 per cent lower than the pre-MiFID I spread: 2011 MiFID II/MiFIR Proposals Impact Assessment, n 93, 40.

[121] 2011 Oxera Report, n 112, finding that trading platforms' costs for on-book trading in shares fell by 60 per cent between 2006 and 2009, although noting significant variation across platforms.

[122] eg London Economics (2010), n 90. Oxera, however, reported that commission rates charged by retail brokers fell by around 35% on a pan-EU basis between 2006 and 2009: 2011 Oxera Report, n 112.

[123] At the outset of the MiFID I Review, two leading trade associations (the Association for Financial Markets in Europe (AFME) and the British Bankers' Association (BBA)) were of the view that liquidity was reducing: AFME/BBA Response to CESR/10-394. The FSA similarly warned that fragmentation had led to concerns relating to liquidity and market efficiency: n 37, 17.

[124] 2010 Celent Report, n 90, 30.

[125] 2009 CESR Equity Market Report, n 106, 12.

[126] The Gresse study (n 90), eg, suggested that fragmentation had affected price quality by increasing short-term volatility. A study of Euronext trading, however, suggested some improvements in market quality for liquid stocks: Soltani, et al, n 90. A study of trading in UK blue chips suggested that a high fraction of trades were executed at best available prices: Storkenmaier, A and Wagener, M, Do We Need a European 'National Market System'? Competition, Arbitrage, and Suboptimal Executions (2011), available at <http://ssrn.com/abstract=1760778>. Stakeholder surveys were also positive: eg Centre for European Policy Studies (CEPS), MiFID I Review: What Next for European Capital Markets (2010), suggesting that there was no evidence that fragmentation had damaged price formation.

V.3 The MiFID I Review and the 2014 MiFID II/MiFIR Negotiations

V.3.1 The MiFID I Review and the Commission Proposals

V.3.1.1 The MiFID I Review

Although the Commission began to review the application of the 2004 MiFID I almost immediately after the Directive's November 2007 application,[127] the massive MiFID I Review[128] (required under MiFID I) got fully underway in 2010, during which CESR presented its technical advice to the Commission on the equity market aspects of the Review,[129] and the Parliament's Resolution on Trading[130] and the Commission's initial MiFID I Review Consultation (in December 2010) were published.[131] The much-anticipated 2011 Proposals for a MiFID II Directive (which contained proposals for the authorization and operational requirements applicable to trading venues) and a new Regulation (which contained the proposals for venue classification and transparency regulation) were published in October 2011.[132] The Proposals were preceded by a series of hearings[133] and the production of a wealth of empirical data, which included a raft of CESR reports[134] and the Commission Impact Assessment for the Proposals and related studies.[135]

The Commission was relatively sanguine with respect to the reform process. It suggested that MiFID I had led to more competition, wider investor choice, a decrease in transaction costs, and deeper integration. It also suggested that the financial crisis experience had

---

[127] eg the Commission-sponsored 'MiFID One Year On' Conference, November 2008 and Commission, Emerging Trends in the European Equity Market (2008). The Commission-sponsored CRA International review of the Financial Services Action Plan (FSAP) reviewed MiFID I, but reported that it was too soon after its implementation to deliver robust findings: CRA International, Evaluation of the Economic Impact of the FSAP (2009).

[128] On the trading venue elements of the MiFID I Review see further Moloney and Ferrarini, n 12 and Clausen, N and Sørensen, K, 'Reforming the Regulation of Trading Venues in the EU under the Proposed MiFID II – Levelling the Playing Field and Overcoming Market Fragmentation' (2012) 9 *ECFR* 275.

[129] CESR/10-802 (2010 CESR Equity Market Technical Advice). The Advice reflected the earlier 2009 CESR Equity Market Report (n 106) and 2010 CESR Equity Market Consultation (n 53). CESR also presented technical advice on the trading of standardized derivatives (CESR/10-1096, Consultation Paper at CESR/10-610); on transparency in non-equity asset classes (CESR/10-799, Consultation Paper at CESR/10-510); and on post-trade transparency (CESR/10-882, relying on the equity market consultation CESR/10-394).

[130] n 102.

[131] Commission, Public Consultation. Review of the Markets in Financial Instruments Directive (2010) (2010 MiFID I Review Consultation). The industry responses to the Consultation are available at: <http://ec.europa.eu/internal_market/consultations/2010/mifid_en.htm>.

[132] COM (2011) 652/4 (2011 MiFIR Proposal) and COM (2011) 656/4 (2011 MiFID II Proposal).

[133] Six Commission round tables were held.

[134] n 129.

[135] n 93. The related and extensive studies for the Commission include Europe Economics, MiFID I Review—Data Gathering and Cost Benefit Analysis. Final Report Phase One (2011) (which quantified the costs and benefits of the Commission's 2010 policy options), PriceWaterhouseCoopers, Data Gathering and Analysis in the Context of the MiFID I Review. Final Report (2010) (which examined market conditions in detail), and the 2011 Oxera Report, n 112 (on trading costs).

'largely vindicated' MiFID I's design.[136] MiFID I's underlying principles were valid, including with respect to competitive order execution, as long as the regulatory playing field was level and transparency requirements were effective; wholesale repair was not, accordingly, required.[137] The Commission's approach to reform was accordingly based on the correction of a series of specific weaknesses which had emerged. The benefits of competition were not flowing efficiently to all market participants. Market fragmentation had made the trading environment more complex and opaque, particularly with respect to the distribution of trade data. The MiFID I classification regime had been outpaced by innovation, and accordingly the 'common interest in a transparent, level playing field between trading venues and investment firms' risked being undermined.[138] The financial crisis had exposed weaknesses in the regulation of trading in non-equity instruments. Finally, rapid innovation and increasing market complexity called for higher levels of investor protection. The Commission thus sought a 'safer, sounder, more transparent and more responsible financial system'[139] by a targeted reform of the trading venue regime; this reform would also respond to the G20 commitment to tackle less regulated and more opaque parts of the financial system and to improve the organization, transparency, and oversight of particular market segments, notably the OTC segment.[140] The major features of the MiFID I Review are outlined in the following sections.

V.3.1.2 Organizational Models for Venue Regulation

From the outset, the organizational model for trading venue regulation which underpinned MiFID I came under scrutiny. This was driven by two developments.

First, the growth of non-MTF organized trading venues for trading in derivatives—which venues operated outside the MiFID I venue regime[141]—and the crisis-driven concern to strengthen market infrastructure for derivatives trading combined to generate a policy concern to extend the regulatory net over a wider range of trading venues and to provide more extensive venue classifications.[142]

Second, experience with MiFID I in the equity markets suggested that the MiFID I classification model was not appropriately capturing all similar trading functionalities in the equity trading space, and was generating related arbitrage risks and competitive distortions. In particular, concerns arose in relation to the OTC equity trading space and in relation to whether investment firms were operating 'MTF-like' structures within the OTC space without being subject to regulation functionally equivalent to that applicable to regulated markets and MTFs. This concern was driven in particular by the emergence of BCSs (although only a small proportion of trading was taking place on these systems).[143]

---

[136] 2011 MiFIR Proposal, n 132, 3, and 2011 MiFID II/MiFIR Proposals Impact Assessment, n 93, 5.

[137] 2011 MiFID II/MiFIR Proposals Impact Assessment, n 93, 5–6.

[138] 2011 MiFID II/MiFIR Proposals Impact Assessment, n 93, 5.

[139] 2011 MiFIR Proposal, n 132, 2–3 and 2011 MiFID II/MiFIR Proposals Impact Assessment, n 93, 5.

[140] 2011 MiFID II/MiFIR Proposals Impact Assessment, n 93, 6.

[141] Such platforms typically fell outside the MiFID I MTF classification as they were not entirely multilateral or non-discretionary in design, being based on some element of bilateral, discretionary, dealer-based trading.

[142] Such as the 'swap execution facility' constructed by the US 2010 Dodd-Frank Act.

[143] CESR estimated that BCS trading represented 1.15 per cent of total EEA trading in 2009 (up from 0.7 per cent in 2008): 2010 CESR Equity Market Consultation, n 53, 27.

While the SI regime applied to the systematic crossing of client orders against a firm's proprietary inventory, this had not prevented the OTC sector from operating BCSs which crossed client orders against proprietary orders but which were not regulated as SIs.[144] More generally, concerns arose as to the extent to which firms were engaging in OTC equity trading (including for small orders[145]) outside the MiFID I trading venue regime, despite the requirement for systematic internalization of orders to be regulated under the SI regime[146] and the MiFID I limitation of the OTC space to large, professional trades.[147] Difficulties also arose in relation to the alignment of the regulated market and MTF regimes. Although both classifications addressed the same trading functionality, the related regulatory regimes were not fully aligned; the MTF regime was, in some respects, lighter.[148]

In the opening salvo of the Review, CESR recommended in its 2010 Technical Advice[149] that the regulated market and MTF requirements be aligned to the more prescriptive regulated market standards, but did not propose radical change to MiFID I's organizational model. With respect to the contested OTC equity trading space, CESR took a careful approach and focused mainly on the SI sub-segment. It did not take a view on the 'appropriate number' of SIs, but suggested that the Commission conduct a review and clarify the SI regime's objectives before major changes were made, and made a number of specific proposals to address the risk that investment firms were using opacities in the regime to avoid classification and regulation as SIs. It also focused on the highly contested BCS segment but did not propose radical change, recommending that a tailored regime apply to firms operating BCSs—defined as internal electronic matching systems operated by an investment firm that execute orders against other client orders or proprietary orders.[150] More controversially, CESR, drawing heavily and problematically on the US 'Alternative Trading System' model but foreshadowing the trading volume limits which would be adopted under the 2014 MiFID II/MiFIR reform, recommended that a limit be posed on the volume of business which could be undertaken by BCSs and that, once the limit was exceeded, BCSs be required to become MTFs.[151] The industry was, with some

---

[144] The merger of SI and crossing functions led the European Banking Federation to call for better enforcement: EBF Response to CESR/10-394.

[145] 2010 Celent Report, n 90, 7. The Report found that some 48 per cent of OTC trades in liquid shares were below 'standard market size': at 18 and 23. It concluded that 'most OTC trades, if analyzed on a trade by trade basis, are rather small and would not face market impact' (at 28).

[146] The requirement for SIs to carry out internalization in accordance with non-discretionary rules (2006 Commission MiFID I Regulation Art 21) led to the potential for arbitrage where a discretionary element could be associated with internalization activity. CESR reported, eg, that the non-discretionary element of the SI classification could provide scope for firms to decide that any discretion they exercised in determining whether or not to execute client orders on own account could take them outside the SI regime: 2010 CESR Equity Market Consultation, n 53, 14.

[147] The reliance on 'non-discretionary trading' as a determining characteristic of an MTF under MiFID I, eg, provided support for the development of automated non-MTF systems in the OTC space which were discretionary in that the firm restricted access to its clients: AFME/BBA Response to CESR/10-394.

[148] 2010 CESR Equity Market Consultation, n 53, 25–6.

[149] 2010 CESR Equity Market Technical Advice, n 129.

[150] 2010 CESR Equity Market Technical Advice, n 129, 36–7. CESR proposed rules addressing: notification by firms of BCS operation; publication of a list of BCSs; and a requirement for a generic BCS identifier in post-trade information which would support better data-gathering on OTC trading.

[151] The trading volume restriction was strongly contested by elements of the investment firm/OTC sector. Arguments included that the MTF business model was fundamentally different to the discretionary, client-orientated BCS business model, and that any requirement to change the business model from a BCS to an MTF would overlook the different trading functions provided by each venue.

flashpoints, relatively supportive of CESR's precursor 2010 Consultation Paper (which shaped its Technical Advice). But particular difficulties arose concerning CESR's proposed BCS definition, with some suggesting that BCS activity should be covered within the MTF/SI categories, others considering the BCS definition too broad,[152] and others calling for clear differentiation between the BCS, MTF, and SI sectors.[153] The brokerage/OTC sector questioned in particular the need for intervention given the low volume of BCS trading,[154] the risk of a reduction in investor choice,[155] and the inappropriateness of targeting systems which were an automation of the manual crossing functions carried out by firms providing execution services to clients.[156]

With respect to the treatment of derivatives trading, CESR separately advised that trading venues for derivatives trading meet a number of criteria[157] and identified regulated markets and MTFs as 'unequivocally' meeting the objectives of the G20 derivatives trading reform; it did not, however, take a position on whether an additional regulatory venue classification was required, although it regarded SIs and BCSs as inappropriate venue models for derivatives trading.[158]

Trading venue regulation was subsequently addressed by the European Parliament in its OTC-hostile 2010 Resolution.[159] The Parliament expressed concern at the scale of OTC trading, called for trading on 'organized trading venues' to be encouraged, and suggested that MiFID I was intended to facilitate a shift to more regulated and transparent venues. It suggested that market fragmentation had generated an 'undesired impact' on liquidity and efficiency, that a related decrease in transaction size had encouraged dark pool trading, that regulated market/MTF waiver-based dark pools were more transparent and better regulated than OTC dark pools, and that the OTC sector enjoyed a comparative advantage under MiFID I. It called for an in-depth investigation of the BCS sector, for ESMA to investigate the SI sector, and for an investigation of OTC trading generally. It also highlighted a need for thorough enforcement of MiFID I, such that BCSs carrying out functionally equivalent activities to SIs, MTFs, and regulated markets were regulated as such, and, like CESR, proposed a related notification system. Also like CESR, it supported the alignment of the regulated market and MTF regimes. More radically, but vaguely, it called for reforms which would lead to a substantial decline in OTC trading.

From an organizational/classification perspective, the key feature of the Commission's subsequent December 2010 Consultation was the introduction of a new trading venue classification—the 'Organized Trading Facility' (OTF)[160] The proposed OTF regime was

---

[152] eg EBF Response to CESR/10-394.
[153] eg IBA Response to CESR/10-394.
[154] Barclays Capital, for instance, was surprised at the inclusion of BCSs, given low trading volumes: Barclays Capital Response to CESR/10-394.
[155] AFME/BBA Response to CESR/10-394.
[156] Deutsche Bank Response to CESR/10-394.
[157] CESR advised that organized platforms for derivatives trading should display high standards of operational efficiency and market transparency, and that the operating requirements should include easy and non-discriminatory market access, objective criteria for efficient order execution, multilaterality, operational resilience, and surveillance of compliance with the venue's rules: CESR/10-1096, n 129, 12.
[158] CESR/10-1096, n 129, 10–13.
[159] 2010 European Parliament Trading Resolution, n 102.
[160] n 131, 9–12.

designed to ensure that all organized trading outside MiFID I venues would be 'suitably regulated', and to capture any facility or system operated by an investment firm or market operator that brought together orders on an organized basis, whether multilateral or bilateral and whether discretionary or non-discretionary.[161] Only 'pure OTC trading' (bilateral trading between counterparties on an *ad hoc* basis, not carried out on an organized venue) would fall outside the new venue regime. The new OTF regime was, however, only thinly justified: the Commission highlighted the need to capture new venues, respond to technological innovation, and address regulatory arbitrage. OTF operators would be subject to a range of rules, including notification and operational requirements. Reflecting CESR's approach to BCSs, the Consultation proposed that all OTFs be required to convert into MTFs when trading volume on the OTF reached a particular (undefined) threshold. The OTF classification was also designed to provide a regulated space for the trading of standardized OTC derivatives by regulating the inter-dealer systems common in this space; to this end, the Commission suggested that a specific sub-regime apply within the OTF regime which would require that these venues provide non-discriminatory access, apply extensive transparency requirements, report transaction data to trade repositories, and have dedicated systems or facilities in place for trade execution.[162]

The market response to the 2010 Commission Consultation was generally hostile, from both the organized venue and the OTC sectors, and particularly with respect to the OTF classification. Criticisms from the OTC sector, at risk of being pulled into the new classification, included the classification's breadth and lack of clarity, its focus on then contentious venue types rather than on core functionality, the danger of a proliferation of different OTF venues, the need for flexibility, the potential risk to bilateral trading, the risk of unintended consequences, and the dangers of dis-proportionality, as the OTC sector was already regulated under the MiFID I investment firm regime.[163] Organized venue concerns included whether a new classification (subject, potentially, to lighter rules) was an appropriate means of dealing with OTC trading and the availability of the MiFID I classification as a means of capturing trading with the same functionality.[164]

Despite the industry concern, the 2011 MiFIR/MiFID II Proposals which followed were similar to those trailed in the 2010 Consultation, although significantly more articulated. The Commission proposed to extend the regulatory perimeter more widely around equity and non-equity trading venues, and to apply the same set of rules to this wider set of venues. Driving concerns were the 'future proofing' of the venue regime against future changes to the nature of organized trading and the effective management of current and potential regulatory arbitrage risks.[165] More specifically, the Commission was concerned to address

---

[161] And would include BCSs and inter-dealer broking systems.

[162] n 131, 12–13.

[163] Variously Deutsche Bank, AFME, Goldman Sachs International, International Capital Market Association (ICMA), and BBA Responses to the 2010 MiFID I Review Consultation.

[164] eg FESE Response to the 2010 MiFID I Review Consultation. Similarly, Nasdaq/OMX Response, suggesting the new category could lead to more dark trading and calling for more careful application of the MiFID I classifications. The London Stock Exchange Group, however, was more sanguine, although it raised concerns as to the absence of pre-trade transparency rules for the OTF sector.

[165] 2011 MiFIR Proposal, n 132, 7 and rec 7. Accordingly, the Commission chose not to treat BCSs as MTFs but relied on the OTF as it provided a more flexible solution: 2011 MiFID II/MiFIR Proposals Impact Assessment, n 93, 33–4.

four developments which were undermining the MiFID I organizational model: the application of less stringent rules to MTFs than regulated markets, despite their comparable functionality; the emergence of new trading venues, notably BCSs[166] and new derivative trading platforms,[167] which were operating outside the regulated market/MTF space and not subject to functionally similar regulation; the scale of the growth of OTC trading, which could threaten the efficiency of price formation; and the need to provide a regulated venue for the trading of standardized OTC derivatives to comply with the G20 commitment.[168]

Accordingly, the 2011 MiFIR/MiFID II Proposals suggested that the regulated market and MTF rulebooks be aligned, as they 'represent the same trading functionality',[169] and that the SI regime be retained, but with clearer and more detailed rules to distinguish SI trading from OTC trading and to minimize regulatory arbitrage.[170] They also proposed a new OTF classification.

The OTF regime was designed to capture all non-regulated market/MTF trading on organized venues, other than *ad hoc* bilateral trading between counterparties which did not take place on an organized venue. It was also designed to address the regulatory arbitrage difficulties generated in relation to equity trading under MiFID I and to provide a regulated venue for the trading of standardized derivatives. Investment firms and market operators operating MTFs and OTFs would be subject to identical transparency regimes (section 3.1.3) and to 'nearly identical' organization and market surveillance rules.[171] While there would be differentiation across the applicable rules, this would be at the level of the asset class traded and not at the level of the venue; transparency rules, accordingly, could differ, but basic organizational and operational requirements would not.

The proposed new regime was accordingly designed to treat regulated markets, MTFs, and OTFs similarly. But it distinguished OTFs in one key respect. While operators of regulated markets, MTFs, and OTFs would all be neutral, only regulated markets and MTFs would be required to offer non-discretionary order execution and non-discretionary access. OTF operators would have a 'degree of discretion' over execution and could route orders to other venues and control access to their order execution systems. They would, accordingly, be subject to some conduct-of-business regulation and would not be permitted (to avoid conflict-of-interest risk) to execute client orders in the OTF against their proprietary capital.[172] The discretionary element of the OTF model was designed to reflect the nature of equity trading in BCSs, as well as the illiquid and discretionary nature of trading in derivatives and the related need to protect the positions of dealers. The proposed OTF regime accordingly allowed dealers to restrict access to their quotes and to provide execution

---

[166] The Commission acknowledged that levels of BCS trading were low, but pointed to the US experience which suggested that BCSs would grow significantly: 2011 MiFID II/MiFIR Proposals Impact Assessment, n 93, 11.

[167] The Commission pointed to the new US regulatory vehicle (the 'swap execution facility') created for such platforms: 2011 MiFIR Proposal, n 132, 11.

[168] 2011 MiFIR Proposal, n 132, 11.

[169] 2011 MiFIR Proposal, n 132, rec 6.

[170] 2011 MiFIR Proposal, n 132, 9–10 and Arts 13–20.

[171] 2011 MiFIR Proposal, n 132, 7.

[172] 2011 MiFIR Proposal, n 132, 7 and rec 8.

on a discretionary basis, but imposed related controls on discretion, notably the prohibition on proprietary trading.[173]

The proposed OTF venue was broadly defined as a system or facility that was not a regulated market or MTF, which was operated by an investment firm or market operator, where multiple third party buying and selling interests in financial instruments were able to interact in a way that resulted in a contract.[174] OTF operators would become subject to authorization requirements, similar to those which applied to investment firms and market operators operating MTFs under MiFID I. Trading process rules and market surveillance rules would apply. The OTF operator would also be required to explain why the system did not correspond to, and could not operate as, a regulated market, MTF, or SI. The earlier 2010 Commission Consultation suggestion that OTFs convert to MTFs when trading volume reached particular thresholds was not pursued.

Although the 2011 MiFIR and MiFID II Proposals were not open to formal consultation, the European Parliament carried out a consultation which suggested considerable industry concern.[175] While most industry participants supported the OTF classification as a means of providing a regulatory space for derivatives trading platforms, its application to equity trading was not supported.[176]

The stage was accordingly set for the MiFID II/MiFIR institutional negotiations to replay the OTC/organized venue clashes with respect to equity trading which shaped the 2004 MiFID I negotiations.

V.3.1.3 Transparency Regulation

The 2014 MiFID II/MiFIR transparency regulation reforms have similar drivers to the organizational reforms: the restriction of dark equity trading, whether in the OTC sector or in the regulated market/MTF sector, and the extension of the regulatory perimeter over trading in non-equity asset classes (which were not covered by the MiFID I transparency regime).[177]

The extent of and the appropriate response to dark equity trading rapidly became one of the most contentious elements of the MiFID I Review. While regulated markets and MTFs could operate 'dark pools' in which dark equity trading could take place, these pools were subject to the MiFID I transparency waiver regime which permitted certain types of dark pool only.[178] By contrast, the OTC equity segment was, with the exception of the calibrated regime which applied to SIs, not subject to pre-trade transparency requirements,

---

[173] 2011 MiFID II/MiFIR Proposals Impact Assessment, n 93, 35.

[174] 2011 MiFIR Proposal, n 132, Art 2(1)(7).

[175] The responses to the Parliament's Consultation, based on an ECON Committee questionnaire, are available at: <http://www.europarl.europa.eu/committees/en/econ/subject-files.html>.

[176] A recurring theme of the consultation was that while the OTF regime would support the better regulation of platforms which traded standardized derivatives, it did not apply effectively to equity trades (eg London Stock Exchange Response).

[177] Although the European Central Bank (ECB) criticized the exclusion of debt securities from the MiFID I regime given the size of the debt markets and the exclusion of a 'very significant asset class' from transparency requirements: European Central Bank Opinion on the MiFID I Proposal [2003] OJ C144/6, para 15.

[178] Under MiFID I, pre-trade transparency waivers were available for 'large-in-scale' trades, reference price systems, negotiated trades, and order management systems (2006 Commission MiFID I Regulation Arts 18–20).

and was dark pre-trade. Regulatory arbitrage concerns accordingly arose where OTC execution functionality was similar to that of regulated market/MTF execution. More generally, policy concerns arose as to whether the volume of dark equity trading had the potential to prejudice price formation.[179]

With respect to non-equity market transparency, the Review was driven by the absence of harmonized transparency rules for non-equity asset classes. Approaches to bond market transparency, for example, varied across the Member States. Transparency requirements were typically only imposed on transactions concluded on regulated markets, and were generally a function of regulated markets' rules, being mandatory in only a few Member States. Considerable execution data, and particularly pre-trade transparency data, was, however, available from market-developed systems[180] and from the associated derivatives markets.[181]

MiFID I had required the Commission to report on whether the regime should be extended to other asset classes. The subsequent (pre-crisis) review stands in stark contrast to the crisis-era MiFID I Review. In July 2007, CESR advised the Commission[182] that there was no evidence of market failure in the EU cash bond markets with respect to transparency levels, and that the market had developed an appropriate level of transparency[183] which met the needs of market participants.[184] The European Securities Markets Expert Group (ESME), which was tasked by the Commission with considering bond market transparency, took a similar view.[185] It highlighted the risks that regulatory intervention posed to liquidity and found there was no convincing evidence of market failure in the bond markets with reference to price dispersion, concentration of market share, persistent excess profits, or investor complaints. The Commission subsequently concluded (reflecting significant market hostility to a mandatory transparency regime)[186] that the market was best placed to drive transparency in non-equity asset classes.[187]

---

[179] Exemplified by the European Parliament's concern on this issue: 2010 ECON Dark Pools Workshop, n 38.

[180] Key industry initiatives included the MTS platform, which supports intra-dealer trading in euro-denominated government bonds, channels for the display of quotes from dealers (such as Bloomberg), bond-market indices (including iBoxx (cash bonds) and iTraxx (derivatives)), and trading platforms for cash bonds, including the Tradeweb dealer-based platforms.

[181] The exponential growth in global credit derivative markets pre-crisis was credited with providing dealers with better risk-management tools and with driving more efficient price formation: FSA, Feedback Statement No 06/04, Trading Transparency in the UK Secondary Bond Markets (2006) 10–11.

[182] CESR, Response to the Commission on Non-equities Transparency (2007) (CESR/07-284b) (which followed the earlier CESR, Non Equity Market Transparency, Consultation Paper (2007) (CESR/07-284)).

[183] CESR concluded that it could not identify an evident market failure in respect of market transparency, with wholesale participants generally content with the operation of the markets.

[184] The evidence suggested that spreads in European corporate bonds were tighter than in their US equivalents, notwithstanding that a post-trade transparency system operated in the US under the TRACE (Trade Reporting and Compliance Engine) mechanism: 2006 CEPR Corporate Bonds Study, n 35.

[185] European Securities Markets Expert Group (ESME), Non-Equity Market Transparency (2007).

[186] Commission, Feedback Statement, Pre-and Post-Transparency Provisions of MiFID in relation to transactions in classes of financial instruments other than shares (2006) 3–4 and 5, noting that even positive responses tended only to be 'open-minded' concerning reform.

[187] Commission, Report on Non-equities Market Transparency pursuant to Art 65(1) of Directive 2004/39/EC on markets in financial instruments (2008).

The crisis, however, radically reshaped the regulatory context, with bond market transparency an early target of the international crisis-era reform programme.[188] In the EU, CESR's crisis efforts included an extensive review of transparency in the corporate bond, structured finance, and credit derivatives markets, from which it came to the new conclusion that while the absence of harmonized transparency requirements was not a determinant of the severe liquidity problems these markets had experienced and a harmonized transparency regime would not have resolved those problems, market-led initiatives to provide transparency had not provided sufficient levels of transparency and harmonized post-trade transparency requirements would be beneficial.[189]

As the MiFID I Review got underway, CESR, in its 2010 Equity Market Technical Advice to the Commission,[190] recommended that the MiFID I pre-trade waiver system which supported regulated market/MTF equity dark pools remain in place but that Member State discretion over its operation be restricted. It also advised that the scope of the equity market transparency regime be extended beyond shares to include 'equity-like' instruments including depositary receipts, ETFs (exchange-traded funds), and certificates.

CESR also provided technical advice on the extension of the transparency regime to cover corporate bond, structured-finance product, and credit derivative markets.[191] In its 2009 analysis of these markets over the crisis period, it had advised that post-trade requirements be imposed, on a phased-in basis as necessary, and with calibrations to address the risks to liquidity.[192] Its 2010 Technical Advice to the Commission additionally recommended that pre-trade requirements apply, appropriately calibrated.[193]

The Commission's initial reform orientations, set out in its 2010 MiFID I Review Consultation, broadly followed CESR's approach.[194] It acknowledged the role of dark equity trading in minimizing market impact costs, but highlighted the risk of damage to price formation. Like CESR, it supported the MiFID I waiver regime for regulated market/MTF dark pool equity trading, but proposed that the regime be tightened and that the grant of waivers be co-ordinated through ESMA.[195] It similarly supported the extension of the equity transparency regime to equity-like instruments.

With respect to transparency for non-equity asset classes, the Commission called for a new pre- and post-trade transparency regime for bonds, structured products, and clearing-eligible derivatives, calibrated to reflect liquidity risks, and argued that such a regime could address information asymmetries, support fair and orderly pricing, and improve overall market efficiency and resilience. It suggested that the new regime apply across the

---

[188] Financial Stability Forum, Enhancing Market and Institutional Resilience (2008).

[189] CESR, Transparency of Corporate Bond, Structured Finance, and Credit Derivatives Markets (2009) (CESR/09-348).

[190] n 129.

[191] CESR, Technical Advice on Non-equity Markets Transparency (2010) (CESR/10-799).

[192] n 189.

[193] n 129.

[194] 2010 MiFID I Review Consultation, n 131, 22–30.

[195] In practice, NCAs co-ordinated their conferral of transparency waivers through CESR, but on an informal basis.

new regulatory perimeter and accordingly to regulated markets, MTFs, and OTFs pre-trade,[196] and to these venues and all investment firms post-trade.

The Commission's subsequent 2011 MiFIR Proposal (which contained the transparency regime proposals) broadly followed the 2010 Consultation and CESR's technical advice. The Commission noted the increasing prevalence of 'dark liquidity' in the equity markets (highlighting that 45 per cent of equity trades were dark pre-trade), the risk that ever-expanding dark pools could come to prejudice price formation, and the need to balance the interest of market participants in managing trading risks with the wider market and public interest in transparency.[197] With respect to the non-equity markets, it argued that the lack of harmonized, mandatory transparency requirements was impeding market efficiency, but accepted the need for calibration to the specificities of each asset class in order to protect liquidity by minimizing dealers' position risks.

It accordingly proposed that a calibrated pre- and post-trade transparency regime for regulated market, MTF, and OTF trading apply to bonds, structured products, and derivatives, and that the waiver regime for equity trading on regulated markets, MTFs, and OTFs be tightened and subject to ESMA oversight.[198] The Commission also proposed that the equity regime apply to equity-like instruments and that the SI pre-trade regime be significantly clarified and tightened to prevent arbitrage risks.

V.3.1.4 Data Consolidation

The data consolidation elements of the MiFID I Review were relatively uncontroversial, reflecting widespread agreement as to weaknesses in this area with respect to data quality, cost, and consolidation.[199]

CESR recommended that new standards address the quality of post-trade information, that publication delays be shortened, and that pre- and post-trade information be unbundled separately by data providers to facilitate onward data distribution. It also suggested that OTC firms be required to publish their post-trade information through an 'Approved Publication Arrangement' (APA) and that APAs be approved and subject to stringent criteria designed to ensure the quality of data and ongoing monitoring. With respect to data consolidation, CESR proposed a 'European Consolidated Tape' of transparency information, which would be developed by the industry within a MiFID-governed data quality and governance framework and time frame. The Commission's subsequent 2010 Consultation and 2011 MiFID II/MiFIR Proposals followed this market-driven approach, rather than a public monopoly model for consolidating and distributing pre- and post-trade data, as being more likely to support innovation and client needs and to be cost-effective.[200]

---

[196] The Commission also suggested that investment firms be subject to a pre-trade obligation to quote prices which did not significantly deviate from pre-trade information available on comparable instruments from regulated markets, MTF, and OTFs, and that quotes be binding at a specific trade size, although these requirements did not appear in the final Proposal.

[197] 2011 MiFID II/MiFIR Proposals Impact Assessment, n 93, 12.

[198] The Commission rejected removing the waivers given the impact this would have on liquidity and on the competitive position of the EU market: 2011 MiFID II/MiFIR Proposals Impact Assessment, n 93, 40.

[199] 2011 MiFID II/MiFIR Proposals Impact Assessment, n 93, 12–13.

[200] 2011 MiFID II/MiFIR Proposals Impact Assessment, n 93, 42.

V.3.1.5 The SME Growth Market

The MiFID I Review was also shaped by the wider EU policy concern to support SME finance-raising. The Commission's 2011 MiFID II Proposal provided for a further venue classification—the SME Growth Market—within the MTF classification, designed to enhance the visibility of SMEs, pool liquidity in SME shares, and support SME financing. This reform is discussed in Chapter II section 7.1.2.

V.3.1.6 Venue Resilience and Regulation

A series of reforms designed to address venue resilience and stability, including with respect to algorithmic trading, market-making, and position management, were also canvassed over the Review and are discussed further in section 7.3 of this Chapter and Chapter VI sections 2.3–2.5.

V.3.2 The 2014 MiFID II/MiFIR Negotiations

The trading venue elements of the 2014 MiFID II/MiFIR negotiations proved very difficult. Sharp points of difference emerged between the European Parliament and Council, and within the Council, with respect to the extent to which the MiFID I regime should be extended; with respect to the balance between dark and lit trading and between organized venue and OTC trading; with respect to the differential treatment of equity and non-equity trading; and as to how the trading venue classifications, and in particular the new OTF classification, should be organized.

The European Parliament's October 2012 negotiating position[201] deviated from the Commission's Proposals in two main respects: with respect to the equity markets, it removed the availability of the OTF trading venue; with respect to the non-equity markets, it restricted the extent to which non-equity asset classes could be traded OTC.

The European Parliament removed the ability of the OTF venue to support trading in shares and equity-like instruments, restricting the venue to the trading of non-equity asset classes (bonds, structured-finance products, emission allowances, and derivatives).[202] It also sought to restrict OTC equity trading by means of a general prohibition on shares/equity-like trading taking place outside a regulated market, an MTF, or an SI; OTC trades would be permissible only where an SI was not available, the transaction was *ad hoc* and irregular, the transaction was between eligible counterparties or professional clients, and the transaction was large-in-scale.[203]

With respect to non-equity trading, the European Parliament took a similarly restrictive approach and required that transactions in bonds, structured-finance products, emission

---

[201] The Parliament's Resolution on the MiFIR Proposal, which was adopted on 26 October 2012 (P7_TA_PROV(2012)0407) (2012 Parliament MiFIR Negotiating Position), reflected the initial draft report of the Parliament's ECON Committee, circulated by the ECON Rapporteur, MEP Ferber, earlier in 2012 (PE485.888v01, 27 March 2012 (Draft 2012 Ferber Report)). The MiFID II Resolution is at P7_TA(2011)406.

[202] This revision was designed to protect the quality of price formation in the equity markets given concerns as to the quality of data from OTFs (given the discretionary nature of OTF trading): 2012 Parliament Negotiating Position, n 201, rec 16.

[203] 2012 Parliament Negotiating Position, n 201, Arts 1(7) and 2a.

allowances, and clearing-eligible derivatives which were not traded on a regulated market, MTF, or OTF be concluded through an SI, unless an SI was not available, the transaction was between eligible counterparties or professional clients, the transaction was large-in-scale, and (with respect to bonds) there was not a liquid market.[204] It also restricted OTF trading for non-derivatives, requiring that where a bond, structured-finance product, or emission allowance was admitted to trading on an MTF or regulated market, it could only be traded on an OTF where the order was large-in-scale.[205]

Otherwise, the European Parliament text was similar to the Commission's 2011 MiFIR Proposal, although its many refinements included the specification (also made by the Council) that the OTF classification apply to multilateral systems only and that the new pre-trade transparency requirements for non-equity asset classes could be temporarily lifted where liquidity levels fell below pre-determined thresholds.

The Council negotiations proved to be long and difficult[206] and did not complete until June 2013.[207] Although the Council was in favour of placing limits on dark trading,[208] sharp divergences arose across the Member States as to the balance of organized (generally lit) venue trading and (dark) OTC trading, which reflected the long-standing differences across the Member States as to the extent to which trades should be centralized on organized venues. The UK, the location of the largest OTC trading market in the EU, was in favour of a liberal OTC model, while France, the standard-bearer for organized, lit trading, sought to restrict the OTC trading space. The OTF venue classification accordingly proved highly controversial, with some Member States in favour of the new venue but calling for less stringent requirements to be imposed on the OTF, others in favour of a strict OTF regime, and others calling for the removal of the OTF venue and for all trading to take place on regulated markets, MTFs, and SIs. Specific difficulties included whether client orders could be executed against proprietary capital in an OTF.[209] The Council ultimately agreed to keep the OTF venue (for organized trading in equity and non-equity asset classes), but resolved the difficulties generated by the Commission's prohibition on proprietary trading by allowing 'matched principal trading' within an OTF for non-equity instruments.[210]

---

[204] 2012 Parliament Negotiating Position, n 201, Art 2a.

[205] 2012 Parliament Negotiating Position, n 201, Art 20(1a).

[206] The negotiations were reported as being fierce, particularly between the UK, France, and Germany: Stafford, P and Fontanella-Khan, J, 'UK Agrees EU Deal on City Regulation', *Financial Times*, 18 June 2013, 1.

[207] Council MiFIR General Approach, 18 June 2013 (Council Document 11007/13) and MiFID II General Approach, 18 June 2013 (Council Document 11006/13). The first Presidency Compromises were issued in June 2012 by the Danish Presidency, and were followed by repeated compromise drafts, which increased significantly in number over the final stages of the Irish Presidency. Summaries of the status of the negotiations were issued at the end of the Cyprus Presidency (Cyprus Presidency Progress Report on MiFID II/MiFIR, 13 December 2012 (Council Document 16523/12)) and the Danish Presidency (Danish Presidency Progress Report on MiFID II/MiFIR, 20 June 2012 (Council Document 11536/12)).

[208] The Irish Presidency described the final Council agreement as showing that the 'Council intends for the EU to lead the way in limiting dark pool trading': Irish Presidency, ECOFIN Press Release, 'Irish Presidency Reaches Breakthrough on new Proposals for Safer and More Open Financial Markets', 17 June 2013.

[209] Danish Presidency MiFID II/MiFIR Progress Report, n 207, 4–5 and Cyprus Presidency MiFID II/MiFIR Progress Report, n 207, 4.

[210] Cyprus Presidency MiFID II/MiFIR Progress Report, n 207, 5.

Difficulties also arose with respect to the proposed SI regime. While most Member States supported a more detailed definition of SI activity in order to minimize arbitrage risks, difficulties arose in relation to the SI pre-trade transparency regime, particularly with respect to the size of quotes to which the SI pre-trade transparency rules and the related 'access-to-quotes' rules (sections 11.3 and 11.4) applied.[211]

The transparency regime generally (for regulated markets, MTFs, and OTFs) was less controversial within the Council, although very significant differences arose across the Member States with respect to the dark pool transparency waivers for these venues, with some seeking to restrict the waivers and others supportive of a more liberal approach. Some Member States were also in favour of empowering ESMA to make binding decisions with respect to waivers, a reform which was strongly opposed by other Member States, including the UK. The Council ultimately adopted a more restrictive approach than the Commission's to dark pool waivers in the equity space, providing for a new volume cap on dark pool equity/equity-like trading. It adopted a significantly more articulated and liberal approach than the Commission's approach to non-equity market transparency, however, and introduced an array of calibrations, including with respect to protecting dealers' holding large positions and empowering national competent authorities (NCAs) to suspend pre-trade transparency requirements for non-equity asset classes when liquidity levels fell below preset thresholds.[212] Overall, the Council sought to protect 'illiquid markets' from transparency; the main thrust of the Council text (which is reflected in the 2014 MiFIR) was to lift transparency requirements from non-equity markets where they became illiquid.

Like the European Parliament, the Council also sought to reduce the OTC trading space in equities (it did not do so with respect to other asset classes). It required that investment firms ensure that all trades in shares admitted to a regulated market or traded on a trading venue take place on a regulated market, MTF, OTF, or SI, unless the trade was systematic, *ad hoc*, irregular and infrequent, or carried out between eligible and professional counterparties, and did not contribute to price formation; it similarly required that any investment firm operating an internal matching system which executed client orders in shares on a multilateral basis must ensure it was authorized as an MTF or OTF.

The subsequent Commission/Council/European Parliament trilogue negotiations (which took place under the shadow of the 2014 closure of the Parliament and Commission terms) proved to be long and difficult. The major points of contention included: the OTF classification and the extent to which it should be limited (or not) to non-equity asset classes; the balance between dark and lit trading, particularly with respect to the transparency waiver regimes and the different calibrations sought by the Council; and the extent to which detailed organizational regulation, orientated to algorithmic trading in particular,

---

[211] Danish Presidency MiFID II/MiFIR Progress Report, n 207, 5.

[212] Particular difficulties arose with respect to the waiver regime for non-equity asset classes and in relation to 'request for quote' and 'voice trading' systems, and with respect to venues restricted to professional participants: Danish Presidency MiFID II/MiFIR Progress Report, n 207, 6. These difficulties reflected the importance of these waivers for supporting trading in smaller markets in which trading was predominantly carried out through these forms of systems. Ultimately, the 2012 Council General Approach provided a specific waiver for these systems, which was designed to protect dealers in these systems holding large positions which exposed them to undue risk as liquidity providers, and which is reflected in the new regime (sect 11).

should be imposed on trading venues (the Parliament sought a restrictive approach; the Council was more liberal).

The complex and detailed 2014 MiFID II/MiFIR compromise as finally adopted reflects the European Parliament's position to a significant extent, particularly with respect to the repatriation of trading on to organized venues: in particular, the OTF classification is not available for equity/equity-like trading and share trading must take place on a regulated market, MTF, or SI.[213] The Parliament's preference for more detailed regulation of trading venues, particularly with respect to algorithmic trading, also prevailed. More generally, the many technical calibrations, nuances, and exemptions[214] introduced by the Council and Parliament were accepted over the trilogue and have finessed the text.

Overall, the 2014 MiFID II/MiFIR trading venue regime is significantly more prescriptive and detailed than the 2004 MiFID I regime.[215] Through the OTF classification device, the regime pulls a wide range of non-equity OTC trading venues into the regulatory net. By prescribing the venues on which share trading takes place, it significantly decreases the OTC space for share trading. By extending the transparency regime to non-equity asset classes, limiting the availability of transparency waivers, and imposing more intrusive operational requirements, the new regime has very significantly extended the reach of venue regulation.

The regime is, however, calibrated, particularly to reflect liquidity risks (a theme which also emerges from the new regime governing the regulation of trading practices (Chapter VI)). The OTF trading venue, for example, is designed to accommodate market structure and practices in the derivatives segment; its regulatory scheme is designed to protect liquidity and to support stability in derivatives trading (section 6.4). Similarly, the transparency regime contains a number of calibrations, particularly with respect to non-equity trading, designed to protect liquidity (section 11). The new operational regime for trading venues also contains calibrations to protect liquidity (section 7.3.2), but the impact of this radical recasting of regulation remains to be seen.

V.4 2014 MiFID II/MiFIR: Harmonization and ESMA

The trading venue regime is scattered across the 2014 MiFID II (directive) and 2014 MiFIR (regulation). MiFID II broadly covers the authorization, organizational, and operational requirements which apply to trading venues. MiFIR broadly covers the transparency regime and transaction reporting, prescribes particular venues for share trading, and establishes the different venue classifications. The allocation of coverage across both

---

[213] The further restrictions which the European Parliament placed on trading by means of restrictions on when an OTF could be used in the non-equity trading space were not accepted.

[214] Including, eg, an exemption from non-equity transparency requirements where the counterparty is a member of the European System of Central Banks and the transaction is in support of monetary, foreign exchange, and financial stability policy, as long as the exemption has been notified to the regulated market, market operator, or investment firm (2014 MiFIR Art 1(6)). The exemption is to be amplified by RTSs and may be extended to other central banks.

[215] The 2014 MiFIR underlines that 'it is important that trading in financial instruments is carried out as far as possible on organized venues and that all such venues are appropriately regulated.' (rec 6). See further sect 6.6.

measures is designed to ensure that areas where some degree of implementation discretion is appropriate are covered by the directive, and that those areas where uniformity is essential to market efficiency are covered by the regulation.

MiFID II accordingly, and for the purposes of this Chapter, applies to investment firms,[216] market operators,[217] and data-reporting service providers[218] (MiFID II Article 1(1)), and establishes requirements in relation to the authorization and operating conditions of investment firms (in relation to their operation of MTFs, OTFs, and SIs), the authorization and operation of regulated markets,[219] and the authorization and operation of data-reporting service providers (MiFID II Article 1(2)). MiFIR, which applies to investment firms and market operators (including any trading venues they operate) (Article 1(2)), establishes uniform requirements, for the purposes of this Chapter, in relation to disclosure of trade data to the public, reporting of transactions to NCAs, and non-discriminatory access to clearing and non-discriminatory access to trading in benchmarks (MiFIR Article 1(1)).[220]

The reliance on a detailed regulation (MiFIR) for much of the trading venue regime has significantly intensified EU trading venue regulation. Further intensification will come through the great number of delegations to ESMA-proposed Binding Technical Standards (BTSs) (which represent the vast majority of delegations) and to Commission administrative rule-making generally.[221] The new administrative rulebook can be expected to be significantly wider and deeper than the MiFID I rulebook.[222] The scale of the harmonization has a number of implications.

Given the great technical complexity of many of the required administrative rules, their untested nature, and the dearth of empirical evidence (particularly with respect to transparency for non-equity asset classes),[223] the effectiveness of the 2014 MiFID II/MiFIR regime will depend in large part on the quality of ESMA's technical advice to the Commission and, in particular, of its proposed Regulatory Technical Standards (RTSs) and Implementing Technical Standards (ITSs) and on the effectiveness of the BTS process.[224] ESMA's influence will be considerable, as the MiFID II/MiFIR negotiations saw many of the delegations change from Commission-led administrative rules to the

---

[216] See Ch IV sect 4.2 on this definition.

[217] A market operator is a person or persons who manages and/or operates the business of a regulated market (the market operator may be the regulated market itself): MiFID II Art 4(1)(18).

[218] See sect 11.6.

[219] See sect 6.2.

[220] A regulation was deployed to provide for the uniform application of a single regulatory framework, strengthen confidence in the transparency of markets across the EU, reduce regulatory complexity and compliance costs, and contribute to the elimination of distortions of competition: 2014 MiFIR rec 3.

[221] The non-Binding Technical Standard (BTS) delegations to Commission rule-making are almost entirely in the form of Art 290 TFEU delegated rules, and the rules will be adopted under the related 2014 MiFIR/MiFID II procedures (which provide for revocation of the delegation by the European Parliament and Council, and empower the Parliament and Council to veto the rule adopted by the Commission within two months of its adoption by the Commission). On administrative rule-making, see Ch X sects 4 and 5.

[222] Which, with respect to the pivotal transparency regime, applied only to shares admitted to trading on a regulated market. Accordingly, only limited reference is made in this Chapter to the MiFID I administrative rules which will be repealed when MiFID II/MiFIR comes into force.

[223] See further sect 11.7 on the challenges.

[224] The scale of the delegations led ESMA to engage in extensive preparatory activity prior to the adoption of the MiFID II/MiFIR legislative texts: ESMA Annual Report (2012) 43–4.

ESMA-led RTSs which form the vast majority of the delegations.[225] The extensive MiFID II/MiFIR review obligation provides a safety valve against regulatory error,[226] but previous experience suggests that review is typically an occasion for an expansion and not contraction/refinement of the EU rulebook.

The scale of the 2014 MiFID II/MiFIR regime, and its capturing of a very wide range of venues and instruments, means that its impact is likely to be asymmetric and to fall most heavily on those Member States with highly developed markets and with high volumes of institutional/OTC trading, and most notably on the UK. Growing political concern in the UK as to the expanding reach of EU regulation over the City of London financial centre, and in particular as to the potential for discriminatory action arising from the *de facto* split between the euro area and the internal market (which is being deepened by Banking Union), led to the UK's insistence on the inclusion of a non-discrimination clause in the recitals to MiFID II/MiFIR: no action by an NCA or ESMA in the performance of their duties should directly or indirectly discriminate against any Member State or group of Member States as a venue for the provision of investment services and activities in any currency (MiFID II recital 139 and MiFIR recital 49). While this clause, which mirrors the non-discrimination provision adopted under the Single Supervisory Mechanism legislation,[227] does not have binding effect and adds little to the fundamental Treaty prohibition on discrimination on grounds of nationality,[228] its inclusion reflects the scale of the reforms which MiFID II/MiFIR has brought.

V.5 2014 MiFID II/MiFIR: Scope

The 2014 MiFID II/MiFIR regime is designed to apply to all organized trading venues. It uses the 'trading venue'[229] concept to capture the different forms of organized venue within MiFID II/MiFIR. The related venue classification regime is calibrated to reflect the different forms of trading on organized venues and the different liquidity risks which regulation can generate (sections 6 and 11).

---

[225] Reflecting Council support for greater engagement by ESMA (Danish Presidency MiFID II/MiFIR Progress Report, n 207, 13). Examples include the new regime governing algorithmic trading on venues (2014 MiFID II Art 48) and the detail of the pre- and post-trade transparency regime for equity and non-equity instruments (2014 MiFIR Arts 3–23). The Commission, however, expressed its concern that this change from its Proposals did not respect the distinction between RTSs and Art 290 TFEU rules: Statement by Commission on the Adoption of MiFID II/MiFIR, 7 May 2014 (Council Document 9344/14). This statement does not augur well for ESMA/Commission relations over the RTS process.

[226] eg 2014 MiFID II Art 90 (requiring review of, *inter alia*, the new OTF regime and developments in prices for pre- and post-trade transparency data) and 2014 MiFIR Art 52 (requiring review of, *inter alia*, the new volume cap on dark trading, the waiver regime for pre-trade transparency, and the effectiveness of the transaction reports regime).

[227] Council Regulation (EU) No 1024/2013 (conferring supervisory tasks on the ECB) [2013] OJ L287/63 Art 1.

[228] Although it was reported as a negotiating victory which could potentially limit the influence of the EU on how the City of London regulates trading on its financial markets: Stafford, P and Fontanella-Khan, J, 'UK Agrees EU Deal on City Regulation', *Financial Times*, 18 June 2013, 1.

[229] With respect to the MiFIR definitions, many of the MiFIR-related definitions are contained in MiFID II (MiFIR Art 2(1) contains the relevant cross references). A trading venue is defined as any regulated market, MTF, or OTF: 2014 MiFID II Art 4(1)(24). See sect 6 on these classifications.

The pivotal transparency regime applies to two broad sets of asset class: equity and non-equity. The equity class includes shares, but also equity-like instruments such as depositary receipts,[230] ETFs,[231] certificates,[232] and other similar financial instruments traded on a trading venue. The non-equity asset classes covered by the transparency regime are bonds, structured-finance products,[233] emission allowances, and derivatives.[234] Particular asset classes, notably sovereign debt,[235] are subject to additionally calibrated rules to protect market liquidity.

In some respects, notably with respect to venues' admission-to-trading rules, the regime applies generally to 'financial instruments'.[236]

V.6 2014 MiFID II/MiFIR: Venue Classification

V.6.1 Regulatory Design

Venue classification is at the heart of the 2014 MiFID II/MiFIR trading venue regime. It was similarly important under the 2004 MiFID I, but had more limited purposes. Under MiFID I, venue classification was designed to ensure that, in a competitive trading environment, trading which was functionally similar was subject to similar regulation; the MiFID I model was essentially facilitative and, in particular, accommodated OTC trading.

The MiFID II venue classification is also designed to ensure that functionally similar trading is subject to similar rules, but it has a distinct market-shaping function in that it is designed to ensure that trading, particularly in the equity market, takes place on organized venues which are open and transparent and subject to similar regulation, and that the OTC trading space reduces.[237]

---

[230] Depositary receipts are those securities negotiable on the capital markets and which represent ownership of the securities of a non-domiciled issuer, while being able to be admitted to trading on a regulated market and traded independently of the securities of the non-domiciled issuer: 2014 MiFID II Art 4(1)(45).

[231] An ETF (exchange-traded fund) is a fund of which at least one unit or share class is traded throughout the day on at least one trading venue, and with at least one market-maker which takes action to ensure that the price of its units or shares on the trading venue does not vary significantly from its Net Asset Value and, where applicable, from its indicative net asset value: 2014 MiFID II Art 4(1)(46).

[232] Certificates are defined as securities which are negotiable on the capital market and which, in case of a repayment of investment by the issuer, are ranked above shares but below unsecured bond instruments and other similar instruments: 2014 MiFIR Art 2(1)(27).

[233] Defined as securities created to securitize and transfer credit risk associated with a pool of financial assets, entitling the security holder to receive regular payments that depend on the cash flow from the underlying assets: 2014 MiFIR Art 2(1)(28).

[234] Defined as any securities which give the right to acquire or sell transferable securities (defined under 2014 MiFID II Art 4(1)(44)—see Ch IV sect 4.3) or which give rise to a cash settlement determined by reference to transferable securities, currencies, interest rates or yields, commodities, or other indices or measures, and which come within the scope of MiFID II/MiFID generally under MiFID II Annex I, sect C paras (4)–(10): 2014 MiFID Art 2(1)(29). See further Ch IV sect 4.3.

[235] Defined as debt instruments issued by a sovereign issuer (sovereign issuer is defined under 2014 MiFID II Art 4(1)(60)): 2014 MiFIR Art 4(1)(61).

[236] This definition applies across MiFID II/MiFIR generally and refers to the instruments listed in 2014 MiFID II Annex I, sect C: see Ch IV sect 4.3.

[237] MiFID II/MiFIR is designed to ensure that all organized trading is conducted on regulated venues and is fully transparent, pre- and post-trade: 2014 MiFIR rec 10.

To achieve this, MiFID II/MiFIR provides for four organized trading venues: regulated markets; MTFs; OTFs; and SIs. The regulated market, MTF, and OTF venues are multilateral[238] and subject to broadly similar rules.[239] The SI venue is essentially bilateral and sits in the OTC space. But, as the SI classification is designed to capture high volumes of internalization activity by investment firms, it is subject to tailored 'venue-like' regulation. The OTC trading space remains undefined (as under MiFID I).[240]

Overall, the 2014 MiFID II/MiFIR classifications are significantly more granular than the MiFID I classifications, in an effort to minimize the regulatory arbitrage and gaming effects associated with MiFID I and to ensure organized trading is carried on in the regulated space. This concern is reflected in the scope of the regime. MiFID II specifies that all multilateral systems in financial instruments must operate under either MiFID II Title II (the investment firm regime, which applies to MTFs and OTFs) or MiFID II Title III (the regulated market regime); that any investment firm which, on an organized, frequent, systematic and substantial basis, deals on own account by executing client orders outside a regulated market, MTF, or OTF operates under the SI-specific transparency rules which apply under MiFIR; and that all order transactions in financial instruments not concluded on multilateral systems or on SIs comply with the relevant MiFIR requirements for OTC trading (MiFID II Article 1(7)).

The classification system can be segmented in three ways. A broad distinction can be made under MiFID II/MiFIR between neutral, organized, multilateral trading venues, subject to similar levels of regulation (regulated markets, MTFs and OTFs); bilateral trading venues in the OTC segment, which are systematized (SIs); and the bilateral OTC sector.

A further distinction can be made with respect to the discretionary/non-discretionary quality of the venue.[241] Where trading on an organized venue has a discretionary element, such as with respect to the operator's decision as whether to admit the order to the venue or to execute it elsewhere (primarily SIs and OTFs), conduct rules, designed to reflect the brokerage element of the service and the agency risks to the investor arising from discretion (and the risks to price formation), apply.

Finally, the regime can be segmented according to whether the trading venue in question is regulated as an investment service or as a market. The provision of MTF, OTF, and SI trading systems are all investment services which can be provided by authorized investment firms under MiFID II/MiFIR. They can also be provided by non-investment-firm 'market operators'[242] where the operator confirms compliance with the relevant investment firm requirements. The provider of the trading system is accordingly regulated as an investment firm, although calibrated venue rules apply. Regulated markets, by contrast, are regulated

---

[238] A multilateral system is any system or facility in which multiple third party buying and selling trading interests in financial instruments are able to interact in the system: 2014 MiFID II Art 4(1)(19).

[239] 2014 MiFID II Art 1(7).

[240] The European Parliament proposed a definition based on the OTC space being limited to bilateral trading carried out by an eligible counterparty on its own account, outside a trading venue or an SI, on an occasional and irregular basis, with eligible counterparties, and always at large–in-scale sizes (2012 Parliament MiFIR Negotiating Position, n 201, Art 1(2c)), which was not adopted.

[241] Non-discretionary rules are rules which leave the regulated market or market operator (or investment operating an MTF) with no discretion as to how trading interests interact: 2014 MiFIR rec 7.

[242] n 217.

under a distinct regulated market regime, which is based on a market operator running the market but which, with respect to the regulation of trading functionality, is broadly the same as the MTF and OTF regimes.

The primary determining feature of an organized trading venue under MiFID II/MiFIR, however, is whether or not it is multilateral.[243]

V.6.2 Regulated Markets

A 'regulated market' is a multilateral system which is operated and/or managed by a market operator, and which brings together, or facilitates the bringing together of, multiple third party buying and selling interests in financial instruments[244] (in the system and in accordance with its non-discretionary rules) in a way that results in a contract, in respect of the financial instruments admitted to trade under its rules and/or systems, and which is authorized and functions regularly in accordance with the 2014 MiFID II/MiFIR rules for regulated markets (MiFID II Article 4(1)(21)).

The classification is therefore 'opt-in' in design and captures the distinct primary market capital-raising and secondary market trading functionalities conferred on 'regulated markets'. In addition to capturing non-discretionary and multilateral trading functionality, the regulated market venue classification provides venues which opt for this status with a capital-raising-related branding mechanism, related to the suite of admission to trading and disclosure rules which apply to regulated markets; these requirements are designed to reduce the cost of capital by signalling to investors that the highest levels of disclosure apply to the admitted issuer, and that instruments admitted to the regulated market meet a series of minimum conditions (see further Chapter II section 7.1.1). By contrast with MTFs, regulated markets operate as primary (issuance) markets as well as secondary trading markets; many MTFs offer only secondary trading. Where MTFs offer primary market trading, they have, by implication, chosen to eschew regulated market status, typically because of the disclosure costs that regulated market admission imposes on issuers and particularly on third country issuers, and in order to compete for SME business in particular: a marked trend has emerged of increased levels of initial public offering (IPO) activity by SMEs on 'exchange-regulated markets' which operate as primary issuance markets within the MTF space.[245]

For the purposes of trading venue regulation, however, the regulated market has the same functionality and is regulated in the same way as the other multilateral, non-discretionary organized venue, the MTF.

V.6.3 Multilateral Trading Facilities

An MTF is a multilateral system, operated by an investment firm or a market operator, which brings together multiple third party buying and selling interests in financial

---

[243] See n 238.
[244] Including orders, quotes, and indications of interest: 2014 MiFIR rec 7.
[245] See further Ch II sect 7.1.2.

instruments (in the system and in accordance with non-discretionary rules) in a way that results in a contract in accordance with the 2014 MiFID II/MiFIR's investment firm rules (MiFID II Article 4(1)(22)).

Although operation of an MTF is characterized as an investment service provided by an investment firm (or market operator), a customized regulatory regime which, with the exception of admission-to-trading requirements, is very similar to the regulated market regime, and which addresses operational and transparency regulation, applies to the operation of an MTF.

Both regulated markets and MTFs are neutral venues and cannot execute client orders against proprietary capital.[246] Similarly, both venue types do not include bilateral systems where a firm enters into every trade on own account, including as a riskless counterparty interposed between the buyer and seller, where the orders are matched simultaneously (matched principal trading).[247]

V.6.4 Organized Trading Facilities

V.6.4.1 The OTF

The new venue, the OTF—which is designed to ensure that all forms of organized trading are captured under 2014 MiFID II/MiFIR[248]—is also a multilateral system, but one which is not a regulated market or MTF, and in which multiple third party buying and selling interests in bonds, structured-finance products, emission allowances, or derivatives (but not, accordingly, equity and equity-like instruments) are able to interact in the system in a way that results in a contract in accordance with the MiFID II/MiFIR provisions for investment firms (MiFID II Article 4(1)(23)).

By contrast with the MTF and the regulated market, the OTF cannot support trading in equity/equity-like securities. In addition, it does not operate under non-discretionary rules, reflecting the discretionary element of the different non-equity venues this classification is designed to capture (primarily the different types of dealer-based platforms for trading derivatives). The OTF venue is not, however, all-encompassing and does not cover, for example, systems where there is no genuine trade execution or arranging (such as bulletin boards for advertising trading interests, electronic post-trade confirmation services, or portfolio compression)[249] (MiFIR recital 8).

V.6.4.2 The OTF and the Exercise of Discretion

OTFs are subject to the rules which apply to MTFs and regulated markets, albeit with two significant calibrations to reflect the discretionary quality of trading on OTFs (and, in particular, the nature of trading on the derivatives platforms which the OTF classification is designed to capture).

---

[246] 2014 MiFIR rec 7.
[247] 2014 MiFIR rec 7.
[248] 2014 MiFIR rec 8.
[249] On portfolio compression services, which apply in relation to derivatives trading, see Ch VI sect 4.3.

First, OTFs, as discretionary venues, are subject to related conduct rules, including best execution requirements (MiFID II Article 20(8)).[250]

Second, OTFs are subject to a series of restrictions on how they exercise discretion and on the trading functions which can they provide (MiFID II Article 20).[251] OTFs must operate on a discretionary basis (MiFID II Article 20(6)), otherwise the MTF classification would apply, but OTF discretion is confined. Given that the venue operator is required to be neutral (in this respect like regulated markets and MTFs), discretion in an OTF operates at two levels only: when deciding to place an order in an OTF or to retract the order and when deciding not to match a client order with other orders in the system at the time, as long as this complies with any specific instructions from the client and with best execution requirements (MiFID II Article 20(6)).[252]

NCAs may require (either at the OTF authorization stage or on an *ad hoc* basis) detailed descriptions of how discretion will be exercised, particularly in relation to when an order may be retracted and how client orders are to be matched (MiFID II Article 20(7)).

As operators of neutral multilateral platforms, OTF operators are also prevented from executing client orders against their proprietary capital (MiFID II Article 20(1)).[253] In a concession to the nature of non-equity trading, however, OTF operators, in order to support stable trading, are permitted to engage in 'matched principal trading' (or riskless principal trading),[254] which is not regarded as proprietary trading under MiFID II/MiFIR (Article 20 (2)). But a series of restrictions apply, given the potential for conflict-of-interest risk and for price formation to be prejudiced. Organizational and NCA monitoring requirements apply.[255] Matched principal trading is only permitted in relation to bonds, structured-finance products, emission allowances, and derivatives which are not subject to the 2012 EMIR clearing obligation,[256] and the client must consent (Article 20(2)).

Reflecting the concern of the Council to support sovereign debt markets, dealing on own account (other than by matched principal trading) by an OTF is permitted in relation to illiquid sovereign debt instruments (Article 20(3)).

---

[250] Although much of the regime will be disapplied where trading is between eligible counterparties (Ch IV sect 5.2).

[251] These restrictions became more nuanced over the trilogue negotiations.

[252] Where an OTF is in the form of a client order crossing system, the firm can decide when and how much of two orders it wants to match. It may also facilitate negotiation between clients so as to bring together two or more potentially compatible trading interests: 2014 MiFID II Art 20(6).

[253] The prohibition applies to the proprietary capital of the investment firm or market operator and/or from any entity that is part of the same corporate group and/or legal person as the firm or market operator: 2014 MiFID II Art 20(1).

[254] Matched principal trading is defined as a transaction where the facilitator (the OTF) interposes between the buyer and the seller in such a way that it is never exposed to market risk throughout the execution of the transaction, with both sides of the transaction executed simultaneously, and where the transaction is concluded at a price where the facilitator makes no profit or loss other than a previously disclosed commission, fee, or charge for the transaction: 2014 MiFID II Art 4(1)(38).

[255] The investment firm or venue operator running the OTF must establish arrangements ensuring adherence to the definition of matched principal trading, and also report to the NCA on its use of matched principal trading: 2014 MiFID II Arts 20(2) and (7). The NCA must monitor the trading to ensure that it complies with the definition of matched principal trading and does not give rise to conflicts of interest (Art 20(7)).

[256] European Market Infrastructure Regulation (EU) No 648/2012 [2012] OJ L201/1 (2012 EMIR) (Ch VI sect 4.2).

The operation of an OTF and an SI cannot take place within the same legal entity;[257] the firm or operator operating an OTF is not, however, prohibited from engaging another investment firm to carry out market-making in the OTF on an independent basis (Article 20(4) and (5)).

These conditions reflect the bias towards multilateral non-discretionary trading under MiFID II/MiFIR, as does the power of the OTF's NCA to require a detailed explanation of why the system does not correspond to and cannot operate as a regulated market, MTF, or SI (Article 20(7)).

V.6.4.3 A Successful Reform?

As one of the most contested elements of the 2014 MiFID II/MiFIR negotiations, the OTF classification warrants some attention.[258]

The Council struggled to reach a position on the OTF. The European Parliament was sceptical from the outset,[259] and sought (successfully) to restrict it to non-equity asset classes. Across stakeholders more generally (and particularly the industry), there was support for the OTF classification as a means of capturing derivatives trading platforms, but concerns relating to its use in the equity segment.[260] Two major difficulties emerged and were related to the application of the OTF to two very different asset classes. First, the use of the OTF in the equity trading space raised a host of objections, among the most fundamental of which was that it potentially prejudiced price formation—given the potentially poor quality of the transparency data such a discretionary venue would produce—while being regulated in a functionally similar manner to non-discretionary, multilateral regulated markets and MTFs.[261] Second, difficulties arose with respect to the Commission's attempt to grapple with the risks posed by OTF discretion by means of a prohibition on proprietary trading within the OTF; such a prohibition, particularly in the non-equity space where it threatened long-established market practices, could have decreased OTF liquidity and stability and ultimately prejudiced investors.[262] Both of these concerns were ultimately addressed over the MiFID II/MiFIR negotiations. By limiting the operation of the OTF to non-equity instruments and accommodating certain exercises of discretion and matched principal trading, the OTF regime as adopted is significantly less risky than the original model. But its untested nature is reflected in the obligation imposed on the Commission to report to the Council and European Parliament on the functioning of OTFs (including

---

[257] An OTF must not connect with an SI in a way that enables orders in an OTF and orders or quotes in an SI to interact.

[258] See further n 12, and n 19.

[259] The 2012 Ferber Report on MiFIR questioned its utility and called instead for a sharper focus on the binary distinction between bilateral and multilateral trading: n 201, Explanatory Statement, 54–5.

[260] Ferrarini and Moloney, n 12.

[261] As OTF operators would have a degree of discretion over execution, could route orders to other venues, and could control access to their execution systems, the pricing information produced would not be of the same order as that produced by the neutral, non-discretionary interplay of third party orders in a non-discretionary, open access, multilateral venue, and data quality risks could arise.

[262] This concern was repeatedly raised during the Parliament's consultation (sect 3.1.2). The UK FSA also expressed concern that liquidity would be withdrawn, particularly with respect to dealer-client trades in the interest rate swaps market, where 95 per cent of trades were against dealers' capital: Lawton, D (FSA), Speech on 'MiFID II: A Regulator's View Point', 30 January 2012.

their use of matched principal trading) and on any necessary adjustments by March 2019 (MiFID II Article 90).

V.6.5 Own-account Dealing: SIs and Investment Firms

In the bilateral OTC space, firms which systematically execute client orders against their proprietary inventory are treated as SIs. The 2014 MiFID II/MiFIR has tightened the SI venue classification to address the regulatory arbitrage difficulties associated with the primarily qualitative 2004 MiFID I SI definition;[263] the definition now has a strongly quantitative quality (MiFID II Article 4(1)(20)). An SI is a firm which, on an organized, frequent, systematic, and substantial basis, deals on own account by executing client orders outside a regulated market, MTF, or OTF, without operating a multilateral system. Whether trading is 'frequent' or 'systematic' is a quantitative assessment, based on the number of OTC trades in the financial instrument carried out by the investment firm on own account by executing client orders. The 'substantial basis' element of the definition is to be measured by either the size of the OTC trading carried out in relation to the total trading of the firm in a specific financial instrument, or by the size of the OTC trading carried out by the firm in relation to the total trading in the EU in a specific financial instrument.[264]

Operating in the bilateral, OTC space and under a lighter operating regime than that which applies to regulated markets, MTFs and OTFs, SIs are not permitted to bring together third party trading interests; accordingly, a single-dealer platform could qualify as an SI, but a multi-dealer platform, where multiple dealers interact for the same financial instrument, could not (MiFIR recital 20). Characterization as an SI is instrument-specific; firms are SIs in relation to particular instruments and not as a general matter (MiFIR recital 19).

All other dealing by investment firms falls outside the regulated trading venue space, although, as discussed further on in the Chapter, an array of general and trading-specific investment firm requirements apply.

V.6.6 Shrinking the OTC Space

The 2004 MiFID I regime was generally facilitative and accommodated OTC trading.[265] The 2014 MiFID II/MiFIR regime is more prescriptive.

---

[263] Under MiFID I, an SI was a firm which, on an organized, frequent, and systematic basis, dealt on own account by executing client orders outside a regulated market or MTF. These criteria were amplified by the 2006 Commission MiFID I Regulation which provided that a firm was an SI where the internalization activity had a material commercial role for the firm and was carried on in accordance with non-discretionary rules and procedures; the activity was carried on by personnel (or by means of an automated technical system) assigned to that purpose (exclusive use was not required); and the activity was available to clients on a regular or continuous basis. A lack of clarity in applying this definition, particularly with respect to the 'material commercial role' element, was associated with only a small number of firms being regulated under the SI regime: 2010 MiFID I Review Consultation, n 131, 17.

[264] Both pre-set limits (for 'frequent and systematic', and for 'substantial') must be crossed for a firm to qualify as an SI.

[265] In its 2010 MiFID I Review Communication, the Commission described the MiFID I regime as not prescriptive about where trades were executed and as providing investors with flexibility and choice about

While the Commission was generally sanguine as to the scale of OTC trading, particularly equity trading, at the outset of the MiFID I Review,[266] this position changed over the Review. In its 2011 MiFID II/MiFIR impact assessment, the Commission argued that the creation of the OTF should 'substantially decrease' the weight of OTC trading in non-equities but also in equities.[267] The European Parliament was hostile to the OTC sector and called for all trades in non-equity instruments, bar large *ad hoc* professional trades, to be executed on organized venues (regulated markets, MTFs, OTFs and SIs), and for equity trading to take place on regulated markets, MTFs, and SIs only. The Council's approach was more liberal, but it nonetheless sought to ensure that as much trading as possible took place on open, transparent, and regulated platforms.[268]

The MiFID II/MiFIR regime represents a compromise between the European Parliament and Council positions. The OTF classification will significantly shrink the non-equity OTC space, but the regime does not otherwise restrict OTC trading in the non-equity sector through trading obligations.

MiFID II/MiFIR is more interventionist in the equity space. In an (admittedly faint) echo of the earlier concentration regime, MiFIR introduces a new requirement for all trading in shares to be located on organized venues (Article 23). An investment firm must ensure the trades it undertakes in shares admitted to trading on a regulated market or traded on a trading venue must take place on a regulated market, MTF, SI, or a third country trading venue which is assessed by the Commission as equivalent, as appropriate (Article 23(1)). The only exception is where the trades are non-systematic, *ad hoc*, irregular, and infrequent, or are carried out between eligible and/or professional counterparties and do not contribute to the price discovery process; the price discovery condition will be amplified through RTSs (Article 23(1)).[269]

Similarly, an investment firm that operates an internal matching system, which executes client orders (in shares, depositary receipts, ETFs, certificates, and other similar financial instruments) on a multilateral basis, must ensure it is authorized as an MTF, and comply with all relevant provisions (Article 23(2)).

This prescriptive approach to equity trading represents a major shift from the MiFID I era. If equity market liquidity is not to move offshore to more accommodating venues, great care will be needed in amplifying the conditions under which equity dark trading can take place on regulated markets, MTFs, and SIs, and in amplifying the exemptions from Article 23.

---

where and how they wished to execute trades: n 131, 9. It similarly characterized MiFID I as neutral as to where a trade was executed.

[266] n 131, 30.
[267] 2011 MiFID II/MiFIR Proposals Impact Assessment, n 93, 36–7.
[268] Cyprus Presidency MiFID II/MiFIR Progress Report, n 207, 5.
[269] ESMA is to take into account trades such as those involving 'non-addressable liquidity trades' or trades where the exchange of shares is determined by factors other than the current market valuation of the shares.

V.7 Operational Regulation of Multilateral Trading: Regulated Markets

V.7.1 A Flexible Regime

The 2014 MiFID II/MiFIR operational regime for regulated markets is broadly similar to the MiFID I regime. The operational requirements have, however, been tightened, particularly with respect to market resilience and liquidity (including by means of new market-making and algorithmic trading requirements) and the governance of the regulated market. The new transparency regime, which applies to regulated markets, MTFs, and OTFs, has also changed the regulatory environment significantly (section 11).

The regulated markets regime is, overall, designed to be flexible and to allow regulated markets to design their own trading rules and access conditions and operate different market segments, subject to any additional local rules, as permitted by MiFID II/MiFIR (the 'public law' governing the trading conducted under the systems of the regulated market is that of the home Member State of the regulated market).[270] Nonetheless, MiFID II/MiFIR subjects regulated markets to a series of operational and organizational requirements and to backstop supervision by NCAs.

V.7.2 Authorization

Authorization is governed by the 2014 MiFID II, which applies a relatively light-touch authorization regime to those venues which seek classification as a regulated market. Under Article 44(1), authorization as a regulated market may only be granted where the NCA (the home NCA)[271] is satisfied that the market operator and the regulated market's systems comply at least with the requirements for regulated markets (MiFID II Title III).[272] NCAs must also keep the regulated market's compliance with MiFID II's requirements and the initial authorization conditions under regular review (Article 44(2)). Authorization is dependent on the market operator providing all necessary information, including a programme of operations which sets out the types of business envisaged and the organizational structure, to enable the NCA to satisfy itself that the regulated market has established, at the time of initial authorization, all the necessary arrangements in place to comply with MiFID II's requirements (Article 44(1)).[273] Authorization must be withdrawn by the NCA where

---

[270] 2014 MiFID II Art 44(4). See n 271 on the home Member State.

[271] The home NCA for a regulated market is the State in which the regulated market is registered or, if under the law of that Member State it has no registered office, the Member State in which the head office of the regulated market is situated: 2014 MiFID II Art 4(1)(55).

[272] Where the market operator is other than the regulated market itself, Member States are to establish how MiFID II's obligations are to be allocated between the regulated market and the market operator.

[273] Each Member State must draw up a list of regulated markets for which it is the home Member State and forward it to the other Member States and ESMA (which is required to publish a list of all regulated markets): 2014 MiFID II Art 56.

the grounds common across EU securities and markets regulation arise, and withdrawals must be notified to ESMA (Article 44(5) and (6)).[274]

The authorization process focuses on the market operator who must perform tasks relating to the organization and operation of the regulated market under the supervision of the NCA (Article 44(2)) and is responsible for compliance with MiFID II's regulated market requirements (Article 44(3)).[275] A new governance regime applies to the management body of the market operator,[276] which reflects the governance regime which applies to the management body of investment firms (Article 45).[277] Accordingly, members of the management body must at all times be of sufficiently good repute; commit sufficient time and comply with the restrictions which apply to cross-directorships;[278] act with honesty, integrity, and independence of mind to effectively challenge the decisions of senior management where necessary; and effectively oversee and monitor decision-making; in addition, the management body must possess adequate collective knowledge, skills, and experience to be able to understand the market operator's activities (including the main risks).[279] The management body must also include a nomination committee[280] which fulfils the specified conditions and functions (Articles 45(4)). The particular functions of the management body are specified (Article 45(6)).[281] The NCA must refuse authorization where it is not satisfied that the members of the management body are of sufficiently good repute, possess sufficient knowledge, skills, and experience, and commit sufficient time, or if there are objective and demonstrable grounds for believing that the management body of the firm may pose a threat to its effective, sound, and prudent management, and to the adequate consideration of the integrity of the market (Article 45(7)).[282] Under Article 46

---

[274] Authorization must be withdrawn where the regulated market: does not make use of the authorization within 12 months, renounces the authorization, or has not operated for the preceding six months (unless the Member State has provided for authorization to lapse in such cases); has obtained the authorization by making false statements or by any other irregular means; no longer meets the authorization conditions; has seriously and systematically infringed MiFID II; or falls within any of the cases where national law provides for withdrawal.

[275] The market operator is also entitled to exercise the rights conferred on the regulated market under MiFID II.

[276] The management body is the body (or bodies) of the market operator, appointed in accordance with national law, which is empowered to set the entity's strategy, objectives, and overall direction, and which oversees and monitors management decision-making (and includes persons who effectively direct the business of the market operator): 2014 MiFID II Art 4(1)(36).

[277] Ch IV sects 6.4 and 8.6.

[278] No more than one executive directorship with two non-executive directorships, or no more than four non-executive directorships. The restriction applies to market operators that are significant in terms of their size, their internal organization, and the nature, scope, and complexity of their activities. An additional non-executive directorship may be authorized by the NCA.

[279] The overall composition of the management body must reflect an appropriately broad range of experience.

[280] The nomination committee requirement is mandatory only where the operator is significant in terms of its size, its internal organization, and the nature, scope, and complexity of its activities. The functions of the nomination committee are specified and reflect those which apply to investment firms generally (Ch IV sects 6.4 and 8.6).

[281] The management body must define and oversee the implementation of governance arrangements that ensure effective and prudent management of the organization, including the segregation of duties in the organization and prevention of conflicts of interest, in a manner which promotes the integrity of the market. The management body must also monitor and periodically assess the effectiveness of governance arrangements and take appropriate steps to address any deficiencies.

[282] ESMA is to adopt guidelines on the governance regime (Art 45(9)).

(which is considerably lighter than the parallel regime which applies to 'qualifying holdings' in investment firms), those persons in a position to exercise, directly or indirectly, 'significant influence' over the management of the regulated market must be 'suitable':[283] this requirement has the potential to become contentious in a politically sensitive takeover, as the controls which apply with respect to the review of qualifying holdings in investment firms do not apply in this situation.[284]

V.7.3 Operating Requirements

V.7.3.1 General Operating Requirements

The 2014 MiFID II operating regime for regulated markets is relatively high-level, but is more interventionist than the MiFID I regime, particularly with respect to market resilience and liquidity. A series of high-level organizational principles apply under Article 47 (which are not subject to administrative rule-making). The regulated market must have arrangements to clearly identify and manage the potential adverse consequences for the operation of the regulated market, or for its members or participants, of any conflict of interest between the interests of the regulated market, its owners or its operator, and the sound functioning of the regulated market. The market must be adequately equipped to manage the risks to which it is exposed, have the appropriate systems to identify all significant risks to its operation, and put in place effective risk mitigation measures. It must also have arrangements for the sound management of the technical operations of the system (including contingency arrangements), transparent and non-discretionary rules and procedures that support fair and orderly trading and efficient execution, effective arrangements for the finalization of transactions, and sufficient financial resources to facilitate its orderly functioning, having regard to its risk profile. Reflecting the 2014 MiFID II/MiFIR concern to reduce regulatory arbitrage risks, market operators of regulated markets are prohibited from executing client orders against proprietary capital and from engaging in matched principal trading in any of the regulated markets which they operate (this activity is reserved to OTFs and SIs and is regulated accordingly).

V.7.3.2 Market Resilience and Liquidity

Under the 2014 MiFID II, a new and detailed regime, which largely reflects the European Parliament's concern to address algorithmic trading, applies to regulated market resilience (it also applies to MTFs and OTFs by virtue of Article 18(5)). While it imposes specific and detailed operational requirements on regulated markets, and significantly ratchets up the level of harmonization in this area, it is also designed to put in place incentives for market

---

[283] The operator of the regulated market must provide the NCA with, and make public, information regarding the ownership of the regulated market and/or the market operator and, in particular, the identity and scale of interests of any parties in a position to exercise significant influence over management. It must also inform the NCA of, and make public, any transfer of ownership which gives rise to a change in the identity of the persons exercising significant influence over the operation of the regulated market. The NCA may refuse to approve changes to the controlling interests in the regulated market and/or the market operator where there are objective and demonstrable grounds for believing the changes would pose a threat to the sound and prudent management of the regulated market.

[284] See Ch IV sect 6.5 on the investment firm regime.

participants to support liquidity through sustainable trading practices, and to support NCA learning in this complex area and NCA monitoring.

A regulated market must have in place effective systems, procedures, and arrangements to ensure its trading systems are resilient, have sufficient capacity to deal with peak order and messaging volumes, are able to ensure orderly trading under conditions of severe market stress, are fully tested to ensure such conditions are met, and are subject to effective business continuity arrangements (Article 48(1)). Effective systems, procedures, and arrangements must be in place to reject orders that exceed pre-determined price and volume thresholds or are clearly erroneous, and to temporarily halt trading or constrain it if there is a significant price movement in a financial instrument on the market (or a related market) during a short period, as well as, in exceptional cases, to cancel, vary, or correct any transaction (Article 48(4) and (5)). Reflecting the concern to support liquidity which is evident across much of the trading venue regime, the trading halt regime is subject to liquidity conditions to protect liquidity levels.[285]

Systems and procedures[286] must also be in place to ensure that algorithmic trading cannot create or contribute to disorderly trading conditions on the market, and to manage any consequent disorderly trading conditions which arise; in particular, markets must have systems which limit the ratio of unexecuted orders to transactions that may be entered into the system by a member or participant, which slow down the flow of orders if there is a risk of system capacity being reached, and which limit the minimum 'tick size'[287] that may be executed on the market (Article 48(6)).

Regulated markets are also subject to conditions governing 'direct electronic access',[288] which include that markets which permit such access must have in place effective systems, procedures, and arrangements to ensure that market members or participants only provide this service where they are authorized under the 2014 MiFID II or the 2013 CRD IV;[289] that appropriate criteria are set and applied regarding the suitability of persons to whom such access can be provided; and that the member in question retains responsibility for orders and trades made through direct electronic access (Article 48(7)).[290] Regulated markets must also identify, through flagging mechanisms, orders generated through

---

[285] The parameters for halting trading must be appropriately calibrated to take into account the liquidity of the different asset classes engaged, the nature of the market model, and the types of market users, and be sufficient to avoid significant disruption to the orderliness of trading. The parameters (and any material changes) must be reported to the NCA (and by the NCA to ESMA). Where any regulated market which is material in terms of liquidity in a particular instrument halts trading, it must have the necessary systems and procedures to notify NCAs so as to co-ordinate a market-wide response and determine whether halts are required on other venues.

[286] Including requiring members or participants to carry out testing.

[287] Or the minimum increments through which price movements can occur.

[288] Direct electronic access (which supports high frequency trading) relates to the access by persons to a trading venue through a member of or participant in a trading venue: 2014 MiFID II Art 4(1)(41). See further Ch VI sect 2.3.

[289] Directive 2013/36/EC [2013] OJ L176/388 (Capital Requirements Directive (CRD) IV) (which governs the authorization of credit institutions).

[290] The regulated market must also set appropriate standards regarding risk controls and thresholds on trading through such access, and must have arrangements in place to suspend or terminate the provision of direct electronic access. Co-location is also addressed, in that rules on co-location must be transparent, fair, and non-discriminatory (Art 48(8)). See further Ch VI sect 2.3.

algorithmic trading,[291] the different algorithms used for the creation of orders, and the persons initiating these orders, and provide this information to NCAs on request (Article 48(10)). Related fee structures are also regulated; *inter alia*, a regulated market must ensure that its fee structures (including execution fees, ancillary fees, and rebates) are transparent, fair, and non-discriminatory, and do not create incentives to engage in the execution of transactions (such as placing, modifying, or cancelling orders) in a way that contributes to disorderly trading (Article 48(9)). NCAs must also be empowered to have access to a regulated market's order book, in order to monitor trading (Article 48(11)).

More generally, the new regime expressly addresses liquidity risks through market-making requirements (Article 48(2) and (3)).[292] A regulated market must have in place agreements with all investment firms pursuing a market-making strategy on the regulated market. It must also have in place market-making schemes to ensure that a sufficient number of investment firms participate in such agreements which require them to post firm quotes at competitive prices with the result of providing liquidity to the market on a regular and predictable basis, where such a requirement is appropriate to the nature and scale of trading on the regulated market.[293] The regulated market must monitor and enforce compliance with these written agreements and inform the NCA (who may request further disclosures) of their content.

By contrast with the Article 47 organizational regime, a wide-ranging delegation to RTSs provides for the Article 48 regime to be extensively amplified with respect to the algorithmic trading rules and the market-making rules (Article 48(12)).

In a significant intensification of the venue regulation regime, driven by the European Parliament, regulated markets must adopt tick-size regimes for identified equity and equity-like instruments (tick sizes for particular instruments must be calibrated to reflect the liquidity profile of the particular instruments); ESMA may propose RTSs on minimum tick sizes (for these and other instruments) where this is necessary to ensure the orderly functioning of markets (Article 49).[294]

V.7.3.3 Market Access

Access to regulated markets is governed by 2014 MiFID II Article 53, which requires regulated markets to establish, implement, and maintain transparent and non-discriminatory rules, based on objective criteria, which govern access to or membership of the regulated market and which cover the constitution and administration of the regulated market, transactions on the market, the professional standards imposed on those operating on the market, and clearing and settlement (Article 53(1) and (2)). Restrictions are also imposed on those who may be admitted to the market. Authorized investment firms and

---

[291] On this definition see Ch VI sect 2.3.

[292] The liquidity regime also relates to the management of the risks of algorithmic trading in that high frequency traders in practice often act as market-makers, but can pull out in conditions of market stress, destabilizing markets.

[293] The minimum content of the written agreement is specified (including that it specify the obligations of the investment firm with respect to the provision of liquidity and the incentives applicable): Art 48(3).

[294] In a further intensification of regulation, and to support monitoring and supervision, all trading venues and their participants must synchronize their business clocks used for recording reportable events (RTSs will develop this requirement): Art 50.

credit institutions may be admitted, but all others must be of sufficient good repute, have a sufficient level of trading ability and competence, have adequate organizational arrangements, and have sufficient resources for the role they are to perform (Article 53(3)). Members and participants are not required to apply to each other the conduct-of-business requirements imposed under Article 24 (fair treatment and disclosure), Article 25 (suitability and reporting), Article 27 (best execution), and Article 28 (order handling), but these obligations are imposed with respect to their clients when members and participants execute orders on their behalf (Article 53(4)).

Remote access, and the ability of markets to place trading screens across the EU, is the subject of a discrete regime. Under Article 53(5), the rules of a regulated market must provide for direct or remote participation by investment firms and credit institutions. Cross-border access by investment firms is subject to passporting rights under Article 36. It provides that Member States (host Member States) must require that investment firms from other Member States, which are authorized to execute client orders or to deal on own account, have the right of membership or access to regulated markets established in their (the host Member States') territory. This can be achieved by direct access through a branch in the host Member State, or through remote membership or access without having to be established in the home Member State of the regulated market (where the trading procedures and systems in question do not require a physical presence). Member States may not impose any additional regulatory or administrative requirements on investment firms exercising this passport right. Member States must also allow regulated markets from other Member States to provide appropriate arrangements on their territory to facilitate access to, and trading on, those markets by remote members or participants established in their territory (Article 53(6)).[295] A discrete supervision regime applies to remote access (section 12).

V.7.3.4 Market Monitoring and Abusive Conduct

Under the 2014 MiFID II, regulated markets must establish and maintain effective arrangements and procedures (including the necessary resources) for the regular monitoring of compliance with their rules on the part of their members or participants; a related NCA reporting and co-operation regime applies to support pan-EU monitoring of trading (Article 54).[296] Regulated markets must monitor orders sent (including cancellations)[297] and transactions undertaken by their members and participants in order to identify breaches, disorderly trading conditions, conduct that may indicate abusive behaviour under the market abuse regime, or system disruptions in relation to a financial instrument (Article 54(1)). Market operators must also immediately inform their NCAs of significant breaches of their rules, disorderly trading conditions, conduct that may indicate abusive behaviour under the market abuse regime, or system disruptions in relation to a financial instrument (Article 54(2)). The NCAs in question must then notify ESMA and the NCAs

---

[295] To support effective supervision, the regulated market must communicate to its home NCA the Member State in which it intends to provide these arrangements, and the home NCA must, at the request of the host NCA, communicate the identity of the members or participants of the regulated market established in the host State.

[296] The reporting and co-operation regime was significantly strengthened under MiFID II to enhance market monitoring and supervision.

[297] In order to capture algorithmic/high frequency trading.

of other Member States. Given the danger of prejudice to the parties concerned, where the conduct in question relates to behaviour which may indicate abusive behaviour—in a potentially troublesome requirement—the NCA in question must be convinced that market abuse is being or has been carried out before it notifies other NCAs or ESMA. Additionally, market operators must supply the relevant information to the authority responsible for the investigation and prosecution of market abuse on the regulated market without undue delay, and provide full assistance to that authority (Article 54(3)).[298]

V.7.3.5 Transparency Rules

Extensive pre- and post-trade transparency requirements apply to regulated markets (and to MTFs and OTFs) under the 2014 MiFIR, and are discussed in section 11.

V.7.4 Admission of Financial Instruments to Trading and Suspension and Removal of Instruments

These requirements relate to capital-raising and are considered in Chapter II section 7.2.1. The most significant reforms introduced by the 2014 MiFID II relate to the procedures governing pan-EU co-ordination between NCAs on the suspension or removal of an instrument from trading on a regulated market.

V.8 Operational Regulation of Multilateral Trading: Multilateral Trading Facilities

The operation of an MTF is characterized as an investment service under the 2014 MiFID II/MiFIR.[299] Investment firms which operate MTFs are accordingly subject to the authorization and operational requirements which apply to the provision of investment services under MiFID II and, with respect to prudential regulation, under the 2013 CRD IV/ CRR.[300] An MTF (or OTF) can be operated by a market operator, but the operator must verify in advance its compliance with MiFID II.[301] In addition, a discrete regime (under MiFID II) which is designed to track the regulated market regime with respect to the regulation of trading functionality applies in relation to the venue-specific risks posed by the operation of an MTF; this regime, with calibrations designed to reflect their non-discretionary trading functionality, also applies to OTFs.

Under MiFID II, where an investment firm (or market operator) seeks to operate an MTF, the usual investment firm authorization process (covering, *inter alia*, firm governance, qualifying shareholders, and initial capital) applies, save that the NCA must also be provided with a detailed description of the functioning of the MTF (or OTF);[302] every

---

[298] Administrative rules will govern the circumstances which trigger the Art 54(1) reporting requirements: Art 54(4).

[299] MiFID II Annex I, sect A (8).

[300] n 289 and Capital Requirements Regulation (CRR) (EU) No 575/2013 [2013] OJ L176/1.

[301] 2014 MiFID II Art 5(2).

[302] Including details of any links to or participation by a regulated market, MTF, OTF, or SI owned by the same investment firm or market operator.

authorization to an investment firm or market operator to operate an MTF (or OTF) must also be notified to ESMA, which must establish a list of all MTFs and OTFs in the EU (Article 18(10)).[303] The Article 16 organizational requirements for investment firms also apply,[304] and are supplemented by the Article 18 trading process requirements (which also apply to OTFs) and by MTF-specific requirements (Article 19).

Article 18 governs the MTF/OTF trading process, admission of financial instruments, venue access, conflicts of interest, and venue resilience. Investment firms or market operators operating an MTF or OTF must, in addition to meeting the Article 16 organizational requirements, establish transparent rules and procedures for fair and orderly trading, and establish objective criteria for the efficient execution of orders; they must also have in place arrangements for the sound management of the technical operations of the facility, including the establishment of effective contingency arrangements to cope with system disruption risks (Article 18(1)). In addition, an MTF (this requirement does not apply to OTFs) must, reflecting the Article 47 regime which applies to regulated markets, and the 2014 MiFID II/MiFIR concern to align MTF and regulated market regulation, be adequately equipped to manage the risks to which it is exposed, have effective arrangements to facilitate the efficient and timely finalization of transactions, and have available, at the time of authorization and on an ongoing basis, sufficient financial resources to facilitate its orderly functioning (having regard to the nature and extent of the transactions concluded on the market, and the range and degree of risk to which it is exposed). The Article 48/49 regime governing regulated markets' systems' resilience also applies to MTFs and OTFs (Article 18(5)). Additionally, reflecting their non-discretionary trading functionality, MTFs must establish and implement non-discretionary rules for the execution of orders in the system (Article 19(1)). MTFs, as non-discretionary multilateral venues (and as is also the case for regulated markets), may not execute client orders against proprietary capital or engage in matched principal trading (Article 19(5)).

MTFs (and OTFs) are not subject to detailed admission-to-trading rules, reflecting their characterization under MiFID II as secondary market trading-services providers (and not, by contrast with regulated markets, as primary market capital-raising-services providers).[305] Investment firms or market operators are subject only to the obligation to establish transparent rules regarding the criteria for determining the financial instruments that can be traded under their systems; they must, however, provide, or be satisfied that there is access to, sufficient publicly available information to enable users to form an investment judgment, taking into account the nature of the users and the types of instrument traded (Article 18(2)).[306] The regime for suspending and removing financial instruments tracks

---

[303] ITSs will govern the content and format of the description and notification required: Art 18(11).

[304] As do the other MiFID II operational requirements (including the Art 23 conflicts of interest regime), although the conduct-of-business regime is dis-applied from transactions between MTF/OTF members, participants, or users (the 2013 CRD IV/CRR regime is also applicable). See further Ch IV sect 7.2.

[305] Although MTFs in the form of SME Growth Markets are exceptions in this regard and are subject to admission conditions. See further Ch II sect 7.1.2.

[306] As under the regulated markets regime, where a transferable security, which is admitted to trading on a regulated market, has been admitted to an MTF (or OTF) without the issuer's consent, the issuer is not subject to any obligations relating to initial, ongoing, and *ad hoc* disclosure with regard to the MTF (or OTF): 2014 MiFID II Art 18(8).

that which applies to regulated markets (Article 32),[307] and accordingly provides for cross-venue and pan-EU suspension or removal of financial instruments (and related derivatives) in certain situations.[308]

Access rules also apply.[309] Investment firms and market operators operating MTFs (or OTFs) must establish, publish, maintain, and implement transparent and non-discriminatory rules, based on objective criteria, governing access to the trading facility (Article 18(3)). MTFs are additionally required to admit as members or participants only investment firms; credit institutions authorized under the 2013 CRD IV/CRR; and other persons who are of sufficient good repute, have a sufficient level of trading ability, competence, and experience, and have adequate organizational arrangements and sufficient resources for the role they are to perform (Article 19(2) and Article 53(3)).[310] A discrete regime governs cross-border/remote access (Article 34(6) and (7)—noted later in the section). As under the regulated market regime, the conduct obligations of Articles 24, 25, 27, and 28 do not apply to transactions concluded under the rules governing an MTF between its members and participants, or between the MTF and its members and participants in relation to the use of the MTF, but they do apply where members or participants act on behalf of clients by executing orders through an MTF (Article 19(4)).

Reflecting the potential for conflicts of interest where a firm operates an MTF (or OTF), arrangements must be in place to clearly identify and manage the potential adverse consequences for the operation of the MTF (or OTF), or for the members or participants and users, of any conflicts of interest between the interests of the MTF (or OTF), its owners, or the investment firm or market operator operating the MTF (or OTF), and the sound operation of the MTF (or OTF) (Article 18(4)).

Reflecting a recurring theme of MiFID II/MiFIR, a liquidity-supporting condition applies which requires that each MTF or OTF has at least three materially active members or users, each having the opportunity to interact with all the others in respect of price formation (Article 18(7)).

MTFs (and OTFs) are also subject to market monitoring rules that replicate those which apply to regulated markets. Accordingly, investment firms and market operators of MTFs (and OTFs) must establish and maintain effective arrangements and procedures, relevant to the MTF (or OTF), for the regular monitoring of compliance with MTF (OTF) rules on

---

[307] Investment firms and market operators operating MTFs and OTFs are also required to comply immediately with any instructions from their NCAs to suspend or remove a financial instrument from trading: Art 18(9).

[308] See further Ch II sect 7.2.1.

[309] MTF/other platform access requirements have been contentious on occasion. Membership of bond-trading platforms, eg, experienced some controversy pre-crisis following the growth of demands from hedge funds for direct access to trading platforms. The demand by US hedge fund Citadel for access to the MTS government bond-trading platform, eg, generated some controversy, with concerns expressed that direct hedge-fund access could result in aggressive trading strategies: Tett, G and Chung, J, 'Hedge Funds are at the Gates of the Eurozone's Cosy Bond Club', *Financial Times*, 13 March 2007, 15. See also Dunne, P, 'Transparency Proposals for European Sovereign Bonds Markets' (2007) 15 *JFRC* 186.

[310] These requirements are broadly similar to the regulated market regime, save that regulated markets are required to adopt rules specifying the obligations of members or participants, and the passporting rules on direct/remote access to regulated markets do not apply (given the discrete MTF/OTF passporting right which applies).

the part of members, participants, or users; they must also monitor the orders sent (including cancellations) and transactions undertaken by their members, participants, or users under their systems in order to identify breaches of those rules, disorderly trading conditions, conduct that may indicate abusive behaviour under the market abuse regime, or system disruptions in relation to a financial instrument. In addition, they must deploy the resources necessary to ensure that such monitoring is effective (Article 31(1)). Investment firms and markets operators operating an MTF (or OTF) must also immediately inform their NCAs of significant breaches of their rules, disorderly trading conditions, conduct that may indicate abusive behaviour under the market abuse regime, or system disruptions in relation to a financial instrument (Article 31(2)). The NCAs in question[311] must then notify ESMA and the NCAs of other Member States; as under the regulated markets regime, where the conduct in question relates to behaviour which may indicate abusive behaviour, the NCA must be convinced that market abuse is being or has been carried out before it notifies other NCAs or ESMA. Additionally, investment firms and market operators operating an MTF (or OTF) must also supply without undue delay the relevant information to the authority responsible for the investigation and prosecution of market abuse, and provide full assistance to that authority (Article 31(3)).

Passport rights in relation to MTFs (and OTFs) (in effect, the right to set up remote screens) are governed by Article 34(6), which, in the context of the investment firm freedom to provide services, allows investment firms and market operators operating MTFs (and OTFs) from other Member States to provide appropriate 'arrangements' in host Member States to facilitate access to and use of their systems by remote users or participants established in the host Member State territory. Article 34(7) imposes a notification obligation, which tracks that imposed on the provision of investment services generally (see Chapter IV section 9), according to which the firm or operator must communicate to its home NCA the State in which it plans to provide such arrangements. The home NCA must communicate the information to the host NCA within one month. The home NCA must also, on the request of the host NCA, communicate the identity of the members or participants in the MTF who are established in the home Member State.

MTFs and OTFs are also subject to broadly the same transparency regime as applies to regulated markets (section 11).

V.9 Operational Regulation of Multilateral Trading: Organized Trading Facilities

The OTF regime is, in nearly all respects, the same as that which applies to MTFs, as outlined above. Accordingly, investment firms or market operators operating an OTF are subject to the 2014 MiFID II/MiFIR authorization and organizational regime and the 2013 CRD IV/CRR prudential regime; they are also subject to the venue-specific

---

[311] On the home NCA of an investment firm see Ch IV sect 6.1. The market operator home NCA is that of the relevant regulated market (n 271).

requirements which apply under MiFID II Article 18 (trading processes and access),[312] Article 31 (market monitoring), and Article 32 (removal and suspension of instruments), as well as to the trading transparency regime which applies to regulated markets and MTFs.

As discretionary venues, however, OTFs are subject to conditions (Article 20) on how discretion can be exercised and on the extent to which they can engage in proprietary trading, as discussed in section 6.4. Similarly, transactions within OTFs are subject to client-facing conduct regulation (Article 20).

V.10 Operational Regulation of the OTC Sector: Dealing on Own Account

V.10.1 Systematic Internalizers

The SI venue sits within the OTC/bilateral space, and accordingly does not trigger the 2014 MiFID II/MiFIR regime for trading venues. SIs are authorized and regulated as investment firms, although they must notify their NCA of their SI status (ESMA must maintain a list of all SIs in the EU) (MiFIR Article 15(1)). Classification as an SI is of critical importance as it subjects the investment firm, dealing on own account by executing client orders, to tailored pre-trade transparency requirements; otherwise, the OTC sector, unlike organized multilateral venues (regulated markets, MTFs, and OTFs) is dark pre-trade. Like all investment firms, SIs are also subject to post-trade transparency requirements. SIs, as investment firms, are subject to the generic authorization, organizational, and conduct rules which apply under MiFID II/MiFIR and 2013 CRD IV/CRR, including the trading rules discussed in Chapter VI. Similarly, they benefit from passporting rights in respect of their internalization activities (Chapter IV section 9).

V.10.2 Dealing on Own Account

Investment firms who deal on own account, but who do not fall within the SI (or other) classification, are not subject to distinct venue-like requirements under the 2014 MiFID II/MiFIR, although post-trade transparency requirements apply under MiFIR (section 11).[313] These firms are subject to the MiFID II/MiFIR authorization, organizational, and conduct regimes (although in practice, many conduct rules are dis-applied where the trades are between eligible counterparties)[314] and benefit from the related passporting rights, and are subject to the 2013 CRD IV/CRR prudential regime. They are also subject to the array of requirements which apply to trading practices generally (including with respect to algorithmic trading and short selling) discussed in Chapter VI.

---

[312] In the case of an OTF, these requirements in practice apply to the firm's clients and, with respect to access, govern how the OTF establishes which clients have access to the OTF.

[313] Under 2014 MiFID II Art 1(7), all transactions in financial instruments which are not concluded on multilateral systems or SIs must be in compliance with the MiFIR post-trade transparency regime.

[314] 2014 MiFID II Art 30. See further Ch IV sect 5.2.

V.11 Transparency Regulation and the 2014 MiFIR

V.11.1 Regulated Markets, MTFs, and OTFs: Equity Market Transparency

V.11.1.1 Pre-trade Transparency

The pre-trade transparency regime for equity and equity-like instruments (MiFIR Articles 3–4) applies to all trading venues (regulated markets, MTFs, and OTFs). Market operators and investment firms operating a trading venue must make public current bid and offer prices and the depth of trading interest at those prices which are advertised through their systems for shares, depositary receipts, ETFs, certificates, and similar financial instruments traded on a trading venue;[315] the transparency requirement also applies to actionable indications of interests (Article 3(1)).[316] The equity trading transparency regime has accordingly been significantly extended from MiFID I, which applied only to shares admitted to trading on a regulated market and excluded shares admitted to MTFs and functionally similar instruments. Reflecting the MiFID II/MiFIR focus on trading-method- and asset-based, not venue-based, calibration, the transparency requirements are to be calibrated to different types of trading system, including order-book, quote-driven, hybrid, and periodic auction trading systems (Article 3(2)). ESMA will shape the new transparency regime, being charged with proposing RTSs which cover the range of bid and offer prices or designated market-maker quotes and the depth of trading interest at those prices, to be made public, taking into account the required Article 3(2) calibration (Article 4(6)). Although the new regime extends beyond shares admitted to trading on a regulated market, the RTSs can be expected to reflect the detailed rules which applied to pre-trade transparency for shares under the 2006 Commission MiFID I Regulation.[317]

---

[315] Some Member States had already extended the MiFID I equity regime to depositary receipts, ETFs, and certificates, but there was a lack of consistency across the EU. CESR accordingly advised that the regime be extended to equity-like instruments, given their economic similarity to shares. 2010 CESR Equity Market Technical Advice, n 129, 25–8.

[316] An actionable indication of interest is a message from one member or participant to another within a trading system in relation to available trading interest, and that contains all necessary information to agree on a trade: 2014 MiFIR Art 2(1)(33).

[317] The 2006 Commission MiFID I Regulation (Art 17) set out transparency requirements according to the three most common forms of trading mechanism employed by MTFs and regulated markets. Pre-trade transparency for continuous auction order book trading systems required publication continuously throughout the system's normal trading hours of the aggregate number of orders and of the shares those orders represented at each price level, for the first five best bid and offer prices. A quote-driven trading system was to make public continuously throughout its normal trading hours the best bid and offer price of each market-maker in the share (published quotes were to represent binding commitments to buy and sell), along with the volumes attached to those prices. Finally, where the system employed a periodic auction trading system, it was to publish the price (for each share) that would best satisfy the system's trading algorithm and the volume which would potentially be executable at that price by participants in the system. Where the system did not fall into one of these categories, it was to maintain a standard of pre-trade transparency that ensured that adequate information would be made public as to the price levels of orders or quotes as well as the level of trading interest in the relevant shares. But the five best bid and offer price levels and/or two-way quotes of each market-maker in that share were to be made public (as long as the system's price discovery mechanism allowed this).

V.11.1.2 Pre-trade Transparency Waivers

Under MiFID I, dark pool share trading within regulated trading venues (then regulated markets and MTFs) was permitted in relation to four pre-trade transparency waivers: the reference price, negotiated trades, order management facility, and large-in-scale waivers. These waivers were designed to provide waivers from pre-trade transparency in circumstances where the risks of prejudice to price formation were reduced but the liquidity and position risks were high if the trades were exposed under transparency requirements.[318] The reference price waiver, for example, covered passive price-taking systems that matched supply and demand, but without price discovery and at a fixed reference price, while the negotiated trades waiver was designed to protect, *inter alia*, orders subject to conditions other than the current market practice and which could not be filled through central trading systems.[319] Over the MiFID I Review, dark pool equity trading under waivers in regulated markets and MTFs came under scrutiny, with the extent to which trading venues should be permitted to operate equity dark pools one of the most contested elements of the MiFID II/MiFIR Council negotiations. Sharp differences arose between those Member States adopting a restrictive approach and seeking to expose as much equity trading as possible to the price-formation process and those concerned to protect dark equity trading and the specialist liquidity and trading needs of traders, particularly institutional investors.[320] The large-in-scale waiver was generally uncontroversial.[321] Most attention focused on the negotiated trades and reference price waivers,[322] in relation to which NCAs had previously clashed as to whether particular waivers permitted by other NCAs under these two waiver categories met the MiFID I conditions, with opinions differing on whether particular waivers prejudiced price formation.[323] The highly detailed compromise finally adopted[324] was to continue to base the waiver regime on the broad categories of waiver available under MiFID I, but to impose more restrictive conditions on the reference price

---

[318] 2006 Commission MiFID I Regulation Arts 18–20 and 2014 MiFID I Arts 29(2) and 44(2).

[319] 2010 CESR Equity Market Consultation, n 53, 11.

[320] As waivers tend to be deployed in a small number of Member States, reflecting the concentration of different types of specialist trading in particular financial markets, the risks for certain Member States were more significant were waivers to be restricted, and political tensions were, as a result, significant. The contested reference price waiver, eg, was only available in four Member States at the time of the MiFID I Review: 2010 CESR Equity Market Consultation, n 53, 10.

[321] CESR reported that the waiver remained justified but was used relatively rarely: 2010 Equity Market Consultation, n 53, 8.

[322] The Commission and several Member States sought to limit the waiver regime to the traditional large-in-scale waiver only. Other Member States were in favour of retaining the other waivers, notably the reference price and negotiated trades waivers: Danish Presidency MiFID II/MiFIR Progress Report, n 207, 6.

[323] Under the CESR-initiated process (noted later in this section) for adopting a common CESR position on the compliance of waivers granted by NCAs under MiFID I, reference price waivers proved problematic, with a qualified majority vote (rather than a consensus position) being required for four waivers, and with France, Italy, and Greece raising objections on the grounds that the CESR position did not ensure that price formation was protected. CESR's equity market consultation noted the growth in reliance on this waiver (which supported the main trading functionality in some MTFs), and related concern that small orders were being transacted under the reference price waiver although it was designed to protect against market impact: 2010 CESR Equity Market Consultation, n 53, 11. The negotiated trades waiver also caused difficulties, with one waiver requiring a qualified majority CESR vote. The order management facility and large-in-scale waivers, however, were not problematic and CESR positions were adopted by consensus: ESMA, Waivers from Pre-Trade Transparency. CESR Positions and ESMA Opinions (2012) (ESMA/2012/206).

[324] The compromise incorporates into the legislative framework much of the operational detail relating to the MiFID I waivers contained in the 2006 Commission MiFID I Regulation, but also contains additional restrictions and finesses which emerged through the trilogue in particular.

and negotiated trades waivers, to subject these waivers to a new volume cap,[325] and to confer ESMA with enhanced powers with respect to waivers. Overall, MiFIR II/MiFIR has restricted the ability of trading venues to operate equity dark pools.

Under the MiFIR pre-trade equity/equity-like transparency waiver regime for trading venues (Article 4), NCAs may waive pre-trade transparency requirements for four types of trading systems. The first waiver (Article 4(1)(a), the reference price waiver) applies to systems which match orders based on a trading methodology by which the price of the equity/equity-like instrument in question is derived from the trading venue where the instrument was first admitted to trading, or the 'most relevant market in terms of liquidity',[326] where that reference price[327] is widely published and regarded by market participants as a reliable reference price. This waiver is subject to the new volume cap, outlined later in this section.

The second waiver (Article 4(1)(b), the negotiated trade waiver) applies to systems that formalize negotiated transactions which are either made within the current volume-weighted spread reflected on the order book or in the quotes of the market-makers of the trading venue operating the system (in this case, the waiver is subject to the new volume cap), or are in an illiquid share, depositary receipt, ETF, certificate or similar financial instrument that does not fall within the meaning of a 'liquid market',[328] and are dealt in within a percentage of a suitable reference price,[329] being a percentage and a reference price set in advance by the system operator, or are subject to conditions other than the current market price of that financial instrument. Trades carried out under the negotiated trades waiver must be carried out in accordance with the rules of the trading venue, and the trading venue must ensure that arrangements, systems, and procedures are in place to prevent and detect market abuse and must establish, maintain, and implement systems to detect attempts to use the waiver to circumvent MiFID II/MiFIR (and to report such attempts to the NCA); the use of the waiver must be monitored by the NCA to ensure the governing conditions are complied with (Article 4(3)).

The third waiver (Article 4(1)(c)) is a classic pre-trade transparency waiver in that it applies to orders that are large-in-scale compared with normal market size. The fourth applies to orders (sometimes termed 'iceberg orders') held in an order management facility of the trading venue pending disclosure (Article 4(1)(d)).[330]

---

[325] The rules governing dark pool waivers, including the volume limit, were regarded by the Council as a major element of its MiFID II/MiFIR agreement and as a significant limitation on dark pool trading: Irish Presidency reaches Breakthrough on New Proposals for Safe and More Open Financial Markets. Irish Presidency Press Release, 17 June 2013.

[326] The conditions imposed on the choice of trading venue from which the reference price is taken represent a tightening of the MiFID I waiver (and were introduced during the trilogue).

[327] The reference price is either the midpoint within the current bid and offer prices of the trading venue where the financial instrument was first admitted to trading or the most relevant market in terms of liquidity, or, where this price is not available, the open and/or closing prices of the relevant trading session (orders may only reference these prices outside the continuous trading phase of the relevant trading session): Art 4(1)(2).

[328] Sect 11.5.

[329] The illiquid instrument category of negotiated trade is an addition from MiFID I and an extension of the original negotiated trade waiver.

[330] These waivers have not changed from MiFID I.

The operational detail of the waiver regime will be contained in RTSs to be proposed by ESMA (Article 4(6)). These are to cover the 'most relevant market in terms of liquidity' for the reference price waiver; the specific characteristics of the negotiated transactions which come within the negotiated trades waiver (in relation to the different ways in which the trading venue member or participant can execute the transaction);[331] the negotiated transactions that do not contribute to price formation and which avail of the negotiated trades waiver as they are subject to conditions other than the current market price of the instrument; the size of orders that are large-in-scale;[332] and the type and minimum size of order held in an order management facility of a trading venue which benefit from the order management facility waiver (Article 4(6)).

A new procedure applies to the waiver regime (Article 4(4)). Under MiFID I, waiver decisions were at the discretion of NCAs but were in practice managed through CESR and, subsequently, ESMA. Under a voluntary arrangement agreed by NCAs, NCAs notified CESR of their proposed waiver, which adopted a common NCA position on the compliance of the proposed NCA waiver with MiFID I; ESMA continued this process, albeit through its powers to adopt opinions under 2010 ESMA Regulation Article 29. While agreement proved difficult to reach with respect to the reference price and negotiated trade waivers,[333] many NCA waivers were subject to positive CESR positions or ESMA opinions. This process has now been formalized. Before granting a waiver under Article 4, an NCA must (not less than four months before the waiver is intended to take effect) notify ESMA and the other NCAs of its proposed waiver decision, and provide an explanation regarding the waiver.[334] Within two months, ESMA must issue a non-binding opinion to the NCA which assesses the waiver's compatibility with MiFIR. Where the NCA grants the waiver and another NCA disagrees, the NCA granting the waiver may refer the waiver to ESMA, and ESMA may exercise its binding mediation powers under 2010 ESMA Regulation Article 19 (Chapter XI sect 5.3.1). The application of the Article 4 waivers is also to be monitored by ESMA, who is to report annually to the Commission on their application in practice; ESMA is also to review all waivers by January 2019 and to issue an opinion to the NCAs concerned on the continued compatibility of the waivers with MiFIR (Article 4(4) and (7)). Although the proposal by some Member States that ESMA be empowered to take a binding decision on waivers was not adopted, reflecting the concern of other Member States as to the validity of such a conferral of power on ESMA, the peer review dynamics exerted by ESMA opinions and the potential for binding ESMA mediation is likely to make it less common that NCAs adopt waivers which are not accepted by the other NCAs.

---

[331] This delegation was also conferred under MiFID I and was amplified by the 2006 Commission MiFID I Regulation Art 19, which set out the types of activities (including dealing on own account with another venue member or participant) which qualified as leading to negotiated transactions.

[332] This delegation was also conferred under MiFID I, but applied only in relation to shares admitted to trading on a regulated market. An order was considered to be large-in-scale where it was equal or larger than the minimum order size set out in the Regulation (all shares admitted to trading on a regulated market were classified in accordance with their average daily turnover): 2006 Commission MiFID I Regulation Art 30.

[333] n 323.

[334] Including with respect to the trading venue from which the reference price is taken for the reference price waiver.

NCAs may withdraw waivers, either under their own initiative or on the request of another NCA, where they observe the waiver is being used in a manner that deviates from its original purpose, or if they consider the waiver is being used to circumvent MiFIR (Article 4(5)).[335]

The most significant change to the waiver regime from MiFID I relates to the new volume cap.[336] The negotiated trades and reference price waivers are subject to a volume cap which is designed to ensure that these waivers do not unduly harm price formation (Article 5). The cap rule provides that the percentage of trading in a financial instrument carried out on a trading venue under these waivers must be limited to 4 per cent of the total volume of trading in that financial instrument on all trading venues across the EU over the previous 12-month period. A further restriction applies in that overall EU trading in the financial instrument and carried out under these waivers must be limited to 8 per cent of the total volume of trading in the instrument on all trading venues across the EU over the previous 12-month period. This restriction does not apply to negotiated transactions in a share, depositary receipt, ETF, certificate or other similar financial instrument for which there is not a liquid market (section 11.5), and which are dealt in within a percentage of a suitable reference price (determined in accordance with the reference price waiver conditions), or to negotiated transactions that are subject to conditions other than the current market price. Where the trading volume exceeds the set percentage in relation to trading on a particular venue (based on data provided by ESMA),[337] the NCA that authorized the waiver must suspend its use for six months (Article 5(2)). Where the percentage limit for all EU trading is exceeded, all NCAs must suspend the waivers for six months (Article 5(3)).

V.11.1.3 Post-trade Transparency

Market operators and investment firms operating a trading venue must also make public the price, volume, and time of transactions executed in respect of shares, depositary receipts, ETFs, certificates, and other similar financial instruments traded on a trading venue (Article 6(1)). RTSs will govern the post-trade transparency information to be made available by trading venues (as well as SIs and investment firms—section 11.3.2) for each class of equity/equity-like financial instrument, including the required identifiers for the different types of transactions (Article 7(2)(a)).

V.11.1.4 Deferred Publication of Post-trade Transparency

Mirroring the pre-trade regime, the equity/equity-like post-trade regime contains publication deferrals designed to protect certain transactions from liquidity and position risk (Article 7). The post-trade regime is not, however, calibrated to the particular functionalities of different market models, as the risks to competition and efficiency are not as acute as they are in the pre-trade context. Nonetheless, liquidity providers face significant market

---

[335] In this case, ESMA and the other NCAs must be notified.

[336] The cap was fiercely resisted by segments of the industry as exposing institutional traders unnecessarily to the risks of lit trading, increasing market impact costs (particularly given the increased risk of exposure to algorithmic traders), and increasing the cost of trading and reducing returns across the EU: Loven, P, 'Proposed EU Regulation Could Risk Savings', *Financial Times, Fund Management Supplement*, 17 June 2013, 6.

[337] Procedures apply to the collation and publication by ESMA of the data needed to monitor trading volumes.

impact risks where a position is being unwound. NCAs are accordingly empowered to authorize market operators and investment firms operating a trading venue to provide for deferred publication of transaction details, based on transaction type or size. In particular, NCAs may authorize deferred publication in respect of transactions that are large-in-scale as compared with the normal market size of that share or equity-like instrument (Article 7(1)). Market operators and investment firms must obtain the NCA's prior approval for deferred publication and clearly disclose these arrangements to market participants and the public. As in the pre-trade context, ESMA is to monitor the application of deferred publication arrangements and to submit an annual report to the Commission. Where an NCA disagrees with a deferral determination by another NCA, the NCA can refer the matter to ESMA binding mediation (2010 ESMA Regulation Article 19) (Chapter XI sect 5.3.1).

The operational criteria governing deferred publication will be governed by RTSs setting out the conditions for authorizing trading venues (and SIs and investments firms) to provide for deferred publication, and the criteria to be applied when deciding the transactions for which, due to their size or the type of instrument involved, deferred publication is allowed.[338]

V.11.2 Regulated Markets, MTFs, and OTFs: Non-equity Market Transparency

V.11.2.1. Pre-trade Transparency

In a major change from MiFID I, a new pre-trade transparency regime applies to specified non-equity instruments (Article 8). Market operators and investment firms operating a trading venue must make public current bid and offer prices and the depth of trading interests at those prices (including with respect to actionable indications of interest) for bonds, structured-finance products, emission allowances, and derivatives traded on a trading venue (Article 8(1)). This requirement does not apply to derivative transactions of non-financial counterparties, which are objectively measurable as reducing risks relating to the commercial activity or treasury financing activity of the non-financial counterparty or its group. This concession reflects the concern across crisis-era EU securities and markets regulation to mitigate the effects of the extension of regulation over the derivatives markets for non-financial counterparties who use derivatives to hedge commercial risks (see also Chapter VI).

The new regime is to be calibrated to reflect the array of different systems engaged in the non-equity space, including order-book, quote-driven, hybrid, periodic auction trading, and voice broking systems (Article 8(2)). The detail of the new transparency regime will be set out in RTSs to be proposed by ESMA, which will cover the range of bid and offer prices

---

[338] Under the 2006 Commission MiFID I Regulation which applied only to shares admitted to trading on a regulated market, a deferral could be granted where the transaction was between an investment firm dealing on own account and a client of the firm, and where the size of the transactions was equal to or exceeded the minimum qualifying size specified in the Regulation (Art 28). The Regulation set out the permitted publication delay for specified classes of shares (classed in terms of their daily turnover/liquidity) and the related minimum qualifying size of transaction for the permitted delays. A 'ladder' model applied, which allowed for increasingly longer delays according to the liquidity of the share in question and the size of the transaction: the greater the size of the transaction, the longer the permissible delay.

or quotes and the depth of trading interests at those prices, or indicative pre-trade bid and offer prices which are close to the price of the trading interest, to be made public for each class of instrument concerned, taking into account the necessary calibrations for different types of trading system (Article 9(5)).

V.11.2.2 Pre-trade Transparency Waivers

The related waiver regime is of critical importance, given the scale of the potential liquidity risks which flow from the dealer-based nature of much of the organized trading in this segment,[339] and the array of instruments and trading systems involved. Under Article 9, NCAs may waive pre-trade transparency requirements in three circumstances: as under the equity regime, with respect to orders which are large-in-scale compared with normal market size and with respect to orders held in an order management facility of the trading venue pending disclosure; with respect to actionable indications of interest in request-for-quote and voice-trading systems that are above a size specific to the instrument, which size would expose liquidity providers to undue risk and takes into account whether the relevant market participants are retail or wholesale investors;[340] and, in a potentially very wide carve-out from the transparency regime, with respect to derivatives which are not subject to the MiFID II/MiFIR trading obligation (Chapter VI section 4.3) and other financial instruments for which there is not a liquid market (Article 9(1)).

Where a waiver is granted in respect of request-for-quote and voice-trading systems, some degree of transparency is provided, as the market operator or investment firm must make public at least indicative pre-trade bid and offer prices which are close to the price of the trading interests advertised through the relevant system; this information must be made available to the public through appropriate electronic means on a continuous basis during normal trading hours, and the arrangements adopted must ensure that the information is provided on a reasonable commercial basis and on a non-discriminatory basis (Article 8(4)).[341]

The ESMA-based waiver process which applies to equity/equity-like pre-trade transparency waivers applies to the non-equity waivers, as does the regime governing the withdrawal of waivers (Article 9(2) and (3)). Extensive RTSs will be adopted on the non-equity pre-trade transparency regime and will cover the size of orders that are large-in-scale and the type and minimum size of orders held in an order management facility which qualify for waivers, the operation of the request-for-quote and voice-trading system waiver,[342] and the financial

---

[339] As was acknowledged by the Commission in its 2011 MiFID II/MiFIR Proposals Impact Assessment: n 93, 12.

[340] This waiver, which was added during the Council negotiations, was contentious, with Member States divided as to its appropriateness: Cyprus Presidency MiFID II/MiFIR Progress Report, n 207, 5. The other waivers, particularly the waiver relating to derivatives, were also contentious, with the Commission, France, and Italy all recording their objections on the adoption of MiFIR: 7 May 2014, Council Document 9344/14.

[341] This additional disclosure obligation reflects the significant Council controversy which attended the availability of the request-for-quote/voice trading waiver.

[342] RTSs will govern the size (specific to the instrument in question) that would expose liquidity providers to undue risk (and taking into account whether the market participants are retail or wholesale). ESMA is to take into account whether, at such sizes, liquidity providers would be able to hedge their risks and, where a market in the instrument (or class of instruments) consists in part of retail investors, the average value of transactions undertaken by those investors.

instruments or classes of financial instrument for which there is not a liquid market (Article 9(5)).

The liquidity risks engaged by the new transparency regime (as well the extent to which the non-equity markets may remain dark) are underlined by the power given to NCAs to suspend transparency requirements where liquidity is compromised (Article 9(4)). The NCA responsible for supervising one or more trading venues on which a class of bond, structured-finance product, emission allowance, or derivative is traded may, where the liquidity of the class of financial instrument falls below a 'specified threshold', temporarily suspend pre-trade transparency requirements; the suspension is valid for an initial period not exceeding three months and may be renewed for further three-month periods if the grounds for suspension continue to be applicable. The threshold is to be based on objective criteria specific to the market for the financial instrument concerned, and will be governed by RTSs.[343] ESMA is closely engaged with any suspension; the relevant NCA must notify ESMA before it takes action (whether to suspend or renew the suspension). ESMA must also issue an opinion to the NCA as soon as is practical on whether the suspension is justified (Article 9(4)).

V.11.2.3 Post-trade Transparency

The new post-trade regime for these specified non-equity instruments follows the equity trading regime, and requires that market operators and investment firms operating a trading venue make public the price, volume, and time of the transactions (Article 10(1)). The details of this regime (which also applies to SIs and investment firms) will be governed by RTSs (Article 11(4)).

V.11.2.4 Post-trade Transparency Deferred Publication

As under the equity/equity-like regime, a deferred publication regime applies. NCAs are empowered to authorize market operators and investment firms operating a trading venue to provide for deferred publication of the details of transactions, based on the size or type of the transaction (Article 11(1)). In particular, NCAs may authorize deferred publication in respect of transactions that are large-in-scale compared with normal market size for the instrument in question or for that class of instrument; are related to an instrument or class of instrument for which there is not a liquid market; or are above a size specific to the instrument which would expose liquidity providers to undue risk, and which size takes into account whether the relevant market participants are retail or wholesale investors. The conditions under which deferrals can be authorized will be governed by RTSs (Article 11(4)).

In addition, and as with the pre-trade transparency regime, NCAs may suspend post-trade obligations where liquidity falls below a specified threshold (Article 11(2)).

The risks to liquidity are further addressed by Article 11(3), which empowers NCAs to require or allow different disclosures in conjunction with the authorization of a post-trade

---

[343] While Member States are to calculate the threshold, RTSs will govern the methods and parameters for calculating the liquidity threshold, and the threshold must be set in such a way that when the threshold is reached it represents a significant decline in liquidity across all venues in the EU for the financial instrument concerned, based on the MiFIR definition of a liquid market (on which, see sect 11.5).

deferral. An NCA may request the publication of limited details of a transaction or details of several transactions in an aggregated form (or a combination thereof) during the time period of the deferral period; allow the omission of the publication of the volume of an individual transaction during an extended time period of deferral; allow (with respect to non-equity instruments that are not sovereign debt) publication of several transactions in an aggregated form during an extended time period of deferral; and (in relation to sovereign debt instruments and reflecting Council concern to protect sovereign debt market liquidity) allow the publication of several transactions in an aggregated form for an indefinite period of time. When the deferral period elapses, the outstanding details of the transactions (bar sovereign debt transactions where, reflecting Council concerns, an indefinite publication concession can apply) must be published.

V.11.3 The Bilateral/OTC Segment: Equity Market Transparency

V.11.3.1 Pre-trade Transparency: Equity Markets

(a) The Pre-trade Quote Publication Obligation

Pre-trade equity/equity-like transparency requirements in the bilateral/OTC segment apply only to SIs. The complex 2014 MiFIR regime reflects the fraught 2004 MiFID I negotiations on the original pre-trade transparency regime for shares admitted to trading on a regulated market, the outcome of which was an SI-specific transparency requirement which sought to ensure functionally equivalent treatment of regulated markets, MTFs, and SIs, but also to reflect the position risks undertaken by SIs. Additional refinements have been introduced by the 2014 MiFID II/MiFIR to limit regulatory arbitrage risks.

The core obligation imposed on SIs is that, with respect to shares, depositary receipts, ETFs, certificates, and other similar instruments traded on a trading venue, for which they are SIs, they publish firm quotes, but only where there is a liquid market[344] in those instruments (Article 14(1)): the liquidity condition is a central feature of the SI regime and a device to protect the trading position of SIs. Where the market in the instruments is not liquid (increasing the risk to the SI of moves against its trading position), quotes are to be provided to clients on request.

To further protect the trading position of SIs, the pre-trade transparency regime for equity/equity-like instruments only applies where the SI is dealing in sizes up to SMS (Article 14(2)). SIs that deal only in sizes above this are not subject to the equity pre-trade transparency regime. SIs may decide the particular size or sizes in which they will quote, but, in an addition to the MiFID I regime, the minimum quote size for a particular instrument must be at least the equivalent of 10 per cent of the SMS of the instrument in question traded on a trading venue (Article 14(3)). Each quote, for a particular instrument, must also include a firm bid and offer price for a size (or sizes) up to SMS for the class of instrument to which the instrument in question belongs.[345] The price must also reflect 'prevailing market conditions' for the instrument in question (Article 14(3)).

---

[344] See sect 11.5.

[345] The tightening of the nature of the quoting obligation, including the 10 per cent size rule and the obligation to provide two-sided (bid and offer) quotes, was designed to provide the market with greater clarity on the trading business within the SI regime: 2010 CESR Equity Market Consultation n 53, 14–15.

For the purposes of the SMS calculation, the equity/equity-like instruments are to be grouped in classes based on the arithmetic average value of the orders executed in the market for the instrument. The SMS for each class of instrument must be of a size representative of the arithmetic average value of the orders executed in the market for the instruments included in each class (Article 14(4)).[346] The market for each instrument is composed of all orders executed in the EU in respect of that instrument, excluding those that are large-in-scale as compared to normal market size (Article 14(5)). The determination of which class a particular instrument belongs to is to be made (at least annually) by the NCA of the 'most relevant market in terms of liquidity' (as determined under MiFIR Article 26—section 12.1), on the basis of the arithmetic average value of the orders executed in the market with respect to that instrument.[347] The quote obligation is to be amplified by RTSs; a widely crafted delegation confers on ESMA the power to develop RTSs specifying the criteria for the application of Article 14(1)-(4) (Article 14(7)).

(b) Execution of Quotes

SI quotes must be made public (in a manner which is easily accessible to other market participants on a reasonable commercial basis) on a regular and continuous basis during normal trading orders; quotes may be updated at any time, and may be withdrawn where exceptional market conditions exist (Article 15(1)).

SIs are required to execute the orders received from clients in relation to financial instruments for which they are SIs at the quoted prices at the time of the reception of the order; in justified cases they can execute those orders at a better price, as long as the price falls within a public range close to market conditions (Article 15(2)).[348] They may, however, offer price improvement (offer different quotes) to professional clients without being required to meet the Article 15(2) justification requirement, in respect of transactions where execution in several securities is part of one transaction or in respect of orders that are subject to conditions other than the market price (Article 15(3)).[349] The quote execution regime is designed to protect the trading position of SIs but also to support price formation and investor protection. A quote, unlike the best price available on a central order book which represents a single order, is a statement of trading interest and can be subject to repeated 'hits', threatening the trading position of the SI. Firms can manage their positions by widening the quote spread and offering price improvement on the published quote. The conclusion of transactions under prices other than published quotes, however, can

---

[346] This calculation formula is based on the 2006 Commission MiFID I Regulation calculation for the standard market size for shares: Art 27.

[347] This information must be made public to all market participants and communicated to ESMA.

[348] Administrative rules will govern the criteria specifying when prices fall within a public range (Art 17(3)). This delegation to Commission rule-making (not BTSs) is designed to ensure the efficient valuation of instruments and to maximise the possibility of investment firms to obtain the best deal for their clients.

[349] In addition, where an SI quoting only one quote, or whose highest quote is lower than the SMS, receives a client order which is bigger than its quote size but lower than the standard market size, it can decide to execute that part of the order which exceeds its quotation size, as long as it is executed at the quoted price (except as otherwise permitted under Art 15(2) and (3)). Where the SI is quoting in different sizes and receives an order between sizes which it chooses to execute, it must execute the order at one of the quoted prices and in compliance with the MiFID II order-handling regime (except as otherwise permitted under Art 15(2) and (3)).

compromise price formation. The Article 15 regime accordingly is designed to accommodate price improvement, but to subject it to conditions to mitigate the related risks. NCAs are to monitor compliance with the Article 15(2) price improvement regime, as well as whether SIs regularly update their bid and offer quotes and maintain prices which reflect prevailing market conditions (Article 16).

(c) Access to Quotes

The Article 15(2) quote obligation implies that SIs are required to stand ready to transact at their quotes and, in effect, to act as market-makers, notwithstanding the risks to their proprietary trading position and their different functionality to multilateral venues. Some protection from the liquidity, counterparty, and credit risks attendant on the Article 15(2) obligation to transact is provided by the access-to-quotes rule (Article 17). It provides that SIs can decide, on the basis of their commercial policy, in an objective, non-discriminatory manner, and in accordance with clear standards, which clients can access their quotes (Article 17(1)). An SI may also refuse to enter into (or discontinue) business relationships with clients on the basis of commercial considerations, which include the client's credit status, counterparty risk, and settlement risk. Article 17(2) is designed to protect SIs against the risk of being exposed to multiple transactions from the same client and allows the SI to limit (in a non-discriminatory manner) the number of transactions from the same client which it undertakes to enter at the published conditions. SIs may also limit the total number of transactions from different clients at the same time where the number and/or volume of orders considerably exceeds the norm.

An extensive Commission delegation governs the quote publication/execution and access-to-quotes obligations (Article 17(3)), and provides for administrative rules governing, when quotes are published on a regular and continuous basis and are easily accessible, how quotes are to be published (Article 15(1)); the criteria specifying the exceptional market conditions which can justify the withdrawal of quotes (Article 15(1)); the criteria specifying those transactions where execution in several securities is part of one transaction or those orders that are subject to conditions other than current market price (Article 15(3)); the criteria specifying when prices fall within a public range close to market conditions (Article 15(2)); and the criteria specifying when the number/volume of client orders 'considerably' exceeds the norm (Article 17(2)).

(d) Limit Orders in Shares and Transparency

Client limit orders—a limit order is an order to buy or sell a financial instrument at its specified price limit or better, and for a specified price (MiFID II Article 4(1)(14))—are generally, although not universally, regarded as an important source of liquidity and price information. Failure by an SI to disclose these orders (which might otherwise contribute to price formation on the price-forming central order book of a multilateral venue) might damage price formation by concealing the real level of trading interest in a share. Competitive order execution also generates the risk that investors will be less inclined to place informative limit orders where they are not filled at a particular venue, although identical orders, submitted at a later time and to a different venue, are. While market forces should ultimately ensure that limit orders are directed to the venue on which they are most likely to be filled in time, the 2014 MiFID II/MiFIR (reflecting MiFID I) intervenes to impose some protection for these orders, and to enhance transparency, through a form of order-routing arrangement under MiFID II Article 28(2).

In a rule inspired by US securities regulation[350] and designed to support market efficiency,[351] where a client limit order in respect of shares admitted to trading on a regulated market or traded on a trading venue is not immediately executed under 'prevailing market conditions', all investment firms (including SIs) must (unless expressly instructed otherwise by the client) 'take measures to facilitate' the earliest possible execution of the order by making the order public immediately in a manner that is easily accessible to other market participants. Member States may decide that this requirement is met by the firm transmitting the order to a trading venue: the MiFID I regime provided for transmission to regulated markets and MTFs only, raising some concerns that this could protect the incumbency of major exchanges.[352] NCAs may waive this obligation where the order is large-in-scale compared with normal market size.[353]

V.11.3.2 Post-trade Transparency and Deferrals

All investment firms, including SIs, are subject to the MiFIR post-trade transparency regime for equity/equity-like instruments (Article 20). Investment firms which, either on own account or on behalf of clients, conclude transactions in shares, depositary receipts, ETFs, certificates, and other similar financial instruments traded on a trading venue must make public the volume and price of those transactions and the time at which they are concluded; the data required corresponds to that required of trading venues under MiFIR Article 6, as do the deferrals available (MiFIR Article 20(2)).

V.11.4 The Bilateral/OTC Segment: Non-equity Market Transparency

V.11.4.1 Pre-trade Transparency

SIs are also subject to a new, calibrated transparency regime under MiFIR governing quotes in bonds, structured-finance products, emission allowances, and derivatives traded on a trading venue, for which the firm is an SI (Article 18). It incorporates the major features of the SI equity/equity-like regime, including with respect to the protections afforded to the SI's quotes, but is more calibrated to liquidity risk.

SIs must make public firm quotes in these non-equity financial instruments for which they are SIs, and for which there is a liquid market,[354] but only when three conditions are met: when they are prompted for a quote by a client of the SI (Article 18(1)); when the SI agrees to provide a quote (Article 18(1)); and where the SI deals in sizes below the size at which the SI, as a liquidity provider, becomes exposed to undue risk (Article 18(10)).[355]

---

[350] Under the US SEC's Display Rule, dealers must display limit orders where they are placed at a price superior to the dealers' quotation. This rule operates in a very different trading environment, however, in which trading information is consolidated into a single data-stream: Ferrarini and Recine, n 60, 259.

[351] The Commission argued that the rule represented an important safeguard for overall market efficiency given the growing preponderance of limit orders and their importance as a source of price-relevant information: 2002 Commission MiFID I Proposal, n 72, 21.

[352] Ferrarini and Recine, n 60, 258–60.

[353] As determined under the MiFIR equity market transparency waiver regime (sect 11.1).

[354] Sect 11.5.

[355] In accordance with the Art 9(5)(d) waiver for trading venues in relation to non-equity trading pre-trade transparency requirements, which waiver is liquidity-risk driven.

In the case of instruments for which there is not a liquid market, SIs must disclose quotes to clients on request if they agree to provide a quote; this obligation can be waived where the Article 9(1) conditions for non-equity transparency waivers are met (Article 18(2)).

The quotes offered must allow the SI to meet its best execution obligations and also reflect prevailing market conditions in relation to the prices at which transactions are concluded for the same or similar instruments on a trading venue (Article 18(9)). An SI can update its quotes at any time and can withdraw its quotes under exceptional market conditions (Article 18(3)).

With respect to access to quotes, quotes published in accordance with Article 18(1) must be available to the other clients of the SI. But, tracking the equity/equity-like transparency regime, SIs are permitted to decide, on the basis of their commercial policy, in an objective non-discriminatory way and in accordance with clear standards, the clients to whom they give access to their quotes; SIs may also refuse to enter into or discontinue business relationships with clients on the basis of commercial considerations such as client credit status, counterparty risk, and settlement risk (Article 18(5)). Price improvement is permitted; in justified cases, SIs may execute orders at a better price, provided that this price falls within a public range close to market conditions (Article 18(9)). The Article 18 quote publication/access requirement does not apply where the instrument in question falls below the liquidity threshold which governs the lifting of pre-trade transparency waivers with respect to the instrument in the trading venue space (Article 18(6)).[356]

With respect to quote execution, SIs must undertake to enter into transactions with any other client to whom the quote is made available under the published conditions, but only when the quoted size is at or below the size at which the SI, as a liquidity provider, would be exposed to undue risk (Article 18(6)).[357] SIs can also establish non-discriminatory and transparent limits on the number of transactions they undertake to enter into with clients pursuant to any given quote (Article 18(7)).

A series of monitoring obligations apply in relation to the new non-equity SI pre-trade transparency regime (Article 19). NCAs and ESMA are to monitor the application of Article 18, including with respect to the sizes at which quotes are made available to SI clients and other market participants relative to the other trading activity of the firm and the degree to which the quotes reflect prevailing market conditions in relation to transactions in the same or similar instruments on a trading venue. ESMA is to review the regime by January 2019.[358]

V.11.4.2 Post-trade Transparency and Deferrals

All investment firms (including SIs) which, either on own account or on behalf of clients, conclude transactions in bonds, structured-finance products, emission allowances, and derivatives traded on a trading venue must make public (through an APA) the volume and price of those transactions and the time at which they were concluded (Article 21(1));

---

[356] Sect 11.2.2.

[357] Administrative rules will specify the sizes at which the SI must enter into transactions with any other client to whom the quote is made available.

[358] It must report earlier in the case of significant quoting and trading activity outside the Art 18 thresholds or outside prevailing market conditions: Art 19(1).

the data published replicates that required for trading venues under Article 10 (Article 21(3)).

Deferrals are provided for by Article 21(4). As under the parallel trading venue deferral regime, NCAs are empowered to authorize investment firms to provide for deferred publication—or may request the publication of limited details of a transaction or details of several transactions in an aggregated form, or a combination thereof, during the time period of the deferral. They may alternatively allow the omission of the publication of the volume for individual transactions during an extended time period of deferral; or, in the case of non-equity instruments that are not sovereign debt, allow the publication of several transactions in an aggregated form during an extended time period of deferral; or, in the case of sovereign debt instruments, allow the publication of several transactions in an aggregated form for an indefinite period of time. NCAs may also suspend post-trade publication obligations where pre-set liquidity thresholds are breached (as is the case under the parallel Article 11 trading venue regime). Otherwise, the regime is broadly similar to that which applies under Article 11.

V.11.5 Liquid Markets

The protection of liquidity is a recurring theme of the transparency regime, reflecting in particular the Council's concern (which was not shared by all Member States—France and Italy in particular sought a stricter regime) to protect liquidity in non-equity asset classes. The extent to which a market is liquid shapes the application of much of the transparency regime and, in particular, the extent to which waivers are available.

Different devices to protect liquidity are used across the transparency regime, as noted earlier in this section 11. In addition, the 'liquid market' concept governs a series of exemptions, particularly with respect to the non-equity segment. With respect to trading venues, a waiver from pre-trade transparency requirements is available for non-equity financial instruments for which there is not a liquid market, while post-trade deferral is available for non-equity financial instruments for which there is not a liquid market (Articles 9(1)(c) and 11(1)(b)). Similarly, the full pre-trade transparency regime for SIs applies only to non-equity instruments for which there is a liquid market (Article 18(1)), while the post-trade transparency regime for SIs and investment firms generally provides for an exemption for non-equity instruments for which there is not a liquid market (Article 21(4)).

For the purposes of these provisions, a liquid market is a market for a financial instrument or a class of financial instruments where there are ready and willing buyers and sellers on a continuous basis, assessed according to specified criteria, and taking into consideration the specific market structures of the particular financial instrument or of the particular class of financial instruments (Article 2(1)(17)). The criteria cover: the average frequency and size of transactions over a range of market conditions, having regard to the nature and life-cycle of products within the class of financial instruments; the number and type of market participants (including the ratio of market participants to traded instruments in a given product); and the average size of spreads, where applicable.

Liquidity is also a key determinant of how the pre-trade equity/equity-like transparency regime applies.[359] For the purposes of the pre-trade equity/equity-like transparency regime for trading venues and SIs (Articles 4 and 14), a liquid market is a market of a financial instrument where the financial instrument is traded daily, and the market is assessed according to the free float, the average daily number of transactions in these financial instruments, and the average daily turnover for these financial instruments.

V.11.6 Publication Requirements and Data Distribution and Consolidation

V.11.6.1 Enhancing Data Quality

One of the major findings of the MiFID I Review related to the poor quality and high cost of execution/transparency data, and to inefficiencies in the distribution and consolidation of such data. In response, the 2014 MiFID II/MiFIR has eschewed price-setting controls (although some light-touch price regulation applies) and infrastructure reforms in favour of a multilayered approach which is designed to prompt market change. A new regulatory and supervisory regime applies to 'data reporting services', which are brought within MiFID II/MiFIR in order to place data distribution within a regulatory and supervisory framework. Market operators and investment firms are subject to a new obligation to unbundle their trading data by offering pre- and post-trade transparency data separately, and administrative rules will establish the parameters within which data charges are to be set. The OTC sector, data feeds from which have proved to be unreliable at times, is subject to a new obligation to report through an APA, which is subject to a range of data quality requirements. These enhancements to the MiFID I distribution regime are designed to enhance the quality of data and ease of access to data, but they are also designed to support data consolidation by making the consolidation process easier.

In addition, MiFID II/MiFIR supports the consolidation of data by providing a regulatory regime within which different 'Consolidated Tape Providers' are to compete to consolidate data. The MiFID I Review canvassed a number of consolidation options, including a public non-profit-making monopoly provider (similar to the US model), a commercial monopoly provider, and a competitive model,[360] and generated intense Council discussions on the merits of the monopoly and competing/commercial models.[361] A commercial model, operating within a regulatory framework governing how consolidation is to take place, was ultimately adopted as affording most flexibility. The consolidation regime applies only in respect of post-trade data; consolidation of pre-trade data, which must be made available under shorter time scales than post-trade data, is technically challenging and costly, and was accordingly regarded as a less pressing policy priority.[362]

---

[359] The full SI pre-trade equity/equity-like pre-trade transparency regime applies only to instruments for which there is a liquid market (Art 14(1)), while waivers are available for trading venues from the pre-trade equity/equity-like transparency regime for instruments which are not liquid (Art 4(1)(b)).

[360] eg 2010 MiFID I Review Consultation, n 131, 34–6.

[361] Council negotiations on the consolidation model for transparency data proved contentious, with some Member States in favour of a single provider and others supportive of a commercially driven model under which multiple providers could compete: Cyprus Presidency MiFID II/MiFIR Progress Report, n 207, 10.

[362] 2010 MiFID I Review Consultation, n 131, 36.

V.11.6.2 Data Publication

The data distribution regime is based on publication requirements. With respect to pre-trade equity/equity-like transparency data from trading venues, it must be made available to the public on a continuous basis during normal trading hours (Article 3(1)). Pre-trade non-equity data must similarly be made available to the public on a continuous basis during normal trading hours (Article 8(1)). Where a waiver is granted in respect of request-for-quote and voice-trading systems, the market operator or investment firm must make public at least indicative pre-trade bid and offer prices which are close to the price of the trading interests advertised through the systems; this information must also be made available to the public through appropriate electronic means on a continuous basis during normal trading hours (Article 8(4)). With respect to post-trade equity/equity-like and non-equity transparency data, trading venues must make details of these transactions public as close to real time as technically possible (Article 6(1) and 10(1)).[363] In each case, market operators and investment firms operating a trading venue must make transparency data available free of charge 15 minutes after the publication of the information. Before that, all trade data required under Articles 3–11 must be available on a 'reasonable commercial basis' (Article 13). In one of the first examples of price regulation in EU securities and markets regulation,[364] the Commission is to provide price guidance by adopting administrative rules clarifying what constitutes a reasonable commercial basis (Article 13). Market operators and investment firms must also unbundle their data, in an effort to reduce costs and support data consolidation, by offering pre- and post-trade transparency data separately (Article 12); RTSs must be adopted on data unbundling, including on the level of data disaggregation.

In the bilateral OTC segment, SIs must make their pre-trade equity/equity-like and non-equity quote data public in a manner which is easily accessible to other market participants on a reasonable commercial basis (Articles 15(1) and 18(8)). The post-trade transparency data required of all investment firms (including SIs) must be published through an APA (Article 21(1)),[365] in a significant change from the MiFID I position which allowed investment firms to report through proprietary channels—a concession which became associated with the poor quality of OTC trading data. In addition, to support data distribution, market operators and investment firms operating a trading venue must give access, on a reasonable commercial basis and on a non-discriminatory basis, to the arrangements they employ for making transparency data public to those OTC investment firms which are required to make public pre-trade transparency data relating to quotes in equity and equity-like instruments and in non-equity instruments (Article 3(3) and 8(3)) (SIs) and post-trade data (all investment firms) (Article 6(2) and 10(2)).

V.11.6.3 Data-reporting Services

Data reporting by trading venues and within the OTC sector now sits within the new regulatory regime governing 'data reporting services' and which addresses data quality; these

---

[363] Under the 2006 Commission MiFID I Regulation, unless a deferral applied, trade information was to be made available as close to real time as possible, and, in any case, within three minutes of the relevant transaction (Art 29).

[364] A limited form of price regulation also applies under the rating agency regime with respect to rating agency fees: Ch VII sect 2.8.2.

[365] Each transaction must be made public once through a single APA to avoid duplication and confusion.

services cover operating an APA,[366] a Consolidated Tape Provider (CTP),[367] and an Approved Reporting Mechanism (ARM).[368] The provision of these services as a regular occupation or business is subject to authorization by the relevant home NCA;[369] an investment firm or market operator of a trading venue can provide these data-reporting services, subject to prior verification of their compliance with the data-reporting regime (Article 59(1) and (2)). All data-reporting service providers must be registered on a publicly accessible register (Article 59(3)).[370] Data-reporting service providers must provide their services under the supervision of the home NCA, who must keep compliance by the provider with MiFID II/MiFIR under regular review, and monitor compliance with the authorization conditions (Article 59(4)). Authorization (which supports a passport for data-reporting services (Article 60)) is governed by light-touch procedures and requirements (Articles 61–3), which essentially require the firm to provide a programme of operations and organizational structure and comply with governance requirements which are related to those which apply to regulated markets and investment firms.[371] NCAs are empowered to refuse authorization where they are not satisfied that the persons who effectively direct the business are of sufficiently good repute, or if there are objective and demonstrable grounds for believing that proposed changes to the management of the provider pose a threat to its sound and prudent management and to the adequate consideration of the interests of its clients and the integrity of the market.

Within this framework, APAs, the new channel for OTC reporting, are subject to distinct organizational and distribution requirements (Article 64). As is the case with trading venues, APAs must make the transparency data they publish available as close to real time as technically possible, on a reasonable commercial basis;[372] it must be available free of charge after 15 minutes. APAs must additionally be able to efficiently and consistently disseminate such information in a way that ensures fast access to the information on a non-discriminatory basis and in a format that facilitates the consolidation of the information with similar data from other sources; RTSs will govern the information to be made

---

[366] An APA is a person authorized to provide the service of publishing trade reports on behalf of investment firms under MiFIR: 2014 MiFID II Art 4(1)(52).

[367] A CTP is a person authorized to provide the service of collecting trade reports and consolidating them into a continuous electronic live data-stream, providing price and volume data per financial instrument: 2014 MiFID II Art 4(1)(53).

[368] An ARM is a person authorized to provide the service of reporting details of transactions to NCAs or ESMA on behalf of investment firms: 2014 MiFID II Art 4(1)(54).

[369] The NCA where the head office (natural person), registered office (legal person), or head office (legal person, no registered office) is situated: 2014 MIFID II Art 4(1)(55).

[370] ESMA is also to establish a list of all data-reporting services in the EU.

[371] The governance regime (Art 63) requires that all members of the management body are at all times of sufficiently good repute and possess sufficient knowledge, skills, and experience, and must act with honesty, integrity, and independence of mind to effectively challenge the decisions of senior management where necessary and to effectively oversee and monitor management decision-making. The management body must, overall, possess adequate collective knowledge, skills, and experience to understand the activities of the provider, and must define and oversee the implementation of governance arrangements that ensure the effective and prudent management of an organization, including the segregation of duties in the organization and prevention of conflicts of interest, in a manner that promotes market integrity.

[372] As with trading venues, administrative rules will set parameters on the nature of 'reasonable commercial basis'.

public[373] and the arrangements to facilitate the consolidation of information. Organizationally, the APA must operate and maintain effective administrative arrangements to prevent conflicts of interests with its clients.[374] Data integrity requirements are also imposed. The APA must have sound security mechanisms designed to guarantee the security of the channels through which information is transferred, minimize the risk of data corruption and unauthorized access, and prevent information leakage prior to publication. The APA must also maintain adequate resources and have appropriate back-up facilities, and have systems in place for checking trade reports. The APA regime will be subject to amplification by RTSs.

The CTP regime (Article 65) is designed to shape the consolidation of transparency data by providing a regulatory framework which sets the parameters for new consolidation channels, but relies on the market to produce the relevant providers. It requires CTPs to have adequate policies and arrangements in place to collect pre- and post-trade transparency data, consolidate it into a continuous electronic data stream, and make it available to the public as close to real time as technically possible, on a reasonable commercial basis. In an effort to shape data consolidation, the different elements of the data stream are specified, including whether the transaction was executed via an SI or OTC. The information must be made available free of charge 15 minutes after the CTP has published it, and the CTP must efficiently and consistently disseminate the information in a way that ensures fast access to the information, on a non-discriminatory basis and in formats that are easily accessible and usable for market participants. The data must be consolidated from at least the regulated markets, MTFs, OTFs, and APAs, and in relation to the financial instruments, to be specified by RTSs. Organizationally, the CTP must comply with the same data security and stability requirements as apply to APAs. The CTP regime will be amplified across a number of dimensions, including administrative rules on the parameters of 'reasonable commercial basis', and RTSs on data formats and standards and on the consolidation process.

The ARMs through which transaction reports can be provided (section 12.1) are also subject to a discrete organizational regime (Article 66) which requires the ARM to have adequate policies and arrangements in place to report the information required under MiFIR Article 26 as quickly as possible, and no later than the close of the working day following the day on which the transaction took place; to have administrative arrangements to prevent conflict of interest (the obligations maps that impose on APAs and CTPs); to have data security arrangements in place (the obligations maps that impose on APAs and CTPs); and to have systems in place for checking transaction reports and for detecting and correcting errors or omissions caused by the ARM. The regime will be amplified by RTSs.

---

[373] Including the financial instrument identifier, price, volume, time, and the code for the trading venue where the transaction was executed (including an SI or OTC code as relevant).

[374] Where the APA is a market operator or investment firm it must treat all information collected in a non-discriminatory manner and operate and maintain appropriate arrangements to separate its different business functions.

V.11.7 An Ambitious Reform

The 2014 MiFID II/MiFIR regime has brought radical change to transparency regulation in the EU. In the equity/equity-like segment, waivers supporting dark pool trading within trading venues have been restricted and a wider range of equity instruments have been subject to transparency requirements. In the non-equity segment, an entirely new and generally untested cross-asset and cross-venue transparency regime, which must appropriately balance liquidity and transparency across a host of trading models—many of which are specific to national markets, and with which the EU has limited experience—will apply.

The likelihood of regulatory error is significant. The evidence base is somewhat shaky;[375] in particular, it has proved difficult to quantify the impact of the non-equity regime.[376] The regime is not conceptually coherent, reflecting the very strong national and institutional interests that are at stake and which have shaped the regime. For example, MiFIR relies heavily on the concept of 'illiquid markets' to shield non-equity markets from transparency requirements; in effect, illiquid non-equity markets will remain dark. But while some calibrations are appropriate given the increased liquidity risk which transparency rules bring to non-equity markets, an asymmetry arises with respect to the significant number of illiquid shares which trade on the EU's markets. The asymmetry is all the more troubling as transparency data supports the monitoring of market abuse. The great technical complexity of the legislative regime, and the extent to which this complexity has been driven by political and institutional compromise, further increases the likelihood of regulatory error.

ESMA will be the engine room in which the operational detail of the new regime is hammered out and where the pivotal liquidity/transparency trade-off will, in practice, be made. ESMA has been charged with proposing a vast array of RTSs which will be of fundamental importance to the calibrated application of the new regime and to the related management of liquidity and position risk. In addition, ESMA will likely adopt guidelines and other supervisory convergence measures.[377] ESMA will also play a pivotal role by overseeing the adoption by NCAs of waivers in the equity/equity-like and non-equity markets, and of suspensions of transparency requirements on liquidity grounds in the non-equity markets. But the technical challenges faced by ESMA are immense, given the vast number of instruments within the regime and the dearth of reliable data sources on

---

[375] The wide-ranging Europe Economics study was somewhat equivocal. It was doubtful as to the benefits of pre-trade transparency requirements, given general market satisfaction with pre-trade transparency levels. It was also doubtful as to the benefits of post-trade transparency in asset classes other than bonds, particularly given liquidity risks, although it suggested that post-trade transparency requirements in the bond markets could be beneficial: n 104, 125–212.

[376] In its 2011 MiFID II/MiFIR Proposals Impact Assessment, the Commission acknowledged that 'it is not possible at this stage to asset the impact of such a regime on the liquidity of the market as this will largely depend on the calibration of the transparency requirements ... in the implementing legislation' but that 'overall, a narrowing of spreads, more reliable pricing, as well as improved valuation' was expected: n 93, 66–7.

[377] CESR adopted important guidance on the operational practicalities of the MiFID I transparency regime with respect to data publication (CESR, Publication and Consolidation of MiFID Market Transparency Data (2007) (CESR/07–043)) and the supporting transaction reporting regime (CESR, Level 3 Guidelines on the MiFID Transaction Report (2007) (CESR/07–301)), and also developed significant operational innovations in the construction and monitoring of the transparency databases which remain in operation under ESMA (with respect to the equity markets).

trading/liquidity patterns and on the likely impact of transparency requirements.[378] The related data collection exercise will be massive in scale, not least given the need to assess the quality and accuracy of the data available and to draw robust conclusions. Highly nuanced analysis will be required of ESMA with respect to the myriad different instruments engaged and their different trading and liquidity patterns.

This rapid and simultaneous intensification and extension of transparency requirements calls for careful post-implementation review. The extensive reviews required of the new transparency regime provide a safety valve[379] and the transaction reports (section 12.1) which will be available to NCAs (and ESMA) suggest that post-implementation review will have a strong evidence base.[380] But much depends on the nimbleness of the review process and on whether the EU has the appetite to remove problematic rules; traditionally reviews have increased and not decreased the intensity of intervention.

V.12 Supervision and Enforcement

V.12.1 NCAs

The supervision of trading venues and of data-reporting services providers is governed by the general 2014 MiFID II/MiFIR supervisory regime (Chapter IV section 11). The harmonized suite of powers required of NCAs is calibrated, however, to reflect the particular concerns of venue and data-reporting services supervision; the required powers must accordingly be available in relation to regulated markets and their market operators, and to data-reporting services providers, as well as in relation to investment firms. In addition, a number of required NCA powers are expressly targeted to venue regulation, including the powers to require information relating to commodity derivative positions (Article 69(1)(j)); require the suspension of trading in a financial instrument (Article 69(1)(m)); require the removal of a financial instrument from trading (whether on a regulated market or under other trading arrangements) (Article 69(1)(n)); request any person to take steps to reduce the size of a position or exposure (Article 69(1)(o)); and limit the ability of any person from entering into a commodity derivative (Article 69(1)(p)).[381]

Distinct supervisory reporting requirements apply in the trading venue context. The transaction recording and daily reporting obligations imposed under MiFID II/MiFIR (and which were initially adopted under MiFID I) are keystone supervisory tools for monitoring market efficiency, transparency, and integrity. Formally, they are designed to support the obligation on NCAs to monitor investment firms to ensure they act honestly, fairly, and professionally, and in a manner which promotes the integrity of the market

---

[378] While some data on bond market transparency is available from the market (including through bond indices and major bond trading platforms), bond market data is generally limited. Data difficulties are immense with respect to the derivatives market, although EMIR trade repositories will act as a source for some data.

[379] The extensive MiFIR review clause (Art 52) requires, *inter alia*, that the volume cap and the waiver regime are reviewed.

[380] The transaction reporting regime requires transaction reports to include details of, eg, whether the transaction took place under a waiver and whether it was OTC or completed through an SI.

[381] See further Ch IV sect 2.5 on position management.

(MiFIR Article 24), but they also support trading venue supervision more generally. The reporting requirements have been significantly expanded by MiFID II/MiFIR to apply to a wider range of venues and asset classes.

Retention and reporting requirements apply. All trading venues are required to keep at the disposal of the NCA, and for at least five years, relevant data relating to orders in financial instruments which are advertised through their systems[382] (MiFIR Article 25(2)).[383]

The pivotal ongoing transaction reporting obligation (MiFIR Article 26) applies to investment firms, but trading venues are required to report details of in-scope transactions which are executed through their systems by firms not within the scope of MiFID II/MiFIR (Article 26(5)), and trading venues may report for firms on the data required of in-scope investment firms (Article 26(7)).

Under Article 26(1), investment firms which execute transactions in financial instruments must report complete and accurate details of such transactions to the NCA as quickly as possible, and no later than the close of the following day. To support supervisory efficiency, the NCA of the 'most relevant market in terms of liquidity' must also receive this information.[384] NCAs must make any information provided under Article 26(1) available to ESMA on request. The Article 26(1) reporting obligation applies widely to the following: financial instruments which are admitted to trading or traded on a trading venue (or for which a request for admission to trading has been made); financial instruments where the underlying is a financial instrument traded on a trading venue; and financial instruments where the underlying is an index or basket composed of financial instruments traded on a trading venue (Article 26(2)).[385] The effect of the regime is to require reporting of all OTC transactions, unless the value of the instrument in question does not depend to some extent on or influence instruments which are admitted to trading.[386]

The transaction reports required under Article 26 are detailed[387] and must include (in addition to names and numbers of instruments, quantities, prices, and times of transactions), *inter alia*, a designation identifying the clients involved, the person or algorithm within the firm responsible for execution, and the firm; a designation identifying the applicable transparency waiver under which a trade has taken place (where relevant); a

---

[382] These records are to contain the relevant data that constitute the characteristics of the order and including the data required for the Art 26 daily NCA report (noted later in this section). The contents of these records is to be governed by RTSs and will include the identification code of the venue participant or member which transmitted the order, the identification code of the order, and the agency or principal capacity in which it was carried out: 2014 MiFIR Art 25(3).

[383] Investment firms are also required to keep at the disposal of the NCA for five years relevant data relating to all orders and transactions in financial instruments which they have carried out, whether on own account or on behalf of a client: 2014 MiFIR Art 25(1).

[384] The determination of this market for different financial instruments will be governed by RTSs.

[385] The reporting obligation applies irrespective of whether or not the transaction is actually carried out on the trading venue, in part to ensure the reporting regime dovetails with the new market abuse regime which applies to a wide range of venues (Ch VIII).

[386] The extension of the reporting regime to OTC derivatives (including credit default swaps) has been described as long overdue: Lawton, n 262.

[387] The content of which will be governed by RTSs: Art 26(9). The new regime is harmonized at a higher level of detail than the previous MiFID I regime and requires additional data in order to address the divergences that emerged across different national regimes under MiFID I: 2010 MiFID I Review Communication, n 131, 47.

designation identifying whether the transaction is a short sale under the 2012 Short Selling Regulation;[388] and, for an OTC transaction in an instrument subject to the Article 26 reporting obligation, a designation identifying the type of transaction (Article 26(3)).[389] A legal identifier regime (to be co-ordinated through ESMA) will identify the type of client engaged (Article 26(6)). In support of the Article 26 regime, trading venues and SIs are required to provide NCAs with identifying reference data for instruments admitted to trading or traded on trading venues (Article 27).[390]

The reporting obligation can be met by direct reporting by the relevant investment firm, reporting through an ARM, or reporting through the trading venue on which the transaction is completed (Article 26(7)).[391] Trade reporting can also be carried out by 2012 EMIR trade repositories (in order to avoid the imposition of double reporting obligations on firms with respect to derivatives transactions) (see Chapter VI section 4.2.12 on trade repositories). Concerns have nonetheless been raised as to the potential for duplication and confusion and related costs, given the extensive reporting required of derivatives transactions under EMIR.

The eligible reporting channels have accordingly been restricted from MiFID I (which allowed an investment firm to report through a non-supervised third party acting on its behalf), reflecting the stronger supervisory oversight of data distribution channels under MiFID II/MiFIR. Trading venues must, in this regard, have sound security mechanisms governing the reporting channel and adequate resources and back-up facilities.

In practice, 'TREM', the ESMA-run Transaction Reporting Exchange Mechanism, is used by NCAs to exchange reports.[392]

V.12.2 Supervisory Co-ordination and Co-operation

The supervisory co-ordination and co-operation regime which applies to NCAs and ESMA under the 2014 MiFID II/MiFIR is calibrated to the trading venue context, in particular to mitigate risks to supervisory effectiveness from the fragmentation of trading across different venues. A distinct co-ordination regime applies, for example, with respect to the suspension or removal of instruments from trading, in which ESMA plays a central role (Chapter II section 7.2.1). Co-ordination is also supported by ESMA's oversight of the adoption by NCAs of pre-trade transparency waivers in the equity/equity-like and non-equity markets, and of temporary liquidity-based suspensions of transparency requirements in the non-equity markets.

---

[388] Regulation (EU) No 236/2012 [2012] OJ L86/1.

[389] The identifying designations distinguish between transactions determined by factors linked primarily to valuation and those determined by other factors.

[390] The mechanics of this new regime are to be governed by RTSs.

[391] Where transactions are reported directly to the NCA by a trading venue or ARM, the firm is not responsible for failures in the reporting which are attributable to the venue or ARM, but must take reasonable steps to verify the completeness, accuracy, and timeliness of reports submitted on its behalf.

[392] TREM requires particular format and coding standards for reports, and a series of related convergence measures have been adopted by CESR initially and since ESMA.

A distinct supervisory co-ordination regime applies to the supervision of trading venues' remote access arrangements under Article 79. In a derogation from the otherwise dominant home-country control principle, shared supervisory arrangements are provided for under Article 79(2). It provides that where, taking into account the situation of the securities markets in the host Member State, the operations of a trading venue that has established arrangements in a host Member State have become of 'substantial importance' for the functioning of securities markets and the protection of investors in the host Member State, the home and host NCAs must establish proportionate co-operation arrangements.[393] A discrete precautionary principle applies to remote arrangements under Article 86. Where the NCA of the host Member State of a trading venue has clear and demonstrable grounds for believing that the venue is in breach of MiFID II/MiFIR obligations, it must refer its findings to the relevant home NCA. Where the venue persists in acting in a manner that is clearly prejudicial to the interests of host Member State investors or the orderly functioning of markets (despite measures taken by the home NCA or where those measures are inadequate), the host NCA may, after informing the home NCA, take all appropriate measures to protect investors and the functioning of the markets.

A distinct co-operation regime applies with respect to NCAs' position management powers.[394] In addition, reflecting the array of financial instruments within the scope of the new trading venue regime, NCAs must report and co-operate with the relevant public oversight bodies in emission allowances markets and agricultural commodities markets (Article 79(6) and (7)).

V.13 2014 MiFID II/MiFIR and Post-trading in the EU

V.13.1 Post-trading

'Post-trading' relates to the process through which ownership in a financial instrument is transferred from the seller to the buyer in return for payment, and involves a number of stages.[395]

The post-trade process[396] starts with confirmation or verification, during which the position of the trading parties is confirmed and settlement instructions are matched. It is

---

[393] The criteria against which the 'substantial importance' of the trading venue's operations are to be assessed will be governed by administrative rules: Art 79(8).

[394] See Ch VI sects 2.5 and 2.6.

[395] The highly technical operational procedures, regulatory risks and responses, and complex private law property and security rules related to post-trading activities are outside the scope of this book, which focuses on the pre-trade and trading process. The new central clearing counterparty (CCP) regime for derivatives clearing is covered in Ch VI. 4.2 given its fundamental importance to the regulation, supervision, and organization of OTC derivatives markets and the changes it has brought to trading in this market. On the post-trade process and the background to the EU's approach see, eg, Conac, P-H, Segna, U, and Thévenoz, L, *Intermediated Securities: The Impact of the Geneva Securities Convention and the Future European Legislation* (2012) and Wymeersch, E, 'Securities Clearing and Settlement: Regulatory Developments in Europe' in Ferrarini, G and Wymeersch, E (eds), *Investor Protection in Europe. Corporate Law Making, the MiFID and Beyond* (2006) 465.

[396] The process has been described as follows: '[a]fter two parties agree to a trade, the terms of the trade may first have to be confirmed by a trade comparison system, which may be run by a specialized institution. Clearance—establishing accountability—may then be carried out by a separate clearinghouse according to a number of different mechanisms such as trade for trade and various forms of bilateral and multi-lateral netting.

often carried out by the relevant trading venue or its participants. The clearing process which follows is concerned with establishing mutual positions and with matching contracts prior to settlement. Positions are typically not dealt with individually, but are pooled in order to minimize the volume of funds and securities that must be transferred and in order to establish net positions. Clearing can happen through a central clearing counterparty (CCP), which becomes a counterparty to every transaction and which, taking on counterparty credit risk, sets off transactions, leaving the net positions which remain for settlement. CCPs concentrate risk, however, and so generate risks to systemic stability, as is discussed further in the context of OTC derivatives markets in Chapter VI section 4. During the final settlement stage, cash and securities are transferred through reciprocal cash and securities book-keeping or transaction processing mechanics (the 'delivery versus payment' process) which ensure that the trading bargain is completed. Settlement typically occurs through accounts maintained within central securities depositaries (CSDs).[397] The account of the trading party (or most likely of a CSD member financial institution) with the CSD is credited or debited, although physical transfers of securities are required in some cases.

CSDs play a central part in the post-trade process by providing a range of services, including the immobilization or dematerialization of securities, the provision of accounts, clearing services, and settlement services, although procedures which are integral to the post-trade process, such as confirmation and clearing, are often carried out elsewhere.

CCPs, at the clearing level, and CSDs, at the settlement level, are integral to the post-trade process and are systematically significant infrastructures on which the post-trade process depends.[398]

Post-trading in the EU has long been fragmented across multiple entities and jurisdictions. Prior to the EU's reform agenda, post-trading systems were highly fragmented and largely nationally based;[399] local providers dominated local markets (with typically one CSD in each Member State), and costly and technologically complex connections were required for cross-border transactions.[400] But a fragmented post-trade system generates stability risks

---

Settlement will then take place.' Steil, B, 'International Securities Market Regulation' in Steil, B (ed), *International Financial Market Regulation* (1994) 197, 216.

[397] Central securities depositaries (CSDs) establish 'book entries' for issues of securities; a particular issue of securities is 'dematerialized' or 'immobilized' within the CSD (securities typically settle in electronic rather than paper form), and transfers between members of the CSD via electronic account entries. The CSD market is fragmented in the EU, with over 30 CSDs in operation. There is typically one in each Member State; two International CSDs (within the Euroclear group and the Clearstream group) specialize in bonds. CSDs may provide services to the issuer whose securities are deposited in the CSD, such as the maintenance of shareholder registers. The membership of a CSD is typically composed of financial institutions who intermediate between trading counterparties and the CSD.

[398] On CCPs and systemic risk see Ch VI sect 4.2. Systemic risk can be generated by a CSD through, eg, legal risk (where the insolvency of a participant disrupts netting arrangements, eg), settlement risk (settlement does not occur), operational risk, and custody risk. CSDs have accordingly been the subject of international standard-setting initiatives since 2001 (CPSS (Bank for International Settlements Committee on Payment and Settlement Systems)-IOSCO, Recommendations for Securities Settlement Systems (2001)). In 2010, the FSB called for an updating of these standards for CSDs. The new standards also cover CCPs: CPSS-IOSCO, Principles for Financial Market Infrastructures (2012).

[399] Schmeidel, H and Schönenberger, A, Integration of Securities Market Infrastructures in the Euro Area, ECB, Occasional Paper Series No 33 (2005).

[400] Three types of costs have been identified as flowing to cross-border investors from fragmentation in the post-trade process: direct costs (higher fees); indirect costs (higher back-office fees); and opportunity costs

and is costly.[401] The EU has therefore been concerned to develop, in tandem with a liberalized and robust pan-EU order execution/trading market, a resilient and efficient pan-EU post-trading system.

Progress has been slow.[402] At the outset, most attention focused on the removal of barriers to access to post-trading services and on the achievement of related efficiencies, given the high costs of clearing and settlement,[403] difficulties with non-discriminatory access, and technical problems relating to linkages between infrastructures. The existence of 'vertical silos' (where clearing, settlement, and trading are owned by the same group) was also a concern; while associated with a safer post-trade process, vertical silos can generate inefficiencies.[404] Prudential risks were also on the EU policy agenda from the outset.[405]

The reform agenda was set by the pioneering 2001 and 2003 Giovannini Reports (for the Commission),[406] which identified the main barriers to efficient pan-EU clearing and settlement (technical issues, taxation, and lack of legal certainty) and set out a related action plan. A Commission Communication followed in 2004[407] which supported non-discriminatory access to post-trade services and relied, for the most part, on industry initiatives. This industry-led approach reached its apotheosis in 2006 with the Commission's support of a remedial industry Code of Conduct;[408] while a 'soft measure', it was something of a hybrid instrument, in that Code compliance was monitored by the Commission[409] and the threat of subsequent intervention was implicit in the Commission's support of the Code.[410]

(inefficient use of collateral, failed trades, and trades not undertaken): Commission, Draft Working Document on Post-Trading (2006) (2006 Commission Working Document) 3.

[401] At an early stage of the development of the EU's post-trade policy, it was observed that settlement costs could impose an implicit tax on trading, hinder the growth of securities markets, and hinder the development of a European capital market: Gros, D and Lannoo, K, *The Euro Capital Market* (2000) 69.

[402] For a review of the EU developments see Expert Group on Market Infrastructure, Report (2011).

[403] For a review of the findings of the swathe of studies which have addressed the cost of post-trading services in the EU see n 402.

[404] As independent post-trade infrastructures can be obstructed in accessing trades/transaction data on the silo's trading venue and the integrated silo provider can engage in unstable, subsidized pricing: 2006 Commission Working Document, n 400, 3.

[405] One of the earliest reviews was set out in the 2001 Lamfalussy Report, which identified the major inefficiencies in the EU's post-trade regime and called for an industry-led restructuring: Final Report of the Committee of Wise Men on the Regulation of European Securities Markets (2001), 16–17.

[406] Giovannini Group, Cross-border Clearing and Settlement Arrangements in the European Union—First Report (2001) and Cross-border Clearing and Settlement Arrangements in the European Union—Second Report (2003).

[407] Commission, Clearing and Settlement: The Way Forward (2004) (COM (2004) 312).

[408] Federation of European Securities Exchange, European Association of Central Counterparty Clearing Houses, and the European Securities Depositaries Association, European Code of Conduct for Clearing and Settlement (2006). The Code of Conduct addressed: price transparency; effective rights of access on a fair, transparent, and non-discriminatory basis and interoperability; and governance (separate accounting and service unbundling by post-trade providers).

[409] Through the Monitoring Group of the Code of Conduct on Clearing and Settlement.

[410] Commissioner McCreevy announced the new strategy in forceful terms: 'I expect full co-operation from the industry on this and a clear timetable. I recognize that this code of practice is not without risks . . . It presents a challenge to the industry . . . if they fail regulators always have the range of measures at their disposal to force changes through.' Commissioner McCreevy, Speech on 'Clearing and Settlement: The Way Forward', Economic and Monetary Affairs Committee of the European Parliament, 11 July 2006.

Although some progress was accordingly being made, if slowly, prior to the financial crisis,[411] the financial crisis reset the policy agenda. A regulatory approach rather than an industry-led approach is now being deployed, and the resilience and stability of post-trade infrastructures has become a policy priority.

The settlement stage will be governed by the new harmonized CSD regime[412] which will address CSD authorization, regulation, and market access.[413] It will operate in tandem with the new 'Target2-Securities' platform, a Eurosystem (European Central Bank and national central banks of the euro area) initiative which is to provide a single technical platform for the settlement of securities in the EU in which CSDs will participate, and which, in effect, will harmonize the operational aspects of securities settlement. The new CSD regime will also operate in parallel with the 1998 Settlement Finality Directive, which deals with insolvency risk within settlement systems.[414] The clearing stage is governed by the 2012 EMIR which addresses CCPs. A proposal for a Securities Law Directive is under development; the proposed regime is designed to remove legal certainty risks and so provide a secure legal platform on which post-trading can take place. While a trading measure, the 2014 MiFID II/MiFIR also forms part of the new post-trade regime by addressing access by post-trade structures to trading venues and vice versa. Its major provisions are outlined in summary in the next section.

V.13.2 2014 MiFID II/MiFIR and Post-trading

With respect to post-trading, the 2014 MiFID II/MiFIR regime is primarily focused on access-related issues and on ensuring that, with respect to CCP access in particular, MiFID II/MiFIR is aligned with the 2012 EMIR, which establishes an access regime for CCPs with respect to OTC (non-regulated-market-admitted) derivatives. It also retains the access requirements initially established under the 2004 MiFID I, which sought to support competition in post-trade services (and, in particular, to address the risks posed by vertical silos) by preventing Member States from discriminating in relation to access to post-trade services. The access regime cascades from Member States, to NCAs, to trading venues and CCPs.

---

[411] A major MiFID I Review study on the costs of trading and post-trading found that CCP costs had decreased on average by 73 per cent, that CSD costs had decreased by 25 per cent (equities) and 35 per cent (bonds), and that new pan-EU CCPs had entered the EU post-trade market: 2011 Oxera Report, n 112.

[412] Commission Proposal for a Regulation on Improving Securities Settlement in the EU and on CSDs (COM (2012) 73). The Council adopted its General Approach in September 2013 and agreement was reached with the European Parliament in February 2014. ESMA has begun work on the related BTSs required (ESMA Discussion Paper ESMA/2013/299).

[413] The main elements of the regime, which is designed to reduce settlement time and to minimize failure over the settlement process, include: harmonization of the settlement period; penalties where securities are not delivered on the agreed settlement date and the imposition of delivery obligations; record-keeping obligations for issuers and investors; organizational, conduct, and prudential requirements for CSDs; and access and passporting rights.

[414] The 1998 Settlement Finality Directive is designed to reduce disruption to securities settlement systems caused by insolvency proceedings against a participant in the system—Directive 98/26/EC [1998] OJ L166/145 (as amended in 2009 by Directive 2009/44/EC [2009] OJ L147/37, primarily to reflect technological developments and to extend the range of assets within the Directive's scope).

The Member-State-facing element (originally established by the 2004 MiFID I) is designed to prohibit Member States from discriminating with respect to access to post-trade clearing and settlement services generally. As under MiFID I, but without prejudice to the 2012 EMIR regime which has since intervened with respect to CCP regulation, under MiFID II Member States must require that passporting investment firms have the right of direct and indirect access to CCP, clearing, and settlement systems generally in their territory for the purposes of finalizing or arranging the finalization of transactions in financial instruments; direct and indirect access by firms to clearing and settlement facilities must be subject to the same non-discriminatory, transparent, and objective criteria as apply to local members. In addition, Member States must not restrict the use of these facilities to the clearing and settlement of transactions in financial instruments undertaken on a trading venue in their territory (MiFID II Article 37(1)). This regime cascades to MTFs and regulated markets. An investment firm or market operator operating an MTF must not be prevented from entering into appropriate arrangements with a CCP or clearing house and a settlement system of another Member State with a view to providing for the clearing and/or settlement of some or all trades concluded by its members or participants under its systems (MiFID II Article 38(1)). In addition, NCAs of investment firms and market operators operating an MTF may not oppose the use of CCP, clearing house, and other settlement systems in another Member State, except where this is demonstrably necessary in order to maintain the orderly functioning of that MTF (Article 38(2)). Similarly, without prejudice to the 2012 EMIR, Member States must not prevent regulated markets from entering into appropriate arrangements with a CCP or clearing house and a settlement system of another Member State, and NCAs may not oppose the use of such facilities in another Member State, except where this is demonstrably necessary to order to maintain the orderly functioning of the regulated market (MiFID II Article 55).

The 2014 MiFIR has extended this regime by addressing access rights between CCPs and trading venues. The 2011 MiFID II/MiFIR Proposals sought to build on the MiFID I non-discrimination provisions by incorporating the 2012 EMIR CCP/trading venue access reforms relating to the OTC derivatives markets,[415] and thereby addressing the discrimination and competition risks of the vertical silo model (under which access by CCPs to trading venues (and vice versa) is controlled by trading venue/CCP groups). Negotiations proved difficult, with some Member States (notably Germany) opposed to non-discriminatory CCP access to trading venues on the grounds of increased fragmentation and reduced liquidity risks, and others (notably the UK) supportive of competition and of requiring CCPs to clear transactions executed in different trading venues (and, in parallel, of requiring trading venues to provide data feeds to CCPs that wished to clear transactions executed on the trading venues).[416] Under the compromise finally adopted, CCP/trading

---

[415] Ch VI sect 4.2.

[416] Cyprus Presidency MiFID II/MiFIR Progress Report, n 207, 11. In practice, the difficulties centred on Deutsche Börse (its derivatives trading exchange, Eurex, operates as a closed vertical silo with its clearing house (Eurex Clearing)) and on whether it would be required to open up its derivatives clearing business to competition: Brunsden, J, 'EU Lawmakers Seek High Frequency Trade Curbs in Markets Law', Bloomberg, 26 September 2012. Earlier, the EU's antitrust authorities had vetoed merger plans between Deutsche Börse and NYSE Euronext on the grounds that the merger could threaten competition for trading in interest rate, single stock, and equity index derivatives, as the merged entity would enjoy a quasi-monopoly in European financial derivatives: Commission Press Release, 1 February 2012 (IP/12/94).

venue access rights have been based on the 2012 EMIR model, although the 2014 reforms have additionally nuanced the original EMIR model (Chapter IV section 4.2.6). Under the new regime, non-discriminatory access requirements (based on requiring CCPs to accept to clear transactions executed in different trading venues, and on requiring trading venues to provide related access to their data feeds) have been imposed on CCPs and trading venues, but subject to conditions designed to protect liquidity and support financial stability; a controversial transitional arrangement (which has been criticized by the Commission as consolidating vested market positions) has also been adopted (MiFIR Articles 35–37).

Without prejudice to EMIR Article 7—EMIR governs access rights in respect of OTC derivatives trading (or trading in derivatives not admitted to a regulated market)[417]—and with respect to trading venue access to CCPs, a CCP must accept to clear financial instruments generally on a non-discriminatory and transparent basis, including as regards collateral requirements and fees, regardless of the trading venue on which a transaction is executed. In particular, the trading venue has the right to non-discriminatory treatment of contracts traded on that trading venue in respect of collateral requirements and netting of economically equivalent contracts, where the inclusion of such contracts in the close-out and other netting procedures of the CCP (based on the applicable insolvency law) would not endanger the smooth and orderly functioning, the validity, and/or the enforceability of such procedures, and in respect of cross-margining with correlated contracts cleared by the same CCP under a risk model which complies with EMIR's requirements (Article 35(1)). A CCP may require that the relevant trading venue comply with the operational and technical requirements established by the CCP, including risk-management requirements (Article 35(1)). The Article 35 access obligation does not apply where the CCP is connected by close links to a trading venue which is subject to transitional access arrangements (these arrangements are noted further ahead in this section). The related process governing trading venue access to a CCP is addressed by Article 35(2)–(4), which provides that the trading venue's access application (which must specify the types of financial instruments con-cerned) must be submitted to the CCP, the CCP's NCA, and the NCA of the trading venue; imposes time limits on the CCP with respect to the application process; makes CCP agreement conditional on NCA (of the CCP or of the trading venue) agreement to access by the trading venue; and requires denials of access by the CCP (which can only be based on the conditions to be specified in RTSs) to be reasoned and notified to the CCP's NCA.[418] The NCA of the CCP (or of the trading venue) can only grant a trading venue access to a CCP where access would not require interoperability arrangements between different CCPs[419] (for derivatives which are not subject to the 2012 EMIR[420]),[421] would

---

[417] Ch VI sect 4.2.6.

[418] The NCA of the trading venue must also be so informed where the trading venue is established in a different Member State to the CCP.

[419] Where the need for interoperability (connections between CCPs) is (or is part of) the reason for a denial, the trading venue must advise the CCP (and inform ESMA) of which other CCPs have access to the trading venue; ESMA must publish this information so investment firms can choose to access those CCPs for clearing purposes.

[420] On the EMIR interoperability regime for CCP clearing of OTC derivatives see Ch VI sect 4.2.10.

[421] Where, however, the request for access requires interoperability and the trading venues and all the CCPs involved have consented to the interoperability arrangement, and where the risks to which the incumbent CCP is exposed arising from inter-CCP positions are collateralized at a third party, access can be granted.

not threaten the smooth and orderly functioning of the markets, in particular due to liquidity fragmentation,[422] or would not adversely affect systemic risk.

Transitional arrangements apply in relation to transferable securities and money-market instruments, and for newly established CCPs for these instruments, who may not be equipped to cope with a large trading venue access obligation; these CCPs may apply to their NCAs for a three-year transitional arrangement. Under this arrangement, an NCA may decide to lift the Article 35 access obligation in respect of transferable securities and money-market instruments for three years. Where a transitional arrangement is granted, the CCP does not benefit from the reciprocal Article 36 rights which apply in relation to CCP access to trading venue data and to other facilities to support CCP clearing of transactions on a trading venue. Similarly, and to address silo risks, trading venues connected by close links to a CCP benefiting from these transitional arrangements do not benefit from access rights under Article 35 or Article 36 over the transitional period.

The operational detail of this access regime will be governed by RTSs, which will address, *inter alia*, the conditions under which trading venue access can be denied by a CCP, the conditions under which trading venue access can be permitted by a CCP, the conditions under which granting access to a trading venue would threaten the smooth and orderly functioning of markets or would adversely affect systemic risk, the conditions for notifying the transitional exemption, and the conditions governing non-discriminatory treatment (Article 35(6)).

A parallel regime applies in relation to CCP access to trading venues (in practice, access to the trading venue data feeds which support CCP clearing of transactions on a trading venue) (MiFIR Article 36).[423] This regime follows the same access model and applies similar conditions as apply to trading venue access, and so requires that trading venues provide trade feeds (in relation to financial instruments traded on the venue) on a non-discriminatory and transparent basis (including with respect to fees) to CCPs. The related transitional regime applies in relation to exchange-traded derivatives[424] and is designed to protect trading venues which have previously not been required to provide CCP access, given the major operational changes required to support CCP access to these trade feeds.[425] A transitional arrangement (for 30 months, and which does not require NCA approval but requires NCA and ESMA notification) is available for a trading venue which falls below the 'relevant threshold'[426] in the calendar year preceding the entry into force of MiFIR, and the

---

[422] Liquidity fragmentation is deemed to occur either when the participants in a trading venue are unable to conclude a transaction with one or more other participants in the venue because of the absence of clearing arrangements to which all participants have access, or when a clearing member or its clients would be forced to hold positions in a financial instrument in more than one CCP, which would limit the potential for the netting of financial exposures (2014 MiFIR Art 2(1)(45)).

[423] The regime applies without prejudice to the 2012 EMIR Art 8, which governs CCP access to trading venue data feeds in the context of OTC derivative clearing.

[424] Defined as a derivative which is traded on a regulated market (or an equivalent third country regulated market) (and so is not an OTC derivative for the purposes of the 2012 EMIR): 2014 MiFIR Art 2(1)(32).

[425] The transitional arrangements acknowledge that, with respect to exchange-traded derivatives, it would be 'disproportionate to require smaller trading venues, particularly those closely linked to CCPs, to comply with non-discriminatory access requirement immediately if they have not yet acquired the technological capability to engage on a level playing field with the majority of the post-trade infrastructure market': MiFIR rec 40.

[426] An annual notional amount traded of €1,000 billion.

arrangement can be extended for a further 30 months on the expiry of the initial transitional period—otherwise, the same conditions apply as govern the CCP transitional regime. A series of review obligations apply to Articles 35 and 36 and their transitional arrangements reflecting the sensitivity of the new access regime and its operational risks, including that, by July 2016, the application of Articles 35 and 36 to exchange-traded derivatives is to be reviewed by the Commission, with respect to whether exchange-traded derivatives should be temporarily excluded from Articles 35 and 36 (Article 52(12)).[427]

Finally, access requirements apply in relation to the bundle of commercial and intellectual property rights related to derivatives, access to which is required to support clearing and trading given the centrality of these rights to establishing the value of derivatives (Article 37). These provisions reflect the approach established under the 2012 EMIR for OTC derivatives; EMIR requires that access to these licences should be available on a proportionate, fair, reasonable, and non-discriminatory basis. The parallel 2014 MiFIR access regime for regulated-market-traded derivatives is based on the CCP and trading venue access models. Under Article 37(1), where the value of any financial instrument is calculated by reference to a benchmark, a person with proprietary rights to the benchmark must ensure that CCPs and trading venues are permitted, for the purposes of trading and clearing, to have non-discriminatory access to relevant price and data feeds; to information on the composition, methodology, and pricing of the benchmark, for the purposes of clearing and trading; and to licences. The access regime requires that access is granted on a fair, reasonable, and non-discriminatory basis and at a reasonable commercial price, taking into account the price at which access is given on equivalent terms to other CCPs, trading venues, or other persons for the purposes of clearing and trading.[428] A 30-month transitional period is available for new benchmarks.[429] In addition, no CCP, trading venue, or related entity can enter into an agreement with a benchmark provider the effect of which would be to prevent any other CCP or trading venue from obtaining access. The benchmark regime will be governed by RTSs, including with respect to the conditions governing access.

The CCP/trading venue regime is subject to specific rules governing access by third country CCPs and trading venues, which is based on equivalence decisions being made by the Commission (MiFIR Article 38).

The 2014 MiFID II/MiFIR regime also addresses clearing and settlement standards more generally, albeit at a high level of generality. At the trading venue level, investment firms or market operators operating an MTF or OTF must clearly inform their participants of their respective responsibilities for the settlement of the transactions executed in that facility; they must also have in place the necessary arrangements to facilitate the efficient settlement of transactions concluded under the MTF or OTF (MiFID II Article 18(6)). With respect to regulated markets, MiFID II Article 47 establishes the general organizational principles

---

[427] Where the Commission comes to the view that a temporary exclusion is not required, a CCP or trading venue may apply to its NCA for a transitional exemption until July 2019 (Art 54).

[428] Different prices can only be charged where they are objectively justified having regard to reasonable commercial grounds, such as quantity, scope, or field of use demanded.

[429] Conditions apply governing when a benchmark is new.

governing the finalization of transactions; regulated markets must also offer all their members or participants the right to designate the system for the settlement of transactions in financial instruments undertaken on that regulated market (MiFID II Article 37(2)).[430] With respect to clearing, the operational regime governing investment firms provides that where an investment firm acts as a general clearing member for other persons (and so supports access to clearing services by other parties), it must have in place effective systems and controls to ensure clearing services are only applied to persons who are suitable and meet clear criteria, and that appropriate requirements are imposed on those persons to reduce risks to the firm and to the market (MiFID II Article 17(6)).

---

[430] Subject to the links and arrangements between the designated settlement systems and any other system or facility as are necessary to ensure the efficient and economic settlement of the transaction in question being in place, and agreement by the NCA responsible for the supervision of the regulated market that technical conditions for settlement of transactions concluded on the regulated market through a settlement system other than that designated by the regulated market are such as to allow the smooth and orderly functioning of financial markets.

VI

TRADING

VI.1 Introduction

VI.1.1 Regulating Trading: Financial Stability and Anti-speculation

This Chapter is concerned with trading (order execution) in financial instruments. Regulation of the trading process has long been associated with the support of market efficiency and efficient resource allocation, and with the related protection of liquidity and the facilitation of risk management.[1] Trading regulation has also long been associated, particularly in the brokerage context, with investor protection, given the significant agency risks, including with respect to competence failures and conflicts of interest, which can arise. EU trading regulation, prior to the crisis-era reforms, was primarily a function of the 2004 MiFID I[2] regime for investment services and activities—broking and dealing investment services/activities were subject to authorization (and remain so under the 2014 MiFID II/MiFIR regime).[3] The trading-specific rules were primarily conduct-orientated, and included order handling and best execution requirements. Trading between dealers or between dealers and professional counterparties, however, was generally exempted from conduct regulation. MiFID I also subjected trading to the prudential requirements which applied to investment services generally, including organizational and trading book capital requirements.

In addition to market efficiency and investor protection risks, trading—and particularly proprietary dealing—can generate systemic risks, particularly where solvency risks generated by severe market losses are passed down a chain of counterparties and disrupt liquidity and stability.[4] But while the EU capital requirements regime addressed trading book risk,[5] the EU regime did not otherwise regulate the stability risks generated by trading in any significant way. The crisis-era reform agenda, however, has re-characterized EU trading

---

[1] See, eg, Amihud, Y and Mendelson, H, 'Asset Pricing and the Bid Ask Spread' (1986) 17 *JFE* 223 and Levine, R, 'Financial Development and Economic Growth: Views and Agenda' (1997) 35 *J of Econ Lit* 685.

[2] Markets in Financial Instruments Directive 2004/39/EC [2004] OJ L145/1.

[3] Markets in Financial Instruments Directive II 2014/65/EU [2014] OJ L173/349 (2014 MiFID II) and Markets in Financial Instruments Regulation EU (No) 600/2014 [2014] OJ L173/84 (2014 MiFIR). On the implementation timeline see Ch IV n 28. The discussion in this Chapter is based on the 2014 MiFID II/MiFIR (MiFID I will be repealed from 3 July 2017 when the 2014 MiFID II/MiFIR applies). Reference is made to MiFID I as appropriate.

[4] For early perspectives see Franks, J and Mayer, C, Risk, *Regulation and Investor Protection. The Case of Investment Management* (1989) 158 and OECD, Report on Risk Management in Financial Services (1992).

[5] Ch IV sect 8.1.

regulation. In addition to addressing market efficiency and investor protection, trading regulation is now closely concerned with the support of financial stability.

Much of the financial stability agenda has focused on derivatives trading and so reflects the related G20 agenda (section 4). The systemic instability which can flow from trading positions in derivatives and from related poor risk management was laid bare by the difficulties which the over-the-counter (OTC) derivatives segment, and in particular credit derivatives, experienced over the crisis. Extensive reforms have followed. As the crisis receded, the massive losses sustained by JP Morgan Chase in 2012 from the controversial 'London Whale' trades in complex credit derivatives ensured regulatory attention remained focused on derivatives trading.[6] In the EU, additional concerns as to the potentially anti-competitive behaviour of major firms in the OTC credit default swap (CDS) market have kept policy attention trained on the derivatives markets.[7]

The financial stability agenda has also led to trading being drawn into the ongoing structural reform of the banking sector, which is designed to address the 'too big to fail' subsidy enjoyed by systemically significant banks which carry out household/commercial deposit-taking and lending functions along with wholesale market intermediation and dealing functions; deposit guarantees and the related 'too big to fail' subsidy have been associated with competitive advantage and with perverse risk-taking incentives in these banks. Ring-fencing and similar structural reforms, designed to reduce incentives for risk-taking by taking trading and other riskier activities outside the scope of deposit protection and of the implicit 'too big to fail' subsidy, to remove the related competitive advantage for large banks, to facilitate resolution, and to reduce the risk to the tax-payer[8] are in train internationally, although they do not form part of the formal G20 reform agenda and reflect domestic initiatives and dynamics.[9]

---

[6] Over 2012, JP Morgan Chase sustained some $6.2 billion of losses arising from very large trades in complex synthetic credit derivatives, which were termed the 'London Whale' trades given their size and impact on credit markets, and which generated close political attention: eg US Senate, Permanent Subcommittee on Investigations, Committee on Homeland Security and Governmental Affairs, JP Morgan Chase Whale Traders. A Case History of Derivatives Risks and Abuses (2013). A co-ordinated global settlement with the leading regulators engaged followed under which JP Morgan Chase was fined $920 million (eg SEC (US Securities and Exchange Commission) Press Release 2013 2013-187e_x2013;187, 19 September 2013).

[7] In July 2013, and following the opening of the investigation in April 2011, the EU published its 'Statement of Objections' relating to its investigation of 13 investment banks, the International Swap Dealers' Association, and the data services provider Markit, setting out its preliminary finding that these actors had colluded to prevent Deutsche Börse and the Chicago Mercantile Exchange from having access to the licences for data and index benchmarks necessary for them to access the CDS market and to support exchange trading in these instruments: Commission, Press Release 1 July 2013 (IP/13/630). As discussed in sect 4.3, a trading venue trading obligation now applies to certain classes of derivative.

[8] eg OECD, Bank Competition and Financial Stability (2011) ch 2.

[9] The US led the way with the highly contested 'Volcker Rule' (2010 Dodd-Frank Act s 619), which prohibits federally insured depository institutions and their affiliates ('banking entities') from engaging in short-term proprietary trading (market-making and hedging activities are permitted), and from acquiring or retaining any equity, partnership, or other ownership interest in or sponsoring a hedge fund or private equity fund (the final rules were adopted in December 2013 and came into force in April 2014).

The UK reforms, which are less intrusive (they do not ban proprietary trading) but which were similarly contested, are derived from the 'Vickers Report' (Independent Commission on Banking, Final Report. Recommendations (2011)), and will lead to a legal ring-fence being erected between, essentially, retail and SME/commercial deposit-taking and lending services, and investment banking services, within major banking groups (2013 Financial Services (Banking Reform) Act). The UK Prudential Regulation Authority is required to review the nature of proprietary trading within in-scope entities; this review will support the required

Structural reform came to form part of the closing stages of the EU's crisis-era reform programme, and was spearheaded by the 2012 Liikanen Group report[10] and supported by the European Parliament.[11] A related Commission Proposal for a regulation on structural measures supporting the resilience of EU credit institutions followed in early 2014.[12] In order to curtail the artificial expansion of banks' balance sheets, particularly through speculative activities; to reduce the risk of bank failure and tax-payer support; and to support efficient resolution where required, the Commission has proposed that a prohibition on 'proprietary trading'[13] and on investing in hedge funds apply to certain banks and entities within the same banking group (Article 6(1)); the proposal therefore requires the divestment of proprietary trading activities.[14] The Commission has also proposed that certain 'trading activities' judged to be at risk of supporting illegal proprietary trading, or with a propensity to endangering financial stability (including market-making, investment in and sponsoring of securitizations, and the trading of certain derivatives), be subject to review by the relevant national competent authority (NCA), and to a subsequent separation requirement by the NCA[15] where the NCA deems it necessary, in accordance with the proposed regime's qualifying metrics and conditions (Articles 8–21);[16] this requirement is designed to separate trading activities from deposit-taking within banking groups. The proposed prohibition regime would apply only (given its concern with mitigating financial

---

subsequent independent review of whether further restrictions should be placed on proprietary trading. On the development of the UK regime see HM Treasury and Department of Business Innovation and Skills, Banking Reform: Delivering Sustainability and Supporting a Sustainable Economy (2012) and Banking Reform: A New Structure for Stability and Growth (2013). Discussion of these reforms, which are directed to the stability of the banking sector, and of the host of complex issues which arise, including with respect to the scope of the separation/ring-fence, is outside the coverage of this work. See, eg, Schwarcz, S, 'Ring-Fencing' (2013) 87 *So Cal LR*, Skeel, D, *The New Financial Deal* (2011) 85–93, Boot, A and Ratnovski, L, Banking and Trading, IMF WP No 12/238 (2012), and Chow, J and Surti, J, Making Banks Safer: Can Volcker and Vickers Do It? IMF WP No 11/236 (2011).

[10] The Liikanen Group report (High-level Expert Group on Reforming the Structure of the EU Banking Sector, Final Report (2012)), which followed a Commission mandate, made a series of recommendations on structural reform of the EU banking sector which included capital-, resolution-, and governance-related reforms, and which also included the recommendation that proprietary trading and other significant trading activities (where they represented a significant share of a bank's business) be assigned to a separate legal entity. See Ojo, M, Volckers/Vickers Hybrid? The Liikanen Report and Justifications for Ring Fencing and Separate Legal Entities (2013), available at <http://ssrn.com/abstract=2211171>.

[11] European Parliament, Report on Reforming the Structure of the EU Banking Sector (2013) (2013/2012 (INI)).

[12] COM (2014) 43, which followed two Commission consultations: Consultation on the Structural Reform of the Banking Sector (2013) and Consultation on the Recommendations of the High Level Expert Group on the Structure of the EU Banking Sector (2012).

[13] Defined in specific terms under the Proposal (Art 5) as using own capital or borrowed money to take positions in any type of transaction to purchase, sell, or otherwise acquire or dispose of any financial instrument or commodities for the sole purpose of making a profit for own account, and without any connection to actual or anticipated client activity or for the purpose of hedging the entity's risk as a result of actual or anticipated client activity, through the use of desks, units, divisions, or individual traders specifically dedicated to such position taking and profit-making.

[14] Although the reform is not projected to require major change within in-scope banking groups, given the global impact of the Volcker Rule on proprietary trading.

[15] The Proposal requires that such trading activities be transferred to a distinct legal entity within the group. Separation requirements apply under the Proposal to ensure these entities are effectively separated, such that the group is organized into subgroups composed of core (deposit-taking) credit institutions and trading entities.

[16] The metrics include relative size, leverage, complexity, profitability, market risk, and interconnectedness. In certain circumstances and where specified thresholds are passed, the NCA must require separation.

stability risks) to the EU's largest banks—those identified as Global Systemically Important Financial Institutions[17]—and banks with total assets exceeding €30 billion or with trading assets and liabilities in excess of €70 billion or 10 per cent of their total assets for three consecutive years.[18] The proposed separation regime focuses in particular on 'core credit institutions'.[19] Overall, some 30 major banking groups are expected to be affected were the reforms to be adopted. Generating mixed reactions,[20] and with a group-wide and extraterritorial reach designed to apply across an EU bank's global corporate group,[21] its fate is uncertain. While the ring-fencing proposals form part of the banking reform agenda and are focused on deposit-taking credit institutions and their groups, they nonetheless underline the close policy focus on the stability risks which trading can generate.

The EU trading reforms can also be associated with the highly politicized anti-speculation agenda which became an early feature of the crisis-era reform programme.[22] It is not unexpected that crisis conditions would pull the trading process into the regulatory net; benign shareholders, traders, and risk managers can quickly become re-characterized as speculators and predators as the economic effects of crisis spread.[23] As noted in Chapter I, the crisis era prompted a concern to monitor and manage financial innovation and generated some scepticism as to the benefit of ever higher levels of market intermediation and of market completeness achieved through the use of derivatives and, in particular, of speculative trading activities.[24] In the UK, for example, the 2009 Turner Review called for regulatory policy to balance the benefits of market completion and market liquidity with

---

[17] The prohibition would apply to any credit institution or an EU parent, including all branches and subsidiaries (including in third countries), where it is identified as a G-SIFI in accordance with the 2013 CRD IV/CRR regime (Directive 2013/36/EU [2013] OJ L176/338 (Capital Requirements Directive (CRD IV)) and Regulation EU No 575/2013 [2013] OJ L176/1 (Capital Requirements Regulation (CRR)): Arts 3 and 6.

[18] In this case, the following entities would be covered: any credit institution operating in the EU which is neither a parent nor a subsidiary (including all branches); an EU parent (including all branches and subsidiaries wherever located); and EU branches of credit institutions in third countries: Art 3.

[19] The separation regime would apply to a core EU credit institution (one which at a minimum takes deposits) which is neither a parent nor a subsidiary (but including its branches); an EU parent (including all branches and subsidiaries, irrespective of location, as long as one group entity is a core credit institution established in the EU); and EU branches of third country credit institutions: Art 9.

[20] eg Barker, A and Fleming, S, 'EU Banking Plan Raises Anxiety', *Financial Times*, 30 January 2014, 6, characterizing the Proposal as cautious, and as steering a careful route across current Member State proposals, but reporting on significant industry anxiety. The 2014 Commission Proposal is in some respects weaker than the 2012 Liikanen Report, particularly with respect to the discretionary model applied to separation, but is tougher with respect to the prohibition on proprietary trading.

[21] Exemptions are available for third country branches and subsidiaries of EU credit institutions, and for EU branches of third country banks, as long as an equivalent regime applies.

[22] The European Parliament's suspicion of trading in derivatives is indicative of this agenda: European Parliament, Resolution on Derivatives Markets: Future Policy Actions, 15 June 2010 (P7_TA(2010)0206), calling on the Commission to look into ways of significantly reducing the overall volume of derivatives so that the volume is proportionate to the underlying securities: para 9.

[23] Hill, J, 'Why did Australia Fare so Well in the Global Financial Crisis' in Ferran, E, Moloney, N, Hill, J, and Coffee, J, *The Regulatory Aftermath of the Global Financial Crisis* (2012) 203, 256. For an example of an anti-speculation analysis see Finance Watch, Investing not Betting. Making Financial Markets Serve Society (2012).

[24] On the policy suspicion of financial innovation and financial market intensity which emerged over the crisis era, and the related anti-speculation movement, see further Ch I and Moloney, N, 'The Legacy Effects of the Global Financial Crisis on Regulatory Design in the EU' in Ferran et al, n 23, 111.

the drawbacks of instability.[25] Similarly, French regulatory policy since the financial crisis has focused on socially inefficient speculation.[26] The Commission has also highlighted its commitment to reducing short-termism and speculative trading activities.[27] The EU's trading reforms reflect this concern to support 'productive' financial markets. But they have also been coloured by a sometimes febrile anti-speculation agenda which has an array of drivers, including long-standing suspicion of Anglo-American capitalism in some Member States, as well as the fiscal impact of turmoil in the EU's sovereign debt markets.[28] This dynamic is most apparent with respect to the new short selling rules, the algorithmic and high frequency trading (HFT) regime,[29] and the proposed Financial Transaction Tax (FTT).

These different influences have combined to produce a trading regime which extends far beyond the original 2004 MiFID I conduct/prudential regime, and which now addresses short selling, algorithmic trading, and position management and includes a host of measures designed to strengthen the stability of OTC derivatives markets. It also applies to a wide range of financial market actors, including non-financial counterparties. The regime promises much, but it has troubling features. Chief among them are the potential risks to liquidity and effective risk management. Liquidity-constraining techniques were in use internationally pre-crisis, typically in the form of short selling curbs and, in some jurisdictions, transaction taxes; however, liquidity is generally promoted by regulators through, for example, disclosure techniques, insider-trading prohibitions, and trading market rules.[30] A concern to protect liquidity is evident across the new trading regime, but liquidity-constraining techniques have also been deployed, notably in the form of short selling curbs, position-management powers, restrictions on algorithmic trading, and the proposed FTT. There are some indications that, reflecting the earlier and long-standing debate on the link between 'excessive liquidity' and 'over-financialization',[31] and wider concerns that 'excessive' liquidity can generate financial instability,[32] the EU regime seems concerned to drain excessive liquidity where it threatens financial stability. But attempts to drain liquidity from the market are fraught with risk, given the importance of liquidity to

---

[25] UK Financial Services Authority (FSA), The Turner Review. A Regulatory Response to the Global Financial Crisis (2009) 41–2.

[26] Authorité des Marchés Financiers (AMF), What are the Priorities for Financial Markets? (2011).

[27] The 2013 Green Paper on Long-Term Financing, eg, notes the EU policy concern to reduce short-term and speculative trading activities and to improve investor protection: Commission, Green Paper on Long-Term Financing of the European Economy (2013) (COM (2013) 150) 11.

[28] See, eg, the Parliament's Resolution on innovative trading practices which supports measures to curb excessive short-termism and speculation: European Parliament, Resolution on Innovative Financing at a Global and European Level, 8 March 2011 (P7_TA(2011)0080).

[29] The algorithmic trading reforms also relate to the G20 agenda. The Seoul Action Plan adopted at the November 2010 Seoul G20 Summit, and in response to a French initiative, added measures to improve market efficiency and integrity to the previously stability-dominated G20 agenda: Seoul G20 Summit, November 2010, Leaders' Declaration, paras 11 and 41. The International Organization of Securities Commissions (IOSCO) responded with, *inter alia*, its 2011 Report on Regulatory Issues raised by the Impact of Technological Changes on Market Integrity and Efficiency, which addresses algorithmic trading.

[30] eg O'Hara, M, Liquidity and Financial Market Stability, National Bank of Belgium WP No 55 (2004), available at <http://ssrn.com/abstract=1691574>.

[31] eg O'Hara, n 30, highlighting the debate on the 'dark side of liquidity' and its leading proponents, including Keynes in the 1930s and Tobin in the 1970s.

[32] For a policy perspective see, eg, Committee on the Global Financial System, Paper No 45, Global Liquidity—Concept, Measurement and Policy Implications (2011).

market efficiency. Particular dangers are associated with the new position limits regime for commodity derivatives trading and with the swingeing reforms to OTC derivatives market trading, given the costs being imposed as a result on hedging and risk-management practices. The pulling of trading by non-financial counterparties into the regulatory net is also potentially troublesome, given the related costs and potential prejudice to effective risk management.

As discussed throughout this Chapter, efforts have been made to calibrate the different rules to support liquidity and effective risk management (the trading venue regime discussed in Chapter V similarly seeks to ensure liquidity is protected, given the potentially prejudicial impact of the new trading venue rules—particularly those related to non-equity asset classes), notably with respect to the non-financial counterparties who use derivatives to hedge commercial risks and with respect to market-makers. In addition, the European Securities and Markets Authority (ESMA) brings a significant technical capacity to bear on the Binding Technical Standards (BTSs) (Regulatory Technical Standards (RTSs) and Implementing Technical Standards (ITSs)) and other administrative rules which will, in effect, operationalize the new regime. Nonetheless, the risks of unintended consequences are considerable. A further challenge relates to the fragmented nature of the regime: the derivatives regime, for example, is fractured across a number of measures, and close alignment between the 2014 MiFID II/MiFIR regime and the regime governing the OTC derivatives market, in particular, is imperative. Difficulties have, however, emerged in this regard (section 4.2.4).

VI.1.2 The EU Trading Regime

The EU trading regime is split across a number of measures. The 2014 MiFID II/MiFIR regime provides the overarching regulatory framework governing order execution (section 2). The 2012 Short Selling Regulation[33] addresses short selling practices (section 3). The 2012 European Market Infrastructure Regulation (2012 EMIR)[34] is the pivotal measure governing trading in the OTC derivatives markets, although an array of new requirements apply to this sector, including the trading venue obligation under MiFID II/MiFIR (section 4). The trading regime is also likely to include a new FTT, albeit that it will only apply within the 'FTT zone' of Member States which agree to implement it (section 5).

The trading regime also includes the universe of rules which govern market efficiency and transparency generally, including the rules governing market abuse and insider dealing considered in Chapter VIII, the reporting rules which require disclosure of certain equity positions (including positions in instruments of similar economic effect under the 2013 Amending Transparency Directive[35]—Chapter II section 5.7), and the transaction reporting and transparency rules which apply to trading activities under the 2014 MiFID II/MiFIR regime (Chapter V section 12.1). The focus of this Chapter, however, is on the subset of rules which focus specifically on the trading process. It does not address the

---

[33] Regulation (EU) No 236/2012 [2012] OJ L86/1.
[34] Regulation (EU) No 648/2012 [2012] OJ L201/1.
[35] Directive 2013/50/EU [2013] OJ L294/13.

regulation of the organized venues or platforms on which trading can occur, which is covered in Chapter V.[36]

Overall, the new trading regime is significantly deeper and wider than the pre-crisis regime. The extensive exemptions previously available to dealers have been scaled back (section 2). A much wider array of financial instruments have become subject to discrete trading rules, including OTC derivatives in general (section 4), commodity derivatives (section 2.5), and CDSs (section 3, with respect to short selling). The regime also deploys more intrusive tools. The new commodity derivatives regime, for example, deploys position-management tools, while the new short selling regime empowers NCAs and ESMA to impose a range of restrictions on short selling. Disclosure and reporting tools, long a feature of order-execution regulation, have been significantly expanded, notably with respect to short positions under the short selling regime and positions in commodity derivatives under the 2014 MiFID II/MiFIR.

The complexity, range, and ambition of the new regime calls for caution, particularly given the liquidity and risk-management risks previously noted. The new regime also demands much of the EU law-making process, particularly at the administrative/ESMA level, given the untested nature of many of the reforms. The new supervisory tools which have been made available at EU level (notably the short selling powers and the position-management powers for the commodity derivatives market) also demand much of supervision and, in particular, of ESMA, which has been conferred with exceptional powers of intervention with respect to position management and short selling (sections 2.5 and 3.9). Careful and holistic post-implementation review will be required.

VI.2 2014 MiFID II/MiFIR: The Regulation of Trading

VI.2.1 2014 MiFID II/MiFIR: Setting the Regulatory Perimeter—Scope and Dealing

The 2014 MiFID II/MiFIR regime provides the regulatory framework which governs the trading process generally. The generic MiFID II/MiFIR authorization, conduct, and prudential regime applies to the reception and transmission of orders, the execution of orders on behalf of clients, and dealing on own account,[37] in each case in MiFID II/MiFIR financial instruments (MiFID II Annex I, section A).[38] While some elements of the original MiFID I regime remain (notably the best execution and order handling requirements), MiFID II/MiFIR is significantly wider and more interventionist, reflecting institutional concern to upgrade MiFID I, close regulatory gaps, and implement the G20 reform agenda; the final trilogue (Commission/Council/European Parliament) negotiations, in particular,

---

[36] Inevitably, there is some overlap between the coverage of both Chapters. The trading transparency rules discussed in Ch V include, eg, the transparency rules which govern bilateral trades away from organized venues in the OTC markets.

[37] Dealing on own account covers a range of practices, including market-making and proprietary dealing.

[38] See Ch IV sect 4.3 on in-scope financial instruments.

saw more intrusive regulation imposed, particularly with respect to algorithmic trading, market-making, and position management.[39]

Its scope, for example (as discussed further in Chapter IV), has extended. The exemption which applies to proprietary dealing activities (in financial instruments other than commodity derivatives, or emission allowances, or derivatives thereof) has been restricted, reflecting the G20 commitment to closing regulatory gaps.[40] While under MiFID I the exemption required that the dealer not engage in market-making activities or deal on own account by executing client orders, MiFID II additionally requires that the dealer not be a member of or participant in a regulated market or multilateral trading facility (MTF) or engage in HFT (MiFID II Article 2(1)(d)).[41] The related exemption for dealers in commodity derivatives, or emission allowances, or derivatives thereof similarly requires that the exempted dealer not engage in HFT (Article 2(1)(j)).[42] More generally, dealers exempted under Article 2(1)(j), as well as the insurance undertakings and collective investment undertakings exempted from MiFID II and certain participants in the energy market, must, where they are participants of regulated markets or MTFs, comply with the new MiFID II requirements relating to algorithmic trading, HFT, and market-making (Article 1(5)).

VI.2.2 Regulating the Order-execution Process: the General Framework

VI.2.2.1 The 2014 MiFID II/MiFIR and the 2013 CRD IV/CRR Framework

The authorization and prudential regime which governs investment services/activities generally under the 2014 MiFID II/MiFIR regime (Chapter IV) applies to trading-related activities. So too do the 2013 CRD IV/CRR[43] prudential requirements (for in-scope firms) governing internal risk management of counterparty, operational, liquidity, and market risk, and which are designed to strengthen incentives (regulatory and other) for prudent risk-taking (Chapter IV section 8). The CRD IV/CRR regime also addresses trading-related capital requirements and has delivered a series of enhancements, including with respect to counterparty credit risk and trading book risk, designed to support prudent risk-taking; extensive capital reforms are expected to apply to the market risk posed by trading portfolios under the trading book reforms under development by the Basel Committee (Chapter IV section 8.7).

Similarly, the MiFID II conduct regime applies to trading-related activities. Where a firm executes an order on behalf of a client (whether retail or professional), the conduct rules which govern the provision of investment services generally, and which include the anchor 'fair treatment' obligation (the obligation to act honestly, fairly, and professionally in accordance with the best interests of clients) and disclosure and record-keeping requirements

---

[39] On the MiFID II and MiFIR negotiations generally see Ch IV sect 2.3.3 (MiFID II) and Ch V sect 3 (MiFID II/MiFIR).

[40] 2011 MiFID II Proposal (COM (2011) 656/4) 7.

[41] See sect 2.3 on the definition of high frequency trading.

[42] The earlier MiFID I exemption (Art 2(1)(k)) for persons whose main business consisted of dealing on own account in commodities and/or commodities derivatives has been removed, reflecting the tightening of regulation over commodity derivatives generally (sect 2.5).

[43] n 17.

(MiFID II Article 24) apply, as do the conflict-of-interest management requirements (Article 16(3) and Article 23). Where the transaction is executed between 'eligible counterparties',[44] however, a lighter regime applies. Where an investment firm brings about or enters into transactions with eligible counterparties (essentially other regulated entities), the conduct regime does not apply (Article 30). The investment firm remains subject, however, to the conflict of interest regime and the disclosure elements of Article 24, and must act honestly, fairly, and professionally and communicate in a way which is fair, clear, and not misleading, taking into account the nature of the eligible counterparty and its business (Article 30(1)).

The conduct regime also contains a number of trading-specific requirements, which will now be discussed.[45]

VI.2.2.2 Best Execution

Best execution rules, which form part of conduct regulation and which address the agency risks of brokerage, can broadly be regarded as requiring execution intermediaries to seek the best possible result for their clients.[46] While the 'best possible result' is often associated with price, it can reflect a range of other factors, including the reduction of market impact costs for large trades. Best execution also serves wider market efficiency functions, particularly where trading is fragmented across competitive order-execution venues, as it requires brokers to tie together execution data from different venues. Prior to the adoption of MiFID I, best execution regulation was not well developed across the EU,[47] given the impact of the 'concentration rule' which, in the Member States where it applied, required retail orders to be routed through the local central stock exchange and, in effect, delivered a form of best execution by requiring the pooling of liquidity on exchanges. MiFID I, however, introduced a harmonized best execution obligation for retail and professional clients.[48] As discussed in Chapter V, the competitive order-execution model imposed by MiFID I generated the risk that trading would become fragmented across multiple venues and that clients could become vulnerable to poor execution quality where intermediaries did not search across a sufficiently wide range of venues. The best execution regime was accordingly designed to ensure that the competitive benefits of a liberalized order-execution market were channelled to clients.[49] The best execution requirement also provided a mitigant against the conflicts of interest inherent in the new competitive order-execution model. In particular, the ability of investment firms to 'internalize' client orders by trading with clients against their proprietary dealing books, and the removal of the obligation to

---

[44] On the classification of eligible counterparties, professional clients, and retail clients see Ch IV sect 5.2.

[45] These requirements are dis-applied from trades between eligible counterparties.

[46] See generally, FSA, Discussion Paper 06/3, Implementing MiFID's Best Execution Requirements (2006) and Macey, J and O'Hara, M, 'The Law and Economics of Best Execution' (1997) 6 *J Fin Intermed* 193.

[47] The pre-MiFID I obligation in most Member States was, typically, simply to match the prevailing price on the local regulated market. The UK's regime was regarded as being considerably more advanced than those of other Member States: Report, 'Could Brussels Drive Share Trading out of Europe?' (2003) 22 *IFLR* 17, 22.

[48] See generally Ferrarini, G, 'Best Execution and Competition Between Trading Venues—MiFID's Likely Impact' (2007) 2 *CMLJ* 404.

[49] The Commission described the MiFID I best execution regime as 'central to the structure and logic of the Directive. [Best execution obligations] not only form a fundamental element of investor protection, but are also necessary to mitigate possible problems associated with market fragmentation': Commission, Background Note to the Draft Commission Directive, February 2006, 24.

route certain orders to stock exchanges, generated conflict-of-interest risks; the best execution obligation, together with the MiFID I fair treatment rules and conflict-of-interest management regime, was designed to protect clients against these prejudicial conflicts of interest.

The design of the MiFID I best execution obligation proved a challenge. As discussed in Chapter V, the MiFID I negotiations on the new competitive order-execution regime were febrile, given the re-allocation of trading benefits between exchanges and other venues which would follow MiFID I. The danger accordingly arose that the best execution requirement could have become a vehicle for favouring one or other class of trading venue. Best execution requirements are also, by their nature, technical and costly, and were all the more so in the new, liberalized MiFID I market, as execution intermediaries could have been required to review trading on and connect to a multiplicity of venues. In addition, poorly designed and overly prescriptive best execution requirements, which, for example, focus on a limited range of execution criteria, run the risk of restricting execution choices and of obstructing the development of competition between execution venues.[50] Best execution obligations should reflect the dependence of best execution on a range of factors and accordingly be flexibly designed;[51] these factors include the impact of trading costs, the importance of speed of execution (particularly where market impact costs arise), and the depth of liquidity, as well as the structure of the market (whether dealer or order-driven—see Chapter V on different market structures), the nature of the instrument (the best execution obligation engages very differently with equities as compared with customized derivatives), and the nature of the order. A flexible approach also allows multiple competing venues to compete on factors other than price—a price-based benchmark, for example, could have the effect of reinforcing the dominant position of incumbent venues where liquidity is deepest.

The MiFID I best execution obligation (composed of the MiFID I legislative regime and the administrative rules set out in the administrative 2006 Commission MiFID I Directive[52] as well as Commission[53] and Committee of European Securities Regulators (CESR) guidance[54]) has, however, been regarded as broadly successful and has not been significantly reformed by MiFID II. Difficulties did arise with respect to the ability of firms to achieve best execution, but these primarily reflected the poor quality of post-trade transparency data[55] rather than the design of the best execution obligation. The MiFID I Review accordingly focused in the main on the quality of trading information flows to investment firms, rather than on the nature of the best execution obligation.

---

[50] Ferrarini, G, 'Contract Standards and the Markets in Financial Instruments Directive' (2005) 1 *Euro Rev Contract L* 19, 38.

[51] Ferrarini, n 48, 407.

[52] Directive 2006/73/EC [2006] OJ L241/26.

[53] Working Document ESC/07/2007, Commission Answers to CESR Scope Issues under MiFID and the Implementing Directive.

[54] CESR, Best Execution under MiFID. Questions and Answers (2007) (CESR/07-320). Of particular note is CESR's approach to the controversial question of whether a firm could include only one execution venue in its policy. CESR suggested that MiFID I did not prohibit firms from selecting only one venue (as long as the choice could be justified as obtaining the best possible result on a consistent basis), and that circumstances could arise where a particular venue would consistently achieve the best possible result, or where the costs of including more than one venue would outweigh any price improvement.

[55] See further Ch V on the impact of MiFID I on trading.

The 2014 MiFID II best execution regime, like the MiFID I regime, is based on a widely cast best execution obligation which is buttressed by execution policy, execution policy-monitoring, execution data collection, and disclosure requirements (MiFID II Article 27(1)). The regime also reflects client autonomy; where there is a 'specific instruction' from the client, the firm must execute the order following the specific instruction (Article 27). As under MiFID I, the best execution obligation applies generically to all trades in financial instruments, although it does not apply to transactions between investment firms and eligible counterparties (including through dealing on own account) (Article 30). It is not calibrated to different instruments, venues, and order handling processes, but leaves determination of the process for the achievement of best execution in particular circumstances to the firm.

Under Article 27(1), investment firms must take all 'sufficient'[56] steps when executing orders to obtain the 'best possible result' for their clients, taking into account price, costs, speed, likelihood of execution and settlement, size, nature, and other relevant considerations. In order to support the achievement of best execution, a new MiFID II obligation requires that for instruments which are subject to the trading venue obligation under MiFIR,[57] each trading venue and systematic internalizer,[58] and for other instruments each execution venue, makes publicly available—without charge—data relating to the quality of execution of transactions on that venue, on at least an annual basis, and including details on price, costs, speed, and likelihood of execution (Article 27(3)).[59]

In support of the core best execution obligation, investment firms must establish and implement 'effective arrangements', including an order-execution policy, to allow them to obtain the 'best possible' result in accordance with Article 27(1) (Article 27(4)). Best execution is therefore a function of a process rather than of a particular price benchmark. Disclosure is also deployed to support best execution; firms must provide information to their clients on their order-execution policy which explains clearly, in sufficient detail, and in a way that can easily be understood by clients, how orders will be executed (Article 27(5)); firms must also obtain the prior consent of clients to the execution policy (Article 27(5)). The investment firm must also inform the client where the order was executed (Article 27(3)). More generally, investment firms must summarize and make public on an annual basis (for each class of financial instrument) the top five venues (in terms of trading volume) where they executed client orders in the preceding year, and provide information on the quality of execution obtained (Article 27(6)).

---

[56] The Proposal applied a 'reasonable' standard (supported by the Council) but the European Parliament inserted a higher 'necessary' standard: MiFID II, Parliament Negotiating Position, 28 October 2012 (P7_TA (2012)0406) Art 27(1). 'Sufficient' was the compromise solution.

[57] This obligation requires shares admitted to a regulated market to be traded on certain classes of trading venue only, and imposes a trading venue obligation on particular derivatives (Ch V sect 6.6 and this Ch sect 4.3).

[58] A systematic internalizer is an investment firm which systematically executes client orders internally through bilateral dealing: Ch V sect 6.5.

[59] The Commission noted that data relating to, eg, speed of execution and number of orders cancelled prior to execution was relevant to the assessment of best execution: 2011 MiFID II Proposal (COM (2011) 656/4) 8. This reform received strong support from the Member States and from the buy-side: 2011 MIFID II/MiFIR Proposals Impact Assessment (SEC (2011) 1226) 55.

Some prescription is imposed on the firm's execution policy (and thereby on the firm's execution practices) under Article 27(5), which requires that the policy include, in respect of each class of instrument, information on the different venues where the investment firm executes its client orders and the factors affecting the choice of execution venue. Firms must include those venues that enable firms to obtain on a 'consistent basis' the 'best possible' result for the execution of client orders. Reflecting the 2014 MiFID II/MiFIR concern that trading be organized on regulated trading venues (Chapter V), investment firms must inform clients where the order-execution policy provides for the possibility of client orders being executed outside a MiFID II/MiFIR trading venue and obtain the 'prior express consent' of clients before executing orders outside a trading venue.[60] Article 27(1) specifies that where there is more than one competing execution venue (in accordance with the firm's execution policy), in order to assess and compare the result for the client, the firm's own commission and costs for execution must be taken into account in the assessment. A specific conflict-of-interest requirement applies: the firm must not receive any remuneration, discount, or non-monetary benefit for routing client orders to a particular venue which would be in breach of the MiFID II conflict-of-interest regime (Article 27(2)).

The more elaborate and complex the best execution policy, however, the greater the likelihood of costs being passed on to clients; the cost burden for retail clients, in particular, where extensive search costs are imposed on firms could become significant. The MiFID I administrative regime therefore established a price benchmark for best execution in the retail markets which has now been incorporated within the legislative text. Under Article 27(1), the best possible execution result for retail clients is to be determined in terms of the 'total consideration', representing the price of the instrument and the execution costs (including all expenses incurred by the client directly related to order execution).

Monitoring obligations apply. Article 27(7) requires firms who execute client orders to monitor the effectiveness of their execution arrangements and policy, and to identify and correct any deficiencies. The monitoring process must include an assessment, on a regular basis, of whether the execution venues included in the policy provide the best possible result for the client, and whether changes are required to firms' execution arrangements (taking account of the information made publicly available under MiFID II on execution quality).

Clients may request the investment firm to demonstrate that their orders have been executed in accordance with the firm's execution policy; investment firms must also be able to demonstrate compliance with the best execution regime to their NCAs on request (Article 27(8)).

The best execution regime is subject to an extensive delegation to administrative rule-making by the Commission (Article 27(9)); ESMA has additionally been empowered to propose RTSs relating to the new data collection and reporting requirements (Article 27(10)). The MiFID II administrative rulebook is likely to reflect the administrative 2006 MiFID I

---

[60] On MiFID II/MiFIR trading venues see Ch V. The earlier and similar MiFID I consent requirement was described as creating a hierarchy among trading venues and as unnecessary for investor protection: Köndgen, J and Theissen, E, 'Internalization under the MiFID: Regulatory Overreaching or Landmark in Investor Protection', in Ferrarini, G and Wymeersch, E (eds), *Investor Protection in Europe. Corporate Law-Making, The MiFiD, and Beyond* (2006), 271, 287.

Directive, which amplified the best execution process and calibrated the best execution obligation to particular situations.

The 2006 Directive followed a flexible approach and set out in general terms the criteria according to which firms were to assess the relative importance of the different best execution factors, thereby eschewing a benchmark-based process—save in the retail markets (now incorporated into the legislative text). The extent of the obligation to select and connect to execution venues, given the potential costs—particularly for smaller brokers— caused very considerable difficulties during the negotiations on the MiFID I best execution regime, and led the Commission to clarify that the core obligation to take all reasonable steps to secure the best possible result was governed by reasonableness and did not require a firm to include all available execution venues in its policy;[61] a 'sufficient steps' test now applies under Article 27(1), but a similar approach, injecting elements of reasonableness, is likely to be followed at the administrative level. The administrative rules did not, however, leave the firm with complete discretion: they set out, for example, the criteria to be taken into account in developing execution policies—the characteristics of the client (including whether retail or professional), the characteristics of the financial instruments, the subject of the order, and the characteristics of the execution venue to which the order could be directed (2006 Commission MiFID I Directive Article 44(1))—and imposed a non-discrimination obligation which required investment firms not to structure or charge their commissions in such a way as to discriminate unfairly between execution venues (2006 Commission MiFID I Directive Article 44(4)).

The administrative regime also addressed the particular best execution risks arising from portfolio management. Under MiFID I (as under MiFID II), the best execution obligation applied to the execution of orders. It did not, therefore, apply to the decision made by an asset manager to route an order to a particular broker for execution. CESR advised that the Article 19(1) 'fair treatment' principle (now MiFID II Article 24(1)) be used to support a discrete best execution regime, designed to address the application of best execution requirements to asset management. Accordingly, under Article 45(1) of the 2006 Commission MiFID I Directive, investment firms, when providing portfolio-management services, were to comply with the Article 19(1) obligation when placing orders generated by decisions to deal in financial instruments on behalf of clients with other entities for execution; Article 45(2) imposed the same obligation on firms which, when providing the service of reception and transmission of orders, transmitted client orders to other entities for execution. In order to comply with this overarching obligation, firms were to take all reasonable steps to obtain the best possible result for clients, taking into account the factors governing best execution (as amplified by the 2006 Commission MiFID I Directive); firms were also required to establish and implement a related best execution policy identifying, for each class of instrument concerned, the entities to which orders would be transmitted, to monitor and review this policy, and to provide related disclosures to clients (Article 45(4) and (5)). These firms were, accordingly, able to rely on the ability of the executing firm,

---

[61] The Commission acknowledged that where the costs of connecting to certain execution venues would be disproportionate and lead to a heavy overall increase in fees, firms would not be expected to connect to such venues: Background Note, n 49, 25. CESR's approach was also facilitative (n 54).

once the choice of firm had been made in accordance with Article 45, to deliver best execution.[62]

Additional calibration was provided with respect to the application of the regime to dealer markets, through an informal MiFID I-related Commission document[63] which responded to CESR's request for clarification on the application of the obligation to markets where dealers provide continuous quotes either continuously, through an online or other limited-access venue, or bilaterally in response to a request for a quote.

VI.2.2.3 Order Handling

The 2014 MiFID II conduct regime also includes order handling rules. MiFID II Article 28(1) addresses the processing of investor orders and the management of conflicts of interest, and requires investment firms to implement procedures and arrangements which provide for prompt, fair, and expeditious execution of client orders, relative to other client orders and the trading interests of the investment firm. It also imposes a time-priority rule which requires firms to execute otherwise comparable orders in accordance with the time of their reception. These rules are designed to enhance confidence in the impartiality and quality of execution services in a competitive trading environment, particularly where retail orders are 'internalized' by investment firms.[64]

The delegations conferred on the Commission to adopt related administrative rules reflect the MiFID I delegations and so can be expected to lead to the adoption of rules similar to those in the 2006 Commission MiFID I Directive. Article 47(1) of the 2006 Directive required that firms comply with a series of overarching conditions when handling client orders. Orders were to be promptly and accurately recorded and allocated. Firms were to carry out otherwise comparable orders sequentially and promptly, unless the characteristics of the order or prevailing market conditions made this impracticable, or where the interests of the client required otherwise. They were also to inform retail clients about any material difficulties relevant to the proper carrying out of orders promptly upon becoming aware of the difficulty. Where the firm was responsible for overseeing or arranging the settlement of an executed order it was to take all reasonable steps to ensure that any client financial instruments or funds received in settlement of the executed order were promptly and correctly delivered to the account of the appropriate client (Article 47(2)). The risk of market abuse and the front running of orders was addressed by Article 47(3), which required that the investment firm not misuse information relating to pending client orders, and take all reasonable steps to prevent the misuse of such information by its employees and management.

Article 48 of the 2006 Commission MiFID I Directive imposed conditions on the aggregation and allocation of orders and required that aggregation and allocation occur only where it was unlikely that it would work, overall, to the disadvantage of any client whose order was to be aggregated, that disclosure of the risk of disadvantage be made to the

---

[62] The lifting of the direct best execution obligation was the result of concerted lobbying by the investment management industry: Stones, R, 'An Introduction to MiFID and its Controversies' (2006) 25(8) *IFLR* 22.

[63] Working Document ESC/07/2007, Commission Answers to CESR Scope Issues under MiFID and the Implementing Directive (2007).

[64] Ferrarini, G and Recine, F, 'The MiFID and Internalisation' in Ferrarini and Wymeersch, n 60, 235, 257.

client, and that an order-allocation policy be established and implemented which provided in sufficiently precise terms for the fair allocation of aggregated orders and transactions. Aggregation and allocation in the risk-prone context of own-account dealing was addressed under Article 49, which provided that where investment firms aggregated own-account transactions with client orders, the allocation was not to be made in a way detrimental to the client. In particular, where orders were allocated and the aggregated order only partially executed, the related trades were to be allocated to the client in priority over the firm. The order-allocation policy was also to cover aggregation of own-account orders with client orders.

VI.2.2.4 Trade and Transaction Reporting

All investment firms which conclude transactions in shares and equity-like instruments and in specified non-equity asset classes, either on own account or on behalf of clients, are subject to post-trade transparency requirements which require disclosure of trade data relating to the volume and price of the transactions and the time at which they were concluded; publication must be made through an 'Approved Publication Arrangement'. Pre-trade transparency requirements apply only where the investment firm acts as a 'systematic internalizer' in that, on an organized, frequent, systematic, and substantial basis, it executes client orders by dealing on own account. Investment firms are also required to keep records on all orders and transactions in financial instruments which they have carried out (whether on own account or on behalf of clients), and to report complete and accurate details of all transactions executed in identified financial instruments to the relevant NCA as quickly as possible, and no later than the close of the following working day. These requirements relate in the main to the EU's regulation of trading venues and of venue efficiency generally, and are considered in Chapter V.

Additionally, investment firms are subject to the general operational and organizational reporting requirements which apply under MiFID II/MiFIR. A trading-specific obligation is imposed by MiFID II which requires that the records kept by firms include mandatory recordings of telephone conversations or electronic communications relating to transactions concluded when dealing on own account, and the provision of client order services relating to the reception, transmission, and execution of client orders (MiFID II Article 16(7)).[65]

VI.2.3 Algorithmic Trading and High Frequency Trading

The MiFID I regime governing trading practices has been significantly expanded by the new regime which applies to algorithmic trading and HFT by investment firms.

HFT has its origins in the recent growth in electronic trading and in competition between trading venues, and in the related fragmentation of execution markets and generation of arbitrage opportunities, all of which are driving innovative trading technologies.[66] It is a

---

[65] The obligation extends to conversations and communications which are intended to result in transactions concluded when dealing on own account and the provision of client order services, even if the communication or conversation does not lead to this outcome. See Ch IV sect 7.2.

[66] eg, Justham, A, (UK FSA), Speech on 'Evolving Market Structures and the Focus on Speed—How Regulators Should try to Keep Pace', 25 November, 2010.

form of 'algorithmic trading', or automated trading based on sophisticated computer technology which dictates trading decisions and which takes advantage of arbitrage opportunities. HFT is latency (or speed of execution) sensitive. It is driven by computer programmes which interpret market signals and execute related trading strategies, and deploying high frequency orders (which are open often for less than a second and are typically market-neutral in effect), in order to take advantage of very short duration arbitrage opportunities; a range of techniques are used, including 'co-location' in, and 'direct'/'sponsored' electronic access to, trading venues.[67] It is typically engaged in by specialist dealers dealing against their own capital (high frequency traders) and is usually deployed to implement particular trading strategies (such as arbitrage, market-making, or short-term/news-driven directional strategies).[68]

The implications of HFT activity, which is significant in the EU,[69] for market efficiency are contested. It can bring significant benefits to markets in the form of deeper liquidity (high frequency traders have come to act as quasi-market-makers by providing continuous 'two-way' (buy and sell) liquidity on major electronic order books[70]), narrower spreads, stronger price discovery, and better price alignment across venues;[71] the liquidity benefits have led trading venues to create incentives in the form of liquidity-sensitive trading fees to support market-making.[72] But risks can be generated, particularly where high frequency traders providing market-making functions withdraw in volatile market conditions and so contribute to a contraction of liquidity.[73] Operational failures with respect to HFT can also threaten orderly trading, as suggested by the 'Flash Crash' on US trading venues on 6 May 2010.[74] Related concerns have arisen as to whether trading venues have appropriately

---

[67] Co-location involves the firm/trader's servers being located within the trading venue in question. Direct electronic access involves a firm/trader connecting directly to a trading venue through a member or participant firm; such arrangements are termed 'sponsored access' where the trader does not place the order through the firm's trading infrastructure. The MiFID II approach is to term both forms of sponsored and direct access as direct electronic access and to treat both forms in broadly the same manner (MiFID II Art 4(1)(41)). Most EU HFT activity is in the form of co-location.

[68] See further Hagströmer, B and Nordén, L, The Diversity of High Frequency Traders (2012), available at <http://ssrn.com/abstract=2153272>.

[69] Estimates of its scale vary. It has been estimated as accounting for in the region of 30–50 per cent of trading: FSA, The FSA's Markets Regulatory Agenda (2010) 18. The European Securities and Markets Authority (ESMA) reported that HFT firms accounted for some 40–70 per cent of total equity trading volume in Quarter 4 2010 in the EU equity market: ESMA, HFT Consultation (2011) (ESMA/2011/224) 49.

More recently, ESMA has reported that HFT firms accounted for some 22 per cent of value traded in EU equity markets in May 2013, and that levels of HFT activity in different trading venues range from 8 per cent to 39 per cent (being higher on multilateral trading facilities (MTFs) (close to 40 per cent) than on regulated markets (close to 20 per cent)). ESMA also found that most orders in EU equity markets (60 per cent) originate from HFT firms (the volume of orders is significantly larger than the number of trades executed (some 22 per cent)): ESMA, Trends, Risks, and Vulnerabilities. Report No 1 (2014) (ESMA/2014/0188) (ESMA 2014(1) TRV), Report on High Frequency Trading Activity in EU Equity Markets (at 41–7).

[70] FSA, n 69, 18.

[71] eg, and from an extensive literature, Hendershott, T, Jones, C, and Menkveld, A, 'Does Algorithmic Trading Improve Liquidity' (2011) 66 *J Fin* 1 and Jovanovic, B and Menkveld, A, Middlemen in Limit Order Markets (2011), available at <http://ssrn.com/abstract=1624329>, examining the Belgian and Dutch markets.

[72] CESR, Impact of MiFID on Equity Secondary Market Functioning (2009) (CESR/09/355) 18.

[73] eg, Grob, S, 'The Fragmentation of the European Equity Markets' in Lazzari, V (ed), *Trends in the European Securities Industry* (2011) 127.

[74] During a 20-minute period starting at 2:40 pm, over 20,000 trades, across more than 300 securities, were executed at prices which were some 60 per cent away from the 2:40pm prices. While the subsequent SEC/CFTC Report identified a series of causes, it highlighted the impact of an automated 'Sell Algorithm'

robust risk-management structures to deal with very high volumes of HFT. Doubts have also been raised as to whether real liquidity benefits are created, as HFT tends to lead to a decrease in trade order size rather than to new liquidity, can lead to other liquidity providers leaving the market, and can result in poor quality liquidity, volatility, and churning.[75] HFT has also been linked with the growth of the dark OTC equity trading which became a major concern of the MiFID I Review of trading venue regulation; HFT trading has been associated with increased demand for dark OTC trading as a protection against the market impact risks which a trader unwinding a large position can face when high frequency traders are active.[76] More generally, while HFT has attracted most attention, it forms only a subset of algorithmic trading generally, which is frequently deployed by investment firms to pursue proprietary dealing strategies as well as agency trading, and which demands careful operational oversight as it can generate the range of risks associated with HFT.[77]

The empirical evidence on the risks and benefits of HFT (and of algorithmic trading generally) is contested[78] and the regulatory design challenges are considerable, not least with respect to how best to capture HFT and algorithmic trading efficiently within robust regulatory definitions. A reasonable case can, however, be made for closer regulatory attention,[79] even if only to assess whether relevant risk management and market integrity rules are correctly applied to traders and venues and appropriately supervised, and to enhance regulatory intelligence on this form of trading. The financial stability implications of HFT, as well as the strong association between HFT and the wider crisis-era concern as to financial market intensity and innovation generally, made HFT a natural target, however, for the expanding crisis-era reform programme[80] and for an interventionist approach.

---

which executed trades in some 75,000 derivative contracts. SEC and CFTC, Findings Regarding the Market Events of May 6 2010 (2010).

[75] Hertig, G, 'MiFID and the Return to Concentration Rules' in Grundmann, S, Haar, B, Merkt, H, Mülbert, P, and Wellenhofer, M (eds), *Festschrift für Klaus Hopt zum 70. Geburtstag am 24 August 2010* (2010) 1989.

[76] London Economics, Understanding the Impact of MiFID in the Context of Global and National and Regulatory Innovation (2010).

[77] On algorithmic trading generally see the UK government-sponsored study into computer-based/algorithmic trading generally: Foresight, the Future of Computer Trading in Financial Markets. Final Project Report (2012).

[78] The UK government's 2012 Foresight study examined the array of evidence and concluded that while some of the commonly-held negative perceptions of HFT and algorithmic trading were not supported by the evidence, and while these trading practices were associated with improvements to market functioning, policymakers were justified in focusing on these forms of trading, given the potential risks in terms of periodic illiquidity, market instability, and market abuse: n 77. Similarly, a Bank of England study has found that high frequency traders can contribute both 'good' and 'excessive' volatility and that it is not immediately clear what the welfare implications of HFT are: Benos, E and Sagade, S, High-frequency Trading Behaviour and its Impact on Market Quality, Bank of England WP No 469 (2012). From the price formation perspective, and finding that HFT facilitates efficient price discovery, see Brogaard, J, Hendershott, T, and Riordan, R, High Frequency Trading and Price Discovery, ECB WP Series No 1602 (2013).

[79] eg, Angel, J, Harris, L, and Spatt, C, Equity Trading in the 21st Century, Marshall School of Business WP No FBE 09 09-10 (2010), available at <http://ssrn.com/abstract=1584026>.

[80] Haldane, A (Bank of England), Speech on 'The Race to Zero', 8 July 2011. Internationally, the examination of HFT quickly acquired some momentum, with the US SEC examining issues related to HFT (SEC, Concept Release 34-61358, Concept Release on Equity Market Structure (2010)), and IOSCO, in response to a G20 mandate, addressing automated trading generally (IOSCO, Regulatory Issues Raised by the Impact of Technological Changes on Market Integrity and Efficiency. Consultation Report (2011) and earlier, IOSCO, Principles for Direct Electronic Access (2010)).

In the EU, the approach adopted can be located at the more interventionist end of the spectrum.[81] The first salvo was fired by ESMA, but its approach was relatively careful. One of ESMA's first major initiatives outside the administrative rulebook was its 2011 guidelines for highly automated trading environments.[82] The Guidelines, which are high-level in nature and systems- and controls-based, are closely based on MiFID I and provide guidance on how MiFID I's operational requirements apply to 'highly automated trading' and in relation to trading venues and investment firms. The MiFID I Review, however, has led to a targeted and more intrusive legislative regime on algorithmic trading generally.

The new 2014 MiFID II regime has three strands: it provides for a new operational regime governing algorithmic trading by investment firms; it extends the scope of MiFID II to include all firms engaging in algorithmic trading and, in particular, specialist firms engaging in HFT; and it imposes new operational requirements on trading venues.[83] Although the Commission, Council, and European Parliament were all in agreement on the need to bring algorithmic trading within the regulatory net, the negotiations proved contentious, with the Parliament, which had been hostile to HFT,[84] adopting a more restrictive approach than the Council,[85] particularly with respect to the regulation by trading venues of the HFT subset of algorithmic trading.[86] Given the uncertain impact of restrictions on algorithmic trading, particularly with respect to liquidity levels when markets are disrupted and there are few incentives to provide liquidity,[87] ESMA's ability to calibrate the regime in order to minimize unintended consequences will have a significant influence on the effectiveness of this new and largely untested regime.

At the core of the new regime are the operational requirements governing 'algorithmic trading' generally (MiFID II Article 17), defined broadly as trading in MiFID II financial instruments where a computer algorithm automatically determines individual parameters of orders (such as whether to initiate the order, the timing, price, or quantity of the order, or how to manage the order after its submission), with limited or no human intervention

---

[81] Pre-empting the EU response and reflecting the more sceptical approach to intense levels of market activity in Germany, in February 2013 Germany adopted the High Frequency Trading Act which imposes a licensing requirement on high frequency traders, imposes conduct-of-business and organizational rules on algorithmic trading generally, and identifies how algorithmic trading can amount to market abuse.

[82] ESMA, Guidelines on Systems and Controls in an Automated Trading Environment for Trading Platforms, Investment Firms and Competent Authorities (2011) (ESMA/2011/456). ESMA's Guidelines build on earlier CESR work, including CESR, Microstructural Issues of the European Equity Markets (2010) (CESR/10-142).

[83] The trading venue requirements are outlined in Ch V.

[84] In its 2011 Resolution on Innovative Financing, the European Parliament highlighted that HFT was associated with excessive price volatility and the persistent deviation of securities and commodity prices from fundamental levels, and linked its control to the highly contested FTT: n 28, para 13 and para D.

[85] Council discussions were relatively smooth and generally supportive of the Commission's approach, with most discussion focusing on the concern of Member States to fine-tune the Commission's proposal that algorithmic traders provide liquidity on a continuous basis (the regime as adopted limits this obligation to market-making algorithms): Danish Presidency Progress Report on MiFID II/MiFIR, 20 June 2012 (Council Document 11536/12) (Danish Presidency MiFID II/MiFIR Progress Report) 9.

[86] The European Parliament called, eg, for minimum resting periods for orders to quell HFT and rules governing the minimum tick size (or minimum price movement increment): 2012 Parliament MiFID II Negotiating Position, n 56, Art 51(1b). These were finally accepted during the trilogue negotiations (Ch V sect 7.3).

[87] The 2012 Foresight Report, eg, cautioned against restrictive requirements, including with respect to continuous liquidity provision, minimum order resting times, and order-to-execution ratios.

(Article 4(1)(39));[88] a subset of rules apply to 'high frequency algorithmic trading'.[89] MiFID II-scope investment firms engaging in algorithmic trading are subject to a targeted operational regime (Article 17(1)) which requires them to have in place effective systems and risk controls, suitable to the business operated, to ensure that trading systems are resilient and have sufficient capacity, are subject to appropriate trading thresholds and limits, and prevent the sending of erroneous orders or the systems otherwise functioning in a way that may create or contribute to a disorderly market. Effective systems and risk controls must also be in place to ensure the trading systems cannot be used for a purpose contrary to the market abuse regime or contrary to the rules of a trading venue to which the firm is connected. The firm must also have in place effective business continuity arrangements to deal with trading system failures, and must ensure its systems are fully tested and properly monitored to ensure compliance with MiFID II.

Regulatory reporting requirements apply, although the regime is proportionate and practical in that MiFID II does not require NCAs to approve the highly complex models used for algorithmic trading or firms to notify all such models. A firm that engages in algorithmic trading must notify the home NCA and the NCA of the trading venue at which the investment firm, as a member or participant, is engaged in such trading; the firm's home NCA may require it to provide, on a regular or *ad hoc* basis, details of its algorithmic trading practices (Article 17(2)).[90] The home NCA must communicate the disclosures received to any NCA of a trading venue at which the firm (as a venue member) is engaged in algorithmic trading on the request of such an NCA (Article 17(2)). Where a firm engages in high frequency algorithmic trading, it must also store, in an approved form, accurate and time-sequenced records of all its placed orders and make them available to the NCA on request (Article 17(2)).

Particular conditions (Article 17(3)), designed to protect market efficiency and avoid a sudden withdrawal of liquidity, apply where the firm engages in algorithmic trading pursuing a market-making strategy.[91] In these circumstances the firm must engage in market-making continuously during a specified proportion of the trading venue's trading hours, except under exceptional circumstances, with the result of providing liquidity on a regular and predictable basis to the trading venue.[92] The firm must also enter into a binding

---

[88] The definition does not include any system used only for the purpose of routing orders to trading venues or for the processing of orders involving no determination of any trading parameters, or for the confirmation of orders or the post-trade processing of executed transactions.

[89] High frequency algorithmic trading is defined as any algorithmic trading technique characterized by: infrastructure intended to minimize network and other types of latencies (including at least co-location, proximity hosting, or high speed 'direct electronic access' (n 93)); system determination of order initiation, generating, routing, or execution, without human intervention for individual trades or orders; and high message intraday rates which constitute orders, quotes, or cancellations: Art 4(1)(40).

[90] Including with respect to trading parameters and limits, testing details, and key compliance and risk controls.

[91] A firm pursues a market-making strategy when, as a member or participant of one or more trading venues, its strategy, when dealing on own account, involves posting firm, simultaneous two-way quotes of comparable size, and at competitive prices, relating to one or more financial instruments on a single trading venue or across different trading venues, with the result of providing liquidity on a regular and frequent basis to the overall market: Art 17(4).

[92] The Commission's earlier version of this provision generated intense industry hostility as it required all algorithmic trading strategies to be in continuous operation during the trading hours of the trading venue in question, and did not reflect the limited nature of many algorithms which are not designed to act as liquidity providers and which are not rewarded accordingly: 2011 MiFID II Proposal, n 59, Art 17(3).

written agreement between the investment firm and the trading venue which at least specifies the obligations of the firm with respect to market-making, and have in place effective systems and risk controls to ensure it can at all times fulfil its market-making obligations. The conditions apply taking into account the liquidity, scale, and nature of the specific market, and the characteristics of the instruments traded.

The regime also imposes specific controls on firms which, as members of trading venues, provide direct electronic access[93] by clients (in effect, high frequency traders) to the venues. These controls, *inter alia*, require that effective systems and controls are in place, that clients are subject to pre-set trading and credit controls, that client trading is monitored, and that risk controls apply to prevent client trading that could generate risks for the firm or create or contribute to a disorderly market—direct electronic access without such controls is prohibited, and firms are also responsible for ensuring that these clients comply with MiFID II and the rules of the trading venues and must monitor transactions to identify breaches of rules (Article 17(5)).[94]

The regime is to be expanded by RTSs governing the organizational requirements (including the requirement for a written agreement governing market-making) and the technicalities of the regime (Article 17(7)).

In tandem with these targeted rules, the scope of MiFID II has been extended to capture proprietary dealers who engage in HFT, reflecting the structure of the HFT industry. The exemptions which apply to proprietary dealers do not apply where the person in question applies a high frequency algorithmic trading technique (Article 2(1)(d) and (j)). In addition, the Article 17 regime applies to members or participants of regulated markets or MTFs who are not required to be authorized under MiFID II by virtue of the exemptions for insurance undertakings, collective investment undertakings, and certain energy market participants.[95]

The regulatory regime for investment firms extends beyond MiFID II, with the new market abuse regime including examples of when algorithmic trading and HFT would amount to market manipulation (Chapter VIII section 8.2.2).

---

[93] Defined as an arrangement where a member or participant of a trading venue permits a person to use its trading code so the person can electronically transmit orders relating to a financial instrument directly to the trading venue (whether or not the person in question uses the infrastructure of the member or participant or any connecting system provided by the member or participant): Art 4(1)(41). The regime does not accordingly differentiate between direct and sponsored access.

[94] Firms must monitor transactions in order to identify breaches of MiFID II and of the trading venue's rules, disorderly trading conditions, or conduct that may involve market abuse and that should be reported to the NCA. The firm must also ensure there is a binding written agreement between the firm and the client regarding the essential rights and obligations arising from the provision of the services; the firm must, under the agreement, retain responsibility under MiFID II. Where the firm provides direct electronic access to a trading venue, it must notify this to its home NCA and the trading venue at which the firm provides direct electronic access (the home NCA may require the firm to provide, on a regular or *ad hoc* basis, a description of the systems and controls used in relation to direct electronic access (this information must be shared with the NCAs of the relevant trading venues when requested)).

[95] Art 1(5) (the direct electronic access requirements) does not apply.

VI.2.4 Market-making

The sensitivity towards market liquidity which is implicit in the new regime governing algorithmic trading is also evident in the attention which the 2014 MiFID II regime gives to market-making[96] (MiFID I did not address market-making and the related risk/reward dynamics and appropriate regulatory supports). Firms engaging in market-making activities cannot be exempted under the MiFID II exemptions for proprietary dealers in instruments other than commodity derivatives, emissions allowances, and related derivatives (Article 2(1)(d)). Specific controls apply where market-makers use algorithmic techniques to engage in market-making, as noted in section 2.3 of this Chapter. The most extensive regulation applies at the trading venue level. As noted in Chapter V section 7.3, MiFID II/MiFIR trading venues must have in place market-making agreements with firms pursuing market-making strategies (the contents of which are subject to minimum conditions) and have schemes in place to ensure that a sufficient number of firms participate in such agreements, which agreements require them to post firm quotes at competitive prices with the result of providing liquidity to the market on a regular and predictable basis, where such a requirement is appropriate to the nature and scale of the trading on that venue (Article 48(2) and Article 18(5)).[97] Similarly, MTFs and organized trading facilities (OTFs)[98] must have at least three materially active members or users, each having the opportunity to interact with all the others with respect to price formation (Article 18(7)).

VI.2.5 Position Management and Trading in Commodity Derivatives

VI.2.5.1 The Commodity Derivatives Agenda

An extensive new position-management regime applies to trading in commodity derivatives under the 2014 MiFID II/MiFIR regime.

As noted in Chapter IV section 4.3, commodity derivative trading and related investment services came within the regulatory net under MiFID I, albeit that exemptions were available for commercial firms deploying commodity derivatives to hedge commercial risks. The regime governing trading in commodity derivatives has become significantly more intrusive over the crisis era. This reflects the expanding perimeter of EU securities and markets regulation and the wider G20 agenda to address unregulated sectors, but it also reflects an international policy concern as to the potentially destabilizing impact of trading by financial institutions in commodity derivatives on world commodity prices. In recent years, concerns have grown as to the increasing volume of trading in commodity derivatives by financial institutions (particularly through commodity index funds) on key benchmark commodity derivatives markets (notably for oil and agricultural products). This trading has

---

[96] A market-maker is a person who holds himself out on the financial markets on a continuous basis as being willing to deal on own account by buying and selling financial instruments against his proprietary capital at prices defined by him: Art 4(1)(7).

[97] RTSs will amplify the market-making conditions: Art 51(12).

[98] An organized trading facility (OTF) is a form of 2014 MiFID II/MiFIR trading venue (Ch V sect 6.4).

been associated with increasing commodity prices and volatility,[99] technical difficulties with pricing dynamics on these markets, and threats to market integrity.[100] Commodity derivatives market efficiency and integrity subsequently became entwined with the global crisis-era reform agenda, with the September 2009 Pittsburgh G20 Summit committing to improve the regulation, functioning, and transparency of financial and commodity markets to address excessive commodity price volatility,[101] and a related International Organization of Securities Commissions (IOSCO) agenda following.[102]

The related EU agenda has a number of elements,[103] including the EMIR-related strengthening of derivatives markets (section 4.2), the new controls on short selling, which also address trading in commodity derivatives (section 3), and the 2014 MiFID II/MiFIR tightening of the exemptions from regulation for commodity and commodity derivatives dealers (Chapter IV section 5.1). It also includes tighter regulation of the organized trading venues on which commodity derivatives are traded (as these markets tend to set the price benchmarks and to serve as the major price discovery channels for commodity prices), mainly through the new 2014 MiFID II/MiFIR position reporting and position-management/control regime.

The new MiFID II/MiFIR regime applies in relation to 2014 MiFID II/MiFIR trading venues and to persons trading in commodity derivatives, whether or not they are otherwise exempted from MiFID II/MiFIR,[104] and in relation to commodity derivatives generally.[105] It is accordingly cast in broad terms given the different dynamics of different types of commodity derivative and trading venue. It has four elements: NCA powers in relation to persons trading in commodity derivatives; related ESMA powers; trading venue position-management powers; and reporting obligations imposed on trading venues and persons.

---

[99] Between 1998 and 2008, the proportion of trading in commodity derivatives accounted for by physical hedgers fell from 77 per cent to 31 per cent, while the proportion accounted for by traditional and index speculators increased from 16 per cent and 7 per cent to 28 per cent and 41 per cent, respectively: Finance Watch, n 23, 39.

[100] eg, from an EU policy perspective, Commission, Public Consultation on the Markets in Financial Instruments Directive Review (2010) 37–9 and 2010 Parliament Resolution on Derivatives Markets, n 22. From the very extensive literature on the impact of derivatives trading on commodity markets and prices see, eg, Nissanke, M, 'Commodity Market Linkages in the Global Financial Crisis: Excess Volatility and Development Impacts' (2012) 48 *J of Development Studies* 732 and Gutierrez, L, 'Speculative Bubbles in Agricultural Commodity Markets' (2012) *European Rev of Agricultural Economics* 1.

[101] Pittsburgh G20 Summit, September 2009, Leaders' Statement, Strengthening the International Financial Regulatory System, para 12. The Communiqué of G20 Finance Ministers and Central Bank Governors of 15 April 2011 similarly called for participants on commodity derivatives markets to be subject to appropriate regulation and supervision, for enhanced transparency in both cash and derivatives markets, and for position management powers (para 15).

[102] eg IOSCO, Principles for the Regulation and Supervision of Commodity Derivatives Markets (2011).

[103] Commission, Tackling the Challenges in Commodity Markets and Raw Materials (2011) (COM (2011) 25) and Commission, A Better Functioning Food Supply Chain in Europe (2009) (COM (2009) 591).

[104] The 2014 position oversight regime applies to persons otherwise exempted under the MiFID II exemption regime: 2014 MiFID II Art 1(6).

[105] Commodity derivatives are defined as those financial instruments related to a commodity or underlying mentioned in 2014 MiFID II, Annex I, sect C(10) or within Annex I, sect C(5), (6), (7), and (10) (2014 MiFIR Art 2(1)(3)). On the scope of Annex I see Ch IV sect 4.3.

VI.2.5.2 NCA Powers

The 2014 MiFID II has introduced mandatory new harmonized powers for NCAs for controlling trading on commodity derivatives markets, primarily in the form of the intrusive power to set and impose position limits.[106] Reflecting the novelty and risks of the new regime and the concern to avoid distortions opening up between different markets and between the spot and derivatives markets, NCA discretion is tightly controlled by the extensive RTSs which will govern this area and by the different ESMA-based devices used to ensure NCAs operate within the harmonized regime. Similarly, the delegations to RTSs are detailed, and include injunctions to ESMA to take into account market and regulatory experience with such limits.

At the heart of the new regime is the highly contested position limit requirement (MiFID II Article 57).[107] NCAs, in line with the calculation methodology to be determined by ESMA, must establish and apply position limits on the size of a net position which a person can hold at all times in commodity derivatives traded on trading venues[108] and in economically equivalent OTC contracts (Article 57(1)). The limits must be set on the basis of all positions held by a person (and those held on its behalf at an aggregate group level) and in order to prevent market abuse and to support orderly pricing and settlement conditions, including preventing market-distorting positions and ensuring convergence between the pricing of derivatives in the delivery month and spot prices for the underlying commodity, without prejudice to price discovery in the market for the underlying commodity (Article 57(1)). The limits must specify clear quantitative thresholds for the maximum size of the position in a commodity derivative that a person can hold (Article 57(2)). In the formula repeatedly used across crisis-era EU derivatives market regulation in order to protect commercial hedging activities,[109] positions limits must not apply to positions held by or on behalf of a non-financial entity and which are objectively measurable as reducing risks directly related to the commercial activity of that non-financial entity (Article 57(1)). RTSs will govern the methodology to be applied by NCAs in establishing the spot month position limits and other position limits for physically settled and cash settled commodity derivatives, based on the characterization of the relevant derivatives.[110]

---

[106] Position limits were strongly resisted by market participants as being arbitrary and as not reducing volatility. They were supported, however, by the EU institutions (albeit with some disagreement as to where the power to set position limits should be located (whether at NCA or trading venue level), and the extent to which limits should be governed by EU rules), and in particular by the European Parliament which saw them as a means for reducing speculation and volatility.

[107] The regime evolved significantly over the negotiations. The Commission proposed the position limits power but provided for the Commission to adopt position limits (through administrative rules). The European Parliament took a restrictive approach, which included the capturing of positions designed to reduce risks from commercial activities, through a 'position check' system (although such positions are typically excluded from regulation across the EU regulatory regime or subject to careful calibration). The Council's position was more light-touch. The trilogue negotiations brought significant nuance to the regime, including with respect to a distinction between person-related position limits and contract-related limits, detailed specification of the RTSs which will govern this area, and a co-ordination mechanism for establishing limits, given that trading occurs across different venues.

[108] The regulated markets, MTFs, and OTFs within the scope of MiFID II/MIFIR: see Ch V.

[109] It is embedded in, eg, the 2012 EMIR regime (sect 4.2) and also applies under MiFID II (eg Ch IV sect 5 on exemptions).

[110] The different factors which ESMA is to consider in developing the RTSs are specified in Art 57(3) and include the maturity of the commodity derivative contract; the overall 'open interest' in that contract (or the total of all futures and options contracts held) and in other financial instruments with the same underlying

In addition, NCAs must set limits for each contract in commodity derivatives traded on trading venues (and including economically equivalent OTC contracts), based on the methodology developed by ESMA for person-related limits (Article 57(4)). As commodity derivatives trade across different venues, a mechanism applies to allocate primary responsibility for determining the single position limit to be applied to all trading in a contract where the same commodity derivative contract is traded in 'significant volumes' on trading venues in more than one jurisdiction; in effect, the limit-setting responsibility lies with the NCA of the venue where the largest volume of trading takes place, but this NCA must co-ordinate with other relevant NCAs (Article 57(6)). NCAs are also to put in place co-operation arrangements, including with respect to the exchange of data to enable monitoring and enforcement of the single position limit.

In an indication of the concern to ensure this novel and interventionist regime is sensitive to market dynamics, NCAs must review position limits whenever there is a significant change in deliverable supply or in open interest, or any other significant change in the market, and reset the limits in accordance with the ESMA methodology (Article 57(4)).

NCAs can impose more restrictive position limits than those established *ex ante*, but only in exceptional cases, where the action is objectively justified and proportionate, taking into account the liquidity and the orderly functioning of the specific market (Article 57(13)).

Generally, position-management limits and controls must be transparent and non-discriminatory, specify how they apply, and take into account the nature and composition of market participants (Article 57(9)).

ESMA is injected into the new position limit process across a number of dimensions, and is to bring expert capacity, as well as operational consistency and convergence, to the regime. It will develop the RTSs governing the pivotal position-limit-setting methodology (Article 57(3). It must also propose an array of other RTSs, including with respect to the scope of the obligation (including with respect to whether a position qualifies as reducing risks directly related to commercial activities, the aggregation determination, and whether a contract is economically equivalent) and the procedure for determining the venue on which the largest volume of trading takes place (Article 57(12)). It is also empowered to review position limits (Article 57(5)). NCAs are to notify ESMA of the exact position limits they intend to set; within two months, ESMA must provide an opinion assessing the compatibility of the limits with the objectives of the position limits regime and with the position-limit-setting methodology. An NCA must modify its limits in accordance with the opinion or provide ESMA with a justification as to why change is not considered necessary; where an NCA imposes limits contrary to an ESMA opinion, it must immediately publish on its website its reasons for doing so. Similarly, where an NCA imposes more restrictive position limits in exceptional cases, ESMA must offer an opinion as to whether the limits are necessary; where an NCA imposes limits contrary to the opinion, it must immediately publish its reasons on its website (Article 57(13)). ESMA is also to monitor, at least

---

commodity; deliverable supply in the underlying commodity; the volatility of the relevant markets (including markets for substitute derivatives and underlying commodity markets); the number and size of market participants; the characteristics of the underlying commodity market; and the development of new contracts. ESMA must also take into account experience with position limits gained by investment firms or market operators operating a trading venue, and in other jurisdictions.

annually, how NCAs have applied the position-limits-setting methodology (Article 57(7)). Where ESMA determines that an NCA position limit is not in accordance with the methodology, it must take action in accordance with its breach of EU law powers under 2010 ESMA Regulation Article 17 (Article 57(5)).[111] With specific reference to contracts traded pan-EU, it is empowered to engage in binding mediation where NCAs cannot agree on a single position limit (Article 57(6)), and is to ensure that a single position limit effectively applies to the same contract, irrespective of where it is traded (Article 57(7)). More generally, it is to perform a facilitation and co-ordination role in relation to NCA action on positions and to ensure a consistent approach is taken by NCAs (2014 MiFIR Article 44(1)).

NCAs are also empowered generally to take specific supervisory/enforcement position-management action to require or demand the provision of information from any person regarding the size and purpose of a position or exposure entered into via a commodity derivative, and any assets or liabilities in the underlying market (Article 69(2)(j)); and, dovetailing with Article 57, to limit the ability of any person from entering into a commodity derivative, including by introducing limits on the size of a position in accordance with Article 57 (Article 69(2)(p)).[112]

VI.2.5.3 ESMA Powers

In addition to its quasi-regulatory and convergence/co-ordination powers, ESMA has—more radically—been conferred with direct position-related powers, akin to the powers it can deploy in relation to product intervention (Chapter IX 7.1) and with respect to short selling (section 3.9.2) under the 2014 MiFIR (Article 45). These powers proved controversial over the negotiations, reflecting Member State concern in some quarters that these powers breached the prohibition on the conferral of discretionary powers on EU agencies.[113]

These powers are not specific to commodity derivatives but apply to all derivative positions, although the regime focuses in particular on commodity derivatives. ESMA may directly request all relevant information regarding the size or purpose of a position or exposure entered into via a derivative from any person; require any such person to reduce the size of or to eliminate the position or exposure; and 'as a last resort' limit the ability of a person to enter into a commodity derivative transaction (MiFIR Article 45(1)). These measures take precedence over any MiFID II Article 69(2)(p) (commodity derivative-specific) or (0) (general) measure (section 2.6) adopted by the NCA (Article 45(1) and (9)).

As is the case with its product intervention and short selling powers, and to ensure compliance with the *Meroni* doctrine which prohibits ESMA from exercising discretionary

---

[111] On these powers see Ch XI sect 5.3.1.

[112] In relation to Art 69(2)(p), the NCA must comply with notification obligations (to the other NCAs and ESMA) and the NCA receiving a notification may take similar action (2014 MiFID II Art 79(5)). ESMA is also conferred with related co-ordination powers, including with respect to collation and publication of all such measures (2014 MiFIR Art 44(2)).

[113] Cyprus Presidency Progress Report on MiFID II/MiFIR, 13 December 2012 (Council Document 16523/1212). The nature of the powers to be granted to ESMA, with respect to the balance between position management and position limit tools, was also the subject of discussion.

powers and accordingly requires that conditions apply to confine discretion,[114] a series of conditions apply to the exercise of these powers. The ESMA measures must address a threat to the orderly functioning and integrity of financial markets, including commodities derivatives markets in accordance with the MiFID II Article 57 objectives and including in relation to delivery arrangement for physical commodities, or to the stability of the whole or part of the financial system in the EU. In addition, either an NCA or NCAs must not have taken measures to address the threat, or the measures taken must have not sufficiently addressed the threat. ESMA must also ensure that the measures taken meet a set of conditions.[115] Administrative rules[116] will specify further the conditions which apply to these powers.[117] ESMA must notify the relevant NCAs before imposing or renewing[118] any measures.[119]

VI.2.5.4 Trading Venue Requirements

The regime cascades to the MiFID II/MiFIR trading venues which trade commodity derivatives, which are required to have in place position-management controls (MiFID II Article 57(8)–(10)).[120] These powers must include, at least, powers for the trading venue to: monitor the open interest positions[121] of persons; access information relating to positions;[122] require the termination or reduction of a position, on a temporary or permanent basis, and to act unilaterally where the position holder does not comply; and, where appropriate, require a person to provide liquidity to the market at an agreed price and volume on a temporary basis with the intent of mitigating the effects of a large or dominant position. Position-management controls must be transparent and non-discriminatory,

---

[114] Case 9/56, *Meroni v High Authority* [1957–1958] ECR 133. See further Ch XI sect 5.8.2.

[115] The action must significantly address the threat to the orderly functioning and integrity of financial markets, including commodity derivatives markets (in accordance with the 2014 MiFID II Art 57 objectives) and including in relation to delivery arrangements for physical commodities, or to the stability of the EU financial system (or part thereof), or significantly improve the ability of NCAs to monitor the threat, as measured in accordance with the Art 45 regime; not create a risk of regulatory arbitrage; and not have the following detrimental effects on the efficiency of financial markets, disproportionate to the benefits of the measure—reduce liquidity in financial markets, restrain the conditions for reducing risks directly related to the commercial activity of a non-financial counterparty, or create uncertainty for market participants. ESMA must also consult with the Agency for the Co-operation of Energy Regulators (ACER) where the action relates to wholesale energy products, and with the public bodies responsible for the oversight, administration, and regulation of physical agricultural markets under the related EU regime, where the measure relates to agricultural commodity derivatives: Art 45(3).

[116] Reflecting the sensitivity of ESMA's powers, these rules do not take the form of RTSs.

[117] Including with respect to the existence of a threat justifying action (and taking into account the degree to which positions are used to hedge positions in physical commodities or commodity contracts, and the degree to which prices in underlying markets are set by reference to the prices of commodity derivatives); the appropriate reduction of a position or exposure; and where a risk of regulatory arbitrage could arise: 2014 MiFIR Art 45(10). These administrative rules are to take into account the RTSs developed under the 2014 MiFID II Art 57 regime.

[118] Measures must be reviewed at appropriate intervals and at least every three months. Where a measure is not renewed, it expires automatically. Renewal decisions are subject to the same conditions as apply to the original decision: Art 45(8).

[119] Notification must be made not less than 24 hours before the measure is intended to take effect (or to be renewed), but shorter notification is permissible in exceptional circumstances.

[120] The venue's position management controls must be notified to the NCA who must communicate this information to ESMA.

[121] An open interest position relates to the total of all futures and options contracts held.

[122] Including in relation to the position's size and purpose, the beneficial or underlying owners, concert arrangements, and any related assets or liabilities in the underlying physical market.

specify how they apply, and take into account the nature and composition of market participants.

VI.2.5.5 Position Reporting

Finally, a new position reporting regime applies to commodity derivatives (MiFID II Article 58). Trading venues which trade commodity derivatives (or emission allowances or derivatives thereof) must make public a weekly report[123] which sets out the aggregate positions held by different categories of persons for the different commodity derivatives (or emission allowances or derivatives thereof) traded on the venue, the number of long and short positions (by category of persons holding positions), changes from the previous report, the percentage of total open interest represented by each category, and the number of persons holding a position in each category (Article 58(1)).[124] This report must be communicated to the NCA and ESMA (Article 58(1)).[125] In addition, trading venues must provide to the NCA a complete breakdown of the positions held by all persons—including venue members or participants and their clients—on the venue, on at least a daily basis (Article 58(1)).

With respect to firms trading in commodity derivatives or emission allowances or derivatives thereof outside a trading venue (OTC trading), these firms must provide the NCA of the trading venue where the relevant commodity derivatives (or emission allowances or derivatives thereof) are traded (or the NCA where the instruments are traded in significant volumes, where more then one jurisdiction is engaged) on at least a daily basis with a complete breakdown of their positions taken in these instruments traded on a trading venue and in economically equivalent OTC contracts, as well as those of their clients and the clients of those clients until the end client is reached (Article 58(2)).[126]

To support monitoring of the Article 57 position limits regime, members or participants of regulated markets and MTFs, and clients of OTFs, must report to the investment firm or market operator operating the trading venue in question the details of their own positions held through contracts traded on the trading venue, on at least a daily basis (Article 58(3)).[127]

The categories of persons against which the reporting obligation applies are designed to allow NCAs to monitor the nature of trading, particularly the nature and prevalence of trading by financial institutions, and include authorized investment firms and credit institutions, investment funds (under the Undertakings for Collective Investment in Transferable Securities (UCITS) or Alternative Investment Fund Managers Directive (AIFMD) regimes),[128] other financial institutions (including insurance undertakings),

---

[123] The reporting obligation applies only where the number of position holders and their open positions in a given financial instrument exceed minimum thresholds.

[124] The report must distinguish between positions identified as positions which in an objectively justifiable way reduce risks directly related to commercial activities; and other positions.

[125] ESMA is charged with centralized publication of position-related information.

[126] The report must distinguish between positions identified as positions which in an objectively justifiable way reduce risks directly related to commercial activities and other positions.

[127] As well as those of their clients and the clients of those clients until the end client is reached.

[128] Directives 2011/61/EU OJ [2011] OJ L174/1 (2011 AIFMD) and Directive 2009/65/EC [2009] OJ L302/32 (2009 UCITS IV Directive).

commercial undertakings, and identified participants in the EU's emission allowances regime (Article 58(4)).

The reporting regime is to be amplified by ITSs governing the format of the trading venue reports to be provided by venue participants, and by administrative rules governing the thresholds below which the venue reporting obligation does not apply (having regard to the total number of open positions and their size, and the total number of persons holding a position).

VI.2.6 General Position Management

In addition to the commodity derivatives-related powers, MiFID II also requires, more generally, that an NCA be empowered to request any person to take steps to reduce the size of a position or exposure (whether or not in commodity derivatives) (Article 69(o)).[129] As noted in section 2.5.3 of this Chapter, ESMA can also exercise general position-management powers.

VI.3 The Regulation of Short Selling

VI.3.1 The EU Regime

The EU's regulation of trading includes a discrete short selling regime which came into force in 2012. The new short selling regime is composed of five legislative and administrative measures. The legislative 2012 Short Selling Regulation[130] has been amplified by four administrative measures: the 2012 Commission Delegated Regulation 918/2012, which contains the majority of the administrative rules;[131] the 2012 Commission Delegated Regulation 826/2012;[132] the 2012 Commission Delegated Regulation 919/2012;[133] and the 2012 Commission Implementing Regulation 827/2012.[134] The regime as a whole applied from 1 November 2012.

---

[129] The NCA must comply with notification obligations (to the other NCAs and ESMA) and the NCA receiving a notification may take similar action (2014 MiFID II Art 79(5)). ESMA is also conferred with related co-ordination powers, including with respect to the collation and publication of all such measures (2014 MiFIR Art 44(2)).

[130] n 33. For an assessment of the Regulation see Payne, J, 'The Regulation of Short Selling and its Reform in Europe' (2012) 13 *EBOLR* 413. The main publicly available elements of the legislative history are: Commission Proposal COM (2010) 482, Impact Assessment SEC (2010) 1055; Parliament Resolution adopting a Negotiating Position, 5 July 2011 (T7-0312/2011) (ECON Report A7-055/2011); and Council General Approach, 11 May 2011 (Council Document 10334/11). The ECB opinion is at [2011] OJ C91/1.

[131] Commission Delegated Regulation (EU) No 918/2012 [2012] OJ L274/1.

[132] Commission Delegated Regulation (EU) No 826/2012 [2012] OJ L251/1 (this Regulation takes the form of an RTS, originally proposed by ESMA).

[133] Commission Delegated Regulation (EU) No 919/2012 [2012] OJ L274/16 (this Regulation takes the form of an RTS, originally proposed by ESMA).

[134] Commission Implementing Regulation (EU) No 827/2012 [2012] OJ L251/11 (this Regulation takes the form of an ITS, originally proposed by ESMA).

VI.3.2 Regulating Short Sales and the Financial Crisis

Short selling involves the selling of a security (typically a share) which the seller does not own with the objective of buying the security prior to the delivery date;[135] it is usually achieved through derivatives or by short sales in the cash market. Where a short sale is 'uncovered' or 'naked', the seller does not borrow the security or enter into an agreement to secure its availability.[136] Short sales serve a number of purposes, including with respect to speculation, hedging and risk management, arbitrage, and market-making. Short selling can also be carried out through CDSs which fulfil similar economic functions to short sales in that they pay the CDS buyer a fee on a decrease in value of the covered (reference) security (corporate and sovereign bonds).[137]

It has long been assumed that short sales support market liquidity through the trades in which the short seller engages, and that they support efficient price formation by correcting over-pricing;[138] the series of autumn 2008 prohibitions internationally on short selling provided extensive evidence of the damage which prohibitions on short sales in shares can wreak on liquidity and on the efficiency of price formation.[139] Short sales can also act as hedging and risk-management devices, allowing the short seller to hedge against price decreases in long positions.[140] This is particularly the case with CDSs, which provide a risk-management function where liquidity is thin in the underlying bond market.[141] CDSs also support liquidity in the sovereign debt markets by standardizing the risk associated with different issues of debt through a single and interchangeable CDS contract.

---

[135] IOSCO, Regulation of Short Selling (2009) 23.

[136] A covered sale, by contrast, has a number of stages, including the borrowing of the shares (to be provided to the buyer at settlement) by the short seller, the shorting of the shares by the short seller, the purchase of the same number of shares to be returned to the original lender, and the return of the shares to the original lender: FSA, Discussion Paper 09/1, Short Selling (2009) 6.

[137] Accordingly, a seller of a CDS takes, in effect, a leveraged long position in the underlying reference bond, while a purchaser of a CDS takes a short position in the bonds: IOSCO, The Credit Default Swap Market (2012) 4.

[138] For a policy view see FSA, n 136, 10.

[139] The extensive literature generally finds that the restrictions contributed to volatility, negative pricing spirals, and a contraction of liquidity. See eg: Klein, A, Bohr, T, and Sikles, P, 'Are Short Sellers Positive Feedback Traders? Evidence from the Global Financial Crisis' (2013) 9 *J of Financial Stability* 337, Bebr, A and Pagano, M, 'Short Selling Banks around the World: Evidence from the 2007–09 Crisis' (2013) 68 *J Fin* 343, Gruenewald, S, Wagner, A, and Weber, R, 'Short Selling Regulation after the Financial Crisis—First Principles Revisited' (2010) 7 *International J of Disclosure and Regulation* 108, and Avgouleas, E, 'A New Framework for the Global Regulation of Short Sales: Why Prohibition is Inefficient and Disclosure Insufficient' (2010) 16 *Stanford J of Law, Business and Finance* 376. An extensive range of studies focus on particular markets. See, eg, Helmes, U, Henker, J, and Henker, T, The Effect of the Bank on Short Selling on Market Efficiency and Volatility (2009), available at <http://ssrn.com/abstract=1568435> (Australia), Arce, O and Mayordomo, S, Short Sale Constraints and Financial Stability: Evidence from the Spanish Ban 2010–2011 (2012), available at <http://ssrn.com/abstract=2089730> (Spain), and Boehmer, E, Jones, C, and Zhang, X, Shackling Short Sellers: The 2008 Shorting Ban (2011), available at <http://ssrn.com/abstract=1412844> (US).

[140] For a policy perspective from the US SEC, see SEC Release No 34-61595, Amendments to Regulation SHO (2010) 13–14.

[141] As is the case in the EU corporate bond market: 2010 Short Selling Proposal Impact Assessment, n 130, 13. CDSs were, presciently, initially analysed in the legal literature, immediately prior to the financial crisis, in Partnoy, F and Skeel, D, 'The Promise and Perils of Credit Derivatives' (2007) 75 *U of Cincinnati LR* 1019, which identified the hedging benefits of CDSs, their potential for bringing greater liquidity into credit markets by allowing banks to hedge their exposure more effectively, and their information transmission mechanism with respect to corporate performance (at 1023–7).

Prior to the financial crisis, a number of market efficiency risks had, however, been associated with short sales,[142] including CDS transactions. Chief among these are the potential short sales have for driving negative price spirals which can lead to disorderly markets and systemic risks; the lack of transparency associated with short sales and the related potential for manipulative conduct and inefficient pricing; and the particular risk of settlement failure[143] and speculation[144] associated with uncovered short sales, where the short seller carries the risk of being unable to close the short position, particularly in illiquid conditions.[145] The crisis era exposed how short selling can contribute to financial instability where negative selling pressure in the securities of a financial institution risks destabilizing an institution and, in conditions of acute market volatility and instability, can generate systemic risks. In addition, poor transparency can hobble regulators in assessing the scale and location of risks to financial stability and market efficiency.

The regulatory toolbox for short sales includes transparency and reporting requirements (including flagging requirements for short sale orders and individual position reporting requirements); conditions on short sales (including 'locate' rules, which are used to determine whether a short sale is covered and so permitted,[146] and 'tick' rules, which govern when short sales can occur);[147] and prohibitions (including 'circuit-breaker' rules which automatically halt trading when prices fall below a set threshold in a set time and prohibitions on uncovered short sales).[148] In the EU, short selling regulation was not common prior to the financial crisis, which has led to a dearth of empirical evidence on short sales[149] and on how to design an optimal regulatory response.

Short selling regulation underwent something of a transformation over the financial crisis as securities and markets regulators worldwide turned to it as a means for supporting financial stability—although it is hard to avoid the impression that a concern to be 'seen to act' and

---

[142] eg FSA, n 136.

[143] The failure of the short seller to deliver the shares to the buyer on the due date.

[144] Uncovered short sales raise similar issues as to the de-coupling of economic ownership and control rights as arise in relation to Contracts for Difference (CfDs) (Ch II sect 5.7).

[145] Although the EU evidence suggests that settlement failures linked to short selling are limited, and were limited over the crisis: 2010 Short Selling Proposal Impact Assessment, n 130, 26–7.

[146] 'Locate' rules, which require that the seller has made arrangements to locate and borrow the security in question (locate rules may, variously, require that the security is reserved for the seller or that best/reasonable efforts are made to ensure that the security is available), and related pre-borrowing rules, are designed to ensure that short sales are covered. They are associated with the reduction of settlement risk and of market disruption risk (in that an economic linkage exists between the demand for short selling activity and the supply of the related securities): IOSCO, n 135, 7–8.

[147] Chief among these is the 'uptick' rule which was a feature of US securities regulation for some 70 years until it was abolished in 2007 (it was replaced by the 'alternative uptick' rule in 2010 (n 155)). Under the uptick rule, a short sale could not be carried out unless the last sale was of a higher price than the sale preceding it.

[148] The US market has long been a laboratory for short selling rules, with short selling regulation a feature of US securities regulation since 1937. The US regime, now set out in Regulation SHO (2004), includes 'locate rules', circuit-breaker rules, an 'uptick' rule (n 155), and transparency rules, including with respect to the flagging of short sales.

[149] In developing the new short selling regime, the Commission struggled to estimate the volume of short selling in the EU market, and drew mainly on proxy evidence from the UK (based on securities lending data) and from Spain in estimating the volume of short sales in shares at approximately 1–3 per cent of EU market capitalization: 2010 Short Selling Proposal Impact Assessment, n 130, 11–13. By contrast, some 50 per cent of total listed equity trading volume in the US market is thought to represent orders marked as short orders under the US flagging regime: SEC Release No-64383, Short Sale Reporting Study Required by Dodd-Frank Act, 3.

to take visible action was also a factor.[150] Certainly, securities and markets regulators worldwide, who had traditionally relied heavily on disclosure tools,[151] had little experience of, and a limited toolbox for dealing with, the massive instability which shook financial markets in autumn 2008.[152] However counterintuitive for regulators who traditionally had not intervened in trading, trading-related regulation was one of the very few tools which could be quickly deployed to support financial stability[153]—however blunt and ineffective a tool it subsequently turned out to be.[154] In the US, for example, the Securities and Exchange Commission (SEC) imposed a temporary prohibition on short sales in the shares of 799 financial institutions on 18 September 2008.[155] On the same day in the UK, the (then) Financial Services Authority (FSA) announced a temporary prohibition on short sales in the shares of 32 financial institutions and related reporting requirements,[156] while similar action was taken by a range of different NCAs across the EU (section 3.3). Australia similarly prohibited short sales on 19 September 2008, although its prohibition originally extended to all listed securities.[157] Short selling did not, however, become a major priority for the G20-led reform agenda. IOSCO subsequently adopted principles on the effective regulation of short selling in response to the action taken worldwide in autumn 2008 and in order to assist regulators and restore and maintain investor confidence, but the principles operate at a high level of generality and did not attract significant political traction.[158]

In the EU, the financial crisis saw the regulatory treatment of uncovered CDS transactions, and particularly CDSs on sovereign debt, also become drawn into the short selling reform agenda; prior to the crisis, the regulation of short selling internationally—to the extent it occurred—was associated with the equity markets and with supporting market efficiency. CDSs are strongly associated with hedging and risk-management activities, and with the

---

[150] Enriques, L, 'Regulators' Response to the Current Crisis and the Upcoming Reregulation of Financial Markets: One Reluctant Regulator's View' (2009) 30 *UPaJIL* 1147.

[151] Hu, H, 'Too Complex to Depict? Innovation, "Pure Information" and the SEC Disclosure Paradigm' (2012) 90 *Texas LR* 1601, at 1687–701, examining the new reliance on short selling regulation as a major departure for disclosure-based regulators.

[152] IOSCO, Mitigating Systemic Risk. A Role for Securities Regulators (2011).

[153] The UK FSA noted in relation to its action that 'We did this at a time of extreme market turbulence, manifested in the form of high and prolonged price volatility and downward pressure on the prices of financial stocks in particular. We were concerned by the heightened risk of market abuse and disorderly markets posed by short selling in these conditions': FSA, n 136, 3.

[154] For a critique of the US, UK, and Australian interventions see Sheehan, K, Principled Regulatory Action. The Case of Short Selling (2009), available at <http://ssrn.com/abstract=1368531>.

[155] The prohibition followed a 15 July 2008 temporary prohibition by the SEC of uncovered short sales in 19 financial institutions, in response to the destabilizing effect of rumours. The SEC subsequently adopted the 'alternative uptick' rule which applies when a share has triggered a circuit-breaker by experiencing a price decline of at least 10 per cent in a day, and which requires that short sales can take place only when the price of the share is the current national best bid price: Regulation SHO, Rule 201, SEC Release No 34-61595, Amendments to Regulation SHO (2010).

[156] The prohibition (on net positions in excess of 0.25 per cent of the issued share capital) extended to uncovered and covered sales and to related transactions through derivatives. See Marsh, I and Payne, R, Banning Short Sales and Market Quality. The UK's Experience (2010), available at <http://ssrn.com/abstract=1645847>.

[157] On the Australian response see Hill, n 23, 256–61.

[158] IOSCO adopted four principles: that short selling should be subject to appropriate controls to reduce or minimize potential risks to the orderly and efficient functioning of markets and the stability of markets; that short selling should be subject to a reporting regime (to markets or to regulators); that an effective compliance and enforcement system apply; and that any rules adopted allow for appropriate exemptions: n 135.

allied support of bond market liquidity. But, as CDS trading is thought to have a strong impact on bond pricing, volatility in the CDS market (particularly where that market is concentrated and cannot quickly respond to demand) can have strong negative effects on bond pricing where bond investors (particularly in illiquid markets) rely heavily on CDS pricing.[159] The structure of a CDS also heightens the speculation risks associated with short selling generally; where the CDS holder does not hold an insurable interest against which the CDS hedges, the holder has strong incentives to drive a default or price decrease against which the CDS pays out.

But intervention in the CDS market, and in the sovereign CDS market in particular, is fraught with risk. CDS trading generally occurs in the global OTC markets; an effective prohibition requires close international co-ordination. Empirical evidence is limited. The empirical evidence as to a link between speculative uncovered trading in sovereign debt CDSs and volatility and instability in sovereign debt markets, for example, is not strong,[160] and it is now clear that the sovereign debt CDS market did not expand materially over the financial crisis.[161] Intervention can bring significant risks to liquidity in the sovereign debt markets, in particular, and to the efficiency with which sovereigns can manage deficits. Similarly, risk management can be prejudiced where market reliance on sovereign CDSs to hedge against a range of assets and liabilities, often on a cross-border basis, is curtailed.[162]

While there were some early indications of appetite for a co-ordinated international response to the treatment of CDSs,[163] the international 'speculation' agenda became largely concerned with the treatment of OTC derivatives and related clearing and venue-trading obligations, and moved away from short selling. The EU agenda, however, became highly politicized and closely associated with addressing the impact of short selling and CDS trades on the troubled sovereign debt market.

---

[159] 2010 Short Selling Proposal Impact Assessment, n 130, 25.

[160] IOSCO's 2012 report on the CDS market found that there was no conclusive evidence on whether taking short positions on credit risk through naked CDSs was harmful for distressed firms or for high yield sovereign bonds: IOSCO, n 137, 32–4. Similarly, the IMF has found that sovereign CDS spreads reflect economic fundamentals and other relevant market factors, that the sovereign CDS market is not prone to higher volatility than other market segments, that increases in sovereign CDS spreads do not cause higher sovereign funding costs, and, overall, that the evidence does not support a ban on uncovered sovereign CDSs and that a ban may reduce sovereign CDS market liquidity to the level at which these instruments become less effective as hedges and as indicators of credit risk: IMF, Global Financial Stability Report, April 2013, 57–92. Although Germany banned uncovered sovereign CDS trades in May 2010 in response to ongoing turmoil in sovereign debt markets in the EU, the BaFIN, Germany's financial regulator, had earlier concluded that CDS trading had not affected Greek bonds: BaFIN, Press Release, 8 March 2010.

[161] IOSCO has reported that globally, notional CDS exposure to private entities is x4 higher than exposure to sovereign entities, and that there has been relative stability in the size of the CDS market for euro-area sovereign debt since 2008: IOSCO, n 137, 7 and 9.

[162] In 2010, the IMF cautioned against prohibiting uncovered sovereign CDS trades given evidence that most dealers in this market were not inclined to take directional bets, and the importance of these instruments, for, eg, hedging against counterparty risks and country corporate risks: IMF, Global Stability Report, April 2010, 49–53. Similarly, cautioning against restricting short sales in sovereign debt given the implications for risk management, Blommestein, H, Keskinler, A, and Lucas, C, The Argument Against Short Selling (2011), available at <http://ssrn.com/abstract=1927787>.

[163] Early indications from the Commission suggested it supported a co-ordinated response through the G20 (Tait, N, Hall, B, and Oakley, D, 'Dilemma over CDS Trades Policing', *Financial Times*, 10 March 2010, 6). In March 2010, then FSB (Financial Stability Board) Chairman Draghi signalled some support for addressing the risks associated with speculation through CDSs: Peel, Q, 'Call for Ban on CDS Speculation', *Financial Times*, 11 March 2010, 6.

VI.3.3 The Evolution of the EU's Response

VI.3.3.1 Initial Developments

Three proximate drivers can be identified for the 2012 Short Selling Regulation: concerns as to regulatory fragmentation and arbitrage consequent on the unilateral and divergent prohibitions on short sales taken by the Member States initially in autumn 2008; a wider concern in some Member States, and particularly in the European Parliament, with respect to perceived excessive speculation and levels of financial market intensity and intermediation; and concerns, notably among the French and German governments, as to speculation in the sovereign debt markets, particularly through the use of CDSs, and as to the consequent pressure on the stability of the euro area and on Member States' ability to raise funds and manage deficits.

Short selling erupted on to the EU agenda in autumn 2008 when a number of Member States (not all)[164] imposed restrictions of varying types on short sales,[165] in an effort to shore up financial stability. Three forms of restriction or condition (which typically, although not always, applied to the shares of identified financial institutions) were used: disclosure requirements related to short positions;[166] prohibitions on naked short sales;[167] and prohibitions on short sales generally.[168] No Member State, until Germany's shock action in May 2010 (noted further on in this section), imposed restrictions on CDS transactions.

The first reform proposal[169] came in July 2009 with CESR's consultation on a pan-EU transparency regime relating to short positions,[170] which was adopted by CESR members in March 2010.[171] The regime, which is reflected in the 2012 Short Selling Regulation, applied to shares only, and recommended disclosure to NCAs where a short position amounted to 0.1 per cent of the issuer's share capital and public disclosure at 0.2 per cent, as well as disclosure at specified incremental steps thereafter.

Political and market conditions intervened in spring 2010 to place more radical regulatory measures on the agenda. Turmoil in the Greek sovereign debt market[172] fuelled political

---

[164] As at September 2010, ten Member States had no restrictions or conditions in place: Cyprus, Czech Republic, Estonia, Finland, Latvia, Malta, Romania, Slovakia, Slovenia, and Sweden.

[165] For a list of the restrictions in place at September 2010 (the majority of which were imposed in autumn 2008) see 2010 Short Selling Proposal Impact Assessment, n 130, Annex 3. A list of restrictions was maintained by CESR (initially CESR/08/742) and since ESMA (ESMA/2011/399). For an examination of the French, German, and UK action see Payne, n 130, 424–8.

[166] This was the most common form of requirement; of the 17 Member States which imposed some form of requirement, 11 imposed reporting requirements.

[167] Imposed by eight Member States, (generally, not always) in relation to identified financial institutions.

[168] Imposed by seven Member States (these prohibitions were typically imposed on shares of financial institutions and were temporary in nature).

[169] The Commission had earlier consulted on whether short selling should be addressed in the market abuse regime reforms in its related 2009 Call for Evidence (a consensus emerged that short selling raised financial stability rather than market abuse risks and should not be addressed under the market abuse regime), and had included risk management procedures related to short selling in its 2009 AIFMD Proposal (COM (2009) 207, Art 11).

[170] CESR, Proposal for a Pan-European Short Selling Disclosure Regime (2009) (CESR/09-581).

[171] CESR, Model for a Pan-European Short Selling Disclosure Regime (2010) (CESR/10-088).

[172] Earlier in May 2009, Greece had imposed a requirement for a flagging of short-sale orders and a circuit-breaker rule.

concerns that speculation in sovereign debt CDSs—in effect, speculation on the likelihood of default—was prejudicing the stability of Member State sovereign debt markets and of the euro area, and damaging the ongoing, strenuous, and politically costly efforts to stabilize the euro area. In March 2010, France and Germany (supported by Luxembourg and Greece) called on the Commission to investigate the effect of speculative trading in CDSs on the sovereign bonds of Member States, to introduce transparency requirements, and to prohibit trades in uncovered CDSs.[173] Ongoing instability led to Greece introducing additional short selling measures in April 2010.[174] Germany's decision to prohibit short selling and CDS transactions in May 2010,[175] which was taken without notification of the Commission or of other Member States, materially ratcheted up the political tensions[176] and the pressure for intervention.[177] It also exposed differences between the Member States as to the optimal approach to short selling (France, in particular, was critical of Germany's unilateral approach), significantly increased tensions between Member States as global equity markets and the value of the euro tumbled in the wake of Germany's action, and generated a call for greater co-ordination from the Financial Stability Board (FSB). The parallel and febrile negotiations on the AIFMD Proposal, and the association between hedge fund activity and short selling,[178] ratcheted tensions up further; the June 2010 recommendation from the European Parliament's economic and monetary committee (ECON) that all naked short sales by fund managers within the proposed AIFMD regime be prohibited underlined the extent of political and institutional hostility to short selling.[179] June 2010 also saw France and Germany take legislative action with respect to short sales.

In this febrile environment, and with consensus on the need to avoid further unco-ordinated action, as well as a strong anti-speculation agenda in some Member States,[180] the Commission engaged in a short consultation[181] before publishing its Proposal (along

[173] Peel, Q, 'Call for Ban on CDS Speculation', *Financial Times,* 11 March 2011, 6.

[174] The Greek regulator banned the short selling of shares listed on the Athens Exchange; while this ban was lifted in August 2010, it was immediately replaced by a ban on uncovered short sales and subsequent measures followed.

[175] Barber, T, Hall, B, and Wiesman, G, 'German Curbs Raise Tensions in Europe', *Financial Times,* 5 May 2010, 1. The prohibition applied to shares of the ten most significant financial institutions in Germany, euro-area sovereign debt, and sovereign debt CDSs: BaFIN Quarterly 2/2010, 3.

[176] Germany's action was widely linked to the domestic political agenda and disquiet in the Christian Democrat party, which reflected hostile feedback from constituents as to the cost of the euro-area bailout: Barber, T and Wiesmann, G, 'Berlin makes Shock Moves without Allies', *Financial Times,* 20 May 2010, 6.

[177] German Finance Minister Schauble was reported as stating that the markets were 'really out of control' and that effective regulation was needed: Barber, T, Hall, B, and Wiesman, G, 'German Curbs Raise Tensions in Europe', *Financial Times,* 5 May 2010, 1.

[178] House of Lords, EU Committee, Directive on Alternative Investment Fund Managers. 3rd Report of Session 2009–2010. Vol 1 (2010) 10 and 20–1.

[179] ECON Committee Gauzès Report on the Alternative Investment Fund Managers Directive Proposal (A7-0171/2010). MEP Gauzès described naked shorting as a 'casino game . . . a tool of pure speculation': Johnson, S and Aboulian, B, 'Europe Plans Ban on Naked Short Selling', *Financial Times Fund Management Supplement,* 24 May 2010, 1.

[180] Hughes, J, 'Political Tide Turns on Regulation', *Financial Times,* 20 May 2010, 6.

[181] Commission, Public Consultation. Short Selling. June 2010. The Consultation addressed, *inter alia,* transparency requirements, restrictions on uncovered short sales, emergency powers, and the appropriate scope of a harmonized regime. Although the consultation responses were generally supportive of a harmonized approach and concerned as to unilateral Member State action, they revealed a lack of support, particularly from the market, for restrictions on uncovered short sales, and only limited support for applying the regime to asset classes other than equity. Although the consultation period was short, CESR had carried out an earlier consultation on short selling, which lasted for almost three months (CESR/09-581).

with the EMIR Proposal) in September 2010. The adoption by the Commission of the Proposal can be strongly associated with the prevailing political climate;[182] Commissioner Barnier, for example, linked the Proposal with efforts to restrain any 'wild west' tendency in financial markets.[183]

VI.3.3.2 The Negotiations

Despite the rhetoric which attended it, the Commission's Proposal was less interventionist than the 2012 Regulation as finally adopted. The Short Selling Proposal was deeply rooted in the crisis-era experience, and accordingly responded to the fragmentation and regulatory arbitrage risks which the Commission associated with the diverging Member State responses to short selling, as well as to the potential for short selling to lead to systemic risks unless transparency was improved and riskier uncovered transactions prohibited.[184] Although less concerned with the international regulatory agenda than the AIFMD Proposal (which had similar drivers in relation to controlling speculation), the Proposal was also designed to ensure the EU regime did not lag the recently reformed US regime.[185] It proposed a transparency regime for short sales in shares based on CESR's model, but extended this model to apply to short sovereign debt positions. It proposed prohibitions on uncovered short sales and on uncovered sovereign debt short sales. It also proposed direct intervention powers for NCAs and for ESMA. All of these elements, albeit significantly nuanced, can be found in the 2012 Short Selling Regulation. The Proposal differed from the Regulation, however, by extending the transparency regime from position reporting to order reporting, through a requirement that all short-sale-related sell orders on trading venues within the scope of the Proposal be 'marked' as short sales, and that venues provide a daily summary of the volume of short sale orders. Most significantly, it did not contain a prohibition on uncovered sovereign CDS transactions; instead, it subjected these transactions to a position reporting requirement.

Although the industry warned of the risks of restricting CDS transactions,[186] the European Parliament, which was concerned as to speculation in the sovereign debt markets,[187] tightened the Commission's text by introducing a prohibition on uncovered sovereign CDS trades, although it provided a more facilitative and nuanced definition than the Commission's Proposal of the nature of a 'covered' trade. The Parliament also lightened the Commission's transparency regime by replacing the reporting requirement relating to short sale orders with a requirement that the daily transaction reports required of trades in in-scope financial instruments include an indication as to whether a transaction was a short sale.

---

[182] The 2010 Short Selling Proposal Impact Assessment drew heavily on the political concern in some Member States as to the potential impact of uncovered CDSs on the sovereign debt markets in justifying the Proposal: n 130, 5–6.

[183] Tait, N, 'Brussels in Bid to Take "Wild West" Markets', *Financial Times,* 16 September 2010, 1.

[184] 2010 Short Selling Proposal Impact Assessment, n 130, 28–30.

[185] 2010 Short Selling Proposal Impact Assessment, n 130, 34.

[186] eg AFME, ISLA, and ISDA, Summary of the AFME, ISLA, and ISDA position on Short Selling (May 2011), expressing the concerns of three major investment banking trade associations.

[187] In its March 2011 Resolution in Innovative Financing it highlighted that short-termism and speculation in EU sovereign debt markets had been important aggravating factors in the euro-area sovereign debt crisis over 2009–2010: n 28, para I.

The European Parliament's prohibition on uncovered CDS transactions quickly became a major point of contention with the Council; through its July 2011 negotiating position, it signalled its determination not to allow the Council a veto in this regard.[188] Internal Council negotiations also proved very difficult, with the Council split between the Member States (the majority) which opposed intervention in the sovereign debt market, given the potential damage to the ability of Member States to raise finance (the most vehement opponents were reportedly the Netherlands, Poland, Italy,[189] the UK,[190] and Luxembourg), and the minority of Member States (including France and Germany) concerned to quell speculation in sovereign debt.[191] ESMA's emergency intervention powers also proved controversial (section 3.9.2). A negotiating position was finally reached by the Council in May 2011 which included a provision providing for a temporary suspension of the prohibition on uncovered short sales in sovereign debt and on uncovered sovereign CDS transactions where sovereign debt markets were disrupted; a more facilitative approach to the characterization of a short sale as 'covered'; and the removal of daily reporting obligations. Very difficult trilogue negotiations followed, with deadlock for some time between the Council and the Parliament on the treatment of the sovereign debt market and of uncovered sovereign CDS transactions.[192] Tensions were exacerbated by ongoing turmoil in the markets, which underlined the divergent views across the Member States and within NCAs as to the appropriate treatment of short selling. On 11 August 2011—as rumours regarding the health of French banks swept EU markets, borrowing costs increased, and emergency financing levels increased—four Member States, supported by ESMA, imposed or extended temporary prohibitions on short selling, which varied in scope.[193] But the Dutch NCA (the AMF) stated that a prohibition was not necessary, and the majority of the EU's NCAs did not act.[194] After difficult negotiations, the Council's modifications to the Parliament's outright ban on uncovered sovereign CDS transactions were finally accepted,[195]

---

[188] As was acknowledged by the Council in its July 2011 report on the negotiations, which noted the view in some quarters in the Parliament that uncovered CDS transactions were riskier than the lotteries permitted in Member States: 3105th Council Meeting, 12 July 2011 (Council Document 12481/2011).

[189] Italy, in particular (whose sovereign debt came under repeated pressure over 2011) was concerned as to the impact of the Parliament's CDS prohibition on its ability to manage its public debt: 'EU Short Selling Talks Collapse amid Sovereign Debt Fears', EurActiv, 22 September 2011.

[190] The UK was opposed to any prohibition on uncovered sovereign CDSs given the potential prejudice to liquidity in the sovereign debt market, pressure on sovereign borrowing costs, damage to the ability of the EU to recover from the financial crisis, and damage to legitimate hedging activities: Wishart, I, 'Council, MEPs at Odds on Short Selling and Supervision' *European Voice*, 7 July 2011 and House of Commons, EU Committee, 20th Report of Sessions 2010–2012, The EU Financial Supervisory Framework: An Update.

[191] Baker & McKenzie, EU Politicians Debate Short Selling Regulation, March 2011.

[192] The European Parliament was initially not prepared to accept any loosening of its prohibition on uncovered sovereign CDS trading, leading to the possibility of the trilogue negotiations failing and the measure proceeding to a second reading: 'EU Short Selling Talks Collapse amid Sovereign Debt Fears', *EurActiv*, 22 September 2011.

[193] Belgium, France, Italy, and Spain. Greece imposed a ban on short sales on 8 August 2011. The supportive ESMA statement is at ESMA/2011/266.

[194] Industry reaction to the series of unco-ordinated prohibitions was hostile. The Managed Funds Association, eg, warned of the damage to risk management and of increased volatility: Letters to the Italian, Spanish, Belgian and German regulators, and to the ECB, the Council, the Commission, and ESMA, 13–15 August 2011.

[195] The Polish Presidency announcement on the successful completion of the trilogue negotiations noted the extensive negotiations and the significant difference between the institutions' positions: Polish Presidency Communiqué on Short Selling, 19 October 2011.

including those relating to when a sovereign CDS would qualify as 'covered' and so would be permitted.[196] A joint text was finally agreed in November 2011.

VI.3.3.3 The Short Selling Regulation

The short selling regime takes the form of a regulation in order to ensure uniform application[197] and to allow for the conferral of powers on ESMA. The Regulation is designed to lay down a common regulatory framework with regard to the requirements and powers relating to short selling and CDSs, and to ensure greater co-ordination and consistency between Member States.[198] The objectives of the Regulation are to: increase the transparency of short positions held in certain securities; ensure Member States have clear powers to intervene in exceptional situations to reduce risks to financial stability and to market confidence arising from short sales and from CDSs; ensure co-ordination between Member States and ESMA in adverse situations; reduce settlement and other risks linked with uncovered short selling; and reduce the risks to the stability of sovereign debt markets posed by uncovered CDS positions.[199] Accordingly, it imposes two sets of obligations on market participants (first, a prohibition on uncovered transactions; second, transparency requirements) and confers a range of powers on NCAs and ESMA.

VI.3.3.4 A Workable Regime?

The crisis-era series of prohibitions and restrictions on short selling internationally has attracted voluminous critical comment.[200] In the EU, the adoption of an effective harmonized regime, or at least a regime which did not unduly prejudice market liquidity, pricing, and risk-management dynamics, faced significant obstacles.[201] The legislative process was highly politicized and often febrile. The empirical evidence which could have mitigated political risks and supported nuanced drafting was limited. While the crisis produced extensive evidence on the impact of prohibitions on short sales in equity[202] (although opinion differed widely as to whether and how uncovered equity short sales

---

[196] This element of the regime was one of the very last points of contention, and was not settled until after the Council and European Parliament had reached agreement on loosening the Parliament's outright prohibition on uncovered sovereign CDSs: Alternative Investment Management Association, Note. EU Short Selling Regulation. October 2011, 6.

[197] The removal of divergence recurs as a major rationale for intervention in the Regulation's explanatory recitals: eg, recs 1, 2, and 5.

[198] 2012 Short Selling Regulation rec 2.

[199] Commission, FAQ. Commission Delegated Regulation on Short Selling and CDSs. 5 July 2012 (MEMO/12/523).

[200] eg n 150, n 154 and the references at n 139.

[201] Even allowing for a degree of industry self-interest, some of the data produced in response to the 2011 Proposal was sobering. The lobby group for the EU investment firm industry, the AFME, suggested that the Commission's requirement that instruments be reserved before a short sale (as part of the 'locate' rule—sect 3.7) could be qualified as 'covered' could drain 95 per cent of securities into reserve accounts, seriously damaging liquidity: AFME, ISLA, ISDA, Short Selling Position Summary. May 2011.

[202] n 139. For an EU review see Bernal, O, Herinckx, A, and Szafarz, A, Which Short Selling Legislation is Least Damaging to Market Efficiency? Evidence from Europe, Centre Emile Berheim WP (2012), available at <http://ssrn.com/abstract=2011435>, finding that the prohibitions on covered short sales raised the bid–ask spread and reduced trading volume, that prohibitions on uncovered short sales raised volatility and the bid–ask spread, and that the new disclosure requirements raised volatility and reduced trading volume. The study concluded that prohibitions on uncovered short sales were the least damaging measures, as they did not impact on trading volume and addressed the risk of failure to deliver securities.

should be restricted),[203] the empirical evidence on prohibitions on sovereign debt short sales and on sovereign CDSs transactions was very limited (only in relation to the German prohibition).[204] Similarly, while some evidence was available on the impact of reporting requirements for short positions (particularly with respect to shares), it was generally limited and did not extend to reporting on sovereign debt and CDS positions.[205] The Commission's Impact Assessment was thinly evidenced[206] and precautionary, particularly with respect to the sovereign debt and CDS measures.[207] It also focused closely on the experience with the Greek sovereign debt markets, rather than on the risks of sovereign debt short selling more generally. The European Parliament's and Council's extensive and operationally sensitive revisions to the Proposal were not the subject of impact assessment.

Ultimately, however, the law-making process delivered a workable compromise.[208] The 2012 Short Selling Regulation does not impose severe constraints on short selling, and the conditions under which NCAs may impose emergency prohibitions are now harmonized, stringent, and subject to ESMA review. The risk of a repeat of the market damage inflicted over the autumn 2008 series of prohibitions should, accordingly, be reduced. The restrictions on uncovered short sales of equity are based in part on tested US practice[209] and address the riskiest form of short selling. The contested restrictions on uncovered sovereign debt short sales and related CDS transactions were untested, but they are, at least, calibrated according to the asset class in question and can be suspended in an emergency, albeit subject to stringent conditions.

The administrative rulebook has also provided a corrective mechanism. It has delivered much-needed nuance, draws on empirical evidence and market practice to a greater extent than the 2012 Regulation, and reflects, within the legislative restrictions imposed by the Regulation, market risk-management practices. Similarly, ESMA's supervisory convergence

---

[203] The evidence from an April 2010 workshop attended by the Commission and NCAs suggests that NCAs were divided as to whether and how uncovered equity short sales should be regulated and how the related 'locate' rule should be designed: 2010 Short Selling Proposal Impact Assessment, n 130, 88.

[204] The regulation of trading in sovereign debt and sovereign CDSs suffers generally from a lack of data, as most market participants take up positions in auctions and maintain them in the secondary markets, and the securities are typically traded OTC: ESMA, Commission Delegated Regulation 918/2012 Technical Advice (2012) (ESMA/2012/236) 51. IOSCO has similarly highlighted the lack of direct research on the CDS market: IOSCO, n 137, 21.

[205] CESR's earlier attempts to develop a pan-EU disclosure regime noted the lack of a strong empirical base on which the new regime could be based. Its initial decision to opt for a 0.5 per cent of share capital threshold for public disclosure, eg, was largely based on applying a higher threshold than the 0.25 per cent threshold at which most of the autumn 2008 reporting requirements had coalesced, given the emergency conditions under which those requirements were adopted, rather than on empirical evidence: CESR Proposal, n 181, 9–10. Industry feedback to CESR's proposal suggested significant disquiet at the lack of empirical evidence: CESR Feedback Statement (2009) (CESR/9-089) 4.

[206] It noted the limited evidence on the impact of CDS trades on the sovereign debt markets and warned that the empirical evidence in favour of a prohibition was not strong: n 130, 25 and 43–4.

[207] The Commission's Impact Assessment Board supported the use of a precautionary model, however, given the lack of evidence. IAB Opinion, 31 August 2010 (Ref.Ares(2010)549585).

[208] For a broadly positive examination of the contested CDS regime, which concludes that it is 'more or less sound' see Juurikkala, O, 'Credit Default Swaps and the EU Short Selling Regulation' (2012) *ECFLR* 307.

[209] For an assessment of US SEC Regulation SHO (2004), which sets out the requirements with which a short sale must comply (including with respect to locating shares), and which is reflected in part in the EU regime, see Hu, n 151.

activities, including its adoption of guidelines in this area, provide a channel through which opacities and ambiguities can be temporarily corrected and market developments reflected.

The regime has also benefited from an early review. The Commission was to report to the European Parliament and Council on the Regulation's main features[210] by end June 2013 (Article 45).[211] As discussed in section 3.13, and allowing for the limitations of a review which took place with less than six months' experience with the measure, it appears that the 2012 Regulation has not generated significant problems, and that market dynamics do not appear to have been prejudicially disrupted. ESMA's extensive report also underlines both the important corrective function which a review clause can deliver and ESMA's capacity to engage in *ex-post* quantitative assessment.

VI.3.4 Harmonization and ESMA

While highly detailed in places, the 2012 Regulation generally operates at a relatively high level of generality. It articulates the hard-fought political compromise on the extent to which short sales of shares and sovereign debt, and transactions in sovereign CDSs, should be restricted. But this compromise was based in part on further calibration and amplification of the regime through extensive administrative rules which would finesse the regime and address the practical implications for risk management and for market liquidity and efficiency. The development of the administrative regime was, accordingly, not only a means for clarifying the regime and addressing matters of great technical detail, but also a critically important process for ensuring that the Regulation, within the parameters set by the political compromise, did not disrupt long-established hedging and risk-management practices.

The sensitivity of the administrative rulebook is reflected in the respective allocation of rules to the traditional Commission-led process for administrative rule adoption, and to the new ESMA-initiated RTS/ITS process for adopting such rules. The most operationally sensitive rules, and those which had the greatest potential to disrupt the political compromise on the legislative text, were adopted through the 2012 Commission Delegated Regulation 918/2012, which was adopted as an administrative measure by the Commission[212] following receipt of ESMA's technical advice[213] and a detailed impact assessment by the Commission.[214] The Regulation addresses highly sensitive operational issues, including in relation

---

[210] The review was to address: the appropriateness of the net short position reporting and disclosure thresholds; the impact of the individual net short position in shares disclosure requirements; the appropriateness of requiring direct, centralized reporting to ESMA; and the operation and appropriateness of the restrictions imposed on short sales and sovereign CDS transactions.

[211] A related Call for Evidence was issued by ESMA in February 2013 (ESMA Call for Evidence on Evaluation of the Regulation (ESMA/2013/203)), following a Commission mandate. ESMA's report was issued in June 2013 (ESMA/2012/614).

[212] In accordance with 2012 Short Selling Regulation Art 42, which, reflecting the procedure for the adoption by the Commission of administrative acts generally (under Art 290 TFEU), provides for revocation of the delegations at any time by the European Parliament or Council, adoption by the Commission, and a veto by the Parliament or Council within three months of the measure's adoption. On the procedure for adopting administrative rules see Ch X sect 4.

[213] n 204.

[214] SWD (2012) 198. The Commission also consulted with the Parliament, the ECB, and the European Securities Committee (on the role of this Committee in rule-making see Ch X): Commission, FAQ. Delegated Regulation on Short Selling and CDS, n 199.

to the type of hedging which renders a sovereign CDS 'covered' and so permitted under the foundation 2012 Short Selling Regulation, the notification thresholds for sovereign debt, the market liquidity thresholds at which the prohibition on uncovered sovereign debt short sales can be suspended, when a 'significant fall in prices' has occurred such that NCAs can temporarily restrict short sales, and the nature of the 'adverse circumstances' which trigger the related emergency powers which can be exercised by ESMA and the NCAs. The two Regulations adopted as RTSs (2012 Commission Delegated Regulations 826/2012 and 919/2012), which were proposed by, and thus driven by, ESMA, albeit adopted by the Commission, address less operationally sensitive issues and are in the main concerned with calculation methodologies and reporting contents and formats. The ITS Regulation (Commission Implementing Regulation 827/2012), which might have been expected to have little impact as a quasi-regulatory measure given the technical and implementation-focused nature of ITSs,[215] is of great operational importance, however, in that it sets out the types of arrangement which qualify under the 'locate' rule, which is used by the 2012 Short Selling Regulation as a key device for assessing whether or not a short sale of shares or sovereign debt is covered.

Despite the acute time pressure under which it was produced,[216] the administrative rule-book has a number of strengths. It reflects a generally good working relationship between the Commission and ESMA and the Commission's willingness to rely on ESMA's technical expertise,[217] a concern to avoid overly burdensome rules,[218] and the significant technical capacity which ESMA has brought to EU law-making. It suffers, however, from the absence of robust empirical data, as was acknowledged by the Commission and ESMA.[219] Nonetheless, Commission Delegated Regulation 918/2012, in particular, was subject to extensive market assessment and empirical review and drew, to the extent it was available, on market intelligence and experience.[220]

---

[215] See further Ch X.

[216] The market consultations on the different administrative rules repeatedly reflected strong concerns as to the limited time for consultation and the time pressure under which the rules were being adopted: eg, Commission Delegated Regulation 918/2012 Impact Assessment (n 214) 66. ESMA also warned that its technical advice for Commission Delegated Regulation 918/2012 was being developed within a significantly compressed process which meant that it was not able to engage in a Call for Evidence, only a short consultation period (three weeks) was possible, and it was not possible to prepare a cost-benefit analysis for the consultation period: n 204, 5.

[217] Commission Delegated Regulation 918/2012 broadly reflects ESMA's advice. One notable departure from ESMA's advice, however, relates to the highly contested question as to how correlation should be assessed in relation to whether a sovereign debt CDS is used for legitimate hedging and so is 'covered'. The Commission adopted a mixed qualitative and quantitative approach, although ESMA (and the market generally) supported a qualitative approach. The Commission underlined, however, that ESMA's approach to the qualitative test incorporated elements of a more quantitative approach: Commission Delegated Regulation 918/2012 Impact Assessment, n 214, 29 and 31. The RTS Regulations and the ITS Regulation were adopted by the Commission without any changes to ESMA's proposals.

[218] This was particularly the case in relation to the development of the notification thresholds for net short sovereign debt positions, where the Commission was keen to avoid onerous reporting obligations which would provide information of only limited systemic relevance: Commission Delegated Regulation 918/2012 Impact Assessment, n 214, 34.

[219] Both the Commission and ESMA noted the paucity of evidence available in relation to the appropriate threshold for reporting of net short sovereign debt positions: Commission Delegated Regulation 918/2012 Impact Assessment, n 214, 33. In particular, no evidence was available on the average size of positions held by market participants in relation to sovereign debt.

[220] The liquidity threshold at which NCAs can suspend the requirement for sovereign debt short sales to be covered, eg, was modelled against real sovereign debt histories for a sample of Member States to assess its resilience: Commission Delegated Regulation 918/2012 Impact Assessment, n 214, 38. Similarly, the rules

ESMA's supervisory convergence activities provide an additional means for ensuring that the regime does not disrupt efficient market practices and that its myriad complexities are clear. In September 2012, ESMA adopted an extensive 'Q&A' document which is regularly updated;[221] it provides a dynamic and responsive method for clarifying the regime and for driving consistent implementation.[222] ESMA has also shown some enthusiasm for adopting 2010 ESMA Regulation Article 16 guidelines (in relation to which NCAs are subject to a 'comply or explain' obligation).[223] Shortly after the application of the 2012 Short Selling Regulation, ESMA adopted important guidelines on the operationally significant market-making exemption. The Guidelines, which are, as noted in section 3.5.2 of this Chapter, notable for their robust tone and highly technical quality,[224] are designed to provide clarity and support a level playing field with respect to a centrally important exemption.[225] But while they underline ESMA's ability to identify and respond to potential weaknesses in the formal rulebook, they have proved problematic as a convergence tool. Similarly, the 2013 Review of the short selling regime highlights ESMA's capacity to engage in quantitative analysis of the regime and to influence its future shape.

VI.3.5 Setting the Perimeter: Scope and Exemptions

VI.3.5.1 Scope

The scope of the 2012 Short Selling Regulation is very widely drawn; the perimeter is set by the wide range of instruments subject to the Regulation, not by the market participants who, by holding positions in these instruments, become indirectly subject to the Regulation.[226] Accordingly, it has wide extraterritorial reach beyond the EU,[227] where short selling activities relate to in-scope instruments.[228]

Under Article 1, the Regulation applies to three sets of instruments. First, it applies to 2014 MiFID II/MiFIR financial instruments (as defined by Article 2(1)(a)) (Chapter IV section 4.3), where those instruments are admitted to trading on a 'trading venue'—a regulated market or MTF (as defined by Article 2(1)(l)) in the EU;[229] these instruments are in scope when traded outside these venues, as long as they are admitted to these venues (Article 1(1)(a)).

---

specifying the 'significant falls in value' of particular instruments which can lead to an NCA taking emergency action drew heavily on market experience.

[221] ESMA, Questions and Answers. Implementation of the Regulation on Short Selling and Certain Aspects of Credit Default Swaps (2012) (ESMA/2012/572). It is regularly updated and addresses technical matters of often significant operational complexity.

[222] It is formally designed to promote common supervisory practices by NCAs and to ensure that supervisory practices converge, but is also designed to assist investors and market participants by providing clarity.

[223] NCAs must also report on their compliance or explain their non-compliance. See further Ch X sect 5.6.

[224] ESMA, Guidelines. Exemption for market making activities and primary market operations under the Short Selling Regulation (2013) (ESMA/2013/74) (2013 ESMA Market-Making Guidelines).

[225] ESMA Annual Report (2012) 52.

[226] The regime typically applies to 'natural and legal persons', termed 'persons' in this discussion.

[227] Extraterritorial reach is not uncommon in the regulation of short sales. The UK autumn 2008 prohibition, eg, applied in relation to the identified UK shares, wherever trading occurred globally.

[228] ESMA's Q&A notes, eg, that the reporting requirements apply wherever a trade in relation to an in-scope instrument is executed or booked globally: n 221, 8.

[229] On regulated markets and MTFs see Ch V.

Second, it applies to financial, commodity, and other derivatives,[230] where those derivatives relate to an Article 1(1)(a) instrument, or relate to an issuer of such an instrument, including when these instruments are traded outside a trading venue (Article 1(1)(b)). Finally, it applies to debt instruments issued by a Member State or the EU, and to Article 1(1)(b) derivatives that relate to or are referenced to debt instruments issued by a Member State or the EU (Article 1(1)(c)). The range of emergency powers which are conferred on NCAs and on ESMA in exceptional market conditions (section 3.9) apply to financial instruments generally, regardless of where they are admitted to trading (Article 1(2)).[231]

While wide in reach, the regime is significantly calibrated (see also section 3.6). It does not, save in exceptional circumstances, apply to financial instruments generally. Its provisions are generally directed to short sales[232] of shares and of sovereign debt,[233] and to sovereign CDSs.[234] Two sets of obligations apply to these instruments: a trading rule which prohibits uncovered short sales of shares and sovereign debt and transactions in uncovered sovereign CDSs; and a reporting rule in relation to net short positions. In neither case is the domicile or establishment of the person entering into the relevant transaction relevant; the scope of the obligation is dictated by whether the related instruments are within the scope of the 2012 Short Selling Regulation.[235]

VI.3.5.2 Exemptions

Two exemptions apply to the 2012 Short Selling Regulation.

The first is efficiency-driven and curtails the extraterritorial reach of the Regulation. The disclosure and notification obligations relating to net short positions in shares, the prohibition on uncovered short sales of shares, and the requirements for buy-in procedures in relation to the settlement of shares do not apply to shares of a company admitted to trading

---

[230] As specified in 2014 MiFID II Annex 1 (see Ch IV sect 4.3).

[231] The Arts 18, 20, and 23–30 powers apply to financial instruments generally.

[232] A short sale in relation to a share or debt instrument is defined broadly as any sale of the share or debt instrument which the seller does not own at the time of entering into the agreement to sell, including a sale where, at the time of entering into the agreement to sell, the seller has borrowed or agreed to borrow the share or debt instrument for delivery at settlement: Art 2(1)(b). Three forms of transaction are excluded from the short sale definition: a sale by either party under a repurchase agreement where one party has agreed to sell the other a security at a specified price with a commitment from the other party to sell the security back at a later date at another specified price; a transfer of securities under a securities lending arrangement; and entry into a future contract or other derivative contract, where it is agreed to sell securities at a specified price at a future date. The nature of 'ownership' for the purpose of the short sale definition has been amplified by the 2012 Commission Delegated Regulation 918/2012 Art 3.

[233] Sovereign debt is defined as a debt instrument issued by a sovereign issuer (Art 2(1)(f)). A sovereign issuer is widely defined as including the EU, a Member State (including a government department, agency, or SPV (special purpose vehicle) of the Member State), a member of the federation in the case of a federal Member State, an SPV for several Member States, an international financial institution established by two or more Member States which has the purpose of mobilizing funding and providing financial assistance to the benefit of its members that are experiencing or threatened by severe financing problems, and the European Investment Bank: Art 2(1)(d).

[234] A CDS is defined as a derivative contract in which one party pays a fee to another party in return for a payment or other benefit in the case of a credit event relating to a reference entity, and of any other default relating to that derivative contract which has a similar economic effect (Art 2(1)(c)). A sovereign CDS is one where a payment or other benefit is paid in the case of a credit event or default relating to a sovereign issuer (Art 2(1)(e)).

[235] As confirmed in ESMA's Q&A, Q1a, 1b and 1e.

on a trading venue in the EU where the 'principal venue' (the venue for the trading of that share with the highest turnover) for the trading of the shares is located in a third country (Article 16(1)). The determination as to whether the principal trading venue for a share is outside the EU is the responsibility of the relevant NCA for the shares,[236] and is carried out on a two-yearly basis in accordance with the delegated rules which govern the calculation.[237] A list of exempted shares is maintained by ESMA.

The second exemption exempts market-making and related activities from the reach of the 2012 Short Selling Regulation (Article 17) in order to ensure that market liquidity, and the related ability of market-makers to take short positions, is not prejudiced. The broadest exemption applies to transactions performed due to 'market-making activities' which are exempted from the reporting and public disclosure obligations relating to net short positions, and from the prohibition on uncovered transactions (Article 17(1)). To benefit from the exemption, the market-maker must (under Article 2(1)(k)) come within the classes of market-maker identified in the Regulation (which include, given the reach of the Regulation, third country actors);[238] be a member of an in-scope trading venue or an equivalent third country market[239] where the actor deals as principal in a financial instrument (whether traded on or outside a trading venue); and act in any one of three capacities.[240] The exemption applies only in relation to market-making activities and does not cover proprietary dealing by the actor in question.[241] With specific reference to sovereign debt, authorized primary dealers[242] are exempted from reporting in relation to net short positions, and from the prohibition on uncovered short sales of sovereign debt and on uncovered sovereign CDSs (Article 17(2)). Notification requirements apply to the relevant home NCA,[243] which is empowered to prohibit reliance on an exemption where it considers the related conditions are not met (Article 17(5)–(8)). The NCA may also

---

[236] Determined in accordance with the rules which determine which NCA is responsible in relation to transaction reporting under MiFID II/MiFIR (see Ch V sect 12.1).

[237] In relation to the calculation of turnover (2012 Commission Delegated Regulation 826/2012 Art 6) and the timing of the calculation and related reviews (2012 Commission Implementing Regulation 827/2012 Arts 8–11).

[238] Including investment firms, credit institutions, and third country entities.

[239] The conditions for the equivalence determination are set out in Art 17(2). Although the actor in question must be a member of a trading venue or third country market, the actor is not required to conduct its market-making activities on that venue/market or to be recognized as a market maker on that venue/market: 2013 ESMA Market-Making Guidelines, n 224, 7. The restriction of the exemption to members of a trading venue has, however, limited the availability of the exemption for OTC market-making activities and has been identified by ESMA as in need of reform (sect 3.13).

[240] The firm can post simultaneous two-way quotes of comparable size and at competitive prices, with the result of providing liquidity on a regular and ongoing basis to the market; it can, as part of its usual business, fulfil orders initiated by clients or in response to clients' requests to trade, or it can hedge positions arising from the fulfilment of the latter two tasks: Art 2(1)(k).

[241] 2012 Short Selling Regulation rec 26.

[242] Defined as a person who has signed an agreement with a sovereign issuer or who has been formally recognized by a primary dealer by or on behalf of a sovereign issuer and who, in accordance with the agreement or recognition, has committed to dealing as principal in connection with primary and secondary market operations relating to debt issued by that issuer: Art 2(1)(n).

[243] Notification in relation to the market-making exemption must be made to the home NCA of the relevant entity (a third country actor must notify the NCA of the main trading venue in the EU on which it trades); notification in relation to the authorized primary dealer exemption must be made to the NCA of the Member State which has issued the sovereign debt in question: Art 17(5)–(8).

request information relating to short positions held or activities conducted under the exemption (Article 17(11)).

The market-making exemption has not been the subject of administrative rules but ESMA has adopted detailed related Guidelines, reflecting significant market uncertainty as to the scope of this operationally critical exemption.[244] Adopted under ESMA Regulation Article 16, the Guidelines are of a harder quality than the ESMA Short Selling 'Q&A': NCAs and financial market participants must make every effort to comply with the Guidelines. NCAs are also required to notify ESMA on whether they have complied with the Guidelines (with reasons for non-compliance); financial market participants are not required to so report.[245] While the Guidelines cover, as might be expected, the format and content of the exemption notification in detail, they are notable for the extent to which they tackle the many operational complexities which the exemption has generated,[246] and for their detailed coverage of the conduct of market-making activities.[247] The scope of the Guidelines has, however, been controversial. Five NCAs, including the NCAs of the largest financial markets in the EU (the markets of the UK, France, and Germany) recorded their non-compliance.[248] While their reasons varied, there was strong NCA disagreement with the scope limitations which the Guidelines imposed with respect to trading venue membership.[249] As discussed in Chapter X section 5.6, the resilience and authority of ESMA guidelines which the NCAs of the largest financial markets in the EU do not support is questionable.

VI.3.6 Calibration and Differentiation

Calibration and differentiation are recurring themes of the 2012 Short Selling Regulation, which seeks to balance between regulating certain aspects of short selling in the interests of supporting financial stability, particularly in the sovereign debt market, on the one hand,

---

[244] n 224.

[245] n 224, 3–4.

[246] The Guidelines highlight, eg, that the exemption applies on a financial instrument basis and that the conditions which apply to the market-making exemption must accordingly be met in relation to each financial instrument in respect of which exemption is sought, reflecting Commission advice to this effect: n 224, 7. Accordingly, where an instrument is not admitted to a trading venue, the exemption is not available as, to qualify for the exemption, the actor must deal as principal in the trading venue in which it is a member in the financial instrument for which the exemption is notified. They also provide that the required notification applies on a per instrument basis, although several financial instruments can be addressed in a single notification (at 16–18). ESMA has also suggested that actors benefiting from the exemption should not hold significant short positions in relation to market-making activities other than for brief periods: at 7.

[247] Detailed guidance applies, eg, to the qualifying criteria for when an actor posts firm two-way quotes with the result of providing liquidity under Art 2(1)(k)(i): 11–14.

[248] ESMA Guidelines Compliance Table (ESMA/2013/765).

[249] The Guidelines provide that to qualify for the exemption, the market-maker must be a member of the market/trading venue in which it deals as principal in the financial instruments for which it notifies the exemption (n 224, paras 19–22 and 35–36). Four NCAs (Denmark, Germany, the UK, and Sweden) disagreed with this interpretation of 2012 Short Selling Regulation Art 2(1)(k), which, as noted (n 246), is based on ESMA's view that the Art 2(1)(k) criteria must be met with respect to every financial instrument in respect of which a notification is made. The UK, eg, based its reasons for not complying on its interpretation of Art 2(1)(k) which, the UK argued, requires trading venue membership, but does not expressly require that the financial instrument in respect of which exemption is sought must be traded on the trading venue in question. The German BaFIN similarly rejected ESMA's interpretation, arguing that it could take market-making in sovereign CDSs outside the exemption as these instruments are often not admitted to trading venues.

and supporting market liquidity and efficiency and not hindering short sales and related transactions which support liquidity and price formation, on the other.[250]

While in principle the scope of the Regulation is very wide, in practice the two main sets of rules—the prohibitions on uncovered transactions and the reporting obligations—apply only to shares, sovereign debt, and sovereign CDSs; the inclusion of sovereign bonds and the exclusion of corporate bonds, and the related fragmentation in the regime, underlines the politicization of the negotiations. The regime applies across all financial instruments only in relation to exceptional circumstances and with respect to the related emergency intervention powers of NCAs and ESMA.

The two main sets of rules are further differentiated between the share, sovereign debt, and sovereign CDS asset classes in order to reflect the different dynamics of trading and risk management in these markets, and to reflect the perceived higher risks to liquidity in the sovereign debt markets from the Regulation's requirements. Generally, exemptions, suspensions of rules, and differentiation between different asset classes are common across the regime.

VI.3.7 Restricting Short Sales: the Uncovered Short Sales Prohibition

VI.3.7.1 The Prohibition

At the core of the 2012 Short Selling Regulation is the prohibition on uncovered short sales of shares and of sovereign debt and on transactions in uncovered sovereign debt CDSs (Articles 4 and 12–13). The conditions which govern whether transactions are 'covered' and so outside the prohibition were the subject of intense negotiations, becoming a focal point for the wider debate on the legitimacy and efficacy of short sales, particularly short sales achieved through sovereign debt CDSs. The resulting regime is complex and technical, as it is designed to balance between the need to protect long-standing market hedging and risk-management practices and the need to reflect the strong political concern, particularly in the European Parliament, to prohibit uncovered short sales and uncovered sovereign CDS transactions.

VI.3.7.2 Uncovered Short Sales in Shares

Under Article 12, a natural or legal person may enter into a short sale of a share admitted to trading on a trading venue only where one of three sets of conditions, designed to ensure the sale is 'covered,' is met. The conditions have been subject to detailed amplification by 2012 Commission Implementing Regulation 827/2012.

A short sale is covered where the person has borrowed the share or has made alternative provisions resulting in a similar legal effect (Article 12(1)(a)).

A sale is also covered where the person has entered into an agreement to borrow the share or has another 'absolutely enforceable claim' under contract or property law to be transferred ownership of a corresponding number of securities of the same class, so that settlement can

---

[250] The 2012 Short Selling Regulation highlights that short selling plays an important role in ensuring the proper functioning of financial markets, particularly with respect to liquidity and price formation: rec 5.

be effected when it is due (Article 12(1)(b)). The Implementing Regulation specifies the range of agreements and claims which can be employed (futures and swaps; options; repurchase agreements; standing agreements and rolling facilities; agreements relating to subscription rights; and other claims or agreements) and the conditions which these agreements must meet (Article 5).

Finally, and significantly in terms of market practice, a sale is covered where the (highly contested)[251] 'locate rule' is met, in that the person has an arrangement with a third party under which that third party has confirmed that the share has been located, and has additionally taken 'measures' vis-à-vis third parties necessary for the person to have a 'reasonable expectation' that settlement can be effected when it is due (Article 12(1)(c)). This 'locate rule' and the related 'measures' were the subject of intense negotiations at legislative and administrative levels. The 2012 Implementing Regulation sets out the three permissible forms of locate arrangements and measures, and the related confirmations required (Article 6).[252] The standard requirement is that the third party (i) confirms, prior to the short sale being entered into by the person, that it considers it can make the shares available for settlement in due time, taking into account the amount of the possible sale and market conditions, and indicates the period for which the share is located, and (ii) confirms, prior to the short sale being entered into, that it 'has at least put on hold' the requested number of shares for the person (Article 6(2)). Reflecting the terms of the legislative delegation,[253] distinct and lighter requirements apply in relation to confirmations relating to intra-day short sales (Article 6(3)) and short sales of liquid shares (Article 6(4)), both of which qualify the short sale as a covered short sale.[254] The 2012 Implementing Regulation also specifies the third party with whom these arrangements can be made (Article 8); in effect, the third party must be a legally separate entity from the short seller.[255]

VI.3.7.3 Uncovered Short Sales in Sovereign Debt

Similar rules govern whether a short sale in sovereign debt is covered, and so permitted, although an exemption regime applies which reflects significant Member State concern as to the potential damage to the sovereign debt market.

---

[251] The Commission and European Parliament took a restrictive approach to the locate rule, requiring that the locate confirmation confirm both that the third party in question had located the securities and that the securities were reserved for lending. The Council's more facilitative approach prevailed in the 2012 Short Selling Regulation as finally adopted.

[252] The different arrangements are based on EU market practice as well as on the US regulatory framework for short sales: Commission FAQ, Short Selling Technical Standards, 29 June 2012 (Memo/12/508).

[253] The Art 12(2) delegation required ESMA in developing the rules to take into account intraday short sales and the liquidity of the shares being sold short.

[254] Lighter conditions apply in relation to Art 6(3) and (4) arrangements. In particular, the third party must provide the locate confirmation, but need only confirm that the share is easy to borrow or purchase in the relevant quantity, taking into account market conditions (the 'put on hold' confirmation does not accordingly apply).

[255] 2012 Commission FAQ, Short Selling Technical Standards, n 252. Art 8 applies to arrangements relating to covered short sales of shares and of sovereign debt, and identifies CCPs, securities settlement systems, central banks (which, respectively, clear, settle, or accept as collateral/conduct open market or repo transactions in relation to the relevant securities), and national debt management entities for the relevant sovereign debt issuers. Investment firms, other persons authorized or registered by a member of the European System of Financial Supervision (ESFS), and equivalent third country persons are also included where they participate in the management of borrowing or purchasing of the relevant shares or sovereign debt, provide evidence of such participation, and, on request, can provide evidence of ability to deliver the shares or sovereign debt on the dates on which they have committed to do so.

Under Article 13 of the 2012 Short Selling Regulation, a short sale of sovereign debt may only be carried out where the sale is covered, in that it meets one of three conditions. First, the relevant person must have borrowed the sovereign debt or have made alternative provisions resulting in a similar legal effect (Article 13(1)(a)). Second, the person must have entered into an agreement to borrow the sovereign debt or have another absolutely enforceable claim under contract or property law to be transferred ownership of a corresponding number of securities of the same class so that settlement can be effected when it is due (Article 13(1)(b)). Finally, a 'locate rule' applies, in that the sale is covered where the person has an arrangement with a third party under which the third party has confirmed that the sovereign debt has been located or (by contrast with the more restrictive confirmation regime which applies to shares), alternatively, otherwise has a reasonable expectation that settlement can be effected when it is due (Article 13(1)(c)).

The restrictions on uncovered short sales of sovereign debt are lighter than those which apply to shares, in order to reflect concern as to the potential detriment to Member States' management of their budget deficits.[256] The 2012 Implementing Regulation 827/2012 accordingly seeks to preserve liquidity in the sovereign debt and related repurchase markets,[257] and sets out the types of arrangements and confirmations necessary to provide a reasonable expectation that settlement can be effected when it is due; these requirements are lighter than those which govern share short sales and the related 'measures' to be taken (Article 7).[258]

The political sensitivities associated with restrictions on the sovereign debt markets are also reflected in the lifting of the requirement for a sovereign debt sale to be covered where the sale hedges a long position in debt instruments of an issuer, the pricing of which has a high correlation with the pricing of the sovereign debt (2012 Short Selling Regulation Article 13(2)).[259]

Additionally, the requirement for short sales to be covered can be temporarily suspended by the relevant NCA[260] where it determines that liquidity has become restricted, in that it has fallen below the threshold set by the 2012 Short Selling Regulation (Article 13(3) and (4)). This exemption is designed to address any potential detriment to the liquidity of sovereign debt markets and any potential prejudice to the ability of Member States to finance public deficits which may arise from the prohibition on uncovered short sales, and to allow NCAs to support liquidity in stressed market conditions. Given the sensitivity of this suspension

---

[256] As was acknowledged by the Commission: 2012 Commission FAQ, Short Selling Technical Standards, n 252.

[257] Concern over prejudice to liquidity in the sovereign debt market led to ESMA being expressly charged with preserving liquidity when developing the regime: 2012 Short Selling Regulation Art 13(5).

[258] In essence, the locate regime for sovereign debt does not require that the securities are placed on hold by the third party. In the standard arrangement, the third party, prior to the sale being entered into, must confirm that it considers that it can make the sovereign debt available for settlement in due time, in the amount requested by the person, taking into account market conditions, and indicate the period for which the sovereign debt is located (Art 7(1)). Art 7 also covers time-limited intraday confirmations, unconditional repo confirmations, and 'easy to purchase' confirmations, all of which qualify the sale as a covered sovereign debt short sale.

[259] Although it is not expressly addressed by the administrative regime, the Commission has suggested that high correlation means a correlation of 80 per cent: 2012 Commission FAQ, Commission Delegated Regulation on Short Selling and CDSs, n 199.

[260] The NCA of the Member State which has issued the debt: Art 2(1)(j)(i).

and the related liquidity calculation, the calculation method has been specified in some detail through administrative rules which are designed to ensure that the suspension only applies where there has been a significant decline relative to the average level of liquidity for the sovereign debt, and that the liquidity threshold is based on objective criteria specific to the relevant sovereign debt market.[261] The 2012 Commission Delegated Regulation 918/2012 sets out the liquidity threshold calculation method, which is linked to turnover, and which is designed to allow NCAs to take pre-emptive action before sovereign debt liquidity problems arise;[262] a temporary suspension may take place where the turnover of a month falls below the fifth percentile of the monthly volume traded in the previous 12 months.[263] The relevant NCA must also notify other NCAs and notify ESMA (which is to issue an opinion within 24 hours on the proposed suspension and its compliance with the related conditions). ESMA is accordingly required to opine, in a likely charged and time-pressured environment, on the validity of potentially highly controversial decisions by NCAs. On the one hand, the opinion obligation suggests a possible endorsement from ESMA which could protect the NCA. On the other, the mechanism is double-edged in that where the NCA proceeds despite an unfavourable ESMA opinion, the political and market volatility risks would be considerable.[264] The insertion nonetheless of ESMA into the process underlines the political sensitivities associated with restricting uncovered short sales and with loosening those restrictions. The suspension is valid for an initial period not exceeding six months, although it may be renewed for an additional six-month period if the qualifying liquidity conditions continue to prevail.

VI.3.7.4 Uncovered Sovereign CDSs

Most controversy attended the prohibition on uncovered sovereign CDSs; accordingly, a complex regime applies governing when a sovereign CDS is 'covered', which is designed to protect legitimate hedging activities. Under the 2012 Short Selling Regulation Article 14(1), a natural or legal person may only engage in a sovereign debt CDS transaction where the transaction does not lead to an uncovered sovereign CDS position. Whether or not a sovereign debt CDS is uncovered and so prohibited is a function of whether it is deployed for the hedging purposes which the 2012 Short Selling Regulation permits.

Two forms of hedging are permitted: hedging against the risk of default of the sovereign issuer, where the person in question has a long position in the debt of the issuer to which the CDS relates; and hedging against the risk of decline of the value of the sovereign debt, where the person holds assets or is subject to liabilities, including but not limited to

---

[261] Including the total amount of outstanding issued sovereign debt for each sovereign issuer: Art 13(4).

[262] Commission Delegated Regulation 918/2012 Impact Assessment, n 214, 35.

[263] Art 22. Turnover is defined as the total nominal value of debt instruments traded, in relation to a basket of benchmarks with different maturities. In performing these calculations the NCA must use representative data readily available from one or more trading venues, from OTC trading, or from both, and inform ESMA of the data used. The NCA must also ensure that the significant drop in liquidity is not as a result of seasonal effects. A basket approach was adopted as providing the best proxy for the liquidity of the sovereign debt market as a whole, given different issues and maturities, and avoiding the complexities engaged with assessing liquidity in relation to every issue: 2012 ESMA Commission Regulation 918/2012 Technical Advice, n 204, 51.

[264] The European Parliament highlighted the political weight which would attach to a negative opinion from ESMA: Parliament Press Release, Crack Down on Short Selling and Sovereign Debt Speculation (Ref 201110181PR29720).

financial contracts, a portfolio of assets, or financial obligations, the value of which is correlated to the value of the sovereign debt (Article 4). The second of these two hedges—the 'proxy hedge'—is of central importance to hedging and risk management in the CDS market. The boundary between legitimate and illegitimate proxy hedges is, however, a difficult one to establish and police, given the complexities related to, for example, the extent to which the exposures should be correlated with the CDS,[265] as well as the dynamism of the exposures, which can change in value over time, affecting the coverage of the hedge. Accordingly, a highly contested and complex regime, designed to ensure consistency in supervisory and market practice, governs the extent to which the CDS is correlated to the proxy hedged assets or liabilities under the 2012 Commission Delegated Regulation 918/2012 (Articles 14–20).

In essence, under the 2012 Commission Delegated Regulation 918/2012, four major conditions govern whether the sovereign CDS is covered, in that it relates to a legitimate proxy hedge under the short selling regime. First, the assets or liabilities must, reflecting the legislative regime (2012 Short Selling Regulation Article 4) be in the sovereign Member State; despite significant market opposition, cross-border proxy hedges are not permitted save to a very limited extent and in relation to cross-border group-related assets and liabilities (Article 15). Second, the hedged assets and liabilities must come within the scope of the identified assets and liabilities (Article 17). Third, a proportionality requirement applies in that the CDS position must be proportionate to the size of the exposures hedged—although a 'perfect hedge' is not required, given the potential volatility of the exposures hedged and the difficulties in exactly capturing the risks in question, and limited over-provisioning is permitted (Article 19). Finally, the nature of the correlation assessment used to ensure the exposures are correlated to the CDS is specified; a quantitative or qualitative assessment may be used (Article 18).[266] Under the quantitative element, there must be a correlation coefficient of at least 70 per cent between the price of the assets or liabilities hedged and the price of the sovereign debt;[267] the 70 per cent correlation requirement is deemed to be met in specified circumstances, which provide a safe harbour.[268] Under the qualitative element, a 'meaningful correlation' (which is based on appropriate data and is not evidence of a merely temporary dependence) must be shown.[269] A person entering into a sovereign debt CDS position must, on the request of the NCA, demonstrate compliance with the applicable conditions (Article 16).

---

[265] A generous approach to correlation could lead to almost any hedge being deemed as 'covered': 2012 Commission Regulation 918/2012 Impact Assessment, n 214, 8.

[266] The Commission considered the relative merits of qualitative and quantitative approaches in some detail and despite ESMA's support for a qualitative approach, chose a mixed approach: 2012 Commission Regulation 918/2012 Impact Assessment, n 214, 22–3 and 26–31.

[267] The correlation is assessed in relation to the price of the assets or liabilities, and the price of the sovereign debt, calculated on a historical basis using data for at least a period of 12 months of trading days immediately preceding the date when the CDS position was taken out: Art 18(1)(a).

[268] The 70 per cent condition is met where the exposure being hedged relates to: an enterprise which is owned, majority owned, or has its debts guaranteed by the sovereign issuer; a regional, local, or municipal government of the Member States; an enterprise whose cash flows are significantly dependent on contracts from a sovereign issuer; or a project which is funded, significantly funded, or underwritten by a sovereign issuer, such as an infrastructure project: Art 18(2).

[269] Art 18(1)(b). The time frame for the calculation of the correlation is specified.

As with the prohibition on uncovered sovereign debt short sales, the prohibition on uncovered sovereign debt CDSs may be suspended in exceptional circumstances, which are designed to capture situations in which the Member States' ability to raise funds might be compromised (2012 Short Selling Regulation Article 14(2)). An NCA may suspend the prohibition[270] where it has objective evidence for believing that its sovereign debt market is not functioning properly and that the prohibition might have a negative impact on the sovereign CDS market, especially by increasing the cost of borrowing for sovereign issuers or by affecting sovereign issuers' ability to issue new debt. Any such decision by the NCA must be based on specified indicators relating to: a high or rising interest rate on the sovereign debt; a widening of interest rate spreads on the sovereign debt compared to the sovereign debt of other issuers; a widening of the sovereign CDS spreads as compared to the sovereign debt's own curve and compared to other sovereign issuers; the timeliness of the return of the price of the sovereign debt to its original equilibrium after a large trade; and the amount of sovereign debt that can be traded.[271] As with the suspension regime for uncovered sovereign debt short sales, ESMA must be informed and provide an opinion within 24 hours and other NCAs must be informed. The suspension applies for an initial 12-month period but can be extended subsequently for six-month periods. Additionally, where a suspension applies, natural or legal persons holding an uncovered position in a sovereign CDS must notify the relevant NCA[272] where the position reaches or falls below the reporting thresholds for sovereign debt (section 3.8) (2012 Short Selling Regulation Article 8).

VI.3.7.5 Buy-in Procedures

Related procedures apply in relation to the settlement of shares,[273] designed to address the settlement risks associated with uncovered short sales and to establish basic standards related to settlement discipline.[274] A central clearing counterparty (CCP) in a Member State that provides clearing services for shares must ensure that 'buy-in' procedures are in place in accordance with 2012 Short Selling Regulation Article 15. Accordingly, where a natural or legal person who sells shares is not able to deliver the shares for settlement within four business days after the day on which settlement is due, procedures must be automatically triggered for the buy-in of the shares to ensure delivery for settlement. Where the buy-in of the shares for delivery is not possible, an amount must be paid to the buyer based on the value of the shares to be delivered at the delivery date, plus an amount for losses incurred by the buyer as a result of the settlement failure. In each case, the person who failed to settle must provide reimbursement of all amounts paid under Article 15. The CCP must also ensure that procedures are in place to ensure that where a person who sells shares fails to deliver the shares for settlement by the date on which settlement is due, that person must make daily payments (which must be sufficiently high to act as a deterrent) for each day that the failure continues.

---

[270] Any uncovered sovereign CDS positions created over the suspension period can be held until maturity: 2012 Short Selling Regulation Art 46(2). Reporting requirements also apply under Art 8.

[271] NCAs may also use other indicators.

[272] The NCA of the relevant sovereign: Art 2(1)(j).

[273] Settlement is also being addressed more generally through the new regime for central securities depositaries (noted in Ch V sect 13).

[274] 2012 Short Selling Regulation rec 23.

VI.3.8 Transparency of Net Short Positions

The restrictions on uncovered short sales are accompanied by disclosure and reporting obligations relating to net short positions. These obligations are designed to enhance NCAs' ability to monitor short selling activities for potential systemic risk or abusive conduct, and to enhance pricing mechanisms by providing disclosure to the market on short positions. Disclosure requirements in relation to short selling typically take two forms: 'flagging' rules, which require that short sale orders are 'marked' as the order is placed and that aggregate daily reports based on the marking of orders are filed with the regulator; and requirements governing reporting by individual investors of significant short positions held by them. Although the Commission and European Parliament initially supported the adoption of a flagging regime, the 2012 Short Selling Regulation is based on individual reporting requirements,[275] reflecting in part the greater operational experience with this approach by NCAs,[276] as well as the data quality risks and limitations of the flagging approach.[277]

By contrast with the restrictions under the 2012 Short Selling Regulation on uncovered short transactions, the reporting measures benefited from some degree of market and NCA experience. Reporting requirements featured heavily in the autumn 2008 actions taken by NCAs, while CESR's 2010 Pan-EU Model for Disclosure provided an opportunity for consultation and for analysis of experience to date with position reporting, albeit only with respect to shares. Accordingly, the reporting regime was significantly less controversial during the negotiations.

In the case of shares, a net short position (subject to the reporting obligation) is the position remaining after deducting the long position held in relation to the issued share capital[278] from any short position held in relation to the share capital (Article 3(4)). An expansive approach has been adopted to the net short position assessment, which is designed to capture the building of positions through derivatives: a short position in shares is one which results from either a short sale of a share issued by a company or (engaging derivative use) from a transaction which creates or relates to a financial instrument other than a share, where the effect (or one of the effects) of the transaction is to confer a financial advantage on the person entering into the transaction in the event of a decrease in the price or value of the share (Article 3(1)). A long position, conversely, arises from holding a share, or from a transaction which confers an advantage in the event of an increase in the price or value of the share (Article 3(2)). Where a position is held indirectly (including through an index, a basket of securities, or an exchange-traded fund (ETF)), the person in question must

---

[275] The flagging model was opposed by the Council. Post-trade transaction reports which identify short sales are, however, required under the 2014 MiFID II/MiFIR reporting regime: Ch V sect 12.1.

[276] Only Poland and Greece applied flagging rules when the 2012 Short Selling Regulation was under negotiation.

[277] In developing its short selling reporting regime for equities, CESR warned of imperfections in flagging-related data, that such data might simply replicate that already available from proxy sources, notably in relation to securities lending, while imposing significant costs, and that this data did not provide disclosure on aggregate individual short positions: 2010 CESR Proposal, n 170, 6.

[278] Defined as the total of ordinary and preference shares issued by the company, but not including convertible debt securities: Art 2(1)(h).

determine whether the reporting requirement applies, acting reasonably having regard to publicly available information as to the composition of the relevant index or other vehicle.[279] The administrative regime amplifies when a person 'holds' a share[280] and provides further detail on how the calculation of net short positions is carried out (with particular reference to the range of derivatives which can be used to build a position),[281] including with respect to when different entities in a group have long or short positions[282] and in the context of fund management activities.[283]

In the case of sovereign debt, a net short position is the position remaining after deducting any long position held in the issued sovereign debt,[284] and also after deducting any long position in debt instruments of a sovereign issuer, the pricing of which is 'highly correlated'[285] to the pricing of the given sovereign debt, from any short position held in relation to the same sovereign debt (Article 3(5)). The calculation of long and short positions in sovereign debt is to be made for each single, sovereign issuer, even if separate entities issue debt on behalf of the sovereign issuer, and sovereign CDSs referenced to the sovereign issuer must be included in the calculation[286] (Article 3(3) and (6)); otherwise the calculation is as for shares (Article 3(1) and (2)).[287]

For net short positions in shares, two reporting thresholds apply: in relation to NCA reporting and in relation to public reporting. A person who has a net short position in relation to the issued share capital of a company that has shares admitted to trading on a trading venue must notify the relevant NCA[288] where the position reaches or falls below 0.2 per cent of the

---

[279] No person is required to obtain any real time information as to such composition from any person (Art 3(3)).

[280] 2012 Commission Delegated Regulation 918/2012 Art 4 (linking the 'holding' of a share to owning the share and having an enforceable claim to be transferred ownership of the share).

[281] Including in relation to the weight to be given to long positions held in shares through a basket of shares, and in relation to the instruments which can generate a long position by conferring a financial advantage in the event of an increase in the share price (essentially, a wide range of derivative instruments (including spread bets and CfDs) which provide exposure to share capital): 2012 Commission Delegated Regulation 918/2012 Art 5. This approach also applies to the calculation of short positions: Art 6. The Commission Regulation also specifies that for the purposes of the net short position calculation it is irrelevant whether cash settlement or physical delivery of the underlying assets has been agreed, and that short positions on financial instruments that give rise to a claim to unissued shares, and subscription rights, convertible bonds, and other comparable instruments, are not to be considered as short positions: Art 7.

[282] 2012 Commission Delegated Regulation 918/2012 Art 13.

[283] 2012 Commission Delegated Regulation 918/2012 Art 12.

[284] Defined as the total of sovereign debt issued by a sovereign issuer that has not been redeemed: Art 2(1)(g).

[285] See n 287.

[286] A sale of a CDS is considered to represent a long position, and a purchase a short position: 2012 Commission Delegated Regulation 918/2012 Art 9(3).

[287] As for shares, the calculation of net short positions in sovereign debt has been amplified by the 2012 Commission Delegated Regulation 918/2012 Arts 8–9, which address similar issues to Arts 5–7 in relation to shares, but additionally address when sovereign debt of another issuer is 'highly correlated' and so included in the calculation of the related long position. It specifies that sovereign debt of non-EU sovereign issuers may not be included in the calculation of the long position, and that instruments are highly correlated where there is an 80 per cent correlation coefficient between the pricing (or yield) of the debt instrument of another sovereign issuer and the pricing of a given sovereign issuer over a 12-month period preceding the position (Art 8(3) and (5)).

[288] The determination of the relevant NCA is carried out according to the rules which govern the relevant NCA for the purposes of transaction reporting under MiFID II/MiFIR (Ch V sect 12.1): Art 2(1)(j).

issuer's share capital initially,[289] and each 0.1 per cent above that (Article 5). Public disclosure of net short positions is required at a higher level,[290] where the position reaches or falls below the higher threshold of 0.5 per cent of the issued share capital, and each 0.1 per cent above that (Article 6[291]).[292]

Article 7 governs reporting on net short positions relating to sovereign debt,[293] which is required of NCAs only. Given the complexities,[294] the relevant thresholds were not set in the Short Selling Regulation, but were specified in the 2012 Commission Delegated Regulation 918/2012 (Article 21). Sovereign debt is classified into three baskets for the purposes of determining which reporting threshold applies.[295] An initial 0.1 per cent (of the total amount of outstanding sovereign debt, regardless of different issues) and a subsequent 0.05 per cent threshold applies where the total amount of outstanding issued sovereign debt is between 0 and 500 billion euro. Where the outstanding debt is above 500 billion euro, or where there is a liquid futures market for the particular sovereign debt, an initial 0.5 per cent and subsequent 0.25 per cent threshold applies. In practice, the reporting threshold is fixed at particular monetary amounts. In accordance with 2012 Short Selling Regulation Article 7(2) and 2012 Commission Delegated Regulation 918/2012, ESMA has placed Member States' sovereign debt in one of these three baskets (0–500 billion euro, 500 billion +, and liquid futures market) and has published the particular monetary amounts, in relation to Member States' sovereign debt, to which the reporting obligation attaches.[296] Public disclosure is not required given the potential for damage to liquidity, particularly in markets which are under liquidity pressure.

---

[289] The model on which CESR consulted was originally more stringent, applying at 0.1 per cent of share capital. CESR revised the threshold upward to 0.2 per cent, given evidence from the UK FSA that a 0.1 per cent threshold could lead to over-reporting and related inefficiencies: CESR Feedback Statement/10-089, 12.

[290] The higher threshold reflects the potential risks to the position holder (who might become vulnerable to moves against the position once it is disclosed) as well as the herding risks which might generate market instability were trading to follow the direction of the disclosed positions to a significant extent. While CESR acknowledged these risks in designing its disclosure model, it also warned that there was limited empirical evidence to suggest the risks were significant in practice: 2010 CESR Proposal, n 170, 7–9.

[291] Art 6 applies without prejudice to rules which may apply at national level, and in accordance with EU law, in relation to the disclosure of positions held in the context of takeover transactions: Art 6(5).

[292] In both cases, ESMA is empowered to provide an opinion to the Commission on adjusting the reporting thresholds, and the Commission is empowered to adopt related revising administrative rules (Art 5(3) and (4) and Art 6(3) and (4)).

[293] The inclusion of sovereign debt (and, in certain circumstances, uncovered sovereign CDSs) reflects the prevailing political climate at the time of the Regulation's adoption. In limiting its reporting regime to shares, CESR simply noted that it was not appropriate to extend the reporting regime to other asset classes, given the specific issues raised by shorting of shares: 2010 CESR Proposal, n 170, 8.

[294] Including in relation to a lack of data, the practical difficulties generated by frequent new issues of sovereign debt and the maturing of issues, differing levels of liquidity in different sovereign debt markets, and the danger of over-reporting where thresholds are set at too low a level.

[295] The classification is based on the need to ensure that the thresholds do not lead to over-reporting of positions of minimal value, to reflect, accordingly, the total amount of each sovereign's debt and the average size of the related positions, and to reflect the relative liquidity of each sovereign's debt: Art 21(5) and 2012 Short Selling Regulation Art 7(3).

[296] The monetary amounts are reviewed on a quarterly basis by ESMA to reflect changes in the total amount of outstanding debt, while the placing of Member States within particular baskets is reviewed annually: 2012 Commission Delegated Regulation 918/2012 Art 21(3) and (9). ESMA has recommended that the thresholds be recalibrated in light of initial experience with the 2012 Short Selling Regulation, and that the current quarterly review of monetary amounts take place on an annual basis, given that amounts of EU issued sovereign debt remain broadly stable (sect 3.13).

The method of NCA notification (and of public disclosure as relevant) is governed by the 2012 Short Selling Regulation (Article 9) and the related administrative rules. Under Article 9(1), the notification or disclosure must set out details of the identity of the person, the size of the relevant position, the issuer in question, and the date on which the position was created, changed, or ceased to be held. Public disclosures must be made in a manner which ensures fast access to the information on a non-discriminatory basis and the information must be posted on a website operated or supervised by the relevant NCA; ESMA also hosts links to these websites (Article 9(4)). Article 9 also addresses the relevant time at which the calculation must be made and the confidentiality of disclosures provided to the NCA. The administrative regime specifies further the content of NCA notifications,[297] the means through which public disclosure can be made in relation to shares, and the format in which NCA reports are to be made.[298]

The reporting regime is cascaded to ESMA, which acts as a central repository for reporting on net short positions. NCAs must provide information in summary form to ESMA on a quarterly basis on net short positions relating to shares and sovereign debt (and uncovered sovereign CDS as relevant) (Article 11(1)). ESMA may also request, at any time and in order to carry out its duties under the Regulation, additional information from NCAs on net short positions related to shares, sovereign debt, or uncovered sovereign CDSs (Article 11(2)). The format and content of these reports has been specified by the administrative regime.[299]

VI.3.9 Intervention in Exceptional Circumstances

VI.3.9.1 NCA Powers

The prohibitions on uncovered short transactions and disclosure/notification requirements are at the core of the 2012 Short Selling Regulation, but apply to specific instruments only. While, as discussed in this section, a series of more wide-ranging intervention powers are conferred on NCAs and on ESMA, they apply in exceptional or emergency conditions. Disorderly market conditions are also addressed by the 2014 MiFID II/MiFIR, which confers new powers in relation to position management (sections 2.5 and 2.6).

The additional and exceptional NCA intervention powers are triggered when there are adverse events or developments which constitute a serious threat to financial stability or to market confidence in the Member State concerned or in one or more other Member States[300] and the measure in question is necessary to address the threat and will not have a

---

[297] 2012 Commission Delegated Regulation 826/2012 Art 2.

[298] 2012 Commission Implementing Regulation 827/2012 Arts 2 and 3.

[299] 2012 Commission Delegated Regulation 826/2012 Arts 4 and 5 and 2012 Commission Implementing Regulation 827/2012 Arts 3 and 4.

[300] The nature of these adverse events or developments has been amplified by the 2012 Commission Delegated Regulation 918/2012 Art 24 which (in outline) identifies any act, result, fact, or event that is or could reasonably be expected to lead to: serious financial, monetary, or budgetary problems which may lead to financial instability concerning a Member State or bank and other financial institution deemed important to the global financial system; a rating action or default by any Member State or bank and other financial institution deemed important to the global financial system; substantial selling pressures or unusual volatility causing significant downward spirals in any financial instruments related to any bank and other financial institution deemed important to the global financial system; any relevant damage to the physical structures of

detrimental effect on the efficiency of financial markets which is disproportionate to its benefits; the NCA's determination in this respect is reviewed by ESMA. Where these threshold conditions are met, the NCA may require persons who have net short positions in relation to a specific financial instrument or class of financial instruments to notify to it, or to disclose to the public, details of the position where the position reaches or falls below a threshold fixed by the NCA (Article 18); the NCA may provide for exceptions, including in relation to market-making and primary market activities.[301] The NCA may also require persons engaged in the lending of a specific financial instrument or class of financial instrument to notify any significant change in the fees requested for such lending (Article 19). More interventionist action is envisaged by Article 20, which empowers the NCA to prohibit or impose conditions relating to persons entering into a short sale or a transaction other than a short sale which creates, or relates to, a financial instrument, and the effect (or one of the effects) of that transaction is to confer a financial advantage on the person in the event of a decrease in the price or value of another financial instrument.[302] Similarly, Article 21 empowers the NCA to restrict the ability of persons to enter into sovereign CDS transactions or to limit the value of sovereign CDS transactions.[303]

A specific 'circuit-breaker' power, which is not subject to the Article 18–21 threshold/ qualifying conditions, applies in relation to the temporary restriction of short sales in financial instruments in the case of a 'significant' fall in price (Article 23), and is designed to prevent disorderly declines in the value of particular financial instruments.[304] Where the price of a financial instrument on a trading venue has 'fallen significantly' during a single trading day (in relation to the closing price on the venue on the previous trading day), the NCA of the home Member State for that venue must consider whether it is appropriate to prohibit or restrict persons from engaging in short selling of the financial instrument on the trading venue, or otherwise to limit transactions in that financial instrument on that trading venue, in order to prevent a disorderly decline in the price of the financial instrument. Where the NCA is satisfied that it is appropriate to do so, it must, in the case of a share or debt instrument, prohibit or restrict persons from entering into a short sale on that trading venue or, in the case of another type of financial instrument, limit transactions in that financial instrument on that trading venue in order to prevent a disorderly decline in the price of the financial instrument.[305] The extent of the falls in value which trigger this power are specified by the 2012 Short Selling Regulation and its supporting administrative rules. The Regulation provides that a fall in value of 10 per cent amounts to a significant fall in

---

important financial issuers, market infrastructures, clearing and settlement systems, and supervisors; and any relevant disruption in any payment system or settlement process.

[301] This power does not apply where the financial instrument is already subject to transparency requirements under the Regulation: Art 18(2).

[302] The NCA may apply the restriction to all financial instruments, financial instruments of a specific class, or a specific financial instrument, and may provide for exceptions (including in relation to market-making and primary dealing activities).

[303] As under Art 20, the NCA may apply the restriction to all sovereign CDS transactions of a specific class, or to specific sovereign CDS transactions, and may provide for exceptions (including in relation to market-making and primary dealing activities).

[304] The circuit-breaker power is designed to empower NCAs to slow a negative price spiral without needing to show, at the same time, the exceptional, emergency conditions on which emergency intervention is otherwise dependent.

[305] Exceptions may be provided for (Art 23(3)).

value for a liquid share. The required fall in value for illiquid shares and other financial instruments is governed by 2012 Commission Delegated Regulation 918/2012.[306] The thresholds are set at levels designed to ensure that NCAs are not required to repeatedly and unnecessarily consider whether Article 23 'circuit-breaker' action should be taken.[307]

The Article 18–21 intervention powers can only be triggered when the threshold conditions are met. The Article 23 powers are also confined in that the required 'significant fall' has been specified in some detail. Procedural requirements also apply to these exceptional powers. The Article 18–21 restrictions may only be valid for an initial period of three months, which may be extended by further three-month periods (Article 24); short time limits also apply to the Article 23 power.[308] Any exercise of power under Articles 18–21 and 23 must also be disclosed on the NCA's website and notified to the other NCAs (Article 26).[309]

Any proposed use of the Article 18–21 and 23 powers (and any renewal of related decisions) must be notified to ESMA (Article 26).[310] ESMA must also issue a publicly disclosed opinion on whether it considers the proposed Articles 18–21 measure necessary to address the applicable exceptional circumstances[311] (Article 27(2)).[312] ESMA's approach thus far has been supportive, although its opinions have been somewhat economically reasoned, as might be expected given the sensitivities of short selling restrictions.[313] An NCA can choose

---

[306] Art 23 specifies the qualifying falls in value in a single trading day as: 10 per cent, 20 per cent, or 40 per cent or more for semi-liquid shares, 'penny shares' (shares with a nominal value of at least 50 cent), and illiquid shares, respectively; an increase of 7 per cent or more in the yield across the yield curve for the relevant sovereign issuer; an increase of 10 per cent or more in the yield of a corporate bond; a decrease of 1.5 per cent or more in the price of a money-market instrument; and a decrease of 10 per cent or more in the price of an exchange-traded fund (ETF). Where a derivative is traded on a trading venue and its only underlying financial instrument is a financial instrument for which a significant fall in value has been specified, a significant fall in value of the derivative is deemed to occur where there has been a significant fall in the underlying financial instrument.

[307] 2012 Commission Delegated Regulation 918/2012 Impact Assessment, n 214, 14.

[308] Art 23 restrictions must initially be imposed for not more than the trading day following the day on which the fall in price occurred and can only be extended for a further two days, and only where a further significant fall in value has occurred (Art 23(2)).

[309] In relation to the Art 18–21 powers, where the NCA taking the action is not the relevant NCA—generally the NCA which receives transaction reports in relation to the financial instrument in question under MiFID II/MiFIR (Art 2(1)(j))—as may be the case where the instrument is traded on a number of venues, the NCA must receive the consent of the relevant NCA before acting: Art 22.

[310] Very tight notification deadlines apply under Art 26 for Arts 18–21 and Art 23 decisions: Art 26(3). In effect, ESMA must be notified not less than 24 hours before an Art 18–21 decision (in exceptional circumstances, shorter notice can be given) and before the Art 23 decision is intended to take effect.

[311] ESMA must also review the measures subject to the opinion obligation regularly and at least every three months.

[312] The opinion must state whether ESMA considers that adverse events or developments have arisen which constitute a serious threat to financial stability or market confidence in one or more Member States, whether the measure is appropriate and proportionate to address the threat, and whether the proposed duration is justified: Art 27(2). The opinion must also state if ESMA considers that the taking of any measures by other NCAs is necessary.

[313] Its initial November 2012, January 2013, and April 2013 opinions on the temporary prohibition by the Greek authority of short sales in shares of credit institutions admitted to the Athens Stock Exchange, and of short selling of shares and units of ETFs admitted to the Athens Stock Exchange generally (November 2012), were short and simply noted that ESMA considered that there were adverse developments which constituted a serious threat to financial stability and market confidence in Greece, and that the measures were appropriate and proportionate to the threat: ESMA/2012/717, ESMA/2013/149, and ESMA/2013/542. It adopted a similar approach in its opinion on the November 2012 restriction by the Spanish NCA on

to take action contrary to the ESMA opinion, but must publicly explain its reasons for doing so; ESMA may also consider whether exercise of its exceptional Article 28 intervention powers (discussed later in this section) is then warranted.

ESMA is less engaged with the Article 23 'circuit-breaker' power, reflecting its time-sensitive nature. ESMA must, however, be notified and is required to co-ordinate where the instrument in question is traded in a number of venues across the Member States. The NCAs of those other venues must be notified by ESMA and where disagreement arises between the NCAs concerned, ESMA must mediate between the NCAs, failing which ESMA can impose a decision in relation to the treatment of the instrument concerned.[314]

VI.3.9.2 ESMA Powers

The political decision to confer direct operational powers on ESMA in relation to short selling was taken prior to the adoption of the 2012 Short Selling Regulation and during the negotiations on the foundation Regulations for the European Supervisory Authorities (ESAs). At the instigation of the European Parliament, an enabling clause was added to the ESAs' founding Regulations which permits the ESAs to prohibit or restrict financial products or services, once the specific power is conferred in the relevant legislation.[315] A specific power to this effect has been conferred under the 2012 Short Selling Regulation, which has the effect of empowering ESMA in a highly sensitive area.

ESMA enjoys a range of powers, however, in relation to short selling, which span the spectrum of intervention from facilitation of Member State action to direct action by ESMA. Under Article 27, ESMA is to perform a co-ordination and facilitation role in relation to emergency (Articles 18–21 and 23) measures taken by NCAs and is to ensure a consistent approach is taken by NCAs. As noted above, ESMA is required to provide an opinion on Article 18–21 action and can facilitate mediation in the case of disputes between NCAs in relation to Article 23 action. ESMA is also empowered to conduct an inquiry (on its own initiative, or at the request of the Council, the Commission, the European Parliament, or one or more NCAs) into a particular issue or practice relating to short selling or into the use of CDSs, in order to assess whether potential threats to financial stability or market confidence in the EU are engaged (Article 31). ESMA is also centrally involved in the adoption of co-operation agreements between NCAs and third countries in relation to information exchange and the enforcement of the 2012 Short Selling Regulation in third countries (Article 38; see section 3.11).

In a precedent-setting extension of ESMA's powers, it is also empowered, subject to strict conditionality, to take direct action with respect to short selling (Article 28). Where the relevant threshold conditions are met, ESMA must either: require persons who have net short positions in relation to a specific financial instrument or class of financial instrument to notify an NCA or to disclose to the public details of any such position; or prohibit or impose conditions on the entry by the person into a short sale or a transaction which

---

transactions which confer a benefit in the event of a decrease in the price or value of shares listed on a Spanish official secondary market: ESMA/2012/715.

[314] Very tight deadlines apply to notification and mediation under Art 23(4) which are designed to ensure agreement is reached by midnight on the day on which the NCA makes the restriction decision.

[315] 2010 ESMA Regulation Art 9(5).

creates, or relates to, a financial instrument (other than sovereign debt or derivatives related to sovereign debt, including CDSs) where the effect (or one of the effects) of the transaction is to confer a financial advantage on such person in the event of a decrease in the price or value of another financial instrument (Article 28(1)).[316] These measures, which are valid for three months in the first instance,[317] prevail over any previous measure taken by an NCA under Articles 18–21 and 23 (Article 28(11)). Before ESMA can act, stringent threshold conditions must be met. The measures must address a threat to the orderly functioning and stability of financial markets or to the stability of the whole of part of the financial system in the EU, and there must be cross-border implications.[318] It must also be the case that no NCA has taken measures to address the threat, or that one or more NCAs have taken measures that do not adequately address the threat (Article 28(2)). In addition, before taking action, ESMA must take into account the extent to which the measure: significantly addresses the threat to the orderly functioning and integrity of financial markets or to the stability of the whole of part of the financial system in the EU, or significantly improves the ability of NCAs to monitor the threat; does not create a risk of regulatory arbitrage; and does not have a detrimental effect on the efficiency of financial markets, including by reducing liquidity in those markets or creating uncertainty for market participants that is disproportionate to the benefits of the measure (Article 28(3)). A number of procedural notification requirements must also be met. The European Systemic Risk Board (ESRB) and, where relevant, 'other relevant authorities'[319] must be consulted before ESMA acts (or decides to renew a measure) (Article 28(4)). The NCAs concerned[320] must also be notified at least 24 hours in advance of ESMA action,[321] and public disclosure made[322] in relation to any Article 28 decision or a renewal of a decision (Article 28(5)–(9)).

While sovereign debt is expressly excluded from the Article 28 power, a somewhat otiose but politically driven declaratory provision states that in the case of an emergency situation as defined in the foundation ESMA Regulation, ESMA's related emergency powers[323] apply (Article 29).

As is implicit in the tight conditions which govern action by ESMA, and by the exclusion of sovereign debt—and although this power was foreseen by the 2010 ESMA Regulation—

---

[316] As with the parallel NCA powers, the measures may apply in particular circumstances or be subject to exceptions, including in relation to market-making activity and primary market activities.

[317] The measure can be renewed for subsequent three-month periods, subject to the Art 28 conditions and procedural requirements being met: Art 28(10).

[318] This condition has been amplified by 2012 Commission Delegated Regulation 918/2012 Art 24(3), which is similar to Art 24(1) of the 2012 Delegated Regulation, which specifies the nature of the threats which can lead to Art 18–21 NCA action (n 300). The conditions differ, however, in that they are related to threats concerning a Member State, or the financial system within a Member State, and do not extend to banks and other financial institutions deemed important to the global financial system, and in that they do not include the condition relating to substantial selling pressures or unusual volatility in financial instruments related to banks or important financial institutions which applies to Art 18–21 action.

[319] Undefined, but designed to capture, eg, authorities responsible for non-financial commodities markets, where necessary (rec 33).

[320] Not defined, but presumably the NCAs of the major venues and markets affected by the ESMA action.

[321] Although a shorter notification period is permissible in exceptional circumstances.

[322] The disclosure (on ESMA's website) must specify the relevant measure(s) and include the reasons why ESMA is of the opinion that it is necessary to impose the measure(s) and the related supporting evidence.

[323] See further Ch XI sects 5.3.1 and 5.4.1.

ESMA's direct powers of intervention were controversial in the negotiations on the 2012 Short Selling Regulation. In particular, while the European Parliament supported powers of intervention for ESMA in the sovereign debt and CDS markets,[324] these powers proved highly contentious during Council negotiations, given the potential impact of any such intervention on a Member State's borrowing costs, and were not supported. Some Member States were also of the view that the short selling powers conferred a wide discretion on ESMA potentially in breach of the Court of Justice's *Meroni* ruling, which prohibits any delegation of powers from an EU institution which involves the exercise of wide discretion by the delegate.[325] In June 2012 the UK launched a challenge to the Article 28 power based on a series of grounds, chiefly relating to the power's breach of the conditions which apply to the delegation of powers to ESMA. In January 2014 the Court rejected the challenge, finding that ESMA's executive discretion was appropriately confined, and underlining the importance of the power in supporting financial stability and the technical capacity which ESMA brought to EU financial system governance.[326]

It remains to be seen how ESMA will shape operational decisions by NCAs in emergency conditions, and how ambitious it will be in deploying its direct powers. Initial indications suggest a cautious approach, supportive of NCA action, although ESMA has yet to be faced with pan-EU market turbulence of a scale that warrants co-ordinated action by NCAs and potential intervention by ESMA. The legal and political sensitivities associated with direct intervention suggest that, notwithstanding the Court's 2014 confirmation of the validity of (and necessity for) its powers, ESMA is likely to be particularly cautious before deploying Article 28.

VI.3.10 Supervision and Enforcement

As with other EU securities and markets regulation measures, the 2012 Short Selling Regulation requires that NCAs be designated for the purposes of the Regulation (Article 32) and addresses NCA powers (Article 33) and ESMA/inter-NCA co-operation, including in relation to on-site inspections or investigations (Articles 35–37).[327]

While the framework for NCA action and co-operation is broadly similar to that which applies across EU securities and markets regulation, a discrete information-gathering power is conferred which empowers NCAs to require a person entering into a CDS transaction (whether a sovereign CDS or otherwise) to provide an explanation for the purpose of the transaction and whether it is for hedging against a risk or otherwise, and to provide information verifying the underlying risk where the transaction is for hedging purposes (Article 33(3)). As discussed in section 3.12 of this Chapter, ESMA's ability to shape supervisory practices is significant given the scale of its supervisory convergence activities and the direct powers it can deploy.

---

[324] European Parliament Press Release, Crack Down on Short Selling and Sovereign Debt Speculation (Ref 201110181PR29720), noting the Council's refusal to accept the Parliament's position.

[325] n 114.

[326] Case C-270/12 *UK v Council and Parliament*, 22 January 2014, not yet reported. See further Ch XI sect 5.8.3.

[327] As is usual, professional secrecy and personal data protection requirements apply (Arts 34 and 39).

The enforcement regime is based on the less articulated model which prevailed prior to the enhancement of enforcement in later crisis-era measures.[328] Accordingly, Member States must establish rules on penalties and administrative measures which must be effective, proportionate, and dissuasive; they must also provide ESMA on an annual basis with aggregated information on penalties and administrative measures imposed (Article 41). ESMA is empowered to adopt guidelines to ensure a consistent approach to penalties and administrative measures.

VI.3.11 Third Countries

The 2012 Short Selling Regulation has significant extraterritorial effects, as its scope is determined by whether the instrument in question is within the scope of the Regulation.[329] The Regulation specifies, for example, that the reporting and disclosure requirements in respect of net short positions apply to persons domiciled or established in the EU or a third country (Article 10), while ESMA has repeatedly underlined that the Regulation's obligations generally are not dependent on the location of the market participant in question.[330]

The regime contains few exemptions from its application to third country actors. While admission to an EU-regulated market or trading venue is required to bring some instruments into scope, it is not a condition for all instruments. Shares are, however, exempted from the 2012 Regulation where the principal venue on which they are traded is outside the EU (section 3.5.2). Third country market-makers benefit from the Article 17 market-making exemption, but only where the Commission has made the related equivalence determination in relation to the legal and supervisory framework of the third country in accordance with Article 17.[331]

The extraterritorial reach, and related exporting effect, of the 2012 Short Selling Regulation is reflected in the obligations imposed on NCAs and on ESMA in relation to third country co-operation arrangements. Under Article 38 NCAs must, where possible, conclude co-operation arrangements with supervisory authorities of third countries concerning the exchange of information.[332] Co-operation arrangements must also, and more radically, address the enforcement of obligations arising under the Regulation in third countries, and the taking of intervention measures similar to Articles 18–21, 23, and 28 in third countries. ESMA is charged with co-ordinating the adoption of co-operation arrangements, although the agreements are executed bilaterally between the relevant NCA and third country

---

[328] See further Ch XI sect 4.1.2.

[329] The international impact was borne out by the 2013 ESMA Short Selling Review which found that around 83 per cent of all reported short positions in shares were held by UK or US domiciled entities: n 211, 10.

[330] eg n 228.

[331] The equivalence framework is designed to ensure that the third country trading venue of which the market-maker is a member complies with legally binding requirements equivalent to the rules which apply to trading venues in the EU, including in relation to venue supervision and transparency, market abuse, issuer disclosure, and transaction reporting: Art 17(2).

[332] Art 38(1) provides that co-operation arrangements must at least ensure an efficient exchange of information that allows NCAs to carry out their duties under the Regulation; professional secrecy guarantees equivalent to those that apply between NCAs must apply (Art 38(4)). Art 40 governs the conditions under which information can be transferred to third countries. Co-operation arrangements must in particular address the information exchange necessary to allow EU NCAs to make the necessary determinations in relation to the principal trading venue for shares, as required under Art 16 (Art 38(2)).

supervisor. ESMA is, however, centrally engaged with the development of these arrangements, being required to co-ordinate the development of co-operation arrangements and to prepare a template for such arrangements (Article 38(3)). ESMA is also charged with co-ordinating information exchange between NCAs and third country supervisory authorities in relation to emergency intervention measures (Article 38(3)).

VI.3.12 ESMA and the Short Selling Regime

As noted in section 3.4, ESMA has been a material influence on the short selling 'rulebook'. It can also deploy significant operational powers which contrast sharply with CESR's comparative impotence in this field. Although short selling came directly within CESR's sphere of competence and influence, CESR was out-gunned by the Member States and their NCAs in the early stages of the financial crisis in autumn 2008. Although CESR included convergence on short selling in its initial own-initiative agenda on the financial crisis,[333] and succeeded in adopting a pan-EU reporting regime (which was ultimately reflected in the Regulation), its ability to co-ordinate in emergency conditions proved limited; it provided only basic co-ordination support to the prohibition of short selling by NCAs in September 2008, although it subsequently established a task force to support co-ordination and consulted with stakeholders on the impact of the restrictions.[334]

Initially, and prior to the adoption of the 2012 Short Selling Regulation, ESMA proved similarly unable to deliver a co-ordinated approach to short selling, particularly during the August 2011 turmoil, reflecting the intense political interests engaged. Since then, ESMA's capacity has been significantly strengthened by the Regulation.

ESMA acts as a central hub for reporting and disclosure on net short positions,[335] is conferred with co-ordination and facilitation responsibilities, and is empowered to provide opinions on the compliance of NCAs' emergency actions in relation to short selling and in relation to the politically charged power of NCAs to suspend restrictions on uncovered sovereign debt short sales and uncovered sovereign CDS transactions. ESMA is also charged with co-ordinating the arrangements between third country supervisors and NCAs in relation to information exchange and the enforcement of the regime in third countries. Most radically, it has been conferred with direct operational powers in emergency situations, and can impose reporting requirements and restrictions on short sales of financial instruments in any Member State.

It remains to be seen whether ESMA can drive a co-ordinated pan-EU response to short selling, particularly in emergency conditions. The disorderly responses in autumn 2008,

---

[333] It announced its intention to investigate further convergence on short selling, to monitor the impact of the crisis on investment funds, to review the impact of the Lehman collapse, and to address the need for guidance with respect to fair value measurement: CESR/08-791.

[334] CESR/08-723, CESR/09-068, and CESR/08-2010.

[335] In outline, ESMA must host links to the websites for public disclosure of net short positions (Art 9(4)); maintain the list of shares for which the principal trading venue is a third country and which accordingly fall outside the Regulation (Art 16(2)); maintain the list of exempted market-makers and authorized primary dealers (Art 17(13)); and maintain a list of all related penalties and administrative measures applicable in the Member States (Art 41). In addition, ESMA must receive aggregated information on net short positions from NCAs on a quarterly basis and can request additional information relating to short sales and CDSs from NCAs (Art 11) and from market participants (Art 28).

May 2010, and August 2011 underline the acutely sensitive political context within which these restrictions are typically imposed, as well as the distinct local market conditions which drive particular NCA responses. Whether or not the extent to which the legal regime relating to short selling has been harmonized, and the new dynamic which ESMA has brought to supervisory convergence generally, can counteract these strong forces remains to be seen. But some degree of variance in this most sensitive of areas seems unavoidable, as well as appropriate. Overall, however, the short selling regime has provided ESMA with the means to exert its nascent authority on the EU's financial markets.

VI.3.13 Impact

In June 2013 ESMA issued a report on the 2012 Short Selling Regulation to the Commission, designed to inform the Commission's required review of the Regulation.[336] ESMA's main findings (in relation to the first five months or so of the Regulation being in force) were broadly positive. Overall, as compared to a control group of US shares, it found a slight decline in the volatility of EU shares, mixed effects on liquidity (a decrease in bid-ask spreads and no significant impact on traded volumes), and a decrease in price discovery effectiveness.[337] It found that the thresholds for NCA reporting and public disclosure in relation to shares were appropriate,[338] and suggested only minor revisions.[339] It recommended, however, that the NCA reporting threshold for sovereign debt be revised, given very limited reporting and reflecting general market unhappiness with the reporting thresholds.[340] With respect to the restrictions on uncovered short sales in shares and in sovereign debt, it found a reduction in the incidence of settlement failure, although it also noted that the securities lending market may have been adversely affected by the locate rule in particular.[341] While it supported maintaining the restrictions on uncovered short selling, it recommended some adjustments to the regime, particularly with respect to the 'locate rule'.[342] The highly contested prohibition on uncovered sovereign CDSs had not had a 'compelling impact' on the liquidity of the EU CDS market or on the related sovereign debt market, although a decline in activity in sovereign CDSs in a few EU Member States and reduced liquidity in EU sovereign CDS indices had occurred. ESMA recommended that the prohibition be kept under review and suggested a number of refinements to the regime to support legal certainty.

---

[336] n 211.

[337] n 211, 9.

[338] ESMA found a reluctance to report to the public (at the 0.5 per cent threshold); in the assessment period (November 2012–February 2013), 74 per cent of notifications were to NCAs and 24 per cent to the public.

[339] Including that indices be required to provide, free of charge, data on index composition to facilitate the calculation of net short positions.

[340] ESMA reported only 148 notifications to NCAs over the assessment period (as compared to 12,603 related to net short share positions). ESMA suggested that, as this level of reporting might not accurately reflect actual short selling activity, a revision was required. Its recommendations included that the threshold calculation method be revised to reflect a wider range of factors (including levels of retail investor participation) and be based on a nominal amount method (rather than the complex, duration-adjusted approach, which reflects the different durations of separate issues held, adopted in 2012 Commission Delegated Regulation 918/2012).

[341] ESMA reported a 'significant reduction in lendable quantities and quantities on loan as compared to the US control group': n 211, 21.

[342] It recommended, eg, that short sellers be able to obtain confirmations from parties within the same legal entity as the seller, as long as the conditions applying to confirmations were met.

The exemption for market-making, however, was found to be problematic in practice, being restrictive in scope and unclear.[343] ESMA's recommendations included that the scope of the exemption be extended to include OTC market-making activities, in order to protect liquidity and avoid higher costs.

Finally, ESMA found that NCA exercise of emergency powers under the Regulation had been necessary and appropriate—although it recommended that the thresholds for Article 23 circuit-breaker intervention be lowered, given evidence that, in certain asset classes, the thresholds were being crossed overly frequently, and that most NCAs did not deem it necessary to impose short sale prohibitions when the threshold was crossed.[344]

The Commission in response concurred with ESMA's findings, concluding that, based on the limited evidence available, the Regulation had a positive impact in terms of greater transparency of short sales and reduced settlement failures, albeit that the economic impact was mixed. While it noted ESMA's proposals for reforms, it decided against taking action, given in particular the limited empirical evidence available, and called for a second review of the Regulation, on the basis of more extensive empirical evidence, by end 2016.[345]

The review of the Regulation suggests that it has not, at least, been disruptive and, broadly, has had positive effects. It also augurs well for the future development of the regime. ESMA's analysis was empirically driven[346] and cautious,[347] as was the Commission in response.

VI.4 Trading in the OTC Derivatives Markets

VI.4.1 The Reform Agenda

The significant expansion in the reach of trading regulation over the OTC markets, and in particular over the OTC derivatives markets,[348] is one of the defining features of the G20 reform programme[349] and of crisis-era EU securities and markets regulation.

---

[343] In particular, the requirement that market-makers be a member of a trading venue was widely regarded as excluding OTC instruments from the exemption, and as limiting OTC market-making in instruments such as interest rate swaps and non-listed derivatives (an OTC market maker in an equity derivative, eg, would not be exempted from the Regulation when hedging by engaging in a short sale in the underlying equity): n 211, 36–7. As noted (n 249), NCA compliance with ESMA's related Guidelines has been problematic in this regard.

[344] This was particularly the case with respect to bonds and sovereign debt, in relation to which ESMA suggested that the threshold be increased.

[345] Commission, Report from the Commission to the European Parliament and Council on the Short Selling Regulation (2013) (COM (2013) 885).

[346] The review was based on a quantitative assessment of the regime's impact and a qualitative assessment based on discussions with NCAs and on responses to a Call for Evidence: n 211, 4 and 7–8.

[347] ESMA warned that its review was based on a short time span (some five months or so), that additional data over a longer period would have generated more robust results, that its findings were subject to model risk and empirical limits, and that its findings might reflect external factors not related to the legal regime and which could distort the results.

[348] For a contrarian perspective, see Stout, L, Helwege, J, Wallison, P, and Pirrong, C, 'Regulate OTC Derivatives by Deregulating Them' (2009) 32 *Regulation* 3, arguing for OTC financial derivatives to be considered as non-legally enforceable gambling contracts, unless the counterparties can prove the transaction has a legitimate hedging purpose.

[349] A significant policy and academic literature has addressed the OTC derivatives market reform programme. Collections of studies (with an EU perspective) include the Special Edition of the Banque de

Prior to the financial crisis, the OTC derivatives market[350] had expanded exponentially.[351] OTC derivatives markets were largely unregulated: trading occurred outside regulated organized venues and often on a bilateral basis between counterparties; transactions were not subject to formal clearing requirements; and risk mitigation and reporting requirements were limited. The financial crisis exposed the very significant transparency and resilience risks which had been building up,[352] notably through the massive increase in reliance on credit derivatives, and in particular CDSs, to manage exposures from asset-backed securitization transactions.[353] The March 2008 Bear Stearns collapse, the September 2008 default of Lehmans, and the September 2008 bailout of AIG[354] triggered widespread market concern as to the extent to which institutions were exposed to CDSs and to the related counterparty risk.

The difficulties in the OTC derivatives market were driven by the opacity of the OTC derivatives market generally[355] and of the CDS segment in particular, and the extent to

---

France's *Financial Stability Review* on OTC Derivatives: New Rules, New Actors, New Risks, Issue 17, April 2013 and the Special Edition of the *EBOLR* on OTC Derivative Market Regulation, 13 (2013) issue 3.

[350] The major classes of OTC derivative are foreign exchange, interest rate (the largest segment), commodity, equity, and credit (particularly CDS) derivatives.

[351] As widely reported in the major crisis-era reports: eg, 2009 Turner Review, n 25, 81–2. The financial crisis did not lead to significant contraction in the market. At the end of 2009, the notional value of the market was $615 trillion—a 12 per cent increase on the end of 2008, although a 10 per cent decrease on the market's peak in June 2008: Commission, 2010 EMIR Proposal Impact Assessment (SEC (2010) 1058/2) 11–12.

[352] The role played by the OTC derivatives market in the financial crisis has been extensively documented. From an EU policy perspective, see Commission, Ensuring Efficient Safe and Sound Derivatives Markets (2009) (COM (2009) 332); it was accompanied by an extensive Staff Working Paper which examined the nature of OTC derivatives market clearing in detail (SEC (2009) 905) and a Consultation (SEC (2009) 914). Similarly, see ECB, Credit Default Swaps and Counterparty Risk (2009). In its extensive Impact Assessment for EMIR, the Commission concluded that 'the crisis has shown that—in certain situations—the combined effect of the very characteristics that make derivatives (in particular leverage) and the OTC derivatives market (high level of customisation, lack of transparency, high market concentration, high interconnection of large market participants, and lack of regulation) so attractive can have devastating consequences for the financial system': 2010 EMIR Proposal Impact Assessment, n 3521, 13. Among the extensive academic studies, see Stout, L, The Legal Origin of the 2008 Credit Crisis, UCLA School of Law Law-Econ Research Paper No 11-05 (2011), available at <http://ssrn.com/abstract=1770082>.

[353] For an assessment see 2009 Turner Review, n 25, 14–16. Although the CDS segment represented only 7 per cent of the global OTC derivatives market, between 2005 and 2007 it had grown by 900 per cent: ECB, n 352, 4 and 13.

[354] The AIG bailout is strongly associated with the systemic risks which CDS exposures triggered. AIG acquired large exposures to the US subprime mortgage market by selling CDSs insuring mortgage-backed securities to major financial institutions. By contrast with most CDS providers, AIG ran a significant short position (rather than a balanced position, as was more common); its net short position amounted to $384 billion. Relying on its strong triple-A credit rating, AIG negotiated favourable collateralization arrangements in relation to the CDSs, which allowed it to avoid posting collateral, as long as it maintained its triple-A rating. A lack of transparency in the CDS market meant AIG's large position was not disclosed, allowing it to build it up its position further (as the CDSs did not price correctly the counterparty risk which AIG represented). When the US housing market collapsed, causing severe downgrades in the ratings of mortgage-backed securities, AIG's rating was cut, triggering a requirement to post additional billions of collateral and tipping it into insolvency; the systemic dangers of a disorderly AIG collapse led to the $182 billion bailout by the US government: eg, Saunders, B, 'Should Credit Default Swaps Issuers be Subject to Prudential Regulation' (2010) 10 *JCLS* 427 and Commission, European Financial Stability and Integration Report 2012 (2013) (SWD (2013) 156) (2012 EFSIR) 105.

[355] Which had been signalled immediately prior to the crisis: Partnoy and Skeel, n 141, 1036.

which the market was concentrated[356]—major institutions, with systemic implications, were closely interlinked through derivatives exposures.[357] The extent of the interlinkages between counterparties, and the degree of concentration of exposure risk among counterparties, transformed counterparty risk (which strongly characterizes OTC derivatives transactions, as counterparty risk can persist for several years)[358] into systemic risk.[359] With respect to opacity risks, the bilateral nature of the market meant that the market was largely opaque; accordingly, the extent to which exposures were concentrated and where they were concentrated was not clear.[360] Demands to post higher quality collateral to cover counterparty exposures as the creditworthiness of counterparties in the OTC derivatives market deteriorated added to the intense pro-cyclical pressure in the market as the financial crisis deepened. It also became clear that OTC derivatives contracts were often under-collateralized,[361] and that operational risks were significant, particularly in relation to asset segregation. In response, financial institutions, and particularly credit institutions, withdrew credit facilities given the potential extent of counterparty risk, thereby aggravating the credit and liquidity contraction over autumn 2008.

Reform of the OTC derivatives market quickly became a central element of the G20 reform agenda. The April 2009 London G20 meeting committed to promoting the standardization and resilience of credit derivatives markets, in particular through the establishment of CCPs subject to effective regulation and supervision.[362] The reform agenda was significantly expanded by the September 2009 Pittsburgh G20 meeting, which made a commitment that all 'standardized OTC derivative contracts' would be traded on exchanges or 'electronic trading platforms' and cleared through CCPs by the end of 2012. It also agreed that OTC derivative contracts would be reported to trade repositories and that non-centrally cleared contracts would be subject to higher capital requirements.[363]

---

[356] The OTC derivatives market is highly concentrated, with a relatively small number of dealer institutions (major financial institutions) providing liquidity to the entire market; the number of potential trading parties is, accordingly, limited: 2012 EFSIR, n 354, 87.

[357] For a recent analysis see ECB, Financial Stability Review, May 2013, 46–8.

[358] By contrast with securities transactions, derivatives transactions are heavily exposed to counterparty credit risk given the longer time horizon over which the reciprocal obligations of the counterparties are open, and the related risk that creditworthiness will fluctuate over that period and become compromised prior to the performance of obligations: Bliss, R and Steigerwald, R, 'Derivative Clearing and Settlement: A Comparison of Central Counterparties and Alternative Structures' (2008) 30 *Economic Perspectives* 22.

[359] ECB, n 352, 20–34.

[360] The lack of transparency had two major impacts. It became difficult to evaluate effectively collateral requirements for exposures; and market distrust, and a related drying up of liquidity, intensified. Regulators also struggled in assessing the nature and location of risk. In 2009, and even allowing for the additional data made available by then, the ECB noted that it found the assessment of counterparty risk 'very challenging': ECB, n 352, 4 and 11–13.

[361] A crisis-era Commission study reported on data which suggested that 66 per cent of credit exposures arising from OTC derivatives were covered by collateral, and that coverage levels were highest in related to fixed income derivatives (71 per cent), but lower in relation to equity (52 per cent), commodities (47 per cent), and foreign exchange (48 per cent) derivatives: 2009 Staff Working Paper, n 352, 13. The IMF has similarly concluded that a large segment of the OTC market was under-collateralized (by some $2 trillion): Singh, M, Collateral, Netting and Systemic Risk in the OTC Derivatives Market, IMF WP No 10/99 (2010).

[362] London G20 Summit, April 2009, Declaration on Strengthening the Financial System.

[363] Pittsburgh G20 Summit, September 2009, Leaders' Statement, Strengthening the International Financial Regulatory System. This commitment was reaffirmed at the June 2010 Toronto G20 meeting which also committed to an acceleration of reform internationally in this area.

The clearing/margin (2012 EMIR), reporting (2012 EMIR), and trading (2014 MiFID II/MiFIR) elements of the G20/EU reform agenda are considered in sections 4.2 and 4.3 of this Chapter. The higher capital requirements for non-centrally cleared contracts have been addressed by the 2013 CRD IV/CRR requirements which implement the Basel III reforms.[364] The EU has also pulled OTC trading in derivatives within the regulatory net through a variety of other regulatory mechanisms, including position controls (including under the short selling regime, particularly with respect to sovereign debt CDSs—see section 3—and under the 2014 MiFID II/MiFIR position-management regime for commodity derivatives—see section 2.5); new transparency requirements for the trading venues on which certain classes of OTC derivatives must now be traded (Chapter V); transaction reporting requirements which now capture transactions in a range of OTC derivatives (Chapter V); and the new market abuse regime (Chapter VIII). More generally, the more intensive prudential regulation of investment firms and the imposition of more demanding risk-management requirements (Chapter IV) can also be associated with a policy concern to manage derivative-related risks. Together, the reforms can reasonably be described as having led to a paradigm shift in the intensity with which OTC derivatives markets are regulated.

VI.4.2 2012 EMIR

VI.4.2.1 Introduction: the 2012 EMIR Regime

(a) 2012 EMIR: Main Features

The 2012 EMIR[365] is an infrastructure-related measure which brings radical change to the regulation of the OTC derivatives market in the EU. It has two major objectives. First, it is designed to reduce risk and strengthen derivatives market resiliency through, first, a CCP clearing obligation and related CCP risk-management requirements (including in relation to the margin which clearing members provide to CCPs as counterparty risk mitigation[366]) and, second, risk-management requirements for non-centrally cleared derivatives, which are designed to strengthen the extent and quality of collateralization of non-cleared derivatives transactions. Second, EMIR is designed to support market discipline and regulatory oversight through the imposition of extensive reporting requirements; EMIR and the 2014 MiFID II/MiFIR (Chapter V) together significantly expand the trading disclosures available to the market and to NCAs.

---

[364] In particular, the CRD IV/CRR reforms apply new counterparty credit risk capital requirements to in-scope institutions. The rules are designed to impose an additional capital charge for possible losses associated with the deterioration in the creditworthiness of a counterparty (in effect, mark-to-market losses), and to address the weakness in the previous regime (it did not address credit valuation adjustment (CVA) risks associated with a deterioration in the creditworthiness of a counterparty). See further Ch IV sect 8.7. The new standards are accordingly designed to address mark-to-market losses through a charge for CVA risk, promote strong risk management and related hedging practices, and provide stronger capital incentives to move bilaterally cleared OTC derivative transactions to CCP clearing (particularly as the margin requirements imposed by CCPs provide a countering disincentive for CCP clearing): 2011 Commission Impact Assessment on CRD IV (SEC (2011) 950) paras 3.4–3.5.

[365] The main elements of the publicly available legislative history are: Commission Proposal COM (2010) 484 and Impact Assessment n 351: Parliament Negotiating Position, 7 May 2011 (T7-0310/2011) (ECON Committee report at A7-022/2011); and Council General Approach, 4 October 2011 (Council Document 15148/11). The ECB Opinion is at [2011] OJ C571/1.

[366] On margin, see further sect 4.2.7.

The behemoth EMIR delegated rulebook is composed of 12 regulations, all highly operational in nature. EMIR has, so far,[367] been amplified by eight administrative RTSs and four administrative ITSs. Chief among these are the 2013 Commission Delegated Regulation 149/2013, which amplifies EMIR in relation to the pivotal CCP clearing obligation and the risk mitigation requirements for non-cleared OTC derivatives, and the 2013 Commission Delegated Regulation 153/2013, which sets out in detail the organizational, conduct, and prudential requirements for CCPs.[368] The administrative regime also includes RTSs on the data to be reported to trade repositories,[369] the application data required for trade repository authorization,[370] the data to be published by trade repositories,[371] the capital requirements for CCPs,[372] the colleges of supervisors for CCPs,[373] and in relation to the application of EMIR's clearing obligation to contracts involving third country counterparties.[374] Four ITSs govern the format of the different reports and applications required under EMIR.[375] The Commission has also adopted administrative rules (not in the form of BTSs) governing the fees charged by ESMA with respect to its supervision of trade repositories, the exemptions available for third country monetary authorities, and the procedures to be followed in relation to ESMA's power to impose penalties on trade repositories.[376]

To achieve its objectives, EMIR imposes three major classes of obligation on market participants. First, certain classes of OTC derivatives (or derivatives which are not traded on a regulated market,[377] and including interest rate, foreign exchange, credit, equity, and commodity derivatives) must be cleared through CCPs which are authorized under EMIR. Not all OTC derivatives are appropriate for CCP clearing, however;[378] non-centrally cleared OTC derivatives are accordingly, second, subject to a range of risk mitigation techniques, including collateral/margin rules. Third, all transactions in financial derivatives within the scope of EMIR (whether cleared or not, and whether traded on a regulated market or not) must be reported to trade repositories.

---

[367] Further Binding Technical Standards (BTSs) are required at the time of writing in a number of areas, notably with respect to the risk mitigation requirements imposed on counterparties with respect to collateral and capital requirements for non-CCP cleared derivatives (n 440).

[368] Respectively, Commission Delegated Regulation (EU) No 149/2013 [2013] OJ L52/11 and Commission Delegated Regulation (EU) No 153/2013 [2013] OJ L52/41.

[369] Commission Delegated Regulation (EU) No 148/2013 [2013] OJ L52/1.

[370] Commission Delegated Regulation (EU) No 150/2013 [2013] OJ L52/25.

[371] Commission Delegated Regulation (EU) No 151/2013 [2013] OJ L52/33.

[372] Commission Delegated Regulation (EU) No 152/2013 [2013] OJ L52/37.

[373] Commission Delegated Regulation (EU) No 876/2013 [2013] OJ L244/19.

[374] Commission Delegated Regulation (EU) No 285/2014 [2014] OJ L85/1. The RTS relates to the rules governing when an OTC derivative contract between two third country counterparties has a direct, substantial, and foreseeable effect within the EU, and so should be subject to the clearing obligation, or where the clearing obligation should be imposed on such contracts to prevent the evasion of EMIR. ESMA proposed the standards in November 2013 following an extension from the Commission (ESMA/2013/1657).

[375] Commission Implementing Regulation (EU) No 1249/2012 [2012] OJ L352/32; Commission Implementing Regulation (EU) No 1248/2012 [2012] OJ L352/30; Commission Implementing Regulation (EU) No 1247/2012 [2012] OJ L352/20; and Commission Implementing Regulation (EU) No 484/2014 [2012] OJ L138/57.

[376] Commission Delegated Regulation (EU) No 1003/2013 [2013] OJ L279/4, Commission Delegated Regulation (EU) No 1002/2013 [2013] OJ L279/2, and Commission Delegated Regulation C(2014) 1537.

[377] On regulated markets see Ch V.

[378] Derivatives which are appropriate for clearing are typically described as standardized, safe, and sound: 2012 EFSIR, n 354, 103. See sect 4.2.6.

In support of this regime, extensive organizational, conduct-of-business, and prudential requirements are imposed on the CCPs which are the centre of EMIR's regulatory design. Trade repositories are also subject to a new regulatory regime.

EMIR has a very wide scope, applying to financial counterparties but also, and controversially, to non-financial counterparties, such as commercial firms which engage in derivative trading incidentally and in order to hedge against risks arising from their commercial and treasury activities. It is accordingly calibrated in order to minimize the costs and any potential prejudice to the efficiency with which firms can engage in risk management.

EMIR has strong market-shaping effects which derive in the main from the pivotal CCP clearing obligation. But EMIR does not intervene more radically in the derivatives market by, for example, taking a position on the optimum number of CCPs.[379] The organizational rules designed to support optimum risk management by CCPs, for example, are also designed to protect the CCP market against risks arising from competition in the CCP segment (section 4.2.10). EMIR does, however, seek to ensure that access to CCPs by market participants is not obstructed by discriminatory conditions; it contains a number of non-discrimination provisions designed to ensure that silo-based CCP structures (or structures which vertically integrate trading and clearing services) do not discriminate (section 4.2.6). EMIR also provides regulatory support to, for example, the development of indirect CCP clearing (Article 4(3)) and CCP interoperability (Articles 51–54), both of which services are projected to develop in response to the new clearing environment.

(b) EMIR and CCP Clearing

The CCP clearing obligation is at the core of EMIR. Clearing in the OTC derivatives markets,[380] which evolved as a means for managing counterparty risk, can happen in two ways. The first method, bilateral clearing, involves the two counterparties to the derivative contract entering into a bilateral clearing arrangement which is supported by risk mitigation techniques, including collateralization; this method dominated prior to the crisis. The second method involves central clearing through a CCP.[381] In CCP clearing, the CCP interposes itself between the two counterparties to the trade. Accordingly, the derivative contract between the counterparties is split into two offsetting transactions, each of which is supported by the CCP, which becomes the legal counterparty to each trade. CCP clearing supports the stability and resilience of the market in cleared derivatives through, first, *ex-ante* centralization within the CCP of counterparty credit risk assessment (and the related assessment of margin and collateral requirements), and, second, in the case of a default, *ex-post* replacement by the CCP of the trades of the failed counterparty and the application of pre-set and orderly procedures (including multilateral netting arrangements) to manage the

---

[379] The Commission has acknowledged the debate on the optimum number of CCPs, but has simply expressed the view that more than one in each market segment is preferable on competition and safety grounds: 2009 Staff Working Paper, n 352, 13.

[380] The clearing process is concerned with establishing mutual positions and with matching contracts prior to settlement (see in brief Ch V sect 13).

[381] An extensive literature canvasses the risks and benefits of CCP and bilateral clearing, and the related design issues (including with respect to the optimum number of CCPs and appropriate CCP market structure). See, eg, Duffie, D and Zhu, H, Does a Central Clearing Counterparty Reduce Counterparty Risk? (2011) 1 *Rev of Asset Pricing Studies* 74; Pirrong, C, The Economics of Clearing in Derivatives Markets: Netting, Asymmetric Information and the Sharing of Default Risk through a Central Counterparty (2009), available at <http://ssrn.com/abstract=1340660>; and Bliss and Steigerwald, n 358.

default and related 'close-out' positions (CCP clearing thereby obviates the need for multiple actions by multiple counterparties).[382]

In order to manage the risk of a default by a CCP clearing member and to ensure it has sufficient resources, the CCP collects margin from the clearing member[383] in the form of high-quality collateral[384] which is designed to allow the CCP to replace the trades of the member if it defaults; accurate assessment of margin requirements is fundamental to effective risk management by a CCP. The mutualization of risk, in the form of a 'default fund' to which all CCP members must contribute and which is available in the event of a member default, also forms a central element of the CCP's risk-management model. In addition, other CCP financial resources stand behind the default fund if it is depleted on a default. This 'waterfall' or hierarchy of resources is designed to ensure the CCP can withstand a major shock to its stability. CCPs also impose a range of risk-management obligations on their members[385] and undertake a range of related risk-management functions (including with respect to the valuation of margin and collateral, monitoring the credit-worthiness of clearing members, and with respect to supporting orderly default—for example with respect to the segregation and orderly recovery of members' and their clients' assets).

(c) The Risks for the EU

Prior to the financial crisis, only a small portion of the OTC derivatives market was cleared centrally through CCPs,[386] and only a limited number of CCPs for OTC derivatives were established in the EU.[387] The 2012 EMIR is projected to lead to a massive increase in the

---

[382] CCPs have the potential to reduce significantly risks to participants through the multilateral netting of trades and by imposing more effective risk controls on all participants: Committee on Payment and Settlement Systems (like the Basel Committee on Banking Supervision, a part of the Bank for International Settlements—(CPSS))-IOSCO, Principles for Financial Market Infrastructure (2012) 9. Similarly, a CCP is a 'centralized, formalized mechanism for sharing default risks on derivative contracts among a coalition of financial intermediaries': Pirrong, n 381, 3.

[383] Margin requirements are designed to protect against defaults and, as a 'defaulter pays' mechanism which imposes costs on counterparties (such as CCP members), to strengthen risk management incentives: eg, Basel Committee on Banking Supervision and IOSCO, Margin Requirements for Non-centrally Cleared Derivatives (2013) 3.

[384] The terms 'margin' or 'collateral' are often used interchangeably. Margin is the difference between the price of a trade at execution and guaranteed by the CCP and the expected price if the CCP had to replace the trade after a default by a member. Collateral is the asset provided by the member to the CCP and which represents the margin; it typically takes the form of highly liquid collateral, such as cash, gold, or government bonds. Margin takes two forms: variation margin, which is assessed on a daily basis, represents profits and losses on open positions and is paid to or collected by the CCP on a daily basis; and initial margin, collected to ensure that sufficient funds are held on behalf of each clearing member to offset any losses incurred should the member default, between the last (marked-to-market) valuation of the position and the close out of the position. See, eg, LCHClearnet, Group Overview and EuroCCP, Q&A.

[385] Including, eg, with respect to credit rating, capital requirements, and operational and risk management abilities in relation to derivatives: Herbert Smith, EMIR: EU Regulation of OTC Derivatives, Central Counterparties, and Trade Repositories (2012) 3.

[386] The FSB reported that as at September 2010, in the OTC market, 31 per cent of interest rate derivatives, 13 per cent of CDSs, 0 per cent of equity derivatives, 20–30 per cent of commodity derivatives, and 0 per cent of foreign exchange derivatives were cleared through CCPs. In the EU, the Commission's 'rough estimates' suggested that 30 per cent of interest rate derivatives, 10–15 per cent of CDSs, and 20–30 per cent of commodity derivatives were cleared through CCPs. Foreign exchange derivatives were not cleared through CCPs: 2010 EMIR Proposal Impact Assessment, n 351, 45.

[387] The 2010 EMIR Proposal Impact Assessment reported that 27 CCPs were established in the EU, but that only a small number cleared OTC derivatives: LCHClearnet (commodity, credit, and interest rate derivatives); European Commodity Clearing AG (commodity derivatives); NASDAQ OMX Stockholm AB

volume of derivatives cleared through CCPs.[388] While some indications augur well for its success,[389] a number of risks follow, chief among them risks related to systemic risk management and to the stability of the CCP market.

The mandatory CCP clearing reform has the effect of concentrating risk to a systemic extent within CCPs.[390] The extent to which CCPs can manage and contain systemic risk is in large part a function of their ability to manage the risks associated with the derivatives which they clear; it is accordingly also a function of the scope of the CCP clearing obligation and of the nature of the derivatives which become subject to the CCP clearing obligation. Particularly in the case of highly complex derivatives, bilateral OTC dealers may be better equipped than CCPs to engage in valuation and in risk assessment, and their incentives to engage in strong risk management may be sharper.[391] Nonetheless, the OTC derivatives market reform agenda quickly adopted a prescriptive, mandatory CCP clearing approach in order to support global convergence and to ensure the G20 commitment was securely implemented.[392] EMIR (reflecting the G20 agenda) recognizes, however, that bilateral clearing of bespoke derivatives remains a centrally important feature of the financial system's risk-management architecture;[393] the EMIR Article 11 risk mitigation standards recognize that segments of the OTC derivatives markets are not appropriate for CCP clearing, and impose functionally equivalent risk-management regulation for bilaterally cleared derivatives. But it remains unclear whether the scope of the CCP clearing obligation has been sufficiently carefully delineated.

In addition, market structure risks, which impinge on systemic stability, arise, particularly as the competition dimension of EMIR (evident in EMIR's support of interoperability between multiple CCPs—see section 4.2.10) and its financial stability objectives may be in tension. The optimum market structure for the CCP market is not clear. On the one hand, the stability risks which CCPs generate suggest that a monopoly structure, based on a single

---

(OTC derivatives); ICE Clear Europe (commodity and credit derivatives); Oslo Clearing (equity derivatives); and NOS Clearing ASA (commodity derivatives): n 351, 120.

[388] The Commission has suggested that some $216 trillion of OTC derivatives will move to CCP clearing from an overall notional amount of $648 trillion ($128 trillion of which was cleared through CCPs) at end 2011: Commission, Consultation on a Possible Framework for the Recovery and Resolution of Nonbank Financial Institutions (2012) 11.

[389] The OTC derivatives market reforms relating to CCP clearing (and the related collateral/margin reforms and the additional capital requirements for derivatives exposures) have been estimated to generate net benefits in the form of 0.13 per cent of GDP annually (in a low-cost scenario) and 0.09 per cent of GDP annually (in a high-cost scenario): Bank for International Settlements, Macroeconomic Impact Assessment of OTC Derivatives Regulatory Reforms (2013).

[390] The resulting concentration of risk has been a major feature of the policy and scholarly debate on CCP clearing (see, eg, IOSCO, Securities Markets Risk Outlook 2013–2014 (2013) 13) and is reflected in the recent policy work on the development of recovery and resolution procedures (n 388 and n 401).

[391] Pirrong, n 381. The appropriate identification of which classes of OTC derivatives should be cleared through CCPs is accordingly a key determinant of the effectiveness of CCPs in managing risk: Sidanius, C and Wetherilt, A, Thoughts on Determining Central Clearing Eligibility of OTC Derivatives, Bank of England Financial Stability Paper No 14 (2012), available at <http://ssrn.com/abstract=2028874>.

[392] eg 2010 EMIR Proposal Impact Assessment, n 351, 46–9 and, similarly, FSB, Implementing OTC Derivatives Market Reform (2010) 25, warning that risk-based incentives and industry-led efforts were not sufficient to achieve the scale of the shift to CCP clearing required.

[393] The foundational FSB report on the OTC derivatives market reforms (n 392) underlined the importance of bespoke derivatives as hedging instruments, and in the development of bespoke investment strategies, and recommended that they not be subjected to CCP clearing: at 19.

(or a small number of) CCP(s) clearing a particular asset class may be the safest model; on the other, where a number of competing CCPs clear derivatives, risk may be dispersed across the different CCPs.[394]

Ultimately, the systemic risks generated by these new and massive 'risk nodes' within the financial system are significant and may heighten the likelihood of a tax-payer bailout being needed.[395] Efforts to develop a common approach to CCP resolution in the case of default underline the strength of EU policy concern that CCP failure does not become an occasion for a tax-payer bailout, as well as the reality that CCP failure would generate a massive risk to systemic stability.[396]

The costs of the new regime represent another source of risk. EMIR generates a range of costs, including in relation to CCP membership and related operational changes, but also in relation to the reporting of trades to trade repositories and in relation to the new risk-management rules for bilaterally (non-CCP) cleared derivatives. These costs are predicted to significantly increase the costs of derivatives transactions, particularly for non-financial counterparties who use derivatives for commercial and treasury (funding) hedging purposes. The most significant costs have been associated with the new margin and collateral requirements.[397] Demand for high-quality collateral is also likely to intensify in response to EMIR (as well as in response to other reforms and given commercial incentives).[398] The margin and collateral costs are not only a function of the new CCP clearing requirement; new margin requirements also apply to non-cleared OTC transactions.[399] Increased margin/collateral costs may lead to a reduction in the volume of hedging transactions through derivatives, and to related prejudice to investor returns. Financial stability may also be implicated as the imposition of higher costs on hedging may lead to less efficient risk management (particularly were counterparties to be driven by EMIR to rely on exchange-traded (non-OTC), non-bespoke instruments which are less calibrated to hedging needs) and reduced market liquidity.

---

[394] Different models have been proposed. See, eg, Duffie and Zhu, n 381, suggesting that it is more efficient to have a single CCP that clears different classes of derivative than to have separate CCPs that clear different classes.

[395] Singh, M, Making OTC Derivatives Safe—A Fresh Look, IMF WP No 11/66 (2011).

[396] 2012 Commission Nonbank Resolution Consultation, n 388. The need to reduce risk to the tax-payer is also adverted to in EMIR rec 52.

[397] One IMF study estimated that were two thirds of the OTC derivatives market to migrate to CCP clearing, the costs would be in the region of $200 billion: Singh, M, Collateral, Netting and Systemic Risk in the OTC Market, IMF WP No 10/99 (2010).

[398] ESMA has estimated additional collateral demand in the EU at €240 billion (in total, and not only in response to EMIR requirements) and warned that the demand for high-quality collateral, driven in part by EMIR, may lead to a scarcity of collateral and to financial stability risks: ESMA, Trends, Risks, Vulnerabilities. Report No 1 (2013) (ESMA 2013(1) TRV) 30–3. Pressure on high-quality collateral has also been highlighted as a risk by the ESMA, EBA, and EIOPA Joint Committee: Joint Committee Report on Risks and Vulnerabilities in the EU Financial System, March 2013, 17–18 and by the Commission (2012 EFSIR, n 354, 5 and 26).

[399] The Basel Committee/IOSCO margin standards for non-CCP-cleared derivatives were adopted in September 2013 (n 383). The EU margin regime for non-CCP cleared transactions (to be contained in BTSs adopted under EMIR Art 11(3), which contains basic principles) will follow. The development process was attended by significant industry concern as to the likely costs: Letter from ISDA, the IIF, AFME and SIFMA to the Basel Committee and IOSCO, April 12, 2013.

The risks of the new regime are exacerbated by the complexity of the issues engaged and the challenges they posed and continue to pose to the efficacy of the EU rule-making process. The design of the new clearing regime generated the most complex of technical challenges for the EU's legislators, across structural (in terms of the shape of the new CCP and trade repository markets, and the impact of related competition and monopoly dynamics), substantive (including with respect to the classes of derivatives which should be subject to CCP clearing, the nature of CCP regulation and risk management, and the standardization of the risk mitigation techniques to be employed in bilateral clearing), and international (in terms of the interaction between the EU regime and other jurisdictions internationally) dimensions. The regulation of clearing and risk management was also something of a *terra incognita* for the EU, as it was for regulators internationally,[400] although international standards were developed as the reform programme progressed.[401] CCP regulation in the EU had previously been developed at national level and varied significantly, reflecting local market features and different CCP business models,[402] while there was almost no experience with trade repository regulation.[403]

The design of EMIR may, however, reduce the risks of regulatory error. EMIR and its related administrative rulebook reflect the standards which have been developed internationally.[404] In addition, the EMIR regime has been designed to support and strengthen the risk-management techniques developed by the OTC derivatives market, and it has accordingly sought to avoid replacing well-tried market practices with untested rules.[405] The extensive calibrations within EMIR which are designed to reduce its costs, particularly for non-financial counterparties, provide a further means for reducing the risks of regulatory error, while the technical capacity which ESMA brought to the administrative rule-making process, and continues to bring to related supervisory convergence measures, provides another. A further corrective mechanism is in place in that an extensive review

---

[400] Braithwaite, J, 'The Inherent Limits of "Legal Devices": Lessons for the Public Sector's Central Counterparty Prescription for the OTC Derivatives Market' (2011) 12 *EBOLR* 8790.

[401] A number of work-streams (operating primarily through IOSCO and the Bank for International Settlements) through the CPSS were initiated following the FSB's foundational report (n 392), which set out 21 recommendations on the practical implementation of the G20 agenda. These work-streams included: the Basel III work-stream on capital requirements for non-centrally/CCP cleared derivatives; the CPSS-IOSCO work-stream on trade repository reporting (leading to, *inter alia*, its Report on OTC Derivatives Data Reporting and Aggregation Requirements (2012)); the CPSS-IOSCO work-stream on review of standards for financial market infrastructures (leading to the 2012 Principles for Financial Market Infrastructures (2012)); IOSCO's work-stream on clearing requirements (leading to its Requirements for Mandatory Clearing (2012)); and initiatives from the OTC Derivatives Supervisors Group (ODSG). For a review see Carney, M, 'Completing the G20 Reform Agenda for Strengthening Over-the-Counter Derivatives Markets' (2013) No 17 *Banque de France Financial Stability Rev* 12. The international standards also include the recommendations issued by CPSS-IOSCO on the resolution and recovery of financial market infrastructures: CPSS-IOSCO, Consultative Report on the Recovery of Financial Market Infrastructures (2013) and Consultative Report on Recovery and Resolution of Financial Market Infrastructures (2012). Summer 2013 saw the adoption of the Basel Committee/IOSCO standards on bilateral margin (n 383).

[402] 2010 EMIR Proposal Impact Assessment, n 351, 25.

[403] By the time of EMIR's development, only two trade repositories were operational: DTCC's Warehouse Trust for credit derivatives, and TriOptima's IR TRR for interest rate derivatives: 2010 EMIR Proposal Impact Assessment, n 351, 81.

[404] These initiatives are noted at n 401.

[405] An extensive literature addresses the interaction between public and private ordering mechanisms in the regulation of the OTC derivatives market. See, eg, Braithwaite, n 400 and Awrey, D, 'The Dynamics of OTC Derivative Regulation: Bridging the Public-Private Divide' (2010) 11 *EBOLR* 155.

must take place before August 2015 (EMIR Article 85), although it remains to be seen whether the institutions will have the appetite for revision and reform.

(d) Timing Issues

Although the 2012 EMIR came into force on 16 August 2012, its application in the market and the imposition of the core CCP clearing obligation has been protracted. The application of many of EMIR's provisions depended on the entering into force of the related EMIR BTSs (which, for the initial swathe, took place on 15 March 2013).[406] The pivotal CCP clearing requirement for particular OTC derivatives cannot come into effect until CCPs have been authorized and ESMA has made the consequent assessment of whether the classes of OTC derivatives which particular CCPs are authorized to clear should be subject to the CCP clearing obligation (section 4.2.6).[407] Overall, the EMIR application timeline is complex, with different obligations being imposed on the market at different times.[408] But the upshot has been that the EU has been relatively slow to move to mandatory CCP clearing: the US market moved to CCP clearing in 2012, but the EU was not expected to do so until the end of 2014—and later for non-financial counterparties.[409]

VI.4.2.2 The Evolution of the 2012 EMIR and the Crisis Context

While it has been shaped by the EU's market, political, and institutional context, the 2012 EMIR is a direct product of the financial crisis and the September 2009 Pittsburgh G20 commitment that 'standardized OTC derivative contracts' would be cleared through CCPs and OTC derivative contracts reported to trade repositories.[410]

The EU had, however, from an early stage and pre-dating the September 2009 G20 commitment, placed OTC derivatives market reform on its crisis-era reform programme. The de Larosière Report of February 2009 called for the simplification and standardization of most OTC derivatives, greater market transparency, and, in a harbinger of the CCP clearing requirement, the establishment of at least one well-capitalized CCP for OTC CDSs.[411] In the early stages of the OTC derivatives market reform programme, the stability

---

[406] In some cases, EMIR applied from the date of its coming into force. The Art 11(3) requirements for counterparties to have in place procedures for the timely, accurate, and appropriate segregated exchange of collateral for non-CCP-cleared OTC derivative contracts came into force immediately, although the detailed BTSs relating to this regime have yet to be adopted. Prior to the adoption of the BTSs, market participants were to apply their own rules: Commission, EMIR FAQ, Q6.

[407] The first CCP authorization decision was made on 18 March 2014 (Nasdaq OMX Clearing AB). On 19 March 2014, ESMA was formally notified of the authorization and of the derivative contracts cleared by the CCP. This notification triggered the EMIR clearing obligation assessment procedure for the first time. ESMA has, accordingly, published the required disclosures relating to the derivative contracts Nasdaq OMX is authorized to clear, and will produce draft RTSs setting out a clearing obligation relating to these CCP-cleared derivative contracts, if they meet the related 2012 EMIR requirements, within six months. ESMA's clearing obligation assessment is triggered each time a new CCP clearing OTC derivatives is authorized; it will accordingly activate in a staggered manner.

[408] For a summary of the different application dates see the ESMA timeline, available at <http://www.esma.europa.eu/page/European-Market-Infrastructure-Regulation-EMIR>, and Commission, EMIR FAQ.

[409] Non-financial counterparties benefit from a three-year phase-in, following negotiations between the European Parliament and Commission: sect 4.2.3.

[410] Pittsburgh G20 Summit, September 2009, Leaders' Statement, Strengthening the International Financial Regulatory System, para 13.

[411] The High Level Group on Financial Supervision in the EU, Report (2009) 25.

and resilience of the CDS segment tended to preoccupy policymakers in the EU.[412] The UK FSA's 2009 Turner Review, for example, supported the establishment of CCP facilities in the CDS market,[413] while the Commission initially focused on encouraging the industry to clear CDSs through CCPs.[414] The drivers of the reform agenda's move from CDS market resilience to the resilience of the OTC derivatives market generally, as it did over 2009, are not clear,[415] and perhaps can be best explained in terms of momentum, a wider suspicion of innovation and speculation, and concerns as to regulatory arbitrage risks. High-level EU political support for OTC derivatives market reform was given by the June 2009 European Council,[416] while the Commission's July 2009 Communication and Consultation on derivatives market reform set out the main elements of OTC derivatives market reform, including central clearing, risk mitigation, and reporting requirements.[417]

Industry action was also taken. As the financial crisis deepened, the industry committed to move more OTC derivative transactions on to CCPs,[418] and significant progress was made with respect to CDS clearing.[419] But while the Commission was supportive of industry efforts to increase CCP clearing levels, it warned that stronger regulatory incentives were required.[420]

Subsequent to the September 2009 Pittsburgh G20 meeting, the Commission outlined the specific action to be taken in the EU on the foot of the G20 agenda.[421] By the end of 2009, the Council had agreed on the need to improve the mitigation of counterparty credit risk, and to improve derivatives market transparency, efficiency, and integrity.[422] The European Parliament similarly supported reform.[423] Following some 18 months of consultation during which the main elements of what would become EMIR were flagged and examined

---

[412] 2012 EFSIR, n 354, 109. Risk management in the interest and foreign exchange segments, by contrast, was regarded as stronger. In the interest rate and foreign exchange segments, pay off structures are shorter, and the markets are more liquid and transparent, less concentrated, and display stronger risk management practices: 2012 EFSIR, n 354, 92–3, 97–8, and 106.

[413] n 25, 82.

[414] 2010 EMIR Proposal Impact Assessment, n 351, 5. It enjoyed some success in this regard (nn 418 and 419).

[415] Braithwaite, n 400, 95.

[416] European Council June 18–19 2009, Conclusions, para 18.

[417] n 352.

[418] In 2009 the Operations Steering Committee (composed of major dealers, buy-side participants, and trade associations) committed to a series of initiatives to strengthen the OTC derivatives market, including in relation to increased use of CCPs, more trade repository reporting, and enhanced collateralization of bilaterally cleared transactions. By August 2009, 7 CCPs for CDSs had launched or were due to: Braithwaite, n 400, 89. In the EU, nine major dealers committed to increasing their use of CCPs (Letter to EU Commissioner McCreevy, 17 February 2009).

[419] Three new CCPs were established in the EU for CDS clearing, while the volume of interest rate derivative transactions cleared through the major interest rate CCP (SwapClear) increased: 2010 EMIR Proposal Impact Assessment, n 351, 26–7. The industry's ability to move to CCP clearing for CDSs relatively quickly reflected the high degree of standardization of CDSs, which was linked to their massive growth pre-crisis: Partnoy and Skeel, n 141, 1032.

[420] 2009 Consultation, n 352, 10.

[421] 2009 Consultation, n 352.

[422] Extensive Conclusions on 'Derivatives Markets and Clearing and Settlement' were adopted by the ECOFIN Council at its 2 December 2009 Meeting: 2981st Meeting, 2 December 2009 (Council Document 16383/09) 26–30.

[423] 2010 European Parliament Resolution, n 22.

in some detail,[424] and extensive industry lobbying,[425] the Commission's Proposal for EMIR was presented in September 2010 (along with the Short Selling Proposal).[426]

The Proposal's main features are reflected in EMIR. It proposed a wide-ranging CCP clearing obligation, applicable to OTC derivative transactions by financial and non-financial counterparties, the reach of which was to be determined through 'top-down' and bottom-up' procedures; the Proposal mitigated the impact of the clearing obligation on non-financial counterparties through a threshold mechanism. The Proposal also contained risk mitigation requirements for non-CCP-cleared OTC derivative contracts and a reporting requirement for all OTC derivative contracts. These obligations were supported by authorization and supervisory regimes for CCPs and trade repositories. The Proposal did not change materially over the negotiations, although its scope became wider and the different calibrations and exemptions more nuanced.

The negotiations focused in the main on how EMIR's costs could be mitigated and, in particular, on the application of the regime to OTC derivatives transactions by non-financial counterparties and the related mitigations and exemptions.[427] The Parliament's July 2011 negotiating position[428] sought to calibrate the Proposal more finely to reflect the costs faced by non-financial counterparties and, ultimately, end investors.[429] It also enhanced the Proposal's provisions in relation to competition and access in the CCP market,[430] and strengthened ESMA's role, including by means of a more extensive set of delegations to BTSs and in relation to ESMA's role in CCP colleges. Council negotiations focused closely on EMIR's scope of application; in particular, the UK strongly supported the application of the CCP clearing obligation to listed derivative contracts traded on regulated markets, in order to ensure competition in relation to exchange-traded derivatives and to protect the City's trading business (this has since followed under the 2014 MiFID II/MiFIR—see section 4.3).[431] The extent of ESMA's powers also proved contentious in the Council, particularly in relation to CCP authorization and supervision. The negotiations were coloured, generally, by the euro-area/internal market divide, with the UK concerned that EMIR would lead to a relocation of CCPs to the euro area. Following concessions to the UK designed to ameliorate its concerns as to

---

[424] Consultations in July and October 2009 were followed by a 2010 Consultation (Commission, Public Consultation on Derivatives and Market Infrastructures (2010)) which immediately preceded the publication of the EMIR Proposal and dealt with four major outstanding issues: clearing and risk mitigation; CCP requirements; interoperability; and trade repositories.

[425] Tait, N and Grant, J, 'EU to Get Tough on OTC Derivative Markets', *Financial Times*, 13 September 2010, 4.

[426] The major texts are referenced in n 365.

[427] Major airline, aerospace, and car manufacturers lobbied strongly against their inclusion in EMIR, given the costs which the clearing and reporting obligations would impose on their hedging activities: Grant, J, 'The Route to Regulation Diverges for Europe and America', *Financial Times*, 12 August 2010, 9.

[428] n 365.

[429] The European Parliament introduced the pension fund exemption, the intra-group exemption, and the inclusion of commercial bank guarantees among the 'highly liquid collateral' required of counterparties for CCP clearing.

[430] It, eg, strengthened the guarantees in relation to CCP access and in relation to CCP access to trading venues trade flow.

[431] The UK's negotiating position was informed by the ongoing negotiations at the time between Deutsche Börse and NYSE Euronext, and related concerns as to a loss of trading business from London to the euro area: Barker, A and Grant, J, 'UK Fears Defeat on Regulation', *Financial Times*, 30 September 2011, 6.

euro-area dominance (these concessions related in particular to restrictions on the powers of CCP colleges in relation to CCP authorization and to easing CCP access to trading venues trade flows—see sections 4.2.9 and 4.2.6), and the UK's agreement to drop its call for EMIR to cover regulated market-traded derivatives,[432] the Council agreed on a compromise text in October 2011.[433] Following difficult trilogue negotiations over October 2011–February 2012[434] which focused in particular on third country CCP access requirements,[435] the extent of the trade repository reporting obligation,[436] and the role of the CCP college and of ESMA in CCP authorization,[437] the European Parliament and Council adopted the text in March and April 2012, respectively.

VI.4.2.3 Harmonization and ESMA

The technical complexity and scale of most of the EU's crisis-era legislative measures challenges the assumption that EU legislative measures are designed to address core regulatory principles and to reflect fundamental political decisions on the nature of market regulation (see further Chapter X section 3). With the 2012 EMIR, however, the crisis-era tendency to encrust legislative measures with technical detail perhaps reached its apotheosis. That said, EMIR's detailed and complex operational rules reflect the scale of the EMIR reforms, the challenges which appropriate differentiation posed, and the technical nature of the risk-management rules on which EMIR is based. A degree of regulatory risk mitigation has been provided by the EMIR BTS rulebook which operationalizes EMIR, but which relies to a significant extent on criteria-based rules designed to build on tested market practice rather than on prescriptive rules. The regulatory risks are intensified, however, by the need to rely on soft law measures, notably the ESMA EMIR Q&A,[438] to clarify the regime's many operational implications, given the danger that NCAs may struggle in ensuring market compliance with operationally critical soft law measures.

The scale of amplification required under EMIR was immense. Some 21 or so of EMIR's provisions were subject to detailed amplification, almost entirely through BTSs; the related EMIR administrative rulebook is currently composed of an array of delegated and implementing regulations.[439] Additional administrative rules will be adopted in relation to the capital and collateral-related risk mitigation techniques for non-cleared OTC derivatives (Article 11(15)).[440]

---

[432] Barber, A, 'Britain Wins Late Concessions on Derivatives Rules', *Financial Times*, 5 October 2011, 9.

[433] n 365.

[434] Commissioner Barnier noted that the negotiations in the Parliament and Council had 'not always been easy': Statement on the EMIR Agreement. 9 February 2009 (MEMO/12/90). A summary of the key issues is available on the European Parliament's EMIR 'Legislative Observatory' procedural file.

[435] Negotiations focused on the nature of the 'recognition' mechanism and the related equivalence assessment for third country CCPs, and on the safeguards for ensuring that the third country access regime for CCPs would not constitute a precedent for other financial sectors in the EU.

[436] The Council's General Approach imposed reporting requirements on non-financial counterparties only where threshold requirements were met.

[437] The Council sought to ensure that NCAs could only be overruled by a CCP college in relation to authorization where all college members so agreed. Under the trilogue compromise (the European Parliament sought a stronger role for the CCP college and for ESMA) this position was retained, but ESMA was given a binding mediation role where a majority of college members raised concerns (see sect 4.2.9).

[438] n 441.

[439] Sect 4.2.1.

[440] The three ESAs are to develop these standards together: a consultation paper was issued in April 2014 (JC/CP/2014/03). The collateral requirements will be based on the 2013 Basel Committee/IOSCO standards (n 383). See also n 364 on capital requirements.

ESMA's supervisory convergence initiatives are also likely to be extensive, further thickening the EMIR regime. ESMA was, for example, quick to deploy the Q&A device in this area,[441] has produced tailored information on EMIR for non-financial counterparties, and has adopted reporting templates.[442] ESMA has also produced guidance on CCP interoperability, as required under EMIR (Article 54),[443] and, on its own initiative, has produced guidance on the operation of the colleges of supervisors for CCPs.[444]

The administrative BTS rulebook, however, is at the heart of the EMIR regime. By contrast with the earlier, and similarly technically complex, 2011 AIFMD process, and in recognition of the growing stature and capacity of ESMA, the EMIR administrative regime took the form of BTSs, proposed by ESMA, rather than administrative rules adopted by the Commission in relation to which ESMA can only provide technical advice. ESMA was, accordingly, the driving influence on the regime.[445]

The BTS adoption process was potentially problematic on a number of grounds. The scale of the task, its complexity, and the short time limits for the adoption of the BTSs (ESMA's initial consultation took place in March 2012 and the proposed BTSs were transmitted to the Commission at the end of September 2013)[446] proved a significant challenge to ESMA, which was at the time also grappling with the rule-making demands of other major crisis-era measures, including the AIFMD. But a number of aggravating factors arose. As noted above, the regulation of OTC derivatives market clearing and risk management presented the EU with an enormous technical challenge, although the development of the BTS regime benefited from the availability, by that stage of the reform process, of international templates and guidance. The administrative regime accordingly reflects the FSB's recommendations on implementing OTC derivatives market reform, and the related guidance and standards in relation to mandatory clearing requirements and CCPs.[447] The international initiatives did not, however, provide the level of operational detail which the EMIR BTSs were charged with delivering.[448] The difficulties were compounded by the lack of empirical evidence on many of the technical design issues.[449]

---

[441] The Q&A was initially adopted in March 2013 (ESMA, Q&A. Implementation of EMIR (ESMA/2013/324)) and is regularly updated. It has become of central importance to the market in interpreting the complex EMIR regime, although its legal basis is relatively insecure.

[442] Relating to the notifications required of non-financial counterparties when they pass EMIR's clearing thresholds and so become subject to a range of obligations, including the CCP clearing obligation.

[443] ESMA, Guidance and Recommendations for establishing consistent, efficient and effective assessments of interoperability arrangements (2013) (ESMA/2013/1390).

[444] ESMA, Guidelines and Recommendations regarding the Written Agreements between Members of CCP Colleges (2013) (ESMA/2013/661).

[445] ESMA's approach to the adoption of BTSs under EMIR is outlined in its September 2012 final report in which it transmitted the BTSs to the Commission: ESMA, Final Report. Draft Technical Standards under EMIR (ESMA/2012/600) (2012 ESMA EMIR Draft BTS Report).

[446] Given the volume of BTSs required, ESMA was required to commence preliminary work before the EMIR text had stabilized, and communicated its concerns as to the timing constraints to the Council, Commission, and European Parliament: ESMA Annual Report (2011) 57.

[447] These initiatives are noted at n 401. ESMA described these initiatives as providing a 'solid basis' for ESMA's work: 2012 ESMA EMIR Draft BTS Report, n 445, 7.

[448] 2012 ESMA EMIR Draft BTS Report, n 445, 27, in relation to the IOSCO-CPSS standards for CCPs.

[449] ESMA noted the difficulties in obtaining sufficient data to perform an in-depth quantitative impact assessment: 2012 ESMA EMIR Draft BTS Report, n 445, 7 and ESMA, Impact Assessment. EMIR BTSs. Annex VIII to ESMA's Final Report on EMIR BTSs (ESMA/2012/600/Annex VIII) (2012 ESMA BTS

The development of the EMIR BTSs also required unusually close co-ordination between ESMA, EBA, the ESRB, the European System of Central Banks (ESCB), and the Agency for the Co-operation of Energy Regulators (ACER). Many of the BTS delegations required ESMA to co-operate with one or more of these authorities,[450] given the systemic implications of the EMIR regime. Careful co-ordination was also needed with authorities with complementary mandates in relation to OTC derivatives market stability. The CCP BTSs, for example, were developed in close co-operation with the ESCB through a joint ESMA/ESCB task force.[451] The ESCB is charged under the Treaty with the 'basic task' of promoting the smooth operation of payment systems (Article 127(2) TFEU). The central bank members of the ESCB accordingly oversee clearing and payment systems. While ESCB activities are closely concerned with payment-related activities and with securities settlement,[452] ESCB members are also engaged with the authorization and monitoring of CCPs and the recognition of third country CCPs. ESCB members accordingly are integrated into EMIR's supervisory oversight regime, forming part, for example, of CCP colleges,[453] and being conferred with access rights in relation to trade repository information.[454] Accordingly, close co-operation was required between ESMA and the ESCB in the development of BTSs in order to avoid the creation of parallel rules.[455]

The compressed BTS process[456] was, however, relatively smooth, despite significant market opposition to some of ESMA's proposals—notably, the approach ESMA took to margin and collateral[457] and the approach it took to the clearing thresholds which govern the extent to which the EMIR CCP clearing obligation applies to non-financial counterparties.[458] ESMA emerged from the process as pragmatic and flexible; while it was responsive to

---

Impact Assessment) 2. Particular difficulties arose in assessing the thresholds which govern whether non-financial counterparties must clear their OTC derivatives contracts through CCPs.

[450] eg, ESMA was to consult with EBA (the European Banking Authority) and the ESCB (the European System of Central Banks) in relation to the RTSs governing CCP governance (Art 26), CCP margin calculations (Art 41), the size of the CCP default fund (Art 42), the nature of 'highly liquid' collateral (Art 46), stress testing (Art 49), and on the nature of trade repository data and reporting frequency, and access by authorities to such data (Art 81). The ESCB was also to be consulted in relation to a CCP's business continuity arrangements (Art 34), liquidity risk management (Art 44), the use of a CCP's own resources in a default situation (Art 45), and the limitations on a CCP's investment policy (Art 47). The European Systemic Risk Board (ESRB) was also to be consulted in relation to particular BTSs, including with respect to the limitations on a CCP's investment policy (Art 47).

[451] 2012 ESMA EMIR Draft BTS Report, n 445, 5 and 6.

[452] Notably with respect to the Target2 system for large value euro payments and with respect to retail payment systems, and in relation to the development of the Target2 Securities system for settlement of securities which is due to operate from June 2015: eg ECB, Annual Report (2012) 126–31.

[453] Art 18(2)(g), providing for CCP college participation by ESCB members responsible for the oversight of the CCP and Art 18(2)(h), providing for CCP college participation by central banks of issues of the most relevant EU currencies of the financial instruments cleared.

[454] Art 81(3)(e).

[455] EMIR rec 11.

[456] ESMA's initial 16 February 2012 Discussion Paper (ESMA/2012/95) was published following political agreement between the Council and Parliament on 9 February 2012. The consultation was open for five and a half weeks, was accompanied by an open hearing, and generated 135 responses. It was followed by a Consultation Paper published on 25 June 2012 (ESMA/2012/379), which was also accompanied by an open hearing and generated 165 responses. The consultation period closed on 5 August, and ESMA's final advice was delivered to the Commission on 27 September 2012 (ESMA/2012/600).

[457] 2012 ESMA EMIR BTS Final Report, n 445, 37–40 and 45–8.

[458] See further sect 4.2.5.

stakeholder concerns,[459] it showed itself to be muscular in defending its position even in the face of opposition from other EU authorities, including the ESRB on occasion.[460] All the required standards (with the exception of those relating to risk mitigation for non-CCP-cleared OTC derivatives and the application of the clearing obligation to contracts between third country counterparties (which were to be adopted at a later stage)) were submitted to the Commission for endorsement on 27 September 2012. They were (with one exception) agreed without change by the Commission on 19 December 2012, and came into force on 15 March 2013. The adoption of the BTS regime represents therefore an early and significant success for the BTS model. Nonetheless, the BTS regime generated significant institutional tensions which underline the stresses to which the BTS process is generally subject, and which tested the resilience of the inter-institutional procedures which are designed to resolve differences over the course of BTS adoption (see further Chapter X section 5.5).

The largely wholesale adoption by the Commission of a raft of rules of great market, operational, and international importance and sensitivity underlines the extent to which the Commission had become comfortable with the technical expertise and consultation capacity which ESMA brings to administrative rule-making. The EMIR BTS process thus stands in contrast to the adoption of the AIFMD administrative rules, in relation to which ESMA's expert 'technical advice' (accordingly, not in the form of proposals for BTSs), which had been subject to impact assessment and market consultation, was in some respects rejected by the Commission, leading to great market disquiet. Two important points of difference arose between ESMA and the Commission under the EMIR process, however. The first relates to ESMA's proposed RTSs on the operation of the colleges of supervisors which are closely engaged with the authorization and supervision of CCPs. ESMA proposed a standard designed to address the potential risk that an NCA could veto the establishment of a college. Under EMIR, a college can only be established once a CCP's application for registration is complete; from that point, the college must be established by the CCP's NCA within 30 days of receipt of the application. The college cannot be established, however, until all participants have agreed in writing the terms on which the college will operate (EMIR Article 18). In order to respond to the risk that a college member might choose not to agree with the written agreement in order to block the establishment of the college, ESMA proposed that the college be constituted in such circumstances, as long as the college could ensure that the voting procedures specified for the college under EMIR Article 19 could be implemented.[461] The Commission rejected this standard[462] on the grounds that it went beyond the mandate given under EMIR for specification of the details of the practical written agreement relating to the establishment and functioning of CCP colleges.[463] It proposed instead that the RTS refer to the Commission's power to take enforcement action, under Article 258 TFEU, where an NCA refused to participate in a college for which it was eligible. The Commission also proposed that the process for adopting the written agreement be strengthened by means of

---

[459] By, eg, introducing a degree of flexibility into the application of the margin rules.
[460] As was the case in particular in relation to the CCP clearing thresholds: sect 4.2.5.
[461] 2012 ESMA EMIR BTS Final Report, n 445, Annex III, Art 2(2).
[462] Commission, Press Release December 2012 (IP/12/1419), 19.
[463] ESMA Opinion, ESMA/2013/312. March 2012, para I.4.

time limits for the adoption of the agreement and procedures for debating its content. As required under the ESMA Regulation, ESMA was given six weeks to amend the relevant CCP college RTSs on the basis of the Commission's amendments and to resubmit the standards in the form of an opinion.

As the first application of the process governing differences between ESMA and the Commission in relation to the adoption of BTSs, the experience with respect to the CCP college RTS warrants some attention. The Commission's decision to reject the standard suggests its sensitivity to overreach at the administrative level and its concern to ensure the parameters of the legislative measure are respected. It also underlines the Commission's concern that national (NCA) discretion could be overridden without a resilient legal framework to support such an override. ESMA's response is also instructive. ESMA was relatively robust in justifying its approach and suggested that Commission enforcement action before the Court of Justice was not compatible with the tight 30 day time limit for the establishment of colleges. It recognized, however, that its mandate was not broad enough to allow it to address appropriately the veto right which had inadvertently been introduced by EMIR, and was of the view that the Commission's revisions were 'sensible' and that the implicit threat of enforcement action (underlined by a new recital to the RTS) was useful. It accepted therefore the Commission's revisions and acknowledged that the veto difficulty could not be addressed until EMIR was reviewed.[464] It is notable, however, that ESMA did not entirely abandon the issue, noting that it would suggest, through guidelines which would provide a template for the college agreement, that NCAs justify their decision not to agree to the terms of a college agreement; the guidelines were subsequently adopted in June 2013.[465]

A sharper BTS rejection, with potentially more serious implications for ESMA/Commission relations, issued from the Commission in relation to ESMA's August 2013 proposal for an ITS to delay the start date for reporting to trade repositories in relation to exchange-traded derivatives (as required under EMIR Article 9). ESMA proposed the delay in order for it to have sufficient time to adopt related guidelines and recommendations governing the Article 9 reporting obligation generally.[466] The Commission rejected the proposed ITS, arguing that it was not necessary to wait for ESMA guidelines, and, in trenchant language, argued that the postponement would 'run counter to the principle of ensuring the stability of the financial system and the functioning of the internal market for financial services'.[467] While the tone may have been unintentionally sharp, the robustness of the Commission's response suggests some Commission concern to underline its primacy as the guardian of the EMIR regime. ESMA's response was similarly robust, repeating its concern that a delay would benefit the application of the EMIR reporting requirement and emphasizing ESMA's commitment to monitoring financial stability using accurate data, but also its concern to ensure EMIR-required data was accurate.[468] While most of the EMIR rulebook

---

[464] The RTS was adopted in May 2013 (n 373).

[465] The Guidelines (n 444) were adopted in the form of ESMA Regulation Art 16 guidance (Art 16 requires NCAs to comply, or explain their non compliance) and are designed to help facilitate the prompt establishment of colleges.

[466] Particularly with respect to the appropriate identification of counterparties and to support consistency between EMIR and the MiFIR regime.

[467] Commission, Communication, 7 November 2013.

[468] Letter from ESMA Chairman to Commission, 14 November 2013 (ESMA/2013/1655).

is now in place, the potential for an uneasy Commission/ESMA relationship, given the tension between the Commission's Treaty primacy as the location of administrative rule-making and ESMA's *de facto* primacy as the location of technical expertise, remains considerable.

Potentially more serious difficulties arose over the BTS adoption process in relation to the European Parliament. Although the Parliament has from the outset been a robust supporter of ESMA, it remains sensitive to any threat to its legislative prerogatives. The scale, importance, and complexity of the EMIR BTS regime, in relation to which the Parliament was to be notified and over which it could exercise a veto, always made it likely that the EMIR BTS process could lead to tensions with the Parliament.

Following the procedure laid down by the 2010 ESMA Regulation (Chapter X section 5.5), the European Parliament had one month to examine the BTSs, which the Parliament extended, as it is empowered to do, by one month. Over that period, the Commission failed to respond to the Parliament's comments on the text of the BTSs and failed to notify the Parliament that it had rejected one of the ESMA BTSs and had revised the timetable for the adoption of the standards (in that two sets of BTSs remained outstanding).

These procedural failures and substantive difficulties led to the European Parliament's ECON committee proposing that the Parliament veto a number of the BTSs,[469] in what would have been a major blow to the new BTS process; the veto would also have significantly delayed the EMIR timetable, complicating negotiations with the US on the interaction of the EU and US regimes.[470] The ECON Committee's concerns were twofold. First, it was concerned at a number of procedural weaknesses, including in relation to the limited time given to the Parliament and to the Commission's failure to communicate effectively with the Parliament.[471] Second, ECON raised a number of substantive concerns in relation to the BTSs. It was concerned in particular as to the impact of the proposed standards on non-financial counterparties[472] and on their ability to manage risk effectively. It opposed, for example, ESMA's method for calculating the thresholds at which a non-financial counterparty would become subject to the CCP clearing obligation as bringing too many non-financial counterparties, without systemic implications, within the costly CCP clearing obligation.[473] It was also concerned that the BTSs did not sufficiently clearly ensure that non-financial counterparties below the CCP clearing threshold were not subject to the mark-to-market obligation which applied to other counterparties as a

---

[469] ECON Committee, Motion for a Resolution, 4 February 2013 (B7-0078/2013).

[470] As was implicit in Commissioner Barnier's subsequent statement once the issue was resolved, in which he noted that he was now free to reassure the US that the EU was meeting its G20 commitments and in a position to apply stringent rules, equivalent to the EU rules, and, thereby, to make progress to the recognition of EU and US rules as equivalent: Statement by Commissioner Barnier on the technical standards to implement the new rules on derivatives, 7 February 2013. ESMA Chairman Maijoor also highlighted that failure to adopt the standards would have 'seriously compromised' the compliance of the EU with the G20 agenda: ESMA Chairman Maijoor, Speech on 'EMIR: A Fair Price for Safety and Transparency', 27 March 2013 (ESMA/2013/428).

[471] Motion, n 469, paras D, G, H, K, and L.

[472] ECON MEP Swinburne, eg, was reported as being concerned as to the impact of EMIR on businesses and as to potential prejudice to the ability of firms to hedge operational risk: Cameron, M, 'EU Parliament poised to reject two ESMA Technical Standards on OTC Derivatives' *Risk Magazine*, 25 January 2013.

[473] Motion, n 469, para N.

form of risk mitigation,[474] and that an overly high standard had been applied to non-financial counterparties in relation to the portfolio reconciliation requirements which form part of the risk mitigation regime for non-CCP-cleared OTC derivatives,[475] in relation to the electronic confirmations which form part of the risk mitigation regime,[476] and in relation to the conditions applicable to the commercial bank guarantees which can be used by non-financial counterparties as collateral.[477]

A plenary debate on the motion which could have led to a European Parliament veto[478] was averted, however, by a compromise between the Commission and ECON,[479] under which the Commission acknowledged the Parliament's concerns, committed to enhancing communications with Parliament in relation to the adoption of BTSs, and agreed to phase in EMIR's obligations in relation to non-financial counterparties over 'an appropriate period of time'.[480] The Commission also acknowledged more generally that the development of BTSs was '*terra nova*' for all the institutions involved and that the process would be refined over time.[481] This led to the plenary vote being cancelled and cleared the way for the coming into force of the EMIR BTSs in March 2013.

These different fracas with respect to the EMIR BTS rulebook underline the instability in the BTS process, the importance of close institutional co-operation and communication, and the readiness of the European Parliament and Commission to flex their muscles. Overall, however, the development of the EMIR BTS administrative rulebook underlines ESMA's capacity to capture and interrogate highly technical market data and to develop a practical set of rules which, by and large, have enjoyed market and institutional support.[482] ESMA has also displayed an ability to capture market-developed risk-management tools and practices and to place them within a regulatory framework, thereby obviating the need for a highly prescriptive and potentially risk-laden rulebook; the BTSs are typically based on the application by the relevant actor of identified criteria rather than on the imposition of prescriptive rules.[483] The BTS process has also underlined ESMA's potential as an agent for ensuring administrative rules are appropriately calibrated in accordance with relevant legislative directions. In the development of the regime for non-financial counterparties, in particular, ESMA showed itself as sensitive to the operational and monitoring costs of the regime for small and medium-sized firms.[484] Procedurally as well as substantively, the EMIR administrative rulebook is of some precedential importance.

---

[474] Motion, n 469, para Q. See further sect 4.2.7 on risk mitigation.

[475] Motion, n 469, para R.

[476] Motion, n 469, para T.

[477] Motion, n 469, para V.

[478] Although it was not clear that a veto would have been passed by the Parliament; the ECON veto vote was passed only narrowly, with the Socialists changing their original 'no' position at the last minute following Commission lobbying: Price, M, 'Emir Vote a Good Compromise', *Financial News*, 8 February 2013.

[479] Statement to the Parliament by Commission Member Hedegaard, 7 February 2013.

[480] Subsequently confirmed as three years: Statement by Commissioner Barnier on the technical standards to implement the new rules on derivatives, 7 February 2013.

[481] A similarly conciliatory approach was adopted by ESMA Chairman Maijoor, who noted that ESMA fully respected the powers of the Parliament and Council to scrutinize its work: 27 March 2013 Speech, n 470.

[482] The ECB described the adoption of EMIR and of the related BTSs as a major achievement: ECB, Annual Report (2012) 130.

[483] 2012 ESMA BTS Impact Assessment, n 449, 3.

[484] Sect 4.2.7.

VI.4.2.4 Setting the Perimeter: Scope

The 2012 EMIR lays down CCP clearing and bilateral risk-management requirements for OTC derivative contracts, reporting requirements for all derivative contracts, and uniform requirements for the performance of the activities of CCPs and trade repositories (Article 1).

Perimeter control under EMIR is in part a function of the contracting parties subject to its requirements. EMIR's clearing and risk management and reporting requirements apply to financial counterparties.[485] Non-financial counterparties[486] are also, and controversially, subject to EMIR,[487] but only when specified thresholds are passed (section 4.2.5).

EMIR takes a similarly broad approach to the derivatives within its scope which are very broadly defined by reference to the 2014 MiFID II/MiFIR regime.[488] This alignment has, however, proved problematic, leading to ESMA raising concerns that difficulties with the consistent application of this core definition might prejudice the application of EMIR unless additional clarifying administrative rules are adopted; the Commission has promised urgent action.[489] In practice, aside from the reporting obligation which applies to all derivatives, EMIR applies to OTC derivatives, or derivatives the execution of which takes place outside a MiFID II regulated market.[490] EMIR accordingly applies to equity, credit, commodity, interest rate, and foreign exchange derivatives, despite significant industry pressure to reduce its scope.[491]

CCPs[492] (and their clearing members[493] and members' clients[494]) and trade repositories[495] also come within EMIR, and are subject to discrete regulatory regimes. Trading venues

---

[485] A financial counterparty is widely defined as, in essence, a regulated financial entity, including investment firms, credit institutions, insurance, assurance, and reinsurance undertakings, UCITSs and their management companies, alternative investment funds authorized under the 2011 AIFMD, and institutions for occupational retirement provision under Directive 2003/41/EC: Art 2(8).

[486] Undertakings other than financial counterparties or CCPs: Art 2(9).

[487] Non-financial counterparties represented the largest volume of respondents to ESMA's different consultations on the EMIR BTS regime, underlining the importance of EMIR for this constituency: ESMA Annual Report (2012) 36–7.

[488] Art 2(5). On the derivatives within the scope of the 2014 MiFID II/MiFIR see Ch IV sect 4.3. The extension of the scope of the derivatives covered under the 2014 MiFID II/MiFIR regime to cover certain physically settled energy derivatives brought these instruments within the scope of the EMIR obligation. Given the potential costs to market participants and disruptions, MiFID II has providing a transitional period of six years before such contracts become subject to EMIR (2014 MiFID II Art 95).

[489] See Ch IV sect 4.3. Particular difficulties have been generated by the definition of foreign exchange derivatives and commodity derivatives.

[490] Art 2(7). MTF-traded derivatives are accordingly OTC derivatives for the purposes of EMIR, as confirmed by the ESMA EMIR Q&A, OTC Q1. ESMA has also confirmed in the Q&A that an OTC-traded derivative does not lose this characterization where it is fungible with an exchange-traded derivative.

[491] Industry stakeholders argued against the inclusion of commodity and foreign exchange derivatives in particular, as they were not implicated in the financial crisis. The Commission, however, underlined the importance of taking a forward-looking approach and of taking an expansive approach: 2010 EMIR Proposal Impact Assessment, n 351, 60.

[492] A CCP is defined as a legal person that interposes itself between the counterparties to the contracts traded on one or more financial markets, becoming the buyer to every seller and the seller to every buyer: Art 2(1).

[493] Defined as an undertaking which participates in a CCP and which is responsible for discharging the financial obligations arising from that participation: Art 2(14).

[494] A client is defined as an undertaking with a contractual relationship with a clearing member of a CCP which enables that undertaking to clear its transactions with that CCP: Art 2(15).

[495] Defined as a legal person that centrally collects and maintains the records of derivatives: Art 2(2).

more generally come within EMIR, mainly with respect to the competition- and access-related provisions.

EMIR's extraterritorial reach is wide. As outlined in section 4.2.13 of this Chapter, third country CCPs and trade repositories operating in the EU must be recognized by ESMA. The clearing, risk management, and reporting obligations imposed on counterparties also have an extensive reach. The CCP clearing obligation applies to contracts between EU financial/non-financial counterparties and an entity established in a third country that would be subject to the clearing obligation if it were established in the EU; it also applies to contracts between two entities established in third countries in these circumstances (Article 4(1)(a)). Similarly, the risk mitigation regime for non-CCP-cleared OTC derivatives has an extensive reach, applying to OTC derivative contracts entered into between third country entities that would be subject to those obligations if they were established in the EU, provided that the contracts have a direct, substantial, and foreseeable effect within EU, or where such obligation is necessary or appropriate to prevent the evasion of any EMIR provision (Article 11(12)). While these requirements are, in practice, anti-avoidance mechanisms designed to prevent EU entities from structuring contracts to avoid EMIR, they underline EMIR's potential reach.

Although the regime is calibrated, particularly in relation to how it applies to non-financial counterparties, there are also three sets of exemption from its scope; while the exclusion of these actors from EMIR reflects different concerns in each case, all three exemptions are broadly related to market efficiency.

Entities engaged in the management of public debt—in particular the members of the ESCB, other Member State bodies performing similar functions, and EU public bodies charged with or intervening in the management of public debt—and the Bank for International Settlements are excluded from EMIR's scope (Article 1(4)) in order to ensure that EMIR does not prejudice the smooth operation of monetary functions. In addition, multilateral development banks, public sector entities, and the European Stability Mechanism are exempted from EMIR, with the exception of the Article 9 reporting requirements (Article 1(5)). Third country central banks and public entities managing public debt were originally not addressed by this exemption, pending greater clarity on how jurisdictions internationally would treat these entities as their OTC derivatives regimes developed. In 2013, the Commission, in the report required under Article 1(6), reported that major third countries typically exempted these entities from the scope of the new OTC derivatives market rules, and recommended that the EU accordingly extend this exemption.[496]

The second exemption has a narrower focus and exempts intra-group derivatives transactions. Such transactions may be used to aggregate risk within a group, and submitting them to the CCP clearing obligation may limit their efficiency. The intra-group exemption is therefore available where conditions designed to mitigate potential systemic risk are met, and in order to support efficient intra-group risk management (Article 3). The exemption is available for non-financial counterparties in relation to an OTC derivative contract entered

---

[496] Commission, The International Treatment of Central Banks and Public Entities Managing Public Debt with Regard to OTC Derivatives Transactions (2013). The report considered the nature of the exemption in the US, Japan, Switzerland, Australia, Canada, and Hong Kong. Related BTSs were adopted in July 2013 (with respect to Japan and the US): Commission Delegated Regulation 1002/2013.

into with another counterparty which is part of the same group, as long as both counterparties are included in the same consolidation on a full basis and are subject to an appropriate, centralized risk evaluation, measurement, and control procedure, and the counterparty is established in the EU (Article 3(1)).[497] The intra-group exemption is also available to financial counterparties, subject to an extensive series of conditions designed to mitigate risks (Article 3(2)). The intra-group exemption applies in relation to the CCP clearing obligation (Article 4) and to elements of the risk mitigation regime for non-CCP-cleared transactions (given the heightened systemic risk thereby engaged, the collateralization requirements are lifted only where specific requirements are met), subject to notification of and agreement by the relevant NCA (Article 11). The exemption does not apply to the Article 9 reporting obligation.

A final and limited exemption applies to pension scheme arrangements.[498] Over the EMIR negotiations, pension funds successfully argued that their derivatives activities are related to the management of inflation and volatility and are not speculative, and that EMIR's requirements, and in particular the CCP margin requirements which would require pension funds to hold significant cash funds, would damage returns to pension holders.[499] A transitional, three-year exemption is accordingly available: identified occupational pension funds[500] benefit from an exemption from the CCP clearing requirement until 15 August 2015 (Article 89). This exemption may be extended for a further two years and a final one-year term, subject to the Commission agreeing, and pending the adoption of a technical solution related to the difficulties posed to the pension fund industry by EMIR's margin requirements (Article 85(2)).

VI.4.2.5 Calibration and non-Financial Counterparties

The wide scope of the 2012 EMIR generated significant industry concern during the negotiations.

Financial counterparties which typically relied on OTC derivatives for hedging purposes, rather than for speculative purposes, raised concerns as to the potential costs and prejudice to efficient risk management arising from the costly collateral and margin requirements. Property fund managers, for example, come within EMIR as AIFMD-scope managers. They use interest rate swaps to hedge interest risk when they fund property investments through floating rate loans. EMIR's CCP clearing and risk-management rules for non-CCP-cleared transactions (particularly in relation to collateral and margin) have the potential to impose significant costs on this core hedging activity and to damage returns.[501] But among financial counterparties, only pension funds were successful in negotiating an exemption from EMIR.

---

[497] Where the counterparty is established in a third country, the exemption remains available as long as the third country has been deemed by the Commission to be 'equivalent': sect 4.2.13.

[498] Defined under Art 2(10) and broadly covering institutions for occupational retirement provision.

[499] EMIR rec 26 notes that the application of EMIR would require pension funds to divest a significant proportion of their assets into cash to meet margin requirements, and that this could lead to a negative impact on the future income of pensioners.

[500] Essentially, occupational pension schemes registered under Directive 2003/41/EC and other similar schemes where the NCA approves an exemption.

[501] The property fund industry suggested that property funds would be required to provide collateral in the region of €65 billion in margin against existing positions: Herbert Smith, n 385, 4.

Greater calibration applies to non-financial counterparties. Non-financial counterparties have not been granted a full exemption from EMIR, given their importance in the OTC derivatives market and the potential for systemic risk from some non-financial counterparties—as well as the regulatory arbitrage risks which could be generated by such an exemption, given the incentives for financial counterparties to operate through non-financial counterparties.[502] But EMIR could potentially impose significant costs on efficient hedging activities related to commercial activities and to treasury/funding activities[503] which do not pose systemic risks;[504] the European Parliament's concern as to the costs which ESMA's proposed BTSs could impose on non-financial counterparties was a major driver of its initial threat to veto the standards.

The calibration of EMIR's application in order to protect commercial and treasury hedging by non-financial firms is achieved by means of the 'clearing threshold' mechanism (calibration is also provided by the extended 'phase-in' of the CCP clearing obligation for non-financial counterparties).[505] This threshold acts as a proxy for sporadic and/or non-systemically significant derivatives activity. Non-financial counterparties under the threshold are subject only to the EMIR reporting obligations and to a lighter risk mitigation regime. But where a non-financial counterparty takes positions in OTC derivative contracts and those positions exceed the threshold, the counterparty must notify ESMA and the NCA immediately, becomes subject to the CCP clearing obligation for all future contracts (and not only in relation to the particular positions which breached the clearing threshold),[506] and must clear all relevant future contracts (whether for hedging purposes or not—hedging contracts within the terms of EMIR are, as noted below, excluded from the clearing threshold calculation)[507] within four months of becoming subject to the clearing obligation (Article 10(1)).

The calculation of the clearing threshold is accordingly pivotal to EMIR's scope of application. It is governed by EMIR Article 10 and its related BTSs. The regime is designed to ensure that non-financial counterparties only become fully subject to EMIR where their activities become systemically significant, and to protect hedging activities related to usual commercial and or treasury financing activities. The concern to protect hedging activities is implicit in the Article 10 calculation procedure, which provides that the position

---

[502] 2010 EMIR Proposal, n 365, 7.

[503] Related to, eg, the management of short and long-term funding, including the management of debt and investment activities, including cash management. The EMIR margin requirements, in particular, could place significant pressure on cash flow, and would likely require that non-financial counterparties have credit lines in place (which could impact on their credit rating). Significant operational costs could also be imposed, as non-financial counterparties could be required to engage in mark-to-market valuations of margin, which valuations generate significant system costs. The exemption of non-financial counterparties was accordingly supported by the FSB: n 392, 28.

[504] eg Confederation of British Industry, Position on Key Elements of EMIR. March 2011.

[505] They benefit from an additional three years, following the February 2013 Commission and Parliament compromise: n 480.

[506] As long as the rolling average position over 30 working days exceeds the threshold. Where the rolling average over 30 days does not exceed the threshold (and this is demonstrated to the NCA), the CCP clearing obligation is lifted: Art 10(2).

[507] 2013 Commission Delegated Regulation 149/2013 rec 24. ESMA explained the wide application of the CCP clearing obligation once the threshold is passed in terms of the systemic relevance of the positions held as a whole, the dangers of uneven risk mitigation were the CCP clearing obligation not to apply consistently, and the importance of the clearing obligation in managing counterparty risk, which is counter-party- and not asset-class-related: 2012 ESMA EMIR Draft BTS Report, n 445, 20.

calculation for the purposes of establishing whether positions exceed the threshold must include all OTC derivative contracts entered into by the non-financial counterparty (or other non-financial entities within the group) which are not objectively measurable as reducing risks directly relating to the commercial activity or treasury financing activities of the counterparty (Article 10(3)). The BTSs which govern whether a derivative transaction meets the Article 10(3) hedging requirement are broadly based,[508] and reflect ESMA's concern that the carve-out reflect the range of risks which commercial and treasury funding operations generate,[509] the flexibility needed by non-financial counterparties,[510] and the need to reduce the costs faced by non-financial counterparties in monitoring their positions for the purpose of the clearing threshold;[511] this concern was also evident in ESMA's development of the clearing thresholds. Nonetheless, the standards generated significant differences of opinion over the consultation process[512] and led to a difference of opinion between ESMA and the ESRB.[513]

The clearing thresholds against which derivative positions are to be monitored were to be established by ESMA by taking into account the systemic relevance of the sum of the net positions and exposures per counterparty and per class of OTC derivative (Article 10(4)). The breadth of the definition of excluded hedging contracts has led to the clearing thresholds being set at a relatively low level,[514] although the thresholds are to be regularly reviewed (Article 10(4)). The clearing thresholds apply in relation to credit derivatives (€1 billion in gross notional value), equity derivatives (€1 billion), interest rate derivatives (€3 billion), foreign exchange derivatives (€3 billion), commodity derivatives (€3 billion), and other OTC derivative contracts (€3 billion).[515] ESMA's tying of the threshold to a

---

[508] 2013 Commission Delegated Regulation 149/2013 provides that a contract falls within the Art 10(3) hedging carve-out where (and whether by itself or in combination with other derivative contracts, and whether directly or through closely correlated instruments) it either: covers the risks arising from the potential change in the value of assets, services, inputs, products, commodities or liabilities that the non-financial counterparty or its group owns, produces, manufactures, processes, provides, purchases, merchandises, leases, sells or incurs, or reasonably anticipates so doing in the ordinary course of business; covers the risks arising from the potential indirect impact on the value of assets, services, inputs, products, commodities or liabilities resulting from fluctuations of interest rates, inflation rates, foreign exchange rates or credit risk; or qualifies as a hedging contract under International Financial Reporting Standards (IFRS). The IFRS definition can be used where the counterparty is not subject to IFRS reporting (Regulation 149/2013 rec 16).

[509] 2013 Commission Delegated Regulation 149/2013 rec 19.

[510] ESMA accepted, eg, that OTC derivative contracts could be used to hedge risks arising in relation to the acquisition of another business: 2012 ESMA EMIR Draft BTS Report, n 445, 17.

[511] ESMA included the IFRS definition of a hedging contract, eg, within the criteria as it would, in practice, exclude a significant number of firms from the CCP clearing obligation and also reduce monitoring costs: 2012 ESMA EMIR Draft BTS Report, n 445, 17.

[512] Some stakeholders called for ESMA to allow hedging in relation to cash and share delivery liabilities in relation to employee share options (which, in a change to its original position, ESMA accepted as part of a non-financial counterparty's normal activities), and to allow reliance on contracts defined as hedging contracts under local GAAP, rather than IFRS (which ESMA rejected given the risks to convergence): 2012 ESMA EMIR Draft BTS Report, n 445, 16–17.

[513] The ERSB was of the opinion, eg, that the IFRS hedging contract definition might not be perfectly matched with the EMIR regime, and called for more detailed specification of commercial and treasury activities. In response, ESMA acknowledged the refinements which the ESRB approach would bring, but rejected it given the implementation difficulties which it would generate for small and medium-sized firms in particular: 2012 ESMA EMIR Draft BTS Report, n 445, 17.

[514] 2013 Commission Delegated Regulation 149/2013 rec 20.

[515] 2013 Commission Delegated Regulation 149/2013 Art 11. Given the limited industry data available, ESMA based its assessment on data provided by the Bank for International Settlement and NCAs. It warned,

gross notional value assessment led to significant industry and European Parliament opposition, and to calls for the calculation to be based on a net, mark-to-market value on the grounds that this would allow the systemic risk represented by OTC derivative positions to be more accurately captured (and would have given non-financial counterparties more leeway to stay under the threshold). Despite the potential for institutional tensions,[516] ESMA argued that a gross notional value was easier to implement and assess than a mark-to-market value and provided greater stability and certainty in the assessment of positions, particularly for small and medium-sized firms. ESMA also underlined that the absence of reliable data on net positions led it to conclude that gross value was a reasonable and practical proxy for systemic relevance.[517]

VI.4.2.6 The Clearing Obligation

At the heart of the 2012 EMIR is the Article 4 obligation on counterparties to clear[518] all OTC derivatives contracts pertaining to a class of OTC derivatives[519] that has been declared subject to the clearing obligation in accordance with the Article 5(2) procedure through a CCP (Article 4(1)). These contracts must be cleared through an EU-established CCP authorized under EMIR (Article 14) or a third country CCP recognized by ESMA (Article 25), in each case authorized to clear the relevant class of OTC derivatives and listed in the Article 6 ESMA-maintained public register (Article 4(3)). In order to support the clearing obligation, the counterparty must become a clearing member or a client, or establish indirect clearing arrangements with a clearing member (Article 4(3));[520] the clearing obligation cannot thus be avoided by a counterparty not engaging with a CCP. Article 4(3), which provides for a range of clearing access models, is designed to respond to the heavy costs associated with becoming a clearing member, given the capital, margin, and default fund requirements which apply (section 4.2.10), and to support structural change within the clearing industry by encouraging the development of new, indirect clearing access routes.

The obligation has a wide reach (Article 4(1)). It applies in relation to contracts concluded between the following: two financial counterparties; a financial counterparty and a non-

---

however, that it did not have sufficient data 'to have a detailed view on the OTC derivative markets and the use of these instruments per asset class by non financial counterparties', and highlighted that the clearing thresholds would be regularly reviewed: 2012 ESMA EMIR Draft BTS Report, n 445, 19.

516 The ESRB supported ESMA's reliance on a gross assessment, but called for a two-step, mark-to-market approach (the first step addressed the assessment of which group a counterparty belonged to, and the second addressed the threshold calculation): 2012 ESMA EMIR Draft BTS Report, n 445, 17. ESMA accepted that the ESRB's approach could have led to a more refined assessment, but highlighted the complexities and costs which this would entail for small and medium-sized firms (at 20).

517 2012 ESMA EMIR Draft BTS Report, n 445, 19. ESMA also highlighted that given that non-financial counterparties are not subject to the daily mark-to-market valuation requirement which applies to financial counterparties and non-financial counterparties for non-CCP-cleared transactions above the clearing threshold, it would be 'paradoxical' to use the mark-to-market approach in setting the clearing thresholds (at 19).

518 Clearing is defined under EMIR as the process of establishing positions, including the calculation of net obligations, and ensuring that financial instruments, cash, or both are available to secure the exposures arising from these positions.

519 A class of derivatives is defined as a subset of derivatives sharing common and essential characteristics including, at least, the relationship with the underlying asset, the type of underlying asset, and currency of notional amount (although maturities may differ): Art 2(6).

520 Indirect clearing arrangements must not increase counterparty risks and must ensure that the assets and positions of the counterparty benefit from protection equivalent to EMIR Arts 39 and 48 (sect 4.2.10).

financial counterparty over the clearing threshold; and two non-financial counterparties over the clearing threshold. The extraterritorial reach of the clearing obligation is supported by its application to contracts between the following: a financial counterparty or non-financial counterparty over the clearing threshold and an entity established in a third country that would be subject to the clearing obligation if it were established in the EU; and two entities established in one or more third countries that would be subject to the clearing obligation if they were established in the EU, as long as the contract has a 'direct, substantial and foreseeable' effect within the EU, or where such an obligation is necessary or appropriate to prevent the evasion of EMIR.[521]

It does not, however, apply to non-financial counterparties below the clearing threshold, pension scheme arrangements (on a transitional basis, Article 89), or intra-group transactions (Article 4(2)). The intra-group exemption is dependent on the counterparties in question having notified their NCAs of their intention to use the exemption and the NCAs not having objected to reliance on the exemption where the conditions governing the exemption (Article 3) are not met.[522]

The identification of the classes of derivatives subject to the clearing obligation has major structural and cost implications for the OTC derivatives market in the EU. It also has implications for CCPs' resilience and their ability to manage the related systemic risks associated with central clearing; the more complex the class of derivative cleared, the greater the pressure on the CCP's risk-management systems—particularly its processes for valuing margin—and, accordingly, on the EMIR rulebook. The process governing which classes of OTC derivatives are subject to the clearing obligation has two elements: the 'bottom-up' (or industry-driven) procedure and the 'top-down' procedure (ESMA-driven). Both procedures were a feature of EMIR from the earliest Commission consultations, and are also a feature of IOSCO's standards on mandatory clearing.[523]

The 'bottom-up' procedure (Article 5(1) and (2)) is driven by the CCP authorization process (section 4.2.9) and so links the clearing obligation to CCP practice, and to whether the CCP has appropriate risk management and other procedures in place to clear identified classes of OTC derivatives safely. Once an NCA has authorized a CCP to clear a class of OTC derivatives, it must inform ESMA of the authorization; public disclosure is made of elements of the related and extensive notification which the NCA must make to ESMA[524] in order to signal to the market that a potential CCP clearing obligation may arise.[525] ESMA is then required to decide whether that class of derivatives should be subject

---

[521] RTSs governing when the clearing obligation applies to contracts between two third country counterparties have been adopted: n 374.

[522] Where NCAs disagree, ESMA may mediate. A similar requirement applies in relation to intra-group transactions involving EU-established and third country-established counterparties.

[523] IOSCO, n 401, 13–31 (the standards reflect the 2010 FSB recommendations).

[524] The extensive information which must be reported to ESMA is set out in 2013 Commission Delegated Regulation 149/2013 Art 6. ESMA's public register must contain information on the class of OTC derivatives notified under the CCP authorization procedure, and the type of OTC derivatives contracts: Commission Delegated Regulation 149/2013 Art 8.

[525] In developing the BTSs related to the CCP clearing obligation, ESMA acknowledged the importance of warning the market of the extent of the likely clearing obligations which would follow as CCPs were recognized: 2012 ESMA EMIR Draft BTS Report, n 445, 11.

to the Article 4 CCP clearing obligation for all relevant counterparties. Procedurally, the determination is made by means of ESMA—following a public consultation, and after consulting the ESRB and, where relevant, competent authorities of third countries—submitting RTSs for Commission endorsement which specify the class of OTC derivatives to be subject to the CCP clearing obligation and the application date (Article 5(2)). In deciding whether to subject a class of OTC derivatives to the CCP clearing obligation, and with the overarching aim of reducing systemic risk, ESMA's assessment must extend beyond the NCA's original assessment of whether the particular CCP can clear the class in question and address the market-wide implications of subjecting the asset class to a general CCP clearing obligation.[526] Accordingly, ESMA must take into consideration the degree of standardization of the contractual terms and operational processes of the relevant class;[527] the volume and liquidity of the relevant class;[528] and, of particular importance to the ability of the CCP to make optimum risk-management decisions, the availability of fair, reliable, and generally accepted pricing information on the relevant class (Article 5(4)).[529] ESMA may also take into consideration the interconnectedness of the counterparties using the relevant class, the anticipated impact on levels of counterparty credit risk,[530] and the impact on competition across the EU (Article 5(4)). There are suggestions within EMIR that the CCP clearing obligation is primarily designed to address counterparty credit risk, and that this may lead to a narrowing of the scope of the clearing obligation; EMIR suggests that for certain classes of OTC derivative the key risk may be settlement risk, and that accordingly CCP clearing, which it identifies as addressing counterparty credit risk, may not be the optimal solution.[531]

EMIR also specifies the criteria which ESMA must take into account in deciding the date from which the CCP clearing obligation should apply.[532]

The changed regulatory environment following the G20 reform agenda, and regulatory pressure on the industry to pre-empt the adoption of binding CCP clearing requirements, has led to a wider range of asset classes and volumes of OTC derivatives being cleared

---

[526] 2013 Commission Delegated Regulation 149/2013 rec 9.

[527] ESMA's approach to standardization was broadly accepted by the market and is based on ESMA taking into consideration: (a) whether the contractual terms of the relevant class of OTC derivatives incorporate common legal documentation, including master netting agreements, definitions, standard terms and confirmations which set out contract specifications commonly used by counterparties; and (b) whether the operational processes of the class are subject to automated post-trade processing and lifecycle events that are managed in a common manner to a timetable which is widely agreed among counterparties: Commission Delegated Regulation 149/2013 Art 7(1).

[528] ESMA will take into consideration: whether the margin or financial requirements of the CCP would be proportionate to the risk that the CCP clearing obligation intends to mitigate; the stability of the market size and depth in respect of the class over time; the likelihood that market dispersion would remain sufficient in the event of default of a clearing member; and the number and value of transactions: 2013 Commission Delegated Regulation 149/2013 Art 7(2).

[529] ESMA is to take into account whether the information needed to accurately price the contracts within the relevant class of OTC derivatives contract is easily accessible to market participants on a reasonable commercial basis, and whether it would continue to be easily accessible if the relevant class of OTC derivatives became subject to the clearing obligation: 2013 Commission Delegated Regulation 149/2013 Art 7(3).

[530] Defined as the risk that a counterparty to a transaction defaults before the final settlement of the transaction's cash flows: Art 2(11).

[531] 2012 EMIR rec 19.

[532] Art 5(5).

through CCPs.[533] The 'bottom-up' procedure, which follows market practice, is likely, as a result, to lead to an extensive CCP clearing obligation.[534]

The 'top-down' procedure, which is designed to follow the 'bottom-up' procedure, has the objective of ensuring that CCP clearing applies to particular classes of OTC derivatives which are not, in practice, cleared through CCPs (and so not picked up through the bottom-up process) but are deemed as systemically relevant—although central to the design of the top-down procedure is the assumption that no CCP will be required to clear derivatives unless it can safely do so. The top-down process can also be associated with regulatory encouragement of the market to provide appropriate clearing facilities.[535] ESMA can independently, and after public consultation and consulting the ESRB (and third country competent authorities, as relevant), identify and notify to the Commission the classes of derivatives that should be subject to the Article 4 clearing obligation, but in respect of which no CCP has received authorization (Article 5(3)).[536] But, given the risks of requiring CCPs to clear instruments which have yet to be cleared in practice by a CCP, the 'top-down' procedure is likely to be more peripheral to the clearing obligation process.

EMIR does not clearly address how the CCP clearing obligation can be withdrawn. Where the conditions which qualify an instrument no longer apply, financial stability demands that the obligation be lifted. ESMA is, however, subject to the usual (cumbersome) RTS procedure when removing an instrument from the obligation. A tailored, accelerated procedure may, accordingly, be required.

A series of allied obligations support the CCP clearing obligation. Least intrusively, public disclosure requirements apply, in that ESMA must maintain a related public register (Article 6).[537] More intrusively, access- and competition-related protections apply in relation to access to CCP clearing, which are designed to promote competition between CCPs and the liberalization of access to CCP clearing services and to protect against discrimination by vertically integrated trading venue/CCP silos.[538] The original provision (EMIR Article 7) has been amended by the 2014 MiFIR (Article 53) to reflect the refinements which MiFIR made to CCP/trading venue access rights generally (noted in

---

[533] Initially, the change was most marked in relation to CDSs and interest rate derivatives. As the reforms developed, industry CCP solutions developed in relation to, eg, CFDs (eg, the CFD clearing platform developed by LCHClearnet and Chi-X in 2010) and, for the first time, foreign exchange derivatives (cleared through LCHClearnet's new ForexClear platform). Globally, the use of CCPs has significantly increased for interest rate derivatives, in particular (60 per cent of which are now CCP-cleared, as compared to 31 per cent in 2010: ESMA 2013(1) TRV, n 398, 7).

[534] ESMA's initial orientations as to procedure and approach were set out in 2013 in ESMA, Discussion Paper, The Clearing Obligation under EMIR (2013) (ESMA/2013/925). ESMA has underlined its concern to adopt an appropriately granular and pragmatic approach, which is attuned to market realities but also avoids circumvention risk. Interest rate and credit derivatives are likely to be candidates for the clearing obligation (reflecting the US approach). The first assessment process was activated in March 2014 (n 407).

[535] IOSCO, n 400, 24.

[536] ESMA is also to publish a call for the development of proposals for the clearing of those classes of derivative.

[537] The register must include, *inter alia*, the classes of OTC derivative subject to the CCP clearing obligation, and the CCPs authorized or recognized for the purposes of the CCP clearing obligation. The coverage of the register is specified in detail by 2013 Commission Delegated Regulation 149/2013 Art 8.

[538] The need to mitigate the risk of unintended competitive distortions arising from the clearing obligation (such as a CCP refusing to clear transactions executed on particular trading venues which compete with the CCP's owner) was noted by 2012 EMIR rec 34. See further Ch V sect 13 on post-trade competition generally.

Chapter V section 13). As revised, Article 7 provides that, with respect to CCP access, where a CCP has been authorized to clear particular OTC derivatives, it must accept the clearing of such contracts on a non-discriminatory and transparent basis, including as regards collateral requirements and fees relating to access, regardless of the trading venue on which the derivative contracts trade. In particular, a trading venue (in practice, an MTF or OTF) has the right to non-discriminatory treatment in terms of how contracts traded on that trading venue are treated in terms of collateral requirements and netting of economically equivalent contracts (where the inclusion of such contracts in the CCP's close-out and other netting procedures, based on the applicable insolvency law, would not endanger the smooth and orderly functioning, the validity, and/or the enforceability of such procedures), and of cross-margining with correlated contracts cleared by the same CCP under a risk model that complies with EMIR Article 41 (which addresses margin and collateral: section 4.2.10).[539] A CCP may, however, require that a trading venue comply with the operational and technical requirements established by the CCP, including risk-management requirements. Refusals of access must be reasoned, and the CCP (and the CCP's NCA) may only refuse access where access would threaten the smooth and orderly functioning of the markets or adversely affect systemic risk (Article 7). Similarly, EMIR protects the provision of trading venues' trade feed data to CCPs, in order to ensure vertical silos do not discriminate against CCPs and to enhance overall liquidity by broadening market participant access to trading venues by means of allowing access by multiple CCPs.[540] Under Article 8, a trading venue must provide trade feeds on a non-discriminatory and transparent basis to any CCP that has been authorized to clear OTC derivative contracts traded on that trading venue (in practice, an MTF or OTF) upon request by the CCP. Access by the CCP to the trading venue can only be granted, however, where it would not require interoperability or threaten the smooth and orderly functioning of markets, in particular due to 'liquidity fragmentation', and the trading venue has put in place adequate mechanisms to prevent such fragmentation.[541]

VI.4.2.7 The Risk Mitigation Obligation for non-CCP-cleared Derivatives

Where OTC derivatives are not subject to the CCP clearing obligation, a series of risk mitigation obligations[542] apply to financial counterparties and to non-financial counterparties above the clearing threshold; a calibrated regime applies to non-financial counterparties below the clearing threshold (Article 11). These risk mitigation requirements are designed

---

[539] The conditions related to non-discriminatory treatment are to be amplified by RTSs.

[540] 2013 Commission Delegated Regulation 149/2013 rec 12.

[541] The liquidity fragmentation requirement relates to a situation in which the participants in a trading venue are unable to conclude a transaction with one or other participants in the venue because of the absence of clearing arrangements to which all participants have access (2013 Commission Delegated Regulation 149/2013, Art 9). Art 9 provides that access by a CCP to a trading venue (which is already served by a CCP) will not give rise to liquidity fragmentation where (and without the need to impose a requirement on all clearing members of the incumbent CCP to become members of the requesting CCP) all participants in the trading venue can clear, directly or indirectly, through at least one CCP in common or through clearing arrangements established by the CCP. In a reflection of the sensitivity of the competition implications, ESMA's approach proved contentious, with some stakeholders calling for a wide approach to liquidity fragmentation risk, but others warning that an overly broad approach could lead to incumbent CCPs being protected from competition (2012 ESMA EMIR Draft BTS Report, n 445, 14).

[542] 2013 Commission Delegated Regulation 149/2013 governs risk mitigation. Additional BTSs are to be developed jointly by the ESAs in relation to collateral and capital (see n 383 on the related IOSCO/Basel Committee standards on margin).

to reduce counterparty risk and operational risk, as well as to enhance and strengthen the collateralization of these transactions and, in so doing, to reflect the risk-management techniques which the OTC markets have developed for bilaterally cleared derivative contracts.[543]

All financial and non-financial counterparties are required to ensure, exercising due diligence, that appropriate procedures and arrangements are in place to measure, monitor, and mitigate operational risk and counterparty credit risk (Article 11(1)). These procedures and arrangements must include timely confirmation, where available by electronic means, of the terms of the contract, and formalized processes, which are robust, resilient, and auditable, to reconcile portfolios, to manage the associated risk, to identify and resolve disputes between parties early, and to monitor the value of outstanding contracts.[544]

Additional and more stringent requirements apply to financial counterparties and non-financial counterparties above the clearing threshold. Financial counterparties and non-financial counterparties above the threshold must mark-to-market on a daily basis the value of outstanding contracts; where market conditions prevent marking-to-market, a reliable and prudent marking-to-model must be used (Article 11(2)).[545]

Collateral requirements also apply. Financial counterparties must have in place risk-management procedures that require the timely, accurate, and appropriately segregated exchange of collateral with respect to OTC derivative contracts (which are entered into on or after 16 August 2012) (Article 11(3)).[546] Non-financial counterparties above the threshold must similarly have collateral exchange procedures in place in relation to contracts entered into on or after the clearing threshold is exceeded (Article 11(3)). Financial counterparties are additionally required to hold an appropriate and proportionate amount of capital to manage the risk not covered by appropriate exchange of collateral (Article 11(4)). The intra-group exemption is available in relation to the collateralization requirements, but only where broadly functional substitutes are in place.[547]

Like the CCP clearing obligation, the risk mitigation regime has an extensive reach, applying to OTC derivative contracts entered into between third country entities that would be subject to those obligations if they were established in the EU, provided that the contracts have a direct, substantial, and foreseeable effect within the EU, or where such obligation is necessary or appropriate to prevent the evasion of any EMIR provision (Article 11(12)).

---

[543] Notably portfolio compression (the process whereby mutually offsetting trades are terminated), exchange of collateral, and portfolio reconciliation (or the management of collateral requirements across a wide range of counterparties): 2012 EFSIR, n 354, 100–1.

[544] The application of these requirements (amplified by 2013 Commission Delegated Regulation 149/2013 Arts 12–15, which address timely confirmation, portfolio reconciliation, portfolio compression, and dispute resolution) to non-financial counterparties generated some controversy over the development process and in the European Parliament, given the costs. In response, ESMA lightened its original proposals for BTSs, including with respect to the portfolio reconciliation requirement which, as adopted, is required only on a quarterly basis for a portfolio of less than 50 OTC derivative contacts (2013 Commission Delegated Regulation 149/2013 Art 13).

[545] The criteria for mark-to-market models, and the market conditions which can prevent marking-to-market, are specified by 2013 Commission Delegated Regulation 149/2013 Arts 16 and 17.

[546] BTSs will be adopted on the Art 11(3) margin requirements, following agreement on the related Basel Committee-IOSCO standards (n 440).

[547] 2013 Commission Delegated Regulation 149/2013: Art 11(5)–(10) and (11).

VI.4.2.8 The Reporting Obligation

The 2012 EMIR's extensive reporting regime for derivatives, which is designed to provide regulators and market participants with significantly greater transparency on the scale and nature of derivatives market activity and related exposures, applies to all counterparties (financial and non-financial) and to CCPs. They must ensure that the details of any derivative contract they have concluded (whether or not OTC and whether cleared or not), and of any modification or termination of the contract, are reported to an ESMA-registered or -recognized trade repository (or to ESMA, where a trade repository is not available) no later than the working day following the contract conclusion, modification, or termination (Article 9).[548] The reporting obligation may be delegated by the counterparty or CCP, but CCPs and counterparties must ensure that contract details are reported without duplication. Counterparties must also keep a record of any derivative contract they have concluded and any modification thereto for at least five years following contract termination.

VI.4.2.9 The CCP Regime: Authorization and the CCP College

The resilience of the new CCP clearing regime depends on the resilience of the CCPs through which a massive volume of OTC derivatives will be cleared. Accordingly, a highly detailed regulatory regime, closely focused on prudential regulation, applies to the CCPs through which the Article 4 clearing obligation is met. Although much of the regime is based on the 2012 CPSS-IOSCO Principles for Financial Market Infrastructure, it is significantly more detailed than the Principles and engages with EU-specific risks, including in relation to cross-border supervision.

The CCP authorization process is distinct from other authorization regimes across EU securities and markets regulation with respect to the significant constraints it places on what is normally the exclusive power of an NCA with respect to authorization decisions. During the early negotiations on what would become the 2010 ESMA Regulation, the possibility of ESMA authorizing and supervising CCPs was raised by the 2009 DLG Report[549] and accepted by the Commission and Council, albeit that some Member States, from the outset, were opposed given the fiscal risk associated with CCPs. The subsequent EMIR negotiations led to a closer focus on the nature, location, and extent of CCP risks, and to a more nuanced authorization process which attempts to balance the national interest in ensuring authorization/supervisory decisions with fiscal implications are located at national level and the cross-border interest in the effective supervision of CCPs.

CCP authorization and supervision remains a national competence, given the very significant fiscal risks which CCP failure would generate for the Member State in which the CCP is based. But the pan-EU systemic risks are acute, with the Member States of the clearing members of a failed CCP likely to be the first impacted by any CCP default.[550] In addition, discriminatory practices with respect to CCP access have the potential to disrupt the EU

---

[548] 2013 Commission Delegated Regulation 148/2013 specifies in detail the data that must be reported to trade repositories. Significant operational concerns have emerged as to the interaction between the EMIR reporting regime and the 2014 MiFIR/MiFIR regime and related duplication of records and confusion of scope (Ch V 12.1).

[549] n 411.

[550] EMIR rec 52.

market. Accordingly, EMIR provides for a CCP college of NCAs which can exercise material powers with respect to CCP authorization. The CCP authorization process triggers the creation of a college of NCAs which is required to adopt an opinion on the authorization, and which can veto the local NCA's decision to authorize the CCP.[551] The operation of the college is addressed by Commission Delegated Regulation 876/2013[552] and co-ordinated through ESMA, whose related activities have included the development of a framework written agreement governing the college, a common risk assessment template, and a model for the composition of CCP colleges.[553]

The CCP authorization application must be made to the NCA of the Member State within which the CCP is established; once granted, authorization is effective pan-EU (Article 14(1) and (2)). As is common across EU securities and markets regulation, and in order to mitigate risks, CCP authorization is tied to particular activities; authorization can be granted only for activities linked to clearing, and the authorization must specify the services in relation to which the CCP is authorized and the classes of financial instrument covered by the author-ization (thereby supporting ESMA's subsequent assessment of whether a mandatory clearing obligation should apply in relation to those financial instruments) (Article 14(3)). Where a CCP wishes to extend its business, express authorization must be granted by the NCA (Article 15). Authorization conditions are not specified in detail under EMIR; Member States are expressly empowered to adopt (or to continue to apply) additional requirements in relation to CCPs established on their territories (Article 14(5)). EMIR simply provides that the applicant CCP must submit an application to the NCA of the Member State where it is established which provides all information necessary to satisfy the NCA that it has estab-lished, at the time of authorization, all the necessary arrangements to satisfy EMIR's requirements (Article 17(1) and (2)). EMIR does require, however, that the CCP be notified as a system under Directive 98/26/EC (Article 17(4)),[554] and specifies the minimum capital requirements for CCPs (Article 16). A CCP must have initial permanent and available capital of €7.5 million. Its capital overall, including retained earnings and reserves, must be proportionate to the risks stemming from its activities, and must at all times be sufficient to ensure an orderly winding down or restructuring of activities over an appropriate time span and an adequate protection of the CCP against credit, counterparty, market, operational, and business risks (which are not already covered by the specific financial resources required of the CCP under Articles 41–44, as discussed later in the Chapter).[555]

The procedure for authorizing a CCP allows the CCP's college of supervisors (acting unanimously) to override the local NCA. The submission of an authorization application by a CCP triggers the formation of a college. With 30 days of the submission of a complete

---

[551] The extent of the CCP college powers proved controversial over the negotiations, with the UK in particular concerned that the college process might lead to a veto being exercised in relation to decisions by UK authorities in relation to a UK CCP.

[552] The Regulation, which is based on EBA's Guidelines for the Operational Functional of Colleges and the Basel Committee's Good Practice Principles on Supervisory Colleges, addresses the procedures governing the establishment of the CCP college, college membership and participation, college governance, information exchange, and the sharing and delegation of tasks.

[553] ESMA Annual Report (2012) 39.

[554] This requirement relates to the 1998 Settlement Finality Directive (Directive 98/26/EC [1998] OJ L166/145) and post-trade regulation: see in summary outline Ch V sect 13.

[555] 2013 Commission Delegated Regulation 152/2013 (which was proposed by EBA) amplifies the CCP capital requirements.

application, the CCP's NCA must establish, manage, and chair a large college of supervisors, the members of which are specified by EMIR (Article 18(1)).[556] The establishment and functioning of the college is based on a written agreement between its members which determines the practical arrangements for the functioning of the college, including detailed voting procedures (Article 18(5)). The CCP's NCA must transmit all information received from the CCP to ESMA and to the college and, after assessing that the application is complete, notify the college, ESMA, and the applicant accordingly (Article 17(3)).

The NCA may grant authorization only where it is fully satisfied that the CCP complies with all the requirements laid down under EMIR and where the CCP college has not exercised its veto (Article 17(4)); in making its decision the NCA must consider the risk assessment required of the college in relation to the CCP (Article 19).[557] Where the NCA does not agree with a positive opinion (risk assessment) from the college, it must provide reasons for its deviation from the assessment. A CCP may not be authorized where all the members of the college (excluding the CCP's NCA) reach a unanimous joint opinion (which sets out full and detailed reasons) that the CCP not be authorized.[558] The CCP NCA may, however, refer the refusal to ESMA for binding mediation. Where the joint opinion against authorization has been adopted by a two-thirds majority of college members, any college member which does not support authorization may request binding ESMA mediation. The CCP's NCA must suspend the authorization decision until ESMA's decision. Underlining the pivotal nature of the authorization decision, ESMA is also expressly (if somewhat otiosely) empowered to take enforcement action[559] against the CCP's NCA where the authority has not applied EMIR or has applied it in a way which appears to be in breach of EU law (Article 17(5)).

The sensitivity of these unusually intrusive college powers is well illustrated by the voting thresholds specified and by the graduated consequences which follow, as well by the requirement for college members not to directly or indirectly discriminate against any Member State or group of Member States as a venue for clearing services in any currency (Article 17(6)).

The CCP college is also engaged with decisions to withdraw authorization.[560] Where the CCP's NCA considers that there are grounds for withdrawal of authorization (which may

---

[556] Composed of: ESMA; the CCP's NCA; the NCAs responsible for the supervision of the clearing members of the CCP that are established in the three Member States with the largest contributions to the CCP's Art 42 default fund (discussed later in the Chapter) on an aggregate basis over a one-year period; the NCAs responsible for the supervision of the trading venues served by the CCP; the NCAs supervising CCPs with which interoperability arrangements have been established; the NCAs supervising central securities depositaries to which the CCP is linked; the relevant members of the ESCB responsible for the oversight of the CCP and the relevant members of the ESCB responsible for the oversight of the CCPs with which interoperability arrangements have been established; and the central banks of issue of the most relevant EU currencies of the financial instruments cleared: Art 18(2).

[557] See n 558.

[558] The process through which the opinion is adopted is governed by Art 19, which requires that the CCP's NCA, within four months of the submission of a complete application by the CCP, conduct a risk assessment of the CCP and report to the college. Within 30 days, the college (facilitated by ESMA) must reach a joint opinion on the compliance by the applicant with EMIR.

[559] In accordance with the 2010 ESMA Regulation (see Ch XI sect 5.3.1).

[560] As across EU securities and markets regulation, the grounds for withdrawal are specified. They cover: failing to make use of the authorization within 12 months (or renouncing the authorization or providing no services or performing no activities in the previous six months); obtaining authorization under false pretences;

be limited to particular services, activities, or classes of financial instrument), it must notify ESMA and college members and consult with the college; the college may not exercise a veto, but where the NCA's decision departs from college members' positions, the NCA must take into account the reservations of college members in adopting its reasoned decision on withdrawal. College members may also request the CCP's NCA to examine whether the CCP remains in compliance with its authorization conditions (Article 20).

Once authorized, a CCP must at all times comply with the authorization conditions and notify the CCP's NCA of any material changes affecting the authorization conditions (Article 14(4)). Where the CCP wishes to extend its business into another Member State, the CCP's NCA must immediately notify the NCA of that State (Article 15(2)).

Third country CCPs may only provide clearing services to clearing members or trading venues established in the EU where they are recognized by ESMA, under a process akin to authorization (section 4.2.13).

VI.4.2.10 CCP Regulation

An extensive organizational, conduct, and prudential regime, which includes detailed administrative rules based in part on the 2012 CPSS-IOSCO Principles for Financial Market Infrastructures and which reflects close co-operation between ESMA and the ESCB, governs authorized CCPs. The regime is designed to contain the significant systemic risks which CCPs pose to the EU financial system and to minimize the risk that a large-scale tax-payer bailout, which a default would likely trigger, could be required. Although CCPs performed well over the financial crisis, the new clearing obligation significantly changes the nature and scale of the risks they face and pose. The potential for radical structural change which the 2012 EMIR brings generates further risks in relation to the CCP industry; a proliferation of CCPs could lead to the generation of poor incentives and hinder transparency.[561]

The organizational rules include a range of requirements designed to enhance risk management and to support the generation of strong CCP incentives to manage risk appropriately, given potentially perverse commercial incentives. These include requirements relating to organizational structure and internal control mechanisms; compliance procedures; continuity; effective resources, systems, and procedures; separation of risk management and other reporting lines; remuneration policy;[562] IT requirements; and frequent and

---

no longer being in compliance with the authorization conditions; or serious and systematic infringement of EMIR: Art 20(1).

[561] Grant, J, 'Conduits of Contention', *Financial Times*, 16 June 2011, 13, reporting on related industry concern.

[562] Reflecting the crisis-era concern across EU securities and markets regulation to break the link between remuneration and incentives for excessive risk-taking, a CCP's remuneration policy must promote sound and effective risk management and not create incentives to relax risk standards: the remuneration requirements have been amplified by 2013 Commission Delegated Regulation 153/2013 Art 8. As was the case with the remuneration rules across the UCITS V, AIFMD, and CRD IV proposals, industry opposition to the remuneration regime was considerable. Many CCPs strongly criticized ESMA's approach (which did not, however, change) as being disproportionate, more restrictive than requirements applying in other regulated sectors, and potentially compromising CCPs' ability to recruit high-calibre employees. ESMA's robust response was that CCPs were systemically important institutions and merited special treatment, which could be more prescriptive than for other regulated entities, and that remuneration could generate severe conflicts of interest: 2012 ESMA EMIR Draft BTS Report, n 445, 32.

independent audit (Article 26).[563] Board governance is addressed through independence and expertise requirements (Article 27); CCPs must also establish an independent risk committee (composed of representatives of clearing members and clients and of the board's independent members, but NCAs may request to attend in a non-voting capacity) to advise the board on a range of risk-management issues (Article 28). Senior management is also addressed, and is subject to a requirement for sufficient experience to ensure the sound and prudent management of the CCP (Article 27). Qualifying shareholders, any close links between the CCP and other natural or legal persons, and the acquisition or disposal of qualifying shareholdings are subject to a review regime similar to that which applies under the 2014 MiFID II (Article 30). The organizational regime also includes record-keeping (Article 29), conflicts of interest management (with respect to conflicts of interest between the CCP and its clearing members and clients) (Article 33), business continuity (Article 34), and outsourcing (Article 35) rules, in all cases tailored to the particular operational risks to which CCPs are exposed.

The conduct-of-business regime addresses the particular conduct risks associated with CCPs and the appropriate protection of CCP clearing members and clients (many of the new rules reflect the asset segregation risks which were exposed by the Lehman Brothers collapse), and so covers fair treatment and complaint handling (Article 36); CCP participation requirements (Article 37);[564] transparency requirements, including with respect to fees and prices, the risks associated with the services provided, and volumes of cleared transactions (Article 38); and segregation and portability of CCP records and accounts (Article 39). EMIR's asset segregation rules also form a central element of EMIR's support of CCP stability by requiring that the assets of clearing members are clearly distinguishable so that in a default the affected assets can be identified and losses contained.

EMIR's prudential regime is primarily concerned with the management of default by CCP members and with the ability of the CCP to replace trades and sustain associated losses. The CCP's ability to absorb losses arising from the default of a clearing member is supported through an array of funding-related measures which together provide a graduated scale of resources that can be called on by the CCP where it is required to replace trades.

At the base of the loss absorption regime are the margin and collateral requirements (described by EMIR as the CCP's 'primary line of defence')[565] which are designed to ensure that the CCP has access to margin in the form of high-quality collateral (and to provide strong risk-management incentives for CCP members, given the costs of margin). Margin and collateral rules must, however tread a fine line between ensuring a CCP is adequately resourced against default and imposing overly stringent and costly rules on CCP members which shrink the pool of available collateral and increase costs. EMIR manages

---

[563] These requirements are amplified by 2013 Commission Delegated Regulation 153/2013 Arts 3–11.

[564] Art 37 establishes the basic requirement that participation rules must be non-discriminatory, transparent, and objective, so as to ensure fair and open access to the CCP, and ensure that clearing members have sufficient financial resources and operational capacity to meet the obligations arising from CCP participation. Criteria that restrict access are only permitted to the extent that their objective is to control the CCP's risk. Art 37 also addresses the management of risk relating to clearing members' financial resources and operational capacity and the suspension and orderly exit of clearing members, and provides for the imposition by the CCP of additional requirements on clearing members, although these rules must be proportionate to the risks engaged and must not restrict participation to certain categories of clearing member.

[565] 2012 EMIR rec 70.

this balance mainly through the EMIR BTS regime, which establishes a number of criteria for the margin assessment by CCPs, but does not specify the particular approach to be adopted by CCPs.[566] The regime is designed to determine the minimum percentages that margins[567] should cover for different classes of financial instruments, to establish principles which CCPs should follow in tailoring margin levels to the characteristics of each financial instrument or portfolio cleared, and to ensure that CCPs do not, in an EMIR-driven competitive CCP environment, reduce margin to a level that compromises safety.[568] The regime is based on the core requirements that: margins are sufficient to cover the potential exposures that the CCP estimates will occur until the liquidation of the relevant positions; margins are sufficient to cover losses from at least 99 per cent of the exposures' movements over an appropriate time horizon; and margins ensure that the CCP fully collateralizes its exposures with clearing members (and CCPs with which it has interoperability arrangements) (EMIR Article 41). The CCP must regularly monitor and (where necessary) revise the level of margins to reflect current market conditions, taking into account any potentially pro-cyclical effects of revisions.[569] While the regime is based on the CCP making the margin decision, the stringency of some of the key criteria[570]—which, in some respects, departed from international standards by imposing more onerous requirements[571]—generated significant industry hostility given the sharp impact of margin requirements on costs, and the heavier cost burden and competitive disadvantages with which the stringent EU margin regime has been associated.[572]

---

[566] 2013 Commission Delegated Regulation 513/2013 rec 23.

[567] Initial and variation margin (see n 384) must be collected. The administrative regime defines initial margin as margin collected by the CCP to cover potential future exposure to clearing members providing the margin and, where relevant, interoperable CCPs, in the interval between the last margin collection and the liquidation of positions following a default of a clearing member or default by an interoperable CCP. Variable margin is defined as margin collected or paid out to reflect current exposures resulting from actual changes in market price: 2013 Commission Delegated Regulation 153/2013 Art 1.

[568] 2013 Commission Delegated Regulation 153/2013 recs 21–22.

[569] Under Art 41, the CCP must also adopt models and parameters in setting its margin requirements that capture the risk characteristics of the products cleared and take into account the interval between margin collections, market liquidity, and the possibility of changes over the duration of the transaction; these margin models and parameters must be validated by the relevant CCP NCA. Margins must be adequate to cover the risk stemming from the positions registered in accounts with the CCP (in accordance with EMIR's account and asset segregation rules); margins may be calculated with respect to a portfolio of financial instruments, as long as the calculation methodology is prudent and robust. The CCP must also call and collect margins on an intraday basis (at least when predefined thresholds are exceeded).

[570] Amplified by 2013 Commission Delegated Regulation 153/2013 Arts 24–28. The margin rules address the margin calculation, the time horizons in respect of which the calculation is made, the determination of the related confidence interval, margining on a portfolio basis, and the incorporation of pro-cyclicality risk management in the margin assessment.

[571] Although a factor-based approach (including in relation to pricing uncertainties, leverage levels, and other risk characteristics related to the class of financial instrument in question), governs the assessment by CCPs of confidence levels for the calculation of margin (Commission Delegated Regulation 513/2013 Art 24(2)), mandatory minimum confidence level requirements also apply. ESMA determined that initial margin be calculated in relation to a minimum confidence interval of 99.5 per cent for OTC derivatives and of 99 per cent for financial instruments other than OTC derivatives (2013 Commission Delegated Regulation 513/2013 Art 24(1)). The CPSS-IOSCO, Principles for Financial Market Infrastructure (2012) (para 3.6.6) and the US 2010 Dodd-Frank Act rules, however, deploy a 99 per cent confidence interval.

[572] eg 2012 ESMA EMIR Draft BTS Report, n 445, 37 and Linklaters, EMIR Update—ESMA Publishes Finalized Technical Standards (2012).

At the heart of the related and extensive regime on the type and quality of collateral which a CCP can accept as margin (and as default fund contributions – noted in this section) is the requirement that the CCP must require 'highly liquid' collateral, with minimal credit and market risk, to cover its initial and ongoing exposure to its clearing members (Article 46);[573] a CCP may also accept, where appropriate and sufficiently prudent, the underlying of the derivative contract or financial instrument that originates the CCP exposure as collateral to cover its margin requirements. As with the margin calculation regime, ESMA's approach to the related BTSs governing collateral[574] proved contentious both with the market and institutionally.[575] The BTSs provide that only cash, financial instruments, commercial bank guarantees (for non-financial counterparties), and gold can be considered as 'highly liquid',[576] despite market support for eligible collateral also to include other commodities, the units of UCITSs and alternative investment funds, and all collateral accepted by central banks or with a minimum credit rating.[577]

Significant controversy attended the rules governing collateral posted by non-financial counterparties, which are designed to provide some flexibility and to minimize the costs of collateral for these actors; specifically, for non-financial counterparties, a CCP can accept commercial bank guarantees (Article 46(1)), but ESMA's approach to the eligibility of commercial bank guarantees[578] generated significant market hostility[579] and the threat of a veto from the European Parliament.

The margin and collateral regime is supported by the requirement for a 'default fund' (Articles 42 and 45). To limit its credit exposure, a CCP must maintain a pre-funded default fund to cover losses that exceed the losses covered by margin requirements; the default fund requirements cover, *inter alia*, contributions to, size of, coverage of, and resilience of the fund.[580]

---

[573] The regime is designed to ensure that collateral can be converted into cash rapidly: 2013 Commission Delegated Regulation 153/2013 rec 34.

[574] Which address the criteria for assessing eligible collateral, the valuation of collateral, haircuts, and concentration limits: 2013 Commission Delegated Regulation 153/2013 Arts 37–44.

[575] ESMA took a more facilitative approach than the ESRB (which it was required to consult). The ESRB recommended, eg, that CCPs only accept listed and publicly traded securities, which advice ESMA rejected as potentially impacting significantly on market liquidity: 2012 ESMA EMIR Draft BTS Report, n 445, 48.

[576] 2013 Commission Delegated Regulation 153/2013 Arts 38–41. In each case, criteria apply to ensure the quality of the collateral. Detailed requirements apply, eg, to financial instruments and address, *inter alia*, the low credit risk of the issuer, the low market risk of the securities, the currency of the securities and their free transferability, and the availability of pricing data; the requirements also include conflict-of-interest rules which exclude securities which have been issued by the clearing member providing the collateral, the CCP, or any entity whose business involves the provision of services to the CCP: Art 39.

[577] ESMA's position with respect to eligible collateral did not shift significantly over the development of the BTSs. It refused, eg, to include investment fund units, as liquidity in these units was dependent on the discretion of the fund manager, and disagreed with criteria linked to ratings, given the G20 and EU commitment to reduce reliance on ratings: 2012 ESMA EMIR Draft BTS Report, n 445, 45–6.

[578] 2013 Commission Delegated Regulation 153/2013 Art 40.

[579] 2012 ESMA EMIR Draft BTS Report, n 445, 45–6. Although some concessions were made, commercial bank guarantees remain subject to stringent collateral requirements.

[580] The default fund must at least enable the CCP to withstand, under extreme but plausible market conditions, the default of the clearing member to which it has the largest exposures (or of the second and third largest clearing members, if the sum of their exposures is larger): Art 42(3). The rules have been amplified by 2013 Commission Delegated Regulation 153/2013 Arts 29–31, which address fund governance, the identification of extreme but plausible market conditions, and the review of extreme but plausible scenarios.

A third line of defence against default is the requirement imposed on a CCP to maintain 'sufficient pre-funded available financial resources' to cover potential losses that exceed the losses to be covered by the margin requirements and the default fund (Article 43).[581] The default fund and the 'other financial resources' must at all times enable the CCP to withstand the default of at least the two clearing members to which it has the largest exposures under extreme but plausible market conditions (Article 43(2)).

Finally, the CCP's capital (Article 16) provides a last-resort resource available to absorb losses from a clearing member's default: the CCP's capital—'other financial resources' cannot be relied on to meet the Article 16 capital requirement (Article 43(1))—is required to be at all times sufficient to ensure an orderly winding down or restructuring of activities over an appropriate time span and an adequate protection of the CCP against credit, counterparty, market, operational, legal, and business risks which are not covered by the specific financial resources related to margin, the default fund, and other financial resources (Article 16(2)).

The priority in which the CCP can call on margin, the default fund, and other financial resources is specified by the 'default waterfall' (Article 45), which determines the order in which contributions by defaulting and non-defaulting members, and the CCP's dedicated own resources, are to be used.[582] Article 48 governs the procedures applicable on a default, including with respect to the management of the default (including in relation to the containment of losses and liquidity pressures and the avoidance of disruption to CCP operations), NCA notification, the enforceability of default procedures (including in relation to the liquidation of the proprietary positions of a defaulting member), the treatment of the clearing member's clients' positions, and the appropriate use of clients' collateral (Article 48).

Extensive related risk assessment and management requirements apply. The exposure management rule (Article 40), for example, requires a CCP to measure and assess its liquidity and credit exposures to each clearing member (or to another CCP, where the CCP has concluded an interoperability arrangement) on a near-to-real-time basis.[583] The liquidity risk control regime is designed to ensure that the CCP has access at all times to adequate liquidity to perform its services and activities, including with respect to credit lines (Article 44[584]). Supporting risk-management rules apply in relation to the CCP's investment policy (which are designed to ensure, *inter alia*, that a CCP invests its financial resources only in highly liquid financial instruments with minimal market and credit risk, and that a CCP's investments can be liquidated rapidly and with minimal adverse price effect, and that secure deposit arrangements are used by the CCP for its financial

---

[581] These funds must include dedicated resources of the CCP, be freely available, and not be used to meet EMIR's capital requirements for CCPs: Art 43(1).

[582] Amplified by 2013 Commission Delegated Regulation 153/2013 Arts 35–36 with respect to the amount of the CCP's own resources which are to be used in the default waterfall (the amount must be at least 25 per cent of its initial minimum capital, including retained earnings and reserves).

[583] A CCP must accordingly have access in a timely manner and on a non-discriminatory basis (and on a reasonable cost basis) to the relevant pricing sources to effectively measure its exposures.

[584] Amplified by 2013 Commission Delegated Regulation 153/2013 Arts 32–34.

instruments and cash deposits)[585] and to settlement.[586] CCPs are, more generally, required to regularly review and stress-test (including by means of back testing and in relation to 'extreme but plausible' market conditions) their risk-management models and the parameters used for, *inter alia*, margin calculations, default contributions, collateral requirements, and other risk control mechanisms (Article 49.[587])[588] Given the obligation on CCPs to continually review and update financial resources and risk-management processes, EMIR seeks to ensure they have timely access to pricing information. The assessment as to whether to subject a class of OTC derivatives to the CCP clearing obligation, for example, includes an assessment as to the availability of fair, reliable, and generally accepted pricing information in the relevant class.[589]

A specific prudential regime applies to CCP interoperability arrangements, which currently apply only to cash securities; this regime is designed to support interconnectivity between CCPs and thus the EU's related wider financial market integration agenda, although there is some industry scepticism as to the feasibility of large-scale CCP interconnectivity, given that OTC derivatives CCP clearing is at an embryonic stage.[590] Interoperability arrangements, which must be approved in advance by the NCAs of the CCPs concerned (following the procedures which govern the authorization of EU-established CCPs), are subject to particular risk management arrangements (Article 52) and margin requirements (Article 53).[591]

EMIR is likely to be buttressed by a specific recovery and resolution regime for CCPs. The extent to which CCPs concentrate risk and can generate systemic risk is underlined by the close focus on CCP resolution in the Commission's 2012 consultation on non-bank recovery and resolution. The Consultation highlights the 'daunting scenario of the failure of a financial market infrastructure' and the systemic consequences which could flow from default by a major CCP member in stressed market conditions.[592] While it acknowledges the regulatory supports provided by EMIR and the *ex ante* risk-management procedures now in place, it highlights the need for an orderly recovery and resolution process which

---

[585] Art 47 and 2013 Commission Delegated Regulation 153/2013 Arts 45–49.

[586] Art 50. A CCP must, where practical and available, use central bank money to settle its transactions; where such money is not used, steps must be taken to strictly limit cash settlement risks. It must also clearly state its obligations with respect to deliveries of financial instruments and, where it has such obligations, eliminate principal risk through the use of delivery-versus-payment mechanisms, to the extent possible.

[587] The model review and stress testing requirements have been amplified by a highly detailed regime (2013 Commission Delegated Regulation 153/2013 Arts 50–63) which governs model validation, back testing, sensitivity testing and analysis, coverage and using test results, reverse stress tests, default procedures, frequencies, time horizons, and public disclosure.

[588] The CCP must also obtain independent valuation (governed by 2013 Commission Delegated Regulation 153/2013 Art 50), inform its NCA and ESMA of the results of the tests performed, and obtain their validation before adopting any significant changes to the models and parameters: Art 49(1) (margin assessment models must be validated by the NCA under Art 41(4)). The adopted models and parameters, and significant changes thereto, are also subject to an opinion of the CCP college. In practice, CCP authorization is also likely to involve a review of the adequacy of risk models: ESMA EMIR Q&A, CCP Q6.

[589] 2013 Commission Delegated Regulation 149/2013 Art 7(3).

[590] Herbert Smith, n 385, 8.

[591] As required by EMIR Art 54, ESMA has adopted related Guidelines (n 443) relating to the assessment of interoperability arrangements by NCAs.

[592] n 388, 11–13.

protects the tax-payer from fiscal risk in the event of a default, and considers the different elements of a recovery and resolution model.[593]

VI.4.2.11 CCP Supervision and Cross-border Co-ordination

The supervision of CCPs is broadly the responsibility of the NCA of the Member State within which the CCP is established, although NCAs across the EU have co-ordination and co-operation powers under the 2012 EMIR and each Member State must accordingly designate an NCA for the purposes of EMIR.[594] EMIR does not follow the enhanced approach to supervisory and enforcement powers in other crisis-era measures, and simply requires that the NCA have the supervisory and investigatory powers necessary for the exercise of its functions and that the Member States ensure that the appropriate administrative measures (which must be effective, proportionate, and dissuasive) can be taken or imposed against natural or legal persons responsible for non-compliance under EMIR (Article 22). Reflecting the emphasis across EMIR on supervisory review and monitoring of CCP resilience, NCAs (without prejudice to the functions conferred on the CCP college) are subject to a specific review obligation: NCAs must review the arrangements, strategies, processes, and mechanisms implemented by CCPs to comply with EMIR and evaluate the risks to which CCPs are exposed (Article 21).[595]

The standard co-operation obligations apply, in that NCAs must co-operate closely with each other and with ESMA, but with the addition of the ESCB, reflecting the potential for systemic risk (Article 23). EMIR also specifies that NCAs, in the exercise of their general duties, duly consider the potential impact of their decisions on the stability of the financial system in all other Member States concerned, in particular in Article 24 emergency situations. Where an emergency situation (undefined, but including developments in financial markets which may have an adverse effect on market liquidity and on the stability of the financial system in any of the Member States where the CCP or one of its clearing members are established) arises relating to a CCP, the CCP's NCA or any other NCA must inform ESMA, the college, the relevant members of the ESCB, and other relevant authorities of the situation without undue delay (Article 24).

CCP colleges are charged with specific co-ordination and co-operation responsibilities under EMIR, notably in relation to authorization, but are also conferred with a series of more general powers with respect to information exchange, the voluntary allocation of tasks between college members, the co-ordination of supervisory examination programmes, and the determination of procedures and contingency plans in relation to Article 24 emergency situations (Article 18(4)). NCAs which are not members of a college may request from the college any information relevant for the performance of their supervisory duties (Article 18(3)).

---

[593] The Consultation considers, *inter alia*, the scope of a recovery and resolution regime (whether common to CCPs and central securities depositaries, or composed of distinct elements, eg), resolution powers, loss allocation models (based on clearing member contributions), and cross-border resolution: n 388, 15–24. CPSS-IOSCO recommendations also apply (n 401).

[594] One or more NCAs may be designated for the purposes of EMIR as the NCA by the Member State in question, although a single authority must be identified for co-ordination with the Commission, ESMA, EBA, members of the ESCB, and other Member States' NCAs: Art 22.

[595] The frequency and depth of the review must reflect the size, systemic importance, nature, scale, and complexity of the activities of the CCPs concerned, but must be carried out on at least an annual basis: Art 21(4).

Co-operation and co-ordination under EMIR is largely a function of the CCP college, although ESMA is also charged with co-ordination between NCAs and across colleges with a view to building a common supervisory culture and consistent supervisory practices; to this end, ESMA must, at least annually, conduct a peer review of the supervisory activities of all NCAs in relation to CCP authorization and supervision, and initiate and co-ordinate EU-wide assessments of the resilience of CCPs to adverse market developments (Article 21(6)).

VI.4.2.12 The Trade Repository Regime

The trade repositories which will hold the massive volume of reporting data required under the 2012 EMIR Article 9 (and which will hold other mandated reports under other EU measures) are subject to a registration and regulation regime which is based on ESMA registration and supervision of trade repositories.[596] The regime is closely based on the credit rating agency regime which provided the operational template for ESMA supervision.

The Article 9 reporting obligation requires counterparties and CCPs within its scope to report the required data to a trade repository registered or (in the case of third country trade repositories) recognized under EMIR. To be eligible for ESMA registration, a trade repository must be established in the EU and meet EMIR's requirements for trade repositories; once registered, a trade repository must comply at all times with the conditions for registration. Registration is effective for the EU (Article 55). The registration process (Articles 56–59 and related BTSs) is based on the rating agency template and requires ESMA to assess the application of the trade repository and to consult (and exchange information) with the relevant NCA where the trade repository is an entity authorized or registered by an NCA in the Member State where it is established. Once registered, trade repositories become subject to a range of ESMA supervisory and enforcement powers, which follow the rating agency model and which empower ESMA to, *inter alia*, request information, carry out investigations and on-site inspections, take a range of supervisory measures, and impose fines (Articles 60–74). The operational procedural devices and third party protection mechanisms developed under the rating agency regime apply, and so include, *inter alia*, ESMA's power to delegate tasks to NCAs, the requirement for supervisory measures and penalty decisions to be assessed by an independent investigation officer within ESMA, and the specification of the particular breaches of EMIR which are subject to particular supervisory measures and penalties.

Once registered, trade repositories become subject to EMIR's requirements. Chief among these are data transparency and access requirements. Trade repositories must calculate positions, by class of derivative and by reporting entity (Article 80(4)); publish specified aggregated position information; and ensure that identified regulatory authorities and

---

[596] The BTSs governing trade repositories are primarily reporting- and information-based and cover: the extensive information required in the trade repository application for registration/recognition (2013 Commission Delegated Regulation 150/2013); the data to be published and made available by trade repositories (2013 Commission Delegated Regulation 151/2013); and the data to be reported by CCPs and counterparties to trade repositories (2013 Commission Delegated Regulation 148/2013).

public authorities have direct and immediate access to their data (Article 81).[597] Trade repositories are also subject to a relatively standard array of operational requirements, including with respect to governance, organizational structure, internal control mechanisms, conflict-of-interest requirements, compliance procedures, business continuity requirements, the separation of functions (where a trade repository provides ancillary services such as trade matching, credit event servicing, and portfolio reconciliation and portfolio compression services), and 'fit and proper' requirements for senior management and board members (Article 78). Like CCPs, trade repositories are also subject to access and related non-discrimination requirements. The strong economies of scale associated with trade repository services have been associated with likely limited competition in this business sector and with a need for related access rules.[598] In particular, a trade repository must have objective, non-discriminatory, and publicly disclosed access requirements. The repository must also grant service providers non-discriminatory access to the information held by the repository, as long as the relevant counterparties have consented. Criteria that restrict access are permitted only to the extent that their objective is to control risk to the data maintained by the trade repository (Article 78). Similarly, trade repositories must also publicly disclose the prices and fees associated with the EMIR services provided (these prices and fees must be cost-related) (Article 78). The regulatory regime is calibrated to the particular risks to which trade repositories are vulnerable, including by means of discrete rules governing operational reliability and disaster recovery (Article 79) and the safeguarding and recording of information (Article 80).

VI.4.2.13 Third Countries

The G20 OTC derivatives market reform agenda, of which the 2012 EMIR forms a part, has a global reach and is supported by a swathe of international standards, as well as by ongoing FSB monitoring. But it has generated complex extraterritorial effects, tensions, and risks, related to how jurisdictions, including the EU, address the cross-border reach of their new rules and deploy related recognition and equivalence mechanisms.[599]

In developing EMIR, the EU frequently adverted to the importance of international convergence.[600] In particular, ESMA's development of the massive EMIR administrative rulebook drew on intensive discussions with third country authorities as well as on the swathe of international principles, reports, and templates available (and in relation to which

---

[597] A trade repository must regularly, and in an easily accessible way, publish aggregate positions by class of derivative on the contracts reported to it. It must also ensure that a wide range of authorities (including ESMA, the ESRB, ACER, the NCAs supervising CCPs which access the trade repository, the NCAs supervising the trading venues of the reported contracts, relevant members of the ESCB, relevant EU securities and markets authorities, and relevant authorities of third countries which have entered into information exchange arrangements with the EU (Arts 75, 76, and 77)) have direct and immediate access to the details of derivatives contracts which they need to fulfil their responsibilities.

[598] 2012 EMIR rec 42, which notes that the trade repository business could take the form of a natural monopoly and that access rules were accordingly necessary.

[599] The difficulties led the IOSCO Chair to call for a new global watchdog with binding powers and competent to resolve disputes between regulators internationally: Jones, H, 'Global Watchdog Says New Body with Teeth Needed to Police Markets' Reuters, 5 November 2013.

[600] EMIR underlines that the Commission should co-operate with third countries to explore 'mutually supportive solutions to ensure consistency' between EMIR and third country requirements: EMIR rec 6.

the Commission was engaged[601]) in order to reflect and preserve the global nature of the OTC derivatives market and to ensure the 'global compatibility' of the EU regime.[602] In another example, the development of the BTSs on the margin and capital requirements to be adopted as risk mitigation mechanisms for non-CCP cleared OTC derivatives (Article 11(3) and (4)) was postponed pending international agreement on the standards to be applied. Similarly, the postponement of the adoption of BTSs on how EMIR would apply in relation to OTC contracts with a 'direct, substantial and foreseeable effect' within the EU (Article 4(1)) reflected the concern to take into account ongoing discussion with third country authorities on the cross-border application of their rules.[603] At the legislative level, particular EMIR provisions also reflect a concern to support global convergence; the decision not to exempt non-financial counterparties fully, for example, was in part driven by the earlier decision by the US not to exempt these actors fully.[604]

Conversely, EMIR negotiations were complicated by US efforts to shape EMIR to the US 2010 Dodd-Frank Act model,[605] reflecting the reality that international co-ordination of OTC derivatives market reforms has proved to be slow and elusive.[606] Overall, the adoption of national rules more stringent than those contained in relevant international standards, 'first mover' and competitive dynamics, and time-lags between the development of the different regimes internationally have all complicated convergence. Above all, the extraterritorial reach of the new CCP clearing regimes proved problematic globally,[607] as it became clear that market actors could become subject to duplicative regimes and be exposed to related costs and legal uncertainties.[608] Particular difficulties arose in relation to the extent of the CCP clearing obligation and with respect to whether jurisdictions required national registration and regulation of actors operating in the cross-border OTC derivatives markets, or relied on recognition and/or equivalence (or 'substitute compliance') mechanisms to, in effect, dis-apply national rules and allow reliance on the relevant third country regime. Difficulties also arose in relation to risk mitigation standards for non-CCP-cleared transactions, in particular in relation to the quality and quantity of margin.[609] A November 2012 meeting of the major international regulators involved sought to generate some degree

---

[601] It had, eg, observer status at the CPSS-IOSCO discussions: 2010 EMIR Proposal Impact Assessment, n 351, 9.

[602] 2012 ESMA EMIR Draft BTS Report, n 445, 7. Similarly, Commission Delegated Regulation 149/2013, 'in view of the global nature of the OTC derivatives market', takes into account globally agreed guidelines and recommendations in order to support convergence: rec 2.

[603] ESMA Chairman Maijoor Speech, 27 March 2013, n 470.

[604] 2010 EMIR Proposal, n 365, 7.

[605] Grant, J and Braithwaite, T, 'Geithner Urges EU to Fall in Line with Derivatives Rules', *Financial Times*, 9 June 2011, 12, reporting on the ratcheting up of EU/US tensions which followed Secretary Geithner's urging of the EU to follow the US approach.

[606] The FSB's first monitoring report on OTC derivatives market reforms warned of significant variation internationally in the pace of reform, and of significant divergences already emerging in national regimes: FSB, OTC Derivatives Market Reforms. Progress Report on Implementation. April 2011.

[607] eg International Centre for Financial Regulation, OTC Derivatives Regulation. Regulatory Briefing. July 2012, 2.

[608] See, eg, Valiente, D, Shaping Reforms and Business Models for the OTC Derivatives Markets: Quo Vadis? ECMI Research Report No 5 (2010).

[609] US Treasury Secretary Geithner's 2011 call for tougher margin requirements generated some concern internationally, particularly from major banks: Braithwaite, T and Tait, N, 'Geithner Warns on Light-touch Oversight', *Financial Times*, 7 June 2011, 1.

of consensus.[610] Despite the November 2012 efforts, significant international tensions were generated by the registration-based approach adopted by the US in relation to derivatives activities by financial counterparties,[611] which led to a co-ordinated call in April 2013 for a more facilitative, equivalence/substitute-compliance-based model,[612] a subsequent warning from the G20 for the reforms to be adopted by summer 2013, and some progress.[613] While further progress was made,[614] the difficulties remained considerable [615] and were acknowledged during the 2013/14 negotiations on the EU–US Transatlantic Trade and Investment Partnership.[616] Agreement was finally reached by the EU and US in February 2014.[617]

The EU's approach has been to apply EMIR expansively, particularly with respect to CCPs and trade repositories, but to support international access through equivalence-based and other mitigation-related mechanisms. The intensity of the EMIR regime, however, has led to the equivalence assessment becoming a lightning rod for tensions related to EMIR's application.

---

[610] In November 2012, the major regulators internationally with responsibility for the regulation of the OTC derivatives markets (in Australia, Brazil, the EU, Hong Kong, Japan, Ontario, Quebec, Singapore, Switzerland, and the US) reached a 'common understanding' as to the potential conflicts, inconsistencies, and duplicative requirements within the new rulebooks internationally, and identified the areas in which further consultation between regulators was required on how divergences could be addressed (the clearing determination; information-sharing and supervisory and enforcement co-ordination; timing of reforms; and scope of application of reforms and reliance on recognition or substitute compliance techniques in the cross-border market): Press Statement on Operating Principles and Areas of Exploration in the Regulation of the Cross-Border OTC Derivatives Market, 28 November 2012.

[611] Particular difficulties arose in relation to the US registration requirement for foreign entities other than CCPs, such as swap dealers. Tensions arising from the perception that the US sought to control the global rulebook on OTC derivatives and to impose its regulatory vision on global markets were a feature of the OTC reform programme from an early stage. Difficulties were compounded by the 'first mover' status of the US, which had acted very early in the OTC derivatives field with the 2010 Dodd-Frank Act, and then pushed other jurisdictions to follow its approach: eg, Braithwaite, T, Masters, B, and Tait, N, 'Global Strains in Push to Regulate Derivatives', *Financial Times*, 8 July 2011, 6.

[612] On 18 April 2013 the finance ministers of a number of leading economies (Brazil, France, Germany, Japan, Russia, South Africa, and Switzerland) and Internal Market Commissioner Barnier wrote to the US Treasury Secretary and the main US authorities (including the SEC and the Commodities Futures Trading Commission (CFTC)) highlighting the dangers of fragmentation, and calling for a substitute-compliance-based approach.

[613] The US SEC ultimately adopted a 'substitute compliance' model with respect to cross-border swap transactions, based on foreign requirements substituting for US requirements where they were deemed to be comparable, and on the SEC examining comparability on the basis of outcomes, not rule-by-rule comparisons: SEC Release 2013–77 and SEC, Fact Sheet—Cross-Border Security-Based Swap Activities. Globally, the OTC Derivatives Regulators Group produced a report in September 2013 on 'agreed understandings', designed to assist the resolution of cross-border conflicts, inconsistencies, and gaps. The September 2013 G20 Summit supported an outcome-based approach, declaring that jurisdictions should defer to each other when justified by the quality of regulatory and enforcement regimes, based on similar outcomes, in a non-discriminatory way, paying due respect to home country regulation: St Petersburg G20 Summit, September 2013, Leaders' Declaration para 71.

[614] Agreement on a 'path forward' was reached between the EU and the US CFTC on the treatment of cross-border derivatives trading in July 2013, based on equivalence-type mechanisms.

[615] US-EU Financial Markets Regulatory Dialogue, 20 January 2014, Joint Statement.

[616] The EU's January 2014 negotiating position on financial services noted that the process leading to the July 2013 agreement with the US CFTC was 'far from optimal': EU-US Transatlantic Trade and Investment Partnership, Co-operation on Financial Services Regulation, 27 January 2014. The EU's position remains based on 'outcomes-based' equivalence (at 3).

[617] The Commission/CFTC deal included agreement that EU trading venues trading derivatives would be exempt from US requirements until the MiFID II/MiFIR regime came into force: Stafford, P and Chon, G, 'Watchdogs Reach Deal on OTC Derivatives Rules', *Financial Times*, 13 February 2013, 15.

As outlined in section 4.2.4, the clearing, reporting, and risk mitigation rules apply where one party to a derivative contract is established outside the EU, and can apply where both parties are established outside the EU; there is accordingly significant potential for extra-territorial overreach, and for costs and uncertainty risks relating to duplicating and conflicting rules. A remedial mechanism is contained in Article 13 which empowers the Commission to adopt an equivalence decision providing that a third country's legal, supervisory, and enforcement arrangements are equivalent to Articles 4 (clearing), 9 (reporting), 10 (application to non-financial counterparties), and 11 (risk mitigation), and are being effectively applied and enforced in an equitable and non-distortive manner so as to ensure effective supervision and enforcement in that third country. Where such a determination has been made by the Commission, the counterparties to the transactions are deemed to have fulfilled the requirements as long as at least one of the counterparties is established in the third country.[618]

Equivalence mechanisms also govern EMIR's third country access regime. Third country CCPs which seek access to the EU market are not subject to EMIR directly, but must meet EMIR's equivalence requirements which apply through the ESMA 'recognition' mechanism; the sensitivity of the CCP access rules is implicit in EMIR's concession that recognition is not required where a third country CCP provides services to EU-established clients through a clearing member established in a third country.[619] Otherwise, CCPs established in a third country may provide clearing services to clearing members or to trading venues established in the EU only where the CCP is recognized by ESMA (Article 25). The credit rating agency regime's third country recognition model has, accordingly, been transplanted to the CCP sphere, albeit with the significant difference that, by contrast with the supervision of rating agencies, NCAs remain responsible for CCP supervision. ESMA's power in this area, given the centrality of CCPs to financial stability, was contested over the negotiations; early versions conferred third country CCP recognition on NCAs. It was only transferred to ESMA after significant industry opposition based on the potential for divergences across the Member States, and related costs and barriers to international access.[620]

ESMA may recognize a CCP (which has applied for recognition) when a series of equivalence-, market access/reciprocity-, and co-operation-based conditions are met (Article 25(2)).[621] Central to the recognition regime is the equivalence determination. The Commission must have adopted an equivalence decision determining that the legal and supervisory arrangements of the third country ensure that CCPs authorized in that country comply with legally binding requirements equivalent to EMIR's CCP requirements[622] and are subject to effective supervision and enforcement, and that the third country's legal

---

[618] The equivalence concession is subject to annual review and may be withdrawn: Art 13(4).

[619] 2012 EMIR rec 59.

[620] Herbert Smith, n 385, 3.

[621] In order to facilitate applications, ESMA has adopted Practical Guidance for the Recognition of Third Country CCPs by ESMA (March 2013).

[622] This requirement is designed to ensure that the third country regime provides for an effective equivalent system, in accordance with the G20 goals and standards for improving transparency in the derivatives market, mitigating systemic risk, and protecting against market abuse: 2012 EMIR rec 7.

system provides for an effective, equivalent system for the recognition of CCPs authorized under other third country legal regimes.[623]

The particular CCP must also be authorized in the relevant third country and, in ESMA's judgment, must be subject to effective supervision and enforcement, ensuring full compliance with the third country's prudential requirements;[624] an attenuated form of equivalence assessment is accordingly required of ESMA[625] which is additional to the full third country equivalence assessment carried out by the Commission and which has, accordingly, generated some market concern.[626] Appropriate co-operation arrangements must also have been established.[627] Finally, the third country must be considered as having equivalent systems for anti-money-laundering action and combating the financing of terrorism to the EU.

Mirroring the CCP authorization regime, which requires extensive pan-EU co-ordination before an authorization decision is made, ESMA must consult with a range of authorities before the recognition decision is made (Article 25(3));[628] ESMA is not, however, subject to veto by other authorities or required to explain where its recognition decision is not in accordance with the views of those consulted. The pan-EU oversight of the third country CCP rests with ESMA.

The trade repository regime for third countries is also governed by ESMA; a trade repository established in a third country may provide services and activities to entities established in the EU only after it has been recognized by ESMA (Article 77(1)). Recognition is conditional on the trade repository submitting to ESMA all the necessary information, including at least the information necessary to verify that the trade repository is authorized and subject to effective supervision in a third country which has been recognized by the Commission as having an equivalent and enforceable regulatory and

---

[623] Art 25(2) and 25(6).

[624] 2013 Commission Delegated Regulation 153/2013 sets out the detailed information requirements which the third country CCP must meet and which support the ESMA assessment.

[625] ESMA's assessment is designed to review the implementation of third country rules in practice, and to ensure that the third country CCP does not disrupt the orderly functioning of EU markets, does not have a competitive advantage compared with authorized CCPs, and will guarantee investor protection: 2012 ESMA EMIR Draft BTS Report, n 445, 29.

[626] While some CCPs supported the equivalence decision being entirely led by ESMA, rather than the Commission, others called for ESMA to rely on the Commission's assessment and for the information-related requirements supporting ESMA's assessment to be dropped: 2012 ESMA EMIR Draft BTS Report, n 445, 29.

[627] The co-operation arrangements must address: information-exchange mechanisms (between ESMA and third country competent authorities); ESMA notification mechanisms where authorization conditions are breached; ESMA notification mechanisms where a CCP has been granted the right to provide clearing services to clearing members or clients established in the EU; and procedures governing the co-ordination of supervisory activities, including on-site inspections: Art 25(7).

[628] ESMA must consult with: the NCA of the Member State in which the CCP provides or intends to provide clearing services and which has been selected by the CCP; the NCAs responsible for the supervision of the clearing members (subject to the threshold requirements related to the CCP default fund which also govern the composition of EU CCP colleges); the NCAs responsible for the supervision of the EU trading venues served or to be served by the CCP; the NCAs supervising CCPs established in the EU with which interoperability arrangements have been established; the relevant members of the ESCB; and the central banks of issue of the most relevant EU currencies of the financial instruments cleared or to be cleared: Art 25(3).

supervisory framework (Article 77(2)). The Commission's equivalence decision must positively determine that the legal and supervisory arrangements of the third country ensure that trade repositories authorized in that country comply with legally binding arrangements equivalent to those under EMIR, that effective supervision and enforcement of trade repositories takes place in the third country, and that guarantees of professional secrecy are in place. Reflecting concern as to adequacy of access to trade repository data internationally, the third country must also have entered into an international agreement with the EU which (Articles 77(2) and 75(2)) governs mutual access to and exchange of information on derivative contracts held in trade repositories established in the third country, and which ensures that the EU authorities, including ESMA, have immediate and continuous access to all the information needed for the exercise of their duties. Finally, recognition is conditional on the third country having entered into a co-operation arrangement which ensures that EU authorities, including ESMA, have immediate and continuous access to all necessary information and which governs, at least, information exchange and procedures concerning the co-ordination of supervisory activities (Articles 77(2) and 75(3)). The concern to ensure access to trade repository data internationally is also evident in the Article 76 co-operation mechanism, which provides that where the relevant authorities in a third country do not have any trade repositories established in their jurisdiction (and so fall outside the Articles 75 and 77 co-operation arrangements), they may contact ESMA with a view to establishing co-operation arrangements with ESMA regarding access to information held in EU trade repositories.

Equivalence is accordingly the means by which the reach of EMIR internationally is determined. ESMA, which was charged with providing the Commission with an assessment of the equivalence of relevant third countries, has described its approach as outcome- rather than rules-based, and highlighted its concern to adopt solutions which avoid potential market disruptions. It has proved to be robust in its approach.[629]

---

[629] ESMA Chairman Maijoor, Speech on 'EMIR: A Fair Price for Safety and Transparency', 27 March 2013 (ESMA/2013/428). ESMA's equivalence assessment of the US, eg, described its approach as being objective-based, holistic, and factual, and as taking into account the consequences for the stability and protection of EU entities and investors (ESMA/2013/1157, 5).

In September and October 2013, eg, ESMA delivered a series of lengthy advice reports to the Commission on the equivalence of a number of countries (Australia, Canada, India, Japan, Hong Kong, Singapore, South Korea, Switzerland, and the US) with respect to different aspects of EMIR (with respect to the equivalence of regulatory regimes governing CCPs (all States) and trade repositories (Australia, Hong Kong, the US, and Singapore), and with respect to duplicative or conflicting rules (Australia, Canada, Hong Kong, Japan, the US, and Singapore)). The advice was extensive and tailored to the different regimes and the different elements (including supervision and enforcement) considered. ESMA tended, overall, to adopt a finding of 'conditional equivalence' with respect to regulation in most cases. Conditional equivalence implies that the third country rules were not equivalent, but that the gaps could be addressed by means of internal policies and procedures by the actors in question which addressed the gaps, as long as the internal policies and procedures could not be changed without local regulatory approval and any departures from the policies and procedures would lead to enforcement action. ESMA tended to find, however, that relevant actors were subject to equivalent supervision and enforcement. For a review see Clifford Chance, ESMA Advises European Commission on Equivalence of non-EU Clearing and Derivative Rules. October 2013. ESMA's careful approach to equivalence reflects its concern to avoid a 'zero-sum' approach to equivalence, where equivalence is assessed as either being met or not: ESMA Chairman Maijoor, Speech on 'International co-ordination of the regulation and supervision of OTC derivatives markets', 17 October 2013 (ESMA/2013/1485).

VI.4.2.14 ESMA and the 2012 EMIR

ESMA has had, and will have, a determinative influence on the 2012 EMIR rulebook, on the nature of CCP clearing in the EU, and on the regulation and supervision of the new clearing environment; EMIR engages all of ESMA's major powers, whether with respect to BTS development, direct supervision, mediation between NCAs, the support of supervisory convergence, college co-ordination, or international co-ordination and engagement.

EMIR represented the first major test of ESMA's capacity for delivering complex technical standards, and for related engagement with the industry, EU institutions, and international bodies; while the 2011 AIFMD regime imposed similar demands, the Commission retained significantly greater control, reflecting the reliance on administrative rules, rather than on BTSs, for the construction of the AIFMD rulebook. While it sustained some bruises over the EMIR BTS process (section 4.2.3), overall ESMA emerged from the EMIR BTS process as a robust but pragmatic standard-setter, able to manage complex institutional dynamics within the EU and to engage with highly technical rule-making. ESMA has been conferred with specific powers in relation to the future development of the EMIR rulebook, notably in relation to the pension exemption (Article 85), but its determination to continue to shape the EMIR rulebook through own-initiative guidance and Q&As in support of supervisory convergence also suggests a considerable commitment to retaining some control over the EMIR rulebook.

EMIR has also conferred on ESMA highly significant powers in relation to the future shape of OTC derivatives clearing in the EU. It is charged with the determination of the derivatives subject to clearing, whether through the 'bottom-up' or 'top-down' procedure (Article 5). Although non-voting, it plays a key role in CCP supervisory colleges—particularly where conflicts arise between the home NCA and the college in relation to the authorization of a CCP (Articles 17–19).[630] It is charged with the recognition of third country CCPs (Article 25) and the supervision of EU trade repositories (and with related enforcement responsibilities where rules are breached) (Articles 55–74) and the recognition of third country trade repositories (Articles 75 and 77). It will also sit at the centre of a web of information on the OTC derivatives market in the EU, including by means of the data collection required for the new public register (Article 6), the notifications which must be made to ESMA in relation to reliance on the intra-group exemption (Article 11(11)), its access rights in relation to trade repositories (Article 81(3)), and its obligation to receive Article 9 reports where a trade repository is not available (Article 9(3)).

ESMA's international responsibilities extend beyond its CCP and trade repository recognition role and include the adoption of related co-operation agreements with third countries (Article 25(7), CCPs; Article 75(3), trade repositories) and the establishment of co-operation arrangements concerning access to EU trade repository data with third countries which do not have trade repositories, in order to ease international access to OTC

---

[630] ESMA participates in the college (Art 18(2)); facilitates in the adoption of the college opinion required on the authorization of a CCP (Art 19(2)); where a two-thirds majority of a college refuses to adopt a positive opinion relating to the authorization of a CCP, any college member within that majority can request ESMA mediation (Art 17(4)); where the college unanimously (save for the CCP's NCA) agrees that the CCP not be authorized, the CCP's NCA may request mediation by ESMA (Art 17(5)); and where the CCP's NCA has not acted in accordance with EMIR, ESMA may take enforcement action (in accordance with ESMA Regulation Art 17) (Art 17(6)).

derivatives market data (Article 76). It has also played a key role in negotiations with international authorities on the extraterritorial application of the EU regime internationally and on third country market access by EU market participants.[631]

EMIR may accordingly significantly enhance ESMA's capacity as a financial market regulator; however, it also poses material challenges to ESMA. Certain of its powers, notably the determination of the scope of the clearing obligation, will have significant market impact and are likely to strengthen ESMA's capacity. But ESMA's highly sensitive role in CCP colleges, given the background fiscal risks, and particularly given tensions between the euro area and the wider internal market—which are unlikely to dissipate as Banking Union develops—will expose the extent to which it can build consensus between NCAs in potentially highly sensitive situations; it will likely have wider ramifications in terms of a consequent strengthening (or weakening) of ESMA's role vis-à-vis its constituent NCAs. Relations with the Commission are also delicate, given the reach and sensitivity of the EMIR legislative regime; certainly, the autumn 2013 disagreement between ESMA and the Commission on the application of the Article 9 reporting regime suggests some tensions between the Commission and ESMA with respect to ESMA's BTS powers.[632] Overall, the nature of ESMA's engagement with EMIR may become a useful bellwether for its future development.

VI.4.3 Derivatives Trading on Organized Venues: 2014 MiFIR

As noted in Chapter V, regulators have long outsourced elements of financial market regulation to major trading venues.[633] But a more ambitious approach to trading venues developed over the crisis era; trading venues were pressed into action as devices for managing the gaps which arise when financial innovation moves ahead of market infrastructure. This policy agenda is particularly marked with respect to OTC derivatives.

The G20 crisis-era reform agenda for OTC derivatives includes, in addition to the CCP clearing reform, a commitment that trading of standardized OTC derivatives move to 'exchanges' or 'electronic trading platforms';[634] like the CCP clearing reform, it is being supported internationally by the FSB and IOSCO.[635] Also like the CCP clearing reform, the trading venue reform has radical market-shaping effects, as most derivatives have typically traded OTC, given their customized quality and the related thin liquidity and limited secondary market trading.[636] The trading venue reform is designed to operate in parallel with the CCP clearing reform and to move trading in standardized derivatives, which are sufficiently liquid to support organized venue-based trading, to trading venues

---

[631] This has particularly been the case in relation to negotiations with the US: eg ESMA Annual Report (2011) 64, reporting on the 'intensive dialogue' in which ESMA engaged internationally.

[632] Sect 4.2.3.

[633] eg Mahoney, P, 'The Exchange as Regulator' (1997) 83 *Va LR* 1453 and Brummer, C, 'Stock Exchanges and the New Markets for Securities Law' (2008) 75 *University of Chicago LR* 1435.

[634] Pittsburgh G20 Summit, September 2009, Leaders' Statement.

[635] eg IOSCO, Report on Trading of OTC Derivatives (2011) and FSB, n 392, 39–43.

[636] In December 2009, some 89 per cent of derivatives were traded OTC (in that trades took place between two contracting parties without an intermediary trading platform). In June 2010, 68.9 per cent of interest rate derivatives were traded bilaterally, 62.6 per cent of credit derivatives, and 82.9 per cent of equity derivatives: IOSCO, n 635, 6.

which are embedded within wider regulatory regimes governing their stability and efficiency. Greater transparency, ease of regulatory monitoring, operational and risk-management efficiencies, and liquidity enhancements should accordingly follow.[637] Mandatory
venue trading should also generate competition between organized venues and reduce
spreads. Like the CCP clearing reform, this reform is targeted to particular OTC derivatives; it applies only to those derivatives which can be safely traded on organized venues.
The reform is accordingly characterized by the imposition of conditions on the classes of
derivatives which are subject to the trading venue obligation (predominantly related to the
degree of standardization and liquidity levels).[638] But the case for mandatory trading is not
as straightforward (in relative terms) as the case for mandatory CCP clearing. OTC
derivatives trading provides an important function given the generally thin liquidity in
derivatives trading markets, and can be regarded as complementary to organized venue
trading.[639]

In the EU, this major reform has proved relatively uncontroversial,[640] although it was
resisted by the industry.[641] The regulatory supports for the reform are set out in the 2014
MiFIR (Articles 28–34) and are based on the regulatory technology developed for the 2012
EMIR; the MiFID II/MiFIR regime is designed to be closely aligned with EMIR. The
trading obligation is also closely related to the wider MiFID II/MiFIR trading venue
reforms. In particular, the new MiFID II/MiFIR OTF classification is largely designed to
provide a regulatory classification and framework for the very wide range of trading venues
on which derivatives have previously traded,[642] to ensure that organized trading venues for
derivatives trading meet appropriate standards,[643] and to respond to the particular risks
which trading venue regulation poses given the structure of trading in derivatives, and
particularly the reliance on dealers (see further Chapter V sections 6.4 and 9 on the OTF).

The new trading venue obligation applies to 2012 EMIR financial counterparties, as well as
the non-financial counterparties which come within the scope of EMIR (under EMIR
Article 10(1)(b)). These parties must conclude transactions (which do not qualify for the
EMIR intra-group transactions exemption, or for transitional exemptions from EMIR)

---

[637] FSB, n 392, 39–43.

[638] eg CESR's advice to the Commission, at the outset of the trading venue reform process, underlined that
standardization (based on legal, process, and product uniformity) was essential, and that traded products must
be sufficiently liquid: CESR, Technical Advice to the Commission on Standardization and Organized
Platform Trading of OTC Derivatives (2010) (CESR/10-1096).

[639] The FSB suggested that OTC and organized trading models responded to different needs and that
complementary models could co-exist: n 392, 43.

[640] Although the Council negotiations on the trading venue aspects of MiFID II/MiFIR were difficult, the
derivatives trading requirements were relatively straightforward: Danish Presidency MiFID II/MiFIR Progress
Report, n 85.

[641] The UK, the major market for OTC derivatives trading, was supportive, as were most Member States
and trading venue operators; market participants, by contrast, were concerned as to a potential reduction in
liquidity, increased costs, and restrictions on their ability to trade customized contracts: 2011 MiFID II/
MiFIR Proposals Impact Assessment, n 59, 36. The industry generally preferred an incentive-based model to a
mandatory trading obligation: 2010 CESR Technical Advice, n 638.

[642] Derivatives trading takes place on a spectrum which extends from full-scale, organized multilateral
trading, to bespoke and entirely bilateral trading, and in the middle of which sits a host of different, typically
dealer-based, trading platforms, which are organized as venues to varying degrees: FSB, n 392, 39.

[643] Benchmarks relating to market access and transparency, trading rules, operational efficiency and
resilience, market surveillance, organizational structure, and public supervision were set out in the 2011
IOSCO Report: n 635, 10–13.

with other financial counterparties or with non-financial counterparties, in relation to a class of derivatives that has been declared to be subject to the trading obligation (and listed in the required ESMA register of such derivatives), only on regulated markets, MTFs, and OTFs (together, MiFIR/MiFID II trading venues) or on third country trading venues, as long as the Commission has made an equivalence determination in relation to the third country (governed by Article 28(4)),[644] and as long as that third country provides for an effective equivalent system for the recognition of trading venues authorized under MiFID II to admit to trading or trade derivatives declared subject to the trading obligation in that third country on a non-exclusive basis (Article 28(1) (discussed further later in this section).

Derivatives can therefore be traded on a very wide range of trading venues, and different market structures can be accommodated. The 2014 MiFID II/MiFIR OTF venue, in particular, is designed to accommodate the distinctive nature of derivatives trading, which is typically thin in the secondary markets, and which often takes place on venues operating under a discretionary, dealer-driven quote model. Derivatives trading venues are also highly sensitive to transparency requirements; dealers provide liquidity to the market and take on related capital risk, but need to protect their proprietary positions as a result. As discussed in Chapter V, calibrated operational requirements (with respect to the exercise of discretion in the OTF) and transparency requirements (in relation to non-equity asset classes) apply as a result to mitigate the risks from the new regulatory regime that are faced by derivatives trading platforms.

As is the case for the determination of the derivatives subject to the 2012 EMIR CCP clearing obligation, the critical determination of the classes subject to the trading venue obligation is to be made by ESMA. Also similarly, the ESMA determination has a 'bottom-up' dimension, being based in part on whether the derivatives are already admitted to trading. The procedure for determining which classes of derivative are subject to the trading obligation (Article 32) is based on ESMA developing draft RTSs to determine which of the classes of derivatives (subject to the EMIR CCP clearing obligation), or a relevant subset thereof, is to be traded on 2014 MiFIR/MiFID II trading venues, and the date from which the obligation is to take effect (including any phase-in arrangements) (Article 32(1)).[645] ESMA is required to conduct a public consultation and, where appropriate, may consult with third country authorities before submitting draft RTSs to the Commission.

For the obligation to take effect, two liquidity-related conditions apply: the class of derivatives (or a relevant subset thereof) must be admitted to trading or traded on at least one 2014 MiFIR/MiFID II trading venue, and there must be sufficient third party buying-and-selling interest in the class of derivatives (or subset) so that the class of derivatives is considered 'sufficiently liquid' to trade on these venues (Article 32(2)). A class will be determined as 'sufficiently liquid' by reference to the average frequency and size of trades over a range of market conditions, having regard to the nature and life cycle of products within the class, the number and type of active market participants (including the ratio of market participants to products/contracts traded in a given product

---

[644] The Commission's decision can be limited to a category(ies) of trading venues.

[645] As under EMIR, ESMA must maintain a register on its website of the derivatives subject to the trading obligation, the venues where they are admitted to trading, and the dates from which the obligation takes effect: Art 34.

market), and the average size of spreads (Article 32(3)).[646] ESMA is also to determine whether the class of derivatives (or subset thereof) is only 'sufficiently liquid' in transactions below a certain size. New RTSs are to be adopted whenever there is a material change in the criteria governing the application of the trading obligation (Article 32(5)).

A 'top-down' procedure also applies. ESMA (on its own initiative) is to identify and notify the Commission of the classes of derivatives or individual derivative contracts that should be subject to the trading obligation but for which no CCP has been authorized, or which have not been admitted to trading or traded on a 2014 MiFID II/MiFIR venue (Article 32(4)). The Commission may then publish a call for the development of proposals for the trading of these derivatives on MiFID II/MiFIR venues.

Derivatives subject to the trading obligation must be eligible to be admitted to trading or to trade on any 2014 MiFIR/MiFID I trading venue on a non-exclusive and non-discriminatory basis (Article 28(3)).

ESMA is to regularly monitor activity in derivatives which have not been declared subject to the trading obligation in order to identify cases where a particular class of contracts may cause systemic risk and to prevent regulatory arbitrage (Article 28(2)).

Organized venue-traded derivatives become subject to the panoply of rules which apply to instruments traded on 2014 MiFID II/MiFIR venues generally, and which now include the new transparency requirements (Chapter V section 11), as well as the new position management and reporting requirements which apply to venue-traded commodity derivatives (section 2.5). But the risk-management techniques employed to manage the risks of derivative positions have required that these requirements be calibrated. In particular, MiFIR calibrates the trading regime to reflect the portfolio compression risk management technique (Article 31). Portfolio compression involves two or more counterparties wholly or partially terminating some or all of the derivatives submitted by the counterparties for inclusion in the portfolio compression and replacing the terminated derivatives with another derivative, whose combined notional value is less than the combined notional value of the terminated derivatives (Article 2(1)(47)). Where investment firms provide portfolio compression, they are not subject to best execution or the MiFIR transparency requirements, the termination or replacement of component derivatives in the compression is not subject to the trading venue obligation, and the MiFID II position management regime does not apply. Firms must, however, make public the volumes of transactions subject to portfolio compression (and the time they were concluded) and keep accurate records of all portfolio compressions, which must be made available promptly to the relevant NCA or ESMA on request.

The 2014 MiFIR trading venue obligation is tied to the 2012 EMIR CCP clearing obligation (only derivatives subject to the CCP clearing obligation come within the obligation). Accordingly, in parallel, a CCP clearing obligation applies in relation to

---

[646] In developing the RTSs which identify the classes of derivatives subject to the trading obligation, ESMA must make the 'sufficiently liquid' determination in accordance with these criteria, and also take into consideration the anticipated impact of the trading obligation on the liquidity of a class of derivatives (or subset) and the commercial activities of end users which are not financial entities. RTSs are also to be adopted governing the criteria for assessing 'sufficiently liquid': Art 32(6).

transactions in derivatives concluded on a regulated market (which are not subject to EMIR):[647] the operator of a regulated market must ensure that all such transactions are cleared by a CCP (Article 29(1)).

In a related obligation, CCPs, trading venues, and investment firms which act as clearing members under the 2012 EMIR must have in place effective systems, procedures, and arrangements in relation to cleared derivatives to ensure that transactions in cleared derivatives[648] are submitted and accepted for clearing as quickly as is technologically practical using automated systems; the conditions governing these systems will be specified in RTSs (Article 29(2)). Indirect clearing is permissible, as long as these arrangements do not increase counterparty risk and ensure the assets and positions of the counterparty benefit from protections with equivalent effect to the relevant EMIR protection (Article 30).[649]

Like the 2012 EMIR CCP clearing obligation, the trading venue obligation has wide extraterritorial effects across a number of dimensions, reflecting the global nature of derivatives trading. The trading obligation applies to counterparties transacting in a class of derivatives subject to the trading obligation with third country financial institutions or other entities that would be subject to the EMIR clearing obligation were they established in the EU; similarly, the trading obligation applies to transactions between two such third country institutions or entities, although, as under EMIR, the trading obligation only applies where the contract has a direct, substantial, and foreseeable effect within the EU, or where such an obligation is necessary or appropriate to prevent the evasion of MiFIR (Article 28(2)).[650]

The trading obligation can be met by trading on non-EU venues, as long as the stringent equivalence requirement is met (Article 28(1)(d)); the combination of the equivalence assessment and the trading obligation has accordingly allowed the EU to export its regulatory approach to trading venues. The equivalence determination is conditional on the Commission finding that the legal and supervisory framework of the third country in question ensures that a trading venue authorized in the third country complies with legally binding requirements which have equivalent effect to the 2014 MiFID II/MiFIR and the EU market abuse regime, and which are subject to effective supervision and enforcement in the third country (Article 28(4)).[651] A reciprocity obligation applies in that the third

---

[647] The 2012 EMIR obligation applies to all derivatives not traded on a regulated market, requiring the loop to be closed by means of a clearing obligation for derivatives trading on a regulated market.

[648] Derivatives subject to the EMIR clearing obligation or derivatives otherwise agreed by the relevant parties to be cleared: Art 29(2).

[649] Art 30(1). RTSs are to govern which types of indirect clearing arrangements comply with Art 30(1).

[650] RTSs are to specify the types of contracts which have the requisite effect in the EU and the cases where the trading obligation is necessary to avoid evasion: Art 28(5). These RTSs are to be identical to the related EMIR RTSs, where possible and appropriate.

[651] The legal and supervisory framework is considered to be equivalent where trading venues in the third country are subject to authorization and effective supervision and enforcement on an ongoing basis; trading venues have clear and transparent rules governing admission of financial instruments to trading so that such financial instruments are capable of being traded in a fair, orderly, and efficient manner and are freely negotiable; issuers of financial instruments are subject to periodic and ongoing information requirements, ensuring a high level of investor protection; and market transparency and integrity are ensured through rules which address market abuse. The stringency of the equivalence regime is mitigated by the mechanism (which also applies under EMIR) for the identification of duplicative and conflicting requirements (Art 33).

country must also provide an equivalent system for the recognition of MiFID II/MiFIR trading venues to admit to trading or trade derivatives subject to a trading obligation in that third country on a non-exclusive basis. The international reach of the obligation is also evident in the encouragement to ESMA to consult with third country authorities when identifying the classes of derivatives subject to the trading obligation (Article 32).

VI.5 The Financial Transaction Tax

VI.5.1 Evolution of the EU FTT

The anti-speculation agenda which can be traced through much of the EU's new trading regime is perhaps most apparent in the proposed FTT.[652] While not strictly part of EU securities and markets regulation, and forming instead part of the EU's taxation regime, it nonetheless has significant implications for trading in the EU. It shares with much of the new trading market regime a concern to dampen perceived excessive speculation and socially wasteful trading activities. The FTT regime has in particular been associated with curbing HFT and speculation in the sovereign debt markets. Accordingly, it has attracted similar political and institutional tensions as have attended the more highly contested elements of the new trading regime.

But tensions have been heightened in this area, and the institutional response has been complex, given the distinct treatment of taxation, as opposed to rule harmonization, under the EU Treaties. The Member States in Council can exercise a veto in relation to the FTT (the EU's competence to act in relation to the harmonization of indirect taxation is conferred under Article 113 TFEU which requires unanimous Council support). The Treaty context, in combination with diametrically opposed views in the Council, led to the FTT creating a significant breach in the internal market-wide nature of financial market governance. The Banking Union project has set the euro area 19 on a closer integration track with respect to financial system regulation than the internal market 28 (Chapter XI section 7). The FTT is exposing a second line of variable integration in that a small group of Member States will, if the FTT is adopted, become more closely integrated, using the Treaty's closer co-operation mechanism. As discussed in Chapter I, these developments represent a potentially epochal shift in the nature of EU financial market governance generally.

The roots of the FTT, in common use in different forms internationally,[653] go back to the 1970s and the oft-discussed Tobin Tax, which was designed to tax foreign exchange transactions and address excessive exchange rate fluctuation and speculation in currency flows. Over the period of the financial crisis, FTT-style taxes and bank levies were canvassed

---

[652] Generally, Cortez, B and Vogel, T, 'A Financial Transaction Tax for Europe' (2011) 20 *EC Tax Review*, 16.

[653] Typically in the form of an *ad valorem* tax on share trades (10–50 basis points): IMF Working Paper 111/54, Taxing Financial Transactions: Issues and Evidence (2011). Prepared by Thornton Matheson (2011 IMF FTT Report) 4.

as financial stability mechanisms and also as funding mechanisms; the Pittsburgh September 2009 G20 meeting, for example, called on the IMF to explore how the financial sector might contribute to the cost of financial system repair.

Bank levies to recover the cost of government rescues and to provide resolution funds are now common across the EU, with a number of Member States imposing some form of bank levy.[654] Co-ordination and arbitrage risks have led the EU institutions to consider the appropriateness of a pan-EU bank levy.[655] But an FTT is associated with much heavier policy lifting and has direct implications for trading. Similar to bank levies, an FTT is a means of yielding revenue from the financial market sector and addressing the costs of recent interventions.[656] It is also, however, associated with the curbing of activities which are perceived to be risky, of markets which are perceived to be excessively large, and of profits which are regarded as economic rents.[657] The design and implementation risks are considerable.[658] So too are the risks of market damage; FTTs have been linked with, *inter alia*, a reduction in trading volume and liquidity, an increase in spreads, and increases to issuers' cost of capital.[659] Competitiveness risks are acute in the absence of international co-ordination. Any crisis-era international enthusiasm for co-ordinated FTT action soon waned. The IMF's response to the Pittsburgh G20 meeting did not endorse FTTs, although it suggested that a profit/wage-related Financial Activities Tax might be used to raise revenue,[660] and the November 2011 Cannes G20 summit subsequently failed to support a global FTT.

VI.5.2 The Closer Co-operation Mechanism and the FTT

In the EU, the FTT question quickly became entwined with wider political tensions regarding the nature of financial market intervention and the extent to which financial markets should be constrained.

Initially the EU proceeded cautiously, although the political environment rapidly became febrile. As the FTT debate began to gather momentum in 2010, the European Council expressed cautious support for an FTT to be explored, but this was typically in the context of the EU 'leading the global debate'[661] rather than in relation to the merits of such a tax for the EU. The Council was similarly careful at the outset, being predominantly concerned with the co-ordination risks were Member States to adopt unilateral positions.[662] The

---

[654] Banks and investment firms will, eg, be required to contribute to resolution funds under the EU's new recovery and resolution regime: Ch IV sect 13.

[655] Commission, Consultation on Financial Sector Taxation (2011).

[656] 2011 IMF FTT Report, n 653.

[657] HM Treasury, Risk, Reward and Responsibility: The Financial Sector and Society (2009).

[658] Particularly with respect to the cascade effect of an FTT as it moves from the original transaction through clearing structures and on to ultimate investors, levying taxes and increasing costs along the chain: Clifford Chance, Financial Transaction Tax: Update (2011) 2.

[659] eg 2011 IMF FTT Report n 653, HM Treasury, n 657, and Honohan, P and Yoder, S, Financial Transaction Taxes: Panacea, Threat or Damp Squib, World Bank Policy Research WP No 5230 (2009), available at <http://ssrn.com/abstract=1505954>.

[660] IMF, A Fair and Substantial Contribution: A Framework for Taxation and Resolution to Improve Financial Stability. Draft Response to G20 (2010).

[661] European Council Conclusions, 24/25 March 2011 and 17 June 2010.

[662] eg 3030th Council Meeting, 7 September 2010, ECOFIN Press Release No 13161/10.

European Parliament, by contrast, robustly supported implementation of an FTT, adopting resolutions calling on the Commission to explore an FTT in 2010 and 2011 and associating an FTT with the curbing of excessive speculation and with burden-sharing by the financial sector.[663]

The FTT debate was brought to a head in September 2011 with the Commission's Proposal for an EU FTT to be adopted in 2014,[664] which followed a 2010 Consultation that had revealed very significant disagreement on the merits of a pan-EU FTT.[665] The widely cast Proposal, which immediately generated widespread industry hostility,[666] was designed to meet three objectives: to avoid fragmentation and arbitrage risks; to ensure that financial institutions made a fair contribution to the costs of the crisis (the Commission estimated the tax would yield revenues of up to €57 billion annually); and, with direct implications for trading, to ensure appropriate disincentives for transactions that do not enhance the efficiency of financial markets.[667] The new FTT was, accordingly, a complement to the crisis-era regulatory programme. Given the significant risks which taxes of this nature can pose, its design sought to avoid or mitigate the significant costs and risks (which the Impact Assessment had identified) in relation to economic growth generally and to market liquidity. The FTT was, for example, designed to apply broadly across a wide range of financial instruments and transactions, but the primary markets on which capital is raised were excluded from its scope. It provided for an FTT on all financial transactions (essentially transactions, broadly defined,[668] in 2014 MiFID II/MiFIR financial instruments—including shares, bonds, derivatives, money-market instruments, UCITS and alternative investment fund units, and structured products), regardless of whether the transaction took place OTC or on a regulated trading venue.[669] The territorial scope of application of the FTT was related to a residence principle, and it was to be levied on financial institutions; it applied where at least one party to the transaction was established in a Member State, and where a financial institution[670] established in a Member State was a party to the transaction (on its own account or for the account of another person), or was acting in the name of a party to the transaction. The major exclusions included primary market transactions, entity-specific exclusions,[671] and, by implication, most household and

---

[663] eg, European Parliament Resolution on 'Financial Transaction Taxes—Making Them Work', 10 March 2010 (T7-0056/2010).

[664] COM (2011) 594 (the 2011 FTT Proposal).

[665] The Commission described reaction to the Consultation as 'strongly polarized': Commission, Results and Survey Report on Consultation, COM (2010) 549 (2011).

[666] Chaffin, J, Pignal, S, and Grant, J, 'Business Lashes Out at Tobin Tax Plans', *Financial Times*, 29 September 2011, 1.

[667] 2011 FTT Proposal, n 664, 2–3.

[668] A financial transaction engaged either: the purchase and sale of a financial instrument, including repurchase and reverse repurchase and securities lending and borrowing agreements; the transfer between entities of a group of the right to dispose of a financial instrument as owner, and any equivalent operation implying the transfer of risk associated with the financial instrument; and the conclusion or modification of derivatives agreements: Art 2.

[669] Arts 1 and 2.

[670] Broadly, regulated entities such as investment firms, credit institutions, insurance undertakings, UCITSs, pension funds, securitization special purpose vehicles, as well as other actors carrying out nominated activities (including proprietary trading) where the activities constituted a significant part of its overall activity.

[671] Including CCPs and central securities depositaries (broadly as these entities were not considered to be engaged in trading activities and were considered as important in relation to the efficient functioning of financial markets).

business financial transactions, including those relating to insurance contracts, mortgage lending, consumer credit, and payment services, as well as currency market spot (non-derivative) transactions. The rate was to be set by the Member States, subject to a minimum of 0.1 per cent for non-derivative transactions and 0.01 per cent for derivative transactions.[672]

From the outset, and unsurprisingly, given the febrile environment which attended its development,[673] the prognosis for a pan-EU harmonized FTT was poor. Empirical studies on the design and potential impact of the FTT were often hostile, with respect to matters including: its likely inability to achieve its objectives; its failure to distinguish between speculative and productive market behaviour; its damaging behavioural and arbitrage-related effects, including in relation to a potential shift from long-term securities market investments to deposits; its potential prejudicial impact on short-term funding sources for banks and so on financial stability; its impact on firms not typically associated with speculative activity, such as pension funds and insurance undertakings, and the related costs to households; its design, including with respect to cascade effects arising from the application of the FTT repeatedly along the transaction chain; and its economic costs, including with respect to increases in the cost of capital (given the higher yield which would likely be demanded by investors to offset the FTT) and the potential movement of business offshore from the EU.[674] The scale of the opposition, and the strength of the empirical arguments, drew an unusual and additional suite of studies from the Commission in May 2012, which provided additional explanations of how the FTT would work in practice and which argued that its risks and costs were not of the magnitude suggested by the stakeholder response to the FTT.[675]

While France and Germany provided strong support from an early stage, and were associated with leading Council discussions and with pushing the EU to provide a global lead,[676] the UK was trenchantly opposed.[677] The proposed Treaty Financial Services Protocol, for example, which the UK had called for as part of its negotiating position during the December 2011 negotiations on the proposed European Stability Treaty, contained a commitment that any such tax be subject to a Member State veto, reflecting UK concern that the FTT, in principle subject to a Member State veto as a matter of taxation policy, could not be

---

[672] The effective rate of the FTT would have been higher in practice, as it was designed to be levied on each in-scope contracting party.

[673] The European Union Committee of the House of Lords in the UK noted the 'feverish atmosphere': House of Lords, European Union Committee, 29th Report of Session 2010–2012, Towards a Financial Transaction Tax (2012) (2012 HL FTT Report). The Report acknowledged the depth of public anger in relation to the financial sector, but warned that an FTT was not the way to proceed.

[674] eg DeNederlansche Bank, Bulletin. Financial Transaction Tax in the EU is Undesirable. 6 February (2012); EFAMA, Impact Assessment of the Commission's Proposal for a Council Directive on a Common System of Financial Transaction Tax (2012); and 2012 HL FTT Report, n 673. For a review of a series of studies on the 2011 Proposal and on FTTs generally see City of London Economic Development, A Financial Transaction Tax—Review of Impact Assessments (2012).

[675] The studies addressed, *inter alia*, territorial application; relocation; revenue estimates; macroeconomic effects; tax collection; and pension funds. The relocation study, eg, examined how the FTT could be applied in practice to minimize the risks of relocation.

[676] Barber, A, 'Britain Attacks Financial Tax as Support Wanes', *Financial Times*, 9 November 2011, 5.

[677] Chancellor George Osborne described the tax as a 'bullet aimed at the heart of London': Parker, G and Peel, Q, 'Germans Criticize UK over Tobin Tax', *Financial Times*, 16 November 2011, 1.

re-characterized as a 'user charge' and so be subject to a QMV.[678] Council negotiations over 2011–12 saw repeated clashes between Ireland, the Netherlands,[679] Sweden, and the UK, in particular, on the one hand, and the Member States in favour of the FTT, notably France,[680] Germany, and Spain, on the other.

As the FTT was proposed under Article 113 TFEU and in relation to the EU's taxation competence, the European Parliament was not a co-legislator in relation to the Proposal, but was consulted. It broadly supported the Commission's 2011 Proposal,[681] but recommended a more stringent approach and significantly extended the reach of the regime, adding an 'issuance principle' which would have required financial institutions located outside the FTT 'zone' to pay the FTT if they traded securities originally issued within the zone.[682] The strong anti-speculation mood in the Parliament which drove its FTT agenda was also evident in its suggestion that a lower rate apply in relation to transactions taking place on a 'stock exchange', rather than OTC. Presciently, it also suggested that the enhanced co-operation mechanism be deployed were it not possible for the Member States to reach agreement.

The Commission's Proposal was abandoned in June 2012 when it became clear that the unanimous Council vote required under Article 113 TFEU to adopt the Proposal could not be achieved; the June 2012 ECOFIN Council concluded that support was not forthcoming for the Commission's Proposal. By now, however, it was clear that a significant number of Member States wished to proceed under the Treaty 'enhanced co-operation' mechanism, although the Council warned that the formal requirements for enhanced co-operation must be met.[683]

Article 20 TEU and Articles 326–334 TFEU allow Member States to establish 'enhanced co-operation' between themselves within the framework of the EU's non-exclusive competences and to use the EU's institutions and competences to do so, as long as the related Treaty conditions are met. Under Article 20 TFEU, enhanced co-operation (which must aim to further the objectives of the EU, protect its interests, and reinforce its integration process) must first be approved by the Council 'as a last resort' and before the enhanced co-operation measure is adopted; acts adopted within the framework of enhanced co-operation apply only to the participating Member States (Article 20(1), (3), and (4) TEU). The Council (acting unanimously) may only authorize enhanced co-operation where it has established that the objectives of the co-operation cannot be attained within a reasonable period by the EU as a whole and where at least nine Member States participate in the arrangement (Article 20(2) TFEU). Additional conditions apply under Article 326–334 TFEU.[684] Following (as required under the Treaties) a request to the Commission from 11

---

[678] Barber, A and Parker, G, 'Cameron's Demands over Financial Regulation Spark French Resistance', *Financial Times*, 9 December 2011, 6.

[679] The Dutch finance minister was reported as describing the FTT as 'completely worthless': Barker, A and Grant, J, 'UK Fears Defeat on Regulation', *Financial Times*, 30 September 2011, 6.

[680] France adopted an FTT in February 2012. It is composed of three different types of FTT which apply to the acquisition of listed shares issued by large French companies, HFT, and CDSs on sovereign debt.

[681] Parliament Resolution on the FTT Proposal, 23 May 2012 (P7_TA-PROV(2012)0217).

[682] The ECON Committee gave the example of the FTT applying where Siemens shares, issued in Germany, were traded between a Hong Kong and US institution.

[683] 3178th Council Meeting, 22 June 2012, ECOFIN Press Release No 11682/12.

[684] Including in relation to the enhanced co-operation not undermining the internal market (Art 326 TFEU); respecting the competences, rights and obligations of non-participating Member States who must not

Member States to proceed in relation to the FTT through enhanced co-operation,[685] the Commission submitted a proposal for a Council Decision approving enhanced co-operation in October 2011, which proposal set out the Commission's assessment of the compliance of the proposed arrangement with the Treaty conditions.[686] The Commission, which highlighted that its preference was for a pan-EU FTT, concluded that enhanced co-operation on an FTT would support the EU's objectives and reinforce the integration process.

Following the European Parliament's consent (required under the Treaty procedures), the proposal for approval was adopted by the Council in January 2013.[687] A Commission proposal for an FTT under the enhanced co-operation mechanism (for 11 participating Member States) followed in February 2013.[688] The Proposal was, at the request of the participating Member States, heavily based on the original September 2011 model, including with respect to scope, the financial-institution-establishment connecting factor, and rates (it was accordingly not subject to a new Impact Assessment). It contained, nonetheless, a number of revisions—mainly designed to reflect the application of the FTT within the participating Member States' 'FTT zone',[689] but also to refine and extend the original FTT model through an issuance principle.[690]

---

impede implementation by participating Member States (Art 327 TFEU); the procedure for the adoption of an enhanced co-operation arrangement, including in relation to the approving Council decision (Arts 329–330 and 333 TFEU); and review and extension of the arrangement (Arts 328 and 331 TFEU).

[685] Austria, Belgium, Estonia, France, Germany, Greece, Italy, Portugal, Slovakia, Slovenia, and Spain: Commission, Enhanced Co-operation on Financial Transaction Tax—Q and A, 23 October 2012 (MEMO/12/799).

[686] COM (2012) 631. The Proposal set out the Commission's positive assessment that the required conditions had been fulfilled in relation to: the enhanced co-operation coming within an area covered by the Treaty (it related to Art 113 TFEU, was broad enough to represent an 'area' covered by the Treaties, and came within an area of shared competence); authorization by the Council representing 'last resort' action (the Commission noted the intensity of opposition in the Council and the preference of one Member State to vote against the Proposal at an early stage); furthering the objectives of the Union, protecting its interests, and reinforcing its integration process (the Commission, *inter alia*, noted the benefits an FTT would bring in terms of reducing distortions to competition, incentives to avoid taxation, and costs); compliance with the Treaties and EU law (the Commission found that enhanced co-operation would respect the EU *acquis* as long as the regime was in compliance with the EU prohibition on indirect taxation on primary market transactions); not undermining the internal market or economic, social, and territorial cohesion, and not representing a barrier to or discrimination in trade or a distortion of competition (the Commission found that all these conditions were met, referring to the benefits of an FTT among participating Member States); and respecting the rights, competences, and obligations of non-participating Member States (the Commission highlighted that the regime would not affect the possibility of non-participating States to adopt their own FTT, and that appropriate connecting factors would apply in relation to the enhanced co-operation FTT): at 4–8.

[687] Council Decision 2013/52/EU ([2013] OJ L22/11) and Parliament Resolution of 12 December 2012 (P7_TA_PROV(2012)0498). The FTT enhanced co-operation proposal is only the third of such arrangements to be launched: 23 January 2013, ECOFIN Press Release No 5555/13.

[688] COM (2013) 71.

[689] The Proposal provided, eg, that where the establishments potentially subject to the FTT were located in a territory of a non-participating Member State, the transaction was not subject to the FTT in a participating Member State, unless one of the parties to the transaction was established in a participating Member State, in which case the financial institution established in a non-participating Member State was deemed to be established in the participating Member State, where the transaction would become taxable: n 688, 10.

[690] In a controversial addition, the 2013 Proposal provided that where none of the parties to the transaction would have been established in a participating Member State (in the FTT zone), but where the parties were trading in a instrument issued in a participating Member State, the FTT would apply to the transaction; the parties to the transaction would be deemed to be established in the Member State of issuance. Where, however, no link existed between the economic substance of the transaction and the territory of the

The wide extraterritorial effect of the new FTT proposal, given in particular the impact of the issuance principle, in combination with the persistence of the features of the FTT which had earlier generated concern,[691] generated an avalanche of criticism. Financial and general industry opposition in the EU,[692] Member State concern outside the FTT zone (particularly in the UK,[693] which in April 2013 launched an unsuccessful challenge to the FTT before the European Court of Justice[694]) and international hostility[695] rapidly became intense, well exemplified by the communication from a group of leading international trade associations to the G20 expressing opposition to the tax.[696] The FTT continued, however, to be supported by the European Parliament,[697] although the ECB was more circumspect.[698] At the time of writing, the future of the FTT is uncertain. Support remains strong from France and Germany, however, and initial agreement was reached on a revised, scaled-back tax in May 2014.[699] But its troubled passage underlines the increasing stresses being placed on the single market (as discussed further in Chapter I).

---

participating Member State, the FTT would not apply: n 688, 11. This aspect of the FTT proved most contentious given its extraterritorial effects.

[691] Including the cascade effect of the tax and the absence of a mitigating intermediary exemption.

[692] eg EFAMA, Potential Impact of the New Version of the FTT on the UCITS Industry (2013), outlining the prejudicial impact of the new FTT on the UCITS industry. The International Securities Lending Association (ISLA) claimed the FTT would effectively close down the securities lending market in the FTT zone: ISLA, Impact of the FTT on Europe's Securities Lending Market (2013). Major German companies also opposed the tax, citing prejudice to their ability to hedge exchange rate risks on exports: Wilson, J, 'German Exporters Attack Plans for Tobin Tax', *Financial Times*, 9 May 2013, 6.

[693] The UK government abstained on the vote on the Council's support for enhanced co-operation, as it was not assured that the proposal would enhance the single market and respect the competences of non-participating Member States: House of Commons European Scrutiny Committee, 38th Report of Session 2012–2013, para 2.10.

[694] Case C-209/13 *UK v Council*, 30 April 2014 (not yet reported). The action for annulment of the Proposal was based on its extraterritorial effect on EU Member States outside the FTT zone, and accordingly its non-compliance with the conditions for enhanced co-operation; its non-compliance with international tax treaties; and its non-compliance with the subsidiarity principle given the failure to provide for the reimbursement of jurisdictions outside the FTT zone for facilitating the tax. On 30 April 2014 the Court rejected the challenge, but not on the substantive grounds raised; the Court found that the action was premature as an FTT had not been adopted under the enhanced co-operation approval decision.

[695] Particularly in the US: Barber, A, 'Brussels Vows to fight Tobin Tax Hurdles', *Financial Times*, February 16, 2013, 6. A coalition of major US business groups (including the US Chamber of Commerce) wrote to the Commission in protest: Barber, A and Politi, J, 'US Banks Fire Warning as EU Prepares to Unveil "Tobin Tax"', *Financial Times*, 14 February 2013, 15.

[696] Letter from the Australian Financial Markets Association, the Global Financial Markets Association, the Investment Industry Association of Canada, the Japan Securities Dealers Association, and the Korea Financial Investment Association to G20 Finance Ministers, 16 April 2013, describing the tax as having 'unprecedented extraterritorial impacts, contrary to G20 principles'.

[697] European Parliament Legislative Resolution on the FTT, 3 July 2013 (T7-0312/2013). The Parliament made a series of revisions, including the application of a higher taxation level to OTC transactions.

[698] It was reported to be concerned as to the impact of the FTT on liquidity in the repurchase agreements (repos) market: Atkins, R, 'ECB Offers to Recast "Robin Hood" Tax Amid Fears Over Market Impact', *Financial Times*, 27 May 2013.

[699] Agreement was not reached on how it would apply, but FTT zone Member States agreed that a revised FTT would be based on the taxation of shares and some derivatives only, and apply from 2016: Barker, A, 'Transaction tax pledge causes outcry', *Financial Times*, 7 May 2014.

VII

GATEKEEPERS

VII.1 Gatekeeper Regulation and the EU

VII.1.1 Gatekeepers and Regulation

Gatekeepers are typically characterized as independent market actors who provide verification or certification services to investors and to the market generally.[1] They include investment analysts, credit rating agencies (CRAs), trading venues (with respect to their admission standards and monitoring functions), auditors, investment banks (particularly with respect to their underwriting function), and lawyers (particularly with respect to their legal opinions on offerings). Gatekeepers have long been associated with mitigating the difficulties and costs that issuers face in signalling that their disclosure is credible, and with minimizing the related risk that securities are discounted (and the costs of capital increased) because investors cannot distinguish between investments.[2] More recently, gatekeepers in the form of CRAs have, by rating the credit risk of securities, become strongly associated with the pricing of risk and, in particular, with the assessment of the capital charge imposed on financial institutions (in effect, the assessment of the internal cost of risk-taking); accordingly, they have become incorporated within the risk regulation framework which supports financial stability.

Although the gatekeeping function is performed by an array of market actors, it is particularly strongly associated with CRAs and with investment analysts. These two forms of gatekeeper have also experienced large-scale failures and have been strongly associated with securities and markets regulation's most recent defining traumas—the Enron-era issuer disclosure and corporate governance scandals (investment analysts) and the global financial crisis (CRAs). In the wake of these crises, these two actors have become subject to discrete regulatory regimes.[3] Regulation in this field can, accordingly, be characterized as archetypal crisis-driven intervention. Prior to their respective defining

---

[1] For an early examination of gatekeepers see Kraakmann, R, 'The Anatomy of a Third Party Enforcement Strategy' (1986) 2 *JLEO* 53.

[2] Black, B, 'The Legal and Institutional Preconditions for Strong Securities Markets' (2001) 48 *UCLA LR* 781, 786–9.

[3] Auditors provide an important gatekeeping function by auditing financial disclosures for market participants. But because the audit function is primarily directed towards shareholders and is strongly associated with company law and corporate governance, it is not further addressed in this Chapter. The crisis era has generated major reform to the EU audit regime as is noted briefly in Ch II sect 6.

On the audit process and EU regulation see generally Anand, A and Moloney, N, 'Reform of the Audit Process and the Role of Shareholder Voice: TransAtlantic Perspectives' (2004) 5 *EBOLR* 223.

crises, however, these two gatekeepers were left to operate, for the most part, outside the regulatory perimeter, given the strong reputational dynamics associated with their business models.

The credibility and related business model of gatekeepers is, at bedrock, based on the value to gatekeepers of their reputational capital. In effect, gatekeepers pledge their reputational capital to vouch for the issuer and for the securities in question. Gatekeepers are repeat verifiers or certifiers and so build their reputational capital over years and over a range of issuers. The risks which gatekeepers face from any market discounting of their reputational capital serve, in theory, as a disciplining mechanism. This disciplining mechanism is based on the market discounting the value of reputation where the gatekeeper's independence and competence, for example, is questioned, and implies that the gatekeeper has a weaker incentive to defraud than has the issuer, given that any benefits from collusion with the issuer should be insignificant by comparison with the erosion of the value of reputational capital.[4]

The effect of this reputational dynamic was that gatekeepers were, until recently, strongly associated with 'new governance' techniques for intervention.[5] The private monitoring function provided by gatekeepers sat comfortably within a wider regulatory environment which was becoming increasingly 'decentred' and drawing on a range of public and private disciplining tools.[6] Gatekeepers were, in effect, 'enrolled' in the regulatory process as self-regulating risk monitors.[7] But the risks to the market are high if disciplining incentives weaken, reputational capital becomes eroded, and gatekeepers fail.

The 2001 Enron collapse provided a paradigmatic example of gatekeeper failure which implicated investment analysts, CRAs, and auditors. In particular, it exposed systemic failures by investment analysts who continued to rate Enron as a 'buy', notwithstanding the evidence publicly available as to its unstable financial position; conflicts of interest were implicated in this failure (see further section 3.1).[8] Gatekeeper failure was also strongly associated with the financial crisis. CRA conflicts of interest and competence failures were implicated in the failure of the CRA industry to correctly rate securitized debt, which failure was an aggravating factor in the system-wide mispricing of risk, inadequacy of capital, and catastrophic drying-up of liquidity in global credit markets over the crisis (see further section 2.1).

In both cases, multiple aggravating factors arose which exacerbated the underlying conflict-of-interest and competence risks and which weakened the importance of reputational capital to gatekeepers. Enron-era investment analyst failure has been attributed to a number

---

[4] eg Coffee, J, 'Gatekeeper Failure and Reform: The Challenge of Fashioning Relevant Reforms' in Ferrarini, G, Hopt, K, Winter, J, and Wymeersch, E (eds), *Reforming Company and Takeover Law in Europe* (2004) 455.

[5] See further Ch X sect 1.2.

[6] eg Black, J, 'The Rise (and Fall?) of Principles Based Regulation', in Alexander, K and Moloney, N (eds), *Law Reform and Financial Markets* (2011) 3, Ford, C, 'New Governance, Compliance, and Principles-Based Securities Regulation' (2008) 45 *American Business LJ*, and Black, J, 'Mapping the Contours of Contemporary Financial Services Regulation' (2002) 2 *JCLS* 253.

[7] Black, J, 'Enrolling Actors in Regulatory Processes: Examples from UK Financial Services Regulation' [2003] *Public Law* 63.

[8] In October 2001, shortly before the Enron bankruptcy, 16 of the 17 analysts covering Enron maintained 'buy' recommendations in respect Enron shares: Coffee, n 4, 466.

of interrelated factors, including market exuberance associated with the dotcom era (1995–2001) which disabled investor caution and caused investors to devalue the gatekeeper function, and specific local factors, such as the weakening of the US legal liability regime. CRA failure over the financial crisis has similarly been associated with a range of factors, including the pre-crisis explosion in financial innovation, which was prompted in part by global macroeconomic conditions which led to a search for yield in a low interest rate environment, and the related exponential growth of structured-finance instruments which were 'ratings-driven'; these developments meant that the impact of CRA failure was ultimately exponential. The regulatory response in both cases was to significantly tighten regulatory oversight over gatekeepers.

VII.1.2 Gatekeeper Regulation and the EU

The EU CRA regime is composed of[9] the three CRA regulations (CRA Regulation I (2009),[10] II (2011),[11] and III (2013)[12]), the 2013 CRA Directive,[13] related administrative rules,[14] and European Securities and Markets Authority (ESMA) supervisory convergence measures.[15] CRAs also come within the extensive prudential regime governing banks and investment firms, particularly with respect to the assessment of capital charges, as 'external credit assessment institutions', and accordingly are subject to discrete requirements under the 2013 CRD IV (Capital Requirements Directive IV)/CRR (Capital Requirements Regulation) regime for the prudential regulation of financial institutions (see further Chapter V on CRD IV/CRR).[16]

---

[9] CRAs are also subject to generic elements of EU securities and markets regulation where they apply, notably the market abuse regime.

[10] Regulation (EU) No 1060/2009 [2009] OJ L302/1. References to the CRA Regulation are to the 2009 Regulation as revised in 2011 and 2013, unless the context dictates otherwise.

[11] Regulation (EU) No 513/2011 [2011] OJ L145/30.

[12] Regulation (EU) No 462/2013 [2013] OJ L146/1.

[13] Directive 2013/14/EU [2013] OJ L145/1.

[14] Commission Delegated Regulation (EU) No 946/2012 [2012] OJ L282/23 applies to the European Securities and Markets Authority's (ESMA) fining powers over rating agencies, and Commission Delegated Regulation (EU) No 272/2012 [2012] OJ L90/6 addresses the supervisory fees which ESMA may charge.

Four Regulatory Technical Standards (RTSs) govern technical aspects of the CRA regime: Commission Delegated Regulation (EU) No 446/2012 [2012] OJ L140/2 (on the content and format of ratings data provided in periodic reports) (2012 Commission Delegated Periodic Ratings Data Reporting Regulation); Commission Delegated Regulation (EU) No 447/2012 [2012] OJ L140/14 (on rating methodologies) (2012 Commission Delegated Methodologies Regulation); Commission Delegated Regulation (EU) No 448/2012 [2012] OJ L140/17 (on the presentation of information required to be provided to ESMA) (2012 Commission Delegated Supervisory Ratings Data Regulation); and Commission Delegated Regulation (EU) No 449/2012 [2012] OJ L140/32 (on the registration and certification process) (2012 Commission Delegated Regulation on Registration and Certification).

[15] Including ESMA/2013/720 (2012 ESMA Guidelines on the Scope of the CRA regime) and ESMA/2011/139 (2011 ESMA Guidelines on the CRA Endorsement Regime). The 'soft' regime also includes the ESMA Q&A on the CRA regime (first issued as ESMA/2013/1935).

[16] CRAs come within the CRD IV/CRR prudential regime (Directive 2013/36/EU [2013] OJ L176/338 (Capital Requirements Directive (CRD IV)) and Regulation (EU) No 575/2013 [2013] OJ L176/1 (Capital Requirements Regulation CRR)) as 'external credit assessment institutions' (ECAIs). Ratings from ECAIs (CRAs regulated under the CRA regime) are used (under the 'Standardized Approach' to capital assessment and with respect to the securitization framework) to establish the risk weighting of assets and thereby the necessary capital requirement. Discrete requirements, additional to the CRA regime, apply to ECAIs under CRD IV/CRR.

EBA (the European Banking Authority), together with ESMA and EIOPA (the European Insurance and Occupational Pensions Authority), is to provide a mapping of credit risk assessments used by and across all

The EU investment analyst regime is unusual in EU securities and markets regulation in that it is almost entirely based on administrative rules. The initial suite of administrative rules were adopted under the 2003 Market Abuse Directive (2003 MAD) and the 2004 Markets in Financial Instruments Directive I (2004 MiFID I).[17] Both legislative measures will be repealed by the 2014 Market Abuse Regulation and the 2014 Markets in Financial Instruments Directive (MiFID II)/Markets in Financial Instruments Regulation (MiFIR) regimes;[18] the related administrative rules will also be repealed. But as the administrative rules are likely to be re-adopted in some form, they are briefly considered in this Chapter. The initial administrative regime was based on the 2006 Commission MiFID I Directive[19] (based on the 2004 MiFID I) and the 2003 Commission Investment Recommendations Directive[20] (based on the 2003 MAD).

The EU's investment analyst and CRA regimes are significantly different in their intensity of intervention, reflecting the development of the former in the pre-crisis period and the latter in the teeth of the financial crisis, as well as the different levels of risk represented by both actors and their different functions in the financial system. The analyst regime is a limited one and relies heavily on disclosure controls. The CRA regime, reflecting the much greater extent to which CRAs are embedded within the financial system, their role in pricing risk and in the application of capital requirements, and the financial stability risks which they accordingly pose, is of a different order, both with respect to the intensity of regulation and with respect to its innovative ESMA-based institutional structure for supervision and enforcement.

VII.2 Rating Agencies

VII.2.1 Regulating Rating Agencies and the Financial Crisis

VII.2.1.1 CRA Regulation and the EU

The EU regime for regulating CRAs[21] was the first pillar of the crisis-era reform programme to be put in place.[22] Composed of three generations of regulations (CRA Regulation

---

ECAIs in order to promote a consistent implementation of the CRR across the EU, given the heavy reliance on ECAI ratings in the assessment of capital requirements (on the initial consultation see the ESA Joint Committee Paper (JC 2014 004 (2014)) (see further sect 2.8 on over-reliance on ratings).

[17] Directive 2003/6/EC [2003] OJ L96/16 and Directive 2004/39/EC [2004] OJ L145/1.

[18] Regulation (EU) No 596/2014 [2014] OJ L173/1 (2014 MAR) (on the implementation timeline see Ch VIII n 3); and Markets in Financial Instruments Directive II 2014/65/EU OJ [2014] L173/349 (2014 MiFID II) and Markets in Financial Instruments Regulation EU (No) 600/2014 OJ [2014] L173/84 (2014 MiFIR) (on the implementation timeline see Ch IV n 28). The discussion in this Chapter is based on the 2014 MAR and 2014 MiFID II/MiFIR regimes; MiFID I will be repealed on the application of the MiFID II/MiFIR regime on 3 July 2017 and the 2003 MAD will be repealed on 3 July 2016 on the application of the 2014 MAR. Reference is made to the earlier 2003 MAD and 2004 MiFID I regimes as appropriate.

[19] Commission Directive 2006/73/EC [2006] OJ L241/26.

[20] Commission Directive 2003/125/EC [2003] OJ L339/73.

[21] On the CRA regime see Johnston, A, 'Corporate Governance is the Problem, not the Solution: A Critical Appraisal of the European Regulation on Credit Rating Agencies' (2011) 11 *JCLS* 395; Möllers, T, 'Regulating Credit Rating Agencies: The New US and EU Law—Important Steps or Much Ado About Nothing?' (2009) 4 *CMLJ* 477; and Amtenbrink, F and de Haan, J, 'Regulating Credit Ratings in the European Union: A Critical First Assessment of Regulation 1060/2009 on Credit Rating Agencies' (2009) 46 *CMLR* 1915.

[22] CRA reform is closely related to the wider banking reform programme which is outside the scope of this work. Accordingly, this section does not cover the interaction between CRA reform and bank capital and liquidity regulation, but focuses on CRA regulation more generally.

I (2009), II (2011), and III (2013)) and a Directive (2013 CRA Directive),[23] its development has been shaped by the progression of the financial crisis and of the related reform agenda in the EU.

The initial 2009 suite of reforms (CRA I) heralded the marked intensification of EU financial market intervention over the crisis and imposed a registration requirement on EU CRAs and applied detailed operational and organizational rules. The 2011 reforms to the 2009 CRA I Regulation conferred all supervisory and enforcement competence over EU CRAs on ESMA (CRA II), following the establishment of the European System of Financial Supervision (ESFS). The 2013 CRA III and CRA Directive reforms drilled more deeply into the nature of CRA risk and focused on market structure and on over-reliance on ratings. The 2013 reforms were also shaped by the then burgeoning euro-area sovereign debt crisis, however, and so addressed the rating of sovereign debt. The regime's development has also tracked the international reform movement, which is discussed later in the Chapter: the CRA I and II reforms reflected the G20 commitment to subject CRAs to registration and oversight, and the CRA III reforms reflected the international drive, since 2010, to reduce reliance on ratings in the regulatory system.

The CRA I Regulation is of central importance in EU securities and markets regulation as one of the first crisis-era measures to be adopted, and because its adoption marked a sharp shift from the prevailing pre-crisis, post-Financial Services Action Plan (FSAP) deregulatory mood. The CRA II Regulation is similarly important because of the radical institutional change it wrought; for the first time in EU securities and markets regulation, supervision and enforcement powers were centralized within ESMA. But, in terms of achieving outcomes, these measures might be regarded as the equivalent of 'picking low-hanging fruit'. Together, CRA I and II impose a procedural rulebook on the EU's CRAs and subject the rating process to a panoply of conflict-of-interest and quality assurance rules, overseen by ESMA. But arguably neither Regulation goes to the heart of the systemic risks which CRAs can generate by virtue of their 'hard-wiring' into the regulatory system, the entrenched market reliance on ratings to price risk and the related pro-cyclical effects, and the weak disciplining of CRAs by the market, as liability risk is limited and the CRA market is oligopolistic in structure (see further section 2.2.3). It is only with the 2013 CRA III reforms that the EU has begun to grapple with the very difficult market structure questions which effective reform requires.

VII.2.1.2 Credit Rating Agency Risk

CRAs have long been regarded as playing a central role in credit markets because they address credit risk and provide a mechanism for its pricing.[24] CRAs issue ratings[25] or opinions on the creditworthiness of a particular issuer or financial instrument and on the likelihood of default on financial obligations. Ratings, which are based on proprietary methodologies, categorize issuers and instruments according to different grades which

---

[23] See nn 10–13 for the references. The consolidated regime will be referred to as the CRA Regulation; distinct reference will be made to the three Regulations which form the regime as appropriate.

[24] For a pre-crisis analysis see generally Levich, R, Majnoni, G, and Reinhard, C (eds), *Ratings, Rating Agencies, and the Global Financial System* (2002).

[25] Described by one commentator as 'an assessment of the likelihood of timely payment on securities': Schwarcz, S, 'The Role of Credit Rating Agencies in Global Market Regulation' in Ferran, E and Goodhart, C (eds), *Regulating Financial Services and Markets in the 21st Century* (2001) 289, 299.

reflect the risk of default, from investment grade to speculative, and allow the market to assess relative risk through standardized risk indicators.[26] Ratings accordingly address the information asymmetries which would otherwise increase the cost of capital and impose costs and inefficiencies on effective risk assessment.

The financial crisis led to a sharp realization of the risks posed by CRAs. But concerns had long been expressed about the CRA industry[27] and the extent to which it could influence financial markets and the pricing of risk.[28] These concerns related to the integrity and quality of the rating process and the independence and objectivity of CRAs, given in particular the impact of conflict-of-interest risk on CRAs' incentives to protect their reputational capital. CRAs generally operate under an issuer-payment model (as ratings are a pre-requisite for debt financing) which generates significant conflict-of-interest risk, although the competing and greater need of the CRA to protect its reputational capital has traditionally been regarded as an effective bulwark against this.[29] Competence failures can also be significant, as the failure of CRAs to signal the increased risk of bankruptcy and the implications of off-balance sheet transactions over the Enron era attested.[30] Risks are exacerbated by the structure of the CRA market. There is limited competition in the market (and thus limited monitoring), which is dominated by three main players (Standard & Poor's, Moody's, and Fitch); the tendency towards oligopoly can be considerable as rated instruments typically must have two ratings.[31] The high barriers to entry and the cost of acquiring reputational capital make market structure weaknesses difficult to address. The risks are also exacerbated by the absence, for the most part, of deterrents in the form of

---

[26] eg Hill, C, 'Regulating the Rating Agencies' (2004) 82 *Washington University LQ* 43, 66–8 and 72–4.

[27] eg Partnoy, F, 'The Siskel and Ebert of Financial Markets? Two Thumbs Down for the Credit Rating Agencies' (1999) 77 *Washington University LQ* 619.

[28] Even prior to the financial crisis, their influence had been vividly highlighted by number of commentators: 'the pronouncements of these high priests of finance...affect the cost of funds for issuers of debt... ratings can single-handedly create or render obsolete particular kinds of securities. A downgrade can even tip countries towards recession or companies towards bankruptcy' (Beales, R, Scholtes, S, and Tett, G, 'Failing Grades? Why Regulators Fear Credit Rating Agencies May Be Out of Their Depth', *Financial Times*, 17 May 2007, 13); 'They are the universally feared gatekeepers for the issue and trading of debt securities' (Schwarcz, n 25, 289); and 'There are two super-powers in the world today, in my opinion. There's the United States and there's Moody's Bond Rating Services. The US can destroy you by dropping bombs and Moody's can destroy you by downgrading your bonds. And believe me, it's not clear sometimes who's more powerful' (Friedman, T, cited in Partnoy, n 27, 260).

[29] Pre-crisis, CRAs defended the issuer-payment model by reference to their attempts to diversify their issuer base and to ensure that no one issuer constituted a significant proportion of an agency's overall revenue, and to the reputational argument that 'ratings from a particular firm are only valuable insofar as the firm maintains a reputation for independence, accuracy, and thoroughness. CRAs would be unwilling to risk damaging their reputations just to retain a single client': International Organization of Securities Commissions (IOSCO), Report on the Activities of Credit Rating Agencies (2003) 11.

[30] On CRA failure in relation to the Enron bankruptcy see Rating the Raters. Enron and the Credit Rating Agencies. Hearings Before the Senate Committee on Governmental Affairs, 107th Congress (2002). In the EU, and with respect to the similar Parmalat bankruptcy, although weaknesses in Parmalat's governance structure were apparent, it enjoyed an investment-grade credit rating which allowed it to borrow ever increasing funds from the market immediately prior to the massive 2003 bankruptcy. See further Ferrarini, G and Giudici, P, 'Financial Scandals and the Role of Private Enforcement: the Parmalat Case' in Armour, J and McCahery, J (eds), *After Enron. Improving Corporate Law and Modernising Securities Regulation in Europe and the US* (2006) 159. In its Communication on the Parmalat scandal, the Commission noted that significant audit failures may have been assisted 'in some way' by CRA failures: Commission, Preventing and Combating Financial Malpractice (2004) (COM (2004) 611) 3.

[31] Hill, n 26, 60.

liability risk; a rating is regarded as an opinion, with the CRA thereby largely insulated from liability claims. The CRA working model further increases the risk of failure; CRAs do not verify disclosures (as an auditor does) but assess the likelihood of default. Overall, considerable pressure can therefore be exerted on the value of reputational capital.

These concerns were magnified by the extent to which, pre-crisis, ratings had become embedded within the financial system and tied to the pricing and management of risk. They had become 'hard-wired' into regulation, most notably by the extensive reliance on ratings under the Basel II capital assessment process,[32] which had led to CRAs being empowered, in effect, to confer a 'regulatory licence' on market participants, which licence led to regulatory consequences in terms of capital requirements.[33] This 'hard-wiring' also had the effect of reducing firms' incentives to monitor credit risk internally and raised the risk of herding effects arising where a change in a rating triggered similar behaviour across the market. Ratings were also used heavily as diversification tools and as triggers to confer rights on creditor counterparties. Above all, the pre-eminence of ratings as risk pricing tools in the credit markets embedded ratings in the global credit market, and allowed ratings to become a primary influence on pricing and, accordingly, on risk management and transmission.

These long-standing weaknesses were exposed to devastating effect by the financial crisis and, in particular, by the toxic interaction between financial innovation (in the form of structured finance), CRA market structure, and the ratings process.[34] Under the 'originate and distribute' banking model which exploded in the period prior to the crisis (including in the EU),[35] debt such as mortgage loans, personal debt, and corporate bonds was 'repackaged' (securitized) and issued as a structured-finance product (based on the original debt and its income flows) through a structured-finance vehicle.[36] The success of the structured product depended heavily on the rating assigned by CRAs. But the rating process placed intense pressure on CRA reputational capital. The CRA was typically involved in the development of the structured-finance product by providing advice to the product's sponsor (the arranging investment bank) on the hypothetical rating a product might receive and the related degree of credit support it would require.[37] The revenue stream from structured

---

[32] eg, Hertig, G, 'Basel II and Fostering the Disclosure of Bank's Internal Credit Ratings' (2006) 7 *EBOLR* 625, Schwarcz, S, 'Private Ordering' (2002) 97 *Northwestern University LR* 301 and Amtenbrink and de Haan, n 21. Rating were used as substitutes for internal credit risk assessment and played a central role in the determination of the risk weight of an asset and the related capital charge.

[33] CRAs have been characterized as selling 'regulatory licences' which allow market participants to purchase favourable regulatory treatment: Partnoy, n 27.

[34] eg Coffee, J, 'What Went Wrong? An Initial Inquiry into the Causes of the 2008 Financial Crisis' (2009) 9 *JCLS* 1 and Hunt, J, 'Credit Rating Agencies and the "Worldwide Credit Crisis". The Limits of Reputation, the Insufficiency of Reform, and a Proposal for Improvement' (2009) *Col Business LR* 109. From a policy perspective, see the Commission's Impact Assessment for what would become the CRA I Regulation (SEC (2008) 2746 (2008 CRA I Proposal Impact Assessment) 12–21) and CESR, The Role of Credit Rating Agencies in Structured Finance (2008) (CESR/08-036).

[35] The volume of related securitizations more than doubled between 2001 and 2005: Commission, European Financial Integration Report (2007) (SEC (2007) 1696) (2007 EFIR) 38. By Q1 2008, there were some €1,200 billion of securitized products outstanding in the EU Market: 2008 CRA I Proposal Impact Assessment, n 34, 7.

[36] Structured finance can be described as the pooling of credit assets and the subsequent sale to investors of tranched claims on the cash flows backed by the asset pool: Bank for International Settlements (BIS), The Role of Ratings in Structured Finance: Issues and Implications (2005) 1.

[37] These structures were accordingly 'ratings-driven' and designed to achieve a particular rating: Hill, n 26, 49.

finance arrangers was significantly higher than that from corporate issuers,[38] increasing the dependence of CRAs on this revenue stream.[39] Revenues also depended on the small group of financial institutions who arranged and issued structured-finance products on a large scale; this concentration of revenue sources led to CRAs becoming dependent on a small number of institutions. In addition, competence risks arose. Risk factors included the lack of track record data on these innovative products, heavy reliance on models although the CRA industry had traditionally relied on the exercise of judgement, insufficiently sensitive default risk tools, and failure to address systemic and correlation risk across these products and the related liquidity risks.[40] Added to this, the pre-crisis exuberance in market conditions led to a destabilization of investor monitoring as a disciplining factor on CRAs, as investors increasingly relied on ratings and did not perform sufficient due diligence on products;[41] this was aggravated by the global search for yield in the then prevailing low interest environment.[42] Investor monitoring was further weakened by technicalities relating to rating labels. The classic 'AAA' rating associated with investment-grade corporate debt was used for structured-finance ratings.

In summer 2007, after rapid growth in the structured-finance market in the first half of the year, liquidity began to evaporate in global credit markets following the exposure of the systemic mispricing of structured-finance instruments as the underlying assets defaulted.[43] While CRAs were initially slow to react, the quickening pace of rating downgrades quickly turned into a catastrophic spiral,[44] deepening the ongoing pro-cyclical collapse in global credit markets as institutions reacted to the loss of value in these instruments and as their capital was accordingly eroded. The reaction and erosion was systemic. Heavy dependence on ratings (exacerbated by the hard-wiring of ratings into the financial system through risk regulation) led to destructive herding effects and to abrupt, large-scale sell-offs of securities ('cliff effects').[45] While it would become apparent that multiple factors had combined to toxic effect to drive the financial crisis, CRAs, a relatively distinct and easy target, bore the initial brunt of policy reaction and reforming zeal, particularly over late 2007.

---

[38] The BIS reported that structured-finance ratings formed the largest and fastest-growing business segment for rating agencies in 2005: n 36, 2.

[39] In 2008, the Commission reported than some 50 per cent of CRA revenues came from structured-finance business: 2008 CRA I Proposal Impact Assessment, n 34, 10.

[40] eg European Central Bank (ECB), Financial Stability Review (2007) 13, Karsenti, R, 'Recent Market Turbulence: Causes and Consequences' ICMA Regulatory Policy Newsletter, Issue No 7 (2007) 3 and Buiter, W, Lessons from the 2007 Financial Crisis, Centre for Economic Policy Research, Policy Insight No 18 (2007).

[41] eg IOSCO, The Role of Credit Rating Agencies in Structured Finance Markets (2008).

[42] The (then) UK Financial Services Authority (FSA) noted the 'self-reinforcing cycle of irrational exuberance' in pricing credit risk: FSA, Financial Risk Outlook 2009 (2008).

[43] The underlying defaults were related to a host of factors but in particular to a collapse in the US subprime mortgage market. See, eg, ESME (European Securities and Markets Expert Group), Role of Credit Rating Agencies (2008).

[44] Between 1 July 2007 and 24 June 2008, some 145,899 downgrades of structured-finance instruments occurred, as compared to 1,455 corporate downgrades: 2008 CRA I Proposal Impact Assessment, n 34, 7–8. See also Moller, n 21, noting very sharp increase in downgrades in autumn 2008, with some instruments downgraded from AAA to investment grade in one step.

[45] FSB, Principles for Reducing Reliance on CRA Ratings (2010) 1.

VII.2.1.3. The International Crisis-era Response to CRA Risk

The financial crisis led to radical change in the regulatory treatment of CRAs. Originally, the nature of the rating process, which produces an opinion rather than a recommendation, the difficulties in distinguishing between the rating process and its outputs, and the traditional association between CRAs and market discipline[46] led to a regulatory treatment which was based on 'enrolling' CRAs in the regulatory apparatus as self-regulating actors.[47] The high barriers to entry, which could be increased by regulatory costs—as well as the potential for moral hazard were ratings to be subject to some form of regulatory imprimatur—lent further support to the prevailing faith in the strength of CRAs' reputational capital.

The initial approach in the US, the home of the three global CRA groups, was to designate CRAs as 'Nationally Recognized Statistical Ratings Organizations', eligible to provide the credit assessments and ratings used to determine net capital requirements for broker-dealers; designation was based on the extent to which agencies were of national repute rather than on assessment by the Securities and Exchange Commission (SEC). Formal regulatory requirements were not imposed until the Enron-era reforms.[48] This model was reflected at international level with the adoption by the International Organization of Securities Commissions (IOSCO), in 2004, of a Code of Conduct for Rating Agencies. Based on a self-regulatory 'comply-or-explain' model, the Code addressed the quality and integrity of the rating process, the independence of agencies and the avoidance of conflicts of interest, and the responsibilities of CRAs to the investing public and issuers through a range of detailed operational and disclosure-based recommendations. While some early difficulties arose, particularly with respect to whether rating advice business, particularly in the structured-finance context, should be separated from core rating business,[49] the Code enjoyed considerable support[50] and experienced reasonably high levels of industry compliance;[51] it was, in a vivid illustration of how dominant the self-regulation model had become, adopted by the EU (section 2.2.1).

---

[46] Ratings developed as private sector support to the construction of the railways: Hill, n 26, 46–7.

[47] See eg Partnoy, n 27, 628–36.

[48] Under the 2006 Credit Rating Agency Reform Act (which followed from a 2002 Sarbanes-Oxley Act mandate), which responded to concerns as to why CRAs had failed to spot the imminent Enron bankruptcy: US Senate Committee on Governmental Affairs, Oversight of Enron: The SEC and Private-Sector Watchdogs (2002).

[49] The Code's requirement that 'other business' be separated from rating business proved problematic, with the industry arguing that the IOSCO separation recommendation did not apply to rating assessment services (associated with structured finance in particular). IOSCO addressed the separation requirement following its 2007 review of industry compliance and clarified that rating assessment services (including with respect to structured finance transactions) fell within core rating business (IOSCO, Review of the Code of Conduct for Credit Rating Agencies (2007) 7).

[50] eg FSA, Discussion Paper 05/4, Hedge Funds: A Discussion of Risk and Regulatory Engagement (2004) 50, highlighting the success of the Code and suggesting it could be a model for aspects of hedge fund regulation.

[51] In its first (2007) monitoring report, IOSCO concluded that the largest CRAs had generally implemented the Code extensively and that variations were noted and explained. Partial and non-implementation, however, was strongly associated with smaller agencies, leading IOSCO to conclude that a risk arose of a two-tier industry structure developing, in which only larger CRAs followed the Code, notwithstanding the market risks: 2007 IOSCO Review, n 49.

The financial crisis dramatically reset the reform dynamics, with CRAs among the first actors to be associated with the crisis.[52] The 2008 report from the (then) Financial Stability Forum[53] provided the first major international review of CRA failure; it took a relatively light-touch approach to reform, however, and called for implementation of the IOSCO Code and review of the role of CRAs rather than for generalized regulation, and also highlighted the importance of investor due diligence. Although reliance on the IOSCO Code became a central plank of the crisis era international reform movement, the resilience of the Code with respect to structured finance was questioned. IOSCO moved quickly to shore up the reputation of the Code,[54] however, adopting a new version in May 2008 which focused on the particular risks posed by structured finance; the Code is still in force, albeit continually subject to reviews and implementation surveys.[55] The industry, clearly seeing regulatory intervention ahead, also adopted reforms.[56] The revised Code quickly became a major element of the international reform movement: the November 2009 Washington G20 Summit recommended that regulators ensure that CRAs met the highest standards of international organizations, avoid conflicts of interests, differentiate between ratings, and provide greater disclosure. It also called on IOSCO to review adoption by CRAs of the Code and suggested CRA registration as a medium-term goal.[57] The April 2009 London G20 meeting hardened this recommendation to a commitment to extend regulatory oversight and registration to CRAs.[58] Since then, the international reform movement has moved to address the systemic risks posed by the embedding of ratings in the financial system, with the G20 repeatedly calling

---

[52] eg FSA, Financial Risk Outlook 2008 (2007) and Financial Stability Forum, Report on Enhancing Market and Institutional Resilience (2008).

[53] Financial Stability Forum, n 52.

[54] Autumn 2007 saw IOSCO convene a task force which focused on the role of CRAs and, in particular, their role in assessing liquidity, as well as credit, risk.

[55] With respect to the major 2008 revision, the reforms to the structured-finance rating process included requirements with respect to: a prohibition on analysts making proposals or recommendations regarding the design of structured-finance products that a CRA rates; the CRA defining the 'ancillary business' not subject to the business separation requirement; disclosure where client revenues represented over 10 per cent of revenues; remuneration; the quality of the rating process, with a particular focus on structured finance but also more generally; rigorous and formal review of methodologies; the CRA refraining from rating where the complexity of a structured product or lack of robust data regarding the underlying assets raises 'serious questions' as to whether a credible rating can be given; the provision of investors and/or subscribers with sufficient information on the CRA's loss and cash-flow analysis so that investors can understand the rating; the differentiation of ratings of structured-finance products from corporate ratings through symbols; the presentation of verifiable, quantifiable, historical information on the performance of CRA ratings; and disclosure of the limitations of ratings. IOSCO's Objectives and Principles for Securities Regulation were also revised in 2010 to include a new principle that CRAs should be subject to adequate levels of oversight, and that CRAs whose ratings are used for regulatory purposes and should be subject to registration and ongoing supervision (para F. 22). Implementation reviews of the Code as revised in 2008 were carried out by IOSCO in 2009, 2010, and 2012. In 2013, IOSCO recommended that colleges of supervisors be established for the largest globally active CRAs (the college for Fitch is chaired by ESMA, while the US SEC chairs the colleges for Moody's and Standard & Poor's). In February 2014, IOSCO launched a major consultation to update the Code to reflect the imposition internationally of regulatory oversight on CRAs (IOSCO, Code of Conduct Fundamentals for CRAs (2014)).

[56] Standard & Poor's, Moody's, and Fitch were all reported as reforming their rating procedures in the early stages of the crisis: eg Tett, G, Hughes, J, and Van Duyn, A, 'S & P Unveils Ratings Overhaul', *Financial Times*, 7 February 2008, 17.

[57] Washington G20 Summit, November 2009, Action Plan to Implement the Principles for Reform.

[58] London G20 Summit, April 2009, Declaration on Strengthening the Financial System.

on members to end mechanistic reliance on ratings.[59] The G20 has also called for market structure reforms in the form of greater transparency and on competition between CRAs.[60] An array of reforms have followed in jurisdictions internationally.[61]

VII.2.2 The Evolution of the EU Regime

VII.2.2.1 Initial Efforts

The EU's CRA regime is a relative newcomer to EU securities and markets regulation and can be dated to 2006 and the Commission's Communication on CRAs.[62] In the wake of the Enron collapse, at the informal ECOFIN Oviedo Council in April 2002, the Commission made a commitment to consider the treatment of CRAs (and investment analysts).[63] The 2003 Parmalat scandal intensified institutional concern,[64] and the initiative shifted to the European Parliament in early 2004, with the Katiforis Report[65] and the subsequent 2004 Parliament Resolution on CRAs;[66] similarly, the Parliament's February 2004 Resolution on the Parmalat scandal also noted its concern that CRAs did not have 'the slightest suspicion' as to the fraud.[67] The 2004 Parliament Resolution on CRAs was broadly supportive of CRAs, but noted instances of inappropriate ratings, conflict-of-interest risk, the contribution CRA failure had made to market destabilization, and the serious implications of downgrades. It called for an interventionist response and requested that the Commission provide an assessment of the need for 'appropriate legislative proposals'.[68] Following extensive advice from the Committee of European Securities Regulators (CESR), which supported reliance on the IOSCO Code,[69] the Commission

---

[59] eg Cannes G20 Summit, November 2011, Final Declaration, and calling for implementation of the related Financial Stability Board (FSB) principles (n 45). In 2013 the FSB launched a peer review on compliance with its principles.

[60] Los Cabos G20 Summit, June 2012, Leaders' Declaration.

[61] See n 307.

[62] Commission, Communication on Credit Rating Agencies (2006) ([2006] OJ L59/2) (2006 CRA Communication).

[63] Commission, Note for the Informal ECOFIN Council, Oviedo, 12 and 13 April 2002, A First Response to Enron-related Policy (2002).

[64] See, eg, European Securities Committee (which, composed of Member State representatives, advises the Commission and plays a role in administrative rule-making; see further Ch X sect 4) Minutes, 15 March 2004, which noted the development of a response towards CRAs as forming part of the EU's post-Parmalat agenda.

[65] Katiforis Report (Economic and Monetary Affairs (ECON) Committee) on the Role and Methods of Rating Agencies, 29 January 2004 (A5-0040/2004).

[66] European Parliament Resolution on The Role and Methods of Rating Agencies, 10 February 2004 (P5-TA(2004)0080).

[67] European Parliament Resolution on Corporate Governance and Supervision of Financial Services—the Parmalat Case, 12 February 2004 (P5-TA(2004)0096) para 3.

[68] Somewhat presciently, it also called for a European Registration Regime, overseen by CESR (which has resonances with the current registration-based and ESMA-supervised regime).

[69] CESR. Technical Advice to the European Commission on Possible Measures Concerning Credit Rating Agencies (2005) (CESR/05-139b). CRAs provided CESR with its first opportunity to influence the strategic direction of a major EU policy initiative and it strongly supported the IOSCO Code, which it regarded 'as the right answer to the issues raised' by the Commission (at 50), particularly with respect to conflict of interest management. Reliance on the IOSCO Code was supported by the impact of the reputational incentives of CRAs, the absence of market failures, and the costs of regulatory initiatives. A 'wait and see' approach, based on the Code, would also, CESR argued, afford the EU the opportunity to assess the combined impact of market forces, the IOSCO Code, the (then new) market abuse regime, the (then new) 2006 Capital Requirements Directive, and the 2006 US reforms to CRA regulation. In an augury of developments to come, a 'distinct

responded by means of the 2006 CRA Communication.[70] In the Communication, the Commission, reflecting widespread support for the IOSCO Code,[71] called for CRA industry compliance with the IOSCO Code, and concluded that no new legislative initiatives were needed, thereby reflecting the driving concern of the post-FSAP period that legislative solutions should only be adopted where strictly necessary. Deploying the 'threat of intervention' mechanism, the Commission warned that it was continuing to monitor developments closely and that CRAs must be 'scrupulous in implementing the provisions of the Code'. In stark contrast to the current institutional arrangement under which ESMA supervises CRAs, compliance with the IOSCO Code was subject to a voluntary agreement between CESR and the CRAs operating in the EU,[72] and supported institutionally by formal Commission requests to CESR to report on compliance.[73] CESR's first report (2006)[74] reported widespread compliance with the Code, leading the Commission to conclude that CESR review was an important and useful basis on which to review industry compliance[75] and that self-regulation was working reasonably well. Nonetheless, CESR warned that while CRAs were 'largely compliant' with the Code, 'there is some room for improvement'.[76]

A number of factors appear to have combined to produce the Commission's ground-breaking reliance on the IOSCO Code. Parallel but separate discussions on the treatment of CRAs under the Basel II/2006 Capital Requirements Directive regime may have provided a safety valve for the release of some of the political pressure to intervene—particularly as the Committee of European Banking Supervisors (CEBS) developed standards for rating agencies under the new capital regime, which relied heavily on ratings to establish risk weightings and related capital assessments.[77] The IOSCO Code provided a convenient template for action, while CESR provided a novel device for policing the Code and strengthening the market monitoring mechanism. Market opinion was strongly in favour

---

minority' of CESR members, however, supported a 'recognition' model under which CRAs would voluntarily register and commit to following the Code. The minority position acknowledged that recognition could not operate through national competent authorities (NCAs), given the costs and duplication risks, but recommended that recognition operate at European level.

[70] n 62.

[71] The IOSCO Code and the EU's incorporation of the Code was, eg, described as 'sett[ing] the stage for an emerging consensus among market participants, regulators, and CRAs around a possible market-driven oversight framework for CRAs': European Parliament Financial Services Forum, Credit Rating Agencies (2006).

[72] Each agency (in an agreement with CESR which pre-dated the 2006 Communication) agreed to make public a letter outlining how it complied with the Code and indicating any deviations, to participate in an annual meeting with CESR to discuss implementation, and to provide an explanation to the national CESR member where any 'substantial incident' occurred with a particular issuer in its market: CESR/05-751.

[73] For an account of the procedure see CESR, Annual Report (2006) 31–3.

[74] CESR/06-545 (2006 CESR Review).

[75] Letter from the Commission to CESR (7 May 2007) attached to CESR, Progress Report on CESR's Dialogue with CRAs to Review how the IOSCO Code of Conduct is being Implemented (2007) (CESR/07-304). CESR's view was that 'the voluntary framework of co-operation between CESR and credit rating agencies has proved a successful way to move forward in an environment where there is an absence of regulation': CESR, Annual Report (2006) 31.

[76] 2006 CESR Review, n 74, 79.

[77] CEBS, Guidelines on the Recognition of External Credit Assessment Institutions (ECAIs) (2006). As noted in n 16, ECAIs, now regulated under the CRA regime, form a central element of the new CRD IV/CRR regime.

of a self-regulatory response.[78] At a time when the international regulatory zeitgeist was to support competition and attract business,[79] it would have been quixotic for the Commission to engage in regulatory warfare with the world's leading and US-based rating agencies. The imprints of the Commission's post-FSAP Better Regulation agenda are also clear in the light-touch approach adopted.

Immediately prior to the crisis, therefore, the EU CRA regime differed from the current regime in a number of respects. There was broad institutional and political consensus as to the appropriateness of market-led discipline, concern to minimize regulatory costs, and faith in the effectiveness of CRA reputational capital. CESR, in stark contrast with ESMA's current robust approach to CRA supervision, was broadly sanguine as to the intensity of CRA risk, particularly with respect to structured finance[80] and including with respect to reliance on ratings in the regulatory architecture,[81] and hostile to regulatory intervention. The Commission was similarly disposed. While there was support in some EU quarters for a degree of intervention, notably through an EU registration system,[82] it was limited,[83] reflecting the EU's weak institutional capacity at the time. While the current CRA regime has revealed the EU's ambition to shape the international rulebook and supervisory practices, the pre-crisis approach was more concerned with ensuring consistency between the EU's nascent approach and the dominant US model. In particular, the 2006 US Credit Rating Agencies Act, which required the registration of CRAs, was followed closely,[84] and there is some evidence of concern to ensure consistency between EU policy and international developments.[85] Early indications of a more combative and independent approach were, however, emerging, with some concern that EU policy should be distinct and reflect EU market conditions,[86] and some evidence of a determination to shape the international agenda (a determination which would strongly characterize the crisis-era response).[87]

---

[78] 'The enormous mass of comments stress that they support the IOSCO Code all the way': CESR, Technical Advice to the European Commission on Possible Measures Concerning Credit Rating Agencies: Feedback Statement (CESR/05-140) 24.

[79] Ch I.

[80] eg in its 2005 Advice to the Commission (n 69), and reflecting strong market opinion (CESR Feedback Statement, n 78, 11), CESR advised that while CRAs played a more active role with respect to structured-finance ratings than with respect to issuer ratings, differential treatment was not required.

[81] With respect to the use of ratings in EU legislation, CESR simply advised that the use of ratings should not be encouraged on a general basis but should be based on a case-by-case analysis of the different techniques possible: CESR Feedback Statement, n 78, 11.

[82] As called for by the European Parliament: n 66.

[83] Only a minority of CESR members, eg, supported registration (n 69), while the Commission's advisory Securities Expert Group was not able to reach a view on whether an EU oversight mechanism was appropriate: Securities Expert Group, Financial Services Action Plan: Progress and Prospectus (2004) 22.

[84] The Katiforis Report also called for a registration system, in part to redress the imbalance between the EU and the US: n 65, 11.

[85] eg 2004 Parliament CRA Resolution, n 66, paras 4 and 6. A similar concern was expressed in the European Securities Committee which called on the Commission to take account of work in other international fora (Minutes, 5 July 2004).

[86] European Securities Committee Minutes, 5 July 2004.

[87] The Parliament's 2004 CRA Resolution highlighted its concern at the dominance of the US as the *de facto* global regulator of CRAs: n 66, paras 4 and F. Hostility towards the US regime was more overt in the Katiforis Report which noted 'a vast de facto imbalance towards the American side . . . created not by design but capable, nevertheless, of upsetting the smooth operation of the market': n 65, 9.

VII.2.2.2 The Financial Crisis

The financial crisis radically reset the EU institutional and political environment, bringing profound change to the substantive and institutional design of the EU CRA regime, as well as to the EU's approach to international engagement in this area.

Although problems with the ratings of structured-finance instruments were clear from 2007, it took some time for EU policy to harden. Over 2007–8, CESR remained broadly sanguine.[88] It remained a supporter of the IOSCO Code or similar self-regulation, albeit that by May 2008, and as the crisis deepened, it was calling for a reinforcement of the Code's compliance mechanism.[89] The Commission's (then) major advisory group on financial markets, the European Securities and Markets Expert Group (ESME), also remained hostile to regulation over summer 2008.[90] But, and reflecting support from France and Germany in particular,[91] political support for regulatory intervention hardened as the crisis deepened. The Council's initial October 2007 roadmap for financial stability included an examination of the role of CRAs.[92] High-level political support for action followed in the European Council, although the European Council saw regulatory intervention as a fallback, in the absence of industry action.[93] The European Parliament, from an early stage of the crisis, also focused on CRA risks,[94] and supported some degree of intervention.[95]

---

[88] Its reaction to the developing crisis can be tracked in its two (Commission-requested) reports on compliance with the IOSCO Code, with particular reference to structured finance (February 2008, CESR/08-036 and May 2008, CESR/08-277). The February review was broadly supportive of the IOSCO Code, while the May 2008 review robustly concluded that 'CESR and market participants believe that there is no evidence that regulation of the credit rating industry would have had an effect on the issues which emerged with ratings of US subprime backed securities and hence continues to support market driven improvement' (at 4).

[89] CESR called for a CRA standard-setting body which would develop and monitor international standards similar to the IOSCO standards, and which would use 'name and shame' techniques.

[90] n 43. The Report followed an extensive Commission mandate which asked for advice on a series of questions (including whether CRA methodologies were robust and whether corporate and structured-finance ratings should be labelled to highlight their differences) in the context of the importance of ratings in structured finance and the appropriateness of the EU's self-regulatory response following the US Credit Rating Agency Reform Act 2006. The Report found that the performance of CRAs was generally satisfactory, save with respect to structured finance; doubted the benefits of a separate EU regime; and proposed a series of recommendations designed to strengthen self-regulation, particularly with respect to governance, transparency, and performance measurement. Reflecting CESR's approach, ESME was sceptical of regulatory intervention.

[91] eg the 6 September 2007 statements by French and German premiers Sarkozy and Merkel which called for greater clarity concerning the role of CRAs: Greater Transparency on the Financial Markets, Press and Information Office of the Federal Government, 6 September, 2007. In a similar vein, the public letter by then French Finance Minister Lagarde to the *Financial Times* argued that 'by rating securitization vehicles... agencies determine prudential limitations based on data they receive from loan originators. This is an unhealthy situation', and suggested that the EU should give serious thought to subjecting CRAs to regulatory oversight on the lines of the US regime: Lagarde, C, 'Securitization Must Lose the Excesses of Youth', *Financial Times*, 9 October 2007, 15.

[92] 2822nd Council Meeting, 7 October 2007, ECOFIN Press Release No 13571/07.

[93] Presidency Conclusions, Brussels European Council, 13–14 March 2008, para 32.

[94] It also commissioned related research, including European Parliament, Study on Financial Stability and Crisis Management in Europe (2007) (IP/A/ECON/IC/2007-069), prepared for the ECON Committee by Alexander, K, Eatwell, J, Persaud, A, and Reoch, R.

[95] It called, eg, for greater transparency on fees and for the separation of rating and ancillary business: European Parliament Van den Burg II Resolution on Financial Services Policy 2005–2010, 11 July 2007 (P6-TA-(2007)0338) para 9.

Reflecting the prevailing political dynamics, the Commission's position shifted significantly as the crisis deepened. While Commissioner McCreevy was initially supportive of the Code and self-regulation, by autumn 2007 the Commissioner had underlined the difficulties in the CRA sector[96] and by September 2008 was 'deeply sceptical,' notwithstanding the 2008 reforms, that the Code was effective.[97] The Commission's proposal for intervention was presented, with some fanfare, in December 2008.[98]

VII.2.2.3 The CRA Regime Negotiations

(a) CRA I: A New Regulatory Regime

Negotiated in the teeth of the financial crisis, the 2009 CRA I Regulation was adopted relatively speedily.[99] The Commission's path-finding July 2008 Consultation, which was open for only four weeks and over the summer period,[100] was followed by a proposal in November 2008 which squarely linked CRAs with the financial crisis,[101] rejected further reliance on self-regulation through the IOSCO Code,[102] and, while relying on the Code as the template for an EU rulebook, sought to consolidate and substantiate its provisions. The basic design of the proposed Regulation did not change very significantly over the negotiations, although its scope of application tightened significantly and the operational design for the cumbersome and temporary supervision arrangement, based on co-ordination between CESR, the home national competent authorities (NCAs), and a college of supervisors, proved difficult to resolve.[103] The Regulation was adopted in April 2009.

The development of the regime revealed a strong concern to respond to, but also shape, the then emerging international agenda.[104] The CRA I Proposal responded to the November 2008 G20 Washington Declaration call for regulators to ensure that CRAs followed the IOSCO Code. But, imposing detailed and binding rules on CRAs, it was considerably

---

[96] In his September 2007 speech to the European Parliament on the then developing crisis, Commissioner McCreevy noted that CRAs had been very slow in downgrading their ratings and that their methodologies had been weak and not well explained. He also pointed to the potential for conflict of interest—'on the one hand credit rating agencies provide objective ratings to investors in asset backed securities, on the other they provide advice to banks on how they should structure their lending to get the best rating': Speech to the European Parliament ECON Committee, 11 September 2007.

[97] Speech on 'Regulating in a Global Market', Dublin, 16 June 2008.

[98] 'Some say it is intrusive, but it is a regulatory approach designed to restore confidence in the ratings process...No other jurisdiction in the world has demanded such changes...we will be encouraging the other leading capital markets in the world to adopt a similar approach to us.' Commissioner McCreevy, 1 December 2008.

[99] The main elements of the publicly available legislative history are: Commission Proposal COM (2008) 704 (2008 CRA I Proposal), 2008 CRA I Proposal Impact Assessment, n 34; and ECON Committee Report A6-0101/2009 (on which the European Parliament's Negotiating Position was based). The ECB Opinion is at [2009] OJ C115/1 and the ECOSOC (now EESC) Report at CES0855/2009.

[100] Generating a hostile response from CESR (CESR/08-671).

[101] 'It is commonly agreed that [CRAs] contributed to recent market turmoil by underestimating the credit risk of structured credit products...furthermore, when market conditions worsened [CRAs] failed to adapt the ratings promptly': 2008 CRA I Proposal, n 99, 2.

[102] 'Self regulation through the IOSCO Code does not appear to offer an adequate, reliable solution to the structural deficiencies of the business': 2008 CRA I Proposal, n 99, 3.

[103] The Commission noted that the supervisory oversight structure, which it described as 'an admittedly complex and heavy structure', was one of the difficult subjects over the CRA I negotiations: 2010 CRA II Proposal Impact Assessment (SEC (2010) 678) 7.

[104] On the international reform context and the factors driving convergence and divergence, particularly between the EU and US, see Brummer, C and Loko, R, The New Politics of Transatlantic Credit Rating Agency Regulation (2012), available via <http://ssrn.com/abstract=2179239>.

more demanding than the IOSCO Code and pre-empted the commitment at the April 2009 G20 London Summit to subject CRAs whose ratings are used for regulatory purposes to a registration regime. On its adoption, the EU saw the Regulation as shaping the global reform movement.[105] The concern to lead the international agenda is also clear from the unwieldy colleges-of-supervisor model of supervision which was adopted initially under the 2009 CRA I Regulation but replaced by the ESMA supervision model by the 2011 CRA II Regulation; the college model was an interim compromise, given the need to comply speedily with G20 obligations concerning rating agencies.[106]

(b) CRA II: ESMA Supervision

Although the CRA I Regulation represents a major *volte-face* in EU policy, and its adoption, at the time, was an important political moment for the EU internationally, its basis in the internationally agreed IOSCO Code dilutes somewhat its importance. Its major significance is its form, rather than its substance. The CRA I Regulation placed the long-established IOSCO Code within a regulatory framework, but it did not radically alter the essentials of, or extend beyond, the Code. It did not address the structural risks in the CRA market, for example, but was concerned with internal, procedural organization by CRAs. A bolder step was taken with the CRA II Regulation, which turned to supervision and enforcement and engaged with sensitive constitutional and operational issues.

CRAs have wide cross-border reach and require large colleges of supervisors;[107] the case for ESMA's involvement was practical. The supervision of CRAs was, for all Member States, a relatively new venture, so the conferral of power on ESMA did not lead to a removal of executive power from the Member States, for the most part. The centralization of operational supervision within ESMA posed only limited direct fiscal risks to the Member States, given that a failure of a CRA would not represent a material threat to systemic stability, and thus supervisory failure by ESMA was unlikely to lead to fiscal consequences in the Member States.[108] The political risks of centralizing CRA supervision were accordingly limited. Nonetheless, and although the principle that CRAs should be supervised centrally had been proposed in the widely supported de Larosière Report[109] and accepted by the 2009 June European Council,[110] its articulation under the 2011 CRA Regulation II,[111] which replaced the cumbersome and temporary CESR/college-of-supervisors model adopted under the 2009 CRA Regulation I, proved a sensitive and complex exercise.[112]

---

[105] Commission President Barosso suggested that 'our G20 partners agreed in London to move in the same direction as the EU has taken today', while Commissioner McCreevy suggested that the 'EU is setting an example to be followed and matched': Commission Press Release 23 April 2009 (IP/09/629).

[106] 2008 CRA I Impact Assessment, n 34, 7.

[107] The Commission's Impact Assessment for the CRA II Regulation (2010) predicted that 14 regulators would participate in Moody's college of supervisors under the CRA I Regulation: n 103, 9.

[108] There was little sign of institutional or Member State dissent on the principle of ESMA supervision: eg European Council, 18/19 June 2009, Presidency Conclusions, para 20.

[109] The High Level Group on Financial Supervision in the EU, Final Report (2009) 19–20 and 53.

[110] European Council Conclusions, 18–19 June 2009, para 20.

[111] The main elements of the publicly available legislative history are: Commission Proposal COM (2010) 289 (2010 CRA II Proposal), Impact Assessment, n 103; and ECON Committee Report A7-0081/2011 (the Klinz Report), on which the European Parliament's Negotiating Position was based. The ECB Opinion is at [2010] OJ C337/1.

[112] Reflected in the Commission's insistence that 'it is not merely political sentiment that goes in favour of considering more centralized EU oversight of CRAs': 2010 CRA II Proposal Impact Assessment, n 103, 8.

Some degree of difficulty could have been predicted, given the constitutional novelty and operational complexities engaged in conferring supervisory and enforcement responsibilities over a segment of the financial markets, for the first time, on an EU agency. Ensuring that ESMA's responsibilities were compliant with the *Meroni* doctrine[113] dominated the development of CRA II,[114] with power moving to and from the Commission over the negotiations, and ultimately led to much greater specification of how ESMA was to exercise its new suite of powers (section 2.10).[115]

(c) CRA III: Market Structure Risks

It is only with the CRA III reforms that the EU has begun to engage with the heavy lifting needed to mitigate CRA risk. The CRA I and II reforms can be regarded as not grappling fully with the need to mitigate the systemic risk which flows from market dependence on ratings to price and to manage risk. These reforms may also deepen difficulties by creating the impression of an ESMA 'regulatory branding' of CRAs, which may decrease the already poor incentives to monitor ratings and CRAs. The final CRA III generation of reforms, however, attempts to pull on a wider range of regulatory levers and, in particular, to address market structure risks.

The CRA industry initially developed slowly in Europe, reflecting the dominance of bank finance and the related location of credit risk monitoring within credit institutions.[116] A total of 33 CRA entities have been registered by ESMA, of which 16 are accounted for by the three major CRA groups—Fitch, Moody's, and Standard & Poor's.[117] These three CRA groups dominate in terms of market share;[118] the other CRAs are small, with less than 50 employees, and focus on domestic markets.[119] Only the three major groups have a pan-EU presence. The three major groups also dominate in the structured-finance field,[120] while only six CRAs rate sovereign debt. Overall, the ratings issued by the three major groups account for 95 per cent of outstanding ratings issued by CRAs registered in the EU.[121] Although smaller rating agencies are being registered,[122] there are few indications of any

---

[113] Case 9/56 *Meroni v High Authority* [1957–1958] ECR 133. The ruling provides that discretionary powers involving a wide margin of discretion which may make possible the execution of economic policy cannot be delegated by an EU institution. See further Ch XI sect 5.8.

[114] Unusually, the Commission Impact Assessment Board called for a new impact assessment of the 2010 CRA II proposal, given fundamental problems with the assessment, including with respect to the *Meroni*-compliance argument. Notably, the Board observed that political support alone was not sufficient: Ref.Ares (2010)108790. A second report, which reiterated many of the earlier concerns, followed the new Impact Assessment (Ref.Ares(2010)205437).

[115] See further Moloney, N, 'The European Securities and Markets Authority and Institutional Design for the EU Financial Markets—a Tale of Two Competences: Part (2) Supervision' (2011) 12 *EBOLR* 177.

[116] Wymeersch, E and Kruithof, M, 'Regulation and Liability of Credit Rating Agencies under Belgian Law' in Dirix, E and Leleu, Y-H (eds), *Belgian Reports at the Congress of Utrecht of the International Academy of Comparative Law* (2006) 355–6, noting that CRAs began to take root in continental Europe only when capital flows began to move away from the banking sector.

[117] ESMA, Report on the Supervision of Credit Rating Agencies 2012 (2013) (ESMA/2013/308) (ESMA 2nd Annual Supervision Report) 7 (CRA numbers are as at the time of writing).

[118] ESMA has reported that the market shares held by Moody's, Standard & Poor's, and Fitch are, respectively, 34.75 per cent, 34.61 per cent, and 17.60 per cent: ESMA/2013/1933.

[119] ESMA, Report on the Supervision of Credit Rating Agencies 2011 (2012) (ESMA/2012/207) (ESMA 1st Annual Supervision Report) 6.

[120] Only the three major groups and one other CRA rate structured products.

[121] ESMA 1st Annual Supervision Report, n 119, 6.

[122] In 2012, eg, ESMA registered smaller CRAs from Slovakia, Spain, and Italy: ESMA 2nd Annual Supervision Report, n 117, 7.

serious challenge to the dominance of the major three groups. Allied to the extent to which ratings are relied on across the EU regulatory framework and in private contracts, and the weakness of liability mechanisms, this market structure limits the extent to which the CRA rulebook can deliver change in the CRA market and thereby enhance risk assessment and management.

The CRA III reforms, however, represent an attempt to address structural market weaknesses. The Commission's Impact Assessment[123] highlighted a series of persistent weaknesses in the CRA market which had not been addressed by the earlier reforms. Regulatory over-reliance on ratings, excessive use of ratings in risk management by investors and in investment strategies, and insufficient information on structured-finance ratings was driving market pro-cyclicality. High concentration in the CRA market, along with high barriers to entry and lack of ratings comparability, was limiting choice and competition. Users of ratings had insufficient rights of redress. Conflict-of-interest risks had not been fully addressed, particularly with respect to risks arising from ownership structures. Specific difficulties were posed by the sovereign debt rating process, including with respect to timing, objectivity, transparency, and completeness, and related contagion risk. Difficulties also persisted with respect to rating methodologies and processes.

Following the completion of the CRA I and II legislative procedures, institutional appetite for ambitious CRA reform remained considerable, with an extensive Commission consultation canvassing an array of options in 2010,[124] and an equally wide-ranging and ambitious European Parliament Resolution on CRAs following in 2011.[125] Political concern over convulsions in the sovereign debt market, and the impact of ratings downgrades on euro-area stability, particularly over 2010, ensured that the reform momentum was sustained. An ambitious and interventionist Proposal followed in November 2011 and, following difficult negotiations, was agreed by the Parliament and Council in December 2012.[126] The Proposal for the CRA III Regulation was accompanied by a related Proposal for a Directive to reduce reliance on ratings in the 2009 Undertakings for Collective Investment in Transferable Securities (UCITS) and 2011 AIFMD regimes.[127]

The CRA III reform has the following main elements: an extension of the scope of the 2009/2011 regime to include, for example, rating outlooks; a range of measures to address ratings over-reliance in regulation and by the market; a further suite of conflict-of-interest

---

[123] 2011 CRA III Proposal Impact Assessment (SEC (2011) 1354).

[124] Commission, Public Consultation on Credit Rating Agencies (2010). The breadth and ambition of the options canvassed, from a European Rating Agency to requiring institutional investors to purchase ratings independently before being permitted to hold a rated investment, attests to the complexity of the market structure problem.

[125] European Parliament Resolution on Credit Rating Agencies: Future Perspectives, 8 June 2011 (P7_TA-PROV(2011)0258). The Commission and Parliament followed a broadly similar CRA III policy agenda from an early stage (particularly with respect to the treatment of sovereign debt and a new civil liability regime), although differences emerged with respect to execution over the negotiations.

[126] The main elements of the publicly available legislative history are: Commission Proposal COM (2011) 747 (2011 CRA III Commission Proposal), 2011 CRA III Proposal Impact Assessment, n 123; and ECON Committee Report A7-0221/2012 (the Domenici Report), on which the European Parliament's Negotiating Position was based. The Parliament's first reading resolution (the text was adopted under the fast-track procedure) highlights the changes introduced by the Parliament and Council to the Commission's Proposal (P7-TA(2013)0012). The ECB Opinion is at [2013] OJ C167/2 and the ECOSOC Report at CES0820/2012.

[127] See sect 2.8.

rules designed to address CRA ownership risks; a further suite of rules on ratings methodologies, designed to address the methodology change process; a series of requirements to support competition in the CRA market, including CRA rotation requirements with respect to structured-finance ratings; new requirements for sovereign debt ratings, focused on timing of release, accompanying disclosures, and rating review; an additional suite of rules on structured-finance ratings, including a requirement for a double rating and disclosure requirements for issuers; enhancement of public disclosure through a new ESMA-supported European Ratings Platform; and a new civil liability regime.

The reach, ambition, and costs of the CRA III reforms, the intractability of the risks addressed, and the highly politicized context, given ongoing convulsion in the sovereign debt market over the negotiations, led to a troubled legislative passage[128] and to a compromise measure which is highly detailed and cumbersome. The Proposal changed significantly over the negotiations, with the main flashpoints including: the Commission's proposal that CRAs be required to rotate from issuers every four years, which was changed, given concerns as to impact on the bond markets, to a complex and awkward compromise rotation regime tied to structured-finance ratings; the Commission's proposal that ESMA be required to approve methodologies (which was removed, reflecting concern as to the risk of interference by ESMA in ratings); the proposed civil liability regime, given concerns as to its reach into national civil procedure regimes, its potential prejudicial chilling effects on CRAs, and its utility, given the availability of the enhanced ESMA enforcement regime; and the proposed treatment of sovereign debt ratings.[129]

(d) An Effective Rulebook?

Overall, the CRA regime has left a troublesome legacy. It is difficult to argue against the raft of organizational rules now imposed on CRAs, given the CRA weaknesses which the crisis exposed and the central role of CRAs in supporting effective risk management and adequate capital provision within financial institutions. But the CRA regime, like the short selling regime in particular (Chapter VI section 3), carries the imprints of politicization in its targeted treatment of sovereign debt ratings.

The new CRA rulebook is also likely to struggle with structural market change.[130] It is essential that the market is weaned from its destructive dependence on ratings to manage and price risk. But while reducing reliance on ratings is a G20 commitment, it is proving a complex commitment to deliver, and depends in particular on the extent to which reliable functional substitutes for ratings can be developed;[131] the sophisticated risk

---

[128] Which was foreshadowed by the difficulties experienced in the Parliament's passing of the 2011 Resolution (n 125), in respect of which the Socialist Party abstained from a number of provisions during the ECON discussions (calling in particular for tighter controls on sovereign debt ratings): ECON Press Release, 16 March 2011.

[129] For an example of the range of concerns raised see, eg, Financial Market Law Committee, Issue 169. Regulation of Credit Rating Agencies (2012); the range of reports produced by the UK House of Commons Scrutiny Committee (eg, 51st Report of Session 2012, sect 3); and Speech by ESMA Chief Executive Verena Ross on 'Credit rating agencies: What are the next steps?', European Parliament ECON Committee Hearings, 24 January 2012 (ESMA/2012/32).

[130] Internationally, radical reform has also struggled; the 'issuer pays' model has not been altered and power remains concentrated in the three major rating agencies which together rate 95 per cent of the world's bonds: Foley, S, 'Outlook Unchanged', *Financial Times*, 15 January 2013, 9.

[131] Sect 2.8.

management systems required are likely to be beyond the competences and resources of all but the largest financial institutions. In addition, the necessary market-structure-related reforms addressing the promotion of competition in the CRA industry and the support of additional CRAs through competition-related measures (such as ESMA's new powers to assess CRA fees) and related transparency measures (such as the new 'European Ratings Platform (ERP)' ratings platform hosted by ESMA), can, by assuming reliance on CRAs, be regarded as in tension with the objective of reducing reliance on ratings.

Given the intractability of CRA market structure weaknesses, the most lasting legacy of the CRA regime may be that it created an incubator for the development of ESMA's supervisory powers (section 2.10). The implications for the institutional organization of EU securities and markets regulation may come to be far-reaching, particularly given the rapid accretion of ESMA's direct supervisory powers which occurred in the wake of the pivotal CRA II reforms (Chapter XI). The capacity of the CRA regime to generate significant institutional, political, operational, and constitutional challenges as it grapples with market structure questions remains considerable. Whether or not the EU should establish an independent EU Rating Agency has been a recurring theme of the crisis-era discussion.[132] While it has, for now, been reduced to an item on which the Commission is to report in 2016,[133] the persistence of this troublesome policy option underlines the increasing ambition of the still embryonic EU CRA regime and the very significant momentum for reform.

VII.2.3 Harmonization and ESMA

The CRA regime, as a product of the financial crisis era, is strongly regulatory in its orientation. Regulation, not the support of passporting, is its concern: the CRA Regulation 'introduces a common regulatory approach' in order to enhance the integrity, transparency, responsibility, good governance, and independence of 'credit rating activities'[134] (Article 1).[135] The detailed Regulation is designed to 'lay down conditions for the issuing of credit ratings' and to set out rules on the organization and conduct of CRAs to promote their independence and the avoidance of conflicts of interest, and accordingly to contribute to the smooth functioning of the internal market and achieve a high level of consumer and investor protection (Article 1). Article 1 also specifies, underlining the centrality of structured-finance ratings to the reform process, that it lays down obligations for issuers, originators, and sponsors established in the EU regarding structured-finance instruments.

---

[132] The 2009 CRA I Regulation (at the initiative of the Parliament) requested the Commission to report on the creation of a public EU CRA (rec 73). An EU CRA was also canvassed, albeit sceptically, in the Commission's 2010 Consultation (n 124, 19–23). The Parliament, from the outset, showed some support for such an agency, particularly from its Socialist Party: 2011 Parliament Resolution, n 125, calling on the Commission to conduct a study on the feasibility of an independent European Credit Rating Foundation (paras 16–21) and ECON Press Release, n 128.

[133] The Commission appears unenthusiastic, particularly given the significant conflict of interest and credibility risks: eg 2011 CRA III Proposal, n 126, 11–12.

[134] Generally defined as data and information analysis, and the evaluation, approval, issuing, and review of ratings: Art 3(1)(o).

[135] The reference to independence was added by the CRA III reforms, which also removed a 2009 reference to reliability.

The CRA regime is also, however, strongly procedurally orientated, given the need to equip ESMA with an operational framework for CRA supervision. The administrative regime is primarily procedural and operational in nature, rather than substantive. The two sets of administrative rules adopted by the Commission address the fees which may be charged by ESMA and set the parameters within which ESMA may impose penalties.[136] The four highly technical Regulatory Technical Standard (RTS) Regulations (which were adopted by the Commission without change to ESMA's proposals) are similarly procedural in orientation, and address the following: the content and format of periodic reporting on ratings data to ESMA; the ESMA assessment of CRA compliance with rating methodologies (based on the earlier CESR guidance adopted under the 2009 Regulation); the presentation of the ratings data required to support ESMA's supervisory responsibilities; and the registration and certification process (based on the earlier CESR guidance adopted under the 2009 Regulation).[137] Additional RTSs will follow under the CRA III Regulation.[138] The regime is being further thickened by less operational and more quasi-regulatory ESMA supervisory convergence measures, including a Q&A on the regime[139] and guidelines on its scope.[140]

ESMA's quasi-rule-making activities have accordingly been mainly technical and operational in nature and have not had major substantive impact on the CRA rulebook—certainly when compared with its activities with respect to the European Market Infrastructure Regulation (EMIR) and the AIFMD.[141] Through its supervisory convergence activities it has, however, shown some determination to shape the rulebook as it develops (section 2.10).

VII.2.4 Setting the Regulatory Perimeter

VII.2.4.1 Scope

The CRA Regulation has a wide scope of application, within and outside the EU. It applies to 'credit ratings' issued by CRAs[142] registered in the EU, and which are disclosed publicly or distributed by subscription (Article 2(1)). ESMA has interpreted this perimeter control as requiring CRAs established in the EU to be registered in order to conduct credit rating activities, independent of whether the ratings are to be used for regulatory purposes (in which case the Article 4(1) application mechanism applies).[143] A CRA is defined as a legal

---

[136] n 14.

[137] n 14.

[138] With respect to the disclosure required with respect to structured-finance ratings, the new 'ERP' (European Ratings Platform) repository managed by ESMA and which holds ratings data, and the fees charged by CRAs to clients. For a preliminary review see ESMA, Consultation Paper (2013) (ESMA/2013/891).

[139] The Q&A was adopted in December 2013 (ESMA/2013/1935).

[140] n 15.

[141] Regulation (EU) No 648/2012 [2012] OJ L201/1 (EMIR) and Directive 2011/61/EU [2011] OJ L174/1 (the 2011 AIFMD).

[142] A rating is 'issued' when it has been published on the CRA's website or by other means, or distributed by subscription and presented and disclosed in accordance with the Regulation's Art 10 presentation regime: Art 4 (2). Following the 2013 CRA III reforms, the regime which applies to ratings also generally applies to 'ratings outlooks' (defined as an opinion regarding the likely direction of a rating over the short and medium term).

[143] 2013 ESMA Scope Guidelines, n 15, 6. ESMA will take enforcement against any CRA which issues, endorses, or distributes ratings in the EU without being registered (or, in the case of a non-EU CRA, certified): at 7 and 10.

person whose occupation includes the issuing of credit ratings (ratings) on a professional basis (Article 3(1)(b)). The Regulation also relies on the concept of a 'rated entity' in the design of the regime, and significantly extends the reach of the regime by bringing 'related third parties' (to rated entities) within the scope of the rules.[144]

A rating is an 'opinion' regarding the creditworthiness of an entity, a debt or financial obligation, a debt security, a preferred share, or another financial instrument,[145] or of an issuer of such obligations or other instruments, using an established and defined ranking system or rating categories[146] (Article 3(1)(a)).[147] Under Article 2(2), the Regulation does not apply to 'private' ratings, provided exclusively to the person requiring the rating and not intended for public disclosure or distribution by subscription. Neither does it apply to credit scores,[148] credit scoring systems, or similar assessments relating to obligations arising from consumer, commercial, or industrial relationships. Ratings produced by export credit agencies or central banks are also excluded.[149] The Regulation also specifies that 'recommendations' within the scope of the 2003 Commission Investment Recommendations Directive and 'investment research' within the scope of the 2006 Commission MiFID I Directive (see further section 3.3), along with opinions related to the value of financial instruments or obligations, are excluded (Article 3(2)).

VII.2.4.2 Application and Reach

Article 3(1) sets the scope of the Regulation's application by applying the regime to CRAs registered in the EU. But a double-lock applies through the application mechanism under Article 4(1), which requires that credit institutions, investment firms, insurance undertakings, assurance undertakings, reinsurance undertakings, UCITSs, institutions for occupational retirement provision, alternative investment funds, and central counterparties, each as defined in the relevant sectoral legislation, may use ratings for 'regulatory purposes'[150]

---

[144] A rated entity is the legal person whose creditworthiness is explicitly or implicitly rated in the rating, whether or not it has solicited the rating and whether or not it has provided related information (Art 3(1)(f)). Third parties related to the rated entity are defined as the originator, arranger, sponsor, servicer, or any other party that interacts with a CRA on behalf of a rated entity, including any person directly or indirectly linked to that rated entity by control: Art 3(1)(i).

[145] The perimeter for financial instruments is, as with EU securities and markets regulation generally, set by reference to the 2014 MiFID II/MiFIR (n 18) definition (Art 3(1)(k)). See further Ch IV sect 4.3 on this definition.

[146] A rating category is a rating symbol used in a rating to provide a relative measure of risk to distinguish the different risk characteristics of the types of rated entities, issuers, and financial instruments or other assets: Art 3(1)(h).

[147] ESMA has suggested additionally that a rating must include sufficient qualitative analysis. A measure of creditworthiness derived from summarizing and expressing data based only a pre-set statistical system or model, without additional substantial rating-specific input from a rating analyst, should not, according to ESMA, be considered a credit rating: 2013 ESMA Scope Guidelines, n 15, 7.

[148] Defined as a measure of creditworthiness derived from summarizing and expressing data, based only on a pre-established statistical system or model, without substantial rating-specific input from a rating analyst (Art 3(1)(y)).

[149] The central bank rating must not be paid for by the rated entity, not be disclosed to the public, be issued in accordance with the principles which govern the integrity and independence of rating agencies under the Regulation, and not relate to financial instruments issued by the central bank's Member State(s) (Art 2(3)). The Commission is empowered to adopt administrative rules specifying that a particular central bank's ratings fall outside the scope of the Regulation (Art 2(4)).

[150] Meaning the use of ratings for the specific purpose of complying with EU law, as implemented by the Member States: Art 3(1)(g).

only if they are issued by CRAs which are, first, established within the EU, and second, registered in accordance with the Regulation (Article 4(1)).[151]

Physical presence in the EU (through the establishment requirement) is a recurring feature of the Regulation's design scheme in order to support ESMA's supervisory activities. While this is most evident with respect to the endorsement and certification regime for non-EU CRAs (section 2.11), it is also clear from ESMA's approach; reliance by EU CRAs on non-EU branches[152] for significant operational functions has been identified by ESMA as a potential threat to its supervisory effectiveness and as potentially triggering enforcement action.[153]

With this form of perimeter control, financial institutions are accordingly brought within the regulatory perimeter as quasi-enforcers of the regime—as is clear under the endorsement process in particular, under which financial institutions are required to ensure that any non-EU ratings used by them for regulatory purposes have been endorsed by an EU-established and -registered CRA (section 2.11).[154] In a similar manner, prospectuses approved under the EU prospectus regime must include 'clear and prominent' information as to whether ratings referenced in the prospectus are issued by an EU-registered CRA (Article 4(1)).

The regulatory perimeter is further secured by the outsourcing regime, which requires that outsourcing of 'important operational functions' must not be undertaken in such a way as to impair materially the quality of the CRA's internal control and the ability of ESMA to supervise the CRA (Article 9); ESMA has similarly suggested that important operational functions should not be carried out through non-EU branches.[155] Finally, the complex endorsement and certification system which applies to third country CRA ratings further tightens the perimeter on the regime (section 2.11).

As the first EU securities and markets regulation measure to confer direct supervisory and enforcement power on ESMA, the CRA Regulation eschews the usual mechanics related to jurisdiction allocation, save with respect to the role which Member States retain with respect to the use of ratings under sectoral EU legislation.[156] The specification of the respective roles of NCAs is therefore significantly more limited, although the identification of NCAs remains relevant. The 'sectoral NCAs', who remain responsible for the use of ratings in areas outside the scope of the Regulation (Article 25a), are the NCAs designated under the relevant EU legislation for the supervision of the Article 4(1) actors whose use of ratings 'for regulatory purposes' is limited to ratings issued by EU-established and -registered CRAs (Article 3(1)(r)),

---

[151] The Commission's CRA I Proposal was broader in reach, requiring investment firms and credit institutions not to execute orders for clients in relation to rated financial instruments, unless the rating was issued by a CRA registered in accordance with the Regulation: 2008 CRA I Proposal, n 34, Art 4.

[152] Any rating issued by a non-EU branch would be regarded as an EU rating for the purposes of the Regulation.

[153] 2013 ESMA Scope Guidelines, n 15, 15–16.

[154] The 'for regulatory purposes' perimeter has taken on considerable significance in this context, as a result, with the Commission confirming that ratings used for the purpose of capital assessment under the internal-model-based approach, typically used by the largest banks and investment firms, are not used 'for regulatory purposes' and, accordingly, that non-endorsed ratings can apply.

[155] 2013 ESMA Scope Guidelines, n 15, 7.

[156] Sectoral EU legislation refers to the range of measures governing, *inter alia*, credit institutions, investment firms, insurance companies, and UCITS and noted in Art 4(1).

with the addition of NCAs responsible for overseeing prospectuses. In addition, and as ESMA's operational powers include the ability to draw on the NCAs, Member States must designate adequately staffed NCAs for the purposes of the Directive (Article 22), and who are the NCAs for the purposes of the Regulation generally (Article 3(1)(p)).

VII.2.5 Differentiation and Calibration

By contrast with other elements of EU securities and markets regulation, the regime is not characterized by a high degree of differentiation, although it does attempt to tailor the regime to smaller CRAs and thereby support competition in the CRA market. A proportionality regime accordingly applies for smaller CRAs (Article 6; see section 2.7.1),[157] while the fee regime is designed to ensure that supervisory fees are not a burden for new entrants and to reflect the lighter supervisory costs of smaller CRAs.[158] More generally, the regime acknowledges the particular challenges which methodology assessment can pose, and provides a specific exemption from the regime's rules relating to the validation of methodologies (section 2.7.2).

VII.2.6 The Registration Process

The mandatory registration process for in-scope CRAs (set out in Articles 14–20) is governed by ESMA, although transitional arrangements applied to the initial series of registrations prior to the 2011 CRA II reforms.[159] ESMA must register the CRA if it concludes that the application meets the requirements imposed under the Regulation (Article 14(4)). Once a CRA has been registered by ESMA, that registration is effective for the EU, and the CRA must comply at all times with its registration conditions (Article 14(2) and (3)).

While the registration procedure is, very broadly, similar to the authorization procedures which apply to financial market actors across EU securities and markets regulation, it is subject to a much higher degree of articulation, given the need to provide ESMA with a procedural basis for registration. The intensity of the procedural specification also reflects the constraints imposed by the *Meroni* doctrine (considered in Chapter XI), which are also implicit in the general direction to ESMA that it not impose registration requirements additional to the Regulation on CRAs (Article 14(5)). The Regulation accordingly addresses the time frames within which ESMA must operate, the treatment of group applications, the language used, the nature of the examination of the application to be

---

[157] Approximately half of the smaller CRAs in the EU have applied for exemptions: ESMA 1st Annual Supervision Report, n 119, 6.

[158] 2012 Commission Delegated Fee Regulation rec 3. Fees are calibrated to the size and complexity of the CRA, and small CRAs (total revenues of less than €10 million annually) are fully exempt from supervisory fees (Art 5). Proportionality filters also apply to the regime which governs the ratings data that must be periodically supplied to ESMA under Art 21(e). While this must be supplied on a monthly basis, smaller CRAs can provide it on a bi-monthly basis: 2012 Commission Delegated Supervisory Ratings Data Regulation.

[159] On the initial process, which was based on co-ordination between CESR, colleges of supervisors, and the relevant home NCAs, see CESR, Annual Reporting according to Art 21 of Regulation (EC) 1060/2009 (2010) (CESR/10-1424) (2010 CESR CRA Report). A total of 23 applications for registration were issued at the outset of the registration process in summer 2010.

carried out by ESMA (ESMA must assess whether the application complies with the Regulation), the communication of registration decisions—whether to register, to reject the application, or to withdraw a registration[160] (ESMA must also maintain a related list of registered CRAs)—and the conditions governing the withdrawal of registration[161] (Articles 15–20). Similarly, the registration (and supervisory) fees which ESMA must charge (Article 19(1)), and which are designed to cover ESMA's necessary expenditures relating to CRA registration and supervision and any necessary reimbursements to NCAs who act on behalf of ESMA, are governed by the related 2012 Commission Delegated Fee Regulation.[162] The rules governing the information which CRAs must provide to ESMA in the registration application are likewise prescribed in some detail in the Regulation's Annex II and in the 2012 Commission Delegated Registration and Certification Regulation.[163]

VII.2.7 Regulating Rating Agencies

VII.2.7.1 Conflict-of-Interest Management and Organizational Requirements

The CRA Regulation can be characterized as an operationally intrusive measure,[164] which represents a radical break with the earlier self-regulatory and disclosure-based approach.

Conflict-of-interest prevention and management relating to the rated entity and ratings quality control are at the core of the Regulation. Article 6 sets out the core conflict-of-interest rule in terms of a wide-reaching, catch-all obligation on CRAs to take all necessary steps to ensure that the issuing of a rating (or rating outlook) is not affected by any existing or potential conflict of interest or business relationship involving the CRA, but also its shareholders, managers, rating analysts,[165] employees, any other natural person whose services are placed at the disposal or under the control of the CRA, or any person directly or indirectly linked to it by control.[166] An intrusive business structure rule, designed to address conflict-of-interest and market structure risks, was added by CRA III which provides that a 5 per cent shareholder in a CRA is prohibited from holding 5 per cent or more of the capital of another CRA (Article 6(a));[167] the restriction does not apply to

---

[160] Including to EBA, EIOPA, the NCAs, and the Commission.

[161] ESMA must withdraw registration where a CRA expressly renounces its registration or has provided no ratings in the previous six months; has obtained the registration through false statements or other irregular means; or no longer meets the condition under which it was registered.

[162] n 14.

[163] Including with respect to ownership, organization, governance, financial resources, staffing, outsourcing, conflicts of interest, and methodologies.

[164] ESMA has reported that EU CRAs had to carry out significant change to their organizational structures and procedures to meet the new requirements: ESMA, Annual Report on the Application of the CRA Regulation (2012) (ESMA/2012/3) 4. This was clear from the initial sequence of registration applications once CRA Regulation I came into force, with CESR reporting difficulties in particular with compliance policies, outsourcing, conflict-of-interest risk management (in relation to small CRAs), and organizational and control functions, particularly with respect to conflict-of-interest risk management (in relation to group-based CRA: 2010 CESR CRA Report, n 159.

[165] A person who performs analytical functions that are necessary for the issuing of a rating: Art 3(1)(d).

[166] As is usual across EU securities and markets regulation, control is defined in terms of the relationship between a parent and subsidiary undertaking or as a close link between any natural or legal person and an undertaking: Art 3(1)(j).

[167] The 5 per cent threshold reflects the 5 per cent threshold for ownership reporting under the EU's major holdings notification regime (Ch II sect 5.7). Conflict-of-interest risk was judged by the Commission to be

group-wide holdings.[168] CRAs are also to maintain an effective internal control structure governing the implementation of conflict-of-interest risk management policies and to ensure independence (Article 6(4)).[169]

The operative detail of these core obligations is largely contained in the very detailed Annex I to the Regulation (sections A and B), which is closely based on the 2008 revised IOSCO Code of Conduct, albeit significantly revised and expanded by CRA I and III. It addresses organizational (section A) and operational (section B) requirements. Following a fairly standard template for addressing conflicts of interest through operational and senior management controls, section A requires that senior management[170] must ensure the sound and prudent management of the CRA, that rating activities are independent, that conflicts of interest are properly identified, managed, and disclosed, and that the CRA complies with the Regulation.[171] CRAs are also subject to the high-level requirement that they be organized in such a way that ensures their business interests do not impair the independence or accuracy of rating activities. Among the key related organizational requirements is the obligation to establish an administrative or supervisory board, with sufficient expertise.[172] The independent members[173] of the board are tasked in particular with monitoring rating policies and methodologies, internal quality control and conflict-of-interest management systems, and compliance and governance processes. A number of organizational and governance requirements apply, including obligations to establish the following: adequate policies and procedures to ensure compliance under the Regulation; sound administrative and accounting procedures, internal control mechanisms, risk management procedures, and information process systems controls; conflict-of-interest risk management procedures;[174] continuity arrangements; and an independent review function, responsible for periodically reviewing methodologies, models, and key assumptions.[175] CRAs must also establish an independent compliance function[176] to assess the adequacy

---

significant as EU CRAs are not admitted to trading and their ownership structure is not transparent: 2011 CRA III Proposal, n 126, 6.

[168] The ownership restriction (which does not apply to holdings through diversified collective investment schemes) extends to related control relationships, including having the right to appoint or remove members of the administrative, management, or supervisory board of another CRA.

[169] CRAs are also to establish 'standard operating procedures' concerning corporate governance, organization, and conflict of interest management. This Art 6(4) reinforcement of conflict-of-interest risk management was added by the 2013 CRA III reforms.

[170] Defined as the person(s) who effectively direct the business of the CRA and the members of its administrative or supervisory board (Art 3(1)(n)), and who must be of good repute and sufficiently skilled and experienced.

[171] Annex, sect A, paras 1 and 2.

[172] The majority of members (including the independent members) must have sufficient expertise in financial services and, where the CRA issues ratings related to structured-finance instruments, at least one independent and one other member of the board must have in-depth knowledge and experience at a senior level of the markets in these instruments: Annex, sect A, para 2.

[173] At least one third, but not less than two, of the members of the board must be 'independent members who are not involved in credit rating activities'. The remuneration of independent members is subject to requirements designed to enhance board member independence, while independent board members are also supported by controls on when dismissal can occur, as well as by fixed-term arrangements: Annex II, sect A, para 2.

[174] Designed to prevent, identify, eliminate, manage, and disclose conflicts of interest.

[175] Annex I, sect A, paras 3–4 and 7–10.

[176] A series of requirements apply to strengthen the robustness of the compliance function, including with respect to resources and authority, a dedicated compliance officer, remuneration arrangements (which must be

and effectiveness of procedures and processes, and to advise rating analysts and other relevant persons.[177]

Section B, which was heavily revised by CRA III to reflect conflicts of interest arising from ownership structures, focuses on conflict-of-interest management and requires a CRA to identify, eliminate, or manage and disclose (clearly and prominently) any actual or potential conflicts of interest that may influence the analysis and judgements of its managers, rating analysts, employees, or other natural persons whose services are placed at the disposal or under the control of the CRA, and who are directly involved in the issuing of ratings or ratings outlooks. Related operational requirements include: disclosure by the CRA of all rated entities or related third parties from which it receives more than 5 per cent of its annual revenue; a prohibition on rating particular entities in specified circumstances—including, reflecting the Article 6a concern to address ownership conflicts, in relation to ratings of entities holding shareholdings in the CRA (or disclosure of the related conflict—including the relevant shareholding, where relevant—where the rating is already issued);[178] remuneration requirements;[179] the contested prohibition on consultancy or advisory services to rated entities or related third parties, which also applies to 5 per cent CRA shareholders;[180] a prohibition on rating analysts making proposals or recommendations regarding the design of structured-finance instruments on which the CRA is expected to issue a rating—which, like the structured-finance rules generally, is redolent of the crisis era; and the establishment of adequate related record-keeping and audit procedures. Section B confirms, reflecting the IOSCO Code, that 'ancillary services' may be provided to rated entities, but characterizes these as services which do not form part of credit rating activities and comprise market forecasts, economic trend forecasts, pricing and general data analysis, and related distribution services. Ancillary services must additionally not present a conflict of interest with rating activities, and their provision must be disclosed in the rating report on the rated entity.[181]

Procedural requirements such as these are costly and represent a challenge to the regime's related concern to promote competition in the CRA market, which ultimately may have

---

independent of the CRA's business performance), and independence of compliance persons from the CRA activities which they monitor: Annex I, sect A, para 6.

[177] Annex I, sect A, para 5.

[178] The prohibition or disclosure requirement applies where: the CRA or any persons within the scope of the conflict-of-interest assessment directly or indirectly own(s) financial instruments of the rated entity (or a related third party), or has any direct or indirect ownership in the entity or party, other than holdings in a diversified collective investment scheme; the rating is issued with respect to a rated entity or related third party directly or indirectly linked to the CRA through a control relationship; any person within the scope of the conflict-of-interest assessment is on the administrative or supervisory board of the rated entity; or a rating analyst who participated in the rating, or person who approved the rating, had a relationship with the rated entity or related third party which may cause a conflict of interest. Restrictions also apply in relation to 5 per cent CRA shareholders. Where these circumstances arise, the CRA must also assess whether there are grounds for re-rating or withdrawing the rating or outlook: Annex I, sect B, para 3. The 2013 CRA III reforms added an additional series of prohibitions, including with respect to where a 10 per cent CRA shareholder holds 10 per cent or more of the rated entity, the rated entity holds 10 per cent or more of the CRA, and a 10 per cent shareholder (or shareholder in a position to exercise significant influence on the CRA) is a member of the rated entity's board (of whatever design).

[179] Fees must be non-discriminatory, based on actual costs, and not depend on the level of the rating: Annex I, sect B, para 3a.

[180] The prohibition applies to consultancy or advisory services regarding the rated entity's (or related third party's) corporate or legal structure, assets, liabilities, or activities.

[181] Annex I, sect B, para 4.

some potential as a disciplining measure. A proportionality mechanism therefore applies which allows ESMA to exempt CRAs from certain of these requirements if the CRA can demonstrate that they are not proportionate in view of the nature, scale, and complexity of its business and the nature and range of its issue of credit ratings (Article 6(3)).[182] The relatively limited exemption regime is further confined in that it can only apply where the CRA has less than 50 employees, the CRA has implemented measures and procedures which ensure effective compliance with the Regulation's objectives, and an anti-avoidance requirement is met in that the size of the CRA is not determined in such a way as to avoid compliance by the CRA (or a group[183] of CRAs).[184]

The Article 6 organizational regime is cascaded to the employee/analyst level by Article 7, which imposes a range of requirements on analysts, employees, and similar persons. The CRA must ensure that rating analysts, employees, and any other relevant natural persons[185] have appropriate knowledge and expertise for the tasks assigned (Article 7(1)). Conflict-of-interest requirements also apply in that these persons are prevented from engaging in fee negotiations with rated entities[186] and are subject to 'an appropriate gradual rotation mechanism'; there is also a remuneration requirement which provides that compensation and performance evaluation must not be contingent on the revenues received by the CRA from rated entities or related third parties (Article 7(1), (4) and (5)). These persons are also subject to the detailed operational requirements set out in section C of the Annex. These include: a multilayered and wide-ranging prohibition on activities which may generate conflict-of-interest risks in rating instruments, particularly, but not exclusively, with respect to investments held;[187] requirements relating to appropriate record-keeping and the professional secrecy obligation; a prohibition on accepting gifts; a whistle-blowing obligation;[188] and rotation requirements in support of the Article 7(4) rotation requirement.[189]

---

[182] The exemption regime applies to Annex I, sect A, paras 2 (general senior management and board requirements), 5, and 6 (the independent compliance function), and the Art 7(4) requirement relating to rotation.

[183] 'Group' is defined by reference to the EU's accounting regime (2013 Accounting Directive 2013/34/EU [2013] OJ L182/19) and relates to parent/subsidiary structures as well as related control structures.

[184] Where the CRA forms part of a group of CRAs, ESMA must ensure that at least one of the CRAs within the group is not exempted under Art 6(3).

[185] Whose, in the formula used across the Regulation, 'services are placed at its disposal or under its control and who are directly involved in credit rating activities'.

[186] And related third parties or persons directly or indirectly linked to the rated entity through control.

[187] Rating analysts, employees, and relevant natural persons must, generally, not buy or sell, or engage in any transaction in any financial instrument issued, guaranteed, or otherwise supported by, any rated entity 'within their area of primary analytical responsibility other than holdings in diversified collective investment schemes (CISs)': Annex I, sect C, para 1. These persons are also prevented from participating in or otherwise influencing the determination of a rating where the person owns financial instruments of the rated entity (other than through a diversified CIS); owns (other than through a diversified CIS) financial instruments of an entity related to the rated entity, the ownership of which may cause or may be generally perceived as causing a conflict of interest; or has had a recent employment, business, or other relationship with the rated entity that may cause, or may be generally perceived as causing, a conflict of interest.

[188] Employees, analysts, and relevant persons must immediately inform the compliance function where they consider conduct by other such persons illegal, without negative consequences to themselves.

[189] Lead rating analysts (the persons with primary responsibility for elaborating a rating, or for communicating with the relevant issuer generally, and for preparing rating committee recommendations, as relevant (Art 3(1)(e)), eg, must not be involved in rating activities related to the same rated entity (or related third party) for a period exceeding four years.

VII.2.7.2 Methodologies

Although ESMA is prohibited from interfering in the content of ratings and their methodologies (Article 23), a core object of the Regulation is to address the quality of ratings, in particular through review of methodologies. This is achieved through a combination of disclosure-related, substantive, and supervisory rules. A general disclosure obligation applies under Article 8(1) which requires CRAs to disclose to the public the methodologies, models, and key ratings assumptions used in rating activities. CRAs must also report to ESMA on the historical performance of their ratings (Article 11(2)); an extensive administrative regime governs the content of and format in which ratings data is provided to ESMA.[190] More generally, CRAs must report to ESMA on ratings data in order to support ESMA's supervisory responsibilities (Article 21(e)).[191]

Article 8(2) requires CRAs to adopt, implement, and enforce adequate measures to ensure that ratings and ratings outlooks are based on a thorough analysis of all the information that is available to the CRA and that is relevant to the analysis.[192] At the core of the methodology regime, however, is the more intrusive requirement[193] that ratings methodologies must be rigorous, continuous, systematic, and subject to validation based on historical experience, including back-testing (Article 8(3)).[194] Article 8(3) operates in tandem with the ratings review function required under Article 6 (Annex I section A). Article 22a specifically empowers ESMA to monitor compliance with Article 8(3). The related 2012 Commission Delegated Methodologies Regulation specifies how ESMA is to exercise its Article 8(3) supervisory powers—in the context of registration applications and on an ongoing basis[195]—in order to ensure transparency, but also to delineate ESMA's sphere of operation given the prohibition on interference in rating methodologies; in particular, ESMA may not decide on the accuracy of ratings related to specific methodologies.[196] Requiring ESMA to apply an appropriate level of assessment—determined, *inter alia*, by whether the CRA has a demonstrable history of consistency and accuracy[197]—the 2012 Commission Delegated Methodologies Regulation establishes a series of benchmarks against which ESMA is to assess whether methodologies are rigorous, systematic, continuous, and subject to validation.[198] It also requires CRAs to provide quantitative evidence of

---

[190] 2012 Commission Delegated Periodic Ratings Data Reporting Regulation (n 14).

[191] The content and format requirements are set out in the 2012 Commission Delegated Supervisory Ratings Data Regulation (n 14).

[192] The CRA must adopt all necessary measures such that the information is of sufficient quality and from reliable sources: Art 8(2).

[193] The new methodologies regime has led to a reinforcement by CRAs of their review procedures: ESMA 2012 CRA Report, n 164, 11. By contrast, in its 2005 technical advice to the Commission on CRA policy, CRA advised against intervention with respect to methodologies, given risks of undue standardization, the obstruction of innovation, and the generation of moral hazard: n 69.

[194] An industry view has been expressed that Art 8(3) 'is one of the most important requirements [in the CRA Regulation] . . . as the methodologies and criteria that underline each . . . rating are among the most essential aspects of a rating decision': ESMA/Feedback Statement/2011/464 (on ESMA's draft RTS for a Commission Methodologies Regulation) 6.

[195] 2012 Commission Delegated Methodologies Regulation, n 14, Art 3.

[196] 2012 Commission Delegated Methodologies Regulation, n 14, rec 4.

[197] 2012 Commission Delegated Methodologies Regulation, n 14, Art 3(3).

[198] The rigour assessment, eg, is based on the methodology being, eg, based on clear and robust controls which allow for suitable challenge, incorporating all driving factors relevant to the rating, and incorporating reliable, relevant, and quality-related analytical models, and on the CRA's explanation of the different

the discriminatory power of the methodology and to, *inter alia*, assess the historical robustness and predictive power of ratings (over appropriate horizons and different asset classes) and the degree to which the assumptions used deviate from actual default and loss rates.[199]

The potentially intrusive assessment regime proved controversial with the industry, given in particular the risks of interference with methodologies, the importance of allowing methodologies to be responsive to market conditions, and the limitations of quantitative evidence and of back-testing in evidencing the predictive power of methodologies.[200] ESMA's related revisions to what would become the 2012 Commission Delegated Methodologies Regulation accordingly included an exemption from the back-testing assessment, where limited quantitative evidence is available to support the predictive power of a methodology, as long as the CRA can demonstrate that the methodology in questions is robust. [201]

CRAs must also monitor ratings and review ratings and methodologies on an ongoing basis and at least annually, particularly where material changes occur which could impact a rating (Article 8(5)).[202] A new review regime was imposed under the CRA Regulation III, which requires CRAs to follow mandated procedures when changing existing or using new methodologies.[203] Where the CRA intends to change materially existing or use new methodologies, models, or assumptions that could have an impact on a rating, they must publish the proposed change for comment (Article 8(5a)) and notify ESMA of the proposed changes or any changes made after the consultation (Article 14(3)). The results of the consultation, and the new methodologies (and a related detailed explanation), must be published on the CRA's website and notified to ESMA (Article 8(6)). ESMA was initially charged with reviewing and approving changes to methodologies under the CRA III Commission Proposal, but a notification requirement was imposed instead, reflecting concern as to the risk of ESMA interfering with the content of methodologies, in contravention of Article 23.[204]

A concern to ensure the robustness of methodologies is also implicit in many of the disclosure requirements which apply to ratings (sections 2.7.3–.5). These include, for example, that a CRA must inform the rated entity at least 12 hours before publication of the rating of the principal grounds on which the rating is based, to allow the entity to raise any factual errors.[205]

Most significantly, where the lack of reliable data, the complexity of an instrument's structure, or the quality of the relevant information is not satisfactory, or raises serious

---

quantitative and qualitative elements of the model: 2012 Commission Delegated Methodologies Regulation, n 14, Art 4.

[199] 2012 Commission Delegated Methodologies Regulation, n 14, Art 7.

[200] ESMA/Feedback Statement/2011/464, n 194, 6.

[201] 2012 Commission Delegated Methodologies Regulation, n 14, Art 8.

[202] Related internal arrangements must be in place to monitor the impact of macroeconomic change or financial conditions on ratings.

[203] New notification procedures (including ESMA notification) also apply where CRAs become aware of methodological errors: Art 8(7).

[204] Concern was widespread, including from ESMA Executive Director Ross: n 129.

[205] Annex I, sect D, para 3.

questions as to whether the CRA can provide a reliable rating, the CRA should refrain from rating or withdraw an existing rating.[206]

VII.2.7.3 Disclosure: Ratings and Ratings Presentation

The CRA Regulation is strongly characterized by its reliance on operational requirements which, particularly with respect to methodologies, allow ESMA to drill deeply in to the operation and governance of a CRA.[207] Nonetheless, disclosure-related rules, and thereby market discipline, remain a central feature of the new regime.

A series of requirements apply to the disclosure and presentation of ratings and ratings outlooks.[208] The core obligation requires that CRAs disclose ratings and ratings outlooks, as well as decisions to discontinue ratings, on a non-selective basis and in a timely manner (Article 10(1)).[209] Unsolicited ratings are subject to specific presentation requirements, including that the CRA's policy in relation to these ratings be disclosed and that where a rating is unsolicited, this (and the extent of the rated entity's involvement) is stated prominently in the rating (Article 10(4) and (5)). Detailed disclosure presentation requirements apply under section D of Annex I,[210] which requires, *inter alia*, the disclosure of: all substantially material sources; the principal methodology used; the meaning of each rating; the date of the rating's release (and updating); whether the rating represents the first time the CRA has rated the instrument in question; and guidance relating to the assumptions and methodologies used. More generally, the CRA must also state clearly and prominently any attributes or limitations of the rating or outlook, whether it considers the quality of the information on the rated entity satisfactory, and the extent to which it has verified information provided to it by the rated entity (or related third party).

VII.2.7.4 Disclosure: Conflict-of-interest Risk

The operational and organizational requirements which apply to conflict-of-interest risk management are supported by related disclosure rules. CRAs must fully disclose to the public (and update immediately) a range of information related to conflict-of-interest risk, and set out in section D of Annex I (Article 10(1)). The required disclosures relate to, *inter alia*, actual or potential conflicts of interest, the listing of ancillary services, the CRA's remuneration arrangements, and material modifications to system and procedures.

---

[206] Annex II, sect D, para 4.

[207] The relative strength of the emphasis placed by the Regulation on methodology and rating review, by comparison with the disclosure-based approach adopted in the US pre-Dodd Frank, was emphasized by CESR in its initial assessment that the US regime was not equivalent to the EU regime: CESR/10-332, 6.

[208] The EU's earlier attempt to address the presentation of ratings (aside from the IOSCO Code) was a function of the complex pre-ESMA institutional dynamics. CRAs were previously the target of an injunction to consider adopting internal policies and procedures designed to ensure that ratings published by them were fairly presented under the 2003 Commission Investment Recommendations Directive (rec 10). CESR had advised that CRAs be subject to the Directive's presentation rules as 'indirect' recommendations, despite the Commission's doubt as to whether a rating could constitute a recommendation. The initial draft of the Directive included CRAs 'in order to respect the [CESR] consensus' (European Securities Committee Minutes, 10 July 2003). Member States, however, regarded ratings as more akin to analysis than recommendation, leading to the rec 10 compromise.

[209] This requirement also applies to ratings distributed by subscription.

[210] The regime is subject to a proportionality filter in that where the relevant disclosures would be disproportionate in relation to the report, the report can 'signpost' the reader to where the relevant disclosures are directly and easily accessible, including on the CRA's website: Annex I, sect D, part II, para 5.

A related Transparency Report must be published annually by CRAs, covering, *inter alia*, the CRA's legal and ownership structure, internal control mechanisms, record-keeping, the annual review by the compliance function, rotation policy, revenue information, the split between rating and non-rating activities, and governance disclosures (Article 12).[211]

VII.2.7.5 Disclosure: ESMA Reports and the Ratings Platform

In addition to the publicly available disclosures, CRAs must also make a series of specific disclosures available to ESMA which address conflict-of-interest risk, but also ratings quality more generally (Article 10(2) and (3)).

A public repository reporting regime is also imposed. The principle of reporting on specific disclosures to a public repository maintained by ESMA is established under Article 11(2), which requires a CRA to make available in a central repository established by ESMA (the publicly accessible 'CEREP') specified information on the CRA's historical performance data and on changes to ratings, which is made accessible to the public by ESMA through CEREP and collated by ESMA in the form of an annual summary on the main developments.[212]

Non-public ratings disclosures must also be reported to ESMA, in support of its supervisory activities (Article 21(3)(e)), to the non-public 'SOCRAT' database. The Regulation specifies two particular disclosures which must be made to ESMA on a periodic basis (Article 11(3)).[213] In an attempt to identify potentially troublesome business relationships, and in a clear reflection of crisis-era concerns, CRAs must disclose annually to ESMA their largest 20 clients by revenue generated, as well as those clients whose contribution to the growth rate in revenue for the previous year exceeded the total revenue growth by a factor of 1.5. CRAs must also disclose on a six-monthly basis data relating to the historical default rates of their rating categories and whether the default rates have changed over time.

The 2013 CRA III reforms enhance the public reporting structure by providing more generally that all CRAs must, when issuing a rating or outlook, submit to ESMA a range of rating information which will be published in the new ERP, which will incorporate CEREP (Article 11a); ERP is more extensive than CEREP, allowing investors real-time access to all ratings on specific instruments issued by in-scope CRAs.[214] These disclosures are designed, in part, to allow ESMA to develop 'mappings' of ratings (Article 21(4b)).

VII.2.7.6 Structured-finance Instruments

The influence of the crisis is most apparent in the close attention given to the rating of structured-finance instruments.[215] In addition to meeting the specific expertise requirements

---

[211] The disclosures are set out in Annex I, sect E, part I.

[212] The 2012 Commission Delegated Periodic Ratings Data Reporting Regulation sets out the content and format of these disclosures.

[213] Set out in Annex I, sect E, part II.

[214] The disclosures, which include the rating, outlook, type of rating action, and time, are subject to amplification by RTSs. The ERP is designed to make available all the ratings issued for an instrument, thereby supporting investor decision-making but, arguably, doing little to decrease investor reliance on ratings.

[215] Defined under Art 3(1)(l) as a financial instrument or other asset resulting from a securitization transaction or other scheme governed by CRR Art 4(36) (which defines these transactions as transactions or schemes whereby the credit risk associated with an exposure or pool of exposures is tranched, and payments in the transaction or scheme are dependent on the performance of the exposure or pool of exposures and the subordination of tranches determines the distribution of losses during the life of the transaction or scheme). This wide definition has the effect of imposing additional disclosure requirements on a range of transactions

which apply to senior management related to structured-finance ratings (section 2.7.1), the CRA must not, where it is using a rating from another CRA with respect to underlying assets or structured-finance instruments, refuse to issue a rating relating to underlying assets or structured-finance instruments because a portion of the entity or instruments had been rated previously by another CRA (Article 8(4)). The CRA must also record whenever it departs from existing ratings provided by another CRA with respect to underlying assets or structured-finance instruments, providing a justification.

In one of the Regulation's more controversial provisions, structured-finance ratings must be clearly differentiated using an additional symbol, differentiating the rating category from those used for other entities, instruments, or obligations (Article 10(3)). Differentiated and detailed presentation requirements also apply to ratings of structured-finance instruments, which focus in particular on the degree of due diligence exercised by the CRA in relation to the underlying assets and the extent to which the rating reflects a stress testing of the instrument.[216]

The CRA III reform intensified the regulation of structured-finance ratings as part of the wider effort to reduce CRA market concentration. CRAs are now subject to a complex rotation requirement where they rate re-securitizations (Article 6b), which requires structured-finance products with underlying securitized assets to be rated by a different CRA every four years; the requirement does not apply to small CRAs or to issuers employing at least four CRAs, each rating more than 10 per cent of total outstanding structured-finance instruments. Additionally, two ratings are required for structured-finance ratings (Article 8c).[217] The concern to address over-reliance and prompt greater investor diligence has also led to a requirement on issuers, originators, and sponsors[218] to disclose publicly a range of disclosures, including with respect to the underlying assets, the securitization transaction, and credit support: the detail will be amplified by RTSs (Article 8b).

VII.2.8 Addressing Market Structure and Reliance on Ratings

VII.2.8.1 Reliance on Ratings

The reduction of reliance on ratings, to reduce pro-cyclicality, herding, and volatility risks, and to promote stronger internal credit risk assessment, has been a recurring theme of the

---

not traditionally regarded as structured-finance transactions, including certain project and asset finance deals and real estate transactions: Clifford Chance, Briefing Note. New Disclosure and Dual Rating Requirements in European Structured Finance (2013).

[216] These are set out in Annex I, sect D, Part II and cover, *inter alia*: disclosure relating to the loss and cash flow analysis performed; the level of assessment performed relating to the due diligence process at the level of the underlying financial instruments or other assets of structured-finance instruments; whether the CRA has relied on a third party assessment; guidance relating to assumptions and methodologies used, including in relation to stress testing; and disclosure relating to all structured products submitted to the CRA for initial review, whether or not the CRA is contracted for the final rating.

[217] A series of restrictions apply to ensure that both CRAs are independent of each other (Art 8b(2)). See also section 2.8.2.

[218] Each as defined under Art 3(1)(s)–(u).

crisis-era reform movement. It is, however, difficult to achieve, given the need to provide reliable, functional substitutes.

From a securities and markets regulation perspective, the CRA III reforms to the CRA Regulation introduced a series of measures designed to reduce over-reliance on ratings and to reflect the 2010 Financial Stability Board (FSB) principles in this area.[219] The regulated undertakings referred to in Article 4(1) are required to make their own credit risk assessment and must not 'solely or mechanistically' rely on ratings for assessing the creditworthiness of entities or instruments. In an example of the regime's split supervision model, this obligation is policed by the sectoral NCAs who must monitor the adequacy of these institutions' processes. NCAs must also assess these institutions' use of contractual references to ratings and encourage mitigation (Article 5a).[220] A proportionality requirement applies in that NCAs must take into account the nature and scale of the institution's activities. More generally, ratings and rating outlooks must specify that they represent the CRA's opinion and are to be relied on to a limited degree (Article 8(2)).

The regime also addresses the embedding of ratings within the regulatory system. The European Supervisory Authorities (ESAs) must not refer to ratings in their guidelines, recommendations, and draft Binding Technical Standards, where such references have the potential to trigger mechanistic reliance on ratings by NCAs and financial market participants, and were also to have removed all existing references, where appropriate, by the end of 2013 (Article 5b).[221]

A wider review process is also underway to reduce reliance on ratings across the legislative structure. The related 2013 CRA Directive[222] provides that UCITS and alternative investment fund managers must not solely or mechanistically rely on ratings and that NCAs must monitor the adequacy of the credit assessment processes of the relevant fund managers, assess the use of ratings, and, where appropriate, encourage mitigation of the impact of such use.[223] The CRA III reforms additionally require that the Commission continues to review references to ratings in EU law, with a view to eliminating all references which may trigger mechanistic reliance by 2020, as long as appropriate credit risk assessment alternatives have been identified and implemented (Article 5c).

VII.2.8.2 Competition and Market Structure

Competition-related tools represent relatively new devices for securities and markets regulation[224] and their effective deployment in the CRA segment (and elsewhere) poses

---

[219] n 45.

[220] The extent to which undertakings rely on ratings in, eg, portfolio management, attracted considerable attention over the development of CRA III, including the suggestion that asset management mandates have a flexibility clause, allowing managers to temporarily deviate from ratings downgrades (eg 2010 Commission Consultation, n 124, 12–13), but a more principles-based approach was finally adopted.

[221] The European Systemic Risk Board (ESRB) is also required not to refer to ratings in its warnings and recommendations where there is potential for the reference to trigger mechanistic reliance. The ESAs have reported on their approach to this requirement. The major revision required of ESMA relates to its use of ratings in its guidelines on money-market funds: EBA, EIOPA, ESMA, Final Report on Mechanistic References to Credit Ratings in the ESAs' Guidelines and Recommendation (2014) (JC-CP-2014-04).

[222] n 13.

[223] The requirements also apply to occupational pension funds.

[224] On the application of EU competition law to CRAs see Gildehaus, H, 'The Rating Agency Oligopoly and its Consequences for European Competition Law' (2012) *ELJ* 269.

significant challenges, given the need for specialist expertise and given the risks of inter-vening in market structure. In addition, while the oligopolistic structure of the EU CRA market is associated with risks to the quality of ratings, competition also bring risks, particularly where the promise of a good rating becomes an instrument of competition.[225]

The CRA III reforms in relation to market structure are, however, tentative and limited in scope.[226] Mandatory CRA rotation is relied on as a device to strengthen competition and to reduce the related co-dependency risks of the issuer-pays model. The difficulties in intervening with respect to market structure were sharply exposed by the scale of market concern as to the Commission's original rotation proposal that CRAs be required to rotate from an issuer every three years.[227] The rotation device was, accordingly, significantly scaled back and restricted to the rating of re-securitized assets in the structured-finance market (Article 6b),[228] although the possible extension of the rotation requirement is the subject of the Commission's review obligations (Article 39).[229] In addition, a somewhat loose direc-tion has been given to issuers to 'consider the possibility' of mandating at least one CRA (where issuers intend to mandate at least two) which does not have more than 10 per cent of the total market share (Article 8d);[230] whether or not such a loosely drafted provision will support greater competition is unclear. CRAs have also been enjoined to ensure that fees are based on actual cost (Annex I, B (3c)); this direction requires that ESMA operate as a quasi-competition regulator and engage with pricing regulation, although it has no prior experi-ence in this field.

VII.2.9 Ratings and the Sovereign Debt Market

The turbulence in the euro-area sovereign debt market over the crisis era has left a mark on the CRA Regulation. The demonstrable impact of sovereign debt rating downgrades on borrowing costs, on euro-area contagion risks, and on the stability of credit institutions exposed to sovereign holdings has shaped the regime.[231] While the effectiveness of the

---

[225] The 2011 European Parliament Resolution, eg, warned that increased competition would not auto-matically imply better quality ratings: n 125, para 15.

[226] Earlier discussions canvassed a range of more intrusive options, including rating by the ECB or a new EU agency: 2010 Commission Consultation, n 124, 19–21.

[227] ESMA Chief Executive Ross, eg, noted the risk that new entrants could compete by offering higher ratings and that mandatory rotation could lead to undue reliance on poorly equipped CRAs: n 129.

[228] This market segment was highlighted as it is regarded as posing the most risks in terms of conflicts of interest, and because, as the credit risk of a securitized transaction is specific to each transaction, the risk of a loss of expertise is less: 2013 CRA III Regulation rec 14. The complex rotation requirement is based on the issuer of structured-finance products with underlying re-securitized assets being required to switch to a different CRA every four years; an outgoing CRA is not allowed to rate re-securitized products of the same issuer for a period equal to the duration of the expired contract, though not exceeding four years. The requirement does not apply to small CRAs or to issuers employing at least four CRAs, each rating more than 10 per cent of total outstanding structure finance instruments.

[229] The Regulation acknowledges in some detail the difficulties in this area, and the importance of trialling the rotation mechanism in the re-securitized assets sphere: rec 7a.

[230] ESMA must publish a list on which the issuer can rely and which identifies relative market shares (on its initial assessment see n 118).

[231] The 2011 CRA III Proposal Impact Assessment rather mutedly suggested that unexpected downgrades had led issuers, investors, and regulators to question the consistency, rationale, and transparency of sovereign ratings (n 123, 7), but also noted some concern as to arbitrariness and subjective bias in sovereign ratings and the risk of CRAs using sovereign rating downgrades as a means of rebuilding their reputational capital (at 15).

sovereign debt rating process was raised internationally,[232] it drew sharp policy and political attention in the euro area, reflecting concerns as to slow and over-reaction by CRAs,[233] competence failures, the effectiveness of methodologies, and failures to reflect the array of euro-area support measures adopted over the crisis.[234] Ultimately, high-level and vocal political concern as to the impact of ratings downgrades, particularly in the cases of Portugal, Greece, and Italy over 2011[235] (which period saw questions raised as to objectivity and quality of the sovereign debt ratings process[236]), and with respect to the high-profile downgrading of the European Financial Stability Mechanism in early 2012,[237] has been reflected in the adoption of a distinct regime for sovereign ratings (Articles 8(5) and 8a).

These rules are designed to improve the transparency and quality of sovereign ratings;[238] the rules which apply to the rating process more generally also continue to apply. Sovereign debt ratings must be reviewed every six months (Article 8(5)), and their release must follow a pre-set calendar, set a year in advance (Article 8a(3) and (4)).[239] Sovereign ratings must also be accompanied by a research report which explains the related assumptions and methodologies.[240] General group ratings of sovereigns are prohibited, unless accompanied by specific research reports (Article 8a(1)).

The regime as adopted is significantly less radical, and more attuned to the conflict-of-interest risks inherent in the Member States' imposing a specific regime on the rating of sovereign debt risk, than the sometimes fanciful range of options canvassed during the development of the regime. The Commission's CRA III Proposal Impact Assessment, for example, assessed options ranging from conferring on ESMA the ability to restrict or ban temporarily sovereign debt ratings, to conferring the rating task on the European Central

---

[232] eg IMF, Global Financial Stability Report, October 2010.

[233] eg Stephens, P, 'Downgrade the Rating Agencies', *Financial Times*, 10 January 2012, 13, querying, in the wake of a series of high-profile sovereign rating downgrades—notably of France—the value represented by ratings, given their failure over the crisis.

[234] eg 2010 Commission Consultation, n 124, 14–16; 2011 European Parliament Resolution, n 125, paras 34–40; and de Santis, R, the Euro Area Sovereign Debt Crisis. Safe Havens, Credit Rating Agencies, and the Spread of the Fever from Greece, Ireland and Portugal, ECB Working Paper No 1419 (2012).

[235] The July 2011 downgrade of Portugal by Moody's led Commission President Barosso to charge Moody's with 'mistakes and exaggerations': reported in Spiegel, P and Oakley, D, 'Brussels Launches Attack on Moody's', *Financial Times,* 7 July 2011, 1.

[236] The downgrades by Standard & Poor's of Greece on 29 March 2011 and of Italy on 21 May 2011, in particular, generated vocal political complaints about the accuracy and timeliness of the downgrades: 2011 CRA III Proposal Impact Assessment, n 123, 16. The Greek downgrade (which generated a hostile reaction from the Greek finance minister: Milne, R and Oakley, D, 'Hard to Credit', *Financial Times*, 28 March 2011) prompted a press release from EU Commissioners Barnier (single market) and Rehn (economic policy), expressing confidence in the fiscal adjustments being achieved by Greece and signalling that CRA regulation would be extended. A Commission Roundtable, held in July 2011, similarly reported market anger and perceptions that some ratings were 'questionable' and 'disruptive and not credible': Roundtable Report, 2.

[237] Chaffin, J and Peel. Q, 'Eurozone Bail-out Fund hit by Downgrade', *Financial Times*, 17 January 2012, 6.

[238] Defined as ratings where the entity rated is a State (or its local or regional authorities), the issuer of the debt security is a State or regional/local authority or special purpose vehicle for these entities, or the issuer is an international financial institution established by one or more States and designed to provide financial assistance to members: Art 3(1)(v).

[239] The calendar must set dates (which must be Fridays) for ratings and ratings outlooks, and deviations from this calendar must be explained. The timing of sovereign ratings was of concern from the outset, with the Commission initially suggesting, eg, that all sovereigns be given three days' notice of a rating, to allow the correction of factual errors (ordinarily, a 12-hour notice period applies): 2010 Commission Consultation, n 124, 15.

[240] The details of the publicly available report are out in Annex I, sect D, III.

Bank (ECB), the Commission, or the European Stability Mechanism, to prohibiting the issuance of sovereign debt ratings.[241] But their airing is more an illustration of the depth of political anger as to the impact of downgrades on euro-area stability than an insight into the Commission's ambitions for EU securities and markets regulation. Certainly, the current transparency-focused regime seems to reflect reasonably strong stakeholder support.[242]

VII.2.10 Supervision and Enforcement: ESMA

VII.2.10.1 Supervision

Under the CRA regime, a direct transfer of 'workaday' supervisory and enforcement competence from the Member States to ESMA has taken place. There are particular specificities to CRAs. They represent a small section of the financial market, they have extensive cross-border reach (some CRAs had, prior to the ESMA regime, up to 14 supervisors in their colleges of supervisors),[243] the impact of ratings extends beyond territorial boundaries, and CRAs do not generate material fiscal risks for the Member States, making the transfer of supervisory power a less risky proposition. Nonetheless, the transfer of direct supervisory power over CRAs is a major development as it has required the EU institutions to design an operational model which may support extensive transfers of direct power to ESMA in the future. The regime for ESMA's supervision of trade repositories under EMIR (Chapter VI section 4.2), for example, is modelled on the CRA regime.

ESMA is charged with ensuring that the Regulation is applied (Article 21). In order to achieve this, an extensive operational and procedural regime is put in place under the Regulation. This is supported by ESMA guidelines[244] and by the RTSs relating to the CRA registration process, the certification process, CRA disclosures to the CEREP/SOCRAT/ERP data repositories, and the assessment by ESMA of CRA compliance with the Article 8(3) requirement that methodologies be rigorous, systematic, continuous, and subject to validation based on historical experience. The reach of ESMA's powers is underlined by the discrete accountability and reporting requirements which apply,[245] but also by the prohibition on ESMA interfering with the content of ratings or with methodologies (Article 23). Reflecting the cross-sector impact of CRAs and the related importance of ESMA's supervision of CRAs, ESMA is also required to co-operate with EBA and EIOPA in performing its tasks under the Regulation and before issuing guidelines and RTSs (Article 21(7)).

While ESMA now exercises exclusive supervisory and enforcement competence over CRAs, the operational structure reflects a degree of power sharing. Member States' sectoral NCAs

---

[241] 2011 CRA III Proposal Impact Assessment, n 123, 34–9.

[242] Roundtable Report, n 236, 3.

[243] 2010 CRA II Proposal Impact Assessment, n 103, 9.

[244] Art 21(2) and (3) direct ESMA to adopt guidance on co-operation between ESMA, the NCAs, and the sectoral NCAs, including with respect to the delegation of tasks, as well as guidance on the endorsement process.

[245] ESMA must publish an annual report on the application of the Regulation (Art 21(5)) and present a report on the supervisory measures taken and penalties imposed under the Regulation annually to the European Parliament, Council, and Commission: Art 21(5) and (6)).

retain responsibility for the supervision of the use of ratings for Article 4(1) regulatory purposes, and under sectoral legislation (Article 25a). These NCAs are accordingly charged with overseeing the new obligations with respect to reducing reliance on ratings and creditworthiness assessments (Article 5a), as well as the issuer-facing obligations with respect to structured-finance instruments (Article 8b–c). ESMA is also, to a degree, dependent on the Commission operationally in certain key respects. Its fee-charging powers, for example, operate within Commission parameters under the 2012 Commission Delegated Fee Regulation, which sets out the type of fees which can be levied on CRAs (registration and supervisory), and which relates fees to, in part, CRA activities (including with respect to structured-finance instruments, endorsement activities, and the extent of international activities) and size.[246] The different RTSs which support the supervisory process[247] have also been adopted by the Commission—albeit that the Commission did not change ESMA's related proposals.

In addition, the NCAs are, in some respects, to act as ESMA's operational arms for direct supervision (although ESMA has developed a distinct and independent supervisory capacity). ESMA may, where it is necessary for the proper performance of a supervisory task, delegate 'specific supervisory tasks' (including information requests and investigations and on-site inspections), in accordance with ESMA guidance, to local NCAs (Article 30).[248] Local NCAs can therefore, as necessary, provide ESMA with additional operational capacity under, in effect, a 'hub and spokes' model. Good ESMA/NCA relations are supported by the requirement for prior consultation (as to scope of supervisory support, timetable, and information transmission) to take place between ESMA and the NCA, and for the NCA to be reimbursed (Article 30(2) and (3)).[249] The delegation of tasks does not affect ESMA's Article 21 responsibility to ensure the Regulation is applied, and must not limit ESMA's ability to conduct and oversee the delegated activity; supervisory responsibilities, including with respect to registration decisions, final assessments, and follow-up decisions concerning infringements, must not be delegated (Article 30(4)).

ESMA's pre-eminence with respect to supervision, however, is reinforced in a number of ways. NCAs are required to co-operate with ESMA under Article 30.[250] NCAs are subject to an obligation to notify ESMA (in 'as specific a manner as possible') where they find breaches of the Regulation have been committed in their territory or in another Member State; where the NCA considers it appropriate for ESMA's investigatory powers to be exercised, it may suggest that ESMA exercise its related powers (Article 31). ESMA is to take 'appropriate action' in response but is not required to follow an NCA request, although it must notify the NCA of the outcome. NCAs may also request that ESMA examines whether the conditions for withdrawal of registration are met (Article 20(2)). Similarly, NCAs notifying ESMA under Article 31 may request that ESMA suspend the use of ratings

---

[246] ESMA provided technical advice, however, on the appropriate fee structure: ESMA/2011/144.

[247] n 14.

[248] Delegations must be reviewed and can be revoked at any time: Art 30(4).

[249] The nature of the reimbursement is set out in the 2012 Commission Delegated Fee Regulation, n 14, Art 9.

[250] Some initial doubts seem to have been raised at an early ESMA Board of Supervisors meeting at which the Commission confirmed that a delegation request must be agreed to by the NCAs: Board of Supervisors, 20 September 2011 (2011/BS/209).

for regulatory purposes in exceptional circumstances.[251] ESMA is not required to follow these requests; under Article 31, it must take 'appropriate measures' to resolve the issue or inform the NCA, setting out its reasons, where it considers the request is not justified. Article 20 similarly requires that full reasons be provided where CRA registration is not withdrawn by ESMA after an NCA request. Some care has been taken to establish ESMA's pre-eminence in on-site inspections (Article 23d—considered below); local officials must, for example, 'actively assist' officials and other persons authorized by ESMA and local enforcement assistance must be made available to ESMA where necessary. A detailed regime also applies to the respective roles of ESMA and the NCA in on-site inspections. The role of local courts has also been carefully delineated. Where authorization from a local judicial authority is required to, for example, compel telephone and data traffic (in relation to ESMA's general investigations power under Article 23c), the national court is to check that the ESMA decision is authentic and that any related coercive measures envisaged are not arbitrary or excessive. But while the national court may request an explanation from ESMA as to its grounds for suspecting an infringement of the Regulation and the seriousness of the infringement, the court may not review the necessity of the investigation or require that it be provided with information on ESMA's files. Review of the lawfulness of ESMA's decision is reserved to the Court of Justice (Article 23b(6)). A similar regime applies where activities related to on-site inspections require judicial authorization (Article 23c(9)). Accordingly, some care has been taken to protect ESMA's pre-eminence.

More generally, ESMA, the NCAs, the sectoral NCAs, and EBA and EIOPA are all required to co-operate where necessary for the purposes of the Regulation (and relevant sectoral legislation) (Article 26). They must also, without undue delay, supply each other with the information required to carry out their duties under the Regulation (and relevant sectoral legislation) (Article 27).[252]

A suite of direct supervisory powers is conferred on ESMA. Reflecting the *Meroni* constraint, the nature of the powers is specified in detail. Under Article 23b, ESMA may either by 'simple request' or by 'decision' require all information necessary to carry out its duties from a range of actors.[253] The 'simple request procedure' is designed for a non-binding request, while the 'decision procedure' is designed for a binding request, failure to comply with which will lead to a penalty.[254] General investigation powers are conferred under Article 23c which empowers ESMA to conduct all necessary investigations of relevant persons,[255] and confers on its officials and authorized persons a range of related powers.[256] The supporting procedural framework covers the procedure governing investigations (including the need for an ESMA decision to launch an investigation and for ESMA to

---

[251] The infringements must be sufficiently serious and persistent to have a significant impact on the protection of investors or the stability of the financial system in the Member State of the NCA in question.

[252] ESMA may transmit confidential information to Member States' central banks and the ECB, the ESRB, and other public authorities responsible for overseeing payment and settlement systems: Art 27(2).

[253] Including from CRAs, rated entities, related third parties, third parties to whom CRAs have outsourced operational functions, and persons 'otherwise closely and substantially related or connected to CRAs': Art 23b(1).

[254] Art 23b(2) and (3), respectively. The relevant procedural and disclosure requirements which apply in each case are specified.

[255] As specified in Art 23b(1): n 253.

[256] Including to examine records and data, to take or obtain certified copies of materials, to summon persons for explanations, to interview persons, and to request telephone and data traffic records: Art 23c(1).

provide written authorizations for those carrying out the investigation), the requirement for relevant persons to submit to ESMA investigations, the assistance of ESMA by home NCAs, and the role of the courts in reviewing authorizations to compel telephone or data traffic records (Article 23c(2)–(6)). Specific powers apply to on-site inspections (Article 23d): ESMA may conduct all necessary on-site inspections at the business premises of the relevant persons,[257] without prior announcement, where the proper conduct and efficiency of the inspection so requires (Article 23d(1)). A suite of related powers are conferred on ESMA's officials and authorized persons.[258] A similar procedural framework applies as governs the general Article 23c investigations power (Article 23d(3)–(9)).[259]

Specific powers apply to CRA methodologies (Article 22a). The European Parliament's Economic and Monetary Affairs (ECON) committee proposed that ESMA be conferred with the power to engage in random sampling of ratings to check rating quality.[260] While this power was downgraded during the final CRA II trilogue negotiations (between the Commission, Council, and European Parliament) to a power to examine CRAs' compliance with their obligation to back-test methodologies under Article 8(3) (Article 22a),[261] it remains an intrusive power, and points to the extent to which ESMA can drill into the operation of CRAs.

ESMA acquired responsibility for CRA supervision in July 2011. By the time of its second annual report on CRA supervision in March 2013, it had registered 19 CRAs and certified one, and had developed an internal supervisory capacity, including a risk assessment model.[262] Its first annual report on CRA supervision, which focused on its first series of 'on-site' investigations of the three major EU agencies—Fitch, Moody's, and Standard & Poor's—suggested a robust approach to supervision and an appetite for driving reforms.[263] Its second annual report in March 2013, which addressed its first full supervisory year, was similarly robust, underlining its commitment to the 'development of a thorough regime with intrusive supervision'[264] and warning that while progress had been made in the CRA sector, further improvements were needed.[265] Initial stakeholder reaction to ESMA's

---

[257] As specified in Art 23b(1): n 253.
[258] Including the power to enter any business premises and exercise the Art 23c(1) powers, and to seal any business premises and books and records for the period of the inspection: Art 23d(2).
[259] Including with respect to reliance on written authorizations, the requirement for relevant persons to submit to ESMA's inspection (and the related ESMA decision needed before an inspection can be launched), and relations with officials from the Member State in question.
[260] n 111.
[261] ESMA is also empowered to verify the execution of back-testing by CRAs, to analyse the results of back-testing, and to verify that CRAs have processes in place to take into account the results of back-testing: Art 22a(2).
[262] ESMA, Annual Report (2011) 29–30, ESMA Annual Report (2012) 19, and ESMA, Second Annual Report on Application of the CRA Regulation—2012 (2013) (ESMA/2013/308).
[263] ESMA 1st Annual Supervision Report, n 119. The Report highlighted, in robust terms, a number of areas where improvements were required, including in relation to the recording of meetings, information flow to the CRAs' risk committees, the monitoring of resources, the strengthening of internal controls, the disclosure of methodologies, and the resilience of IT systems.
[264] ESMA 2nd Annual Supervision Report, n 117, 30.
[265] Particularly with respect to the consistent application and comprehensive presentation of rating methodologies, the empowerment and resourcing of analytical and control functions, the monitoring and surveillance of ratings, and the reliability of IT infrastructures: ESMA 2nd Annual Supervision Report, n 117.

approach to supervision has generally been positive.[266] Most indications suggest that ESMA has the appetite for a robust supervisory approach[267] which is executed through a range of supervisory tools, including ongoing, risk-based, and proactive day-to-day supervision, thematic assessment of risks, and risk analysis.[268] It also appears ready to address politically sensitive elements of CRA regulation, notably with respect to sovereign debt ratings.[269] ESMA therefore appears to have embraced its first set of direct supervisory powers with an enthusiasm that might suggest some institutional ambition.

VII.2.10.2 Enforcement and ESMA

ESMA's suite of enforcement powers (and in particular its power to impose fines) generated considerable controversy over the CRA II Regulation negotiations, on the part of certain Member States[270] as well as the Commission,[271] with respect to compliance with the *Meroni* doctrine and the related prohibition on the delegation of wide-ranging discretionary executive powers. The regime evolved significantly over the negotiations; the CRA II Regulation as adopted is considerably more sophisticated than the Commission's original, cumbersome model, which conferred fining powers on the Commission, reflecting the Commission's view of the *Meroni* constraints.[272] While the Regulation as adopted confers more extensive powers on ESMA, particularly with respect to enforcement, it also confines ESMA's discretion to a greater extent.

ESMA's enforcement activities must take place within the detailed procedural framework established under the Regulation (Article 23e), which is based on investigation by an

---

[266] eg Mazars, Review of the New European System of Financial Supervision. Part 1: The Work of the European Supervisory Agencies. Study for the ECON Committee (2013) (IP/A/ECON/ST/2012-23) 97, reporting on the view that 'ESMA has efficiently established the process and organization to professionally execute' its responsibilities, and IMF, Financial Sector Assessment Program, European Union. European Securities and Markets Authority. Technical Note. March 2013. Support also came (if indirectly) through the rejection by the ESA Board of Appeals of a procedural and substantive challenge to ESMA's decision not to register a CRA (although ESMA lost on some points, overall the appeal against the ESMA decision was not allowed): Decision of the Board of Appeal, BoA 2013-14, 10 January 2014.

[267] ESMA's 2013 CRA supervision and policy work plan identified the importance of a credible regime that encourages registered CRAs to embed good practices and of 'engaged and intrusive' supervision: ESMA 2013 CRA Supervision and Policy Work Plan (2013) (ESMA/2013/87).

[268] n 267.

[269] ESMA's December 2013 report on the issuing of sovereign debt ratings, which followed a targeted supervisory review of practices by Fitch, Moody's, and Standard & Poor's, was critical, particularly with respect to independence and the avoidance of conflicts of interests, timing, confidentiality procedures, and resources: ESMA/2103/1775.

[270] Notably the UK: House of Commons European Scrutiny Committee, 7th Report, Session 2010–2011, 70–2, citing the Financial Services Secretary to HM Treasury as noting that 'the legality of delegating discretionary powers to [ESMA] is of vital importance and has been a priority for the Government throughout the negotiations'.

[271] The Commission's Impact Assessment Board reports on the proposed 2011 CRA II Regulation raised *Meroni* concerns related to the Commission's justification for ESMA's supervisory and enforcement powers: see reports at n 114.

[272] The Commission noted the complexities engaged in splitting enforcement intervention between the Commission and ESMA, but suggested that conferring fining powers on ESMA, while bringing efficiencies, 'could raise some concerns of consistency with the Community acquis and notably . . . the Meroni case': 2010 CRA II Proposal Impact Assessment, n 103, 31. The Commission's model also reflected earlier agency precedent: the fining regime under the European Aviation Safety Agency Regulation reserves fining powers to the Commission (Regulation (EC) No 216/2008 [2008] OJ L79/1).

independent investigation officer within ESMA of the relevant breach[273] and the adoption of a final decision by the ESMA Board of Supervisors, in accordance with the CRA Regulation Annex III rules, which set out the specific infringements which are susceptible to enforcement action. Although the Regulation does not provide for criminal sanctions, matters for criminal prosecution are to be referred to the relevant national authorities where there are serious indications of the possible existence of facts liable to constitute criminal offences (Article 23e(8)).

Article 24 specifies the range of non-monetary enforcement measures which can be taken by ESMA as follows: withdrawal of registration, temporary prohibition of the CRA from issuing ratings throughout the EU and/or suspension of the use of the CRA's ratings for regulatory purposes until the infringement has been brought to an end, requiring the CRA to bring the infringement to an end, and public notices. The application of the relevant measure is subject to procedural constraints in that ESMA must take into account the nature and seriousness of the infringement, having regard to a series of factors.[274] A concern to avoid market instability and for the related fiscal implications for Member States is implicit in the enforcement regime. Where ESMA decides to suspend the use of a rating for regulatory purposes or to withdraw a CRA registration, the rating can be used for ten days after the ESMA decision; where another rating is not available, a three-month period applies, and this period may be extended by three months in exceptional circumstances related to the potential for market disruption or financial instability (Article 24(3)). EBA and EIOPA must also be informed of any ESMA decisions to withdraw CRA registrations or to suspend the use of particular ratings (Article 24(3)). Article 24 decisions, which must be notified to the relevant person and communicated to EBA, EIOPA, the NCAs, and the sectoral NCAs (Article 24(5)), have third-party effects, and must be subject to the right of the person concerned to be heard (Article 25).

The monetary penalties regime (fines and periodic penalties) is particularly carefully confined, reflecting the significant concern as to the *Meroni* risks which it generated over the negotiations. ESMA's power to impose fines (Article 36a) arises only where the Board of Supervisors finds that a rating agency has, negligently or intentionally,[275] committed an infringement identified in Annex III. A minimum and maximum fine range applies to each of the Annex III infringements (Article 36a(2)). The Regulation also sets out how ESMA should decide whether fines 'should be at the lower, the middle, or the higher' end of these limits, specifies when the fining ranges should be adjusted by means of mitigating or aggravating factors,[276] and places an overall cap on fines of 20 per cent of the CRA's annual turnover in the preceding business year.[277] This highly detailed regime is supported by the 2012 Commission Delegated Penalties Regulation, which lays down procedural rules

---

[273] During this process, the relevant person has the right to be heard and file access rights: Art 23e(3)–(4).

[274] These are: the duration and frequency of the infringement, whether the infringement revealed serious or systemic weaknesses in the undertaking's management systems or internal controls, whether financial crime was facilitated, and whether the infringement was intentional or negligent: Art 24(2).

[275] An intentional infringement is considered to arise where ESMA finds objective factors which demonstrate that the CRA or its senior management acted deliberately to commit the infringement: Art 36a(1).

[276] Art 36a(3) and Annex IV. Annex IV, eg, provides that if the infringement has been committed repeatedly an additional co-efficient of 1.1 must apply to each repetition.

[277] Where the CRA has benefited financially, directly or indirectly, from the infringement, the fine must be at least equal to the financial benefit: Art 36a(4).

governing the imposition of fines (and periodic penalties), including with respect to the right to be heard by an ESMA investigation officer and by the ESMA Board of Supervisors, access to documents, limitation periods, and the collection of monetary sanctions. In the case of continuing infringements or lack of co-operation, ESMA may also impose periodic penalties, which are designed to compel action by CRAs or relevant persons[278] (Article 36b). ESMA is empowered to impose periodic penalties which are effective and proportionate, imposed on a daily basis until compliance is achieved, but for no longer than six months. The amount of the penalty is specified in the Regulation.[279] As with Article 24 enforcement generally, decisions relating to monetary penalties under Articles 36a and 36b are subject to the right to be heard (Article 36c). All fines and periodic payments imposed must be publicly disclosed by ESMA, absent exceptional circumstances (Article 36d(1)).[280]

Of particular importance is the Regulation's delineation of how enforcement proceedings are to be carried out. On general principles, the Treaty loyalty obligation (Article 4(3) TEU) suggests that national courts should accept ESMA as a party to any enforcement proceedings, although Treaty difficulties may arise given that the Commission exercises direct enforcement powers under the Treaty with respect to breaches of EU law.[281] The CRA Regulation provides, however, that administrative sanctioning powers—including the power to levy fines and periodic penalties (Article 36d(2))—can all be directly exercised by ESMA, subject to the general review, hearing, and appeal regime for decision-making which applies under the foundation 2011 ESMA Regulation. It also specifies that fines and periodic penalties are to be enforceable, and that enforcement is to be governed by the rules of civil procedure in force in the Member State in the territory of which enforcement is carried out, once the authenticity of the ESMA decision has been verified by the local authority so designated by the Member States (Article 36d). Only the Court of Justice can (reflecting the foundation ESMA Regulation) review ESMA's decisions to impose monetary sanctions (Article 36c)). In the case of potential criminal prosecutions, ESMA is, as noted above, to refer matters for prosecution to the relevant national authorities where it finds that there are serious indications of the possible existence of facts liable to constitute criminal offences (Article 23d).

Notwithstanding the constitutional sensitivities, ESMA has shown some appetite for enforcement action. It has warned that it has 'no tolerance' for entities engaging in rating activities which should be registered but are not, and that it will take appropriate enforcement action.[282] But this might best be regarded as ESMA testing the deterrent effects of its powers, rather than ESMA signalling its appetite for direct action.

---

[278] Penalties can be imposed to compel a CRA to put an end to an infringement, and to compel a person to supply complete information, to submit to an investigation and produce related information, or to submit to an on-site inspection: Art 36b(1).

[279] The amount is set at 3 per cent of the CRA's average daily turnover in the preceding business year or, in the case of natural persons, 2 per cent of average daily income in the preceding calendar year: Art 36b(3).

[280] Art 36d does not apply where disclosure would seriously jeopardize the financial markets or cause disproportionate damage to the parties involved.

[281] The Commission's 2008 report on agencies, eg, argued that agencies could not be entrusted with powers which had been conferred on the Commission by the Treaty: The European Agencies—The Way Forward (2008) (COM (2008) 135).

[282] ESMA 2nd Annual Supervision Report, n 117, 7. The Report also noted that investigations were underway in relation to possible enforcement action: at 18.

VII.2.10.3 Civil Liability

The imposition by the 2013 CRA III reforms of a harmonized civil liability regime (independent of the contractual rights of action which may otherwise be available to issuers who contract with CRAs) represents a new departure for EU securities and markets regulation.[283] Hitherto, private liability mechanisms have been regarded as a Member State preserve, given the embedding of liability actions within national procedural regimes (Chapter XI section 4.1). The new Article 35a regime, however, is designed to provide CRAs with strong compliance incentives—albeit that ESMA's enforcement powers should also have this effect. A new liability action is, nonetheless, a double-edged sword, carrying the risk of increased costs,[284] of 'chilling' CRAs, and of prompting vexatious litigation— although the relatively confined nature of the action, which is linked to specific infringements of the Regulation, may limit its impact.

The new action provides that that where a CRA commits 'intentionally' or 'negligently' any of the infringements specified in Annex III, an investor or issuer may claim damages from the CRA in respect of damage 'due to that infringement'. An investor may claim damages where it has established that it 'reasonably relied', in accordance with the Article 5a(1) reliance regime[285] or otherwise with due care, on a rating for a decision to invest in, hold, or divest financial instruments covered by the rating. A lower threshold of proof applies to the rated issuer, who can claim damages where it establishes that it or its financial instruments are covered by the rating and the relevant infringement was not caused by misleading and inaccurate information provided by the issuer, directly or through information publicly available. The burden is on the issuer or investor to present accurate and detailed information (the nature of which is to be determined by the relevant national court) indicating that an infringement has occurred and the infringement has had an impact on the rating. Civil liability may be limited in advance by the CRA, but only where the limitation is reasonable and proportionate and the limitation is allowed under applicable national law.

The regime is crafted in loose terms, particularly with respect to the damage which the infringement must cause. Operationally, it depends on national civil liability regimes, with the key determinants for the action—including 'damage', 'intention' 'due care', and 'reasonably relied'—all to be interpreted in accordance with applicable national law, and all relevant matters not covered by the Regulation to be determined by applicable national law. It is accordingly a framework regime which will depend almost entirely on national interpretation. The possibility for forum shopping is therefore significant.[286]

VII.2.11 Third Countries

One of the defining features of the CRA Regulation is the extent to which it requires the physical presence within the EU of CRAs if their ratings are to be used for regulatory

---

[283] A liability mechanism was also introduced in the US under the 2010 Dodd-Frank Act, leading to a 'ratings strike' by CRAs with respect to structured finance.

[284] The cost of liability insurance was acknowledged by the Commission: 2011 CRA III Proposal, n 126, 5.

[285] As noted earlier in the Chapter, Art 5a(1) requires certain regulated actors to make their own credit risk assessment and not to solely or mechanistically rely on ratings for assessing creditworthiness.

[286] 2010 Commission Consultation, n 124, 24.

purposes. Ratings originating from third country CRAs who are within a group with the EU CRA can be used, but only subject to an 'endorsement' process which requires the 'requirements' of the third country regime to be 'as stringent as' the EU regime, and as long as there is an objective reason for the rating to be elaborated in a third country and supervisory co-operation arrangements are met (Article 4(2)–(6)). Where a rating originates from a CRA without this group connection, it can only be used for regulatory purposes within the EU where the legal and supervisory framework of the third country is 'equivalent' to the EU regime, where co-operation arrangements are in place, where the CRA does not have systemic importance for the stability or integrity of financial markets in one or more Member States, where the rating relates to a non-EU issuer or instrument, and where the CRA has been 'certified' by ESMA (Article 5). Given the international nature of the rating business, this adoption of a 'fortress Europe' approach has had the effect of extending the reach of the EU regime significantly. While it reflects the EU's concern to lead the way on CRA reform, this approach also suggests a concern to ensure that ESMA, as the untested EU-level supervisor, has as secure as possible a territorial base for supervising CRAs.

The Article 4 rating endorsement mechanism is designed to address the heavy reliance across the EU on ratings issued in third countries, particularly by members of the three large CRA groups (Fitch, Moody's, and Standard & Poor's), and the related potential for significant market disturbance were a prohibition to apply to the use of these ratings in the EU for regulatory purposes.[287] Although the necessary 'requirements as stringent as' assessment is related to the Article 5 equivalence assessment (for third country CRAs, outside an EU CRA group, and without a physical presence in the EU), the Article 5 Commission-driven equivalence process takes significantly longer than the Article 4 ESMA-driven 'requirements as stringent as' process, as the equivalence process addresses legal and supervisory equivalence more generally. The Article 4 endorsement process, which is focused on regulatory requirements, accordingly became the major channel for protecting non-EU ratings for use for regulatory purposes in the EU. Despite significant market concern as to the potential risk of disruption were the endorsement process to be delayed[288]—which is reflected in the Regulation's provision for transitional periods to address the risk of market disruption or financial instability where ratings could not be used[289]—and ESMA's related warnings as to the need for precautionary action by market participants were all endorsement assessments not completed by the end-April 2012 deadline for endorsement,[290] ESMA recognized the major jurisdictions from which ratings are issued for use in the EU as having requirements 'as stringent as' the EU requirements by the deadline.[291]

---

[287] Particular concerns arose with respect to the capital requirements of banks relating to rated securitization exposures originating in the US and rated in the US.

[288] Tait, N, 'SEC and EU in Talks to Resolve Ratings Impasse', *Financial Times*, 24 April 2011, 10, reporting on market concerns as to the capital changes which major banks could have faced were they prevented from relying on third country ratings, and on the efforts by third country authorities to meet the requirements of the endorsement and equivalence regime.

[289] CRA Regulation Arts 24(2) and 40. Prior to the end of April 2012, transitional arrangements applied which protected the use of non-endorsed ratings while ESMA concluded the related necessary co-operation agreements: ESMA Press Release 22 December 2011 (ESMA/2011/460).

[290] ESMA Press Release, 22 December 2011 (ESMA/2011/460).

[291] ESMA Press Release, 27 April 2012 (ESMA/2012/274); a list of the jurisdictions from which applications have been endorsed is set out in the 2nd Annual Supervision Report, n 117, 23. ESMA

A series of conditions apply to the Article 4 endorsement mechanism which together are designed to ensure the third country regime is broadly equivalent and that the EU CRA can accordingly endorse the rating (Article 4(3)(a)–(h)). The CRA must verify, and be able to demonstrate on an ongoing basis, to ESMA that the conduct of credit rating activities by the third country CRA resulting in the rating to be endorsed fulfils requirements 'as stringent as' the Regulation's Articles 6–12 regulatory regime.[292] ESMA's ability to assess and monitor the compliance of the third country CRA with these requirements must not be limited. The EU CRA must also make available on request to ESMA all the information necessary to enable ESMA to supervise compliance on an ongoing basis with the Regulation. There must also be an objective reason for the rating to be elaborated in a third country, the third country regulatory regime must prevent interference by competent and public authorities with rating content and methodologies,[293] and appropriate co-operation arrangements must exist between ESMA and the relevant competent authority of the third country CRA.[294] Once the rating has been endorsed, it is considered to be a rating issued by an EU-established and registered CRA (Article 4(4)). Anti-avoidance measures apply in that CRAs established and registered in the EU must not use endorsement to circumvent the Regulation (Article 4(4)). The endorsing CRA remains responsible for the rating (Article 4(5)). It is also clear that ESMA expects regulated entities subject to Article 4(1) on the ratings which can be used for regulatory purposes to take careful note of whether endorsement of a rating is required and has been carried out; as the transitional period has passed and all non-EU ratings must be endorsed under Article 4(3), this assessment has become of critical importance.[295]

The certification regime (Article 5)—which is equivalence-driven—allows a third country CRA, whose activities are not considered to be of systemic importance to the financial stability or integrity of the financial markets of one or more Member States, to enable its ratings to be used for regulatory purposes in the EU; accordingly, Article 5 supports the use of ratings issued by smaller CRAs, who do not have the worldwide group operations of the CRAs addressed by the Article 4 endorsement process.

Under Article 5, where the rating relates to entities established in third countries, or to financial instruments issued in a third country,[296] and is issued by a third-country-established CRA but is not endorsed, it may still be used for regulatory purposes within the EU, subject to an equivalence-driven procedure (Article 5(1)). The third country CRA

---

accordingly urged financial institutions to take precautionary steps with respect to non-endorsed jurisdictions, given the Art 4(1) prohibition on the use of such ratings.

[292] Exemptions apply, however, to most of the CRA III reforms, including with respect to ownership restrictions, rotation, and sovereign ratings.

[293] This requirement is dis-applied where a general equivalence decision has been adopted by the Commission (under the Art 5 procedure) in relation to the third country: Art 4(6).

[294] The co-operation arrangement must cover a mechanism for the exchange of information and procedures governing the co-ordination of supervisory activities, such that ESMA can monitor the credit rating activities resulting in the issuing of the endorsed rating on an ongoing basis: Art 4(3)(h).

[295] In its decisions on the status of third country regimes, ESMA highlighted that financial institutions must carefully consider all information made available by CRAs regarding the endorsement status of their ratings, and that precautionary measures should be taken in relation to non-endorsed ratings: eg ESMA/2011/274 (the Brazil decision).

[296] The certification regime cannot accordingly be used for ratings of EU issuers and instruments, in respect of which the Art 4 endorsement process or full EU establishment and registration is required.

must be authorized or registered and subject to supervision in the third country, the Commission must have adopted an equivalence decision relating to the legal and supervisory framework of the third country, and co-operation arrangements between ESMA and the third country authority[297] must be in place (Article 5(1)). The ratings must additionally not be of systemic importance to the financial stability or integrity of the financial markets of one or more Member States (Article 5(1)) and the third country CRA must be 'certified' in accordance with Article 5(2). The certification process, which is based on ESMA ensuring compliance with the Article 5(1) conditions, is run by ESMA and follows similar procedural steps as apply to CRA registration. The necessary equivalence decision is taken by the Commission (Article 5(6)), where it is satisfied that the legal and supervisory framework of the third country ensures that CRAs comply with 'legally binding requirements' equivalent to the Regulation[298] and are subject to 'effective supervision and enforcement' in the third country.[299] A third country CRA may, however, apply for an exemption from the operational requirements (Annex I section A) and the rotation requirements (Article 7(4)) where the CRA can demonstrate that the requirements are not proportionate given the nature, scale, and complexity of the business, and the nature and range of its issuing of credit ratings. The CRA may also be exempted from the requirement for physical presence in the EU where this would be similarly disproportionate (Article 5(4)). Certified CRAs are subject to the public disclosure requirements of the Regulation with respect to reporting to CEREP and the ERP (Articles 11(2) and 11a).

The combined effect of the Article 4 endorsement and the Article 5 equivalence/certification regimes is to exert significant pressure on third country regimes to conform to the EU model—not only with respect to regulation, but also (for equivalence/certification) with respect to operational supervision and enforcement. ESMA has taken a robust approach to Article 4 endorsement decisions, particularly with respect to the core 'as stringent as' requirement, which ESMA has interpreted as requiring that the third country's measures are legally binding, in the face of very significant market opposition.[300] It has been similarly robust with respect to Article 5 equivalence assessments (on which it provides the Commission with technical advice).[301] Early indications of an uncompromising approach, and of the related capacity of the EU regime to shape regulation internationally, came from

---

[297] The arrangements track those required under the endorsement mechanism: Art 5(7).

[298] Exemptions apply, however, to most of the CRA III reforms, including with respect to ownership restrictions, rotation, and sovereign ratings.

[299] A third country regime can be considered equivalent where: CRAs are subject to authorization or registration and are subject to effective supervision and enforcement on an ongoing basis; CRAs are subject to legally binding rules equivalent to Arts 6–12 and Annex I; and the third country regime prevents interference by supervisory and other public authorities of that third country with the content of ratings and methodologies.

[300] 2011 ESMA Endorsement Guidelines, n 15. Given the dangers of non-endorsement, there were calls from the market for ESMA to adopt a more flexible and less stringent approach, which would recognize self-regulatory measures and the ultimate responsibility of the EU CRA for the rating and also reflect a distinction between 'equivalent to' under the Art 5 certification process and 'as stringent as' under the Art 4 endorsement process (at 4–5). In response, ESMA confirmed that its position stood, and was based on consultation with stakeholders and the Commission (at 8).

[301] Its equivalence assessment follows an objective approach, based on the capacity of the third country regime to meet the objectives of the EU regime, and focuses in particular on the scope of the regulatory and supervisory framework, corporate governance, conflicts of interest management, organizational requirements, quality of methodologies and of ratings, disclosure, and effective supervision and enforcement: ESMA, Technical Advice on CRA Equivalence—US, Canada, and Australia (2012) (ESMA/2012/259) 5–6.

CESR's initial 2010 finding that the US regime (prior to the 2010 Dodd-Frank Act reforms) was not equivalent to the EU regime, particularly with respect to the quality of methodologies and ratings and with respect to disclosure of ratings, where significant differences obtained. CESR also signalled the need for US reforms, observing that a reduction in the outstanding differences between regimes could be achieved by revisions to the relevant SEC rules.[302] As the subsequent Commission decision (based on ESMA's advice) to find the US regime equivalent illustrates, ESMA changed the CESR position following the Dodd-Frank reforms.[303]

Initial evidence suggests substantial convergence to the EU model is taking place—albeit also reflecting the wider G20 agenda in this area. ESMA has found a number of jurisdictions to be 'as stringent as' the EU regime for the purposes of the Article 4 endorsement process;[304] the majority of non-EU issued ratings are now recognized by ESMA as being subject to a broadly EU-equivalent regime.[305] A number of regimes have also been declared formally equivalent, following ESMA's advice to the Commission,[306] reflecting recent reforms in these jurisdictions.[307]

Associated with the changes to the EU's international engagement relating to rating agencies, a shift has taken place with respect to the central place of the IOSCO Code in EU regulation, although ESMA is actively engaged with IOSCO on the Code's development.[308] While the CRA I Regulation relied heavily on the IOSCO Code as the template for the new rulebook, it also extended and substantiated those rules. A delegation for administrative rules applies to the detailed rules contained in Annex I to the Regulation, which gives the Commission the capacity to further refine the regime. Although the early phase of the development of the CRA regime saw close contact with IOSCO, every subsequent reform is likely to see significant change to the Annex I rulebook and to greater distance from the IOSCO regime; conversely, the EU rulebook is coming to shape the IOSCO Code.[309]

The regime for third countries also underlines ESMA's distinct capacity in the international sphere, as distinct from its constituent NCAs. It is empowered to enter into co-operation

---

[302] CESR/2010/332. In a reflection of the sensitivities, CESR emphasized that its report did not take account any consideration of a political nature' (at 4).

[303] n 301, noting that the Dodd-Frank Act, together with the SEC's related rule-making powers 'provide a solid background for a positive decision' on US equivalence (at 3).

[304] Japan, Australia, US, Canada, Hong Kong, Singapore, Mexico, Argentina, and Brazil.

[305] ESMA Press Release, 27 April 2012 (ESMA/2012/274).

[306] In October 2012, eg, the Commission adopted equivalence decisions relating to the US, Canadian, and Australian regimes: respectively, Commission Decisions 2012/628/EU [2012] OJ L274/32, 2012/630/EU [2012] OJ L278/17, and 2012/627/EU [2012] OJ L274/30. ESMA has also advised that the regimes of Argentina, Brazil, Mexico, Hong Kong, and Singapore are equivalent (ESMA/2013/626). Commission equivalence decisions have followed.

[307] Notably, the 2010 Dodd-Frank Act (US), the 2012 National Instrument 25–101 Designated Ratings Organizations (Canada), and a series of 2010 reforms to the Corporations Act and the Australian Securities and Investment Commission (ASIC) Act (Australia).

[308] ESMA 2nd Annual Supervision Report, n 117, 23 and ESMA, Annual Report (2012) 33.

[309] The CRA III Regulation reforms, eg, led to a significant extension of the conflict of interest management rules to address the risks posed by CRA ratings of major shareholders and to new disclosure requirements for raters of sovereign debt. As noted in n 55, however, the 2014 consultation on review of the IOSCO Code was designed to reflect the reforms undertaken in jurisdictions internationally, including the EU.

arrangements in support of the endorsement mechanism under Article 4,[310] but is also empowered more generally to enter into information-exchange agreements with third country authorities (Article 34) and to disclose information received from third country authorities (Article 35). ESMA is also the chair of the global college of CRA supervisors for Fitch (the US SEC is the chair of the Moody's and Standard & Poor's colleges).

VII.2.12 ESMA and the CRA Regime

Along with the EMIR regime (Chapter VI section 4.2), the CRA regime has conferred an extensive array of direct operational powers on ESMA. ESMA has not, however, been closely engaged with the development of the CRA rulebook, which was mainly constructed at the legislative level. But it has been conferred with precedent-setting direct supervisory and enforcement powers, and has been placed at the centre of the EU's international engagement in relation to CRAs. The CRA regime has, accordingly, very significant potential to strengthen ESMA's capacity more generally. Initial indications also point to some ESMA enthusiasm for robust and expansive application of its powers, and some appetite for grappling with political contentious issues, notably with respect to sovereign debt risk.

VII.3 Investment Analyst Regulation

VII.3.1 The Rationale for Intervention

Investment analysts who assess issuer-disclosure and produce investment recommendations (typically 'buy, 'sell,' 'hold', and variations thereof) are frequently termed 'the engine of market efficiency', given their role in supporting effective price formation.[311] They are particularly important for small and medium-sized enterprises (SMEs) as they can raise a firm's profile and thereby reduce the cost of capital;[312] the recent series of reforms to the EU issuer-disclosure regime in support of SME access to equity finance are in part designed to address the difficulties SMEs face in generating analyst coverage over the reporting 'bottleneck' period, over which quarterly/interim and half-yearly reports are issued and during which analysts can be swamped with issuer disclosures.[313]

---

[310] And has entered into a series of Memoranda of Understanding in this regard, including with the US SEC and the Australian ASIC.

[311] Coffee's seminal work on the role of analysts justified the imposition of mandatory issuer-disclosure requirements in part by the informational efficiencies and cost reductions mandatory requirements would generate for analysts, who would accordingly be able to cover a wider range of issuers: Coffee, J, 'Market Failure and the Economic Case for a Mandatory Disclosure System' (1984) 70 *Va LR* 717. The view has become mainstream opinion among regulators. IOSCO, eg, has argued that the volume and complexity of issuer disclosure can be overwhelming and confusing for investors and that research analysts accordingly play an important role in the relationship between firms and investors: IOSCO, Report on Analyst Conflicts of Interest (2003) (2003 IOSCO Analyst Report) 2.

[312] Forum Group, Financial Analysts: Best Practices in an Integrated Market (2003) 13. See also McVea, H, 'Research Analysts and Conflicts of Interest—the Financial Services Authority's Response' (2004) 4 *JCLS* 97, 105–10.

[313] Ch II sect 3.3.2.

But investment analysts are exposed to significant conflict-of-interest risks which can devalue their reputational capital and reduce their incentives to protect that capital.[314] In particular, sell-side investment research,[315] or research typically produced within a multi-service investment firm and disseminated to clients, is prone to conflicts of interest. Although buy-side, in-house analysts (who provide in-house research for pension funds and collective investment schemes, for example) are less vulnerable to conflict-of-interest risk as their incentives are more closely aligned with the interests of their 'in-house' clients, the potential exists for conflict-of-interest risks.[316] Independent research houses which produce independent research on a fee basis are not as yet a major feature of the EU financial market landscape.

The scale of the conflict-of-interest risk to which sell-side investment research is exposed came into sharp focus over the Enron crisis-era. Although analysts appear to have a bias towards positive assessments,[317] the 'dotcom' era, which came to an abrupt end with the Enron-era series of equity market scandals, saw a significant bias towards positive 'buy' recommendations. This bias was driven by perverse incentives caused by the deep conflict-of-interest risks to which investment research activities can be exposed in the integrated, sell-side multiservice firm, and by the related weakening of reputational capital as a disciplining mechanism.[318] In principle, four major and interrelated groups of conflicts can be identified within firms, relating to the range of business activities within the firm, analyst remuneration arrangements, financial interests in the issuers reviewed by analysts, and reporting relationships within firms.[319] These conflicts of interest deepened over the dotcom era. In particular, sell-side investment research became driven by the business interests of investment firms as a whole and by the need to engage and retain issuer clients. Particularly severe conflicts arose with respect to corporate finance (particularly underwriting) business. Pro-issuer reports (to which retail investors were particularly vulnerable) were used to build relationships with issuers and to secure corporate finance/underwriting mandates, while analysts came under pressure to promote offerings. Particular conflicts of interest arose with respect to venture capital. A firm (and its employees and analysts) might

---

[314] The role of gatekeepers (primarily auditors and investment analysts) in the Enron-era equity market scandals and the nature of the subsequent regulatory reform movement generated a vast scholarship, particularly on the US experience. See, eg, Coffee, J, *The Role of the Professions in Corporate Governance* (2006); Choi, S, 'A Framework for the Regulation of Securities Markets Intermediaries' (2004) 1 *Berkeley Business LJ*; Macey, J, 'Efficient Capital Markets, Corporate Disclosure and Enron' (2004) 89 *Cornell LR* 394; Coffee, J, 'Understanding Enron: It's the Gatekeepers, Stupid' (2002) 57 *Business Law* 1403; Langevoort, D, 'Taming the Animal Spirits of the Stock Markets: A Behavioural Response to Securities Regulation' (2002) 97 *NorthWestern University LR* 135; Gordon, J, 'What Enron Means for the Management and Control of the Modern Business Corporation: Some Initial Regulations' (2002) 69 *University of Chicago LR* 1233; and Ribstein, L, 'Market v Regulatory Responses to Corporate Fraud: A Critique of the Sarbanes-Oxley Act of 2002' (2002) *J Corp L* 1.

[315] The sell side of the market concerns the origination, marketing, and sale of securities. The buy side concerns the trading and investment activities of major institutional investors.

[316] A buy-side firm might, through its analysts' relationships with the sell side, eg, exert pressure on the sell side to provide and distribute recommendations which enhance the buy side's investment products: 2003 Forum Group Report, n 312, 38.

[317] The FSA reported that in June 2002 only 16 per cent of UK analysts had issued sell recommendations: Discussion Paper 15, Investment Research. Conflicts and Other Issues (2002) 23.

[318] On the range of conflicts of interest raised by investment research within the multi-service firm see the 2003 IOSCO Analyst Report, n 311, 7–11 and FSA, n 317, 16–23.

[319] 2003 IOSCO Analyst Report, n 311, 8.

acquire a significant stake in a start-up company by investing in discounted, pre-Initial Public Offering (IPO) shares; sharp and destructive incentives were then generated to produce favourable reports.[320] Analysts also came under pressure from broking and proprietary trading business divisions. Proprietary trading positions generated particular risks with respect to the front-running of research (or dealing ahead of a recommendation) and with respect to the use of recommendations to influence the price of a security. Risks also arose of price-sensitive information as to changes in a recommendation leaking across information barriers and being passed on to favoured clients. Risks were exacerbated by the linkage of analyst remuneration to underwriting or broking revenues.

The regulatory design risks raised by regulation of investment analysts are, however, considerable.[321] Investment analysis is a costly process[322] and excessive costs in the production of investment research represent a risk to the effectiveness of price formation. The imposition of onerous and costly regulation on multiservice firms, which might result in a firm not following smaller issuers where trading activity in the securities does not justify the costs of coverage, is particularly risky in the absence of a strong independent research industry (as is the case in the EU).[323] In particular, stringent conflict-of-interest rules run the risk that the only viable methods of coverage for some issuers are threatened.[324]

Nonetheless, in the wake of the dotcom collapse and the Enron-era scandals, a high degree of consensus emerged internationally as to the nature of analyst risk and the key principles which should govern investment research.[325] Management of the risks generated in the multiservice firm to the quality of investment recommendations, particularly with respect to analyst remuneration and the marketing of new issues, whether through disclosure or organizational arrangements, is now common to the US regime,[326] the EU

---

[320] 2003 IOSCO Analyst Report, n 311, 9.

[321] eg Romano, R, 'The Sarbanes-Oxley Act and the Making of Quack Corporate Governance' (2005) *Yale LJ* 1521 and Ribstein, n 314.

[322] Choi, n 314, 5–6, noting that public-good dynamics prevent analysts from capturing fully the costs of their work from the investment community.

[323] On the risks posed by harmonization in terms of 'chilling' investment research see Cervone, E, 'EU Conduct of Business Rules and the Liberalization Ethos: The Challenging Case of Investment Research' (2005) *EBLR* 421.

[324] The 2003 Forum Group Report noted that smaller issuers are often only followed by their corporate broker and that, although the perception of a loss of independence and conflict-of-interest risks reduced the impact and value of this research, it was still 'extremely valuable' to the issuer and investors, as long as investors were aware of the relationship between issuers and their corporate brokers: n 312, 23.

[325] eg FSA, Consultation Paper 205, Conflicts of Interest: Investment Research and Issues of Securities (2003), highlighting international developments.

[326] The New York Stock Exchange (now NYSE Euronext) and the National Association of Securities Dealers (now the Financial Industry Regulatory Authority (FINRA)) originally adopted prescriptive SEC-approved rules governing the integrity of investment research in 2002 which addressed, *inter alia*, business separation (including the removal of linkages between analyst remuneration and the performance of other business units and the separate supervision of analysts). Following the Sarbanes-Oxley Act requirement that the SEC adopt rules addressing analyst conflicts of interest, 2003 also saw the adoption of SEC rules which require analysts to certify their reports. The US response was, however, multilayered, and included the December 2002 Global Settlement under which investment firms agreed to a number of conflict-of-interest prevention arrangements, including the severance of all links between analysts and investment banking, that analysts would not accompany bankers on roadshows, and that analyst remuneration would be divorced from the performance of other business units. The industry also agreed to allocate over $400 million to fund independent research and to allocate $80 million to investor education.

regime, and the international standards adopted by IOSCO,[327] which shaped the EU response.[328]

Although the Commission committed to monitoring the (then) new harmonized regime for investment analysts which was in place by the end of the FSAP period, and to reconsidering its position if new circumstances arose or if the regime proved to be inefficient,[329] the regulatory framework for analysts has remained stable. It remains to be seen, however, how the administrative regime will change when the 2014 MiFID II/MiFIR and 2014 MAR regimes come into force.

VII.3.2 The Evolution of the EU Regime

VII.3.2.1 The Enron Effect

The harmonized investment analyst regime has had a very different evolution to that of the CRA regime, reflecting the much lesser role of investment analysis in risk regulation and in supporting financial stability, and its close association with equity market efficiency.

Although not of as recent a vintage as the CRA regime, the regulation of investment analysis is a relative newcomer to EU securities and markets regulation. The EU's initial policy decision to address investment analysts pre-dated the Enron scandal by some months and can be dated to the Commission's 2001 Proposal for the 2003 Market Abuse Directive,[330] which contained a precursor of the 'fair presentation' obligation imposed on the dissemination of investment research contained in the 2003 Market Abuse Directive (Article 6(5)) and which led to the 2003 Commission Investment Recommendations Directive. The influence of the Enron scandal and the related US response was nonetheless determinative. Reflecting the reality that the extensive US response to the Enron scandal (and particularly the adoption of the Sarbanes-Oxley Act) was always likely to have had some repercussions in the EU,[331] even if only through a 'copycat' dynamic,[332] the Oviedo ECOFIN Council (April 2002) discussed the related issues and risks and requested that the Commission consider possible regulatory action.

The regulatory design risks were therefore considerable. By contrast with the financial crisis (in relation to which regulatory and market failures were often similar internationally), many of the structural market conditions (and related regulatory failures) which led to the

---

[327] IOSCO, Statement of Principles for Addressing Sell-Side Securities Analyst Conflicts of Interest (2003) (the IOSCO Principles). The Principles remain in force.

[328] The Commission noted that IOSCO's work helped to shape the regulatory debate in the EU: Commission, Communication on Investment Research and Financial Analysts (2006) (COM (2006) 789) (the 2006 Investment Research Communication) 3.

[329] Commission, White Paper on Financial Services Policy 2005–2010 (2005) (COM (2005) 629), Annex II Impact Assessment, 22.

[330] COM (2001) 281.

[331] A considerable literature addresses the impact of Enron on the development of EU policy, although predominantly with respect to company law and corporate governance reforms. See, eg, Enriques, L, 'Bad Apples, Bad Oranges: A Comment from Old Europe on Post Enron Corporate Governance Reforms' (2003) 38 *Wake Forest LR* 911.

[332] Hertig, G, 'On-Going Board Reforms: One Size Fits All and Regulatory Capture' (2005) 21 *Oxford Review of Economic Policy* 269. See also McVea, n 312, 115, noting the inevitability of the FSA 'joining the fray' post-Enron.

Enron-era series of bankruptcies in the US, and which were associated with gatekeeper failure, were not replicated in the EU. This is not least because of the dominance of the bank finance model in continental Europe, and the related prevalence of large block-holding shareholders.[333] Where large block-holding shareholders dominate, the need for investment analysis is less strong, as large block-holders are better equipped than dispersed shareholders (the market finance model) to monitor managers effectively; the gatekeeper function remains important, however, in monitoring appropriation risks (to which minority shareholders are vulnerable), as became clear from the Parmalat scandal.[334] The risks to retail investors from investment research, which drove much of the US policy concern, were also of a different order in the EU, given limited household exposure to direct equity investments and the absence of a 'star analyst' culture.[335] The regulatory orientation of the FSAP and the availability (and, then, novelty) of the Lamfalussy process for administrative rule-making also increased the risks of a heavy-handed regulatory response and of related regulatory design errors.

Political pressure for action was, however, not overwhelming, in part due to the absence of a strong retail market constituency to drive a regulatory response and to increase the likelihood of Member State support for a concerted response.[336] By contrast, regulatory and political reaction to the Enron-era scandals in the US was shaped by the powerful political constituency represented by its deep retail markets.[337] The piecemeal development of the new investment analysts regime also mitigated the risks of intervention. The timing and the structure of the FSAP reform agenda dictated that the regime split into, first, the administrative fair presentation and disclosure rules designed to support market integrity under the market abuse regime (adopted in 2003) and, second, the administrative conflict-of-interest rules designed to support investor protection and the investment services passport under the 2004 MiFID I regime (adopted in 2006). Accordingly, by the time the MiFID I administrative rule-making process was underway (2004–6), the sharpest concerns generated by the dotcom collapse had receded, and concerns were beginning to emerge as to the dangers of the US's prescriptive approach under the Sarbanes-Oxley Act. Risks were also reduced by the particular dynamics of the development of the administrative market abuse and MiFID I regimes. The 2003 Commission Investment Recommendations Directive, for example, was among the first of the administrative rules to emerge from the then novel Lamfalussy process; institutional concern to ensure the stability of the

---

[333] See Ch I.

[334] See Coffee, J, 'A Theory of Corporate Scandals: Why the US and Europe Differ' in Armour and McCahery, n 30, 215, 228–9.

[335] The EU did not experience mass retail-market exuberance over the dotcom period (on retail investment patterns, see Ch IX sect 1.2). Even in the UK market, investment research risks were regarded as lower, notwithstanding its more dispersed ownership model, given the dominance of institutional investors who were less susceptible to the 'cult of the star analyst' which distorted the US market: 2002 FSA Discussion Paper, n 317, 3 and 36–7.

[336] Moloney, N, 'Building a Retail Investment Culture Through Law: The 2004 Markets in Financial Instruments Directive' (2005) 6 *EBOLR* 341.

[337] Langevoort, D, 'Structuring Securities Regulation in the European Union: Lessons from the US Experience' in Ferrarini, G and Wymeersch, E (eds), *Investor Protection in Europe: Corporate Law Making, the MiFID and Beyond* (2006) 485. See also Coffee, J, 'Law and the Market. The Impact of Enforcement' (2007) 156 *UPaLR* 229, arguing that retail investors are a 'potent political force' which demands 'reforms and retribution' following scandals, and noting that in Europe, by contrast, the dotcom and post-Enron market crash fell more on institutional investors than individual shareholders.

process may have distracted the institutions from over-zealous intervention. In addition, a degree of *schadenfreude* informed the initial EU response to the Enron-era scandals, with the EU seeking to distance the then nascent EU regulatory regime from the US's difficulties;[338] this may have quenched any over-enthusiasm for a regulatory response to investment research. Finally, the investment analysts regime developed in a very different regulatory climate to the crisis-era climate: the policy environment was generally supportive of industry discipline as an oversight mechanism and of principles-based intervention, the latter of which came to be associated with the MiFID I conflict-of-interest administrative regime in particular.

VII.3.2.2 Developing a Response

(a) The Enron Response

The Commission's initial response to the Enron scandals took the form of a report on the implications of Enron for the Oviedo ECOFIN Council.[339] Its specific recommendations with respect to investment research were low-key and based on the (then) 2003 Market Abuse Directive, which was at the time under negotiation, and on consideration of whether the emerging MiFID I regime should address investment analysts.[340]

The Commission subsequently constituted the Forum Group on Financial Analysts, which was composed of representatives from industry and the regulatory community, to assess investment research. Their 2003 Report[341] focused on the prevention, management, monitoring, and disclosure of conflicts of interest relating to investment research, particularly with respect to analyst involvement in new issues and other corporate finance business, best practice for issuers, analyst remuneration, and own-account dealing in securities. Although the Forum Group Report did not recommend how its reforms should be addressed, it emphasized self-governance, recommended that best practice be allowed to evolve, and called for any new regulation deemed necessary to be in the form of framework principles developed in collaboration with the industry.

(b) The 2003 Commission Investment Recommendations Directive

The 2003 Market Abuse Directive required that investment recommendations be presented fairly, and provided for a related delegation for administrative rules. Although CESR's overall approach to investment recommendations in its subsequent technical advice[342] was broadly accepted by the Commission, major revisions were made to CESR's treatment of journalists,[343] as well as in relation to the exclusion of CRAs, which CESR had included within the scope of its proposed investment recommendations regime.[344]

---

[338] The Commission's Financial Services Action Plan (FSAP) policy assessment took care to highlight that the Enron-era crisis had not impacted directly on the direction of the EU's wider company law and corporate-governance programme on which most post-Enron attention had focused in the US: Commission, FSAP Evaluation. Part I: Process and Implementation (November 2005).

[339] Commission, Note for the Informal ECOFIN Council Oviedo, 12 and 13 April. A First Response to Enron-related Policy Issues (2004).

[340] n 339.

[341] n 312.

[342] CESR, Market Abuse Directive Technical Advice (2002) (CESR/02/089d).

[343] CESR's prescriptive approach was changed in favour of a more facilitative regime, designed to protect the dissemination of investment recommendations by journalists.

[344] See n 342.

CESR's adoption of an essentially prescriptive approach to presentation was accepted, however, by the Commission, although it generated a hostile response from the market, which argued that the extensive disclosure requirements could inhibit transparency and increase market volatility.

(c) The 2006 Commission MiFID I Directive and Investment Research

The administrative MiFID I regime on conflict-of-interest management relating to investment research followed in 2006 and was contained within the 2006 Commission MiFID I Directive. In contrast to the 2003 Investment Recommendations Directive, it was principles-based.

The delegation for the administrative investment recommendations/investment analysts regime related to MiFID I Article 13(3) (and was set out in Article 13(10)) (now 2014 MiFID II Article 16(3) and 16(12)),[345] which required investment firms to maintain and operate effective organizational and administrative arrangements to prevent conflicts of interests from prejudicing client interests. The investment recommendations/analyst provisions of the subsequent 2006 Commission MiFID I Directive had a troublesome gestation at the CESR level, and evolved considerably throughout the process. After two rounds of consultation in 2004,[346] CESR was required to delay its technical advice to the Commission on investment analysts until April 2005 in order to assess the hostile market response to its proposals.[347] CESR's technical advice was subsequently subject to considerable revision by the Commission, although some care was taken by the Commission to explain where it diverged from CESR's advice.[348] Most significantly, the Commission adopted a principles-based approach, and recast CESR's investment research-specific proposals into a regime which was based on the application of general conflict-of-interest rules and on the imposition of only a limited number of investment recommendations/analyst-specific rules (addressing, for the most part, dealing restrictions).

VII.3.3 Investment Analysts and Conflicts of Interest: The MiFID I/II and 2006 Commission MiFID I Directive Regime

VII.3.3.1 Scope

(a) The 2014 MiFID II Regime

Investment research is included within the 2014 MiFID II list of 'ancillary services'.[349] As a result, an entity which engages solely in investment research and which does not provide

---

[345] The 2014 MiFID II Art 16(3) obligation uses the same formula as the 2014 MiFID II Art 13(3) obligation with respect to conflicts of interest. The 2006 Commission MiFID I Directive is accordingly likely to be reflected in the new set of administrative rules to be adopted under MiFID II (under Art 16(12)).

[346] CESR/04-261b (June 2004) and CESR/04-603b (December 2004). CESR noted the 'very difficult' negotiations in its April 2005 Feedback Statement on the final advice: CESR/05-291b, 17.

[347] CESR 05-290b (April 2005). Particular points of contention included CESR's original definition of 'investment research' and its proposal that Chinese walls be required between investment analysts and all other investment banking business.

[348] European Securities Committee Working Document ESC/17/2005 (July 2005), Explanatory Memorandum, 5.

[349] Listed in the 2014 MiFID II Annex I, sect B(5).

any of the MiFID II core investment services[350] cannot be authorized under MiFID II (Article 6(1)) and is not subject to its regulatory regime.[351] But an investment firm which comes within the scope of MiFID II and which includes investment research among the investment services it provides is subject to MiFID II. Similarly, the MiFID II passport is not available in respect of investment research alone, although, as an ancillary service, investment research may be provided under the investment firm passport together with core investment services.

Like MiFID I, MiFID II does not expressly address investment research. A new set of administrative rules will follow, and these are likely to reflect the administrative conflict-of-interest rules relating to investment research contained in the 2006 Commission MiFID I Directive, outlined in the following sections.

(b) Investment Research

The 2006 Commission MiFID I Directive defined 'investment research' as research or other information which recommended or suggested an investment strategy (explicitly or implicitly) and which concerned one or several MiFID I financial instruments (or the issuers of financial instruments),[352] including any opinion as to the present or future value or price of the instruments, and which was intended for distribution channels[353] or for the public (Article 24(1)).

The definition was further refined to narrow the scope of the research caught by the definition: (i) the research was to be labelled or described as investment research (or in similar terms) or, in an anti-avoidance measure, was to be otherwise presented as an objective or independent explanation of the matters contained in the recommendation,[354] and (ii) where the recommendation was made by an investment firm to a client, it was not to come within the (MiFID I) definition of 'investment advice'.[355] The labelling requirement was designed to support investor understanding of the nature of the communication and develop investors' ability to distinguish between different communications, as well as to focus the firm's attention on the regulatory regime activated by the provision of 'investment research'.[356] But failure to label research as 'investment research' did not lift the obligations which applied under the 2006 Commission Directive where the research appeared to be presented as objective. An examination of the context and content of the research was therefore required of firms.

---

[350] 2014 MiFID II Annex I, sect A.

[351] Research was included in the 2004 MiFID I regime on an ancillary basis to avoid bringing specialized and independent research within the Directive and to focus regulatory attention on the risks posed by research in the multiservice firm: MiFID I Proposal (COM (2002) 625) 71).

[352] The 2014 MiFID II 'financial instruments' regime is broadly similar to the 2004 MiFID I regime: see Ch IV sect 4.3.

[353] Defined by reference to the 2003 Commission Investment Recommendations Directive Art 1(7). See sect 3.4.

[354] The investment research definition underwent a number of changes after the initial and controversial proposal by CESR in its original June 2004 consultation paper that research be classified as either 'objective' or 'non-objective'. The Commission, however, changed this approach to safeguard the status of 'investment research' as a 'gold standard', and to require all investment research to be objective: n 348, 5.

[355] At the legislative level, this definition has not changed under the 2014 MiFID II (MiFID II Art 4(1)(4)). See further Ch IX sect 5.

[356] CESR April 2005 Feedback Statement, n 346, 19.

The investment research regime was bedevilled by confusion as to the interaction between the 2006 Commission MiFID I Directive rules which addressed 'investment research' and the wider category of investment 'recommendations' covered by the 2003 Commission Investment Recommendations Directive.[357] As discussed in section 3.4, the 2003 Commission Investment Recommendations Directive imposed rules on the presentation of investment research and the disclosure of conflicts of interest for all entities which produced 'recommendations'. The 2006 Commission MiFID I Directive provided, however, that 'investment research' under the 2006 Directive was a subset within the wider 'recommendations' covered by the 2003 Commission Investment Recommendations Directive.[358] It also clarified that a 'recommendation' for the purposes of the 2003 Investment Recommendations Directive which did not meet the requirements of Article 24(1) and accordingly was not classified as 'investment research' under the 2006 Directive was to be treated as a 'marketing communication' for the purposes of MiFID I and its related administrative rules.[359]

VII.3.3.2 Conflict-of-Interest Management: Organizational Arrangements

(a) Investment Research-specific Requirements
Reflecting the MiFID I focus on structural control of conflicts of interest and its move away from disclosure as a remedial tool, which is also apparent in MiFID II, the 2006 Commission MiFID I Directive required firms to establish procedural and structural arrangements to protect the objectivity and independence of investment research. These requirements were based on the generic requirements which governed conflict-of-interest risk management under the 2006 Directive and which applied to investment firms generally.

Article 25 was designed to focus investment firms' conflict-of-interest management systems (particularly with respect to organizational arrangements) on the particular risks posed by investment analysts. It was based on the generic conflict-of-interest regime which applied under Article 22 to the organizational procedures which were to be set out in a firm's conflicts policy and followed to manage conflicts of interest (Article 22(2)). Under Article 25(1), Member States were to require investment firms which produced (or arranged for the production of) investment research to ensure the implementation of the general organizational requirements set out in Article 22(3) in relation to the analysts involved in the production of the investment research, and in relation to other 'relevant persons'[360] whose responsibilities or business interests might have conflicted with the interests of the

---

[357] Considerable market concern as to the nature of the interaction was expressed in the UK: FSA, Policy Statement 07/6, Reforming Conduct of Business Regulation (2007) 75.

[358] See also rec 28.

[359] On the 2014 MiFID II marketing regime see Ch IX sect 5.This category of communications might have included short-term investment recommendations from sales or trading departments, including sales notes, market or trader commentary, and other short-term recommendations: MiFID Connect, Guidelines on the Application of the Investment Research Requirements under the FSA Rules Implementing MiFID in the UK (2007) 8.

[360] 'Relevant person' was defined as a director, partner/equivalent, manager or tied agent of the firm (or of any tied agent of the firm), an employee of the firm or of a tied agent of the firm, as well as any other natural person whose services were placed at the disposal, and under the control, of the firm (or a tied agent of the firm) and who was involved in the provision by the firm of investment services and activities, and a natural person who was directly involved in the provision of services to the investment firm (or its tied agent) under an outsourcing arrangement: 2006 Commission MiFID I Directive Art 2.

persons to whom the investment research was disseminated. Reflecting the particular conflicts of interest to which analysts are subject, these persons included corporate finance personnel and those involved in sales and trading on behalf of clients or the firm (recital 30). The regime did not, therefore, enumerate the specific organizational steps to be taken with respect to investment research[361] or impose specific prohibitions with respect to particular activities (such as new issue marketing), but required firms to apply the generic investment firm conflict-of-interest management regime to the particular risks posed by financial analysts.

(b) The Application to Analysts of Generic Organizational Arrangements under Article 22

Article 22(3) of the 2006 Commission MiFID I Directive required that firm procedures to manage conflicts of interest be designed to ensure that persons engaged in business activities (such as analysts) which involved a conflict of interest carried on those activities at a level of independence appropriate to the size and activities of the investment firm (and of the group to which it belonged) and appropriate to the materiality of the risk of damage to client interests. The regime was therefore designed to be calibrated to reflect specific risks, such as the risks posed by investment research, but it also set out a list of the procedures which might be necessary and appropriate to ensure the requisite degree of independence.

Article 22(3)(a) covered effective procedures to prevent or control the exchange of information (Chinese walls). Article 22(3)(b) addressed supervision risks and the separate supervision of relevant persons (such as analysts). Remuneration risks were addressed by Article 22(3)(c), which covered the removal of any direct link between remuneration of relevant persons in an investment firm (such as analysts) and the remuneration of or revenues generated by persons principally engaged in other activities, where a conflict of interest could arise in relation to those activities. Article 22(3)(d) addressed the prevention or limitation of the application of inappropriate influence over the way in which relevant persons (such as analysts) carried out their duties.

Article 22(3)(e) was a key provision and concerned measures to prevent or control the simultaneous or sequential involvement of the relevant person (such as an analyst) in separate activities where involvement might impair the proper management of conflicts of interest—the classic risk concerning the participation of analysts in the marketing of new issues. Recital 36 to the 2006 Commission MiFID I Directive amplified this provision and stated that analysts should not become involved in activities other than the preparation of investment research where involvement was 'inconsistent with the maintenance of objectivity'. Reflecting the 2003 IOSCO Principles, the recital also highlighted participation in corporate finance business and underwriting, participating in pitches for new business or roadshows, and being otherwise involved in the preparation of issuer marketing as involvements which would ordinarily be considered as inconsistent with the maintenance of objectivity. Article 22(3)(e) was opaque, however, as to whether participation in new issue business was prohibited or whether 'quiet periods' during which research could be distributed were required. The design of the conflicts regime (and CESR's earlier technical advice),[362] and its emphasis on investment firm judgement, suggested, however, that it

---

[361] Unlike the IOSCO Principles.

[362] CESR's original consultation on investment research suggested that analysts be prohibited from participation in the marketing of new issues. Market opinion was strongly opposed to a ban on the basis of

remained within the discretion of the investment firm to assess whether its internal arrangements (whether through Chinese walls, disclosure, quiet periods, or otherwise) were sufficiently robust to permit analyst participation without 'impairing the proper management of conflicts of interests' and ensure the 'maintenance of objectivity'.

The Article 22(3) procedures were to be calibrated to reflect the nature, scale, and complexity of a firm's business (Article 22(1)). Firms therefore retained discretion as how to manage specific analyst conflict-of-interest risks, although these generic procedures were to be followed as necessary and appropriate to ensure the necessary degree of independence for analysts (Article 22(3)). A safeguard clause applied, however, in that Member States were to require investment firms to adopt alternative or additional measures where these procedures did not ensure the requisite degree of independence (Article 22(3)).

(c) Exemptions

An exemption applied to investment firms which disseminated third party investment research produced by another person to the public or clients, given the related reduction in conflict-of-interest risk. Under Article 25(3), the Article 25(1) requirements did not apply where the person who produced the investment research was not a member of the firm's group, where the firm did not substantially alter the recommendations within the investment research, and where the firm did not present the research as having been produced by it; however, the firm was required to verify that the producer of the research was subject to the 2006 Commission MiFID I Directive's requirements with respect to the production of the research or had established a policy which imposed the Directive's requirements. Conversely, where a firm substantially altered investment research produced by a third party, the requirements which applied to investment research were activated.

VII.3.3.3 Dealing Rules

Dealing with knowledge of investment research which amounts to insider dealing or market manipulation comes within the scope of the market abuse regime (Chapter VIII). Dealing by analysts and firms was also dealt with by the 2006 Commission MiFID I Directive from a conflict-of-interest perspective.

Under Article 25(2), investment firms were to have in place arrangements which addressed the dealing restrictions set out in Article 25(2). Front-running was addressed by Article 25(2)(a), which provided that analysts (the prohibition was not limited to analysts but included all other investment firm 'relevant persons') could not undertake personal transactions or trade on behalf of any person (including the investment firm) in financial instruments to which the investment research related or in any related financial instruments. The prohibition applied where the analyst (or relevant person) had knowledge of the likely timing or content of the investment research which was not publicly available or available to clients and which could not readily be inferred from information that was so available. The dealing restriction extended until the recipients of the research had a reasonable opportunity to act on it. The prohibition did not apply to transactions or trades carried out in the capacity of market-maker where the individuals engaging in

---

the valuable commercial role performed by analysts. CESR agreed that situations could arise where there was no apparent conflict, as long as the analyst was not an active participant in marketing activities and could display appropriate independence and impartiality: April 2005 Feedback Statement, n 346, 21.

market-making had 'knowledge' of the likely timing or content of the research (they were likely, as a result, to have been brought over a Chinese wall), as long as the individuals engaging in market-making were acting in good faith and in the ordinary course of market-making. Neither did it apply to the execution of client orders.

A more general restriction was imposed by Article 25(2)(b) which provided that financial analysts and other relevant persons (although only where they were involved in the production of investment research) could not undertake personal transactions in financial instruments to which the investment research related, or in any related financial instrument, where the transaction was contrary to a current recommendation.[363] An exemption was available where exceptional circumstances[364] existed and where the analyst had obtained prior approval from the firm's compliance function.

VII.3.3.4 Inducements and 'Bundled' Research

Under Article 25(2) of the 2006 Commission MiFID I Directive, the investment firm, analyst, and other relevant persons involved in the production of investment research were prohibited from accepting inducements from those with a material interest in the subject matter of the investment research.[365]

This prohibition sat alongside the more general inducements regime (Article 26) which had particular implications for investment firms, such as asset managers, which received investment research under 'bundling' or 'softing' arrangements with their brokers which combined research (and other services and products) with execution services and which resulted in the fee for the research being passed on to the manager's clients through often opaque commission structures. Under Article 26, acceptance by a MiFID I investment firm of a fee, commission, or non-monetary benefit which fell outside the conditions imposed by Article 26,[366] and was in relation to the provision of an investment or ancillary service to a client, was a breach of the MiFID I Article 19(1) requirement to act honestly, fairly, and professionally in accordance with the best interests of a client. The Commission's 2006 Communication noted that the receipt of softed or bundled research could continue only if it met the inducement requirements.[367] MiFID II imposes a new inducements regime for investment firms generally (Ch IX sect 5.2).

VII.3.3.5 The Integrity of Investment Research

Articles 25(2)(d) and (e) of the 2006 Commission MiFID I Directive sought to protect the integrity of investment research more generally. Under Article 25(2)(d), the investment firm, analysts, and other relevant persons could not promise favourable research coverage. Inappropriate influence was also addressed by Article 25(2)(e), which provided that where a draft recommendation included a recommendation or target price, issuers, relevant persons

---

[363] A current recommendation was one which had not been withdrawn or lapsed: rec 34.

[364] These included circumstances where, for personal reasons relating to financial hardship, the analyst was required to liquidate a position: rec 31.

[365] Small gifts or minor hospitality below a level specified in the firm's conflicts policy and disclosed in the policy were not considered to be inducements: rec 32.

[366] Art 26 imposed disclosure obligations and a requirement that the inducement be designed to enhance the quality of the service to the client and not impair compliance with the firm's duty to act in the best interests of the client.

[367] 2006 Investment Research Communication, n 328, 6.

other than analysts, and other persons could not be permitted to review a draft of the investment research before the research was disseminated—whether for the purpose of verifying the accuracy of factual statements made in the research or for any other purpose, other than verifying compliance with the firm's legal obligations.

VII.3.3.6 Disclosure of Conflicts of Interest

The disclosure rules under the 2006 Commission MiFID I Directive dovetailed with the 2003 Commission Investment Recommendations Directive by addressing disclosure of conflicts of interest. The disclosure regime was a function of the generic MiFID I conflict-of-interest regime, which required, at the legislative level, under Article 18(2) of the MiFID I Directive that, where organizational or administrative arrangements were not sufficient to ensure with reasonable confidence that risks of damage to client interests would be prevented, the firm was to clearly disclose the general nature and/or sources of the conflict of interest to the client before undertaking business on its behalf; the parallel MiFID II requirements (Article 23(2) and (3)) are broadly similar, but require additionally that the disclosure be in sufficient detail to enable the client to take an informed decision.

At the administrative level, the conflict-of-interest risks posed by investment research were also to be identified in the firm's conflict-of-interest policy, under the 2006 Commission MiFID I Directive Article 22(2).

VII.3.4 The 2003 MAD/2014 MAR and Investment Recommendations

VII.3.4.1 The 2014 MAR and Investment Recommendations

The market abuse regime (the 2014 MAR) is designed to support market integrity and the efficiency of price formation. Its primary focus is on the prohibition of insider dealing and market manipulation, both of which are engaged by the access analysts have to inside information.[368] The related prohibitions on dealing, tipping, and disclosure are therefore relevant, as are the market manipulation prohibitions (Chapter VIII).

The 2014 MAR also contains extensive obligations with respect to the dissemination of information which are designed to support market efficiency and to limit the opportunities for market abuse. These include rules on the fair presentation of investment research and the disclosure of related conflicts of interest (2014 MAR Article 20(1)). A version of Article 20(1) was initially contained in the precursor 2003 MAD (Article 6(5)). The Commission's proposal for the 2003 MAD,[369] which included a version of Article 6(5), pre-dated the Enron series of scandals (it was published in 2001), but over the 2003 MAD's legislative passage the importance of the new regime for addressing gatekeeper failure in the wake of the Enron scandal was highlighted.[370]

---

[368] On insider-dealing risk and investment research generally see Fischel, D, 'Insider Trading and Investment Analysts—An Economic Analysis of Dirks v SEC' (1984) 13 *Hofstra LR* and Langevoort, D, 'Investment Analysts and the Law of Insider Trading' (1990) 76 *Va LR* 1023.

[369] COM (2001) 281.

[370] In its second reading on the Proposal, the European Parliament's ECON Committee noted the failures in investment research exposed by the Enron scandal and the importance of addressing the risks of biased research: A5-0343/2002, Explanatory Memorandum, 9.

Article 20(1) of the 2014 MAR requires that persons who produce or disseminate 'investment recommendations' or other information recommending or suggesting an investment strategy must take reasonable care to ensure that such information is 'objectively presented', and to disclose their interests or indicate conflicts of interest concerning the financial instruments or the issuers to which that information relates. The scope of this obligation is widely cast. An 'investment recommendation' is any information recommending or suggesting an investment strategy, explicitly or implicitly, concerning one or several financial instruments, or the issuers of financial instruments, including any opinion as to the present or future value or price of such instruments, intended for distribution channels or for the public (Article 3(1)(35)). 'Information recommending or suggesting an investment strategy' is similarly widely defined as information produced by an independent analyst, an investment firm, a credit institution, any other person whose main business is to produce investment recommendations, or a natural person working for them, under a contract of employment or otherwise, that directly or indirectly expresses a particular investment proposal in respect of a financial instrument or issuer of financial instruments (Article 3(1)(34)). It also, in a catch-all provision, includes information produced by any other person which directly proposes a particular investment decision in respect of a financial instrument (Article 3(1)(34)). RTSs will govern the 'objective presentation' requirement and the disclosure of conflicts of interest (Article 20(3)).

The 2014 MAR Article 20(1) requirement is broadly similar to the precursor 2003 MAD Article 6(5) requirement, although it refers to 'objective presentation' while the 2003 regime required 'fair presentation'. The legislative 2003 MAD Article 6(5) obligation was supported by a Commission delegation which led to an extensive administrative disclosure regime, set out in the 2003 Commission Investment Recommendations Directive, which will be repealed by the 2014 MAR.[371] Elements of this regime have been incorporated in the 2014 MAR in the form of the definitions of 'investment recommendation' and 'information recommending or suggesting an investment strategy', which follow the 2003 Commission Directive.

The new RTSs are likely be very similar in design to the requirements imposed by the 2003 Commission Investment Recommendations Directive, particularly given the extensive reporting and disclosure requirements which now apply to CRAs under CRA I-III and which suggest that the investment analysts/investment recommendations regime is unlikely to be lightened. The main elements of the 2003 Commission Directive are outlined next.

VII.3.4.2 The 2003 Commission Investment Recommendations Directive

(a) Relevant Persons

The 2003 Commission Investment Recommendations Directive had a broad scope. It applied to 'relevant persons', defined as a natural or legal person producing or disseminating 'recommendations' (the definition of which tracked the 2014 MAR definition of investment recommendations) in the exercise of his profession or the conduct of his business. The Directive therefore extended far beyond the investment firms (and credit institutions which provide investment services) subsequently covered by the 2006 Commission MiFID I Directive. General, high-level obligations were imposed on 'relevant persons'. More detailed

---

[371] The repealing provisions come into force on 3 July 2016.

obligations were imposed on a group composed of investment firms, credit institutions, independent analysts, and any related legal persons. The most onerous obligations (with respect to conflict-of-interest disclosure) were imposed on investment firms and credit institutions. The Directive also distinguished between the production of recommendations (including the substantial alteration of research) and their dissemination, with a considerably lighter regime applying to the dissemination of recommendations.

(b) Website Disclosure

The new 2014 MAR RTSs are likely to reflect the concern of the 2003 Commission Directive to manage the costs of disclosure. In particular, Member States were to adapt the Directive's requirements to non-written recommendations to ensure they were not disproportionate and, where the required disclosures would be disproportionate in relation to the recommendation, it was sufficient that the recommendation made a clear and prominent reference to where the disclosure could be easily accessed by the public (including websites).

(c) The Presentation of Investment Research and Conflicts of Interest Disclosure

Detailed rules applied under the Directive to the presentation of investment research.

The general regime which applied under Article 3(1) required Member States to ensure that appropriate regulation was in place which required all relevant persons to take reasonable care to ensure that (i) facts were clearly distinguished from interpretations, estimates, opinions, and other types of non-factual information, (ii) all sources were reliable—where there was any doubt as to reliability, this was to be disclosed, and (iii) all projections, forecasts, and price targets were to be clearly labelled as such and the material assumptions made in producing or using them indicated. Member States were also to require that all relevant persons took reasonable care to ensure that any recommendation could be substantiated as reasonable, on a request by the NCAs (Article 3(3)).

Investment firms, credit institutions, independent analysts, any related legal person, any other relevant person whose main business was to produce recommendations, or a natural person working for them under a contract of employment or otherwise were subject to more rigorous requirements. Under Article 4(1), these persons were to take reasonable care to ensure that: (i) all substantially material sources were indicated, as appropriate (including the relevant issuer), together with whether the recommendation had been disclosed to the issuer and amended following this disclosure; (ii) the basis of the valuation or methodology used to evaluate a financial instrument (or an issuer of a financial instrument) or to set a price target for a financial instrument was adequately summarized; (iii) the meaning of any recommendation made (such as 'buy', 'sell', or 'hold') was indicated—this disclosure could include an explanation of the time horizon of the investment in question and risk warnings as to the assumptions made; (iv) reference was made to the planned frequency (if any) of updates to the recommendations and to any major changes to the relevant coverage policy; (v) the date at which the recommendation was first released for distribution was indicated clearly and prominently (as well as the relevant date and time for any financial instrument price mentioned); and (vi) disclosure of any changes to a recommendation was indicated clearly and prominently.

Conflicts of interest were subject to extensive disclosure requirements which are likely to be reflected in the 2014 MAR RTSs. Article 5 set the general standard for disclosure by all entities which produced recommendations. Under Article 5(1), Member States were to ensure that there was appropriate regulation in place to ensure that relevant persons disclosed all relationships and circumstances 'that may reasonably be expected to impair the objectivity of the recommendation'. The disclosure obligation arose in particular where the relevant person had a 'significant financial interest' in one or more of the financial instruments the subject of the recommendation, or a 'significant conflict of interest' with respect to an issuer to which the recommendation related. Where the relevant person was a legal person, the disclosure was to include at least (i) any interests or conflicts of interest of the relevant person or of related legal persons accessible or reasonably expected to be accessible to the persons involved in the preparation of the recommendation, and (ii) any interests or conflicts of interests known to persons who, although not involved in the preparation of the recommendations, had or could reasonably be expected to have had access to the recommendation prior to its dissemination to customers or the public. Where the disclosures would be disproportionate in relation to the recommendation, it was sufficient that the recommendation made a clear and prominent reference to where the disclosure could be easily accessed by the public (including websites) (Article 5(3)). Similarly, Member States could adapt the disclosure requirements to non-written recommendations to ensure they were not disproportionate (Article 5(4)).

Enhanced disclosure obligations applied to independent analysts, investment firms, credit institutions, any related legal persons, or any other relevant person whose main business was to produce recommendations. Article 6 listed the specific information required of these entities, which was to be disclosed clearly and prominently. Article 6(1)(a) required disclosure of 'major shareholdings' between the relevant person and the issuer, including at least shareholdings in excess of 5 per cent of the total issued share capital of the issuer held by the relevant person (or any related legal person), and holdings of the same magnitude by the issuer in the relevant person. Member States could provide for lower thresholds. Similarly, under Article 6(1)(b), 'other significant financial interests' held by the relevant person (or any related legal person) in relation to the issuer were to be disclosed.

Business relationships were addressed by Article 6(1)(c)–(e), which covered disclosure of market-making or liquidity provision by the relevant person in the issuer's financial instruments, lead managing or co-lead managing by the relevant person of any publicly disclosed offer of financial instruments by the issuer over the previous 12 months, and any agreement to provide any other investment banking services to the issuer by the relevant person. Article 6(1)(f) also required disclosure where the relevant person was party to an agreement with the issuer related to the production of the recommendation.

Under Article 6(2), Member States were also to require disclosure in the recommendation, in general terms, of the 'effective organizational and administrative arrangements' set up within the investment firm or credit institution for the prevention and avoidance of conflicts of interests. Public disclosure in the recommendation was also required of whether the remuneration of those involved in preparing the recommendation was tied to investment banking transactions (Article 6(3)). Disclosure was also required where persons working for the firm received or purchased the shares of the issuer prior to a public offering of such shares and was to include the price at which the shares were acquired and the date of the acquisition.

The most revealing disclosures, perhaps, were required by Article 6(4). Member States were to require that investment firms and credit institutions disclosed, on quarterly basis, the proportion of recommendations which were 'buy', 'hold', or 'sell' (or equivalent), as well as the proportion of issuers corresponding to each of these categories to which the firm had supplied material investment banking services over the previous 12 months.

(d) Dissemination of Recommendations Produced by Third Parties

The 2003 Commission Investment Recommendations Directive also addressed the dissemination of third party recommendations (of particular significance for journalists), in unaltered and 'substantially altered' forms. The core obligation was imposed by Article 7, which provided that Member States were to require that whenever a relevant person, under his own responsibility, disseminated a recommendation produced by a third party, the recommendation was to clearly and prominently indicate the identity of the relevant person.

Additional presentation and disclosure requirements were imposed on 'substantially altered' recommendations under Article 8. Member States were to ensure that whenever a third party recommendation was 'substantially altered' within disseminated information, that information was to clearly indicate the substantial alteration in detail. Where the substantial alteration consisted of a change to the direction of the recommendation, Articles 2–5 on the fair presentation of research applied. Conflicts of interests were additionally addressed through a linkage to the disclosure made by the original producer. Where the recommendation was substantially altered, it was to be possible to direct those persons receiving the information to where they could access the identity of the original producer of the recommendation, the recommendation, and the disclosure concerning the producer's interests or conflicts of interests (as long as this information was publicly available).

Two provisions had particular implications for journalists under Article 8. First, these requirements did not apply to news reporting on recommendations produced by a third party where the substance of the recommendation was not altered. Second, where a summary of a third party recommendation was disseminated, the relevant person disseminating the summary was to ensure that the summary was clear and not misleading, and mention the original recommendation and where the required disclosures related to the recommendation could be directly and easily accessed by the public.

Additional requirements applied to investment firms and credit institutions under Article 9. Whether or not the recommendation had been substantially altered, the name of the NCA of the investment firm or credit institution was to be clearly and prominently indicated and the Article 6 disclosure requirements were to be met by the firm (if the producer had not already disseminated the recommendation through a distribution channel). The requirements of Articles 2–6 were to be met by the firm where the recommendation had been substantially altered.

VIII

MARKET ABUSE

VIII.1 Introduction

This Chapter covers the EU regime which governs the prohibition of market abuse. In common with regulatory regimes internationally, the regime has expanded beyond an original prohibition on insider dealing to include prohibitions on a range of different market abuses, well illustrated by the crisis-era extension of the regime to include abuses related to high frequency trading and the abuse of benchmarks. It deploys an array of regulatory mechanisms, including prohibitions and disclosure-related techniques.

The 2003 Market Abuse Directive (the 2003 MAD),[1] which was a central pillar of the Financial Services Action Plan (FSAP), was the cornerstone of the EU's market abuse regime[2] until the adoption of the 2014 Market Abuse Regulation (the 2014 MAR), which will replace the 2003 MAD;[3] the 2014 MAR is accompanied by the 2014 Market Abuse Directive (the 2014 MAD), which requires Member States to impose criminal sanctions for specified acts of market abuse.[4] Previously, the 2003 MAD had been significantly amplified by four administrative Commission measures: the 2003 Commission Definitions and Disclosure Obligations Directive; the 2003 Commission Investment Recommendations Directive; the 2003 Commission Buy Backs and Stabilization Safe Harbour Regulation; and the 2004 Commission Accepted Market Practices Directive.[5] The 2003 MAD was

---

[1] Directive 2003/6/EC [2003] OJ L96/16 (the 2003 MAD).

[2] See, eg, Ferrarini, G, 'The European Market Abuse Directive' (2004) 41 *CMLR* 711; Hansen Lau, J, 'MAD in A Hurry: The Swift and Promising Adoption of the EU Market Abuse Directive' (2004) *EBLR* 183; Reynolds, C and Rutter, M, 'Market Abuse—a Pan European Approach' (2004) 12 *JFRC* 306; and Coffey, J and Overett-Somnier, J, 'The Market Abuse Directive—the First Use of the Lamfalussy Process' (2003) *JIBLR* 370.

[3] Regulation (EU) No 596/2014 [2014] OJ L173/1 (2014 MAR). The 2014 MAR applies from 3 July 2016. The delegations for administrative rule-making, however, apply from 2 July 2014 to allow for the preparation of the related administrative rulebook. To allow for the later application of the related MiFID II/MiFIR regime (n 9) (most of which applies from 3 January 2017), references in the 2014 MAR to the 2014 MiFID II/MiFIR are to be read as references to the 2004 MiFID I (Directive 2004/39/EC OJ L145/1) regime until 3 January 2017, and similarly, references in the 2014 MAR to 2014 MiFID II/MiFIR concepts (such as the organized trading facility) do not apply to the relevant entities until that date (Art 39). This Chapter is based on the 2014 MAR regime but makes reference to the earlier regime as appropriate.

[4] Directive 2014/57/EU [2014] OJ L173/179 (2014 MAD). The 2014 MAD must be implemented by and applied from 3 July 2016 (Art 13). The original proposals for both 2014 MAR and MAD measures were amended in 2012 to address market abuse relating to benchmarks in the wake of the Libor scandal (COM (2012) 421 (revising the 2014 MAR) and COM (2012) 420 (revising the 2014 MAD)) (sect 8.2.3).

[5] Respectively, Commission Directive 2003/124/EC [2003] OJ L339/70; Commission Directive 2003/125/EC [2003] OJ L339/73; Commission Regulation (EC) No 2273/2003 [2003] OJ L336/33; and Commission Directive 2004/72/EC [2004] OJ L162/70.

amended at the legislative level in 2008 to reflect adjustments to the administrative rule-making process,[6] and again in 2010 to reflect the establishment of the European Securities and Markets Authority (ESMA).[7] The 2014 MAR will repeal the 2003 MAD and its related supporting administrative rules.[8] It incorporates, however, elements of the original set of administrative rules and provides for new delegations to administrative rule-making, primarily in the form of ESMA-proposed Binding Technical Standards (BTSs).

The market abuse regime is multilayered, extending beyond the 2014 MAR/MAD regime. Detection is supported by the extensive 2014 MiFID II transaction reporting regime,[9] discussed in Chapter V section 12.1. Market abuse is also addressed, more tangentially, under the takeover regime,[10] while a discrete regime applies to market abuse in the wholesale energy market.[11] The 2012 Short Selling Regulation[12] has implications for the prevention of market abuse where short selling has abusive qualities, but it is primarily directed towards the financial stability implications of trading; it is accordingly addressed in Chapter VI section 3.

VIII.2 The Rationale for Prohibiting Insider Dealing and Market Manipulation and the EU

VIII.2.1 The Rationale for Prohibiting Insider Dealing and Market Manipulation

VIII.2.1.1 Insider Dealing

The insider-dealing element of securities and markets regulation has remained broadly stable for some time, and was largely immune from the reform pyrotechnics of the crisis era. But this is not to say the area is robust and settled. Notwithstanding the prevalence of insider-dealing prohibitions in systems of securities and markets regulation internationally,[13] attempts to identify a robust rationale for prohibiting insider dealing have generated a vast literature.[14] This brief discussion does not attempt to canvass all the legal and

---

[6] Directive 2008/26/EC [2008] OJ L81/42.

[7] Directive 2010/78/EU [2010] OJ L331/120 (the 2010 Omnibus I Directive).

[8] 2014 MAR Art 37 (from 3 July 2016).

[9] Markets in Financial Instruments Directive II 2014/65/EU [2014] OJ L173/349 (2014 MiFID II) (on the implementation timeline see Ch IV n 28). MiFID II operates as a regulatory package with the Markets in Financial Instruments Regulation (MiFIR) EU (No) 600/2014 OJ [2014] L173/84.

[10] Directive 2004/25/EC [2004] OJ L142/12. Art 3(1)(d) requires Member States to ensure that false markets are not created in the securities of the offeror, offeree, or any other company concerned with a takeover bid, while Art 8 requires that a bid must be made public in such a way as to ensure market transparency and integrity for the securities of the offeror, offeree, or any other company affected by the bid. As the Takeover Directive is more a creature of company law and corporate governance than of securities and markets regulation, it is not considered further.

[11] Regulation (EU) No 1227/2011 [2011] OJ L326/1 (the 2011 REMIT Regulation).

[12] Regulation (EU) No 236/2012 [2012] OJ L86/1.

[13] One oft-cited study reported that of the 103 countries studied, 87 had adopted insider-dealing prohibitions: Bhattacharya, U and Daouk, H, 'The World Price of Insider Trading' (2002) 57 *J Fin* 75. See also International Organization of Securities Commissions (IOSCO), Insider Trading. How Jurisdictions Regulate It (2003), which noted that 'nearly every jurisdiction' had enacted a prohibition on insider dealing: at 1.

[14] For a review of the major controversies see Beny, L, 'Do Insider Trading Laws Matter? Some Preliminary Comparative Evidence' (2005) 7 *ALER*, Bainbridge, S, 'Insider Trading' in *The Encyclopedia of Law and*

economic arguments raised by the prohibition on insider dealing, but is limited to identifying the main features of the debate in order to contextualize the EU's approach.

Although the related arguments embrace protestations as to amorality and unfairness[15] and concerns about organized crime, the underlying rationale for prohibiting insider dealing[16] can be described, very broadly, as two-pronged and as composed of contrasting relationship-based and market-based theories.[17] The first rationale for insider-dealing regulation has a micro focus. It characterizes insider dealing as a breach of the fiduciary relationship of trust and confidence (a related strand characterizes insider dealing in terms of the allocation of property rights[18]), where one can be established, between, typically, the insider and the company concerned. The macro focus of the second theory (which has shaped the EU regime) is on market efficiency, and on the support of efficient price formation and deep liquidity. Insider dealing is prohibited to support the efficiency with which the market allocates resources through the price-formation mechanism; this argument is typically made by regulators with little by way of reasoning or empirical support,[19] although some evidence of the impact of enforcement on market efficiency is emerging.[20] If investor confidence in the price-formation process is compromised, goes the argument, liquidity can be damaged and the cost of capital increased as investors price in the risk of trading against inside information.[21] While investor confidence in the marketplace is notoriously difficult to assess,

Economics (2000) 772, Suter, J, The Regulation of Insider Trading in Britain (1989) 14–49, and Hopt, K, 'The European Insider Dealing Directive' in Hopt, K and Wymeersch, E (eds), European Insider Dealing (1991) 129, 129–30.

[15] Schepple, K, 'It's Just Not Right: The Ethics of Insider Trading' (1993) 56 Law & Contemporary Problems 123.

[16] Although in reviewing the rationale for insider dealing it should be noted that in this area '[t]o cross between the doctrinal and policy discussion is to risk disorientation; in the policy debate even the settled legal rule against open trading by corporate insiders dissolves into a decidedly unsettled account of price behaviour and compensation contracts': Kraakmann, R, 'The Legal Theory of Insider Trading Regulation in the United States' in Hopt and Wymeersch, n 14, 39, 47.

[17] For an exposition of the relationship and market approaches see, eg, Loke, A, 'From the Fiduciary Theory to Information Abuse: the Changing Fabric of Insider Trading Law in the UK, Australia, and Singapore' (2006) 54 Am J Comp L 123; Black, J, 'Audacious But Not Successful: A Comparative Analysis of the Implementation of Insider Dealing Regulation in EU Member States' (1998) 2 CFILR 1, 3; Rider, B, Abrams, C and Ashe, M, Guide to Financial Services Legislation (3rd edn, 1997) 221–3; and Davies, P, 'The European Community's Directive on Insider Dealing: From Company Law to Securities Market Regulation' (1991) 11 OJLS 92. The two approaches have been described in terms of the contrasting interests at stake—the ownership rights of the information holder, and the interest of investors in the integrity of the marketplace as a whole: Davies, P, 'The Take-over Bidder Exemption and the Policy of Disclosure' in Hopt and Wymeersch, n 14, 243, 251.

[18] See, eg, Macey, J, 'From Fairness to Contract: The New Direction of the Rules Against Insider Trading' (1984) Hofstra LR 9 and Bainbridge, S, 'Insider Trading Regulation: The Pathdependent Choice Between Property Rights and Securities Fraud' (1999) 52 Southern Methodist University LR 1589.

[19] For a classic example see the assertion by IOSCO that 'insider trading undermines investor confidence in the fairness and integrity of securities markets': n 13, 1. Similarly, the UK Financial Services and Markets Tribunal (now the Upper Tribunal) argued that 'the vice of insider dealing, and the reason why it is prohibited, is that it reduces confidence in the integrity and transparency of the market in the particular security which is being abused': Financial Services and Markets Tribunal, Philippe Jabre and Financial Services Authority (10 July 2006) para 28.

[20] Sect 9.

[21] '[I]n a stock market in which insiders trade with impunity... [t]he liquidity providers in such a market would protect themselves by increasing their sell price and decreasing their buy price. This increases the transaction costs, which in turn induces a stock trader to require an even higher return on equity': Bhattacharya and Daouk, n 13, 76.

in the insider-dealing context it is often linked to confidence in market egalitarianism or the confidence of investors in the equality of access to information in the marketplace.[22] Market egalitarianism, which has been influential on the EU regime,[23] requires that in the context of impersonal markets and trading venues, investors should deal on a relatively equal basis with equal opportunities to access information, and should not be unfairly disadvantaged by dealings on the part of those with special access to non-public information.[24]

Market-efficiency-based arguments have been subject to voluminous critique, in particular since the publication of Manne's seminal 1966 work. In a controversial and agenda-setting work, Manne argued against the prohibition of insider dealing given its beneficial effects on price formation and given its efficiency as an executive compensation device in providing entrepreneurs with stronger performance incentives and in overcoming agency costs.[25] Manne argued that insider dealing ultimately moved prices steadily in the right direction,[26] benefited long-term investors (including uninformed investors), harmed only speculators, and increased confidence in the price-formation mechanism. The stage was then set for a long-running and largely inconclusive debate on the impact of insider dealing on market efficiency and price formation.[27]

In particular, it is difficult to establish whether insider-dealing prohibitions have an impact on the efficiency of price formation, on the depth of market liquidity, and on market development.[28] Although the international momentum driving the adoption of

---

[22] See Scott, K, 'Insider Trading, Rule 10-b(5), Disclosure and Corporate Privacy' (1980) 9 *J Legal Studies* 801 and Brudney, V, 'Insiders, Outsiders and Informational Advantages Under the Federal Securities Laws' (1979) 93 *Harv LR* 322.

[23] The EU's first attempt at prohibiting insider dealing (the 1989 Insider Dealing Directive 89/592/EEC [1989] OJ L334/30 (the 1989 IDD)) linked investor confidence to the assurance afforded to investors that they would be on an equal footing and protected against the improper use of inside information (recs 4 and 5). Egalitarianism was influential on the Court of Justice's interpretation of key IDD concepts in Case C-391/04 *Oikonomikon and Amfissas v Georgakis* [2007] ECR I-3741 and Case C-384/02 *Grøngaard and Bang* [2005] ECR I-9939. Market egalitarianism is also implicit in the 2014 MAR disclosure regime (sect 7.1). See further Moalem, D and Hansen Lau, J, 'Insider Dealing and Parity of Information—is Georgakis Still Valid?' (2008) 19 *EBLR* 949.

[24] Complete equality is impossible to achieve, given the superior ability of certain (typically professional) investors legitimately to access and decode publicly available information: Gilson, R and Kraakmann, R, 'The Mechanisms of Market Efficiency' (1984) 70 *Va LR* 549, 571.

[25] Manne, H, *Insider Trading and the Stock Market* (1966). For a summary see Manne, H, 'In Defense of Insider Trading' (1966) *Harv B Rev* November–December 113.

[26] The thesis is based on the notion that buying activity by insiders with price-sensitive positive information about the company will drive the price up, reflecting more accurately the status of the company and allowing non-insiders to trade at a more accurate price.

[27] See generally Bainbridge, n 18 and Beny, n 14. For the argument that insider-dealing prohibitions slow down the rate at which securities prices adjust to new information see Carlton, D and Fischer, D, 'The Regulation of Insider Trading' (1983) 35 *Stanford LR* 857. For a challenge to this view, based, *inter alia*, on the argument that the inside information driving the insider's trading decision cannot be decoded by the marketplace (through 'derivatively informed' trading which supports market efficiency), see Gilson and Kraakmann, n 24, 629–34. In the EU context, for a robust response to the price-formation argument for permitting insider dealing, based on the fact that while a positive impact on prices may be observed empirically, the fact remains that 'essential information relevant to price is not supposed to reach the Stock Exchange slowly, indirectly and with a prior profit for insiders but immediately, directly and with due regard to equality of opportunity, thus through timely disclosure', see Hopt, K, 'Insider Regulation and Timely Disclosure', *Forum Internationale*, No 21 (1996) 4.

[28] Prior to the enforcement of insider-dealing rules in the 1960s, the US had developed strong securities markets: Black, B, 'The Legal and Institutional Preconditions for Strong Securities Markets' (2001) 48

insider-dealing regimes internationally in the mid-1980s was generated in part by pressure from the markets (and in part by pressure from the US Securities and Exchange Commission (SEC)[29]), the relationship between insider-dealing regulation and financial market development remains unclear, although evidence has emerged that the enforcement of insider-dealing prohibitions can have quantifiable positive effects on markets; 'laws on the books' governing insider dealing, however, appear to have no appreciable effect on market development.[30]

VIII.2.1.2 Market Manipulation

Market manipulation[31] controls typically address the misuse of material information (and so supplement or include insider-dealing rules), the dissemination of false or misleading information, and practices which distort the trading price or trading volume of a security. One of the difficulties inherent in tackling market manipulation effectively is that such activity can range from relatively straightforward instances of fraudulent misrepresentation to highly complex and difficult-to-detect trading practices designed artificially to increase or decrease a security's trading volumes and/or to distort its price or to interfere with market forces of supply and demand; legitimate market practices might also risk being characterized as manipulative, absent careful regulatory design. Market manipulation practices are also continually evolving as new products are developed, as new participants enter the marketplace, and, as markets become ever more interconnected, the opportunities for cross-border manipulation increase; the crisis-era benchmark-fixing scandal represents only one example of a persistent problem (section 8.2.3). Prior to the financial crisis, the explosive increase in hedge fund activity, for example, was linked to an increased risk of market abuse, including market manipulation.[32]

Misuse of information can affect confidence, as can misrepresentations and false statements concerning securities and issuers by market participants (and their dissemination). The latter can include the intentional spreading of untrue rumours concerning securities or their issuer in order to depress the market price and so enable the market abuser to buy the securities at an artificially low price.

Manipulative behaviour which distorts volumes and prices encompasses a vast range of abusive conduct. While difficult to define conceptually, it is often regarded as covering two overlapping activities: conduct which creates an artificial and misleading impression about

---

University of California LR 781, 803. For a similar argument in the UK context, see Cheffins, B, 'Does Law Matter: the Separation of Ownership and Control in the United Kingdom' (2001) 30 *J Legal Studies* 459.

[29] Enriques, L, 'EC Company Law Directives and Regulations: How Trivial Are They?' (2006) 27 *UPaJIEL* 1, 21 and Pitt, H and Hardison, D, 'Games Without Frontiers: Trends in the International Responses to Insider Trading' (1992) 55 *Law & Contemporary Problems* 199.

[30] Bhattacharya and Daouk, n 13. See also Fernandes, N and Ferreira, M, 'Insider Trading Laws and Stock Price Information' (2009) 22 *Rev of Financial Studies* (2009) 1845.

[31] See generally Avgouleas, E, *The Mechanics and Regulation of Market Abuse. A Legal and Economic Analysis* (2005).

[32] In its first major (2005) report on hedge fund activities, the UK Financial Services Authority (FSA) reported that hedge fund managers 'might be testing the limits of acceptable practice in relation to market manipulation' and might be tempted to use their trading position or start market rumours to deliberately move the market and committed to close surveillance and tough enforcement where necessary: FSA, Discussion Paper 05/4, Hedge Funds: A Discussion of Risk and Regulatory Engagement (2005) 53–4.

the real market in or price or value of a security,[33] and conduct which, by interfering with the usual forces of supply and demand, distorts the market. The former typically involves engaging in trades or a series of trades in order to create a false impression of a liquid market in particular securities or in order to maintain or position prices at an artificial level. Speculative investors, in particular, are vulnerable to this form of manipulation and may sustain severe losses when the manipulating traders offload their securities when a particular price level is reached. The latter practices (which manipulate the market and the forces of supply and demand more generally) include 'abusive squeezes'. In an abusive squeeze, a person who exercises significant influence over the supply of a security enters into transactions under which that person has the right to require others to deliver that security or to take delivery of it, and uses those deals to distort the market by setting abnormal prices for the discharge of the obligations owed. More generally, the market can be distorted by a trader taking advantage of a shortage in a security by controlling supply and exploiting congestion in the marketplace in such a way as to create artificial prices.[34]

The design of an effective prohibition of market manipulation poses a series of challenges for regulators. The establishment of robust indicators for when a security price is artificial, as evidence of manipulative conduct, can be difficult.[35] The assessment of whether the forces of supply and demand have been distorted is equally complex, particularly when it comes to establishing whether the manipulator had control over the supply of the security in question. The establishment of the range of persons liable to market manipulation controls can also be difficult. Where an order or a series of orders is given to a broker, it is clear that liability still remains with the client/party placing the orders and initiating the abusive transaction. Where the broker is aware, however, that the client is engaging in market manipulation, it may be appropriate to impose liability on the broker also. The freedom of action of intermediaries may be compromised, however, where overly onerous conditions are imposed on them with respect to monitoring clients' orders. Further, a number of trading practices which have the purpose of maintaining prices at an artificial level are legitimate. Stabilization, market-making, arbitrage activities, and hedging practices are legitimate activities which enhance the efficiency of the marketplace but may be vulnerable to a catch-all market manipulation prohibition. So too may legitimate, large price-moving trades. Transparency rules play an important part in protecting legitimate conduct; if the market is aware of the artificial activity engaged in by the trader, then it is not misled.

Although the rationale for prohibiting market manipulation is similarly, if less intensely, as contested as the rationale for prohibiting insider dealing,[36] prohibitions on market

---

[33] The efficiency of prohibitions based on price-distorting effects has been queried given the difficulties in establishing the correct level at which a security should trade: Fischel, D and Ross, D, 'Should the Law Prohibit "Manipulation" in Financial Markets?' (1991) 105 *Harv LR* 503.

[34] IOSCO, Investigating and Prosecuting Market Manipulation (2000) (2000 IOSCO Market Manipulation Report) 6.

[35] IOSCO has suggested that: 'The key question is whether there appears to be any logical trading pattern to the security's price and volume, or whether it seems erratic. If it is erratic, the question is whether the pattern coincides with the activities of the promoter, broker, or other participant in the potential manipulation': n 34, 13.

[36] Not all commentators are convinced of the need for controls on market manipulation. See Fischel and Ross, n 33.

manipulation are likewise typically based on supporting market efficiency and on lowering the cost of capital.[37] Manipulative practices are typically characterized as a form of market failure which ultimately leads to an inefficient allocation of resources and damages the role of the marketplace in capital allocation. Where the manipulative behaviour results in a misleading impression being given to the marketplace of the demand for, and liquidity in, a particular security, or results in the dissemination of misleading or untrue information about the security or its issuer, the price-formation mechanism is distorted.[38] More generally, market manipulation controls typically seek to enhance investor confidence in the fairness, honesty, and integrity of the marketplace, and in its freedom from fraudulent practices.

VIII.2.2 The EU and the Prohibition of Market Abuse

The EU market abuse regime, by contrast with EU securities and markets regulation generally, was from the outset concerned with regulation rather than with passporting. Its most recent iteration—the 2014 MAR—reflects the 2003 MAD and the initial 1989 Insider Dealing Directive (the 1989 IDD) in justifying intervention by identifying market integrity as essential for an integrated and efficient financial market, linking the smooth functioning of securities markets and public confidence in markets to economic growth and wealth, and finding that market abuse harms the integrity of financial markets and public confidence in securities and derivatives (recital 2). Similarly, under Article 1 the 2014 MAR is designed to ensure the integrity of financial markets in the EU and to enhance investor protection and confidence in those markets. The support of market integrity and related market efficiency accordingly is the main driver of the EU regime, reflecting the rationales typically associated with insider dealing and market manipulation prohibitions.

Notwithstanding the by now extensive experience with market abuse regulation in the EU, the 2014 MAR is, however, largely unsupported by empirical evidence as to the impact of the earlier 2003 MAD regime on market integrity[39]—although this evidence is difficult to establish.[40] In particular, there is little evidence as to the impact of the market abuse

---

[37] Enriques, L and Gatti, M, 'Is there a Uniform EU Securities Law After the Financial Services Action Plan?' (2008) 14 *Stanford J of Law, Business and Finance* 43.

[38] 'Anti-manipulation regulation focuses on maintaining the integrity of the market price of securities, of derivatives contracts and of the assets underlying such contracts. The rules attempt to ensure that a price is set by the unimpeded collective judgment of buyers and sellers': 2000 IOSCO Market Manipulation Report, n 34, 8.

[39] The Impact Assessment for the 2011 Proposal for the 2013 MAR noted, however, the significant difficulties in building an evidence base. It also noted the generally reducing levels of criminal prosecutions (albeit from a very limited data set) and presented tentative evidence of the cost to the market of abusive conduct, in the form of an estimation of a cost of €13.3 billion to EU equity markets in 2010: 2011 MAR Proposal Impact Assessment (SEC (2011) 1217) 14–17. The 2009 Commission Call for Evidence on review of the 2003 MAD also noted the significant lack of empirical evidence in this regard, although it drew on the tentative evidence from the UK FSA's 2006–8 market cleanliness surveys (which examined the extent of suspicious transactions prior to significant market announcements in the FTSE 350), and from the Dutch regulator which suggested that a decline in suspicious activity prior to significant market announcements had occurred: Commission, Call for Evidence. Review of Directive 2003/6 (2009) (2009 Commission Call for Evidence) 4.

[40] The UK Financial Conduct Authority (previously part of the UK FSA) remains the only national regulator to collate market cleanliness data, based on assessment of abnormal price movements in the two days prior to a regulatory announcement in FTSE 350 shares. The levels of abnormal price movement in the UK

prohibitions on market efficiency, although there is some evidence of a positive effect on market liquidity in the wake of the implementation of the 2003 MAD.[41] The uncertain impact of insider-dealing regulation in particular prompts the question as to whether the EU's regime can deliver quantifiable benefits in terms of financial market development.[42]

It is clear, however, that the market abuse regime is following the trajectory of other elements of EU securities and markets regulation by becoming ever more dense and multilayered, as it expands to address new market sectors and as, through the ESMA, it becomes more operational.

VIII.3 The Evolution of the Regime

VIII.3.1 Early Developments

Insider dealing was, from a very early stage, associated with the EU's regulation of financial markets, being highlighted by the seminal 1966 Segré Report, which primarily addressed insider-dealing risks in terms of unequal access to information (and so adopted a fiduciary-driven approach), but also identified the risks to efficient pricing.[43] But in the context of widespread Member State resistance to a statutory prohibition on insider dealing, particularly in Germany,[44] and given the slower development of market finance in the EU as compared to the US—where insider-dealing prohibitions were, by then, long established[45]—progress towards an EU regime was slow. The 1977 Code of Conduct[46] promoted equality of access to information and the avoidance of market imperfections by fair and adequate disclosure, reflecting the market-orientated approach adopted by a 1976 Commission working group on harmonizing insider-dealing rules.[47] The Code was, however, largely ignored by the Member States and had little impact on the control of insider dealing.[48] Nonetheless, the precedent for market-orientated insider-dealing controls had been set.

FTSE 350 remained largely level over 2005–9. They dropped substantially, however, in 2010, 2011, and 2012: FCA, Annual Report 2012–2013, 37. Previously, the then FSA noted that while this downward trend could be related to the FSA's sharper focus on deterrence and to more aggressive enforcement, it was not possible to determine with certainty whether the reduction in abnormal pricing activity was linked to the market abuse regime generally and its enforcement: FSA, Annual Report 2011–2012, 44–5.

[41] Christensen, H, Hail, L, and Leuz, C, Capital-Market Effects of Securities Regulation: Prior Conditions, Implementation and Enforcement, ECGI Finance WP No 407/2014 and Chicago Booth Research Paper No 12-04 (2013), available at <http://ssrn.com/abstract=1745105>.

[42] For a critique of the impact of the original 1989 IDD regime which cast doubts on its impact on the development of the EU equity market see Ferran, E, *Building an EU Securities Market* (2004) 30–4.

[43] Report of a Group of Experts Appointed by the EEC Commission, *The Development of a European Capital Market* (1966) 248–9.

[44] For the view that in Germany it was commonly held that insider trading was simply a part of doing business see Standen, D, 'Insider Trading Reforms Sweep Across Germany: Bracing for the Cold Winds of Change' (1995) 36 *Harv Int LJ* 177, 177–8.

[45] Hopt, n 27, 4.

[46] Commission Recommendation 77/534/EEC concerning a European Code of Conduct relating to transactions in transferable securities [1977] OJ L212/37.

[47] Working Paper No 1, 'Coordination of the Rules and Regulations Governing Insider Trading', EC Commission XV/206/76-E.

[48] In its comments on the proposal for the 1989 IDD, ECOSOC's support for a harmonized regime was based partly on the Code of Conduct 'not [being] the success that was hoped for' [1988] OJ C35/22, para 1.2.

VIII.3.2 The 1989 Insider Dealing Directive

Although continued resistance from certain Member States to a statutory treatment of insider dealing slowed progress,[49] a series of insider-dealing scandals in the late 1980s, together with a movement across the EU to address insider dealing[50]—particularly as market finance began slowly to gain traction[51]—created conducive conditions for the Commission's first proposal for an insider-dealing regime (1987),[52] which was replaced by a lightly revised proposal in October 1988.[53] The Insider Dealing Directive was finally adopted in November 1989 (the 1989 IDD).[54]

Although radical in that it was the EU's first 'regulatory' measure in the securities and markets sphere (in that it was not anchored to a market access/passporting mechanism), the 1989 IDD did not drive significant regulatory change,[55] given the extent to which the Member States had already introduced insider-dealing regimes while the 1989 IDD was under negotiation.[56] It has proved relatively resilient, however, providing the basic template for initially the 2003 MAD's and then the 2014 MAR's insider-dealing prohibitions. It also provides a very early example of how the local, political benefits of EU-led intervention can facilitate an extension of the EU's reach over financial markets[57]—as the crisis era has shown to dramatic effect.

Nonetheless, the 1989 IDD suffered from a number of weaknesses from the outset. The scope of the regime was limited in terms of the securities and markets covered; the sanctions and enforcement regime was weak, as was the supporting structure for supervisory co-operation; and, most significantly, it did not, in a reflection of a less sophisticated regulatory environment, address market manipulation. The limitations of the 1989 IDD regime were made clear in the Court of Justice's *Georgakis* 2007 ruling.[58] It concerned the interpretation of the insider-dealing prohibition under the 1989 IDD and whether a decision by a group of majority shareholders to support trading in the shares of a publicly quoted company on the advice of their financial advisers, and at a time when the share price was coming under downward pressure, breached the Directive. Although a classic example of market manipulation, it could,

---

[49] The Commission accordingly took some time to decide whether insider dealing should be addressed through a directive or a recommendation: Tridimas, T, 'Insider Trading: European Harmonisation and National Law Reform' [1991] 40 *ICLQ* 919, 920.

[50] See generally Ferran, n 42 and Enriques, n 29, 21–2.

[51] Fornasier, R, 'The Directive on Insider Trading' (1989–1990) 13 *Fordham Int LJ* 149, 149, noting increased merger and acquisition activity, and related demand for insider dealing protections.

[52] [1987] OJ C153/8 (the Original Proposal); Explanatory Memorandum at COM (87) 11.

[53] [1988] OJ C277/13 (the Revised Proposal); Explanatory Memorandum at COM (88) 549.

[54] n 23.

[55] On the manner in which the Directive was implemented see Wymeersch, E, 'The Insider Trading Prohibition in the EC Member States: A Comparative Overview' in Hopt and Wymeersch, n 14, 65; Tridimas, n 49, and Black, n 17.

[56] For a review of the pre-IDD position see British Institute of International and Comparative Law, Comparative Implementation of EU Directives (I)—Insider Dealing and Market Abuse (2005), Corporation of London, City Research Series No 8 (the 2005 BIICL Report).

[57] Ferran has questioned why Germany, which engaged in a large-scale reform of its capital market regulation during the 1990s, waited for EU intervention before adopting an insider-dealing regime and suggested it may have been that, with an EU-led initiative, Germany was able to avoid direct confrontation with powerful domestic lobbies: n 42, 32.

[58] n 23.

in the circumstances of the case, only be dealt with under the insider-dealing regime, which the Court refused to stretch to cover this conduct. The Court acknowledged that the practices were liable to provoke a loss in investor confidence but highlighted that 'the fact remains that the scope of [the IDD]—the sole Community measure applicable to the facts in the case ... is limited to taking advantage of inside information ... it is not applicable to transactions designed to determine artificially, by concerted means, the price of certain transferable securities'.[59]

The risks associated with the absence of a harmonized regime on market manipulation, both in terms of the rules applicable and the optimal supervisory and enforcement tools, became more acute as the EU trading environment changed over the 1980s and 1990s. In particular, as trading began to fragment across different venues, greater pressure was brought to bear on regulation and on supervision, and the potential for prejudicial cross-border effects was magnified.[60] The parallel growth in derivatives trading exacerbated the risks,[61] given the potential for manipulation where the underlying interest is trading in a different jurisdiction from the one in which the derivative interest was trading.[62]

VIII.3.3 The FSAP

The 1999 FSAP contained a commitment to the adoption of a directive designed to address market manipulation and enhance market integrity 'by reducing the possibility for institutional investors and intermediaries to rig markets'. It was also to establish 'common disciplines for trading floors in order to enhance investor confidence in an embryonic single securities market'.[63] Support for EU-wide regulation of market abuse was also provided by the 2000 Lamfalussy Report, which highlighted the absence of regulation in this area as one of the factors hindering the development of the integrated securities market.[64]

VIII.3.4 The 2003 MAD Negotiations

In May 2001 the Commission presented a proposal for a new market abuse regime.[65] In addition to proposing a new market manipulation regime, the Proposal restructured and consolidated the 1989 IDD regime within a single market abuse directive. The subsequent

---

[59] n 23, para 41.
[60] In its report on the emergence of 'alternative trading systems' FESCO (the Federation of European Securities Commissions) noted the risk of 'the ability to monitor overall trading in the market for an investment instrument being impaired, with implications for effective deterrence and policing of market abuse': FESCO, The Regulation of Alternative Trading Systems in Europe. A Paper for the EU Commission (2000) (Fesco/00–064c) 15.
[61] For an early discussion see FESCO, FESCO's Response to the Call for Evidence from the Securities Regulators under the EU's Action Plan for Financial Services (2000) (FESCO/00–0961) (2000 FESCO Market Abuse Report) 4.
[62] 2000 IOSCO Market Manipulation Report, n 34, 3.
[63] Communication from the Commission, Implementing the Framework for Financial Markets: Action Plan (COM (1999) 232) (FSAP) 18.
[64] Final Report of the Committee of Wise Men on the Regulation of European Securities Market (2001) (2001 Lamfalussy Report) 10 and 12.
[65] Proposal for a Directive on insider dealing and market manipulation (market abuse) (2001 MAD Proposal), COM (2001) 281 (including the Explanatory Memorandum) and [2001] OJ C240/265.

2003 Directive,[66] which was the first FSAP measure to emerge under the then novel Lamfalussy process, provided an early procedural success for the institutions. The Directive was adopted in January 2003, some 20 months after the publication of the Commission's Proposal, and was to be implemented by the Member States by October 2004; adoption of the 1989 IDD, by contrast, had taken over two and a half years. The relatively smooth and speedy institutional passage of the Directive (the European Parliament made a number of important refinements which were accepted by the Council)[67] reflected wider political commitment to the FSAP, the transfer of detailed issues to the administrative rule-making process,[68] and, more generally, the ramifications of the 11 September 2001 attacks which revealed market abuse as a tool of international terrorism.[69] In one important respect, however, the Directive represented an early failure for the Lamfalussy process in that the Commission failed to consult on the Proposal.[70] The Parliament's close review of the Proposal and its tabling of extensive revisions in its readings in effect substituted for widespread public consultation. The Commission at the time and since has acknowledged that this was a serious mistake.[71] The development of the 2014 MAR stands, accordingly, in stark contrast.

VIII.3.5 The Crisis Era and Reform

The 2003 MAD, initially at least, was broadly regarded as a success, although weaknesses in implementation and in supervisory consistency emerged from the outset. Extensive reports from the Committee of European Securities Regulators (CESR)[72] and the European Securities Markets Expert Group (ESME)[73] over 2007–9 suggested that while the Directive

---

[66] The main publicly available elements of the legislative history are: European Parliament first reading (T5–0113/2002 ([2003] OJ C47/417) (the First Reading ECON (Economic and Monetary Affairs Committee) Report is at A5–0069/2002)), Parliament second reading (T5–0513/2002 ([2003] OJ C300/442) (the Second Reading ECON Report is at A5–0343/2002)); ECOSOC opinion [2002] OJ C80/61; and Council Common Position at [2002] OJ C228/19.

[67] It proposed 77 revisions to the Commission's Proposal, 60 of which were fully incorporated and ten of which were partially incorporated in the Council's Common Position: Common Position, n 66, 29.

[68] Inter-Institutional Monitoring Group, Second Interim Report on the Lamfalussy Process (December 2003) 8 and Third Interim Report on the Lamfalussy Process (November 2004) 13.

[69] Coffey and Overett-Somnier, n 2, 371.

[70] The market took the opportunity to comment on the Directive during CESR's (the Committee of European Securities Regulators) first consultation on the related administrative regime, although CESR acknowledged that it could not engage with these comments within the terms of its mandate: First Level 2 Advice, Feedback Statement (2002) (CESR 02-287b) 4.

[71] The Commission acknowledged the inadequacies of the consultation process in its Explanatory Memorandum in which it argued that, in view of the need for urgent action in the market-abuse area and given that it had consulted with Member States' governments, regulators, and the financial industry, it decided to present the Proposal rather than to delay it by using more formal consultative procedures. Explanatory Memorandum to the Proposal, n 65, para 1. The weaknesses in the 2003 MAD consultation procedures were also acknowledged by the Commission in its FSAP review: Commission, FSAP Evaluation. Part I: Process and Implementation (2005) 12.

[72] In 2007, CESR published a wide-ranging report on supervisory powers under the MAD (CESR, An Evaluation of Equivalence of Supervisory Powers in the EU under the Market Abuse Directive and the Prospectus Directive. A Report to the Financial Services Committee (2007) (CESR 07-334) (2007 CESR FSC Supervisory Powers Report). This was followed in 2009 by CESR's review of Member States' exercise of options and derogations under the MAD (CESR/09-1120) (2009 CESR Options and Derogations Report).

[73] ESME, The Market Abuse EU Legal Framework and its Implementation by Member States: a First Evaluation in July 2007 (2007 ESME Report).

was not under serious strain,[74] and enjoyed significant support (save with respect to the issuer-disclosure regime—see section 7.1), practical divergences in interpretation were weakening the regime, as was poor supervision and enforcement.[75] Unlike other FSAP measures, the 2003 MAD was not subject to a review obligation. It benefited, however, from the post-FSAP commitment to Better Regulation, with the Commission committing to reviewing the implementation and functioning of the Directive by the end of 2008.[76]

Review of the 2003 MAD quickly became incorporated within the wider crisis-era reform programme. The 2011 MAR Proposal[77] followed early Commission discussions launched in the teeth of the crisis in November 2008;[78] a 2009 call for evidence;[79] and a 2010 Consultation on reform of the 2003 MAD.[80] It also reflected parallel and early crisis-era consultations related to sanctioning and on the derivatives markets. The major weaknesses identified included gaps in the regime's regulation of trading venues and of instruments (notably weaknesses in the treatment of abusive behaviour in commodity derivatives and related spot or physical markets); enforcement problems linked to limited national competent authority (NCA) powers; legal certainty risks arising from implementation divergences; and administrative burdens, particularly for the small and medium-sized (SME) sector, arising from the 2003 MAD's range of reporting and monitoring obligations. The Proposal's related proposed extension of the 2003 MAD perimeter (including with respect to derivatives and trading venues other than regulated markets), its engagement with financial market innovation (including high frequency trading), and its close focus on enforcement and sanctioning accordingly reflected these weaknesses. But these proposed reforms also reflected the wider themes of the crisis-era reform movement, which were by then clear, as did the concern in the Proposal to calibrate the proposed new regime to the SME sector. In addition, although market abuse was not strongly associated with the financial crisis in the EU, the crisis brought a sharp focus to bear on the efficiency and integrity of information dynamics in certain market segments, including the credit default swap (CDS) segment, which was reflected in the Proposal's reforms.[81] The MAR Proposal also responded to the G20's call for a strengthening of financial market integrity and related regulation and supervision, and, by proposing a new suite of rules for derivatives markets, reflected the G20's wider commitment to strengthening oversight of over-the-counter (OTC) derivatives markets.

---

[74] ESME reported that 'the market abuse legislation represents an important achievement on the road to a further integration of EU financial markets: it has led to an increased level of harmonisation across Member States and is contributing to creating a common level playing field for all the involved stakeholders': n 73, 3.

[75] 2009 CESR Options and Derogations Report, n 72.

[76] European Securities Committee (on the role of the Committee see Ch XI) Minutes, 14 February 2007.

[77] COM (2011) 651 (2011 MAR Proposal).

[78] Commission Conference on Review of the Market Abuse Directive.

[79] 2009 Commission Call for Evidence, n 39.

[80] Commission, Public Consultation on a Revision of the MAD (2010) (2010 Commission MAD Consultation).

[81] The Commission referenced significant equity market volatility, greater reliance on contracts for difference (CfDs), and the acute sensitivity of the sovereign debt market to information flows through CDS trading over the 2003 MAD Review: eg 2009 Commission Call for Evidence, n 39, 2 and 6 and 2010 Commission MAD Consultation, n 80, 2. CESR similarly highlighted the importance of applying the 2003 MAD to CfDs and CDSs: CESR, Response to the Commission MAD Call for Evidence (CESR/09-635 (2009) (2009 CESR MAD Review Response) 3.

The negotiations[82] were relatively smooth, certainly compared with the negotiations on other crisis-era measures. European Parliament and, in particular, Council discussions led to a significant finessing of the Proposal and a widening of its scope.[83] But while the main elements of the Commission's Proposal persisted in the text as adopted, sharp points of difference arose in certain areas over the Parliament and Council negotiations, and the text as adopted differs from the Proposal in some key respects. The Council negotiations, in particular, exposed Member State resistance to the Commission's proposal that a new definition be employed for the 'inside information' subject to the issuer-disclosure obligation (the Commission's proposal in this regard was not ultimately adopted); Member State disagreement with the Commission's proposal that the 'accepted market practice' defence to market manipulation be removed (it has been retained in the text as adopted); Member State concern that market efficiency not be disrupted;[84] and differences across the Member States as to the level of pecuniary sanctions and the nature of the NCA reporting obligation with respect to sanctions.[85] The Council also supported significantly greater reliance on Binding Technical Standards (BTSs) in preference to traditional administrative rules.[86] The European Parliament's position was close to the Council's in many places (including with respect to the retention of the accepted market practice defence and the 'legitimate purposes' regime which protects certain actions from the insider-dealing prohibition), but it was concerned in particular to address abuses arising from algorithmic trading and to impose tough sanctions.[87] Overall, the 2014 MAR broadly reflects the Council position.

The reforms are functionally radical, in that the 2003 MAD regime and its related administrative rules will be repealed and replaced by the new directly applicable Regulation. Some elements of the 2003 MAD administrative regime are incorporated within the legislative 2014 MAR; otherwise, the Commission is conferred with a fresh set of delegations, many of which cover the 2003 MAD administrative regime, but some of which address new areas.

The reforms are also substantively significant, across three dimensions in particular. The 2014 MAR addresses three weaknesses, which reflect crisis-era concerns but also more general concerns with the 2003 MAD: an overly narrow regulatory perimeter in light of the extent of market innovation, particularly with respect to the derivatives and trading venues covered; a lack of clarity, and related implementation and supervisory convergences failures;

---

[82] The main elements of the publicly available legislative history are: 2011 Commission MAR Proposal, n 77 and Impact Assessment, n 39; ECON Report, 22 October 2012 (A7-0347/2012) (on which the European Parliament's Negotiating Position was based); and Council General Approach, 26 June 2013 (Council Document 11383/13).

[83] The European Parliament and Council, eg, both introduced wider and more nuanced definitions of the instruments subject to the 2014 MAR, which are reflected in the final text.

[84] The Council introduced the new 'market soundings' regime which is designed to protect from the insider-dealing prohibition certain statements made in the context of fund raising (sect 6.3.3).

[85] Danish Presidency Progress Report on MAR, 21 June 2012, Council Document 11535/12 (Danish Presidency MAR Progress Report).

[86] On administrative rule-making see Ch X sects 4 and 5.

[87] The main differences between the Council, European Parliament, and Commission texts can be traced in the tabular analyses produced over the negotiations, including Differences Table, 20 March 2013. The Parliament sought, eg, the introduction of a specific prohibition on 'abusive order entry' (which was not adopted) and higher sanctions than the Council (it proposed an unlimited pecuniary sanction for natural persons and pecuniary sanctions of up to 20 per cent of turnover for legal persons; lower thresholds were finally adopted).

and weaknesses in supervisory and enforcement powers.[88] In response, the 2014 MAR has adopted a number of substantive reforms. The major perimeter reforms include an extension and clarification of the venues which come within the market abuse regime; in effect the regime applies to all types of organized trading and to OTC trading which impacts on organized venues, and so is aligned with the new 2014 MiFID II/MiFIR perimeter.[89] They also include an extension of the regime's reach over derivatives markets (particularly commodity derivatives markets, where the regime now covers cross-market abuse and thereby captures abusive behaviour relating to the underlying physical or spot market) and the inclusion of the manipulation of benchmarks as a specific form of manipulation. Greater clarity is supported by a streamlining and enhancing of key reporting requirements, including the insiders' lists and managers' transactions reporting regimes, which had been shown to suffer from a lack of legal clarity. Clarity is also supported by a calibration and finessing of the 2003 regime generally, particularly with respect to the various defences and safe harbours available, including by means of the recast 'legitimate behaviour' regime governing insider dealing and the recast 'accepted market practices' regime which provides a defence to market manipulation. The 2014 MAR also significantly reduces the options and derogations available to the Member States and accordingly seeks to establish a single rulebook in this area, including by incorporating previous administrative rules within the 2014 MAR, adopting the form of a Regulation, and providing for a significant number of delegations, to BTSs in particular. Finally, the 2014 MAR seeks to enhance supervision, investigation, and enforcement in a number of ways, including by strengthening the suspicious transaction reporting regime and the managers' transactions reporting regime, by prohibiting attempts to engage in market manipulation, by introducing a new 'whistle-blowing' regime, and by strengthening the powers of NCAs, enhancing NCA/ESMA co-operation, and introducing a new administrative sanctions regime.

VIII.4 Harmonization and ESMA

Harmonization in the market abuse field has a distinctive quality, given the acute dependence of the effectiveness of EU rules on operational supervision and enforcement. Under the 2003 MAD, the combination of a principles-based legislative text and a dense administrative rulebook[90] and an extensive set of 'softer' supervisory convergence measures adopted by CESR[91] was designed to allow NCAs an appropriate degree of flexibility in applying the regime, while at the same time providing them with detailed examples and directions in support of pan-EU operational consistency and convergence. This approach was not, however, successful in supporting pan-EU consistency in the application of the regime; CESR's 2009 report on Member States' exercise of options and derogations under the 2003 MAD found a 'remarkably heterogenous' approach to the 2003 MAD in practice across the EU.[92] The regime also suffered from a lack of clarity, particularly with respect to

---

[88] 2011 MAR Proposal, n 77, 3.
[89] n 9.
[90] Sect 1.
[91] n 99.
[92] n 72.

issuers' disclosure and reporting obligations and managers' transaction reporting requirements.[93] Signficantly more intense harmonization has accordingly followed.

At the legislative level, a radical reorganization of the regime has followed with the 2014 MAR, which has intensified the EU rulebook by extending the regime's perimeter (and calibrating the rules to discrete market segments and, in particular, their pricing dynamics, including markets for commodity derivatives and emission allowances) and removing Member State implementation discretion.

At the administrative level, new administrative rules in the form of Regulatory Technical Standards (RTSs) and Implementing Technical Standards (ITSs) will amplify a range of pivotal matters, including the stabilization and buy-back exemption, the new 'market soundings' regime which protects the disclosure of certain inside information, the accepted market practices regime which protects certain practices which might otherwise amount to market manipulation, the insiders' lists regime and the investment recommendations/ analysts regime.[94] The 2014 MAR negotiations saw administrative rules move from the standard administrative rule-making process, dominated by the Commission, to the BTS process in which ESMA plays a key role by proposing rules and across which its prerogatives are protected, although the Commission adopts the rules. But although only a small number of the administrative rules required under the 2014 MAR do not take the form of BTSs, these areas are often of major importance, notably the new managers' transactions reporting regime and the related prohibition on trading during closed periods.

The 2014 MAR will also be supported by ESMA's 'soft' supervisory convergence activities, which will remain important given the persistence of ambiguities within the 2014 MAR. ESMA is charged with developing guidance in specific areas under the 2014 MAR. Own-initiative supervisory convergence measures can also be expected from ESMA. Amplification through supervisory convergence measures, and particularly guidance, was strongly associated with the somewhat porous 2003 MAD regime from the outset, and the legacy from the CESR era is significant.[95] ESMA's initial activities (under the 2003 MAD)[96] were limited, reflecting the intense resource pressure exerted by the

---

[93] 2011 MAR Proposal Impact Assessment, n 39, 28.

[94] Prior to the 2014 MAR text being adopted, in November 2013 the European Securities and Markets Authority (ESMA) published an early Discussion Paper on its policy orientations on delegated rules under the MAR once the Council and European Parliament had reached agreement: ESMA, Discussion Paper. ESMA's Policy Orientations on Possible Implementing Measures under the Market Abuse Regulation (2013) (ESMA/ 2013/1649). While ESMA is likely to build on the precursor 2003 MAD administrative rules (where relevant) the Discussion Paper makes clear that significant refinements and nuancing can be expected, reflecting in part the extended scope of the 2014 MAR.

[95] CESR May 2005 Guidance (CESR/04-505b); CESR July 2007 Guidance (CESR/06-562b); and CESR May 2009 Guidance (CESR/09-219). CESR's Guidance addressed a range of issues, including the following: the operational template which NCAs used to decide whether particular practices were 'accepted market practices' and so exempt, the type of practices that NCAs would consider as constituting market manipulation, the 'signals' of suspected insider dealing or market manipulation transactions which might trigger the 2003 MAD's 'suspicious reporting' obligation to the relevant NCA, and a common format for reporting suspicious transactions (2005); guidance on the nature of inside information, when it was legitimate to delay inside information, when information relating to a client's pending orders constitutes inside information, and the operation of the insider lists regime (2007); and further guidance on the insider lists regime, the suspicious transactions reporting obligation, stabilization, and the nature of inside information for the purposes of issuer disclosure (2009).

[96] The 2014 MAR was not yet adopted during ESMA's early years.

crisis-era administrative rulebook and CESR's extensive earlier work on the 2003 MAD, and were largely confined to a new FAQ[97] and to ongoing assessments of operational supervisory convergence.[98] But the capacity of supervisory convergence measures to extend the reach of the EU market abuse rulebook became clear in early 2013, with the joint ESMA, EBA (European Banking Authority), and EIOPA (European Insurance and Occupational Pensions Authority) initiative on the development of guidance relating to benchmarks, pending adoption of a legislative regime (section 8.2.3). More generally, ESMA is inserted into the supervisory and enforcement process through a number of channels (including the sensitive 'accepted market practices' process), through which it can be expected to shape how the market abuse regime develops.

By contrast with most other EU securities and markets regulation measures, the Court of Justice has also played a significant role in the development of the regime, particularly with respect to its disclosure obligations, as discussed in section 7.1.

VIII.5 Setting the Perimeter: Scope

The 2014 MAR establishes a common regulatory framework on insider dealing, misuse of inside information, and market manipulation, as well as on measures to prevent market abuse to ensure the integrity of financial markets in the EU and to enhance investor protection and confidence in those markets (Article 1). The scope of the 2014 MAR is governed by two widely cast concepts: financial instruments, and the venues on which they trade. These two devices are designed to capture the market abuse risks which arise where trading is fractured across multiple trading venues and where abuse can be hidden by the manipulation of complex financial products.

VIII.5.1 Financial Instruments and Commodities

Under Article 2(1), the Regulation applies to a wide range of 'financial instruments'[99] defined by reference to MiFID II.[100] These instruments only come within the regime, however, when the venue-related scope restrictions are met (section 5.2). The extension of

---

[97] ESMA/2012/9. The FAQ, which is designed to support convergence in supervisory practices is, thus far, very limited and addresses only issuer-disclosure obligations with respect to dividend policy.

[98] Sect 9.2.3.

[99] The 2014 MAR does not apply to transactions, orders, or behaviours carried out in pursuit of monetary, exchange rate, or public debt-management policy, by a range of public institutions including Member States, the Commission, the European System of Central Banks, and relevant national agencies, or to actions by the EU, Member State special purpose vehicles, the European Stability Mechanism, the European Investment Bank, or other international financial institution established by two or more Member States which has the purpose of mobilizing funding and providing funding to members experiencing or threatened by severe financing problems (Art 6). The exemption also extends to actions by the Commission and Member States in pursuit of climate policy (given the extension of the regime to emission allowances) or actions in pursuit of the EU's Common Agricultural Policy or Common Fisheries Policy (given the potential for commodity trading to come within the MAR): Art 6. The Commission is empowered to adopt administrative rules establishing equivalent exemptions for third country public bodies and central banks.

[100] Art 3(1)(1). On the 'financial instruments' covered by the 2014 MiFID II see Ch IV sect 4.3.

the scope of MiFID I[101] 'financial instruments' by MiFID II has led to a related extension under the 2014 MAR; in particular, emission allowances now come within the scope of the market abuse regime[102] and have required a series of calibrations to be made, given the particular nature of these instruments and of the markets on which they are auctioned and trade.[103]

The 2014 MAR does not contain a definitive list of in-scope financial instruments, although the negotiations saw some discussion on whether ESMA should be empowered to propose BTSs establishing a list of in-scope instruments. In a Council amendment designed to support enforcement, the 2014 MAR provides instead for a more flexible device, which requires that market operators of regulated markets, and investment firms and market operators operating a multilateral trading facility (MTF) or organized trading facility (OTF) (see the next section), notify their NCAs of each financial instrument when it is first admitted to trading or traded, or when a request for admission has been made, and when the instrument ceases to be traded or admitted; these notifications must be transmitted by NCAs to ESMA, which must publish and update the list of related instruments (Article 4). The list does not, however, limit the scope of the 2013 MAR.[104]

The 2014 MAR prohibitions on market manipulation also apply to spot (or physical) commodity contracts[105] which are not wholesale energy products (these are covered under the 2011 REMIT Regulation), where the transaction, order, or behaviour has or is likely or intended to have an effect on the price or value of an in-scope financial instrument (see further section 6.1.2) (Article 2(2)(a)). They also apply to types of financial instruments, including derivative contracts or derivative instruments for the transfer of credit risk, where the transaction, order, bid, or behaviour has or is likely to have an effect on the price or value of a spot commodity contract where the price or value depends on the price or value of those financial instruments (Article 2(2)(b)). As discussed in section 8.2.3, the prohibitions on market manipulation also apply to behaviour in relation to benchmarks (Article 2(2)(c)).

---

[101] n 3.

[102] Arts 3(1)(19) and 2(1), bringing in scope behaviour or transactions, including bids, relating to the auctioning of emission allowances or other auctioned products covered by Commission Regulation (EU) No 1031/2010 [2010] OJ L302/1, which governs emission allowances (the EU's emission allowance regime is based on Directive 2003/87/EC [2003] OJ L275/32).

[103] The trading of emission allowances engages the EU's climate policy and the operation of the related carbon market under Commission Regulation 1031/2010. In order to avoid disruption to EU climate policy, and to reflect the particular structural features of the emission allowances trading market, the application of the 2014 MAR is calibrated to the distinct features of this market: eg obligations typically imposed on issuers of financial instruments apply to 'emission allowance market participants' (persons who enter into transactions, including the placing of orders to trade, in emission allowances—in effect, companies with large installations which fall within the regime) under the governing Regulation 1031/2010: Art 3(1)(20). Exemptions also apply (in relation to the MAR's disclosure obligations) where emission allowance market participants fall below particular emission thresholds (Art 3(1)(20) and Art 17(2)) (sect 7.1).

[104] The information required in the notification includes names and numbers of instruments, and date and time of first trade. The ESMA list is additionally to include details of the trading venues on which the instruments are traded for the first time, and the date and time when the instrument in question ceases to trade. RTSs and ITSs will govern the content, format, and other modalities of the notifications and the ESMA list: Art 4(4) and (5).

[105] A spot commodity contract is any contract for the supply of a commodity traded on a spot market which is promptly delivered when the transaction is settled, as well other contracts for the supply of a commodity (such as physically settled forward contracts) that are not financial instruments. A spot market is any commodity market in which commodities are sold for cash and promptly delivered when the transaction is settled, as well as other non-financial markets, such as forward markets for commodities (Art 3(15) and (16)).

VIII.5.2 Venues

Perimeter control under the 2014 MAR eschews the 'regulated market' model[106] on which the 2003 MAD perimeter was based; the 2003 MAD only applied to instruments admitted to trading on a regulated market. The weakness of the regulated market as the perimeter control for market abuse prohibition was apparent from the outset[107] given the range of instruments admitted to other organized venues and the capacity for abusive behaviour to involve arbitrage between different venues. The recent explosion in trading on venues outside the regulated market segment, and including exchange-regulated markets, multilateral trading facilities more generally, broker crossing systems, and specialist venues such as swap execution platforms, as well as the massive increase in OTC bilateral trading, meant that very large segments of the EU financial market operated outside the 2003 MAD, even though the 2003 MAD applied irrespective of whether or not the transaction in question actually took place on a regulated market, as long as the instrument was admitted to trading on a regulated market.[108] The crisis-era regulatory programme for trading venues, which is in part designed to repatriate trading in much of the OTC derivatives market on to formal venues (see Chapter VI section 4), has further increased the importance of trading venues generally in maintaining market integrity and the need for robust regulation of abuse.

In response, the 2014 MAR perimeter is significantly wider than the 2003 MAD perimeter. The 2014 MAR covers financial instruments admitted to trading on a regulated market (or for which a request for admission has been made),[109] but also financial instruments traded on an MTF, admitted to trading on an MTF or for which an admission request has been made, and financial instruments traded on an OTF (each as defined under the new 2014 MiFID II regime).[110] It also, in a very significant extension of the perimeter, applies to instruments traded OTC (not covered by 2014 MAR 2(1)(a)–(c)), where those instruments can have an effect on trading on an in-scope venue.[111] More generally, the Regulation also applies to any transaction, order, or behaviour concerning in-scope financial instruments, irrespective of whether the transaction, order, or behaviour takes place on a trading venue (Article 2(3)). While the capacity for regulatory arbitrage should significantly diminish, this perimeter extension amounts to a radical reorganization of the scope of the market abuse regime and will place significant pressure on the supervisory and enforcement process if it is to have appropriate deterrent effects.

---

[106] See Ch V sect 7 on the 'regulated market' trading venue.

[107] eg Enriques and Gatti, n 37, 8.

[108] The Commission reported that of the 41 or so multilateral trading facilities (MTFs) (as defined under MiFID I) trading shares in the EU in 2010, 25 admitted shares not admitted to trading on a regulated market and so fell outside the 2003 MAD. As only three Member States fully applied the 2003 MAD to these facilities, a large segment of trading fell outside the MAD: 2011 MAR Proposal Impact Assessment, n 39, 19. Similarly, CESR's 2009 Options and Derogations Report found significant differences across the Member States with respect to the extension or otherwise of the 2003 MAD to MTFs (n 72).

[109] 2014 MAR Art 2(1)(a).

[110] 2014 MAR Art 2(1)(b) and (c).

[111] Art 2(1)(d) catches financial instruments not covered by Art 2(1)(a)–(c) the price or value of which depends or has an effect on the price or value of a financial instrument covered by those provisions, including, but not limited to CDSs or CfDs. This provision in particular has the hue of crisis-era reform, reflecting as it does concerns as to the potential for abuse through bilateral trading in CDSs, which were closely implicated in the crisis: 2011 MAR Proposal, n 77, 7.

VIII.5.3 Transactions, Orders, and Behaviours

Across the Regulation, and in a refinement to the 2003 MAD, the Regulation uses the catch-all concept of 'transactions, orders to trade, or other behaviours' to capture behaviour which may otherwise fall outside the Regulation, particularly with respect to derivatives.

VIII.5.4 Jurisdictional Scope

The 2014 MAR confers wide-ranging jurisdiction on NCAs, reflecting the cross-border reach of abusive activities. Member States must designate a single NCA under the 2014 MAR responsible for ensuring that the Regulation is applied on its territory, and regarding all actions carried out on its territory as well as those actions carried out 'abroad' relating to instruments admitted to trading on a regulated market or trading on an MTF or OTF operating within its territory (Article 22).

Under Article 2(4), the 2014 MAR has significant extraterritorial reach, applying to actions and omissions carried out in the EU or outside the EU, as long as the instruments are in scope; whether or not the conduct in question affects the EU market or takes place on an EU venue will be irrelevant.[112] Indications of the extraterritorial ambition of the 2014 MAR can also be taken from the Commission's suggestion that the consolidation of the market abuse regime within a regulation would facilitate its international export as a regulatory standard.[113] The 2014 MAR's supporting supervision framework is similarly ambitious, requiring NCAs to conclude co-operation arrangements with third country authorities to ensure the enforcement of obligations which arise in third countries, and to co-ordinate with ESMA and follow an ESMA template when so doing (Article 26).

VIII.6 The Prohibition on Insider Dealing

VIII.6.1 Inside Information

VIII.6.1.1 The Core Definition: Inside Information and Financial Instruments

A reorganized and expanded definition of 'inside information', based on the 2003 MAD definition and its related administrative rules, is at the heart of the 2014 MAR prohibition of insider dealing. Notwithstanding some uncertainties as to its scope, particularly following the Court of Justice's 2009 *Spector* ruling,[114] the core 2003 MAD definition of inside information was generally regarded as working reasonably effectively,[115] which augurs well for the reorganized 2014 MAR definition. But the 2003 MAD definition also, and more

---

[112] Clifford Chance, Market Abuse: European Commission Proposes New Regime. Briefing Note. October 2011, 2. Notably, the extensive Art 6 exemption (n 99) does not extend to monetary and related activities by non-EU governmental actors.

[113] 2011 MAR Proposal Impact Assessment, n 39, 69–70.

[114] Case C-45/08 *Spector Photo Group NV and Chris Van Raemdonck v Commissie voor het Bank-, Financie-en Assurantiewezen (CBFA)* [2009] ECR 12073.

[115] 2007 ESME Report, n 73, 5 and 2009 Commission Call for Evidence, n 39, 8.

problematically, governed ongoing issuer disclosure of material events under the Directive; in this respect it was much less successful. The 2014 MAR has, however, retained the dual purpose function of 'inside information', reflecting difficult negotiations in the Council; related attempts have been made to restrict the potential prejudicial impact of the 'dual-function' definition on issuers, but difficulties remain (section 7.1). The 2003 definition has also been expanded to address pricing and trading dynamics, and thus the nature of inside information, in relation to particular market segments. Previous iterations of the definition (under the 2003 MAD and 1989 IDD), by contrast, were heavily concerned with more standard market transactions, and in particular with the types of takeover-related information which could be characterized as inside information and the treatment of investment analysts' reports. The recast definition will likely continue to be placed under pressure as opportunities for insider dealing increase, as financing techniques and market products become more complex.

Under Article 7(1)(a), inside information is information of a precise nature which has not been made public, relating, directly or indirectly, to one or more issuers of financial instruments or to one or more financial instruments and which, if it were made public, would be likely to have a significant effect on the prices of those financial instruments or on the price of related derivative financial instruments. Each of these elements raises very considerable definitional challenges[116] and are discussed later in this section 6, following discussion of the specific applications of the definition under the 2014 MAR.[117]

VIII.6.1.2 Inside Information and Commodities

The 2014 MAR makes special provision for transactions in commodity derivatives in order to reflect the particular dynamics of information production and price formation in the commodity derivatives markets, which have a different function to securities markets in that their main purpose is to support risk transfer between professional traders.[118] Their interaction with the underlying physical (spot) commodity markets is also complex. The spot markets, which vary considerably in their structure and in whether they are centralized or based on bilateral trading, can, for example, be regulated (or not) to different degrees, including with respect to the prohibition of market abuse; display different levels of transparency; and impose different reporting obligations on participants.[119] Although the 2003 MAD provided a distinct definition of inside information in relation to commodity

---

[116] For a discussion of the range of interpretations possible see IOSCO, n 13.

[117] The Commission additionally proposed a general catch-all definition of inside information not otherwise covered by the foundational Art 7(1)(a) definition and the sector-specific definitions noted, designed to catch information related to one or more issuers of financial instruments, or to one or more financial instruments, not generally available to the public but which, if it were available to a 'reasonable investor' who regularly deals on the market and in the financial instrument (or related spot commodity contract) concerned, would be regarded by that investor as relevant when deciding the terms on which transactions in the financial instruments (or related spot commodity contract) should be effected (2011 MAR Proposal, Art 6(1)(e)). This was removed during the negotiations. The definition was designed in part to limit issuers' disclosure obligations with respect to inside information.

[118] The notion of the issuer, eg, is different, while the pricing of commodity derivatives is closely related to the transactions and positions of market users, the terms and conditions of traded contracts, and the underlying commodity; eg, in developing its technical advice on inside information for commodity derivatives for the original 2003 MAD administrative regime, CESR noted that it was neither possible nor desirable to import equity-market disclosure rules into these markets: CESR, First Level 2 Advice (2002) (2002) (CESR 02-089d) 10–11.

[119] The Impact Assessment noted the sharp divergences across commodity (or spot) markets with respect to, *inter alia*, information flows and governing legal regimes: 2011 MAR Proposal Impact Assessment, n 39, 20–3.

derivatives, it was troublesome, raising difficulties with respect to legal certainty and with respect to the linkage between trading on the commodity/spot markets and on the related financial and derivative markets (which may have come within the scope of the 2003 MAD, depending on where the instrument was admitted).[120]

Trading on the underlying commodity/spot markets is not governed by the 2014 MAR, given the distinct structures of these markets and their different underlying regulatory and self-regulatory frameworks.[121] The EU is, however, gradually extending its reach over these markets through instruments such as, for example, the 2011 REMIT Regulation on energy market transparency and integrity.[122] But in the absence of distinct market abuse frameworks, the capacity for a leakage of abuse potential from spot to derivative/financial markets, and back again, is significant, particularly given limited co-operation between spot and derivative/financial market regulators.[123] The new regime is designed to reduce the risks of such leakage.

Inside information in relation to commodity derivatives is specified as information of a precise nature, which has not been made public, relating directly or indirectly to one or more of such derivatives or relating directly to the related spot commodity contract,[124] and which, if it were made public, would be likely to have a significant effect on the prices of such derivatives or related spot commodity contracts, and where this is information which is reasonably expected to be disclosed or required to be disclosed in accordance with legal or regulatory provisions at EU or national level, market rules, contracts, practices, or customs, on the relevant commodity derivatives or spot markets (Article 7(1)(b)).[125]

A distinct regime applies to emission allowances (and related auctioned products), in respect of which inside information is defined as information of a precise nature, which has not been made public, relating directly or indirectly to one or more such instruments and which, if it were made public, would be likely to have a significant effect on the prices of such instruments or related derivative financial instruments (Article 7(1)(c)).[126]

---

[120] Leading NCAs to regard the 2003 MAD legal framework as not being suited to addressing manipulative strategies that extended across physical and financial markets: 2011 MAR Proposal Impact Assessment, n 39, 116.

[121] CESR accordingly advised against applying the 2003 MAD to physical markets and in particular to the energy and gas market: 2009 CESR MAD Review Response: n 81, 4.

[122] n 11.

[123] And was highlighted by NCAs during the 2003 MAD review process: 2011 MAR Proposal Impact Assessment, n 39, 112.

[124] Defined as any contract for the supply of a commodity traded on a spot market (or commodity market in which commodities are sold for cash and promptly delivered when the transaction is settled) (Art 3(16)), which is promptly delivered when the transaction is settled (and including derivative contracts which must be settled physically): Art 3(1)(15).

[125] ESMA is charged with issuing guidelines on the indicative information which would come within this provision: Art 7(5).

[126] This definition is designed to capture the nature of inside information in this area, which typically arises in relation to companies with large installations regulated by the EU emissions trading system: Commission, European Parliament's Endorsement of the Political Agreement on the Market Abuse Regulation, 10 September 2013 (MEMO/13/774). Similarly, these companies, rather than the issuers of emission allowances, are the subjects of the issuer-disclosure obligation in relation to emission-allowance-related inside information (sect 7.1). See also n 103.

VIII.6.1.3 Inside Information and Execution Information

Insider dealing and the management of inside information raises particular risks within multiservice investment firms, particularly where mere possession of inside information triggers the prohibition: traders, investment analysts, portfolio managers, and corporate finance advisers can all become 'insiders' in possession of inside information, and so become subject to the prohibitions, by virtue of the exercise of their employment, profession or duties (section 6.2). It also generates a complex interaction between conflict-of-interest management and insider-dealing rules, particularly with respect to whether conflict-of-interest management structures, such as Chinese walls, can prevent the attribution of inside information.[127]

The 2014 MAR makes specific provision for the information produced by the trading process on the direction of trading and order flow. Article 7(1)(d) provides that inside information covers information conveyed by a client and related to the client's pending orders, which is of a precise nature, relates directly or indirectly to one or more issuers of financial instruments or to one or more financial instruments, and which, if it were made public, would be likely to have a significant effect on the prices of those financial instruments, the price of related spot commodity contracts, or the price of related derivative financial instruments. Proprietary trading on the basis of the information provided by advance knowledge of client dealing is therefore prohibited. A series of provisions, however, protect 'legitimate behaviour' and protect different functions against the attribution of knowledge within the multiservice firm (section 6.3.4).

VIII.6.1.4 Inside Information: Of a Precise Nature, Relating to One or Several Issuers of Financial Instruments

The characterization of inside information as 'precise', which is designed to ensure that mere speculation, opinion, and rumours are not treated as inside information, is a frequent one across insider-dealing regimes. It is a key concept for supporting self-assessment of sensitive information and for deciding when information should be promptly disclosed by an issuer under 2014 MAR Article 17(1). What is meant by 'precise', however—and, in particular, the point at when rumour hardens into concrete information—can evade clarification.

Article 7(2), which is drawn from the 2003 Commission Definitions and Disclosure Directive, and which provides a rather unwieldy but reasonably pragmatic formula which incorporates a price impact assessment, governs the nature of 'precise'. Information is of a precise nature if (i) it indicates a set of circumstances which exists (or may reasonably be

---

[127] See, eg, the controversial action taken by ASIC (the Australian regulator) against Citigroup concerning alleged breaches of fiduciary duties in relation to a proposed takeover by its client, proprietary trading in the target's shares, failure to manage conflict of interests, and insider dealing. In a closely followed ruling, the Australian Federal Court, on appeal, confirmed in July 2007 that fiduciary relationships can be contractually excluded and that effective Chinese walls can prevent the attribution of insider knowledge. The control and transmission of insider dealing and the transmission of inside information within multiservice firms and its interaction with conflict-of-interest management, duties owed to clients, and attribution of inside information is a complex area outside the scope of this discussion. See generally Henderson, A, 'Misuse of Information, Chinese Walls, and Changes to the FSA's Code of Market Conduct' (2005) 20 *JIBLR* 1 and Rider, B, 'Conflicts of Interest: An English Problem' in Ferrarini, G and Wymeersch, E (eds), *European Securities Markets. The Investment Services Directive and Beyond* (1998) 149.

expected to come into existence) or an event which has occurred (or may reasonably be expected to do so); and (ii) the information is specific enough to enable a conclusion to be drawn as to the 'possible' effect of that set of circumstances or event on the prices of financial instruments (or the related spot commodity contracts, or auctioned products based on emission allowances). In an attempt to clarify the scope of the related obligation on issuers to disclose 'inside information'—particularly where sensitive negotiations, for example, are ongoing—the 2014 MAR, in a Council amendment, specifies that in the case of a protracted process intended to bring about, or that results in, a particular circumstance or a particular event, not only may that future circumstance or future event be regarded as precise information, but also the intermediate steps of that process which are connected with bringing about or resulting in that future circumstance or event; it also specifies that an intermediate step in a protracted process can be inside information if, by itself, it satisfies the criteria of inside information (Article 7(2) and (3)). This finessing of the definition reflects the Court of Justice's *Daimler* ruling, which took a wide approach to when the related issuer-disclosure obligation activates with respect to 'inside information' arising from a process;[128] difficulties remain in relation to the interaction between the 'inside information' definition and the related issuer-disclosure obligation, as discussed in section 7.1.

The elastic concept of 'relating directly or indirectly' to financial instruments or issuers has not been amplified under the 2014 MAR (and was not in the earlier generation of 2003 MAD administrative rules), although this distinction is of considerable significance, given that only inside information relating directly to the issuer is subject to the Article 17 prompt disclosure requirement.[129]

VIII.6.1.5 Inside Information: Information which Has Not Been Made Public

The 2014 MAR does not specify the extent to which information must be disseminated before it shakes off the taint of 'inside information'. A wide articulation of 'not been made public' would ensure the maximum availability of information and respond to the market egalitarianism rationale for prohibiting insider dealing. Market egalitarianism could also suggest, however, that investors trade on an equal basis, in that the price-formation process on which they are relying efficiently reflects the available information. Sectoral disclosure to an influential group of institutional investors with power to move the market price might therefore suffice. Setting the boundaries to 'not been made public' also requires consideration not only of the disclosure process but also of how quickly information is disclosed and of the related efficiency of information transmission.[130] But Article 7 does not specify

---

[128] See sect 7.1. The recitals to the 2014 MAR additionally suggest that inside information which may form part of a protracted process can relate to, eg, the state of contract negotiations, provisional agreed terms, the possibility of a placement of financial instruments, the conditions under which a financial instrument will be marketed, and the consideration of the inclusion of a financial instrument in a major index (or its deletion): rec 17. The new specification of 'precise' is not, however, intended to prohibit discussions of a general nature regarding the business and market developments between shareholders and management, which the 2014 MAR recognizes as essential for the efficient functioning of markets: rec 19. Whether or not the new regime will hinder or support firms remains to be seen.

[129] CESR's July 2007 Guidance (n 95) suggested that inside information related to the issuer included general market information such as government-driven information including interest rate, regulatory, and taxation information, and upcoming and market-produced information, including ratings and changes to indices.

[130] The dynamics of information disclosure and its impact on price are the subject of a rich scholarship which considers the implications of the efficient-market hypothesis and, more recently, the impact of the

whether a particular span of time must elapse before the information ceases to be inside information. If equality of access is the concern, it seems arguable that insiders must, once the information is disclosed or published, wait until it can be said that the information can be accessed by all investors and that they have had a reasonable opportunity to react to it.

VIII.6.1.6 Inside Information: Likely to have a Significant Effect on Prices

The 2014 MAR relies on the extent to which the information might impact on price movements as an indicator of the information's materiality.[131] But price impact indicators for insider dealing generate difficult assessments as to the degree of probability with which a price impact could have been expected.

Article 7(4), which is based on the 2003 Commission Definitions and Disclosure Directive, adopts a micro 'reasonable investor' model,[132] rather than a macro market impact model.[133] It characterizes price-sensitive information as information which a 'reasonable investor'[134] would be likely to use as part of the basis of his investment decision.[135] Although this model is considerably more flexible than a blunt model based on fixed price thresholds (which was earlier rejected by CESR),[136] it demands considerable convergence in supervisory practices if a consistent approach is to emerge. Recital 14 to the 2014 MAR, however, emphasizes that any assessment of whether a reasonable investor would take particular information into account must be made on the basis of the information available *ex ante*.[137] It also asserts that the assessment as to the investor's decision must take into account the anticipated impact of the information, in light of the totality of the related issuer's activities, the reliability of the source of the information, and 'any other market variables likely to affect' the related

---

findings of behavioural finance for rational decision-making and price formation. For an extensive review of the issues see the collection of articles in the 2003 special issue of the *Journal of Corporation Law* (29 *J Corp L*, issue 4 Summer 2003) marking the 21st anniversary of Gilson and Kraakmann's seminal analysis (cited in 24) and, for a crisis-era perspective, see Gilson, R and Kraakman, R, Market Efficiency After the Financial Crisis: It's Still a Matter of Information Costs (2014), ECGI Law WP No 242/2014, available at <http://ssrn.com/abstract=2396608>.

[131] Some limited guidance earlier came from the Court of Justice. In the *Georgakis* case, which addressed the closely related 1989 IDD definition of inside information, it found that a prior decision to engage in trading to support a share price was likely to have a significant impact on the shares and was capable even of leading to a stock market collapse, leading to the decision amounting to inside information: n 23.

[132] It reflects the US approach which is based on whether a reasonable investor would consider the omitted fact important in taking an investment decision: Ferrarini, n 2, 721, discussing *Basic v Levinson* 485 US 224.

[133] This approach attracted some controversy given the well-known decision-making failures associated with retail investors who might be regarded as 'reasonable investors' (Coffey and Overett-Somnier, n 2, 373), with the Commission agreeing to this approach only later during European Securities Committee discussions on the Directive (Minutes, 10 July 2003). CESR initially called for views on whether a professional or reasonable investor model was appropriate, and adopted the reasonable investor as a balanced solution given the very high standard which would apply were a professional-investor approach adopted, although there was strong market support for an approach based on the overall market effect: CESR First Level 2 Advice, Feedback Statement, n 70, 7–8.

[134] Although this central concept is not defined, CESR's earlier technical advice on the related 2003 Commission Directive suggests an approach based, to some degree, on retail-investor competence.

[135] This model is used in a range of jurisdictions worldwide: IOSCO, n 13, 4. The rule is calibrated to emission allowances to reflect MAR's use elsewhere of a threshold-based exemption for emission allowances which reflects the particular dynamics of this market.

[136] CESR July 2007 Guidance, n 95, 6.

[137] *Ex-post* information may be used to check the presumption that the *ex-ante* information was price sensitive, but should not be used to take action against persons who drew reasonable conclusions from *ex-ante* information available to them: rec 15.

financial instrument, spot commodity contract, or emission allowance-related product. This recital reflects the Court of Justice's interpretation of the precursor 2003 Commission Definitions and Disclosure Directive amplification of 'price sensitive' in the *Spector* ruling, in which the Court ruled that the capacity of the information to have a significant effect on price must be assessed in light of the content of the information at issue and the context in which it occurred, and that it was not necessary, accordingly, to assess whether the disclosure actually had a significant effect on the price of the instrument in question.[138]

VIII.6.2 Persons Subject to the Prohibition

The 2014 MAR imposes dealing, recommending/inducing, and disclosure prohibitions on persons in possession of inside information (Articles 8, 10, and 14) (section 6.3). While a market-based approach to insider dealing implies that further differentiation is not required once the person in question is in possession of inside information,[139] the 2014 MAR, based on the 2003 MAD, imposes the prohibitions on five categories of persons.

Under 8(4), the prohibitions apply to any legal[140] or natural person who possesses inside information as a result of being a member of the administrative, management, or super-visory bodies of the issuer (or emission allowance market participant), having a holding in the capital of the issuer, having access to such information through the exercise of an employment, profession, or duties, or being involved in criminal activities.

While the scheme is well settled and largely based on the 2003 MAD regime,[141] some opacities persist. Article 8(4) does not, for example, specify how large the relevant holding must be before the prohibition attaches. The holding must be such, however, that 'as a result' of that holding the person in question possesses inside information. It is unlikely that small shareholders who do not enjoy a close relationship with the company will be affected by this provision. Rather, it has in its sights large institutional shareholders who, either due to their influential relationship with the company arising from their voting power (which may in certain cases entitle them to board positions bringing them within the first category) or, for example, in the course of company briefings to institutional shareholders, acquire inside information. Difficulties also persist with respect to persons who hold inside information 'through the exercise of an employment, profession or duties'. The 2014 MAR is silent on whether, or the degree to which, a connection back to the company or the securities in question is required. It appears (given the 2014 MAR's market orientation and the wide definition of inside information as including market-related as well as issuer-related information) that those persons unconnected with the company but in possession of inside information, who acquire such information due to a direct link between the inside

---

[138] n 114, ruling of the Court, paras 67–69.
[139] The point has been made that, articulated to its logical conclusion, the market approach to defining the insider would mean that 'there would be no need to distinguish different categories of insider; anyone possessing inside information would be the target of the regulation. The classic distinction between "primary" and "secondary" insiders would thus be otiose': Black, n 17, 11.
[140] In conformity with national law, where the person in question is a legal person, the insider-dealing prohibitions also apply to the natural persons who participate in the decision to carry out the acquisition or disposal or cancellation or amendment of an order for the account of the legal person: Art 8(5).
[141] The 2003 MAD was based on the information being 'by virtue of' rather than 'as a result of'.

information and the nature of their occupation, are covered. These persons may include a stock exchange employee aware of changes to the composition of an index, an investment analyst who has received price-sensitive information from a company's investor-relations department, a civil servant in possession of market-sensitive company taxation law-reform information, a central bank official aware of market-sensitive interest rate changes, or an employee of a rating agency aware of a forthcoming change in a company's bond rating. The picture becomes blurred where the inside information is not related to the employment or profession in question and is acquired by chance, albeit in the course of that occupation.[142] This view, which does not require a connection of any kind between the employment/profession and either the issuer, its securities, or the nature of the information, had its supporters with respect to the 1989 IDD regime.[143] The market orientation of the 2014 MAR and its focus on the protection of confidence[144] suggests that a broad reading of this provision, which would downplay the source of the information and the connection or lack thereof with the company and focus more sharply on the mere possession of inside information, would be appropriate. The lack of a knowledge requirement for these classes of person also suggests such a reading. The Court of Justice remains the final arbiter on this question; a wide approach might be tentatively predicted following the *Grøngaard* ruling on the 1989 IDD.[145]

Under Article 8(4), the insider-dealing prohibitions also apply in relation to any inside information obtained by a legal or natural person in circumstances other than the situations which otherwise place persons within the scope of the prohibition, and which the person 'knows or ought to know that it is inside information'. This extension of the chain of liability sits well with the 2014 MAR's market orientation (and is based on the 2003 MAD).

VIII.6.3 The Prohibition: Dealing, Recommending, and Disclosing

VIII.6.3.1 Dealing

Save for persons outside the nominated categories, who must know or ought to know that the information which they have obtained is inside information before they can become liable, a strict liability regime applies to dealing by persons in possession of inside information. Under Article 14(a) a person (as defined in Article 8(4)) must not engage or attempt to engage in 'insider dealing', which, under Article 8(1), arises where a person possesses inside information and uses that information by acquiring or disposing of,[146] for

---

[142] Classic examples include the taxi driver or waitress who overhears, or the employee of a financial printer who reads, inside information which he or she would not have had access to if he or she did not perform those particular roles.

[143] See the discussion in Tridimas (who ultimately supports the need for some degree of connection), n 49, 926 and Davies, n 17, 102.

[144] eg Art 1 and rec 2.

[145] The Court argued that the objectives of the 1989 IDD with respect to ensuring the proper functioning of securities markets and protecting investor confidence called for a strict interpretation of the exemption: n 23, Ruling of the Court, para 34.

[146] Art 8(1) also specifies that the use of inside information to cancel or amend an order concerning a financial instrument to which the information relates, where the order was placed before the person concerned possessed the information, is also inside information. As across much of the 2014 MAR, a calibration addresses

his own account or for the account of a third party, either directly or indirectly, financial instruments to which the information relates.[147]

VIII.6.3.2 Recommending and Inducing

The core dealing prohibition is supplemented by Article 14(b), which extends the prohibition to recommending that another person engages in insider dealing or inducing another person to engage in insider dealing, activities which are driven by inside information.[148] Where a person uses the recommendation or inducement, this amounts to insider dealing where the person 'using the recommendation or inducement' knows or ought to know that it is based on inside information (Article 8(3)).

VIII.6.3.3 Improper Disclosure and 'Market Soundings'

The final element of the prohibition relates to disclosure. Under Article 14(c), persons within the scope of Article 8(4) must not 'unlawfully disclose' inside information; unlawful disclosure arises where a person who possesses inside information discloses that information to any other person, except where the disclosure is made in the normal exercise of an employment, a profession, or duties (Article 10(1)). The onward disclosure or recommendations or inducements also amounts to unlawful disclosure when the person disclosing knows or ought to have known that it was based on inside information (Article 10(2)).

The Court of Justice took a strict approach to the scope of the 1989 IDD's parallel exemption, which is almost identical, in *Grøngaard*.[149] The 2005 ruling concerned disclosure by a company board member (who was appointed to represent employee interests) of inside information concerning the company's (a major Danish financial institution quoted on the Danish stock exchange) upcoming merger to the general secretary of a Danish trade union for financial sector employees. The board member had also been appointed by the trade union to the company's 'liaison committee', on which he represented the trade union, and was secretary to one of the union's local sections. The general secretary passed the information on to employees of the trade union, one of whom dealt on the basis of the information and was successfully prosecuted. The Court noted that the exemption was to be interpreted strictly as an exception to the general prohibition on disclosure and in light of the objectives pursued by the 1989 IDD. As a result, a 'close link' was required between the disclosure and the exercise of the employment, profession or duties. Further, the Directive's objectives of ensuring the proper functioning of the secondary market in transferable securities and protecting investor confidence (particularly as to the equal footing of investors) required that the disclosure be strictly necessary and comply with the principle of proportionality. The Court also found that in determining whether disclosure was justified, account should be taken of the sensitivity of the information (and that merger information was particularly sensitive) and that each additional disclosure was liable to

---

the emission allowances market, in that the use of inside information also comprises submitting, modifying, or withdrawing a bid by a person for its own account, or for the account of a third party.

[147] Attempting to engage in insider dealing is not expressly defined but should track Art 8(1).

[148] Recommending or inducing is clarified by Art 8(2) as the recommendation or inducement of another person, in possession of inside information and on the basis of that inside information, that another person acquire or dispose of financial instruments to which that information related, or induces that person to make such an acquisition or disposal (or so recommends or induces a cancellation or amendment of an order).

[149] n 23.

increase the risk of the information being exploited in breach of the 1989 IDD. With respect to the disclosure by the board member (and the secretary general), the Court found that whether the disclosure was within the normal exercise of their duties depended, to a large extent, on the rules governing those duties in the national legal system. But it also found that the disclosure had to meet the conditions established by the Court. Accordingly, a close link was required between the disclosure and the exercise of the employment, profession, or duties; the disclosure must be strictly necessary for their exercise; and, in interpreting the relevant national rules, national courts were required to consider that the exception was to be interpreted strictly, to consider that each additional disclosure was liable to increase the risk of breach of the Directive, and to consider the sensitivity of the inside information.[150]

The strictness of the unlawful disclosure obligation has been mitigated somewhat by the 2014 MAR's introduction of a novel 'market soundings' regime, which protects the communication by firms and other actors of certain information (in effect, inside information) and is designed to support fund-raising (Article 11): where a disclosure of inside information is 'made in the course of a market sounding', and as long as the relevant conditions are complied with, the disclosure is deemed to have been made in the normal course of the exercise of a person's employment, profession, or duty (Article 11(4)). The regime covers the communication of information, prior to the announcement of a transaction, to one or more potential investors, by an issuer,[151] a secondary offeror of a financial instruments,[152] an emission allowances market participant, or a third party acting on behalf of these persons, in order to gauge the interest of potential investors in a possible transaction and the related conditions (including size and pricing) (Article 11(1)). 'Market soundings' also cover the disclosure of inside information by a person intending to make a takeover bid for the securities of a company (or engage in a merger), as long as the information is necessary to enable the parties entitled to the securities to form an opinion on their willingness to offer their securities and the willingness of the parties entitled to the securities is reasonably required for the decision to make the takeover bid or merger (Article 11(2)). The 'disclosing market participant'[153] must consider, prior to conducting the sounding (and for each disclosure made in the course of a sounding), whether it will involve the disclosure of inside information and make a written record of the conclusion drawn and its reasons; the records must be made available to NCA on request (Article 11(3)). A number of conditions apply prior to the making of the disclosure, including that the consent of the person receiving the sounding to receiving inside information is obtained and that person is informed of the prohibitions and requirements which follow under the 2014 MAR for those in possession of inside information[154]

---

[150] n 23, Ruling of the Court, para 48.

[151] Defined widely as a legal entity governed by private or public law, which issues or proposes to issue financial instruments (in the case of depositary instruments, the issuer is the issuer of the financial instruments represented): Art 3(1)(21).

[152] The offer must be of such quantity or value that it is distinct from ordinary trading and involves a selling method based on the prior assessment of potential interest from potential investors.

[153] The natural or legal person who discloses information in the course of a market sounding, and is covered by Art 11(1) or (2): Art 3(1)(32).

[154] The 'receiving person' must also be told when the information is no longer inside information: Art 11(6).

(Article 11(5)).[155] The persons receiving the information remain responsible for determining whether they are in possession of inside information or when they cease to be in possession of inside information (Article 11(7)). ESMA will be a key influence on the shape of this new regime, being charged with proposing RTSs and ITSs on the modalities of the record-keeping obligations and with developing guidelines for those receiving market soundings, including the related steps such persons should take if inside information has been disclosed (Article 11(9)–(11)).

VIII.6.3.4 Legitimate Behaviour

Reflecting the attempt under the new 'market soundings' regime to protect legitimate market behaviour and to support market efficiency, a second new feature of the insider-dealing regime under the 2014 MAR is the 'legitimate behaviour' safe harbour regime, the introduction of which was largely driven by the Council.[156] The new regime is designed in part to engage with the difficulties associated with the precursor 2003 MAD regime with respect to the intention element of the insider-dealing prohibition,[157] and particularly with respect to whether a person 'used' inside information to make an acquisition or disposal.

Proof of intention is not expressly required under Article 14(a)/Article 8(1), which adopt an effects-based approach, although a causality qualification seems to apply in that the insider must 'use' the information when dealing. Prior to the Court of Justice's important ruling in *Spector* on the nature of the intention element under the 2003 MAD regime, Member States tended to adopt either a restrictive approach (under which simple possession of inside information triggered the prohibition) or a more intention-based approach (under which the decision to deal was influenced by the inside information).[158] In the *Spector* ruling, the Court of Justice adopted a restrictive, possession-based approach,[159] although it ruled that the presumption as to prohibited conduct could be rebutted. The ruling related to share purchases, under a share option programme, by Spector and its chief executive, subsequent to which the share price rose. The Belgian authorities imposed fines on Spector and its chief executive for breach of the insider-dealing prohibition.[160] In assessing the nature of the

---

[155] The disclosing market participant must also make a record of all information given to the person receiving the market sounding and the identity of the potential investors to whom the information has been disclosed.

[156] Member States were concerned to ensure defences were organized within a specific MAR provision, although there was concern to ensure that the new regime did not reverse the burden of proof: Danish Presidency MAR Progress Report, n 85, 3.

[157] Although the Commission had also earlier raised concerns in this regard, and with respect to the different approaches Member States had taken to whether the prohibition applied simply on possession, or required that the inside information exerted an influence on the decision: 2009 Commission Call for Evidence, n 39, 11.

[158] The UK being an example of the latter (adopting a 'material influence' model), and Belgium of the former. See, eg, Financial Markets Law Committee, Issue 154, Market Abuse Directive (2010) and Klöhn, L, 'The European Insider Trading Regulation after the ECJ's Spector Photo Group decision' (2010) 7 *ECFLR* 347. On the UK approach see, eg, Band, C and Hopper, M, 'Market Abuse: A Developing Jurisprudence' (2007) 20 *JIBLR* 23 and, on the nature of the influence exerted by insider information, Financial Services and Markets Tribunal, *Arif Mohamed and FSA* (29 March 2005) paras 68–72.

[159] For an extensive analysis of the use/possession distinction in the context of the *Spector* ruling see Langenbucher, K, 'The 'Use or Possession' Debate Revisited—Spector Photo Group and Insider Trading in Europe' (2010) 5 *CMLJ* 452.

[160] In particular as the last in the series of share repurchases was quickly followed by a positive results announcement, and the announcement of a possible takeover, which led to a share price rise.

mental element required for insider dealing, and whether simple possession of inside information triggered the prohibition in terms of the information being 'used',[161] the Court found the prohibition did not require that dealing take place with full knowledge of the facts, set out subjective conditions in relation to intention, or require that the inside information be decisive in relation to the dealing decision, noting the legislative history of the provision.[162] The absence of an intention element reflected the construction of the prohibition, which presumed a mental element once the constituent elements of the prohibition were in place;[163] the absence also reflected a concern to strengthen the effectiveness of administrative sanctions (the enforcement mechanism deployed under the 2003 MAD).[164] The Court also found, however, that, in order not to extend the prohibition beyond what was appropriate and necessary to attain the 2003 MAD's goals, the prohibition was not to be interpreted as applying automatically to persons in possession of inside information, and that the presumption of breach of the prohibition could be rebutted.[165] The Court also noted the range of legitimate market transactions which could be prohibited by its approach, and sought to protect these by reference to the purpose of the 2003 MAD which, it argued, was to ensure equality between contracting parties, prevent those in possession of inside information from obtaining an advantageous position or unfair advantage, and avoid the undermining of the principle that all investors must be placed on an equal footing.[166] The insider-dealing prohibition accordingly applied where the person in possession of the information took an unfair advantage; accordingly, 'certain situations' could require a 'thorough examination of the factual circumstances, enabling it to be ensured that the use of the inside information is actually unfair'.[167]

The Court's restrictive approach,[168] which is somewhat cavalier with respect to the due process concerns arising from using a possession-based approach to support enforcement,[169] generated significant concern with respect to the operation of the rebuttal.[170]

---

[161] The action was taken against persons within the identified persons class, and so the knowledge requirement which would otherwise be required relating to the possession of inside information did not apply.

[162] Ruling of the Court, n 114, paras 31–32. The 2003 MAD provision was more restrictive than the precursor IDD prohibition which included a 'with full knowledge of the facts' qualifier. Similarly, the 2003 MAD replaced 'taking advantage' of inside information with 'using' information, to remove the notion of intention from the dealing prohibition, leading the Court to rule that the prohibition defined insider dealing objectively, without reference to intention, and in order to support harmonization: at para 34.

[163] The Court noted that the status of the person in possession of the information assumed, under the legislative scheme, a responsibility in relation to the information, that the nature of a dealing transaction makes it possible to exclude the possibility that the person could have acted without being aware of his actions, and that, where the person is in possession of the inside information, it could, in principle, be inferred that the information played a role in the decision-making: at para 36.

[164] The Court suggested that the effectiveness of the 2003 MAD's enforcement regime could be weakened by a requirement for systematic analysis of the existence of a mental element, and that the prohibition was accordingly based 'on a simple structure': para 38.

[165] Paras 44 and 55.

[166] Paras 46–53.

[167] Para 55.

[168] By contrast, the Advocate General suggested a general exception where the information did not influence the action of the person. See Hansen Lau, J, What Constitutes Insider Dealing? The Advocate General's Opinion in Case C-45/08 Spector Photo Group (2009), available at <http://ssrn.com/abstract=1499093>.

[169] eg Langenbucher n 159.

[170] eg Financial Market Law Committee, n 158, calling for the 2003 MAD reform to provide a clear set of exemptions from the dealing prohibition, and highlighting the particular difficulties generated by share buy-back programmes which may become interrupted, and the market disrupted, when the issuers become aware

The 2014 MAR, however, retains the 2003 MAD language, but clarifies which actions fall outside the regime by means of the new Article 9 'legitimate behaviour' regime.[171] Many of the protected situations had, however, previously been acknowledged through specific legislative provisions or through recital references, and as such the 'legitimate behaviour' regime does not represent a major change to the approach previously taken to insider dealing, although it does bring some degree of legal certainty.

The risks posed to multiservice firms are addressed under Article 9(1), which provides that a legal person in possession of inside information will not, in itself, be deemed to have 'used' that information or consequently to have engaged in inside dealing on the basis of an acquisition of disposal, where the legal person has established, implemented, and maintained adequate and effective internal arrangements and procedures that effectively ensure that neither the natural person who dealt in the instruments to which the inside information relates, nor any other natural person who may have had any influence on that decision, was in possession of the inside information; and the legal person did not encourage, recommend to, induce, or otherwise influence the natural person. In effect, Article 9(1) protects dealing where an effective Chinese wall prevents the flow of inside information. Under Article 9(2), a market-maker[172] in a financial instrument to which inside information relates, and in possession of the inside information, is not, in itself, deemed to have 'used' that information or consequently to have engaged in inside dealing, on the basis of an acquisition or disposal, where the acquisition or disposal to which the information relates is made legitimately in the normal course of exercise of its function as a market-maker or a counterparty for the financial instrument; a person authorized to execute orders on behalf of third parties is similarly protected where the acquisition or disposal is made to carry out such an order legitimately in the normal course of the exercise of the person's employment, profession or duties. Under Article 9(3), the person in possession of inside information is not, in itself, deemed to have 'used' that information (or consequently to have engaged in insider dealing) where the person engages in an acquisition or disposal of financial instruments where the transaction is carried out in discharge of an obligation that has become due in good faith and not to circumvent the prohibition on insider dealing, and the obligation results from an order placed or agreement concluded before, or to satisfy a legal or regulatory obligation that arose before, the person concerned possessed inside information. Takeovers are specifically addressed: insider dealing is deemed not to arise in itself where a person possessing inside information obtained in the conduct of a public takeover or merger uses that information solely for the purpose of proceeding with that takeover or merger, provided that, at the point of approval of the merger or acceptance of the offer by the relevant shareholders, any inside information has made public or ceased to be inside information (Article 9(4)). 'Stakebuilding'[173] using inside information is, however,

---

of inside information, as well as the difficulties posed by the attribution of the possession of inside information in multiservice firms. Similarly, Klöhn, n 158, noting the range of practical difficulties for market participants.

[171] The new regime was added by the Council, reflecting its concern to provide certainty to the market but also to avoid significantly re-casting the core insider dealing definition, given the difficulties of achieving consensus across the Member States on any such re-cast. The 2011 MAR Proposal, by contrast, had limited the exemptions available, but adopted a more nuanced approach to the definition of inside information, adopting a specific definition for the purposes of the disclosure obligation (n 77).

[172] 'Market-maker' is defined by reference to the 2014 MiFID II (2014 MAR Art 3(1)(30)). See Ch VI sect 2.4.

[173] Defined as the acquisition of securities in a company which does not trigger a legal or regulatory obligation to make an announcement of a takeover bid (Art 3(1)(31)).

expressly excluded from this protection and is not deemed to constitute legitimate behaviour in accordance with Article 9. Finally, the mere fact that a person uses their own knowledge that they have decided to acquire or dispose of financial instruments does not constitute in itself the 'use' of inside information (Article 9(5)). A breach of the Article 9 prohibition can still be deemed to have occurred if the NCA establishes that there was an illegitimate reason behind the orders to trade, transactions, or behaviours concerned (Article 9(6)).

VIII.7 Disclosure Obligations

VIII.7.1 Issuer Disclosure

VIII.7.1.1 Article 17(1) and Ongoing Issuer Disclosure

Among the most significant of the 2003 MAD's innovations was its introduction of an ongoing disclosure obligation for issuers admitted to regulated markets, cast in terms of the disclosure by the issuer 'as soon as possible' of 'inside information' which directly concerned the issuer. This obligation supported the prohibition on inside information by limiting the opportunities for insider dealing, but more importantly it completed the issuer-disclosure matrix by requiring ongoing disclosure to the market of, in effect, material information.[174]

Issuer-disclosure obligations can be related to the prevention of market abuse in that they limit opportunities for abuse. But the location of this ongoing, materiality-driven issuer-disclosure obligation within a measure designed to prohibit market abuse was, in principle, problematic, given the different functions of issuer disclosure (support of market efficiency and of related pricing mechanisms through optimal information disclosure) and of market abuse prohibitions (support of market efficiency through the prohibition of certain abusive behaviours by persons).[175] The 2003 MAD's inside information definition soon emerged as ill-equipped to set the perimeter of the obligation on issuers to make disclosure of material information.[176]

The difficulties with the 2003 MAD issuer-disclosure obligation arose from its linkage to the 2003 MAD definition of 'inside information' and the 'dual function', accordingly, of

---

[174] The 2003 MAD obligation has been described as the missing part of the issuer-disclosure puzzle: Ferran, n 42, 197. Although the 1989 IDD imposed an ongoing disclosure obligation with respect to material, *ad hoc* disclosure (Art 7), Member States varied considerably with respect to their treatment of *ad hoc* material disclosure in terms of how materiality was determined and how the information was disseminated: Lannoo, K, 'The Emerging Framework for Disclosure in the EU' (2003) *JCLS* 329, 355–6.

[175] See Hansen, J, The Hammer and the Saw: A Short Critique of the Recent Compromise Proposal for a Market Abuse Regulation (2012), available at <http://ssrn.com/abstract=2193871>. Hansen notes that while insider-dealing prohibitions and issuer-disclosure obligations both serve market efficiency, they do so in different ways, and highlights the potential damage to market efficiency where an overly wide disclosure obligation leads to an issuer not being able to protect sensitive disclosures (particularly information the disclosure of which may prejudice its competitive position) and where torrents of potentially unreliable disclosures feed market volatility.

[176] eg Hansen Lau, J and Moalem, D, 'The MAD Disclosure Regime and the Twofold Notion of Inside Information: the Available Solution' (2009) 4 *CMLJ l* 323 and di Noia, C and Gargantini, M, 'Issuers at Midstream: Disclosure of Multistage Events in the Current and in the Proposed EU Market Abuse Regime' (2012) *ECFR* 484.

the inside information definition in establishing the scope of the prohibition on insider dealing, and in determining when ongoing disclosures were required of issuers with respect to sensitive/material information. Although this linkage suggested regulatory coherence in the treatment of insider dealing given the preventative role of issuer disclosure with respect to market abuse,[177] it generated significant difficulties. These related in part to the specific strains experienced by financial institutions over the crisis, particularly with respect to when disclosures related to financial support, and at risk of generating instability, could be delayed.[178] The 2003 MAD delay regime allowed an issuer to delay disclosure of inside information, but only where delay would not be likely to mislead the public. Given that the definition of inside information was (and is now) cast in terms of whether a reasonable investor would take it into account, the circumstances in which delay was legitimate were accordingly very limited. More generally, difficulties also emerged with respect to when information was sufficiently 'precise' (and so 'inside information') as to trigger the issuer-disclosure obligation, particularly with respect to ongoing negotiations. The extensive definition of inside information, and, in particular, the alignment of 'precise' with indicating a set of circumstances which 'exist or may reasonably be expected to come into existence',[179] placed issuers at risk of being required to disclose and continually correct fast-changing information, with consequent implications for market volatility,[180] particularly given the restrictions on the delay mechanism.

Additionally, the 2003 MAD did not contain an express jurisdiction allocation clause for the disclosure obligation. In principle, the home Member State is the anchor for issuer disclosure (see Chapter II). But Article 10 of the 2003 MAD required a Member State to apply its requirements to actions carried out in its territory, or elsewhere, concerning financial instruments admitted to a regulated market on its territory or to actions carried out in its territory concerning financial instruments admitted to trading on a regulated market in another Member State; this approach reflects the territorial orientation of the 2003 MAD, which (like the 2014 MAR) was not a passporting measure, and did not adopt a home Member State model.[181] But this regime raised the possibility of multiple rules applying to issuers with respect to, for example, how disclosures were disseminated and, in particular, of the application of different liability and enforcement regimes, thereby generating significant risk for issuers.[182]

The 2003 MAD administrative regime provided some comfort for issuers by suggesting a distinct approach to the treatment of 'inside information' for the purposes of the issuer-disclosure obligation. The 2003 Commission Definitions and Disclosure Directive clarified that the 2003 MAD Article 6(1) issuer-disclosure obligation was met where 'upon the coming into existence of a set of circumstances, or the occurrence of an event, albeit not yet

---

[177] Karmel, R, 'Reform of Public Company Disclosure in Europe' (2005) 26 *UPaJIEL* 379, 400.

[178] 2007 ESME Report, n 73, 5–6 and n 203.

[179] 2003 Commission Definitions and Disclosure Directive Art 1(1).

[180] Hansen and Moalem, n 176, 325, noting the potential for a flood of disclosures and for disruption to markets. Similarly, Hansen, n 175, highlighting the risks in terms of the promotion of short-term speculation.

[181] Ferran, n 42, 199.

[182] Concerns were raised in the UK by the Financial Markets Law Committee (Financial Markets Law Committee, Paper 119, Conflicts Between FSAP Directives (December 2005)) paras 4–12 and the London Stock Exchange (Letter from the London Stock Exchange to David Wright, Commission (14 October 2005), annexed to the Financial Markets Law Committee Report).

formalized' the issuer promptly informed the public.[183] Accordingly, although the scope of the information subject in principle to the disclosure obligation remained very wide, the timing of the disclosure was linked to crystallized information.[184]

Nonetheless, the breadth of the issuer-disclosure obligation and confusion as to its scope,[185] and the limitations of the related delay mechanism, generated significant market concern,[186] became associated with issuers choosing to admit securities to exchange-regulated markets,[187] and led to widespread calls for reform and for a distinction between inside information for the purposes of disclosure and for the purposes of the insider-dealing prohibition.[188] The Court of Justice ruling in *Daimler*,[189] issued over the 2003 MAD review process,[190] had been anticipated to provide clarity, but it did not. It concerned the failure by Daimler to disclose the resignation of its Chairman in time, given that the disclosure took place after a series of intermediate, internal steps related to the Chairman's resignation, including the communication of the Chairman's intention to members of the supervisory and management boards, the preparation of a press release, and the appointment of a successor. At issue before the Court was the nature of the inside information definition for the purposes of issuer disclosure and, in particular, whether, in the case of a protracted process intended (over a series of steps) to bring about a particular event or circumstance (as with respect to the Chairman's resignation), account was to be taken of whether the relevant future event or circumstance was to be regarded as 'precise' (for the purposes of the determinative inside information definition), or whether intermediate steps could constitute precise information. The Court did not take the opportunity to address the dual function of inside information (or refer to the approach adopted by the 2003 Commission Definitions and Disclosure Directive and its use of the notion of the crystallization of events to determine when the issuer-disclosure obligation arose). The Court instead focused narrowly on the issue at hand, finding that an intermediate step could constitute a set of circumstances or an event, and so could be 'precise' for the purposes of the general definition of inside information.[191] The Court also took an expansive approach to the related question as to whether circumstances or events were 'reasonably likely' to come into existence or occur, finding that a 'highly probable' standard could not apply, as this would undermine the objectives of the 2003 MAD.[192] The Court acknowledged, however, that there was a need to ensure legal certainty, and ruled that information would not be precise where it concerned events and circumstances the

---

[183] 2003 Commission Definitions and Disclosure Directive Art 2(2).

[184] Hansen and Moalem, n 176, 329, suggesting that the obligation to disclose only arose accordingly where the circumstances were certain and reliable and the inside information, accordingly, certain.

[185] ESME criticized the limited scope of the delay regime as obstructing issuers in completing sensitive negotiations and transactions and as not being in the interests of market efficiency: n 73, 8.

[186] As noted by CESR in its 2008 consultation on MAD Guidance: CESR/08-717.

[187] Ferran, n 42, 19; 2007 ESME Report, n 73, 6.

[188] eg 2007 ESME Report, n 73 ibid, 7. The difficulties were also noted by the Commission in its 2009 Call for Evidence (n 39, 9–10).

[189] Case C-19/11 *Markus Getl v Daimler AG*, 28 June 2012, not yet reported.

[190] Council discussions on this issue were postponed pending the ruling: Danish Presidency MAR Progress Report, n 85, 2.

[191] The Court argued that to find otherwise would undermine the purpose of the 2003 MAD with respect to placing investors on an equal footing, as parties could be placed in an advantageous position with respect to other investors: n 189, Ruling of the Court, paras 33–36.

[192] n 189, paras 45–47.

occurrence of which was implausible. The 'reasonably likely' element of the inside information definition inferred that there was a 'realistic prospect' that the circumstances or events would come into existence or occur.[193]

The 2014 MAR negotiations on this question proved troublesome, with wide variations across key stakeholders as the MAR regime was developed.[194] The Commission supported a dual-function approach; its 2011 Proposal made a distinction between 'inside information' for the purposes of the insider-dealing prohibition and 'inside information' which was not sufficiently precise to be subject to the issuer-disclosure obligation.[195] While there was some support in the Council for a dual-function approach, this approach did not prevail, with many Member States opposed to changing the definition of inside information and supporting instead a clarification of the definition.[196]

Accordingly, under the 2014 MAR Article 17(1), the issuer-disclosure obligation maps the 2003 MAD issuer-disclosure obligation: an issuer of a financial instrument must inform the public as soon as possible of inside information (defined in accordance with the 2014 MAR dual-function definition) which directly concerns the issuer. In an amplification of the 2003 MAD obligation, the issuer must ensure that the inside information is made public in a manner which enables fast access and complete, correct, and timely assessment of the information by the public and, where applicable, in the relevant Officially Appointed Mechanism.[197] The disclosure obligation applies only to issuers who have requested or approved the admission of their financial instruments to trading on a regulated market in a Member State or, in the case of financial instruments only traded on an MTF or OTF, issuers who have approved the MTF/OTF trading or request the admission to trading of their financial instruments on an MTF in a Member State. A calibrated disclosure obligation of similar design applies to emission allowances market participants, who are required to publicly, effectively, and in a timely manner disclose inside information concerning emission allowances which they hold in respect of their businesses (Article 17(2)).[198]

---

[193] n 189, paras 48–50.

[194] CESR, eg, did not support any change to the 2003 MAD approach: 2009 CESR MAD Review Response, n 81, 4.

[195] The Commission had proposed a new and broader definition of inside information which would have incorporated information which was not precise or price sensitive, but which would be regarded by a reasonable investor as relevant (n 117), but excluded this new category of inside information from the issuer-disclosure obligation: 2011 MAR Proposal, n 77, Art 12(3).

[196] Danish Presidency MAR Progress Report, n 85, 2–3. Council working party discussions revealed a lack of common understanding across the Member States as to the type of inside information which triggered the dealing prohibition and the type of information which triggered the issuer-disclosure obligation. This was particularly the case with respect to multistaged processes.

[197] Officially Appointed Mechanisms (OAMs) are the official conduits for mandated issuer disclosures (see Ch II sect 8). The issuer must also post and maintain on its official website all inside information which it is required to publish (for a period of five years). In addition, Art 17(1) specifies that the issuer must not combine the disclosure of inside information to the public with the marketing of activities. ITSs will govern the modalities of public disclosure (Art 17(10)).

[198] The calibration to the emission allowances market includes a *de minimis* exemption for participants, which lifts the disclosure obligation where the relevant installations or aviation activities that the market participant owns, controls, or is responsible for, do not exceed a minimum threshold of carbon dioxide equivalent, and a similar exemption in relation to thermal inputs; the details of this exemption are to be specified by the Commission through administrative rules.

The greater specification of the notion of 'precise' under Article 7(2), which follows the *Daimler* ruling and which addresses processes with multiple stages and how they can generate inside information,[199] intensifies the risk to the issuer of breach of the Article 17(1) disclosure obligation, although the recitals to the 2014 MAR acknowledge that the MAR is not intended to disrupt discussions of a general nature between the board and company shareholders. The delay regime has, however, also been finessed, and may mitigate the risks to issuers.

VIII.7.1.2 Delaying Article 17(1) Disclosure

The Article 17(1) issuer-disclosure obligation is partnered by a delay mechanism which is based on the 2003 MAD version, but which has been finessed. Under Article 17(4), an issuer of a financial instrument (or emission allowances market participant) who does not otherwise benefit from an NCA-permitted delay may, under its own responsibility, delay the public disclosure of inside information, provided a series of conditions are met: the immediate disclosure would likely prejudice its legitimate interests; the omission would not be likely to mislead the public; and the issuer (or emission allowances market participant) is able to ensure the confidentiality of the information. In a nuance to the 2003 delay regime, which is designed to acknowledge the risks generated by the *Daimler* ruling, Article 17(4) confirms that, subject to these conditions, in the case of a protracted process, which occurs in stages, intended to bring about or which results in a particular circumstance or particular event, an issuer may under its own responsibility delay the public disclosure of inside information relating to this process. The issuer or market participant is also required to inform the NCA of the delay and provide an explanation of how the conditions were met, immediately after the information is disclosed.[200] Under the 2003 MAD regime, notification was optional, but it has been made mandatory to facilitate *ex post* review of delay decisions.[201]

The original 2003 MAD delay mechanism came under close scrutiny over the financial crisis given the market instability which followed disclosures by certain banks of liquidity support from central banks, and related concerns as to the inability of financial institutions to delay the disclosure.[202] In a Council amendment, the 2014 MAR clarifies that, in order to preserve the stability of the financial system, an issuer that is a credit institution or

---

[199] Sect 6.1.4.

[200] Alternatively, national law may provide that the information be submitted only at the request of the NCA.

[201] The technical modalities of the delay mechanism will be governed by ITSs (Art 17(10)). In addition, and mitigating the jurisdiction allocation risks, the NCA to which notifications must be made will be specified by administrative rules (Art 17(3)). Further, ESMA has been charged with issuing guidelines which set out a non-exhaustive indicative list of 'legitimate interests' and of situations where omitted disclosures would be likely to mislead the public (Art 17(11)). The new regime might be expected to reflect the earlier 2003 Commission Definitions and Disclosure Directive which provided (Art 3(1)) that legitimate interests could be related to two non-exhaustive 'catch-all' circumstances: (i) negotiations in course, or related elements, where the outcome or normal pattern of the negotiations would be likely to be affected by public disclosure; and (ii) decisions taken or contracts made by the management body of an issuer which need the approval of another body of the issuer to become effective, as long as public disclosure, together with the simultaneous announcement that approval is pending, would jeopardize the correct assessment of the information by the public.

[202] The delay regime generated some controversy with respect to the collapse in the share price of UK bank Northern Rock and the run on its deposits in autumn 2007, following disclosure of the liquidity support provided by the Bank of England. Criticisms that disclosure of this support had led to a run on the bank were met by arguments that disclosure was required under EU market-abuse rules.

investment firm may, under its own responsibility, delay the public disclosure of inside information (including information related to a temporary liquidity problem and related to temporary central bank/lender of last resort liquidity assistance), where disclosure entails a risk of undermining the financial stability of the issuer and the financial system, its delay is in the public interest, confidentiality can be ensured, and the relevant NCA has consented to its delay on the basis that the conditions are met (Article 17(5)).[203] Where the NCA does not consent, the issuer must disclose the inside information.

Whether the inside information is delayed under Article 17(4) or (5), in both cases, where the confidentiality of the information is no longer ensured, the issuer must inform the public as soon as possible (Article 17(7)).[204]

VIII.7.1.3 Selective Disclosure: Article 17(8)

The market egalitarianism tenor of Article 17 and its related promotion of retail investor interests via equal-access techniques is most clear in Article 17(8). It addresses selective disclosure and reflects the controversial Regulation Fair Disclosure (FD) adopted by the US SEC in 2000. Regulation FD was designed to eliminate selective issuer disclosure to market professionals, particularly with respect to the disclosure of quarterly earnings forecasts to analysts, to place retail investors on an equal footing with the professional sector with respect to access to material information, to prevent selective disclosure from becoming pervasive, and to reduce the risk of analyst independence being undermined through selective disclosure. But analyst assessment of issuer disclosure is now well established as a key factor in efficient price formation and as an engine of market efficiency,[205] notwithstanding the conflict-of-interest risk to which analysts are vulnerable (Chapter VII). Regulation FD was heavily criticized as potentially 'chilling' issuer disclosure, reducing the flow of information to the marketplace, increasing analysts' costs, increasing the risk of damage to price formation (and the cost of capital) were analysts to follow a smaller range of issuers, and as being based on the illusory premise that retail investors operate on the same playing field as professional investors.[206] Regulation FD is, however, deeply rooted in the SEC's retail investor-protection mission and reflects a concern to address the perceived inequality of selective disclosure and to promote equality, thereby supporting investor confidence—an oft-wielded objective which defies empirical testing.[207] The similar 2014 MAR Article 17(8) disclosure obligation, originally introduced by the 2003 MAD, accordingly serves as a striking example of the influence exerted by US regulatory policy in the early stages of the

---

[203] The NCA must ensure that the delay is only for such period as is necessary in the public interest, and evaluate the conditions on a weekly basis.

[204] Art 17(7) also specifies that public disclosure is required where a rumour is explicitly related to undisclosed inside information and the rumour is sufficiently accurate to indicate that the confidentiality of the inside information is no longer ensured.

[205] Coffee, J, 'Market Failure and the Economic Case for a Mandatory Disclosure System' (1984) 70 *Va LR* 717.

[206] See, eg, Goshen, Z and Parchomosky, K, 'On Insider Trading, Markets and Negative Property Rights in Information' (2001) 87 *Va LR* 1229 and Choi, S, 'Selective Disclosure in the Public Capital Markets' (2002) 35 *University of California (Davis) LR* 533.

[207] It was criticized for being justified on the grounds of investor confidence (Final Adopting Release No 33–7881), without empirical evidence of how the change to disclosure practices would impact on confidence: Choi, S and Pritchard, A, 'Behavioural Economics and the SEC' (2003) 56 *Stanford LR* 1.

FSAP. It might also be regarded as an expression of the depth of the FSAP concern to promote the retail markets and build an equity culture.[208]

Under the Article 17(8) selective disclosure rule, where an issuer or emission allowance market participant (or a person acting on either actor's behalf) discloses any inside information to any third party in the normal course of the exercise of an employment, profession, or duty[209] (as referred to in Article 10(1)), that person must make complete and effective public disclosure of the information, simultaneously in the case of an intentional disclosure and promptly in the case of a non-intentional disclosure. This obligation does not apply where the person receiving the information owes a duty of confidentiality.

VIII.7.1.4 The SME Segment

As is the case with the prospectus and transparency regimes discussed in Chapter II, the issuer-disclosure regime reflects a concern to manage the costs of disclosure for SME issuers. The extension by the 2014 MAR of the market abuse regime's perimeter beyond regulated markets has significant cost implications for SME issuers admitted to trading in markets other than regulated markets who become subject to the Article 17 disclosure requirements.[210] The 2014 MAR makes a limited concession to these issuers by allowing trading venues operating an 'SME growth market'[211] to disclose Article 17(1) disclosures for issuers of financial instruments admitted to trading on such a market on their website (rather than on the issuer's website) (Article 17(9)). In practice this concession is of limited value (certainly by comparison with the lifting of the insiders' list obligation—see section 7.2 below), and the extension of the issuer-disclosure obligation beyond regulated markets sits uneasily with the regulated markets focus of the bulk of the issuer-disclosure regime.

VIII.7.2 Insider Lists

The insider-list regime proved to be one of the most costly and controversial of the 2003 MAD's innovations, for all market segments, but particularly for SMEs, given in particular significant differences in national rules.[212] The 2014 MAR has streamlined and clarified the regime, and is designed to ensure that the content of these lists is tightly specified.[213]

---

[208] See further Ch IX.

[209] The 2014 MAR regime (and earlier 2003 MAD) is more widely drawn than Regulation FD, which, in an effort to reduce 'chilling effects', only prohibits selective disclosure to enumerated persons, including analysts.

[210] As was highlighted by CESR at an early stage of the MAD Review: 2009 CESR MAD Review Response, n 81, 3.

[211] See Ch II sect 7.1.2.

[212] EMSE reported on market concern over the significant administrative costs imposed by the list obligation: 2007 ESME Report, n 73, 10–13. CESR's Market Participants Consultative Panel also noted that the regime was overly bureaucratic and that overly lengthy lists were ineffective: CESR, Annual Report (2006) 7. Similarly, 2011 MAR Proposal Impact Assessment, n 39, 29–30.

[213] Commission Memo, n 126. The Proposal and the 2014 MAR differ significantly. The Proposal was based on a thin legislative obligation which would have been amplified by administrative rules on content and by ITSs on format. The Council revised this approach, expanding the legislative regime (specifying those subject to the obligation and setting out a brief set of content requirements) and removing the delegation relating to content rules (but retaining the more limited ITSs on format).

Under Article 18(1), issuers and emission allowance market participants[214] (and persons acting on their behalf or for their account) must draw up a list of all persons who have access to inside information, where such persons work for them under a contract of employment or otherwise perform tasks through which they have access to inside information, such as advisers, accountants, or credit rating agencies.[215] The 'insider list'[216] must be regularly updated and transmitted to the NCA whenever it is requested; lists must be retained for at least five years (Article 18(5)).

Issuers whose securities are admitted to an SME Growth Market are exempt from this requirement, as long as the issuer takes all reasonable steps to ensure that any person with access to inside information acknowledges the legal and regulatory duties which follow and is aware of the sanctions applicable, and the issuer is able to provide the NCA, on request, with the insider list (Article 18(6)).[217]

Article 18 does not allocate jurisdiction in respect of the insider-list obligation. Member States applied the precursor 2003 MAD obligation to issuers whose financial instruments were admitted to trading on their regulated markets and to domestic issuers, resulting in multiple and overlapping insider-list obligations being imposed on issuers. CESR's July 2007 Guidance, however, recommended that all NCAs recognize the insider lists prepared according to the requirements of the Member State where the issuer in question had its registered office, although it emphasized that each NCA remained empowered to request the lists.[218]

The insider lists regime reflects the well-established market practice of maintaining 'watch lists', particularly in investment firms and with respect to mergers and acquisitions advice. But this practice is usually deal-specific and is based on access to confidential information and on managing conflict-of-interest risk more generally. While robust internal information-management procedures provide an important bulwark against insider dealing, the volume of information produced by issuers under the insider lists regime, who will tend to adopt an over-inclusive approach in fear of supervisory action, is unlikely to be of significant use to NCAs.[219] The braver approach for reform under the 2014 MAR might have been a high-level issuer obligation to adopt effective internal procedures tailored to the risk profile of the issuer, anchored to robust supervision and enforcement.

---

[214] The obligation applies to market participants and auction platforms, auctioneers, and auction monitors relating to the auction of emission allowances under Regulation 1031/2010: Art 18(8).

[215] Issuers must also take all reasonable steps to ensure that any person on the list acknowledges in writing the legal and regulatory duties entailed and is aware of the sanctions applicable to the misuse or improper disclosure of such information.

[216] Art 18(3) specifies that the list include at least the identity of the person having access to inside information, the reason for including the person on the list, the date and time at which the person obtained access to the information, and the date at which the list was created. ITSs will govern the precise format of the lists and the format for their updating.

[217] Issuers who have not requested or approved the admission of their financial instruments to trading on an in-scope venue are also exempt: Art 18(7).

[218] CESR July 2007 Guidance, n 95, 14–15.

[219] ESME reported that in practice issuers produce long lists of names (over 1,000 names listed is common for larger companies) which provide no real guidance as to whether a particular person has in fact received particular information: n 73, 12.

VIII.7.3 Disclosure of Insider Transactions: Managers' Transactions

Insider (manager) trades are regarded as (at least somewhat) informative for price formation,[220] but as vulnerable to insider-dealing risk. As such, they are typically subject to discrete disclosure and dealing requirements designed to enhance price formation and to deter insiders from insider dealing.[221] Notwithstanding the doubt over the extent to which insider trades enhance price-formation and insider-disclosure requirements deter insider dealing,[222] the 2003 MAD introduced a harmonized regime for insider transactions under Article 6(4) which was heavily influenced by the US experience.

This regime has been recast and clarified by the 2014 MAR,[223] reflecting concerns as to the costs of the 2003 MAD regime, particularly for SME issuers, and its effectiveness.[224] Article 19(1) provides that persons discharging managerial responsibilities[225] within an issuer or an emission allowances market participant[226] (and those 'closely associated'[227] with them[228]) notify the issuer and emission allowance market participant (as relevant) and the NCA of

---

[220] An extensive but inconclusive financial economics literature assesses the extent to which insider trades are informative and whether outsiders can profit from following publicly-disclosed insider transactions. For a wide-ranging review, and an examination based on a sample of over one million trades from 1975–1995 (which concludes that the market initially largely ignores valuable information in insider trades), see Lakonishok, L and Lee, L, 'Are Insider Trades Informative?' (2001) 14 *Rev Fin Studies* 79.

[221] See, eg, Fried, J, 'Reducing the Profitability of Insider Trading through Pre-Trading Disclosure' (1998) 71 *Southern California LR* 303. They are long established in the US, which also limits the opportunities for insiders to earn short-term profits under the 'short-swing rule' (Securities Exchange Act 1934, s 16(a)—which requires company directors, officers, and 10 per cent equity holders to file forms with the SEC which indicate their holdings in the issuer's stock and to report most changes within two business days (Rule 16a-3g) and s 16(b) (the short-swing rule)).

[222] The effectiveness of reporting rules appears to depend on enforcement: Wisniewski, T and Bohl, M, 'The Information Content of Registered Insider Trading under Lax Enforcement' (2005) 25 *Int'l Rev of Law and Econ* 169.

[223] Primarily reflecting Council revisions. The 2011 MAR Proposal was less articulated; the Council amplified the regime, including by extending the obligation from shares and specifying the issuer's obligations and the content of the notification.

[224] 2009 Commission Call for Evidence, n 39, 13 and 2011 MAR Proposal Impact Assessment, n 39, 29–30.

[225] Defined under 2014 MAR Art 3(1)(25) as a person within an issuer, an emission allowance market participant, or another entity referenced in Art 19(10) (essentially, identified auction market actors) who is a member of the administrative, management, or supervisory bodies of that entity, or a senior executive, who is not a member of these bodies, but has regular access to inside information relating directly or indirectly to that entity, and having the power to make managerial decisions affecting the future developments and business prospects of that entity.

[226] Where the Art 17(2) exemption related to carbon dioxide and thermal input thresholds (n 198) does not apply (Art 3(1)(20)).

[227] In essence, spouse or equivalent partner, dependent children, other relatives who have shared the same household as the person for at least one year on the date of the transaction concerned, and any legal person, trust, or partnership whose managerial responsibilities are discharged by the relevant person (or associated persons) or that is set up for the benefit of such a person, or whose economic interests are substantially equivalent to the relevant person: 2014 MAR Art 3(1)(26).

[228] In the case of the emission allowance market, it applies to those 'closely associated' with market participants, in so far as their transactions involve emission allowances (and derivatives thereof or auctioned products based thereon). The regime also covers persons discharging managerial responsibilities within any auction platform, auctioneer, and auction monitor, and persons closely associated with them in so far as their transactions involve emission allowances (and derivatives thereof or auctioned products based thereon): Art 19(10).

every transaction[229] conducted on their own account relating to shares or debt instruments of the issuer[230] (or derivatives or other financial instruments linked to them)[231] or in emission allowances or related derivatives.[232] The issuer or emission allowance market participant must ensure that the Article 19(1) information is made public promptly, and no later than three business days after the transaction, in a manner which enables fast access on a non-discriminatory basis (Article 19(3)).[233]

Reflecting the concern to reduce excessive costs, the obligation applies only where the relevant thresholds are met. The obligation applies to any subsequent transaction once a total amount of €5,000 (calculated without netting) has been reached in a calendar year; an NCA may, however, decide to increase the threshold to €20,000[234] (Article 19(8) and (9)).[235]

The 2014 MAR additionally introduces a 'closed period', or a prohibition on persons discharging managerial responsibilities within an issuer on conducting any trading (related to shares or debt instruments of the issuer, or derivatives or financial instruments linked to them) on the person's account or for the account of a third party, directly or indirectly (Article 19(11)). This requirement, which is common practice in major capital markets and a means of addressing potentially high-risk periods for insider dealing, covers the period of 30 calendar days before the announcement of an interim financial report or year-end report which the issuer is required to make public. Trading may be permitted during the closed period by the issuer, either on a case-by-case basis, due to the existence of exceptional circumstances which require the immediate sale of shares (such as severe financial difficulty), or due to the characteristics of the dealing involved (such as dealings under an employee share scheme, savings schemes, or dealings where the beneficial interest in the security does not change). The Commission has been empowered to amplify the new 'closed period' regime through administrative rules.

VIII.7.4 Investment Research

Article 20 addresses the dissemination of investment research and is discussed in Chapter VII on gatekeepers.

---

[229] Art 19 specifies the content of the notification, including the price, volume, and nature of the transaction (Art 19(6)).

[230] The 2003 MAD obligation applied only to shares.

[231] The transactions covered by Art 19(1) have, in order to support market certainty, been specified to include the pledging or lending of financial instruments, and transactions undertaken by any person professionally arranging or executing transactions on behalf of the person discharging managerial responsibilities, including where that person exercises discretion: Art 19(7). The type of transactions which trigger the obligation are to be amplified by the Commission through administrative rules.

[232] As noted in n 228, under Art 19(10) the obligation also applies to any auction platform, auctioneer, or auction monitor in relation to the auction of emission allowances.

[233] The issuer or emission allowance market participant must use such media as may reasonably be relied on for the effective dissemination of information to the public throughout the EU and, where applicable, must use the relevant Officially Appointed Mechanism (Ch II sect 8).

[234] The Commission originally proposed a €20,000 threshold; the text as adopted reflects the Council's position.

[235] The NCA must inform ESMA of its decision and the related justification, with specific reference to market conditions; ESMA must publish the threshold and the related justification.

VIII.7.5 Public Statistics

Article 20 links to the wide definition of inside information as including market information which indirectly relates to issuers by providing that public institutions disseminating statistics or forecasts liable to have a significant effect on financial markets disseminate them in an objective and transparent way.

VIII.7.6 Disclosure or Dissemination of Information in the Media

Special consideration is given to the role of the media in that, for the purpose of applying the 2014 MAR's rules on information dissemination, where information is disclosed or disseminated, and where recommendations are produced for the purpose of journalism or other form of expression in the media, such disclosure or dissemination of information is to be assessed taking into account rules governing the freedom of the press and freedom of expression in other media, and the rules or codes governing the journalist profession (Article 21). This will not be the case where the persons concerned, or persons closely associated with them, derive (directly or indirectly) an advantage or profits from the disclosure or dissemination or where the disclosure or dissemination is made with the intention of misleading the market.

VIII.8 Prohibition on Market Manipulation

VIII.8.1 The Prohibition on Market Manipulation and Identification of Market Manipulation

Article 15 of the 2014 MAR prohibits any person from engaging in market manipulation or, in a significant extension of the 2003 MAD, attempting to engage in market manipulation.[236]

Capturing market manipulation within a regulatory scheme presents a series of challenges. Formal, detailed definitions are unlikely to capture the full range of manipulative activity and are likely to become outdated rapidly. They also provide perverse incentives to potential abusers to develop practices which fall outside the scope of the prohibition. Under the 2003 MAD regime an extensive and multilayered rulebook applied to the definition of market manipulation in an attempt to capture a diffuse and difficult concept. At the legislative level, the 2003 MAD adopted a high-level, definitional approach. The administrative regime (the 2003 Commission Definitions and Disclosure Directive) and CESR's supervisory convergence measures recognized the limits of definitions in capturing

---

[236] Attempts to engage in market manipulation were not covered under the 2003 MAD, and were introduced in the 2014 MAR to align the market manipulation rules with the insider-dealing regime and to ease the burden on supervisors (who are otherwise required to produce evidence of the relevant transactions or orders): 2011 MAR Proposal, n 77, 8. Similarly, CESR highlighted the difficulties supervisors faced in building enforcement cases given the complexity of manipulative structures: 2009 CESR MAD Review Response, n 81, 6.

the range of activity which can be classed as manipulative. These measures accordingly focused on indications, signals, and examples of potential market manipulation in order to build market understanding of which practices breached the 2003 MAD,[237] and were designed to provide NCAs with flexible tools for investigating manipulative practices. Under the 2014 MAR, much of the administrative rulebook has been brought within the Regulation and its Annex (which sets out indicators for different types of abuse), leading to a highly detailed and directly applicable legislative regime. A new delegation empowers the Commission to adopt administrative measures specifying in more detail the different indicators set out in the 2014 MAR Annex (Article 12(5)).

The 2014 MAR, like the 2003 MAD, adopts an effects-based approach,[238] the breadth of which has been scaled back somewhat by the accepted market practice regime (section 8.3.1) and by the intention requirement which applies to manipulation through the dissemination of information. Market manipulation is defined as encompassing three major classes of behaviour. In line with the approach commonly taken internationally, market manipulation is defined in terms of (i) trading practices (Article 12(1)(a) and (b)) and (ii) the dissemination of false or misleading information (Article 12(1)(c)). Article 12(1)(d) addresses market manipulation through benchmark manipulation (section 8.2.3).

Under Article 12(1)(a), market manipulation covers entering into a transaction, placing an order to trade, or any other behaviour which has the following consequences: it gives, or is likely to give, false or misleading signals as to the supply of, demand for, or price of a financial instrument, a related spot commodity contract or an auctioned product based on emission allowances; or it secures, or is likely to secure, the price of one or several financial instruments or related spot commodity contracts or auctioned products based on emission allowances at an abnormal or artificial level (behaviour typically termed 'price positioning').[239] As discussed further in section 8.3.1, an important defence applies where the person who entered into the transaction (or who issued the orders to trade) establishes that his reasons for so doing were legitimate, and that the transactions or orders to trade conform to 'accepted market practices'. Under Article 12(1)(b), market manipulation also covers entering into a transaction, placing an order to trade, or any other activity or behaviour which affects or is likely to affect the price of one or several financial instruments or a related spot commodity contract or an auctioned product based on emission allowances, which employs a 'fictitious device' or any other form of 'deception or contrivance'.

Article 12(1)(c) addresses manipulative activities related to information, and covers the dissemination of information through the media, including the internet, or by any other means which gives or is likely to give false or misleading signals as to the supply of, demand

---

[237] The 2003 MAD prohibition was designed to 'encourage and guide the responsible behaviour' of market participants rather than to set out detailed rules on what behaviour was not permitted: Explanatory Memorandum to the 2001 Proposal, n 65, para 2.

[238] For a critique of the effects approach, given its weaknesses with respect to protecting legitimate behaviour (and with particular reference to the commodities markets), see Ferrarini, n 2, 724–7.

[239] The Court of Justice has ruled that the prohibition on behaviour which secures prices at an abnormal or artificial price level is not qualified by a duration requirement and can capture a single abusive transaction, as otherwise the objectives of the market abuse regime to protect the integrity of markets and enhance investor confidence (under the 2003 MAD) would be undermined (in the case in question, the impact of the manipulative behaviour on prices did not last for more than one second): Case C-445/09 *IMC Securities BV v Stichting Autoriteit Financiële Marketen* [2011] ECR 5917.

for, or price of a financial instrument or a related spot commodity contract or an auctioned product based on emission allowances, or secures, or is likely to secure, the price of one or several financial instruments or a related spot commodity contract or an auctioned product based on emission allowances at an abnormal or artificial level, including the dissemination of rumours. Unlike Articles 12(1)(a) and (b), an intention requirement applies: the person who made the dissemination must know, or ought to have known, that the information was false or misleading.

This framework regime is supported by Article 12(2), which sets out the types of behaviour which will be considered as market manipulation, and which covers 'abusive squeezes',[240] market open/close abuses,[241] abuses relating to algorithmic and high frequency trading (section 8.2.2), and information-related abuses, involving taking advantage of occasional or regular access to the traditional or electronic media.[242] Specific behaviours in the emission allowance market are also covered (Article 12(2)(e)).

The framework regime is also supported by the non-exhaustive indicators set out in the 2014 MAR Annex I related to the employment of fictitious devices (or any other form of deception or contrivance), false or misleading signals, and price securing (Article 12(3)).[243] Reflecting the restrictions posed by the framework- and effects-based legislative regime, the indicators are not dependent on intention (although manipulative intent is implied in the nature of the signals). The regime recognizes, however, that the existence of the indicators should not necessarily be deemed in itself to indicate an instance of market manipulation (Annex), given that the practices in question may be legitimate in a particular context.[244]

The indicators, which are objective and focus on market effects, include: the extent to which the orders to trade or transactions undertaken represent a significant proportion of the daily transaction volume in the relevant financial instrument, related spot commodity contract, or auctioned emission allowance (in particular when these activities lead to a significant change in the price of the instrument); the extent to which the orders or transactions are undertaken by persons with a significant buying or selling position and lead to significant changes in the price; whether any change in beneficial ownership occurs; the extent to which the orders or transactions (or orders cancelled) include position reversals

---

[240] Conduct by a person (or persons acting in collaboration) to secure a dominant position over the supply of or demand for a financial instrument (or related spot commodity contract or auctioned product based on emission allowances) which has, or is likely to have, the effect of fixing, directly or indirectly, purchase or sale prices, or creates or is likely to create other unfair trading conditions: Art 12(2)(a).

[241] The buying or selling of financial instruments at the opening or close of the market, which has or is likely to have the effect of misleading investors acting on the basis of the prices displayed, including the opening or closing prices: Art 12(2)(b).

[242] This provision captures the taking advantage of such access by voicing an opinion about a financial instrument or related spot commodity contract or auctioned product based on emission allowances (or indirectly about its issuer), while having previously taken a position on those instruments or contracts and profiting subsequently from the impact of those opinions without having simultaneously disclosed the conflict of interest to the public in a proper and effective way: Art 12(2)(d).

[243] These indicators or 'signals' are drawn from the 2003 Commission Definitions and Disclosure Obligations Directive. As originally designed, the signals were to allow NCAs to adjust their methods of diagnosing, evaluating, and sanctioning manipulative behaviour: CESR First Level 2 Advice, n 118, 15.

[244] During the development of the original administrative regime, there was considerable market resistance to the absence of an intention element. CESR acknowledged legitimate fears over the scope of the regime but pointed to the constitutional limits posed by the legislative effects-based approach: CESR First Level 2 Advice, Feedback Statement, n 70, 12–13.

in a short period and represent a significant proportion of the daily volume of transactions and might be associated with significant changes in the price; the extent to which the orders or transactions are concentrated within a short time span and lead to a price change which is subsequently reversed; the extent to which orders to trade change the representation of the best bid or offer price, or more generally the representation of the order book available to market participants, and are removed before they are executed; and the extent to which orders or transactions are undertaken at or around a specific time when reference prices, settlement prices, and valuations are calculated, and lead to price changes which have an effect on such prices and valuations. Non-exhaustive indicators also apply with respect to the employment of fictitious devices or any other form of deception or contrivance.[245]

In its technical advice for the earlier administrative regime on which the 2014 MAR Annex I is based, CESR acknowledged that many issues relating to the characterization of market manipulation (and particularly those relating to market-specific issues such as market structure and liquidity) could be dealt with through supervisory convergence measures. Accordingly, its May 2005 Guidance attempted to be flexible and practical and was designed to build a common understanding of what constitutes market manipulation. The examples of false and misleading transactions, for example, included wash trades (where no change in beneficial ownership occurs), 'painting the tape' (engaging in trans-actions which are shown on a public-display facility to give the impression of price movement), improper matched orders (matched buy and sell orders carried out by colluding parties, and placing orders with no intention to execute them. This guidance is likely to remain relevant for the 2014 MAR.

VIII.8.2 Extending the Perimeter: Derivatives, Algorithmic Trading, and Benchmarks

VIII.8.2.1 Financial Derivatives and Commodity Derivatives

The 2014 MAR extends the regulatory perimeter around financial derivatives and commodity derivatives in order to capture manipulative behaviours which might otherwise fall outside the regime. In particular, it seeks to capture cross-market manipulation between the relevant derivative market and the related (often unregulated) spot market, given the capacity for transactions in derivatives markets to manipulate prices on spot markets, and conversely.[246] Wholesale energy products, however, fall outside the market manipulation prohibitions, being subject to the 2011 REMIT Regulation. The 2014 MAR also attempts to ensure co-ordination between the market abuse regime and the developing sectoral spot regimes, requiring, in particular, a co-ordinated approach to enforcement under the market

---

[245] These cover whether orders to trade or transactions undertaken by persons are preceded or followed by the dissemination of false or misleading information by the same persons (or persons linked to them), and whether orders or transactions are undertaken by persons before or after the same persons or persons linked to them produce or disseminate research or investment recommendations which are erroneous or biased or demonstrably influenced by material interest.

[246] As noted in sect 5.1, the prohibitions on market manipulation apply additionally to transactions, orders to trade, or other behaviour relating to spot commodity contracts (excluding wholesale energy products, covered by the 2011 REMIT Regulation), where the action has, or is likely or intended to have an effect on an in-scope financial instrument.

abuse regime and under the wholesale energy market regime.[247] The 2014 MAR also seeks to capture abusive conduct related to financial derivatives which otherwise might fall outside the scope of the regime.[248]

VIII.8.2.2 Algorithmic Trading

The imprints of the financial crisis on the 2014 MAR can be seen most clearly in the inclusion of practices related to algorithmic trading. As discussed in Chapter VI, algorithmic and in particular high frequency trading (HFT) has emerged as a crisis 'poster child' for 'excessive' financial market innovation and intensity, and is subject to a range of reforms under MiFID II in particular. The policy concern to address this form of trading is reflected in the 2014 MAR, which, somewhat unnecessarily,[249] specifies the behaviours concerning algorithmic and HFT strategies which are to be considered to amount to market manipulation.[250]

VIII.8.2.3 Benchmark and Index Manipulation

The global rate-fixing scandal relating to the manipulation of major interest rate benchmarks[251] (notably Libor and Euribor[252])[253] which, following the initiation of investigations by regulators worldwide in 2009, erupted over 2012,[254] exposed the vulnerability of the benchmark management and related index-setting process to manipulation, and the related impact on market confidence and integrity. Indices, and the benchmarks which they

---

[247] Art 25, requiring co-operation between ESMA, NCAs, and ACER—the new EU Agency for the Co-operation of Energy Regulators.

[248] The market manipulation regime applies additionally to types of financial instruments (including derivatives for the transfer of credit risk), where the transaction, order, bid, or behaviour has, or is likely to have, an effect on the price or value of a spot commodity contract where the price or value depends on the price or value of those financial instruments: Art 2(2)(b).

[249] As is implicitly acknowledged by the 2011 MAR Proposal which notes that the market manipulation definition is very broad and capable of applying to such abusive behaviour, but suggests that it is nonetheless appropriate to address trading specifically: n 77, 8.

[250] The placing of orders to a trading venue, including any cancellation or modification thereof, by any available means of trading, including electronic means, such as algorithmic trading and high frequency trading strategies, and which has one of the effects covered by Art 12(1)(a) or (b) by: disrupting or delaying the functioning of the trading system of the trading venue or which is likely to do so; making it more difficult for other persons to identify genuine orders on the trading system of the trading venue or which is likely to do so, including by entering orders which result in the overloading or destabilization of the order book; or creating or being likely to create a false or misleading signal about the supply of, or demand for, or price of a financial instrument, in particular by entering orders to initiate or exacerbate a trend: Art 12(2)(c).

[251] Where an index is used as a reference price for a financial instrument or contract it operates as a benchmark.

[252] The London interbank offered rate and the Euro interbank offered rate.

[253] Which was followed over 2013–14 by the global foreign exchange rate-setting scandal which led to international regulatory investigations into allegations of manipulation of key exchange rates and benchmarks.

[254] The Libor and Euribor rates were set through submissions from banks based on their borrowing and lending in the interbank market. The abuse related to banks providing estimates of lending rates for the purpose of benchmark-setting which were different from the rates they would have accepted in practice. Among the many impacts was the misleading of the market generally as to banks' cost of funding. In the UK, the scandal led to a fine of £59.9 million being imposed on Barclays (reduced from £80 million because of early settlement) for making interest rate submissions in relation to the setting of the benchmark rates which took into account requests made by its derivative traders, which requests sought to benefit Barclays' trading positions: FSA, Final Notice, Barclays Bank, 27 June 2012. One estimate has placed the potential penalty bill for major global banks at $22 billion: Masters, B and Barber, A, 'Banks Face $22 Libor Bill', *Financial Times*, 13 July 2012, 1.

provide,[255] are embedded into the pricing and structure of financial instruments internationally[256] and serve a host of functions in financial markets,[257] including with respect to risk management and asset management, which have led to their being 'hard-wired' into financial markets.[258] The Libor/Euribor scandal has led to a cascade of reforms and initiatives internationally, most notably the International Organization of Securities Commissions (IOSCO) reforms,[259] and in key jurisdictions impacted by the scandal,[260] which reforms have extended significantly beyond the regulation of the interbank lending rates implicated in the scandal.

The process through which the indices which act as benchmarks are constructed can be vulnerable to process and conflict-of-interest failures,[261] and the momentum for reform, and stakeholder support, is considerable.[262] But the scale of the benchmark industry,[263] the multiplicity of benchmarks and indices and the range of public and private purposes they serve,[264] the range of providers,[265] the different means through which data of very different types is gathered, and the very significant instability risks where an index which acts as a benchmark is withdrawn from use or radically changed[266] make appropriate reform

---

[255] The major indices used as benchmarks in financial markets include those related to interbank interest rates (eg Euribor and Libor), equities (eg FTSE 100 and Dow Jones), and commodities. A vast array of indices are, however, produced by index providers and financial institutions for private consumption/benchmarking generally.

[256] The Libor and Euribor reference rates, eg, are fundamental to the operation of the massive market in euro, US dollar, and sterling interest rate derivatives contacts (OTC and venue-traded). Underlining the importance of the integrity of the rate-setting process, the UK FSA highlighted the notional outstanding of OTC interest rate derivatives contracts in the first half of 2011 as being some US\$554 trillion: Barclays Final Notice, n 254, para 4.

[257] As well as in other markets; variable rate mortgages, eg, are based on the Libor and Euribor benchmarks.

[258] The UK FSA warned that the integrity of benchmark reference rates such as Libor and Euribor was of fundamental importance to UK and international financial markets: Barclays Final Notice, n 254, para 6.

[259] Over 2013, IOSCO produced two major consultations on Principles for Financial Benchmarks—a consultation report in January 2013 and a consultation paper in April 2013—and in July 2013 adopted its Principles for Financial Benchmarks.

[260] Including the major UK Wheatley Review into Libor: The Wheatley Review of LIBOR. Final Report. September 2012.

[261] While the UK Wheatley Review into the Libor scandal concluded that Libor should continue to be based on daily estimates from a panel of submitting banks, it recommended a range of process and governance-related proposals which included: statutory regulation of the administration of, and submission to, Libor and the related application of criminal and civil sanctions; the transfer of responsibility for administering Libor from the industry-based British Bankers' Association to a new administrator, subject to governance, transparency, and data quality requirements; and a code of conduct governing submission of rates to Libor: Wheatley Review, n 260. In July 2013, it was announced that NYSE Euronext was to take over the management of Libor from the BBA: Masters, B and Stafford, P, 'Scandal-plagued Libor Moves to NYSE as Part of Reforms', *Financial Times*, 10 July 2013.

[262] In autumn 2012, as the reform movement gathered momentum internationally, the Global Financial Markets Association produced its Principles for Financial Benchmarks, as a potential basis for international standards.

[263] The size of the markets impacted by benchmarks has been estimated at €1,000 trillion: Commission 2013 Benchmark Proposal Impact Assessment (SWD (2013) 337/2).

[264] Which can extend from market-wide price-setting (as in the case of Libor and Euribor) to tailored risk and performance management for individual firms and in relation to particular products (such as exchange-traded fund (ETF) indices). A significant element of the benchmark/index production market relates to the production of bespoke products for clients, which products, designed for proprietary use often in the OTC market, are often based on non-public information and are not disclosed.

[265] Which range from public authorities to specialist index providers.

[266] As was highlighted by the Wheatley Review, which decided accordingly against a radical reform or withdrawal of the Libor benchmark.

a challenge, particularly given the importance of market discipline and competition in driving quality in index and benchmark production.

The EU response,[267] the speed of which underlines the extent to which, since the crisis era, the EU now commands the regulatory space for EU securities and markets regulation and also seeks to shape reform internationally,[268] has been multilayered. For the purposes of this discussion,[269] the main initiative was the revision of the original 2011 MAR Proposal to address manipulation through benchmarks.[270] In order to address any potential regulatory gaps, and to ensure the market manipulation prohibition is appropriately tailored to benchmark manipulation,[271] the 2014 MAR accordingly applies the prohibition on market manipulation to benchmarks (Article 2(2)(c)),[272] and the definition of market manipulation includes transmitting false or misleading information or providing false or misleading inputs where the person who made the transmission or provided the input knew or ought to have known that it was false or misleading, or any other behaviour which manipulates the calculation of a benchmark (Article 12(1)(d)). The 2014 MAD Directive similarly applies the requirement for criminal sanctions to benchmark manipulation. The extraterritorial reach of the 2014 MAR (section 5.4) implies that the EU's approach will have implications for the treatment of benchmark and index abuse globally.

More generally, in September 2012 the Commission launched a consultation on the production and use of indices used as benchmarks[273] which addressed the process through which indices and benchmarks are developed and, in particular, the governance and transparency of these processes. A relatively ambitious Proposal for a regulation on indices used as benchmarks in financial instruments and financial contracts (particularly with respect to its potential international reach through the proposed equivalence regime)[274] followed in September 2013.[275] The Proposal is designed to improve the governance of and

---

[267] Which has included enforcement action by the EU's competition authorities related to illegal cartel activity. The Commission levied fines worth €1.71 billion on eight international financial institutions: Commission, Press Release 4 December 2013 (IP/13/1208).

[268] The EU's engagement with the international benchmark reform process appears, however, constructive. The Commission's September 2012 Consultation on Benchmarks and Indices, eg, called for a consistent and co-ordinated approach internationally (Commission, Consultation Document on the Regulation of Indices (2012) 25) (2012 Commission Indices Consultation).

[269] Benchmarks are already addressed under the prospectus regime, which requires that where a prospectus refers to an index, specific disclosures should be made, while the UCITS regime imposes asset-allocation rules on index-related investments. The MiFID II reforms introduce a new regime governing the licensing of benchmarks (with respect to clearing and trading) (Ch V sect 13). In the energy markets, the 2011 REMIT regulation provides that the manipulation of benchmarks used for wholesale energy products is illegal.

[270] n 4.

[271] The introduction of a specific prohibition relating to benchmark manipulation arose from concerns that the 2011 MAR Proposal (then under negotiation) did not capture this form of manipulation, and to remove the necessity of NCAs making enquiries into the price impact of this form of manipulation, given the very severe challenges this would pose: 2013 Benchmark Proposal (COM (2013) 641) 1.

[272] A benchmark is defined as any rate, index, or figure, made available to the public or published, that is periodically or regularly determined by the application of a formula to, or on the basis of: the value of one or more underlying assets or prices, including estimated prices, actual or estimated interest rates, or other values or surveys, and by reference to which the amount payable under a financial instrument or the value of a financial instrument is determined: Art 3(1)(29).

[273] 2012 Commission Indices Consultation, n 268.

[274] n 280.

[275] n 271. As the Proposal is at a very early stage and will likely be on the agenda of the new European Parliament and Commission term (2014–19), it is considered in outline only.

controls over the benchmark process, and to ensure that benchmark administrators avoid conflicts of interest; to improve the quality of the data and methodologies used in benchmark production; to ensure contributors to benchmarks are subject to adequate controls (particularly with respect to conflicts of interest); and to ensure adequate protection for consumers and investors, including through transparency and suitability requirements. The proposed regime is designed to apply a common framework to ensure the accuracy of 'indices' used as 'benchmarks' in financial instruments and financial contracts[276] (Article 1), and is directed towards the provision of benchmarks, the contribution of data to benchmarks, and the use of benchmarks within the EU (Article 2). The indices which can form benchmarks are broadly defined in terms of any figure published or made available to the public,[277] regularly determined (entirely or partially) through a formula or other method of calculation, or by an assessment, where the determination is made on the basis of the value of one or more underlying assets or prices or other values. Benchmarks are similarly broadly defined in terms of any index by reference to which the amount payable under a financial instrument or contract, or the value of a financial instrument, is determined, or an index used to measure the performance of an investment fund (Article 3).

The proposed regime is broadly designed to ensure effective oversight of the provision of the benchmark[278] by the benchmark administrator (the person with control over the provision of the benchmark) and of the contribution of data to the benchmark. In terms of scope, the regime follows the mechanism which the credit rating agency regime deployed for setting the scope of that regime; a 'supervised entity'[279] may only use a benchmark as a reference to a financial instrument or financial contract, or to measure the performance of an investment fund, if the benchmark is provided by an authorized administrator (or a third country administrator which is registered with the ESMA in accordance with the relevant equivalence requirements)[280] (Article 19); the potential impact on the use of benchmarks is accordingly significant and portfolio reallocations may be required. An EU benchmark administrator must apply for authorization if it provides indices which are used or intended to be used to reference financial instruments or financial contracts, or to measure the performance of an investment fund; authorization is the responsibility of the home NCA (Articles 22–23). Authorized administrators become subject to the proposed regime for administrators which includes governance and outsourcing requirements (Articles 5–6),

---

[276] Financial instruments are defined by reference to the MiFID II regime; the instruments must also have been admitted to trading on a trading venue, or a request for admission to trading on a trading venue (likely to be a MiFID II/MiFIR trading venue, but not defined) must have been made. Financial contracts are, broadly, defined as credit agreements (including some consumer credit and mortgage loans, but excluding corporate and wholesale loans: Clifford Chance, The New EU Benchmark Regulation, September 2013, 3).

[277] Privately contracted indices are therefore excluded.

[278] Defined as administering the arrangements for determining the benchmark; collecting, analysing, or processing input data; and determining the benchmark through a formula or otherwise (Art 3).

[279] In essence, a wide range of EU-regulated financial institutions, including credit institutions, investment firms, insurance undertakings, UCITS managers, alternative investment fund managers, trade repositories, and central clearing counterparties (CCPs).

[280] The proposed equivalence regime reflects the equivalence regimes which apply across crisis-era EU securities and markets regulation, and includes that the Commission has adopted an equivalence decision relating to the equivalence of the third country's legal regime and supervisory framework governing benchmarks, the authorization and supervision of the administrator in the third country, the notification by the administrator of ESMA that it consents to the use of its benchmarks by supervised entities in the EU, the registration of the administrator with ESMA, and supervisory co-operation requirements. Benchmark regulation is, however, new to most States, although the 2013 IOSCO Principles provide a template.

addresses the process through which input data is identified and collated (Articles 7–8),[281] and requires administrators to adopt and follow a code of conduct for each benchmark specifying administrator and contributor responsibilities (and reflecting the proposed Regulation's requirements (Article 9)). In order to protect index producers from becoming benchmark providers without their consent, where an NCA becomes aware that an index is being used as a reference in respect of a financial instrument admitted to trading on a trading venue supervised by the NCA (or an instrument in respect of which an admission application has been made), it must notify ESMA, and ESMA must request the relevant benchmark administrator to confirm that it consents to the use of the benchmark (Article 25).[282] While supervision of authorized benchmark administrators is the responsibility of the home NCA (despite earlier suggestions that ESMA would be empowered to supervise benchmarks), the Proposal suggests that a college of supervisors be established to support consultation and information-sharing with respect to 'critical benchmarks' (noted later in this section), including between NCAs of benchmark contributors, ESMA, and the benchmark administrator's NCA.

The proposed regime also imposes governance and control requirements on 'supervised contributors' (essentially, regulated entities) (Articles 9 and 11), imposes specific require-ments for particular key benchmarks (interbank interest rate and commodity benchmarks) (Article 12), and applies mandatory contribution rules to 'critical benchmarks'[283] designed to ensure these benchmarks remain stable where major contributors cease providing data (Article 13–14). In addition, supervised entities are required to produce written plans addressing the action to be taken in the event a benchmark materially changes or ceases to be produced (Article 17).

Disclosure and transparency requirements are also proposed, primarily through a 'bench-mark statement' to be provided by the administrator for each benchmark (Article 15). Consumer protection is addressed by means of a requirement that where a supervised entity intends to enter into a financial contract with a consumer, it must follow a suitability assessment designed to assess that the benchmark to which the contract is referenced is suitable for the consumer (Article 18). Structurally, the regime is designed to be operation-ally detailed; the proposed Regulation's general principles are amplified by a detailed Annex and are to be further amplified by administrative rules.

Unsurprisingly, given the opportunity the management of benchmark risk generated for strengthening their credibility as nascent regulators, ESMA (which has begun to closely monitor benchmark risks)[284] and EBA also seized the initiative,[285] both operationally with

---

[281] Including requirements that the data be sufficient to represent reliably and accurately the market or economic reality the benchmark is designed to measure, that data be provided from a reliable and represen-tative panel or sample of contributors, and that conflict of interests/data quality risks related to the position of the contributor in the market which the benchmark is designed to measure are addressed.

[282] This requirement affords index providers the opportunity to refuse consent for an index to be used as a benchmark (and so to lift the application of the proposed regime).

[283] To be identified by the Commission, and the majority of contributors to which are supervised entities and which reference financial instruments with a notional value of at least €500 billion.

[284] Its second Trends, Risks, and Vulnerabilities report examined the risks posed by financial benchmarks to EU securities markets, particularly with respect to benchmark continuity and the quality of contributions to benchmarks: ESMA, Trends, Risks, and Vulnerabilities. Report No 2 (2013) (ESMA/2013/1138) (ESMA 2013(2) TRV) 28.

[285] Including by highlighting the risks posed by a lack of confidence in financial market benchmarks in the first joint report by ESMA, EBA (European Banking Authority), and EIOPA (European Insurance and

respect to Euribor and more generally with respect to the development of principles for the setting of benchmarks, pending legislative reform. Operationally, ESMA and EBA, somewhat along the lines of the UK Libor review process, reviewed the operation of Euribor and made a series of recommendations to improve its governance and transparency,[286] while EBA made recommendations to the relevant NCAs of banks making submissions to Euribor.[287]

ESMA and EBA also produced principles on the benchmark-setting process in 2013[288] which are designed to mitigate governance and incentive issues relating to benchmarks, in the absence of a distinct legislative measure and pending the adoption of an EU response (now in train). Here the two European Supervisory Authorities (ESAs) proved imaginative, as the range of actors and conduct captured by the principles extends significantly beyond the regulated actors and the legislative framework within the ESAs' remit.[289] Designed to provide an interim and immediate response to benchmark risk pending legislative action by the EU, the principles are acknowledged not to have binding effect and to depend on market discipline for enforcement, but are declared to provide relevant market participants with a consistent and common framework.[290] As discussed further in Chapter X, the principles illustrate ESMA's strengthening ability to respond to market developments and to grasp emerging issues, and thereby to consolidate its institutional position.[291] The principles also underline ESMA's growing influence on EU rule-making and in the international sphere. With respect to the former, they provided the Commission with a potential template for action, tested through market consultation (the 2013 Benchmarks Proposal reflects the principles in many respects), and thereby strengthen the ability of ESMA to shape the legislative process. They also strengthen ESMA's influence at the international level, given the extent to which action on benchmarks has been internationally co-ordinated (through IOSCO)[292] and ESMA's role in this process. The principles are declared to promote consistency in the international standard-setting process and smooth

---

Occupations Pensions Authority) on risks and vulnerabilities in the EU financial sector: Joint Committee, Risks and Vulnerabilities in the EU Financial Sector, March 2013 (JC 2013-010) 20–2.

[286] EBA/ESMA, Letter to the European Banking Federation, 13 January 2013, and EBA/ESMA, Report on the Administration and Management of Euribor (2013). The subsequent EBA/ESMA Joint Review of implementation of the recommendations reported on good progress: ESMA/2014/207.

[287] EBA, Recommendations on Supervisory Oversight of Activities Related to Banks Participation in the Euribor Panel (2013) (EBA/REC/2013/01).

[288] ESMA/EBA, Principles for Benchmark-Setting Processes in the EU (2013) (ESMA/2013/659) (Consultation Paper, ESMA/2013/12). The Principles are designed to cover all stages of the benchmark-setting process and cover data submission, benchmark administration, benchmark calculation, benchmark publication, the use of benchmarks, and the continuity of benchmarks. They also establish a general framework for benchmark setting, which covers methodology; governance structure; supervision and oversight; and transparency. The Principles are designed to be applied proportionately, in a manner appropriate to the size, nature, and complexity of any specific benchmark.

[289] Including, eg, benchmark publishers, administrators, and calculation agents, who may not be regulated actors.

[290] The principles are designed to bridge a gap, pending the adoption of a legislative framework, and to provide a 'common framework to work together and provide a glide path to future obligations that are likely to be binding': ESMA/EBA Consultation Paper, n 288, 3.

[291] The 2013 Joint Committee Risks and Vulnerabilities Report captures EBA's and ESMA's concern to seize this reform agenda, noting that ESMA and EBA 'took decisive action' in this area, in co-ordination with the Commission and IOSCO, pending legislative developments: n 285, 20.

[292] The relevant IOSCO Taskforce was chaired by the Chairs of the UK FCA and US CFTC, both of which regulators were closely engaged with the reform process.

transition to the application of international standards, and were developed in close collaboration with IOSCO;[293] IOSCO's July 2013 Principles for Financial Benchmarks also took the ESMA/EBA Principles into account.[294]

VIII.8.3 Calibration and Differentiation

VIII.8.3.1 Accepted Market Practices

Under Article 13, an important defence to a finding of market manipulation with respect to trading practices (under Article 13(1)) applies where the person who entered into the transaction (or who placed the orders to trade or engaged in any other behaviour) establishes that the action was carried out for 'legitimate reasons' (an intention-based element) and (ii) the transactions or orders to trade conform to 'accepted market practices' (or are an accepted market practice or AMP), established in conformity with the Article 13 AMP regime.[295] The AMP defence does not apply to Article 12(1)(b) as there can never be a legitimate reason for entering into 'fictitious devices' or any other form of 'deception or contrivance'.

The AMP concept reflects the reality that in certain markets certain practices have evolved which are accepted as legitimate.[296] The AMP defence applied under the 2003 MAD. AMPs were determined by NCAs in accordance with the 2004 Commission AMP Directive which addressed the NCA decision-making process and did not harmonize AMPs. The Directive set out non-exhaustive factors which NCAs were to take into account, and required NCAs to review their AMPs regularly. The factors were designed to focus NCA attention on how a practice which might have constituted market manipulation impacted on price formation and how it could be justified. The 2004 AMP Commission Directive also imposed a stakeholder consultation requirement (including of other NCAs, although permission was not required from other NCAs). Diverging national AMP were respected, although there was some implicit pressure in the 2004 AMP Commission Directive for convergence. CESR additionally established a template for assessing AMPs, a reporting system, and a publication mechanism, as well as a market-facing FAQ document.[297]

Some variation in AMPs was always to be expected given the different features and specializations of domestic markets. But the significantly diverging approaches which emerged had the potential to generate arbitrage risks and prejudice to supervisory convergence.[298] CESR originally called for an 'organic convergence' which would respect national autonomy while encouraging stronger convergence.[299] The AMP process was driven by the

---

[293] 2012 Commission Indices Consultation, n 268, 5.

[294] n 259, 2.

[295] The defence was added by the European Parliament during the first reading of the 2003 MAD: First ECON Report, n 66, 19.

[296] The Commission described the 2003 MAD AMP regime as reflecting the existence of behaviours that could reasonably be expected in a national market due to, eg, local, long-established customs, while potentially constituting market abuse in others: 2011 MAR Proposal Impact Assessment, n 39, 28.

[297] CESR/05-365.

[298] CESR, First Progress Report on Supervisory Convergence in the Field of Securities Markets Report (2005) (CESR/05-202).

[299] CESR noted that given that it would publish the different AMPs, NCAs might come under pressure to accept a practice which they initially found inappropriate: n 298, 6.

NCAs, however, and consistent pan-EU AMPs did not emerge.[300] The Commission, concerned as to divergence in AMPs and a related lack of legal certainty, proposed the removal of the AMP regime in the 2011 MAR Proposal.[301] Following significant hostility within the Council (which supported national discretion and flexibility in this area),[302] the AMP regime has been retained but has been significantly recast, primarily by means of the incorporation of the original 2003 MAD AMP administrative regime within the 2014 MAR Regulation and the conferral of a range of oversight powers on ESMA.

The conditions under which an NCA can establish an AMP are set out in Article 13(2). An NCA can establish an AMP taking into account that: the specific market practice has a substantial level of transparency to the market; the practice ensures a high degree of safeguards to the operation of market forces and the proper interplay of the forces of supply and demand; the practice has a positive impact on market liquidity and efficiency; the practice takes into account the trading mechanism of the relevant market and enables market participants to react properly and in a timely manner to the new market situation created by that practice; the practice does not create risks for the integrity of (directly or indirectly) related markets, whether regulated or not, in the relevant financial instrument within the EU; the outcome of any investigation of the practice by any NCA or other authority, in particular whether the practice breached rules or regulations designed to prevent market abuse, or codes of conduct, be it on the market in question or on directly or indirectly related markets within the EU; and the structural characteristics of the relevant market, including whether it is regulated or not, the types of financial instrument traded, and the type of market participants, including the extent of retail investor participation in the relevant market. Article 13(2) also confirms that a practice that is accepted as an AMP by the NCA in one market is not considered applicable to other markets unless the NCAs have officially accepted that practice. RTSs will amplify the Article 13(2) criteria (Article 13(7)).

These conditions map those which applied under the 2004 Commission AMP Directive. The most significant change relates to the role of ESMA. In a model now familiar from other elements of crisis-era EU securities and markets regulation, but in a significant change to the CESR-era, NCA-driven, AMP model, an NCA must, not less than three months before the AMP is intended to take effect, notify ESMA and other NCAs of its intention to establish an AMP and provide details of its assessment of the criteria which must be reviewed (Article 13(3)). ESMA must issue (and publish) an opinion on the compatibility of the proposed AMP with the Article 13(2) criteria and related RTSs; the opinion must also consider whether the AMP would threaten market confidence in the EU's financial market (Article 13(4)). ESMA must publish a list of all AMPs and the Member States in which they are applicable; NCAs must review their AMP regularly and at least every two years (Article 13(8) and (9)).

---

[300] Some 11 AMPs specific to different Member States were in place when the 2014 MAR was adopted in 2014. In its FAQ on the AMP regime under the 2003 MAD, CESR emphasized that AMPs did not provide a safe harbour for market participants as they were the responsibility of individual NCAs: CESR/05-365.

[301] 2011 MAR Proposal Impact Assessment, n 39, 28 and 57.

[302] Danish Presidency MAR Progress Report, n 85, 3; most Member States were, however, of the view that an AMP was limited, and could only apply within the particular Member State and could not be transposed to other Member States.

ESMA is central to the new AMP process and is likely to drive convergence. Where an NCA establishes an AMP contrary to an ESMA opinion, it must publish (within 24 hours) its reasons for doing so, including why the AMP does not threaten market confidence (Article 13(5)). In addition to this 'comply or explain' disciplining method, where another NCA considers that an NCA has not met the Article 13(2) criteria, ESMA is to assist in the reaching of an agreement, using its ESMA Regulation Article 19 mediation powers (Article 13(6)). In addition, ESMA-proposed RTSs will govern the AMP procedure (Article 13(7)), while ESMA is also to monitor the application of AMPs and to report annually to the Commission on their application in the markets concerned (Article 13(10)).[303] The continued tolerance of local AMPs cuts against the single rulebook for market abuse regulation sought by the 2014 MAR, but reflects significant political sensitivities; the filtering of AMPs through ESMA, however, has the promise of supporting an appropriate degree of convergence in this area.

VIII.8.3.2 Stabilization and Buy-Backs

Stabilization involves trading in securities by the lead managers of a primary distribution of securities for a limited period of time after the offering in order to support the price against excessive volatility which may arise under the initial pressure of early sell orders. It is designed to ensure that the price reflects the security's real, as opposed to speculative, value. *Prima facie*, it can be regarded as an artificial manipulation of the market price. It is usually permitted, albeit subject to strict controls which are designed to minimize the risk that it maintains prices at an artificial level for too long and to avoid the potential for insider dealing. These controls typically involve time and price requirements and disclosure obligations. The dispensation is based on stabilization's contribution to the development of a stable market in the securities in question and to increasing investor confidence in new issues of securities.[304] Prior to the 2003 MAD, however, considerable divergences existed between Member States and markets with respect to stabilization, with stabilization unknown in some domestic markets. Share buy-back programmes similarly raise potential risks in terms of market manipulation.

One of the key innovations of the 2003 MAD was its establishment of the foundations for a pan-EU stabilization and buy-backs regime under Article 8, which established a framework within which stabilization and buy-back regimes could be constructed through administrative rules.[305] The subsequent 2003 Commission Buy Backs and Stabilization Safe Harbour Regulation was designed to act as a 'safe harbour' and so took the form of a Regulation to ensure uniformity across the Member States.[306]

---

[303] With respect to pre-existing AMPs, NCAs are to submit their AMPs to ESMA within 3 months of the relevant RTSs coming into force, and they will continue to apply in the Member State concerned until the NCA concerned has made a decision under the new procedure as to their continuation: Art 13(11).

[304] eg FESCO, Stabilisation and Allotment, A European Supervisory Approach, Consultative Paper (2000) (Fesco/00–099b) (2000 FESCO Stabilisation Paper) 8.

[305] For a detailed analysis see Lombardo, S, 'The Stabilization of the Share Price of IPOs in the United States and in the European Union' (2007) 8 *EBOLR* 521.

[306] The decision to employ a regulation was not without controversy (European Securities Committee Minutes, 17 March 2003 and 10 July 2003). Finland abstained from the final vote as it objected to the use of a regulation on subsidiarity grounds (Minutes, 29 October 2003).

Particular difficulties arose with the stabilization regime, however. While the stabilization regime was designed to calibrate the 2003 MAD to long-established practices in the public offering market, difficulties emerged with its application to non-equity asset classes, and with respect to market liquidity. Foreshadowing the widespread concern which would emerge with respect to the impact of crisis-era measures on market liquidity,[307] concerns emerged that restrictions under the 2003 Commission Regulation designed from an equity market template were too blunt for all markets, and that liquidity and short-term trading performance could be affected.[308] It also became clear that NCAs had adopted widely varying approaches to the 2003 Commission Regulation, even though it should have delivered a uniform regime across the Member States.[309]

The detailed regime established under the 2003 Commission Regulation[310] has now been replaced by the 2014 MAR and a new set of delegations for administrative rules. Under Article 5, the insider dealing and market manipulation prohibitions do not apply to trading in own shares in buy-back programmes, or to the stabilization[311] of securities more generally (Article 5(1) and (4)). The regime broadly reflects the earlier 2003 MAD regime and incorporates elements of the earlier administrative rules.

The buy-back exemption (Article 5(1)–(3)) applies to trading in shares, and requires that full details of the buy-back programme are disclosed prior to the start of trading, trades are reported as being part of the buy-back programme to the NCA and subsequently disclosed to the public, and adequate limits regarding price and volume are respected (Article 5(1)). The trading must also be carried out in accordance with the RTSs which will govern this area. In addition, the sole purpose[312] of the buy-back programme must be to reduce the capital of an issuer (in value or number of shares) or to meet an obligation arising from either debt financial instruments exchangeable into equity instruments or share option programmes or other allocations of shares to employees or to members of the administrative, management, or supervisory bodies of the issuer or an associate company (Article 5(2)). The issuer must also have in place mechanisms for ensuring that it fulfils related trade

---

[307] Particularly under the MiFID II trading transparency reforms: Ch V.

[308] Particularly with respect to the Regulation's 5 per cent short position limit for over-allotments; positions in the subordinated debt market were typically held in the 8–12 per cent region.

[309] ESME reported that some Member States allowed stabilization to exceed the 5 per cent short-position limit, others prohibited the stabilization of debt securities, while still others did not appreciate the notion of a 'safe harbour' or recognize that failure to meet the requirements of the Regulation did not automatically render the conduct abusive: 2007 ESME Report, n 73, 15–16. CESR, however, found the regime to be broadly convergent: 2009 CESR MAD Review Response, n 81, 7.

[310] CESR's 2009 Guidance attempted to address market concerns on a range of questions, including technical issues related to certain of the Regulation's terms, reporting mechanisms, inconsistencies between the EU regime and third countries, and the extent to which the Regulation provided a safe harbour: n 95, at 11–13.

[311] Defined as any purchase or offer to purchase relevant securities, or any transaction in associated instruments equivalent thereto, by investment firms or credit institutions, which is undertaken in the context of a 'significant distribution' of such relevant securities, exclusively for supporting the market price of the securities for a predetermined period of time, due to selling pressure in those securities. A 'significant distribution' is an initial or secondary offer of securities distinct from ordinary trading, both in terms of the amount in value offered and the selling method to be employed: Art 3(2)(c) and (d).

[312] The 'sole purpose' restrictions on buy-backs (and on stabilization), which are an addition to the 2003 MAD, were added by the Council and incorporate the earlier administrative regime.

reporting requirements to the NCA of the regulated market on which the shares have been admitted to trading.

Article 5(4) governs stabilization, and exempts trading in securities[313] or associated instruments[314] for the stabilization of securities, when the stabilization is carried out for a limited time period, relevant information about the stabilization is disclosed, the stabilization is notified to the relevant NCA,[315] adequate limits with regard to price are respected, and the trading complies with the RTSs which will amplify the regime.[316]

RTSs will amplify the stabilization and buy-back exemptions, and are to cover, *inter alia*, conditions for trading, restrictions regarding time and volume, disclosure and reporting obligations, and price conditions. The new administrative regime is likely to reflect some at least of the detailed rules adopted under the 2003 Commission Regulation,[317] while responding to the difficulties which have since emerged.[318]

VIII.9 Supervision and Enforcement

VIII.9.1 Context

Although the exact impact of the EU's market abuse regime on market integrity and on the wider efficiency, growth, and liquidity of the EU financial market remains uncertain, it does seem clear that success depends on enforcement. A considerable body of evidence suggests that the enforcement of market abuse prohibitions can have quantifiable positive effects on markets.[319] But insider-dealing and market manipulation prohibitions are notoriously difficult to enforce.

---

[313] For the purposes of the stabilization regime, 'securities' covers shares and securities equivalent to shares, bonds, and other forms of securitized debt, or securitized debt convertible or exchangeable into shares or into other securities equivalent to shares (Art 3(2)(a)).

[314] Including contracts or rights to subscribe for, acquire, or dispose of the securities, financial derivatives on the securities, and, where the securities are convertible or exchangeable debt instruments, the securities into which the relevant securities can be converted or exchanged: Art 3(2)(b).

[315] The details of all stabilization transactions must be notified by issuers, offerors, or entities undertaking the stabilization acting (or not) on behalf of such persons, to the NCA of the relevant market, no later than the end of the seventh daily market session following the date of execution of the transactions.

[316] Including with respect to conditions for trading, restrictions regarding time and volume, disclosure and reporting obligations, and price conditions.

[317] The Regulation imposed, with respect to stabilization, time restrictions, disclosure and reporting requirements, price conditions, and conditions for 'ancillary stabilization' (or the use by investment firms or credit institutions of additional 'greenshoe' allotments and overallotment facilities which support hedging by investment firms and credit institutions during the offer, often in volatile conditions). It provided that securities could only be overallotted during the subscription period and at the offer price. With respect to buy-back programmes, the Regulation covered, *inter alia*, programme disclosure requirements and trading conditions.

[318] ESMA's initial policy orientations suggest that some refinements can be expected: ESMA/2013/1649, n 94, 8–17.

[319] Bhattacharya and Daouk, n 13, and Bhattacharya, U and Daouk, H, 'When No Law is Better than a Good Law' (2009) 13 *Rev of Finance* 577, pointing to an increase in the cost of capital where such rules are adopted but not enforced. Similarly, Fernandes and Ferreira n 30, showing how the enforcement of insider trading laws has an impact on price informativeness, but only in developed markets, and Beny, L, 'Do Insider Trading Laws Matter? Some Preliminary Comparative Evidence' (2005) 7 *American Law & Economics Rev* 144, linking indicators of financial market development to, broadly, the deterrent strength of insider-dealing

The difficulties which arise in enforcing insider-dealing rules are well known. These include the complex, multilayered nature of the insider-dealing prohibition, the evidentiary and procedural requirements of the criminal law (where insider dealing is criminalized as opposed to being subject to administrative or civil sanctions), and the difficulties which can be experienced by the enforcement authorities in understanding the often complex financial context in which insider dealing must be examined.[320] Administrative sanctions can facilitate enforcement, but they may lack sufficient deterrent effect. Their effectiveness also depends on how easily they may be employed by supervisors and on whether the imposition of financial penalties requires additional recourse to the courts. Private causes of action, where available, typically face high evidentiary hurdles as well as the conceptual difficulties inherent in applying individual remedies to a form of activity which, under the terms of the 2014 MAR at least, is regarded as damaging the marketplace as a whole, rather than particular investors or the company to which the inside information relates.

The enforcement of other market abuse prohibitions is also problematic. The detection of market manipulation and its control is heavily dependent on action by market actors, in particular with respect to the use of trading-surveillance programmes directed towards picking up unusual and possibly manipulative trading activity. The need for efficient co-operation between regulatory authorities, anti-fraud agencies (where relevant), financial, derivative, and spot markets, market participants, and market supervisors is acute.[321] If market abuse is criminalized, its enforcement becomes subject to the evidentiary and procedural hurdles of the criminal law. The difficulties in detecting and enforcing insider dealing and market manipulation are exacerbated in the EU's integrated market, as will be discussed.

VIII.9.2 Supervision

VIII.9.2.1 NCAs

As under the 2003 MAD, supervision of the 2014 MAR is conducted through a network of NCAs; each Member State must designate a single administrative competent authority[322] for the purposes of the Regulation (Article 22).[323] The jurisdictional reach of these authorities is wide: an NCA is responsible for ensuring the 2014 MAR is applied on its territory regarding all actions carried out on its territory, as well as those actions carried out

---

rules, characterized in terms of, *inter alia*, the scope of the prohibition and the enforcement powers of the supervisor. In the EU, there is some evidence to suggest that the intensity of enforcement impacts on the extent to which market abuse rules support strong markets: Christensen et al, n 41.

[320] See Rider, B, 'Policing Insider Dealing in Britain' in Hopt and Wymeersch, n 14, 313, 327–9.

[321] Davies, H, 'Financial Regulation and the Law' (1999) 3 *CFILR* 1, 9–10.

[322] The 2003 MAD, on which these provisions are based, drove significant institutional change to the structure of supervision. Prior to the MAD's application, operators of regulated markets exercised considerable powers with respect to the prevention of market abuse. By 2007, these powers had transferred to administrative authorities, although in practice supervisory tasks were frequently delegated to stock exchanges: 2007 CESR FSC Supervisory Powers Report, n 72, 2.

[323] These authorities are to exercise their functions directly, but can also act in collaboration with other authorities or with market undertakings, by delegation to such authorities or undertakings, or by application to the competent judicial authorities (Art 23(1)).

'abroad' relating to instruments admitted to or trading on in-scope venues within its territory (Article 22).

The extent to which this network-based model can support effective intra-Member State and cross-border supervision depends in large part on the suite of supervisory powers conferred on NCAs, and on how they are applied. While pre-crisis CESR had highlighted the importance of equivalence in supervisory powers to effective home/host supervisory organization,[324] greater convergence of and consistency in supervisory practices emerged as a major policy preoccupation over the crisis era, as discussed in Chapter XI. But the market abuse regime was an early pathfinder in this regard, reflecting the symbiosis between the harmonization of market abuse rules and convergence in operational practices and related cross-border co-operation; supervisory convergence with respect to the suite of supervisory powers conferred on NCAs and how they are deployed appears strong (section 9.2.3).

The 2014 MAR has, however, brought enhancements to NCA powers. The powers with which NCAs are conferred have been strengthened from the 2003 MAD (Article 23) and reflect the strengthening of NCA powers across the crisis-era reforms to EU securities and markets regulation. Member States must generally ensure that appropriate measures are in place so that NCAs have all the supervisory and investigatory powers necessary to fulfil their duties, but a minimum suite of powers is also specified. This suite includes the power to have access to documents and other data in any form, to require or demand information from any person,[325] to carry out inspections or investigations at non-private premises with or without warning, and, in an enhancement to the 2003 MAD, to enter into private premises in order to seize documents and other data in any form, as long as prior authorization is received from the relevant judicial authority and reasonable suspicion exists that the documents or other data may be relevant to prove insider dealing or market manipulation,[326] to request the freezing and/or sequestration of assets, to suspend trading in the financial instrument concerned, to require the temporary cessation of any practice the NCA considers contrary to the 2014 MAR, and to take all necessary measures to ensure that the public is correctly informed (including the correction of false or misleading information). NCAs must also be empowered to require telephone and data traffic from telecommunications operators (as well as from investment firms), where reasonable suspicion exists that such records may be relevant to prove insider dealing or market manipulation. Reflecting the strengthening of enforcement under the 2014 MAR (section 9.3), NCAs must be able to refer matters for criminal investigation. In a significant strengthening of the 2003 MAD, but reflecting the 2014 MAR focus on addressing cross-market abuse, NCAs must also be empowered to request information from related spot market participants directly according to standardized formats, obtain transaction reports, and have direct access to traders' systems.[327]

---

[324] See generally CESR, Preliminary Progress Report. Which Supervisory Tools for the EU Securities Market? An Analytical Paper by CESR (2004) (CESR 04-333f).

[325] Including from those successively involved in the transmission of orders or conduct of the operations concerned, and their principals.

[326] Due process conditions apply to reflect the Charter of Fundamental Rights of the European Union.

[327] As these markets may not be subject to mandatory reporting requirements or have centralized supervision of information. The new power is designed to allow NCAs access to continuous spot market data, and to allow them to monitor real-time data flows, by requiring such data to be submitted directly to them in a specified format and by giving NCAs access to spot market traders' systems: 2011 MAR Proposal, n 77, 11.

VIII.9.2.2 Supervisory Co-operation

Extensive co-operation obligations are imposed under the 2014 MAR, based on those set out in the 2003 MAD.[328] ESMA is to propose ITSs relating to the procedures and forms for co-operation (Article 25(9)), and co-operation is to take place in accordance with the ESMA Regulation (Article 25(1)), but the core legislative requirement is for NCAs to co-operate with each other and ESMA where necessary for the purpose of the Regulation, unless a relevant exception applies (Article 25(1)). In particular, NCAs are to render assistance to each other and to ESMA and, without undue delay, exchange information[329] and co-operate in investigation, supervision, and enforcement activities (Article 25(1)).[330] Reflecting the new focus on enforcement, and with specific reference to criminal sanctions, where a Member State applies criminal sanctions, their NCAs must have all necessary powers to liaise with relevant judicial authorities to receive specific information related to criminal investigations under the 2014 MAR and provide the same to other NCAs and ESMA, in fulfilment of the co-operation obligations. In a similar vein, NCAs must co-operate with respect to facilitating the recovery of pecuniary sanctions. NCAs may also require the assistance of other NCAs regarding on-site inspections or investigations; ESMA must be informed and can, where requested, co-ordinate the investigation or inspection (Article 25(6)).[331]

The limited and exceptional conditions under which an NCA may refuse to act on an information or co-operation request are specified as: where the communication might adversely affect the security of the Member State, compliance would be likely to adversely affect the NCA's own investigation or enforcement activities or, as relevant, a criminal investigation; judicial proceedings have already been initiated in respect of the same persons and action; and a final judgement has already been delivered in relation to the same persons and action (Article 25(2)). Otherwise, an NCA whose request is not acted on within a reasonable time or rejected may refer this to ESMA, who may exercise its ESMA Regulation mediation and enforcement powers (Article 25(6) and (7)).

NCA co-operation with ESMA is expressly addressed under Article 24, which requires NCAs to co-operate with ESMA and to provide ESMA, without delay, with all necessary information; ESMA is to prepare ITSs governing the relevant procedures and forms.

In an attempt to prevent abusive behaviour slipping through jurisdictional loopholes, an NCA is also required to inform the relevant NCAs and ESMA[332] where it is convinced that acts contrary to the 2014 MAR are being, or have been, carried out on the territory of another Member State, or that acts are affecting financial instruments traded on a trading

---

[328] Professional secrecy and data protection requirements apply to NCAs generally and in the cross-border co-operation context.

[329] NCAs must, on request, immediately supply information required under Art 25(1): Art 25(4).

[330] The co-operation obligations extend to the relevant supervisory authorities at national and EU level under the 2011 REMIT Regulation for the energy markets, and to the Commission, as appropriate, with respect to spot markets for agricultural commodities.

[331] The NCA in receipt of the request may provide assistance in various forms, including by carrying out the investigation or inspection itself, allowing the requesting NCA to participate in the investigation or inspection, allowing the NCA to carry the investigation or inspection out independently, appointing auditors or inspectors to carry out the investigation or inspection, or sharing tasks relating to the investigation or inspection with other NCAs (Art 25(6)).

[332] And the ACER, in relation to wholesale energy products.

venue situated within another Member State. The NCAs involved and ESMA must consult each other where this situation arises on the appropriate action to take, inform each other of significant interim developments, and co-ordinate their actions in order to avoid duplication and overlap when applying sanctions in cross-border cases (Article 25(5)).[333]

Specific co-operation obligations address the relationship with spot market authorities. NCAs are to co-operate and exchange information with relevant national and third country regulatory authorities where they have reasonable grounds to suspect that abusive acts under the 2014 MAR are being or have been carried out; ESMA is to play a facilitation and co-ordination role in this regard (Article 25(8)).[334]

Given its extraterritorial reach, the 2014 MAR also addresses co-operation with third countries, imposing, in a significant extension of the 2003 MAD, a co-operation framework on NCAs with respect to their third country relations. Under Article 26, NCAs are, where necessary, to conclude co-operation arrangements (co-ordinated and facilitated, where possible, through ESMA—who, with the other NCAs, must be informed where an NCA proposes such an arrangement—and following an ESMA template), with third country competent authorities concerning information exchange and enforcement of MAR obligations in third countries;[335] ESMA is also, where possible, to facilitate and co-ordinate information exchange between NCAs and third country supervisory authorities. These arrangements are also to include third country spot markets and their authorities (Article 25(8)).

VIII.9.2.3 Supervisory Convergence and ESMA

The extent to which co-operation operates effectively in practice and NCAs deploy their powers effectively is in large part a function of the quality of supervisory convergence with respect to how formal powers are deployed and on the effectiveness of co-operation. In the market abuse area, supervisory convergence and co-operation have been relatively strong, and can be expected to intensify further, given ESMA's suite of supervisory convergence powers (Chapter XI).

CESR monitored levels of supervisory convergence closely in the market abuse field. In its 2005 Annual Report CESR noted generally that differences in applicable laws and processes across the Member States had exposed 'collective weaknesses' in the ability of CESR to take action.[336] Subsequently, and as the 2003 MAD bedded in, the level of formal equivalence in supervisory powers became relatively high. CESR's 2007 Report on Supervisory Powers under the 2003 MAD reported that almost all NCAs had the powers required under the 2003 MAD.[337] NCAs had also developed sophisticated IT tools for direct market surveillance and the detection of market abuse, and were also co-operating with stock exchanges, engaging in on-site inspections, and examining disclosures and reports.[338] Nonetheless, while most difficulties with respect to operational powers arose with respect to enforcement

---

[333] These obligations also apply to authorities responsible for the wholesale energy markets under the REMIT Regulation.

[334] The 2014 MAR specifies the form this co-operation is to take under the emission allowances regime (under Regulation 1031/2010).

[335] Professional secrecy and data protection requirements apply.

[336] CESR, Annual Report (2005) 56.

[337] 2007 CESR FSC Supervisory Powers Report, n 72, 2 and 3.

[338] 2007 CESR FSC Supervisory Powers Report, n 72, 4 and 6–7.

(section 9.3), gaps and weaknesses also emerged with respect to supervisory powers, particularly with respect to the power to compel data from telecommunication operators generally and the power to enter into private premises, which were not available in a number of Member States and which were associated with supervision and enforcement difficulties,[339] and which led to the 2014 MAR enhancements.

But even where supervisory powers and practices are broadly consistent, it is not necessarily the case that co-operation with respect to market abuse investigations is straightforward. Where divergences arise in the expertise and experience of NCAs, for example, a smaller group of NCAs, with sophisticated surveillance tools and large markets, could be required to bear the brunt of the information exchange burden and become net exporters of information.[340] NCA will to co-operate has, however, generally been strong.[341]

Over the CESR era, CESR-Pol, a permanent operational group within CESR responsible for the surveillance of securities markets and the exchange of information, provided operational support to co-operation. Its Surveillance Intelligence Group was designed to foster simultaneous and comprehensive intelligence sharing and to provide a forum for discussion of practical issues of concern arising in the day-to-day supervision of firms and markets. Issues addressed included best practice in dealing with insider-dealing rings, the management of trading halts, suspicious transaction reporting, market manipulation in low-liquidity markets, and investigation techniques. CESR also established an Urgent Issues Group system which allowed CESR-Pol members to co-ordinate and jointly conduct investigations in specific cases, and which was designed to ensure a rapid regulatory response to potential and actual threats to the single market. Joint investigations under the market abuse regime were generally conducted according to the CESR paper on Requests to Open an Investigation and Joint Investigations which was agreed by CESR members in 2005. It established flexible guidelines for the procedures to be followed.

Supervisory convergence is likely to strengthen over the ESMA era. The largely successful CESR co-operation structures have been retained by ESMA (now through ESMA-Pol), and can be expected to benefit from the changed dynamic which ESMA has brought to NCA co-operation generally. ESMA has also sought to support supervisory convergence through peer review of NCA powers and practices. Its 2013 peer review of supervisory practices under the market abuse regime (the 2003 MAD) examined how NCAs assessed whether investment firms and trading venues had appropriate structural provisions in place to ensure compliance with the 2003 MAD, investment firms' handling of insider lists, and NCA handling of rumours.[342] The peer review was positive, finding generally strong supervisory practices across the NCAs and reliance on a wide range of investigative tools.

---

[339] 2011 MAR Proposal Impact Assessment, n 39, 24–5.

[340] The UK FSA, eg, acted as a co-ordinator for the exchange of data among supervisors with respect to the Citigroup bond-trading case: Mayhew, D, 'Market Abuse: Developing a Law for Europe' (2006) 3 *European Company Law* 1.

[341] CESR reported in 2007 that there were no cases of refusals by CESR members to assist another CESR member under the 2003 MAD: 2007 CESR FSC Supervisory Convergence Report, n 72, 10.

[342] ESMA, Supervisory Practices under the Market Abuse Directive: Mapping Report (2013) (ESMA/2013/806) and ESMA, Supervisory Practices under the Market Abuse Directive: Peer Review Report and Good Practices (2013) (ESMA/2013/805).

The peer review is notable for its granular and practical approach,[343] however, which suggests an ESMA determination to review and shape operational practices and monitor best practice.

VIII.9.2.4 Harnessing Market Actors to Supervision

(a) Firm Systems and Suspicious Transaction Reports

Effective control of market abuse requires a number of mechanisms in addition to regulatory prohibitions and supervisory powers, including controls within investment firms, the imposition of reporting requirements on traders, position limits on derivatives which reduce the possibility of unusually large exposures, and the use of trading suspensions as 'circuit-breakers' when necessary to blunt the impact of unusual market volatility. Over the crisis era, the EU regime governing trading has become significantly more sophisticated, and now includes the 2012 Short Selling Regulation as well as the new MiFID II/MiFIR position management and transaction reporting regimes.[344] Although the new trading regime is primarily addressed to supporting market stability, it also supports the integrity of the EU marketplace.

The 2014 MAR does not impose particular trading requirements beyond the prohibitions on insider dealing and market manipulation, but it requires that trading venues and brokers maintain monitoring systems and imposes reporting obligations; these have been strengthened from the 2003 MAR regime. Under Article 16(1),[345] market operators and investment firms that operate a trading venue must establish and maintain effective arrangements, systems, and procedures, aimed at preventing and detecting market abuse and attempts to engage in market abuse, in accordance with MiFID II/MiFIR. These persons must also report orders and transactions that might constitute insider dealing, market manipulation or an attempt to engage in insider dealing or market manipulation to the relevant NCA without delay; the breadth of this obligation, engaging unexecuted orders and attempts, represents a significant strengthening of the 2003 MAD.

A related and controversial monitoring obligation (based on the 2003 MAD) applies to persons professionally arranging or executing transactions in financial instruments; in a strengthening of the 2003 MAD, they must have systems in place to detect and report suspicious orders and transactions.[346]

While such persons had been subject to a reporting obligation under the 2003 MAD, this has been strengthened: where such a person has a 'reasonable suspicion' that an order or transaction in any financial instrument, whether placed or executed on or outside a trading venue, 'might constitute insider dealing or market manipulation' or an attempt to engage in either, it must notify the NCA without delay.[347] These persons are subject to the notification

---

[343] The best practice guidelines, eg, are practical in nature, including that NCAs ensure the quality of market abuse detection systems is appropriately assessed (with 'deep attention') during the investment firm authorization process, while the questionnaire against which NCA supervisory practices were assessed was detailed and practical: eg, 2013 Peer Review Report, n 342, 13–14 and 51–2.

[344] Ch VI.

[345] Which is to be amplified by RTSs.

[346] The 2003 MAD equivalent provisions were the subject of the 2013 peer review (n 342).

[347] During the original 2003 MAD negotiations, the Commission proposed a prohibition on dealing where the relevant person had suspicions about the transaction. This was changed to a notification requirement by the European Parliament on the basis that a dealing prohibition was inappropriate as firms did not

rules of the Member State in which they are registered, and the notification is made to that NCA;[348] NCAs must transmit the notifications made to the NCAs of the trading venues concerned. While broadly similar to the 2003 MAD reporting regime, the inclusion of suspicions relating to attempts at insider dealing or market manipulation, the extension to orders and to OTC trading, and the requirement for related monitoring systems extends its scope considerably. RTSs will amplify the related necessary arrangements, systems, and procedures, and the notification templates for reports.

The original regime (termed the Suspicious Transaction Reports (STR) regime), which applied only to persons professionally arranging transactions, was amplified by extensive administrative rules by the 2004 Commission AMP Directive which addressed when the notification obligation arose, the relevant time-frame, the content of the notification, and the related liability and professional secrecy regimes. It provided that relevant persons consider, on a 'case by case basis', whether there were 'reasonable grounds' for suspecting that a transaction involved insider dealing or market manipulation, and required the necessary notification to be made without delay once the relevant person became aware of facts or information which gave reasonable grounds for suspicion. The administrative regime provided little guidance, however, as to when suspicion should arise, save to refer to the constituent elements of market manipulation and insider dealing and to note that while certain transactions could by themselves appear innocent, they might provide indications of market abuse when regarded in conjunction with transactions, certain behaviour, and other information. The RTSs to be adopted under the new regime might be expected to follow a similar model, but also to reflect the significant market concern as to the effectiveness of the 2003 MAD STR regime, which not all NCAs found to be useful.[349]

(b) Whistle-blowing

In addition, the 2014 MAR, reflecting international trends as well as the inclusion of similar measures in other crisis-era securities and markets measures,[350] engages with 'whistle-blowing'[351] (Article 32). Member States are to ensure NCAs establish effective mechanisms to enable reporting of actual or potential breaches of the 2014 MAR to NCAs.[352] The MAR specifies that these must include procedures for receipt of reports and follow-up (including secure communication channels), employment protections for reporting persons, and protection of the personal data of the reporting and accused persons, including with respect to preserving the confidentiality of relevant persons. Employers engaging in activities which are regulated for financial services purposes must have in place appropriate internal procedures for reporting breaches. Financial incentives may be granted

---

have the expertise to make a judgement over whether the transaction amounted to insider dealing or market manipulation: First ECON Report, n 66, 33.

[348] Or the rules of where the branch is located, in the case of a branch (and to the branch NCA).

[349] 2009 CESR Options and Derogations Report, n 72, 14–15. Most NCAs, however, regularly communicate with the market relating to the importance of these reports and take enforcement action on the foot of failures with respect to the reports: 2013 Peer Review, n 343, 22–4.

[350] Including the 2014 MiFID II/MiFIR.

[351] See, eg, Fleischer, H and Schmolke, K-U, Financial Incentives for Whistleblowers in European Capital Markets Law? Legal Policy Considerations on the Reform of the Market Abuse Regime, ECGI Law WP No 189/2012 (2012), available at <http://ssrn.com/abstract=2124678>.

[352] The new regime is designed to address the appropriate design of incentives and how to mitigate fear of retaliation: rec 74.

in conformity with national law, and where reporting persons do not already have an obligation to report, the information is new, and it results in the imposition of an administrative measure or sanction, or a criminal sanction, for breach of the 2014 MAR. The new regime is to be amplified by administrative Commission acts.

VIII.9.3 Enforcement

VIII.9.3.1 Enforcement and the Market Abuse Regime

The success of the market abuse regime depends heavily on effective enforcement; diverging levels of enforcement can damage market integrity, diminish trust between NCAs, and lead to prejudicial regulatory arbitrage. But enforcement has only recently become a concern of EU securities and markets regulation, under the crisis-era reform programme (Chapter XI).[353] Enforcement and sanctions have, however, long been a concern of the market abuse regime: divergences across, and weaknesses within, Member States' sanctioning regimes were, from an early point in the application of the 2003 MAD,[354] recognized as a threat to its effectiveness.

This was borne out in CESR's 2007 Supervisory Convergence Report which noted considerable differences in the range of civil and criminal sanctions available to NCAs and in the form and content of sanctions.[355] There was little consistency in the application of sanctions, with some NCAs deploying sophisticated approaches including expedited settlement mechanisms, others applying administrative sanctions only to breaches of reporting obligations and relying heavily on criminal sanctions, other authorities inexperienced in dealing with market abuse issues,[356] and considerable differences with respect to the size of financial penalty which could be imposed. CESR's Chairman highlighted the market abuse regime as an area in which supervisory co-operation between NCAs was working reasonably well, but in which co-ordination difficulties had arisen over the imposition of penalties in different Member States.[357]

Very considerable divergences also emerged between Member States in the procedures applicable to enforcement actions, leading to cross-border market participants finding it difficult to navigate a Member State's enforcement procedures, whether through a regulatory tribunal or other mechanism. There was no consistency on access to decisions, making it difficult for market participants to predict how enforcement operated in practice and obstructing the evolution of a body of practice and case law on the market abuse regime.[358]

---

[353] The new approach to sanctioning was set out initially in Commission, Communication on Reinforcing Sanctioning Regimes in the Financial Sector (2010) (COM (2010) 716).

[354] While the 2003 MAD adopted a light-touch approach to sanctioning, rec 39 of the 2003 MAD cautioned Member States on the need to remain alert when determining sanctions to the need to ensure a degree of uniformity of regulation from one Member State to another.

[355] 2007 CESR FSC Supervisory Powers Report, n 72, 4. CESR also produced a distinct report on sanctions: CESR, Report on Administrative Measures and Sanctions as well as the Criminal Sanctions available in Member States under the Market Abuse Directive (2007) (CESR/07-693).

[356] ESME also reported on great disparity in enforcement practices: 2007 ESME Report, n 73, 19.

[357] European Securities Committee Minutes, 26 June 2006.

[358] Mayhew, D and Anderson, K, 'Whither Market Abuse (In a More Principles-Based Regulatory World)?' (2007) 22 *JIBLR* 516, 522–3. The authors argued that a body of case law was required to inform market participants of the scope and meaning of the regime and pointed to the increasing volume of decisions emerging from national supervisors (particularly from the French AMF) which should be subject to consistent disclosure.

Neither was there convergence on the level of reasoning disclosed by authorities on typically fact-driven enforcement actions and where the final decision could reflect a settlement between the parties.[359] More generally, a lack of consistency in the publication of settlements, where used, raised the risk of a perception that market abuse was not enforced, while the inability to adopt a settlement (subject to some public disclosure) limited the ability of supervisors to achieve quick results.[360]

Sanctions and enforcement procedures aside, the consistency with which the market abuse regime is applied and enforced pan-EU, and its related effectiveness, depends on the complex range of institutional, resource, experience, and political dynamics which influence how NCAs operate and take enforcement action. In the UK, for example, the (then) Financial Services Authority's enforcement efforts in the market abuse field increased sharply shortly after the crisis, reflecting the (then) UK Financial Services Authority (FSA's) move to a more intense 'credible deterrence' enforcement strategy. Over 2010, for example, 16 'Final Notices', concerning enforcement action in the market abuse sphere, were issued by the FSA, as compared to eight in total over 2009 and six in 2008.[361] While data of this nature is raw, it points to a change in enforcement behaviour (which has continued)[362] which is hard not to relate to the pressure the FSA came under with the eruption of the financial crisis and the prospect (since realized) of its being dismantled. Different levels of experience between NCAs, particularly with respect to sophisticated market practices, also militate against a consistent approach to the treatment of market abuse. In addition, the harmonized regime is based on subtle and complex concepts, which are often unclear, and which require the exercise of careful judgement. Under the 2003 MAD, the high-profile Citigroup 'Dr Evil' bond trade, for example, generated different regulatory responses across the EU to the same conduct.[363] Operational factors also drive divergence. Resource allocation to NCAs is an important determinant of the extent to which effective action can be taken against market abuse.[364] But resource allocation is often a function of local market and political conditions.[365]

Pan-EU divergences with respect to enforcement appear to be persistent. ESMA's 2012 report on sanctioning under the 2003 MAD revealed persistent and strong divergences in enforcement.[366] It reported on a host of divergent rules and practices, including differences

---

[359] Mayhew, D, 'Market Abuse: Developing a Law for Europe' (2006) 3 *European Company Law* 1, 4.

[360] ESME was particularly concerned as to the limited use of settlement mechanisms as a quick and effective means of enforcement, and about inconsistencies in the public disclosure of settlements: n 73, 19.

[361] Data available via <http://www.fsa.gov.uk/pages/About/What/financial_crime/market_abuse/index.shtml>.

[362] In its Annual Report for 2011–2012, the FSA reported that it was continuing to pursue its credible deterrence strategy forcefully to combat insider dealing and market abuse, and its related step up in enforcement activity (at 45). The 2012–2013 Annual Report reported on a 'successful year that has seen the culmination of many years' work in several criminal and non-criminal investigations' and the conclusion of a 'record number' of insider-dealing trials: 37–38. The Financial Conduct Authority (which has replaced the FSA as the new conduct regulator since April 2013) has committed to robust enforcement of market abuse violations: FSA, Journey to the FCA (2012) 38–9.

[363] One commentator suggested that the different responses could have reflected different levels of exposure to sophisticated trading strategies: Mayhew, n 359, 2.

[364] Jackson, H and Roe, M, 'Public and Private Enforcement of Securities Laws: Resource-Based Evidence' (2009) 93 *J Fin Econ* 207.

[365] Enriques and Gatti, n 37, 10.

[366] ESMA, Actual Use of Sanctioning Powers under the MAD (2012) (ESMA/2012/270).

relating to: legal frameworks, including with respect to the relationship between NCAs and judicial authorities; the range of powers available for the detection of market manipulation and insider-dealing abuses; procedural approaches to the pre-investigation, investigation, and sanctioning stages; the factors determining whether enforcement action would be taken; resources and NCA specialization and organization; the use of settlement procedures; levels of pecuniary sanction; and standards of proof. Prior to the 2014 MAR reforms, major gaps existed in the pan-EU pecuniary sanctioning regime, with administrative pecuniary sanctions not available for insider dealing in four Member States or for market manipulation in eight Member States.[367]

While ESMA can drive stronger convergence with respect to enforcement, convergence operates within and is constrained by the supporting legal framework. Radical legislative action has also, however, followed with respect to the sanctioning process.

VIII.9.3.2 The New Sanctions Regime

The 2014 MAR was the first crisis-era measure to grapple with the optimum way to harmonize sanctions, and provided the template for the new approach to sanctioning across EU securities and markets regulation generally. At the heart of the new regime is a concern to avoid regulatory arbitrage and to support the 2014 MAR rulebook in driving market transparency and integrity.[368]

The core requirement placed on Member States reflects the earlier, and more basic 2003 MAD regime.[369] Under Article 30, and without prejudice to criminal sanctions, Member States must provide for NCAs to have the power to take 'appropriate administrative measures and sanctions' required under the 2014 MAR; the measures and sanctions available must be notified to the Commission and ESMA.

In a step change from the 2003 MAD, the 2014 MAR specifies the specific breaches of the MAR which, at a minimum, must be subject to administrative measures (Article 30(1)); [370] Member States may choose not to apply administrative sanctions where criminal sanctions apply. In a similarly significant innovation, the 2014 MAR also specifies in detail the types of measure and sanction which must be available (Article 30(2)).[371] In another major reform, Article 30(2) specifies that pecuniary sanctions must be available and sets the

---

[367] 2011 MAR Proposal Impact Assessment, n 39, 25–6. The Commission reported that the range of administrative pecuniary sanctions ranged from €200 or less (four Member States with respect to insider dealing and nine Member States with respect to market manipulation) to €1 million or more (ten Member States with respect to insider dealing and 14 Member States with respect to market manipulation): at 26.

[368] 2011 MAR Proposal, n 77, 12.

[369] The 2003 MAD's approach, which was an advance from the 1989 IDD in that it ventured into sanctioning territory, was tentative. It simply required that administrative sanctions be employed. While novel at the time, its weaknesses rapidly became apparent.

[370] The list is extensive, covering the key elements of the 2014 MAR and addressing breaches of the insider dealing and market manipulation provisions, but also failures to comply with, eg, the disclosure, insider lists, managers' transactions, and investment recommendations/statistics requirements, and failures to co-operate or comply in an investigation, or with an inspection or request.

[371] Injunctions; orders for the disgorgement of profits gained or losses avoided through the breach; public warnings; withdrawal or suspension of investment firm authorization; temporary bans against persons discharging managerial responsibility in an investment firm or any other natural person who is held responsible, from exercising management functions, and, in the event of repeated breaches of Arts 14 and 15, a permanent ban on such persons; and a temporary ban on such persons from dealing on own account. The banning powers represent a significant enhancement from the 2003 MAD.

minimum quantam.[372] A maximum administrative pecuniary sanction of at least three times the amount of the profits gained or losses avoided because of the breach must be available. The 2014 MAR also specifies for natural persons maximum administrative pecuniary sanctions of at least €5 million in respect of breaches of Articles 14 and 15, €500,000 for breaches of Articles 18-20, and €1 million for breaches of Article 16 and 17. In respect of legal persons, the maximum sanctions must be at least €15 million or 15 per cent of total annual turnover,[373] €1 million, and €2.5 million or 2 per cent of total annual turnover, respectively. This obligation is not a maximum harmonization obligation; NCAs may have other sanctioning powers and impose higher levels of pecuniary sanction. The 2014 MAR also specifies how administrative measures and sanctions are to be applied (Article 31); NCAs are to take into account all relevant circumstances, including, where appropriate, the gravity and duration of the breach, the degree of responsibility of the relevant person, the financial strength of the person,[374] the importance of the profits gained or losses avoided, the level of co-operation by the relevant person and previous breaches by that person, and measures taken, after the breach, by the relevant person to prevent the repetition of the breach.

A highly controversial[375] 'name and shame' mechanism, designed to harness market discipline dynamics in this area,[376] attaches to sanctioning (Article 34). Each decision imposing an administrative measure or sanction must be published by the NCA on its website immediately after the person sanctioned is informed (and ESMA notified; ESMA must also accordingly update its register of investment firms (Article 33 (4)).[377] The reporting obligation does not apply to investigatory measures.[378] Where publication of the identity of legal persons or personal data of natural persons is considered by the NCA to be disproportionate, following a case-by-case assessment as to proportionality, or as jeopardizing the stability of financial markets or an ongoing investigation, NCAs can either delay publication, publish on an anonymous basis, or not publish.[379] The outcome of any appeal must also be published.

The new sanctions regime is also subject to an NCA/ESMA reporting obligation to enhance monitoring and support convergence.[380] NCAs must provide ESMA annually with aggregated information regarding all administrative measures, sanctions, and fines imposed under the 2014 MAR, which must be published by ESMA in an annual report. NCAs must also

---

[372] Negotiations on the quantam were difficult. The Member States, in particular, disagreed as to the level, with some concerns that the proposed levels were too high and disproportionate in relation to other offences in the Member State, and others arguing that they were too low and lacked deterrent effect. The compromise solution was to allow Member States to adopt higher levels than the 2014 MAR's minimum thresholds: Danish Presidency MAR Progress Report, n 85, 4.

[373] Calculated by reference to the formula set out in Art 30.

[374] As indicated in particular by total annual turnover or annual income.

[375] The Council struggled to reach agreement on this issue, with some Member States opposed and others regarding it as a necessary deterrent: Danish Presidency MAR Progress Report, n 85, 4.

[376] CESR had earlier identified convergence in the use of 'naming and shaming strategies' as of considerable importance, given the importance of these strategies in placing pressure on market participants: 2007 CESR FSC Supervisory Convergence Report, n 72, 9.

[377] The report must identify the person concerned and the type and nature of the breach.

[378] While the 2003 MAD contained a similar regime, it was optional.

[379] The decision not to publish can be taken where the NCA decides that delayed or anonymous publication is insufficient to ensure that the stability of financial markets would not be jeopardized, or that publication would be disproportionate, where the measure in question is deemed to be minor.

[380] The process is to be governed by ITSs.

provide ESMA annually with anonymized and aggregated data on all related administrative investigations undertaken (Article 33). Where criminal sanctions apply to the relevant breaches of the 2014 MAR which require administrative measures, NCAs must provide ESMA annually with anonymized and aggregated data on all criminal investigations undertaken and criminal penalties imposed by judicial authorities; data on criminal sanctions must be published annually by ESMA (Article 33).

VIII.9.3.3 Criminal Sanctions

As noted above, considerable divergences exist with respect to the availability of criminal sanctions; neither in the case of insider dealing nor that of market manipulation do all Member States provides for a criminal sanction.[381] In a striking reform,[382] Member States must impose criminal sanctions on insider dealing and market manipulation, in accordance with minimum standards and as required under the 2014 MAD, which accompanies the 2014 MAR.[383]

The 2014 MAD is the first legislative proposal to be adopted under Article 83(2) TFEU, which provides for the adoption of common minimum rules on criminal law (where this is essential to ensure the effective implementation of a harmonized EU policy) and is a landmark measure with respect to the pan-EU enforcement of EU securities and markets regulation.[384] The 2014 MAD is deeply rooted in the crisis-era policy concern to strengthen the enforcement of EU securities and markets regulation generally, and the market abuse regime specifically. The related 2011 MAD Proposal[385] was designed to strengthen the sanctions available across the EU and their dissuasive effect, remove the significant divergences across the Member States with respect to the deployment and availability of criminal sanctions, and strengthen the market abuse regime by 'demonstrating social disapproval of a qualitatively different nature compared to administrative sanctions'.[386] Despite its pioneering nature, the crisis era (and in particular the Libor scandal)[387] created supportive political conditions for criminalizing market abuse, although the negotiations were not straightforward, given in particular the implications of the regime for Member States' criminal justice systems (including with respect to the privilege against self-incrimination)[388] and difficulties (in the Council in particular) relating to the distinction between administrative offences under the 2014 MAR and criminal offences under the

---

[381] 2011 MAR Proposal Impact Assessment, n 39, 27.

[382] Which divided stakeholders over the MAD review process. Industry and some NCAs tended to be hostile or sceptical: 2011 MAR Proposal Impact Assessment, n 39, 56.

[383] See generally Herlin-Karnell, E, 'White-collar Crime and the European Financial Crisis: Getting Tougher on EU Market Abuse' (2012) *ELJ* 481.

[384] The UK chose to exercise its opt-out under this provision, given that its criminal justice regime already provides for offences with respect to market abuse. Its decision was primarily motivated by concerns as to sequencing with the MAR, and not with the substantive elements of the regime. It is expected to opt-in in the future: House of Commons, Ministerial Statement, 20 February 2012.

[385] COM (2011) 654. It was amended in 2012 to incorporate offences related to the manipulation of benchmarks.

[386] n 385, 3.

[387] The European Parliament strongly supported the Proposal and strengthened it (notably by introducing minimum terms of imprisonment), frequently adverting to the need for strong enforcement following the Libor scandal: eg, European Parliament Press Release 4 February 2014 (following the Parliament and Council agreement on the text). The Libor scandal is also referenced in the Directive: rec 7.

[388] Council discussions were accordingly carried on in the Justice and Home Affairs (JHA) Council in co-ordination with ECOFIN discussions on the 2014 MAR.

2014 MAD and to whether intention alone should be the governing factor, or whether criteria to determine whether an offence was sufficiently serious to constitute a criminal offence should be included in the MAD (these criteria were not ultimately added to the text but were noted in the recitals).[389] The Proposal did not change significantly over the negotiations, although the regime became more extensive, with the final text including minimum harmonized standards governing imprisonment terms and the criminal offences being extended to include unlawful disclosure of inside information. Progress was slowed by the parallel negotiations on the 2014 MAR; following the final MAD trilogue negotiations between the Commission, Council, and European Parliament, political agreement was finally reached between the Council and Parliament in December 2013.

The 2014 MAD is a minimum harmonizing measure which requires Member States to provide criminal sanctions for insider dealing, unlawful disclosure of inside information, and market manipulation, to ensure the integrity of financial markets in the EU and to enhance investor protection and confidence in those markets (Article 1(1));[390] Member States are also required to ensure appropriate training is provided to the authorities and staff involved in criminal proceedings and investigations with respect to the Directive's objectives (Article 11). Its scope maps that of the 2014 MAR: the Directive applies to financial instruments (as defined under the 2014 MAR and by reference to the 2014 MiFID II/MiFIR) admitted to trading on a regulated market (or for which a request for admission to trading has been made); financial instruments traded or admitted to trading on an MTF (or for which a request for admission to trading on an MTF has been made); OTF-traded financial instruments; and financial instruments not otherwise covered, but the price or value of which depends on, or has an effect on, the price or value of in-scope financial instruments (including, but not limited to CDSs and CfDs) (Article 1(2)). It also applies to the auctioning on an auction platform of emission allowances or other auctioned products. More generally, the Directive applies to any transaction, order, or behaviour which has an effect on the price or value of an in-scope financial instrument, irrespective of whether the activity in question takes place on a trading venue (Article 1(4)). Trading in buy-back programmes and for the stabilization of securities, in each case in accordance with the 2014 MAR, falls outside the Directive.[391] The jurisdictional scope of the Directive is wide to support enforcement. Member States must take the necessary steps to established their jurisdiction over the offences established by the Directive where the offence has been committed in whole or in part within their territory, or by one of their nationals, at least in cases where the act is an offence where it was committed (Article 10).[392]

The 2014 MAD criminal offences are closely based on the 2014 MAR regime which supports administrative offences, although the criminal offences are distinctly defined under the MAD (and in particular include a 'serious' element and an intention requirement, which do not

---

[389] Presidency Report, Proposal for a Directive on Criminal Sanctions—Outstanding Issues, 3 July 2012 (Council Document 12089/12).

[390] Member States can adopt more stringent systems; rec 21, eg, suggests that Member States may provide that the offence of market manipulation is committed where the conduct is reckless or seriously negligent.

[391] As do transactions, orders, and behaviours in support of monetary, exchange rate, or public debt management policy, the EU's climate policy, or its common agriculture and fisheries policies.

[392] A Member State must inform the Commission where it decides to establish jurisdiction over an offence committed outside its territory where the offender has his or her habitual residence in its territory or the offence is committed for the benefit of a legal person established in its territory.

apply to sanctions under the 2014 MAR); the 2014 MAD is accordingly designed to complement the MAR. The required insider-dealing offence (Article 3) (Member States must take the necessary measures to ensure it is a criminal offence) applies to insider dealing and recommending or inducing another person to engage in insider dealing, at least in 'serious cases'[393] and where committed intentionally. Article 3 defines insider dealing for the purposes of the criminal offences in accordance with the 2014 MAR, and as arising where a person possesses inside information and uses that information by acquiring or disposing of, for his own account or the account of a third party, either directly or indirectly, financial instruments to which that information relates, and with respect to persons who possess inside information as a result being a member of the issuer's governance bodies, having a holding in the issuer's capital, having access to the information through the exercise of an employment, profession or duties, or being involved in criminal activities (as well as persons who obtain inside information under other circumstances, but where the person knows it is inside information) (Article 3(1)–(3)). For the purposes of the criminal offence, the use of inside information by cancelling or amending an order, where the order was placed before the person possessed the inside information, is also considered as insider dealing (Article 3(4)). The recommending or inducing offence arises where the person possesses inside information and recommends, on the basis of the information, that another person acquire or dispose of financial instruments to which the information relates (or induces that person to make such an acquisition or disposal), or recommends, on the basis of the information, that another person cancel or amend an order covering a financial instrument to which that information relates (or induces that person to make such a cancellation or amendment) (Article 3(6)).[394] Under Article 4, Member States must also take the necessary measures to ensure that the unlawful disclosure of inside information constitutes a criminal offence, at least in serious cases and when committed intentionally. The offence arises where a person (within the scope of Article 3) in possession of inside information discloses it to another person (except where disclosure is made in the normal course of an employment, profession, or duties, and including where the disclosure takes the form of a 'market sounding' under the 2014 MAR). The onward disclosure of recommendations or inducements (under Article 3(6)) amounts to unlawful disclosure when the person disclosing knows that the recommendations or inducements were based on inside information. This offence must be applied, however, in accordance with the need to protect the freedom of the press and of expression (Article 4(5)).

Market manipulation must also be treated as a criminal offence, at least in serious cases[395] and when committed intentionally (Article 5). The 2014 MAD follows the 2014 MAR approach, defining market manipulation as comprising: entering into a transaction, placing

---

[393] This key distinguishing factor for the criminal offence is not specified, allowing Member States significant discretion. Rec 11, however, suggests (in general terms) that insider dealing (and unlawful disclosure) should be deemed to be 'serious' in cases such as where the impact on market integrity, the actual potential profit derived or loss avoided, the level of damage to the market, or the overall value of the instruments traded is high. Whether the offence has been committed within the framework of a criminal organization, or by a person who has previously committed an offence, are also identified as relevant factors.

[394] The use of the recommendations or inducements amounts to insider dealing when the person so using knows that it is based on inside information (Art 3(7)).

[395] Rec 12 identifies the same factors governing 'serious' as apply to insider dealing and unlawful disclosure (n 393), with the addition of whether the level of alteration of the value of the instruments or the funds deployed is high, and whether the person in question is employed in the financial sector or in a supervisory or regulatory authority.

an order to trade, or any other behaviour which either gives false or misleading signals as to the supply of, demand for, or price of, a financial instrument or a related spot commodity contract, or secures the price of one or several financial instruments or a related spot commodity contract at an abnormal or artificial level—in each case unless the reasons for so doing of the person are legitimate, and the transactions or orders are in conformity with accepted market practices on the relevant trading venues; entering into a transaction, placing an order to trade, or any other behaviour which affects the price of one or several financial instruments or a related spot commodity contract, which employs a fictitious device or any other form of deception or contrivance; dissemination of information through the media, including the internet, or by any other means which gives false or misleading signals as to the supply of, demand for, or price of a financial instrument (or a related spot commodity contract), or secures the price of one or several financial instruments (or a related spot commodity contract) at an abnormal or artificial level, where the person in question derives for themselves or another person an advantage or profit from the dissemination of the information; or transmitting false or misleading information, or providing false or misleading inputs or another behaviour which manipulates the calculation of a benchmark.[396]

Inciting, aiding, or abetting these offences, and attempts to engage in insider dealing or market manipulation must also be punishable as criminal offences (Article 6).

The relevant criminal penalties for natural persons must be punishable by 'effective, proportionate and dissuasive criminal penalties' (Article 7). A minimum-harmonization requirement applies in that the insider dealing and market manipulation offences must be punishable by at least a maximum term of imprisonment of at least four years, and the unlawful disclosure offence by a maximum term of imprisonment of at least two years. A distinct regime applies to legal persons. Under Article 8, Member States must take the necessary measures to ensure that legal persons can be held liable for offences committed for their benefit by a person, acting either individually or as part of an organ of the legal person, and having a 'leading position' with the legal person.[397] Legal persons must also be held liable where a lack of supervision or control by a person in a leading position has made possible the commission of an offence for the benefit of the legal person, under its authority.[398] Legal persons must be subject to effective, proportionate, and dissuasive sanctions, which must include criminal (or non-criminal) fines and may include other sanctions such as exclusion from entitlement to public benefits or aid, temporary or permanent disqualification from the practice of commercial activities, being placed under judicial supervision, judicial winding-up, or temporary or permanent closure of establishments used for committing the offence.

---

[396] Art 5 also covers behaviours relating to the auctioning of emission allowances (or other auctioned products based thereon) (Art 1(2)) and similarly also extends to spot commodity contracts (apart from wholesale energy products) where the transaction, order, or behaviour has an effect on the price of value of an in-scope financial instrument, and to types of financial instruments including derivative contracts or instruments for the transfer of credit risk where the transaction, order, bid, or behaviour has an effect on the price or value of a spot commodity contract where the price or value depends on the price or value of those financial instruments, and to behaviour in relation to benchmarks (Art 1(4)).

[397] This position being based on a power of representation of the legal person; an authority to take decisions on behalf of the legal person; and authority to exercise control within the legal person.

[398] Liability of legal persons does not exclude criminal proceedings against natural persons who are involved as perpetrators, inciters, or accessories in the offences.

IX

THE RETAIL MARKETS

IX.1 Investor Protection, Regulation, and the EU

IX.1.1 Regulation and the Retail Markets

Retail market-orientated[1] regulation in the securities and markets sphere can be associated with two objectives: the traditional objective of protecting investors and the objective of promoting long-term household saving through the markets, which is more recent in origin.

With respect to the first objective, investor protection-directed regulation in the retail markets has long been concerned with addressing market failures arising from the wide information asymmetry between retail investors and professional market actors, and from the related risks and costs.[2] These risks and costs are exacerbated first by the agency relationship which strongly characterizes retail investor engagement with the markets,[3] and second by the severe behavioural risks to which retail investors are exposed. With respect to the latter, a massive canon of literature and a rapidly growing empirical data set make clear that retail investors are vulnerable to significant decision-making weaknesses and to biases which damage optimum decision-making.[4] Retail investors are vulnerable to these weaknesses and biases being exploited and, absent exploitation, to making poor investment decisions.[5]

---

[1] Retail-orientated regulation is often termed household-orientated regulation; the terms retail investor and household investor are used throughout this Chapter.

[2] eg Howells, G, 'The Potential and Limits of Consumer Empowerment by Information' (2005) 32 *J of Law and Society* 349 and Garten, H, 'The Consumerization of Financial Regulation' (1999) 77 *Washington University LQ* 287. Consumer financial markets generally have been described as providing 'the textbook case of market failure due to information asymmetries': Campbell, J, Jackson, E, Madrian, B, and Tufano, P, 'Consumer Financial Protection' (2011) 25 *J Econ Perspectives* 91.

[3] Given in particular heavy reliance on investment advisers and similar distribution channels (eg Choi, S, 'A Framework for the Regulation of Securities Market Intermediaries' (2004) 1 *Berkeley Business LJ* 45) and on collective investment schemes (CISs) (eg Mahoney, P, 'Manager-Investor Conflicts in Mutual Funds' (2004) 18 *J of Econ Perspectives* 161).

[4] For an extensive review of the literature see Decision Technology, Chater, N, Huck, S, Inderst, R, and Online Interactive Research, Consumer Decision Making in Retail Investment Services: A Behavioural Economics Perspective (2010) (2010 Consumer Decision Making Study) 24–84.

[5] In the crisis-era context see, eg, Barr, M, Mullainathan, S, and Shafir, E, 'Behaviourally Informed Regulation' in Shafir, E (ed), *Behavioural Foundations of Policy* (2012) 442, Kingsford Smith, D, 'Regulating Investment Risk: Individuals and the Global Financial Crisis' (2009) 32 *University of New South Wales LJ* 514, and Avgouleas, E, 'Reforming Investor Protection Regulation: The Impact of Cognitive Biases' in Faure, M, and Stephen, F (eds), *Essays in the Law and Economics of Regulation. In Honour of Anthony Ogus* (2008). Pre-crisis see, eg, Campbell, J, 'Household Finance' (2006) 61 *J Fin* 1553, Stout, L, 'The Mechanisms of Market

These risks to retail investors are generated through a number of channels. Retail investors typically rely heavily on market intermediation in the form of investment product distribution (whether through advice or other distribution channels). But investment product distribution is vulnerable to deep conflict-of-interest risks, arising from the limited ability of retail investors to monitor the incidence of commission and other incentive risks in the sale of third party products and equivalent risks related to the distribution of proprietary products. Investment products themselves can be poorly designed, overly complex, and have a tendency to proliferate, reflecting a failure of market discipline which in turn reflects retail investor decision-making difficulties and commission risk in the product distribution chain. Retail investors can also face severe difficulties with product and distribution-related disclosures.

The classical response to market failures of this type is to correct information failures by means of disclosure requirements, and thereby to support investors in achieving efficient bargains. But in the retail market, regulation has long had a more paternalistic dimension and has been more interventionist and supportive of the investor decision.[6] Regulation accordingly typically seeks to address the major failures which beset the retail markets through product design rules, distribution rules (including conduct rules relating to fair treatment, the quality of advice, and conflict-of-interest management), and disclosure requirements.

With respect to the second objective, retail investor protection regulation also has a less defensive and more proactive dimension. Greater responsibility for financial planning and welfare provision is being imposed on individuals and households; welfare is increasingly being privatized and governments are seeking stronger individual financial independence.[7] Retail market investment is increasingly necessary to finance retirement, education, and other social needs, and is becoming more of a mass market, consumer activity than a speculative, wealth accumulation activity reserved to the few;[8] households and individuals are being 'empowered' and 'financialized',[9] and markets are being 'democratized' through large-scale public participation, whether direct or indirect.[10] While this phenomenon is particularly associated with the pre-crisis era, the financial crisis and the EU's related fiscal crisis led to the need to monetize EU household savings as part of the response to the sovereign debt crisis and to the related socialization of bank and sovereign debt. And while

---

Efficiency: An Introduction to the New Finance' (2003) 28 *J Corp L* 635, Gilson, R, and Kraakman, R, 'The Mechanisms of Market Efficiency Twenty Years Later: the Hindsight Bias' (2003) 28 *J Corp L* 215, and Prentice, R, 'Whither Securities Regulation? Some Behavioural Observations Regarding Proposals for its Future' (2002) 51 *Duke LJ* 1397.

[6] See, eg, Ogus, A, 'Regulatory Paternalism: When is it Justified' in Hopt, K, Wymeersch, E, Kanda, H, and Baum, H (eds), *Corporate Governance in Context* (2005) 303.

[7] eg Borio, C, Change and Constancy in the Financial System: Implications for Financial Distress and Policy, BIS WP No 237 (2007), available via at <http://ssrn.com/abstract=1022874> and Ageing and Pension System Reform: Implications for Financial Markets and Economic Policies (2005) (a report prepared at the request of the Deputies of the G10 by an experts' group chaired by Visco, I, Banca d'Italia) (the 2005 G10 Report). See further Moloney, N, *How to Protect Investors. Lessons from the EC and the UK* (2012) 47–3.

[8] Zingales, L, 'The Future of Securities Regulation' (2009) 47 *J of Accounting Research* 391.

[9] eg Kingsford Smith, n 5; Ertürk, I, Froud, J, Johal, S, Leaver, A, and Williams, K, 'The Democratization of Finance? Promises, Outcomes and Conditions' (2007) 14 *Rev of International Political Economy* 553, and Ireland, P, 'Shareholder Primacy and the Distribution of Wealth,' (2005) 68 *MLR* 4981.

[10] eg Shiller, R, *The Subprime Solution* (2008).

the crisis wrought destruction to household savings,[11] it remains the case that financial markets allow households to smooth consumption over lifetimes, providing the means to accumulate and de-cumulate assets.[12] Derivative products, for example, carry the promise of allowing households to hedge against future fluctuations in house prices.[13]

In this regard, retail investor protection regulation can be regarded as playing a more proactive role and as having 'marketing' undertones[14] and 'responsibilizing' functions,[15] and as promoting the importance of financial independence though long-term market-based savings.[16] The capable and informed retail investors which should be the outcome of this form of investor protection regulation can also be 'enrolled' in the regulatory process, monitoring the market, exerting competitive pressures, and accepting responsibility for their actions.[17] The responsibilities of regulators can accordingly be reduced.[18]

Both objectives can be associated, to greater and lesser degrees, with different regulatory strategies. The more traditional investor protection objective, concerned with preventing malfeasance, can be associated with typical interventionist regulatory strategies, such as process-related controls on distribution and advice, marketing restrictions, and product authorization requirements. The more proactive marketing and independence-based objective can be associated with empowering strategies, typically disclosure-, choice-, and financial-literacy-based. But whatever the objective(s) or combination of objectives pursued and the blend of regulatory devices deployed, retail investor regulation poses myriad and often intractable difficulties.

The 'retail investor' (or 'household' investor) targeted by intervention, for example, is an elusive character.[19] Regulation has struggled for some time with how to differentiate between different types of household investor in an attempt to identify how regulation in the retail markets, which is typically costly, can best be targeted.[20] Characterization matters

---

[11] See sect 2.3 on the crisis and EU retail markets.

[12] eg Dynan, K, Changing Household Financial Opportunities and Economic Security (2009), available via <http://ssrn.com/abstract=1508864>.

[13] As has long been argued by economists Case and Shiller, who have promoted the development of an appropriate and tradable futures contract: eg Shiller, R, Derivatives Markets for House Prices, Yale Economics Department WP No 46 (2008), available at <http://ssrn.com/abstract=1114102> and Case, K and Shiller, R, 'The Efficiency of the Market for Single Family Homes' (1989) 79 *Am Econ Rev* 125.

[14] As argued in the work of Donald Langevoort in the context of the US Securities and Exchange Commission (SEC). See, eg, Langevoort, D, 'Managing the Expectations Gap in Investor Protection: The SEC and the Post-Enron Reform Agenda' (2003) 48 *Villanova LR* 1139.

[15] See, eg, Kingsford Smith, n 5, Pearson, G, 'Reconceiving Regulation: Financial Literacy' (2008) 8 *Macquarie LJ* 45, Williams, T, 'Empowerment of Whom and for What? Financial Literacy Education and the New Regulation of Consumer Financial Services' (2007) 29 *Law & Policy*, Gray, J and Hamilton, J, *Implementing Financial Regulation. Theory and Practice* (2006) 49–50 and 192–7, and Ramsay, I, 'Consumer Law, Regulatory Capitalism and New Learning in Regulation' (2006) 28 *Sydney LR* 9.

[16] eg Gray and Hamilton, n 15, 192–7 and Kingsford Smith, n 5, 518–26.

[17] Black, J, 'Decentring Regulation: Understanding the Role of Regulation and Self Regulation in a "Post Regulatory World"' (2001) 54 *Current Legal Problems* 103.

[18] eg Williams, n 15, 242.

[19] Fisch, J and Wilkinson-Ryan, T, Why do Retail Investors Make Costly Mistakes? An Experiment on Mutual Fund Choice, ECGI Law WP No 220/2013 (2013), available at <http://ssrn.com/abstract=2086766>, noting the importance of evidence to inform regulatory intervention.

[20] See, eg, in the Canadian context, Deaves, R, Dine, C, and Horton, W, How Are Investment Decisions Made, Research Report Prepared for the Task Force to Modernize Securities Legislation in Canada. Evolving Investor Protection (2006) (2006 Deaves Report).

as it tends to determine the intensity of intervention in the investor decision and in the retail markets. A 'consumer'-driven approach, for example, might suggest a policy acknowledgement that the investment products in question are essential to daily life, that consumption is a consequence of government withdrawal from welfare, and that protection of the consumer with respect to potential losses and risks is warranted.[21] An 'investor'-driven approach, by contrast, might be more easily associated with discretionary activities, speculation and asset accumulation, *caveat emptor*, and personal responsibility, and with capital supply.[22] This approach might also be associated more strongly with disclosure and with market-based mechanisms for protection, including hedging and diversification tools, and privilege investor choice. A 'consumer'-based approach might lead to a more interventionist approach, particularly with respect to product testing, and privilege investor protection.

Regulation must also be carefully adapted to the reality of investor behaviour. An extensive literature charts the limited ability of retail investors to decode disclosures, to exercise informed choice, and to monitor market actors, and underlines that behavioural weaknesses can be intractable and impervious to regulatory action.[23] But despite a fast-expanding data set, regulators are often grappling in the dark in this area: the determinants of retail investor engagement with the markets, for example, are not clear.[24]

More generally (and as discussed throughout this Chapter), retail market regulation is not easy to design or to apply. Disclosure is a very limited tool given the behavioural weaknesses to which retail investors are vulnerable. Distribution regulation poses complex problems given the range of issues engaged, from industry structure and incentive issues (particularly with respect to commission payments), to investor access-to-advice difficulties, to the ability and/or willingness of retail investors to engage with investment advice. Product intervention was, until the financial crisis, largely overlooked (in the EU and its Member States). Financial literacy strategies are best deployed as very long-term solutions to retail market risks. The regulatory perimeter can be difficult to fix, particularly with respect to the perimeter within which investment products can be distributed to retail investors, and its appropriate design can require often fine decisions as to the appropriate level of risk in the retail market, the level of investor responsibility which can be expected, and the extent to which choice can be supported. Regulatory arbitrage risk is typically significant, given the ever-expanding universe of investment products distributed to retail investors. The pressure on regulation is all the greater as the beleaguered retail investor cannot easily

---

[21] For a leading analysis of the need for protection with respect to consumer finance products, given their necessity and ubiquity, see Warren, E, 'Product Safety Regulation as a Model for Financial Services Regulation' (2008) 42 *J of Consumer Affairs* 452. In a similar vein, and arguing for more standardized product regulation of US mutual funds, see Fisch, J, 'Rethinking the Regulation of Securities Intermediaries' (2009–2010) 158 *UPaLR* 1961.

[22] Karmel, R, 'Reconciling Federal and State Interests in Securities Regulation in the US and Europe' (2003) 28 *Brooklyn J Int Law* 495.

[23] eg Campbell, n 5 and Barr, Mullainathan and Shafir, n 5.

[24] From the extensive literature which identifies factors such as peer influence, tax incentives, behavioural factors, household wealth, education, financial literacy, the housing market, and pension provisions see, eg, Guiso, L, Haliassos, M, and Japelli, T, Household Stockholding in Europe: Where do we Stand and Where do we Go? CEPR DP No 3694 (2003). The impact of trust, eg, on retail investor decision-making has been extensively studied. See, eg, the findings of the Chicago Booth/Kellogg School, Financial Trust Index (available at <http://www.financialtrustindex.org>) and Guiso L, Sapienza, P, and Zingales, L, Trusting the Stock Market, NBER WP No 11648 (2005).

support regulation, having limited ability to monitor firms and products and to use disclosures effectively.

The challenge to the regulator is all the greater as retail market regulation rarely benefits from the reform movements which typically follow crisis and which create space for regulatory innovation and experimentation. The high costs of retail market regulation mean that reforms tend to be incremental and to reflect public reaction to particularly egregious episodes of malfeasance, typically related to mis-selling. In its early stages, for example, the financial crisis had little impact on the resolution of long-standing and intractable retail market problems in the EU, notably those relating to distribution and mis-selling. It was only in the later stages of the reform programme that attention turned to the retail markets (section 2.3).

IX.1.2 Investor Protection, Regulation, and the EU

IX.1.2.1 The EU Retail Market

The EU investor protection regime grapples with the two major objectives of retail market regulation considered in section 1.1 above and with the related design difficulties. But the EU retail market also raises distinct challenges.

EU retail market regulation has long been more concerned with regulation than with market integration, by contrast with EU securities and markets regulation more generally. There is little evidence of cross-border retail investor activity.[25] A host of factors, including language, taxation, the home bias, savings and investment cultures and preferences, familiarity with and preference for local distribution structures (particularly the multifunction banks (financial supermarkets) which dominate in continental Europe), and the costs to the industry have long militated against the development of a cross-border retail market.[26] The example of the 2002 Distance Marketing Directive is instructive.[27] The Directive was designed to support the cross-border supply of financial services to consumers, but two extensive 2008 studies found that there was no significant cross-border marketing of financial services through 'distance' mechanisms (such as online and phone marketing) and that the failure of the market to develop was linked not to legal difficulties but to a range of factors including taxation, language, cultural factors, and the nature of financial services.[28] As noted in section 2.2, by 2007 the EU had largely accepted that retail market integration would not be easily achieved,[29] and had embraced a regulatory rather

---

[25] eg Commission, European Financial Integration Report (2009) (SEC (2009) 1702) (2009 EFIR) 14–17, reflecting a consistent trend which can be dated back to the first Integration Report (Commission, Financial Integration Monitor (2004) (SEC (2004) 559)). More recently, a 2012 Eurobarometer study reported that almost 94 per cent of respondents had never purchased a financial product or services from another Member State, and 8 in 10 would not consider so doing: Commission, Special Eurobarometer 373, Retail Financial Services (2012) (Special Eurobarometer 373) 5.

[26] eg Commission, Financial Integration Monitor (2005) (SEC (2005) 927) 10.

[27] Directive 2002/65/EC [2002] OJ L271/16.

[28] Reifner, U, et al, Financial Report: Part I: General Analysis: Impact of Directive 2002/65/EC. Project No. SANCO/2006/B4/034 (2008) and Civic Consulting, Analysis of the Economic Impact of Directive 2002/65/EC: Final Report (2008).

[29] The Commission's 2007 Green Paper on Retail Financial Services acknowledged that integration had not reached its potential, with only modest cross-border activity, wide variations in price, restricted product

than integrationist agenda. But a regulatory agenda, largely disconnected from passporting, faces myriad difficulties, as the justification for EU intervention is weaker, the ousting of national regimes is more troublesome, and greater pressure is placed on the quality of the harmonized rulebook.

Particular difficulties are posed by the nature of retail investment in the EU. It is clear that individuals and households in the EU are participating in the financial markets.[30] Household market participation has been increasing since the early 1970s,[31] although the first major cycle of household market investment is most strongly associated with the period 1980–2000 and the related cycles of equity market exuberance and of stock market privatization.[32] But it is also clear that levels of market investment are not high.[33] Deposits and pension/life insurance assets still dominate in the financial asset portfolios of EU households. The European Central Bank (ECB) has reported that household financial assets in the euro area are primarily composed of deposits (42.98 per cent) and voluntary (non-occupational) pensions and life insurance policies (26.3 per cent); bonds, publicly listed shares, and collective investment schemes (CISs) account for 6.6 per cent, 7.9 per cent, and 8.7 per cent, respectively, of household financial assets.[34] Only 5.3 per cent, 10.1 per cent, and 11.4 per cent of households in the euro area hold bonds, quoted shares, and CISs, respectively.[35] But levels of market investment, while low, seem broadly stable. While the financial crisis has led to a general retrenchment by retail investors and a flight to deposits, it has not led to a major withdrawal from market-based investments. The Commission's European Financial Integration and Stability Report on 2011 reported a significant drop in household financial assets in most Member States and a strong increase in deposits; but while holdings of securities dropped, they remained broadly stable.[36] Similarly, the European Securities and Markets Authority (ESMA) has reported on the

---

diversity and choice, and large variations in the profitability of retail providers: Commission, Green Paper on Retail Financial Services in the Single Market (2007) (COM (2007) 226) 4–5.

[30] For an extended examination of the empirical evidence see Moloney, n 7, 30–41.

[31] Between 1970 and 2003, household savings in bank deposits as a proportion of household portfolios dropped from 54 per cent, 60 per cent, 49 per cent, and 34 per cent in Italy, Germany, France, and the UK, respectively, to 27 per cent, 36 per cent, 30 per cent, and 26 per cent. Over that period, institutionalized savings increased from 8 per cent, 15 per cent, 6 per cent, and 23 per cent in Italy, Germany, France and the UK, respectively to 28 per cent, 41 per cent, 39 per cent, and 54 per cent: 2005 G10 Report, n 7, 18.

[32] eg Ertürk et al, n 9, 10–11 and Guiso et al, n 24.

[33] It is difficult, however, to construct a clear and detailed pan-EU picture of household financial assets, as the major studies (including those by central banks) often use different variables.

[34] ECB, The Eurosystem Household Financial and Consumption Survey, Results from the First Wave, Statistics Paper Series No 2 (2013) 46, Table 2.6. The remaining financial assets relate to money owed to households (2.2 per cent) and 'other financial assets' (including non-listed shares and derivatives) (5.3 per cent). Similar results, although based on a different sample of Member States and constructed from different data sets, emerged from the major 2010 Commission-commissioned study into consumer decision-making (n 4), which found, overall, that relatively liquid and safe assets (primarily deposits) dominated in household portfolios and that riskier assets (such as quoted shares or CISs) were much less common: 93–4.

[35] n 34, 36, Table 2.4.

[36] Commission, European Financial Stability and Integration Report 2011 (2012) (SWD (2012) 103) (2011 EFSIR) 99. The increase in deposits was related to a concern to safeguard principal, lower risk aversion across households, higher deposit rates reflecting banks' efforts to shore up deposits, and a flight-to-safety dynamic, reflecting the increase in the EU deposit guarantee to €100,000 in 2010: 99–101. Similarly on the dominance of deposits in EU household portfolios see European Supervisory Authorities (ESAs) Joint Committee, Report on Risks and Vulnerabilities in the EU Financial System (2014) (JC/2014/018) (2014 ESA Joint Committee Report) 16.

return of positive returns in the retail market, although it has noted that sentiment seems unstable.[37] It is also clear that across the Member States patterns of investment vary very sharply,[38] reflecting the myriad different drivers of retail investment and the different ways in which these drivers seem to operate across the Member States.[39] The retail bond markets are significantly stronger in Italy and Germany, for example.[40] CIS investment patterns and equity patterns also diverge very significantly.[41] Generally low levels of market investment, coupled with sharp variations in investment patterns, do not together provide the securest of empirical bases for supporting an extensive harmonized rulebook for the retail markets.

Further, while there is a degree of clarity now on the composition of household portfolios, over most of its development EU retail investor regulation was adopted in the absence of evidence as to the predominant features and competences of retail investors on a pan-EU basis, although a significant data set has been developed at Member State level.[42] The first major composite study was produced only in 2006, by the Council's Financial Services Committee, which identified a 'currently unsophisticated and unprepared retail mass market'.[43] Since then, empirical evidence has strengthened. The Commission's subsequent pan-EU Optem (2008) and BME (2007) Reports[44] provided the first close-up look at pan-EU investment patterns and investor competence; they found an unsophisticated retail investor with poor decision-making skills, poor awareness of diversification benefits, and limited understanding of the investment process, who struggled to understand disclosures and rarely reviewed investment decisions. This position was confirmed by the major 2010 Commission study on consumer decision-making in retail investment services.[45] Its

---

[37] ESMA, Report on Trends, Risks, and Vulnerabilities. No 1 (2013) (ESMA 2013(1) TRV) 21, reporting on positive returns and on strengthening sentiment. The second TRV, however (ESMA Report on Trends, Risks, and Vulnerabilities. No 2 (2013) (ESMA 2013(2) TRV)), reported that investor sentiment was weakening although returns remained above the long-term average: at 22.

[38] For an extensive review of individual country profiles, and based on the relative proportion of cash, mutual fund, equities, fixed income, insurance/pension, and other assets, see 2010 Consumer Decision Making Study (2010), n 4, 96–113 and 2013 ECB Eurosystem Household Financial Survey, n 34, 37–45.

[39] 2010 Consumer Decision Making Study, n 4, 93–4.

[40] Fixed-income holdings represent 7.29 per cent of household financial assets in Germany and 9.86 per cent in Italy but are significantly lower in France (1.93 per cent) and in the UK (0.84 per cent): 2010 Consumer Decision Making Study, n 4.

[41] While CIS holdings represent in the region of 10 per cent of household financial assets in Poland and Sweden, they represent in the region of 3 per cent in the UK and the Netherlands. Holdings of quoted shares similarly diverge, with shares representing in the region of 13 per cent of French and Austrian, 12 per cent of Swedish, and 10 per cent of UK financial assets, but only in the region of 2 per cent of Dutch household financial assets: 2010 Consumer Decision Making Study, n 4.

[42] Particularly with respect to the UK, Dutch, French, and Italian markets where the UK Financial Services Authority (now Financial Conduct Authority (FCA)), AMF (Autorité des Marchés Financiers), AFM (Autoriteit Financiële Markten), and CONSOB (Commissione Nazionale per le Società e la Borsa), respectively, have been particularly active in engaging in empirical studies. Major studies include, eg, TNS Sofres, Report for the AMF, Investigations of Investment Information and Management Processes and Analysis of Disclosure Documents for Retail Investors (2006). For an examination of the results of local empirical studies see Moloney, n 7, 71–4.

[43] Financial Services Committee, Subgroup on the Implications of Ageing on Financial Markets, Interim Report to the FSC (FSC4180/06) (2006) 21.

[44] Optem, Pre-contractual Information for Financial Services. Qualitative Study in the 27 Member States (2008) (2008 Optem Report) and BME Consulting, The EU Market for Consumer Long-Term Retail Savings Vehicles. Comparative Analysis of Products, Market Structure, Costs, Distribution Systems, and Consumer Savings Patterns (2007) (2007 BME Report).

[45] 2010 Consumer Decision Making Study, n 4.

headline findings included that retail investors in the EU typically struggled to make optimal investment decisions,[46] that decisions were prejudiced by behavioural weaknesses, and that the efficacy of disclosure was strongly context dependent.[47] It also found high levels of retail investor confusion, very limited searching for information, and difficulties in processing the conflict-of-interest disclosure essential to alerting investors to commission and other conflict-of-interest risks, but very heavy reliance on and trust in investment advice.[48] Users of financial services in the EU (including investment services) also tend to display high levels of inertia and rarely switch products or service providers.[49]

Harmonization is therefore a precarious business. The evidence suggests that the retail investor in the EU requires significant regulatory support.[50] But retail market regulation is not easy to design or apply. It is all the more difficult in the EU where investment patterns vary considerably across the Member States, where market structures often diverge,[51] and where generally low levels of pan-EU retail market participation suggest that the risks of harmonization, and of ousting local market regulation, may not be outweighed by the benefits.

Overall, retail market risks in the EU market tend to be local, cross-border activity is very limited, and the optimum regulatory response is likely to be one deeply rooted in the local market. CONSOB, the Italian regulator, for example, has long been concerned with retail bond market risks, the Dutch (AFM) with structured products, and the UK authorities with commission risk in the distribution process, in each case reflecting local market features.[52] Nonetheless, the EU has moved decisively into the retail market space, with relatively little Member State resistance and with some evidence of popular support for this shift in the location of regulatory control. A 2008 survey found that retail investors were generally supportive of Commission action in the retail markets—seeing the Commission

---

[46] The Report characterized the majority of investment decisions (34 per cent) as emerging through a 'Confused Mainstream' process in the course of which investors expended a moderate amount of effort in searching for information, canvassed an average number of options, and relied on advice, but were often confused by the choices and information available. In all, 22 per cent of investment decisions emerged through a 'Self Sufficient' process (characterized by high levels of knowledge but limited reliance on advice), 27 per cent through 'Advice Sought' (characterized by an in-depth purchase process with high levels of knowledge, research, advice, and shopping around), and 17 per cent through 'Limited Search' (characterized by low involvement and effort and limited reliance on advice): 2010 Consumer Decision Making Study, n 4, 183–211.

[47] 2010 Consumer Decision Making Study, n 4, 8–10, reporting that only 56 per cent of funds were invested optimally, that poorer investment decisions were made where the choice was 'framed' in particular ways (where, eg, greater reliance was placed on per cent data), and that investors were disproportionately averse to uncertainty, ambiguity, and product complexity.

[48] Almost 40 per cent of investors in equities believed their investment to be protected, only 33 per cent of investors compared investments from more than one provider, awareness of conflict of interest risk was poor, and 80 per cent of investments were purchased in a face-to-face setting, with 58 per cent of investors reporting that their final choice was influenced by an advisor: 2010 Consumer Decision Making Study, n 4, 7.

[49] 2012 Special Eurobarometer 373, n 25, 5–6.

[50] In addition, EU investors tend not to have significant levels of satisfaction in investment products and services. At end 2012, the market for 'investment products, private pensions, and securities' ranked, for the third year in a row, lowest among 51 different consumer markets: Commission, Consumer Markets Scoreboard, 8th Edition, December 2012.

[51] Distribution systems and related incentive risks, eg, vary. In the UK, for example, independent advice is the dominant distribution channel, while across most of continental Europe investment products are distributed as proprietary products through the major bank-based 'financial supermarkets' (sect 5.1).

[52] See further Moloney, n 7, 36–9.

as a champion against fraud and local regulatory failures.[53] But it remains the case that the risks of harmonization are particularly high in this segment of EU securities and markets regulation.

IX.1.2.2 Scope

The EU retail market regime is composed of a number of measures, discussed in the following sections.

The cornerstone 2014 MiFID II/MiFIR regime governs the provision of investment services and accordingly addresses related distribution and disclosure regulation; it also governs product oversight and confers supervisory powers in this regard on the national competent authorities (NCAs) and on ESMA.[54] While it covers a wide range of financial instruments, MiFID II/MiFIR does not comprehensively address the distribution of insurance-based investment products, which are governed by the Insurance Mediation Directive I (IMD I);[55] IMD I is currently being reformed by the 2012 IMD II Proposal.[56] Targeted enhancements to the distribution of insurance-based investment products have, however, been made by MiFID II, in advance of the IMD II Proposal reforms. MiFID II has revised IMD I to impose additional conflict-of-interest and disclosure-related obligations on direct sales and insurance mediation activities (distribution/advice) of 'insurance-based investment products' by insurance undertakings (previously outside the IMD I regime), and on insurance mediation by insurance agents and brokers (subject to IMD I but now subject to additional requirements under MiFID II) (section 5.3).

Additionally, with respect to disclosure, the 2009 Undertakings for Collective Investment in Transferable Securities (UCITS) IV regime governs product disclosures relating to UCITS funds;[57] its ground-breaking Key Investor Information Document (KIID) for summary regulated disclosures is being extended to a wide range of 'packaged' investment products under the Packaged Retail Investment Products (PRIPs) disclosure reforms.[58] The 2003 Prospectus Directive,[59] as reformed in 2010,[60] governs summary disclosure for securities issued by issuers (including structured securities issued by financial institutions) within its scope.

Access to compensation schemes is governed by the 1997 Investor Compensation Schemes Directive.[61]

---

[53] 2008 Optem Report, n 44, 117.

[54] Markets in Financial Instruments Directive 2014/65/EU OJ [2014] L173/349 (2014 MiFID II) and Markets in Financial Instruments Regulation (EU) No 600/2014 OJ [2014] L173/84 (2014 MiFIR) (on its implementation timeline see Ch IV n 28). The retail market provisions are to be applied from 3 July 2017. MiFID I (Directive 2004/39/EC OJ L145/1) will be repealed from 3 July 2017. The discussion in this Chapter is based on MiFID II/MiFIR although reference is made to MiFID I as appropriate. Most retail-market-orientated protections (those relating to distribution and conduct regulation) are contained in 2014 MiFID II Arts 24-25; the product oversight regime is contained in 2014 MiFIR Arts 39–43.

[55] Directive 2002/92/EC [2003] OJ L9/3.

[56] COM (2012) 360/2.

[57] Directive 2009/65/EU [2009] OJ L302/32. The detailed KIID rules are set out in Commission Regulation (EU) No 583/2010 [2010] OJ L176/1.

[58] COM (2012) 352/3.

[59] Directive 2003/71/EC [2003] OJ L345/64.

[60] Directive 2010/73/EC [2010] OJ L327/1.

[61] Directive 97/9/EC [1997] OJ L84/22.

The horizontal marketing and contracting protections which apply to consumer transactions generally under the 2002 Distance Market of Financial Services Directive, the 2005 Unfair Commercial Practices Directive and the 1993 Unfair Contract Terms Directive[62] also apply in the retail markets.

IX.1.2.3 A Silo-based Regime

Retail investors in the EU invest in a range of often complex products which are functionally similar, including UCITS CISs, non-UCITS CISs, insurance-linked investments, and, particularly immediately before and over the financial crisis, structured securities or products.[63] Internationally, these broadly substitutable investment products are often subject to discrete, silo-based regulation. The related risks of regulatory arbitrage, and of the poor investor outcomes which differential regulation of functionally similar products can generate, has led to an international policy concern[64] as to the effectiveness of sectoral regulation of retail investment products. EU retail market policy currently shares this concern.

Silo-based regulation has long been a feature of the EU retail market regime. This segmentation reflects the origins of the regime at a time when products were segmented for regulatory purposes according to their different insurance (insurance), savings (deposits) and investment (UCITS) functions and profiles, were often subject to different tax treatment, and were distributed through different channels.[65]

With respect to distribution, the 2004 MiFID I regime[66] contained the most rigorous distribution rules, including quality-of-advice rules and rules governing disclosure of commission and the treatment of inducements, but applied only to MiFID I-scope investment products. MiFID I did not, therefore, cover deposit-based investments (structured deposits)[67] or, reflecting international practice,[68] insurance-linked investment products. Deposit-based investment products were not, accordingly (until addressed by the 2014 MiFID II/MiFIR reforms), subject to distribution regulation, save the horizontal protections under the EU's general marketing regime. The 2002 IMD I regime covered the distribution of insurance-related investment products through insurance agents and brokers, but not through insurance companies. IMD I has been revised by MiFID II to apply to distribution by insurance companies, and to impose high-level distribution requirements on insurance companies and agents and brokers with respect to insurance-based investment products. But, even allowing for the 2014 MiFID II reforms to IMD I, the IMD I distribution regime (pending the IMD II reforms) is a lighter regime than the MiFID

---

[62] Respectively, Directive 2002/65/EC [2002] OJ L271/16; Directive 2005/29/EC [2005] OJ L149/22; and Directive 93/13/EC [1993] OJ L95/29.

[63] See further sect 2.3 on structured products. Together, 'packaged products' of this type represent a market of some €10 trillion in the EU: Commission, Key Information Document for Packaged Retail Investment Products. Frequently Asked Questions (2012) (MEMO/12/514), 1.

[64] eg the 2008 Joint Forum Report: Basel Committee on Banking Supervision, International Organization of Securities Commission, International Association of Insurance Supervisors, Customer Suitability in the Retail Sale of Financial Products and Services (2008) (2008 Joint Forum Report).

[65] Commission, Need for a Coherent Approach to Product Transparency and Distribution Requirements for 'Substitute' Retail Investment Products (2007) (2007 Commission Substitute Products Call for Evidence) 3 and 8.

[66] n 54.

[67] On structured products, see sect 2.3.

[68] 2008 Joint Forum Report, n 64.

II/MiFIR regime, particularly with respect to quality-of-advice rules and commission/ inducement requirements. Direct distribution of UCITS units through the UCITS is not covered by the MiFID II/MiFIR regime (which excludes UCITS), but a high-level marketing requirement applies under UCITS IV in that all UCITS marketing communications must be fair, clear, and not misleading (UCITS IV Article 77). Where a UCITS management company engages in investment advice or discretionary asset management, however, the MiFID II/MiFIR regime applies (UCITS IV Article 6(4)).[69]

The disclosure regime governing financial instruments is also fragmented. The 2014 MiFID II regime imposes extensive disclosure requirements on the distribution of 'financial instruments' within its scope. But this regime does not extend to insurance-based investment products. MiFID II has revised the 2002 IMD I to impose the foundational 'fair, clear and not misleading' obligation on disclosures (including marketing communications) related to 'insurance-based investment products' within its scope. Otherwise, such products are subject to the less extensive disclosure regime which applies under the 2009 Solvency II Directive, which requires the publication of generic information concerning the insurance company and the insurance contract, but which is not calibrated to reflect the market-facing risks of insurance-related investment products, although it does require an indication of the nature of the underlying assets.[70] Structured securities, however, are governed by the EU's prospectus regime (where they come within the scope of the requirement for issuers of securities, which includes financial institutions, to produce a prospectus) and MiFID II. But the MiFID II regime is not complete. While it imposes extensive disclosure requirements on the distribution of in-scope investments, it does not address standardization or format, or how retail-orientated summary disclosures should be designed. Sophisticated, retail-orientated summary disclosure requirements apply elsewhere, but only with respect to UCITS CISs under the UCITS IV KIID regime.

Accordingly, until the crisis-era MiFID II reforms different distribution and disclosure rules applied to functionally similar investments, with the most pronounced differences between MiFID I investments, insurance-linked investment products, and investment-linked deposit products, with respect to distribution, and between UCITS and all other investment products, with respect to disclosure. Silo-based and differential regulation of this type generates a number of risks. In particular, retail investors can struggle to recognize the different levels of protection attached to functionally similar products. Differential treatment of substitutable products also generates incentives for product providers to design products which respond to arbitrage possibilities rather than to investor needs.[71]

---

[69] The Commission committed to monitoring the UCITS IV distribution regime at the time of its development: Commission, UCITS IV Impact Assessment (COM (2008) 2263) 13. On UCITS distribution see further Ch III sect 3.11.4.

[70] Directive 2009/138/EC [2009] OJ L335/1 Art 185. It provides that additional national requirements can be imposed only where necessary for proper policy-holder understanding of the essential elements of the commitment (Art 36(3)).

[71] As was frequently noted by the EU institutions during the development of the EU's policy on silo-based retail market regulation: eg, European Parliament, Resolution on Asset Management II (2007 Klinz II Resolution), 13 December 2007 (P6_TA-PROV(2007)0627 (2007) paras 12–19. The Delmas Report (Delmas-Marsalet, J, Report on the Marketing of Financial Products for the French Government (2005)), to take another example, highlighted the case of a French product provider who was able to avoid regulatory oversight of its complex and high-risk investment product by repackaging a UCITS product as an identical structured product, within a unit-linked insurance product issue, listed by a subsidiary in another Member State.

The Commission, following a Council request in May 2007,[72] initially broached the treatment of substitutable investment products in a silo-based regime with a 2007 Call for Evidence.[73] From the outset, there was stakeholder support from the retail and supervisory sectors for a degree of cross-sector harmonization.[74] But the risks of a massive re-engineering of the EU design, distribution, and disclosure regimes to apply to a notional wide class of investment products are considerable. A key threshold question concerns whether the risks of regulatory arbitrage and of gaps in the harmonized regime are outweighed by the costs of intervention. The cross-border market in investment products is limited and cross-border distribution structures are only developing. The development of a harmonized regime provides a focal point for industry lobbying efforts which, given the competitive territory at stake, can increase the risks of poor regulatory design. Substitute products are an elusive class to define; whether or not investment products are in practice substitutable can be unclear.[75]

Following an extensive consultation,[76] the Commission's 2009 Packaged Products Communication[77] suggested that the 'fragmented regulatory patchwork' be replaced by a coherent, cross-sector, horizontal 'selling' regime for PRIPs, which would address conflict of interests, inducements, and conduct-of-business regulation. This initiative was based on reform of the 2002 IMD I and the 2004 MiFID I. While the Commission had suggested a new cross-sector selling regime for packaged products, this was abandoned in favour of targeted reforms to MiFID I[78] and large-scale reform of IMD I. The Commission also proposed a new summary disclosure regime for PRIPs generally. The PRIPs disclosure initiative became one of the central planks of the EU's retail market agenda over the crisis era,[79] although progress was slow before the final agreement on the measure in April 2014.

A series of related reforms are now underway. With respect to distribution, the 2014 MiFID II/MiFIR reforms have brought structured deposits within the MiFID regime and imposed minimum, high-level requirements on the distribution of insurance-based investments, while the 2012 IMD II Proposal seeks to reform the IMD I regime to align it with MiFID II/MiFIR (section 5.3). With respect to disclosure, after significant delays, the 2012 PRIPs Disclosure Proposal is designed to apply a KIID-style summary disclosure reform to a wide range of packaged investment products (section 6.3). The risks of silo-based

---

[72] 2798th Council Meeting, 8 May 2007, ECOFIN Press Release No 9171/07, 11.

[73] 2007 Commission Substitute Products Call for Evidence, n 65.

[74] Commission, Feedback Statement on Contributions to the Call for Evidence on Substitute Retail Investment Products (2008) 29–30.

[75] The European Banking Federation, eg, argued during the policy debate that UCITSs operate under a collective mandate and expose investors to the risks of investment management, while structured products offer a return linked to the product's design: EBF, Response to Call for Evidence (2008) 1 and 3. The European Derivatives Association similarly argued that structured products represent a contractual obligation while CIS management involves a fiduciary obligation to act in the best interests of investors: Commission, Minutes of the Industry Workshop on Retail Investment Products (2008) 3.

[76] Which included the 2007 Call for Evidence, which was followed by a Feedback Document, a 2008 Industry Workshop and a 2008 Open Hearing.

[77] Commission, Communication from the Commission to the European Parliament and the Council. Packaged Retail Investment Products (2009) (COM (2009) 204) (2009 PRIPs Communication).

[78] The Commission hailed MiFID I as a 'sophisticated regime' for the management of conflict of interest risk: 2009 PRIPs Communication, n 77, 7 and 10.

[79] It was highlighted, eg, in the roadmap for reform set out in Commission, Driving European Recovery (2009) (COM (2009) 114), Annex, 4.

regulation are also being mitigated by the Joint Committee of the European Supervisory Authorities (ESAs), which has adopted a specific work programme with respect to the retail markets and which includes cross-sector product oversight.[80] At the time of writing, progress on the IMD II proposal is slow, reflecting significant industry resistance.

IX.2 The Evolution of EU Retail Market Law and Policy

IX.2.1 Initial Developments

The EU's embrace of retail investor protection regulation and policy is a relatively recent phenomenon. The seminal 1966 Segré Report did not address retail investor protection in any detail.[81] The early phases of EU securities and markets regulation (from the late 1970s) were concerned with supply-side market access. The initial series of detailed securities directives were designed to support cross-border capital-raising by issuers and were not constructed as investor protection measures. In the wake of the 1985 Commission White Paper on the Internal Market,[82] and the arrival of minimum harmonization and mutual recognition, however, regulation came to embrace market intermediaries and CISs, and thus the retail markets; the major measures of relevance to retail market protection were the now-repealed 1985 UCITS Directive,[83] the now-repealed 1993 Investment Services Directive (ISD) on investment services,[84] and the 1997 Investor Compensation Schemes Directive (ISCD).[85] But these measures were primarily designed to support passporting. The ISD, for example, asserted in a recital reference that one of its objectives was to protect investors. But this assertion sat very uneasily in a Directive which was primarily focused on the investment firm, the investment services passport, and achieving the minimum level of harmonization required to support home Member State control of cross-border investment firm activity, and which did not establish robust minimum standards for conduct of business and marketing. The UCITS regime as originally conceived was primarily designed to facilitate the cross-border marketing of the UCITS (Chapter III). While the Investor Compensation Schemes Directive (ICSD) had a strong investor protection orientation, it was primarily designed to ease the regulatory costs associated with cross-border activity by investment firms, and had significant gaps and omissions (section 8).

The first significant moves towards a harmonized investor protection regime came in the late 1990s when supporting the confidence of retail investors in the single financial market acquired some traction as a means of promoting integration.[86] The first hint of a retail-investor-facing approach came in 1996 with the Green Paper on Financial Services

---

[80] Sect 10.
[81] Report by a Group of Experts Appointed by the EEC Commission, The Development of a European Capital Market (1966) (Segré Report).
[82] Commission, Completing the Internal Market (COM (85) 310).
[83] Directive 85/611/EC [1985] OJ L357/3.
[84] Directive 93/22/EEC [1993] OJ L141/27.
[85] n 61.
[86] Moloney, N, 'Confidence and Competence: the Conundrum of EC Capital Markets Law' (2004) 4 *JCLS* 1.

Consumers[87] which highlighted a number of retail market concerns, including aggressive marketing by investment firms and poor disclosure. A separate development outside the financial market policy sphere, the adoption of the 2000 E Commerce Directive,[88] further sharpened the focus on the retail markets. The Directive anchored cross-border online services (including online investment services) to the 'Member State of origin' (essentially the State of establishment) and removed the ability of host Member States to apply their protective rules to cross-border online services (subject to an investor protection derogation), but did not engage in parallel rule harmonization. The subsequent 2001 Communication on E Commerce and Financial Services[89] called for further convergence of protective rules, including conduct-of-business rules, in order to address the risk that Member States would rely on the Directive's derogations to the Member State of origin principle to protect investors and consumers where the Member State of origin's rules were not regarded as offering adequate protection, and that online service delivery would be obstructed. But the Communication also adopted an investor-facing agenda. It linked market integration to the demand side and noted that 'consumer confidence' depended on sufficiently harmonized levels of protection. An initial response came in the form of the 2002 Distance Marketing of Financial Services Directive,[90] which, still in force, addresses disclosure, marketing, contractual rights (including withdrawal rights), and redress in the distance marketing context, and which applies to a range of financial services, including investment services. It was the EU's first sustained attempt to grapple with retail investor protection.

IX.2.2 The FSAP, the Pre-crisis Period, and the Retail Markets

Over the Financial Services Action Plan (FSAP)[91] era (1999–2004), the EU agenda would embrace retail market law and policy to a significantly greater extent. The first indications of the adoption of a retail market agenda came with the 2003 Prospectus Directive.[92] As discussed in Chapter II, while this is designed to support cross-border capital-raising by issuers, it is also designed to build the confidence of 'small investors' in financial markets and has a strong retail orientation. Distribution regulation also became considerably more sophisticated. The sectoral Insurance Mediation Directive (IMD I)[93] addressed distribution risks in the context of sales of insurance-based investment products. The most radical developments occurred under MiFID I,[94] which applied to a wide range of investment services (notably investment advice) and products, but did not cover insurance-linked investments or deposit-based investments. The massive MiFID I regime was expressly designed to support investor protection and addressed conduct-of-business regulation (including marketing, disclosure, and suitability requirements), conflict-of-interest management, best execution, and order execution. MiFID I was also notable for the

---

[87] Commission, Green Paper on Financial Services. Meeting Consumers' Expectations (COM (96) 209).
[88] Directive 2000/31/EC [2000] OJ L178/1.
[89] Commission, Communication on E Commerce and Financial Services (2001) (COM (2001) 66).
[90] n 62.
[91] Commission, Communication on Implementing the Framework for Financial Markets Action Plan (COM (1999) 232) (FSAP).
[92] n 59.
[93] n 55.
[94] n 54.

Commission's policy rhetoric which claimed investor protection (domestically and cross-border) as a legitimate concern of EU securities and markets regulation,[95] and which appeared to break the link between investor protection-based harmonization and market integration; under MiFID I, investor protection became an end in itself. The MiFID I Proposal was designed to address the failure of the precursor ISD to provide a 'bedrock of harmonized investor protection',[96] while the pivotal conduct-of-business regime was described as a 'mainstay of investor protection'.[97]

Post-FSAP and pre-crisis, the policy focus on the retail markets continued. Integration was typically a subsidiary concern over this period; effective regulatory design for the retail markets became the primary concern. As discussed in Chapter III, in the UCITS sphere radical reforms to the design of UCITS disclosure in the form of the KIID were proposed under what would become the 2009 UCITS IV reforms.[98] This period can also be strongly associated with a more holistic appreciation of retail market policy, and with a related concern to promote financial literacy (section 9), easier access to redress (Chapter XI), and stronger retail involvement in the law-making process (section 9).[99] Belated efforts were also made to understand retail investor behaviour, with the publication of important reports on long-term retail saving patterns[100] and on retail market disclosures.[101] The establishment of the Committee of European Securities Reguators (CESR), and its claiming of a retail market agenda, led to a range of initiatives, particularly with respect to financial education and retail investor engagement with rule- and policy-making (section 9).

The maturing of the retail market agenda over this period is well illustrated by the Commission's post-FSAP 2007 Green Paper on Retail Financial Services.[102] Its earlier 2005 White Paper on Financial Services Policy had identified the retail market as a key element of the 2005–2010 financial services agenda and committed to a series of investor-facing initiatives, including with respect to investor education, investor governance, and redress.[103] The 2007 Green Paper was concerned with ensuring that the integrated financial services market (including investment services) delivered products that met consumer needs, with enhancing consumer confidence by ensuring consumers were properly protected, and with empowering consumers to take the right decisions.[104] Retail financial services markets (including investment services) were also a theme of the Commission's wider 2007 internal market policy initiative which addressed the distribution of investment products, financial education and redress.[105]

---

[95] Speech by Internal Market Director General Schaub on 'Economic and regulatory background to the Commission proposal for revision of the ISD', 15 October 2002.

[96] 2002 MiFID I Proposal (COM (2002) 625), 23.

[97] n 96, 25.

[98] n 57.

[99] Engagement devices included, for example, simpler and tailored consultation documents and the creation of a new EU stakeholder body (FIN-USE). The Committee of European Securities Regulators (CESR) also engaged in muscular efforts to build better retail investor governance through, for example, specialist consultations and retail workshops. See further Moloney, n 7, 398–425.

[100] 2007 BME Report, n 44.

[101] 2008 Optem Report, n 44.

[102] n 29.

[103] Commission, White Paper on Financial Services Policy (2005–2010) (2005) (COM (2005) 629) 7–8.

[104] 2007 Retail Financial Services Green Paper, n 29, 2–3.

[105] Commission, A Single Market for 21st Century Europe (COM (2007) 725), Staff Working Paper on Initiatives in the Area of Retail Financial Services.

Overall, the FSAP/pre-crisis period grappled with the traditional investor protection objective of retail market regulation, primarily through sector-specific distribution rules (MiFID I and IMD I) and calibrated summary disclosure techniques (Prospectus Directive and UCITS IV). But it also embraced the empowerment/financialization agenda. The Commission's 2005 White Paper on Financial Services linked regulation to more effective engagement with financial products as Member States limited social security.[106] The 2007 Green Paper on Retail Financial Services included investment products among the savings products 'essential for the everyday lives of EU citizens' and necessary for long-term planning and protection against unforeseen circumstances.[107] The Council called on governments to strengthen the tools with which they monitored household savings and to increase their efforts to raise households' awareness of financial education and information needs;[108] its Financial Services Committee engaged in a wide-ranging review of the implications of ageing populations for financial markets, highlighting the macroeconomic and demographic trends which were leading to pressure on households to increase market-based savings.[109] The European Parliament, often sceptical of the financial markets, acknowledged that societal and lifestyle changes demanded sound management of private finances, and related better financial literacy to lower levels of problem debt, increased savings, and adequate retirement provision.[110] Support of market investment by households is implicit across the FSAP programme, but particularly in two cornerstone measures: the Prospectus Directive and MiFID I. As discussed in Chapter III, the Prospectus Directive was in part designed to promote a pan-EU retail equity market. The Commission placed MiFID I in the context of 'investors turn[ing] to market-based investments as a means of bolstering risk-adjusted returns on savings and for provisioning for retirement'.[111] The promotion of market engagement is also evident in the pervasive FSAP-era investor confidence rhetoric,[112] which survived the early stages of the financial crisis;[113] in its 2009 Communication on packaged products, for example, the Commission highlighted the collapse in investor confidence and the need to rebuild confidence, and argued that 'the foundations for future investor re-engagement with packaged retail investment products will need to be laid; people will continue to need to save and invest'.[114]

In tandem with the promotion of market engagement, the policy agenda also sought to support active and empowered investors. The UCITS reforms, for example, focused on the KIID disclosure reforms and took a facilitative approach to product development, including the stretching of the UCITS 'gold standard' retail market label to include hedge-fund

---

[106] 2005 White Paper, n 103, 7 and Annex III, 10–11.
[107] 2007 Retail Financial Services Green Paper, n 29, 4.
[108] 2798th Council Meeting, n 72, 10–11.
[109] n 43.
[110] European Parliament, Resolution on Improving Consumer Education and Awareness on Credit and Finance, 18 November 2008 (P6_TA_PROV(2008)0539) paras A and B.
[111] 2002 MiFID I Proposal, n 96, 3.
[112] The wealth of policy and regulatory examples includes the Prospectus Directive, which associates disclosure regulation with increasing confidence in securities (rec 18), and the Commission's Explanatory Memorandum to MiFID which emphasized the need to support investor confidence in the wake of the dot-com era scandals: 2002 MiFID Proposal, n 96, 4.
[113] The European Parliament in late 2008 noted that 'educated and confident investors' can provide additional liquidity to the capital markets: European Parliament, Resolution on Improving Consumer Education and Awareness on Credit and Finance, n 110, para 4.
[114] 2009 PRIPs Communication, n 77, 1 and 12.

related products.[115] In December 2007, the Commission's then newly constituted consultative Financial Services Consumer Group noted that transparency, the provision of information, and education were all key elements of the current policy debate.[116] Signs also began to emerge of financial literacy strategies substituting for regulatory intervention, notably in the retail bond markets.[117]

IX.2.3 The Financial Crisis

Immediately prior to the financial crisis, the harmonized EU retail market rulebook had become significantly more sophisticated, but it was incomplete. Advances had been made with respect to distribution, but regulatory arbitrage risks were considerable in what was a silo-based regime. Important outcome-driven reforms had been made with respect to retail market summary disclosure, but only with respect to UCITSs. Product intervention was generally limited. Regulatory innovation remained at Member State level, where advances were being made, particularly with respect to supervisory techniques in the retail markets.[118]

Over the financial crisis, household and individual savers across the EU sustained massive losses.[119] Equities,[120] bond investments,[121] and CISs[122] were all affected. The Commission estimated that assets invested in the most common retail packaged products fell in value from €10 trillion at the end of 2007 to around €8 trillion at the end of 2008.[123] EU retail market regulation does not, however, claim or seek to protect investors from market risk, however short-sighted a policy this may be.[124] But the crisis also exposed weaknesses in the EU's regulation of distribution and of disclosure, and the persistence of mis-selling, despite the MiFID I and IMD I reforms. The incentive risks to which the EU's different distribution channels were exposed (section 5.1) were highlighted by the pan-EU

---

[115] See Ch III sect 3.8.8.

[116] Financial Services Consumer Group Minutes, 12 December 2007.

[117] In 2008, the Commission decided against imposing mandatory transparency requirements on the EU debt market (DG Internal Market and Services Working Document, Report on non-Equities Market Transparency pursuant to Article 65(1) of Directive 2004/39 (2008) 12–13), relying, in part, instead on industry-led investor education initiatives.

[118] See Moloney, n 7, Ch 1.

[119] The largest losses of value occurred in Greece (a drop of 76 per cent in the value of household financial assets) and Spain (a drop of 37 per cent): 2011 EFSIR n 36, 100.

[120] eg the market capitalization of European stock exchanges fell by €5.6 trillion in the 12 months prior to October 2008: Federation of European Securities Exchanges, Share Ownership Structure in Europe (2008) 5, noting 'the loss of financial wealth has been massive'.

[121] As the crisis heightened, reports emerged of issuers defaulting on or delaying meeting their redemption obligations: Davies, P and Wilson, J, 'Deutsche Bank Faces Buyer Strike over Decision Not to Redeem Bond', *Financial Times*, 19 December 2008, 15.

[122] Equity schemes, eg, shrank dramatically in 2008, reducing from €350 billion to €188 billion over 2008, and massive investor withdrawals took place in the first and third quarters of 2008: Johnson, S, 'Hopes of Return to Calmer Times', *Financial Times, Fund Management Supplement*, 5 January 2009, 1. The picture became significantly worse in the final quarter of 2008, with outflows reaching €142 billion, making that quarter the worst in the sector's history: European Fund and Asset Management Association (EFAMA), Quarterly Statistical Release No 36 (2008) 2 and 5.

[123] 2009 PRIPs Communication, n 77, 1.

[124] In favour of regulation addressing market risk see Moloney, N, 'Regulating the Retail Markets: Law, Policy and the Financial Crisis' in Cinnéide, C and Letsas, G, *Current Legal Problems 2009–2010* (2010) 375.

mis-selling of structured products[125] and, as the crisis took root, the mis-selling of proprietary products designed to shore up financial institutions' balance sheets (particularly in Spain)[126] and of complex interest rate hedging products (particularly in the UK).[127]

The mis-selling of structured products, in particular, came to define the failure of retail market regulation over the crisis.[128] Retail investor appetite for structured, and particularly capital-protected, products had been strong immediately prior to the crisis,[129] reflecting retail investors' search for yield in a low-interest environment. Demand increased over the crisis in response to extreme market volatility[130] and historically low interest rates. Structured products can offer attractive returns and allow retail investors diversified and hedged access to assets which may not otherwise be available, particularly in the commodities and derivatives markets. They also provide investors with opportunities for increased gains (and increased risks) through leverage. The capital protection associated with these products also proved popular, particularly for investors close to retirement. But structured products can be complex and opaque. Liquidity risks can be considerable, as the secondary market for structured products tends to be illiquid, and difficult market conditions can cause product providers to withdraw from market-making, increasing the potential for investor losses. Distribution risks and mis-selling risks can be considerable; retail investors are acutely vulnerable to products marketed as 'low-risk' and 'capital-protected' and may not appreciate the impact of capital protection on returns, or that protection depends on the guarantee's resilience. Many of these risks crystallized over the financial crisis. In the UK, for example, a review of sales of Lehman-backed structured products found evidence of significant advice failures and of serious disclosure deficiencies[131] and led to related enforcement action;[132] similarly, in Germany, a series of actions was brought against banks and investment firms in relation to Lehman debt certificates.[133] CESR's review of

---

[125] Structured products are typically bonds issued by specialist vehicles and marketed by the banks/investment firms who construct them, the return on which is derived from a range of underlying or embedded assets, including securities, indices, foreign exchange, commodities, derivatives, or debt, and combinations thereof. See generally Benjamin, J and Rouch, D, 'Providers and Distributors: Responsibilities in Relation to Structured Products' (2007) *LFMR* 413.

[126] A major mis-selling scandal arose with respect to banks' sale of high-risk preference shares to their retail depositors which generated massive losses, estimated in the region of over €3.8 billion: Dowsett, S, 'Insight: Spain Bank Rescue Signals Legal Battle for Duped Savers', Reuters, 16 October 2012.

[127] The mis-selling of interest-rate hedging products led to investigative action by the UK and the appointment of independent reviewers to oversee the compensation of investors: FCA, Interest Rate Hedging Products Review April 2013.

[128] Which occurred on a global basis and was associated with the G20's recommendation that conduct rules be reviewed to protect markets and customers: G20 Washington Summit, November 2008. In response, IOSCO adopted Suitability Requirements with Respect to the Distribution of Complex Financial Products (2013) and a Report on the Regulation of Retail Structured Products (2013) which sets out a regulatory toolkit to be used by regulators to address the risks of retail structured products.

[129] Société Generale, The European Retail Structured Investment Product Market. Panorama and Trends (2006).

[130] EFAMA reported a demand shift from UCITSs to structured products (and deposits) over the worst of the market turbulence: Quarterly Statistical Release No 36, n 122, 2.

[131] UK Financial Services Authority (FSA) Press Release, 27 October 2009.

[132] eg UK FSA, Quality of Advice on Structured Investment Products (2009).

[133] Herbert Smith, A Changing Landscape. Regulatory Developments in the Distribution of Retail Investment Products (2010) and (2012) and CESR, The Lehman Brothers Default: An Assessment of the Market Impact (2009) (CESR/09-255) 3.

the Lehman collapse also raised concerns as to the quality-of-advice in the EU concerning structured products.[134]

More generally, mis-selling actions and regulatory enforcement action,[135] along with complaints to Ombudsmen services and to alternative dispute resolution schemes across the EU, increased over the crisis.[136] A 2012 Eurobarometer study of retail financial services similarly found low levels of disclosure to consumers related to commissions and evidence of potential conflict-of-interest risk.[137]

Regulatory weaknesses can be associated with these failures. As noted in section 5.1, the EU investment product distribution market is vulnerable to significant market failures. These derive from: the dominance of complex packaged products as household investments; persistent conflict-of-interest risk arising from the 'financial supermarket' business model (which is based on the distribution of proprietary products) or arising from the commission-based adviser business model; a proliferation of complex products; and limited investor ability to decode complex product disclosures and often opaque and incomplete disclosures related to conflicts of interest. In this environment, MiFID I's process-based quality-of-advice rules struggled to engage in the heavy lifting required of them. MiFID I also generated significant regulatory arbitrage risks as it did not apply to insurance-based investment products or to deposit-based investment products. Similarly, MiFID I did not prove to be entirely robust in dealing with the incentives which product providers had to use household products, and related revenue streams, to repair broken balance sheets.[138]

The first wave of crisis-era regulatory reform, however, was almost entirely concerned with financial system stability and prudential regulation. The initial reform agenda contained only two retail market measures: the 2009 PRIPs Communication for the retail markets, which reflected discussions which predated the crisis but received some impetus from the crisis (section 6.3), and a proposal for reform of the ICSD which was driven by the policy concern to reform the related Deposit Guarantee Directive (section 8.3.2). The position of retail stakeholders was also shown to be insecure: most notably, the de Larosière Group, whose seminal 2009 Report provided the foundation for the ESAs, consulted widely with the industry but signally failed to engage with any retail stakeholders.[139]

---

[134] 2009 CESR Lehmans Report, n 133.

[135] Herbert Smith (2012), n 133, noting increased litigation by retail clients in the Netherlands, litigation in Spain following mis-selling of products such as bank preferred stock and subordinated bonds, intervention by the UK regulator with respect to unregulated collective investment schemes, and the French AMF's placing of retail distribution of financial products among its top three priorities and the discovery by the AMF of deficiencies in the provision of advice: at 4.

[136] 2011 MiFID II/MiFIR Proposals Impact Assessment (SEC (2011) 1226) Annex 8 and FIN-NET, Activity Report for 2011 (2012), reporting an 80 per cent increase in the complaints handled by FIN-NET's members (alternative dispute resolution bodies dealing with financial services). Similarly, 2014 ESA Joint Committee Report, n 36, noting the intensifying risk to consumer confidence in the EU from increasing incidences of misconduct, and the related increase in redress costs and settlement payment: at 23–24.

[137] 2012 Special Eurobarometer 373, n 25.

[138] Skypala, P, 'What Will the Banks Think of Next', *Financial Times, Fund Management Supplement*, 14 November 2011, 6.

[139] The High Level Group on Financial Supervision in the EU, Report (2009). The oversight generated a strong protest from the EU consumer stakeholder body, FIN-USE: Letter to José Manuel Barosso Concerning User Representation in the de Larosière Group, 3 February 2010.

Financial literacy more or less evaporated from the EU policy agenda,[140] notwithstanding the urgent need for reassurance and advice and related co-ordinated action from the EU's regulators.

The crisis era would, however, ultimately lead to the adoption of a series of important retail market reforms and to a renewed focus from the Commission on the retail markets,[141] and continued attention from the European Parliament.[142] Distribution regulation is being tightened under the 2014 MiFID II reforms; further distribution reforms are expected under the insurance-related IMD II reforms. Disclosure is being enhanced under the 2014 MiFID II, the 2010 Prospectus Directive summary prospectus, and the cross-sector PRIPs reforms (agreed in 2014). Product intervention has become part of the EU's retail market toolbox under MiFID II/MiFIR (section 7). The arrival of ESMA has brought a new dynamic to retail market law and policy, with respect to rule-making and the construction of a single rulebook, but also with respect to supervisory convergence in the retail markets. Governance reforms have followed with the establishment of the Commission's Financial Services User Group (which replaces the earlier FIN-USE) and the stakeholder groups attached to the ESAs, including ESMA; investor access to redress is also under consideration, including through the proposed reforms to collective action (Chapter XI).

The combined effect of these measures is a stronger degree of 'consumerization' in EU retail market regulation. A precautionary, *ex-ante* approach to the retail markets has emerged, particularly with respect to product-design-related intervention, but also as regards product distribution.[143] The investor autonomy typically associated with the investor empowerment model is being restricted by, for example, the new product intervention regime (section 7) and the more restrictive approach to execution-only sales (section 5.2). The drivers of this approach are not entirely clear. The renewed enthusiasm for retail market regulation can be associated with the wider crisis-era reform agenda; pre-emptive action, a widening of the regulatory perimeter, and distrust of market mechanisms, all features of the new consumerization phase, reflect the financial stability reform agenda generally. Similarly, the shift in approach may reflect the wider suspicion of financial innovation and financial intensity which can be associated with the crisis era more generally. The wider political environment was and remains favourable. The political risks associated with retail market failures are considerable, particularly following the publicly funded bailouts of the EU banking industry, as the

---

[140] Expert Group on Financial Education, The Financial Crisis and Financial Education (2009).

[141] In its 2011 EFSIR, eg, the Commission acknowledged that households' limited capacity to compare products and assess risk profiles had made it more difficult for them to adjust over the crisis to volatile market and economic conditions, and that it was vital that measure be taken to 'enable them to make informed decisions in a marketplace free of deceptions and abuse': n 36, 108.

[142] As discussed further in this Chapter, the European Parliament drove a number of enhancements to MiFID II/MiFIR. Its ECON (Economic and Monetary Affairs) Committee produced a wide-ranging report in 2014 on Consumer Protection Aspects of Financial Services (IP/A/IMCO/ST-2013-07) which was primarily focused on banking, insurance, and pension products, but noted, eg, widespread instances across the Member States of lower than expected returns on investment products (particularly structured products) and that information provision and the suitability of investment products was a 'problem area in a large number of Member States' (63–5 and 69–70), and made a series of related recommendations.

[143] The 2011 MiFID II/MiFIR Proposals Impact Assessment adopted a precautionary approach in places, particularly with respect to retail market intervention which, while queried, was accepted by the Commission's Impact Assessment Board: 2011 MiFID II/MiFIR Impact Assessment Board Report (20 April 2011) (Ref.Ares (2011)55344).

Commission's Eurobarometers suggest.[144] NCAs also were and remain willing to manage retail policy through the EU, perhaps as a result of the industry costs which inevitably follow reforms and the related attractions for NCAs of associating these reforms with the EU. France's AMF, for example, adopted a new retail market agenda over the crisis era, which it pursued at EU level.[145] The emergence of an invigorated new generation of retail market stakeholders also cannot be discounted. Effective retail governance has long been a problem in the EU and remains so; for example, of the some 4,200 replies to the 2010 MiFID I Review Consultation, only ten or so directly represented the consumer interest.[146] The establishment of EuroInvestors (now EuroFinuse) in 2009, however, in direct response to the need to provide a strong consumer voice in crisis-era reform discussions, has brought a new dimension to policy-making. The institutional landscape is also changing with the establishment of the new ESAs, and particularly ESMA (section 10).

Conversely, however, a more robust approach has been taken by the Commission's 2013 Proposal for a new European Long-Term Investment Fund (ELTIF). The Proposal, the first proposal for a harmonized retail market alternative investment vehicle, is designed to prompt retail investor demand for long-term and illiquid investments (and thereby to deepen the pool of capital available for long-term infrastructure projects), and to allow retail investors access to the related illiquidity premium which these funds generate. While market reaction remains to be seen, the ELTIF Proposal can be strongly associated with a policy construction of the retail investor as competent capital-supplier, and with a relatively high level of policy tolerance of risk in the retail market (Chapter III section 5.2).

The main elements of the current investor protection regime are discussed in the following sections.

IX.3 Harmonization

The harmonized retail markets regime is highly prescriptive. This is related in part to the proliferation of administrative rules in this sphere, but also to the prevalence of maximum harmonization.

The 2002 Distance Marketing of Financial Services Directive contained an augury of what was to come by employing a maximum harmonization model and removing Member State ability to apply additional local rules to domestic actors; recital 13 of the Directive provides that Member States should not be able to adopt provisions other than those laid down by the Directive in the field it harmonizes. To take another example, the prospectus regime, while not formally a maximum harmonization regime, significantly constrains the extent to which Member States can use prospectus requirements to address local retail markets risks. Maximum harmonization has also been deployed with respect to the horizontal consumer rights which can be relevant for retail investors. The 2005 Unfair Commercial Practices

---

[144] Evidenced, eg, by the significant pan-EU support for a tax on bank profits (81 per cent of respondents), the regulation of bankers' bonuses (80 per cent) and a tax on financial transactions (61 per cent): Commission, Eurobarometer 74. Autumn 2010. Europeans, the European Union and the Crisis.

[145] Outlined in AMF, The AMF's New Strategy Proposals (2010).

[146] 2011 MiFID II/MiFIR Proposal Impact Assessment, n 136, Annex 13.

Directive adopts a maximum harmonization model, although financial services, given their complexity and the risks to consumers (recital 9) are subject to a specific derogation which permits national super-equivalent rules (Article 3(9)).

The extent to which the cornerstone 2014 MiFID II regime is regarded as deploying *de facto* maximum harmonization is clear from the express power conferred on Member States to adopt additional restrictions in certain cases. Notably, the pivotal Article 24 conduct regime permits Member States to adopt additional rules, subject to notification obligations; this concession is designed in particular to preserve the more restrictive approach to investment firm commission and inducements adopted in some Member States, particularly the UK.[147] A Member State may impose additional requirements on investment firms in respect of matters covered by Article 24, but only in 'exceptional cases' and where the rules in question are objectively justified and proportionate so as to address specific risks to investor protection or to market integrity which are of particular importance in the circumstances of the market structure of the Member State in question; these rules must not restrict or otherwise affect investment firms' passporting rights (Article 24(12)).[148] The rules must be notified to the Commission (which is empowered to adopt an opinion on the proportionality of and justification for the additional requirements).[149]

IX.4 Calibration and Segmentation: Classifying the Retail Investor

Segmentation strategies, based on classifying investors and products, are frequently deployed in retail market regulation. They typically place restrictions on the products which can be marketed to retail investors (for example, the UCITS and Prospectus regulatory regimes) and on the related distribution channels (for example, the 2014 MiFID II execution-only regime); more radical segmentation strategies might engage with, for example, investor testing.[150] Segmentation allows regulators to target regulation, to mitigate the costs of regulation, and to construct a regulatory space within which innovations can be developed.[151]

---

[147] House of Commons, European Scrutiny Committee, 31 October 2012, Letter on MiFID II/MiFIR from the Financial Secretary to the Treasury.

[148] Under the MiFID I regime, a similar regime applied, albeit that it was regarded as restricting Member States rather than as supporting local difference, and required Commission approval (not simply the delivery of an opinion) of the rules in question. This 'goldplating' prohibition applied to the administrative rulebook generally under the 2006 Commission MiFID I Directive (Commission Directive 2006/73/EC [2006] OJ L241/26) (Art 4).

[149] The notification must be made within two months of the relevant rules coming into force and the Commission opinion must be provided within two months of the notification. Requirements previously notified under the precursor regime can remain in force, as long as the relevant conditions of that regime are met.

[150] The Commission's first working draft on the 2004 MiFID I administrative conduct-of-business regime proposed an investor-aptitude test which was designed to 'explore a more effective and targeted solution', and would have allowed qualified investors to choose to opt-out of aspects of the disclosure regime: ESC/23/2005 Art 9 and July 2005 Explanatory Note (ESC/24/2005), 2.

[151] eg Zingales, L, *A Capitalism for the People. Recapturing the Lost Genius of American Prosperity* (2012) 231–2.

But segmentation can be a problematic regulatory device and must be carefully deployed. Segmentation can be associated with troublesome regulatory determinations that certain products or markets are 'too risky' for direct retail market access, or as to the design of 'appropriate' retail market products, and with complex trade-offs between access/choice and protection. As discussed in section 7, the line between 'safer' and 'too risky' products is a difficult one to draw: in addition, the perimeter within which 'safer' retail market products are contained can be porous and allow 'excessive' risk to flow to the retail market. Conversely, segmentation may place undue restrictions and costs on the retail market. Segmentation may also underestimate the monitoring discipline which can come through institutional investor monitoring of traditionally riskier investments.[152]

Similarly, investor classification demands nuanced decisions. It is difficult to choose appropriate proxies for sophistication, competence, and risk appetite, and changes to investor classifications, driven by deregulatory and liberalization objectives, can lead to a leakage of undue risk to the retail sector. Unintended effects may also follow; for example, the segmentation by the Prospectus Directive of retail and professional markets has reduced retail market access to the bond markets (Chapter III).

Segmentation is a marked feature, however, of EU retail market regulation, and particularly of MiFID II. The 2014 MiFID II classification system, which is, broadly, based on distinguishing between retail investors and professional investors, calibrates the application of MiFID II's conduct-of-business protections based on whether the investor is a retail client,[153] who benefits from the full range of protections; a professional client; or an eligible counterparty.[154] Retail clients, like professional clients, benefit from the full range of MiFID II conduct-of-business rules. But they are also likely to be targeted by more detailed administrative rules. The administrative rules which governed the conduct regime under MiFID I were designed to apply additional protections to services provided to retail clients; these protections included significantly more detailed disclosure requirements and more stringent suitability/appropriateness quality-of-advice requirements. Although these rules will be replaced under the new set of MiFID II delegations to administrative rule-making, a similar approach can be expected.[155] When eligible persons, which include 'private individual investors', seek to 'opt in' to professional client status and so to reduce the level of protection, extensive classification and notification requirements apply, which include minimum experience and asset tests.[156] Accordingly, while the MiFID II classification regime allows retail clients to progress to professional client status, the stringency of the conditions suggests that very few retail clients will be in a position to make

---

[152] Mahoney, P, 'The Development of Securities Law in the United States' (2009) 47 *J of Accounting Research* 325.

[153] Defined by default as a client who is not a professional client: 2014 MiFID II Art 4(1)(11).

[154] This sect examines the classification system from a retail perspective. For its impact on the provision of investment services generally see Ch IV sect 5.2.

[155] The delegations which apply to 2014 MiFID II Arts 24 and 25, which Articles are at the heart of the MiFID II conduct regime, provide that the administrative rules take into account the retail or professional nature of the client or the client's classification as an eligible counterparty (Arts 24(14) and 25(8)).

[156] The waiver assessment includes the requirement that two of three conditions be met: the client has carried out transactions, in a significant size, on the relevant market at an average frequency of ten per quarter over the previous four quarters; the client's financial instrument portfolio (including cash deposits and financial instruments) exceeds €500,000; and the client works or has worked in the financial sector for at least one year in a professional position, which requires knowledge of the transactions or services envisaged.

the transition. MiFID II also deploys segmentations strategies in the form of product restrictions. Only identified products (generally non-complex products) can be distributed through execution-only channels (section 5.2.6).

IX.5 Distribution and Investment Advice

IX.5.1 The EU Distribution Market and Distribution Risks

IX.5.1.1 Distribution in the EU

Since the adoption of MiFID I in 2004, the investment advice and product distribution process has been at the centre of EU retail market law and policy, reflecting the heavy dependence of retail investors in the EU on advice and other intermediated distribution channels.[157]

Investment advice and product distribution typically occurs through commission-based tied agents of product providers (for example Germany), multi-tied agents who advise on a range of products (for example the Netherlands), and integrated banc-assurance (financial supermarket) banking models (for example Germany, France, Spain, Italy, and Poland). Overall, banks are key suppliers of advice and investments, particularly CIS units and bonds.[158] Long-standing cultural practices, such as the familiarity of consumers with local branch networks and agents, have driven these advice and distribution practices; so too have different savings patterns, with greater wealth associated with more complex investment needs and more sophisticated advice structures. Although 'independent' advisers are slowly becoming more popular across Europe, they are generally uncommon, although prevalent in the UK, Poland, and the Czech Republic.[159] Overall, distribution structures vary significantly across the Member States, and a wide range of different structures can be deployed within Member States.

IX.5.1.2 Distribution Risks: Incentives and Commission

Principal-agent risks can be acute in the distribution context. They include fraud, misuse of investor funds, and incompetence.[160] The behavioural weaknesses which bedevil retail investor decision-making may simply be replaced by adviser weaknesses, and not displaced.[161] Overall, however, remuneration-based conflict-of-interest risk poses the greatest

---

[157] This was a recurring finding of the initial series of pan-EU retail market studies (eg 2007 BME Report, n 44, 175 and 2008 Optem Report, n 44, 88 and 93–4). The 2010 Consumer Decision Making Study (based on a sample of 6,000 investors across the EU) found that advice was 'ubiquitous' in the retail market with nearly 80 per cent of investments made in a face-to-face setting, 79 per cent of purchasers obtaining information or advice from a financial professional, and 58 per cent of investors reporting that their final choice of product was influenced by an adviser: n 4, 7 and 223. Levels of trust in advisers were high but levels of awareness of conflict-of-interest risk low: at 178.

[158] The 2010 Consumer Decision Making Study found that bank-based financial supermarkets were the dominant providers of advice, with almost half of the sample canvassed (6,000) having some contact with such an entity for advice or information: n 4, 170 and 223.

[159] n 4, 169 and 172.

[160] Odean, T, 'Are Investors Reluctant to Realise Their Losses' (1998) 53 *J Fin* 1775.

[161] Langevoort D, 'Selling Hope. Selling Risk. Some Lessons from Behavioural Economics about Stockbrokers and Sophisticated Investors' (1996) 84 *California LR* 627.

threat to good investor outcomes and is the most significant driver of mis-selling and poor-quality advice.[162]

Remuneration structures have very considerable potential to misalign incentives in the distribution process.[163] The well-documented detriment which can follow includes biased advice, failure to provide debt reduction advice, poor product selection, inappropriate advice to switch products, and ultimately mis-selling. The risks are all the greater given the difficulties retail investors face in identifying conflict-of-interest risk and in assessing relevant disclosures. In addition, retail investors are unlikely to gain experience as investment decisions tend to be irregular, over-reliance on and excessive trust in advisers is common, and the well-documented reluctance of retail investors to pay a fee for advice entrenches remuneration-related risks.[164] Commission and incentive risk in the distribution process is a common problem internationally and is increasingly the subject of strenuous reforms efforts,[165] including those proposed by international standard-setters.[166] In the EU, the regulation of remuneration-related incentive risk poses particular challenges given the range of distribution channels which are used across the Member States and the related varying ways in which incentive risks arise. The bank-based distribution channel is vulnerable to deeply embedded conflict-of-interest risk arising from the distribution of proprietary products whose sale is often driven by internal remuneration incentives.[167] In the other major distribution channel, severe commission risks arise with 'open-architecture', commission-based product distributors, whether in the form of 'independent' advisers or networks of agents.[168]

---

[162] As has been repeatedly acknowledged in major studies: eg the French 2005 Delmas Report, n 71, 9 and FSA, Discussion Paper No 07/1, A Review of Retail Distribution (2007), Annex 3, 12.

[163] eg Krausz, M and Paroush, J, 'Financial Advising in the Presence of Conflicts of Interest' (2002) 54 *J of Economics and Business* 55.

[164] n 219.

[165] In Australia, eg, the protection of retail investors became a major political priority over the financial crisis, following a series of failures in the financial sector and mis-selling scandals; the subsequent Future of Financial Advice reforms included bans on a range of payments to advisers which were regarded as creating conflict of interest risk (including a ban on commissions), new fiduciary duties imposed on advisers, and an enhanced disclosure regime: Hill, J, 'Why did Australia Fare so Well in the Global Financial Crisis', in Ferran, E, Moloney, N, Hill, J, and Coffee, JC *The Regulatory Aftermath of the Global Financial Crisis* (2012) 203, 270–6. In the US, the 2010 Dodd-Frank Act led to a series of SEC studies into the workings of the US retail investment advice/brokerage market, including SEC, Study on Investment Advisers and Broker Dealers (2011), which led to the SEC recommending that reforms be introduced such that a uniform fiduciary standard be applied to broker-dealers and investment advisers where advice was provided, and to related impact assessment studies over 2013 (SEC Release No 34–69013 and IA-3558).

[166] eg 2008 Joint Forum Report, n 64, and 2013 IOSCO Suitability Requirements for Complex Financial Products, n 128. The 2012 G20 High Level Principles on Financial Consumer Protection highlight that 'the provision of advice should be as objective as possible' (at 6) and that remuneration structures 'should be designed to encourage responsible business conduct, fair treatment of customers and to avoid conflicts of interest' (at 7).

[167] eg Jansen, C, Fischer, R, and Hackenthal, A, The Influence of Financial Advice on the Asset Allocation of Individual Investors (2008), available at <http://ssrn.com/abstract=1102092> (suggesting, based on an examination of German banks, that bank advisers have incentives to promote equity-concentrated asset allocation as equity products have higher margins).

[168] Commission-based distribution has been associated with a range of failures, including poor quality advice and mis-selling, particularly in the UK. Repeated cycles of mis-selling led to the radical 2013 'Retail Distribution Review' (RDR) reforms, which have imposed a prohibition on commission payments and required extensive labelling as to the nature of the advice/distribution service provided. Notwithstanding the RDR, the management of incentive risks remains a key priority for the UK authorities given persistent evidence of incentive-based failures in the advice process: eg FSA, Guidance. Consultation. Risks to Customers

At EU level, a major 2011 study for the Commission, based on 1,200 'mystery shops' conducted across the 27 Member States, provided the first in-depth examination of distribution across the EU.[169] It found evidence of limited information-gathering, and that advisers often did not adhere to the MiFID requirements (MiFID I) with respect to 'know your client' and information-gathering.[170] Risk profiling was often weak; almost 50 per cent of advisers did not record any information related to the investor's risk appetite and only 30 per cent of investors were asked about their ability to deal with investment risk. Information provided on product risk was often not comprehensive; explanations of the associated risk levels were often vague.[171] Advisers were often more interested in the funds investors had available to invest than in their capacity to finance the investments given other financial commitments. Very few advisers disclosed the existence of conflicts of interest or inducement payments.[172] Overall, only 43 per cent of investment recommendations were deemed to be 'suitable', in accordance with MiFID I; the main driver of unsuitability was relatively high levels of investment risk. Risks were generated across the independent advice and bank/financial supermarket distribution channels: the independent advice channel, however, tended to produce riskier investment recommendations, while the bank/financial supermarket channel tended to lead to the recommendation of proprietary products.[173] The Report also suggested that unsuitable recommendations may have been driven by limited product ranges carried by banks/financial supermarkets and by failures to address properly the investor's needs and risk/financial profile.[174] Similarly poor outcomes and practices were reported in the Commission's 2012 Eurobarometer on retail financial services.[175] As noted in section 2.3, the financial crisis underlined the scale of mis-selling risk in the EU.

Some very heavy lifting is demanded of regulation in delivering incentive alignment and good-quality advice in a commission-based and proprietary product sales-based environment. While NCAs, operating in a MiFID I-shaped regulatory environment, were focusing increasingly on distribution risks prior to the crisis,[176] the 2014 MiFID II reforms have led to a significant enhancement of the EU rulebook and should support NCAs in addressing

---

from Financial Incentives (2012) and FCA, Final Guidance. Risks to Customers from Financial Incentives (2013).

[169] Synovate, Consumer Market Study on Advice within the Area of Retail Investment Services—Final Report (2011) (2011 Synovate Report).

[170] The Report found that only in the region of 8 per cent of advisers followed all the 2004 MiFID I requirements: n 169, 60.

[171] The Report found that only 10 per cent of advisers covered all aspects of risks associated with financial instruments: n 169, 66.

[172] The Report found that advisers were generally reluctant to discuss commissions and suggested that the limited disclosure typically provided could indicate failure to comply with the 2004 MiFID I requirements: n 169, 9–10.

[173] Almost 80 per cent of products recommended by banks were proprietary: n 169, 12. The report highlighted that this did not necessarily point to incentive risks, but could suggest that only a limited range of products were offered (at 90).

[174] n 169, 15.

[175] It found that in 50 per cent of cases, the consumers surveyed had not been informed as to whether the firm was being paid a bonus, commission, or other form of remuneration: n 25, 12.

[176] eg the Dutch AFM isolated the quality of advice as a priority issue (AFM, Policy and Priorities for the 2007–2009 Period (2007)), the German BaFIN highlighted the risks posed by commission sales (BaFIN, Annual Report (2006)), the Italian CONSOB targeted sales networks, suitability assessments and conflict-of-interest rules (CONSOB, Annual Report 2006), and the UK FSA proposed the major RDR reforms (n 168).

distribution risks; further reforms are likely under the IMD II reforms. But the difficulties are significant given the range of distribution structures and very limited reliance on fee-based independent advisers.

IX.5.2 Distribution and the 2014 MiFID II

IX.5.2.1 From the 1993 ISD to the 2014 MiFID II

The 1993 ISD was a landmark measure in that it was the first EU measure to address conduct regulation. But it was a limited measure. It contained high-level principles which were designed to inform how Member States regulated the conduct of investment firms, but disclosure, marketing, and incentive/conflict-of-interest management were not addressed in any detail. Investment advice only came within the scope of the ISD as an ancillary service where it was provided by firms already within the scope of the ISD; stand-alone advice firms were not covered.

The 2004 MiFID I brought major reforms to the regulation of distribution. It included stand-alone investment advice as a MiFID I service and imposed a new set of harmonized conduct, disclosure, and conflict-of-interest management rules on investment advice and product distribution which were subject to detailed amplification by the MiFID I administrative rulebook. More generally, MiFID I embraced a 'conduct-shaping' style of regulation,[177] which emphasizes the firm/investor fiduciary relationship and which limits the extent to which disclosure and investor consent are used to deliver good outcomes. While disclosure was an important element of MiFID I (and remains so under MiFID II), the Commission sought to limit disclosure and to 'reinforce the fiduciary duties of firms' through the conduct-of-business regime.[178] Disclosure was generally limited to those elements essential for retail investors to understand the nature of the investor/firm relationship, and the Commission was concerned to 'avoid overloading clients with information of no immediate use'.[179]

The new 2014 MiFID II/MiFIR[180] regime is most strongly associated with the wide-ranging reforms to trading and trading venues which have followed, and which are discussed in Chapters V and VI. But it has also, under MiFID II, brought material change to the EU's regulation of investment product distribution; MiFID II and MiFIR have also introduced new requirements governing product intervention (section 7).[181]

---

[177] The Commission described the 2004 MiFID I as entailing 'reinforced fiduciary duties [which] protect consumers by enhancing responsible behaviour by firms': 2007 Retail Financial Services Green Paper, n 29, 12.

[178] Commission Working Document EC/24/2005, Explanatory Note to ESC/23/2005 (July 2005) 1.

[179] The Commission FAQ document issued on the eve of the application of the 2004 MiFID I stated that MiFID I was designed not to flood consumers 'with reams of information which may not be relevant to them and which they may have difficulty understanding. Instead, the emphasis will be on the fiduciary duties of firms towards their clients': Commission, Markets in Financial Instruments Directive: Frequently Asked Questions (2007).

[180] n 54.

[181] The main elements of the publicly available legislative history of the 2014 MiFID II/MiFIR are: MiFID II Commission Proposal (COM (2011) 656/4), MiFIR Commission Proposal (COM (2011) 652/4), and MIFID II/MiFIR Proposals Impact Assessment, n 136; MiFID II Council General Approach, 18 June 2013 (Council Document 11006/13) and MiFIR Council General Approach 18 June 2013 (Council Document 11007/13); and European Parliament Resolution adopting a Negotiating Position on MiFID II, 26 October 2012 (P7_TA (2012)0406) and on MiFIR, 26 October 2012 (P7_TA (2012)0407).

The Commission's 2011 MiFID II Proposal had three main features with respect to investment product distribution. First, it brought structured deposits in scope to address the arbitrage risks which the exclusion of these investment products had generated under MiFID I.[182] Second, it closed the non-advice execution-only distribution channel to structured UCITSs, and prohibited firms from offering lending (margin) services in conjunction with execution-only services.[183] Third, and most radically, it introduced a new category of 'independent investment advice' and required that where advice was so labelled, the firm was required to advise on a cross-market selection of financial instruments and commission payments were prohibited; it also imposed a commission prohibition on discretionary asset management. The independent investment advice reform, which was trailed by the Commission in the 2010 Commission MiFID I Review as being necessary given concerns as to the quality of advice,[184] was based on the then emerging empirical evidence as to incentive and mis-selling problems in the distribution market.[185] A ban on all inducements, across all distribution channels, was rejected on cost grounds.[186]

The proposed reforms reflected growing concern, pre- and over the crisis, at EU level and across the Member States, as to the persistence of mis-selling and conflict-of-interest risk,[187] and benefited from extensive *ex-ante* empirical analysis[188] and consultation.[189] They were, accordingly, relatively uncontroversial, save with respect to the proposed commission prohibition. The proposed prohibition generated severe tensions within and between the Council and the European Parliament, reflecting the very significant industry interests at stake. In the Council, although some Member States supported a more wide-ranging commission prohibition than the Commission's independent-advice-related proposal (which extension was called for by leading consumer stakeholders given the arbitrage risks from limiting the prohibition to independent advisers and the need to address incentive risks in proprietary product distribution,[190])[191] most Member States (with France a leading member of this group) did not, reflecting local industry structures, and supported instead enhanced disclosure requirements.[192] The final Council General Approach retained the Commission's proposed prohibition on commission with respect to independent advice (and discretionary asset management),[193] and did not extend it. The Council also, however,

---

[182] See Ch IV sect 4 on the scope reforms.
[183] 2011 MiFID II Proposal Art 24. See further sect 5.2.6.
[184] Commission, Consultation on the MiFID I Review (2010) 56–7 and 60.
[185] 2011 MiFID II/MiFIR Proposals Impact Assessment, n 136, 16.
[186] n 136, 55.
[187] 2011 Synovate Report, n 169, 5.
[188] Including the 2011 Synovate Report, the 2010 Consumer Decision-Making Study (n 4), and the raft of studies which, by then, NCAs had engaged in. The Commission also drew on CESR's technical advice on the MiFID I Review generally, including its advice related to investor protection and intermediaries (CESR/10-589).
[189] The pre-Proposal consultation process included six roundtables as well as the 2010 Consultation (n 184).
[190] Woolfe, J, 'Widespread Belief MiFID II Set to Fail Retail Investors', *Financial Times, Fund Management Supplement,* 30 January 2012, 8.
[191] Notably the UK and the Netherlands: Sullivan, R, 'European States at Odds over Commission', *Financial Times Fund Management Supplement,* 18 July 2011, 3.
[192] Cyprus Presidency Progress Report on MiFID II/MiFIR, 13 December 2012 (Council Document 16523/12) 8 (but reporting that a smaller group of Member States 'seems firmly committed to introducing a general ban on inducements'); and House of Commons, European Scrutiny Committee, 31 October 2012, Letter on MiFID II/MiFIR from the Financial Secretary to the Treasury.
[193] Council General Approach, n 181, Art 24(5) and Art 24(6).

strengthened the Commission's Proposal by addressing remuneration governance and structures more generally, and requiring that remuneration not conflict with a firm's duty to act in the best interests of clients.[194] Within the European Parliament, while some MEPs supported a general prohibition on commission-type payments across all distribution channels, there was also significant opposition, including in relation to the proposed prohibition of commission in relation to independent advice; the initial report from the Economic and Monetary Affairs Committee (ECON) removed the Commission's independent investment advice-related prohibition in favour of a disclosure-based approach.[195] After intense negotiations,[196] the final Parliament Negotiating Position re-introduced the prohibition on commission in relation to independent investment advice (although it removed the prohibition with respect to discretionary asset management)[197] and, like the Council's General Approach, introduced rules governing remuneration structures generally.[198] It went further than the General Approach, however, by adding a new legislative requirement governing inducements[199] and imposing specific disclosure requirements for inducements paid in the context of investment advice.[200] The European Parliament and Council were both, however, supportive of allowing Member States to impose general bans on inducements/commissions across all distribution channels—a concession which was of central importance to the UK, which applies such a prohibition under its Retail Distribution Review reforms, and to Denmark and the Netherlands, which both have similar prohibitions.[201]

During the final Commission/Council/European Parliament trilogue discussions, the obligations imposed on firms were tightened, with the acceptance, for the most part, of the Council and European Parliament enhancements. The major additions to the text made during the trilogue discussions included: requirements governing inducements and remuneration for all investment services; more detailed specification of the nature of 'independent investment advice'; more detailed cost disclosure requirements; more extensive obligations concerning the firm's understanding of the investments distributed; and greater specification of the nature of the 'suitability' assessment (particularly with respect to the client's risk tolerance, and with respect to the 'suitability letter' required to be given to retail clients) required in relation to investment advice and discretionary asset management. More generally, the trilogue negotiations led to an embedding of client interests more securely within firm governance and to a stronger client orientation in the MiFID II regime generally. The new MiFID II firm governance regime, for example, places

---

[194] Council General Approach, n 181, Art 24(6A).

[195] Ferber Report on MiFID II (A7-0306/2012) Art 24.

[196] The final amendments on commission were reportedly added on the day of the plenary vote on the Parliament's Negotiating Position: Malhère, M, 'MiFID II-MiFIR: EP Confirms Negotiating Mandate for Rapporteur', EuroPolitics, 29 October 2012.

[197] Leading BEUC, the leading EU consumer lobbying group, to note that the Parliament had 'at least reversed the ECON committee's dramatic decision to allow commission if disclosed to clients, which represented a considerable backwards step from current standards': n 196.

[198] Although the European Parliament text was more specific than the Council text, and expressly required that remuneration not be based on sales or profitability targets, and that remuneration and performance incentives not provide incentives to recommend particular products: Negotiating Position, n 181, Art 24(1b).

[199] This approach was (broadly) accepted during the trilogue discussion (see sect 5.2.5).

[200] Parliament Negotiating Position, n 181, Art 24(3a).

[201] Financial Secretary Letter, n 192.

responsibilities on the investment firm's management body[202] with respect to the design, oversight, and implementation of governance arrangements and policies relating to, *inter alia*, conflict-of-interest management and the services and products offered, which reflect the interests of clients and their characteristics and needs (Article 9(3)). The trilogue negotiations also led to enhancements to the 2002 IMD I regime with respect to insurance-based investment products (section 5.3).

IX.5.2.2 2014 MiFID II: Scope

Reflecting the coverage of MiFID I, the 2014 MiFID II regime applies to specified 'investment services' with respect to a wide range of simple and complex 'financial instruments'.[203] These include structured products, which come within the scope of the 'transferable securities' which are included as financial instruments. A wide range of derivatives, including commodity derivatives, also come within MiFID II's scope. The MiFID II-scope reforms include the inclusion of deposit-based investments (structured deposits) and the removal thereby of a source of regulatory arbitrage risks. MiFID II does not, however, cover insurance-based investments (which are addressed by the significantly lighter-touch IMD I regime, which has, however, been enhanced by reforms made by MiFID II—section 5.3).

MiFID II governs broking-related trading services (Chapter VI) and discretionary asset management (Chapters III and IV). Of most direct relevance to the EU retail market, however, is its coverage of product distribution, through 'investment advice' and through execution-only channels, including, in a scope clarification added by MiFID II, sales by credit institutions and investment firms of proprietary products.[204] 'Investment advice' is defined as the provision of 'personal recommendations' to a client, either on its request or at the initiative of the investment firm, in respect of one or more transactions relating to financial instruments (Article 4(1)(4)).[205] The personalization of the advice to the client's personal situation, and the specificity of the advice given, are central to its regulatory characterization as regulated 'investment advice'.

---

[202] Defined as the body or bodies appointed in accordance with national law which is empowered to set the firm's strategy, objectives, and overall direction, and which oversees and monitors management decision-making and includes persons who effectively direct the business of the entity (in effect, the board of directors) (2014 MiFID II Art 4(1)(36)).

[203] 2014 MiFID II Art 4(1)(2) and Annex I sects A and C. On the scope of the 2014 MiFID II see Ch IV sect 4.

[204] Under the 2004 MiFID I, it was not clear whether sales by investment firms of proprietary products issued by them came within the regulatory regime. Following a series of high-profile mis-selling scandals related to bank securities in particular (notably in Spain), the 2014 MiFID II has clarified that the 'execution of orders on behalf of clients' includes the conclusion of agreements to sell financial instruments issued by a credit institution or an investment firm at the moment of issuance (Art 4(1)(5)). See further Ch IV sect 4.

[205] Further clarification of the nature of investment advice is likely to come from the Art 4(2) delegation which empowers the Commission to amplify the 2014 MiFID II definitions. Under the 2006 Commission MiFID I Directive (Art 52) a personal recommendation was defined as one made to a person in his capacity as an investor or potential investor, presented as suitable for that person or based on a consideration of the circumstances of that person, and constituting a recommendation to: (a) to buy, sell, subscribe for, exchange, redeem, hold, or underwrite a particular financial instrument; or (b) to exercise, or not to exercise, any right conferred by a particular financial instrument to buy, sell, subscribe for, exchange, or redeem a financial instrument.

As discussed in Chapter IV, MiFID II contains a number of exclusions, but it tightens the MiFID I exemption which allowed Member States to exempt from MiFID I firms which did not hold client funds or assets, and which accordingly took many investment advisers outside the scope of MiFID I.

IX.5.2.3 2014 MiFID II: Fair Treatment—Article 24(1)

A foundation fiduciary-style obligation to act fairly in the client's best interests is imposed on investment firms under Article 24(1). The 'fair treatment' principle requires a firm, when providing investment services to clients, to act honestly, fairly, and professionally in accordance with the best interests of its clients, and to comply with the Article 24 and 25 conduct-of-business requirements.

The original adoption of the fair treatment obligation under MiFID I (Article 19(1)) marked a significant shift towards a more interventionist approach and away from disclosure. Although its inchoate nature carries risks, including with respect to *ex-post* enforcement action,[206] a fair treatment obligation provides NCAs with a useful, catch-all mechanism for reviewing investment firm behaviour, for capturing emerging risks, and for proactively addressing the asymmetry in bargaining power which characterizes the firm/client relationship. In practice, however, the management of incentive-related remuneration risk is more likely to be achieved by robust supervision and enforcement of specific quality-of-advice and related conflict-of-interest rules.

The fair treatment obligation is supported by two additional obligations (added during MiFID II trilogue discussions) which exemplify how the investor protection regime became stricter over the trilogue. Reflecting the injection of product oversight requirements into the MiFID II investor protection regime, and in particular the concern to ensure distribution channels are chosen appropriately (section 7), investment firms which manufacture financial instruments for sale to clients must ensure those instruments are designed to meet the needs of an identified target market of end clients within the relevant category of clients, that the strategy for the distribution of those instruments is compatible with the identified target market,[207] and that the firm takes reasonable steps to ensure the instruments are distributed to the identified target market (Article 24(2)).

In addition, the investment firm must understand the financial instruments it offers or recommends, assess the compatibility of the financial instruments with the needs of the clients to which it provides investment services (taking into account the identified target market), and ensure that financial instruments are only offered or recommended when this is in the interest of the client (Article 24(2)). While a related and more detailed 'suitability/appropriateness' assessment regime applies in relation to particular types of investment service (section 5.2.5), the new Article 24(2) obligation has the effect of imposing an overarching obligation on firms to consider clients' interests when distributing products through any distribution channel.

---

[206] *Ex-post* fairness assessments may become an occasion for value judgments on the investment process: Park J, 'The Competing Paradigms of Securities Regulation' (2007) 57 *Duke LJ* 625.

[207] The 'target market' concept is a function of the new product oversight regime, noted in sect 7.

IX.5.2.4 2014 MiFID II: Marketing—Article 24(3)

Marketing communications typically represent the first stage in the investment process, carry disproportionate impact, and are a key risk point for retail investors who are typically ill-equipped to decode marketing strategies and are trusting of firm communications. The evidence suggests that retail investors tend to over-rely on 'simpler' marketing disclosures where product disclosures are complex and can over-react to how marketing frames the investment decision, particularly as communications tend to accentuate opportunities rather than risk. The risks can be exacerbated in a cross-border context; the Equitable Life mis-selling scandal, which affected retail investors in a number of Member States, highlighted not only the risk of misleading marketing communications, but also the tendency of cross-border investors to rely on marketing.[208]

Although the 2002 Distance Marketing of Financial Services Directive and the horizontal consumer protection regime provide ancillary support (section 5.4), retail investor protection against marketing risk is largely a function of MiFID II's requirements. Article 24(3) addresses marketing risks through an overarching, conduct-shaping rule which requires that all information, including marketing communications, which is addressed by a firm to (potential) clients must be 'fair, clear and not misleading'. It governs all communications between the firm and the investor, but has particular significance for marketing communications.

Article 24(3) will be amplified by administrative rules.[209] These are likely to reflect the precursor MiFID I administrative regime under the 2006 Commission MiFID I Directive, which imposed standards on the content and presentation of marketing communications, but did not provide for more interventionist mechanisms, such as the prohibition of marketing communications. Similarly, it did not require pre-approval of marketing communications or prescribe their content. The overarching MiFID I obligation that communications must be 'fair, clear and not misleading' was amplified by a series of administrative rules broadly designed to address the more acute risks which marketing can generate. Firms were to ensure that information be presented in such a way that it was likely to be understood by the 'average member' of the group addressed (2006 Commission MiFID I Directive Article 27(2)). Marketing communications were to be accurate and were not to emphasize the potential benefits of an investment without also giving a fair and prominent indication of risk, and communications were not to disguise, diminish, or obscure important items, statements, or warnings (Article 27(2)). Particular requirements applied to a range of marketing techniques prone to investor over-reaction, such as suggestions of endorsement by a regulatory authority (prohibited under Article 27(8)), tax information (Article 27(7)), simulated historic returns (Article 27(5)), past performance disclosure (Article 27(4)), comparisons (Article 27(3)), and projections (Article 27(6)). This broadly facilitative regime can be expected to be reflected in the new generation of MiFID II administrative rules.

---

[208] European Parliament, Committee of Inquiry into the Crisis of the Equitable Life Assurance Society, Report on the crisis of the Equitable Life Assurance Society (2007) (A6-0203/2007) 255–7.

[209] Art 24(13) empowers the Commission to adopt administrative rules governing the conditions which information must comply with in order to be fair, clear, and not misleading.

Retail investors are particularly vulnerable to cold calls, particularly where the calls relate to 'boiler room' frauds which seek to sell worthless shares. Unusually, given investor vulnerability in this context—but reflecting a long-standing approach which dates to the 2002 Distance Marketing of Financial Services Directive, which only curtails the use of automatic-calling machines and fax machines[210] and does not prohibit cold calls[211]—MiFID II does not directly address cold calls. In one of the few examples of an area of significant importance to the retail markets which falls outside the EU regime, the treatment of cold calls remains with the Member States; the *Alpine Investments* ruling suggests, however, that the Court of Justice will be sympathetic to Member State rules in this area, even where they pose an obstacle to the Treaty freedoms.[212] Where the calls are made by MiFID II-scope firms, they are, however, subject to the general fair treatment obligation and to the Article 24(3) requirement that any information communicated during a call be fair, clear, and not misleading. In addition, the 2005 Unfair Commercial Practices Directive characterizes 'persistent and unwanted solicitation' by phone, email, and fax as 'unfair' (and so prohibited), although this is without prejudice to the 2002 Distance Marketing of Financial Services Directive.[213] But retail investors are typically most vulnerable to cold calls from overseas 'boiler rooms' which are usually beyond the reach of EU regulation and national enforcement.

Overall, the MiFID II marketing regime, if its administrative rules follow the MiFID I approach, is likely to avoid the risks of over-prescription and related 'tick-the-box' compliance, as it focuses on core principles rather than on prescribing content and requiring 'laundry lists' of risk warnings which are of limited use to investors. It should also give NCAs the flexibility to design related supervisory and enforcement strategies calibrated to local market needs and to respond to emerging risks, although ESMA has a key role to play in the communication of strong supervisory practices and in exhorting NCAs not to neglect strong supervision and enforcement.

IX.5.2.5 2014 MiFID II: Quality of Advice—Articles 24 and 25

(a) Investment Advice and Independent Investment Advice (MiFID II Article 24)
MiFID I significantly strengthened pan-EU investor protection in the retail markets by including 'investment advice' as a passportable core service, subject to MiFID I's conduct regime. The regulation of 'investment advice' remains pivotal to retail market protection under MiFID II. But MiFID II moves away from the broadly process-based model which defined the MiFID I approach, and which relied on investment firm application and senior management oversight of principles-based suitability and conflict-of-interest rules to deliver good investor outcomes, and adopts a more intrusive approach—primarily by means of a new 'independent investment advice' regime, but also by means of a more prescriptive and remuneration-focused conflict-of-interest regime.

---

[210] Art 10(1) requires the consumer's prior consent before the use of automatic-calling machines and fax machines is permitted.

[211] Art 10(2) appears to leave the issue of prior consent to the discretion of the Member States under an opt-in/opt-out model.

[212] Case C-384/93 *Alpine Investments v Minister van Financiën* [1995] ECR I-1141.

[213] Annex I, para 26.

Structural reform of the EU distribution sector through support of fee-based 'independent advice' (and the related prohibition of commission payments) has been a recurring feature of EU retail market policy for some time and has been strongly supported by retail market stakeholders.[214] The Commission, which had shown an earlier, if poorly executed, enthusiasm for an independent advice model during the MiFID I negotiations,[215] warned in its 2007 Green Paper on Retail Financial Services that the sales and distribution infrastructure '[was] not always optimal'.[216] The European Parliament similarly highlighted the importance of access to 'unbiased investment advice',[217] while a key report by the Council's influential Financial Services Committee warned that the capacity of existing distribution channels to deliver the required advisory and sales services was underdeveloped and posed a risk to effective retirement provision.[218]

As long as retail investors struggle to decode commission risks but depend on advice services, the use of more muscular regulatory/supervisory devices to influence the structure of the advice industry by supporting fee-based independent investment advice seems reasonable. But the risks of an EU strategy are considerable. Delivery channels for advice across the EU vary. A fee-based model must grapple with very considerable investor resistance to fee-based investment advice.[219] The risks in terms of access to advice are considerable; some evidence suggests that commission-based advisers are more receptive to retail investors who might, initially at least, be unprofitable.[220]

MiFID II, however, has seen the EU engage with structural reform of the advice industry. As under MiFID I, investment advice generally is subject to a suitability/know your client requirement (discussed in this section 5.2.5) and to conflict-of-interest requirements (discussed in this section 5.2.5). But in a new requirement, appropriate information must be provided to clients or potential clients, and in good time before the investment advice is provided, as to whether the advice is provided on an 'independent' basis or not; whether it is based on a broad or more restricted analysis of different types of financial instruments and, in particular, whether the range is limited to financial instruments issued or provided by entities having close links with the investment firm, or any other legal or

---

[214] FIN-USE, Opinion on the European Commission Green Paper on the Enhancement of the EU Framework for Investment Funds (2005).

[215] The Commission's 2001 'Initial Orientations' for ISD reform suggested that 'advice' could be defined as 'independent investment advice' paid for by the client, and distinguished from the provision of advice through tied agents (Commission, Overview of Proposed Adjustments to the ISD (2001) 11). The Commission somewhat helplessly acknowledged that the treatment of advice in the sale of proprietary products was 'unclear'. Following support during the MiFID I consultation process for the independence of advice to be supported through background conflict-of-interest and disclosure techniques (Commission, Revised Orientations on ISD Reform (2002) Annex 4, 16), the latter model was followed in MiFID I.

[216] n 29, 17.

[217] European Parliament, Resolution on Financial Services Policy (2005–2010) White Paper, 11 July 2007 (P6_TA(2007)0338) (2007) (2007 Van den Burg II Resolution) para 36.

[218] n 43, 21.

[219] The extent of retail investor reluctance to pay a fee for advice was a recurring theme of major policy reviews and studies across the EU including at national level—eg France's 2005 Delmas Report (n 71, 9) and the UK's RDR (FSA, Accessing Investment Products, Consumer Research No 73 (2008) 2). Similar results have been found at pan-EU level: the 2008 Optem Report found that inexperienced consumers did not envisage paying a fee for advice (n 44, 100), while the 2010 Consumer Decision Making Study found that a 'significant minority' (26–30 per cent of its research sample) were 'disproportionately averse' to paying an upfront fee for advice and regarded it as an immediately incurred loss: n 4, 9 and 338–9.

[220] Deloitte and Touche, Costing Intermediary Services. A Report for the FSA (2008).

economic relationships with the firm, such as a contractual relationship, so close as to pose a risk of impairing the independent basis of the advice provided (in effect, whether the advice relates to proprietary or otherwise 'tied' products); and whether the firm will provide the client with a periodic assessment of the financial instruments recommended to clients (Article 24(4)).

Where advice is provided on an 'independent' basis, two constraints apply (Article 24(7)). First, the firm must assess a 'sufficient range' of financial instruments available on the market, which financial instruments should be 'sufficiently diverse' with regard to their type and issuers or product providers to ensure that the client's investment objectives can be suitably met, and should not be limited to instruments issued or provided by the investment firm itself or entities having close links to the investment firm, or by entities with which the firm has such close legal or economic relationships (such as a contractual relationship) so as to pose a risk of impairing the independent basis of the advice provided.[221]

Second, and more radically, the firm cannot accept and retain fees, commissions, or any monetary and non-monetary benefits paid or provided by any third party (or person acting on behalf of a third party) in relation to the provision of the service to clients. A *de minimis* exception applies in that minor non-monetary benefits that are capable of enhancing the quality of service provided to the client, and which are of a scale and nature that they could not be judged to impair compliance with the investment firm's duty to act in the best interest of the client, should be clearly disclosed, but are not subject to the prohibition.[222] A prohibition on commissions also applies in relation to discretionary asset management (Chapter III sect 2). Recital 74 to MiFID II suggests that, accordingly, where a payment is received (the recital highlights in particular payments from issuers and product providers) it must be returned in full to the client as soon as possible after receipt, and that the firm may not offset any such payments from fees owed by the client to the firm, and that a policy must be set up to ensure that any such payments are allocated and transferred to clients.

A related structural reform directed towards the prevention of conflict-of-interest risks is designed to address product/service 'bundling'—a practice which is vulnerable to conflict-of-interest risk: where products or services are bundled together, firms are to inform the client as to the possibility and cost of buying the different components separately (Article 24(11)).[223]

The independent advice reform, and in particular the related commission prohibition which reflects a current trend to ban incentives (in the EU and internationally),[224] represents an attempt to address the deep-seated conflict-of-interest risks which trouble the EU product distribution market. It also represents an attempt at structural reform, by

---

[221] Administrative rules will address the criteria governing this assessment (Art 24(13)).

[222] The conditions governing these permissible inducements are to be amplified by administrative rules: Art 24(13).

[223] Where the risks resulting from the bundle are likely to be different from the risks of the separate components, the firm must provide an adequate description of the different components of the bundle and the way in which the interaction modifies the risks in question. ESMA (in conjunction with the European Banking Authority (EBA) and the European Insurance and Occupational Pensions Authority (EIOPA)) is to develop guidelines for the assessment and supervision for related cross-selling practices.

[224] Commission payments have been banned in the UK, the Netherlands, and Australia since 2013.

linking 'independent investment advice' to fee-based advice. Given the extent to which suitability and generic conflict-of-interest management rules struggle to deliver good outcomes, as the persistent evidence of mis-selling under MiFID I suggests, more radical intervention is warranted. But the reform is limited and targets only independent investment advice. As a result, the reforms will affect only a very small segment of the EU product distribution market, most of which is in the UK; some 16–18 per cent of what the Commission describes as the 'mass affluent' sector in the EU (some 40–45 million persons) receive independent advice, and most of this population of clients is based in the UK (60 per cent of all EU independent advisers are based in the UK).[225] But the UK distribution sector has already been the subject of swingeing and radical reforms under the Retail Distribution Review reforms, which came into force in January 2013 and which ban commission in the distribution of packaged investment products generally, impose strict labelling requirements as to whether investment advice is 'independent' or 'restricted' given the nature of the 'relevant market' on which investment advice is based, and introduce strict new qualification rules for investment advisers.[226]

In addition, distribution problems in the EU are primarily a function of the 'financial supermarket' model and of advice on/sales of proprietary products, which are not addressed by the commission prohibition, although the general constraints on remuneration (Article 24(10), discussed in this section 5.2.5) will apply to these distributors. The reform accordingly sits uneasily in an EU market dominated by sales of proprietary products.

(b) Suitability and Appropriateness (2014 MiFID II Article 25)

All investment advice, whether or not it is independent, is subject to the suitability requirement initially introduced under MiFID I (MiFID II Article 25).

Suitability rules have long been associated with a paternalistic approach to the retail investor.[227] More recently, they have been associated with minimizing the behavioural weaknesses which can disable optimal investor decision-making.[228] Suitability rules are process-based and do not prescribe a particular outcome, but they require that an adviser 'knows the client' and makes a personalized recommendation which reflects the investor's profile. A mandatory suitability assessment can accordingly also support investor access to a wider range of products which might otherwise be restricted through public marketing restrictions, and can thereby support diversification and increase investors' ability to hedge against market risks.

The suitability assessment required under MiFID II takes two forms: (i) the assessment of 'suitability' (Article 25(2)) and (ii) the assessment of 'appropriateness' (Article 25(3)). Whether the assessment is to suitability or appropriateness depends in each case on the degree of client reliance on the adviser. Execution-only services in 'non-complex products' are not subject to the requirement to apply a suitability assessment (section 5.2.6).

---

[225] 2011 MiFID II/MiFIR Proposals Impact Assessment, n 136, 190.
[226] n 168.
[227] Markham, J, 'Protecting the Institutional Investor—Jungle Predator or Shorn Lamb' (1995) 12 *Yale J Reg* 345.
[228] Cunningham, L, 'Behavioural Finance and Investor Governance' (2002) 59 *Washington & Lee LR* 767, 798–9.

Under Article 25(2), where the firm provides investment advice or portfolio management services, a suitability assessment is required.[229] The process-based requirement allows firms a significant degree of flexibility; the process is calibrated to the nature of the client, the service, and the investment. This flexibility allows the suitability assessment to apply to the range of choices which may be made by the firm; it captures, for example, any decision by the firm to choose a particular platform on which to manage an investor's portfolio. The suitability rule requires that the firm must obtain the 'necessary information' regarding the client's knowledge and experience in the investment field, which must be relevant to the specific type of product or service, and regarding the client's financial situation (including ability to bear losses) and investment objectives (including risk tolerance),[230] so as to enable the firm to recommend the investment services and financial instruments 'suitable' for the client and, in particular, in accordance with the client's risk tolerance and ability to bear losses.[231] Where an investment firm provides investment advice recommending a package of services or 'bundled' products, the assessment must consider whether the overall bundle or package is suitable.

Where the necessary information is not provided, a firm can only proceed with the transaction in question on a non-advised basis, under the execution-only regime, as long as the conditions of that regime and the Article 24(1) fair treatment principle are met; the same strategy could be adopted where a firm determines that a transaction is unsuitable for the investor. The MiFID II suitability regime is broadly based on the MiFID I template, with the addition of the requirement to consider risk tolerance and ability to bear losses, and finessing in relation to bundled products and services. But it contains a useful innovation in the form of the requirement for a suitability statement, which sets out how the advice offered meets the preferences, needs, and other characteristics of the client, and which should strengthen firms' compliance incentives and support investor monitoring (Article 25(6)).[232]

A lighter-touch 'appropriateness' regime (Article 25(3)) applies where services 'other than Article 25(2)' (investment advice and discretionary asset management) services are provided. These services include in particular execution-only transactions in complex products

---

[229] The suitability regime is to be amplified by administrative rules (Art 25(8)). These rules can be expected to follow the administrative rules adopted under the 2006 Commission MiFID I Directive on the suitability regime.

[230] The MiFID I administrative regime provided that the information to be collected concerning the investor's financial situation include, where relevant, information on the investor's source and extent of regular income, assets, investments and real property, and regular financial commitments (2006 Commission MiFID I Directive Art 35(3)), while the information with respect to investment objectives covered the investor's time horizon, risk-taking preferences, risk profile, and the purposes of the investment (Art 35(4)). Information related to knowledge and experience included the level of education, profession, or former profession of the investor (Art 37).

[231] Under the MiFID I administrative regime, the firm was to obtain such information as was necessary for it to understand the 'essential facts' about the client, and for the firm to have a 'reasonable basis for believing', given due consideration of the nature and extent of the service provided, that the transaction satisfied three suitability criteria: it met the client's investment objectives; the client was able financially to bear the related investment risks consistent with his investment objectives; and the client had the necessary experience and knowledge in order to understand the risks involved in the transaction or in the management of the portfolio (2006 Commission MiFID I Directive Art 35).

[232] The Art 25(6) rules governing the suitability statement provide, *inter alia*, for the provision of the statement in the distance services context.

(which cannot be sold through the non-advised MiFID II execution-only channel). The appropriateness assessment requires the firm to ask the client to provide information only regarding the investor's knowledge and experience in the investment field[233] relevant to the specific type of product or service demanded, so as to enable the firm to assess whether the service or product is 'appropriate'; to this end, the firm must simply assess whether the client has the necessary experience and knowledge in order to understand the risks involved in relation to the specific type of product or service offered or demanded.[234] By contrast with the suitability regime, an assessment of the client's financial situation or investment objectives is not required. Where the service relates to a bundle of services or products, the assessment must consider whether the overall bundle or package is appropriate.

Suitability requirements are an essential element of the regulatory distribution toolkit, but they have limitations.[235] Where only lip service is paid to the different elements of the suitability test, suitable recommendations are less likely to be made.[236] The quality of advice depends in particular on the existence or absence of remuneration-related incentives, as discussed later in section 5.2.5. It also depends on the myriad behavioural and other factors which shape the exercise of an adviser's investment judgement,[237] including herding dynamics, which are very difficult to displace through regulation. Suitability requirements are also problematic in terms of supervision and enforcement. Suitability assessments are based on context, information, experience, judgement, and the nature of the client, all of which pose considerable *ex-ante* assessment and enforcement difficulties. Supervisory fact-finds are complex and may require troublesome, *ex-post* benchmarking of advice and a considerable commitment of supervisory resources and expertise. The importance of supervision is recognized under MiFID II, which provides that Member States must require investment firms to ensure (and demonstrate to NCAs on request) that natural persons giving investment advice or information about financial instruments or services possess the necessary knowledge and competence to fulfil their obligations under Article 25 and Article 24 and publish the criteria used to assess knowledge and competence (Article 25(1)).

Given the strenuous supervisory and enforcement action which the embedding of strong suitability practices seems to require,[238] the difficulties in achieving strong supervision and enforcement, and significant divergences across the Member States with respect to the embedding of good practices,[239] ESMA has a key role to play in supporting NCAs. The

---

[233] This information was specified under Art 37 of the 2006 Commission MiFID I Directive.

[234] As was specified under the 2006 Commission MiFID I Directive Art 36.

[235] The 2011 Synovate Report underlined the difficulties, finding that there was no significant difference between firms which followed MiFID I and those which did not with respect to whether their investment recommendations were suitable or unsuitable: n 169, 100.

[236] The 2011 Synovate Report underlined that MiFID I's risk profile requirements, in particular, might have been applied in a superficial manner, given the evidence that most advisers were neither methodological nor comprehensive in applying the risk profile requirement: n 169, 61.

[237] The Synovate Report recommended that 'advisory engagement should not be viewed as a "checklist" of MiFID guidelines ... the actual diagnosis of "investment suitability" is a complex and relatively cognitive process, subject to the adviser's own personal experience and judgment': n 169, 13.

[238] eg FSA, Assessing the Quality of Investment Advice in the Retail Banking Sector. A Mystery Shopping Review (2013).

[239] The 2011 Synovate Report found significant cross-Member State variation in levels of compliance with the MiFID I know-your-client requirements: n 169, 60. Member States with more developed financial markets (and in particular the UK, France, and Finland) displayed stronger due diligence practices.

initial indications augur well. ESMA's 2012 guidelines on suitability[240] are detailed, practical, and robust, and are designed to ensure that the investment firm remains responsible for the suitability assessment and that the responsibility is not devolved to the investor by means of, for example, signature of complex suitability questionnaires or of online assessment tools.[241] ESMA has also taken targeted action in relation to complex products with an opinion on the application of the MiFID I regime (including its suitability rules) to the sale and marketing of complex products.[242]

(c) Conflicts of Interest and Inducements (2014 MiFID II Articles 23 and 24)

The retail investor is exposed to myriad conflict-of-interest risks in the investment firm/client relationship generally, including in the asset management and brokerage contexts. For most retail investors, however, the main source of conflict-of-interest risk is the advice/sales channel and the related remuneration structures. The new MiFID II prohibition on commissions is designed to materially reduce conflict-of-interest risk with respect to independent investment advice. But the commission prohibition is limited. The delivery of good outcomes for investors who engage with firms through other distribution channels, and in particular through financial supermarket advisers who advise on proprietary products, will continue to be dependent on the effectiveness of the MiFID II suitability regime, and of the MiFID II conflict-of-interest management regime more generally. An obligation to avoid prejudicial conflicts of interest is implicit in the Article 24(1) fair treatment principle. But conflict-of-interest management is additionally addressed by the MiFID II conflicts regime—Article 16(3) and Article 23—and by the discrete MiFID II regime governing remuneration and inducements. In further support of strong conflict-of-interest management, the new investment firm governance regime requires the management body of an investment firm to define, oversee, and be accountable for the implementation of governance arrangements that ensure effective and prudent management of an organization, including the segregation of duties in the organization and the prevention of conflicts of interest, in a manner that promotes the integrity of the market and the interests of clients. Client interests and conflict-of-interest management have accordingly been placed at the heart of the management body's responsibilities and linked to the oversight duties of senior management (Article 9(3)).

The conflict-of-interest regime (which broadly follows the MiFID I template, albeit with a number of enhancements directed towards remuneration and inducements) is designed to contain damaging conflicts *ex-ante* through identification and management techniques.[243] Firms must take 'all appropriate steps' to identify, to prevent, and to manage conflicts of interests including (in a MiFID II trilogue addition) those caused by the receipt of inducements from third parties or by the firm's own remuneration and other incentive structures (Article 23(1)), and to adopt organizational and administrative arrangements with a view to taking 'all reasonable steps' to prevent conflicts of interest from adversely

---

Conversely, the Report found that unsuitable recommendations tended to be more prevalent in more developed financial markets: at 86.

[240] ESMA/2012/387.

[241] And include warnings, eg, with respect to the fitness for purpose of online suitability assessment tools and practical guidance as to how the risk tolerance of clients can be established, including that levels of potential loss should be indicated.

[242] ESMA/2014/146.

[243] See further Ch IV sect 7.3 on the conflict-of-interests regime, which is noted here in outline.

affecting client interests (Article 16(3)). Where the organizational and administrative arrangements adopted are not sufficient to ensure 'with reasonable confidence' that risk of damage to client interests will be prevented, the firm must clearly disclose the general nature and/or the sources of the conflicts of interest to the client before undertaking business on its behalf (Article 23(2)).

In an addition to MiFID I, conflicts of interest arising from remuneration structures are specifically addressed by Article 24(10).[244] It provides that a firm must ensure it does not remunerate or assess the performance of staff in a way that conflicts with its duty to act in the best interests of clients. Additionally, it must not make any arrangements by way of remuneration or otherwise that could incentivize its staff to recommend a particular financial instrument to a retail client when the firm could offer a different financial instrument which would better meet that client's needs. This requirement is bolstered by the MiFID II firm governance regime, which requires that the management body define, approve, and oversee a remuneration policy aimed at encouraging fair treatment of clients as well as at avoiding conflicts of interest in relationships with clients.[245]

In addition, MiFID II contains a general prohibition on all inducements, save those which meet the applicable conditions, as was called for by the European Parliament (Article 24(9)); the prohibition broadly reflects the administrative regime which governed inducements under MiFID I.[246]

The conflict-of-interest regime has accordingly been significantly strengthened with respect to remuneration/inducements and related incentive risks, which were not expressly addressed under MiFID I. The effectiveness of the conflict-of-interest regime remains heavily dependent on rigorous supervision and enforcement, however, given the powerful perverse incentives to which retail product distribution is vulnerable. While it appears that NCAs are increasingly focusing on conflict-of-interest risk, ESMA provides an important resource for supporting strong NCA practices. CESR had previously followed a muscular approach, adopting strict guidelines on inducements in 2010.[247] ESMA looks set to be

---

[244] The remuneration restrictions were added during the trilogue discussions.

[245] 2014 MiFID II Art 9(3). On the governance regime, see Ch IV sect 6.4.

[246] Under Art 24 (9) where a firm pays or is paid any fee or commission, or provides (or is provided with) any non-monetary benefit in connection with the provision of an investment service or ancillary service), it will be regarded as not fulfilling the Art 23 conflict of interest obligation or the Art 24(1) fair treatment obligation unless the payment is designed to enhance the quality of the service and does not impair compliance with the firm's duty to act honestly, fairly, and professionally in the best interests of the client. In addition, the existence, nature, and amount of the payment (or, where the amount cannot be ascertained, the method of calculating the amount) must be clearly disclosed to the client, in a manner that is comprehensive, accurate, and understandable, prior to the provision of the related investment or service. In a final condition, and where applicable, the firm must inform the client of mechanisms available for transferring the payment in question to the client (these mechanisms are not mandatory). Payments or benefits necessary for the provision of services (such as those related to custody costs and settlement fees) and which, by their nature, cannot give to conflicts with the firm's Art 24(1) duty to act honestly, fairly and professionally in accordance with the best interests of clients are not subject to this regime. Inducements are, therefore permitted, although the Art 24(1) require-ment, in particular, should act as a mitigant to the risks to which investors are exposed. This provision is heavily based on the 2004 MiFID I administrative regime on inducements, but adds the requirement for disclosure relating to repayment possibilities.

[247] CESR, Inducements under MiFID (2007) (CESR/07-228b). The Guidelines included recommenda-tions on when an inducement was designed to enhance the quality of the service and would not impair compliance with the firm's obligation to act in the best interests of clients.

similarly robust. Its own-initiative decision to adopt guidelines on remuneration practices under MiFID I augurs well for its commitment to addressing incentive risks. The 2013 Guidelines on Remuneration are designed to ensure the consistent application of the MiFID I Article 19(1) and Articles 13(3) and 18 requirements (reflected in MiFID II Articles 24(1) and 16(3) and 23) with respect to remuneration policies as they apply to employees who engage with clients in particular.[248] The Guidelines are notable for their close focus on quality-of-advice risks[249] and their strongly operational dimension.[250] In the absence of robust supervision and enforcement, however, previous experience suggests that the long-standing conflict-of-interest problems which trouble distribution may persist.

IX.5.2.6 2014 MiFID II: Execution-Only Distribution and Trading—Article 25

(a) Product Distribution

Low-cost, non-advised distribution is supported by the 2014 MiFID II through the execution-only regime which provides that execution-only services are exempt from the potentially costly suitability requirements (Article 25(4)). Execution-only distribution channels allow investors to access low-cost distribution services and provide informed investors with a speedy and flexible means for acquiring investments. The execution-only distribution channel is, however, an inherently risky one, even allowing for the incentive risks which trouble intermediated distribution. A series of restrictions accordingly apply.

The MiFID II execution-only regime (Article 25(4)) is more prescriptive than the MiFID I regime and has limited the range of instruments which can be sold through execution-only channels.[251] There are six classes of instruments which may be sold in this manner. Shares admitted to trading on a regulated market, or on an equivalent third country market, or on a multilateral trading facility (MTF) may be sold execution-only,[252] but only where these are shares in companies; shares in non-UCITS collective investment undertakings and shares that embed a derivative are excluded, given the higher risk they represent. So too may bonds or other forms of securitized debt admitted to trading on a regulated market or on an equivalent third country market or on an MTF, but excluding those instruments which embed a derivative or incorporate a structure which makes it difficult for the client to understand the risk involved. Money-market instruments can be sold execution-only, but not those money-market instruments that embed a derivative or incorporate a structure which makes it difficult for the client to understand the risk involved. Shares or units in

---

[248] ESMA Guidelines on Remuneration Policies and Practices (MiFID) (2013) (ESMA/2013/606).

[249] The Guidelines provide, eg, that remuneration should not be designed in such a way as to create incentives to favour a firm's proprietary products (including sales of more lucrative products); that where a direct link is made between remuneration and sales of specific financial instruments, the firm is unlikely to be able to demonstrate compliance with MiFID; and that the qualitative indicators used to assess remuneration should include review of compliance with suitability requirements and the findings of reviews of the outcomes of sales/advice activities.

[250] The Guidelines contain detailed practical examples of good and bad practices.

[251] The Commission originally proposed only the exclusion of structured UCITSs from execution-only channels. The Council negotiations led to a significantly more restrictive regime and, in particular, to the requirement that instruments sold execution-only should not incorporate structures which make it difficult for clients to understand the risks involved.

[252] A multilateral trading facility is a form of organized venue which includes many of the EU's leading 'second tier' markets on which shares in smaller companies are traded. See further Ch V.

UCITSs may also be sold execution-only, but not structured UCITSs.[253] Structured deposits may be sold execution-only, but not if they incorporate a structure which makes it difficult to understand the risk of return or the cost of exiting the product before term. Finally, other 'non-complex' financial instruments can be sold execution-only.[254]

In addition, the service must be provided at the initiative of the client, who must be clearly informed that the firm is not required to assess the appropriateness of the instrument or service offered, and that the client does not accordingly benefit from the corresponding protection of the relevant conduct-of-business rules. The firm must also comply with its background conflict-of-interest obligations under Article 23. Where the requirements for an execution-only sale are not met (for example, all transactions in derivatives fall outside the execution-only regime), the appropriateness-based suitability assessment must be undertaken. An additional requirement to MiFID I, added by MiFID II, provides that the provision of credits or loan services to clients (margin services) takes the execution of related orders outside the execution-only regime, given the increased risks of such transactions.

While the execution-only regime has become more restrictive under MiFID II, particularly with respect to the requirement that the structure of the instrument not make it difficult for the client to understand the risk involved,[255] the exclusion of structured UCITSs represents the most significant change from the MiFID I regime. As discussed in Chapter III, the expansion in the range of investments which can be undertaken through the UCITS structure, in combination with the MiFID I inclusion of UCITSs as qualifying instruments for the execution-only channel, meant that highly risky products could be sold to the retail markets through the MiFID I execution-only channel—although simple derivatives, disqualified as 'complex instruments' for the purposes of the execution-only regime, could not. This asymmetry was addressed at the outset of the MiFID I Review. The Commission's 2010 MiFID I Review consultation queried whether the execution-only regime should be abolished, or whether it should be retained but with the exclusion of particular UCITSs which employed more complex portfolio management techniques.[256] The 2011 MiFID II Proposal ultimately took a more limited approach, excluding structured UCITSs from the execution-only regime and retaining the channel.[257] This

---

[253] Structured UCITSs are defined under the UCITS regime as UCITSs which provide investors, at certain predetermined dates, with algorithmic-based payoffs that are linked to the performance or to the realization of price changes or other conditions, of financial assets, indices, or reference portfolios, or UCITS with similar features: Commission Regulation (EU) No 583/2010 [2010] OJ L176/1 Art 36.

[254] A delegation provides for administrative rules to amplify when a financial instrument is non-complex: Art 25(8); in addition, ESMA is to provide related guidelines. The precursor 2004 MiFID I administrative regime defined 'non-complex instruments' as instruments which: were not derivatives; in relation to which there were frequent opportunities to dispose of, redeem, or otherwise realize the instrument at prices publicly available to market participants and which were market prices or prices made available, or validated, by valuation systems independent of the issuers; did not involve any actual or potential liability for the client that exceeded the cost of acquiring the instrument; and in relation to which adequately comprehensive information on the characteristics of the instrument was publicly available and likely to be readily understood so as to enable the average retail client to make an informed judgement as to whether or not to enter into the transaction: Art 38.

[255] In respect of which ESMA is to provide guidelines: Art 25(10). This requirement reflects CESR's earlier advice over the MiFID I Review on reform of the 2004 MiFID I execution-only regime (CESR/10-589).

[256] 2010 MiFID I Review Consultation, n 184, 54–6.

[257] 2011 MiFID II Proposal, n 181, Art 25.

approach, with additional refinements and restrictions in relation to other financial instruments, was followed in the final MiFID II text—although it was initially resisted by the European Parliament, which did not support a distinction between UCITSs and structured UCITSs,[258] and the Council negotiations proved difficult.[259] The issues raised by any change to the designation of UCITSs as 'non-complex' financial instruments are many and complex. The risk of detriment to the retail sector, following the 'stretching' of the UCITS brand to include funds deploying complex and high-risk portfolio management techniques (in particular hedge-fund-like funds), is potentially significant, but industry opposition is considerable, given the potential damage to the UCITS brand globally (Chapter III section 3.8.8). The MiFID II execution-only regime accordingly can be regarded as adopting an ambitious approach,[260] reflecting the generally consumer-orientated nature of the MiFID II crisis-era retail market reforms.

(b) The Trading Process

The execution-only channel also supports direct trading by retail investors. Direct trading by retail investors is not common across the EU, although technological advances have made the trading process accessible to the retail market.[261] The trading process generally is subject to principal/agent risks arising from the broker/investor relationship. But retail investor trading is also often associated with poor investor outcomes from ill-advised trading decisions.[262] Intermediated investment is likely to deliver the best outcomes for most investors, given the prejudicial impact of trading costs, market risk, and behavioural weaknesses (notably the over-confidence bias) in the trading context.[263]

The generic MiFID II conduct rules, including the fair treatment principle, disclosure requirements, and conflict-of-interest management rules, apply to the trading process. As discussed in Chapter VI on the trading process, a series of additional requirements also apply to the trading process, and address order handling and the execution process. These rules are generally not calibrated to the retail sector, although a discrete regime applies to best execution, in the form of a price-based retail benchmark for best execution and

---

[258] European Parliament Negotiating Position, n 181, Art 25(3)(a)(iv).

[259] While most Member States agreed that certain UCITSs were too complex for retail investors to trade in through execution-only channels, there was disagreement on how to address the issue, particularly with respect to the criteria which would disqualify particular UCITSs from execution-only sales: Danish Presidency Progress Report on MiFID II/MiFIR, 20 June 2012 (Council Document 11536/12) 8.

[260] The Commission in its Impact Assessment acknowledged that the execution-only channel was strongly supported by investors, but argued that 'precautionary' intervention was necessary given the evidence from the financial crisis that access to more complex instruments needed to be strictly conditional on a proven understanding of risk and that the ability of investors to borrow funds solely for investment purposes needed to be tightly controlled, given the potential for risks to be magnified, as well as of the need to review the classification of UCITSs for the purposes of execution-only sale, given the array of complex products which could be sold under the UCITS label: 2011 MiFID II/MiFIR Proposals Impact Assessment, n 136, 16.

[261] eg 2007 BME Report, n 44, 115 and 145. See further Moloney, n 7, 345–6.

[262] eg in the EU context and from an extensive literature on trading decisions: Anderson, A, 'All Guts, No Glory: Trading and Diversification Among Online Investors' (2007) 13 *European Financial Management* 448 (based on a Swedish sample and pointing to failures to diversify, aggressive trading, and market underperformance linked to trading costs).

[263] eg French, K, 'Presidential Address: the Cost of Active Investing' (2008) 63 *J Fin* 1537; Barber, B and Odean, T, 'The Internet and the Investor' (2001) 15 *J of Econ Perspectives* 41; and Barber, B and Odean, T, 'Trading is Hazardous to Your Wealth. The Common Stock Investment Performance of Individual Investors' (2000) 55 *J Fin* 773.

targeted related disclosure requirements (Chapter VI section 2.2). Retail investors who trade through execution-only channels are also supported by the EU's product disclosure regime and the enhancements which have been delivered under the prospectus and UCITS regimes and which are in train under the PRIPs reform (section 6). More generally, the MiFID I and MiFID II reforms to the order execution process, and the related restructuring of order execution across multiple competing platforms, have reshaped the trading environment within which retail investors operate, potentially lowering costs and increasing diversification possibilities for the subset of retail investors engaged in direct trading (Chapter V).

The EU regime does not address the difficult regulatory questions which 'over-trading' and 'excessive' speculation by retail investors generate. Only limited trading 'frictions' are built into the MiFID II execution-only regime, although the new prohibition on providing margin services without advice represents a significant reform. MiFID II's focus on product distribution and relative lack of focus on retail market trading is, however, warranted given the current shape of retail market investment in the EU; where local markets experience high levels of this form of activity, a local response is likely to be the most efficient one. This is all the more the case as the policy levers available to dull excessive trading are limited and the risks of intervention are considerable.[264]

IX.5.2.7 2014 MiFID II: Disclosure and Record-keeping—Article 24(3) and (4) and 25(5) and (6)

As discussed in section 6, disclosure is a limited tool for delivering good investor outcomes in the retail markets, particularly where disclosure requirements do not address the 'processability' of disclosure. The MiFID II disclosure regime is, at the legislative level, traditional (although some enhancements, particularly with respect to cost disclosure, have been made from the MiFID I regime) and focuses on the identification of the types of disclosures which must be provided to clients; it contrasts sharply with the summary disclosure reforms delivered under the UCITS KIID reform and in train under the PRIPs reform, which focus to a materially greater extent on how key disclosures are delivered and designed.

The high-level Article 24(3) requirement that communications be 'fair, clear, and not misleading' governs all communications between the firm and investor, including those made in the advice context. More specifically, Article 24(4) requires that 'appropriate information' be provided to clients or potential clients 'in good time' (recital 83 to MiFID II notes that the time available should reflect the client's need for sufficient time to read and understand disclosures and should reflect the complexity of the product/service and the client's experience) regarding: the nature of the services (and including the nature of the investment advice provided, as noted in section 5.2.5); the financial instruments and proposed investment strategies, including appropriate guidance on and warnings of the risks associated with these instruments or particular investment strategies and, in a MiFID II enhancement reflecting the new product oversight regime, whether the financial instrument is intended for retail or professional clients, taking account of the intended target

---

[264] Mahoney, P, 'Is There a Cure for Excessive Trading' (1995) 81 *Virginia LR* 713, 715–16.

market; execution venues; and all costs and associated charges (related to investment services and ancillary services), which must include the cost of advice (where relevant) and the cost of the financial instrument recommended or marketed to the client and how the client may pay for it, and encompass any third party payments. Information about costs and charges, including costs and charges in relation to investment services and financial instruments which are not caused by the occurrence of underlying market risk, must be aggregated to allow the client to understand the overall cost as well as the cumulative effect on the return of the investment, and, where the client so requests, an itemized breakdown must be provided. This information must be provided in a comprehensible form in such a manner that the client is reasonably able to understand the nature and risks of the investment service and the specific type of financial instrument being offered and, consequently, to take investment decisions on an informed basis. Information may be provided in a standardized form.

The Article 24(4) disclosure requirements are subject to a delegation to administrative rule-making which is likely to generate extensive administrative rules governing the content and format of information (Article 24(13)). Under the precursor MiFID I administrative regime, the litany of firm disclosures required formed an extensive catalogue of disclosures relating to the firm and the service, the financial instruments in question (including past performance requirements), the risks engaged, costs and charges, and the firm's conflict-of-interest policy. But the administrative regime was traditional and did not engage with formats, standardization, or processability generally, and rapidly came to lag behind the summary disclosure reforms adopted under the UCITS regime in particular. The MiFID I conflict-of-interest disclosures proved limited and were not successful in bringing greater transparency to the distribution process.[265] Whether or not the MiFID II administrative regime will be more imaginative and draw on the processability reforms introduced under the UCITS regime remains to be seen.

In addition, investment firms are subject to record-keeping requirements. An investment firm must establish a record that includes the document(s) agreed between the firm and the client and that sets out the rights and obligations of the parties and the other terms on which the firm will provide services to the client (Article 25(5)). The firm must also provide ongoing reports to the client. These must include periodic communications, taking into account the type and the complexity of the financial instruments involved and the nature of the service provided, and include, where applicable, the costs associated with the transactions and services undertaken (Article 25(6)). The nature of the record-keeping obligation will be amplified by administrative rules (Article 25(8)).

---

[265] 2011 Synovate Report, n 169, 68–9. The Report found that only 5 per cent of advisers discussed conflicts of interest and inducements. While it acknowledged that this did not necessarily mean that 95 per cent of advisers breached the 2004 MiFID I (as inducements may not have been relevant, or conflicts of interest may have been appropriately managed), it warned that 'it is likely that a number of firms may have failed to comply with MiFID'. Similarly, the 2010 Consumer Decision Making Report found that 40 per cent of investors in the sample (6,000) did not know about the adviser's financial incentives and that uncertainty and confusion was higher where the adviser was an investment provider such as a bank or insurance company: n 4, 180–1.

IX.5.3 Distribution and the 2002 IMD

The distribution of insurance is governed by the 2002 Insurance Mediation Directive (the 2002 IMD I)[266] regime. The IMD I regime is currently being reformed through the IMD II reforms,[267] and has also been reformed by MiFID II.

The 2002 IMD I applies to insurance agents and brokers (insurance intermediaries) but not to employees of insurance companies (undertakings); proprietary sales of insurance-based investment products are accordingly not subject to most of the IMD I's rules (MiFID II has brought some change, as noted later in this section 5.3). In addition to imposing registration requirements on insurance agents and brokers, it imposes limited disclosure and quality-of-advice/conflict-of-interest rules. Prior to contract conclusion, brokers must provide investors with certain disclosures concerning the firm[268] and its status (Article 12(1)). The latter disclosures, which have since been reflected in MiFID II, address the independence or otherwise of the intermediary. The intermediary must disclose: whether advice is given on a 'fair analysis' basis; whether the broker is under a contractual obligation to conduct insurance mediation business exclusively with one or more insurance undertakings (and their identities); or whether the intermediary is not under a contractual obligation to conduct insurance mediation business exclusively with one or more insurance undertakings and does not give advice on a 'fair analysis' basis (in which case the identities of the undertakings with which the intermediary may and does conduct business must be supplied).

This disclosure obligation is supplemented by controls on the nature of 'fair analysis' advice, which must be given on the basis of a 'sufficiently large' number of insurance contracts available on the market to enable the intermediary to make a recommendation, in accordance with professional criteria, regarding which contract would be 'adequate' to meet the customer's needs (Article 12(2)). The MiFID II regime reflects this more nuanced approach to advice in the investment context.

Otherwise, however, the IMD I regime is less nuanced than the MiFID II regime. In a quasi-know-your-client requirement, prior to the conclusion of any specific contract the intermediary must at least specify, on the basis of information provided by the customer, the demands and needs of that customer as well as the underlying reasons for any advice given to the customer on a given insurance product (Article 12(3)). The considerably more extensive fair treatment, marketing, suitability, conflict-of-interest/commission risk, and contract requirements which apply under MiFID II do not apply to insurance brokers or to insurance products.

MiFID II has strengthened the IMD I regime by imposing new requirements in relation to 'insurance-based investment products' (MiFID II Article 91).[269] In relation to these

---

[266] n 55.

[267] n 56.

[268] Art 12 requires, *inter alia*, that the intermediary disclose whether the intermediary has a holding, direct or indirect, representing more than 10 per cent of the voting rights or capital of a given insurance undertaking, whether a given insurance undertaking (or parent undertaking) has a holding, direct or indirect, representing more than 10 per cent of the voting rights or the capital in the insurance intermediary, and provide disclosure concerning complaints and redress (Art 12(1)(a)–(e)).

[269] Defined under the revised Art 2 of the 2002 IMD I as an insurance product which offers a maturity or surrender value, and where that maturity or surrender value is wholly or partially exposed, directly or indirectly, to market fluctuations (and excluding specified products, including pension products).

products, IMD I-scope insurance agents and brokers, but also insurance undertakings (in relation to insurance mediation and direct sales) are now subject to a high-level conflict-of-interest management requirement[270] and to fair treatment and disclosure requirements.[271] Member States are empowered (but not required) to prohibit commission payments.[272]

The more extensive IMD II reforms are designed to expand the scope of the IMD I regime to all insurance distribution channels, to strengthen conflict-of-interest risk management, to enhance the suitability and appropriateness of advice, and to raise the level of professional qualifications. The proposed reforms to the distribution of insurance-related investment products are broadly based on the MiFID II template and are designed to align the IMD I regime with the MiFID II regime as regards the distribution of these products. They include a fair treatment principle, enhanced disclosure requirements, conflict-of-interest management requirements, a suitability/appropriateness regime, and requirements governing whether the provision of advice related to insurance investment products is independent (which follow the MiFID II approach and impose a prohibition on commission and a requirement to assess products across the market).[273]

IX.5.4 Distribution and Horizontal Consumer Protection

The 2002 Distance Marketing of Financial Services Directive[274] represented the EU's first major foray into the distribution process and the management of marketing risks. Although overtaken initially by MiFID I and since by MiFID II, it remains a useful if basic investor protection measure, particularly for products and, more particularly, services which fall outside MiFID II as a result of the MiFID II exemption regime. It addresses the risks posed to clients[275] in the context of the distance marketing of financial (including investment) services.[276] In this context, clients' informational disadvantages and monitoring difficulties may be intensified given the lack of personal interaction, and clients may be unable to assess the product or service and the rights and obligations involved. As an FSAP measure, the Directive is heavily based on investor/client-facing disclosure requirements concerning the firm, the distance service, the contract, risk warnings, and redress (Article 3). Disclosure

---

[270] The intermediary or undertaking must maintain and promote effective organizational and administrative arrangements with a view to taking all reasonable steps designed to prevent conflicts of interest from adversely affecting the interests of its customers (2002 IMD I Art 13a and 13b). Under Art 13c, intermediaries and undertakings must take all appropriate steps to identify conflicts of interest between themselves (including their managers, employees, and tied insurance intermediaries), or any person directly or indirectly linked to them by control, and their customers (or between one customer and another), that arise in the course of carrying out insurance distribution. Where these arrangements are not sufficient to ensure with reasonable confidence that risks of damage to customer interests will be prevented, a disclosure obligation applies. The conflicts regime is subject to a delegation for administrative rules.

[271] An insurance intermediary or undertaking must act honestly, fairly and professionally in accordance with the best interests of customers, and all information (including marketing communications) must be fair, clear, and not misleading: Art 13d.

[272] 2002 IMD I Art 13d.

[273] 2012 IMD II Proposal, n 56, Arts 22–25. As the IMD II Proposal relates to insurance products generally and thus addresses a range of risks specific to insurance, it is not covered in detail in this section.

[274] n 62.

[275] The Directive applies to the 'consumer' (any natural person who, in distance contracts covered by the Directive, is acting for purposes outside his business, trade, or profession): Art 2(d).

[276] Arts 2(a) and (e).

delivery obligations are imposed, although formats are not addressed: the supplier must communicate to the consumer all the contractual terms and conditions, and the required disclosures, on paper or, with respect to non-paper communications, on another 'durable medium',[277] in good time before the consumer is bound by any distance contract or offer (Article 5(1)). But by providing a mandatory 14-day withdrawal right,[278] the Directive also takes a more interventionist approach to investor protection. This protection is, however, of limited relevance, as it does not apply where the price of a product or service reflects market fluctuations which may occur during the withdrawal period,[279] although the withdrawal right does apply to contracts to receive investment advice or portfolio management services.

Ancillary protections are also available under the 2000 E Commerce Directive[280] concerning online services—largely with respect to disclosure, but online commercial communications[281] are also subject to clarity requirements.[282] The Directive also engages with contractual requirements and imposes rules on the conclusion of contracts by electronic means which are designed to ensure that contracts concluded by e-commerce are electronically workable.[283]

Retail investors are also protected by the horizontal consumer protection directives which address marketing—chief among them, from the retail investor perspective, the 2005 Unfair Commercial Practices Directive.[284] The Directive,[285] which has its roots in EU consumer law and policy,[286] represents a significant addition to the arsenal available to the retail investor. Like the 2002 Distance Marketing of Financial Services Directive, its protections apply to 'consumers'.[287] It adopts a considerably more interventionist approach to marketing than MiFID II, which for the most part, does not prohibit particular forms of marketing, but relies heavily on firm compliance with the overarching requirement that communications are 'fair, clear, and not misleading'; the 2005 Unfair Commercial Practices Directive, by contrast, prohibits certain types of marketing outright.

It applies to 'unfair' business-to-consumer commercial practices, before, during, and after a commercial transaction in relation to a product (Article 3(1)). The wide and generic definitions of business-to-consumer commercial practices (Article 2(d)) and products (Article 2(c)) bring investment services within the Directive's scope, although commercial

---

[277] Any instrument which enables the consumer to store information addressed personally to him in a way accessible for future reference for a period of time adequate for the purposes of the information and which allows the unchanged reproduction of the information stored (Art 2(f)). This could include website disclosure, but only as long as the Art 2(f) conditions are met.

[278] Arts 6 and 7.

[279] These include services relating to: foreign exchange; money-market instruments; transferable securities; units in CISs; financial futures contracts; forward interest rate agreements; interest rate, currency, and equity swaps; and options to acquire any of these instruments, including equivalent cash-settled instruments.

[280] n 88.

[281] Any form of communication designed to promote, directly or indirectly, the goods, services or image of the provider (Art 2(f)).

[282] Art 6.

[283] Arts 9–11.

[284] n 62.

[285] See, eg, De Groote, B and De Vulder, K, 'European Framework for Unfair Commercial Practices: Analysis of Directive 2005/29' (2007) *J of Business* 16 and Weatherill, S and Bernitz, U (eds), *The Regulation of Unfair Commercial Practices under EC Directive 2005/29/EC: New Rules and Techniques* (2007).

[286] Commission, Green Paper on EU Consumer Protection (2001) (COM (2001) 531) 11–15.

[287] Any natural person who, in commercial practices covered by the Directive, is acting for purposes outside his trade, profession, or craft (Art 2).

practices which are not directly designed to influence transactional decisions,[288] such as annual reports and corporate promotional literature, are excluded (recital 7). The risks posed by misleading marketing of financial products are expressly addressed by recital 10, which highlights the Directive's importance for complex products with a high level of risk to consumers, and particularly financial services products, where a trader seeks to create a false impression of the product's nature.

'Unfair' commercial practices are prohibited (Article 5), although a reasonableness regime applies. A practice is 'unfair' if it is contrary to the requirements of professional diligence[289] and materially distorts,[290] or is likely to materially distort, the economic behaviour with regard to the product of the 'average consumer' whom it reaches or to whom it is addressed (or the average member of the group where the practice is directed to a particular group of consumers). Reasonableness is supported by the 'average consumer' device.[291] A commercial practice is, by default, characterized as 'unfair' and so prohibited where it is 'misleading', within the terms of Articles 6 and 7, or 'aggressive',[292] within the terms of Article 8 and 9. 'Misleading' practices are those which contain false information and are untruthful or in any way, including overall presentation, deceive or are likely to deceive the average consumer across a number of different dimensions,[293] or are likely to cause the consumer to take a transactional decision which would not otherwise have been taken (Article 6). Of particular relevance to the investor protection context is the determination that practices can be misleading where material information (including required invest-ment-related disclosures)[294] is omitted which the average consumer, according to the context, needs in order to take an informed transactional decision, and the omission causes, or is likely to cause, the average consumer to take a transactional decision that would not otherwise have been taken (Article 7(1)). This provision, and the consequent prohibition of the related commercial practice or marketing communication and the prospect of enforce-ment action,[295] dovetails with MiFID II's imposition of positive disclosure requirements on

---

[288] Any decision taken by a consumer concerning whether, how, and on what terms to purchase, make payment in whole or in part for, retain or dispose of a product, or exercise a contractual right in relation to the product, whether the consumer decides to act or to refrain from acting: Art 2(k).

[289] These requirements relate to the standard of special skill and care which a trader may reasonably be expected to exercise towards consumers, commensurate with honest market practices and/or the general principle of good faith in the trader's field of activity.

[290] Behaviour is materially distorted where the practice appreciably impairs the consumer's ability to make an informed decision, causing the consumer to take a transaction decision that would not otherwise have been taken (Art 2(e)).

[291] The 'average consumer' concept is based on the European Court of Justice's consumer law jurispru-dence, and assumes a consumer 'who is reasonably well-informed and reasonably observant and circumspect, taking into account social, cultural and linguistic factors': rec 18.

[292] Aggressive practices are of less direct relevance to the investor protection context; a practice is aggressive if by harassment, coercion, or undue influence it significantly impairs or is likely to significantly impair the average consumer's freedom of choice or conduct with regard to the product and causes the consumer to take a transactional decision which would not otherwise have been taken (Art 8).

[293] These are listed in Art 6(1) and include the existence or nature of the product, its main characteristics, the extent of the trader's commitments, the motives for the practice and the nature of the sales process, the price, and the nature, attributes, and rights of the trader, including qualifications.

[294] Art 7(4) lists information which is to be regarded as material, including the main characteristics of the product, the price, and withdrawal rights, where they apply. MiFID II's disclosure requirements are also regarded as material under Art 7(5).

[295] The Directive requires that penalties are effective, proportionate, and dissuasive (Art 13) and that actions for injunctions can be brought by persons and organizations with a legitimate interest in combating unfair commercial practices (Art 11).

the investment firm. Of similar importance is the determination that a practice is misleading where a trader hides material information or provides material information in an unclear, unintelligible, ambiguous, or untimely manner, or fails to identify the commercial intent of the practice, and where, in either case, this causes, or is likely to cause, the average consumer to take a transactional decision which would otherwise not have been taken (Article 7(2)). This requirement chimes well with MiFID II's overarching requirements that disclosure be 'fair, clear and not misleading' (Article 24(3)) and 'comprehensible' (Article 24(4)). It also imposes discipline on UCITS product providers with respect to UCITS marketing. The Directive's key concepts are challenging from a legal certainty perspective (certainly by comparison with the process-based suitability protections which characterize MiFID II, and even by comparison with the 'fair, clear, and not misleading' concept which governs MiFID II's marketing regime and the overarching Article 24(1) 'fair treatment' principle). In an attempt to provide legal certainty, the 'misleading' and 'aggressive' regime is supplemented by Annex I to the Directive, which sets out a 'black list' of commercial practices which, in all circumstances, are to be regarded as unfair.[296]

IX.6 Disclosure and the Retail Markets

IX.6.1 The EU Disclosure Regime

Effective disclosure design for the retail markets presents one of the most intractable of regulatory problems. Disclosure is an investor-facing tool, but a wealth of evidence underlines the severe difficulties which retail investors face in decoding disclosure and how behavioural dynamics can disable disclosure.[297] The EU evidence, at Member State[298] and EU level,[299] suggests that disclosure is a very limited tool which struggles to enhance the investor decision and support investor monitoring.[300] And even where strenuous efforts are expended in the attempt to deliver effective disclosure, it does not follow that decision-making will be optimal,[301] as research on conflict-of-interest related disclosures

---

[296] These are the only practices which can be deemed 'unfair' without a case-by-case assessment against Arts 5–9 (rec 17). Practices of particular importance to the retail investor include: falsely claiming to be a signatory to a code of conduct; falsely claiming that a code of conduct has an endorsement from a public or other body; falsely claiming that a trader or product has been approved, endorsed, or authorized by a public or private body; and stating or otherwise creating the impression that a product can be legally sold when it cannot.

[297] From the extensive literature see, eg, Williams, n 15; Gray and Hamilton, n 15, 207–8; and Paredes, T, 'Blinded by the Light: Information Overload and its Consequences for Securities Regulation' (2003) 81 *Washington University LQ* 417.

[298] eg 2006 TNS-Sofres Report, n 42 (on the French market) and FSA, Consumer Research No 5, Informed Decisions? How Consumers Use Key Features: A Synthesis of Research on the Use of Product Information at the Point of Sale (2000) (on the UK market).

[299] eg 2010 Consumer Decision Making Report, n 4, reporting on the limitations of conflict of interest disclosures; 2008 Optem Report, n 44, on the limited impact of product disclosures; and Commission, Special Eurobarometer No 203, Public Opinion in Europe on Financial Services. Summary (2005), finding low levels of satisfaction with financial services disclosure generally.

[300] Generally, Schwarcz, A and Wilde, L, 'Intervening in the Market on the Basis of Imperfect Information: A Legal and Economic Analysis' (1978–1979) 127 *UPaLR* 630.

[301] Rachlinski, J, 'The Uncertain Psychological Case for Paternalism' (2003) 97 *Northwestern University LR* 1165.

suggests.[302] To the extent disclosure is useful, its utility is a function of its 'processability', or of the extent to which it can be used by investors and achieves the outcomes sought;[303] repeated extensions and refinements of the types of disclosure which must be provided are of limited value unless processability is addressed. Effective retail market disclosure accordingly requires much more than fiddling with content; it demands deep drilling into investor needs and risks, and close engagement with the dynamics of information processing. In the EU the challenges become acute, as harmonized rules may not only prove ineffective but may obstruct productive national innovation; arbitrage risks are also significant given the silo-based nature of the EU regime and the dangers which arise where disclosures are product-specific and product innovation outstrips the perimeter of regulation.

Disclosure has long been a key element of EU retail market regulation. But the period between the close of the FSAP and the crisis era saw an overdue recognition of the limits of disclosure. The post-FSAP 2007 Green Paper on Retail Financial Services revealed some scepticism concerning disclosure, and highlighted concerns that investment product disclosure was too complex, inadequate, difficult to understand, and did not support informed choice;[304] the Commission's related commitment to reviewing the disclosure regime, given the risk that the 'current variety and accumulation' of information could confuse both the industry and consumers,[305] generated the important 2008 Optem Report. The UCITS review, which commenced as the FSAP closed, led to the ground-breaking UCITS KIID reform which produced a requirement for a summary disclosure document that was highly standardized and deployed an array of mechanisms to support processability, including a standardized risk indicator and composite cost disclosures.[306] The main focus of the crisis-era reforms has been on closer intervention in the retail market, whether with respect to the distribution process or in relation to product intervention. Disclosure has accordingly been less heavily relied on to support good investor outcomes, and is becoming more of a background, education-based tool. But overall, and while pockets of difficulty remain (notably with respect to distribution-related conflicts of interest), product disclosure in particular has become more sophisticated.

IX.6.2 Scope of the Disclosure Regime

The EU's distribution regime (MiFID II Articles 23-25) has a significant disclosure component, including with respect to the conflict-of-interest regime (which includes disclosure requirements) and the quality-of-advice regime (notably the suitability letter). Discrete disclosure requirements also apply to financial instruments and products. The EU retail market disclosure regime also includes the summary disclosure requirements which accompany the following: the detailed prospectus which is required on the issuance of

---

[302] Investors can fail to understand and also over- and under-react to these disclosures: 2010 Consumer Decision Making Report, n 4, 9 and 22.

[303] eg Kozup, J and Hogarth, J, 'Financial Literacy, Public Policy and Consumers' Self Protection—More Questions Fewer Answers' (2008) 42 *J of Consumer Affairs* 127.

[304] n 29, 16.

[305] n 29, 6–7.

[306] See Ch III sect 3.11.3.

securities (the summary prospectus under the prospectus regime);[307] the marketing of UCITSs (the UCITS IV KIID);[308] and the marketing of PRIPs (the PRIPs reform).

IX.6.3 Disclosure for Packaged Retail Investment Products

The UCITS summary KIID is currently the most advanced of the required EU retail market disclosures in terms of 'processability'. But, while a major breakthrough, it sits uneasily with the reality that functionally similar products which substitute for UCITSs, and particularly non-UCITS CISs (including alternative investment-based schemes), structured products, and insurance-based investment products, can be highly complex, are popular with retail investors, but are not subject to a similar summary disclosure regime. Accordingly, comparability across substitutable products is difficult to achieve. Regulatory arbitrage risks are significant. In particular, the variable treatment of cost disclosure under the fragmented UCITS IV/investment distribution/prospectus/insurance regimes, and the ability of product providers to avoid more stringent requirements by constituting products slightly differently, has been identified as a particular risk to retail investors, particularly with respect to cost disclosures.[309] Disclosures for substitutable, non-UCITS investments (governed by the prospectus regime and/or MiFID II) may also be inadequate or not present key risk information clearly, as has been highlighted with respect to structured products in markets across the EU including the Danish,[310] Dutch,[311] French,[312] German,[313] and UK[314] markets, and by the impact of the Lehman collapse on capital-protected structured products.[315]

Designing an effective, summary harmonized product disclosure regime is, however, difficult. The complexities of structured products, for example, might be difficult to capture in a two-page UCITS KIID-style summary, which might lead to moral hazard risks for the inexperienced retail investor. Comparability is not always achievable or even desirable where products have distinct features. Investment products are often designed to reflect local market influences; local disclosure requirements may be more effective in addressing disclosure risks. On the other hand, while extensive harmonization of product disclosure across the universe of investment products is neither practical nor desirable, significant gaps remain—particularly with respect to structured deposits, but also with respect to insurance-based investments. The EU's design technology has also improved immeasurably following the UCITS IV KIID experience.[316] Economies of scale, particularly for less well-resourced and experienced NCAs, can follow from a centralized approach.

---

[307] See Ch II sect 4.5.1.

[308] See Ch III sect 3.11.3.

[309] Aboulian, B, 'Brussels Mulls Common Information Form', *Financial Times Fund Management Supplement*, 16 February 2009, 11.

[310] The Danish market has seen concerns as to disclosure concerning the costs of index-linked bonds and their option components: Rang Rasmussen, A S, 'Index-Linked Bonds' in *Danish Central Bank Monetary Review, Second Quarter 2007*, 51.

[311] AFM, Exploratory Analysis of Structured Products (2007) 37, 8.

[312] 2005 Delmas Report, n 71, 9 and 20–3.

[313] BaFIN, Annual Report 2006, 27.

[314] eg FSA, Financial Risk Outlook 2008, 51.

[315] See sect 2.3.

[316] Discussed in Ch III sect 3.11.3.

Cross-product summary disclosure harmonization has emerged as the EU policy preference, although industry resistance has been significant. The Commission proposed a recasting of the harmonized summary disclosure regime such that a coherent regime would apply to all 'packaged products' under the 2012 PRIPs Regulation Proposal.[317] The Proposed Regulation[318] applied to investment products, defined as products where, regardless of the legal form of the investment, the amount payable to the investor was exposed to fluctuations in reference values or in the performance of one or more assets not directly purchased by the investor (Article 4); this definition was designed to capture investment funds of all types (UCITSs and non-UCITSs), structured products (whether packaged as insurance policies, funds, securities, or deposits), investment-linked insurance products, and derivatives.[319] Traditional, pure protection, non-investment insurance products which do not offer a surrender value (which are not exposed to market risk), 'plain' shares and bonds (as they are not packaged), deposits with a rate of return related to an interest rate (which are not exposed to market risk), and occupational pension schemes and pension products for which a financial contribution is paid by the employer and where the employee has no choice as to the provider (workplace pensions) were excluded (Article 2).

The Proposal took a 'factory gate' approach in that the manufacturer of an in-scope investment product[320] was to draw up a Key Information Document (KID) for each investment product produced; the obligation applied only in relation to retail investors[321] (Article 4).[322] Like the UCITS KIID,[323] the proposed PRIPs KID was designed to be a standardized document. The Proposal accordingly set out the format and content of the KID (Articles 6–8); detailed administrative rules were envisaged to follow to specify the KID requirements in detail. The KID was to be 'fair, clear and not misleading' and

---

[317] n 58 (2012 PRIPs Proposal Impact Assessment (SWD (2012) 187)). The Proposal was preceded by extensive consultation and assessment, including a Commission Consultation in 2010, a 2009 Issues Workshop, and a report from the CESR, CEBS (Committee of European Banking Supervisors), and CEIOPS (Committee of European Insurance and Occupational Pension Supervisors) Taskforce on PRIPs: Report of the 3L3 Task Force on PRIPs (2010) (CESR/10-1136). See also sect 1.2.3.

[318] The Proposal took the form of a regulation in order to ensure uniformity and to impose direct obligations on private parties (the manufacturer) with respect to the preparation of the required disclosures: 2012 PRIPs Proposal, n 58, 6.

[319] The disclosure regime was designed to capture 'manufactured' products which address capital accumulation needs and are indirectly exposed to fluctuations in the market value of assets. Key to the notion of an investment product for the purposes of the Proposal was the notion of 'wrapping' or 'packaging', as products of this type are economically similar and share similar risks in terms of complexity, costs, and opacity: 2012 PRIPs Proposal, n 58, 7.

[320] The manufacturer was defined as any natural or legal person who manufactures an investment product or makes changes to an existing investment product by altering its risk and reward profile or the costs associated with an investment in an investment product (Art 4). This definition was designed to capture the wrapping or other reconstruction of investment products.

[321] The investment products within scope, however, were not limited to those designed for retail use: 2012 PRIPs Proposal, n 58, 8.

[322] Defined in accordance with the 2014 MiFID II/MiFIR and in accordance with 'customers' under the 2002 Distance Marketing of Financial Services Directive (Art 4).

[323] The proposed PRIP's KID was designed initially to operate in parallel with the UCITS KIID regime; for a transitional period of five years, UCITS management companies and investment companies were to be exempt from the KID regime (Art 24), following which the scope of the KID was to be assessed, including with respect to whether it should replace the UCITS KIID (Art 25). The regime was designed to operate in parallel with the Prospectus Directive's summary prospectus regime where the manufacturer was also subject to that regime; the interaction of two regimes was not, however, made clear.

designed to operate as a stand-alone document clearly separate from marketing materials[324] (Article 6(1)). Like the UCITS KIID, the proposed PRIPS KID was to be drawn up as a short document and subject to clarity requirements (Article 6(2));[325] it was to be written in the official language of the Member States in which the product was sold (Article 7).[326]

The proposed PRIPs KID was, like the UCITS KIID, designed to be a highly standardized document which supported comprehensibility, but also comparability, across a range of products. The proposed legislative specification of the KID's content was more rigorous than that in the UCITS IV legislative regime; the Proposal specified that its content cover, in addition to the name of the product and the identity of the manufacturer, disclosures related to the questions: 'what is this investment?'; 'could I lose money?'; 'what is it for?'; 'what are the risks and what might I get back?'; what are the costs?'; 'how has it done in the past?'; and (for in-scope pension products) 'what might I get when I retire?' (Article 8). Within these categories, the Proposal specified the information to be included, such as disclosures relating to capital protection and guarantees under 'could I lose money?', risk and reward profile under 'what are the risks?', past performance under 'how has it done in the past?', and investment objectives and performance scenarios under 'what is this investment?' Additional information could only be included where it was necessary for the retail investor to take an informed investment decision. Under the Proposal the PRIPs KID was to be highly standardized and to follow the exact order and content specified in the legislative text. The Proposal provided for the content of the KID to be shaped by an administrative rulebook[327] which would address the particular risks and features of different products within the packaged product asset class.[328] The Proposal provided that the KID be subject to a regular review obligation, in accordance with the administrative rules to be adopted governing review (Article 10).

Unusually, the Proposal made provision for causes of action by retail investors; where a KID did not comply with the requirements, and the retail investor had relied on it when making an investment decision, the Proposal provided that the investor could claim from the manufacturer damages for any losses caused through the use of the KID (Article 11). How this private cause of action was to be operationalized in different Member States' legal regimes was not made clear.[329] As discussed in Chapter XI, private causes of action have not

---

[324] Like the UCITS KIID, the proposed PRIPs KID was to carry a mandatory legend specifying its status as regulatory disclosure and not marketing material, and advising the investor to read it so that an informed decision was made: Art 8.

[325] Including that it be presented and laid out in a way that was easy to read and was clearly expressed and written in a language that facilitated the retail investor's understanding (the language used was to be clear, succinct, and comprehensible, and jargon and technical terms were to be avoided).

[326] Alternatively, it could be written in a language accepted by the NCA of the Member State. Where it was written in another language, it was to be translated into one of these languages.

[327] In addition to making provision for Commission-led administrative rules, the Proposal also empowered ESMA, EBA, and EIOPA to develop RTSs governing the methodology underpinning the presentation of risk and reward and the calculation of costs.

[328] The Commission was to take into account the differences between investment products and the capabilities of retail investors, as well as the features of investment products which allow retail investors to select between different underlying investments or other options provided by the product.

[329] The 2012 PRIPs Proposal simply stated that where an investor demonstrated a loss resulting from use of the information contained in the KID, the manufacturer was to prove the KID had been drawn up in compliance with the proposed Regulation.

been a significant feature of EU securities and markets regulation. Their inclusion in the Proposal reflects the growing concern to sharpen enforcement mechanisms.

The Proposal also addressed the distribution of the PRIPs KID. It was to be provided (and not simply offered), free of charge, by a person selling the investment product to retail investors in good time before the conclusion of a transaction relating to the product (Articles 12 and 13), although exceptions were available where transactions were not carried out face-to-face, which exceptions permitted the supply of the KID immediately after the conclusion of the transaction.

With respect to enforcement, the proposed administrative sanctions and redress regime (Article 18-22), was broadly similar to the enhanced regimes which now apply under, for example, MiFID II/MiFIR (see Chapter IV section 11.6) and required, *inter alia*, that NCAs be empowered to make orders suspending or prohibiting the marketing of an investment product, deliver warnings, and make orders requiring the publication of a new KID (Article 19).

Despite its very slow gestation, the PRIPs Proposal struggled and became something of a casualty of the EU's complex inter-institutional law-making process. Industry opposition—particularly from the insurance sector, which would become subject to a new disclosure regime[330]—was fierce, and institutional negotiations were difficult. Parliamentary negotiations quickly became bogged down in discussions on the scope of the Proposal, with strong support for the KID to be a radically wider document, extending to shares and bonds,[331] and for the Proposal to extend beyond disclosure to include distribution and product governance reforms. A complex series of amendments was ultimately adopted by the European Parliament in late 2013 which led to a significant recasting and, in many respects, muddying of the Commission's text. The amendments significantly extended the Proposal to cover corporate bonds (despite the Proposal's focus on packaged and substitutable products), prescribed often highly contested and elusive disclosures (including a requirement for the label 'complex' to be used in certain circumstances), and introduced product distribution and product governance requirements (thereby creating alignment difficulties with MiFID II).[332] The Council reached a position earlier in June 2013 which was relatively close to the Commission's Proposal and which restricted the KID to packaged products.[333] The Council and European Parliament positions therefore differed sharply, with the Council treating the KID as supporting comparability across broadly substitutable products and thereby limiting its scope, and the Parliament regarding the KID as a general

---

[330] During the European Parliament negotiations, strong representations from the insurance industry led to a series of amendments to exclude insurance-related investment products from the Proposal; these amendments were defeated in the November 2013 vote on the Parliament amendments.

[331] The initial draft ECON Committee Report on the Proposal extended its application to shares, interest rate savings products, sovereign debt, bank term accounts, and life insurance: A7-0368/2013.

[332] After fierce negotiations, the European Parliament voted on a set of amendments in November 2013 (P7-TA(PROV(2013)0489)).

[333] PRIPs Regulation Council General Approach, 24 June 2013 (Council Document 11430/13). The main differences from the Commission's Proposal related to: more detailed specification of the insurance products excluded; variations as to the information specified (including the addition of a synthetic risk indicator, reflecting the UCITS KIID); a requirement for separate KIDs for each underlying product where an investment product offers an investor different options; the removal of the private right of action and its replacement by the standard exclusion as to civil liability contained in the UCITS KIID; and the re-characterization of all administrative rules related to the KID content as RTSs.

information document designed to support investors in understanding particular products and recasting the PRIPs Proposal as a more general investor protection measure.

The Commission's Proposal, adopted after an intensive preparation and consultation period, provided a broadly workable template for substitutable product summary disclosure[334] but risked being significantly distorted over the negotiations. Ultimately, however, the Commission's original model prevailed (for the most part), following intense trilogue negotiations over spring 2014.[335] Despite the fraught negotiation process, experience with the UCITS KIID augurs well for the proposed PRIPs KID. A positive outcome might also be predicted given the role the ESAs are likely to play in the development of the new regime and the cross-sector and empirical capacity they will likely bring.

IX.7 Product Oversight and Product Intervention

IX.7.1 A New Product Intervention Regime: 2014 MiFID II/MiFIR

Prior to the financial crisis, harmonized EU regulation (and Member State rules) tended to eschew product regulation (which can extend across a spectrum from *ex-ante* product authorization, to oversight of product development processes, to the prohibition of products) in favour of disclosure and distribution rules.[336] This reflects the significant risks associated with product intervention[337] and which include arbitrage, damage to innovation and investor choice, and moral hazard, given the strong implication of regulatory approval which product authorization, in particular, can generate and the related risk that the product provider (and investor) takes less care in monitoring the product.[338] The association between product intervention and 'over-regulation' is also considerable.[339] Product regulation had not been entirely overlooked by EU retail market regulation, but it was primarily a function of the portfolio-shaping and risk management rules which apply to the UCITS. And, as discussed in Chapter III, the UCITS regime is more a function of liberalization and the extension of the UCITS market than of retail investor protection requirements, as is clear from the extension of the UCITS product to include complex and often hedge-fund-like funds.

Prior to the financial crisis, there were some tentative moves towards product-related intervention at Member State level, including the (then) UK Financial Services Authority's

---

[334] Although the private rights of action regime and the interaction between the KID and other disclosure requirements was problematic, while the omission of a 'who is it for' segment sat uneasily with the emphasis elsewhere under MiFID II on product targeting.

[335] Agreement was reached by the Parliament and Council just as the Parliament's 2009-2014 term finished. The new regime was adopted by the Parliament at its last plenary session in April 2014 ('Super Tuesday' 15 April). At the time of writing, the formal text as adopted was not available.

[336] On the emergence of product intervention as a retail market tool in the EU see further Moloney, N, 'The Legacy Effects of the Financial Crisis in the EU' in Ferran et al, n 165, 111.

[337] Karmel, R, 'Mutual Funds, Pension Funds and Stock Market Volatility—What Regulation by the Securities and Exchange Commission is Appropriate' (2004–2005) 80 *Notre Dame LR* 909, 918.

[338] Stronger arguments can be made in relation to the consumer finance markets given the ubiquity and necessity of basic banking and credit products. For a leading analysis see Warren, n 21.

[339] eg Epstein, R. 'The Neoclassical Economics of Consumer Contracts' (2008) 92 *Minnesota LR* 808 and Bar Gill, O, 'The Behavioural Economics of Consumer Contracts' (2008) 92 *Minnesota LR* 749.

(FSA's) 'Treating Customers Fairly' supervisory initiative which applied to the 'product life cycle' and to the respective responsibilities of product providers and distributors.[340] The crisis era, however, has led to product-related intervention coming to the fore in many NCAs as an additional tool for addressing retail market risk and in response to persistent mis-selling risks, which are often exacerbated by the complex and illiquid structure of some products sold through retail distribution channels.[341] A range of product-related techniques are now being deployed by NCAs, including oversight of the product development process and prohibitions on the marketing of certain products.[342]

The 2014 MiFID II/MiFIR reforms have followed this striking trend. The Commission proposed emergency product intervention powers for NCAs and for ESMA (the latter on a temporary basis only), which would allow NCAs and ESMA (temporarily only) to prohibit or restrict the marketing of financial instruments (and prohibit or restrict other services and activities);[343] most NCAs did not have powers of this type and, where they did exist, the lack of co-ordination mechanisms raised the risk of prejudice to the single market where an NCA took unilateral action.[344] The proposed new powers were related to insufficient risk control over products and the need for improvements in the design and launch of new products, the need to address mis-selling, and the dangers of 'socio-economic impacts' were consumers to lose confidence in investment products.[345] Less radically, the Commission also proposed product governance/oversight requirements, proposing that investment firm management boards be required to define, approve, and oversee a policy as to the services, activities, products, and operations offered or provided by the firm and in accordance with the risk tolerance of the firm and the characteristics and needs of the clients to whom they would be offered, including appropriate stress-testing.[346]

---

[340] FSA, Policy Statement No 7/11, The Responsibilities of Providers and Distributors for the Fair Treatment of Customers (2007).

[341] For a summary of product-related failures across the EU see ESMA, EBA, EIOPA, Joint Position of the ESAs on Manufacturers' Product Oversight & Governance Processes (2013) (JC-2013-77) Annex 1. The Joint Committee reported on an NCA survey which exposed failures with respect to complex and illiquid alternative investment products (UK), structured products (Denmark), equity instruments issued by banks (Spain), and complex products generally (Italy).

[342] In an October 2010 'position' (AMF Position No 2010-05) the French AMF in effect prohibited the marketing of complex structured products to investors: Jory, R, 'New Regulations Leave Retail Structured Products on Shaky Ground in France', *Financial Risk Management News and Analysis*, 21 April 2011. In 2011, the Belgian regulator (the FSMA) called for the voluntary suspension by the industry of the retail distribution of structured products which it deemed to be 'needlessly complex'. 2011 also saw the Dutch government announce proposals for the Dutch regulator to supervise the development of new financial products. The Polish regulator has published recommendations governing offerings of structured products (September 2012). In the UK, a new product intervention strategy was adopted by the FCA which is designed to bring a more intrusive approach to retail market regulation (n 340) and which has been supported by other NCAs: FSA, Feedback Statement No 11/3, Product Intervention. Feedback (2011) 20. The UK strategy is based on regulatory oversight of the product design process and on more intrusive product intervention techniques which culminate, as a last resort, in pre-approval and prohibition techniques for specific products. Some industry anxiety concerning the current direction of travel in the EU can be read in the 2011 re-release of the principles which the industry Joint Association Committee adopted in 2008 concerning the distributor/investor relationship and provider/distributor relationship with respect to structured products (Joint Associations Committee, Combined Principles for Retail Structured Products (2011)).

[343] 2011 MiFIR Proposal, n 181, Arts 31–32.

[344] 2011 MiFID II/MiFIR Proposals Impact Assessment, n 136, 44.

[345] 2011 MiFID II/MiFIR Proposals Impact Assessment, n 136, 17–19.

[346] 2011 MiFID II Proposal, n 181, Art 9(6)(c).

Oversight of the product development process was strongly supported by the European Parliament during the MiFID II/MiFIR negotiations. In addition to the Commission's management-board-focused, product oversight/product governance requirement, it significantly strengthened the proposed organizational regime for firms to require that product development policies, *inter alia*, assessed the compatibility of the product with the needs of clients targeted, that products met the need of an identified target market, and that marketing strategies ensured that the product be marketed to clients within the target group. It also required that product approval processes be adopted, that all relevant risks be assessed during the approval process, and that existing products be continually reviewed to ensure they continued to meet the needs of the identified target market.[347] It similarly strengthened the proposed MiFID II conduct regime to provide that products designed by investment firms be designed to meet the needs of an identified target market, within the relevant categories of retail or professional clients, that investment firms take all reasonable steps to ensure that products were marketed and distributed to clients within the target group, and that sales targets and other reward schemes or inducements not provide incentives for distributing products outside the target group. The Council followed the Commission's more light-touch approach to product governance/oversight, limiting product oversight requirements to oversight by the management board.

The position of the European Parliament on product governance, however, generally prevailed over the MiFID II trilogue discussions. An overarching new governance requirement now applies under MiFID II Article 9(3) which requires the firm's management body to take responsibility with respect to product governance: the management body must define, approve, and oversee a policy as to services, activities, products, and operations offered or provided, in accordance with the risk tolerance of the firm and the characteristics and needs of the clients of the firm to whom they will be offered or provided (including with respect to stress-testing, where appropriate). Strong product governance processes accordingly become the responsibility of senior management. Similarly, the overarching Article 24 fair treatment principle now includes a product governance-specific component: investment firms which manufacture financial instruments for sale to clients must ensure those instruments are designed to meet the needs of an identified target market of end clients within the relevant category of clients, that the distribution strategy is compatible with the identified target market, and that reasonable steps are taken to ensure the instrument is distributed to the identified target market (Article 24(2)). In addition, the firm must understand the financial instruments offered or recommended, assess the compatibility of the financial instruments with the needs of the clients to whom investment services are provided—taking into account the identified target market of end clients—and ensure that financial instruments are only offered or recommended when this in the interests of clients (Article 24(2)).

Specifically with respect to product development, a new product oversight regime applies under MiFID II Article 16(3). An investment firm which manufactures financial instruments for sale to clients must maintain, operate, and review a process for the approval of each instrument (or significant adaptations of existing financial instruments) before it is marketed or distributed to clients. The approval process must specify an identified target

---

[347] European Parliament MiFID II Negotiating Position, n 181, Art 16(3).

market of end clients within the relevant category of clients for each product, and ensure that all relevant risks to such identified target market are assessed and the intended distribution strategy is consistent with the identified market. The firm must also regularly review financial instruments offered or marketed by the firm, taking into account any event that could materially affect the potential risk to the identified target market, to assess at least whether the financial instrument remains consistent with the needs of the target market and whether the intended distribution strategy remains appropriate. Firms which manufacture financial instruments must also make available to any distributor all appropriate information on the financial instrument and the product approval process, including the identified target market. Where a firm offers or recommends financial instruments which it does not manufacture, it must have in place adequate arrangements to obtain the information required to be made available by the manufacturer and to understand the characteristics of the intended target market of each financial instrument.[348] As noted in section 5.2.5, the identified target market concept is also used to strengthen the distribution regime. The product governance regime is supported by specific supervisory powers: NCAs are empowered to, for example, suspend the marketing or sale of financial instruments or structured deposits where the firm has not developed or applied an effective product approval process or otherwise failed to comply with Article 16(3) (Article 69(2)).

The Commission's more radical proposals for direct NCA and ESMA product intervention powers (under MiFIR) proved more contentious over the MiFID II/MiFIR negotiations. While the Commission's Proposal was limited to emergency, *ex-post* restriction/prohibition powers, the European Parliament extended the regime to require NCAs and ESMA to monitor the marketing, distribution, and sale of investment products in their jurisdictions, and to suggest that NCAs and (somewhat unrealistically, given its resource base) ESMA could proactively investigate new investment products before they were marketed. The Parliament also proposed that the intervention powers be used pre-emptively, on a precautionary basis, before products were marketed or sold to clients.[349] Within the Council, although most Member States supported the intervention powers, the negotiations revealed tensions between the Member States as to whether ESMA could be conferred with direct temporary intervention powers and as to the degree of discretion which could be exercised by ESMA,[350] reflecting the similar concerns of some Member States as to the legitimacy of ESMA's short selling powers under the 2012 Short Selling Regulation;[351] the legitimacy of these product prohibition powers has since been given a more secure foundation following the ruling of the Court of Justice with respect to ESMA's similar short selling powers.[352] The final position agreed by the Council imposed tighter conditions on ESMA's temporary powers and its related exercise of discretion, including

---

[348] The Art 16(3) product governance regime applies without prejudice to the other requirements of MiFID II in relation to disclosure, quality of advice, and conflict of interest management.

[349] Parliament Negotiating Position, n 181, Art 31.

[350] Danish Presidency MiFID II/MiFIR Progress Report, n 259, 11. The UK in particular was concerned as to the legality of the proposed powers which it viewed as conferring ESMA with a degree of discretion which was incompatible with the *Meroni* (Case 9/56 *Meroni v High Authority* [1957–1958] ECR 133) restrictions: Letter from Financial Secretary, n 192.

[351] See Ch VI sect 3.9.2.

[352] Case C-270/12 *UK v Council and Parliament*, 22 January 2014, not yet reported. See Ch XI sect 5.8.3.

that they only be exercised where the relevant conditions were fulfilled,[353] and specification of the nature of the administrative rules to be adopted by the Commission governing how the ESMA (and NCA) powers were to be exercised.[354] The trilogue negotiations led to the Parliament and Council positions being broadly reflected in the final text.

The new MiFIR product (and services) prohibition regime confers product intervention powers on NCAs and similar temporary intervention powers on ESMA. They are designed as 'last resort' powers which should only be required where organizational and conduct rules have failed. They also operate *ex-post*; the Commission, reflecting regulatory practice internationally, rejected *ex-ante* product licensing controls given the costs, the potential risk to innovation, the moral hazard risks were authorization to imply regulatory approval, and the resource strain which would be placed on NCAs.[355]

NCAs are required to monitor the market for financial instruments and structured deposits which are marketed, distributed or sold in or from their Member States (MiFIR Article 39(3)). More radically, NCAs are given the power to prohibit or restrict, in or from the Member State, the marketing, distribution, or sale of certain financial instruments or structured deposits, or financial instruments or structured deposits with certain specified features, or a type of financial activity or practice (MiFIR Article 42(1)) where a series of conditions are met (Article 42(2)).[356] The NCA must be satisfied (on reasonable grounds) either: that a financial instrument, structured deposit, or activity or practice gives rise to significant investor protection concerns, or poses a threat to the orderly functioning and integrity of financial markets or commodity markets or to the stability of whole or part of the financial system within at least one Member State; or that a derivative has a detrimental effect on the price formation mechanism in the underlying market. The criteria by which NCAs are to assess these factors will be governed by administrative rules to be adopted by the Commission, which will include the degree of complexity of the financial instrument or structured deposit and the relation to the type of client to whom it is marketed and sold; the size or notional value of the issuance in question; the degree of innovation of a financial instrument, structured deposit, activity, or practice; the leverage a product or practice provides; and, in relation to the orderly functioning and integrity of financial markets or commodity markets, the size of the notional value of an issuance of financial instruments or structured deposits (Article 42(7)).

Under Article 42(2), the NCA must also be satisfied that existing regulatory requirements under EU law (which are applicable to the financial instrument, structured deposit, or activity or practice) do not sufficiently address the risks in question and that (reflecting the crisis-era focus on strengthening supervision) the issue would not be better addressed by improved supervision or enforcement of existing requirements. The action must be proportionate taking into account the nature of the risks identified, the level of sophistication of the investors or market participants concerned, and the likely effect of the action on investors and market participants who may hold, use, or benefit from the financial

---

[353] The 2011 MiFIR Proposal proposed that ESMA be empowered to act where it was satisfied on reasonable grounds that the relevant conditions were met.

[354] Council MiFIR Proposal General Approach, n 181, Arts 31 and 32.

[355] 2011 MiFID II/MiFIR Proposals Impact Assessment, n 136, 45.

[356] The prohibition or restriction may apply in particular circumstances, or be subject to exceptions, specified by the NCA.

instrument, structured deposit, activity, or practice, and must not have a discriminatory effect on services or activities provided from another Member State. The NCA must also consult properly with NCAs in other Member States that may be significantly affected by the action, and also with the public bodies competent for the oversight, administration, and regulation of physical agriculture markets (given that the prohibition could apply to commodity derivatives), where a financial instrument, activity, or service poses a serious threat to the orderly functioning and integrity of these agriculture markets. The NCA may impose the prohibition or restriction on a precautionary basis, before a financial instrument or structured deposit has been marketed or sold to clients (Article 42(2)). The prohibition or restrictions must be removed when the conditions no longer apply (Article 42(6)).

Procedural requirements apply which require the NCA to give not less than one month's written notice (or notice through another agreed medium) to the other NCAs and ESMA[357]—in exceptional cases where urgent action is necessary to prevent detriment, an NCA can act on a provisional basis with no less than 24 hours written notice, as long as a series of conditions are met (Article 42(4))[358]—and to publish written notice of any decision to intervene on its website (Article 42(3) and (5)).

ESMA's product intervention powers relate to market monitoring, direct temporary intervention powers, and co-ordination of NCA action. ESMA, reflecting its powers under the foundation 2010 ESMA Regulation, is to monitor the market for financial instruments (EBA is conferred with these powers in relation to structured deposits) which are marketed, distributed, or sold in the EU (MiFIR Article 39(1)). ESMA's temporary intervention powers, which mark a significant ratcheting-up of ESMA's direct powers over EU financial markets, are similar to the NCA powers, albeit that tighter conditions apply (MiFIR Article 40), and are designed to limit ESMA's discretion and thereby to ensure compliance with the *Meroni* restrictions on agencies[359] and respect NCAs' competences in this new and sensitive area. ESMA, acting under the foundation enabling prohibition power conferred on it by the 2010 ESMA Regulation Article 9(5),[360] and where the relevant MiFIR conditions are fulfilled, may temporarily prohibit or restrict in the EU the marketing, distribution, or sale of certain financial instruments, or financial instruments with certain specified features, or a type of financial activity or practice (Article 40(1)).[361] Although ESMA's powers are designed to complement the NCAs' powers, action by ESMA prevails over any previous action taken by an NCA; the potential for conflict—in a highly charged context, given the political attention which large-scale retail market mis-selling often attracts—therefore arises (Article 40(7)). Any prohibitions or restrictions must, reflecting the need to constrain ESMA's discretion, be reviewed at appropriate intervals

---

[357] The notice must include the financial instrument, activity or practice engaged; the precise nature of the proposed prohibition and when it is intended to take effect; and the evidence on which the NCA has based its decision and which leads it to conclude that the conditions for intervention are met. Notification is made to EBA in the case of action related to structured deposits.

[358] The NCA must meet all the relevant Art 42 criteria and, in addition, it must be clearly established that the one-month notification period would not adequately address the specific concern or threat. The NCA may not take action on a provisional basis for a period in excess of three months.

[359] See Ch XI sect 5.8.2.

[360] See Ch XI sect 5.4.3.

[361] The prohibition or restriction may apply in particular circumstances, or be subject to exceptions, specified by ESMA.

and at least every three months; where a measure is not reviewed after a three-month period, it expires (Article 40(6)).

ESMA may act only where: the proposed action addresses a significant investor protection concern, or a threat to the orderly functioning and integrity of financial markets or commodity markets or to the stability of the whole or part of the financial system in the EU; regulatory requirements under EU law applicable to the financial instrument or activity do not address the threat;[362] and an NCA (or NCAs) has not taken action to address the threat, or the action which has been taken does not adequately address the threat (Article 40(2)). ESMA must also ensure that the action does not have a detrimental effect on the efficiency of financial markets or on investors that is disproportionate to the benefits; that it does not create a risk of regulatory arbitrage; and that it has consulted with the public bodies responsible for the oversight, administration, and regulation of physical agricultural markets (Article 40(3)). Where the conditions are met, ESMA may impose the prohibition or restriction on a precautionary basis, before the financial instrument has been marketed or sold to clients. Procedurally, ESMA must notify the other NCAs before acting and provide written notice of its decision (Article 40(4) and (5)).

Less controversially, ESMA is also conferred with co-ordination powers relating to the NCAs' powers (MiFIR Article 43). It must perform a facilitation and co-ordination role in relation to NCA action and ensure that action taken by an NCA is justified and proportionate and that, where appropriate, a consistent approach is taken by NCAs. To that end, the 'ESMA opinion' mechanism (which also applies in relation to, for example, NCA short selling measures, NCA action under the Alternative Investment Fund Managers Directive (AIFMD) leverage regime, and NCA action under MiFIR II/MiFIR with respect to transparency waivers and position management powers) applies. On receipt of notification from an NCA of an NCA Article 42 action, ESMA must adopt an opinion on whether the action is justified and proportionate and, where it considers that action by other NCAs is necessary to address the risk, state this in the opinion. Where an NCA proposes to take, or takes, action contrary to an ESMA opinion, or declines to take action, it must publish its reasons—thereby potentially allowing ESMA to take direct action under Article 40.

A parallel suite of temporary intervention and co-ordination powers are conferred on EBA with respect to structured deposits (MiFIR Articles 39(2), 41, and 43). While this silo-based approach reflects the allocation of banking and financial market competences to EBA and ESMA respectively, it underlines the risks of the EU's sectoral approach to regulation and the need for close co-ordination between ESMA and EBA in this nascent area (section 10).

ESMA appears ready to embrace these new powers, although it is likely to deploy them cautiously, not least given the strict conditionality which applies; the initial, agenda-setting statements by ESMA's then newly appointed Chairman in early 2011 suggested that ESMA Regulation Article 9 (the enabling power for product intervention) was a priority power for ESMA, and that ESMA would be willing to take action against high-commission

---

[362] The criteria governing these conditions are to be adopted by the Commission and will follow the criteria specified in relation to NCAs' intervention powers: Art 40(8).

products where negative outcomes were likely for investors.[363] Auguring well for ESMA/
EBA co-ordination, product oversight has been a major priority for the Joint Committee of
the ESAs,[364] which, following an NCA mapping exercise, has adopted a Joint Position
which sets out high-level principles on product oversight and governance processes within
firms, and which is designed to strengthen the process controls of product providers, both
with respect to product design and to the selection of distribution channels.[365] The ESAs
(including ESMA)[366] are to develop sector-specific and more detailed provisions based on
these principles. The new powers can also be expected to be actively deployed by NCAs,
given the crisis-era enthusiasm for product oversight.

IX.7.2 Product-specific Initiatives

Horizontal measures under 2014 MiFID II/MiFIR aside, more specific product intervention initiatives have been taken with respect to two classes of retail market product,
structured UCITS funds; and exchange-traded funds (ETFs), which have been mainly
driven by ESMA.

Structured UCITSs are akin to structured products in that the pay-off to investors is linked
to the performance of underlying assets.[367] Their distinct risks are increasingly being
addressed by specific rules. The UCITS KIID, for example, contains distinct requirements
for 'structured UCITS'.[368] Structured UCITS are also addressed by ESMA's 2012 Guidelines on UCITS and Exchange Traded Funds, which highlight the need for such funds to
comply with the diversification and risk management rules which apply to UCITSs
generally.[369] At the legislative level, the new MiFID II execution-only regime addresses
the particular risks posed by structured UCITSs, prohibiting their sale through execution-
only channels. ESMA has also undertaken own-initiative research action with its 2013
study on the sale of complex products to retail investors, which suggested that certain types
of complex product (structured products and alternative investment UCITS) produced
relatively low returns, and highlighted the need for enhancements to product disclosure.[370]
Further action has followed, with ESMA producing an opinion in early 2014 on the
marketing and sale of complex products under MiFID and the application of relevant
rules.[371]

---

[363] Tait, N, 'ESMA Watchdog Prepared to Clash with Brussels', 2 March 2011, available at <http://www.
FT.com>. Similarly, ESMA Executive Director Verena Ross welcomed the proposed powers as a 'major leap
forward': Speech on 'Strengthening Investor Protection', 5 December 2011.

[364] Product oversight and governance has been a priority for the Joint Committee which established a
subgroup to deal with product-related issues: Joint Committee, 2013 Work Programme (2013) (JC-2013-
002).

[365] n 341.

[366] Which committed to 'undertaking substantial further work' on product governance and distribution:
n 341, 5. An opinion on product governance for structured retail products followed (ESMA/2014/332).

[367] On the definition of a structured UCITS, see n 253.

[368] 2010 UCITS KIID Regulation n 253, Art 36. In particular, the KIID must include explanations of the
pay-out formula and different performance scenarios.

[369] ESMA, Guidelines on ETFs and other UCITS Issues (2012) (ESMA/2012/832) (2012 ETFs and
UCITS Guidelines).

[370] ESMA, Retailization in the EU (2013) (ESMA/2013/326).

[371] ESMA/2014/146.

The emerging EU agenda for ETFs also illustrates the growing importance of product-related intervention. As discussed in Chapter III, ETFs are open-ended UCITS funds which track an index or benchmark and have experienced very strong growth. Internationally, the Financial Stability Board (FSB) and the International Monetary Fund (IMF) have highlighted the potential stability risks arising from ETF exposure to counterparty risk and from market illiquidity, and called for careful monitoring.[372] The EU has addressed the stability risks posed by ETFs, primarily through the 2012 ESMA Guidelines on ETFs and UCITSs.[373] Notwithstanding the relatively small size of the EU ETF market and its predominantly institutional base,[374] the regulatory agenda has also focused on retail market risk. At Member State level, the UK and Dutch authorities have highlighted the increased retailization of these products and the complexity risks which they pose.[375] ESMA's ETFs and UCITSs Guidelines have also addressed retail market risk. Although the Guidelines are based on the disclosure model predominant pre-crisis, indications of a more robust approach which may come are evident in the identification of ETFs as a product in need of closer attention, and in the warning that ESMA may require product prohibition powers in this field.[376]

IX.7.3 An Ambitious Reform

At first glance, the 2014 MiFID II/MiFIR product intervention tools seem promising, particularly as there are few indications that the EU is inclined to move to a full-scale *ex-ante* product licensing regime, with its attendant risks. Product regulation, and intervention at a higher level in the product supply cycle, may provide a means of ensuring better outcomes for those retail investors who do not access advice, and mitigate quality-of-advice risks for retail investors in an advice relationship. This is particularly the case with respect to robust and clear product governance/oversight requirements which seek to ensure that firms focus on developing products which meet investors' needs and on the selection of appropriate distribution channels which reduce the risk of mis-selling. Product-related regulation also takes the pressure from distribution regulation and provides investors with an additional source of support. But product regulation is a new and untested tool for the EU and may have unexpected effects.

The new powers may come to energize NCAs, as seems to be suggested by the ESA Joint Committee's focus on product governance. But product intervention, whether *ex-ante* governance-based or *ex-post* prohibition-based, implies that the regulator can second-guess weaknesses in the retail product market. Expectations may be unrealistically high, not least as the incentive risks associated with product design are significant—particularly in the current climate, as banks turn to product design to support revenues—and are likely to be no easier to resolve than incentive risks in the distribution process.[377] The very novelty

---

[372] See Ch III sect 3.14.2.

[373] n 369.

[374] Amenc, N, Ducoulombier, F, Goltz, F, and Tang, L, *What are the Risks of European ETFs?* EDHEC-Risk Institute Paper (2012).

[375] eg FSA, Retail Conduct Risk Outlook 2011, 69–71 and AMF, 2011 Risk and Trend Mapping for Financial Markets and Savings (2011) 6.

[376] Noted in the earlier ESMA, Discussion Paper (ESMA/2011/220) 6.

[377] eg FSA, Retail Product Development and Governance. Structured Product Review (2011), reporting on persistent difficulties in the structured product design process and, overall, that firms were emphasizing their commercial position at the expense of consumer outcomes.

of product intervention may also lead to an overly ambitious and heavy-handed approach. While the new emergency intervention powers are subject to stringent (if somewhat open-ended) conditions, they may prove attractive to NCAs seeking 'quick wins' in the retail markets. The risks to supervisory effectiveness will be all the greater if the new regime enmeshes NCAs in complex, detailed, and resource-intensive oversight of industry product development processes, with the attendant moral hazard and resource risk to NCAs.

Product intervention can also be associated with a more intrusive approach to retail investor risk-taking. The placing of restrictions on the distribution of products to the public is a common feature of retail marketing regimes, but the perimeter for retail marketing is usually drawn very widely. The most high-profile example in the EU relates to the restrictions which apply in most Member States to hedge-fund-related investments and which have been preserved by the 2011 AIFMD.[378] The MiFID II/MiFIR product intervention powers, however, imply that a wider group of products might face restrictions on retail distribution. Making a determination as to whether a product is not suitable for retail distribution, whether through governance/design oversight powers or *ex-post* prohibition powers, demands of the regulator that choices are made as to the optimum levels of risk and choice in the retail market. It implies that investor choice and autonomy can be trumped by a regulatory decision (*ex-ante* or *ex-post*) that certain products should not be distributed to retail investors, and a more precautionary, consumerist approach to potential detriment.

Difficult regulatory design choices also arise. Governing concepts can be elusive. Complexity risk is emerging as a key theme of the wave of EU and Member State product-related reforms, with complexity becoming something of a proxy for 'excessive' retail market risk.[379] The degree of complexity of a product is, for example, a determinant of whether it should be subject to *ex-post* prohibitions or restrictions under the new MiFIR product intervention regime. But prejudicial complexity is difficult to capture through the regulatory system. The UK, for example, has struggled for years with how to use regulatory and market mechanisms to deliver 'simple' investment products which can be price-capped and sold through a simplified advice process,[380] while the French AMF's 2010 prohibition of the distribution of complex structured products has been criticized for relying on subjective criteria.[381] And some degree of complexity in the markets is good for investors, and can deliver strong outcomes.[382] Important determinants of investor outcomes also arise beyond complexity. The extent to which market risks were borne by households over the crisis suggests that close attention should be paid to diversification. The extent to which conflict-

---

[378] Alternative Investment Fund Managers Directive (2011 AIFMD) (2011/61/EU [2011] OJ L174/1) Art 31.

[379] ESMA and the European Systemic Risk Board (ESRB), eg, have both produced extensive reports on the retailization of complex products and the related risks: ESRB, Systemic Risk due to Retailization (2012), raising concern as to product mis-pricing and illiquidity and the risk of mis-selling, and ESMA, n 370.

[380] For the most recent iteration see Sergeant Review of Simple Financial Products (2013).

[381] Jory, n 342.

[382] As has been repeatedly highlighted by Robert Shiller who has suggested that the necessary democratization of finance post-crisis calls for a focus on 'creatively extending the capitalist principles of risk management so that they really work for everyone ... [i]t means an adventure in financial innovation': Shiller, R, 'Democratizing and Humanizing Finance' in Kroszner, R and Shiller, R, *Reforming US Financial Markets. Reflections Before and Beyond Dodd-Frank* (2011) 43.

of-interest risk can lead to mis-selling also suggests that how commission and costs are embedded into a product's return should be addressed.

The difficulties should not, however, detract from the merits of the new approach. Given repeated failures in the EU retail markets, and the extent to which distribution and disclosure regulation has struggled to address mis-selling, the new suite of powers may represent a fresh approach. As is the case with much of the new MiFID II/MiFIR regulatory regime, ESMA has a critical role to play in shaping the new suite of powers. Initial indications augur well. The 2012 Guidelines on ETFs and other UCITS[383] are measured, as is the 2013 report on retailization,[384] while the Joint Position on product oversight produced by the ESA Joint Committee[385] suggests that a practical and restrained approach is likely to be adopted.

IX.8 The Investor Compensation Schemes Directive

IX.8.1 Compensation Schemes, Retail Investor Protection, and the EU

Compensation schemes, by now a well-established if somewhat controversial feature of the securities and markets regulation landscape, act as an *ex-post*, last-resort safety net for investors when investment firms fail.

Many regulatory systems choose to shield clients of intermediaries who have entrusted assets or funds to such intermediaries from the consequences of insolvency. The financial crisis has brought into sharp relief the role which deposit guarantees play in supporting financial stability; the new focus on bank rescue and resolution mechanisms has also led to a reconsideration of the role of deposit protection in bank resolution, and of the extent to which depositors can be subject to 'bail-in' obligations.[386] But deposit protection is of a fundamentally different nature to investor compensation. Deposit protection has an important consumer protection dimension, but it is primarily a device for supporting financial stability by insuring against the risk of a run on a bank;[387] the well-known asymmetry between liquid liabilities (customers can withdraw their deposits at short notice) and illiquid assets (loans make up the greater part of a credit institution's assets) renders credit institutions liable to mass withdrawals when a default on deposit repayments is suspected. The guaranteeing of deposits was one of the first regulatory levers to be deployed by the EU as the financial crisis intensified in autumn 2008; the increase of the guarantee to €100,000 was designed to protect the EU's troubled credit institutions from a run on retail deposits.[388]

---

[383] n 369.

[384] n 370.

[385] n 341.

[386] As the fraught efforts to rescue Cypriot banks—which initially included a 'bail-in' element for all depositors, however small—in early 2013 underline.

[387] See, eg, from the pre-crisis era, Campbell, A and Cartwright, P, 'Co-insurance and Moral Hazard: Some Reflections on Deposit Protection in the UK and USA' (2003) 5 *J IBR* 9. On the role of deposit protection in the financial crisis see, eg, Lannoo, K, and Gerhardt, M, Options for Reforming Deposit Protection in the EU, ECMI Policy Brief No 4 (2011) and LaBrosse, J, Olovares-Caminal, R, and Singh, D, (eds), *Financial Crisis Management and Bank Resolution* (2009) 155.

[388] Deposit protection across the EU is harmonized by Directive 2014/49/EU on deposit guarantee schemes [2014] OJ L173/149.

The rationale for investor compensation schemes is less clear-cut. On the insolvency of a firm, funds and assets should be available if the firm has complied with asset-protection rules and own-account trading rules. They may, however, have been fraudulently mis-appropriated, or operational failures may have resulted in a failure to segregate funds and to record client assets. The client will then simply have a claim in bankruptcy over part of the assets of the bankrupt firm. Compensation schemes typically intervene to short-circuit bankruptcy proceedings (which are likely to be lengthy as well as to produce uncertain outcomes in terms of the retrieval of assets) and to return cash and/or securities to investors. But the funds entrusted to investment firms are typically discretionary. The dangers of systemic instability in the event of a loss of investor confidence are significantly less material as compared with the systemic risks associated with a bank run. Investor compensation schemes (like deposit protection schemes) can generate moral hazard risk. Other distorting effects may arise. Where schemes are funded by a mandatory industry-wide levy, this quasi-taxation may result in sound, prudent firms underwriting improvident and reckless firms and/or act as a barrier to new entrants.

A more paternalistic approach to retail market protection, however, suggests that retail investors are vulnerable to firm failure where assets and funds are entrusted to an invest-ment firm,[389] or where outstanding claims remain against the insolvent investment firm (including with respect to mis-selling), and that a degree of protection in the form of a safety net is appropriate; a retail investor is unlikely to be in a position to assess the soundness and probity of a firm and to minimize the risk of fraud and insolvency. Retail investor awareness and understanding of compensation schemes can be low, and compen-sation schemes are typically capped, making it less likely that schemes can disable retail investors' incentives to take due care. There is also a financial stability dimension to investor compensation, although to a significantly lesser extent than with respect to deposit protection. Investor losses (or the potential for losses) sustained through operational and financial failures run the risk of damaging confidence in market investment, particularly where there is a strong culture of mass retail participation in the financial markets; in particular circumstances, for example where major money-market funds become insolvent, the financial stability risks may become acute.[390]

In the EU, a harmonized regime for investor compensation schemes has been in place since 1997 under the ICSD.[391] Compensation scheme proposals were included among the prudential rules to be drawn up and enforced by the Member States in the Commission's original proposal for the 1993 ISD, but did not survive the negotiation process.[392] The

---

[389] Funds may be held following a firm's receipt of the proceeds of a sale of securities, dividends, or interest payable on securities. Cash deposits may be made by clients before a purchase order is made. Fully paid securities may be entrusted by the client to a firm for safekeeping or held through a discretionary asset management portfolio. Where securities have been purchased on margin, the firm may advance part of the price of the securities and then hold the securities as collateral for loans and re-pledge the securities to a third party to secure its own future borrowings.

[390] See further Ch III sect 3.14.1 on money-market funds.

[391] n 61. See generally Wessel, N, 'Directive on Investor Compensation Schemes' (1999) 10 *EBLR* 103, Landsmeer, A and van Empel, M, 'The Directive on Deposit-guarantee Schemes and the Directive on Investor Compensation Schemes in View of Case C–233/94' (1998) 5 *EFSL* 143, and Lomnicka, E, 'EC Harmon-isation of Investor Compensation Schemes' (1994) 1 *EFSL* 17.

[392] Member States were opposed to the difference in treatment between compensation arrangements for investment services carried out on a services basis, which were subject to the home Member State regime, and

Commission's original 1993 proposal for the ICSD[393] proved relatively uncontroversial, not least because at the time of the Proposal's presentation all but two of the Member States had some form of compensation scheme.[394] The adoption of the original Deposit Guarantee Directive (DGD)[395] in mid-1994 triggered a substantial re-working of the Proposal to align it to the DGD.[396] The measure stalled due to the European Parliament's concerns that the measure did not adequately protect investors, and was further delayed by Germany's challenge to the DGD. Following the Advocate General's initial rejection of Germany's challenge in late 1996,[397] a compromise between the Parliament and the Council was reached, and the Directive was finally adopted in March 1997.

The ICSD was primarily designed to support passporting by investment firms. Adopted before the retail market agenda took root over the FSAP, it suffers from a number of design defects, particularly with respect to its scope, regarded as a retail investor protection measure. Nonetheless, it represents a landmark in the development of retail market policy, in that it was the first measure specifically directed to retail investors. It is also a landmark measure, as one of the first securities and markets regulation measures to acknowledge the need to address financial stability.

IX.8.2 The 1997 ICSD

IX.8.2.1 Scope and Claims

By sharp contrast with FSAP- and crisis-era measures, the ICSD is a minimum standards measure; Member States are free to prescribe wider or higher coverage than the minimum requirements, while rules concerning the structure, funding, and operation of compensation schemes are not harmonized.

Article 2(1) provides that each Member State must ensure that one or more investor compensation schemes are introduced and officially recognized within its territory. An investment firm authorized in that Member State may not carry on 'investment business'[398] unless it is a member of such a scheme; MiFID II Article 14 provides that investment firms must comply with the ICSD prior to authorization under MiFID II. Credit institutions which come within MiFID II by providing investment services also come within the scope of the ICSD;[399] MiFID II additionally specifies that where a credit institution issues

---

through branches, which were subject to the host Member State regime. Member States favoured home country control, as the home authorities were responsible for authorization and prudential supervision, and harmonization of compensation schemes. The complexities involved in harmonizing compensation schemes meant, however, that to avoid further delays to the adoption of the ISD compensation schemes were excluded from its scope and reserved for a future directive.

[393] [1993] OJ C321/15. Explanatory Memorandum at COM (93) 381.

[394] Explanatory Memorandum, n 393, 14–15.

[395] Directive 94/19/EC [1994] OJ L135/5.

[396] [1994] OJ C382/27. Explanatory Memorandum COM (94) 585.

[397] The Court would not deliver its judgment rejecting the challenge until May 1997: Case C–233/94 *Germany v Parliament and Council* [1997] ECR I–2405.

[398] Defined under Art 1(2) originally by reference to the 1993 ISD.

[399] Where a single scheme meets the requirements of both the ICSD and the DGD, it is not necessary that a credit institution belong to two separate schemes (ICSD rec 9). It may, however, be difficult to distinguish between funds held on deposit covered by the DGD and funds held in connection with investment business

structured deposits, the compensation scheme requirement is met where it is a member of a 2014 DGD scheme (Article 14). The instruments and firms within the scope of the ICSD are thus aligned to MiFID II. The linkage between MiFID II activities and the ICSD's scope means that CIS managers and custodians are excluded from the ICSD; losses sustained in connection with the management of CISs through, for example, custody failures, the possibility of which was graphically made clear by the Madoff scandal,[400] are not covered by the ICSD, although the enhanced depositary regime which applies to UCITS investments (Chapter III) provides *ex-ante* protection. Some controversy arose in the early days of the ICSD as to whether wholesale-market-orientated investment firms could be required to participate in ICSD schemes as these schemes are (as noted below) directed towards retail investors; in practice, most Member States confine participation to retail market firms.[401]

ICSD compensation schemes are directed to retail investors. Coverage extends in principle to the 'investor', broadly defined under Article 1(5) as 'any person who has entrusted money or instruments to an investment firm in connection with investment business'. Under Article 4(2), however, Member States may exclude certain investors regarded as sophisticated (listed in Annex I) from the scheme completely or limit their degree of protection.[402] Also open to exclusion, albeit with a somewhat different motivation, are investors who have any responsibility for or who have taken advantage of certain factors related to an investment firm which gave rise to the firm's financial difficulties or contributed to its deterioration. The retail orientation is also reflected in the minimum compensation requirement. A relatively low minimum level of compensation of €20,000 per investor was adopted (Article 4(1)), as this level was regarded as being 'sufficient to protect the interests of the small investor' (recital 11).[403] Co-insurance is also permitted; under Article 4(4), Member States may, in the interests of promoting a degree of co-responsibility among investors and 'in order to encourage investors to take due care in their choice of investment firms' (recital 13), limit the cover to a specified percentage of an investor's claim. The percentage covered, however, must be equal to or in excess of 90 per cent of the claim where the amount claimed is under €20,000.

---

which are covered by the ICSD (rec 9). In such cases, it is within the discretion of the Member State to decide which scheme applies. In addition, double recovery under the DGD and ICSD is prohibited (Art 2(3)).

[400] Earlier, significant losses were sustained by funds run by Morgan Grenfell Asset Management in 1996. Although investors sustained considerable losses, they were fully covered by Morgan Grenfell and its parent (Deutsche Bank).

[401] There was some litigation in continental Europe as to whether wholesale market firms could be required to participate in compensation schemes. Although the Dutch courts, eg, exempted market-makers from the Dutch scheme, the German courts ruled that firms without eligible clients benefited from the general increase in market trust and confidence and should participate: Oxera, Description and Assessment of the National Investor Compensation Schemes Established in Accordance with Directive 97/9/EC: Report Prepared for the European Commission (2005) (2005 Oxera Report) 18–19.

[402] Annex I is closely related to the original 2004 MiFID I classification system and includes professional and institutional investors, governmental, local and municipal authorities, and larger firms.

[403] This figure can be traced to the Original Proposal in which the Commission noted that a figure of 20,000 would only be significant for the small investor. The Commission also relied on evidence that individual holdings of securities in investment accounts tended on average to be greater than individual holdings of cash held on deposit with credit institutions. In order to protect the small investor, it was therefore essential that the level of compensation be at least as high as that originally set out in the DGD (€20,000): Explanatory Memorandum to Original Proposal, n 393, 8 and 10.

Compensation is available in respect of two types of claim. Investors may request compensation for claims arising out of a firm's inability to repay money owed or belonging to investors and held on their behalf in connection with investment business (Article 2(2)). Claims may also be made under Article 2(2) in respect of the inability of an investment firm to return to investors any instruments belonging to them and held, administered, or managed on their behalf in connection with investment business. Compensation is accordingly available only for a loss of money or instruments arising from the inability of the firm to meet its obligations to investors, whether that arises through fraud or operational failures. Investors may not claim in respect of damages for negligence, breach of statutory or fiduciary duty, or other forms of civil liability. Claims in respect of conflict-of-interest breaches, negligent advice (mis-selling), or misleading advertising are all excluded. In all these cases, investors with a cause of action will simply have a claim over the assets of the bankrupt firm. This represents a major gap in the regime. The risk of loss related to a firm's inability to repay monies or return instruments seems to be low.[404] But the risk of mis-selling is considerably higher and the risk of an investor being unable to pursue a claim against a bankrupt firm accordingly considerable.

The right to compensation is triggered when the relevant NCA determines that an investment firm appears for the time being, for reasons directly related to its financial circumstances, to be unable to meet its obligations arising out of investor claims, and has no early prospect of being able to do so (Article 2(2)). Compensation is also payable where a judicial authority makes a ruling, for reasons directly related to an investment firm's financial circumstances, which has the effect of suspending the ability of investors to make claims against it (Article 2(2)); the earlier in time determination (whether by the NCA or the judicial authority) activates the compensation process. By severing the compensation process from formal bankruptcy procedures in this way, the ICSD speeds up the payment process. The procedures governing the calculation and payment of claims are largely left to Member State discretion.[405]

The ICSD also imposes information requirements. Member States must ensure that each investment firm takes 'appropriate measures' so that 'actual and intending' investors are aware of the compensation scheme to which the firm belongs (Article 10(1)). Information must also be made available concerning the provisions of the compensation scheme, including the amount and scope of cover. The ICSD also requires Member States to establish rules limiting the use in advertising of information relating to compensation schemes, in order to prevent such advertising from affecting the stability of the financial system or investor confidence (Article 10(3)).

---

[404] 2005 Oxera Report, n 401, 93–94.

[405] Only certain aspects are subject to minimum harmonization. Art 2(4) addresses the calculation of the value of claims; Art 8(1) addresses the aggregation of claims; Art 8(2) addresses claims related to joint business by more than one firm; and Art 9 imposes minimum time periods. Under Art 9(1) the time period within which a claim must be made cannot be less than five months from the determination of the firm's inability to meet its obligation; Art 9(2) requires that eligible claims be paid 'as soon as possible' and within three months of the establishment of the validity of the claim, although a further three-month extension can be applied.

IX.8.2.2 Scheme Governance and Funding

The governance and funding of schemes is largely left to the discretion of Member States. The ICSD does not, for example, require that the compensation scheme be placed on a statutory footing (it leaves the form of the scheme to the Member States)[406] or address the composition and independence of the scheme's governing bodies.

The ICSD does, however, impose basic requirements related to the investment firms covered by ICSD schemes. Under Article 5(1) where an investment firm does not meet the obligations of the scheme, the NCA which authorized that firm must, in co-operation with the compensation scheme, take all measures appropriate to ensure that the firm meets its obligations. If the default continues, the compensation scheme may (where permitted under national law and with the express consent of the NCAs) give not less than 12 months' notice of its intention to exclude the firm from the scheme (Article 5(2)). In the interests of investor protection, the scheme must continue to provide cover in respect of investment business transacted during this 12-month period. The ultimate sanction for failure to comply with scheme obligations is loss of authorization, as Article 2(1) sets out that an authorized investment firm may not carry out investment business unless it is a member of a recognized compensation scheme (as also required by MiFID II Article 14).[407]

The ICSD is similarly largely silent on the sensitive question of funding models. Recital 23 indicates that the cost of funding schemes be borne by the investment firms themselves, but this is not the subject of a binding provision. It also suggests that the funding capacities of a scheme must be in proportion to its liabilities and that the funding arrangements adopted must not jeopardize the stability of the financial system of the Member State in which the scheme is recognized.

Schemes may as a result levy fixed or variable premiums. They may alternatively operate without premiums and levy charges based on the actual commitments to be met by the scheme. Risk-weighting may or may not be adopted by schemes in assessing contributions. Funding requirements may, for example, reflect cross-sector risk profiles and assess contributions on a sectoral basis, given that within the universe of investment services some activities are likely to generate more claims than others and cross-subsidies may emerge between sectors engaged in different activities, such as the discretionary portfolio management and brokerage sectors, for example.

The right of investors under Article 13 to sue compensation schemes where compensation is not forthcoming suggests that schemes must be in a position to meet all investors' claims up to the ICSD's minimum threshold and, accordingly, that they may not impose maximum pay-out limits for particular time periods. It is possible that a catastrophic series

---

[406] Art 13 stipulates, however, that Member States must ensure that the investor's right to compensation may be the subject of an action by the investor against the compensation scheme, and its legal form must therefore allow such an action to be taken.

[407] The *Peter Paul* case on the parallel provisions under the DGD has clarified that the purpose of these provisions (in the DGD context) is to guarantee to depositors that the credit institution in which they make their deposits belongs to a deposit guarantee scheme, in order to ensure protection of their right to compensation in the event that deposits are unavailable in accordance with the Directive's rules on recovery. These provisions only relate to the introduction and proper functioning of the deposit guarantee scheme and do not support private rights of actions against the NCA responsible for supervising the credit institution in question: Case C-222/02 *Paul, Sonnen-Lütte, and Mörkens v Germany* [2004] ECR I-9425.

of investment-firm failures could drain the resources of a scheme completely and place considerable funding strains on member firms. It is not entirely clear in such circumstances how the requirement that funding arrangements must not jeopardize the stability of the financial system and the apparent obligation on a scheme to meet all claims can be reconciled. The financial crisis, however, has led to radical reforms being proposed to funding arrangements and to a significant increase in the level of prescription (section 8.3).

IX.8.2.3 Cross-border Claims

The pan-EU retail market remains an aspiration, not a reality, and cross-border claims are accordingly relatively unusual. But—and foreshadowing the stresses which the allocation of fiscal responsibility would place on the EU's ability to respond to the financial crisis—the Directive struggles, nonetheless, to allocate responsibility between home and host schemes efficiently.

The ICSD operates on a home Member State model. Under Article 7(1), an investor compensation scheme recognized in a Member State also covers investors at branches set up by investment firms belonging to that compensation scheme in other Member States. This model, combined with minimum harmonization, allows home Member States to increase the level of compensation provided. It follows that investors in the same Member State may be protected to varying degrees depending on whether the investment firm is authorized in that State or passporting from another Member State. In addition, branches may suffer from a competitive disadvantage if they cannot offer the same level of coverage in an insolvency as home firms. Although the impact of the scale of compensation available on the exercise of investor choice is debatable, and the level of cross-border activity very low, the ICSD contains a 'top-up' mechanism designed to address these potential distortions.[408] Where the level or scope of the scheme offered by the host Member State exceeds the coverage of the home Member State's scheme, the host Member State must provide that visiting branches may voluntarily join the host scheme (Article 7(1)). Despite its investor protection benefits, the top-up rule represents a distortion of the home Member State control principle. More generous host schemes are exposed to claims in respect of firms the solvency of which they are not in a strong position to monitor. Claims may be made on the host scheme which have arisen due to a failure of supervision by the home NCA responsible for prudential control. In addition, the host scheme faces the additional costs of assessing the appropriate premium to charge the branch. The ICSD does, however, seek to reduce the risks faced by host schemes, in that a host scheme may subject the branch to objective and generally applied membership conditions and may, after a 12-month notice period, expel the branch from the scheme if it does not meet its obligations (Article 7(1) and (2)). Risks have also been reduced by the shift under MiFID I originally (and, since, MiFID II) to branch control for some aspects of investment services supervision, and particularly conduct-of-business and record-keeping rules, although prudential supervision remains a

---

[408] The ICSD also contained a transitional 'export ban' (where the home Member State's scheme was more extensive in scope than that offered in the host Member State in which a branch provided services, the cover provided by that branch's scheme to its investors in the host Member State was not permitted to exceed the cover provided by the host Member State's scheme) which was discontinued, following the Commission's review, in 1999.

home NCA competence. The top-up regime also raises complex issues both for investors seeking compensation (as the payment of claims will be split between two schemes) and for the administration of the host scheme with respect to the additional premium charged to branches voluntarily joining the scheme.[409]

More generally, the ICSD's home Member State model is vulnerable. In theory, home Member State control has the advantage of providing the home Member State's authorities with an incentive to ensure adequate supervision, as the home Member State scheme will carry the consequences of firm failure; it also lessens the exposure of host Member States to inadequate home Member State supervision. In practice, the home Member State is vulnerable to failures in the host State which can lead to significant calls on the home scheme.

IX.8.3 Reviewing the 1997 ICSD

IX.8.3.1 The FSAP/Pre-crisis Era

The ICSD remained untouched by the wider FSAP reforms and was generally regarded as a robust measure until the crisis-era period. CESR's important 2004 Himalaya Report on supervisory convergence did not report any major problems in convergence in the powers required under the ICSD,[410] although it presciently acknowledged the strain that extensive host Member State activity could place on a home Member State compensation scheme were genuine pan-EU investment firms to emerge;[411] the financial crisis would dramatically reveal the extent of the risks to which the parallel deposit protection scheme was exposed in this regard. The ICSD was notable by its absence from the extensive reviews of EU financial market regulation which occurred post-FSAP and from the 2007 Green Paper on Retail Financial Services.

The ICSD was, however, reviewed by the Commission in 2000[412] (in the context of the now defunct 'export ban'), and its practical operation was subject to extensive review in 2005.[413] The 2005 report addressed how the ICSD had been implemented at national level and was broadly positive,[414] although it noted recurring procedural weaknesses, particularly with respect to the timeliness of compensation payments, and made a series of reform recommendations. The report found there had been very few cases of firm failure that triggered the operation of national schemes, and that in many countries no failures had occurred. This finding was closely related, however, to the exclusion of claims related to investment advice/mis-selling by national schemes; the UK scheme, which covers such claims, experienced significantly higher volumes of activity.[415] The report also found,

---

[409] Guiding principles to support host authorities are set out in Annex I.
[410] CESR, Preliminary Progress Report, Which Supervisory Tools for the EU Securities Market? An Analytical Paper by CESR (2004) (CESR/04–333f), 29.
[411] n 410, 19.
[412] Commission, Report on the Application of the Export Prohibition Clause, Article 7(1) of the Directive on Investor Compensation Scheme. COM (2000) 81 (the 2000 ICSD Report).
[413] n 401. For the Commission's response see Commission, Evaluation of the ICSD, DG Internal Market and Services—Executive Report and Recommendations (2005) (2005 Commission Report).
[414] The Commission interpreted the report as suggesting that compensation schemes were working 'fairly well' and played an important complementary role in providing last-resort protection: n 413, 10.
[415] n 401.

reflecting the ICSD's minimum-harmonization model, significant variations in how schemes were designed and funded. Schemes diverged across a range of criteria, including organizational structure, relationship with national NCAs, participation requirements, definition of eligible investors, types of losses covered, compensation limits, and funding arrangements.[416] While schemes were principally financed through industry levies, there were considerable differences with respect to when contributions were collected, how they were calculated, contribution limits, and whether funds were pooled across participating firms.[417] The report also considered whether funding was adequate and found that none of the EU-15 schemes reviewed had suffered funding shortfalls, although the report presciently expressed concern at the failure of most schemes to assess potential loss exposures, to engage in stress-testing, and to assess their state of readiness to deal with major defaults. While the report made a series of recommendations, relating in the main to the mitigation of delays in making payments, to supporting the resilience of schemes' funding structures, and to the assessment of the exclusion of claims relating to investment advice failures, major reform would not follow until the financial crisis. The Commission's response to the 2005 report was unusually low-key but reflected the post-FSAP and pre-crisis concern to minimize regulatory intervention. It identified three options to address the report's findings: legislative action, a Commission Communication or Recommendation, and dialogue between the Member States concerning best practice. Rejecting legislative intervention as a 'last resort', it supported dialogue between the Member States as the best means for enhancing national schemes.[418]

IX.8.3.2 The Financial Crisis and the 2010 Proposal

Immediately prior to the financial crisis, the ICSD was accordingly regarded as relatively resilient—although it was something of an oddity as a minimum-harmonization measure. The most significant difficulties related to the exclusion of claims against insolvent firms relating to mis-selling and the exclusion of claims relating to CIS custody failures. While it was always vulnerable to serious destabilization if significant cross-border claims became more common, the very limited cross-border activity in the retail market masked this weakness. Reform of the ICSD has since followed under the crisis-era reform agenda, but this has been primarily a function of the spillover and momentum dynamics of the stability-related reforms to deposit protection.[419]

The earliest of the EU's interventions in the crisis in autumn 2008 were concerned with the DGD. The 1994 Directive set the minimum level of protection at €20,000, contained a co-insurance provision which allowed Member States to limit recovery to 90 per cent of a claim, allowed for lengthy pay-out periods, and left the operation and funding of schemes, for the most part, to Member State discretion. Turmoil in the EU banking market, along with unilateral intervention by some Member States to increase the level of coverage provided to depositors, and consequent significant risk of competitive distortions in the

---

[416] Oxera concluded that there was no favoured model for implementation and that schemes varied, in particular, according to the investors eligible for coverage, the nature of the claims covered, and the instruments covered: n 401, 38–39.

[417] n 401, 63–90.

[418] 2005 Commission Report, n 413, 11.

[419] The crisis era also saw efforts to introduce a guarantee system for insurance, but this initiative languished.

EU banking market, led the October 2008 ECOFIN Council to support an increase in minimum deposit guarantee levels. The Directive, after an extraordinarily short legislative process, was revised in February 2009 to provide for a €100,000 minimum coverage limit in all Member States by end 2010, the removal of co-insurance, and a reduction in the pay-out period.[420] A major review of the Directive was then launched[421] to address scheme resilience and funding, given the demands which the crisis placed on deposit protection, as well as the risk, which the Icelandic banking failure exposed, of home authorities unilaterally closing schemes to host depositors. The early stages of the crisis also saw some indications of support for a common EU deposit protection scheme.[422] This proposal did not gain traction, reflecting the significant institutional design and fiscal complexities, even as the sovereign debt crisis and the subsequent Banking Union agenda intervened; the institutional structure of Banking Union is currently based on the Single Supervisory Mechanism and the Single Resolution Mechanism, but on Member State-based deposit protection, albeit subject to detailed harmonized rules.[423] The proposed new regulatory regime for deposit protection was set out in the 2010 DGD Proposal.[424] In addition to procedural refinements (primarily in relation to shorter time limits for pay-outs, as well as scope clarifications), it proposed a new harmonized funding model based on: a pre-funding requirement for all schemes, requiring coverage of 1.5 per cent of covered deposits; an *ex-post* funding mechanism, based on risk-based contributions by banks, where a scheme was not fully funded for a bank failure; a mechanism for mutual borrowing between EU schemes; and, as a last line of defence, alternative funding sources. The Proposal also suggested that schemes could be used for bank resolution purposes, albeit that a ring-fence would apply to deposit protection funds. The scale of the harmonization envisaged by this new regime led to very difficult negotiations.[425] The European Parliament and Council became deadlocked, leading to the Parliament adopting a first reading of the Proposal in February 2012,[426] thereby closing off the fast-track ordinary legislative procedure employed for all other major crisis-era reforms.[427] Particular difficulties arose with respect to the time-

---

[420] Directive 2009/14/EU [2009] OJ L68/3.

[421] The 2010 Proposal (n 424) was the subject of a barrage of assessment and consultation, including an informal roundtable of experts in March 2009, three meetings of the Working Group on Deposit Guarantee Schemes, and a range of reports from the Commission's Joint Research Centre and the European Forum of Deposit Insurers.

[422] eg the Commission's pathfinder 2009 Communication on DGD reform: Commission, Consultation Document, Review of Directive 94/19/EC (2009) 11–12.

[423] The Banking Union proposals were originally set out in Commission, A Roadmap towards a Banking Union (2012) (COM (2012) 510). The roadmap envisaged that within Banking Union deposit protection be organized at Member State level, albeit subject to enhanced harmonized rules (at 5). Similarly, the European Council in October 2012 called for rapid adoption of the stalled proposal to reform the DGD, but did not refer to a common scheme: European Council 18/19 October 2012, Conclusions. The President of the European Council's 2012 Interim Report on Towards a Genuine Economic and Monetary Union (October 2012) noted the important pre-emptive role of deposit protection schemes in supporting financial stability, but called for progress on the Commission's proposal and not for a new EU scheme. The ECB also supported a 'more harmonized deposit guarantee mechanism': ECB, Financial Stability Review (2012) 124.

[424] COM (2010) 368.

[425] The European Parliament, eg, was concerned with the proposed harmonization levels, while the Commission's Impact Assessment Board called for the Proposal to present more evidence concerning the necessity for harmonization, given the scale of the policy changes and their costs: IAB Opinion, 26 March 2010 (Ref.Ares(2010)163905).

[426] T7-0049/212.

[427] See further Ch X sect 3.3.2 on the fast-track process.

scale for the new funding model, the level of pre-funding required, and the extent to which schemes could engage in preventive intervention in failing banks.[428] The advent of Banking Union increased the pressure to finalize negotiations,[429] and agreement was finally reached between the Parliament and Council in December 2013.[430]

While the need for reform to the ICSD had been identified over the FSAP period, the crisis-era and momentum effects relating to the DGD drew it into the wider reform programme. The ESA negotiations, for example, saw the imposition of an obligation on ESMA (ESMA Regulation Article 26) to contribute to strengthening the European system of investor compensation schemes, with the aim of ensuring that national schemes were adequately funded and provided a high level of protection to all investors; to that end, ESMA was expressly empowered to adopt guidelines and recommendation and, where the relevant delegation was conferred, to propose Binding Technical Standards (BTSs). The 2010 ESMA Regulation also included in its review clause the extent of convergence of national compensation schemes.

The crisis-era ICSD review commenced with the pathfinder 2009 Commission Communication,[431] which related the reform process to the need to review the Directive after over ten years of operation, but also in light of the financial crisis and the parallel reforms to deposit protection. Many of the issues canvassed related to the scope of the ICSD and, in particular, to whether it should be extended to include failures by third parties to which custody of assets and funds had been delegated by investment firms, and failures by UCITS custodians. The Commission also addressed the limited range of claims possible under the ICSD, and queried whether the claims within the scope of the ICSD could include claims arising from breaches of conduct-of-business rules, opening up the possibility of claims relating to mis-selling. The need for a higher minimum compensation level was also canvassed, as was the need to reduce pay-out delays. Reflecting the parallel DGD reforms, the Communication also raised whether scheme funding should be addressed.

The 2010 ICSD Proposal[432] largely followed the Communication. Much of the Proposal is relatively uncontroversial. It proposes a series of extensions to the scope of the ICSD, notably with respect to failure by a third party custodian to which client financial instruments have been entrusted by a MiFID II firm, and with respect to custody failures by a UCITS depositary or sub-custodian. It also aligns the ICSD formally and more carefully with MiFID II/MiFID I, including with respect to the definition of the sophisticated

---

[428] eg the European Parliament called for a 15-year implementation period for the funding model (the Commission for ten) and for schemes to be permitted to use nearly all their funds for preventive intervention (the Commission limited this to one third of funds). The 1.5 per cent level of pre-funding generated considerable opposition from the Member States.

[429] Commissioner Barnier, Speech on 'The European Banking Union, a precondition to financial stability and a historical step forward for European integration', 17 December 2012.

[430] The compromise includes a reduction of the pre-funding level to a minimum harmonized level of 0.8 per cent of covered deposits (to be achieved within ten years) (the level can be reduced to 0.5 per cent by the Commission where a banking sector is highly concentrated) and a voluntary mutual borrowing arrangement. Other reforms include consumer-orientated reforms, relating to a reduction of the repayment deadline from 20 days to 7 days (by 2024) and a mandatory information sheet for depositors on deposit protection, and resolution-orientated reforms. The Directive was adopted by the Council and Parliament in March and April 2014, respectively.

[431] Commission, Directive 1997/9/EC on Investor Compensation Schemes. Call for Evidence (2009) 8.

[432] COM (2010) 317. Impact Assessment at SEC (2010) 845.

investors who may be excluded by Member States from the Directive, and provides that all MiFID I (now MiFID II) activities and services are subject to the Directive, regardless of whether the instruments or funds are held in contravention of a firm's authorization. The Proposal also proposes an increase in the level of minimum compensation from €20,000 to €50,000, in order to reflect the effects of inflation and an increase in the average value of investments held by retail investors,[433] removal of the co-insurance possibility, and procedures to reduce the delays which currently can attach to compensation payments.

Its claim to strengthen retail investor protection is weakened by the failure to extend the claims which can be pursued to include outstanding claims relating to breaches of conduct requirements.[434] The Proposal also suffers from acute spillover risks from the parallel deposit guarantee reforms, which are at bedrock concerned with financial stability. In particular, the new ICSD funding model is closely based on the DGD model, albeit with a lower 0.5 per cent funding target. The Proposal (like the DGD Proposal) proved divisive, earning the distinction of being the first crisis-era financial market measure not to be passed by means of a first reading by the European Parliament under the fast-track procedure, but moving into the second reading phase in July 2011,[435] following failure by the Council and European Parliament to reach an initial agreed position.[436] At the root of the problem is the Proposal's failure to distinguish between the different functions of deposit protection and compensation schemes,[437] despite the Proposal's acknowledgement of the different purposes of both schemes.[438] Investor compensation schemes are not directly concerned with financial stability. The Commission's Proposal, however, assumes that a stringent, harmonized pre-funding regime is necessary on financial stability grounds, notwithstanding the limited nature of, and consequences of, investor claims under the Directive and, in particular, the absence of a cross-border market and the related lower likelihood of strain on home schemes.

The financial stability context also seems to have distracted policy attention from the main weakness in the Directive; its failure to address compensation for outstanding claims arising from a firm's liability, whether with respect to mis-selling, negligence, or other forms of statutory or civil liability.[439] The Commission's Impact Assessment raised the possibility of extending the ICSD to cover civil liability claims but decided against, given, *inter alia*, the discretion of Member States to extend schemes, the likely costs, the protections provided elsewhere in the regulatory regime, and market structure divergences.[440] The failure of the Proposal to support investors by means of a compensation regime for mis-selling claims suggests, nonetheless, a lack of joined-up thinking given the MiFID II distribution reforms.

---

[433] 2010 ICSD Proposal, n 432, 8.

[434] Such an extension was supported by the European Parliament in its First Reading.

[435] T7-0313/2011.

[436] Significant differences emerged between the European Parliament and the Council concerning the necessity for a pre-funding regime, its intensity, and its level.

[437] A theme which also emerged during the European Parliament's discussions: ECON Committee, Safeguarding Investors Interests by Ensuring Sound Financing of ICSs. Compilation of Briefing Notes (2011).

[438] n 432, 5.

[439] The financial stability agenda, and the extensive preparatory work carried out for the DGD reforms may have weakened the quality of the ICSD analysis and proposals. Notably, the Commission's Impact Assessment Board rejected the initial impact assessment prepared for the Proposal and requested a more extensive and evidenced review: IAB Opinion, 12 March 2010, Ref.Ares(2010)134796.

[440] 2010 ICSD Proposal Impact Assessment, n 432, 15–16 and 41–3.

IX.9 Supporting the Rulebook: Education and Engagement

Investor education and more general financial literacy strategies have recently become embedded within retail market law and policy internationally.[441] This marked trend is well illustrated by the US Securities and Exchange Commission's (SEC) efforts,[442] the Organization for Economic Co-operation and Development's (OECD) financial education agenda[443] and the International Organization of Securities Commissions' (IOSCO) investor education initiatives which have increased in intensity since the financial crisis broke out.[444] Financial literacy strategies must form part of any retail market regime which, as the EU's regime does, seeks to promote stronger engagement with market investment.[445] They also offer the prospect of a more informed retail cohort developing which can, in time, take some of the pressure from regulation by engaging in more effective market monitoring.[446] The construction of an effective literacy/education strategy requires, however, that a number of challenges are addressed.[447] The over-selling of the merits of market investment[448] must, for example, be avoided, and undue weight must not be placed on the ability of literacy strategies to empower investors, given the persistence of behavioural weaknesses[449] and the often poor outcomes associated with literacy strategies.[450] The muscular regulatory and supervisory strategies needed in the retail markets must not be sidelined. Appropriate mechanisms for feedback and for providing individual support must be designed; static disclosure-based techniques should be avoided.[451] Additionally, and with particular reference to the EU, investor education and financial literacy strategies must be deeply rooted in the cultural and social fabric of the Member State and reflect local savings patterns, distribution channels, and national education systems.

EU engagement in this sphere[452] is accordingly best directed to supporting the sharing of best practices and supervisory learning, and to prodding national authorities and Member

---

[441] Lusardi, A, Financial Literacy and Financial Education: Review and Policy Implication, NFI Policy Brief No 2006-PB-11 (2006), available at <http://ssrn.com/abstract=923437>.

[442] As required under the 2010 Dodd-Frank Act, the SEC produced a major study in 2012 on financial literacy: SEC, Staff Study Regarding Financial Literacy Among Investors (2012).

[443] The OECD programme, launched in 2003, includes its Recommendations on Principles and Good Practices for Financial Education and Awareness (2005), review of national programmes, sector-specific principle for different financial sectors, and a governmental financial education network. Financial education and awareness also forms part of the OECD-developed G20 High-Level Principles on Financial Consumer Protection (2011).

[444] eg the 2013 launch of IOSCO's 'Investor Education Gateway' which supports information-sharing between IOSCO members on investor education.

[445] eg Jackson, H, 'To What Extent Should Individual Investors Rely on the Mechanisms of Market Efficiency: A Preliminary Investigation of Dispersion in Investor Returns' (2003) 28 *J Corp L* 671 and Van Rooij, M, Lusardi, A, and Alessie, R, Financial Literacy and Stock Market Participation, NBER WP No w13565 (2007), available at <http://ssrn.com/abstract=1024979>.

[446] Choi, S and Pritchard, A, 'Behavioural Economics and the SEC' (2003) 56 *Stanford LR* 1.

[447] Willis, L, Against Financial Literacy Education (2008), available at <http://ssrn.com/abstract=1105384>,

[448] eg Black, B and Gross, J, 'The Elusive Balance between Investor Education and Wealth Creation' (2005) 25 *Pace LR* 24.

[449] Kozup and Hogarth, n 303.

[450] FSA, Report by Atkinson, A, Evidence of Impact: An Overview of Financial Education Evaluations, Consumer Research Paper No 68 (2008).

[451] Willis, n 447.

[452] See further Moloney, n 7, 374–98.

States to take effective action. Despite its pre-crisis enthusiasm for investor empowerment, which likely acted as a spur to its initial move into investor education in 2007, the Commission's initiatives have been directed in the main to co-ordination. They include a Communication on financial education,[453] a range of studies,[454] a new Expert Group on Financial Education,[455] and other co-ordination-based initiatives.[456] These initiatives are directed to financial literacy in its broadest sense and have not been noticeably successful.[457] ESMA, however, is well placed to support more targeted supervisory learning in this area.[458] There may also be scope for ESMA to take a more interventionist role, particularly with respect to requiring NCAs to produce investor alerts or warnings, whether on a national or a pan-EU basis, particularly in times of crisis.

EU retail market policy has also engaged with the intractable problem of how to engage retail investors in the law-making process, albeit with very limited success.[459] Direct retail investor engagement with the law-making process strengthens accountability and increases the credibility and legitimacy of regulation (which is of acute importance where 'responsibilized' and 'financialized' investors are sought). It may also lead to more empirically informed regulation, reduce capture risks, stiffen what can be a flabby governmental resolve to reform where industry 'backlash' risks arise, and mute the familiar industry clamour against regulation.[460] But retail investors (or the 'panicked mass public',[461] in one vivid characterization) are ill-informed and poorly organized,[462] particularly when compared to the behemoth industry lobbies, and typically only come to bear on the law-making process in times of immense turbulence—even then their influence can wane very quickly, as the financial crisis period suggests.[463] The difficulties are all the greater in the EU's polycentric law-making process (Chapter XI)[464] and because retail investors do not yet form a cohesive or politically influential group. But the need is all the sharper, particularly as retail market protection can become a cover for national interests and as law-making for retail markets is increasingly an EU function.

The FSAP period and the greater focus over that period on adequate consultation, associated in particular with the Lamfalussy process,[465] saw the Commission become alive to the need to

[453] Commission, Communication from the Commission, Financial Education (2007).

[454] Including, Evers & Jung, Survey of Financial Literacy in the EU 27 (2007).

[455] Commission Decision 2008/365/EC [2008] OJ L125/36.

[456] The European Database for Financial Education, eg, was established in January 2009 (IP/09/69).

[457] Commission, Review of the Initiatives of the Commission in the Area of Financial Education (2011), reporting that the Expert Group and Database had not been particularly effective and noting that financial literacy programmes were lagging behind in many Member States.

[458] ESMA has highlighted that while primary responsibility for investor education is best placed at NCA level, it is well placed to raise awareness across NCAs and to encourage and communicate best practices. Its initial initiatives included the ESMA Guide to Investing, directed to retail investors, and preparatory work on the development of Financial Education Best Practices: ESMA, Annual Report (2012) 27.

[459] See further Moloney, n 7, 398–425.

[460] Black and Gross, n 448, 34–6.

[461] Braithwaite, J and Drahos, P, *Global Business Regulation* (2000) 122–3 and 159.

[462] See Black, J, Involving Consumers on Securities Regulation. Report for the Taskforce to Modernize Securities Regulation in Canada (2006).

[463] Coffee, J, 'The Political Economy of Dodd-Frank: Why Financial Reform Tends to be Frustrated and System Risk Perpetuated' in Ferran et al, n 165, 301.

[464] FIN-USE, The Consumer's Voice in the European Financial Services Sector (2007).

[465] See Ch X sect 2.3.4.

strengthen retail investor engagement with the law-making process, and its establishment of the consultative groups FIN-USE in 2004 and the Financial Services Consumer Group in 2006. Short 'citizen summaries' were also deployed to encourage stronger retail participation. Outside the legislative process, CESR engaged in a series of initiatives to promote retail investor engagement.[466] These efforts largely went into abeyance over the financial crisis and as the EU rulebook was reset at the legislative level; the inter-institutional legislative process became dominated by often titanic institutional, political, and market interests. But even in calmer conditions, the legislative process, with its varying entry points, opaque procedures, and shifting locations of power as legislation progresses between the Commission, Council, and European Parliament, is almost un-navigable by the retail interest. The 2010 establishment by the Commission of the new Financial Services User Group,[467] which replaces FIN-USE and the Financial Services Consumer Group, has led to the arrival of a vocal and relatively well-resourced stakeholder body.[468] But there are limits to what single-issue stakeholder groups can achieve, particularly given the resources at the disposal of industry groups.[469]

The distinction between 'input' legitimacy and 'output' legitimacy, which distinguishes between, for example, legitimacy based on representation and legitimacy based on the achievement of particular goals or outcomes, may provide something of a compromise solution for the EU, given the challenges posed by traditional representation,[470] at least at ESMA level. The conferral on ESMA of an express objective relating to consumer protection marks the first time that a specific retail market mandate has been conferred on an actor in the EU legislative apparatus. As discussed in section 10, the initial indications suggest that ESMA may become an effective advocate for retail interests generally, although it has been less effective in supporting direct retail representation. Ultimately, the extent to which the retail interest is engaged in the EU's law-making process, and particularly in the legislative process, is likely to be a function of the extent to which individuals and households become more closely engaged with market investing and, accordingly, a politically cohesive and influential group.

IX.10 The Retail Markets and ESMA

As discussed in Chapters X and XI, CESR exerted significant influence on the development of the EU rulebook and on convergence in supervisory practices from 2001 until its replacement in January 2011 by ESMA. In so doing, and to a striking extent, it embraced

---

[466] n 99 and Ch X sect 2.3.4.

[467] [2010] OJ C199/12.

[468] For a review of its extensive activities, which include the commissioning of research on retail market failures, see, eg, FSUG, Annual Report (2012).

[469] 2013 saw the outbreak of a fracas between the fund management industry and major consumer stakeholders following consumer concerns that the fund industry was aggressively lobbying against investor-protection-orientated reforms, and concern from influential MEP Giegold that a disproportionate amount of lobbying was being engaged in: Marriage, M, 'Fund Lobby Groups Attacked by Investors', *Financial Times, Fund Management Supplement*, 17 June 2013, 1.

[470] eg Esty, D, 'Good Governance at the Supranational Scale: Globalizing Administrative Law' (2006) 115 *Yale LJ* (2006) 1490.

a retail market agenda.[471] It significantly strengthened the Commission's capacity to develop nuanced legislative proposals for the retail markets, particularly through its wide-ranging research and testing activities on the UCITS KIID.[472] It adopted a raft of soft law guidance for the retail markets.[473] It developed an innovative retail governance agenda, engaging in a range of activities to support greater retail investor involvement (including Consumer Days and Workshops), and developed an investor education programme.[474] It was much more attuned to the retail markets than was the Commission in the early stages of the crisis, and moved quickly to address the Madoff failure and to co-ordinate a response on enforcement of retail investor claims.[475] It is not surprising that retail market interests would be prioritized by CESR in the days before financial stability acquired central importance, and given the prominence given to retail market protection over the FSAP era. CESR's insecure foundations and its need to construct both an accountability model and strong institutional relations[476] made the retail agenda an attractive one; in particular, it allowed CESR to build close relations with the generally pro-retail European Parliament, to acquire the 'colour' of a market regulator, and to develop a sense of institutional mission.[477] It is not entirely clear that ESMA, which has a materially stronger legislative basis, will, with respect to its discretionary activities, engage with retail market interests to the same extent.

ESMA is a securities markets regulator and as such would be expected to engage closely with retail market concerns. But it was constructed in the teeth of the financial crisis. Its primary objective is to 'protect the public interest by contributing to the short, medium, and long-term stability and effectiveness of the financial system, for the Union economy, its citizens and businesses' (ESMA Regulation Article 1(4)). The overwhelming preoccupation with financial stability as the ESA reform was negotiated, and the decision to use the same legal text for all three ESAs, notwithstanding their different spheres of operation, led to a lack of differentiation and to the dominance of the financial stability objective. ESMA has a subsidiary obligation to contribute to 'enhancing consumer protection', but this appears after its obligation to contribute to improving the functioning of the internal market, ensuring the integrity, transparency, efficiency, and orderly functioning of financial markets, strengthening international supervisory co-ordination, preventing regulatory arbitrage, and ensuring the taking of investment and other risks are appropriately supervised and regulated (ESMA Regulation Article 1(5) (a)–(f)). ESMA also has strong incentives to prioritize its novel financial stability mandate (Chapter XI section 7). The retail market agenda may be less attractive. The retail markets are, however, expressly addressed by Article 9, which contains a number of retail-market-oriented obligations and was inserted by the European Parliament, which has since shown a commitment to monitoring the

---

[471] Which was repeatedly referred to in its Annual Reports.

[472] Ch III sect 3.11.3.

[473] Including, eg, a Q&A on the contested question of whether certain investment products were 'complex' or 'non-complex' and so could be sold execution-only under MiFID I (CESR/09-559) and on the definition of 'advice' under MiFID I (CESR/10-293); a report setting out good and poor practices relating to inducements (CESR/10-295); guidance on the treatment of inducements (CESR/07-228b); and guidance on best execution (CESR/07-320).

[474] See Moloney, n 7, 396–8 and 419–25.

[475] CESR/09-089.

[476] See further Ch X sect 2.3.2 and 2.3.3.

[477] eg, in the context of the US SEC, Langevoort, D, 'Re-reading Cady Roberts: the Ideology and Practice of Insider Trading Regulation' (1999) 99 *Columbia LR* 1319.

exercise of these powers.[478] It is a somewhat muddled provision, combining workaday powers with radical product intervention powers. Article 9 requires ESMA to 'take a leading role' in promoting 'transparency, simplicity, and fairness' in the market for consumer financial products, including by examining consumer trends, reviewing and co-ordinating financial literacy initiatives, developing training standards, and contributing to the development of common disclosure rules (Article 9(1)). It also empowers ESMA to issue warnings where a financial activity poses a series threat to its objectives (Article 9(3)), requires ESMA to monitor financial innovation (through a dedicated Committee) in order to achieve a co-ordinated approach (Article 9(4)), and contains the enabling power for product intervention (Article 9(5)).

ESMA has accordingly, and for the first time within the EU legislative apparatus, been conferred with an express retail market mandate. While it has the capacity to shape the EU's retail market rulebook through its technical advice on administrative rules and its proposals for BTSs, its discretionary activities will prove particularly revealing as to its retail market agenda.[479] Early evidence suggests some enthusiasm for the retail markets, despite the gravitational pull of the stability agenda. ESMA's developing 'soft rulebook', for example, includes robust, detailed, and practical guidelines on MiFID I remuneration and on MiFID I suitability requirements,[480] which underline ESMA's publicly expressed commitment to addressing mis-selling risks,[481] as well as 'Q&As', supervisory briefings, and opinions.[482] ESMA was quick to use its power to issue warnings.[483] ESMA has also engaged with the slowly emerging international agenda on retail market protection which is being driven by the OECD.[484]

A number of governance initiatives have been taken to embed ESMA's coverage of retail market risks. During its first year of operation, an Article 9 'Implementation Task Force' was established to ensure ESMA was equipped to fulfil its Article 9 responsibilities; its early work included an assessment of the different approaches taken by national NCAs to the retail markets.[485] The Task Force and ESMA's Article 9 Financial Innovation Committee

---

[478] Hearing of the Chairs of the European Supervisory Authorities. 19 September 2012. Written Questions from ECON Coordinators. Joint Answers from the ESAs (JC 2012 090). The Art 9 powers featured prominently in the Hearing.

[479] Its first Annual Report suggested a commitment to the retail markets, highlighting ESMA's ESMA Regulation Art 9 investor protection responsibilities: Annual Report 2011, 12.

[480] ESMA/2013/606 (MiFID I remuneration) and ESMA/2012/827 (MiFID I suitability).

[481] ESMA Chairman Maijoor committed to using all ESMA's available powers to address incentive risks and bias in product distribution in the event that the Commission's proposed MiFID II ban on commission in advice and discretionary asset management was not adopted: Speech, ESMA Investor Day, 12 December 2012 (ESMA/2012/818). Similarly, ESMA Executive Director Ross supported the MiFID II reforms designed to support the quality of advice: Open Statement, ECON Public Hearing on the MiFID I Review, 5 December 2011 (ESMA/2012/77).

[482] eg MiFID I Q&A investor protection and intermediaries (ESMA/2012/328), Supervisory Briefings ESMA/2012/851 (appropriateness and execution only) and ESMA/2012/850 (suitability), and an opinion on product governance processes for structured retail products (ESMA/2014/332).

[483] Four warnings have been issued at the time of writing, with respect to: foreign exchange products (ESMA/2011/412); online investing (ESMA/2012/557); contracts for difference (ESMA/2013/267); and the risks posed by complex products (ESMA/2014/154).

[484] Maijoor Speech, 12 December 2012, n 481. At the core of this agenda are the G20 High Level Principles on Financial Consumer Protection (2011), which were developed by the Organization for Economic Co-operation and Development (OECD) in consultation with the Financial Stability Board (FSB).

[485] ESMA Annual Report (2011) 35.

have focused in particular on product intervention powers.[486] ESMA has also established a permanent Operational Working Group to promote common practices in investor protection.

The Commission's 2013 Review of the European System of Financial Supervision (and of the ESAs) suggested some concern as to the more limited attention given by ESMA to retail market investor protection, as compared to financial stability-related matters.[487] But while in some respects ESMA has been less successful (notably with respect to investor education,[488] research on the retail markets,[489] and investor engagement[490]) this can be related to the monumental weight of the crisis-era administrative rule-making agenda.[491] Overall, the early evidence suggests that ESMA has the appetite and the capacity to develop a strong retail agenda, assuming the financial stability agenda leaves it with sufficient space to do so.

Effective retail market protection is, however, ill-served by the split of financial consumer market issues across the three sector-specific ESAs, given the cross-sector nature of retail market risk and the prevalence of substitutable products. Nonetheless, the ESA Joint Committee may support a more co-ordinated approach. It has established retail-market-focused subgroups, including for consumer protection generally, for product oversight and governance, and with respect to the PRIPs reforms. The operational and practical quality of its agenda thus far[492] suggests that it has the potential to shape a more co-ordinated approach to retail market risk across the EU. More radical institutional reforms can, of

---

[486] In advance of its being conferred with direct intervention powers under MiFID II, ESMA, *inter alia*, mapped the powers available to national NCAs and began to develop a possible ESMA approach: ESMA Annual Report 2011, 35–6. This review informed the subsequent work by the ESA Joint Committee on product intervention.

[487] eg Response by EuroFinuse to the 2013 Commission Consultation on Review of the ESFS (responses available at <http://ec.europa.eu/internal_market/consultations/2013/esfs/contributions_en.htm>).

The Parliament's ECON Committee also noted its concern as to the coverage of consumer protection across the ESAs: ECON Committee, Draft Report with Recommendations to the Commission on the ESFS Review, 11 October 2013 (PE521.510v01-00). The IMF also noted that stronger information-gathering in the products sphere would allow ESMA to make a 'qualitative leap' in this area: IMF, Financial Sector Assessment Program. ESMA. Technical Note, March 2013, 5.

[488] Its first initiative was a traditional Guide to Investing (ESMA/2012/682), which was relatively unsophisticated as compared to the financial literacy efforts at national level.

[489] Although it has been engaged in data collection with respect to complaints, thematic work, and product sales (European Parliament Hearing, n 478, 18), and with respect to the drivers of investment behaviour (ESMA, Annual Report (2012) 27), at the time of writing, ESMA has produced only one major report on the retail markets which addressed the sale of complex products to retail financial consumers (n 370). Trends with respect to retail structured product sales and retail investment trends generally are, however, tracked (in outline) in its regular Trends, Risks, and Vulnerabilities Reports (TRVs): eg, n 37, 22, reporting on returns on a representative portfolio of retail investor wealth. EBA, by contrast, has produced key reports on consumer protection and financial innovation, and has committed to monitoring emerging risks in these areas: EBA, Financial Innovation and Consumer Protection. An Overview of the Objectives and Work of the EBA's Standing Committee on Financial Innovation (SCFI) in 2011–2012 (2012). See, eg, EBA Consumer Trends Report (2014). EIOPA has produced a Methodology Report for Collecting, Analysing, and Reporting on Consumer Trends (2012) (EIOPA-CCPFI-12-037).

[490] While the Securities and Markets Stakeholder Group supports engagement with the retail sector, ESMA as yet has not actively support engagement with this sector by means of, eg, retail-friendly summaries of consultation of particular interest to the retail sector (by contrast with EIOPA).

[491] eg Statement by ESMA Chairman Maijoor, ECON Public Hearing, 20 September 2013 (ESMA/2013/1363).

[492] Its consumer protection subgroup, eg, has focused on cross-selling and complaints handling: 2013 Work Programme of the Joint Committee (JC-2013-002).

course, be imagined, particularly given the current popularity of 'twin peaks' institutional design, based on the separation of prudential and of conduct/financial consumer protection. In particular, the establishment of the Single Supervisory Mechanism and the location of prudential supervision of euro-area banks within the ECB might suggest some policy momentum towards a 'twin peaks' institutional structure and the possible location of conduct/investor-protection-related regulation and/or supervision in a distinct EU agency, whether an EU Financial Consumer Protection Authority or otherwise.[493] But the very distinct political, market, and legal dynamics of Banking Union caution against predictions of spillover effects in the financial markets sphere and of any radical institutional reforms related to the retail markets (see further Chapter XI section 7).

---

[493] The 2013 ESFS Review Consultation revealed some support for a movement to EU-level twin peaks institutional organization generally, and specifically for a discrete EU Financial Consumer Protection Authority. See, eg, the Responses to the Commission ESFS Consultation from (from the consumer sector) BEUC and EuroFinuse and (from the public sector) the Finnish Ministry of Finance: responses available at n 487.

X

LAW-MAKING

X.1 Introduction

X.1.1 A Complex and Evolving Process

This Chapter addresses the law-making process for EU securities and markets regulation.[1]

Securities and markets regulation develops in an empirical manner; it responds to observed events, often crisis-driven.[2] But its development is not entirely haphazard. It is a truism that process matters. The process or institutional risks to effective regulation—at legislative and administrative levels—are many. The standard roll-call includes information asymmetries with respect to the regulated sector, capture, bureaucratic inertia, perverse incentives, political risks, organizational weaknesses, and limited resources,[3] all of which can distort the delivery of efficient outcomes. These risks are exacerbated in crisis conditions, as the recent reform period has highlighted. The need to address system oversight, for example, has exposed the vulnerabilities of polycentric law-making environments, particularly in the international market.[4] The heightened dependence on highly technical rules, to take another example, has exposed the effectiveness risks which administrative rule-making poses.[5] The short-termism which can afflict crisis-driven law-making has, again, been

---

[1] It is, accordingly, concerned with institutional structures and procedures. The range of other factors which shape the nature and intensity of EU intervention over financial markets is discussed in Ch I.

[2] Allen, F and Gale, D, *Understanding Financial Crises* (2007) 190–215—from a financial economics perspective, examining the 'empirical process' through which financial regulation develops 'as a matter of trial and error, driven by the exigencies of history rather than by formal theory' (at 190).

[3] eg Enriques, L and Hertig, G, 'Improving the Governance of Financial Supervisors' (2011) 12 *EBOLR* 357.

[4] See eg Verdier, P-H, 'The Political Economy of International Financial Regulation' (2013) 83 *Indiana LJ* 1405, Brummer, C, *Soft Law and the Global Financial System* (2012), Kelly, C and Cho, S, 'The Promises and Perils of New Global Governance: A Case of the G20' (2012) 12 *CJIL* 491, Black, J, 'Restructuring Global and EU Financial Regulation: Capacities, Coordination and Learning' in Ferrarini, G, Hopt, K, and Wymeersch, E (eds), *Rethinking Financial Regulation and Supervision in Times of Crisis* (2012) 3, and Arner, D, 'Adaptation and Resilience in Global Financial Regulation' (2011) 89 *N Carolina LR* 101.

[5] For different perspectives on whether administrative rule-making can lead to a productive correction of legislative error or stymie political choices, in the context of rule-making under the 2010 Dodd-Frank Act, see Coffee, J, 'The Political Economy of Dodd-Frank: Why Financial Reform Tends to be Frustrated and Systemic Risk Perpetuated' (2012) 97 *Cornell LR* 1019 (and in Ferran, E, Moloney, N, Hill, J, and Coffee, J, *The Regulatory Aftermath of the Global Financial Crisis* (2012) 301) and Romano, R, Regulating in the Dark, Yale Law & Economics Research Paper No 442 (2012), available at <http://ssrn.com/abstract=1974148>.

observed.[6] The difficulties multiply where, as over the current period, substantive reform is accompanied by parallel institutional and process reform.[7]

It is also a truism that the EU law-making process similarly matters; the extent to which it engages with and manages the risks to effective regulation shapes the EU securities and markets rulebook. The EU process also dictates the location and intensity of regulation; the extent to which the process supports administrative rule-making, for example, has had a determinative shape on the balance of power between the EU and the Member States.

The law-making process for EU securities and markets regulation is based on the institutional framework and processes set out in the Treaties and which govern law-making in the EU generally. But it is also based on an incremental and pragmatic recycling of the Treaties' institutional structures and processes, which reflects changing perspectives on the nature and location of securities and markets regulation.[8] EU agencies and the EU's 'comitology' oversight process for administrative rule-making, for example, both provided 'off the shelf' institutional and process templates from which the EU's administrative rule-making process for securities and markets regulation has been designed. The effectiveness of the EU law-making process for securities and markets regulation accordingly depends in large part on how well it manages the general risks associated with EU law-making (and particularly administrative rule-making)[9] and the particular risks from the fitting of this law-making process into the securities and markets sphere.[10]

Some optimism is warranted on this front, as the incremental lurches forward which have characterized changes to the institutional structure and processes for adopting EU securities and markets regulation have usually been accompanied by significant institutional learning. Nonetheless, procedural inefficiencies and sources of institutional tensions tend to reappear and are often exacerbated in each cycle of reform. But overall the law-making process can be described as pragmatic and evolutionary, and as increasingly responsive to the specialist needs of securities and markets regulation. It is becoming increasingly specialized and

---

[6] From an extensive scholarship and in the context of the regulation of short selling see Enriques, L, 'Regulators' Response to the Current Crisis and the Upcoming Reregulation of Financial Markets: One Reluctant Regulator's View' (2009) 30 *UPaJIL* 1147.

[7] eg in the US and UK contexts, where parallel institutional reforms have occurred in tandem with substantive reform: Coffee, J and Sale, H, 'Redesigning the SEC – Does the Treasury Have a Better Idea?' (2009) 95 *Va LR* 707 and Ferran, E, 'The Break Up of the Financial Services Authority' (2011) 31 *OJLS* 455.

[8] An extensive political science literature charts the development of securities and markets law-making structures in the EU. See, eg, Mugge, D (ed), *Europe and the Governance of Global Finance* (2014), Thatcher, M and Coen, D, 'Reshaping European Regulatory Space: an evolutionary analysis' (2009) 31 *Western European Politics* 806, Thatcher, M and Coen, D, 'Network Governance and Multi-level Delegations. European Networks of Regulatory Agencies' (2008) 28 *Journal of Public Policy* 49, and de Visscher, C, Maisocq, O, and Varone, F, 'The Lamfalussy Reform in the EU Securities Markets: Fiduciary Relationships, Policy Effectiveness, and the Balance of Power' (2008) 28 *Journal of Public Policy* 19.

[9] The governance dynamics and risks of the 'comitology' (administrative rule-making) process have been subject to extensive review. On the pre-Lisbon Treaty model see, eg, Curtin, D, 'Holding (Quasi-) Autonomous EU Administrative Actors to Public Account' (2007) 13 *ELJ* 523 and Harlow, C, *Accountability in the European Union* (2002) and, post-Lisbon Treaty, Héritier, A, Moury, C, Bischoff, C, and Bergström, C, *Changing Rules of Delegation. A Contest for Power in Comitology* (2013) and the special edition of the *ELJ* (2013) 19(1).

[10] See, eg, Everson, M, A Technology of Expertise: EU Financial Services Agencies (2012) LEQS WP No 49/2012.

refined, certainly at the administrative level, and typically generates a pragmatic willingness to engage in 'learning by doing'.

X.1.2 Levels and Forms of Intervention

Regulatory intervention in the financial markets is multilayered. A legislative rulebook, designed to reflect normative policy choices, is typically adopted by representative bodies and through the political process. In the EU, the Treaty-based, inter-institutional law-making process, which balances intergovernmental (the Council), representative (the European Parliament), and supranational/executive elements (the Commission), produces binding rules in the form of 'legislative' directives and, increasingly, regulations;[11] law-making at this level is designed to produce high-level principles but, as discussed in this Chapter, frequently becomes more akin to detailed administrative rule-making given the intensity of the interests engaged.

As discussed in section 4, the modern nation-state also relies heavily on technocratic governance and on technical rule-making by expert administrative agencies; this is particularly the case in the securities and markets regulation sphere, where administrative rule-making is typically carried out by the financial market regulator(s). In the EU, administrative rule-making is located in the Commission and based on a delegation of law-making power from the co-legislators (the European Parliament and Council), but specialist agencies and committee-based structures are engaged to different degrees. In the securities and markets sphere, technical administrative rules are adopted by the Commission, but produced through a process in which agency-based (the European Securities and Markets Authority (ESMA)) and committee-based structures play a determinative role.

The regulatory toolkit in the securities and markets sphere also includes a plethora of 'soft law' measures, such as guidance, recommendations, Frequently Asked Questions (FAQs), Q&As, agency letters, and so on. These typically have different levels of coercive effect and are rarely wilfully ignored by financial market participants, but they are not directly binding or enforceable. While a long-standing component of the regulatory toolkit,[12] soft law became particularly associated with the 'new governance' techniques in the ascendant internationally prior to the financial crisis.[13] These techniques reflected a governing view of financial regulation as arising from an iterative process between private parties and regulators, developed in a series of regulatory dialogues, and resulting in a 'decentred' regulatory environment in which a range of public and private disciplining tools were relied on.[14] Principles-based regulation,[15] a central element of the new governance model, was

---

[11] On the different types of EU measure see Ch I.

[12] Soft law is a central feature of international financial regulation in particular, where distinct dynamics serve to 'harden' soft international standards. See, eg, Brummer, C, 'How International Financial law Works (and How it Doesn't)' (2011) 99 *Georgetown LJ* 257 and Alexander, K and Ferran E, 'Can Soft Law Bodies be Effective? The Special Case of the European Systemic Risk Board' (2010) *ELR* 751.

[13] An extensive social sciences literature considers the nature of 'new governance'. For an early and leading discussion see Ayres, I and Braithwaite, J, *Responsive Regulation. Transcending the Deregulation Debate* (1992).

[14] Black, J, 'Mapping the Contours of Contemporary Financial Services Regulation' (2002) 2 *JCLS* 253.

[15] Principles-based regulation typically involves: the articulation of regulatory objectives and outcomes through high-level principles which are supported, where necessary, by rules but also by guidance; a commitment to paring back unnecessary or ambiguous rules; a focus on the achievement of outcomes; and

typically accompanied by an array of soft measures used to amplify principles and to develop industry understanding of the outcomes sought by the regulator.[16]

Soft law carries a number of advantages in the securities and markets sphere. It can be more flexible and open-textured than binding rules which need to respond to legal certainty requirements, it can be adopted with less procedural formality, and it can be more responsive to market innovation. The coercive effect of soft law can, usefully, operate through multiple channels. Compliance may, for example, make a 'safe harbour' available. Soft law can also generate deterrent effects in that compliance may head off the adoption of a more restrictive binding rule. But soft law also carries risks, not least among them that the regulator can 'reverse-engineer' into firms' practices, without being subject to the formalities and disciplines which govern formal law-making, a blurring of the distinction between binding rules and best practice, increasing opacity and uncertainty in the regulatory environment, legitimacy and accountability risks, and, potentially, a disabling of strong enforcement by the regulator where ever more dense explanatory soft law measures become a panacea for addressing failures.[17]

The financial crisis has changed the nature of intervention. While soft law will always form part of the regulatory toolkit, traditional, rules-based 'command and control' regulation is now dominant internationally.[18] The changing fortunes of soft law have, however, had less impact in the EU. EU securities and markets regulation is predominantly a creature of binding law, reflecting the requirements of single market construction. Nonetheless, soft law has long formed part of the EU regulatory toolkit, and can be traced back to the 1977 Code of Conduct.[19] Immediately prior to the financial crisis (2005–7), soft measures were (briefly) in the ascendant, as the Commission embraced the post-Financial Services Action Plan (FSAP) 'regulatory pause' and the wider deregulatory zeitgeist, most notably with respect to credit rating agencies, where the Commission relied on the International Organization of Securities Commissions (IOSCO) Code of Conduct in preference to a binding regime.[20] Since then, soft law has, more or less, been removed from the EU policy agenda, at least at the inter-institutional level. Soft law is, however, strongly associated with the institutional structure which supports administrative rule-making. As discussed in this Chapter, initially CESR (the Committee of European Securities Regulators) and, since, ESMA have developed extensive 'soft rulebooks'. While this form of EU soft law carries the

---

engagement by industry and senior management with the delivery of outcomes. See, eg, Black, J, Hopper, M, and Band, C, 'Making a Success of Principles-Based Regulation' (2007) 1 *LFMR* 191 and Ford, C, 'New Governance, Compliance, and Principles-Based Securities Regulation' (2008) 45 *American Business LJ* 1.

[16] The UK Financial Services Authority (FSA) flagship 'Treating Customers Fairly' (TCF) strategy, eg, was heavily based on soft law, which amplified the 'fair treatment' principle in the FSA Handbook on which the TCF initiative was based. See further Moloney, N, *How to Protect Investors. Lessons from the EU and the UK* (2010) 219–23.

[17] See, eg, Hopper, M and Stainsby, J, 'Pause for Thought: the FSA Needs to Decide What Status it Intends to Ascribe to Industry Guidance' (2007) 26 IFLR 40 and Black et al, n 15.

[18] Black, J, 'The Rise (and Fall?) of Principles Based Regulation', in Alexander, K and Moloney, N (eds), *Law Reform and Financial Markets* (2011) 3 and Ford, C, 'New Governance in the Teeth of Human Frailty: Lessons from Financial Regulation' (2010) *Wisconsin LR* 441.

[19] Commission Recommendation 77/534/EEC concerning a European Code of Conduct relating to transactions in transferable securities [1977] OJ L212/37.

[20] See further Ch VII sect 2.2.

risks and benefits associated with soft law generally, it also generates distinct accountability and legitimacy risks related to the EU's institutional settlement for law-making.

X.1.3 Chronology of Developments

The process for adopting securities and markets regulation in the EU operates through three channels. First, at the legislative level, primary choices as to the nature of regulation are made by the co-legislators (the European Parliament and Council) by negotiating and adopting legislative proposals presented by the Commission. Second, rule-making occurs through administrative channels. Legislative measures typically contain extensive delegations to the Commission for related non-legislative administrative rule-making. These administrative rules can take the form of, first, 'delegated' or 'implementing' rules, which are proposed and adopted by the Commission and subject to oversight procedures (designed to protect the Council and Parliament's legislative prerogatives) which depend on the form of rule; or, second, 'Regulatory Technical Standards' (RTSs) or 'Implementing Technical Standards' (ITSs) (together, Binding Technical Standards (BTSs)), proposed by ESMA and adopted by the Commission, subject also to oversight procedures. Finally, ESMA can adopt a range of 'soft' supervisory convergence measures, including guidelines (in relation to which national competent authorities (NCAs) may be required to 'comply or explain'), recommendations, opinions, and a host of similar measures, chief among them FAQ/Q&A measures. The Commission also adopts soft measures, typically in the form of recommendations and Q&As, although ESMA is the primary source of soft law.

Four broad stages can be identified in the development of the law-making process for EU securities and markets regulation (see further section 2). In some respects, the process can be regarded as revolutionary and as characterized by game-changing institutional reforms which have responded to shifts in the EU's approach to securities and markets regulation and to related shifts in the balance of power between the Member States and the EU. In other respects, the process can be regarded as evolutionary, incremental, and driven by wider EU institutional reforms.

The first stage can be associated with the very early efforts in the 1970s and early 1980s to integrate and regulate the EU's nascent financial markets, and with the initial and failed attempts to establish maximum harmonization measures in the capital-raising sphere. During this period, a limited suite of legislative measures were adopted under Treaty-based institutional law-making procedures under which the Council was dominant, which conferred veto powers on the Member States in Council, and which led to a sclerotic law-making process. Delegation to administrative rule-making was not associated with this period.

The second stage was triggered by the 1987 Single European Act Treaty reforms which provided for single market legislation to be adopted by a Council qualified majority vote, and by the wider commitment, spearheaded by the Court of Justice in the *Cassis de Dijon* ruling,[21] to mutual recognition and minimum harmonization. This period can also be associated with the slow emergence of the European Parliament as a co-legislator and thus

---

[21] Case 120/78 *Rewe-Zentral AG v Bundesmonopolverwaltung für Branntwein (Cassis de Dijon)* [1979] ECR 649.

with the injection of a new institutional dynamic. The 1993 Maastricht Treaty reformed the Treaty to provide for the co-decision process, a variant of which still governs the adoption of legislation (the 'ordinary legislative procedure'), and which elevated the Parliament to the status of co-legislator. During this period, the pace of legislative intervention quickened, although the rulebook remained embryonic by today's standards. This period can also be associated with the slow emergence of administrative rule-making by the Commission (exercising delegated powers), and with the related early attempts to apply the 'comitology' oversight system,[22] which, based in legislation and not (by contrast with the current post-Lisbon Treaty position) the Treaties, then applied to EU administrative rule-making generally. The comitology system was then based on review of Commission rule-making by committees composed of Member State representatives, and reflected a concern to protect the Council's prerogatives with respect to law-making, rather than the Parliament's, which asymmetry generated ongoing tensions with respect to the comitology system.[23]

The third stage relates to the first of the two major reform eras in EU securities and markets regulation (to date). Wider market exuberance, and stakeholder and Member State support, driven by the coincidence of a range of factors,[24] led to the EU's ambitious FSAP-era reform agenda (1999–2004) and to the first major re-balancing of law-making power in this sphere between the Member States and the EU in favour of the EU. This was driven in particular by process reforms to administrative rule-making under the Lamfalussy process for financial markets law-making. But the Lamfalussy reform was dependent on wider reforms to the EU law-making process. The 1999 reforms to the comitology process generally[25] provided a framework within which a distinct model for the adoption of administrative rules in the securities and markets regulation sphere could be adopted. Earlier, the 1997 establishment of FESCO (the Federation of European Securities Commissions) provided a potentially useful institutional vehicle. The institutional conditions were therefore in place for the Lamfalussy Report[26] to make its seminal recommendation that the law-making process for financial markets be categorized as involving: 'level 1' high-level rules adopted by the co-legislators; 'level 2' technical (or administrative) rules adopted by the Commission under a delegation of power from the co-legislators, advised by CESR (based on FESCO) and overseen by a new committee of Member State representatives (the European Securities Committee) which would act within the 1999 comitology framework; 'level 3' non-binding supervisory convergence measures adopted by CESR; and 'level 4' enforcement activity by the Commission. Over the FSAP era, and as discussed later in the Chapter, the institutions would learn to play a new rule-making game. The European Securities Committee, and CESR in particular, would mature, and administrative rule-making would become embedded, leading to a paradigmatic shift in the intensity of EU intervention and in the balance of power between the Member States and the EU.

This period also, however, witnessed significant tensions in the foundational relationship between the Council and European Parliament co-legislators, as the new administrative

---

[22] Council Decision 87/373/EEC [1987] OJ L197/33.
[23] See further sect 2.3.2.
[24] See Ch 1 sect 4.
[25] Council Decision 99/468/EC [1999] OJ L184/23.
[26] Final Report of the Committee of Wise Men on the Regulation of European Securities Markets (2001) (2001 Lamfalussy Report).

rule-making model increased the strain on the unstable institutional settlement which governed the delegation of law-making powers generally. These tensions injected significant instability into the FSAP in the form of the four-year 'sunset clauses' which, demanded by the Parliament, applied to the delegations granted to the Commission under FSAP 'level 1' measures. Resolution of these wider tensions in 2006 with the establishment of the new 'regulatory committee with scrutiny' comitology procedure, which enhanced the Parliament's position in the comitology process,[27] led to the sunset clauses being removed from FSAP measures in 2008.[28]

A period of relative calm followed, during which the EU committed to a 'legislative pause' (2005–7).[29] During this phase, as the shadows of the financial crisis began to lengthen, incremental and largely 'tinkering' changes were made to the Lamfalussy model.

The current stage (to date) is unusual in that, for the first time, process reform has been crisis-driven. But the process changes are less radical and crisis-driven than at first might appear. As under the FSAP era, wider Treaty and institutional developments have had a determinative effect.[30] The 2009 Lisbon Treaty provided a Treaty settlement to the long-running battle between the European Parliament and Council on the nature of, and control over, administrative rule-making, and on the relative spheres of competence of the institutions and the Member States with respect to executive (or implementing) acts.[31] The Lisbon Treaty classified EU law-making as engaging 'legislative' rules (Article 289 TFEU, adopted by the co-legislators and equivalent to the 'level 1' stage of the Lamfalussy process) and 'delegated' and 'implementing' administrative rules (Articles 290 and 291 TFEU, equivalent to 'level 2' of the Lamfalussy process), and adopted oversight procedures for Articles 290 and 291 rules.

The facilitation by the Lisbon Treaty of administrative rule-making, in combination with the EU's agency infrastructure, the availability of the Lamfalussy committees of regulators (CESR, the Committee of European Banking Supervisors (CEBS), and the Committee of European Insurance and Occupational Pensions Supervisors (CEIOPS)) as 'off the shelf' institutional vehicles, and institutional confidence in administrative rule-making (expressed over the 2007 Lamfalussy Review),[32] meant that the institutional conditions were favourable when the crisis led to political pressure for law-making reform with respect to financial system regulation generally. Specifically, the recommendation by the 2009 de Larosière High Level Group Report for a recasting of CESR, CEBS, and CEIOPS into EU agencies—the European Supervisory Authorities (ESAs)—conferred with a range of quasi-regulatory (and supervisory) powers[33] became institutionally feasible. As discussed in

---

[27] Council Decision 2006/512/EC [2006] OJ L200/11.

[28] See sect 2.3.2.

[29] Commission, White Paper on Financial Services Policy 2005–2010 (2005) (COM (2005) 629) (2005 White Paper).

[30] At the launch of the European Banking Authority (EBA), European Parliament Economic and Monetary Affairs Committee (ECON) Chair Bowles suggested that the establishment of the European Supervisory Authorities (ESAs) was 'not merely a crisis response; it is part of an evolutionary process which was dictated by logical needs in a single market for financial services': Speech by ECON Chair Bowles, EBA Launch, 1 April 2011.

[31] See, eg, Mendes, J, 'Delegated and Implementing Rule Making: Proceduralisation and Constitutional Design' (2013) 19 *ELJ* 22.

[32] Sect 2.3.

[33] The High Level Group on Financial Supervision in the EU, Report (2009) (the 2009 DLG or de Larosière Group Report).

section 2.4, 2010 saw agreement on the establishment of the ESAs, empowered to wield a range of quasi-rule-making powers. Since its establishment in 2011, ESMA has come to exercise a decisive influence on EU rule-making.

Overall, therefore, while resetting shocks have driven institutional change to the law-making process for securities and markets regulation in the EU, wider institutional and Treaty-based reforms, and pragmatic reliance on and the reshaping of available institutional formats, have been similarly determinative in shaping the law-making process for securities and markets regulation.

X.2 The Evolution of the Law-making Process and Institutional Change

X.2.1 Early Developments and Comitology

The institutional process for securities and markets regulation did not develop significantly until the FSAP era and the adoption of the Lamfalussy reforms. Administrative rule-making, the primary location for innovation in the process for adopting EU securities and markets regulation, had, however, long been an element of the EU law-making landscape. In 1999, immediately prior to the commencement of the FSAP period, administrative rule-making was based on (then) Article 202 EC, which permitted the Commission to adopt administrative rules under a delegation of powers from the Council, and the (now repealed) 1999 Council Comitology Decision,[34] which governed the related 'comitology' (or committee-based) oversight procedures which were designed to ensure that the administrative rule-making process was sufficiently transparent and that there was accountability towards the Council, in particular, but also towards the European Parliament.

The comitology process was based on the supervision of the Commission by various committees. The greatest degree of control over the Commission was exercised by 'regulatory committees' (the Lamfalussy process was originally based on a regulatory committee model). The 1999 Comitology Decision provided that the regulatory committee procedure be used with respect to the adoption by the Commission of measures of general scope designed to 'implement' or 'apply' 'essential' provisions of basic instruments, and measures designed to 'adapt' or 'update' 'non-essential' provisions of basic instruments; the core legislative functions located in the European Parliament and Council could not, therefore, be delegated.[35] Regulatory committees (composed of Member State representatives) could significantly obstruct Commission proposals and ultimately require the Commission to submit the proposal to the Council; the Parliament did not exercise veto powers and was not in an equivalent position to the Council.

---

[34] Council Decision 99/468/EC [1999] OJ L184/23. The Decision replaced Decision 87/373/EC [1987] OJ L197/33. See generally Lenaerts, K and Verhoeven, A, 'Towards a Legal Framework for Executive Rule-making in the EU? The Contribution of the New Comitology Decision' (2000) 37 *CMLR* 645.

[35] The references to implementing and applying 'essential' provisions and adapting 'non-essential' provisions reflected the controls the Court of Justice has long placed on the delegation of law-making functions. See, eg, Case 25/70 *Einfuhr-und Vorratsstelle v Köster* [1970] ECR 1161 and the opinion of the Advocate General in Case C-270/12 *UK v Parliament and Council*, 22 January 2014, not yet reported.

EU securities and markets regulation would not deploy the administrative comitology process in any material way until the adoption of the Lamfalussy process in 2001. From its earliest days, however, EU securities and markets regulation had relied on a network of advisory committees to support law-making, if informally. The initial securities directives, for example, were monitored by a Securities Contact Committee, composed of Member State and Commission representatives. It was to undertake consultations on problems arising from the application of the directives and to facilitate the establishment of a 'concerted attitude' between Member States on the adoption of more stringent or additional conditions at national level. The influence of the Contact Committee on law-making was, however, heavily circumscribed in that its role was advisory only. The banking regime, by contrast, had from an early stage adopted a comitology-based model by means of the Banking Advisory Committee (BAC), which assisted the Commission in ensuring the proper implementation of the banking regime, carried out the specific tasks required of it across the banking regime, and assisted the Commission in the preparation of new proposals. In its alternative guise as a comitology committee, the BAC also exercised oversight functions over the Commission when the Commission amended the banking regime using delegated rule-making powers.

Although the 1993 Investment Services Directive (ISD)[36] referred to the setting up of, variously, a 'securities market committee' and a 'transferable securities committee',[37] it was not until 1995 that the Commission proposed to amend the ISD to provide for the establishment of a Securities Committee and to empower the Commission to make technical adaptations to the ISD through administrative rules, overseen by the Committee.[38] Although the Council reached a common position on this proposal in 1997, it was abandoned.

In its pre-FSAP 1998 Communication, however, the Commission suggested that the legislative process for financial services regulation generally be streamlined by means of reliance on administrative rules.[39] The related establishment of a Securities Committee to oversee the Commission formed part of the subsequent FSAP reforms.[40] This modest proposal was overtaken by the more radical Lamfalussy reforms to administrative rule-making.

X.2.2 The Lamfalussy Model

The drivers of the FSAP noted in Chapter I, and the related political consensus on EU-led financial market intervention, provided the conditions within which the pre-existing comitology-based procedures could be more fully deployed in relation to securities and markets regulation under the Lamfalussy model.[41]

---

[36] Directive 93/22/EEC [1993] OJ L141/27 (the ISD).
[37] Art 7(1).
[38] The Commission proposal and explanatory memorandum are at COM (95) 360.
[39] Communication from the Commission, Financial Services: Building a Framework for Action, COM (1998) 625 (the 1998 Communication) 3.
[40] COM (1999) 232.
[41] For early assessments see, eg, Ferrarini, G, 'Contract Standards and the Markets in Financial Instruments Directive. An Assessment of the Lamfalussy Regulatory Architecture' (2005) 1 *Euro Rev Contract L* 19; Ferran, E, *Building an EU Securities Market* (2004) 61–126; Mogg, J, 'Regulating Financial Services in Europe: A New

In the FSAP, the Commission reviewed the EU's approach to law-making in light of the challenging FSAP reform agenda. It identified three weaknesses in particular. First, and in an echo of the difficulties which have recurred, a piecemeal and reactive approach was followed in designing legislation which was inadequate in an era of financial conglomeration which required a cross-sectoral approach to regulation. Second, the inter-institutional legislative process was often protracted. Finally, the tendency to rely on overly detailed, inflexible, and prescriptive measures carried the danger of stultifying market structures and behaviour. The Commission proposed a number of rather unambitious initiatives which did not entail radical institutional reform, including a Securities Committee to support administrative rule-making under the ISD regime, the establishment of a political forum to forge consensus on emerging challenges, closer and earlier engagement with the European Parliament, and the creation of a high-level forum to take soundings from major market stakeholders.

Although the Commission therefore diagnosed the difficulties with the law-making process, the most significant remedial action was initially taken outside the EU institutional sphere. In 1997, EU securities regulators took the initiative by establishing a forum for co-operation and policy development, FESCO. Notwithstanding its informal structure, the consensus-driven nature of its operation, and the non-binding status of measures, FESCO became a prime mover in sustaining momentum under the FSAP, particularly in the wholesale markets area, by adopting common standards which its members committed to implement in their home jurisdictions.[42]

As the FSAP period began to unfold, concern intensified that the glacial pace of and cumbersome institutional structure for EU law-making would seriously prejudice its timely delivery. In summer 2000, the Council accordingly appointed a 'Committee of Wise Men' under the chairmanship of Baron Lamfalussy to investigate the regulation of securities markets.[43] The subsequent Lamfalussy Report was a dismal indictment of the legislative process; the Report's trenchant conclusion was that 'the chances of delivering the FSAP on time are close to zero'.[44] The process of adopting legislation was criticized as being too slow, with the average time taken for the co-decision procedure, even where political agreement existed, amounting to two years in general and to longer in the financial services area. The Council was criticized for its tendency to over-complicate legislation 'often in an attempt to try to fit [then] 15 sets of national legislation into one Community framework'.[45] Over-reliance on directives, attributed to subsidiarity pressures, was leading to uneven and delayed implementation of rules. The Report's conclusion was that the legislative process was too slow and too rigid to respond to changing market conditions, inclined to produce

Approach' (2003) 26 *Fordham Int LJ* 58; Hertig, G and Lee, R, 'Four Predictions on the Future of EU Securities Regulation' (2003) 3 *JCLS* 359; McKee, M, 'The Unpredictable Future of European Securities Regulation' (2003) 18 *JIBLR* 277; Moloney, N, 'The Lamfalussy Legislative Model: A New Era for the EC Securities and Investment Services Regime' (2003) 52 *ICLQ* 509; and Avgerinos, Y, 'Essential and Non-Essential Measures: Delegation of Powers in EU Securities Regulation' (2002) 8 *ELJ* 269.

[42] A process described by the first Chairman of the Committee of European Securities Regulators (CESR) as 'narrowing the bandwidth of EU rules': Norman, P, 'Regulators Pick Up the Integration Baton', *Financial Times, Fund Management Supplement,* 22 March 2004, 7.

[43] An Initial Report was published in November 2000.

[44] n 26, 12.

[45] n 26, 14.

ambiguous texts, and unable to distinguish between core essential framework principles and detailed implementing rules.

The Lamfalussy Report's (then) ambitious recommendation was based on a rethinking of the form which securities and markets regulation should take, but it was based on pre-existing comitology procedures. The Report characterized securities and markets regulation as composed of two layers: (i) basic political choices which could be articulated as framework rules and (ii) detailed technical administrative rules. A four-level approach based on this duality was set out in some detail in the report. Under the Lamfalussy vision, the Commission would adopt technical 'level 2' rules for financial markets based on mandates in the related 'level 1' measure (adopted under normal inter-institutional procedures), advised by CESR (composed of national regulators and based on the already available FESCO model) and supervised by the European Securities Committee (composed of Member State representatives and, based on the pre-existing comitology structure, acting as a 'regulatory committee'). Level 3, driven by CESR (often termed a 'level 3' committee), would address supervisory convergence and consistency in the implementation and application of level 1 and level 2 rules. Level 4 related to the enforcement (by the Commission) of Member State obligations.

The Lamfalussy Report benefited from the wider political and market zeitgeist (as would the establishment of the ESAs in a very different context). It was welcomed by industry stakeholders[46] and was quickly endorsed by the Member States at the March 2001 Stockholm European Council,[47] although acute institutional tensions would soon arise (section 2.3.2).

As an enthusiastic supporter of the new model from the outset (and the actor with the most to gain), the Commission was quick to establish the Lamfalussy committees.[48] In 2001 the Commission established the oversight-based European Securities Committee, composed of 'high level representatives of the Member States',[49] and the advisory CESR, established as an independent advisory body for 'reflection, debate and advice' and composed of the NCAs.[50] The work previously carried out by FESCO was transferred to CESR, with FESCO adopting a Charter which was adopted by CESR at its first meeting in September 2001.[51] A revised CESR Charter was adopted in July 2006, which reflected the significant changes to CESR after five years' experience with the Lamfalussy process; the Charter was

---

[46] Norman, P and Bolland, V, 'Caution Over the Pace of Market Regulation', *Financial Times*, 16 February 2001.

[47] Presidency Conclusions, Stockholm European Council, 23 and 24 March 2001, Annex 1, Resolution on More Effective Securities Market Regulation (the 2001 Stockholm Resolution), para 1. Agreement on the wording of the Resolution required some negotiation, given the inter-institutional interests at stake and also the concerns of some Member States that the Commission's approach to market regulation (which in some quarters was seen as being Anglocentric) would become too dominant.

[48] Mogg, n 41, 75.

[49] Commission Decision 2001/528/EC [2001] OJ L191/45 (the European Securities Committee Decision), Proposal and Explanatory Memorandum at COM (2001) 1493.

[50] Commission Decision 2001/527/EC [2001] OJ L191/43 (the 2001 CESR Decision), Proposal and Explanatory Memorandum at COM (2001) 1501.

[51] FESCO/01-070e, which was designed to set out the operational arrangements of CESR and to 'reflect the wish of the network of national securities regulators, that have successfully worked within FESCO in the last three years, to go a step further and fully play the role assigned to them in the Lamfalussy Report': Wittich, G, FESCO Chairman, FESCO Press Release, 19 June 2001, FESCO/01-095. The Charter was adopted by CESR at its first meeting on 11 September 2001 (CESR/01-002).

revised again in 2008 following the 2007 Lamfalussy Review.[52] CESR commenced operations in September 2001 and opened its first consultation (on harmonizing conduct-of-business rules—a project initiated by FESCO) some weeks later.[53] The first meeting of the European Securities Committee also took place in September 2001 and addressed the need for smooth co-operation with CESR, the need for effective transparency and consultation mechanisms throughout the new structure, rules of procedures, and Member States' priorities for mandates to CESR.[54]

The administrative 'level 2' rule-making cycle, at the heart of the Lamfalussy process, started with the Commission's mandate to CESR, based on the delegation in the relevant level 1 measure (during the time-pressured FSAP period mandates were often provisional, in that they were issued before the level 1 measure was adopted and were confirmed on the adoption of the level 1 measure; the related 'parallel working' technique, which involved CESR working on level 2 issues before the level 1 text had stabilized and was much criticized as a necessary but inefficient evil, would repeat itself in the early stages of the crisis-era programme in relation to ESMA's work). The mandate was also transmitted to the European Parliament, in practice the ECON (Economic and Monetary Affairs) committee. This was followed by an initial public call for evidence from CESR. At least one round of consultation followed, including public hearings, followed by CESR's final 'technical advice' to the Commission. At the same time, CESR issued a feedback statement, explaining its approach and why it had taken or rejected feedback from the consultation process. This process typically completed over 9–12 months, according to the timetable set out in the Commission mandate, although extensions were granted. The Commission then published draft rules open to public comment, and at times (not always) accompanied by an impact assessment, which were discussed in the European Securities Committee. Comparative tables were provided to the European Securities Committee which explained where the Commission's position differed from CESR's. The Commission's publicly available working documents also explored these differences. A formal proposal was then adopted and considered in the European Securities Committee under comitology procedures (which were revised in 2006—see section 2.3.2) and opened to public comment. Following Committee agreement, the Commission formally adopted the measure as a level 2 administrative rule. The draft rules and subsequent formal proposal were also considered by the Parliament (through the ECON committee). Following the 2006 revisions to the comitology process, the Parliament could adopt a resolution on the rules within three months of receipt of the draft rules and with respect to whether the measure exceeded the level 1 mandate, within one month of the European Securities Committee vote.

---

[52] CESR 06/289c. The Charter addressed a range of operational matters including relationships with the European Securities Committee and the Commission, the establishment of operational groups, working procedures, and consultation and transparency procedures. Key aspects of the 2006 Charter (which reflected CESR's tendency to acquire soft power) included the establishment of a Review Panel to oversee peer review and the hardening of decision-making procedures through Qualified Majority Vote (QMV) procedures (under the original Charter, CESR was to 'identify and elaborate' any dissenting opinions of individual members with respect to advising the Commission at 'level 2', and was to operate by consensus for all other tasks). The 2008 Charter reform was primarily directed to decision-making and to more extensive QMV requirements, notably with respect to CESR's supervisory convergence measures, including guidance.

[53] CESR/01-003.

[54] Commission Press Release, 24 September 2001.

Early support for the new model came from its extension in 2004 to the banking and insurance/occupational pensions sectors, and the establishment of the necessary oversight and advisory committees (the latter CEBS and CEIOPS—with CESR, the '3L3' committees).[55] Consequential amendments were made to the relevant level 1 measures in 2005 by the 2005 Financial Architecture Directive.[56] The 3L3 committees developed a cross-sector work agenda and operated under a Joint Protocol which co-ordinated their activities and which was a precursor to the ESAs' Joint Committee. The remit of CESR was expanded in 2004 to cover the Undertakings for Collective Investment in Transferable Securities (UCITS)/asset management regime.[57] In September 2006, the Lamfalussy process reached a major milestone with the completion of the FSAP-era level 1 and level 2 reforms;[58] the level 2 process would be activated again in 2009 with the UCITS IV reforms.[59] CESR's informal standard-setting activities, through guidelines and similar measures, would get underway in 2006 and had generated, by the time of CESR's replacement by ESMA at the end of 2010, a substantial but informal 'soft rulebook'.

X.2.3 Learning from Lamfalussy

X.2.3.1 Did it Work?

The Lamfalussy process delivered a securities and markets-specific reform process, albeit within the well-tested, comitology-based institutional model. Did it work? Output-wise, an exponential increase in the intensity of EU securities and markets regulation occurred between 2001 and the outbreak of the financial crisis, driven in large part by the production of level 2 administrative rules and level 3 supervisory convergence measures.[60] Technically, the new administrative rules marked a significant departure in their sophistication,

---

[55] Commission Decisions 2004/10/EC ([2004] OJ L3/36) and 2004/9/EC ([2004] OJ L3/34) addressed the level 2 banking and insurance/occupational-pension political committees, respectively, while Decisions 2004/5/EC ([2004] OJ L3/28) and 2004/6/EC ([2004] OJ L3/30) created the level 3 committees for banking (CEBS) and insurance/occupational pensions (CEIOPS), respectively. Considerable difficulties arose over the location of the new level 3 committees, with CESR expressing concern that a proposed compromise (based on locating all three bodies in Brussels where they would potentially form the nucleus of a European financial regulator) threatened its position, could disrupt its work programme as the Lamfalussy process was bedding down, and could undermine its independence.

[56] Directive 2005/1/EC [2005] OJ L79/9.

[57] Commission Decision 2004/7/EC [2004] OJ L3/32.

[58] Level 2 measures had by then been adopted in relation to the 2004 MiFID I (Commission Directive 2006/73/EC [2006] OJ L241/26 and Commission Regulation (EC) No 1287/2006 [2006] OJ L241/7); the 2003 Market Abuse Directive (Commission Definitions and Disclosure Obligations Directive 2003/124/EC [2003] OJ L339/70, Commission Investment Recommendations Directive 2003/125/EC [2003] OJ L339/73, Commission Regulation (EC) No 2273 on Buybacks and Stabilization 2003 [2003] OJ L336/33, and Commission Directive 2004/72/EC [2004] OJ L162/70); the 2004 Transparency Directive (Commission Directive 2007/14/EC [2007] OJ L69/27); the 2003 Prospectus Directive (Commission Prospectus Regulation 809/2004/EC [2004] OJ L149/1) and the pre-Financial Services Action Plan (FSAP) 1985 UCITS Directive (Commission Directive 2007/16/EC [2007] OJ L79/11).

[59] A range of level 2 administrative measures were adopted in 2010 (Commission Regulation (EU) No 583/2010 [2010] OJ L176/1, Commission Regulation (EU) No 584/2020 [2010] OJ L176/16, Commission Directive 2010/42/EU [2010] OJ L176/28, and Commission Directive 2010/43/EU [2010] L176/42) on a range of issues including prudential and conduct-of-business regulation of UCITS managers, notification and other procedural matters, and the Key Investor Information document (KIID).

[60] Leading one commentator to note the risks of excessive innovation and market exhaustion: Enriques, L, 'EC Company Law Directives and Regulations: How Trivial Are They?' (2006) 27 *UPaJIEL* 1, 52.

reflecting CESR's capacity to inject regulatory and market intelligence into the rule-making process; this is well exemplified by the 2010 level 2 UCITS reforms, adopted towards the end of the CESR era, which grappled with technically complex conduct-of-business and risk management rules and the novel Key Investor Information Document (KIID), and by the 2006 MiFID I level 2 rules on market transparency, which similarly engaged with highly technical issues related to market structure. Procedurally, the process was generally regarded as a success. Although the Commission argued that 'the Lamfalussy process was not introduced in order to spark a revolution in financial markets',[61] the explosive combination of the Lamfalussy process reform linked to the FSAP regulatory reform agenda led to large-scale reforms to EU securities and markets regulation.

Overall, most reviews of the process (which was exhaustively reviewed, including by the Inter-Institutional Monitoring Group (IIMG) which was set up to review the new process[62])[63] were positive. Although by the eve of the financial crisis the process was still evolving,[64] the final 2007 review,[65] which led to the positive December 2007 ECOFIN Council

---

[61] Commission, FSAP Evaluation. Part I: Process and Implementation (2005) (2005 FSAP Report) 10.

[62] Initially established in October 2002 in order to ensure effective inter-institutional co-operation throughout the Lamfalussy process, this group (the IIMG) was composed of independent experts appointed by the European Parliament, Council, and Commission. A new Group was constituted in December 2005 with a renewed review mandate to assess progress on the Lamfalussy model. The second group was a key actor during the 2007 Lamfalussy Review.

[63] The reviews took place in a number of phases.
   The initial series of reviews was undertaken by the IIMG: IIMG, First Interim Report Monitoring the New Process for Regulating Securities Markets in Europe (May 2003) (May 2003 IIMG Report); Second Interim Report Monitoring the Lamfalussy Process (December 2003) (December 2003 IIMG Report); and Third Interim Report Monitoring the Lamfalussy Process (November 2004) (November 2004 IIMG Report). The proposed extension of the process from securities to other financial sectors led to review by the Council's Economic and Financial Committee (EFC, established under the Treaties and charged with supporting Member State co-ordination and, in particular, supporting the Council (Art 134 TFEU)): EFC Report on Financial Regulation, Supervision and Stability (October 2002) (2002 EFC Report). 2004 saw the Commission's first review of the Lamfalussy process: Commission, Working Document on Application of the Lamfalussy Process to EU Securities Market Legislation (November 2004) (2004 Commission Lamfalussy Report). Key responses included that of the European Central Bank: European Central Bank (ECB), Review of the Application of the Lamfalussy Framework to EU Securities Market Legislation (2005) (2005 ECB Lamfalussy Report).
   As the FSAP closed, the Lamfalussy process was subject to further review, including, eg, the Commission-mandated FSAP 'Expert Group' Reports (made by the expressly constituted industry Securities, Banking, Asset Management, and Insurance Expert Groups). Major private sector reviews from that period include that by the Centre for European Policy Studies, Task Force Report No 54, January 2005, EU Financial Regulation and Supervision Beyond 2005 (2005 CEPS Report). Finally, a second IIMG was constituted in 2006 to address the extended Lamfalussy model, which subsequently fed into the 2007 Lamfalussy Review: IIMG First Interim Report Monitoring the Lamfalussy Process (March 2006) (2006 Interim IIMG Report) and Second Interim Report (January 2007) (2007 Interim IIMG Report). The major Lamfalussy Review reports are noted at n 65.

[64] Ferran, E and Green, D, Are the Lamfalussy Regulatory Networks Working Successfully, European Financial Forum Paper (2007) 3–4.

[65] The original extension of the Lamfalussy process from the securities sector to cover the banking, insurance, and pensions sectors was linked to a review of the process being carried out in 2007: Directive 2005/1/EC [2005] OJ L79/9 Art 12. Key institutional reviews included: the final review by the IIMG (IIMG, Final Report Monitoring the Lamfalussy Process (October 2007) (2007 Final IIMG Report)), the Commission Communication on Review of the Lamfalussy Process. Strengthening Supervisory Convergence (2007) (2007 Commission Lamfalussy Report), the European Parliament Van den Burg II Resolution on Financial Services Policy 2005–2010, 11 July 2007 (P6-TA-(2007)0338), and CESR, A Proposed Evolution of Securities Supervision Beyond 2007 (2007) (CESR/07-783) (2007 CESR Securities Supervision Report). Major industry reports included: Deutsche Bank, Towards a New Structure for EU Financial Supervision. EU

Conclusions on the Lamfalussy process,[66] revealed broad satisfaction with the model[67] from the institutions and stakeholders.[68] The process was generally regarded as delivering shorter time-frames for the adoption of legislation,[69] better working relationships between the institutions, a greater level of transparency, and much closer engagement by key stakeholders, notably market participants (the retail sector remained under-represented), in the law-making process.[70] The general perception was that the quality of legislation had improved,[71] although the crisis era would expose the catastrophic weaknesses in the EU rulebook. The Lamfalussy process was also regularly described as a pragmatic, 'learning by doing' process for all involved,[72] which underwent continuous refinement and improvement.[73] CESR,[74] the Commission,[75] and the European Central Bank (ECB)[76] were all supportive, as was the Council.[77] The European Parliament's support was more qualified, however,[78] reflecting a history of considerable inter-institutional tensions related to the Parliament's involvement in administrative rule-making.

Monitor 48 (2007) and City of London Group, Level 3 of the Lamfalussy Process. Submission to IIMG Group By a Group in the City of London (2007).

[66] 2836th Council Meeting, 4 December 2007, ECOFIN Press Release No 15698/07, 13–21.

[67] Some earlier predictions had suggested that the model risked failure, given political risks: Hertig and Lee, n 41.

[68] The IIMG's Final 2007 Report stated, after widespread consultation, that 'it had helped to deliver the [FSAP] on time, and has contributed to the improvement of the quality of legislation through improved consultation processes': n 65, 8. The UK perspective was that 'the Lamfalussy arrangements have made a significant positive contribution to the EU's regulatory and supervisory framework ... and played an integral role in delivering many of the measures contained in the [FSAP]. Had these arrangements not been adopted, many of the measures might still be under negotiation': HM Treasury and FSA, Strengthening the EU Regulatory and Supervisory Framework: A Practical Approach (2007) 17 and 21.

[69] The average negotiation time for the four cornerstone FSAP level 1 measures, the 2003 Prospectus Directive, the 2003 Market Abuse Directive, the 2004 MiFID I, and the 2004 Transparency Directive, was 20 months: 2007 Commission Lamfalussy Report, n 65, 3. For a stark comparison with pre-FSAP measures see the November 2004 IIMG Report, n 63, 7, which noted time periods from 2.5 years to nine years.

[70] 2005 FSAP Evaluation Report, n 61, 11.

[71] 2004 Commission Lamfalussy Report n 63, 2007 ECOFIN Conclusions, n 66, and 2007 Final IIMG Report, n 65. This assessment also emerged from the Securities Expert Group Report on the FSAP, which pointed to an increase in speed and flexibility and a 'new dynamic involving greater interaction, consultation, and transparency': n 63, 8. The consumer sector was also supportive, with FIN-USE (the forum for consumer interests) reporting that the process had 'made a promising start in terms of its speed, efficiency and ability to reach consensus', albeit that it was concerned over poor levels of retail involvement. FIN-USE, Financial Services, Consumers and Small Businesses. A User Perspective (2004) 16–17.

[72] See, eg, 2006 Interim IIMG Report, n 63, 5.

[73] eg although weaknesses in retail governance were noted in the first series of IIMG Reports, the 2007 Interim Report stated 'with satisfaction' that the representation of consumers was increasing (n 63, 10), and the 2007 Final Report noted that consumers were recognized by the Commission and CESR as one of the targets of their consultation practices (n 65, 11).

[74] '[T]he process of shaping EU legislation at level 1 and 2 can still be improved in terms of process but should be regarded as a success that should be continued based on a stable inter-institutional agreement': 2007 CESR Securities Supervision Report, n 65, 1.

[75] 'Overall experience with the Lamfalussy Process has been positive—a view broadly shared by Member States, the European Parliament, market participants and regulators ... the overall decision making process is more efficient and inclusive and has speeded up': 2007 Commission Lamfalussy Report, n 65, 3.

[76] It described the process as effecting a substantial improvement in the regulation of the securities sector: n 63, 3.

[77] The December 2007 ECOFIN Council concluded that overall experience with the process had been positive, stakeholders had repeatedly expressed support, and the process had significantly increased the efficiency and effectiveness of the Community's regulatory framework: n 66, 15.

[78] See, eg, the Parliament's 2005 Van den Burg Resolution which noted that it was necessary to consider the overall political and democratic accountability of the process: Van den Burg I Resolution on the Current

X.2.3.2 Managing Institutional Tensions

In an augury of what would come with the crisis-era ESA negotiations, the Lamfalussy reforms sparked acute institutional tensions which shaped the new process. These were evident from an early stage with the European Council's 2001 Stockholm Resolution, which emphasized that the 'prerogatives of the institutions concerned and the current institutional balance' must be respected.[79] The European Council acknowledged the critical fault-line between level 1 and level 2 measures, and emphasized that the level 1/ level 2 split was to be determined in a clear and transparent manner.[80] Its Resolution also placed a brake on the Commission's exercise of delegated rule-making powers, noting that in order to find a balanced solution to measures acknowledged to be 'particularly sensitive', the Commission 'has committed itself... to avoid going against predominant views which might emerge within the Council'.[81] The Resolution did not expand on these sensitivities but the wording (the 'aerosol clause') was clearly an early shot across the bows from the Member States to the Commission. In practice, the failure to adopt level 1 measures as high-level principles meant that sensitive questions were addressed, often in great detail, at level 1 and that the aerosol clause was not activated over the FSAP period.[82]

The aerosol clause did, however, heighten the need to provide equivalent protection for the prerogatives of the European Parliament, which by then had emerged aggressively as a force to be reckoned with[83]; the Stockholm Resolution noted that the Commission also 'commits itself to expeditiously re-examine' draft level 2 measures where the Parliament believed that they exceeded the bounds of the rule-making power granted in the relevant level 1 measure.[84] At the heart of the Parliament's difficulties was its concern about its removal from the level 2 process and its fear that the European Securities Committee would become too powerful. In particular, it sought a right of appeal against Commission rule-making at level 2. A parliamentary veto was, however, rejected in the Lamfalussy Report as not being envisaged in the Treaty, and rejected by the Council as disturbing the institutional balance.[85] Discussions on this issue were to dog the early stages of the Lamfalussy model. Following an 11-month struggle between the Commission and the Parliament, an initial

---

State of Integration of EU Financial Markets, 28 April 2005 (T6-0153/2005) para E (based on the 2005 Van den Burg Report by the Committee on Economic and Monetary Affairs (ECON) (A6-0087/2005)). A similar view was taken in the 2007 Van den Burg II Resolution which welcomed the work of CESR and the level 3 committees, but raised accountability concerns: n 65.

[79] n 47, Introduction.

[80] n 47, para 2.

[81] n 47, para 5.

[82] This was the case even at the outset when the institutions were testing the procedure. See the May 2003 IIMG Report, n 63, 10 and 14.

[83] Apart from a 'dreadful lapse' with respect to the Takeover Directive, the Parliament was described over the FSAP as 'on the side of the angels in seeking to create an open and honest European Union-wide financial market. It has generally improved the legislation placed before it': Norman, P, 'Credit Due to Brussels' Achievement', *Financial Times Fund Management Supplement*, 19 April 2004, 8.

[84] 2001 Stockholm Resolution, n 47.

[85] The 2001 Lamfalussy Report attempted to assuage the Parliament's concerns by pointing to the close contact which would be maintained by the European Securities Committee and CESR with the Parliament: n 26, 34. The Report's conclusion at 34 was that 'it is in everybody's interest that the European Parliament be given an adequate role in the procedure... [w]ere Parliament not to be satisfied, the consequences would be felt the next time co-decision legislation (Level 1) conferring implementing powers on the Securities Committee is proposed. This point would no doubt not be lost on the Commission or on the Securities Committee'.

and rather brittle settlement[86] was agreed between the Parliament, the Commission, and the Council in February 2002 on the operation of level 2.[87] The settlement included a range of procedural and transparency-related guarantees for the Parliament, and the major concession that all delegations would be subject to time limits in the form of 'sunset clauses'. The related collapse of level 2 powers after four years injected very considerable instability into FSAP law-making, which instability became more apparent as the FSAP progressed.[88] Particular concerns arose, for example, that the removal of level 2 law-making powers under the Prospectus Directive would have serious implications for international negotiations on equivalence between International Financial Reporting Standards (IFRS) and third country GAAP.[89] July 2006, however, saw resolution of the wider comitology issue, following inter-institutional agreement on a new comitology 'regulatory procedure with scrutiny'.[90] As part of the wider inter-institutional settlement, it was also agreed that the Commission's delegated powers would no longer be subject to time limits, and that Parliament would not call for such clauses in the future. Reform of the related level 1 measures in the securities and markets sphere followed in February 2008 (under the 'comitology alignment legislative package') to reflect the Parliament's new powers and to remove the sunset clauses.[91]

At level 2, strong inter-institutional relationships developed, notwithstanding earlier tensions and the novelty of the process.[92] But flash-points were a recurring feature, typically linked to perceptions of overreach by an institution; this was particularly the case with respect to European Parliament/CESR relations. Commission/Parliament relations, for example, quickly stabilized, with considerable efforts made by the Commission, outside the formalities of the comitology process, to engage closely with Parliament.[93] This approach bore fruit; the Parliament did not obstruct the adoption of any level 2 measure

---

[86] Although described as a 'fair and honourable compromise' by Commissioner Prodi when affirming the settlement to a plenary session of the European Parliament on 5 February 2002.

[87] Set out in a letter from Commissioner Bolkestein to the Chairman of the European Parliament's ECON Committee (2 October 2001) and in the 5 February 2002 Prodi Declaration to the European Parliament. The settlement was accepted by the Parliament in a Resolution (European Parliament Resolution on the Implementation of Financial Services Legislation, 5 February 2005 (P5_TA(2002)0035)) proposed by MEP von Wogau, who had supported acceptance of the compromise in the earlier von Wogau Report (Report on the Implementation of Financial Services Legislation (A5–0011/2002)). The Resolution also set out the procedural steps under which the Parliament expected the process to be run.

[88] The clauses were regarded as threatening the future of the Lamfalussy process in the 2006 Interim IIMG Report, n 63, 11.

[89] See, eg, Speech by Commissioner McCreevy to the European Parliament's Open ECON Coordinators Meeting, 10 July 2007.

[90] Council Decision 2006/512/EC [2006] OJ L200/11.

[91] See generally Commission, Single Market in Financial Services Progress Report 2006 (SEC (2007) 263). As part of the settlement, the Council, European Parliament, and Commission agreed to align 25 'basic acts' to the new procedure as a matter of urgency, including 13 financial-services directives. Proposals to this effect were adopted by the Commission in December 2006 (COM (2006) 900). A package of directives amending key FSAP directives to refer to the new procedure and to remove the sunset clauses (including MiFID I, the Prospectus Directive, and the Market Abuse Directive) was subsequently adopted by the Council and European Parliament in February 2008: Directive 2008/11/EC [2008] OJ L76/37 (Prospectus Directive); Directive 2008/10/EC [2008] OJ L76/33 (MiFID I); Directive 2008/22/EC [2008] OJ L76/50 (Transparency Directive) and Directive 2008/26/EC [2008] OJ L81/42 (MAD).

[92] See Ferran and Green, n 64.

[93] 2004 Commission Lamfalussy Report, n 63, 5. Close informal contacts also developed between the ECON committee and the Commission, with ECON rapporteurs given much of the credit for the timely completion of the FSAP at levels 1 and 2: November 2004 IIMG Report, n 63, 11.

over the FSAP era. The lengthy MiFID I level 2 process, for example, resulted in a positive resolution from the Parliament which accepted the administrative rules as a 'workable compromise' and the 'best achievable outcome'.[94] The Parliament/Commission relationship remained somewhat fragile, however, over the FSAP/Lamfalussy era.[95] European Parliament/CESR relations were, however, often fraught; the fracas which erupted in relation to the 2004 European System of Central Banks (ESCB)–CESR clearing and settlement standards exposed the Parliament's concern to protect its law-making prerogatives from CESR's burgeoning ambitions with respect to supervisory convergence.[96] The Parliament also repeatedly raised concerns in relation to CESR's accountability model.[97]

The Commission/European Securities Committee/CESR dynamic was broadly effective, with the Prospectus, Market Abuse, Transparency, and MiFID I administrative level 2 regimes all passing without a single opposing vote in the European Securities Committee. While the Commission regularly showed itself to be concerned to protect its right of initiative, and radically altered CESR's technical advice on occasion, this does not appear to have translated into a default position of scepticism towards CESR, although some tensions inevitably remained[98] and became sharp during the MiFID I administrative rule-making process.[99] Within the European Securities Committee, relations between the Member State delegations were generally strong.[100] The Commission/European Securities Committee/CESR dynamic was nonetheless fundamentally awkward, given that technical advice based on extensive rounds of market consultation by CESR could be overturned by the Commission or during European Securities Committee discussions.

Internal tensions within CESR also shaped the process. CESR, unlike ESMA, operated under a consensus model for much of its existence. At level 2, CESR's strenuous efforts to seek consensus[101] generated the risk of technical advice following a 'lowest common denominator' approach, potentially inimical to good quality rule-making,[102] and constrained the

---

[94] European Parliament Resolution on the MiFID Draft Implementing Measures, 13 June 2006 (P6-TA (2006)071) paras A.2, A.15, and A.10.

[95] Lingering suspicion can be seen in the letter sent by Commissioner McCreevy to the ECON Committee, assuring it that the Commission's Background Note prepared in conjunction with the first Commission drafts of the 2004 MiFID I level 2 measures was simply designed for discussion and could not add new conditions to the level 2 measures: Letter from Commissioner McCreevy 26 March 2006, cited in the 2006 European Parliament MiFID I Resolution (n 94, para A.6).

[96] Discussed later in this section.

[97] Discussed later in this section.

[98] See, eg, the 2006 Interim IIMG Report, which noted a concern of the level 3 committees generally that implementing measures often differed from their technical advice 'in a way that is not fully understandable to them': n 63, 12.

[99] The Commission significantly revised CESR's technical advice, notably by adopting a maximum harmonization model although CESR had proposed a minimum approach which would allow Member States discretion. It was reported that, following the indications that the Commission was to depart from CESR's advice in some significant respects, CESR took a 'strong collective position' attacking the Commission. This was undermined by a number of CESR members then breaking away and undertaking confidential bilateral negotiations with the Commission: McKee, M and Aubry, N, 'MiFID: Where Did it Come From and Where is it Taking Us?' (2007) *JIBLR* 177, 182.

[100] eg European Securities Committee Minutes, 14 February 2007.

[101] CESR's level 2 technical advice on the market abuse regime provides one of the very few examples of a publicly disclosed disagreement between CESR members: CESR/03-213b, 15–17. It concerned the threshold at which trades by insiders (company managers) in their companies' shares should be publicly disclosed.

[102] CESR's first consultation on the market abuse regime, eg, was not well received by the market: 'They were perceived as assortments of best practices in each Member State rather than drafts for genuine technical

development of a distinctly EU approach to regulation. The consensus model also clothed CESR in considerable opacity and made it difficult to assess which Member States, political considerations, and regulatory traditions were influential during CESR's formative years, or whether national interests or prestige dynamics trumped objective regulatory positions. At level 3, the consensus model added to the accountability and legitimacy risks which CESR's burgeoning 'soft rulebook' soon generated. Consensus decision-making reflected, however, CESR's embryonic nature and the need to build trust between CESR members as it developed; two waves of reforms in 2006 and 2008 would see CESR ultimately move to qualified majority voting (QMV).[103]

While the Lamfalussy process therefore became (for the most part) institutionally stable, similar institutional tensions would recur (and become acute) over the subsequent ESA construction period, however; as with the Lamfalussy era, they have shaped the new rule-making process.

X.2.3.3 Establishing the Space for Administrative Rule-making

The establishment of the dividing line between level 1 (legislative) and level 2 (administrative) measures was, from the outset, problematic (and remains so). Little science seems to have attended FSAP-era decisions as to how the line was drawn—they were generally politically driven.[104] The supporting comitology framework limited level 2 to applying the essential elements of basic instruments and adapting and updating non-essential provisions. By implication, level 1 was limited to 'essential measures', but there was little guidance as to what this involved. The Lamfalussy Report provided only limited direction, characterizing level 1 rules as 'framework principles', 'basic political choices', 'core political principles', and the 'essential elements of each proposal'.[105] But the combination of a massive increase in the regulatory ambitions of the EU under the FSAP, the burgeoning political sensitivities of financial market regulation (particularly as the FSAP began to address contested policies, such as support of competition in order execution),[106] the growing sophistication of influential market actors in lobbying national government and building pan-EU coalitions,[107]

---

advice,' December 2003 IIMG Report, n 63, 27. The 2006 Interim IIMG Report similarly saw a 'potential danger in the fact that the results...may be more "consensus" than "best practice" driven' and questioned whether a 'common good or European reflex by national supervisors and the capacity to act collectively' could develop: n 63, 14–15.

[103] The 2006 Charter reforms provided that level 2 technical advice could be subject to a QMV where the Chair considered there was a split of views or if more than one member asked for a vote, and that level 3 measures could be the subject of a unanimous vote (or veto) where a CESR member so required. The 2008 reforms followed the 2007 Lamfalussy Review and provided for a QMV on all CESR decisions where consensus could not be established.

[104] 'Decisions on the final split are not a matter of institutional or legal orthodoxy. Instead it depends on political negotiations': May 2003 IIMG Report, n 63, 27.

[105] 2001 Lamfalussy Report, n 26, 19 and 22.

[106] For an analysis of the 2004 MiFID I's controversial and detailed level 1 transparency regime as representing a failure of the Lamfalussy process see Ferrarini, G and Recine, F, 'The MiFID and Internalisation' in Ferrarini, G and Wymeersch, E (eds), *Investor Protection in Europe. Corporate Law Making, the MiFID and Beyond* (2006) 235. The Commission was also of the view that MiFID I's pre-trade transparency regime should have been dealt with at level 2, but that this proved impossible given industry lobbying: November 2004 IIMG Report, n 63, 19.

[107] The November 2004 IIMG Report laid much of the blame squarely at the door of market interests, noting that it was 'paradoxical that market participants cling on to the proven mechanisms of inserting their detailed requirements in the legislative sequence at the first opportunity': n 63, 19.

inter-institutional tensions,[108] the perceived risks by stakeholders of a loss of control were issues to move to level 2,[109] and the simple novelty of the process always militated against the limitation of level 1 to high-level rules. The final 2007 report of the IIMG, while concerned as to the level of detail in level 1 (and level 2) measures and calling for a commitment to 'regulatory self-restraint', was ultimately sanguine as to the level 1/level 2 split. While it recognized that the split between basic principles and technical implementing measures was an 'important and open issue', it called for a practical, flexible approach, and cautioned against the adoption of a one-size-fits-all approach.[110]

This question is still unresolved in the ESMA era, and has become all the more sensitive given the five forms of measure (legislative measure, delegated rule, implementing rule, RTS, and ITS) under the current model (section 4).

X.2.3.4 Consultation and Engagement

One of the major objectives of the Lamfalussy process was to secure an improvement in consultation procedures and greater engagement with a wide range of stakeholders, but particularly end-users, in policy development.[111] Prior to the FSAP, widespread public consultation at level 1 was not standard, with consultation exercises largely based on the 'sounding out' of key industry representatives prior to the adoption of formal legislative proposals. The initial signs did not augur well, with the initial drafts of the Market Abuse and Prospectus Directives (although both proposals predated the formal establishment of the Lamfalussy model) not being subject to pre-legislative consultation.[112] By contrast, MiFID I experienced an extensive pre-consultation process.[113] By the November 2004 IIMG Report, consultation procedures were widely regarded as having considerably improved.[114] Enhancements[115] included repeated rounds of pre-legislative consultations, publication of responses, open hearings, and reliance on expert and advisory groups.[116] Retail engagement remained, however, problematic.

At the level 2 administrative level, CESR's extensive consultation procedures on its technical advice were based on three elements: public consultation on particular mandates, including a call for evidence, a full consultation paper(s), open hearings, and a feedback document, closing the consultation loop; establishment of specific stakeholder working groups for particular mandates; and more general consultation through the Market Participants Consultative Group, which was designed to act as a 'sounding board' for CESR.[117]

---

[108] CEPS argued that the Council resisted devolving power to the Commission at level 2: n 63, 26.

[109] This was a particular concern in the Parliament: November 2004 IIMG Report, n 63, 19.

[110] 2007 Final IIMG Report, n 65, 8.

[111] The 2007 Interim IIMG Report described consultation as the 'cornerstone of the Lamfalussy process': n 63, 9.

[112] December 2003 IIMG Report, n 63, 21–3. No formal consultation took place on the Prospectus Directive proposal, while the Market Abuse Directive proposal was only subject to discussion within a forum group of market participants and regulators.

[113] See Ch V.

[114] December 2003 IIMG Report n 63, 21–3 and 25. The Report found that procedures had become substantially more extensive and systematic, while market participants generally regarded the system as sufficient and appropriate.

[115] For a review see the 2005 FSAP Evaluation Report, n 61, 15–16.

[116] While the Commission had long been a user of expert groups, the Parliament's ECON committee also established an Advisory Panel of Financial Services Experts to advise on the FSAP.

[117] Established in July 2002 (CESR/02-111).

The Commission also opened working drafts of level 2 rules (usually containing explanatory statements and, on occasion, impact assessments) and the final proposals to consultation. Formally at least, extensive consultation procedures were followed. Retail engagement remained, however, a significant challenge. CESR consultations were almost entirely dominated by industry and wholesale market interests.[118] But, and by contrast with the early days of ESMA, retail engagement quickly became a source of institutional concern. CESR repeatedly underlined its commitment to improve retail governance generally[119] and adopted a series of remedial measures, including investor conferences,[120] Consumer Days,[121] consumer-friendly versions of its consultation papers,[122] and efforts to build communication links with retail investor associations.[123] But while the IIMG reported that progress had been achieved and the Council was supportive,[124] effective retail governance remained a significant challenge for the Lamfalussy process at all levels.[125] Consultation fatigue was also a recurring problem of the FSAP period, particularly given the increase in consultations across levels 1–3 of the Lamfalussy process.[126]

Consultation risks, including retail governance risks, remain in place in the ESMA era, however, with retail governance continuing to be troublesome.[127]

X.2.3.5 Institutional Design Risks and the CESR Experience: the Soft Law Issue

CESR's dynamic evolution and its uneasy fit within the EU's traditional legitimacy and accountability controls for comitology-based administrative rule-making[128] presented

---

[118] Across all the consultations held by CESR from October 2002 until June 2005 on various FSAP measures, including the MiFID I conduct-of-business regime, there were 1,680 responses, of which only 13 represented consumer groups: McKeen-Edwards, H and Roberge, I, Efficiency Over Democracy? The Case of Monetary and Financial Services Sector Integration in Europe (2005). Of the 77 responses to CESR's First Draft Level 2 Advice on the MiFiD I regime (CESR/04-261b) (which included advice on the disclosure provided by investment firms to investors), only one (the Danish Shareholders' Association) formally represented the interests of private investors.

[119] CESR's 2006 Annual Report noted that, following the steps it had taken to increase 'active dialogue' with the retail sector, participation rights had risen from 1.7 per cent of consultations in 2005 to 3.1 per cent in 2006 and acknowledged that more needed to be done to increase retail engagement with the consultation process.

[120] Conferences with retail investor associations were held in November 2005 and in February 2007.

[121] It ran a 2004 MiFID I Consumer Day in March 2005 which was supported by a user-friendly discussion paper which highlighted issues of particular concern to retail investors. A specific hearing was also held for consumers on transparency and on CESR's approach to the storage of issuers' financial information. CESR members were also asked to liaise with their national consumer associations and to explain the background to CESR's approach: CESR, Annual Report (2006) 25.

[122] eg during the extensive consultation on the reforms to the UCITS prospectus regime, CESR produced a discrete consultation document for retail investors: CESR, Summary of Key Points for Retail Investors Arising From CESR's Consultation on Key Investor Information Disclosures for UCITS (2007) (CESR/07-753).

[123] CESR, 2007 Interim Report on the Activities of CESR (2008) (CESR/07-671) 8–9.

[124] 2007 Interim IIMG Report, n 63, 10. The 2007 ECOFIN Council Conclusions welcomed the improvement in consultation procedures but highlighted the need to strengthen consumer input: n 66, 16.

[125] The 2007 Final IIMG Report acknowledged that it was difficult to target consumers and that it was necessary to be realistic as to the extent to which consumers could participate in technical consultations: n 65, 11.

[126] 2005 CEPS Report, n 63, 7, which described the consultation process as laborious, complicated, time-consuming and resource-absorbing.

[127] Ch IX sect 9.

[128] eg Lavrijssen, S and Hancher, L, European Regulators in the Network Sectors. Revolution or Evolution. TILEC DP No 2008-024 (2008), available via <http://ssrn.com/abstract=1162164>.

something of a constitutional conundrum in the closing years of the CESR era. In many respects CESR provided a pragmatic and effective response to the challenge of setting standards for a highly complex and rapidly evolving marketplace within the constraints imposed by the EU's law-making processes. But it also presented a considerable challenge to the EU's governance of law-making.

While the level 2 process generated some institutional difficulties, these were generally resolved relatively easily. Most difficulties arose in relation to level 3 and the novel supervisory convergence/soft law element, which represented a departure from the relatively well-tested delegated rule-making/comitology model. The instabilities associated with the uneasy fit between CESR's formal powers and the dynamism and momentum which became associated with its accretion of soft power over rule-making have, to some extent, been resolved by the institutional framework which now applies to ESMA. But opacities remain and the legacy effects of the CESR era on ESMA have, in some cases, been strong.

As noted in section 1.2, soft law measures provide a convenient and pragmatic channel for standard-setting and for shaping market behaviour where formal institutional procedures and competence limitations may stymie action by regulators. In the EU, the complex dynamics of the institutional formalities for law-making, combined with strong incentives for institutional aggrandizement and fast-moving market developments, always made it likely that CESR would seize on soft law as a key tool for building its regulatory capacity and shaping the EU rulebook. But its soft law activities presented a host of accountability and validity conundrums.

Under the Lamfalussy vision, level 3 was designed to support convergence and consistency in the implementation and application of level 1 and level 2 rules. Over the CESR era, it acquired a quasi-regulatory dimension which allowed CESR to exert soft influence over the shape of EU securities and markets regulation, and which generated legitimacy and accountability risks deriving from the absence of the formal oversight controls which applied at level 2. CESR's quasi-regulatory activities operated across a number of dimensions, including with respect to agenda-setting activities generally, inter-institutional interaction, and international activities.[129] Chief among them, however, and attracting most controversy, was CESR's construction of a 'soft rulebook', formed from a plethora of guidance, recommendations, briefings, and 'level 3 papers' generally; what started as a fairly thin trickle in 2004, as CESR began to extend its activities from the massive level 2 technical advice programme, became a full spate from 2006,[130] which would not abate until ESMA was established. The market abuse 'soft' regime was limited to guidance on the application of the market abuse rules,[131] while the prospectus and transparency regimes were similarly economical.[132] But the later MiFID I regime, for example, included a

---

[129] For discussion see Moloney, N, 'The Committee of European Securities Regulators and level 3 of the Lamfalussy Process', in Tison, M, de Wulf, H, Van der Elst, C, and Steennot, R (eds), *Perspectives in Company Law and Financial Regulation* (2009) 449.

[130] CESR's 2006 Annual Report noted the shift in its activities from level 2 to level 3: at 5.

[131] CESR/04-505b, CESR/06-562b and CESR/09-219.

[132] The soft prospectus regime contained guidance (CESR/05-054b) but was mainly concerned with the extensive Q&A. The soft transparency regime was limited to a Q&A document (CESR/09-168) and standard forms for large shareholding notifications (CESR/08-066), reflecting little stakeholder enthusiasm for quasi-regulatory intervention following CESR's 2007 consultation on potential level 3 activities.

regularly updated Q&A,[133] 'supervisory briefings',[134] 'statements of policy',[135] reports,[136] and recommendations.[137] The UCITS regime, on which CESR focused over the final years of its operation, produced the greatest volume of level 3 quasi-regulatory material, typically termed 'guidance' and related to the UCITS IV reforms, and including: guidance on the UCITS eligible assets regime;[138] risk management guidance;[139] a raft of measures on the production of the KIID,[140] risk measurement guidance;[141] and money-market fund guidance.[142] While these interventions were, until 2008, typically closely related to the level 1 and level 2 framework, the financial crisis saw CESR addressing areas which were only sketchily (if at all) addressed in the legislative regime (including money-market funds,[143] contracts for differences,[144] and short selling),[145] finessing EU rules,[146] and seeking to shape the EU legislative response to the crisis. CESR's 2009 review of transparency in the corporate bond, structured-finance product, and credit derivatives markets,[147] for example, was prompted by the 2008 Financial Stability Forum Report on market resilience[148] and not by (as was typical, until then, of CESR's reviews) a Commission request. CESR was also one of the few EU actors to highlight the retail investor cause over the crisis, notably with respect to the Madoff scandal[149] and the Lehman collapse.[150]

CESR's 'soft rulebook' activities developed organically from the original 2001 Commission Decision[151] establishing CESR as part of the Lamfalussy process and as an independent advisory group on securities within the Community, to advise the Commission, either on

---

[133] Initially, CESR/08-266.

[134] In 2008, CESR adopted three supervisory briefings designed to summarize key elements of MiFID I and to indicate how NCAs might approach supervision (CESR/08-733 (conflicts of interest); CESR/08-734 (inducements); and CESR/08-735 (best execution)).

[135] CESR adopted a Q&A on the nature of complex and non-complex investments for the purposes of the 2004 MiFID I appropriateness test which it described as a statement of policy (CESR/09-559) and a Q&A on the nature of 'advice' under MiFID I, which it described as a 'level 3 paper' and statement of policy (CESR/10-293).

[136] In 2010, CESR adopted a report on inducements, designed to highlight good and bad practices (CESR/10-295).

[137] CESR adopted, eg, a recommendation on the MiFID I inducement and passporting regimes in 2007 (CESR/07-2286 and CESR/07-337 and 337b) and on MiFID I record-keeping in 2006 (CESR/06-552c).

[138] CESR/07-044b.

[139] CESR/09-178.

[140] Including CESR/10-1318 (performance scenario disclosures for UCITSs); CESR-10/1319 (the transitional regime from the simplified prospectus to the KIID); CESR-10/1320 (clear language); CESR-10/231 (the KIID template); and CESR-10/673 (the KIID synthetic risk indicator).

[141] CESR/10-788.

[142] CESR-10/049.

[143] The 2009 guidance (CESR/10-049) was adopted in response to the financial crisis.

[144] CESR/09-1215b.

[145] CESR produced a model for the regulation of short selling, which its member NCAs committed to voluntarily adhere to: CESR/10-453 and CESR/10-088 (which followed an earlier consultation (CESR/09-581)).

[146] The UCITS risk management guidance, eg (CESR/09-178), was designed to respond to market turbulence, as well as (more traditionally) to prevent regulatory arbitrage, foster mutual confidence and strengthen investor protection.

[147] CESR/09-348.

[148] CESR related the need for its review to the pivotal 2008 Financial Stability Forum (FSF) Report on Enhancing Market and Institutional Resilience and also to the range of international initiatives being taken concerning market transparency: n 147, 7–10.

[149] CESR/09-089.

[150] CESR/09-255.

[151] n 50.

the Commission's initiative or on its own initiative, in particular with respect to level 2 (Article 2). The Decision did not refer directly to supervisory convergence activities, although these were covered in CESR's Charter.[152] Formal accountability or procedural requirements were not established. CESR, which declared itself independent,[153] was not, under its founding Decision, accountable to the Member States or the EU institutions and was only loosely tethered to the institutional structure.[154] By contrast, at level 2, oversight by the European Securities Committee and Commission, and European Parliament engagement, reduced accountability risks.

The status of the informal level 3 CESR 'soft rulebook' was, from the outset, unstable. The legal nature of the 'soft rulebook' was never clear, nor were the addressees, nor the extent of the obligations which followed.[155] Level 3 measures were developed by consensus, until the closing stages of CESR's operation, and were not subject to 'comply or explain' or similar commitments from CESR's member NCAs. Nonetheless, exhortations to CESR members to follow guidance, and to market participants to reflect CESR policy, recurred across the CESR 'soft rulebook'. Peer reviews of level 3 measures were undertaken,[156] although the variable results underlined the uncertain status of the soft rulebook.[157] CESR also became increasingly assertive in relation to level 3, suggesting, in the context of the MiFID I Q&A, that while level 3 was not legally binding, its 'legal effects' could include providing a 'safe harbour' to be used by courts and tribunals in interpreting level 1 and level 2 measures, being 'of relevance' in enforcement action taken by an NCA, and 'creating relevant considerations and legitimate expectations', particularly with respect to the predictability of actions taken by NCAs.[158] While an element of 'wishful thinking' can be associated with

---

[152] Art 4 provided that CESR was to 'foster and review' common and uniform day-to-day implementation and application of Community legislation, issuing guidelines, recommendations, and standards to be adopted by CESR members in their regulatory practices on a voluntary basis (Art 4.3).

[153] eg CESR, Annual Report (2004) describing CESR as 'an independent Committee of European Securities Regulators': 66.

[154] The foundation Decision establishing CESR simply required CESR to present an annual report to the Commission (Art 6) and to maintain close operational links with the Commission and the European Securities Committee (Art 4).

[155] With respect to MiFID I, eg, the 2010 inducements report (CESR/10-295) was described laconically as designed to assist firms in better understanding good inducement practices and to support firms in benchmarking their activities. The 2007 Inducements Recommendation (CESR/-228b), by contrast, was explained in some detail as being designed to facilitate supervisory convergence and the consistent implementation of MiFID I, as being applied by CESR members on a voluntary basis, and as not imposing new or additional obligations, not taking the form of EU legislation, and not prejudicing the Commission's position as guardian of the Treaties. In the UCITS sphere, the status of the different measures adopted was similarly varied. The status of important 2010 money-market funds guidance (CESR/10-049), eg, was not addressed, while the 2010 risk measurement guidance (CESR/09-178) was described as providing stakeholders with detailed methodologies and designed to foster a level playing field.

[156] And have continued in the European Securities and Markets Authority (ESMA) era. The 2010 CESR measure on money-market funds, eg, was subject to peer review over 2012: ESMA/2013/476.

[157] Peer reviews of the UCITS passporting guidance (eg CESR/09-1034) and of CESR's guidelines on the enforcement of financial reporting standards (CESR/09-374 and CESR/09-212) delivered mixed results. A striking feature of the 2009 peer review assessment of CESR's standards on enforcement of financial reporting standards was the divergence between the peer review findings and the related supervisory self-assessment. With respect to Standard No 1, the peer review found that less than half of regimes (45 per cent) were fully compliant, but the self-assessment suggested that more than half were fully compliant. Similarly, the peer review of Standard No 2 found that slightly less than one third of regimes were fully applying the standards but that the self-assessment suggested that 45 per cent of regimes were in full compliance.

[158] CESR, MiFID Level 3 Work Plan for Q4 2007–2008 (2008) (CESR/07-704c) 3.

CESR's approach, CESR's soft rulebook, representing authoritative pronouncements from the EU's NCAs and largely unmoored from the EU's governance controls, had a troublesome quasi-binding quality.

Difficulties also arose in relation to the relationship between CESR's level 3 activities and the level 1 and 2 framework which provided a basis for CESR's level 3 quasi-rule-making activities. In practice, CESR's level 3 measures tended to be rooted in the relevant level 1 and level 2 regime. They were often (although not consistently) stated not to conflict with or subvert level 1 and level 2 rules. The decision to adopt guidance or a similar measure was, in some cases, driven by a Commission/European Securities Committee decision over level 2 negotiations to move particular standards to level 3, as was the case with the UCITS III regime. The fracas which attended the ill-fated 2004 CESR/European System of Central Banks standards on clearing and settlement,[159] which did not have a basis in level 1 or 2 and which saw the European Parliament deliver a stinging rebuke to CESR on the need for its actions to have a legal base and for stronger accountability,[160] was not repeated. But CESR pushed against the level 1 and level 2 framework again over the crisis era, moving into areas outside the rules adopted by the institutions.

Institutional tensions were quick to follow the organic growth of CESR's quasi-rule-making activities,[161] reflecting the risks of CESR activities taking place in a 'grey zone where political accountability is unclear'.[162] The European Parliament, for example, in the 2005 Van den Burg I Resolution, urged all 3L3 committees 'to pay the utmost attention to providing a sound legal basis for their actions, avoid[ing] dealing with political questions and prevent [ing] prejudice to upcoming Community law'.[163] The Commission also raised accountability concerns[164] (as did the ECB[165]); in its 2004 Report on the Lamfalussy Process, the Commission called for a clearer articulation of the role of level 3, particularly with respect to protecting the institutional prerogatives of the Council, Parliament, and Commission.

CESR's level 3 activities generated, however, a range of pragmatic and incremental CESR-driven and other reforms designed to support the legitimacy and accountability of level 3. CESR's efforts to construct a related accountability model[166] engaged all the major

---

[159] CESR/04-561.

[160] European Parliament Resolution on Clearing and Settlement in the EU, 7 July 2005 (P6-TA(2005) 0301).

[161] Prior to the explosion in level 3 activities, the reaction was more sanguine. The EFC reported in 2002 that the accountability mechanisms employed by CESR (in the form of reporting obligations and consultation procedures) were adequate: 2002 EFC Report, n 63, 19.

[162] As described by certain (unidentified) European Securities Committee delegations. European Securities Committee Minutes, 15 December 2004.

[163] n 78, para B.19.

[164] Writing in 2005 Internal Market Director General Schaub warned that level 3 could not prejudice the political process: Schaub, A, 'The Lamfalussy Process Four Years On' (2005) *JFRC* 110, 116.

[165] n 63, 7–8.

[166] CESR initially related the legitimacy of its level 3 role, rather tenuously, to the 'fact that CESR members take decisions on a daily basis that create jurisprudence. This "bottom-up" approach relates to the normative nature of concrete decision-making activities of the supervisors. The impact of precedents on decisions is determined by the law and cannot be fully controlled by legislators. In addition, in an integrated European market, the jurisprudence created by supervisors produces effects that cannot be limited to national jurisdictions and therefore must be considered at EU level': Van Leeuwen, A-D (first CESR Chairman) and Demarigny, F (CESR Secretary General), 'Europe's Securities Regulators Working Together Under the New EU Regulatory Framework' (2004) 12 *JFRC* 206.

stakeholders on which its capacity depended, and included extensive market consultation on proposed level 3 agendas,[167] outreach to the retail investor constituency,[168] a commitment to report to the European Parliament regularly,[169] closer engagement with the Commission on the content of level 3 measures,[170] a framework for the adoption of level 3 guidance,[171] and (despite its uncompromising view that it was 'master of its own agenda' at level 3)[172] a pulling back from guidance which was not related to level 1 measures. The first series of Charter reforms in 2006 also saw CESR, which had been reluctant to disturb its consensus-based model by adopting voting requirements,[173] commit to operating by unanimous vote (in effect, allowing a veto) in relation to level 3 work, where a member(s) so requested.[174] Further reforms followed the 2007 Lamfalussy Review and the December 2007 ECOFIN Council Conclusions; the ECOFIN Council requested that the 3L3 committees enhance the efficiency and effectiveness of their decision-making procedures by introducing the possibility of QMV. The Council acknowledged, however, that level 3 decisions must remain non-binding but suggested that, as proposed by CESR, a 'comply or explain' model be used to drive compliance.[175] CESR's 2008 Charter reforms, adopted in the teeth of the financial crisis and soon to be superseded by the ESMA reforms, accordingly provided that its decisions (whether in relation to level 2 or 3 or internal matters) be taken by consensus, that a QMV be deployed where consensus could not be attained, and that 'comply or explain' requirements apply to NCAs in relation to level 3 measures. Immediately prior to the publication of the 2010 de Larosière Group Report which would change the institutional context by proposing the ESAs, the Commission adopted new founding decisions for the 3L3 committees which reflected the range of activities and powers which the committees, and particularly CESR, had acquired organically, required the QMV to be used, and formalized the 3L3 committees' powers to issue non-binding guidelines, recommendations, and standards in order to fulfil their tasks and to contribute

---

[167] It consulted on, eg, its proposed level 3 agenda for the transparency regime, and scaled back its agenda in response to market reaction: CESR-07/487 and CESR-08/066.

[168] Sect 2.3.4.

[169] A new accountability framework (with respect to the European Parliament) was formalized in September 2005.

[170] The 2007 MiFID I Inducement Recommendation, eg, noted that the Commission participated in CESR's development of the recommendations on inducements as an observer, that CESR discussed the interpretation of relevant MiFID I legal obligations with the Commission, and that the Commission agreed with CESR's interpretations and considered that the recommendations did 'not go beyond the MiFID regime but flow[ed] from a normal, natural reading of MiFID and the Level 2 Directive': n 155, 3.

[171] CESR committed to only undertake level 3 work which met: (i) a risk threshold (in that the issue addressed at level 3 represented a significant market failure or a repeated or major regulatory or supervisory failure); (ii) an EU threshold (in that the issue was likely to have an EU-wide impact on market participants or end-users and on the smooth functioning of the single market); and (iii) an effectiveness threshold (in that CESR could contribute positively by creating change or 'collective direct action' by CESR members): CESR, 2006 Report on Supervisory Convergence in the Field of Securities Markets (2006) (CESR/06-259b) 2–3.

[172] n 171, Summary.

[173] In its 2004 Report on the Lamfalussy Process, the Commission had earlier raised the possibility of voting, arguing that transparency and democratic accountability could be increased were CESR to adopt a 'more transparent set of procedures for adopting their advice and opinions': n 63, 9. CESR proved resistant to this initially, arguing that there would not be any benefit in moving to majority voting, particularly at level 3 where standards were not binding: European Securities Committee Minutes, 18 November 2004. Later discussions in the Committee raised the possibility of an 'accountability board' to support CESR's accountability: Minutes, 15 December 2004.

[174] Charter of the Committee of European Securities Regulators (2006) (CESR/06-289c) Art 5.

[175] n 66, 17.

to the common and uniform implementation and consistent application of Community legislation.[176]

The difficulties generated by CESR's 'soft rulebook' were particular to CESR's informal status. The pragmatic solution which was under development before the crisis broke was similarly particular, reflecting institutional and Member State concern to achieve a compromise governance model which would acknowledge the utility of soft measures in supporting supervisory convergence, but which would avoid the 'opening of Pandora's Box' which any attempt to formalize the status of the 'soft rulebook' as binding law would have created.[177] ESMA, as discussed later in the Chapter, operates under a materially stronger institutional framework. But the status of 'soft' measures adopted by ESMA has yet to be fully resolved.

X.2.4 The Financial Crisis: Recalibrating the Law-making Process

X.2.4.1 The Financial Crisis and the Single Rulebook

Immediately prior to the deepening of the global financial crisis in autumn 2008, the law-making process for EU securities and markets regulation was relatively stable. The FSAP had completed. Market actors and the EU institutions were, with one or two flash-points,[178] enjoying the 'regulatory pause' for which the Commission had called in 2005.[179]

As the crisis was taking hold earlier in 2007, attention was initially trained on the 2007 Lamfalussy Review. The December 2007 ECOFIN Council Conclusions broadly supported the institutional status quo and were reflected in the Commission's January 2009 recasting of CESR's founding Decision to identify more clearly its core tasks,[180] and in the earlier September 2008 revisions to CESR's founding Charter.[181] As the crisis created the space for more radical institutional reform, two approaches to law-making emerged: 'more Europe' or 'less Europe'.[182] The early stages of the crisis saw some support for 'less Europe', based on a limitation of passporting and a retrenchment towards national regulation and supervision, but, as discussed further in Chapter I, 'more Europe' has followed. A solid political and institutional consensus quickly emerged in favour of a 'single rulebook'; this in turn drove the establishment of the ESAs and led to changes to the process for the adoption of administrative rules. The financial crisis also saw changes to the foundational legislative process and, in particular, to heavy reliance on the 'fast-tracking' of legislation. But the

---

[176] Commission Decision C9 (2009) 176, January 2009 (CESR).

[177] The reluctance of CESR members to engage with this issue is clear from the CESR contribution to the 2007 Lamfalussy Review: 2007 CESR Securities Supervision Report, n 65.

[178] Notably the stand-off between a regulation-sceptical Commission and an interventionist European Parliament with respect to hedge funds. See further Ch III sect 3.4.

[179] 2005 White Paper, n 29.

[180] Commission Decision C (2009) 176.

[181] CESR/08-375d.

[182] The 2009 Turner Review, eg, queried whether a 'less open single market' might be required, in the form of granting powers to host supervisors to require local subsidiarization in certain circumstances, although it also posited the alternative solution in the form of 'more Europe': FSA, The Turner Review. A Regulatory Response to the Global Banking Crisis (2009) 101–2. In a similar vein, the *Financial Times* argued that 'there must either be more harmonised regulation . . . or . . . a shallower common market in which all banks are separately regulated or capitalized': Editorial, 'The City has Little to Fear from the EU', *Financial Times,* 4 December 2009, 14.

pressure of the massive crisis-era reform programme also exposed long-simmering tensions across the Member States and the institutions with respect to the nature and location of financial market regulation (section 3.3.1).

The foundations for the decisive crisis-era move to the single rulebook and the related institutional reforms[183] were laid in the seminal February 2009 de Larosière Group (DLG) Report on the financial crisis.[184] It highlighted that while the 'areas for regulatory repair' which it identified were relevant for all major jurisdictions internationally, the EU suffered from an additional difficulty in the form of the absence of a single set of rules. The Report underlined that a lack of cohesiveness in the regulatory framework disrupted the internal market, generated the risk of regulatory arbitrage and of competitive distortions, imposed costs and inefficiencies on cross-border groups, and made cross-border crisis management difficult. At the core of the rulebook problem was the persistence of options in legislative measures and the inability of the level 3 process to provide legally robust solutions.[185] Accordingly, 'institutionalized and binding arrangements' were needed, as well as a 'set of consistent core rules'. To achieve this, the Group called for the reconfiguration of the 3L3 committees into European Authorities which would 'play a decisive role in the technical interpretation of level 1 and level 2 measures and in the development of level 3 technical standards'.[186]

The single rulebook consensus which the 2009 DLG Report reflected,[187] and which the International Monetary Fund (IMF) supported,[188] was an outcome of myriad factors, including the need to address the G20 reform agenda and consensus on the weaknesses in the EU's regulation of financial markets.[189] But chief among these factors was the crisis-driven re-characterization of the dominant single market priority. Over the pre-crisis FSAP period, the construction of a single deep and liquid financial market provided the justification for the massive liberalizing and re-regulating regulatory regime. The crisis, by contrast, exposed the pathology of the single market and the destructive consequences which follow where regulatory liberalization is not matched by supervisory co-ordination. The crisis saw rule-making become partly re-characterized as a hedge against weaknesses in home/host Member State supervision, and as a mechanism for supporting stronger supervision (which emerged, after years in obscurity, as a primary concern of the EU) and for protecting the cross-border market from financial stability risks.[190] Similarly, regulatory

---

[183] The term 'single rulebook' was somewhat loosely employed over the crisis, but was characterized by the Commission as reflecting 2 important goals—the more consistent application of EU legislation and, as far as possible, the removal of transposition risks—and as engaging the construction of one harmonized set of core standards, composed of level 1 and 2 measures: 2009 ESA Proposals Impact Assessment (SEC (2009) 1234) 8.

[184] n 33.

[185] n 33, 27.

[186] n 33, 49–56, and 53.

[187] The Report was generally warmly received by the industry and the EU institutions: Tait, N, 'Brussels Left to Finish "Mission Impossible"', *Financial Times,* 25 February 2009, 6.

[188] International Monetary Fund (IMF), IMF Country Report No 11/186, Lessons from the European Financial Stability Framework Exercise (2011) (2011 IMF Report) 6.

[189] See, eg, Moloney, N, 'EU Financial Market Regulation after the Financial Crisis: "More Europe" or More Risks?' (2010) 47 *CMLR* 1317. See further Ch I.

[190] The Commission argued that the single rulebook 'should provide a common legal basis for supervisory action in the EU—ensuring strengthened stability, equal treatment, lower compliance costs for companies, as well as removing opportunities for regulatory arbitrage': eg Commission, Financial Supervision Package—Frequently Asked Questions, 22 September 2010 (MEMO/10/434), Q 9.

diversity and competition (which had previously been tolerated in the EU regime) were recast as prejudicial regulatory arbitrage.

X.2.4.2 Negotiating the ESAs and Rule-making

The ESMA Proposal, along with the proposals for the two other ESAs and the European Systemic Risk Board (ESRB), and the related construction of a new European System of Financial Supervision (ESFS) based on these actors and the NCAs, was presented by the Commission in September 2009.[191]

The main elements of ESMA's quasi-rule-making powers were flagged in the earlier May 2009 Commission Communication[192] on which the Proposal was closely based. The Communication also set out ESMA's governance design, which was closely based on the EU's template for agency governance design, and thus was based on a decision-making Board of Supervisors (composed of the NCAs) and an executive Management Board, on both of which the Commission would be represented. The independence and accountability elements of ESMA's governance design were also trailed, as were its decision-making procedures, including the application of the QMV to ESMA's quasi-rule-making powers.

The 2010 ESMA Regulation as finally adopted is a product of struggles between the Council and the European Parliament (the Parliament presented some 242 amendments to the Commission's ESMA Proposal in its initial ECON Report in February 2010)[193] with respect to the extent of ESMA's powers. Most attention, however, focused on operational supervision, the most innovative element of the ESA reform generally.[194] ESMA's quasi-rule-making powers were not heavily contested.[195] They were, however, fine-tuned over the Council and Parliament negotiations (as they were not fully articulated in the Commission Proposal).[196] Both institutions shared a concern to protect ESMA's nascent powers in relation to the proposal of BTSs, and to ensure Council and Parliament oversight, in accordance with the governing Article 290 and 291 TFEU framework for administrative rule-making which came into force with the Lisbon Treaty in December 2009.

The initial European Parliament ECON committee report, for example, specified the nature of BTSs in more detail and applied the Article 290/291 TFEU framework to the adoption of BTSs, and introduced a 'comply or explain' mechanism for supporting compliance with ESMA guidelines.[197] The Parliament's final July 2010 Negotiating Position included a further finessing of the BTS regime, including the introduction of two

---

[191] COM (2009) 503 (ESMA); COM (2009) 501 (EBA); COM (2009) 502 (European Insurance and Occupational Pensions Authority) (EIOPA)); and COM (2009) 499 (European Systemic Risk Board (ESRB)); Impact Assessment (for all three ESAs), n 183.

[192] Commission, Communication on European Financial Supervision (2009) COM (2009) 252 (2009 Communication).

[193] 2010 Giegold Report (PE438.409v01-00).

[194] Initial reaction to the Commission's 2009 Proposal focused on the ESA's supervisory and enforcement powers: Tait, N, Wilson, J, and Masters, B, 'Common Rules Likely to be Enforced', *Financial Times*, 24 September 2009, 6.

[195] The rule-making provisions were not included in the final July 2010 Council position, which was used during the trilogue negotiations and which set out the most contested provision.

[196] The Commission's original model did not, eg, relate the adoption of Binding Technical Standards (BTSs) to the Art 290 and 291 TFEU framework, did not protect ESMA's position where the Commission declined to endorse, or revised, an ESMA BTS, and did not address the nature of a BTS.

[197] 2010 Giegold Report, n 193, amendments 45–53, amendment 56.

types of BTSs (RTSs and ITSs) and their respective oversight procedures, thereby adjusting the regime fully to the Article 290/291 TFEU framework. The Council followed a broadly similar approach. Its December 2009 General Approach introduced enhancements to the BTS process, including procedural protections for ESMA where the Commission did not endorse or changed ESMA's proposed BTSs. The Council did not, however, support the application of 'comply or explain' disciplines to ESMA guidance, although it ultimately followed the Parliament's approach. ESMA's scope of action was also finessed over the negotiations.

Structurally, the sectoral design of the new system (based on three ESAs) was never seriously in doubt, given the availability of the 3L3 committees. Whatever the efficiencies which may or may not have derived from a more radical institutional design, based, for example, on the 'twin peaks', cross-sectoral, conduct and prudential regulation models,[198] it was always likely that the 3L3 model would have been recycled. In its May 2009 Communication, the Commission recognized the debate on the optimal organizational structure but took the pragmatic view that it was preferable to build on existing structures, in the absence of persuasive evidence that another structure would be more efficient.[199]

The Council reached initial political agreements in October (on the ESRB) and December (ESMA and the other ESAs) 2009.[200] In July 2010, the European Parliament and Council adopted positions designed to facilitate the final negotiations and a single reading of the proposals.[201] Although close inter-institutional contacts had been maintained between the Council and Parliament (which led to the Council's July 2010 position focusing only on those areas where difference existed with the Parliament),[202] considerable differences remained between the July 2010 Council and Parliament positions, albeit with respect to supervision and not rule-making.[203] Intense 'trilogue' discussions (Commission/Council/ Parliament) accordingly took place over the summer of 2010. On 2 September 2010, agreement was reached in the trilogue on the European Banking Authority (EBA) Regulation text,[204] which served as the basis for finalizing the ESMA (and European Insurance and Occupational Pensions Authority (EIOPA)) Regulation texts. Following the

---

[198] See sect 5.2.6.

[199] Similarly, the 2010 ESA Proposals Impact Assessment pragmatically argued that the ESAs were not to be 'built from scratch': n 183, at 5.

[200] Council (ECOFIN) Meeting, 2 December 2009, Council Document 16571/1-09 (ESMA); Council Document 16748/109 (EBA); and Council Document 16749/1/09 (EIOPA); and Council Meeting, 20 October 2009, Council Document 14491/1/09 (ESRB).

[201] Parliament Debate 6 July 2010 outcomes: T7-0270/2010 (ESMA); T7-0272/2010 (EBA); T7-0273/ 2010 (EIOPA); and T7-0271 (ESRB). The Council adopted a General Approach on 13 July 2010 on aspects of the EBA proposal which were critical to the negotiations across all three ESAs: Council Document 11669/10.

[202] The Council noted that 'there is now a large degree of convergence between the two institutions thanks to the negotiations which have already taken place, but it has not proved possible to find an official agreement in time to enable the first reading on 8 July, as originally intended': 13 July 2010, ECOFIN Press Release No 12020/10.

[203] See further Ch XI.

[204] Report from the Presidency to the Council, 6 September 2010, Proposal for a Regulation of the European Parliament and the Council establishing a European Banking Authority—Presidency Compromise Text (Council Document 13070/1/10 Rev 1).

Presidency's recommendation,[205] the trilogue position was accepted by the Council at its 7 September 2010 meeting.[206] The final Parliament plenary vote on the ESMA Regulation took place on 22 September 2010,[207] and the Council's final formal adoption of the Regulation took place on 17 November 2010.[208] The ESMA Regulation was published in the Official Journal on 15 December 2010,[209] and ESMA (and the other ESAs and the ESRB) were established in January 2011.

X.2.4.3 A Brave New World?

The institutional and political rhetoric which attended the establishment of the ESAs certainly suggested that something very new was afoot. The 22 September 2010 inter-institutional agreement on the ESAs, for example, was welcomed in fulsome terms: Commission Barnier called it 'a fundamental moment for the evolution of financial regulation in Europe',[210] while the European Parliament claimed that the new structure would 'see a fundamental shift in the way banks, stock markets and insurance companies are policed'.[211]

As discussed in Chapter XI, ESMA's operational supervisory powers represent a new departure for EU securities and markets regulation. In the law-making sphere, however, the establishment of ESMA can be regarded as more of an incremental step from the 2001 establishment of CESR. ESMA is a creature of the administrative rule-making process, like CESR, and, also like CESR, cannot adopt binding rules. As discussed in section 5, the agency and comitology models on which ESMA's institutional structure and quasi-rule-making powers are based may not be optimal for rule-making efficiency.

X.3 The Legislative Process

X.3.1 Legislation and the Treaty: Competence to Act

The breadth and depth of the EU securities and markets regulation rulebook suggests that the EU has untrammelled powers to intervene in financial markets. This is not the case. EU securities and markets regulation measures must have a basis in a law-making competence granted to the EU and set out in the Treaties, and must respect the Treaty-based subsidiarity and proportionality requirements.

Article 5 TEU requires the EU to act within the limits of the powers conferred upon it and of the objectives assigned to it. The EU must also respect the proportionality and subsidiarity principles, in that the EU can take action in areas of shared competence between the EU and the Member States[212] only and insofar as the objectives of the action

---

[205] Report from the Presidency to the Council on Financial Supervision Reforms, 6 September 2010, Council Document No 13179/10.

[206] 3030th Council Meeting, 7 September 2010, Council Document 13161/10.

[207] P7_TA-PROV(2010)0339.

[208] 3045th Council Meeting, 17 November 2010, Council Document No 16369/10.

[209] Regulation EU (No) 1095/2010 [2010] OJ L331/84.

[210] MEMO/10/436.

[211] European Parliament, Press Release 20100921PR83190.

[212] Which includes securities markets regulation; Art 4(2) TFEU identifies the internal market as an area of shared competence.

cannot be sufficiently achieved by the Member States and can therefore, by reason of the scale or effects of the proposed action, be better achieved by the Union.

Legislation in this area has, for the most part, been based on: Article 50(2)(g) TFEU (directives designed to co-ordinate the safeguards required by Member States of companies or firms); Article 53(1) TFEU (directives designed to co-ordinate Member States' rules on the taking up and pursuit of activities as self-employed persons and the provision of services); Article 115 TFEU (directives for the approximation of Member States' rules which directly affect the establishment or functioning of the common market); and Article 114 TFEU (measures for the approximation of Member States' rules which have as their object the establishment and functioning of the internal market). The free movement of capital competence (Articles 63-66 TFEU) has also been called in aid.

The competence, subsidiarity, and proportionality constraints have, at times, been a source of inter-institutional tension and challenge in EU law-making generally.[213] In the securities and markets sphere (and while compliance with these requirements is typically carefully justified in recitals to legislative measures), however, they have rarely, if ever, provided a brake on the adoption of legislation. An elastic interpretation by the Court of Justice of the foundational free movement and, in particular, Article 114 TFEU, competences,[214] which has limited the extent to which the Treaties confine legislative competence in practice,[215] combined with a broadly facilitative political and institutional status quo, has led to only one (banking) measure ever being challenged, and then unsuccessfully.[216]

---

[213] eg Case C-70/81 *European Parliament v Council* [1990] ECR I-2041.

[214] Since the seminal 2000 *Tobacco Advertising* ruling, the Court has repeatedly ruled that the Art 114 TFEU competence does not confer a general competence to regulate the internal market, but requires that the measure must genuinely improve the conditions for the establishment and functioning of the internal market, and that a mere finding of disparities between national rules and the abstract risk of infringements to fundamental freedoms or distortions to competition is not sufficient. But it has taken a facilitative approach in examining whether, as required, legislation addresses barriers to free movement or distortions to competition (including accepting that the potential for disruption, and the prevention of the emergence of obstacles can be considered). It has also ruled that broad discretion is required where legislative action under Art 114 involves political, economic, and social choices, and complex assessments. See, eg, Case C-376/98 *Germany v Parliament and Commission* [2000] ECR I-8419; Case C-491/01 *British American Tobacco (Investments) Limited and Imperial Tobacco v Secretary of State for Health* [2002] ECR I-1453; Cases C-210/03 and C-434/02 *The Queen, on the application of Swedish Match and Others v Secretary of State for Health and Others* [2004] ECR I-11893; Case C-380/03 *Germany v European Parliament and Council* [2006] ECR I-11573; and Case C-58/08 *Vodafone, O2 et al v Secretary of State* [2008] ECR I-4999. The Court only rarely addresses securities and markets measures, but a sympathetic approach might be assumed from the leading *Alpine Investments* ruling in which it accepted that a link existed between 'investor confidence' and the smooth functioning of the internal market: Case C-384/93 *Alpine Investments v Minister van Financien* [1995] ECR I-1141.

[215] It has been argued that the Treaty rules governing competence, and in particular Art 114 TFEU, are ill suited in practice to give real meaning to the principle that the EU has only limited competence granted by the Treaties: Weatherill, S, 'The Limits of Legislative Harmonization Ten Years after Tobacco Advertising: How the Court's Case has become a 'Drafting Guide' (2011) 12 *German LJ* 827.

[216] The German government unsuccessfully challenged the 1994 Deposit Guarantee Directive on the grounds that it should have been adopted under the then Treaty consumer protection competence and not under the internal market competence, as the measure was not a free movement measure but was consumer-protection-driven. The Court found that in eliminating obstacles to free movement the EC was to have regard to the public interest aims of the Member States, and to adopt a level of protection for those interests which seemed acceptable in the EC. It also assumed that consumer protection was relevant to the free-movement competence and that consumer (and investor) interests could not be disregarded: Case C-233/94 *Germany v Parliament and Council* [1997] ECR I-2405.

Although the reach of the massive FSAP-era legislative programme might have generated some concern as to whether it went significantly beyond what was necessary to construct and protect the functioning of the internal financial market, the strong political consensus which attended the liberalization-driven FSAP era muted any concerns.[217]

Similarly, the titanic market convulsions which triggered the crisis-era reform agenda, in combination with the strength of the international reform agenda and the EU's commitment to a single rulebook, meant that potential competence difficulties were not a major feature of the institutional negotiations. Like the FSAP-era programme, the crisis-era legislative programme is largely based on Article 114 TFEU and Article 53(1) TFEU[218] and, formally at least, is closely tied to the functioning of the internal market, albeit that the market liberalization rationale associated with these competences over the FSAP era has been replaced with a market protection rationale.[219] The toxic pathologies of the internal financial market which the crisis exposed made the Treaty-required link to supporting the internal market through remedial measures a relatively easy one to establish.[220] The scale and intensity of intervention, and the removal of Member State discretion, might, nonetheless, have generated some constitutional queasiness around compliance with the Treaties' proportionality and subsidiarity principles. But, absent unusual circumstances, the political likelihood of challenge by a disgruntled Member State (bound under a QMV) was always unlikely over the crisis period.

Nonetheless, the scale of EU intervention, and in particular the institutional reforms, sharply exposed the underlying tensions across the Member States as to the location and intensity of intervention, as outlined in Chapter I. These tensions became sharply apparent in 2012 when the UK challenged the validity of Article 114 TFEU as the competence supporting ESMA's powers under the 2012 Short Selling Regulation.[221]

Most EU agencies have been established under Article 352 TFEU under which Member States have veto powers;[222] Article 114 operates under a Council QMV, however, which made it a more attractive competence given the urgency with which ESMA was established. But ESMA's dynamism and the reach of its powers from the outset rendered it vulnerable to Treaty challenge by a disgruntled Member State. The competence vulnerability is

---

[217] In the context of the EU's retail market agenda see further Moloney, N, 'Confidence and Competence: the Conundrum of EC Securities Regulation' (2004) 4 *JCLS* 1.

[218] The European Market Infrastructure Regulation (Regulation (EU) No 648/2012 [2012] OJ L201/1 (2012 EMIR) and the Short Selling Regulation (Regulation (EU) No 236/2012 [2012] OJ L86/1 (2012 Short Selling Regulation)), eg, were based on Art 114 TFEU, while the Alternative Investment Fund Managers Directive (Directive 2011/61/EU [2011] OJ L174/1 (2011 AIFMD)) was based on Art 53(1) TFEU.

[219] Rec 14 to the 2012 EMIR, eg, argued that it was likely that Member States would adopt divergent national measures which could create obstacles to the smooth functioning of the internal market and be to the detriment of market participants and financial stability. It also argued that uniform application of the clearing obligation in the EU was necessary to ensure a high level of investor protection and to create a level playing field between market participants.

[220] Nonetheless, the recitals to the major crisis-era measures underline the institutional care taken to address, formally at least, the subsidiarity, proportionality, and competence requirements, as do the preparatory documents: eg 2012 EMIR, recs 14 and 99; 2010 EMIR Proposal (COM (2010) 484) 5–6; and 2010 EMIR Proposal Impact Assessment (SEC (2010) 1058/2) 30–1.

[221] Case C-270/12 *UK v Council and Parliament*, 22 January 2014, not yet reported. See Ch XI sect 5.8.3 on the challenge.

[222] Geradin, D and Petit, A, The Development of Agencies at EU and National Levels: Conceptual Analysis and Proposals for Reform, Jean Monnet Working Paper 01/04 (2004) 42–3.

underlined by the explicit reference in the 2010 ESMA Regulation to the 2006 *ENISA* (European Network and Information Security Agency) ruling[223] in support of the Article 114 competence (recital 17).[224] In the *ENISA* ruling, which relates to the establishment of the European Network and Information Security Agency, the Court supported ex Article 95 EC, now Article 114, as the basis for the Agency. The UK had challenged the Treaty basis of ENISA on the grounds that Article 95 was concerned with harmonizing laws and not with the setting up and conferring of powers on bodies; it also argued that being of benefit to the functioning of the internal market did not also mean that the relevant body constituted a harmonizing measure under Article 95: Article 308 (now Article 352) was the appropriate competence in such a case. The Court disagreed and found that Article 95 conferred discretion on the EU legislature as to the method of approximation which was appropriate, particularly in fields with complex technical features. The legislature could deem it necessary to provide for the establishment of a body which was responsible for contributing to the implementation of a 'process of harmonization' in situations where, in order to facilitate the uniform implementation and application of acts based on Article 95, the adoption of non-binding supporting and framework measures was appropriate.[225] The Court also emphasized that the body's tasks must be closely linked to the subject matter of the acts, and that this would be the case where the body provided services to national authorities and/or operators which affect the homogenous implementation of harmonizing instruments and which are likely to facilitate their application.[226] ENISA's powers fit this model, being largely concerned with data collection, advice, co-operation, best practice, and consultation activities. But the ESAs powers are significantly greater and include the power to impose binding decisions on NCAs and market participants.[227]

The *Short Selling* challenge provided, accordingly, an important test case for the Treaty resilience of ESMA's precedent-setting direct supervisory powers, in the context of ESMA's short selling-related powers. As discussed in Chapter XI, the Court adopted a liberal approach to Article 114 TFEU which acknowledged the financial stability context as well as the technical expertise which ESMA brought to EU financial market governance.[228] While the Advocate General found that ESMA's powers could not come within Article 114 (as they replaced Member State action, provided for an EU-level decision-making mechanism, and so did not constitute harmonization), the Court ruled that Article 114 could

---

[223] Case C-217/04 *UK v Council and Parliament (ENISA)* [2006] ECR I-3771.

[224] The Commission's original Communication on the new institutional structure (2009 Communication, n 192, 9) and the ESMA proposal (n 191, 3–4) also considered the justification for Art 114 TFEU in some detail, relying in particular on the need to protect the stability of the internal market and on the *ENISA* ruling, while the European Parliament added in a justificatory recital to the ESMA proposal based on the *ENISA* ruling (adopted as 2012 ESMA Regulation rec 17).

[225] Kokott AG, by contrast, advised that the ENISA Regulation be annulled as ENISA's contribution to the approximation of laws was not clear.

[226] Similarly, outside the agency context, the Court found that Art 114 TFEU accommodated the EU legislature's discretion to choose the appropriate method of harmonization where the proposed approximation required highly technical and specialist analysis, and so supported a centralized comitology-like mechanism for evaluating and authorizing smoke flavourings in foodstuffs: Case C-66/04 *UK v Parliament and Council (Smoke Flavourings)* [2005] ECR I-10553.

[227] See further van Meerten, H and Ottow, A, 'The Proposals for the European Supervisory Authorities: The Right (Legal) Way Forward?' (2009), available at <http://ssrn.com/abstract=1517371> and Fahey, E, 'Does the Emperor have Financial Crisis Clothes? Reflections on the Legal Basis of the European Banking Authority' (2011) 74 *MLR* 581.

[228] Ch XI. sect 5.8.3.

support measures which empowered ESMA to take individual decisions. Although the ruling was located in the particular features of ESMA's short selling powers, the Treaty competences for the securities and markets regime now seem relatively secure—although further challenges cannot be ruled out, particularly given the increasingly asymmetric impact of EU securities and markets regulation in particular markets where specialized, wholesale market activities are carried out, and the potential for Member State concern.

X.3.2 The Legislative Process: the Ordinary Legislative Process

Legislative rules in the securities and markets sphere are adopted under the Article 294 TFEU 'ordinary legislative procedure'; the dominant single market competence for law-making (Article 114 TFEU) provides that rules be adopted under Article 294.

The ordinary legislative process has been through a number of Treaty changes and is now central to EU law-making as the main procedure for adopting legislative rules. It is based on the principle of parity between the European Parliament and Council (the co-legislators) and is designed to ensure that legislation cannot be adopted without the assent of each institution. The procedure (initially termed co-decision) was established under the Maastricht Treaty and has been subject to repeated refinements, generally designed to enhance the Parliament's position, under the Treaty of Amsterdam, the Nice Treaty, and the Lisbon Treaty. The main refinements introduced most recently by the Lisbon Treaty related to the extension of the procedure to most major spheres of EU law-making[229] and to the conferral on national parliaments of the power to assess Commission proposals for compliance with the subsidiarity principle.

The ordinary legislative procedure is multistaged and based on multiple readings by the European Parliament, prior to the adoption of an agreed text by the Council (ECOFIN, in the securities and markets sphere) and Parliament. The process is initiated by the Commission's adoption of a proposal. Proposals are typically adopted after repeated rounds of consultation (including through Green and White Papers) and engagement with stakeholders, including through expert groups. An impact assessment of the proposal is also undertaken and reviewed by the Commission's Impact Assessment Board.

Commission proposals in the securities and markets sphere typically form part of a wider regulatory agenda driven by the political priorities set by the European Council and the Council, although the Commission plays a central steering role, as the FSAP era[230] and the crisis era have made clear.[231] The crisis has also underlined the influence the European Parliament brings to bear on agenda-setting, as well on particular proposals.[232] The crisis-era institutional reforms have brought the ESRB into the agenda-setting environment; its

---

[229] Under the Lisbon Treaty, 85 spheres of activity became subject to the ordinary legislative procedure; 44 areas had been subject to the precursor co-decision procedure: European Parliament, Codecision and Conciliation. A Guide to how the Parliament Co-legislates under the Treaty of Lisbon (2012).

[230] On the Commission's central role over the FSAP see Quaglia, L, *Governing Financial Services in the European Union. Banking, Securities, and Post-trading* (2010).

[231] See Ch I and sect 3.3 on the crisis experience.

[232] At the outset of the crisis, eg, it set out a general reform agenda (rolled into its 2008 Resolution on Hedge Funds and Private Equity: Resolution with Recommendations to the Commission on Hedge Funds and Private Equity, 23 September 2008 (P6_TA-PROV(2008)0425)), and also adopted more specific reform

initial recommendations have included a recommendation to the Commission to secure legislative action in relation to money-market funds (MMFs).[233] Recommendations of this nature cannot easily be ignored by the Commission, given the need to support the institutional position of the ESRB as the EU's independent macroprudential oversight authority, and as ESRB recommendations are subject to ongoing reporting and review requirements.[234]

National parliaments are empowered to send a reasoned opinion on the proposal's compliance with the subsidiarity principle to the Council, European Parliament, and Commission.[235] In the securities and markets sphere, opinions can also be delivered by the ECB and the Economic and Social Committee (EESC).[236]

The ordinary legislative procedure is based on the European Parliament reaching a first reading on the proposal.[237] In practice, a rapporteur is appointed whose report, which sets out amendments to the proposal, is debated within the relevant committee (in the securities and markets sphere, the Economic and Monetary Affairs (ECON) committee);[238] the approved report,[239] following negotiations on any additional amendments offered by MEPs, is adopted by the Parliament's plenary meeting.[240] The Commission may amend the legislative proposal to incorporate Parliament amendments at this stage. The Council, which typically operates under a QMV,[241] then finalizes its position[242] on the basis of the Commission's proposal and in light of the Parliament's first reading. Where the Council

---

programmes, including in relation to shadow banking: eg, October 2010 ECON Report on Shadow Banking (A7-0354/2012).

[233] ESRB Recommendation on Money Market Funds (2012) (ESRB/2012/01).

[234] See further Ch XI sect 6.

[235] A series of procedural steps follow where national parliaments contest a proposal; ultimately, and if the Council or European Parliament are of a majority view that the proposal does not comply with the subsidiarity principle, the proposal is abandoned. These procedures have yet to be tested in the securities and markets sphere.

[236] The European Economic and Social Committee (EESC) (previously ECOSOC) (Art 300 TFEU) provides opinions on legislative initiatives and represents civil society generally. While EESC/ECOSOC opinions carried some weight in the pre-FSAP period, they did not feature heavily over the FSAP and crisis eras. The ECB is to be consulted on all EU acts within its field of competence (Art 127 TFEU). It does not opine on all financial market proposals, but typically engages in relation to financial stability issues.

[237] The process is governed by the European Parliament's Rules of Procedure.

[238] Files can be of interest to more than one committee; opinions from other committees are, therefore, delivered to the committee responsible and considered in the adoption of the rapporteur's report. The Legal Affairs committee, eg, will typically examine securities and markets proposals.

[239] The relevant committee (ECON) examines the report, and amendments to the proposal from the different MEPs and parties represented on the committee are debated.

[240] In the course of the plenary debate, the Commission explains its position on the amendments tabled.

[241] The QMV can result in a Member State being bound against its will, however important its financial market and long its experience in securities and markets regulation. A QMV is 55 per cent of Council members, comprising at least 15 of them, and representing Member States comprising at least 65 per cent of the EU population. A blocking minority for a measure must include at least four Council members, absent which the QMV is deemed to be attained (Art 16 TEU).

[242] In practice, negotiations take place in Council working groups which are chaired by the Council Presidency and which report to the influential COREPER (the Committee of Permanent Representatives, composed of Member States' permanent delegations to the EU), which prepares the Council's work. While the Council negotiations can take place concurrently with the Parliament's work, the Council position can only be adopted after the Parliament's first reading. The common position is adopted under a QMV; where the common position differs from the proposal, a unanimous vote is required. In practice, to ease negotiations, the Commission typically revises its proposal to allow the Council to use a QMV.

accepts a Commission proposal which has not been amended by Parliament, the proposal can be adopted. Where the Council accepts all the Parliament's amendments which have been incorporated by the Commission in an amended proposal, the act can be adopted. In all other cases the Council adopts a common position.

The adoption of the Council common position, which is accompanied by a Commission Communication which sets out the Commission's view of the Council position, triggers the second reading stage. During this stage, where the Parliament approves the common position as it stands, or fails to act within the relevant time limits, the proposal is adopted in accordance with the common position. Where the Parliament rejects the common position, the act is deemed not to have been adopted.[243] Where the Parliament proposes amendments,[244] the Commission must provide an opinion and the Council engages in a second reading. Where the Council agrees all the Parliament's amendments, the proposal is deemed to be adopted. Where the Council does not agree, the proposal enters the conciliation process. During this process, a Conciliation Committee (composed of Parliament, Council, and Commission representatives) seeks agreement (the Commission plays a mediation role) on a compromise 'joint text' to be adopted by the co-legislators. Where agreement is reached, the Parliament and Council adopt the proposal in accordance with the joint text; if the co-legislators fail to agree, the proposal is deemed not to be adopted and the procedure ends. Voting majority requirements are specified for each stage of the procedure; once the first reading stage has passed, strict time limits apply.

In practice, the crisis era saw this complex and multistage procedure being eschewed in favour of the 'fast-track' process,[245] which is based on the conclusion of an agreement at the first reading stage[246] and which is becoming more widely used.[247] Under this procedure, before the European Parliament reaches a first reading, informal tripartite meetings attended by the Parliament, the Council, and the Commission (the 'trilogues') are held, on the basis of the Parliament's and Council's previously agreed negotiating texts.[248] During the trilogues, agreement is sought on the Parliament's amendments, such that they can be adopted in a plenary Parliament session and accepted by the Council. In practice, and as outlined in earlier Chapters, trilogue negotiations can be bruising and, over the crisis era, took place under severe time pressure, which continued to build until the final raft of measures was finally adopted on 15 April 2014 ('Super Tuesday') during the final plenary session of the Parliament's 2009–2014 term. The process tends to be dominated by the Parliament and requires that the Council negotiators revert continually to the Council to confirm any changes in negotiating positions.

---

[243] An absolute majority of the European Parliament is required.

[244] An absolute majority of the European Parliament is required.

[245] The fast-track procedure became technically possible after the Amsterdam Treaty revisions.

[246] The procedures governing the fast-track process are set out in the Joint Declaration on Practical Arrangements for the Codecision Procedure (2007) and in the 2008 Code of Conduct for negotiating co-decision files, set out in Annex XXI of European Parliament's Rules of Procedure.

[247] Over the 2004–9 Parliamentary term, 72 per cent of procedures were concluded at the first reading; the first half of the 2009–14 term saw 78 per cent of procedures concluded at the first reading. By contrast, 28 per cent were concluded over the 1999–2004 term: Codecision and Conciliation Guide, n 229, 14.

[248] Termed the General Approach, in the case of the Council text.

X.3.3 The Legislative Process and the Crisis-era Reform Agenda

X.3.3.1 Heightened Political (Intergovernmental) and Institutional (Supranational) Tensions

The legislative process was generally regarded as having worked reasonably effectively over the FSAP/Lamfalussy era, and as having benefited from the Lamfalussy process. On the eve of the financial crisis the process was relatively battle-hardened; it was familiar with complex regulatory dossiers, and had become accustomed to the conferral of administrative rule-making powers on the Commission, although the potential for institutional tension remained significant. Over the crisis era, however, the legislative process became the key battleground for contesting the nature and location (both with respect to the EU/Member State balance of power, and in relation to legislative and administrative rules) of securities and markets regulation in the post-crisis era.

At the intergovernmental level, the Council, reflecting high-level political support from the European Council which provided overarching direction to the crisis agenda,[249] but also the fiscal implications of the crisis, quickly became embroiled in the identification and implementation of policy priorities, although it was relatively slow to develop a reform agenda. A broad-brush Council reform roadmap was adopted in October 2007,[250] along with rather vague principles for cross-border crisis management which would be of little use in autumn 2008.[251] The Council then focused on the Lamfalussy Review[252] and would not closely engage with regulatory reform until October 2008,[253] although it can be credited with some degree of prescience in mandating the Economic and Financial Committee (EFC),[254] at its June 2008 meeting, to simulate a pan-EU crisis in spring 2009.[255] Once the regulatory reform agenda got underway, the Council took a markedly more engaged

---

[249] The June 2010 European Council, eg, called for the necessary reforms to restore soundness and stability to the EU financial system to be completed urgently, and called on the Council and European Parliament to rapidly adopt the relevant legislative proposals: Presidency Conclusions, para 14. Earlier, the October 2008 European Council, which took place in the teeth of the crisis, affirmed that the Council would take co-ordinated and thorough action to restore the smooth running of the financial system, and supported the range of regulatory reforms being proposed: Presidency Conclusions, paras 1 and 8–9.

[250] The roadmap addressed market transparency (particularly with respect to securitizations and off-balance sheet items); valuation standards (particularly with respect to illiquid assets); the prudential framework (including the treatment of large exposures, capital requirements for securitizations, and liquidity risk management); and structural market issues, including the role of rating agencies and the 'originate to distribute' model: 2822nd Council Meeting, 7 October 2007, ECOFIN Press Release No 13571/07.

[251] Including that public money not be taken for granted, that direct budgetary costs be shared among affected Member States, that collective costs be minimized, and that national authorities take into account financial stability considerations in other Member States.

[252] 2836th Council Meeting, 4 December 2007, ECOFIN Press Release No 15698/07, adopting Conclusions on the 2007 Review and 2872nd Council Meeting, 14 May 2008, ECOFIN Press Release No 8850/08, reviewing progress on the recommendation of the 2007 Review.

[253] 2894th Council Meeting, 7 October 2008, ECOFIN Press Release No 13784/08. This meeting focused on the immediate response of the EU and the Member States to the financial crisis, and on the EU's commitment to supporting the stability of the banking system. ECOFIN also supported the Commission's proposals to reform the deposit guarantee and capital adequacy regimes.

[254] See n 63 on the EFC and see further Quaglia, n 230, 27–8.

[255] 2872nd Council Meeting, 3 June 2008, ECOFIN Press Release No 10014/08.

approach to securities and markets regulation than it had over the FSAP period.[256] Taken as a whole, crisis-era Council negotiations are notable for the close attention given to the minutiae of regulatory reform and for the repeated rounds of Council compromise positions prior to the adoption of final negotiating positions for European Parliament and Commission trilogue negotiations; for frequent agenda-setting requests to the Commission to consider issues for potential action;[257] and for the repeated exhortations to the Commission and Parliament to achieve progress speedily. Completion of particular dossiers became strongly associated with the six-monthly rotating Council Presidencies, which generated significant pressure for agreement to be reached within the time frames of particular Presidencies; financial regulation was typically identified as a priority by the different Presidencies over the crisis era (broadly 2008–13).

The nature of the Council's engagement with the reform programme reflects, of course, the significant national interests at stake as the shape of the EU financial market was redrawn and as the location of regulatory power moved to EU level, particular controversies on key dossiers, and particular Member State concerns. Long-standing divergences across the Member States relating to the optimum intensity of and appropriate regulation of financial markets, reflecting deeply rooted economic models,[258] led to fiercely contested battles on key elements of the reform programme.[259] As documented in earlier Chapters, alliances shifted as national interests changed on different dossiers and it is not possible to identify consistent positions across and between Member States. Overall, however, the crisis-era programme can be associated with the ascendancy of the market-sceptical coalition of Member States.[260] The Council's closer engagement also reflected a new dynamic in the form of the internationalization of the EU's regulatory agenda. The EU's concern to shape the international regulatory agenda, supranational EU and intergovernmental Member State incentives to use the G20 agenda to achieve particular ends, and, on a procedural level, the greater engagement by the committees which support the ECOFIN Council (notably the Financial Services Committee (FSC)) on G20 matters,[261] all intensified the Council's focus on the minutiae of regulatory reform.

At the supranational level, the Commission—traditionally a dominant actor in the setting of policy priorities, particularly over the FSAP era[262]—was initially rather sanguine about the scale of the crisis, suggesting in spring 2008 that 'financial markets are well regulated in the EU' and that 'long before the current turmoil' the EU had supported financial stability through a range of measures.[263] By autumn 2008, however, the Commission was calling for

---

[256] Even allowing for the spats which key FSAP measures generated (notably the MiFID I order execution provisions), FSAP Council negotiations did not probe the intensity and nature of financial market regulation to the extent they did over the crisis era.

[257] eg 2922th Council Meeting, 10 February 2009, ECOFIN Press Release No 6069/09, requesting the Commission to examine short selling and signaling ECOFIN's support for CESR's actions in this area.

[258] On the impact of political economy on financial regulation in the EU see Ch I.

[259] For an extensive assessment see Ferran, E, 'Crisis-driven Regulatory Reform: Where in the World is the EU Going' in Ferran et al, n 5, 1.

[260] The political science literature has termed this group the 'market shaping' States: see Ch I.

[261] The FSC is composed of representatives from the Commission and the Member States, and is designed to provide the Council (ECOFIN) with high-level strategic input, distinct from the legislative process.

[262] Quaglia, n 230, 134–5.

[263] Commission, Europe's Financial System: Adapting to Change (2008) (COM (2008) 122) 3.

the EU's regulatory model to be redefined,[264] and in March 2009 it called for ambitious reform of the EU financial system.[265] It is too easy to associate the Commission's enthusiastic support for reform with regulatory opportunism, particularly as the reform agenda reflects myriad forces, not least among them Council and the European Council priorities, technical input from the 3L3 committees, and the international agenda. Nonetheless, the Commission was a prime mover in intensifying the EU rulebook. With respect to rating agency regulation, for example, the battle for international regulatory share, as well as strong Member State political interests,[266] influenced the Commission's dramatic about-turn from supporting a soft code of conduct to proposing a hard regulation.[267] But it is not unreasonable to assume that the Commission was also concerned to stamp its authority on the developing EU reform agenda by means of what was a relatively straightforward and confined measure. It is difficult, however, to discern the Commission's vision for securities and markets regulation, although Commission rhetoric remained uncompromising over the reform programme, particularly following the appointment of Commissioner Barnier in 2009. In relation to certain dossiers, a clear Commission interest can be discerned. It had a strong institutional interest in the new ESAs, for example, and incentives to protect its institutional position, and its imprints are clear on the new structures. But on substantive dossiers, and as documented in earlier Chapters, it is more difficult to identify a consistent Commission position. Blunt characterizations of the Commission as pro- or anti-market certainly cannot be easily made; while the Commission's original proposal for the 2011 Alternative Investment Fund Managers Directive (AIFMD)[268] was, particularly with respect to leverage controls, watered down during the Council/Parliament negotiations, its proposal for the 2012 Short Selling Regulation, by excluding the credit default swaps which the Parliament would subsequently insert, was lighter than the text as finally adopted. What is clear, however, is the extent to which the Council and Parliament (often radically) reshaped Commission proposals.

Also at supranational level, the emergence of the European Parliament as a force to be reckoned with[269] is perhaps the most striking feature of the crisis-era legislative process. The Parliament, which had previously acquired some considerable technical expertise over the FSAP period, quickly—and perhaps reflecting the increase in its powers with the adoption of the Lisbon Treaty[270]—became something of a standard-bearer for reform[271]

---

[264] Commission, From Financial Crisis to Recovery: A European Framework for Action (2008) (COM (2008) 706) 4.

[265] Commission, Driving European Recovery (2009) (COM (2009) 114) 5.

[266] eg the 6 September 2007 statements by French and German premiers Sarkozy and Merkel which called for greater clarity concerning the role of rating agencies: Greater Transparency on the Financial Markets, Press and Information Office of the Federal Government, 6 September 2007. The October 2007 ECOFIN Council included examination of rating agencies in its roadmap (2822nd Council Meeting, 7 October 2007, ECOFIN Press Release No 13571/07).

[267] See Ch VII.

[268] n 218.

[269] Chaffin, J and Spiegel, P, 'MEPs Turn New Clout at Fiscal Reform', *Financial Times*, 27 October 2010, 12. The FSAP era had previously seen the Parliament emerge as an influential force, typically in favour of intervention: Quaglia, n 230, 136.

[270] Piris, JP, *The Lisbon Treaty. A Legal and Political Analysis* (1 edn, 2010) 118–19 and 235–6.

[271] The July 2010 Parliament Negotiating Position on the ESMA Regulation, eg, included a somewhat self-serving recital (1a) stating that 'long before the financial crisis', the Parliament had been regularly calling for the reinforcement of a true level playing field, while pointing out 'significant failures' in the EU supervisory regime.

and was generally supportive of the G20 reform agenda.[272] In October 2008, for example, it was quick to adopt a reform agenda which, while very similar to the other institutional and international templates, nonetheless underlined its concern to shape the reform process.[273] As discussed in earlier Chapters, it was an assertive actor over the legislative process and proved particularly dominant in the critical trilogue negotiations, which it has tended to lead.[274] As the reform programme entered its final stages, it called for faster progress and for stagnant proposals to be progressed and for enhancements to the rule-making process.[275] It is not unfair to associate the Parliament with the crisis-era intensification of regulation, some overheated reaction to financial market turbulence, and a sceptical perspective on financial market intensity, as well as with a strong preference for supranational EU-level solutions. But it also achieved important accommodations and refinements to key measures—most notably, perhaps, with the 2012 European Market Infrastructure Regulation (EMIR),[276] where it championed the cause of protecting non-financial firms from EMIR's costly requirements,[277] and with the 2011 AIFMD, in relation to which it has been associated with brokering a compromise on the highly contested third country access regime.[278] The Parliament, like the Council, struggled, however, to adopt coherent positions. The crisis era saw greater engagement by the Parliament's disparate political groupings with securities and markets regulation, often sharp clashes between different parties, and the production of frequently unreasonable and impractical numbers of amendments to key dossiers.[279]

X.3.3.2 Procedural Innovation: Fast-tracking Legislation

The crisis-era reform programme was adopted under conditions of extreme time pressure, reflecting a host of factors, not least among them the pressure of the G20 reform agenda and the need to stabilize the EU financial system.[280] Major measures were adopted in unprecedentedly quick time frames. The 2010 ESA reform, for example, was proposed in September 2009 and agreed in September 2010, the 2011 AIFMD proposed in April 2009 and agreed in November 2010, and the 2012 EMIR proposed in September 2011 and agreed in March 2012. This was achieved through heavy reliance on the accelerated/fast-track ordinary legislative procedure, based on one reading by the European Parliament.

---

[272] It adopted supportive resolutions on, eg, the pivotal G20 Pittsburgh and London Summits: 8 October 2009 P7-TA(2009)28 and 24 April 2009 (P6-TA(2009)330).

[273] Resolution with Recommendations to the Commission on Lamfalussy follow-up: future structure of supervision, 9 October 2008 (A6-0359/2008) Annex.

[274] Although the Parliament's addition of the controversial 'bonus cap' to CRD IV (Directive 2013/36/EU [2013] OJ L176/338) received particularly close attention (eg Editorial, 'Bonus Cap is a Bad Omen for Britain', *Financial Times*, 19 February 2013, 10), it was closely engaged on all aspects of the crisis-era reform programme.

[275] European Parliament Resolution on Financial Services: Lack of Progress in the Council and Commission's Delay in the Adoption of Certain Proposals, 13 June 2013 (P7_TA2013)0276) and ECON, Enhancing the Coherence of EU Financial Services Legislation (2014).

[276] n 218.

[277] See further Ch VI.

[278] See further Ch III.

[279] Over 1,300 amendments were originally proposed to the 2011 MiFID II/MiFIR proposals prior to the adoption of the Parliament's negotiating position.

[280] eg 3015th Council Meeting, 18 May 2010, ECOFIN Press Release No 9804/10 and Conclusions of the Brussels European Council, 18/19 June 2009, calling for progress on a range of legislative proposals.

Although the fast-track procedure was recommended by the 2001 Lamfalussy Report and the related 2001 Stockholm European Council,[281] it was not a feature of the FSAP, save for the adoption of the 2002 IAS Regulation (which was relatively uncontroversial)[282] and the 2004 Transparency Directive (which was adopted under severe time pressure given the pending dissolution of the Commission and Parliament). Despite the concerns raised over the FSAP period that fast-tracking might prove impractical and controversial,[283] and the Commission's post-FSAP concern that it be limited to measures with strong institutional backing,[284] it became the default law-making procedure over the crisis era.[285] All crisis-era securities and markets proposals, with the exception of the Investor Compensation Schemes Directive Proposal,[286] were adopted under the fast-track procedure.

In its favour, the fast-track procedure, which has been identified as an inevitable consequence of the expansion of the areas subject to the ordinary legislative procedure under the Lisbon Treaty,[287] demands close and intense co-operation between the Commission, Council and European Parliament during the 'trilogue' which follows the adoption by the Council and Parliament of their negotiating positions,[288] and generates a concentrated focus which has the potential to enhance the quality of legislation. A speedy legislative process also has the potential to minimize the extent to which highly organized market interests can stymie political choices as to the nature of regulation. On the other hand, the multistaged ordinary legislative procedure has the potential to brake the legislative process, inject challenge, and provide some protection against the hasty adoption of flawed regulation, particularly with respect to highly complex and largely untested measures. While the impact of the crisis-era programme remains to be seen, it is already clear that the coherence weaknesses which have always troubled EU securities and markets regulation may be increasing, as experience with the core definition of 'derivatives' suggests (Chapter IV section 4.3); time-pressured and simultaneous but not linked negotiations on closely-related measures are unlikely to have supported coherence.

The impact of fast-tracking and trilogue dynamics on the quality of legislation cannot easily be disentangled from the myriad factors which have shaped the post-crisis securities and markets EU rulebook. It did have the effect of concentrating institutional positions, and of forcing compromises on key issues. It also, however, injected very significant opacity into the rule-making process, excluded all but the most connected of lobbyists and interested parties (typically industry interests), and has generated some discomfort in the European Parliament,[289] although in practice the Parliament typically leads trilogue discussion in the

---

281 n 47, para 3.

282 Regulation (EU) No 1606/2002 [2002] OJ L243/1.

283 May 2003 IIMG Report, n 63, 8 and 26.

284 2005 FSAP Report, n 61, 25.

285 The 2008 Code of Conduct which governs the fast-track procedure provides that it is to be used on a case-by-case basis, taking into account the distinctive features of each individual file and must be politically justified with respect to, eg, political priorities, the file's uncontroversial or technical nature, urgent situations, or the attitude of a particular Presidency to a particular file: n 246, para 2.

286 See Ch IX sect 8.

287 Piris, n 270, 118.

288 On the dynamics of the trilogue see, eg, Häge, F and Kaeding, M, 'Reconsidering the European Parliament's Legislative Influence: Formal vs Informal Procedures' (2007) 29 *J of European Integration* 341.

289 The European Parliament's official position is lukewarm on the fast-track process. It has noted that while the process illustrates the greater degree of trust and willingness to cooperate between the institutions,

securities and markets regulation sphere, working closely with Committee of Permanent Representatives (COREPER). Trilogue discussions are not, however, transparent; by sharp contrast with the earlier Parliament and Council discussions, negotiating drafts and progress reports are not made public. It is difficult, accordingly, to pinpoint the location of influence at a critical stage in the legislative process.

X.3.3.3 Impact Assessment and Consultation

Immediately prior to the financial crisis, consultation processes and impact assessment protocols had been enhanced, at least at Commission level. But although the crisis-era institutional consensus on intervention, combined with the acceleration of the law-making process, increased the importance of challenging impact assessment and consultation, the performance of the legislative process in this regard over the crisis was mixed.

Extensive Commission impact assessments were, with one exception,[290] carried out on the crisis-era measures. Impact assessment disciplines now seem securely embedded within the Commission; review by the Commission's Impact Assessment Board has also led to material changes to the quality of impact assessments.[291] Early stage reviews by CESR and subsequently ESMA have also supported Commission impact assessments.[292] But, as discussed in earlier Chapters, and reflecting the intense politicization of particular dossiers, is less clear that impact assessments are always appropriately evidence-based. Of greater concern, however, is the failure to engage in impact assessment once the legislative process is underway, given the radical revisions which many measures sustain over the process.

While the extensive reports by ECON rapporteurs provide some background on the rationale for European Parliament revisions, these revisions are not subject to impact assessment.[293] Some empirical basis for Parliament revisions can be located in the extensive hearings and workshops which it held over the crisis era.[294] But impact assessment remains a major weakness in the Parliament's engagement. To take one example, as discussed in Chapter IX section 6, Parliament discussions on the 2012 Commission proposal for a new disclosure regime for packaged retail investment products led to the proposal, which had

---

'concerns have been expressed . . . about the potential lack of transparency inherent in the informal first and second reading negotiations, the lack of democratic legitimacy and clarity concerning appropriate procedural steps and not least about the institutional gains for the European Parliament': Codecision and Conciliation Guide, n 229, 14.

[290] The 2008 Deposit Guarantee Directive Proposal was not subject to impact assessment, given the crisis conditions under which it was adopted: MEMO/08/622.

[291] The Board's Report on the UCITS V Impact Assessment, eg, called for better substantiation of the scope and scale of the problem addressed and for closer examination of the costs of the Proposal (Report on the UCITS V Proposal, Ref.Ares(2012)249941). The Board's Report on the European Venture Capital Regulation similarly called for a significant strengthening of the Impact Assessment, including with respect to the nature of impediments to SME fundraising (Report on the European Venture Capital Proposal, Ref.Ares (2011)1127519.

[292] As was the case with the 2014 MiFID II/MiFIR reforms (Markets in Financial Instruments Directive 2014/65/EU OJ [2014] L173/349 (2014 MiFID II) and Markets in Financial Instruments Regulation (EU) No 2014/ 600 OJ [2014] L173/84 (2014 MiFIR) (on the implementation timeline see Ch IV n 28).

[293] eg while the ECON Gauzès Report (PE430.709) on the 2009 AIFMD Proposal made a large number of material revisions, the Report did not engage in impact assessment.

[294] eg ECON Committee Report, Derivatives, Central Counterparties and Trade Repositories. February 2011 (IP/A/ECON/NT/2010-14) and ECON Committee Report, Rating Agencies—Role and Influence of their Sovereign Credit Risk Assessment in the Euro Area. December 2011 (IP/A/ECON/NT/2010-04).

emerged from an extensive fact-finding process undertaken by the Commission between 2007 and 2011, being radically recast, but without empirical assessment. Similarly, Council revisions—which often reflect specific and special national interests, as well as political compromises on more wide-reaching issues—are not subject to impact assessment. For example, the unusually detailed legislative rules which now govern the transparency of trading under the 2014 MiFID II/MiFIR[295] and which, at the behest of the Council, address such detailed and arcane matters as 'volume caps' for 'dark' equity trading, have not been subject to any impact assessment.

In mitigation, reflecting the FSAP era, all crisis-era measures have been subject to detailed review clauses[296] and in many cases require the Commission and ESMA to report on different aspects of key measures. ESMA has also significantly enhanced the capacity of the EU to engage in quantitative impact assessment of legislation, as its 2013 review of the Short Selling Regulation suggests (Chapter VI section 13). Correction and the refreshing of legislation have accordingly been built into the crisis-era reforms. But EU securities and markets regulation has to date struggled with the removal of measures; review tends to lead to an encrustation of additional rules. And while *ex-post* quantitative analysis has been strengthened through ESMA, *ex-ante* assessment of legislative measures remains patchy.

Similarly, the experience with consultations has been mixed. Initial pre-proposal consultation periods were often short; the initial June 2010 short selling consultation, for example, lasted for under four weeks, as did the initial June 2010 consultation on what would become the 2012 EMIR. The initial December 2008 consultation on what would become the 2011 AIFMD lasted four weeks, as did the initial July 2008 consultation on rating agencies. Account must, however, be taken of the Commission's engagement with different advisory bodies; the Commission regularly drew on, for example, technical advice from the European Securities and Markets Expert Group (ESME),[297] from specialist industry groups,[298] and arising from CESR's initiatives in related areas.[299] Depending on the nature of the dossier, the Commission also consulted with the ECB and CEBS, particularly where market stability issues arose.[300] The Commission also typically engaged in extensive pre-proposal consultations and with different groups of stakeholders.[301] Technical expertise was

---

[295] See further Ch V sect 11.

[296] Review clauses are a long-standing element of EU securities and markets regulation and respond to the compromises and opacities which are typically generated during the inter-institutional law-making process, as well as to the obsolescence risks to which legislation is vulnerable.

[297] ESME was established as an advisory group to the Commission in 2006. Its mandate expired at the end of 2009 and was not renewed. Over its operation it produced a number of reports on EU securities and markets regulation and over the crisis era addressed, *inter alia*, short selling and rating agencies.

[298] Notably the Derivatives Working Group, which was established to advise on OTC derivative market clearing and EMIR.

[299] eg CESR carried out an earlier consultation on short selling, which lasted for almost three months (CESR/09-581).

[300] This was particularly the case in relation to the 2012 EMIR.

[301] The pre-proposal consultations on the 2012 EMIR, eg, stated: 'Since October 2008 the Commission has been engaged in almost continuous, extensive consultation with representatives from the great majority of stakeholders. The interaction has taken the form of bilateral and multilateral meetings, two written public consultations and a public conference. Through this process the Commission has obtained a wealth of information about the functioning of the derivatives market and its various segments, as well as views on the issues to be solved and how to solve them': 2010 EMIR Proposal Impact Assessment (SEC (2010) 1058/2). The Commission's consultation activities included engagement with the industry-based Derivatives Working Group,

therefore available to the Commission, as can be read in its decision not to extend ESME's mandate; ESMA is now the primary source of technical market expertise for the Commission. The Commission has also reconfigured the European Securities Committee and formed a related subgroup, the Expert Group of the European Securities Committee; while its primary role is to advise the Commission with respect to the adoption of administrative rules, it provides an additional technical capacity for the Commission.

But the consultation process was less effective in responding to the accountability function associated with consultation. The cacophony of market protest which many of the key measures generated, and the muscular lobbying efforts of major industry groupings, underline the extent to which industry engaged with the legislative process. As discussed in Chapter IX section 9, the household constituency, as in the pre-crisis era, remained largely marginalized.

X.4 Administrative Rule-making

X.4.1 Administrative Rule-making, Securities and Markets Regulation, and the EU

Reliance on technocratic bodies (agencies) conferred with delegated powers in order to deliver the expert administrative functions required by the modern State has long been a central feature of modern regulatory governance. Administrative agencies should bring efficiencies in the form of, for example, technical expertise, freedom from bias, an ability to reduce information asymmetries, distance from the political process, and a longer-term perspective—as well as political benefits in the form of their capacity to shift blame for unpopular decisions from the political to the administrative level.[302] In order to achieve an appropriate balance between the dictates of administrative efficiency ('output'-orientated governance) and the imperatives of legitimate, representative government ('input'-orientated governance), administrative agencies are typically designed to operate within carefully confined mandates which attach conditions to their discretionary powers, in order to support review and to constrain the taking of decisions with redistributive effects.[303]

The conferral of technical rule-making powers on administrative agencies of various hue is not new to financial market governance. The benefits which administrative agencies bring in terms of technical and expert capacity, nimbleness, their distance from the political process, and their ability to engage stakeholders is reflected in the rule-making mandates conferred on regulatory authorities worldwide.[304]

---

the Member States Working Group on Derivatives and Market Infrastructures, the ECB and CEBS, as well as with a range of international organizations, two public consultations in 2009 and 2010, and a conference in 2009: at 8–10.

[302] Griller, S and Orator, A, 'Everything Under Control? The "Way Forward" for European Agencies in the Footsteps of the Meroni Doctrine' (2010) *ELR* 3. An extensive political science literature examines the EU administrative space in terms of principal/agent theory and the incentives which the EU's institutions have to delegate functions to agencies. See, eg, Coen and Thatcher (2009) and (2008) n 8.

[303] eg Everson, n 10.

[304] For an analysis in the context of the new US Consumer Financial Protection Bureau see Barkow, E, 'Insulating Agencies: Avoiding Capture Through Institutional Design' (2010) 89 *Texas LR* 15.

In the EU, the regulatory demands of the single market have led to a massive expansion in the 'administrative state'[305] and to a material 'agencification' of EU governance;[306] a multiplicity of agencies now exercise quasi-rule-making powers to varying degrees. The establishment of ESMA in 2011 forms part of this trend. But under the EU Treaties, the Commission is the constitutional location for administrative rule-making (exercising powers delegated from the Council and European Parliament) (Articles 290 and 291 TFEU). However functionally desirable it may be from an 'output' perspective, agencies may not adopt administrative rules, given the prohibition which the need to respect the institutional balance established by the Treaties places on any 'sub-delegation' of discretionary rule-making power from the Commission to agencies.[307] These restrictions have had a decisive influence on how ESMA, as an EU agency, engages with administrative rule-making for EU financial markets (section 5).[308] In addition, as an administrative rule-maker, the Commission is subject to restrictions on the nature and extent of the rule-making power which can be delegated to it, and to related procedural requirements. These constraints are designed to protect the institutional balance established by the Treaties and, in particular, to locate the power to adopt legislative rules which have a normative colour and which engage wide discretionary choices in the democratically accountable Council and European Parliament (section 4.2).

Accordingly, administrative rule-making procedures for EU securities and markets regulation are designed to meet the efficiency and accountability requirements of administrative rule-making for financial markets generally. But these procedures are situated within a *sui generis* EU constitutional framework for administrative rule-making which is shaped by the need to respect the institutional balance established by the Treaties. The consequent location of administrative rule-making power in the Commission, however, can lead to an uneasy relationship between functional dictates and constitutional imperatives.

The *sui generis* nature of administrative rule-making in the EU also means that while the nature, extent, and appropriateness of administrative delegation for EU securities and markets regulation are contested, the grounds of contestation are often different to those which typically apply to administrative rule-making in this area. For example, the relative efficiency of principles (typically associated with law-making by political institutions) and

---

[305] As examined in Majone's seminal work: Majone, G, *Regulating Europe* (1996).

[306] The Commission's support of the agency model is most strongly associated with its 2000 White Paper on European Governance (COM (2001) 428). See Everson, n 10. The Lisbon Treaty recognized the position of agencies through Art 236 TFEU, which provides for the Court of Justice's review powers over agencies.

[307] Agencies can, however (reflecting Arts 263 and 277 TFEU which provide for the review by the Court of Justice of acts of general application adopted by agencies), adopt measures of general application having the force of law, as long as these acts respect the conditions which the *Meroni* ruling (Case 9/56 *Meroni v High Authority* [1957–1958] ECR 133, sects 5.2.1 and 5.5.1) imposes with respect to the exercise of discretion by agencies: Case C-270/12, n 221, paras 63–8.

[308] A massive literature examines EU agencies, including from governance, political science, and legal perspectives. For reviews of the main features of EU agencies, their risks and benefits, and the control mechanisms used to support accountability and legal resilience see, eg, Chiti, E, 'European Agencies' Rule-making: Powers, Procedures, and Assessment' (2013) 19 *ELJ* 93; Griller and Orator, n 302; Chiti, E, 'An Important Part of the EU's Institutional Machinery: Features, Problems and Perspectives of European Agencies' (2009) 46 *CMLR* 1395; Vibert, F, 'Better Regulation and the Role of EU Agencies' in Weatherill, S (ed), *Better Regulation* (2007) 387; Geradin and Petit, n 222; and Vos, E, 'Refoming the European Commission: What Role to Play for EU Agencies?' (2000) 37 *CMLR* 1113.

rules (usually adopted by agencies)[309] received close attention in the pre-crisis era, as principles-based intervention became associated with the then dominant 'new governance' approach to regulating financial markets. In the EU, this debate had much less traction. The location of securities and markets law-making in the EU has been less a function of choices as to the appropriate design of rules and more a function of the shifting balance of power between the EU and its Member States and between the EU institutions, and of the need to bring procedural efficiencies to the law-making process. The Lamfalussy process, which heralded the arrival of large-scale administrative rule-making, arose from concerns as to the ability of the cumbersome inter-institutional law-making process to deliver the FSAP, and took root given political support for greater EU control over securities and markets regulation. Similarly, the institutional refinements to administrative rule-making which occurred over the crisis, chief among them the establishment of ESMA, reflect the decisive shift of regulatory power from the Member States to the EU which occurred with the financial crisis.

The effectiveness, transparency, and accountability risks often associated with administrative rule-making for financial markets have, however, resonance in the EU. Administrative rule-making takes place through Treaty-based structures and processes primarily designed to accommodate institutional interests and Treaty constraints, and which have frequently been challenged.[310]

The following sub-sections examines the role of the Commission in administrative rule-making. The role of ESMA in administrative rule-making is considered in section 5.

X.4.2 The Commission and Administrative Rule-making

X.4.2.1 The Current Framework: Article 290 and 291 TFEU

Administrative rule-making has long been a feature of the EU law-making landscape, but its organization and its nature have been heavily contested. Delegation from the co-legislators to Commission administrative rule-making requires that limits are placed on the delegation to prevent the risk of any threats to the democratic process and to the EU institutional balance of powers. But while delegations of rule-making power are accordingly limited, they nonetheless generates significant inter-institutional tensions, given the related loss of power by the co-legislators and the gain by the Commission; they similarly generate Member State and market sensitivities, as administrative rule-making implies a shift in regulatory power from the Member States to the EU.[311] The process has accordingly been the subject of major revisions over time. Following a series of Treaty and legislative

---

[309] eg Cunningham, L, 'A Prescription to Retire the Rhetoric of "Principles-based Systems" in Corporate Law, Securities Regulation, and Accounting' (2007) 60 *Vanderbilt LR* 1411.

[310] From an extensive literature see, eg, the discussions in (2013) 19 *ELJ*; Curtin n 9; Majone, G, *Dilemmas of European Integration* (2005) 83–106; and Dehousse, R, 'Regulating by Networks in the European Community: the Role of European Agencies' (1997) 4 *JEPP* 246.

[311] Delegation has accordingly, across the EU administrative space generally, tended to be uneven, often reflecting the strength of national authorities, who often resist the establishment of EU agencies, in particular: Thatcher, M, 'The Creation of European Agencies and its Limits: a Comparative Analysis of European Delegation' (2011) 18 *JEPP* 790.

revisions, since March 2011, administrative rule-making is governed by Articles 290 and 291 TFEU and by Regulation 182/2011.[312]

Two forms of administrative rule-making are supported by the Treaties.

First, the Article 290/291 TFEU process (introduced by the Lisbon Treaty) permits a direct delegation of (Article 290) or conferral of (Article 291) rule-making power to or on the Commission. Article 290 provides for a delegation of rule-making power to the Commission by the co-legislators which empowers the Commission to adopt acts of general application which are of a legislative/normative nature; in effect, it discharges the co-legislators from amending or supplementing non-essential elements of legislative acts, the adoption of which is reserved to the co-legislators.[313] Article 290 provides that a legislative act may delegate to the Commission the power to adopt 'non-legislative acts of general application to supplement or amend certain non-essential elements of legislative act' (Article 290 (1)). Article 290 also specifies that the 'essential elements' of an act must be reserved to the legislative act and not be delegated. The nature (objectives, content, scope, and duration) of the delegation, and, by contrast with the earlier comitology-based regime, the oversight mechanism, must be specified in the relevant legislative measure which confers the delegation. Article 290(3) provides, however, that the relevant legislative acts are to explicitly lay down the conditions to which the delegation is subject and specifies that these conditions may be as follows: the European Parliament or the Council may revoke the delegation, and the delegated act may enter into force only if no objection has been expressed by the Parliament or Council within the period set by the legislative act. In each case, the Parliament acts by a majority of its members and the Council by a qualified majority. The Commission has, accordingly, significant freedom to operate.[314] In practice, ESMA is engaged in this process by providing technical advice, although this is not specified in Article 290.

Article 291, by contrast, addresses executive powers and related implementing rules. These powers are primarily located with the Member States, who are required to adopt all measures of national law to implement legally binding Union acts (Article 291(1)). But Article 291 provides that the Commission (and exceptionally the Council), where uniform conditions for implementing legally binding EU acts are needed, may be conferred, through a legislative act, with 'implementing' powers to adopt implementing rules of general application (or individual administrative decisions).[315] The line between 'delegated rules' and 'implementing' rules can be a fine one and the distinctive features of both rules have been sharply contested.[316] But arguably, the defining feature of an Article 290 rule is its legislative nature (although this is an elusive quality); Article 291 rules are executive in nature and designed to support implementation.

---

[312] Regulation (EU) No 182/2011 [2011] OJ L55/13. The new settlement for the delegation of rule-making powers to the Commission has been described as the most significant reform in a long line of changes, in terms of procedures, legal basis, and institutional balance: Hardacre, A and Kaeding, M, Delegated and Implementing Acts. The New Comitology, EIPA Essential Guide (2011) 1.

[313] As examined in the Opinion of Jääskinen AG in Case C-270/12, n 221.

[314] The Commission has emphasized its procedural autonomy under Arts 290 and 291: Mendes, n 31.

[315] Opinion of Jääskinen AG (Advocate General) in Case C-270/12, n 221.

[316] eg Mendes, n 31 and Craig, P, 'Delegated Acts, Implementing Act, and the New Comitology' (2011) 36 *ELJ* 671.

By contrast with the Article 290 TFEU procedure, the procedural framework for the adoption of Article 291 TFEU 'implementing' acts is set out in Regulation 182/2011, the adoption of which was envisaged in the Treaty (Article 291(3)). Regulation 182/2011 provides for two committee-based oversight procedures: the 'advisory' procedure, which cannot result in Commission action being blocked;[317] and the more intrusive 'examination' procedure.[318] Article 291 implementing measures in the securities and markets sphere are adopted under the examination procedure. Under this procedure, oversight is exercised by a committee composed of Member State representatives and chaired by the Commission (the European Securities Committee). Where the Committee delivers a positive opinion, the Commission adopts the implementing rule. Where the Committee delivers a negative opinion, the Commission cannot adopt the rule, but can either submit a revised rule to the committee (within 2 months) or submit the original rule to an appeal committee for further deliberation (within a month).[319] Where the appeal committee (composed of Member State representatives and chaired by the Commission) delivers a positive opinion or does not deliver an opinion, the rule is adopted by the Commission. Where the committee delivers a negative opinion, the Commission's rule is vetoed, although the rule may still be adopted in exceptional circumstances.[320] In practice, ESMA is also engaged in this process by providing technical advice, although this is not specified in Article 291.

A second, related form of administrative rule-making applies in the securities and markets sphere. Delegated rule-making can also take the form of the adoption by the Commission of BTSs. Under this distinct process, which is based on Article 290/291 TFEU, the delegation/conferral to the Commission is more indirect (although the Commission remains the constitutional delegate) and ESMA is heavily engaged. ESMA proposes the relevant administrative rules which are subsequently adopted by the Commission, and the distinct procedures set out in the ESMA Regulation apply. The BTS process is discussed in section 5.

X.4.2.2 Applying the Model

The Article 290/291 TFEU framework has been deployed in the securities and markets sphere through a series of legislative measures.

The 2010 Omnibus I Directive[321] aligned the major FSAP-era legislative measures to Articles 290 and 291 TFEU. It revised these measures to characterize the pre-existing, FSAP-era powers conferred on the Commission to adopt 'implementing rules' as powers to adopt Article 290 'delegated rules.'[322] Common oversight procedures were also added to reflect Article 290. Three forms of control accordingly apply under these measures. First,

---

[317] Under the advisory procedure (Art 4), the relevant committee adopts an opinion on the implementing rules proposed by the Commission. The Commission decides on the act to be adopted 'taking utmost account of the conclusions drawn from the discussions within the committee and of the opinion delivered', but is not required to follow the committee's opinion.

[318] Regulation 182/2011 Art 5.

[319] The same procedure applies where the committee does not deliver an opinion: Art 5(4).

[320] Set out in Art 7, which provides for the adoption of implementing acts by the Commission in limited and specified circumstances related to significant disruption of agricultural markets or to the financial interests of the EU in relation to combating fraud.

[321] Directive 2010/78/EU [2010] OJ L331/120.

[322] The reforms related to the Prospectus Directive, however, were carried out by the 2010 Amending Prospectus Directive.

and by contrast with the 2006 comitology settlement which removed such clauses, time limits (or sunset clauses) govern the delegations in question.[323] Second, a veto power applies. When the Commission adopts a delegated act under these measures it must notify the act simultaneously to the European Parliament and Council, who then have three months within which to object to the act. The three-month period can be extended by a further three months; if either institution objects, the act cannot be adopted. Third, the Council or Parliament can revoke the delegation(s) at any time.[324]

The new generation of measures adopted since the crisis have also followed this model, albeit with greater nuance. As noted in earlier Chapters, the initial series of crisis-era measures relied heavily on Article 290 TFEU delegated rules, often in highly sensitive areas, to build the new EU rulebook. The complexity of the reform programme, the untested nature of many of the legislative choices and the related dearth of empirical evidence, and the need for extensive calibration and finessing of legislative choices to different market segments made extensive delegations to administrative rule-making inevitable. Familiarity with the Lamfalussy process, and acceptance of the technical capacity which ESMA provided by means of its technical advice to the Commission, along with recognition of the need for a channel which could engage with the extensive international standard-setting agenda, can also be associated with the relative comfort which the legislative process displayed with the extent of the Article 290 delegations.[325]

The 2011 AIFMD, for example, contains very extensive conferrals of power to the Commission to adopt delegated rules, which led to the massive 2013 Commission AIFMD Regulation.[326] The exercise of the AIFMD Article 290 TFEU delegations is subject to AIFMD Articles 56–58, which follow the 2010 Omnibus I Directive model by employing sunset clauses, the Council/European Parliament revocation power, and the Council/Parliament veto power as Commission oversight mechanisms. The AIFMD additionally requires the Parliament and Council to provide reasons for their objection to a delegated act (Article 58(3)). The 2012 Short Selling Regulation, which also contains extensive Article 290 delegations which have led to the 2012 Commission Delegated Short Selling Regulation,[327] is very similar to the AIFMD with respect to Commission oversight (Article 42), although it does not impose sunset clauses on the different Article 290 delegations or require the Council/Parliament to provide reasons when objecting to a delegated act. The 2012 EMIR,[328] by contrast, contains only limited direct delegations of power to the Commission to adopt Article 290 delegated rules[329] and instead relies

---

[323] Typically four years from December 2010 or January 2011.

[324] eg the 2010 Omnibus I Directive revisions to Art 27 of the 2004 Transparency Directive, and the additions of new Arts 24a, b, and c to the 2003 Prospectus Directive.

[325] The Commission's rationales for proposed delegations, however, were, typically, very economical and based on assertions (eg 2009 AIFMD Proposal (COM (2009) 507) 8; 2010 EMIR Proposal (COM (2010) 484) 11–12; and 2010 Short Selling Regulation Proposal (COM (2010) 482) 10). During negotiations, the European Parliament typically extended the Commission's power to adopt administrative rules, albeit that it typically also specified in more detail the mandate for administrative rule-making.

[326] n 218 and Commission Delegated Regulation (EU) No 231/2013 [2013] OJ L83/1.

[327] n 218 and Commission Delegated Regulation (EU) No 918/2012 [2012] OJ L274/1. RTSs and ITSs have also been adopted.

[328] n 218.

[329] The Art 290 TFEU delegation applies in relation to ESMA's power to impose fines on trade repositories, and relates to the calculation of penalties (2012 EMIR Art 64(7) and Art 70).

heavily on ESMA-proposed BTSs. It follows the 2012 Short Selling Regulation's oversight model (Article 82), but with one major difference: it is the only measure to include an express reference to ESMA. Under Article 82(3), the Commission must endeavour to consult ESMA when adopting Article 290 delegated rules. The rating agency regime has similarly relied more heavily on RTSs and deploys direct delegations under Article 290 only in limited circumstances.[330]

The behemoth 2014 MiFID II/MiFIR regime relies heavily on extensive direct Commission delegations under Article 290 TFEU, although the negotiations saw ESMA's influence increase with a large number of delegations transferred to the BTS process, particularly with respect to highly technical (but substantively significant) matters in relation to trading venue regulation under MiFIR (section 5.5). The MiFID II/MiFIR oversight regime for Article 290 rules does not employ the sunset clause oversight device (delegations are granted for an indeterminate period of time), but delegations can be revoked at any time by the Council or European Parliament, who can also exercise veto powers.[331] By contrast with EMIR, MiFID II/MiFIR does not require that the Commission endeavour to consult ESMA.

Article 291 TFEU has not had a significant influence on EU securities and markets regulation to date. To the extent administrative implementing measures are used, they primarily take the form of ITSs proposed by ESMA and endorsed by the Commission, and in relation to which European Securities Committee oversight does not apply and a light-touch governance procedure applies under the ESMA Regulation.[332] Its use so far has been mainly confined to the adoption of equivalence decisions by the Commission.[333] Where Article 291 has been relied on, the relevant legislative measure conferring the power has provided for the Regulation 182/2011 examination procedure and for the European Securities Committee to act as the relevant oversight committee.[334]

X.4.2.3 Early Lessons?

Early experience with the Article 290/291 TFEU process suggests that strong legacy effects can be identified from the Lamfalussy/FSAP era, although the new process has also benefited from experience over that era.

The nature of administrative rule-making, and the distinction between legislative rules and Article 290 TFEU administrative rules in particular, remains unclear. Although the formula typically adopted across crisis-era legislative acts is that the Article 290 rules 'specify' identified aspects of the legislative rule, the delegations are typically drafted in very broad terms, and it is not easy to draw a distinction, in terms of substantive import and impact, normative quality, and political sensitivity, between many of the legislative rules and the related Article 290 administrative rules. For example, while the threshold at which short sales in shares must be reported is specified in the legislative 2012 Short Selling Regulation,

---

[330] Related to ESMA's fining powers in relation to rating agencies, and the imposition of fees.

[331] 2014 MiFID II Art 89 and 2014 MiFIR Art 50. The veto period extends for three months following the Commission's adoption of the measure.

[332] I am grateful to Professor Pierre-Henri Conac for discussions on this point.

[333] eg 2012 Short Selling Regulation Art 17(2); 2012 EMIR Arts 13(2), 25(6) and 75(1); 2011 AIFMD Art 37(14) and (15); and 2014 MiFIR Arts 24(18) and 25(8).

[334] eg 2011 AIFMD Art 59, 2012 Short Selling Regulation Art 44, and 2012 EMIR Art 86(2).

the threshold for reporting on sovereign debt and sovereign debt credit default swaps (CDSs) is specified in the administrative 2012 Commission Regulation. Both sets of thresholds, however, have major ramifications for market participants and it is difficult to distinguish the respective legislative/non-legislative quality of each; the governing factor seems to be the empirical reality that setting the threshold in relation to sovereign debt and sovereign debt CDSs was technically complex, particularly given the lack of empirical data.[335] Elsewhere, the 2011 AIFMD provides significant detail at the legislative level on the depositary regime.[336] But substantively, it is not clear why much of the technical detail (which might be regarded as 'non-essential') was not addressed through Article 290 delegated rules. Politically, however, the depositary regime was one of the most contested elements of the AIFMD. As under the FSAP era, expediency and political realities seem to be the primary driver for the choice of legislative or Article 290 rule.

The Article 290 TFEU process has, however, benefited from the impact assessment and consultation protocols developed for administrative rule-making over the FSAP era. The 2010 Amending Prospectus Directive Article 290 administrative rules, for example, which were adopted over 2012–13,[337] were subject to independent impact assessment by the Commission,[338] and were additionally subject to technical consultation and impact assessment during the ESMA technical advice stage (section 5.4). Similarly, the 2012 Short Selling Regulation Article 290 administrative rules were subject to Commission impact assessment,[339] in addition to an ESMA assessment, as were the 2011 AIFMD Article 290 rules.[340] Consultation processes are, however, relatively opaque. For the most part, the Commission seems to rely on consultation at the ESMA technical advice stage;[341] it can, however, engage in informal consultations with market stakeholders.[342]

Institutional relations remain, as over the pre-crisis era, generally good, but vulnerable to tensions. The main crisis-era legislative measures typically assert the importance of the Article 290 TFEU oversight procedures and of related relationships with the Council and European Parliament,[343] and the Commission appears careful to ensure that Article 290 delegated rules do not risk distorting legislative choices. Thus far at least, neither the Council nor Parliament have exercised their Article 290 veto or revocation powers, underlining the 'last resort' nature of these powers but also the degree of institutional trust in the Article 290 process. The Commission also regularly consults the European Securities Committee, thereby engaging with Member State interests.[344]

---

[335] See further Ch VI sect 3.

[336] 2011 AIFMD Art 21.

[337] Commission Delegated Regulations 486/2012 [2012] OJ L150/1; 862/2012 [2012] OJ L256/4; and 759/2013 [2013] OJ L213/1.

[338] SWD (2012) 77.

[339] SWD (2012) 198.

[340] SWD (2012) 386.

[341] Although crisis-era measures typically underline the importance of the Commission undertaking appropriate consultation during its preparatory work: eg, 2012 Short Selling Regulation rec 43.

[342] eg the impact assessment on the 2012–2013 Prospectus Directive delegated rules (SWD (2012) 77, 6) and on the 2012 Short Selling Regulation delegated rules (SWD (2012) 198, 4).

[343] eg 2012 Short Selling Regulation rec 43 and 2011 AIFMD rec 87.

[344] The European Securities Committee Minutes of its 76th Meeting on 15 November 2011, eg, record discussion on the 2011 AIFMD delegated rule-making process and the Commission's invitation for members to raise possible concerns on the proposed text at an early stage.

The pivotal Commission/ESMA relationship seems relatively stable. As discussed in section 5.4, the Commission always mandates ESMA to provide technical advice on delegated and implementing administrative rules. The transition from CESR to ESMA did not, at the outset at least, disturb the previously strong Commission/CESR dynamic. As noted in earlier Chapters, the Commission has, as a general rule, tended to accept ESMA's technical advice, reflecting the extensive consultation and assessment to which ESMA's technical advice is subject. The Commission's internal Impact Assessment Board has also required the Commission to explain the extent to which its administrative rules follow the ESMA technical advice, and to provide 'clear arguments' justifying any deviations.[345] European Securities Committee discussions also suggest some Member State concern to ensure that ESMA's technical advice is generally followed.[346]

But the Commission has overridden ESMA on occasion, thereby subverting the regulatory design choices which ESMA has made after expert technical assessment and consultation, and appears concerned to protect its hierarchical position with respect to administrative rule-making (see further sections 5.4 and 5.5 on ESMA/Commission relations). With respect to the prospectus regime, for example, the Commission, in the context of small and medium-sized enterprise (SME) disclosure, overruled strongly worded technical advice from ESMA that prospectus requirements for issuers admitted to regulated markets not be weakened.[347] The Commission's strong policy attachment to deregulation as a means of supporting the SME sector accordingly trumped ESMA's technical advice. The 2012 Short Selling Regulation administrative regime also saw the Commission reject ESMA's technical advice, albeit this time in relation to largely technical issues, most notably in relation to the injection of a quantitative approach into ESMA's entirely qualitative approach to the pivotal determination of when a sovereign CDS was 'covered' and thus free of many of the Regulation's restrictions.[348] Most controversy, however, attended the extensive revisions which the Commission made to ESMA's technical advice on the 2011 AIFMD administrative rules. As discussed in Chapter III section 4.5, while the Commission's action generated a market outcry, ESMA's reaction was sanguine[349]—reflecting, perhaps, the delicacy of the Commission/ESMA relationship and ESMA's concern not to disrupt the relationship at a relatively early stage. Since then, however, ESMA has become more assertive in its relationship with the Commission (section 5.5). Further pressure on the Commission may come from the 2013 ESFS review, which, as discussed in section 5.10 below, has seen calls for ESMA's technical advice to be protected and for the BTS process, in which ESMA's position is stronger, to be privileged.

---

[345] eg Impact Assessment Board Opinion on the Commission Delegated Short Selling Regulation (Ref. Ares(2012)529435). The Board required that 'given the special role that has been given to ESMA in the Short Selling Regulation the report should carefully present the agency's arguments and provide clear explanations for all instances in which the Commission proposes to deviate from ESMA's advice'. The Board also required that relevant elements of ESMA's advice be 'carefully quoted' and the most important sections attached as annexes.

[346] eg European Securities Committee Minutes, 15 November 2011 on the 2011 AIFMD administrative rule-making process.

[347] See further Ch II sect 4.4.3.

[348] Commission Delegated Regulation 918/2012 Impact Assessment (2012) (SWD (2012) 198) 29–31.

[349] At a Board of Supervisors meeting, ESMA Chair Maijoor noted that the differences between the Commission's and ESMA's position were not as substantial as implied by the media, and the Board discussion noted that ESMA and the Commission would diverge on issues, and that ESMA's advice would not always be followed, but that transparency was key: Board of Supervisors Meeting, 17 April 2012 (ESMA/2012/BS/66).

The Commission's dominance over Article 290 TFEU rule-making reflects the Treaty settlement on administrative rule-making and any call for radical change accordingly risks charges of naïveté. But the untrammelled ability of the Commission to revise and/or ignore technical advice which has been produced by a technically expert agency with robust consultation and impact assessment procedures, and after engagement, as appropriate, with international standard-setters, underlines the starkness of the conflict which can arise between functional 'output' effectiveness and constitutional 'input' resilience. Notwithstanding the crisis-era commitment to, and need for, a dense and technically sophisticated rule-book, rule-making governance for the EU financial market still lacks resilience. While the BTS process, in which ESMA's position is more secure, may come to dominate administrative rule-making, this process also lacks resilience, as is discussed in the following section.

X.5 ESMA and Administrative Rule-making

X.5.1 Introduction

With the 2011 establishment of ESMA,[350] administrative rule-making for EU financial markets has come a step closer to the regulatory agency model for financial market rule-making in common use internationally.

Although their supervisory powers have attracted most attention, the ESAs' powers in relation to quasi-rule-making and the single rulebook[351] were, from the outset, regarded by the ESAs themselves as representing a material and significant change to the 3L3 committee powers.[352] The experience of the 3L3 committees with standard-setting, the rule-making territory at stake, the potential for quickly strengthening their 'capacity' (or ability to pursue the outcomes sought),[353] the pace and depth of the crisis-era administrative rule-making agenda, and the constitutional, market, and political uncertainty which the new supervisory powers generated all made it likely that the ESAs would initially prioritize their quasi-rule-making powers.[354]

---

[350] On ESMA see, eg, Everson, n 10; Spendzharova, A, 'Is More "Brussels" the Solution? New European Union Member States' Preferences about the European Financial Architecture' (2012) 50 *JCMS* 315; Ferran E, 'Understanding the Shape of the New Institutional Architecture of EU Financial Market Supervision' in Ferrarini et al (n 4) 111; Wymeersch, E, 'Europe's New Financial Regulatory Bodies' (2011) 11 *JCLS* 42; Schammo, P, 'The European Securities and Markets Authority: Lifting the Veil on the Allocation of Powers' (2011) 48 *CMLR* 1911; Moloney, N, 'The European Securities and Markets Authority: A Tale of Two Competences. Part (1) Rule-Making' (2011) 12 *EBOLR* 41; and Wymeersch, E, 'The Reforms of the European Financial Supervisory System – An Overview' (2010) 7 *ECFLR* 240.

[351] For further discussion see Busuioc, M, 'Rule-making by the European Financial Supervisory Authorities: Walking a Tight Rope' (2013) 19 *ELJ* 111, Moloney, n 350, and Everson, n 10.

[352] On the reaching of inter-institutional agreement on the ESA package, the CEBS Chairman highlighted that one of EBA's priorities would be the development of technical standards which would apply directly to banks and bank supervisors, and that this innovation would contribute to the establishment of a common EU rulebook. The CESR Chairman similarly underlined that the powers given to the ESAs would greatly enhance their capacity to deliver a single rulebook for Europe: CESR, CEBS, and CEIOPS Press Release, 22 September 2010.

[353] The notion of regulatory capacity is now well-established as a means for examining the effectiveness of regulators. See, eg, Black, J, 'Enrolling Actors in Regulatory Processes: Examples from UK Financial Services Regulation' [2003] *Public Law* 62.

[354] EBA Chairman Enria, eg, underlined that 'the single rulebook is the true power': Masters, B and Jenkins, P, 'EU banks to get "single rulebook"', 14 February 2011, available at <http://www.FT.com>.

ESMA's first Annual Report illustrates the importance of the rulebook-related powers: ESMA highlighted its role in 'building a single rule book for EU financial markets' as a key element of its mission, and described itself as a 'standard setter in relation to securities legislation'.[355] Its second Annual Report also underlined the importance of its rulebook functions.[356] Similarly, in their first Joint Report on risks and vulnerabilities in the EU financial sector, the ESAs asserted in robust terms the fundamental importance of the single rulebook in reversing what they described as a harmful trend towards fragmentation in the single market, and highlighted their roles in the development of the rulebook.[357]

In practice, this ambition has been fulfilled. The 2013 review of the ESFS revealed strong stakeholder support for the ESAs' 'single rulebook' activities. ESMA (to take a representative example) was regarded as having demonstrated an efficient capacity to develop draft technical standards, recommendations and guidelines, and as having engaged in intensive and innovative regulatory activity.[358]

ESMA has been conferred with an array of quasi-rule-making functions. Article 8(1) of the ESMA Regulation specifies ESMA's tasks. While quasi-rule-making is inherent to many of the Article 8(1) tasks, it is closely engaged with the task of contributing to the establishment of high-quality common regulatory and supervisory standards and practices, in particular by providing opinions to the EU institutions and by developing guidelines, recommendations, and draft BTSs (Article 8(1)(a)); with the task of monitoring and assessing market developments and undertaking economic analysis of markets (Article 8(1)(f) and (g)); and with the task of fostering investor protection (Article 8(1)(h)). ESMA's related powers are specified in Article 8(2), which, with respect to quasi-rule-making, identifies the power to develop BTSs and to issue guidelines and recommendations under Article 16 (Article 8 (2)(a)–(c)).

These powers represent a material but incremental hardening of CESR's quasi-rule-making powers. Like CESR, ESMA cannot adopt rules independently. But a series of factors, discussed further below, have established it as a *de facto* standard-setter. These include: the formalization of its role in administrative rule-making, particularly with respect to BTSs; its demonstrated technical capacity in relation to the crisis-era administrative rulebook; its relatively robust procedural governance, particularly with respect to consultation and impact assessment; relatively consistent institutional support, although Commission relations can be unstable; and its engagement with the international standard-setting process. Additionally, and like CESR before it, ESMA, from the outset, has deployed the range of soft law tools at its disposal to shape the regulatory environment more generally and without the constraints posed by the administrative rule-making process.

---

[355] ESMA Annual Report (2011) 9 and 11.

[356] ESMA Annual Report (2012) 12 and 13, noting that ESMA achieves its aims with respect to investor protection and the promotion of stable and well-functioning financial markets by building a single rulebook, and 'serves as a standard-setter in relation to securities legislation', and again highlighting ESMA's 'role as a standard-setter'.

[357] ESMA, EBA, EIOPA, Joint Committee Report on Risks and Vulnerabilities in the EU Financial Sector, March 2013, 16.

[358] Mazars, Review of the New European System of Financial Supervision. Part 1: The Work of the European Supervisory Agencies. Study for the ECON Committee (2013) (IP/A/ECON/ST/2012-23) (2013 Mazars ESA Review) 119 and 123.

But ESMA has also inherited many of the difficulties which troubled the CESR era, notably with respect to the legitimacy and validity of its soft law activities, and is afflicted by distinct difficulties arising from its agency status. Above all, the Treaty constraints on administrative rule-making risk that its effectiveness is undermined and its independence is threatened. This is particularly the case with respect to the Commission's ability to reject ESMA's technical advice and proposed BTSs, which the 2013 review of the ESFS identified as potentially undermining ESMA's independence.[359]

X.5.2 ESMA Structure and Governance

X.5.2.1 Agency Design and *Meroni*

As an EU agency, ESMA's quasi-rule-making (and other) powers have been shaped by the pivotal 1958 *Meroni* ruling.[360] It provides, *inter alia*, that discretionary powers implying a wide margin of discretion (which may, according to the use made of them, make possible the execution of economy policy) cannot be delegated by an EU institution, given the risk of prejudice to institutional balance; only clearly defined executive powers, subject to strict review in light of objective criteria determined by the delegating authority, may be delegated.[361] While the 2014 Court of Justice ruling in the *Short Selling* case seems to suggest that agencies can adopt measures of general application where strict conditionality applies, it has also underlined that the exercise of delegated powers by agencies must respect the *Meroni* restriction and that discretionary powers implying a wide margin of discretion cannot be delegated.[362] The *Meroni* ruling and its related jurisprudence limits ESMA's rule-making capacity,[363] but it has also had a related and decisive influence on how ESMA is organized and controlled,[364] as it has on agency design generally.[365]

ESMA is an agency but is not designated as such; it is described as a 'Union body with legal personality' (ESMA Regulation Article 5). It shares a number of features with the traditional EU agency in that it has legal personality, has a degree of independence, is established under

---

[359] The 2013 Mazars ESA Review, eg, noted that 'the regulatory roles of the ESAs are fully dependent on successful co-operation with the European Commission' and stakeholder opinion that the ESAs were not independent from the Commission: n 358, 42 and 49.

[360] n 307. On *Meroni* and EU agencies generally see, eg, Chit (2013) and (2009), n 308.

[361] As specified in *Meroni*-related case law, including Case C-154/04 *R ex p Alliance for Natural Health v Secretary of State for Health and National Assembly Wales* [2005] ECR I-6451.

[362] n 221, ruling of the Court: eg, paras 45 and 66.

[363] The *Meroni* ruling applies to delegated powers; the ESAs' governance design and powers were based on the assumption that their powers, including quasi-rule-making powers, were situated in a delegated context. But whether or not ESA powers, including the power to adopt a measure of general application, are conferred or delegated can be unclear, particularly where the measure has executive/implementing features. In the *Short Selling* ruling, the Court of Justice characterized ESMA's executive powers in relation to short selling as conferred, but did not rule more generally on this question.

[364] The Commission has been highly sensitive to *Meroni* issues, as is clear from their prominence in the opinions of the Commission Impact Assessment Board (eg, the Board's opinion on the first Rating Agency Proposal, Ref.Ares 2010)108790 and has been concerned in particular to ensure that the ESAs are not delegated the power to 'take decisions which require difficult choices in reconciling various objectives laid down in the Treaty amounting to the execution of actual economic policy'. This formula recurs across the main policy discussions: eg, 2010 Rating Agency Proposal Impact Assessment (SEC (2010) 678) 13.

[365] eg Chamon, M, 'EU Agencies Between Meroni and Romano or the Devil and the Deep Blue Sea' (2011) 48 *CMLR* 1055; Curtin, n 9; and Geradin and Petit, n 222. Implementing/executive supervisory powers and *Meroni* are considered in Ch XI.

secondary EU law, and is designed to inject expert technical capacity into the rule-making process.[366] But its range of powers takes it far beyond the traditional agency.[367] In the rule-making sphere, EU agencies have hitherto exercised only limited powers with respect to rules of general application; the most advanced agencies have been characterized as 'pre-decision-making agencies with *de facto* decision-making powers' in that they can influence the Commission.[368] Typically, agencies advise the Commission on administrative rule-making and adopt soft law measures.[369] ESMA is qualitatively different. It has not been (and cannot be) conferred with the delegated power to adopt binding rules of general application and of normative effect, and thereby exercise powers delegated from the co-legislators which engage discretionary choices and which risk disturbing the current institutional balance established in the Treaties.[370] But the BTS proposal power, in particular, brings ESMA closer to the position of rule-maker than any other agency.[371] So does the 'comply or explain' mechanism and the related devices which 'harden' non-binding ESMA guidelines and recommendations adopted under ESMA Regulation Article 16.

Nonetheless, the *Meroni* constraint remains a real control on ESMA's operation and, together with the related devices used in EU agency design, has exerted a decisive influence on ESMA's governance and rule-making powers, limiting ESMA's freedom of operation and its *de facto* independence.[372]

X.5.2.2 ESMA's Status, Structure, and Governance, and the Independence Problem

In its initial January 2011 FAQ on its role, ESMA—which, like CESR, is based in Paris[373]—describes itself as 'an independent EU authority that contributes to safeguarding the stability of the European Union's financial system by ensuring the integrity, transparency, efficiency and orderly functioning of securities markets, as well as enhancing investor protection'.[374] Formally, however, the ESMA Regulation, which otherwise uses the term 'Authority', describes ESMA as an independent Union 'body' with legal personality (ESMA Regulation Article 5(1)). Although the term 'agency' has not been formally deployed, ESMA is a *de facto* agency, as has been recognized by ESMA itself.[375]

---

[366] On the features of EU agencies see the sources at n 308.

[367] The ESAs have been characterized as agencies in that they have legal personality, are 'relatively independent', and are established under secondary EU law: Griller and Orator, n 302, 7–9. But they have also been characterized as a 'genuinely different arrangement' (Chiti (2009), n 308, 1431) and 'as some of the most powerful autonomous institutions ever established at EU level' (Everson, n 10, 17).

[368] Griller and Orator, n 302, 13.

[369] See further Chiti (2009), n 308, 1403–7 and Vibert, n 308, 392.

[370] In Case C-270/12, however, the Advocate General suggested that agencies could be empowered to adopt Art 291 TFEU rules as, by contrast with Art 290 rules, these rules do not have a normative legislative content and can be adopted by bodies other than the co-legislators, without prejudice to the institutional balance, and as agencies are subject to judicial review under Art 267 TFEU. This point was not addressed by the Court.

[371] The ESAs' quasi-rule-making powers have been described as constituting 'a culmination of agency rule-making powers': Busuioc, n 351, 113.

[372] The *Meroni* ruling has generated a largely hostile literature critiquing the efficiency constraints which it imposes on the development of an effective administrative arm. See, eg, Geradin and Petit, n 302.

[373] The Parliament's somewhat incendiary proposal to locate all three ESAs in Frankfurt met with little Member State enthusiasm and with particular hostility from the UK: Ferran, n 350.

[374] ESMA, Frequently Asked Questions. A Guide to Understanding ESMA (2011) (2011 ESMA FAQ).

[375] The foreword by ESMA Executive Director Ross to ESMA's 2011 Annual Report noted that 'as an EU agency, ESMA needs to ensure that its financial, procurement, and other administrative procedures follow the strict rule laid down under EU legislation': at 7. Elsewhere, the Report highlighted the need for ESMA 'to

ESMA's governance design is based on that of EU agencies generally[376] and is accordingly designed to support efficiency and operational independence (thereby legitimating the delegation of powers), accountability (to the Commission, European Parliament, and Council), transparency (reinforcing accountability), and technical capacity.[377] ESMA is, however, in a number of respects *sui generis*.[378] The typical agency is composed of a director, an administrative board responsible for ensuring the obligations of the founding regulation are met (formed of representatives of the Commission, Council, and Parliament), and an expert, scientific board.[379] While ESMA's governance design very broadly follows this structure, its governance is calibrated to reflect the need for intergovernmental dominance given the quasi-rule-making powers which ESMA exerts, and for expert, independent judgement to drive its rule-making activities.

ESMA is composed of a series of components.[380] The Board of Supervisors (Articles 40–44) is ESMA's decision-making body and is composed of the heads of the NCAs responsible for the supervision of financial markets;[381] the ESMA Chairperson also sits on the Board and chairs its meetings but, reflecting typical agency design, is non-voting. The Board also includes the Commission (a feature of agency governance), the ESRB, EBA, and EIOPA as non-voting members.[382] The ESMA Executive Director may also participate in meetings on a non-voting basis (Article 40). By contrast with standard agency design, therefore, the double-headed scientific/expert board function and political oversight board function has not been deployed; both these functions are combined in the Board of Supervisors.[383] Commission representation, a key element of agency governance,[384] remains, however, of central importance. The Board may establish internal committees for specific tasks and delegate certain clearly defined tasks to internal committees or panels, the Management Board, or the Chairperson (Article 41). Its tasks include giving guidance to the work of ESMA, the adoption of opinions, recommendations, decisions, and advice, and adoption of

work effectively and efficiently an EU agency' and described the procedural, financial, and administrative steps required to establish ESMA 'as an EU agency': at 13 and 28.

[376] On agency structure and the tensions generated by the need to accommodate supranational and intergovernmental interests see Busuioc, M, 'European Agencies and their Boards: Promises and Pitfalls of Accountability beyond Design' (2012) 19 *J EPP* 719.

[377] Everson, n 10, 14–16 and Vibert, n 308.

[378] Everson, n 10, 22–4.

[379] eg Chiti (2009), n 308, 1396 and Everson, n 10, 14–15. The Agency for the Cooperation of Energy Regulators (ACER), established in 2009 (Regulation (EC) No 713/2009 [2009] OJ L211/1), has an Administrative Board (composed of representatives of the Commission, European Parliament, and Council) and a Regulatory Board (composed of representatives of the national competent authorities and a non-voting Commission representative): Arts 3, 12, and 14. The European Aviation Safety Agency, established in 2008 (Regulation (EC) No 216/2008 [2008] OJ L79/1), is closest in structure to ESMA, in that its main body is its Management Board (composed of Member States representatives and one Commission representative): Arts 33 and 34.

[380] A Board of Supervisors, a Management Board, a Chairperson, an Executive Director, and a Board of Appeal: Art 6.

[381] Where more than one authority is relevant in a Member State, the different national authorities must agree as to which authority sits on the Board of Supervisors (Art 40(4)); representation may be changed where the subject under discussion is not within the competence of the agreed representative. NCAs must also arrange for high-level alternates who can replace the head of the authority (although the heads must meet in person twice a year): Art 40(1) and 40(3).

[382] The NCAs of Norway, Iceland, and Liechtenstein are, as members of EFTA, permanent observers.

[383] Everson, n 10, 22.

[384] Chiti (2009), n 308, 1397.

ESMA's annual and multi-annual work programme(s), budget, and Annual Report (Article 43). By sharp contrast with CESR, the Board operates under a simple majority vote, for the most part.[385] A QMV applies, however, to its quasi-rule-making activities (related to the proposing of BTSs and the adoption of Article 16 guidelines and recommendations, but not to Article 29 'soft law' activities) (Article 44).[386]

Operational management is provided by an executive Management Board (Articles 45–47) which is composed of the Chairperson and six Board of Supervisor members, elected by and from the voting members of the Board of Supervisors;[387] the Commission and the Executive Director are non-voting members (Article 45(2)), although the Commission, in a traditional agency feature, is empowered to vote on the adoption of ESMA's budget (Article 45(2) and (63)). The Management Board operates on a simple majority basis (Article 45(2)). It is tasked with ensuring that ESMA carries out its mission and performs the tasks assigned to it in accordance with the ESMA Regulation (Article 47). In particular, it must propose (for adoption by the Board of Supervisors) an annual and multi-annual work programme, the draft budget, and the Annual Report, and adopt a staff policy plan, provide access to document rules, and appoint and remove members of the Board of Appeal.

ESMA is represented by a 'full-time, independent professional' Chairperson (Articles 48–50); the Chairperson[388] represents ESMA and is not a representative of the Member States or a Commission appointee,[389] as ESMA has been careful to highlight.[390] The Chairperson is responsible for preparing the work of the Board of Supervisors and chairs meetings of the Boards of Supervisors and Management (Article 48(1)). A 'full-time, independent professional' Executive Director (Articles 51–53), appointed by the Board of Supervisors,[391] is in charge of the management of ESMA, preparing the work of the Management Board, and implementing ESMA work programmes.

A Board of Appeal, common to the three ESAs (Article 6), is empowered to review ESMA decisions, on appeal by affected parties (Articles 58-60).[392]

---

[385] Each Board member has one vote: Art 44(1).

[386] Under Art 44(1), BTS/guidance activities (Arts 10–16), and the power to prohibit temporarily products and services (Art 9—see Ch IX sect 7), are subject to a QMV. Special 'blocking minority' rules apply to ESMA's Art 19 binding mediation power to impose decisions on NCAs in cases of disagreement, and in the particular case of mediation concerning colleges of supervisors and consolidating supervisors.

[387] Management Board members are appointed for a term of two and a half years, which may be extended once. The composition of the Board must be balanced and proportionate and reflect the EU as a whole.

[388] Appointed for a five-year term, which may be extended once: Art 48(3).

[389] Although the Chairperson is appointed by the Board of Supervisors on the basis of merit, skills, knowledge and experience, based on an open selection procedure, the European Parliament may object to the appointee following a hearing (Art 48(2)), and the first Chairperson was to be selected from a shortlist drawn up by the Commission (rec 55); the shortlist review procedure is, however, to be reviewed. On the fracas generated by the appointment of the first Chairperson see sect 5.2.5.

[390] 2011 ESMA FAQ, n 374, 9.

[391] The Executive Director is appointed by the Board of Supervisors, after confirmation by the European Parliament, on the basis of merit, skills, knowledge and experience and for a five year term which may be extended once: Art 51(2).

[392] See further Ch XI sect 5.

ESMA has also established a consultative Securities and Markets Stakeholder Group (SMSG), as required under Article 37, to facilitate consultation with stakeholders.[393] The composition of the SMSG is dictated by Article 37 and is designed to be representative of the major stakeholders in the EU financial market.[394] The SMSG is consulted on ESMA's proposed BTSs and Article 16 measures (Article 37(1)) and in practice is consulted generally by ESMA on a range of its activities, including in relation to technical advice; the SMSG may submit opinions and advice on any issue related to the tasks of ESMA, with a particular focus on its BTS and Article 16 guidance activities and on its supervisory convergence, peer review, and market assessment activities (Article 37(5)).

ESMA is formally accountable[395] to the European Parliament and Council (Article 3), and subject to a range of related reporting requirements.[396] Accountability is also supported by budgetary controls (Articles 62–64), the review powers which the Court of Justice can exercise over ESMA decisions (Article 61),[397] and the range of consultation requirements imposed on ESMA, including with respect to the SMSG.

ESMA enjoys a formal independence guarantee, both as a body[398] and with respect to the Board of Supervisors, Management Board, Chairperson, and Executive Director.[399] Its

---

[393] A second Group was constituted in January 2014, following the completion of the first Group's two-and-a-half-year term of office.

[394] The Group is composed of 30 members appointed by the Board of Supervisors, and must, under Art 37(2), represent, in balanced proportions, financial market participants operating in the EU, their employees' representatives, consumers, users of financial services, and representatives of SMEs; ten of its members must represent financial market participants. In addition, five of its members must be independent top-ranking academics. In appointing the SMSG, the Board must also, to the extent possible, ensure an appropriate geographical and gender balance and representation of stakeholders across the EU. The composition of the ESAs' SMSGs has been the subject of significant controversy, particularly with respect to perceptions as to the under-representation of consumers (which led to a challenge to the European Ombudsman), and received close stakeholder attention over the European System of Financial Supervision (ESFS) Review.

[395] An extensive political science literature considers the accountability mechanisms used to control EU agencies. See, eg, Curtin, D, 'Delegation to EU Non-Majoritarian Agencies and Emerging Practices of Public Accountability' in Geradin, D and Petit, N (eds), *Regulation through Agencies in the EU. A New Paradigm of European Governance* (2008) 87.

[396] Including an annual report to the Commission, European Parliament, Council, Court of Auditors and ECOSOC/EESC (Art 43(5)). Work programmes must also be submitted to these institutions for information. The ESMA Chair may be invited to make a statement by the Parliament or Council, and must report on the main activities of ESMA to the Parliament when requested (Art 50).

[397] Member States, the EU institutions and any natural or legal person who meets the standing requirements may initiate proceedings (under Art 263 TFEU) in relation to a Board of Appeal decision or an ESMA decision (where there is no appeal to the Board of Appeal).

[398] ESMA is to act independently and objectively and in the interest of the Union alone (Art 1(6)).

[399] Arts 42, 46, 49, 52, and 59. In relation to the Board of Supervisors and the Management Board (Arts 42 and 46), the independence guarantee is cast in terms of the Board acting independently and objectively in the sole interest of the EU as a whole and not seeking or taking instructions from EU bodies or institutions, any Member State government, or any other public or private body. Similarly, neither the Member States, EU institutions or bodies, nor any other public or private body are to seek to influence the Board in question. With respect to the Chairperson and the Executive Director (Arts 49 and 52), the independence guarantee is cast in terms of the person neither seeking nor taking instructions from the EU institutions or bodies, from any government of a Member States, or from any other public or private body; neither Member States, the EU institutions or bodies, nor any other public or private body are to seek to influence the Chairperson in the performance of tasks. The Chairperson and Executive Director are also, after leaving service, bound by the duty to behave with integrity and discretion as regards the acceptance of certain appointments or benefits.
The Chairperson's independence is additionally protected by the requirement that the Chairperson can only be removed from office by the European Parliament, following a decision of the Board of Supervisors (Art 48(5)); the Executive Director's removal requires a decision from the Board of Supervisors (Art 51(5)).

independent status is underlined by its funding model (Article 62). It is funded by a mixture of Member State and EU funding, derived from the Commission's budget and from Member State funding, and any fees paid to ESMA (thus far, from credit rating agencies)[400]. This funding model is designed to support its independence (recital 59).

But while formal supports for independence are in place, there are weaknesses in ESMA's independence model, recognized in the 2013 ESFS Review, which derive in the main from the Commission's involvement, albeit that such involvement is a key feature of agency design.[401] The Commission (in a non-voting capacity) is represented on ESMA's Board of Supervisors and Management Board; although this supports the development of good inter-institutional relations, it might also be expected to exert something of a 'chilling' effect.[402] ESMA is not formally accountable to the Commission, but it is subject to an array of reporting requirements.[403] The Commission plays a central role in the adoption of ESMA's budget. The complex budgetary procedures (Articles 62–64) are based on ESMA proposing its estimated revenue and expenditure for the year, but on the Commission transmitting the estimates to, and negotiating ESMA's budget (as part of the overall budget of the EU) with, the Council and European Parliament.[404] The Commission is also closely engaged with decisions on how personnel funds are expended under the Staff Regulations which govern ESMA's personnel but apply generally to persons employed by the EU institutions. Similarly, ESMA's financial rules were adopted only after consultation with the Commission, given the application of the EU's financial rules to agencies (Articles 64 and 65). Perhaps above all, the Commission endorsement mechanism which applies to ESMA's proposed BTSs sits very uneasily with ESMA's formal independence guarantee.

Controls also apply with respect to the appointments process. While the Board of Supervisors appoints the Chairperson and exerts disciplinary authority over the Chairperson, the European Parliament may object to the designation (Articles 43(3), 43(8), and 48(2)). Similarly, while the Board of Supervisors appoints the Executive Director and exerts

---

[400] The initial funding settlement was based on 40 per cent EU funds and 60 per cent Member State contributions: 2010 ESMA Regulation rec 68. The mixed model was designed (by including Member State funds) to support ESMA's independence from the institutions, and to ensure appropriate risk controls and support pan-EU solidarity (by including EU funds and thereby subjecting the budget to EU budgetary controls): 2009 ESA Proposals Impact Assessment, n 183, 35–6.

[401] From the outset, the Commission warned that 'while the ESAs should enjoy maximum independence to objectively fulfil their mission, the Commission has to be involved where institutional reasons and the Treaty so require' (2009 ESMA Proposal, n 191, 4), although it also suggested that 'in order to limit as much as possible interference in the technical work of supervisors', the Commission's participation in the governance of the ESAs be kept to the minimum: 2009 ESA Proposals Impact Assessment, n 183, 35.

[402] Board of Supervisor Minutes suggest that the Commission plays an active role and is particularly concerned to highlight where ESMA action may conflict with legislative measures—eg, with respect to ESMA's Short Selling Q&A and a proposed Q&A on the prospectus regime: Board of Supervisor Meetings, 29 January 2013 (ESMA/2013/BS/30) and 6 November 2012 (ESMA/2012/BS/143). It is also concerned to ensure that ESMA does not encroach on its rule-making prerogatives—eg, Board of Supervisor Meeting, 17 December 2013 (ESMA/2014/BS/1), noting, in the context of an ESMA draft opinion, the Commission stating that ESMA should not engage in work on definitions (in relation to difficulties with respect to the definition of derivatives) and that the Commission would address the definitional difficulties with respect to derivatives once the 2014 MiFID II/MIFIR negotiations were complete (see further Ch IV sect 4.3 on the derivatives issue).

[403] n 396.

[404] The Commission determines the budgetary amount it deems necessary to be charged to the General Budget of the EU: Art 63(3).

disciplinary authority over the Director (Articles 43(8) and 51(2)), the Parliament must confirm the appointment.

The location of decision-making at the intergovernmental Board of Supervisors, which can be at risk from national interests,[405] while politically and practically necessary, also has the potential to undermine ESMA's institutional independence.[406] Similarly, the non-voting status of the ESMA Chairman on the Board of Supervisors undermines the ability of ESMA to project an independent 'ESMA position'.

These features reflect the *ex-ante* and *ex-post* accountability controls which have developed as mechanisms for controlling and legitimizing EU agencies' powers, as well as the specific solutions deemed necessary to establish ESMA, and to protect its quasi-rule-making powers, within the *Meroni* constraints. But independence is a defining feature of institutional design for regulatory agencies.[407] If experience with the ECB is anything to go by, particularly with respect to the ECB's somewhat ill-judged defence of its independence in the *OLAF* case,[408] ESMA might be expected vigorously to assert its independence.[409] But the extent to which the Commission is injected into ESMAs's governance structure and operation limits ESMA's *de facto* independence. In practice inter-institutional relations seem good, but the potential for tension is real. As discussed in section 5.10, the role of the Commission in particular has been questioned by the 2013 review of ESMA under the ESFS Review.

X.5.2.3 Hubs and Spokes

ESMA has a double-sided structure. On the one hand, it is an independent body, charged with a range of tasks to support the EU financial market and, in particular, with the building of an EU rulebook; it is to act 'in the interest of the Union alone' (ESMA Regulation Article 1(5)). It regards itself as having a distinct mission as an EU authority and has highlighted its 'independent' and 'European' characteristics.[410] On the other hand, ESMA's governance has a strong intergovernmental quality in that decision-making is located in the Board of Supervisors; incentives for NCAs on the Board to promote distinct national positions are strong. In addition, ESMA's limited resources (section 5.2.4) means that in practice its working model is dependent on strong liaison with the NCAs who resource the Standing Committees through which ESMA works,[411] as well as on the range of working

---

[405] Clear from the UK government's priority 'to ensure that there is a strong and credible voice to promote the UK's interests in these new institutions': HM Treasury, A New Approach to Financial Regulation: Building a Stronger System (2011) para 7.11.

[406] Busuioc, n 351, 120–1 examining the risk of agency boards 'serv[ing] as a platform for mobilisation around narrowly-drawn national interests'.

[407] In the EU context, Hupkes, E, Quintyn, M, and Taylor, M, 'The Accountability of Financial Sector Supervisors—Principles and Practice' (2005) *EBLR* 1575 and Tison, M, 'Do Not Attack the Watchdog: Banking Supervisor's Liability after Peter Paul' (2005) 42 *CMLR* 48.

[408] Case C-11/00 *Commission v ECB* [2003] ECR I-7147.

[409] ESMA Chairman Maijoor was clear from the outset that independence was a key characteristic of ESMA and could lead to conflict with the markets, politicians, and the Commission: Tait, N, 'ESMA Watchdog Prepared to Clash with Brussels', March 2 2011, available at <http://www.FT.com>.

[410] ESMA has identified six characteristics which describe it and how it achieves its mission and objectives: European, independent, co-operative, accountable, professional, and effective. ESMA Annual Report (2011) 9.

[411] ESMA has established the following Standing Committees (SCs), each chaired by an NCA Board of Supervisors member (ESMA staff act as rapporteurs): Secondary Markets; Investment Management; Post-Trading; Credit Rating Agencies; Corporate Finance; Corporate Reporting; ESMA-Pol (market surveillance);

groups, task forces, panels, and networks in which ESMA staff and NCA staff work. Tussles over 'who holds the pen' are, at the outset at least, more likely to be resolved in the favour of the national or intergovernmental interest than of the ESMA or supranational interest, particularly as the pivotal Standing Committees are chaired by senior NCA representatives. The QMV decision-making model for quasi-rule-making activities is similarly conducive to the dominance of national/intergovernmental interests, as alliances and groupings form and re-form as NCAs seek to protect their positions. This double-sided model has, accordingly, the potential to generate unhelpful tensions, to increase the likelihood of 'lowest common denominator' measures, and to prejudice ESMA's capacity to develop technical advice, proposed BTSs, and soft law which reflects the elusive EU interest or, at least, does not respond to particular national interests.

On the other hand, the relative ease with which the vast array of technical advice and proposed BTSs were adopted over ESMA's first three years of operation suggests that national interests were not obstructive, and that either the Board of Supervisors became comfortable with QMV decision-making or that consensus was relatively easy to achieve.[412] The ESFS Review also suggests that 'EU decision-making' is beginning to characterize the Board of Supervisors and that national interests have not been detrimental.[413]

X.5.2.4 Technical Capacity and Strains

While closely based on the typical agency design, ESMA's governance structure and operating framework contains a number of features designed to enhance its capacity with respect to rule-making.

As outlined in earlier Chapters, ESMA is the recipient of vast amounts of regulated information, primarily channelled through the NCAs, which strengthens its rule-making capacity and credibility. It is also charged with a range of reporting obligations (generally, ESMA Regulation Article 8(1)(f) and (g)), including with respect to consumer market trends (Article 9) and market developments more generally, in relation to which it must assess microprudential trends and potential risks and vulnerabilities (Article 32).[414] These obligations demand a related technical capacity, which ESMA is developing,[415] but also strengthen ESMA's ability to engage in forward-looking rule development. ESMA was also charged with establishing 'as an integral part of the Authority' a Financial Innovation

---

Investor Protection and Intermediaries; Financial Innovation; Review Panel; Economic and Markets Analysis; and IT Management: ESMA Annual Report (2012) 70.

[412] Board of Supervisor Minutes suggest that consensus is often achieved, but that a QMV vote is regularly deployed (eg Board of Supervisors Meeting, 18 December 2012 (ESMA/BS/4), noting that a QMV was not yet in place on ESMA's Short Selling Guidelines on the Market Making Exemption).

[413] The 2013 Mazars ESA Review reported that the ESA governance model managed to strike an effective balance between the need for an EU-wide perspective and for NCA 'buy in', and that while national bias had been a challenge and decisions tended to be heavily influenced by the major NCAs (and the Commission), the QMV was operating effectively and the EU and NCA interests were neither fixed nor binary: n 358, 14 and 34.

[414] ESMA must report annually (and in practice reports semi-annually) to the European Parliament, Council, Commission, and ESRB on trends, potential risks, and vulnerabilities, and include a classification of the main risks and vulnerabilities: Art 32(3). The first report and related risk dashboard was published in February 2013: ESMA, Report on Trends, Risks, and Vulnerabilities. Report No 1 February 2013 (ESMA/2013/212), and ESMA, Risk Dashboard. No 1 February 2013.

[415] Through ESMA's Standing Committee on Economic and Financial Market Analysis, which also oversees impact assessment.

Committee to achieve a co-ordinated approach to the regulation and supervisory treatment of new or innovative financial activities, and to provide related advice to present to the Parliament, Council, and Commission (Article 9).[416] Institutional support has accordingly been given to 'horizon-scanning' by ESMA, which augurs well for its ability to engage with emerging risks.

Consultation and impact assessment were, from the outset, ESMA priorities. ESMA is required to engage in consultation and cost-benefit analysis in quasi-rule-making (Articles 10(3), 15(1), and 16(2)), and must consult with its SMSG (Article 37). As outlined in earlier Chapters, consultation exercises have typically been extensive and generated qualitative and (to a lesser degree) quantitative market intelligence.

ESMA is also, and for the first time in EU securities and markets regulation, subject to a clearly defined set of regulatory objectives (Article 1(5)) which should give direction to its quasi-rule-making activities. ESMA decision-making is also subject to discipline through the Board of Appeal and Court of Justice review processes which apply to ESMA decisions (Articles 60 and 61). CESR, by contrast, was a soft law body and not formally subject to Court of Justice review.

Resource strain, however, is a risk.[417] It has in part been driven by the intensity of the crisis-era rule-making programme and the short deadlines which legislative measures often imposed for the adoption of administrative rules,[418] and which led to ESMA raising its concerns with the Commission and co-legislators.[419] ESMA's SMSG has similarly called for ESMA to be given appropriate timescales within which to develop technical advice and/or proposed BTSs.[420] Budgetary strains have also emerged. ESMA's budget rose from €16.9 million in 2011 to €28.2 million in 2013, while its staffing levels have risen from 35 on 1 January 2011 to 195 (planned for end 2014).[421] But despite these increases, budgetary strain has been repeatedly identified as a risk.[422] The nature of ESMA's funding is, however, a contested and sensitive issue. Additional funding calls on Member States, particularly smaller Member States, are unlikely to be warmly received, while ESMA's ability to levy fees on market participants is very limited.

---

[416] The Committee initially focused on product intervention and the related powers of NCAs and on the collection of data on investor protection risks: ESMA, Annual Report (2011) 35–6.

[417] The scale of the administrative rule-making programme and ESMA's ability to respond raised concerns from the outset: Tiernan, R, 'Little Body with a Big Agenda', *Financial World*, April 2011, 18.

[418] The 2012 Short Selling Regulation, eg, required that the Commission adopt all necessary administrative acts by November 2012, which required the related ESMA process and consultations to be 'significantly compressed' (ESMA, Annual Report (2011) 49).

[419] In relation to the 2012 EMIR BTS agenda, ESMA wrote to the European Parliament, Council, and Commission, highlighting the importance of it having sufficient time to develop the standards, and calling for a postponement of the BTS adoption deadline (with respect to measures not essential to the G20 commitment): ESMA, Annual Report (2011) 57.

[420] Letter from ESMA SMSG to Commissioner Barnier, ECON Committee Chair Bowles, JURI Committee Chair Lehne and Council Presidency, 2 February 2012 (2012/SSMG/6).

[421] 2013 Mazars ESA Review, n 358, 49 and 93.

[422] eg from the industry perspective, Letter from Afme, AIMA, EACH, EBF, FOA, ICMA, and ISDA, 17 January 2012, to the Danish Council Presidency, the ECON Parliament Committee Chair, and Commissioner Barnier, and 2013 Mazars Review, n 358, 48, noting that current ESA funding arrangements seemed to have 'reached their limit' (53).

X.5.2.5 Inter-institutional Strain

ESMA operates in a complex and fragile institutional ecosystem in which relations with the Commission and European Parliament are potentially difficult. The Commission has been supportive of governance through agencies, which, overall, leads to an increase in its administrative powers. But the leaching away of technical, expert authority to an agency generates risks to the Commission's authority.[423] Related Commission/ESMA tensions may, as discussed further below, prejudice efficient rule-making. The Parliament also poses a risk to rule-making efficiency. The Parliament has long been suspicious of the agency model. It has embraced it for financial markets,[424] reflecting its concern to centralize rule-making power over financial markets and impose its vision for EU financial markets. Residual tensions remains, however, particularly with respect to the Parliament's law-making prerogatives, and have the potential to destabilize ESMA as a nascent rule-maker.

X.5.2.6 Cross-sectoral Liaison

ESMA forms part of a fragmented, silo-based institutional structure, along with EBA, EIOPA, and the ESRB. A consolidated European Financial Authority was always unlikely; the silo structure is an outcome of pragmatic political considerations and the availability of the sectoral '3L3' model. But a sectoral model fits awkwardly in a financial market which does not respect silos; the financial crisis has graphically illustrated the interconnection between credit and market risk and how systemic risks transmit cross-sector. It is all the more a problem as ESMA's silo-based model sits atop NCAs which can take the form of twin peak supervisors, consolidated supervisors (the dominant model) or sectoral supervisors.[425] From a governance perspective, the composition of ESMA's Board of Supervisors may be unstable—although one NCA must be nominated for ESMA membership, an alternate may sit on the Board where the subject matter demands different expertise (Article 40(4)), potentially making it more difficult for ESMA to establish cohesion, trust, and a sense of mission in its decision-making body.

More generally, co-ordination difficulties may arise with EBA and EIOPA. Institutional support of co-ordination has, however, been provided by the Joint Committee of the European Supervisory Authorities (Article 54).[426] The Joint Committee, which has a separate secretariat resourced by the ESAs, acts as a forum in which the ESAs co-operate regularly and is designed to ensure cross-sectoral consistency. While the potential for inter-ESA tension was significant given the institutional territory at stake, cross-sectoral co-operation seems to be operating relatively smoothly,[427] with the 2013 EBA/ESMA Principles for Benchmarks[428] an early success of the process. But co-ordination risks remain potentially significant, as the ESMA/EBA experience in relation to the sensitive question of financial

---

[423] eg Everson, n 10, 14, describing the Commission as 'an institutionally powerful if sometime reluctant proponent' of the agency model.

[424] Everson, n 10, 9, noting that the Parliament 'in the face of crisis dropped its longstanding opposition to the further consolidation of EU governance by means of supranational "agencification"'.

[425] On the models currently adopted in the EU see Ferran, n 350.

[426] The Joint Committee was based on the CESR-era 'Joint Task Force', which supported co-operation between the 3L3 committees.

[427] Four sub-committees have been established: financial conglomerates; cross-sector developments, risks, and vulnerabilities (which produced its first cross-sector risk report in 2013 (2013-04-12JC)); anti-money-laundering; and consumer protection and financial innovation.

[428] See further Ch VIII sect 8.2.3.

institution reporting on forbearance measures attests.[429] Cross-sectoral co-ordination has also been supported by the crisis-era legislative programme which, in identified instances, requires co-ordination between the ESAs (typically ESMA and EBA) in relation to the proposal of certain BTSs.

Relations with the ESRB may potentially become more troublesome.[430] There does not appear to be a material degree of co-ordination between the ESRB and ESMA with respect to standard-setting. Both institutions have, for example, taken different approaches to money-market funds, which are not simply a function of the different legal instruments at their disposal, but also reflect different positions on how these funds should be treated.[431]

X.5.3 Objectives and Scope

ESMA's objective is to 'protect the public interest by contributing to the short, medium, and long-term stability and effectiveness of the financial system, for the Union economy, its citizens and businesses' (ESMA Regulation Article 1(5)). To that end, it is charged with contributing to a range of specified activities: improving the functioning of the internal market, including in particular a sound, effective, and consistent level of regulation and supervision; ensuring the integrity, transparency, efficiency, and orderly functioning of financial markets; strengthening international supervisory co-ordination; preventing regulatory arbitrage and promoting equal conditions of competition; ensuring the taking of investment and other risks are appropriately regulated and supervised; and enhancing consumer protection (Article 1(5)). It is conferred with a range of related powers which can be broadly categorized as quasi-rule-making powers (considered in this Chapter) and operational/supervisory powers (Chapter XI), which are set out in Article 8, which identifies its tasks[432] and powers[433] in detail.

---

[429] In 2012 and 2013, ESMA and EBA independently addressed forbearance reporting by financial institutions (ESMA, Public Statement on Forbearance Practices in IFRS Financial Statements (ESMA/2012/853) and EBA, Consultation Paper on Supervisory Reporting on Forbearance and Non-Performing Exposures (EBA/2013/06)). Despite references to co-ordination and co-operation between both institutions in each measure, the two measures were not fully aligned, including with respect to the definition of forbearance. The ESMA and EBA positions became aligned, however, as the process developed (as was acknowledged by EBA: EBA, Final Draft Implementing Standards (EBA/ITS/2013/03) 44).

[430] See further Ch XI sect 6.

[431] The ESRB's 2012 intervention (ESRB Recommendation on Money Market Funds (2012) (ESRB/2012/01)) takes the form of a recommendation addressed to the Commission and calling for legislative action, while ESMA's action has taken the form of a non-binding guideline. The ESRB has also been significantly more risk-averse, calling for certain funds to be prohibited. See further Ch III sect 3.14.1.

[432] Under Art 8(1) ESMA is to: contribute to the development of high-quality common regulatory and supervisory standards and practices; contribute to the consistent application of legally binding EU acts (including through supporting a common supervisory culture, preventing regulatory arbitrage, mediating between supervisors, acting in emergency situations and ensuring the coherent functioning of colleges of supervisors); stimulate and facilitate delegation by NCAs; co-operate with the ESRB; engage in peer review; monitor and assess market developments; undertake economic analyses of markets; foster investor protection; and engage in a range of tasks concerned with the support of colleges of supervisors and crisis resolution.

[433] Under Art 8(2) ESMA is empowered to: develop binding technical standards; issue guidelines and recommendations; issue specific recommendations; take individual decisions addressed to NCAs in nominated cases; take individual decisions addressed to financial market participants in nominated cases; issue opinions to the EU institutions; collect information; develop methodologies concerning the assessment of products and distribution processes; and maintain databases.

In exercising its powers, ESMA must operate within its scope restrictions. Article 1(2) empowers ESMA to act within the scope of identified EU legislative acts, and all administrative measures based on those acts (essentially, the acts forming EU securities and markets regulation); it is also to act 'in the field of activities of market participants' in relation to issues not directly covered by those measures, including corporate governance, auditing, and financial reporting, as long as such action is necessary to ensure the effective and consistent application of those acts. In a significant hostage to fortune, it is to take 'appropriate action' in the context of takeover bids, clearing and settlement, and derivative issues. In practice, the ever-increasing scope of the legislative regime means that ESMA's scope is unlikely to materially restrict its rule-making activities.

X.5.4 ESMA and Technical Advice

X.5.4.1 The Procedure

ESMA plays a key role in the adoption of Article 290/291 TFEU administrative rules by providing the Commission with technical advice, following receipt of a mandate from the Commission.[434] Procedurally, like CESR before it, ESMA engages in market consultation prior to delivering its advice, typically based on a public call for evidence and a subsequent consultation paper, and on consultation of the SMSG.[435] ESMA also draws on advice from various standing expert groups. The extent to which ESMA engages in impact assessment usually depends on the Commission mandate; typically, the mandate for technical advice simply requires ESMA to justify its action or to provide sufficient factual data to support its analysis. ESMA's technical advice often, however, includes quantitative analysis derived from the extensive consultations it carries out in preparing technical advice.[436] Procedurally, ESMA has shown itself sensitive to inter-institutional dynamics, transmitting its advice to the Commission, the Chair of the European Securities Committee, and the Chair of the European Parliament's ECON Committee.[437]

X.5.4.2 Early Lessons

By contrast with the new BTS process, the institutions were familiar with the technical advice process from the CESR era. Nonetheless, the change from CESR to ESMA, and the material reconfiguration of powers and status which followed, had the potential to destabilize inter-institutional relations. Inter-institutional relations have generally been smooth, however, although the Commission has shown no reluctance to revise ESMA's technical

---

[434] The ESMA Regulation does not refer directly to the technical advice function, but ESMA Regulation Art 8(1)(a) empowers ESMA to provide opinions to the EU institutions, and Art 8(1)(l) empowers ESMA to take over, as appropriate, all existing and ongoing tasks from CESR.

[435] The 2011 AIFMD process, eg, which commenced at the end of the CESR era, involved a December 2010 call for evidence (CESR/20-1459) and hearing, two consultation papers in the course of 2011 (ESMA/2011/121 and ESMA/2011/209), and two hearings. ESMA provided feedback on the consultation process in its Final Advice: ESMA Final Technical Advice. ESMA/2011/379, Annex IV.

[436] See in relation to technical advice on the Prospectus Directive, eg, ESMA's Final Technical Advice, ESMA/2012/137, 8 and Final Technical Advice, ESMA/2011/323, 7. A rather skeletal cost-benefit analysis was provided in relation to the AIFMD technical advice which, while lengthy, was short on quantitative analysis, reflecting the difficulties ESMA experienced in sourcing quantitative evidence during its consultations (ESMA Final Technical Advice, ESMA/2011/379, Annex II).

[437] As it did in November 2011 in relation to its extensive AIFMD technical advice.

advice and appears concerned to reinforce its dominant position in the administrative rule-making hierarchy, notwithstanding the rule-making inefficiencies which can follow.

In its scale, technical complexity, and requirement for engagement with often hostile market stakeholders, the strenuous 2011 AIFMD technical advice process posed an early challenge for ESMA.[438] As discussed in Chapter III, ESMA succeeded in delivering a technically robust set of advice with which the market was broadly comfortable. The Commission's subsequent revision of ESMA's advice led to a relatively sanguine (publicly at least) response from ESMA.[439] The cacophony of complaints from the market, however, delivered a blow to the perceived efficiency and effectiveness of the administrative rule-making process generally, and threatened to undermine ESMA's credibility as a nascent standard-setter. The fracas was short-lived and does not seem to have materially damaged either ESMA's standing or Commission/ESMA relations. But ESMA was then a very new actor in the institutional space. As its capacity grows, and as it establishes itself as the primary location of technical expertise in the rule-making structure, it can be expected to exert itself more forcibly. But this early eruption of tension underlines the inefficiencies to which the Article 290/291 TFEU administrative rule-making process is vulnerable, given the facility with which the Commission can trump ESMA's consultation-based and empirically-informed technical advice. As noted in section 5.10, the 2013 review of the ESFS has exposed significant stakeholder concern as to the Commission's untrammelled ability to reject or revise ESMA's technical advice.

X.5.5 Binding Technical Standards

X.5.5.1 The Procedure and the *Meroni* Constraint

ESMA is also empowered to propose BTSs which are endorsed (enacted) by the Commission. The relatively complex BTS procedure, detailed in the ESMA Regulation, reflects the Article 290/291 TFEU framework within which the BTS regime sits. It is also designed to reflect the Treaty requirements governing notional 'delegations' of rule-making powers from the Commission and associated with the *Meroni* ruling and Article 290 TFEU administrative rule-making in particular. But, while protecting the Commission's position, the procedures also support ESMA's prerogatives as the independent initiator of BTSs, the seat of technical expertise, and the location of extensive stakeholder consultation.

The BTS procedure is defined by two elements in particular: the location of rule-making power with the Commission through the endorsement process,[440] and the constraints placed on the Commission where it rejects or revises ESMA's proposed BTSs. The procedures differ for RTSs (which have a normative/legislative character and derive from Article 290 TFEU delegated rule-making powers) and ITSs (which have an executive/implementing character and derive from the Article 291 TFEU allocation of power in relation to implementation). RTSs are characterized as technical and not implying strategic

---

[438] The final technical advice ran to some 500 pages.

[439] n 349.

[440] The Commission from the outset argued that the ESAs could not be empowered to adopt BTSs as to do so would confer discretionary powers on the ESAs and conflict with responsibilities conferred on the Commission under the Treaties: 2009 ESA Proposals Impact Assessment, n 183, 13.

decisions or policy choices, and their content is described as being delimited by the legislative acts on which they are based (ESMA Regulation Article 10(1)). ITSs are similarly designed to be technical and not to imply strategic decisions or policy choices, but, in contrast to RTSs which have a quasi-legislative quality, their content is to determine the conditions of application of legislative acts.

RTSs (ESMA Regulation Articles 10–14), which can take the form of regulations or decisions, are adopted by the Commission where a delegation has been made by the co-legislators in a legislative measure (Article 10(1)). But ESMA plays a key role in the process. Under Article 10(1), ESMA is empowered to develop draft RTSs. It must engage in public consultations and engage in impact assessment, unless it would be dispropor-tionate in relation to the scope and impact of relevant RTSs or given the particular urgency of the issue in question; ESMA must also consult with the SMSG.

The procedural steps which follow are derived, in the case of Council and European Parliament oversight, from the Article 290/291 TFEU framework. The Commission must immediately forward draft RTSs received from ESMA to the Parliament and Council (Article 10(1)). Once a standard is adopted, the Commission must notify the Council and Parliament (Article 11(2)). The Parliament and Council are empowered to object to an RTS within three months of the date of notification (this period can be extended by a further three months at the initiative of either institution); where an RTS adopted by the Commission is the same as the draft RTS proposed by ESMA, the review period is reduced to one month (Article 13(1)). If on the expiry of the review period neither the Council or Parliament have objected, the RTS enters into force; it may enter into force before this period where the Council and Parliament inform the Commission of their intention not to object (Article 13(2)). Where an objection is raised (the relevant institution must state reasons), the RTS does not enter into force (Article 13(3)). The Council and Parliament are also empowered to revoke the Article 10 delegation at any time (Article 12).[441] The Council and Parliament are also engaged where the Commission does not endorse an RTS or revises it (Article 14); in these cases, the Commission must inform ESMA, the Council, and Parliament, stating its reasons, and, where appropriate, the Parliament or Council may invite the responsible Commissioner, together with the ESMA Chairperson, for an *ad hoc* meeting of the competent committee of the Parliament or Council to present and explain their differences. The power to adopt RTSs is subject to a sunset clause; the Article 10 power was conferred on the Commission for four years from 16 December 2010, before which the Commission was to report on the delegated power (Article 11) (in practice, as part of the ESFS Review (section 5.10)). The Article 10 delegation is automatically extended for successive four-year periods, unless the Parliament or Council revoke the power under Article 12.

A series of procedures govern the relationship between ESMA and the Commission (Article 10 and 14). The Commission must decide whether or not to endorse draft RTSs within three months, and may endorse, or endorse in part or with amendments. Under Article 10(1), the power to endorse in part or with amendments can only be exercised where the interests of the Union so require. Where the Commission intends not to endorse an RTS or to endorse

---

[441] The institution which has commenced revocation proceedings must endeavour to inform the other institution and the Commission within a reasonable time before the final decision to revoke is taken.

in part or with amendments, it must remit the RTS to ESMA, with reasons. Within six weeks, ESMA may amend the draft RTS on the basis of the Commission's revisions and resubmit it to the Commission, in the form of a formal opinion (which must also be sent to the Council and European Parliament). Where ESMA does not act within the six-week period, or submits an RTS which is not consistent with the Commission's amendments, the Commission may adopt the RTS with the amendments it deems relevant or reject it. Underlying this procedure is the Article 10(1) requirement that the Commission may not change the content of an RTS without prior co-ordination with ESMA.

Particular procedures apply where ESMA does not submit an RTS proposal when required to do so (Article 10(2) and (3)). Where ESMA does not submit an RTS proposal within the time limit set out in the relevant legislative measure, the Commission may request a draft; it is only when a draft is not supplied that the Commission may adopt an RTS without an ESMA proposal. The preparation of this draft by the Commission is subject to impact assessment and consultation requirements (including consultation of the SMSG) and to transmittal of the draft to the Council and European Parliament. The draft must also be submitted to ESMA, which may, within a six-week period, amend the RTS (and must send the related formal opinion to the Council and Parliament). Where ESMA does not submit an amended draft to the Commission within the review period, the Commission may adopt the standard. Where ESMA provides revisions, the Commission may amend the standard accordingly or adopt such amendments as it considers relevant. As with the normal procedure, the Commission must not change the content of a draft RTS prepared by ESMA without prior co-ordination with ESMA.

A truncated procedure, with significantly less European Parliament and Council oversight, applies to ITSs. The procedures governing the relationship between ESMA and the Commission track those which apply to the adoption of RTSs, with the distinction that the Commission may add an additional month on to the three-month period at the end of which the Commission must decide its approach to the ESMA draft (Article 15(1)). In terms of Parliament and Council oversight, the Commission must simply forward draft ITSs (whether based on an ESMA draft or a Commission draft) to the Parliament and Commission (Article (1) and (2)).

X.5.5.2 Early Lessons: Classifying BTSs

Strong legacy effects from the pre-ESMA era can be seen in the opacities relating to the status of BTSs. The distinction between RTSs, which have a quasi-legislative quality, and ITSs, which are generally concerned with detailed implementing and procedural matters (such as reporting formats), is now relatively clear after experience with the initial sets of delegations. But the wider characterization of BTSs as 'technical rules which do not require policy choices'[442] and the distinction between BTSs and other Article 290/291 TFEU rules remains troublesome.

---

[442] The 2010 Omnibus I Directive additionally claims that identification of the areas subject to technical standards should strike an appropriate balance between building a single set of harmonized rules and avoiding unduly complicated regulation and enforcement, and that technical standards are to contribute significantly and effectively to the achievement of legislative objects, while ensuring policy decisions remain with the institutions: rec 11.

In particular, the distinction, if any, between RTSs and other delegated Article 290 TFEU rules is problematic. The Article 290 administrative rules adopted by the 2013 Commission AIFMD Directive are, in terms of their quasi-legislative/normative nature no different to the RTSs adopted under the 2012 EMIR regime. An important procedural distinction applies, however. ESMA's technical advice on the AIFMD rules, and its proposed RTSs on the operation of central clearing counterparty (CCP) colleges of supervisors under EMIR—both of which were rejected (in part) by the Commission—were of a broadly similar quality in terms of their substantive impact on regulation and supervision and normative quality. But very different procedural outcomes followed in each case. The Commission was not required to engage with ESMA in relation to its rejection of ESMA's technical advice, but the rejected ESMA EMIR standard was subject to procedural checks and balances.[443]

It appears, notwithstanding the Commission's concern in this regard, that BTSs (and in particular RTSs) are likely to be used in preference to standard Article 290/291 TFEU administrative rules more generally as the Council and Parliament become more familiar with the BTS process, and as ESMA's technical capacity becomes apparent. Under the Omnibus I Directive 2010 which revised FSAP measures to reflect the establishment of ESMA, BTSs are limited to highly technical matters.[444] The 2011 AIFMD contains delegations to BTSs, particularly with respect to the complex third country regime which the AIFMD establishes for non-EU alternative investment fund managers and funds, although most delegations take the form of Article 290 delegations.[445] The 2012 Short Selling Regulation[446] provides for a range of delegations to BTSs, many of which have a strongly substantive quality, although most delegations relate to Articles 290 and 291.[447] By the 2012 EMIR, however, the balance had switched in favour of BTSs.[448]

Institutional trust by the Council and Parliament in the BTS procedure continues to grow. The summer 2012 Council Presidency Progress Report on the 2014 MiFID II/MiFIR negotiations, for example, noted that a number of Member States were supportive of relying more heavily on BTS delegations.[449] The 2014 MiFID II/MiFIR regime accordingly relies heavily on BTS delegations, particularly with respect to trading venue regulation under MiFIR where BTSs, for the most part, are used to amplify the highly technical trading venue regime, particularly with respect to market transparency. But Article 290 TFEU measures are also relied on heavily across MiFID II/MiFIR[450] (and particularly

---

[443] See further Ch VI sect 4.2.3.

[444] n 321.

[445] Some 21 or so Articles are subject to Art 290/291 delegations and some 22 Articles to ESMA-proposed BTS delegations; the BTS delegations are, however (certainly as compared to the EMIR BTS delegations), highly technical and procedural.

[446] n 218.

[447] Approximately 11 Articles are subject to Art 290/291 delegations, while eight or so are subject to ESMA-proposed BTS delegations.

[448] Some 26 or so Articles are subject to ESMA-proposed BTS delegations and some seven or so to Art 290/291 delegations; the substantive rules which amplify EMIR almost entirely take the form of RTSs.

[449] Danish Presidency Progress Report on MiFID II/MiFIR, 20 June 2012 (Council Document 11536/12) para 64.

[450] In some (limited) cases, the negotiations saw a BTS delegation become an Art 290 delegation (eg the 2014 MiFID II Art 31 delegation for administrative rules governing when an investment firm or market operator must notify its NCA in respect of significant breaches of its rules or disorderly conditions or conduct that may indicate behaviour in breach of the market abuse regime or system disruptions, which was originally in the form of an RTS delegation).

under MiFID II and with respect to investment firm regulation[451]). It is often not clear why one form is used over another; the Commission, however, has expressed its concern at the reliance on RTSs, in particular, and, implicitly, as to the relative preference shown by the Council and Parliament for ESMA-proposed RTSs.[452] Similarly the negotiations on the 2012 PRIPs Proposal[453] saw the Council support greater reliance on RTSs than on Commission rule-making more generally.[454] The ESFS Review has also revealed stakeholder support for BTSs to be privileged.[455]

Ultimately, the distinction between BTSs and other Article 290/291 TFEU rules is fine. It may be that pragmatism will come to define the classification; the extent to which a rule requires technical expertise (BTS) or sails close to the policy border and/or engages politically controversial issues (Commission-led Article 290/291 rule) is likely to be determinative. There is, however, a risk of legal challenge on the grounds of the incorrect choice of measure, to the potential detriment of the clarity and stability of the rulebook.[456] The procedural anomalies are also significant in relation to the relative degree of protection given to ESMA as the location of technical expertise in EU financial market governance, as is the potential for tension between the Commission and the Council and Parliament on how to deploy both sets of rules.

X.5.5.3 Early Lessons: Effectiveness, Institutional Balance, and the *Meroni* Effect

The BTS endorsement requirement, and the Commission's related veto and revision powers over proposed BTSs, had, from the outset, the potential to destabilize Commission/ESMA relations to the detriment of rule-making efficiency, particularly given the Commission's documented unhappiness at the restrictions placed on its BTS rule-making powers.[457]

---

[451] Art 290 rules dominate as the amplification vehicle under 2014 MiFID II Arts 24–30, which set out the extensive conduct regulation regime; they are also used in relation to organizational requirements (Art 16).

[452] The Art 290 route, eg, is used under the 2014 MiFIR to amplify the size of trade quote at which 'systematic internalizers' are required to enter into transactions with clients, although quote-related regulation is highly technical and heavily based on empirical evidence (ESMA is required to monitor the size of the quotes made by systematic internalizers (Art 19(1)): 2014 MiFIR Art 19(2). Elsewhere, the driver for reliance on Art 290 is clearer. The MiFIR requirement for trading venues and systematic internalizers to make trade data available on a 'reasonable commercial basis', eg, is to be amplified by administrative rules under the standard Art 290 TFEU route (2014 MiFIR Arts 13 and 15), reflecting, perhaps, the sensitivity of price-control-related regulation and its relative novelty for EU securities and markets regulation. Similarly, the reliance on Art 290 for administrative rules governing the conditions under which ESMA can take direct product intervention and position management measures (Arts 40(8)) and 45(10)) reflects the contested nature of ESMA's direct supervisory powers and the significant related institutional sensitivities. The Commission has, however, expressed its concern that the movement to RTSs over the negotiations does not reflect the technical nature of an RTS under the ESMA Regulation: Commission Statement on the Council Adoption of MiFID II/MiFIR, 7 May 2014 (Council Document 9344/14).

[453] COM (2012) 352/3.

[454] PRIPs Regulation ECOFIN General Approach, 24 June 2013, Council Document 11430/13.

[455] 2013 Mazars ESA Review, n 358, 15.

[456] The IMF, at an early stage, called for greater clarity as to the nature of BTSs and warned of the dangers of possible challenge: 2011 IMF Report, n 188, 15.

[457] At the time of the adoption of the ESA Regulations, the Commission issued a statement underlining its concern, and has re-asserted this concern over the crisis-era legislative programme. The 2012 PRIPs Proposal, eg, states: 'In this respect the Commission refers to the Statements in relation to Articles 290 and 291 TFEU it made at the adoption of the Regulations establishing the European Supervisory Authorities according to which: "As regards the process for the adoption of regulatory standards, the Commission emphasises the unique character of the financial services sector, following from the Lamfalussy structure and explicitly

There are few formal restraints on the Commission's powers to reject/revise BTSs. Neither impact assessment nor consultation is required, although ESMA's BTS proposals are subject to both. BTSs should be amended only 'where the Union's interests so require' and RTSs 'in very restricted and extraordinary circumstances', reflecting ESMA's status as the 'actor in close contact with and knowing best the daily functioning of financial markets'.⁴⁵⁸ These circumstances are potentially wide, however, including where the RTS is incompatible with EU law, does not respect the proportionality principle, or 'run[s] counter to the fundamental principles of the internal market for financial services as reflected in the acquis'.⁴⁵⁹ ESMA's initial sensitivities to the Commission's power were made clear from the outset: the 2011 ESMA FAQ asserts that the role of the Commission is to 'check that these draft laws are in the Union interest and are compatible with EU law and then to adopt these draft technical standards with minimal amendments, if at all possible'⁴⁶⁰ and 'the substance of the creation of [BTSs] has been delegated by the legislator to the supervisory community'.⁴⁶¹

The Commission had considerable incentives to ensure ESMA's effective operation, as one of its major architects, as a beneficiary of the intensification of EU intervention consequent on ESMA's activities, and as a consumer of ESMA's technical expertise. The likely hostility from the financial markets if the Commission was too quick to veto ESMA BTS proposals provided an additional brake. But the Commission also had the most to lose in terms of a loss of control over administrative rule-making; the potential for tension was aggravated by ESMA's reporting and communication links to the European Parliament.⁴⁶²

In practice, the risks associated with a poor ESMA/Commission relationship have not crystallized. At the time of writing, all but three of the swathe of BTSs proposed since January 2011 have been adopted without revision or veto by the Commission. Two of the rejected BTSs relate to the 2012 EMIR (one relates to the EMIR CCP college of supervisors and one to the EMIR implementation process (both 2013)); the other (2013) relates to the 2011 AIFMD and the identification of different types of AIF.⁴⁶³ The public record suggests that the Commission was not concerned to second-guess regulatory design choices made by ESMA (as has been the case with respect to ESMA technical advice). The three exceptions underline, nonetheless, the Commission's dominant position, its concern to protect its institutional prerogatives and the integrity of legislative measures (all three were concerned with differences between ESMA and the Commission on the foundation legislative text), and the potential for destabilizing tensions.

---

recognised in Declaration 39 to the TFEU. However, the Commission has serious doubts whether the restrictions on its role when adopting delegated acts and implementing measures are in line with Articles 290 and 291 TFEU".': COM (2012) 352/3, 6.

⁴⁵⁸ 2010 ESMA Regulation Arts 10(1) and 15(1) and rec 23.

⁴⁵⁹ 2010 ESMA Regulation rec 23.

⁴⁶⁰ 2011 ESMA FAQ, n 374, 4–5.

⁴⁶¹ 2011 ESMA FAQ, n 374, 5.

⁴⁶² The background tensions were alluded to by ECON Chair Bowles on the launch of EBA, when she highlighted that the dialogue with the ESAs would flourish 'given that we are actually meant to engage with you—perhaps I ought to explain to the uninitiated that in times past, the Commission was a little jealous of others getting advice from the advisory committees': Speech by ECON Chair Bowles, EBA Launch, 1 April 2011.

⁴⁶³ See Ch VI sect 4.2.3 and Ch III sect 4.5.

The AIFMD RTS rejection underlines the potential for institutional tensions.[464] The draft RTS was rejected by the Commission, at the very end of the period given to the Commission to revise/reject the RTS, as it did not conform to the Commission's analysis of the AIFMD legislative text.[465] ESMA subsequently revised the RTS to respond to the Commission's position.[466] But it was robust in response, justifying its original approach in detail, highlighting that the Commission's approach was not the only reasonable way of interpreting the AIFMD, and underlining that draft RTSs should only be revised by the Commission in 'very restricted and extraordinary circumstances'.[467] ESMA also highlighted that its original approach was designed to be flexible and to reflect market practice and investor expectations. It revised the RTS, however, in order to ensure timely implementation of the AIFMD administrative regime. ESMA's robust approach can also be seen from its proposal of the RTS, although the Commission's concern had been well flagged in advance.[468] It may not be unreasonable to suggest that ESMA is becoming concerned to assert its institutional position as expert regulator, to force the Commission into publicly stating its opposition, to activate the review process and, thereby, to restate its objections and reinforce its position. Equally, the determination of the Commission to reject the proposed RTS, despite familiarity with the debate at the ESMA Board of Supervisors, suggests some Commission determination to retain control over the process. But the public rift between ESMA and the Commission underlines the potential for destabilizing tensions between ESMA, as the expert markets regulator and location of technical expertise, and the Commission, as the location of competence with respect to administrative rule-making. Thus far, however, these episodes remain rare.

Relations with the European Parliament are also potentially problematic. It was, and remains, the driving force behind the conferral of new supervisory powers on ESMA. But supervisory powers do not directly impinge on the Parliament's law-making prerogatives, in relation to which the Parliament has, historically, been intensely protective. The possibility arose, therefore, of Parliament exercising its veto rights in relation to BTSs. The precedents were troubling. Although the Lamfalussy-era 'level 2' rule-making process ultimately became workmanlike, the relationship between CESR and the Parliament was fractious

---

[464] On the friction generated by the rejected EMIR BTS see Ch VI sect 4.2.3.

[465] Commission Letter to ESMA, 4 July 2013 (Ref.Ares(2013)2569526). The draft ESMA RTS (ESMA/2013/413) was designed to identify different types of alternative investment fund manager for the purposes of appropriate differentiation of the AIFMD requirements (as required by AIFMD Art 4(4)), and identified managers of open- and closed-ended funds as appropriate for differentiation. ESMA differentiated between open- and closed-ended funds by means of redemption frequency: open-ended funds provided for redemption on at least an annual basis; closed-ended funds provided for redemption at intervals longer than annually. This approach, ESMA argued, would ensure flexibility and proportionality in the application of the AIFMD, particularly with respect to liquidity and valuation, and reflected market practice. It would not, ESMA argued, be proportionate to require funds with infrequent redemption intervals of more than one year to be subject to the full set of liquidity management obligations. The Commission argued that this approach did not conform to the legislative text which treated closed-end funds as those which did not redeem.

[466] ESMA, Opinion on the Draft RTS on types of AIFM (2013) (ESMA/2013/119).

[467] n 466, 6. Subsequently, ESMA Chairman Maijoor noted that ESMA was of the view that the RTS draft was 'valid and legally sound', 'but in order to move the process forward—and recognizing that the Commission ultimately holds the pen', had presented a revised draft: Speech on ESMA—Issues and Priorities, 5 November 2013 (ESMA/2013/1582).

[468] Board of Supervisors Meetings, 14 March 2013 (ESMA/2013/BS/30) and 6 November 2012 (ESMA/2012/BS/143).

on occasion.[469] The Parliament's ECON committee's muscular approach to the nomination of the first set of ESA chairs in February 2011 set down a marker for its intention to protect its institutional powers.[470] The Parliament's ECON committee initially, and somewhat provocatively, rejected the nominations. The nominations were subsequently approved by the Parliament's plenary session, but only after it had extracted a series of written commitments from the Commission and Council with respect to the independence of the ESAs, the composition of their Boards of Supervisors, budgetary resources, and the appointment procedure.[471]

The risks which tensions with the European Parliament could pose to effective rule-making were exposed to dramatic effect in January 2013, when the Parliament's ECON committee threatened to veto the swathe of EMIR BTSs, on substantive grounds as well as procedural grounds related to the Commission's failure to communicate effectively with the Parliament over the BTS adoption process. Although the Commission's subsequent commitment to enhancing relations with the Parliament, and its acknowledgement that the BTS process was a new process which would become refined over time, removed the veto threat, the episode underlines that the Parliament's veto power is not a paper tiger.[472]

Ultimately, the BTS process is delicately balanced. It must inject ESMA's technical expertise while respecting the Commission's status as the administrative rule-maker under the Treaty and ensuring the Parliament's prerogatives are respected. Most difficulties lie with Commission endorsement. Were the Commission to automatically endorse all ESMA's proposals, the BTS process would generate significant constitutional uncertainty relating to the *de facto* location of rule-making power,[473] but rejections and revisions generate tensions and market uncertainty. At present, the process seems to be working relatively well. The Commission has, for the most part, not sought to substitute its regulatory design choices for ESMA's (as it has done in relation to ESMA's technical advice) but has limited rejections/revisions to where it has concerns as to fit with the legislative text. The process is highly transparent and thus imposes discipline on both institutions. The ESFS Review did not suggest significant stakeholder concern with the endorsement process in principle; greater concern was reported with respect to revisions of ESMA's technical advice and proposed BTSs and with respect to the scale of ESMA's soft law activities.[474]

Further difficulties may, however, emerge. The BTS process is cumbersome and is ill suited to facilitating efficient revisions of BTSs where market developments require that BTSs are speedily revised or withdrawn. The process can be lengthy, particularly where the

---

[469] Well illustrated by imbroglio concerning CESR's adoption of 'standards' concerning clearing and settlement in 2004: see further sect 2.3.

[470] As did an earlier revision by the European Parliament to the ESA Proposals to identify the Parliament as the sole institution to which the ESAs were accountable (July 2010 Parliament Negotiating Position, n 201, Art 1b).

[471] European Parliament Press Release, 20110203IPR13128. The release noted that the Council was 'roundly criticised' during the plenary debate.

[472] See further Ch VI sect 4.2.3.

[473] It has been suggested that any abdication by the Commission of its oversight powers would generate legal certainty and transparency risks, negatively impact the rights of affected parties, and raise significant issues related to the control of delegated and implementing rules: Busuioc, n 351, 123.

[474] See further sect 5.10.

institutions exercise their ability to extend the deadlines for review of proposed BTSs. Where legislative mandates for BTSs are highly technical and detailed, reflecting political compromises which can be muddled, the ability of ESMA to inject technical expertise can be prejudiced. And the potential for destabilizing institutional conflict is real. In particular, as the rule-making ecosystem becomes more fragile, and if tensions emerge between the single market and the euro area under Banking Union, endorsement may come to represent an unhelpful additional source of tension.

Overall, the potential damage to ESMA's capacity and to the Commission's credibility were institutional relations to deteriorate such that the BTS process came into doubt, as well as experience with other agencies where the potential for destabilizing conflict has not arisen,[475] suggests that both institutions have strong incentives to ensure the BTS process is effective. While procedural efficiency would be best served by the removal of the Commission endorsement shackle, this is not a realistic proposition given the current Treaty settlement. Some procedural enhancements may, however, enhance the BTS process, as the ESFS review has suggested (section 5.10).

X.5.6 Guidelines and Recommendations

X.5.6.1 Article 16 and the 'Hardening' of Soft Law

Under ESMA Regulation Article 16, ESMA is empowered to issue guidelines and recommendations, addressed to NCAs or to financial market participants, and with a view to establishing consistent, efficient, and effective supervisory practices within the ESFS.

Non-binding soft law measures such as guidelines have traditionally formed a key part of the financial market 'rulebook', loosely termed. In the EU, these soft measures fulfil the standard-setting and disciplining functions associated with soft law generally. But they also provide a channel through which ESMA can side-step the formal Treaty constraints which shape the binding rulebook, and thereby extend and shape the EU regulatory environment in response to evolving market conditions and correct, or at least smooth over, errors in the binding rulebook which cannot easily be addressed. At the same time, they provide a potentially powerful mechanism for strengthening ESMA's capacity as a nascent standard-setter. They generate, accordingly, troublesome opacities in relation to status and legitimacy.

As outlined in section 2.3.5, CESR, with few legal supports, developed a vast array of soft law of doubtful status. ESMA's Article 16 measures had (and have been shown to have) the potential to be qualitatively different. The ESMA Regulation acknowledges the need for a 'soft rulebook' to support the binding regime: 'in areas not covered by regulatory or implementing standards, ESMA should have the power to issue guidelines and recommendations on the application of Union law' (recital 26). The procedural requirements for Article 16 measures are akin to those which apply to binding rules. As with proposals for BTSs, public consultations and impact assessment must be carried out,[476] and the SMSG

---

[475] Everson, n 10, 19.

[476] Although only 'where appropriate', and consultations and impact assessment exercises must be proportionate to the scope, nature, and impact of the guidelines or recommendations.

consulted (Article 16(2)). In a material change to the CESR era, NCAs and financial market participants are injuncted to 'make every effort' to comply with guidelines and recommendations (Article 16(3)).

Most importantly, Article 16 has been subject to a novel 'comply or explain' requirement[477] which, like the QMV, brings a new dynamic to bear on NCA relations within ESMA. It also has the capacity to strengthen significantly ESMA's ability to steer its soft law measures into binding rules or into *de facto* binding supervisory practices at national level. Within two months of the issuance of a guideline or recommendation, each NCA must confirm whether it complies or intends to comply with the guideline or recommendation—where it does not comply, or intends not to comply, it must inform ESMA providing reasons (Article 16(3)). ESMA must publish the fact of non-compliance (or intended non-compliance) and, on a case-by-case basis, may also decide to publish the NCA's reasons (Article 16(3)). ESMA must also address NCA compliance in its annual report to the Council, European Parliament, and Commission; ESMA must also inform the institutions of the Article 16 measures which have been issued, identify non-compliant NCAs, and outline how it 'intends to ensure' that the NCA follows Article 16 measures in the future (Article 16(4)). The Parliament, in particular, can be expected to take a keen interest in how ESMA responds to explanations of failures to comply (Article 16(4)). ESMA may also, at its discretion, require financial market participants to 'report in a clear and detailed way whether they comply' with Article 16 measures.

The 'comply or explain' mechanism is novel and its implications should not be underestimated.[478] In principle, the 'comply or explain' mechanism accommodates non-compliance and allows NCAs, defeated under a QMV, to disregard a measure and explain the non-compliance by reference to, for example, local market conditions or a difference of interpretation. But the public quality of the 'explain' element makes it more difficult to disregard Article 16 measures on narrow national interest grounds. Reluctance to disclose particular national interests, and the significant cultural shift which the 'explain' requirement may require of many NCAs, further strengthens the binding quality of Article 16. NCAs may also be reluctant to undermine ESMA publicly and thereby weaken ESMA's ability to support NCAs at national level. The formal mechanisms for hardening Article 16 measures are also coupled with a hardening of the wider environment, given QMV-based decision-making and the hierarchical dimension which ESMA's operational supervisory and enforcement powers have brought to the ESMA/NCA relationship.[479]

The 'hard' quality of ESA guidelines has recently been acknowledged by the ESA Board of Appeals. In its first decision, it relied on EBA guidelines to interpret the (now repealed) 2006 Capital Requirements Directive I (CRD I) as potentially requiring NCAs to impose management suitability requirements on the management of a bank branch. EBA had argued that such an obligation was not required under EU law under CRD I and that its Guidelines were not binding and could not extend the scope of EU law. The Board relied

---

[477] Which was introduced by the European Parliament during the ESA negotiations. By the end of the CESR era, CESR members had formalized their commitment to this principle in the 2008 CESR Charter, but it was not required as a matter of EU law.

[478] ESMA has identified the 'comply-or-explain' requirement as a 'key difference' from the CESR regime: 2011 ESMA FAQ, n 374, 5.

[479] See further Ch XI.

on the guidelines and a wider interpretation of CRD I to find that a breach of EU law could have taken place. It argued that even if the EBA guidelines were not binding, they addressed the matter in question from a practical perspective and assisted in the interpretation of CRD I.[480] The Commission has similarly suggested that non-compliance with guidelines could indicate an underlying breach of EU law.[481]

The co-legislators have also formally acknowledged the role of soft law. The crisis-era rulebook (including the ESMA Regulation)[482] contains a series of specific directions to ESMA to adopt guidelines, often in relation to technical and procedural matters, but also with respect to substantively significant areas.[483] So too do the reforms to the FSAP-era measures under the 2010 Omnibus I Directive[484] and the reforms adopted during the 'second wave' of crisis-era reforms, including the 2014 MiFID II/MiFIR regime.[485]

X.5.6.2 Early Lessons

ESMA has adopted a range of Article 16 measures which clarify the rulebook (often building on earlier CESR measures)[486] or are expressly required by the crisis-era legislative

---

[480] Decision of the Board of Appeal. BoA 2013-008. 24 June 2013. Ref. EBA C 2013 002. At issue was whether the failure by the NCAs in question to impose suitability requirements on branch management was a breach of EU law, and whether the related Art 17 complaint which was the subject of the appeal was thereby admissible (ESA Regulation Art 17 empowers the ESAs to take action where an NCA is in breach of EU law). Art 11 CRD I, which imposed fit and proper management requirements, applied only to those directing the business of the credit institution and in the authorization context. Art 22, however, required NCAs more generally to ensure that credit institutions had robust governance arrangements. EBA's 2012 Guidelines on the Assessment of the Suitability of Members of the Management Body and Key Function Holders, which relate to Arts 11 and 22, were designed to be broader in scope than Art 11 and to apply beyond the authorization context, and, in particular, to address a wider range of persons, including key function holders. EBA relied on the restrictive scope of Art 11 and the non-binding quality of its Guidelines to argue that the complaint was inadmissible as a breach of EU law had not occurred. The Board of Appeal concluded that the complaint was admissible given that Art 22, as interpreted in light of the EBA Guidelines, could be read as requiring that failure to assess the ongoing suitability of branch management was a breach of EU law.

[481] In relation to the reporting by a group of NCAs of their non-compliance with ESMA's guidelines on the exemption for market-makers under the Short Selling Regulation: Commission, Report from the Commission to the European Parliament and Council on the Short Selling Regulation (2013) (COM (2013) 885) 6. The Commission also indicated to ESMA that it might request it to take action: Board of Supervisors Meeting, 4 July 2013 (ESMA/2013/BS/125).

[482] Which suggests that ESMA develop Art 16 guidelines to promote convergence in supervisory functioning and best practices adopted in colleges of supervisors.

[483] ESMA has, eg, been directed to adopt guidelines (in conjunction with EBA) in relation to the remuneration structures used by alternative investment fund managers and in relation to the complex array of required third county co-operation arrangements: 2011 AIFMD Arts 13, 35(12), 36(4), 37(16), 40(12), and 42(4). The 2012 EMIR, eg, requires ESMA to adopt guidelines in relation to interoperability (Art 64(7)). See nn 487 and 488.

[484] Under the 2010 Omnibus I Directive, ESMA has been encouraged to adopt guidance in relation to the reputation and experience requirements which apply to investment firms' management (rec 34).

[485] The 2014 MiFID II directs ESMA to adopt guidance with respect to, eg, the cross-selling of proprietary products to investors and the suitability assessment: 2014 MiFID II Directive Arts 24 and 25.

[486] This category includes ESMA's Art 16 measures under crisis-era measures (eg, Guidelines on Exemptions for Market Making Activities and Primary Market Operators under the Short Selling Regulation (ESMA/2013/74); and Guidelines on Key Concepts of the AIFMD (ESMA/2012/845)) and under earlier measures, chief among them MiFID I (Guidelines on Certain Aspects of the MiFID Compliance Function (ESMA/2012/388) and on the MiFID I Suitability Function (ESMA/2012/387)) and the UCITS regime (Guidelines on ETFs (Exchange-Traded Funds) and other UCITS Issues (ESMA/2012/832); Guidelines on Repurchase and Reverse Repurchase Agreements (ESMA/2012/722); and Guidelines and Recommendations on Risk Measurement and Calculation of Global Exposure for Structured UCITS (ESMA/2012/197)).

regime.[487] As under the CESR era, these measures are typically described as being designed to promote greater convergence across NCAs and to achieve clarity in the application of the rulebook. They are also typically closely tied to the rulebook.[488]

More controversially, ESMA has adopted Article 16 measures which are tied to the binding rulebook but which push against it, in that they are designed to apply the rulebook to emerging risks not contemplated when the rules were adopted. Chief among these are ESMA's 2011 guidelines on automated trading, which address the contested area of high frequency trading (HFT);[489] ESMA's NCA members became subject to the Article 16 'comply or explain' reporting obligation in February 2012 and market participants were 'expected to comply' by May 2012.[490] Algorithmic trading and HFT have developed exponentially in recent years and are the subject of regulatory attention internationally, including under the 2014 MiFID II/MiFIR reforms (Chapter VI section 2.3). But at the time of the adoption of the 2011 ESMA Guidelines, the EU had not adopted discrete rules in this area. The Guidelines arose from CESR's earlier fact-finding on EU equity market microstructure which highlighted the rapid growth in automated trading, and ESMA's subsequent concern that, pending the adoption of binding rules under the MiFID II/ MiFIR and market abuse reforms, and given the risks associated with automated trading and the focus of EU and international regulators on this issue, it was necessary to clarify how the current legislative regime applied to automated trading.[491] The Guidelines are, however, closely tied to MiFID I and the market abuse regime. They address automated trading from the perspective of trading platforms and of firms engaging in this form of trading, and do not address the panoply of regulatory issues raised by automated trading, focusing instead on MiFID I-related organizational requirements.[492] They are described as setting out ESMA's view of how EU law should be applied and of appropriate supervisory practices within the ESFS, and as having the purpose of ensuring a common, uniform, and consistent application of MiFID I and of the market abuse regime.[493] Application of the existing MiFID I rulebook, and not a soft law extension, was the overriding concern in this first major application of Article 16. Specific guidelines are, in each case, referenced to the relevant binding rules (typically a MiFID I organizational rule). ESMA also repeatedly reiterated its concern to operate within the binding rulebook,[494] as well as the non-binding nature of the Guidelines.[495]

---

[487] Including ESMA's Guidelines on Interoperability (required under EMIR Art 54(4)) (ESMA/2013/ 323) and its Guidelines on Alternative Investment Fund Manager Remuneration (required under AIFMD Art 13(2)) (ESMA/2013/201).

[488] ESMA's EMIR Interoperability Guidelines, eg, are declared not to involve new requirements and to respect the related Art 51(3) legislative requirements on interoperability: ESMA/2012/323.

[489] ESMA/2012/122.

[490] ESMA Press Release 24 February 2012 (ESMA/2012/128).

[491] Consultation Paper ESMA/2011/224 (ESMA Automated Trading Consultation Paper) 7–8 and Final Report ESMA/2011/456 (ESMA Automated Trading Guidelines Final Report) 7–8.

[492] See further Ch. VI sect 2.3.

[493] ESMA Automated Trading Guidelines Final Report, n 491, 3 and 5.

[494] ESMA Automated Trading Guidelines Final Report, n 491, Feedback Statement, 62. Accordingly, it declined to deal with issues which engaged revision of the binding rulebook.

[495] eg ESMA Automated Trading Guidelines Final Report, n 491, Feedback Statement, 62, highlighting that the Guidelines were non-binding and did not have the legal authority of legislation.

ESMA does not appear to have any appetite for using Article 16 for measures which do not have any direct connection to the EU rulebook.[496] This is clear from the high-profile ESMA/EBA initiative in response to the Libor and benchmarks scandal. The 2013 ESMA/EBA Principles for Benchmarks[497] are addressed to the activities of reference-rate and other benchmark administrators, publishers, and market participants, as well as to competent authorities and users of reference-rates and other benchmarks. They are designed to bridge the interim period until binding rules are adopted in the EU. The measures were not adopted as quasi-binding Article 16 guidelines, however, but as 'principles'. ESMA and EBA 'consider it important' that the 2013 Principles are applied by relevant market participants and national supervisory authorities, but their coercive force is a function of the extent to which the market and national authorities have incentives to follow these principles. The earlier consultation made this explicit, arguing that the proposed principles were designed to address problems in the areas of benchmarks until a formal regulatory and supervisory framework was devised, and describing the principles as providing a 'glide path to future obligations that are likely to be binding'.[498] Similarly, ESMA has deployed a 'code of conduct' mechanism in relation to proxy advisers. Concluding after a review of the proxy adviser market and a related consultation[499] that there was no evidence of a market failure demanding either legally binding intervention by the EU or 'quasi-binding EU regulatory instruments' such as Article 16 guidelines,[500] ESMA called on the industry to address the concerns it had identified by means of a code of conduct, based on the principles and operating within the governance structure ESMA recommended.[501] ESMA accordingly proved reluctant to deploy Article 16 and also displayed some sensitivity to the scope restrictions which apply to ESMA's operation generally.[502]

Early evidence also suggests that ESMA's capacity to build a 'soft rulebook' which acquires coercive force through national supervisory practices is considerable. Article 16 guidelines all make reference to their basis in Article 16 and to the requirements for NCAs and financial market participants to 'make every effort to comply', and underline the reporting obligations which apply to NCAs who must also incorporate the guidelines in their supervisory practices (to date, ESMA has not required financial market participants to report on compliance). The change in status from the CESR era is clear from ESMA's appetite for using the Article 16 channel to achieve similar effects where the binding route is closed off; on the Commission's rejection of its proposed RTS on the operation of CCP colleges of supervisors under EMIR, it suggested that it would proceed through the Article 16 guideline route.[503] The change in status is also underlined by ESMA's care in addressing CESR-era guidelines; the 2013 and 2011 re-issues and updates of CESR's extensive

---

[496] The MiFID I Remuneration Guidelines, eg, were embarked on after confirmation from the Commission that there was scope for ESMA to clarify these rules under MiFID I: ESMA, Annual Report (2011) 45.

[497] ESMA-EBA Principles for Benchmark-Setting Processes in the EU (ESMA/2013/659); Consultation Paper ESMA/2013/12.

[498] n 497, 2–3.

[499] ESMA, Discussion Paper on the Role of the Proxy Adviser Industry (2012) (ESMA/2012/212).

[500] n 499, 7.

[501] ESMA, Final Report. Feedback Statement on the Consultation Regarding the Role of the Proxy Adviser Industry (2013) (ESMA/2013/84).

[502] 2012 ESMA Proxy Advisor Discussion Paper, n 499, 35, highlighting that any Art 16 initiative would need to come within ESMA's scope of activity.

[503] See Ch VI sect 4.2.3.

guidelines on the 2004 Prospectus Regulation are expressly stated as not taking the form of Article 16 guidelines, and as not being subject to the NCA 'comply or explain' requirement.[504] CESR's Guidelines on the Enforcement of Financial Information, by contrast, have been re-issued as Article 16 guidelines and subject to the 'comply or explain' reporting requirement.[505]

But the reality of non-compliance is real. ESMA's Guidelines on the Exemption for Market-Making Activities under the 2012 Short Selling Regulation triggered non-compliance from five NCAs: Denmark (in part), France (in whole), Germany (in part), Sweden (in part), and the UK (in part).[506] Although reasons varied, Denmark, Germany, Sweden, and the UK[507] all shared the view that ESMA's interpretation of the 2012 Short Selling Regulation as limiting the availability of the exemption (by means of the market maker's trading venue membership) was incorrect, although the Guidelines expressly referred to the Commission's support of ESMA's position. The reasons offered were based on textual interpretation, the objectives of the Short Selling Regulation, and the NCAs' concern that liquidity in their markets would be damaged. By contrast, France refused to comply on entirely different grounds, making its compliance conditional on all NCAs fully applying the Guidelines in order to avoid competitive distortion between the French financial industry and that of other Member States. NCA non-compliance in this case seems to have been a function of a difference of interpretation rather than of national interests. But the failure of the NCAs of five major financial markets, including the NCAs of the EU's largest three markets, to comply with a key element of operationally critical Guidelines points to a significant failure in ESMA Board of Supervisors' decision-making, while France's adoption of a conditional compliance model may become a serious threat to Article 16. The Commission's subsequent highlighting of the potential distortion to competition which could arise, and of the possibility of enforcement action where NCAs were in breach of the regime, underlines the dangers which arise where guidelines are not applied consistently.[508]

There are further difficulties. Different forms of guidelines co-exist, generating legal certainty risks. ESMA Article 16 guidelines apply alongside, for example, CESR-era guidelines which have been re-issued by ESMA but not adopted under Article 16, and CESR-era guidelines which remain in force but have not been re-issued by ESMA. These three forms of guidelines have all emerged from different procedures and have different degrees of coercive effect. ESMA has, for example, engaged in a peer review of the important 2010 CESR Guidelines on Money Market Funds,[509] suggesting these Guidelines carry some coercive effect, but the Article 16 'comply or explain' mechanism does not apply.

The Article 16 channel may also inject significant uncertainty into the EU regulatory environment. The Money Market Fund Guidelines Peer Review highlights that in some Member States NCAs do not have the legal power to implement ESMA guidelines, leading

---

[504] ESMA/2013/319 and ESMA/2011/81.

[505] The Guidelines are under review: ESMA/2013/1013.

[506] Guidelines Compliance Table (ESMA/2013/765).

[507] The UK refusal was described as a 'significant milestone' in the context of the UK's attempts to minimize the negative impact on the City of EU measures: Masters, B, 'New Watchdog Snubs Brussels to Adopt Rules that Favour Bankers', *Financial Times*, 27 August 2013, 1.

[508] n 481.

[509] ESMA, Peer Review Money Market Funds (2013) (ESMA/2013/476).

in some cases to the NCA simply informing the industry of the guidelines; in other cases, guidelines have been implemented through the relevant NCA's binding rulebook.[510] National courts may also take different approaches to the status of guidelines. Legitimacy difficulties arise,[511] although they are mitigated by the insertion of the NCA as the channel through which compliance is, in practice, achieved.[512] Effectiveness risks also arise, particularly where market participants challenge the ability of NCAs to impose 'soft' guidelines on a national market and NCA capacity to act is thereby challenged.

The possibility for institutional tension is also strong. The Commission, protecting its rule-making prerogatives, has taken a close interest in ESMA's Article 16 activities, and has repeatedly warned where it regards a measure as not being in conformity with the related legislative measure,[513] raised the possibility of it producing interpretative communications where ESMA action conflicts with the legislative text, and highlighted that ESMA is not empowered to interpret legislative measures.[514] Legitimacy within the EU framework generally also remains problematic, however, as does *Meroni* compliance given the norm-generating effects of ESMA soft law, although the close connection to the EU rulebook acts a mitigant, as does ESMA's accountability framework.

But however messy the status of the measures it produces, and however uncertain the consistency of pan-EU application, Article 16 remains a pragmatic response to the strains which the EU's constitutional arrangements place on ESMA's ability to clarify a highly technical rulebook and to support its consistent application.

X.5.7 Supervisory Convergence Measures: Article 29 and Beyond

ESMA is empowered to adopt an array of 'soft' supervisory convergence measures which, in practice, have quasi-regulatory effects. The main competence for the vast array of supervisory convergence measures it can adopt is Article 29, which requires ESMA to play an active role in building a common EU supervisory culture and consistent supervisory practices and in ensuring uniform procedures and a consistent approach throughout the EU. It also expressly empowers ESMA to provide opinions to NCAs and to contribute to the development of high-quality and uniform supervisory standards. ESMA's related activities include: 'opinions' to NCAs;[515] 'principles' addressed to market participants

---

[510] n 509, 6–7.

[511] As is clear from the ESFS Review (sect 5.10).

[512] NCAs implement guidelines in a variety of ways, including through binding administrative rules, soft circulars and other measures, and supervisory practices. The 2010 CESR Guidelines on Money Market Funds, eg, were implemented by NCAs through mandatory rules but also by means of soft measures, compliance with which by the market was achieved by an NCA statement that failure to comply would be interpreted as a breach of a specific binding rule: n 509, 6–7.

[513] eg with respect to ESMA's proposed guidelines on AIFMD reporting (Board of Supervisors Meeting, 22 May 2013 (ESMA/2013/BS/86)); ESMA's proposed guidelines on the Short Selling Regulation market-maker exemption (Board of Supervisors Meeting, 18 December 2012 (ESMA/2013/BS/4)); and ESMA's proposed Q&A on a tripartite base prospectus under the prospectus regime (Board of Supervisors Meeting, 6 November 2012 (ESMA/2012/BS/143)).

[514] Board of Supervisors Meetings, 14 March 2013 (ESMA/2013/BS/30) and 18 December (2012 ESMA/2013/BS/4), relating to ESMA's short selling market-maker guidelines and short selling Q&A, respectively.

[515] ESMA has, eg, addressed an opinion to NCAs which sets out a framework within which third country prospectuses can be assessed (ESMA/2013/317), an opinion to NCAs on the base prospectus (ESMA/2013/

and NCAs;[516] 'Q&As'/'FAQs';[517] 'supervisory briefings',[518] and 'public statements'.[519] Finally, ESMA's powers to impose individual decisions on financial market participants and on NCAs (discussed in Chapter XI section 5) can be expected to generate norm-setting effects.

Article 29 measures are generally designed to support supervisory convergence. The Q&A/FAQ device, for example, is typically described by ESMA as a response to questions raised by the public and NCAs, and as a 'practical convergence tool' designed to promote common supervisory approaches and practices and to assist market participants by providing clarity.[520] Like Article 16 guidelines, Article 29 measures operate within the EU rulebook and have not (typically) been used to extend ESMA's sphere of operation.[521] They are usually addressed to NCAs, although not always, and market participants are frequently identified as benefiting from the clarity which the measure in question provides. While Q&As/FAQs have come to be relied on heavily by the market, particularly in new and complex areas (as has been the case with the EMIR FAQ), the binding quality ascribed to these measures varies, although, overall, ESMA has made efforts to cloak these measures with some degree of quasi-binding quality. The proxy adviser 'Principles', for example, have been cloaked with a deterrent mechanism to support compliance.[522] That they have a weaker binding quality than Article 16 measures is clear from ESMA's characterization of these measures as potential launchpads for subsequent Article 16 intervention.[523]

1944), an opinion to NCAs on the application of the UCITS Directive requirement that only 10 per cent of a UCITS's assets can take the form of non-eligible assets (ESMA/2012/721), and an opinion to NCAs on the late transposition of the UCITS IV Directive and the practical arrangements to be deployed by NCAs (ESMA/2011/342).

[516] Notably the Benchmark Principles (ESMA/2013/659) and the Proxy Adviser Code of Conduct Principles (ESMA/2013/84).

[517] 'New' Q&As have been adopted under the 2011 AIFMD (ESMA/2014/163), the rating agency regime (ESMA/2013/1935), the 2012 Short Selling Regulation (ESMA/2013/159), the 2012 EMIR (ESMA/2013/324), the market abuse regime (ESMA/2012/9), and the UCITS regime (an array of Q&As have been adopted, including in relation to ESMA's Guidelines on UCITS ETF and other issues (ESMA/2013/314), on the UCITS KIID (ESMA/2012/592), on UCITS risk management and the calculation of global exposures and counterparty risk (ESMA/2012/429), on the UCITS notification system (ESMA/2012/428), and on the earlier CESR Money Market Fund Guidelines (ESMA/2012/113)). ESMA has also continued to update and revise CESR-era Q&As in relation to the prospectus regime, the transparency regime, and the 2004 MiFID I.

[518] Supervisory briefings, addressed to NCAs and designed to support supervisors, have been adopted in relation to MiFID I and with respect to its suitability requirements (ESMA/2012/850) and appropriateness and execution-only requirements (ESMA/2012/851).

[519] These are typically deployed in relation to the International Financial Reporting Standards (IFRS) reporting regime and set out ESMA's stance on various reporting issues: eg, ESMA/2012/853 on the treatment of forbearance practices in the IFRS financial statements of financial institutions, ESMA/2012/397 on sovereign debt treatment in financial statements, and ESMA/2011/211 on retrospective adjustments to financial statements.

[520] eg Short Selling Q&A (ESMA/2013/159) 3.

[521] The MiFID I Supervisory Briefings, eg, are asserted to be not exhaustive, not constituting new policy, and not promoting any particular way of supervising MiFID I's rules: Suitability Supervisory Briefing (ESMA/2012/850) 2.

[522] ESMA warned that it would review industry developments within two years, and that 'it may reconsider its position' if substantial progress was not made in that time: ESMA Press Release on Proxy Advisers (ESMA/2013/240).

[523] ESMA highlighted, eg, that its Q&A on its UCITS ETF and other UCITS Issues Guidelines could be converted into an Art 16 measure: n 517, 4.

Article 29 allows ESMA to deploy an array of flexible tools to support supervisory convergence and gives ESMA the necessary freedom to respond to market developments and provide market participants with some degree of certainty and clarity. Nonetheless, where these measure are associated with related enforcement strategies, as is the case with the 'public statements' on the accounting regime, they raise troubling questions as to their validity. Similar difficulties arise as to their relationship with the binding rulebook where opacities or inconsistencies arise, and with respect to whether compliance provides any form of 'safe harbour'.

X.5.8 Shaping the Rulebook: Reviews

The ESMA Regulation envisages a specific role for ESMA in 'upstream' policy development with respect to the strengthening of the EU investor compensation system and the development of an EU resolution and recovery system (Articles 25–27). This policy role was the outcome of a political compromise designed to placate the European Parliament, which sought more extensive ESMA powers over cross-border actors.

But there are a number of other channels through which ESMA can shape the legislative framework upstream. Article 16 (guidelines) and Article 29 (supervisory convergence measures) allow ESMA to shape legislative reform.[524] Its demonstrated technical capacity, and its ability and obligation to capture market intelligence, particularly with respect to systemic risk,[525] makes it a key resource for the EU institutions, and particularly the European Parliament, which does not have the technical resource base of the Commission. Its obligation to provide reviews and reports to the Parliament, Commission, and Council, on request,[526] places it in a strong position to shape policy development as well as to strengthen its reputation across the law-making institutions. It has already shown its capacity and enthusiasm for upstream shaping of legislative action by its soft law measures, particularly with respect to algorithmic trading and benchmarks. ESMA might also be expected to enthusiastically exercise its power to issue own-initiative opinions to the EU institutions (ESMA Regulation Article 34(1))—opinions of this nature might also prove a useful means for bolstering relations with the Parliament.

ESMA is also injected into the review process which applies to EU securities and markets regulation. Under ESMA Regulation Article 26, ESMA is expressly empowered to review the application of BTSs and of Article 16 measures and to propose amendments where appropriate. The crisis-era legislative programme has required ESMA to review a host of

---

[524] The development process for the 2011 Automated Trading Guidelines, eg, contains repeated references to stakeholder concern that the Commission engage with ESMA on how the Guidelines would interact with the MiFID I Review and the market abuse reforms, as well as to ESMA's close co-operation with the Commission on the development of the Guidelines and to ESMA's position on how the legislative regime might develop: eg n 491, Impact Assessment, 62–3. Ultimately, the Guidelines shaped the new 2014 MiFID II/MiFIR regime (as acknowledged in 2014 MiFID II rec 47).

[525] eg Arts 9(1) (consumer trends), 22 and 23 (systemic risk), 32 (assessment of market conditions and risks generally), and 35 (general information gathering powers). On its extensive systemic risk-related surveillance activities see Ch XI sect 5.5.3.

[526] Art 22(4) requires ESMA to conduct enquires into systemic risk on the request of the Parliament, Commission, or Council (and confers own-initiative powers to do so), and Art 34(1) more generally requires it to provide opinions to the Parliament, Council, or Commission on their request.

areas which were highly contested at the time of their adoption, including the reporting thresholds for short positions and the operation of the circuit-breaker regime under the 2012 Short Selling Regulation,[527] the 2011 AIFMD's third country access regime,[528] and the 2012 EMIR's exemption for pension funds.[529] ESMA will also be closely engaged with the mandatory reviews required of the Commission in respect of all the crisis-era legislative measures.[530] As discussed in Chapter VI, ESMA's 2013 review for the Commission of the Short Selling Regulation did not shy away from proposing reforms.

X.5.9 The International Context and ESMA

EU agencies typically have an international dimension to their operation, which can be troublesome given the Commission's competences internationally.[531] ESMA's quasi-rule-making activities similarly have an international dimension,[532] implicit in the ESMA Regulation Article 1(5) objective of strengthening international supervisory co-ordination, and reflecting ESMA's strong incentives to establish a presence on the international stage.[533] ESMA's quasi-rule-making activities include expert assistance to the Commission on equivalence determinations, negotiations with, in particular, the US Securities and Exchange Commission (SEC) on the application of EU and US regulation extraterritorially, and, of most direct relevance to rule-making, engagement with international standard-setters. The 2012 EMIR BTS process, for example, saw ESMA closely engaged in the development of standards internationally in relation to the over-the-counter (OTC) derivatives market, while it has also engaged with international standard-setters, in particular IOSCO, in relation to, for example, automated trading[534] and the treatment of benchmarks.[535] ESMA is also developing a distinct international presence, sitting on IOSCO as an associate member, alongside the NCA members of IOSCO.

ESMA's developing international activities provide another channel through which it can strengthen its capacity as a rule-maker. But they also open up a further line of potential tension with the Commission, which typically represents the EU on international standard-setters, notably the Financial Stability Board (FSB). This may particularly be the case where ESMA's technical expertise trumps that of the Commission and where ESMA has built up a strong relationship with the members of standard-setters through, for example, its information exchange, equivalence, and co-operation activities or where the

---

[527] 2012 Short Selling Regulation Arts 5(3) and 6(3) and Art 23(6).

[528] 2011 AIFMD Arts 67 and 68.

[529] 2012 EMIR Art 89.

[530] While in practice ESMA will be consulted by the Commission, its involvement is expressly required by EMIR (Art 85) and the Short Selling Regulation review (Art 45).

[531] Chiti (2009), n 308, 1413–16.

[532] See Ch XI sect 5.7 on the international dimension of its supervisory activities.

[533] ESMA's initial activities in January 2011 suggested an early concern to establish a strong international presence. It, eg, wrote to the SEC to express its concerns at proposed SEC rules concerning Swap Data Repositories (ESMA/2011/16).

[534] Throughout the development of the related 2011 Guidelines, ESMA emphasized its incorporation of and engagement with international developments and its close relationship with the SEC, in particular: n 491, Feedback Statement, 25 and 26.

[535] The Principles were designed to be aligned with IOSCO's (the International Organization of Securities Commissions) standards: 2013 Discussion Paper, n 497, 3.

Commission's position is insecure. The potential for destabilizing tension with standard-setters, however, also exists. This is particularly the case with respect to the International Accounting Standards Board (IASB), ESMA's recent clarification efforts in relation to IFRS may be taking it perilously close to interpreting IFRS, which remains the prerogative of the IASB (Chapter II section 6).

X.5.10 The ESFS Review, ESMA, and Rule-making

ESMA has been granted considerable powers with respect to rule-making, and there are promising signs that it may be an effective 'quasi-rule-maker' and can dilute some of the risks associated with the increasingly monolithic EU rulebook. The level 1 process remains problematic and struggles, in particular, to produce a coherent set of interlocking level 1 rules, to differentiate appropriately between the diversity of actors in the financial markets, and to engage in effective impact assessment. ESMA's ability to correct legislative errors is very limited. But it injects an important technical capacity into level 2 and, thereby, into the process through which the level 1 rulebook can be refined and differentiated.

It remains to be seen whether the ESFS Review will lead to major changes. As required under the ESA Regulations, a review of the ESAs was launched in 2013 with the Commission's April 2013 ESFS Review Consultation.[536] Extensive stakeholder[537] and institutional consultation[538] informed the Review, which also saw interest from international bodies, notably the IMF.[539] Major change is not expected from the Review, not least given the limited period of time for which the ESAs have been operating and the need to gain additional experience, the need for institutional stability, and the need to allow the ESFS to accommodate the institutional change being wrought by the establishment of the Single Supervisory Mechanism.[540]

Although supervision was the major concern of respondents to the ESFS Review (see Chapter XI section 5.10), the efficacy of the ESAs in supporting rule-making was addressed, with reaction broadly positive. Notwithstanding the difficulties posed by the endorsement process and by the Commission's ability to reject ESMA's technical advice, ESMA appeared relatively sanguine in relation to its rulebook powers,[541] and highlighted how its quasi-rule-making powers had led to a 'clear and substantial improvement' in the

---

[536] Commission, Consultation on the Review of the ESFS (2013) and Background Document (2013). The Consultation did not assess the ESAs or the European Systemic Risk Board (ESRB), but posed an extensive series of questions on their operation (including with respect to effectiveness and governance) and on ESA/ESRB interaction.

[537] The extensive responses to the Commission Consultation are available at <http://ec.europa.eu/internal_market/consultations/2013/esfs/contributions_en.htm>. Some 94 responses were made publicly available. The 2013 Mazars ESA Review (n 358) for the European Parliament also canvassed stakeholder opinion.

[538] eg, European Parliament, Resolution on the European System of Financial Supervision, 11 March 2014 (P7_TA-PROV(2014)020), based on ECON Committee, Giegold Report with Recommendations to the Commission on the ESFS Review, February 2014 (A7-0133/2014).

[539] IMF, Financial Sector Assessment Program, European Union. European Securities and Markets Authority. Technical Note. March 2013.

[540] ESMA Chairman Maijoor suggested that the Review should not trigger a fundamental overhaul but be used to strengthen the ESFS: n 467.

[541] ESMA, Review of the European System on European Financial Supervision, Letter from Chairman Maijoor to Commissioner Barnier, 31 October 2013 (ESMA/2013/1561).

EU rulebook.[542] The enhancements it suggested were not radical, focusing in the main on strengthening its budgetary position,[543] on consultation of the ESAs during the negotiation of level 1 measures with respect to the timetable for and nature of administrative measures,[544] and on the possibility for ESMA to temporarily suspend BTSs where their application could lead to unintended consequences.[545]

The European Parliament, while critical with respect to supervisory issues, emerged as broadly supportive with respect to rule-making, noting that the ESAs had fulfilled their mandate to contribute to legislative procedures and propose BTSs, that the Article 16 guidelines power was 'useful and necessary', but that the ESAs were limited in fulfilling their mandates by limited resourcing.[546] It sought to strengthen the independence of the ESAs, supporting RTSs as guaranteeing the involvement of the ESAs in areas in which they have technical expertise, and calling on the Commission to provide detailed reasons when departing from BTS proposals (accompanied by fully evidenced cost-benefit analysis), and, more generally, for the nature of the Commission's engagement with the ESAs to be more transparent (such that ESA independence was not threatened) and for the independence of the ESAs from the Commission to be enhanced (including by means of an independent budget line). It also sought a greater role for the ESAs in the legislative process, suggesting that they provide formal opinions on legislative proposals and assess related impact assessments. It made a series of governance recommendations of relevance to rule-making, including, in what would be a major change to ESA governance but in order to strengthen the 'EU interest' on the ESAs, a recasting of the Management Board into an independent body (composed of three Parliament appointees, the ESA Chairperson, and the ESA Executive Director), the members of which would have the right to vote on the Board of Supervisors.

The IMF similarly reported that ESMA was building 'a strong institution with adequate expertise' and, 'within its resource envelope', had performed well during its first two years, particularly with respect to the single rulebook, noting the significant number of BTSs which had been proposed and the volume of technical advice.[547] It noted stakeholder support for ESMA's QMV-based decision-making governance (and recognition that this represented a major change from the CESR consensus-based era) and reported that stakeholders were of the view that destructive blocking minorities had not emerged to prejudice effective rule-making. It also found that ESMA's influence over quasi-rule-making was strengthening relative to NCA influence, in particular through ESMA's growing influence on its Standing Committees. It called, however, for ESMA's independence to be enhanced (in particular to reduce the influence of domestic NCA interests)

---

[542] ESMA Chairman Maijoor, Public Hearing on Financial Supervision in the EU, 24 May 2013 (ESMA/2013/603).

[543] By means of increasing the fees received from ESMA-supervised entities and an independent EU budget line.

[544] The ESMA Board of Supervisors had earlier noted the need to approach engagement with level 1 'in a careful manner': Board of Supervisors Meeting, 24 September 2013 (ESMA/2013/BS/155).

[545] ESMA acknowledged that 'strong democratic control' by the Parliament and Council would be required.

[546] n 538.

[547] n 539, 4 and 14, although the IMF noted the significant time pressure under which ESMA had been placed.

through mechanisms such as the addition of independent members to the Board of Supervisors or delegation to the ESMA Management Board, and for stronger resourcing.[548] More radically, it described the Commission's ability to change or veto proposed BTSs as 'troublesome', although it noted the transparency requirements to which the Commission was subject.[549]

Similar themes emerged from the Commission's Consultation and the 2013 Mazars ESA Review for the European Parliament. While respondents to the Commission Consultation generally preferred modification and nuancing over radical reform, and supported the ESAs, there was support for stronger Board of Supervisor independence from the Commission and from NCAs,[550] and for some engagement by the ESAs (as observers) with the legislative process in order to strengthen the administrative rule-making process.[551] Concern was frequently raised as to the Commission's ability to change or veto BTSs developed by ESMA and/or to reject ESMA's technical advice,[552] as were concerns as to the inability of the ESAs to amend BTSs quickly, where necessary.[553] Concerns were also raised as to guidelines being used to extend the EU rulebook beyond the legislative framework,[554] although other respondents supported guidelines and similar measures as a means of ensuring the integrity of the rulebook.[555] The 2013 Mazars Review similarly reported that the ESAs were 'well-functioning organizations', but called for—reflecting stakeholder opinion—stronger and independent resourcing, ESA engagement with proposed legislation by means of a mandatory ESA opinion, and greater clarity on the use of guidelines.

Whatever the outcome of the Review, ESMA has brought rule-making for financial markets in the EU considerably closer to the technocratic governance model common to most major financial markets worldwide. The EU's capacity to engage in the sophisticated rule design which the financial crisis has demanded has been significantly enhanced. ESMA is only one element, however, of a much larger law-making ecosystem. The governance inefficiencies and fragilities at level 2, and the persistent weaknesses of the level 1 legislative process, underline that major frailties still beset the institutional process for law-making. They also underline, however, that in the EU market, the functional imperatives of securities and markets regulation must be managed within an institutional structure which operates within a distinct political settlement and constitutional environment.

---

[548] The IMF suggested that alternative budget models (including models based on industry levies) be explored, given the burden which ESMA funding could represent for NCAs: n 539, 12.

[549] The IMF warned that any interventions from the Commission must be 'motivated and grounded on technical reasons': n 539, 23.

[550] eg responses from trade associations AFME (Association for Financial Markets in Europe), British Bankers' Association (BBA), Assonime (Italian listed companies), and EuroFinuse (consumer interests).

[551] eg responses from trade associations AFME and the European Fund and Asset Management Association (EFAMA), and Deutsche Bank.

[552] eg responses from trade associations BBA, EFAMA, ICMA (International Capital Markets Association), and the European Private Equity and Venture Capital Association. Deutsche Bank similarly called for stronger challenge from the ESAs where their advice was not taken.

[553] eg Deutsche Bank response.

[554] eg responses from trade associations ABI (Association of British Insurers), BBA, EFAMA, and the German Banking Industry Committee.

[555] eg response by Barclays.

XI

SUPERVISION AND ENFORCEMENT

XI.1 The European System of Financial Supervision

The supervision of the EU's financial system is carried out through the European System of Financial Supervision (ESFS), which was established in January 2011. It is composed of: the national competent authorities (NCAs) which form the basis of the system; the three European Supervisory Authorities (ESAs)—the European Securities and Markets Authority (ESMA), the European Banking Authority (EBA), the European Insurance and Occupational Pensions Authority (EIOPA)—and their co-ordinating ESA Joint Committee; and the European Systemic Risk Board (ESRB).[1] From November 2014, it also includes the European Central Bank (ECB) as the authority responsible for the supervision of the euro-area's banks under the Single Supervisory Mechanism (SSM).[2] The ESAs, the ECB, and the NCAs are primarily concerned with microprudential (and conduct) oversight (or the supervision of individual financial system participants); the ESRB (in collaboration with the ECB in particular) is responsible for macroprudential oversight and so for safeguarding the stability of the financial system as a whole, by strengthening its resilience and reviewing the build up of systemic risk.[3] All of the ESFS entities must co-operate with trust and full mutual respect, in particular to ensure that appropriate and reliable information flows between them.[4]

---

[1] The composition of the European System of Financial Supervision (ESFS) is detailed in the founding regulations of the European Supervisory Authorities (ESAs) and of the European Systemic Risk Board (ESRB): eg, European Securities and Markets Authority (ESMA) Regulation (Regulation (EU) No 1095/2010 [2010] OJ L331/84) Art 2. The national competent authorities (NCAs) are defined as those authorities defined in and required by the legislative measures which form EU securities and markets regulation (Art 4(3)). More generally, the institutional system which supports the internal financial market includes the national resolution authorities required under the 2014 Bank Resolution and Recovery Directive (Directive 2014/59/EU [2014] OJ L173/149 (2014 BRRD).

[2] Two legislative instruments support the Single Supervisory Mechanism (SSM): Council Regulation (EU) No 1024/2013 [2013] OJ L287/63 (conferring specific tasks on the European Central Bank (ECB)) (2013 ECB/SSM Regulation) and Regulation (EU) No 1022/2013 [2013] OJ L287/5 (revising the governance of the European Banking Authority (EBA) to reflect the ECB/SSM) (2013 EBA Regulation). The SSM is based on supervision of euro-area banks by the ECB and by banking NCAs. The process for allocating banks to ECB and NCA supervision is set out in the 2013 ECB/SSM Regulation (in effect, the largest and most systemically risky banks will be directly supervised by the ECB and others will be supervised by the relevant NCA, in conjunction with the ECB). The ECB remains responsible for the SSM as a whole. Non-euro-area Member States may join the SSM on a voluntary basis.

[3] The ESRB operates in collaboration with a range of authorities, including the specialist national authorities responsible for macroprudential oversight: ESRB, Annual Report (2011) 9.

[4] eg 2010 ESMA Regulation Art 2(4) and 2010 ESRB Regulation (Regulation (EU) No 1092/2010 [2010] OJ L331/1) Art 1(4). The 2013 ECB/SSM Regulation imposes distinct co-operation obligations on the ECB with

The ESFS operates on a sectoral basis. In the financial markets, supervision is carried out by the NCAs for financial markets, ESMA, and the ESRB, and is largely decentralized; operational supervision (and enforcement) remains, for the most part, at Member State level with the NCAs. The principle of centralized supervision of financial markets at EU level has, however, been conceded with the 2011 establishment of ESMA and the conferral on it of limited, enumerated direct supervisory powers.

By contrast, significantly greater centralization has occurred in the banking sector with the establishment of Banking Union's SSM for euro-area banks.[5] But the drivers for institutional reform and supervisory organization are distinct in the banking field. The SSM forms part of the wider Banking Union project, which in addition includes a Single Resolution Mechanism (SRM) (designed to provide a centralized mechanism for the resolution of ailing euro-area banks, and including an intergovernmental Single Resolution Fund),[6] and an intensively harmonized (albeit not centralized) deposit protection regime, and which is supported by the single banking 'rulebook', based primarily on the 2013 CRD IV/CRR and the 2014 resolution regime.[7] The roots of Banking Union are in the EU's fiscal and sovereign debt crisis and the destructive feedback loop which developed between bank failure, sovereign rescue of banks, sovereign fragility, and the viability of the euro, and the consequent overwhelming political imperative to break the link between sovereigns and banks.[8] Notably, the SSM is a precondition for empowering the European Stability Mechanism to capitalize banks directly, thereby protecting the sovereign from the costs of bank rescue.[9]

Supervisory organization for the EU financial market has developed differently and has relied to a much greater extent on a decentralized approach; the different trajectories of the banking and financial market approaches reflect in particular the acuteness of the fiscal risk to the sovereign following bank (and supervisory) failure. But prior to the euro-area sovereign debt crisis, which became acute in 2010, and the related dramatic materialization of the fiscal risk which banks generate, the organizational model for financial market supervision evolved, for the most part, in lockstep with the model applicable to banking. Accordingly, it was based on national supervision by NCAs, supplemented by cross-border co-ordination and co-operation mechanisms. Variations did emerge, however, between the banking and financial market models. The significantly greater reliance on subsidiaries,

---

respect to its relations with the ESAs, the ESRB, and NCAs responsible for markets in financial instruments (Art 3 (1) and (3)).

[5] The SSM applies to euro-area 'credit institutions'—deposit-taking institutions as defined under the 2013 Capital Requirements Regulation (EU) No 575/2013 [2013] OJ L176/1 (2013 CRR) Art 4(1) (ECB/SSM Regulation Art 1 and 2(3)). See sect 7.

[6] See in brief Ch IV sect 13. SSM Chairman Nouy has made clear that she expects that weak euro-area banks should be allowed to die: Jones, C, Ross, A, and Fleming, S, 'Let Weak Banks Fail, Says New Regulator', *Financial Times*, 10 February 2014, 1.

[7] On the deposit protection regime (in brief) see Ch IX sect 8. On the main elements of the banking rulebook (2013 CRR (n 5), 2013 CRD IV (Directive 2013/36/EU [2013] OJ L176/38), and 2014 BRRD (n 1)) see, in brief, Ch IV sects 8 and 13. For an early policy articulation of the elements of Banking Union see Commission, Communication on a Roadmap Towards a Banking Union (2012) (COM (2012) 510) and ECB, Financial Stability Review, June 2012, 11.

[8] eg Pisani-Ferry, J and Wolff, G, The Fiscal Implications of a Banking Union. Bruegel Policy Brief, Issue 2012/02, September 2012.

[9] As reinforced by the October 2012 European Council: European Council Conclusions, 18–19 October, para 12.

supervised by home NCAs, for cross-border activity in the banking sector (cross-border financial market activity is typically carried out on a services basis or through branches)[10] placed greater demands on pan-EU co-ordination and co-operation structures for banking groups, and led to earlier experimentation in the banking sector with group-focused mechanisms such as colleges of supervisors. The sharper systemic risks associated with banks also led to a closer (if still somewhat weak) focus on financial stability.

The financial crisis led to supervisory reform being cast in terms of the EU financial system generally.[11] The ESAs were all designed to the same institutional template, which was designed to reinforce supervision and to protect the EU financial system from a subsequent systemic crisis. The ESAs were also, however, constrained by a range of institutional limitations designed to protect national treasuries from any fiscal costs generated by an ESA supervisory decision. But the minimal fiscal impact of particular financial market infrastructures and actors, combined with a supportive political and institutional climate, led to ESMA being the sole ESA to be conferred with direct and exclusive supervisory powers over particular financial market participants (notably rating agencies and trade repositories for over-the-counter (OTC) derivatives market data).

The recognition of the need to mutualize the management and costs of bank rescue in order to protect the sovereign led to a further recasting of the institutional model, however, following the euro-area sovereign debt crisis, and to the establishment of the SSM and SRM for euro-area banks. But in the financial markets sphere, fiscal neutrality remains the defining characteristic of EU-level supervision, and supervision, accordingly, remains decentralized.

Nonetheless, and as discussed throughout this Chapter, the extent to which supervision over financial markets should be further centralized at EU level remains contested.

XI.2 Achieving Outcomes: From Rules on the Books to Rules in Action

XI.2.1 Supervision and Enforcement

Regulation does not operate in a vacuum; it must be operationalized through supervision,[12] which is a 'hands on' business. Supervision requires granular engagement with firms and the taking of decisions which carry risk to the markets, the supervisor, and the tax-payer. The crisis era has led to supervision, enforcement, and the achievement of the outcomes sought by regulation achieving a much greater prominence than previously.[13] Institutional

---

[10] Wymeersch, E, 'The institutional reforms to the European Financial Supervisory System' (2010) *ECFLR* 17.

[11] See sect 3.3.

[12] 'Simply because something is enacted into law, clearly or not, does not tell us much about how strongly it will influence economic behaviour': Langevoort, D, 'The Social Construction of Sarbanes-Oxley' (2007) 105 *Michigan LR* 1817, 1818.

[13] eg: 'supervision and enforcement are fundamentally important to the credibility of any regulatory regime . . . without effective supervision and enforcement, the rules will ultimately lack credibility': HM Treasury, A New Approach to Financial Regulation: Judgment, Focus and Stability (2010) 28.

reform, in part designed to achieve stronger supervisory outcomes, has been a feature of reform agendas internationally.[14] The international peer review programme, spear-headed by the Financial Stability Board (FSB) and designed to support international compliance with the G20 reform programme,[15] is another indicator of the new focus on the achievement of outcomes;[16] it is not limited to 'rules on the books' and is engaging with whether particular outcomes are being achieved.[17] Equivalence strategies, used to manage third country access, are also increasingly replying on equivalence assessments of supervisory practices.[18]

The sharper focus on supervision reflects the limitations of rules which the crisis exposed. Regulation is now recognized as only a part of the toolkit which is needed to capture the dynamic and complex risks of financial markets.[19] Careful *ex-ante* monitoring and supervision of emerging risks and the deploying of risk-based approaches[20] has been widely recognized as central to the prevention of destabilizing financial system risks.[21] The new focus on supervision also reflects the 'retooling' of financial market supervisors to engage with systemic risks and related risks to financial stability. While financial markets remain different to banking markets with respect to their capacity to generate systemic risks,[22] as discussed in Chapter I, the financial crisis exposed the failure of financial market supervisors to identify and monitor systemic risk. Accordingly, in tandem with the expansion of the scope of market regulation to address systemic risk, financial market supervisors are being tasked with new responsibilities with respect to the application and monitoring of rules designed to contain systemic risk and to support financial stability and being conferred with related new powers.

More generally, as the financial system becomes subject to an increasingly detailed and complex rulebook and as the related risk of herding and homogeneity in the financial

---

[14] On the UK and US institutional reforms, eg, see, respectively, Ferran, E, 'The Break Up of the Financial Services Authority' (2011) 31 *OJLS* 455 and Skeel, D, *The New Financial Deal. Understanding the Dodd-Frank Act and its (Unintended) Consequences* (2011).

[15] Based on FSB, Framework for Adherence to International Standards (2010).

[16] Gilligan, G, The Financial Stability Board II: A Tale of Sherpas and Traffic Lights—An Uphill but Positive Track for the Financial Stability Board (2012).

[17] Notably, the Basel III implementation review is not only based on formal implementation, but also on whether Basel III signatories are achieving the outcomes sought: Basel Committee on Banking Supervision. Progress Report on Basel III Implementation (2012).

[18] This is the case in the EU (see, eg, Ch VII sect 2.11 on the rating agency regime) but also in the US, where the application of the 2010 Dodd-Frank Act's provisions relating to OTC clearing is subject to a substitute compliance/equivalence assessment which includes supervisory review.

[19] Ford, C, 'New Governance in the Teeth of Human Frailty: Lessons from Financial Regulation' (2010) *Wisconsin LR* 441 and Lo, A, 'Regulatory Reform in the Wake of the Financial Crisis of 2007-2008' (2009) 1 *J of Financial Economic Policy* 4.

[20] Risk-based supervision has been defined in terms of a systematized framework of inspection or supervision which is primarily designed to manage regulatory or institutional risk and which allows a regulator to prioritize its supervisory activities. Risk in this context is typically cast in terms of the risk of the supervisor not achieving its objectives: eg Black, J, 'Risk Based Regulation: Choices, Practices and Lessons Being Learned' in OECD, *Risk and Regulatory Policy: Improving the Governance of Risk* (2010).

[21] The UK regulatory authorities, eg, have adopted a 'judgement-based' supervisory model, which is based on a more proactive, intrusive, and *ex-ante* approach to financial market intervention. See, eg, Financial Services Authority (FSA), Journey to the Financial Conduct Authority (2012) and Bank of England and FSA, The Prudential Regulation Authority's Approach to Banking Supervision (2012).

[22] Langevoort, D, 'Global Securities Regulation after the Financial Crisis' (2010) 13 *JIEL* 799.

system increases,[23] judgement-based supervision is increasingly being deployed as a miti-gant.[24] Supervision, by contrast with rule-making, also offers the prospect of being less prone to the capture risks which threaten rule-making.[25] In addition, given that crisis-driven rules tend to 'fight the last war',[26] proactive, battle-hardened, nimble, and imagina-tive *ex-ante* supervision, and careful application of new rules to particular situations, may remain the best first line of defence for the financial system.

But the determinants of effective financial market supervision can be elusive, and the design choices required are many and complex.[27] Financial systems globally have experimented with a range of institutional models, classically the 'twin peaks' model (an institutional split of conduct and prudential supervision); the consolidated model (omnibus supervision by one authority); the sectoral supervision model (typically based on segmenting the insur-ance, markets, and banking sectors); and the central bank-based model. The financial crisis has led to significant institutional redesign internationally and to something of a preference for the twin-peaks-based model.[28] While these institutional models are exposed to different effectiveness risks (including with respect to organizational dynamics and incentives),[29] the crisis did not reveal a 'best in class' model; economies which weathered the crisis did not follow a common institutional model.[30]

Similarly, the intensity of resource allocation to supervision has an impact on outcomes, but the optimum allocation of resources is not clear.[31]

The style of supervision also has a bearing on supervisory effectiveness, but much depends on how supervisory styles are deployed and how they are shaped by, for example, regulatory mandates, political factors, and relationships with the regulated sector. While risk-based supervision is currently in the ascendant,[32] it is not without difficulties.[33] It demands, and

---

[23] Romano, R, Against Financial Regulation Harmonization: A Comment, Yale Law & Economics Research Paper No 414 (2010), available at <http://ssrn.com/abstract=1697348>, Haldane, A (Bank of England), Rethinking the Financial Network, Speech to Financial Student Association, Amsterdam, 28 April 2009 (2009) and Avgouleas, E, 'The Global Financial Crisis, Behavioural Finance and Financial Regulation. In Search of a New Orthodoxy' (2009) 9 *JCLS* 23.

[24] Haldane, A and Madouros, V, The Dog and the Frisbee, Bank of England Paper, 31 August 2012.

[25] In the US Securities and Exchange Commission (SEC) context, Langevoort, D, 'The SEC as a Lawmaker: Choices about Investor Protection in the Face of Uncertainty' (2006) 84 *Washington University LR* 1591.

[26] Enriques, L, 'Regulators' Response to the Current Crisis and the Upcoming Reregulation of Financial Markets: One Reluctant Regulator's View' (2009) 30 *UPaJIEL* 1147.

[27] See generally, Moloney, N, 'Supervision in the Wake, of the Financial Crisis: Achieving Effective Law in Action – a Challenge for the EU' in Wymeersch, E, Hopt, K, and Ferrarini, G (eds), *Financial Regulation and Supervision. A Post Crisis Analysis* (2012) 71.

[28] eg Coffee, J, and Sale, H, 'Redesigning the SEC – Does the Treasury Have a Better Idea?' (2009) 95 *Va LR* 707, Jackson, H, A Pragmatic Approach to the Phased Consolidation of Financial Regulation in the US, Harvard Public Law WP No 09-19 (2009), available at <http://ssrn.com/abstractid=1300431>, and Pan, E, 'Four Challenges to Financial Regulatory Reform' (2009) 55 *Villanova LR* 101.

[29] eg Pan, n 28.

[30] FSA, The Turner Review. A Regulatory Response to the Global Banking Crisis (2009) (2009 Turner Review) and Regling, K and Watson, M, A Preliminary Report on the Sources of Ireland's Banking Crisis (2010).

[31] eg Jackson, H and Roe, M 'Public and Private Enforcement of Securities Laws: Resource-Based Evidence' (2009) 93 *JFE* 207 and Jackson, H, 'Variations in the Intensity of Financial Regulation: Preliminary Evidence and Potential Implications' (2007) 24 *Yale J Reg* 253.

[32] eg International Organization of Securities Commissions (IOSCO), Guidelines to Emerging Market Regulators Regarding Requirements for Minimum Entry and Continuous Risk-Based Supervision of Market Intermediaries (2009).

[33] Including with respect to model (design) risk, operational risk, and cultural risk: Black, n 20, 23.

makes transparent, troublesome determinations as to the level of risk which the supervisor is prepared to tolerate and as to the prioritization of supervisory resources, and requires acceptance of the reality that failures will arise. Political risk can, accordingly, be considerable.[34]

More generally, opportunities for correction and for supervisory learning can be limited, as the factors which shape supervision and which have a bearing on how optimum outcomes can be achieved are often context-dependent and reflect local markets, cultures, and political features.[35] The outcomes achieved from the mix may not necessarily be the product of clearly observable factors, but can arise instead from the often opaque environmental dynamics which shape how the supervisor engages with the regulated sector.[36]

Nuanced judgements must also be made as to the extent to which outcomes can be achieved through self-regulation techniques—or through the 'enrolment' of private actors and of market-based monitoring techniques in the process for achieving outcomes.[37] Self-regulation became something of a poster boy for failure over the crisis, with lightly or non-regulated sectors (such as the OTC derivatives markets) strongly associated with the crisis; market-based gatekeeper functions were also regarded as failing in some cases.[38] Similarly, market discipline dynamics generally, whether with respect to governance-related risk management systems, executive pay devices, or monitoring by institutional investors, or with respect to market efficiency and pricing dynamics generally (the failure of credit default swap (CDS) spreads and of bank share prices to reflect risk being a case in point), became regarded as not being effective.[39] But self-regulation, or at least nuanced self-regulation, remains a necessary part of any well-calibrated supervisory system, not least as supervisors, operating with limited resources, must rely on regulated actors' ability to self-regulate.[40]

The *ex-post* enforcement devices which regulatory systems deploy also have a bearing on the achievement of outcomes. But, and despite some evidence of a policy preference for private enforcement,[41] the extent to which enforcement should deploy public enforcement mechanisms[42] or private liability mechanisms, or draw on softer mechanisms,[43] is not

---

[34] Black, n 20.

[35] The Turner Review, eg, attempted to benchmark the FSA's post-crisis supervisory model against international comparators, but concluded that the crisis had not identified which supervisory models were best equipped to deal with the crisis, given the range of political, market, regulatory, societal and other variables which influence supervision: 2009 Turner Review, n 30, 89–90.

[36] Baldwin, R and Black, J, 'Really Responsive Regulation' (2008) 71 *MLR* 59.

[37] Black, J, 'Enrolling Actors in Regulatory Processes: Examples from UK Financial Services Regulation' [2003] *Public Law*, 63–91.

[38] Coffee, J, 'What Went Wrong? An Initial Inquiry into the Causes of the 2008 Financial Crisis' (2009) 9 *JCLS* 1.

[39] 2009 Turner Review, n 30, 45–7 and 92.

[40] Black, J, 'Managing Regulatory Risks and Defining the Parameters of Blame: A Focus on the Australian Prudential Regulation Authority' (2006) 28 *Law & Policy* 22.

[41] World Bank, The Institutional Foundations for Financial Markets (2006).

[42] On the complexities of effective public enforcement see Baldwin and Black n 36 and Bird, H, Chow, D, Lenne, J and Ramsay, I, 'Strategic Regulation and ASIC Enforcement Patterns: Results of an Empirical Survey' (2005) 5 *JCLS* 191.

[43] One influential model for regulatory decision-making suggests a model based on a graduated application of regulatory techniques, including voluntary compliance, supported by dialogue, education, and the threat of intervention: Ayres, I and Braithwaite, J, *Responsive Regulation—Transcending the Deregulation Debate* (1992).

clear [44] and is context-dependent.[45] The optimum intensity of enforcement is also not clear, with the extent to which high levels of private enforcement, in particular, can prejudice market efficiency contested.[46]

XI.2.2 Achieving Outcomes in the EU

XI.2.2.1 Cross-border Supervision: Managing Decentralization Risks

The supervisory challenges outlined above must, in the EU financial market, be met within a structure which also responds to the particular supervisory difficulties posed by cross-border activity. Cross-border financial market supervision can draw on a number of organizational devices including: the allocation of 'home' (typically the State of registration)/'host' (the State in which cross-border activities are taking place) supervisory jurisdiction and of fiscal responsibility to different supervisors, and the related identification of the supervisory powers and best practices which local supervisors must employ domestically and with respect to cross-border supervision; co-operation and information-sharing obligations to tie home and host supervisors together; delegation structures; colleges of supervisors; cross-border resolution and rescue mechanisms; and, ultimately, the allocation of supervision to a central authority.[47]

There is no easy formula for an optimal organizational design for EU financial market supervision. Decentralization (and reliance on NCAs) allows for geographic proximity to the supervised entity and supports the application of local knowledge and expertise. It supports experimentation and innovation in supervisory practices and locates fiscal responsibility with the supervising Member State. It sidesteps the institutional, political, and legal pyrotechnics associated with the construction of a single central supervisor. But anchoring the supervision of the cross-border activity of a financial market actor to the home NCA exposes the pan-EU market to any weaknesses in the quality of home supervision. It also exposes the pan-EU market to the home bias of supervisors, which bias reflects a range of factors, including political accountability to the domestic market, technical difficulties with

---

[44] The debate has been framed in terms of how enforcement relates to strong financial markets. Leading contributions include: La Porta, R, Lopez-de-Silanes, F, and Shleifer, A, 'The Law and Economics of Self Dealing' (2008) 88 *JFE* 430; Coffee, J, 'Law and the Market: The Impact of Enforcement' (2007) 156 *UPaLR* 229; Jackson and Roe, n 31; and La Porta, R, Lopez-de-Silanes, F, and Shleifer, A, 'What Works in Securities Laws' (2006) 61 *J Fin* 1.

[45] In the context of the achievement of outcomes in the UK market which exhibits lower levels of public and private enforcement than other systems internationally see Armour, J, Black, B, Cheffins, B, and Nolan, R, 'Private Enforcement of Corporate Law: An Empirical Examination of the UK and US' (2009) 6 *J of Empirical Legal Studies* 701; Ferran, E and Cearns, K, 'Non-Enforcement Led Public Oversight of Financial and Corporate Governance Disclosure and of Auditors' (2008) 8 *JCLS* 191; and MacNeil, I, 'The Evolution of Regulatory Enforcement in the UK: A Case of "Less is More"'? (2007) 2 *CMLJ* 345.

[46] Well illustrated by the debate generated by the 2006 Paulson Report, which related a perceived drop in the competitiveness of the US capital market to aggressive private enforcement: Committee on Capital Market Regulation, Interim Report (2006). See, eg, Zingales, L, Is the US Capital Market Losing Its Competitive Edge? ECGI Finance WP No 192/2007 (2007), available via <http://ssrn.com/abstract=1028701> and Coffee, n 44.

[47] In its impact assessment for the ESAs, the Commission noted the 'hierarchy of possibilities', including national supervision for national entities, colleges of supervisors for cross-border entities, and EU supervision for entities with an EU-wide reach: 2009 ESA Proposals Impact Assessment (SEC (2009) 1234) 26.

respect to enforcement, and resource constraints,[48] particularly where financial market participants engage to a disproportionate extent in cross-border activity relative to home activity.[49] These risks increase with intensifying levels of cross-border activity, as key risk management functions become centralized within home business units,[50] and as the potential for systemic risk increases as cross-border risk transmission channels develop. The decentralized system must accordingly operate to consistent standards; information exchange and related co-ordination arrangements must be robust; supervisory incentives to ensure high-quality supervision of cross-border activity must be strong; and resilient rescue and resolution arrangements, with clear allocations of fiscal responsibility, must be in place.

Centralization through a single central authority provides a potentially cleaner and simpler organizational model. Prior to the financial crisis, the policy agenda had periodically flirted with the 'Euro-SEC/single supervisor' model, albeit that it never gained serious political or market traction.[51] But the legion of legal[52] and political difficulties and of organizational risks,[53] in addition to the complex allocation decisions which must be made with respect to the location of fiscal responsibility, which were not fully apparent until the financial crisis, make it a highly troublesome organizational choice. While the banking sector has proceeded in this direction, the drivers for the SSM are distinct and the ECB was already in place as an independent, Treaty-based body with extensive decision-making power.

In practice, the EU financial market is likely to be best served by a judicious blend of co-ordination devices which respond to the local and supranational interests which EU

---

[48] Langevoort, D, 'Structuring Securities Regulation in the European Union: Lessons from the US Experience' in Ferrarini, G and Wymeersch, E (eds), *Investor Protection in Europe. Corporate Law Making, the MiFID and Beyond* (2006) 485, 491–501.

[49] This is particularly the case where a branch is systemic to the host Member State but not to the home Member State, and the related risk of a divergence of interests arises: eg, Commission, European Financial Integration Report 2007 (2007) (SEC (2007) 1696) 40.

[50] This was recognized as a threat to supervision prior to the financial crisis: Commission, Financial Integration Monitor 2003 (2004) (SEC (2004) 559) 18–19 and Deutsche Bank, Towards a New Structure for EU Financial Supervision, EU Monitor 48 (2007) 3.

[51] eg Lastra, R, 'The Governance Structure for Financial Regulation and Supervision in Europe' (2003) 10 *Col J Euro L* 49; Hertig, G and Lee, R, 'Four Predictions about the Future of EU Securities Regulation' (2003) 3 *JCLS* 359; Avgerinos, Y, *Regulating and Supervising Investment Services in the European Union* (2003); Andenas, M and Avgerinos, Y (eds), *Financial Markets in Europe. Towards a Single Regulator* (2003); Pan, E, 'Harmonization of US–EU Securities Regulation: The Case for a Single European Securities Regulator' (2003) 34 *L Pol Int Bus* 499; and Karmel, R, 'The Case for a European Securities Commission' (1999) 38 *Col J T'nal Law* 9.

[52] Including with respect to the Treaty competence for such an entity. The legal foundation of the ESAs is based on the general internal market competence (Art 114 TFEU) and on the *Meroni* doctrine (Case 9/56 *Meroni v High Authority* [1957–1958] ECR 133) which provides the framework within which powers can be delegated from the EU institutions. Both of these restraints significantly constrain the operational freedom of the ESAs (sects 5.8.2 and 5.8.3 and Ch X sects 3.1, 5.2.1, and 5.5.5). The greater freedom of action which a fully fledged supervisor for financial markets would require would most likely demand a Treaty revision.

[53] The litany of risks associated with centralized supervision in the EU includes that the supervisor risks being over-powerful, costly, prone to capture, not equipped to deliver a calibrated response to different market sectors, unresponsive, distanced from the markets and prone to severe information-asymmetry risks, unable to deal with local, retail-market difficulties, and vulnerable to accountability risks. The design difficulties are immense and include the resolution of how fiscal support is organized (which, as the Banking Union negotiations exposed, requires very sophisticated institutional technology as well as deep political support which is unlikely to be forthcoming, absent an overwhelming imperative to act). Sanctioning and enforcement systems must also be designed.

supervision engages. But the current model is the product of a messy combination of political compromise, legal constraints, and the searing influence of the financial crisis; it also builds on the largely decentralized model, based on home Member State control and co-ordination through the Committee of European Securities Regulators (CESR), employed prior to the crisis. It is organizationally untidy. The dynamics of the pivotal ESMA/NCA relationship and the complex ESRB/ESMA/NCA relationship are still evolving. The extent to which ESMA can engage in centralized supervision is not clear. Incentive and consistency risks remain in place as the marketplace is, for the most part, supervised by local supervisors. Nonetheless, the current model, operating through the ESFS, represents a pragmatic and practical response to a fractured institutional environment, complex legal constraints, and a lack of consensus on how fiscal responsibility for supervisory decisions with cross-border implications should be allocated. It builds on NCAs, battle-hardened, more strongly resourced, and retooled after the financial crisis.[54] It strengthens co-ordination and consistency mechanisms very considerably. It also has a dynamic quality and has significant capacity to evolve over time.

XI.2.2.2 Private Enforcement

Private enforcement through civil liability mechanisms has the potential to substitute for and complement supervisory action.[55] Some glancing attempts to promote private enforcement were made prior to the financial crisis. The 2003 Prospectus Directive and 2004 Transparency Directive[56] each contained tentative steps towards a civil liability regime by requiring that Member States impose their civil liability regimes on those responsible for issuer disclosure—but the very limited rules (still in force) do not engage with the range of potential plaintiffs, the nature of liability, causation, or the quantum of damages. The 2009 UCITS IV disclosure regime addresses liability for the Key Investor Information Document (KIID), but only to limit the extent to which the KIID provider is liable (Chapter III section 3.11.3).[57]

Limited moves were also made towards supporting consumer associations and other trade associations in taking action for breach of national rules implementing key retail-invest-ment-services directives,[58] for example, while access to justice more generally was promoted through exhortations to the Member States to develop alternative dispute resolution (ADR) mechanisms and by the FIN-NET network for cross-border ADR.[59]

Overall, however, the initial Financial Services Action Plan (FSAP)-era intensification of EU securities and markets regulation was associated with investor protection being re-characterized

---

[54] Sect 5.9.

[55] On private enforcement and financial market discipline see Jackson and Roe, n 31.

[56] Directive 2003/71/EC [2003] OJ L345/64 and Directive 2004/109/EC [2004] OJ L390/38.

[57] Directive 2009/65/EC [2009] OJ L302/32.

[58] 2004 MiFID I Directive 2004/39/EC [2004] OJ L145/1 Art 52(2) and 2002 Distance Marketing of Financial Services Directive 2002/65/EC [2002] OJ L271/16 Art 13(2). This requirement continues to apply under the 2014 MiFID II (Markets in Financial Instruments Directive 2014/65/EU [2014] OJ L173/349 (2014 MiFID II) (Art 74)). On the implementation timeline see Ch IV n 28. The discussion in this Chapter is based on the 2014 MiFID II regime, although reference is made to MiFID I as appropriate.

[59] Established in 2001, FIN-NET provides a pan-EU redress network for cross-border disputes involving financial services. All FIN-NET members are required to follow the Commission's 1998 Recommendation on Out of Court Settlement of Consumer Disputes (Commission Recommendation 98/257/EC [1998] OJ L115/31). FIN-NET operates as a filtering system; the local FIN-NET member either transfers the complaint to the relevant body in another Member State or advises the consumer as to the appropriate FIN-NET member. See further Moloney, N, *How to Protect Investors. Lessons from the EU and the UK* (2010) 456–8.

from being a function of contract/fiduciary law and enforced through private rights of actions, to being a function of public supervisory and enforcement action.[60] As discussed in section 4.1.3, this position broadly still obtains after the crisis-era reforms.

XI.3 The Evolution of the EU's Supervisory Model for Financial Markets

XI.3.1 The pre-CESR Era

The first major change to the organization of EU supervision over financial markets took place over the FSAP period in 2001 with the establishment of CESR. Prior to that, the primary focus of EU securities and markets regulation was on the construction of an integrated marketplace by means of a harmonized regulatory framework which supported passporting and which supported the principle of home Member State control, but which also provided for host Member State intervention. Pre-FSAP measures accordingly allocated supervisory jurisdiction between home and host NCAs, although often with a significant degree of opacity.[61] Supervisory co-operation obligations, sanctioning and enforcement requirements, and the specification of the minimum powers required of NCAs were all generally underdeveloped.

The establishment of the European System of Central Banks (ESCB) and the ECB under the 1992 Maastricht Treaty enhanced the EU's ability to address financial stability, at least in the banking sector. Under the 1992 Maastricht Treaty, the ECB was conferred with a financial stability mandate, and required to contribute to the smooth conduct of policies pursued by the competent authorities relating to the prudential supervision of credit institutions and the stability of the financial stability.[62] In pursuit of this mandate, the ECB's Banking Supervisory Committee brought together the EU's central banks and supervisors to discuss issues related to financial stability. The ECB also brought its analytical and statistical capacity to bear on financial stability, producing financial stability reports and opinions on, *inter alia*, legislative proposals.

XI.3.2 The FSAP, the CESR Era, and Supervisory Convergence

XI.3.2.1 The FSAP era

Over the FSAP period, the securities and markets legislative framework became considerably more sophisticated with respect to supervisory powers and co-operation, and the policy

---

[60] Tison, M, 'Financial Market Integration in the Post FSAP Era: In Search of Overall Conceptual Consistency in the Regulatory Framework' in Ferrarini, G and Wymeersch, E, *Investor Protection in Europe. Corporate Law Making, the MiFID and Beyond* (2006) 443, 458–9 and Ferrarini, G, 'Contract Standards and the Markets in Financial Instruments Directive' (2005) 1 *Euro Rev Contract L* 19.

[61] Most notably in relation to the 1993 Investment Services Directive (Directive 93/22/EC [1993] OJ L197/58) under which it was not clear which NCAs had jurisdiction with respect to conduct-of-business regulation and supervision.

[62] Now Art 127(5) TFEU.

agenda, for the first time, began to focus closely on supervision.[63] FSAP-era measures intensified the level of harmonization of supervisory powers, addressed sanctioning and enforcement in more detail, and adopted a more sophisticated approach to supervisory co-operation. In order to support the regulatory passport, the home/host allocation of power was clarified, and the host NCA limited to precautionary intervention, for the most part. In particular sectors where cross-border risks were judged to be particularly acute, closer attention was given to supervisory co-operation (notably with respect to the 2009 UCITS IV regime for the supervision of management companies).[64] Provision was also made in some sectors, notably under the 2003 Prospectus Directive, for delegation of powers between NCAs, but this mechanism was rarely activated.[65]

Financial stability discussions, dominated by the ESCB and the ECB, continued through a number of institutional channels, including the Financial Stability Table of the Treaty-based Economic and Financial Committee,[66] the ECOFIN Council's Financial Services Committee,[67] and the Banking Supervision Committee of the ESCB.[68] Initial steps towards an operational structure for crisis management were also taken over this period to formalize crisis co-ordination arrangements,[69] but limited progress was made.

XI.3.2.2 CESR and Supervisory Convergence

With the establishment of CESR in 2001 and the subsequent establishment of the Committee of European Banking Supervisors (CEBS) and the Committee of European Insurance and Occupational Pensions Supervisors (CEIOPS), the supervision of the EU financial system generally became framed within a 'supervisory convergence' model and, for the first time, within a centralized institutional structure.[70]

The supervisory convergence model was developed originally for financial markets and can be traced to CESR's first major foray into supervision in 2004 with the important Himalaya Report.[71] The Report concluded that an 'adaptive' supervisory strategy which could manage the progressive integration of securities markets was necessary. CESR did not

---

[63] See, eg, the 2000 Commission Communication on Upgrading the Investment Services Directive (COM (2000) 729).

[64] 2009 UCITS IV Directive Arts 16–21.

[65] 2003 Prospectus Directive Art 13(5).

[66] The Economic and Financial Committee (EFC) undertakes a range of co-ordination tasks but primarily supports the Council: Art 134 TFEU.

[67] The Financial Services Committee is composed of representatives from the Commission and the Member States, and is designed to provide the Council (ECOFIN) with high-level strategic input, distinct from the legislative process.

[68] Recine, F and Teixeira, PG, The New Financial Stability Architecture in the EU, Paolo Baffi Research Paper No 2009-62 (2009), available at <http://ssrn.com/abstract=1509304>.

[69] In 2003, the Banking Supervision Committee of the ESCB produced recommendations designed to assist banking supervisors and central banks to respond to a financial crisis which led to a Memorandum of Understanding (MoU) (between banking supervisors and central banks) later in 2003. In May 2005, a second MoU was signed between the EU's banking supervisors, central banks, and finance ministries: Alexander, K and Ferran E, 'Can Soft Law Bodies be Effective? The Special Case of the European Systemic Risk Board' (2010) *ELR* 751.

[70] The Commission described supervisory convergence as 'one of the most innovative elements of the Lamfalussy architecture': Commission, Review of the Lamfalussy Process. Strengthening Supervisory Convergence (2007) (COM (2007) 727) (2007 Commission Lamfalussy Report) 7.

[71] Committee of European Securities Regulators (CESR), Preliminary Progress Report. Which Supervisory Tools for the EU Securities Market? An Analytical Paper by CESR (2004) (CESR 04-333f) (2004 Himalaya Report).

propose to create a new supervisory model,[72] but to 'pragmatically adapt the EU supervisory arrangements to what will occur in European securities markets'.[73] CESR presented a wide range of possible supervisory tools, which included the adoption of a 'co-ordinating supervisor' model, on a case-by-case basis and for particular supervisory tasks or investigations; identification of the role of supervisors in crisis management; discussion at CESR level of supervisory priorities and resource allocation; and the adoption of a standard Memorandum of Understanding (MoU) for the supervision of 'trans-European' entities. Enforcement initiatives included more active use of joint investigations, a sanctions database, and a more active co-ordination role for CESR. CESR's main proposal, however, related to the encouragement of a European 'supervisory mindset' such that NCAs would, in effect, become 'mini EU supervisors', exercising similar powers, sharing information freely, and making supervisory decisions based on a common approach to resource allocation, risk management, and supervisory objectives. Realization of this objective became the primary objective of EU financial market (and wider financial system) supervision policy, which became framed in terms of 'supervisory convergence'.

Pragmatic, evolutionary, and not requiring radical institutional change or any destabilization of fiscal responsibilities, the supervisory convergence model came to enjoy significant institutional support. It was supported by the European Parliament[74] and formed a central element of the Commission's post-FSAP strategy in its 2005–2010 White Paper.[75] The White Paper identified specific objectives for the new EU supervision agenda,[76] which included the clarification of home and host NCA responsibilities, the exploration of delegation mechanisms, and the development of a pan-EU supervisory culture through staff exchanges, joint training programmes, joint inspections, and peer reviews. Political support from the Council was also strong. The 2006 Francq Report of the Council's advisory Financial Services Committee isolated supervisory convergence as critical, and highlighted the importance of CESR's role. It was endorsed by the important Council Conclusions of May 2006,[77] which underlined that the success of the FSAP depended on the intensification of supervisory convergence.

Like its quasi-standard-setting activities, CESR's activities in the supervision/supervisory convergence sphere were strongly dynamic and foreshadowed many of the activities in which ESMA now engages.

As discussed in Chapter X sections 2.2 and 2.3, CESR engaged in an array of quasi-standard-setting activities designed in part to promote convergence in supervisory practices by NCAs as well as industry compliance.

---

[72] CESR noted that 'the mention of transnational options is risky in the sense that the focus of attention is likely to move too soon into this field': n 71, 3.

[73] n 71, 2.

[74] Parliament Van den Burg I Resolution on the Current State of Integration of EU Financial Markets, 28 April 2005 (T6–0153/2005) (2005 Van den Burg I Resolution) paras A.2, B.10, and B.12.

[75] Commission, White Paper on Financial Services Policy 2005–2010 (2005) (COM (2005) 629) (2005 White Paper), Impact Assessment Annex, 9.

[76] Supervision was also discussed extensively in the precursor Green Paper, which called for agreement on overall policy objectives, a maximizing of the current framework and the identification of gaps, and the development of new structures as a last resort: Commission, Green Paper on Financial Services Policy (2005–2010) (2005) (COM (2005) 177) (2005 Green Paper) Annex 1, 19–11.

[77] 2726th Council Meeting, 5 May 2006, ECOFIN Press Release No 8500/06.

It developed a capacity to co-ordinate supervisory/regulatory reporting. The centralization and streamlining of supervisory reports was identified at an early stage of the supervisory convergence discussion as central to promoting convergence and was highlighted by the 2006 ECOFIN Council Conclusions. CESR became, for example, a key player in the initial efforts to develop an electronic network of Officially Appointed Mechanisms to consolidate the distribution of issuer disclosure. The 2004 MiFID I's transparency and transaction-reporting regime saw considerable operational innovation, led by CESR-Tech; in particular, the TREM (the Transaction Reporting Exchange Mechanism) project, although problematic, led to the construction of a system which allowed NCAs to exchange reports.[78] CESR also maintained a series of databases which supported MiFID I obligations. Chief among these was the Database on Shares Admitted to Trading on a Regulated Market[79]—this included the important list of 'liquid shares', the determination of which was key to the application of MiFID I's transparency regime.

CESR also significantly strengthened co-operation and co-ordination with respect to enforcement in relation to market abuse and International Financial Reporting Standards (IFRS) reporting. Through CESR-Pol, a permanent operational group within CESR, CESR addressed the surveillance of financial markets and co-operation concerning enforcement and information exchange. Key operational developments included the establishment of the Urgent Issues Group and the Surveillance and Intelligence Group and the construction of an enforcement database. Operational innovation was also evident in the financial reporting sphere, where CESR-FIN, a permanent operational group which co-ordinated enforcement of IFRS by CESR members, established the European Enforcers' Co-ordination Sessions as well as a database on enforcement decisions.

There was also a more radical and coercive dimension to CESR's supervisory convergence activities. It developed a peer review capacity: CESR's Peer Review Panel reviewed the implementation by NCAs of CESR guidelines and standards and, where requested by the Commission, of EU rules. Although, as noted in section 5.6.4, it was not a noticeable success, it brought a new quasi-coercive dynamic to CESR's supervisory activities. The Panel also played a significant role in support of supervisory convergence by identifying inconsistencies in supervisory powers.[80] CESR also developed a Mediation Protocol, based on a 'comply or explain' mechanism, to support supervisory convergence and resolve supervisory disputes between NCAs.[81]

Throughout the CESR era, the relatively stable institutional and market environment meant there was limited policy and institutional enthusiasm for any conferral of direct supervision powers on CESR, although the hardy 'Euro-SEC' policy annual appeared and re-appeared over this period. CESR, however, initially harboured far-reaching ambitions in this regard. Although the 2004 Himalaya Report rejected the central supervisor model, it initially floated whether CESR should acquire a capacity for 'EC decision-making', including with respect to pre-clearance of innovative products and approval of, for example,

---

[78] CESR/07-739 and CESR/07-627b.
[79] CESR/07-718.
[80] In 2007 it examined (for the Council's Financial Services Committee) the range of powers available to members under the Prospectus and Market Abuse Directives (n 56 and Directive 2003/6/EC [2003] OJ L96/16).
[81] Protocol for a Mediation Mechanism (2006) (CESR/06-286b).

standardized UCITSs, and the supervision of 'trans-European infrastructures'.[82] By 2007, however, a sharper awareness of the legitimacy risks to its position, and perhaps a realization of the possibilities afforded through supervisory convergence, had reduced CESR's enthusiasm for the political maelstrom that any such transfer of power would (then) have generated.[83]

Nonetheless, and foreshadowing the agenda-setting impact of the rating agency sector over the crisis era, CESR made tentative steps towards more direct supervisory intervention in the rating agency sphere. It was brought within the supervisory framework for rating agencies by the Commission, which in 2006 built EU rating agency policy on industry compliance with the 2004 International Organization of Securities Commissions (IOSCO) Code of Conduct for Rating Agencies (Chapter VII section 2.2.1). A subsequent innovative joint venture between CESR and the industry, based on a voluntary agreement, empowered CESR to review industry compliance with the Code and gave CESR something of the quality of a direct supervisor.[84]

XI.3.2.3 Prior to the Financial Crisis and the 2007 Lamfalussy Review

Supervisory convergence provided an organic, pragmatic, and incremental response to the challenges which the optimal organization of post-FSAP supervision posed. But despite its dynamic quality and the advances it delivered, the CESR-led supervisory convergence model was an inadequate and unstable response to the integrated financial market which had developed by 2007.

NCAs had differing resource levels, different suites of supervisory and enforcement powers (including with respect to their ability to exchange information), and different mandates which shaped their supervisory priorities; employed different supervisory styles; and had different levels of experience, depending on the market structure in question. They were also organized in myriad ways which shaped supervisory practices accordingly.[85] The consequent lack of convergence in the application of supervisory powers, in related supervisory practices, and in sanctioning powers emerged as a serious threat to effective supervision and enforcement, and to the management of pan-EU risks.[86] The 2004 Himalaya Report had at an early stage identified failure to converge on supervisory powers as a key risk to effective supervision. In its subsequent 2005, 2006, and 2007 Reports on

---

[82] 2004 Himalaya Report, n 71, 17.

[83] In 2007, CESR stated clearly that it was 'not advocating for the creation of an EU single regulator embedded within the Treaty': CESR, A Proposed Evolution of Securities Supervision Beyond 2007 (2007) (CESR/07-783) (2007 CESR Securities Supervision Report) 6.

[84] Its first report in January 2007 included, eg, a warning to the industry concerning the lack of progress in the separation of rating business from other business lines in order to manage conflicts of interests (CESR/06-545).

[85] On the diverging features of NCAs immediately prior to and in the early stages of the financial crisis see, eg: Ferran, E, 'Understanding the Shape of the New Institutional Architecture of EU Financial Market Supervision' in Ferrarini, G, Hopt, K, and Wymeersch, E (eds), *Rethinking Financial Regulation and Supervision in Times of Crisis* (2012) 111; CESR Factbook (CESR, Factbook on Markets and Supervision (2007) (CESR/07-306)) 20–1; 2007 CESR Securities Supervision Report, n 83; Wymeersch, E, 'The Structure of Financial Supervision in Europe: About Single Financial Supervisors, Twin Peaks and Multiple Financial Supervisors' (2007) 8 *EBOLR* 23; and Lannoo, K, Supervising the European Financial System. CEPS Policy Brief 21 (2002).

[86] Inter-institutional Monitoring Group, First Interim Report Monitoring the Lamfalussy Process (2006) 15.

supervisory convergence to the Council's Financial Services Committee,[87] CESR revealed considerable concern as to the failure to converge, including with respect to resources, application of powers, levels of supervisory intensity, and NCA views on the purposes and nature of market regulation and supervision, including with respect to which risk levels were acceptable. Despite CESR's supervisory convergence agenda, the threats to consistency in supervision were many, as were the threats to mutual trust between NCAs and, accordingly, to effective co-ordination. The risks of destabilizing supervisory competition were also significant.[88] The treatment of multijurisdictional actors, including trading markets, posed particular difficulties. Although some *ad hoc* college-of-supervisor models had developed outside the EU structures (notably with respect to the supervision of Euronext and LIFFE), multijurisdictional actors were typically supervised under the standard home/host NCA relationship, and the particular co-ordination, operational, and governance mechanisms necessary to support colleges of supervisors were not in place.

Overall, the supervisory convergence model was not sufficiently robust to respond to these weaknesses. It was dependent on a voluntary commitment from NCAs and based on reputational dynamics and peer pressure. As the financial crisis would reveal, it was not equipped to deal with financial stability risks or crisis conditions. The IMF's July 2007 review was eerily prescient: it warned that as national supervisory authorities' fiduciary responsibilities were towards national treasuries, this limited their incentives to work towards a common EU financial stability framework, and that, in a crisis, they were likely to look to protect the national treasury, using informational advantages, notwithstanding co-operation and information-exchange arrangements—a 'scramble for assets' was accordingly likely.[89]

But the 2007 Lamfalussy Review,[90] which took place under the shadow of the emerging financial crisis, did not lead to radical change and reflected the evolutionary approach which had long characterized the organization of supervision for the EU's financial market.[91] Support for any material strengthening of the EU's engagement with operational supervisory practices was limited,[92] and appetite for radical institutional change almost entirely

---

[87] CESR, First Progress Report on Supervisory Convergence in the Field of Securities Markets for the Financial Services Committee (2005) (CESR/05-202), CESR, 2006 Report on Supervisory Convergence in the Field of Securities Markets (2006) (CESR/06-259b), and CESR, An Evaluation of Equivalence of Supervisory Powers in the EU under the Market Abuse and Prospectus Directive. A Report to the Financial Services Committee (2007) (CESR/07-334).

[88] CESR argued that supervisory arbitrage within an integrated market was detrimental for the fair and safe functioning of the market and investor protection, that 'referees should not compete', and that a 'strong team spirit' was required among supervisors: 2007 CESR Securities Supervision Report, n 83, 3.

[89] International Monetary Fund (IMF), Country Report No 7/260, Euro-area Policies (2007) 18–21.

[90] The major reports and reviews included: European Parliament, Van den Burg II Resolution on Financial Services Policy (2005–2010) White Paper, 11 July 2007 (P6_TA(2007)0338) (2007 Van den Burg II Resolution); the Commission's 2007 Lamfalussy Report, n 70; Inter Institutional Monitoring Group, Final Report Monitoring the Lamfalussy Process (October 2007) (2007 Final IIMG Report), and CESR's 2007 Securities Supervision Report, n 83. See further Ch X sect 2.3.

[91] Immediately prior to the intensification of the financial crisis, Commissioner McCreevy described the Commission's approach to supervision as evolutionary rather than revolutionary: Speech on 'Challenges to the Further Integration of EU Financial Markets', EUROFI Conference, 4 December 2007.

[92] 2007 Council discussions saw some tensions, eg, over the extent to which supervisory practices should converge. The UK, in particular, was hostile to any centralization of supervisory practices: Tait, N and Barber, T, 'UK Set to Reject Italy Plan on Financial Standards', *Financial Times*, 4 December 2007, 8.

absent.[93] The 'Euro-SEC' model, which had little traction over the FSAP period, got short shrift over the Lamfalussy Review.[94]

The Review accordingly focused on stronger convergence in supervisory powers[95] and the strengthening of the supervisory convergence powers of CESR, CEBS, and CEIOPS (the '3L3' committees), primarily through 3L3 qualified majority voting (QMV) and a requirement for national supervisory mandates to refer to supervisory convergence obligations.[96] The Review revealed some support for the conferral on the 3L3 committees of formal powers in relation to cross-border co-operation, including delegation,[97] the adoption of multilateral MoUs to support home/host NCA relationships,[98] and greater use and oversight of colleges of supervisors.[99]

The review process culminated in the important December 2007 ECOFIN Council Conclusions,[100] which broadly reflected these themes. The Conclusions did not support major institutional change, preferring the supervisory convergence model. The Council supported use of the QMV within the 3L3 Committees and greater reliance on the 'comply or explain' mechanism to promote compliance with convergence measures. It also supported the adoption of supervisory convergence mandates in NCA supervisory mandates, although it was not prescriptive and simply recommended that Member States consider including in the mandates of NCAs the task of co-operating within the EU and working towards supervisory convergence. The Council also addressed convergence in supervisory powers and called on the Commission to study differences in supervisory powers and whether there was sufficient equivalence in how powers were used. More radical changes to the status quo included the Council's support of delegation and of colleges of supervisors, in relation to which the Council called for the adoption of a common set of 3L3 operational guidelines for colleges of supervisors and called on the 3L3 committees to monitor the coherence of the practices of different colleges and share best practice.

---

[93] The Commission, eg, argued that more ambitious institutional changes, such as the granting of independent rule-making power to CESR, CEBS (the Committee of European Banking Supervisors), and CEIOPS (the Committee of European Insurance and Occupational Pensions Supervisors), were not feasible given lack of agreement among Member States and stakeholders: n 70, 3. The IMF similarly noted that while there was general agreement that Europe's financial stability framework needed to be strengthened, views differed how this could be achieved, particularly with respect to co-ordinated action and burden-sharing: n 89, 20.

[94] It had been repeatedly ruled out by the Commission since the closure of the Financial Services Action Plan (FSAP). The 2005 Green Paper argued that no new structures would be proposed unless compelling evidence arose (2005 Green Paper, n 76, Annex, 11), while the 2005 White Paper contained the strong statement that 'the central policy of the Commission is to keep faith with the [Lamfalussy] process' and that the Commission (in the context of prudential supervision) 'advocates an evolutionary approach, responding to demonstrated problems': n 75, 9 and 10. ECB President Trichet similarly stated that the Lamfalussy structures provided the appropriate institutional vehicle for supporting a decentralized supervisory model: Trichet, J-C, Speech on 'Enhancing the EU Regulatory and Supervisory Framework—the Eurosystem's Perspective', EUROFI Conference on Achieving the Integration of European Financial Markets in a Global Context, 3 December 2007.

[95] 2007 Commission Lamfalussy Report, n 70, 10.

[96] 2007 Final IIMG Report, n 90, 18 and 2007 Commission Lamfalussy Report, n 70, 8.

[97] 2007 Final IIMG Report, n 90, 16 and 2007 Commission Lamfalussy Report, n 70, 11.

[98] 2007 Commission Lamfalussy Report, n 70, 11.

[99] 2007 Commission Lamfalussy Report, n 70, 11–12 and 2007 Van den Burg II Resolution, n 90, para 60.

[100] 2836th Council Meeting, 4 December 2007, ECOFIN Press Release No 15698/07, 13–21.

The Council restated its support for its December 2007 Conclusions in May 2008, albeit that it additionally called for the 3L3 committees to report on financial stability risks.[101] The attachment to decentralized supervision remained very strong, even as the crisis deepened over 2007 and 2008.[102] The governance changes called for by the Lamfalussy Review and supported by the Council would be made to CESR's organization over 2008 and 2009.[103] But these changes and the supervisory convergence model would rapidly be overtaken by the deepening of the financial crisis over summer and autumn 2008.

XI.3.3 The Financial Crisis

XI.3.3.1 The Financial Crisis and Supervisory Weaknesses

The EU's decentralized, supervisory convergence-based model for the organization of supervision over the EU's financial system came under great strain and buckled over the financial crisis.[104]

Although financial stability had been on the EU's agenda for some time, supporting pan-EU structures were not in place. The Council had adopted Conclusions on financial stability at the outset of the crisis in October 2007,[105] the Commission followed a somewhat sanguine financial stability agenda in its early 2008 Communication on financial stability,[106] and the

---

[101] 2866th Council Meeting, 14 May 2008, ECOFIN Press Release No 8850/08.

[102] ECB President Trichet suggested that the EU's financial stability strategy should build on national responsibility for financial stability, and that the Lamfalussy structures provided the appropriate institutional setting by supporting the geographical proximity of supervisors and a sharing of local experience and expertise: Trichet, J-C, Enhancing the EU Arrangements for Financial Stability, European Parliament, Session on European Financial Supervision. Crisis Management on Financial Markets, 23 January 2008. In a similar vein, Commissioner McCreevy argued in December 2007 that while the need for improved crisis management which emerged in the wake of the UK's Northern Rock crisis and during the 2007 turbulence in credit markets might suggest greater centralization in supervision, his 'political antennae' suggested that political circumstances would prevent any such initiative: n 91.

[103] See Ch X sect 2.3.

[104] See, eg, Moloney, N, 'EU Financial Market Regulation after the Financial Crisis: "More Europe" or More Risks?' (2010) 47 *CMLR* 1317; Ferrarini, G and Chiodini, F, Regulating Multinational Banks in Europe. An Assessment of the New Supervisory Framework, ECGI Law WP No 158/2010 (2010), available at <http://ssrn.com/abstract=1596890>; Dabrowski, M, The Global Financial Crisis: Lessons for European Integration, Case Network Studies and Analysis No 384/2009, available at <http://ssrn.com/abstract=1436432>; Cotterli, S and Gualandri, E, Financial Crisis and Supervision of Cross Border Groups in the EU (2009), available at <http://ssrn.com/abstract=1507750>; and Fonteyne, W, et al, Crisis Management and Resolution for a European Banking System, IMF Working Paper WP/10/70 (2010), available at <http://www.imf.org/external/pubs/ft/wp/2010/wp1070.pdf>. For the EU institutional view, see The High-Level Group on Financial Supervision, Report (2009) (the 2009 de Larosière or DLG Report) and EFC, High-Level Working Group on Cross-Border Financial Supervision Arrangements, Lessons from the Crisis for European Financial Stability Arrangements (2009) (2009 EFC Report).

[105] The October 2007 ECOFIN Council Conclusions (2822nd Council Meeting, 7 October 2007, ECOFIN Press Release No 13571/07) saw the Council adopt a work programme which addressed enhancing transparency, improving valuation standards for complex financial products, strengthening the prudential framework (including exchange of information between supervisors and central banks), and credit rating agencies. Stability was discussed again in the December 2007 Conclusions (2836th Council Meeting, 4 December 2007, ECOFIN Press Release No 15698/07) and was a feature of the spring 2008 European Council and the May 2008 ECOFIN Council (2866th Council Meeting, 14 May 2008, ECOFIN Press Release No 8850/08).

[106] The Commission's February 2008 Communication, which was prepared for the spring 2008 European Council, was somewhat relaxed as to the risks posed by the EU's supervisory and regulatory structure, and placed long-term financial stability and efficiency in the context of international co-operation. Commission,

European Council's March 2008 meeting also addressed financial stability.[107] But these efforts were not operational in nature, and the subsequent June 2008 Memorandum of Understanding on Financial Stability[108] was almost irrelevant when disaster struck in autumn 2008. As has been extensively documented, the intensification of the financial crisis in autumn 2008 placed the home/host decentralized model under intense pressure, arising primarily from banking failures and from poor co-ordination of pan-EU banking group supervision and related rescue and resolution. As noted in Chapter I, at the core of the banking crisis in autumn 2008 was a destructive imbalance in the regulatory and supervisory architecture; while the regulatory structure facilitated cross-border activity by large banking groups, it did not adequately address cross-border supervision, co-ordination, crisis resolution, and deposit protection. Chaotic rescue efforts, which often paid little heed to pan-EU financial stability consequences, followed.

Institutionally, the 3L3 committees proved ill equipped to deal with crisis management and co-ordination, although CESR and CEBS, in particular, took on more operational roles. CEBS co-ordinated pan-EU bank stress tests, at the Council's request, in 2009 and 2010, assessed banks' supervisory and public disclosures, examined the supervisory implications of national stabilization plans, and was closely involved with the new supervisory colleges established over the crisis.[109] In the financial markets sphere, CESR was only able to provide very basic co-ordination support to the chaotic prohibition of short selling by NCAs in September 2008.[110] Almost two years later, during the sovereign debt crisis, the unilateral prohibition of short selling in sovereign debt by Germany in May 2010, which shocked the markets, further underlined CESR's difficulties in co-ordinating NCAs.[111] CESR subsequently embraced the reform agenda and undertook more operational functions, including the review of disclosure by listed banks and insurers,[112] but its supervisory and co-ordinating capacity proved to be limited.

Consensus on the nature of the failures emerged rapidly. The 2009 DLG Report[113] highlighted poor supervisory co-ordination, co-operation, and information-sharing across the EU financial system, as well as diverging supervisory practices and sanctions, supervisory error, ineffective 3L3 committee peer review, and an absence of crisis decision-making mechanisms, crisis resolution devices, and macroprudential (or system oversight) powers. The 2009 Report of the Economic and Financial Committee[114] similarly found that the distribution of tasks between home and host NCAs was not clear, host NCAs had limited

---

Europe's Financial System: Adapting to Change, Contribution of the Commission to the European Council (2008) (COM (2008) 122).

[107] The Council called for improvements in the prudential framework and in risk management of individual institutions, and for full and prompt disclosure of exposure to distressed assets. While it emphasized that primary responsibility remained with the private sector, it also highlighted that the relevant authorities should stand ready to take supervisory and regulatory action: Presidency Conclusions, Brussels European Council, 13–14 March 2008, paras 31 and 32.

[108] ECB, MoU on Co-operation between the Financial Supervisory Authorities, Central Banks, and the Finance Ministries of the EU on Cross-Border Financial Stability (2008).

[109] CEBS, Annual Report (2009) 9–10, 13, and 17–20.

[110] It attempted to co-ordinate national actions, produced a table of national restrictions, and reported to the Council on the prohibitions.

[111] Ch VI sect 3.3.

[112] CESR, Annual Report (2009) 47.

[113] n 104.

[114] n 104.

powers, NCAs were not mandated to consider pan-EU financial stability, and there were significant inconsistencies in Member States' intervention and rescue powers. The Commission warned that the EU's institutional capacity, based on the 3L3 committees, was inadequate and had to improve.[115]

Although the immediate impetus for reform came from the chaotic attempts to rescue the EU banking sector in late 2008, the institutional reform movement almost immediately extended to the EU financial system generally, although the particular fiscal consequences of the banking rescue had a decisive influence on the negotiations. But while consensus on the need for some form of institutional reform was generally strong, the crisis exposed the depth of the institutional and political tensions with respect to fiscal burden-sharing and the appropriate intensity of EU supervisory intervention.

XI.3.3.2 Legislative Reform: Enhancing Supervision and Enforcement and Strengthening Co-ordination

While the establishment of the ESAs and the ESRB was the major outcome of the financial crisis, the crisis also led to an enhancement of supervision more generally. Reflecting the recommendation of the 2009 DLG Report that a more harmonized set of supervisory powers be deployed by NCAs, and its call for supervisory powers to be aligned to the most comprehensive system in the EU, the crisis-era reforms have led to greater prescription of supervisory powers (section 4.1).

Although enforcement has long been regarded as a national competence, sanctioning powers have also been subject to more prescriptive harmonization. The 2009 DLG Report called for more consistent sanctioning regimes and warned that supervision could not be effective with 'weak, highly variant' sanctioning regimes.[116] As outlined in section 4.1, the crisis-era programme has accordingly led to greater prescription of the types of sanctions which must be available and how they must be applied with respect to particular breaches.

The financial crisis also led to significantly greater reliance on formal co-ordination and co-operation through colleges of supervisors and to an enhancement of their role, as discussed in section 4.2.2.

XI.3.3.3 Institutional Reform: the ESA Negotiations

From October 2008, institutional and political support for some degree of institutional reform was strong.[117] Political support for the oft-mooted 'single regulator' remained limited, however, as was support for any significant enhancement of the powers of

---

[115] The Commission warned that 'the EU cannot remain in a situation where there is no mechanism to ensure that national supervisors arrive at the best possible supervisory decisions for cross-border institutions; where there is insufficient cooperation and information exchange between national supervisory authorities; where joint action by national authorities requires a tour de force to take account of the patchwork of regulatory and supervisory requirements; where national solutions are often the only feasible option in responding to European problems, where different interpretations of the same legal text abound'. Commission, Communication on European Financial Supervision (2009) (COM (2009) 252) (2009 European Financial Supervision Communication) 8.

[116] n 104, 50–1.

[117] Tait, N and Hughes, J, 'Trichet Calls for Supervision of All Institutions', *Financial Times*, 24 February 2009, 7, reporting on a 'swelling chorus' of support for institutional reform, and Barber, T and Mallet, V, 'Call from BBVA for Single Regulator', *Financial Times*, 19 January 2009, reporting on industry support.

ECB.[118] From the outset, reliance on the 'off the shelf' 3L3 model was politically attractive as well as operationally sensible.

The 2009 DLG Report's reform prescription was based on the establishment of a European Systemic Risk Council (ESRC), to provide macroprudential oversight, and of an ESFS, responsible for microprudential-supervision and composed of the NCAs and the proposed three new supervisory authorities, based on the precursor 3L3 committees. The DLG Report's vision[119] was based on NCAs remaining the primary location of operational supervisory power and retaining most of their competences, but on the conferral of discrete powers on the new supervisory authorities.[120] The new authorities would carry out the supervisory convergence activities of the 3L3 committees, including peer reviews; exercise co-ordination functions, including in crisis situations; and would have an international role, including with respect to equivalence determinations and the representation of the EU's interests with respect to supervision. More radically, the authorities would be empowered to engage in legally binding mediation (which would include the power to impose supervisory decisions directly on financial market participants), to exercise quasi-enforcement powers,[121] and to supervise 'some specific EU-wide institutions such as credit rating agencies and post-trading infrastructures'.[122]

The Commission, which supported the DLG model in its 2009 Communication on Driving European Recovery,[123] amplified it in its May 2009 Communication on European Financial Supervision,[124] which proposed a twin-pillar-based system based on macroprudential oversight by the ESRC and a 'robust network of national financial supervisors working in tandem with the new ESAs' and within the ESFS. The authorities would take on the functions of the 3L3 committees, but would additionally, and as a 'last resort', exercise binding mediation powers (reflected in 2010 ESMA Regulation Article 19); be empowered to investigate breaches of EU law by NCAs, adopt recommendations, and, in the event of continued non-compliance, address decisions to financial market participants (reflected in Article 17); adopt 'some emergency decisions' in specific crisis situations (reflected in Article 18); and have full supervisory powers over 'certain entities with pan-European reach', such as rating agencies and central clearing counterparties (CCPs).[125] Like the 2009 DLG Report, the Commission highlighted that the focal point for day-to-day supervision would remain at national level. The Commission's subsequent September 2009 Proposals for the new structures followed the May 2009 Communication for the most part, but provided more articulated detail.[126]

---

[118] Tait, N and Atkins, R, 'Pressure to Adopt the Least Worst Option', *Financial Times*, 22 January 2009, 5.

[119] n 104, 42–56.

[120] n 104, 47.

[121] The Report suggested that the authorities be empowered to issue rulings aimed at ensuring that national supervisors corrected weaknesses that had been identified, failure to comply with which could ultimately lead to fines and to Commission enforcement action: n 104, 54.

[122] n 104, 53.

[123] COM (2009) 114.

[124] n 115.

[125] n 115, 10–11. On central clearing counterparty (CCP) supervision see Ch VI sect 4.2.9 and 4.2.10.

[126] The ESMA Proposal is at COM (2009) 503 (Impact Assessment n 47). The ESRB reform is discussed in sect 6. See also Ch X sect 2.4 on the different stages of the inter-institutional negotiations.

By the September 2009 adoption by the Commission of the Proposals, a significant degree of consensus had coalesced on the main elements of the proposed new institutional structure. The main lines of conflict, however, had also been established. The Member States' wariness with respect to any transfers of power which would entail fiscal conse-quences (reflecting the costs of the ongoing bank rescue efforts[127]), and which would frame the negotiations,[128] was clear. While the June 2009 European Council supported 'binding and proportionate decision-making powers', it also stated that ESA decisions should not impinge on the fiscal responsibilities of Member States, given the risks of contingent liabilities.[129] Similarly, the June 2009 ECOFIN Council meeting supported the establish-ment of the ESAs but warned that the framework for the ESAs' powers was to be exhaustively specified, and it underlined the need for a fiscal safeguard which would allow Member States to veto ESA actions.[130]

Tensions between the Member States also emerged. The UK and the 'new' Central and Eastern European Member States were particularly concerned to ensure that the ESAs could not take decisions with fiscal consequences; the new Member States, whose financial services industries were dominated by cross-border branches and subsidiaries, were con-cerned in particular that they would be required to fund the costs of rescues of cross-border actors operating in their jurisdictions.[131] But, prior to the June 2009 ECOFIN Council and European Council declarations, not all Member States were committed to a rigid prohib-ition on any ESA decision carrying fiscal consequences.[132]

The Commission was concerned as to the damage which over-reliance by the Member States on fiscal risk arguments could wreak on its ESA Proposals.[133] Nonetheless, it was (and remains) sceptical of transfers of operational power to the ESAs,[134] reflecting the *Meroni* risks engaged[135] as well as the related threats to the Commission's executive powers.[136]

---

[127] The UK's resistance was driven by concern that an ESA could force a government to bailout a bank: Barber, T and Benoit, B, 'EU Set to Agree on Tighter Rules for Markets', *Financial Times*, 18 June 2009, 8.
[128] eg Tait, N, Wilson, J, and Masters, B, 'Common Rules Likely to Be Enforced', *Financial Times*, 24 September 2009, 6.
[129] European Council Conclusions, 18–19 June 2009, 8.
[130] 2948th Council Meeting, 9 June 2009, ECOFIN Press Release No 10737/09, 11–14.
[131] Spendzharova, A, 'Is More "Brussels" the Solution? New European Union Member States' Preferences about the European Financial Architecture' (2012) 50 *JCMS* 315.
[132] The main conflict line was reportedly between the UK (rigidly opposed), often supported by Spain and the Czech Republic, and France, often supported by Italy, Portugal, and the Netherlands: Spendzharova, n 131, 318–19. Significant discord was reported at the June 2009 ECOFIN Council meeting which preceded the June 2009 European Council, and which saw the Council divided between the majority of Member States in favour of ESA powers of intervention, and a minority of Member States, led by the UK, concerned to limit the impact on fiscal sovereignty: Barber, T, 'EU Impasse Over More Powers for Bank Supervisors', *Financial Times*, 10 June 2009, 6.
[133] The Commission's concern to ensure that fiscal risk arguments would not unduly hinder the ESAs is clear from its Impact Assessment in which it underlined that it was of 'high importance' that the 'fiscal safeguard' clause, which allows Member States to veto certain ESA actions, was not abused, be used sparingly, and be limited to well-justified cases: n 47, 29.
[134] eg from the outset it highlighted that it would only consider making a proposal for the supervision by the ESAs of pan-EU entities where there was a 'clear added value': Commission, Financial Supervision Package—Frequently Asked Questions (MEMO/10/434), 22 September 2010 (2010 Commission FAQ) Q 15.
[135] n 52. See sect 5.8.2.
[136] See further sects 5.8 and 5.9.

The European Parliament, by contrast, saw the proposed ESAs as an institutional vehicle for the greater concentration of supervisory power at EU level.

Most attention focused on ESMA's[137] contested powers to issue recommendations to NCAs in breach of EU law, to engage in binding mediation, and to take emergency action, and in all these cases to address related decisions to financial market participants (now 2010 ESMA Regulation Articles 17–19). The Article 17 enforcement power as finally adopted did not differ significantly from the Commission's proposal, drawing support from the European Parliament and the Council, which reflected the need for a mechanism to deal with non-compliance with EU law. The more intrusive Article 18 emergency power, however, was heavily negotiated. The Commission's position was close to that as finally adopted, save that the Commission initially proposed that it be empowered to declare an emergency for the purposes of triggering ESMA's powers.[138] The Council, however, in its December 2009 General Approach,[139] reserved the power to declare an emergency to itself, introduced review obligations, tightened the conditions for the exercise of emergency powers,[140] and removed the Commission's proposal for a related emergency power to impose decision on financial market participants. The European Parliament's July 2010 Negotiating Position[141] located the declaratory power with the Commission and supported the related power to address decisions to financial market participants. The Article 19 binding mediation power was also contentious, inter-institutionally and within the Council, as it empowered ESMA to interpose its will in contested situations between NCAs, and became associated with the ability of ESMA to impose decisions with respect to the respective liabilities of NCAs in rescue situations and to override the exercise of NCA discretion.[142] The Council's December 2009 General Approach also removed the Commission's proposal that ESMA be empowered to address decisions to financial market participants in the binding mediation context—but this power was supported by the Parliament. The related fiscal safeguard (which in effect allowed Member States a veto over ESA decisions) was also the location of major differences between the institutions and within the Council.[143] The Council, in its December 2009 General Approach, reduced the related Council voting majority required to overturn an ESMA decision (on fiscal grounds) from a QMV to a simple majority vote, and introduced the possibility of a final appeal by the Member State in question where the Council did not overturn an ESMA decision.

---

[137] Broadly the same set of issues arose with respect to each ESA; this discussion accordingly refers to ESMA, although the issues in question were raised with respect to the ESA reform generally.

[138] The Commission argued rather thinly that 'the determination of a cross-border emergency situation involves a degree of appreciation and should therefore be left to the Commission': 2009 ESMA Proposal, n 126, 6.

[139] Council Document 16571/1-09, 2 December 2009.

[140] Including that, in addition to the declaration of an emergency by the Council, 'exceptional conditions' obtained which demanded co-ordinated action to respond to adverse developments.

[141] 6 July 2010 (T7-0270/2010).

[142] 'Europe's Growing Co-ordination Pains', Editorial, *Financial Times*, 11 June 2009, 10 and Barber, T, 'EU Impasse Over More Powers for Bank Supervisors', *Financial Times*, 10 June 2009, 6, reporting on disagreement within the Council on whether the ESAs should have the power to impose a binding decision, which was related to the fiscal risk thereby engaged for Member States. The binding mediation power was particularly contested with respect to the banking sector and EBA.

[143] The UK led a small group of Member States anxious to retain the fiscal safeguard in the face of opposition from France and Germany in particular: Barber, T and Benoit, B, 'EU Set to Agree on Tighter Rules for Markets', *Financial Times*, 18 June 2009, 8.

Major differences also arose (specific to ESMA) with respect to ESMA's proposed powers to supervise cross-border actors. The Commission, which initially supported ESMA's exercise of supervisory powers over rating agencies and CCPs,[144] supported the conferral of powers as agreed by the institutions, and proposed that ESMA 'execute any exclusive supervisory powers over entities with Community-wide reach or economic activities with Community-wide reach' entrusted to it by the binding rulebook.[145] But despite the breadth of this proposed enabling clause, the Commission was supportive only of transfers of power involving 'added value', and was sensitive to the need for all such transfers to be decided by the European Parliament and Council.[146] The Council, sceptical towards—and internally divided with respect to—ESMA supervision of pan-EU entities, replaced this enabling provision with a narrowly drawn conferral of power with respect to rating agencies only.[147] The Commission's original position was, however, supported by the Parliament in its July 2010 Negotiating Position, which additionally empowered ESMA to: 'supervise those financial market participants that are not subject to the supervision of competent authorities'; temporarily prohibit or restrict certain types of financial activities where the orderly functioning and integrity of financial markets or the stability of the financial system was threatened; support resolution of cross-border institutions through a Resolution Unit; and supervise cross-border institutions that may pose systemic risk.[148] The Parliament also proposed the establishment of a 'European Stability Fund for Securities and Markets' to provide funding for crisis resolution.[149]

The final summer 2010 trilogue negotiations between the Commission, Council, and Parliament focused on the considerable distance between the Council and European Parliament positions, and were based on the Council's July 2010 EBA-based political approach.[150] The Council conceded the Parliament's proposal for an ESA power to temporarily restrict or prohibit certain financial activities and for an ESA power to address decisions to financial market participants in emergency conditions and in relation to binding mediation (albeit that the Council required that these powers be subject to tougher conditions). It maintained its position, however, with respect to the removal of all references to the supervision of pan-EU entities (bar rating agencies) but proposed that ESMA instead be required to engage in a range of monitoring and policy development activities related to systemic risk and cross-border resolution. After difficult negotiations, an agreement which reflected, for the most part, the Council's position was reached in September 2009.[151]

XI.3.3.4 A Brave New World?

As noted in Chapter X section 2.4.3, the initial agreement on and subsequent establishment of the ESAs was attended by a rich institutional rhetoric. The ESAs' potential ability to

---

[144] eg 2009 ESA Proposals Impact Assessment, n 47, 26.

[145] 2009 ESMA Proposal, n 126, Art 6(3).

[146] 2010 Commission FAQ, n 134, Q14.

[147] December 2009 General Approach, n 139, Art 6(3).

[148] July 2010 Parliament Negotiating Position, n 141, Arts 6(1) (fc) and (ga), 6a(5), 12a, 12b, and 12c.

[149] July 2010 Parliament Negotiating Position, n 141, Art 12f.

[150] The Council adopted a political approach on 13 July 2010 on aspects of the EBA Proposal which were critical to the negotiations across all three ESAs: Council Document 11669/10.

[151] Report from the Presidency to the Council, 6 September 2010, Proposal for a Regulation of the European Parliament and the Council establishing a European Banking Authority—Presidency Compromise Text (13070/1/10 Rev 1).

transform supervision was loudly trumpeted.[152] The European Parliament claimed that the new supervisory structure would 'see a fundamental shift in the way banks, stock markets and insurance companies are policed'.[153] ESMA Chairman Maijoor, in ESMA's first Annual Report, suggested that the establishment of ESMA marked the 'beginning of a new era in how we go about protecting investors and ensuring we have well-functioning and stable markets across the European Union'.[154] Expectations were high and scrutiny from key stakeholders intense. The IMF, for example, suggested that the ESAs generally would need to move quickly to establish their credibility with national authorities and financial institutions, and that this would be best achieved by early and decisive action.[155] The Commission, in its 2011 European Financial Stability and Integration Report, suggested that ongoing market turbulence and the ongoing Greek sovereign debt crisis emphasized the need for the ESAs and gave them an opportunity to show their added value.[156] An extensive hearing by the European Parliament in September 2012 underlined the intense institutional interest in their development and in their supervisory powers in particular.[157]

The nature of ESMA's powers is considered in section 5.

XI.4 The ESFS: NCAs

XI.4.1 NCAs: Supervision and Enforcement

XI.4.1.1 Supervision

Notwithstanding the injection of ESMA into the organization of EU financial market supervision, the supervision of the EU financial market remains based on a network of NCAs.[158] This organizational principle was never in doubt over the crisis-era reconfiguration of the institutional structure. The 2009 DLG Report's core recommendation that the ESFS 'would be a largely decentralized structure' in which national authorities, closest to the markets and institutions supervised, would continue to carry out day-to-day supervision and preserve the majority of their competences[159] reflects not only the efficiency attractions of decentralization, but also the very significant political, fiscal, operational, and legal complexities of centralized supervision, which were long acknowledged, but which the ESA negotiations sharply exposed.

---

[152] eg Statement of the Commission following the final agreement on financial supervision reform, 22 September 2010 (MEMO/10/436), suggesting that the EU was the first region in the world to put in place 'top-notch' supervision, up to the challenges of the future.

[153] European Parliament, Press Release 20100921PR83190.

[154] ESMA, Annual Report (2011) 5.

[155] IMF, IMF Country Report No 11/230, July 2011. United Kingdom: The Future of Regulation and Supervision Technical Note, 12–13.

[156] Commission, European Financial Stability and Integration Report 2011 (2012) (SWD (2012) 103) (2011 EFSIR) 54.

[157] Written Answers to the 19 September 2012 ECON Hearing of the ESA Chairs (JC/2012/090).

[158] eg 2010 ESMA Regulation rec 9, describing the ESFS as an integrated network of national and EU supervisory authorities 'leaving day-to-day supervision at the national level'.

[159] 2009 DLG Report, n 104, 47. The Commission's subsequent 2009 European Financial Supervision Communication underlined that the 'new network' was based on nationally-based supervision and the centralization of only specific tasks at EU level: n 115, 3. Similarly, the Commission argued that day-to-day supervision was best done at national level and that NCAs would play a pivotal role: 2010 Commission FAQ, n 134.

With some very limited exceptions, NCAs remain responsible for the authorization of financial market participants, for ongoing supervision, and (depending on local procedural arrangements) for enforcement. While ESMA is increasingly drilling into how NCAs engage in the business of supervision, it remains a primarily local function. The EU legislative framework which governs the powers and supervisory activities of NCAs has, however, become increasingly granular and outcomes-focused.

As discussed in earlier Chapters, the legislative measures which form EU securities and markets regulation require Member States to appoint NCAs (the legislative framework usually requires that they are public authorities,[160] but not always[161]) to carry out the functions identified. They also typically identify the supervisory powers with which authorities must be conferred. The 2011 Alternative Investment Fund Managers Directive (2011 AIFMD),[162] for example, requires that NCAs have the power to: have access to any documents; require information from any person related to the activities of alternative investment funds and managers and, if necessary, summon and question persons; carry out on-site inspections, with or without prior announcements; require existing telephone and existing data traffic records; require the cessation of any practice contrary to the AIMFD; request the freezing or sequestration of assets; request the temporary prohibition of professional activities; require authorized AIFMD depositaries or auditors to provide information; adopt any type of measure to ensure that fund managers or depositaries continue to comply with the requirements of the AIFMD; require the suspension of the issue, repurchase, or redemption of units in the interest of unit-holders or the public; withdraw the authorization granted to a manager or depositary; refer matters for criminal prosecution; and request that auditors carry out verifications or investigations (Article 46). This model re-appears across EU securities and markets regulation,[163] albeit calibrated to the particular supervisory territory in question.[164] Despite the crisis-era commitment to removing divergences between the supervisory powers granted to NCAs, overall, the degree of prescription has not changed significantly since the FSAP era.[165] Administrative rules, including Binding Technical Standards (BTSs), are, however, addressing supervisory

---

[160] eg 2011 AIFMD (Directive 2011/61/EU [2011] OJ L174/1) Art 44; 2009 UCITS IV Directive Art 99, and 2014 MiFID II Art 67.

[161] The 2012 European Market Infrastructure Regulation (Regulation (EU) No 648/2012 [2012] OJ L201/1 (2012 EMIR)) and the 2012 Short Selling Regulation (Regulation (EU) No 236/2012 [2012] OJ L86/1 (2012 Short Selling Regulation)), eg, do not specify the status of the authority. The 2003 Prospectus Directive requires that the NCA is 'completely independent from all market participants' but does not require that it be a public authority (Art 21(1)).

[162] n 160.

[163] A similar model applies under the 2009 UCITS IV Directive (Art 98) and 2014 MiFID II (Art 69). The 2012 EMIR, however, does not enumerate the powers of NCAs, simply requiring (in an echo of the pre-FSAP approach) that NCAs have the supervisory and investigatory powers necessary for the exercise of their functions (Art 22(2)).

[164] The 2012 Short Selling Regulation, eg, contains a shorter list, reflecting the particular powers needed with respect to short selling, and includes specific powers with respect to requesting explanations relating to the purpose of particular credit default swap transactions (Art 33). The 2003 Prospectus Directive, to take another example, requires that NCAs be empowered to deploy a range of tools related to public offers and admissions to trading, including the suspension of offers and admissions, and the suspension and prohibition of trading: Art 21(3).

[165] The prospectus regime, eg, remains based on the list of powers contained in the 2003 Prospectus Directive, which list was not enhanced by the 2010 Amending Prospectus Directive (Directive 2010/73/EU [2010] OJ L327/1) reforms.

powers and how they are exercised. ESMA's supervisory convergence powers, and in particular its peer review powers, are similarly shaping the exercise of supervisory powers (section 5).

XI.4.1.2 Enforcement and Sanctions

Enforcement has long been a very weak point of EU securities and markets regulation, but major change is now underway. FSAP-era legislative measures typically required Member States to ensure, in conformity with their national law, that the appropriate administrative measures could be taken or administrative sanctions imposed against the persons responsible, and to ensure that those measures were 'effective, proportionate, and dissuasive'.[166] Member States were often also directed to provide that NCAs could use 'name and shame' techniques and disclose to the public any measure or sanction imposed, unless to do so would seriously jeopardize the financial markets or cause disproportionate harm to those involved.[167]

The crisis-era has led to a significantly greater degree of prescription with respect to sanctions. The Commission's December 2010 Communication on sanctioning[168] initially envisaged a legislative measure which would govern the design of administrative sanctions and related measures.[169] Specific reforms have since followed. The approach has evolved across the different reforms, with the earliest crisis-era measures adopting a lighter approach. The 2011 AIFMD, for example, follows the FSAP-era model, with the addition of a requirement that NCAs report to ESMA annually on the application of administrative sanctions and measures and the imposition of penalties (Article 48); the 2012 EMIR tracks this approach, albeit with the finessing requirement that the administrative sanctions and measures available to NCAs include requests for remedial action within a set time frame (Article 22(3) and (4)). The 2012 Short Selling Regulation is similar in design, being largely based on the FSAP model, with the addition of the ESMA reporting requirement as well as a direction that ESMA may adopt guidelines to ensure a consistent approach is taken by NCAs concerning penalties and sanctions (Article 41). By contrast, a significantly more articulated model applies in relation to ESMA's direct sanctioning powers under EMIR (in relation to trade repositories) and the rating agency regime.[170]

The second wave of crisis-era reforms, however, has seen a significantly more prescriptive approach to sanctioning emerge. These reforms were spearheaded by the autumn 2011 proposal to reform the market abuse regime (the 2011 MAR Proposal),[171] which contained the template that would, once refined over the MAR negotiations, come to apply across the new sanctioning regimes. It proposed a new harmonized regime based on a requirement for administrative sanctions and on identification of the particular breaches to which an

---

[166] eg 2003 Prospectus Directive Art 25.
[167] eg 2004 MiFID I Art 51 and 2009 UCITS IV Directive Art 99.
[168] COM (2010) 716.
[169] The Commission proposed that harmonized standards apply to: the minimum range of administrative sanctions which should be available; the publication of sanctions; the level of fines; those persons on whom sanctions can be imposed; the criteria for imposing sanctions; the mechanisms supporting the application of sanctions (such as 'whistle-blowing' regimes and leniency regimes for those who admit wrong-doing); and, potentially, the imposition of criminal sanctions for the most serious violation.
[170] See further Chs VI sect 4.2.12 and VII sect 2.10.
[171] 2011 Market Abuse Regulation Proposal (COM (2011) 651).

administrative sanction was to apply, the range of sanctions to be made available, and how the determination as to the appropriate sanction and level of sanction was to be made. The template also provided for a mandatory 'name and shame' public reporting obligation on the imposition of a sanction, and for related reporting to ESMA, annual reporting to ESMA on aggregated sanctions disclosure, and protection of whistle-blowers. The proposed new sanctions template was applied across a series of other legislative proposals, with the institutions seeking to ensure the same template applied to all relevant measures. Negotiations on the 2011 MAR Proposal template ultimately led to the template being refined and applied to a series of other measures.

The new sanctions regime was initially adopted in the 2013 Amending Transparency Directive (Chapter II section 5.9.2), the 2014 Market Abuse Regulation (Chapter VIII section 9.3.2), and the 2014 MiFID II/MiFIR regime (Chapter IV section 11.6).[172] It has also been applied to the 2012 packaged retail investment products (PRIPs) disclosure proposal and to the 2014 UCITS V reforms.[173]

Criminal sanctions remain the preserve of the Member States save under the market abuse regime, where a new requirement for criminal sanctions applies (Chapter VIII section 9.3).

XI.4.1.3 Civil Liability

Private enforcement mechanisms have not traditionally formed part of EU securities and markets regulation. Member States differ considerably with respect to the design of causes of action and the extent to which private enforcement is engaged.[174] These differences are not simply a function of the well-documented divergences which arise from diverging cultural approaches to private litigation and, in particular, the differing roles of courts and ombudsmen and other forms of ADR across the EU, particularly with respect to retail market disputes;[175] the differences also arise at the more granular level of how causes of action are designed and how they relate to the EU rulebook. The overlooking of private enforcement mechanisms might be regarded as problematic: harmonized private enforcement might support the achievement of outcomes and take pressure from public enforcement, as well as reduce legal uncertainty and arbitrage risks. But it is not easy to design an effective private liability regime, private liability actions can be costly and slow, and the risk arises of penalizing shareholders for wrongdoing by corporate insiders and of inefficiently enriching the litigation industry.[176] A harmonization exercise would be all

---

[172] Respectively, Directive 2013/50/EU [2013] OJ L294/13; Regulation (EU) No 596/2014 OJ [2014] L173/1; 2014 MiFID II (n 58) and Markets in Financial Instruments Regulation (EU) No 600/2014 [2014] OJ L173/84 (2014 MiFIR). On the implementation timeline for the 2014 MiFIR see Ch IV n 28. This discussion is based on the 2014 MiFIR although reference is made to the 2004 MiFID I as appropriate. Similarly, for the implementation timeline for the 2014 MAR see Ch III n 3.

[173] COM (2012) 352/3 (Ch IX sect 6.3) and Council Document 7411/14, 13 March 2013 (not yet published in the OJ) (Ch III sect 3.13.4), respectively.

[174] eg in the asset management context, see Busch, D and DeMott, D (eds), *The Liability of Asset Managers* (2012).

[175] eg the report for the Commission of the Study Centre for Consumer Law, Centre for European Economic Law, Katholieke Universiteit Leuven, An Analysis and Evaluation of Alternative Means of Consumer Redress Other than Redress through Ordinary Judicial Proceedings. Final Report (2008). Similarly, Cherednychenko, O, 'The Regulation of Investment Services in the EU: Towards the Improvement of Investor Rights' (2010) 33 *J of Consumer Policy* 403.

[176] eg Jackson and Roe, n 31, 5–9.

the more complex. The national legal and procedural complexities, as well as the choice of law issues, are considerable, and make harmonization a complex and resource-intensive proposition.

There is some evidence of change, however. The Commission is examining private liability under the prospectus regime (Chapter II section 4.10.4), while the UCITS and AIFMD depositary regimes address depositary liability (Chapter III sections 3.10 and 4.10). The 2012 PRIPs proposal saw the Commission propose that direct rights of action be available for investors, but this was not supported by the Council.[177]

The EU is also pursuing a collective redress agenda for consumers, but this agenda is directed to consumer disputes generally, and does not engage with the particular procedural and risk-bearing complexities associated with class actions and other form of collective redress in the financial markets sphere.[178] ADR mechanisms are, however, being promoted. While support of ADR was a feature of the 2004 MiFID I (and now the 2014 MiFID II),[179] it has also featured in the 2012 PRIPs proposal.

More radically, the 2013 Credit Rating Agency III Regulation[180] reforms provide, for the first time, for an EU civil liability regime (Chapter VII section 2.10.3). The new cause of action provides that that where a rating agency commits 'intentionally' or 'negligently' any of the infringements specified in the Regulation, an investor or issuer may claim damages from the rating agency in respect of damage 'due to that infringement'. But the reform is unlikely to provide a template for the future. EU rating agency regulation attracts complex political and institutional dynamics, related in part to the sovereign debt crisis, which drive intense intervention in this sector.

The Commission's pathfinder 2010 Consultation on the reform of MiFID I, however, canvassed whether a harmonized civil liability regime might be developed for breaches of the new regime, including the disclosure, suitability, and best execution rules.[181] But this proposal did not survive. The responses to the 2010 Consultation suggested relatively little enthusiasm for a harmonized private liability mechanism, although the consumer sector was generally supportive. A recurring concern from the NCA sector was related to how a harmonized regime would fit with well-established domestic liability mechanisms. Industry concerns related to, for example, the likely costs in the form of higher indemnity insurance, which might ultimately be carried by consumers; the practicability of a pan-EU regime; and the role played by ADR mechanisms.

Private enforcement and liability is likely to remain a function of national law across the EU, in the medium term at least. There is, however, a need for an EU Securities and Markets Law Acquis Database to be established. For some time, the Commission has hosted an EU Consumer Law Acquis Database, which collates court rulings from across the EU on, for example, the Unfair Contract Terms regime. The complexity and variety of

---

[177] See Ch IX sect 6.3.
[178] eg Commission Consultation, Towards a Coherent European Approach to Collective Redress (2011) (SEC (2011) 173). On the EU's collective redress policy and its potential application to the financial markets see Moloney, n 59, 458–63.
[179] 2014 MiFID II Art 75.
[180] Regulation (EU) No 462/2013 [2013] OJ L146/1.
[181] Commission, Public Consultation. Review of the Markets in Financial Instruments Directive (2010).

Member States' private liability regimes, and their potential importance for the achievement of regulatory outcomes, suggests that legal certainty and regulatory effectiveness would be well served by such an initiative.

XI.4.2 NCAs and the Home/Host Model

XI.4.2.1 Home/Host Co-ordination

Cross-border activity in the EU financial market tends to be carried out through branch structures and through cross-border service delivery, which both demand close home/host NCA co-operation. By contrast, cross-border activity in the banking field is typically carried out through subsidiaries, which require home/home NCA co-operation and which generate a somewhat different set of co-ordination challenges.

The supervision of cross-border activity in the EU financial market is managed through a range of different co-ordination mechanisms. At the base of the co-ordination system is the allocation of supervisory competence. Although some opacities remain, the main legislative measures typically clarify the NCA which has supervisory competence. Cross-border activity is generally anchored to the home Member State in which the financial market participant is authorized. The home NCA is the location of operational supervisory control over the actor, with respect to authorization, prudential, and conduct elements. Host intervention is typically limited to the exercise of precautionary powers, which activate only where serious threats to investor protection, financial stability, or market integrity arise, where the home State/NCA has not acted, and where notification obligations (to the Commission, ESMA, and host State) are met.[182] There are exceptions to this model. The 2014 MiFID II regime allocates conduct supervision to the host NCA of a branch.[183] Similarly, the 2011 AIFMD locates prudential supervision of the fund manager with the home NCA, but locates supervision of conduct with the NCA of the branch.[184] The 2009 UCITS IV regime, to take another example, requires extensive co-ordination between the home NCA of the UCITS and the home NCA of the management company.[185] But for the most part, the home NCA is responsible for pan-EU supervision.

To support intelligence sharing, effective cross-border supervision, and the establishment of trust between home and host NCAs, the main legislative measures which govern EU financial markets also contain a foundational co-operation and information-exchange obligation, which is typically supported by more detailed information-exchange requirements and procedures governing operationally sensitive issues, such as the carrying out by the home NCA of on-site inspections in the host State. The foundation co-operation obligation typically requires that NCAs co-operate where necessary for the purposes of the measure, and supply each other, without undue delay, with information relevant for the purposes of carrying out their duties under the measure in question. More specific

---

[182] eg 2011 AIFMD Art 45(7) and (8); 2003 Prospectus Directive Art 23 (as amended by the 2010 Amending Prospectus Directive); 2004 Transparency Directive Art 26 (as amended by the 2010 Omnibus I Directive (Directive 2010/78/EU [2010] OJ L331/120)), and 2009 UCITS IV Directive Arts 21 and 108 (as amended by the 2010 Omnibus I Directive).

[183] 2014 MiFID II Art 35(8).

[184] 2011 AIFMD Art 45(2)–(6).

[185] 2009 UCITS IV Arts 16–21.

obligations govern information exchange[186] and on-site inspections and investigations.[187] Refusals to exchange information or to co-operate with inspections and investigations can usually only be justified by reference to the potential adverse impact, or to ongoing or completed judicial proceedings.[188] NCAs are also often enjoined to exchange information with respect to suspected breaches of the measure in question to the NCA with supervisory competence.[189] The exact nature of the co-operation and co-ordination regime differs across the different segments of EU securities and markets regulation; the 2011 AIFMD regime, for example, contains specific information-exchange obligations with respect to systemic risk.[190] The procedural modalities of co-operation, particularly with respect to information exchange, have been amplified by a series of sector-specific BTSs.

The main legislative measures also impose co-operation, co-ordination, and information exchange obligations with ESMA[191] and, in particular areas, with the ESRB.[192] Specific ESMA notification obligations are imposed on NCAs with respect to a host of supervisory actions, ranging from the standard (typically linked to authorization and delegation decisions[193]) to the more unusual (including with respect to short selling and the imposition of leverage limits on alternative investment fund managers).[194] Dispute settlement between home, host, and other NCAs can, where the relevant legislative authority has been given in the related legislative measure,[195] be subject to binding mediation by ESMA under

---

[186] Professional secrecy, data protection, and information gateway arrangements (which specify the entities with which exchanged information can be transmitted) typically apply.

[187] eg 2014 MiFID II Arts 79 and 81 (co-operation, including information exchange) and Art 80 (on-site inspections and investigations); 2012 EMIR Art 23 (co-operation with NCAs) and Art 84 (information exchange); 2012 Short Selling Regulation Art 35 (co-operation with NCAs, including with respect to information exchange) and Art 37 (co-operation with respect to on-site inspections and investigations); 2011 AIFMD Art 50 (co-operation with NCAs, including information exchange) and Art 54 (co-operation with on-site inspections and investigation); and 2009 UCITS IV Art 101 (UCITS co-operation, including information exchange and notification of breaches and on-site inspections and investigation) and Arts 109–110 (management company co-operation, information exchange, and onsite inspections and investigations).

[188] eg 2011 AIFMD Art 55.

[189] eg 2011 AIFMD Art 50(5).

[190] eg 2011 AIFMD Art 53.

[191] eg 2014 MiFID II Art 87; 2012 Short Selling Regulation Art 36; 2011 AIFMD Art 50; 2009 UCITS IV Directive, Art 101, as amended by the 2010 Omnibus I Directive; and 2003 Prospectus Directive, Art 21, as amended by the 2010 Omnibus I Directive.

[192] eg the 2011 AIFMD requires NCAs to co-operate with the ESRB where necessary (Art 50) and specifically requires information on fund manager leverage (including any limits imposed) to be made available to the ESRB (Art 25). Under the 2009 UCITS IV Directive, NCAs must ensure that risk management information related to derivatives transmitted to them under Art 51 is accessible to ESMA and to the ESRB for the purposes of systemic risk monitoring (Art 51, as amended by the 2010 Omnibus I Directive). The ESRB is also typically identified as an entity with which NCAs can exchange information.

[193] eg 2014 MiFID II Art 5 (investment firm authorization); 2012 EMIR Art 17–21 (CCP authorization); 2011 AIFMD Art 7 (alternative investment fund manager authorization); 2009 UCITS IV Directive Art 7 (UCITS authorization); and 2003 Prospectus Directive Art 13 (prospectus and prospectus supplement approval and delegation of prospectus approval) and Art 18 (prospectus approval certification for passporting (as amended by the 2010 Omnibus I Directive)).

[194] 2012 Short Selling Regulation Art 26 and AIFMD Art 25.

[195] eg 2011 AIFMD Art 55, providing that disagreements between NCAs on an assessment, action, or omission of one NCA, in areas where the Directive requires co-operation or co-ordination between NCAs from more than one Member State, can be referred to ESMA which can exercise its Art 19 mediation powers. Similarly, 2014 MiFID II Art 82, providing for binding mediation in relation to refusals to co-operate (including with respect to on-site verification/inspection activities and information exchange). The 2003 and

2010 ESMA Regulation Article 19. ESMA's ability to take enforcement action against an NCA (under 2010 ESMA Regulation Article 17) has also been noted in certain measures with respect to failures to co-operate.[196]

XI.4.2.2 Colleges of Supervisors

The financial crisis has led to an enhancement of the structures which support co-ordination, chiefly colleges of supervisors.[197] Colleges of supervisors are most strongly associated with the supervision of cross-border groups, in relation to which co-ordination between different 'home' NCAs of group subsidiaries is required. The college-of-supervisors mechanism was, accordingly, embedded at an early stage of the crisis-era reform of banking regulation through the 2009 CRD II reforms, which required that supervisory colleges be established, clarified their roles, and gave a larger role to the supervisors of systemically significant branches.[198] The college-of-supervisors model has had less traction in the financial markets given the dominance of branch and cross-border services activity, and the reliance on the home/host co-operation model. The 2010 ESMA Regulation, however, requires that ESMA contribute to promoting and monitoring the efficient, effective, and consistent functioning of colleges of supervisors where they are established under the legislative framework (section 5.5.1). While colleges of supervisors have yet to become an integral part of the financial markets' supervisory infrastructure, the very significant potential which CCPs hold for cross-border risk transmission and systemic failure has led to the application of the college-of-supervisor model in this field (under the 2012 EMIR), as discussed in Chapter VI section 4.2.9, and may herald more extensive reliance on colleges, particularly given stakeholder support, notably with respect to the cross-border supervision of regulated markets.[199]

XI.4.2.3 Delegation

Delegation structures have also been enhanced. Delegation has long been mooted as a means of addressing home/host NCA co-ordination risks, particularly where significant cross-border activity takes place in the host State, and was originally provided for in the 2003 Prospectus Directive.[200] But liability and reputation risks to the home NCA and the lack of a clear framework within which delegation can take place[201] have severely limited the utility of delegation.

2004 Prospectus and Transparency Directives provide that binding mediation can take place where a request for co-operation, in particular in relation to information exchange, has been rejected or not acted on in a reasonable time (Arts 22 and 25, respectively, each as amended by the 2010 Omnibus I Directive). Similarly, the 2009 UCITS IV Directive provides that binding mediation can take place in similar circumstances: Art 101, as amended by the 2010 Omnibus I Directive.

[196] eg 2009 UCITS IV Directive Art 101 (as amended by the 2010 Omnibus I Directive).

[197] Colleges of supervisors were highlighted by the 2009 DLG Report as a key mechanism for strengthening cross-border supervision, particularly in the banking field: n 104, 47. The Report called for a strengthening of their roles and for the 3L3 committees to establish colleges: at 52.

[198] Directive 2009/111/EC [2009] OJ L302/97 (now within the CRD IV regime (n 7)). See in outline Ch IV sect 12.

[199] Mazars, Review of the New European System of Financial Supervision. Part 1: The Work of the European Supervisory Agencies. Study for the ECON Committee (2013) (IP/A/ECON/ST/2012-23) (2013 Mazars ESA Review) 98–9.

[200] Art 13(5).

[201] Wymeersch, E, Delegation as an Instrument of Financial Supervision (2007), available at <http://ssrn.com/abstract=952952>.

The 2010 ESMA Regulation now provides a framework within which delegation can be carried out, and tasks ESMA with stimulating and facilitating the delegation of tasks and responsibilities among NCAs (Article 8(1)(c)). The delegation framework (Article 28), which is designed to support delegation to the NCA best placed to take action in the matter in question,[202] provides that NCAs may, with the consent of the delegate, delegate tasks and responsibilities to other NCAs or ESMA, subject to the Article 28 conditions. These conditions provide that any delegation results in a reallocation of competences under the EU legislative framework, and that the law of the delegate NCA governs the procedure, enforcement, and administrative and judicial review relating to the delegated responsibilities. Member States may set out specific arrangements regarding delegation which must be complied with, and may limit the scope of any delegations to what is necessary for the effective supervision of cross-border financial market participants or groups. NCAs must also inform ESMA of delegation agreements. The new delegation model is based on ESMA playing a co-ordination role: it must stimulate and facilitate delegation by identifying the tasks and responsibilities that can be delegated and by promoting best practices, and may also provide an opinion on delegation agreements. Thus far, however, delegation has not been deployed by ESMA and the NCAs.[203]

XI.5 The ESFS: ESMA

XI.5.1 ESMA and Supervision: A New Model

From a supervisory perspective, ESMA's exact position within the ESFS is difficult to pin down.[204] In some respects, the ESMA/NCA relationship can be regarded as hierarchical, given ESMA's ability to impose decisions on NCAs, to intervene in national markets in exceptional circumstances, and to subject its supervisory guidelines to 'comply or explain' dynamics. In other respects, ESMA sits on the same level as the NCAs as a 'peer supervisor', but with discrete responsibility for particular market actors (rating agencies and trade repositories). ESMA can also be regarded as the hub at the centre of a circle of NCA spokes, co-ordinating NCA activity, managing international relationships, collating and sharing intelligence, developing and sharing best practices, and providing overall system oversight. It therefore can be regarded as hovering 'above' and 'beside' the NCAs. It might also be regarded as a form of 'supervisor of supervisors' or 'system supervisor',[205] overseeing the quality, consistency, and effectiveness of supervision in the EU financial market. The elusive quality of its position within the ESFS underlines that the optimum location of financial market supervision within the EU remains unresolved (and may not be amenable

---

[202] 2010 ESMA Regulation rec 39 suggests that a reallocation of responsibilities would be appropriate, eg, for reasons of economies of scale or scope, of coherence in group supervision, and of optimal use of technical expertise.

[203] 2013 Mazars ESA Review, n 199, 99, noting its potential as a 'pragmatic tool'.

[204] On ESMA and supervision see further: Schammo, P, 'EU Day to Day Supervision or Intervention-Based Supervision: Which Way Forward for the European System of Financial Supervision' (2012) 32 *OJLS* 771 and Moloney, N, 'The European Securities and Markets Authority and Institutional Design for the EU Financial Markets – a Tale of Two Competences: Part (2) Supervision' (2011) 12 *EBOLR* 177.

[205] For an analysis of ESMA as a 'system supervisor' and of its role in 'system management' see HM Treasury, Response to the Commission Services Consultation on the Review of the ESFS (2013).

to a clear resolution) and that tidy institutional solutions and allocations of competences are likely to remain also elusive.

There are a number of dimensions to ESMA's supervisory functions. First, ESMA builds on CESR's work by engaging in a range of cross-border co-ordination activities, including with respect to the support of financial stability.[206]

Second, in a significant change, it is empowered to act as a direct supervisor. Through ESMA, the EU now has a capacity to enhance NCA compliance with EU law (2010 ESMA Regulation Article 17), to take co-ordinated action in a crisis (Article 18), and to break through NCA deadlock with binding mediation (Article 19). ESMA also has direct and exclusive sector-specific supervisory powers over two entities with extensive cross-border reach, rating agencies and trade repositories. It also has (more limited) direct operational powers with respect to short selling (2012 Short Selling Regulation) and product/position intervention (2014 MiFID II/MiFIR). ESMA can also exercise direct supervisory powers over financial market participants more generally in cases of NCA breach of EU law (Article 17), emergency situations (Article 18), and where ESMA is empowered to mediate between NCAs (Article 19). Although all these powers are subject to strict conditionality of various types, they represent the first time that an EU body has been conferred with direct and binding operational authority over financial market participants and NCAs.

Third, and finally, ESMA is empowered to support supervisory convergence by shaping day-to-day local supervision by NCAs, reflecting the 2009 DLG Report's concern that insufficient supervisory resources, combined with an inadequate mix of skills and different national systems of supervision, had aggravated the financial crisis in the EU, and that additional resources and more sophisticated detection mechanisms were required of NCAs.[207] ESMA is, accordingly (slowly), developing a consistent 'EU approach' to supervision, beyond the co-ordination and management of cross-border and home/host risks, and has the ability to drill deep into operational practices by NCAs. The nascent ESMA 'supervision manual' is not yet in the form of the 'Single Supervisory Handbook' which is being associated with Banking Union,[208] but ESMA has the potential to develop and support a 'harmonized' approach to operational supervision across the EU, and in so doing to enhance supervisory effectiveness, quality, and consistency.

XI.5.2 ESMA Structure and Operation

ESMA's governance and operating model is discussed in Chapter X section 5; as is the case with its quasi-rule-making activities, ESMA's supervisory decisions are made through its Board of Supervisors, decision-making on which is made by the NCAs. Supervision is at the

---

[206] Robust institutional support for stronger cross-border co-ordination, particularly in crisis conditions, was, as senior Commission figures have suggested, part of ESMA's core mission from the outset: Merlin, M, 'Financial Supervision in Europe after the Crisis' in Balling, M, et al (eds), *New Paradigms in Banking, Financial Markets and Regulation* (2012) 13 and Faull, J, Some Legal Challenges of Financial Regulation in the EU, Ninth Slynn Foundation Lecture, 7 March 2011.

[207] 2009 DLG Report, n 104, 39–42 and 49.

[208] Sect 7.

heart of ESMA's operation.[209] Its 2010 ESMA Regulation Article 1(5) objectives include that ESMA contribute to the functioning of the internal market, including in particular a sound, effective, and consistent level of supervision, and the strengthening of international supervisory co-ordination, while its Article 8(1) tasks and powers are closely focused on supervision.[210] ESMA's supervisory powers, like its quasi-rule-making powers, are constrained by the scope restrictions which apply to its activities, although in practice these restrictions do not represent a significant constraint on ESMA's operational freedom.[211]

Reflecting the coercive effect of many of ESMA's supervisory powers, as well as the oversight models established for earlier EU agencies with decision-making powers,[212] the 2010 ESMA Regulation establishes a distinct review system to protect third party interests. Addressees of a decision must be informed of ESMA's intention to adopt a decision and given an opportunity to respond. Decisions must also be reasoned (and, absent exceptional circumstances, made public), addressees must be informed of their legal remedies under the 2010 ESMA Regulation, and decisions must be reviewed at appropriate intervals (Article 39). Decisions can be appealed (by addressees and by those directly and individually concerned by the decision) to the independent ESA Board of Appeal (Article 60)[213] and to the Court of Justice under Article 263 TEU (Article 61). The distinct supervisory regimes which apply to rating and trade repositories provide for specific procedural protections for third parties, including with respect to internal ESMA decision-making on related supervisory and enforcement decisions.

---

[209] ESMA's first annual report highlighted that ESMA 'was created as an independent EU authority to improve harmonization in both supervisory rules and practices', and identified direct supervision, supervisory convergence, investor protection, and the safeguarding of financial stability as among its objectives: ESMA, Annual Report (2011) 11–13. ESMA's two key objectives are typically identified by ESMA as the construction of the single rulebook and the achievement of supervisory convergence and consistent application and enforcement of the single rulebook: eg, ESMA Executive Director Ross, Speech on 'ESMA's role in Markets Reform', 4 December 2012 (ESMA/2012/800).

[210] ESMA's Art 8(1) tasks include: to contribute to the establishment of high-quality supervisory standards and practices (Art 8(1)(a)); to contribute to the consistent application of legally binding acts, in particular by contributing to a common supervisory culture, ensuring consistent, efficient and effective application of the EU rulebook, mediating disagreements between NCAs, ensuring effective and consistent supervision of financial market participants, ensuring a coherent functioning of colleges of supervisors, and taking action, *inter alia*, in emergency situations (Art 8(1)(b)); to stimulate and facilitate delegation of tasks and responsibilities among NCAs (Art 8(1)(c)); to co-operate closely with the ESRB (Art 8(1)(d)); to organize and conduct peer reviews (Art 8(1)(e)); to foster investor protection (Art 8(1)(h)); and to contribute to the consistent functioning of colleges of supervisors (Art 8(1)(i)).

[211] ESMA's powers must be exercised within the scope of the binding EU rulebook (Art 1(2)), although ESMA must also 'act in the field of activities of market participants' in relation to issues not covered by Art 1(2), including matters of corporate governance, auditing, and financial reporting, as long as ESMA's actions are necessary to ensure the effective and consistent application of those binding acts. ESMA must also 'take appropriate action' in the context of take-over bids, clearing and settlement and derivative issues: Art 1(3).

[212] Geradin, D and Petit, N, The Development of Agencies at EU and National Levels: Conceptual Analysis and Proposals for Reform, Jean Monnet WP 01/04 (2004) 52.

[213] Appeals do not have suspensive effect, although the Board of Appeal may suspend a decision if it considers the circumstances so require. The first Board of Appeal decision (in relation to an EBA action) is considered in sect 5.3.1. The second decision (January 2014) related to an ESMA refusal to register a rating agency—the appellant contested ESMA's decision on a range of procedural and substantive grounds. The Board supported ESMA's decision not to register the rating agency: Decision of the Board of Appeal, BoA 2013–14, 10 January 2014. On the Board of Appeal see Blair, W, 'The Board of Appeal of the European Supervisory Authorities' (2013) 24 *EBLR* 165.

XI.5.3 Directing NCAs

XI.5.3.1 Directing NCAs: Horizontal Articles 17–19 Powers

ESMA's controversial powers to 'address decisions' to NCAs (in effect, overrule them) arise in three situations: where a breach of EU law has occurred (2010 ESMA Regulation Article 17) (ESMA action takes the form of a 'recommendation' in this case); in 'emergency situations' (Article 18); and where disagreements arise between NCAs and ESMA mediation is provided for in the relevant measure (Article 19). While representing in theory a radical change, these powers are envisaged to act as emergency or last-resort powers, as was repeatedly underlined over the negotiations,[214] are subject to strict conditionality, and are not designed to unseat the NCAs as the primary location of supervisory power.

Article 17 represents a significant enhancement of the weak peer review mechanisms previously used by CESR to support NCA compliance with EU law. It applies to NCA failure to apply the 2010 ESMA Regulation 'Article 1(2) rulebook' which defines the scope of ESMA's activities (in effect, the wide range of measures which regulate EU financial markets),[215] and to applications of the rulebook which appear to be in breach of EU law, in particular with respect to NCA failures to ensure financial market participant compliance (Article 17(1)). Article 17 empowers ESMA to undertake investigations, make recommendations, and ultimately address decisions to market actors, subject to strict time limits. As interpreted by ESMA, the Article 17 procedure 'is intended to place the national competent authority under considerable pressure more quickly'.[216]

ESMA is empowered to investigate alleged breaches of EU law by an NCA (on its own initiative or following a request by an NCA, the European Parliament, Commission, Council, or its Stakeholder Group). Not less than two months after initiating the investigation, ESMA may issue a 'recommendation' to the NCA, setting out the remedial steps necessary to comply with EU law (Article 17(2) and (3)). Where the NCA does not comply within a month of the recommendation (it should inform ESMA of the steps it is to take within ten days of receipt), the Commission, on its own initiative or after notification by ESMA, may issue a formal opinion (within three months of the ESMA recommendation), taking into account ESMA's recommendation, requiring the NCA to take the necessary remedial action (Article 17(4)). Within ten days of receipt of the opinion, the NCA must inform the Commission and ESMA of the steps it has taken. Where the NCA does not comply with the formal opinion, ESMA may address a decision to a financial market participant (section 5.4.1). ESMA must also report on NCA failures to comply in its Annual Report to the Commission, Council, and Parliament. ESMA, through its Board of Supervisors, acts under a simple majority vote for the purposes of Article 17 (Article 44).

---

[214] The 2009 European Financial Supervision Communication, eg, highlighted that the proposed mediation powers were to be exercised as a 'last resort' and that recourse to the Art 17 enforcement power was to be 'rare', and characterized the emergency intervention power as limited: n 115, 10–11. Similarly, 2010 ESMA Regulation, recs 29 and 32, describing ESMA's powers to address decisions to financial market participants under Arts 17 and 19 as 'last resort' powers.

[215] 'Art 1(2) rulebook' is used hereafter as shorthand for the range of binding measures which define ESMA's scope under ESMA Regulation Art 1(2), and which, in practice, cover the measures addressed by EU securities and markets regulation.

[216] ESMA, Frequently Asked Questions. A Guide to Understanding ESMA (2011) (2011 ESMA FAQ) 5.

A 2012 ESMA Decision amplifies the Article 17 process;[217] the same Decision is applied by all three ESAs.[218] The Decision suggests some ESA nervousness as to the potential risks which recourse to this power could generate in terms of the pivotal ESA/NCA relationship. The Decision carefully clarifies the scope of this controversial power, reserves this power to serious breaches of EU law,[219] and identifies the other mechanisms, such as peer review or binding mediation, which can act as alternative channels for addressing breach of EU law difficulties where appropriate.[220] It seems clear that the ESAs regard Article 17 as a last-resort power and as sitting at the apex of an enforcement pyramid which includes a host of softer convergence-related powers; in practice, breaches of EU law by NCAs are unlikely to represent a threat to supervisory effectiveness in the EU—divergences in supervisory judgements as to how rules apply have the potential to be more troublesome, but are not addressed by Article 17. A similarly careful approach has been taken by the ESA Board of Appeal, which has emphasized the discretionary nature of the Article 17 power. Its first Decision related to an appeal by an individual from a decision by EBA not to take Article 17 enforcement action against the Finnish and Estonian NCAs, following a request by the individual for EBA to take enforcement action related to alleged suitability failures with respect to the management of a branch of a Finnish bank in Estonia.[221] The appeal turned on the admissibility of the individual's request to EBA,[222] but the Board of Appeal emphasized that the Article 17 power was discretionary, that EBA, as a small body, was not in a position to investigate every admissible complaint, and that, following the correct application of its discretion, EBA was empowered not to take action even where the request was admissible and related to a breach of EU law.[223]

Article 18 governs ESMA's highly contested emergency powers. To a greater extent than Article 17, Article 18 operates within a constrained procedural framework, which reflects the significant resistance from certain Member States as to the conferral of powers of this nature on the ESAs. Like the Article 17 power, ESMA's freedom to act is constrained by the need for prior action by an EU institution (the Commission, in the case of Article 17). ESMA's powers are triggered where the Council determines that an 'emergency situation'[224] exists, through a decision addressed to ESMA (Article 18(2)).[225] The trigger factor is accordingly

---

[217] ESMA/2012/BS/87. It addresses issues such as the admissibility criteria for Art 17 action and, overall, defines carefully the scope of the Art 17 power.

[218] EBA DC 054 and EIOPA-BOS-11-017.

[219] The 'investigation factors' which ESMA will consider prior to taking Art 17 action include whether the alleged breach undermines the foundations of the rule of law, concerns a repeated infringement, and whether it may have a significant, direct impact on ESMA's objectives: 2012 Art 17 Decision, n 217, Annex 2.

[220] n 217, Annex 2.

[221] Decision of the Board of Appeal, BoA 2013-008, 24 June 2013.

[222] EBA rejected the appellant's request for Art 17 action on the grounds that it was inadmissible as there was no breach of EU law as the relevant banking rules (under the now repealed CRD regime) applied the suitability requirement only to the authorization process and with respect to those who directed the business of the credit institution, and not to ongoing supervision and in relation to branches. The Board upheld the admissibility appeal, finding that the CRD regime more generally required that credit institutions have robust governance structures and that EBA's related guidelines could potentially be regarded as applying to the management of branches.

[223] At paras 30 and 34.

[224] In consultation with the Commission, the ESRB and, where appropriate, the ESAs, and, following a request by an ESA, the Commission or the ESRB.

[225] The Council decision must be reviewed at 'appropriate intervals' and at least once a month; where a decision is not reviewed at the end of a one-month period, it automatically expires. The Council may declare the discontinuation of the emergency situation at any time.

controlled by the Council, although the Council must take this decision in consultation with the ESRB and the Commission and, although only 'where appropriate', the ESAs. The ESRB and the ESAs are empowered to issue a confidential recommendation to the Council where they consider an emergency situation may arise (Article 18(2)).[226] The European Parliament and Commission must be informed of a declaration of an emergency by the Council. Where an emergency has been declared, ESMA's Article 18 emergency powers (Article 18(2)–(5)) are activated, but only where a second condition is met: exceptional circumstances, where co-ordinated action by national authorities is necessary to respond to adverse developments which may seriously jeopardize the orderly functioning and integrity of financial markets or the stability of the whole or part of the financial system in the EU, must arise (Article 18(3)). ESMA is not granted the wide-ranging powers which the emergency context might suggest. ESMA may only adopt individual decisions requiring NCAs to take the necessary action, in accordance with the Article 1(2) rulebook, to address 'any such developments' by ensuring that NCAs (and financial market participants—see section 5.4.1) comply with the relevant legislation (Article 18(3)). ESMA acts under a simple majority vote for the purposes of the Article 18 (2)–(5) procedure.

Article 19 empowers ESMA to impose binding mediation decisions on NCAs in cases of disagreement and represents a considerable step up from CESR's soft mediation powers; ESMA has highlighted the difference between CESR's mediation powers and its new powers to 'settle sectoral disputes'.[227] Where an NCA disagrees about the procedure or content of an action or inaction of an NCA of another Member State, in cases specified in the Article 1(2) rulebook, ESMA, at the request of one or more of the NCAs concerned, may assist the NCAs in reaching an agreement through the Article 19 mediation process (Article 19(1)). As with Articles 17 and 18, own-initiative action by ESMA is constrained. ESMA may only mediate on its own initiative where it is provided for in the relevant legislation,[228] and where, on the basis of objective criteria, disagreement between the NCAs can be determined (Article 19(1)). The binding mediation procedure requires ESMA to set a time limit for conciliation (Article 19(2)).[229] Where the NCAs fail to reach an agreement, ESMA may take a decision requiring them to take specific action or to refrain from action in order to settle the matter, with 'binding effects for the competent authorities concerned' in order to ensure compliance with EU law (Article 19(3)).[230] Article 19 decision-making is made in the first place by an independent panel of the Board of the Supervisors,[231] which

---

[226] On receipt of such a recommendation, the Council is to assess the need for a Council meeting.

[227] 2011 ESMA FAQ, n 216, 6.

[228] Under the securities and markets regulation regime, binding mediation is typically provided for in relation to failures of home NCA supervision which activate host NCA precautionary powers, failures to co-operate (including with respect to on-site inspections), and failures to exchange information (n 195). It also applies more specifically in relation to, eg, NCA failure to agree on 2014 MiFIR transparency waivers and to NCA decisions on MiFID II position limits where related trading takes place pan-EU; NCA failure to agree on 2014 MAR 'accepted market practices' (a defence to market abuse); and in the context of decision-making failures by 2012 EMIR colleges of supervisors. Binding mediation is more central to supervision in the banking regime, where it is deployed in relation to colleges of supervisors and with respect to failures by colleges to take joint decisions and, accordingly, to exercise effective supervision over banking groups.

[229] Taking into account the relevant rules in dispute and the complexity and urgency of the issue: Art 19(2).

[230] A discrete voting regime applies to this procedure under Art 44: Arts 17 and 18 are subject to a simple majority vote.

[231] Composed of the Chairperson and two Board of Supervisor members, who are not representatives of the NCAs concerned and who have neither any interest in the conflict nor direct links to the NCAs concerned: Art 41(2).

must facilitate an impartial settlement of the disagreement and which operates by a simple majority vote; the panel must propose a decision for adoption by the Board of Supervisors (Article 41(2) and (3) and Article 44(1)).[232] Decision-making powers also apply in relation to financial market participants (section 5.4.1). ESMA must report on Article 19 activity in its annual report to the Commission, Council, and European Parliament (Article 19(6)).

Articles 17–19 confer on ESMA the ability to make potentially serious incursions into Member State and NCA sovereignty; in theory, they bring radical change to the supervision of EU financial markets. But they are subject to strict conditionality and address unusual circumstances. In each case, ESMA's ability to take own-initiative action is constrained, including by prior institutional action in the case of Article 17 and 18 (the Commission and Council, respectively), and by prior legislative grant in the case of Article 19. The powers which can be exercised are limited, and their exercise is closely tied to ensuring compliance with the Article 1(2) rulebook; Articles 17–19 do not confer on ESMA the ability to make decisions other than those related to compliance with rules previously adopted through the legislative and administrative processes. The fiscal check (Article 38), which requires ESMA to ensure that no decision adopted under Articles 18 or 19 impinges in any way on the fiscal responsibilities of Member States (Article 38(1)) and sets out procedural protections for the Member States (section 5.9.2), also applies. These powers are also attended by significant political risks and, given the restraints which the *Meroni* doctrine places on discretionary action by agencies, constitutional sensitivities, which can be expected to limit their use.

At the time of writing, none of the 2010 ESMA Regulation Article 17–19 powers had been deployed by ESMA.[233] As an emergency power triggered by Council action, Article 18 is unlikely to feature heavily, even as the ESAs focus more closely on supervision in their next phase of development.[234] But Articles 17 and 19 are unlikely to be 'paper tigers'. The early indications suggest that ESMA has the appetite to deploy Article 17 where it deems it appropriate,[235] but that Article 17 is most likely to be used as a deterrent, in that ESMA has linked its 2010 ESMA Regulation Article 29 power to address opinions to NCAs to subsequent Article 17 action.[236] There are some indications, however, that the legislative regime will come to embed Article 17 as a disciplining device, particularly in new and sensitive areas: the new position limits regime under the 2014 MiFID II, for example,

---

[232] A different procedure applies where a consolidating supervisor is subject to the Art 19 procedure. For decisions taken by the consolidating supervisor, the panel decision is considered as adopted if approved by a simple majority of the panel, unless it is rejected by panel members representing a blocking minority in votes, in accordance with Art 16(4) TEU.

[233] ESMA appears alive to the restrictive nature of the Art 18 power in particular. Board of Supervisor discussions on Art 18 reveal a Board concern that ESMA could be perceived as having more powers than it does and as to the procedural complexity of the power: Board of Supervisors Meeting, 20 December 2011 (ESMA/2012/BS/4).

[234] Although ESMA has engaged in planning for particular crisis scenarios: 2013 Mazars ESA Review, n 199, 103.

[235] In 2012, ESMA assessed some 30 requests for it to take Art 17 action; 12 of these led to further interaction between ESMA and the relevant NCA but none led to full Art 17 action: n 199, 101.

[236] In its December 2013 opinion on the correct application of the prospectus regime's base prospectus rules, eg, ESMA warned that it could pursue non-compliant NCAs under Art 17: ESMA Opinion on the Base Prospectus Format 2013. 18 December 2013 (ESMA/2013/1944).

requires ESMA to take Article 17 action where an NCA does not set position limits in accordance with the new harmonized regime (2014 MiFID II Article 57). The extent to which Article 19 will be deployed is more uncertain. It empowers ESMA to intervene in 'greyer' areas short of breach and to address divergences in supervisory judgements, but its scope is elusive. While it is of considerable practical importance in supporting supervisory convergence and effective cross-border supervision (particularly in colleges of supervisors where joint decisions are required (as under the 2012 EMIR)), and where convergence in supervisory decisions is required (as under the 2014 MiFIR regime for NCA decisions on trading venue transparency waivers), its exact scope and relationship with Article 17 is contested. Particular difficulties attend whether ESMA can, under Article 19, replace an NCA decision, taken by means of a legitimate exercise of discretion, by directing it to act in a particular way. Some interpretations of Article 19 suggest that it applies solely where one NCA is in breach of EU law and that it only allows an ESA to establish the breach and set out the conditions which the NCA must comply with to remedy the breach; wider discretionary judgements by the ESAs, under this interpretation, would breach the *Meroni* prohibition on discretionary action, particularly as Article 19, by contrast with Articles 17 and 18, is not subject to specific conditionality.[237] On the other hand, Article 17 addresses breach and such a limited interpretation would render Article 19 ineffective; the Article 38 fiscal condition restricts Article 19 (but not Article 17) and so implies action by ESMA; and Article 19 can be regarded as being necessary to allow ESMA (and the other ESAs) to break through cases of supervisory deadlock where differences in supervisory judgement arise or where it is necessary to establish clear best practice standards.[238] While the Court's 2014 *Short Selling* ruling suggests a facilitative approach to the exercise of discretion by ESMA (section 5.8.3), and while the European Parliament is supportive of binding mediation being deployed in relation to exercises of discretion (section 5.10), the scope of Article 19 remains unclear.

While Articles 17 and 19 are likely to be deployed, if carefully, they remain reserve powers and the extent of their practical importance is likely to be a function of the hierarchical and deterrent dynamic which they bring to the ESMA/NCA relationship more generally. This dynamic is likely to strengthen ESMA's supervisory capacity[239] generally as a 'supervisor of supervisors' and to enhance its ability to strengthen the quality of pan-EU supervision through 'softer' measures.

XI.5.3.2 Directing NCAs: ESMA Opinions and Advice

A softer suite of powers allows ESMA to provide opinions with respect to specified sensitive supervisory decisions and to require NCAs to, in effect, 'comply or explain'. Supervisory

---

[237] This interpretation is supported by rec 32 of the 2010 ESMA Regulation which was inserted towards the end of the ESA negotiations to allay the fears of some Member States that the ESAs would be empowered to exercise extensive supervisory discretion and to displace NCA judgment. Rec 32 provides that in cases where the relevant EU law confers discretion on NCAs, decisions taken by ESMA under Art 19 cannot replace the exercise in compliance with EU law of that discretion.

[238] EBA Chairman Enria has accordingly called for a clarification of the ESA Regulations to remove textual ambiguities which restrict the practical effectiveness of Art 19: Speech on 'The Single Market after Banking Union', 18 November 2013.

[239] The notion of capacity is associated with a supervisor's ability to achieve outcomes and depends on, *inter alia*, reputational capital, resources, expertise, relationships with the regulated sector and the nature of the regulated sector, and enforcement and supervisory powers: Black, J, 'Enrolling Actors in Regulatory Processes: Examples from UK Financial Services Regulation' *Public Law* (2003) 62.

action by NCAs under the 2012 Short Selling Regulation (including with respect to reporting requirements and prohibitions) must be notified to ESMA, who must provide an opinion on whether the action is necessary to address the exceptional circumstances in question; where the NCA does not follow the ESMA opinion, it must publish a notice explaining its reasons (2012 Short Selling Regulation Articles 26–27). The primacy of the ESMA opinion is underlined by the direction to ESMA to consider whether its powers of intervention with respect to short selling should be employed where an NCA does not follow the opinion (Article 27(3)). Similarly, under the 2011 AIFMD, decisions by NCAs to impose leverage limits on alternative investment fund managers must be notified to ESMA, and ESMA must provide 'advice', including with respect to whether the conditions for taking action are met and the appropriateness and duration of the measures; where the NCA does not follow the advice, it must inform ESMA of its reasons and ESMA may publish the non-compliance and the reasons for non-compliance (2011 AIFMD Article 25). ESMA may also advise an NCA to impose leverage limits where it has not done so; the 'comply or explain' obligation similarly applies here (Article 25). ESMA may also 'request' NCAs to take specified action in relation to third country fund managers, but in this case the 'comply or explain' mechanism does not apply (Article 47(4)).

A similar regime governs the exercise by NCAs of position management powers under the 2014 MiFID II regime. Where an NCA imposes more restrictive position limits for commodity derivatives than those set under its position limits regime, it must notify this action to ESMA, which is required to issue an opinion on whether it regards the limits as necessary; where an NCA acts contrary to an ESMA opinion, it must publicly explain its reasons for doing so (MiFID II Article 57 (8)). The opinion mechanism also applies to the underlying NCA position limits which normally apply (NCAs must put in place position limits under MiFID II Article 57).[240] ESMA in this case must assess whether the limits adopted by the NCA are compatible with the objectives of Article 57 (which governs position limits) and the methodology for calculating such limits (Article 57 (5)); the NCA must either modify its limits in accordance with the opinion or provide a justification as to why it will not modify the limits. The opinion review (and NCA response) mechanism also applies to the new NCA product intervention powers (2014 MiFIR Article 42). The 2014 MiFIR trading venue transparency regime similarly deploys ESMA opinions to shape NCA decision-making with respect to the waivers which can be granted from pre-trade transparency requirements, and with respect to the NCAs' related powers to suspend pre-trade transparency requirements when liquidity is threatened (MiFIR Articles 4 and 9); the opinion relates to the compatibility of NCA waivers (and suspension) with the MiFIR regime.[241]

A softer form of the opinion model is deployed under the 2014 MiFID II/MiFIR with respect to the suspension or removal of financial instruments from trading. NCAs are required to suspend/remove instruments from trading where they are notified by an NCA of its decision in this regard in relation to instruments trading on a regulated market within its jurisdiction; while NCAs may decide not to do so, within the conditions imposed by

---

[240] See Ch VI sect 2.5.
[241] Given the sensitivity of the transparency regime, and the very difficult negotiations on the waiver regime in particular, Art 4 (the equity market waiver) specifies that the opinion is 'non-binding' and NCAs (under both Art 4 (equity) and 9 (non-equity)) are not required to 'comply or explain'.

MiFID II, they must provide an explanation of their reasons to ESMA and the other NCAs (2014 MiFID II Article 52).

More generally, ESMA is empowered to adopt opinions addressed to NCAs under 2010 ESMA Regulation Article 29(1)(a), which power it has used to ensure NCAs interpret EU law correctly.[242]

Although considerably less intrusive than the Article 17–19 powers, these softer powers can be expected to promote greater consistency in supervisory practices and to establish ESMA as the natural forum for assessment of sensitive national supervisory decisions.

XI.5.4 Directing and Supervising Market Participants

XI.5.4.1 Horizontal Article 17–19 Powers

ESMA is also empowered to address decisions to financial market participants under 2010 ESMA Regulation Articles 17–19, subject to a series of conditions.

Under Article 17, where an NCA does not comply with the Commission's formal opinion, and where timely remedying of the non-compliance is necessary to maintain or restore neutral conditions of competition or ensure the orderly functioning and integrity of the financial system, ESMA may address a decision to a financial market participant requiring the action necessary to comply with its obligations under EU law, including the cessation of any practice; the relevant EU measure in relation to which compliance is directed must, however, come within Article 1(2) and be directly applicable and in conformity with the Commission's earlier formal opinion (Article 17(6)). Any such decision adopted by ESMA prevails over a previous decision adopted by the NCAs on the same issue, and the NCAs must, when taking action in relation to issues which are subject to a related Commission formal opinion or an ESMA decision addressed to a financial market participant, comply with the relevant formal opinion or ESMA decision (Article 17(7)). This regime allows ESMA to bypass the considerable difficulties raised where NCAs ignore ESMA decisions under Article 17 and where a serious breakdown in ESMA/NCA relations has occurred.

A similar regime applies under Article 18 where an NCA does not comply with an Article 18 ESMA emergency decision. ESMA may, where the Article 1(2) rule(s) engaged by the Article 18 decision directed to the defaulting NCA are directly applicable to financial market participants, adopt an individual decision addressed to a financial market participant requiring the necessary action to comply with its obligations under the rule(s) in question, including the cessation of any practice. This power only applies where the NCA does not apply the Article 1(2) rule(s) or applies them in a way which appears to be a manifest breach of those acts, and where urgent remedying appears to be necessary to restore the orderly functioning and integrity of financial markets or the stability of the whole or part of the EU financial system (Article 18(4)). Any such decision adopted by ESMA prevails over a previous decision adopted by the NCAs on the same issue, and any action by the NCAs in relation to issues subject to an Article 18 decision (whether

---

[242] eg n 236.

addressed to an NCA or a financial market participant) must be compatible with the ESMA decision (Article 18(5)).

Under Article 19, where an NCA does not comply with an ESMA binding mediation decision and thereby fails to ensure that a financial market participant complies with directly applicable Article 1(2) rules, ESMA may adopt an individual decision addressed to a financial market participant, requiring the action necessary to comply with its EU law obligations, including the cessation of any practice (Article 19(4)). These ESMA decisions prevail over any previous decisions adopted by the NCAs on the same matter, and any action by the NCAs in relation to facts subject to an Article 19 mediation decision (whether directed to the NCA or a financial market participant) must be compatible with those decisions (Article 19(5)).

These eye-catching direct supervisory powers represent a step change in the nature of EU intervention in the financial markets. But, like the NCA-related powers, they are activated in unusual circumstances and are generally concerned with escalating circumstances, whether emergency-driven or where relations between NCAs, and between ESMA and NCAs, have broken down to a very significant degree. In practice, ESMA's ability to direct financial market participants is more likely to be a function of the discrete powers with which it has been conferred in particular areas, noted in the following sections. But the deterrent effect of these powers, and the hierarchical dimension they bring to ESMA/NCA relations, have the potential to strengthen ESMA's capacity as a 'supervisor of supervisors' and its ability to shape, enhance, and bring consistency to local supervisory decisions.

XI.5.4.2 Direct Supervision: Credit Rating Agencies and Trade Repositories

The conferral of direct and exclusive day-to-day supervisory powers on ESMA with respect to particular financial market participants represents one of the most radical of the differences between the ESMA and CESR eras.

The 2010 ESMA Regulation does not expressly address direct, day-to-day supervision by ESMA over particular market segments. These powers are implicitly conferred by Article 8 (1)(j) which requires ESMA to fulfil specific tasks set out in the Regulation or other legislative acts. The extent to which ESMA can engage in direct supervision is accordingly controlled by the co-legislators who can make specific grants in discrete legislative measures, and the Commission, which can make such proposals. The ESMA Regulation negotiations initially framed direct supervision in terms of the supervision of 'pan-EU' or 'cross-border actors', reflecting the 2009 DLG Report proposals; the Commission envisaged centralized supervision of entities 'with a clear Community dimension', where it would not be optimal for one national authority to be responsible for supervision.[243] As discussed in section 5.9, whether or not ESMA is empowered to supervise particular actors is a function of a number of factors. Chief among them is the fiscal risk of the actor in question, the extent of which is typically a major driver of the Council's position. Thus far, ESMA has been conferred with exclusive operational supervisory powers over two actors: credit rating agencies and trade repositories.

---

[243] 2009 ESA Proposals Impact Assessment, n 47, 26.

The credit rating agency regime represents a watershed as the first time that exclusive supervisory competence over an aspect of financial market regulation has passed to an EU body from the Member States (even allowing for the reality that few Member States already regulated or supervised rating agencies directly); ESMA Chief Executive Ross has described ESMA's move into direct supervision of rating agencies as a 'milestone achievement'.[244] As discussed in Chapter VII section 2.10, the rating agency regime confers supervisory powers on ESMA and establishes an operational template under which ESMA holds exclusive operational powers but can require NCAs to carry out a range of supervisory tasks, and which delineates the respective roles of NCAs and local courts in supporting ESMA. The template also confers enforcement powers on ESMA (including fining powers) within a procedural framework which addresses the following: the role of NCAs in supporting investigations, inspections, and subsequent enforcement action; the pecuniary penalties which apply and how they are to be assessed; the procedure under which enforcement action is to be taken through national courts; and due process requirements for the protection of third party rights, including with respect to procedural requirements which apply to the taking of supervisory and enforcement decisions by ESMA.

This template has also been deployed for the conferral of exclusive registration, supervisory, and enforcement powers on ESMA in relation to trade repositories under EMIR (Chapter VI section 4.2.12).

XI.5.4.3 Direct Supervision: Discrete Powers of Intervention

ESMA's direct supervisory powers also include operational powers directed to the prohibition or restriction of identified activities. These stem from 2010 ESMA Regulation Article 9 which empowers ESMA to temporarily prohibit or restrict certain financial activities that threaten the orderly functioning of financial markets or the stability of the whole or part of the financial system in the Union; this power applies to particular cases specified in EU law and also, if required, in Article 18 emergency situations (Article 9(5)).

As discussed in Chapter VI section 3.9.2, ESMA has been conferred with a related suite of discrete, direct supervisory powers with respect to short selling under the 2012 Short Selling Regulation, albeit in particular and limited circumstances. ESMA is empowered to, *inter alia*, require natural or legal persons to notify to an NCA, or disclose to the public, details of net short positions, and to prohibit or impose conditions on short sales; short sales of sovereign debt and transactions in sovereign debt CDSs are excluded from these powers, but the ESMA Regulation Article 18 emergency powers are expressly declared to apply where the Article 18 conditions are met. A range of procedural requirements (including notification obligations) and conditions (including with respect to the severity of the related threat to the stability of the EU market and the failure of local NCAs to act) apply, and are designed to limit ESMA's discretion given the *Meroni* constraint. The 2014 MiFID II/MiFIR reforms have also conferred direct intervention powers, albeit subject to strict conditionality to limit ESMA's discretion, with respect to the temporary restriction or prohibition of financial instruments and of services and activities (Chapter IX section 7.1), and with respect to position management in relation to derivatives markets (Chapter VI section 2.5).

---

[244] Speech on 'ESMA's Role in Europe and International Regulatory Co-operation', 12 June 2012 (ESMA/2012/367). Similarly, ESMA Chairman Maijoor, Speech, 'Key Note Address, ISDA AGM', 13 April 2011 (ESMA/2011/115).

These powers are of a similar order to the ESMA Regulation Article 17–19 powers in that they are intrusive, activate in unusual circumstances where NCA action is deemed inadequate and significant threats arise to the EU market, and are subject to strict conditionality. As such, they can be expected to be used but rarely. But while they provide the EU with an important reserve supervisory capacity for emergency situations, like Articles 17–19, they also significantly enhance ESMA's supervisory capacity more generally.

XI.5.4.4 Quasi-Supervision and Norm-Setting Effects

As discussed in Chapter X, ESMA is developing a significant 'soft rulebook' through which it can exert coercive effects on market participants, particularly where ESMA uses its power to require market participants to report on their compliance with guidelines or recommendations (2010 ESMA Regulation Article 16(3)).

In discrete areas, ESMA is also employing informal, soft law tools to exert quasi-supervisory/enforcement power over market participants. This is most marked in the financial reporting sphere. As discussed in Chapter II section 6, ESMA, through its European Enforcers Co-ordination Sessions, has become the main EU vehicle for supporting national convergence across NCAs in the application and enforcement of IFRS. But it also addresses market participants directly, through reviews of particular reporting requirements and 'public statements' on reporting issues. In 2012, for example, it produced a public statement on the treatment by financial institutions of their forbearance practices; while a soft law measure, ESMA stated that issuers 'should take [the Statement] into due consideration'.[245] Similarly, its earlier public statement on IFRS disclosures related to sovereign debt holding encouraged issuers to make full disclosures in this regard, although it acknowledged that the measure was not an official IFRS interpretation[246] but designed to assist issuers;[247] ESMA also carried out a review of IFRS reporting practices relating to Greek sovereign debt holdings by a sample of major EU financial institutions.[248]

A similar dynamic can be associated with the 2010 ESMA Regulation Article 9(3) power to issue warnings where a financial activity poses a threat to ESMA's objectives, given the potential coercive effects of such a warning on targeted market participants and the likelihood of close attention from the NCA, particularly as ESMA typically highlights the risks of dealing with unauthorized firms and of aggressive marketing strategies.[249]

These 'quasi-supervisory' powers are significantly less sensitive than ESMA's direct powers although, like ESMA's 'soft rulebook' more generally, their norm-setting dynamic is troublesome given the somewhat shaky legitimacy foundation on which these soft law measures rest.[250] Nonetheless, they provide ESMA with an important mechanism for responding to emerging risks and thereby strengthening its credibility as a supervisor.

---

[245] ESMA/2012/853.
[246] The power to issue definitive guidance is reserved to the IASB: see Ch II sect 7.
[247] ESMA/2011/226, 1.
[248] ESMA/2012/482.
[249] eg ESMA Warnings on Complex Products (ESMA.2014/154), Contracts for Differences (ESMA/2013/267), Online Investing (ESMA/212/557), and Foreign Exchange Trading (ESMA/2011/412).
[250] On the legitimacy and validity risks associated with the ESMA 'soft rulebook' see Ch X sect 5.6.

XI.5.5 Supervisory Co-ordination: Colleges of Supervisors, Cross-border Co-operation, and Cross-sector Co-operation

XI.5.5.1 Colleges of Supervisors and Cross-border Co-ordination

As noted in section 4.2.2, colleges of supervisors are increasingly forming part of the supervisory architecture of EU securities and markets regulation. ESMA is conferred with a range of powers to support supervisory colleges. It is to contribute to promoting and monitoring the efficient, effective, and consistent functioning of colleges of supervisors established under the 2010 ESMA Regulation Article 1(2) rulebook, and to foster the coherence of the application of EU law among colleges (Article 21(1)). ESMA staff are empowered to participate in the activities of colleges, including on-site examinations, carried out jointly by two or more NCAs (Article 21(1)). ESMA is also to take the lead in ensuring a consistent and coherent functioning of colleges, taking account of the systemic risk posed by financial market participants (Article 21(2)). In support of these powers, ESMA may establish and manage information systems for colleges, initiate and co-ordinate EU stress tests to assess the resilience of financial market participants,[251] and promote effective and efficient supervisory activities. ESMA may also request further deliberation by a college where it considers a college decision would lead to an incorrect application of EU law or not contribute to convergence in supervisory practices (Article 21(2)). Specific legislative measures confer discrete powers on ESMA with respect to colleges: the 2012 EMIR confers ESMA with tailored mediation powers with respect to the CCP authorization decisions in relation to which the mandatory CCP college of supervisors plays a key role under EMIR, and with peer review powers over these colleges (Chapter VI section 4.2.9).

Colleges aside, ESMA is also conferred with a suite of powers designed to enhance cross-border co-ordination. The 2012 Short Selling Regulation, for example, provides that ESMA may (and if requested must) co-ordinate cross-border on-site inspections or investigations (Article 37), while the 2003 Prospectus Directive, following the 2010 Omnibus I Directive reforms, empowers ESMA to participate in on-site inspections carried out by two or more NCAs (Article 5(10)).

More informally, ESMA is also to 'stimulate and facilitate' the delegation of supervisory tasks and responsibilities between NCAs and to be informed of all delegation agreements entered into by NCAs (2010 ESMA Regulation Article 28).

XI.5.5.2 Co-ordination in Crisis Conditions

Under Article 18(1), in the case of adverse developments which may seriously jeopardize the orderly functioning and integrity of financial markets or the stability of the whole or part of the financial system in the EU, ESMA must actively facilitate and, where deemed necessary, co-ordinate any actions undertaken by NCAs; to this end, it must be fully informed of any relevant developments and invited to participate as an observer in any relevant gathering of national authorities. More generally, Article 31 requires ESMA to fulfil a general co-ordination role between NCAs, in particular in situations where adverse developments could potentially jeopardize the orderly functioning and integrity of financial

---

[251] See sect 5.5.3.

markets or the stability of the EU financial system, including by means of: facilitating information exchange; determining the scope and verifying the reliability of information to be made available to the NCAs concerned; carrying out non-binding mediation (outside Article 19) where requested or on its own initiative; centralizing information received from NCAs; and, with particular reference to crisis conditions, notifying the ESRB of any potential emergency situations without delay and taking all appropriate measures in the case of developments which may jeopardize the functioning of the financial markets, with a view to facilitating the co-ordination of actions taken by relevant NCAs.

XI.5.5.3 System Oversight and Systemic Risk

In a new departure for securities regulators, but reflecting the paradigmatic crisis-era focus on financial stability,[252] ESMA has been conferred with a range of powers and duties related to financial stability in the form of macroprudential system oversight and the containment of systemic risk, and with respect to co-operation and co-ordination with the ESRB. From the outset, and reflecting ongoing turmoil in the sovereign debt markets in its first year of operation, it was clear that ESMA regarded the support of financial stability and market surveillance of systemic risk as a core part of its mission.[253]

ESMA is subject to an overarching obligation to duly consider systemic risk, defined by reference to the 2010 ESRB Regulation,[254] and to address any risk of disruption in financial services that is caused by an impairment of all or parts of the financial system and has the potential to have serious negative consequences for the internal market and the real economy (Article 22(1)). A number of related and generally cast obligations are imposed on ESMA. It must, *inter alia*, in collaboration with the ESRB, develop a common approach for the identification and management of systemic risk, including quantitative and qualitative indicators (Article 22(2) and Article 23); draw up, as necessary, additional guidelines and recommendations for key financial market participants which take account of systemic risk (Article 22(3)); ensure that systemic risk is taken into account in its BTS development activities (Article 22(3)); conduct inquiries (at its own initiative, or following a request from the European Parliament, Council, or Commission) into activities or products in order to assess potential systemic risk and make related recommendations (Article 22(4)); and develop a permanent capacity to respond to the materialization of systemic risk (Article 24).

At the core of ESMA's systemic risk-related functions, however, are its monitoring and surveillance activities, where it has quickly built a significant capacity and signalled its ability to engage in empirically driven analysis. ESMA is required to monitor and assess market developments and, where necessary, inform EBA, EIOPA, the ESRB, the Council, the Commission, and the European Parliament about relevant microprudential trends, potential risks, and vulnerabilities; it is required, at least annually and more frequently as necessary, to provide assessments to the Parliament, Council, Commission, and ESRB of

---

[252] See, eg, 2013 Mazars ESA Review, n 199, 89.

[253] ESMA, Annual Report (2011), Foreword by ESMA Chairman Maijoor, highlighting ESMA's EU-wide market surveillance (in co-ordination with NCAs, EBA, EIOPA (the European Insurance and Occupational Pensions Authority), and the ESRB), at 5 and ESMA, Annual Report (2012) 13, highlighting ESMA's surveillance and trend analysis activities. Similarly, ESMA Chairman Maijoor, 'Key Note Speech, IFRS Conference', 5 July 2011 (ESMA/2011/202), acknowledging that financial stability was a new area of activity for securities market supervisors, and highlighting ESMA's important role in this regard.

[254] See sect 6.

trends, potential risks, and vulnerabilities in its area of competence (Article 32(1) and (3)). ESMA accordingly publishes a bi-annual report on Trends, Risks, and Vulnerabilities in EU Securities Markets,[255] issues a quarterly Risk Dashboard for securities markets, and conducts daily market surveillance which supports its Weekly Financial Monitor, which is distributed to national and regional public bodies.[256] Cross-sector risk assessments are published by the three ESAs through the ESA Joint Committee. ESMA also issues regular thematic reviews of market sectors, which include reviews of the CDS market, of the hedge fund/prime broker relationship, and of the retailization of complex investment products.[257]

More controversially, stress testing was included among ESMA's systemic risk-related obligations, reflecting the policy and political focus on bank stress testing and its inclusion within the ESFS structure through EBA's parallel powers. ESMA must, in co-operation with the ESRB, initiate and co-ordinate Union-wide assessments of the resilience of financial market participants to adverse developments and develop related methodologies (Article 32(2)). Thus far, stress testing has been confined to the banking sector, and co-ordinated through EBA and, since the establishment of the SSM, the ECB. ESMA's competence in this area, however,[258] confers on it a potentially significant influence, particularly were the outcomes of stress tests to take the form of Article 16, 'comply or explain'-based recommendations to NCAs.

ESMA's pivotal relationship with the ESRB with respect to systemic risk oversight is formalized under Article 36, which requires ESMA to co-operate closely and on a regular basis with the ESRB (Article 36(1)): ESMA must 'take the utmost account' of ESRB warnings and recommendations in discharging its tasks (Article 36(6)). ESMA is subject to a range of related co-operation obligations with respect to the supply of information to the ESRB (Article 36(2)), and with respect to follow-up of ESRB warnings (Article 36(3)–(6)).[259] As discussed in section 6, the relationship between the ESRB and ESMA appears reasonably stable, although the potential for institutional tensions is not insignificant.

---

[255] At the time of writing, three 'TRVs' have been issued: ESMA, Report on Trends, Risks, and Vulnerabilities. Report No 1 2013 (2013) (ESMA/2013/212) (ESMA 2013(1) TRV), ESMA, Report on Trends, Risks, and Vulnerabilities. Report No 2 2013 (2013) (ESMA/2013/1138) (ESMA 2013(2) TRV), and ESMA, Trends, Risks, and Vulnerabilities. Report No 1 (2014) (ESMA/2014/0188) (ESMA 2014(1) TRV). The TRVs assess trends in securities markets (with respect to markets in a wide range of different asset classes, different classes of investor, and market infrastructures); risks (systemic stress, liquidity, market, contagion, and credit risk); and vulnerabilities (the 2013(2) TRV, eg, assessed vulnerabilities arising from short selling, the CDS market, the UCITS industry, and bail-in securities and contingent capital securities). The TRVs are becoming increasingly sophisticated and granular as the methodology for assessing risks to the EU securities market develops. The second 2013(2) TRV, eg, examined new risk indicators, including with respect to credit quality, securities lending, and short selling, and expanded the coverage of market infrastructures to include financial benchmarks and rating agencies.

[256] For a summary see ESMA, Annual Report (2012) 20–4.

[257] ESMA, Annual Report (2012) 21–4.

[258] Which is most likely to be exercised in relation to CCPs and alternative investment fund managers: 2013 Mazars ESA Review, n 199, 103.

[259] Where an ESRB recommendation or warning is addressed to ESMA, ESMA must convene a meeting of the Board of Supervisors without delay and assess the measure and decide on the action to be taken; where it does not act, it must explain its reasons to the ESRB and the Council. Where the recommendation or warning relates to an NCA, ESMA must use its powers to ensure a timely follow-up; where the NCA intends not to follow the recommendation, it must inform the Board of Supervisors and discuss its reasons for not acting, and take due account of the views of the Board of Supervisors when responding to the ESRB.

XI.5.6 Supervisory Convergence and Co-ordination and an EU Supervisory 'Approach': the 'Supervisory Handbook'

XI.5.6.1 Supervisory Convergence

ESMA's ability to shape supervisory convergence, and to ensure that a consistent and high quality of supervision obtains across the EU, is in practice a function of all of its supervisory powers, as together these powers support ESMA's capacity to influence the behaviour of NCAs. A number of its powers, however, are expressly directed to support of supervisory convergence.

ESMA Regulation Article 29 expressly requires ESMA to play an active role in building a common EU supervisory culture and consistent supervisory practices, as well as in ensuring uniform procedures and consistent approaches throughout the EU. It identifies the providing of opinions to NCAs, promoting information exchange, contributing to the development of high-quality and uniform supervisory standards, reviewing the application of BTSs, guidelines, and recommendations, and establishing training programmes as key convergence tools.[260] ESMA is also empowered to develop 'as appropriate' new practical instruments and convergence tools to promote common supervisory approaches and practices.

XI.5.6.2 Shaping Supervisory Decision-Making: Quasi-Rule-Making

ESMA's quasi-rule-making powers also support supervisory convergence. CESR's 'soft rulebook' was concerned in particular with promoting convergence in supervisory decision-making. As discussed in Chapter X section 5, ESMA has a significantly more stable basis for quasi-rule-making, which allows it to shape supervisory decision-making; proposals for BTSs, Article 16 guidelines and recommendations, and other 'soft' measures (such as 'Q&As') can all be used to build a *de facto* 'Supervisory Handbook'.

Many of the BTSs which ESMA must or can propose address operational supervisory practices. BTSs have already been produced on, for example, when NCAs should require a supplementary prospectus under the 2003 Prospectus Directive and in relation to the operation of colleges of supervisors under the 2012 EMIR. Similarly, Article 16 guidelines are often concerned with operational supervision,[261] as are the array of soft measures which ESMA produces, notably the 'Q&As' which are typically described as directed to NCAs and as supporting supervisory convergence.[262]

XI.5.6.3 Common Decision-Making

The extent to which NCAs engage in common decision-making is in part determinative of the extent to which supervisory practices and judgements converge. Generally, ESMA's

---

[260] ESMA has developed, in conjunction with EBA and EIOPA, a training manual for supervisors, and delivers regular training sessions which are seen by ESMA as a channel for 'strengthening our common supervisory culture': ESMA, Annual Report (2011) 38.

[261] eg 2010 ESMA Regulation Art 21(3), which provides that ESMA may issue Art 16 guidelines and recommendations to promote convergence in supervisory functioning and in best practices adopted by colleges of supervisors.

[262] The 2013 EMIR Q&A, eg, is designed to 'promote common supervisory practices and approaches in the application of EMIR' and is directed to NCAs: ESMA/2013/324, 3.

Article 16 power to adopt guidelines provides a vehicle through which NCAs bind themselves to common supervisory practices through the 'comply or explain' mechanism.

In addition, ESMA is also, in particular areas, promoting common decision-making by the NCAs. In the financial reporting sphere, for example, the European Enforcers Co-ordinators Sessions (EECS) co-ordinate enforcement practices across the NCAs with respect to IFRS compliance (Chapter II section 6). Common decision-making is also taking place with respect to market transparency supervision. As discussed in Chapter V, CESR had developed an informal review process whereby NCAs adopted a common opinion on the validity of waivers from MiFID I transparency requirements sought in national markets.[263] ESMA has since formalized the waiver process; the Board of Supervisors has agreed that when a market operator seeks a waiver, it is considered at ESMA level, at the initiative of the relevant NCA.[264] The adoption of the subsequent ESMA 'opinion' is considered by ESMA as part of its role in building a common supervisory culture and consistent supervisory practices.[265] The 2014 MiFIR regime has now formalized this practice, empowering ESMA to issue an opinion on the compatibility of the different waivers which national supervisors may apply in respect to the trading transparency rules which otherwise apply to securities market trading (MiFIR, Articles 4 and 9).

The ESA Joint Committee is also promoting common decision-making. Its initial mapping exercises on product intervention and product governance powers across the EU, for example, led to the development of a set of high-level principles governing the product approval process at national level.[266]

XI.5.6.4 Peer Review

Peer review has become an important element of the crisis-era supervisory environment. In the EU context, peer review gives ESMA significant potential to shape and enhance operational supervision by NCAs; ESMA's more radical powers to direct NCAs under 2010 ESMA Regulation Articles 17 and 19 are ill suited to directly supporting the embedding of good supervisory practices, being directed towards exceptional intervention by ESMA. In practice, peer review procedures, which identify and embed good practices, are likely to be significantly more effective in strengthening supervisory judgement and practices and pan-EU consistency. The IMF, for example, has called for the ESAs to play a significant role in the dissemination of best practices, including through intrusive and publicly disclosed peer review.[267]

CESR's experience with peer review was mixed. Its 2007 Protocol on Peer Review[268] identified the objectives of the CESR peer review process as supporting a consistent and timely application of supervisory provisions and enhancing supervisory convergence. It also

---

[263] The different positions are set out in ESMA/2011/241.

[264] ESMA, Annual Report (2011) 40.

[265] n 264, noting that while the legal authority to confer a waiver remains with the NCA, the Board of Supervisors had agreed to consider waivers at ESMA level.

[266] ESMA, EBA, EIOPA, Joint Position of the ESAs on Manufacturers' Product Oversight & Governance Processes (2013) (JC-2013-77).

[267] IMF, Financial Sector Assessment Program, European Union. European Securities and Markets Authority. Technical Note. March 2013 (2013 IMF ESMA Report) 14.

[268] CESR 07/070b.

identified a range of review techniques, including self-assessment and peer review exercises, as well as less interventionist 'mapping' and survey exercises. CESR's 2008 Annual Report regarded the related Panel as a 'peer pressure group' which could exercise peer pressure by reviewing NCAs against benchmarks. In practice, however, CESR's peer review activities tended to be limited, examining the technical operation of the UCITS passporting regime[269] and the application of CESR's guidelines with respect to the enforcement of financial reporting standards and related supervisory co-operation (CESR Standards Numbers 1 and 2 on Financial Information).[270] Mapping exercises of supervisory powers and practices were undertaken with respect to the 2004 Transparency Directive,[271] the 2004 MiFID I,[272] the 2003 Market Abuse Directive,[273] and the 2003 Prospectus Directive.[274] CESR's mapping exercises (and the peer review exercises) were largely directed to 'powers on the book'. The market abuse regime exercises (2010, 2009, and 2007), for example, focused for the most part on the formal powers which NCAs could exercise rather than on the operational exercise of these powers, although the 2008 MiFID I mapping contained some general discussion of different approaches to risk-based supervision.

ESMA peer review is designed to be more granular and intrusive. The 2010 ESMA Regulation Article 30 peer review regime requires ESMA periodically to organize and conduct peer review analyses of NCAs' activities to further strengthen consistency in supervisory outcomes (Article 30(1)). ESMA must develop methods to allow for objective assessment and comparison between NCAs (Article 30(1)). Peer review should assess (but not exclusively): the adequacy of resources and governance arrangements, including with regard to the effective implementation of EU securities and markets regulation and capacity to respond to market developments; the degree of convergence in the application of EU law and supervisory practices and the extent to which supervisory practices achieve the objectives of EU law; and good practices developed by some NCAs which might be of benefit to other NCAs (Article 30(2)). Overall, there is a granular concern not only with convergence in supervisory practices but with the 'capacity of supervisors to achieve high quality supervisory outcomes' (recital 41). The coercive effect of peer review is also addressed, in that ESMA may subsequently issue guidelines and recommendations (under Article 16) to NCAs, and NCAs are under an obligation to 'endeavour to follow' these guidelines and recommendations (Article 30(3)). The results of the peer review may also be disclosed publicly, subject to the agreement of the relevant NCA (Article 30(4)). The peer review process is linked to ESMA's quasi-rule-making activities in that ESMA is to take into account the outcomes of peer review when developing technical standards (Article 30(3)). ESMA peer review is becoming a feature of EU securities and markets regulation more generally; the 2011 AIFMD, for example, grants ESMA a specific peer review function with respect to how competent authorities supervise non-EU alternative investment fund managers.[275]

---

[269] Most recently, CESR/09-1034.

[270] Including CESR/09-374 (peer review and self-assessment of Standard No 1), CESR/09-188 (peer review of Standard No 2), and CESR/09-212 (self-assessment of Standard No 2).

[271] CESR/09-058 and CESR/08-514b.

[272] CESR/08-220.

[273] CESR/10-262, CESR/09-1120, and CESR/07-380.

[274] CESR/07-383.

[275] 2011 AIFMD Art 38.

Peer review is carried out through a Review Panel (composed of NCAs) and in accordance with the ESMA Protocol and Methodology on Peer Review.[276] ESMA's initial approach was based on the CESR approach, in that it was based on self-assessment by NCAs and on benchmarking by the Review Panel. Despite its peer-driven quality, it had nonetheless a robust quality. The first series of peer review reports addressed the market abuse regime, the prospectus authorization process, and the application of the important Money Market Fund Guidelines;[277] a mapping exercise on contingency powers for crises has also been completed.[278]

The 2012 Prospectus Peer Review, to take an example, examined the practical procedures adopted to review prospectuses, and found full application of the relevant 'Good Practice Principles' in 25 Member States. But the peer review is notable for its focus on operational reality and on the particular practices which NCAs use in reviewing prospectuses. Similarly, the April 2012 report on the mapping exercise on the use of sanctioning powers under the market abuse regime examined, at a high level of detail, divergences between supervisors with respect to, for example, organizational structure, staff, degree of specialization, use of settlements, and the relationship between administrative and criminal law sanctions; a similarly operational approach was taken in the 2013 review of supervisory practices under the market abuse regime.[279] The 2013 peer review on the application of the Money Market Fund Guidelines was also operational, reviewing, for example, internal organization within NCAs, technical expertise, resources, reliance on risk-based supervision, and supervisory tools employed.

While these exercises drilled much deeper into supervisory practices than did CESR's peer reviews, a more robust approach can be expected in the future given the autumn 2013 reforms to ESMA's Peer Review Methodology, which are designed to move peer review away from peer/NCA assessment and towards independent assessment by ESMA, and to remove the risk that NCA interests could distort the outcomes of peer review and dilute its effectiveness.[280] ESMA's 'supervisor of supervisor' function and its related hierarchical position are, accordingly, likely to be strengthened.

XI.5.7 Supervision and the International Market

ESMA's early years suggest that its international engagement has the potential to significantly strengthen its capacity by extending its supervisory reach, conferring on it an international presence, and allowing it, potentially, to become the EU 'face' of financial market supervision.

The 2010 ESMA Regulation envisages a co-ordination-based role for ESMA in the international market. Under Article 33, ESMA may develop contacts and enter into administrative arrangements with supervisory authorities, international organizations, and the administrations of third countries (Article 33(1)). In practice, ESMA plays a

---

[276] ESMA/2011/BS/229 and ESMA, ESMA Review Panel Methodology (ESMA/2013/1709 (revised from the 2012 version)).

[277] ESMA 2012/270 and ESMA/2013/805; ESMA 2012/300; and ESMA/2013/476, respectively.

[278] ESMA/2011/261.

[279] The review assessed the treatment of rumours, insider lists, and the obligations of investment firms and trading venues to have in place structural provisions to meet the requirements of the market abuse regime.

[280] A risk which was raised in the 2013 Mazars ESA Review, n 199, 100–1, which called for a more independent approach, akin to the IMF's FSAP (Financial Sector Assessment Programs) reviews.

co-ordinating role in the conclusion of international co-operation agreements by NCAs, adopting, in effect, template agreements which are executed bilaterally between NCAs and third country authorities. The 2011 AIFMD is a landmark measure in this respect. Under the AIFMD, ESMA centrally negotiated co-operation arrangements (MoUs) between NCAs and 42 third country authorities (in effect, more than 1,000 bilateral MoUs) based on an ESMA MoU template agreed by the Board of Supervisors.[281] The mass adoption of these agreements by the Board of Supervisors represents a major success for ESMA and a significant advance for international supervisory co-ordination at EU level.[282] The economies of scale which ESMA-led conclusion of the swathe of agreements delivered were significant; so too was the signal sent as to ESMA's ability to act on behalf of its NCAs in international negotiations, and the NCAs' willingness to confer a mandate on ESMA in this regard.

Additionally, ESMA must assist in the preparation of equivalence decisions (Article 33(2)); as discussed in previous Chapters, it has become closely engaged with equivalence decisions, particularly in relation to the credit rating agency regime (Chapter VII section 2.11). It also registers certain actors established in third countries.[283]

The potential for ESMA to strengthen its supervisory capacity through international activities is all the greater given some evidence that the 'substitute compliance' model may become more common as a means for managing international regulatory and supervisory co-ordination. Although this model was initially developed by the US SEC prior to the financial crisis, it subsequently went into abeyance until it was resurrected in relation to the 2010 Dodd-Frank Act, and the application of its rules for OTC derivatives trading in particular.[284] As NCAs become more accustomed to ESMA's international role,[285] ESMA can be expected to assume a central co-ordination role in relation to any potential substitute compliance assessments, further strengthening its capacity.

XI.5.8 ESMA's Operating Environment and Effectiveness

XI.5.8.1 The Treaty Context

If construction of the single rulebook was the defining feature of the first three years of ESMA's operation, its next phase of development is likely to be defined by its role in

---

[281] ESMA, Annual Report (2012) 46. The ESMA MoU template was adopted in the form of an Art 16 guideline (ESMA/2013/998). It was developed originally by means of consultation with all IOSCO members (more than 80 third country regulators) and subsequently by focused discussions with particular regulators. ESMA Chairman Maijoor has described the AIFMD MoU process as an important step which helped the EU to speak with one voice, ensured a level playing field and greater negotiation efficiency, and 'was in some ways a perfect illustration of what the new ESFS can achieve': 'Speech on ESMA—Issues and Priorities', 5 November 2013 (ESMA/2013/1582).

[282] ESMA Press Release 30 March 2013 (ESMA/2013/629). ESMA Chairman Maijoor described the successful completion of the negotiations as a 'key achievement for ESMA in its co-ordinating role for EU securities markets'.

[283] eg 2012 EMIR, Art 25 (CCPs) and Art 77 (trade repositories) and Credit Rating Agency Regulation Arts 4 and 5 (rating agencies established in a third country).

[284] Ch VI sect 4.2.13.

[285] Some tensions clearly persist, particularly with respect to the respective roles of ESMA and the NCAs in international meetings: eg, in the context of OTC derivatives markets supervision, Board of Supervisors Meeting, 14 February 2012 (ESMA/2012/BS29).

supervision and in supporting the consistent implementation and application of the single rulebook. Stakeholder reaction to the 2013 ESFS Review underlined strong support for the ESAs to intensify their supervisory activities, while the complex Banking Union dynamics, which demand that EBA intensively polices pan-EU supervisory consistency in the application of the banking rulebook as a hedge against euro-area/internal market fragmentation risks, are likely to further sharpen the focus on ESMA as a 'supervisor of supervisors' (sections 5.10 and 7).

But supervision by ESMA poses a number of constitutional conundrums. Supervisory powers are primarily implementing or executive in nature and typically rest at Member State level (Article 291 TFEU). Accordingly, it is not necessarily clear whether supervisory powers conferred on an agency such as ESMA are conferred directly by the co-legislators or represent a form of delegated power, and which modes of constitutional analysis accordingly apply to any assessment of their validity. The norm-setting effects of executive powers which are of general application (such as a supervisory decision addressed to a class of persons) pose potential difficulties with respect to the Court's *Romano* ruling (which prohibits the conferral of legislative powers on bodies other than the EU legislature).[286] Difficulties arise with respect to the Article 290/291 TFEU framework within which the Commission can be conferred with the power to adopt 'delegated' (non-legislative) acts and executive 'implementing' acts (Chapter X section 4.2.1), if this framework is regarded as the exclusive means through which the co-legislators can delegate or confer powers to adopt acts of general application or, in the case of implementing acts, individual application.

Whether or not the conferral on and exercise of supervisory powers by ESMA is supported by a Treaty competence can also be unclear, not least given the novelty of agency-exercised supervisory powers and the precedent-setting operational powers allocated to the ESAs. While Article 114 TFEU, the competence on which the ESMA Regulation and ESMA's distinct supervisory powers have been based, is elastic,[287] it is not endlessly so, and is relatively untested outside the rule-making context.

XI.5.8.2 The Treaty Context: *Meroni*

Above all, the difficulties posed by the *Meroni* doctrine[288] (should it apply, in that the supervisory powers in question can be regarded as delegated rather than conferred)[289] are potentially acute.[290] The *Meroni* doctrine provides that discretionary powers involving a wide margin of discretion which may make possible the execution of economic policy cannot be delegated by an EU institution; only clearly defined executive powers, subject to strict review in light of objective criteria determined by the delegating authority, may be delegated. But supervision can (and typically does) involve discretionary decisions as to how rules are applied and can (and, increasingly in the crisis-era environment,

---

[286] Case 89/90 *Romano* [1981] ECR 1241.

[287] See Ch X sect 3.3.1 on Art 114.

[288] n 52.

[289] ESMA's operating framework for supervision is based on the assumption that *Meroni* applies. The *Meroni* constraint on delegated powers informed, eg, the rating agency regime.

[290] On *Meroni* and operational supervision generally see, eg, Curtin, D, 'Delegation to EU Non-Majoritarian Agencies and Emerging Practices of Public Accountability' in Geradin, D, Muñoz, R and Petit, N (eds), *Regulation through Agencies in the EU. A New Paradigm of European Governance?* (2005) 87.

is expected to have) normative effects on market behaviour, potentially breaching the *Meroni* prohibition.[291]

The *Meroni* risks arise primarily in relation to ESMA's direct powers of intervention in relation to which the political intention has been described as to create 'clear hierarchical authority'[292] over NCAs. These powers take two forms; the horizontal powers of intervention conferred under 2010 ESMA Regulation Articles 17–19 and the specific powers conferred on ESMA with respect to discrete market sectors and activities, such as its powers of intervention under the 2012 Short Selling Regulation and its powers to supervise rating agencies and trade repositories under the rating agency regime and the 2012 EMIR, respectively.

The *Meroni* difficulty derives from the tension between the political decision to empower ESMA to intervene and the reality that the practical execution of this decision requires a degree of discretion. The need to exercise a degree of discretion or judgement in making a supervisory decision does not, in itself, risk a *Meroni* breach, as long as the conditions under which the discretion is exercised are clear and a wide margin of discretion is not afforded to ESMA. But multiple difficulties of nuance arise in an area which demands absolute operational certainty.

Difficulties arise in relation to how much discretion along a spectrum is valid and whether the margin of discretion is overly wide where policy choices are, to some extent, engaged. Similarly, a *Meroni* breach might arise where ESMA's operating environment is uncertain or unstable, where sensitive choices are required, or where the governing factors or conditions are necessarily subjective, so as to support judgement-based supervision.

Further difficulties arise with respect to the conditionality deployed to support *Meroni*. Delegations of operational power to ESMA have been subject to tight conditions on their operation to control discretion. ESMA's supervisory powers over rating agencies and trade repositories, for example, sit within an extensive binding rulebook, are delineated in detail, and are supported by enforcement powers which are carefully enumerated. ESMA's discretion has been curtailed to a significant extent: the binding rulebook details, for example, the conditions which govern when and how information can be requested of rating agencies, the supervisory fees which can be charged to rating agencies, the factors which ESMA is to take into account in quantifying and applying pecuniary penalties, and the range of pecuniary penalties which can be applied (Chapter VII section 2.10). Similarly, the 2012 Short Selling Regulation imposes a range of conditions on ESMA's powers to prohibit short sales (Chapter VI section 3.9.2). These operational conditions reflect *Meroni* and the templates it has produced for agency design rather than the dictates of operational effectiveness. This is all the more the case as the conditions tend to veer between a high degree of prescription (as under the rating agency regime), which can obstruct ESMA's

---

[291] *Meroni* risks are not only associated with the ESAs; the *Meroni*-resilience of the (then) proposed Single Resolution Mechanism was the subject of intense institutional discussions over the negotiations and the subject of a controversial (and widely-leaked) Council Legal Service Opinion which suggested that the Commission's proposal breached *Meroni* given the discretion given to the proposed Resolution Board (Opinion, 7 October 2013).

[292] Case C-270/12 *UK v Council and Parliament*, 22 January 2014, not yet reported, Opinion of Advocate General Jääskinen, para 24.

operational freedom, and a high degree of subjectivity (as under the short selling regime) which may, given the legal risks it may run when taking action, restrain ESMA from taking action where it is necessary.

To take a contrasting example, different conditionality difficulties trouble the horizontal 2010 ESMA Regulation Article 19 power to impose binding mediation, which is a key power for supporting supervisory consistency and for breaking through deadlock, particularly in colleges of supervisors. Article 19 is not, save with respect to the related ESMA power to impose decisions on third parties, subject to limiting conditions. It thereby allows ESMA to choose from a range of options to resolve NCA disputes. This approach seems functionally correct as it reflects the need for ESMA to be empowered to take action where NCAs disagree, and a backstop limiting condition applies through the overarching fiscal condition (2010 ESMA Regulation Article 38). But the lack of more specific conditions may risk undermining the validity of this power. Given that ESMA Regulation Article 17 is designed to address breaches of EU law by NCAs, it seems reasonable that Article 19 addresses divergences short of breach, where divergences in supervisory practices or judgements lead to failures to act or disrupt supervisory convergence. But the lack of conditionality risks undermining ESMA's operating effectiveness in this highly sensitive area and the inviting of legal challenges.

Overall, *Meroni*-driven conditionality may provide a useful braking device as ESMA learns to exercise operational powers, but it sits uneasily with ESMA's status as an independent authority and with the degree of operational freedom typically enjoyed by supervisory agencies, particularly given the crisis-era emphasis on judgement-based supervision.

A further difficulty arises. Member States diverge on the extent to which operational powers should be conferred on ESMA (section 5.9.2). While negotiations on allocations of power to ESMA have typically been framed by the *Meroni* ruling, this often masks fundamental differences as to the extent to which power should be located within ESMA. The *Meroni* constraint has therefore become the location of significant institutional and Member State conflict on ESMA's role in supervision, and has led to ESMA's operational powers resting on an unstable foundation, given the incentives to deploy *Meroni* to undermine ESMA's powers.

Most EU agencies do not cause difficulties in this regard as they are designed to support co-operation between national authorities, collate information, or provide administrative support or technical expertise to the Commission.[293] A handful of EU agencies at the top of the agency 'hierarchy' are 'decision-making' authorities in that they can impose decisions on third parties. But even these advanced agencies exercise more limited decision-making powers and typically operate within discrete and specialist EU regimes, usually concerned with licensing. The Community Plant Variety Office (CPVO) exercises licensing and right-conferral powers.[294] The Office for Harmonisation in the Internal Market (OHIM) administers the Community trade mark regime and exercises related trade mark-conferral powers.[295] The European Aviation Safety Agency (EASA) exercises powers with respect to

---

[293] eg Chiti, E, 'An Important Part of the EU's Institutional Machinery: Features, Problems and Perspectives of European Agencies' (2009) 46 *CMLR* 1395, 1403–4.

[294] Regulation (EC) No 2100/94 [1994] OJ L227/1.

[295] Regulation (EC) No 40/94 [1994] OJ L11/1.

safety licensing under the aviation regime.[296] The European Chemicals Agency registers, evaluates, and authorizes chemicals under the EU's 'REACH' regime.[297] All of these decision-making powers are limited and closely related to particular EU regimes.[298] A step change occurred in 2009 with the Agency for the Cooperation of Energy Regulators,[299] which can take 'individual regulatory decisions' with potentially discretionary and economic implications with respect to cross-border energy infrastructures and exemptions from the energy regime.[300]

ESMA, however, is particularly vulnerable to challenge for breach of the prohibition on delegation of discretionary powers; the sensitive nature of the economic interests potentially at stake when ESMA exercises power is reflected in the 2010 ESMA Regulation Article 38 fiscal safeguard clause. This is all the more the case given the open-textured nature of the typical conditions which govern its supervisory powers, which often relate to competition being distorted, the orderly functioning and integrity of the market being affected, or market stability being threatened.[301] The *Meroni* constraint may also lead to the risk of ESMA not exercising powers in cases where it should, fearful of triggering litigation.

From the outset, the resilience of the controls on ESMA's exercise of operational power came under close scrutiny. The Commission's original proposal for what would become the 2011 CRA Regulation II[302]—the main operational template for ESMA's direct supervisory activity (and used for ESMA's powers under the 2012 EMIR)—led to significant concern from the Commission's Impact Assessment Board, which called for additional discussion of how ESMA's enforcement and fining powers met the *Meroni* conditions.[303] The Regulation as finally adopted shows significant sensitivity to the *Meroni* constraint (Chapter VII section 2.10). The 2014 MiFIR negotiations on ESMA's temporary prohibition and restriction power over financial instruments and services and activities similarly reveal the institutional sensitivities. The original Commission proposal placed a series of conditions on ESMA's exercise of this power, and empowered the Commission to adopt related administrative rules which would set out the factors governing when threats to investor protection and financial stability would warrant exercise of the proposed new power. The Council negotiation extended these conditions and specified in more detail the particular conditions under which the power was to be exercised, including with respect to the degree of complexity of the instrument in question, its size/notional value, and degree of innovation (Chapter IX section 7.1).

Institutionally, the Commission was, from the outset, reasonably confident as to the *Meroni*-resilience of these conferrals of power,[304] although its Impact Assessment Board repeatedly called for more intense discussion in Commission proposals of why the conferral

---

[296] Regulation (EC) No 216/2008 [2008] OJ L79/1.
[297] Regulation (EC) No 1907/2006 [2006] OJ L396/1.
[298] Geradin and Petit note the 'clear trans-European component': n 212, 39.
[299] Regulation (EC) No 713/2009 [2009] OJ L211/1.
[300] Arts 8 and 9.
[301] eg 2010 ESMA Regulation Art 17(6) and Art 18(3); Short Selling Regulation Art 28(2).
[302] Regulation (EU) No 513/2011 [2011] OJ L145/30.
[303] Reports of the Impact Assessment Board Ref.Ares(2010)108790 and 205437.
[304] One senior official has suggested that ESMA's powers with respect to rating agencies, eg, are 'circumscribed executive powers' which operate within a clearly defined regulatory framework, including with respect to the sanctions which can be applied: Faull, n 206.

of particular powers on ESMA was necessary.[305] But it is generally wary of ESMA's operational, executive powers. It resisted the transfer of operational fining powers to ESMA under the rating agency regime, for example[306] and originally suggested that it exercise the temporary prohibition powers conferred on ESMA under the 2014 MiFIR,[307] despite the 2010 ESMA Regulation enabling clause (Article 9(5)). The European Parliament, by contrast, has been a champion of conferring additional powers on ESMA. During the ESA negotiations, it proposed that all three ESAs have direct supervisory powers over systemically significant cross-border actors and called for ESA resolution units.[308] Since then, it has been an enthusiastic supporter of the conferral of additional powers on ESMA and rarely appears troubled by *Meroni* restrictions;[309] over the 2014 MiFIR negotiations, for example, it supported ESMA's temporary intervention powers and called for an enhancement, suggesting that ESMA be additionally empowered to engage in product pre-approval in particular circumstances (Chapter XI section 7.1). Unlike the Commission, however, the Parliament is not a location of executive power in the EU, and has little to fear from ESMA in this regard.

Council negotiations, however, have often been the occasion of additional restrictions being placed on ESMA's operational supervisory powers, typically in the name of *Meroni*. The 2011 CRA Regulation II negotiations, for example, revealed significant Member State concern, and in particular from the UK, on the *Meroni*-resilience of ESMA's sanctioning powers.[310] Similar dynamics emerged under the 2014 MiFID II/MiFIR negotiations. The June 2012 Presidency Progress Report on MiFID II/MiFIR, for example, suggested that one Member State (the UK)[311] was concerned at the legality of the temporary product/service prohibition and restriction powers and the position management powers being proposed for ESMA.[312]

XI.5.8.3 The 2014 *Short Selling* Ruling

The nature of the *Meroni* constraint and of the relationship between ESMA's operational powers and the Treaties became clearer, however, following the Court's important January 2014 ruling in the *Short Selling* case.[313]

---

[305] eg Commission Impact Assessment Board Report on Impact Assessment Board Report on MiFID II (2010) (Ref. Ares(2010)549585).

[306] Wishart, I, 'MEPS Want to Give More Power to Securities and Markets Authority', *European Voice*, 25 November 2011.

[307] 2010 Commission MiFID I Review Consultation, n 181, 80–1.

[308] Sect 3.3.3.

[309] eg in relation to the rating agency regime, it added the ESMA power to undertake random sample tests on the validity of ratings (later diluted to a power to oversee back-testing by rating agencies) and argued for ESMA (rather than the Commission) to exercise the power to impose fines; and, in relation to the 2012 Short Selling Regulation, called for additional ESMA information-gathering powers and a hardening of ESMA's power to offer an 'opinion' on an NCA short-selling decision to the power to make a binding 'decision' (this proposal was not adopted).

[310] The relevant UK government minister noted that the issue of the legality of delegating discretionary decisions was 'of vital importance' and a 'priority for the Government', and that the UK government sought to ensure a 'tight legal framework': House of Commons, European Scrutiny Committee, 7th Report, November 2010.

[311] See, eg, House of Commons, European Scrutiny Committee, 31 October 2012, Letter on MiFID II/MiFIR from the Financial Secretary to the Treasury.

[312] Danish Presidency Progress Report on MiFID II/MiFIR, 20 June 2012, Council Document 11536/12, para 25.

[313] n 292.

In June 2012, the UK government lodged a challenge to ESMA's powers under the 2012 Short Selling Regulation to require market participants to notify to the relevant NCA or disclose to the public details of a net short position, or to prohibit or impose conditions on short sales (2012 Short Selling Regulation Article 28(1)), subject to a range of conditions linked to threats to market integrity, functioning, and stability, and NCA failure to act appropriately, and also governing the nature of the measures taken by ESMA (2012 Short Selling Regulation Article 28(2) and (3)).[314] The UK's *Meroni*-related challenge was based on: ESMA's intervention powers entailing a large measure of discretion; ESMA being given a wide range of choices as to which measures to impose and which measures would have very significant policy implications; the factors which ESMA was required to take into account before acting being highly subjective; the ongoing ability of ESMA to renew measures imposed being without any overall time limit; and, overall, the conferral of broad discretion on ESMA to apply policy in a particular case. The UK also argued, with respect to the norm-setting potential of the powers, that they illegally empowered ESMA to adopt measures of general application which had the force of law in breach of the *Romano* ruling; that they illegally empowered ESMA to adopt administrative rules of general application in breach of Articles 290 and 291 TFEU which, exclusively, set out the allocation of power with respect to the adoption of such rules; and that, to the extent that the 2012 Short Selling Regulation empowered ESMA to take individual decisions directed at natural or legal persons, it breached Article 114 TFEU, being without a sound competence.[315]

The case rapidly achieved political and market prominence (Spain, France, and Italy intervened against the UK), being regarded as an early test case for the resilience of the ESAs' direct intervention powers and for whether crisis-era political choices with respect to regulation and supervision had placed insupportable strain on the underpinning Treaties. The fate of the proposed Single Resolution Mechanism also became linked to the outcome of the challenge, given the similar (if more acute) *Meroni* risks posed by the proposed powers of the Mechanism.[316]

The Advocate General's (AG) opinion proved liberal on *Meroni*. The AG recast *Meroni* in light of the clarification which the Lisbon Treaty had brought to the distinction between normative delegated acts (Article 290 TFEU) and executive implementing powers (Article 291) and the Treaty's formal extension of judicial review at EU level over agencies, and the related addressing by the Treaties, accordingly, of the concerns as to institutional balance and judicial review which, the AG argued, had shaped *Meroni*. The AG argued that agencies could not be empowered to act directly under Article 290 (as to do so would empower an agency to change the normative content of a legislative act and so offend the principle of democratic accountability), but they could be so empowered in relation to delegations of Article 291 executive/implementing acts (including such acts of general application), as long as the implementing powers were not different to those conferred on the delegating authority, whether the Council or Commission, and the powers were sufficiently well defined so as to avoid arbitrary exercise. But while this analysis suggested

---

[314] On the applicable conditions see Ch VI sect 3.9.2.
[315] Case C-270/12, n 292, Pleas in Law and Main Arguments and Ruling of the Court.
[316] n 291.

that ESMA's powers to act could be Treaty-compliant, the AG found that the powers in question were not delegated but conferred directly by the EU institutions, and *Meroni* did not apply.[317] In conferring powers, however, the legislature was required to ensure that the powers were sufficiently specific such that institutional balance and the need for effective judicial control were safeguarded, and that ESMA was not empowered to take policy decisions, in order to protect the primary democratic role of the EU legislature. On an analysis of the conditions governing ESMA's powers, the AG found that they were sufficiently specific and that these constitutional principles were met.

But in what came to be regarded as an existential threat to a range of ESMA's powers (and to the Single Resolution Mechanism then under negotiation), the AG argued that Article 114 TFEU was not a valid competence. The AG interpreted the Article 114 case law as providing that the conferral of powers on ESMA to adopt measures in substitution for assessments by NCAs could not be considered a measure for the approximation of Member States' laws, as required by Article 114. ESMA's powers elevated to the EU level powers to intervene which were equivalent to the powers of NCAs under the 2012 Short Selling Regulation, which activated only where NCAs had failed to act (or to act adequately) and which prevailed over previous NCA measures; its powers accordingly allowed it to intervene in the conditions of competition in a financial market, otherwise the remit of an NCA, albeit in defined and exceptional circumstances, and did not involve the development of specific and detailed rules relating to financial products or services. The AG also found that ESMA's powers bore little resemblance to the agency powers which the Court had previously found to be Article 114-compliant under the *ENISA* ruling,[318] being legally binding and 'lifting implementation powers' from NCAs to ESMA where disagreement arose.[319] In effect, ESMA's powers created an 'EU level emergency decision-making mechanism';[320] the outcome of action by ESMA was not harmonization but the replacement of national decision-making. The AG noted that such powers could be conferred under the EU's residual competence (Article 352 TFEU), given the need for action at EU level in the circumstances addressed by the 2012 Short Selling Regulation powers, but acknowledged the political difficulties posed by the unanimous Council vote required.

The widely anticipated Court ruling, which did not follow the AG's opinion, proved a decisive victory for the Council and European Parliament.[321] By contrast with the AG, the Court treated ESMA's powers as delegated powers (it did not address the conferral argument) subject to *Meroni*, and highlighted the difference between valid, clearly defined executive powers, subject to strict review in the light of objective criteria, and invalid, discretionary powers involving a wide margin of discretion which could make possible the exercise of actual economic policy. ESMA's powers under the 2012 Short Selling Regulation, Article 28 did not go beyond the regulatory framework established by the 2010 ESMA Regulation. They were also circumscribed by the various conditions and criteria which

---

[317] The AG noted that in this respect the EU legislature was not acting as a delegating actor, but as a constitutional actor exercising its legislative competence.

[318] See Ch X sect 3.3.1.

[319] Opinion of the AG, n 292, para 50.

[320] Opinion of the AG, n 292, para 52.

[321] It was reported as a 'serious defeat' to the UK's campaign to limit the power of the 'EU financial watchdogs': Barber, A, 'London Loses Short Selling Case', *Financial Times*, 23 February 2013, 4.

limited ESMA's discretion. ESMA could only adopt measures where the conditions laid down in the 2012 Short Selling Regulation (Article 28(2)) were met and where NCA action was absent or inadequate; and conditions applied to the measures taken by ESMA under 2012 Short Selling Regulation Article 28(3). Accordingly, a significant number of factors governed the ESMA decision. The Court additionally underlined the amplification of the conditions governing the ESMA decision under the 2012 Commission Delegated Regulation 918/2012, which placed 'even greater emphasis on the technical factual assessment' by ESMA.[322] The Court also related the Article 28 powers to the enabling power relating to intervention under ESMA Regulation Article 9(5), and found that ESMA's powers were strictly confined to those set out in Article 9(5). The Court also pointed to the consultation obligations imposed on ESMA, as well as to the temporary nature of the ESMA decision and the related need to review any measure imposed on a three-month review cycle. Accordingly, ESMA's powers were 'precisely delineated and amenable to judicial review in light of the objectives established by the delegating authority' and complied with *Meroni*; they did not imply that ESMA was vested with a large degree of discretion incompatible with the TFEU.[323]

The Court also dismissed arguments relating to the alleged illegal norm-setting impact of quasi-legislative action by ESMA, in the form of supervisory action taken by ESMA with respect to short selling through measures of general application (where its supervisory action related to an entire class of persons engaging in transactions in an instrument that was the subject of ESMA action, for example). It found, in an economically argued section of the ruling, that ESMA was empowered (in strictly circumscribed circumstances) to adopt such measures of general application under the 2012 Short Selling Regulation Article 28. But the *Romano* ruling did not prevent ESMA from being conferred with the power to adopt measures of general application, as long as the *Meroni* conditions were met; Articles 263 and 277 TFEU (which govern judicial review) expressly permitted agencies to adopt measures of general application.

Similarly, the Court rejected the Article 290/291 TFEU argument, rejecting the premise that Article 290/291 was the exclusive framework within which the power to adopt administrative measures of general application (whether executive/implementing or delegated) could be delegated or conferred. The Court found that Article 28 of the 2012 Short Selling Regulation did not delegate powers to the Commission (as provided for under Articles 290 and 291) but to an agency, and that while the Treaties did not expressly provide for the conferral of powers on agencies, a number of provisions, including Article 263 TFEU which provides for judicial review of acts of agencies, presupposed that such a possibility existed. The conferral of powers on ESMA under Article 28 related to a sphere in which the deployment of specific technical and professional expertise was required, and did not correspond to the situations defined in Articles 290 and 291. The legal framework for Article 28 was based on, *inter alia*, the 2012 Short Selling Regulation, the 2010 ESMA Regulation, and the 2010 ESRB Regulation, which formed part of a series of regulatory instruments designed to allow the EU 'to endeavour to promote financial stability'.[324]

---

[322] Ruling of the Court, n 292, para 52.
[323] Ruling of the Court, n 292, paras 53–54.
[324] The Court made reference to the 2010 ESRB Regulation rec 7 in this regard (at para 84).

Accordingly, Article 28 could not be considered in isolation, but formed part of a series of rules designed to endow NCAs and ESMA with powers of intervention in order to address adverse developments which threatened market stability within the Union and market confidence. Therefore, Article 28, read in conjunction with the 2010 ESMA and ESRB Regulations, could not be regarded as undermining Articles 290 and 291 TFEU.

Finally, the argument that ESMA's powers, in so far as they empowered ESMA to adopt individual decisions directed at natural or legal persons breached Article 114 TFEU, was dispatched. The Court followed the liberal approach to Article 114 which it had adopted in earlier rulings.[325] Addressing first the Article 114 requirement that the measures in question 'approximate' provisions laid down by law, regulation, or administrative action in the Member States, it found that Article 114 TFEU conferred on the EU legislature discretion as to the most appropriate method of harmonization for achieving the desired result, particularly in fields with complex technical features; this discretion could be used to choose the most appropriate method of harmonization where the proposed approximation required highly technical and specialist analysis.[326] The legislature could also deem it necessary to provide for the establishment of an EU body responsible for contributing to the implementation of the process of harmonization.[327] Accordingly, the legislature could delegate to an agency powers for the implementation of the harmonization sought, particularly where the measures to be adopted were dependent on specific professional and technical expertise and on speedy reaction. The Court rejected the argument that Article 114 could not support the adoption by such an agency of measures which were legally binding on individuals, noting, *inter alia*, that nothing in the Article implied that the addressees of related measures could only be the Member States and that the 'measures for approximation' supported by Article 114 could go beyond the approximation of laws where it was necessary to ensure the unity of the market, and could relate to a specific product, class of product, or individual measures relating to products.[328] Examining the nature of the contested Article 28 power, the Court found that it was a last-resort power which applied in very specific circumstances, that Member States had adopted divergent approaches in this area, that the power addressed the risk of divergences arising across the Member States, took the form of a regulation to ensure a uniform approach, was designed to address fragmentation risks by adopting a harmonized approach, and so was directed to the harmonization of Member States' laws, regulations, and administrative provisions related to short selling.

With respect to the Article 114 TFEU requirement that the measure have as its object the establishment and functioning of the internal market, the Court did not engage in extensive analysis but drew on the recitals to the 2012 Short Selling Regulation in finding that the purpose of the Regulation was to ensure the proper functioning of the internal financial market by means of the adoption of a common regulatory framework to address short selling and ensure greater co-ordination and consistency where measures must be taken in

---

[325] See Ch X. sect 3.3.1.
[326] The Court drew on Case C-66/04 *UK v Parliament and Council (Smoke Flavourings)* [2005] ECR I-10553.
[327] The Court drew on the *ENISA* ruling (Case C-217/04 *UK v Council and Parliament* (ENISA) [2006] ECR I-3771). See Ch X sect 3.3.1.
[328] The Court drew on Case C-359/92 *Germany v Council* [1994] ECR I-3681.

exceptional circumstances. The harmonization undertaken was therefore intended to prevent the creation of obstacles to the proper functioning of the internal market and the continuing application of divergent measures by Member States. The purpose of the Regulation was accordingly to improve the conditions for the establishment and functioning of the internal market in the financial field.

Although the Court's ruling is framed by the particular qualities of ESMA's powers under the 2012 Short Selling Regulation and the related conditionality, a liberal reading might suggest that it has significantly stabilized ESMA's constitutional basis and that the *Meroni* restraint is, in practice, somewhat limited. The ruling might also be read as suggesting a judicial sensitivity to the operational realities of supervisory decision-making and acceptance of the need for ESMA's technical capacity. A more restrictive reading, however, might be that nothing, fundamentally, has changed. The Court did not take the opportunity to follow the AG's liberal reading of *Meroni*, and the persistence of 'discretion' as the touchstone for assessments of the legality of ESMA's operating powers may well lead to a closer Commission (at least) focus on the conditions which contain ESMA's operating freedom.

Overall, the persistent political sensitivities suggest that ESMA is likely to tread carefully when exercising direct supervisory powers which replace NCA action. The ruling has, however, re-ignited the European Parliament's enthusiasm for conferring direct powers of intervention on the ESAs, and so may come to shape the trajectory of ESMA (and the ESAs) more generally.[329]

XI.5.8.4 ESMA's Governance

As discussed in Chapter X section 5, the effectiveness of ESMA's governance depends on a co-operative relationship between ESMA and its constituent NCA members. In the supervisory context, the potential for tension and inefficiencies is considerable. ESMA was constructed in a political climate which reflected a broad consensus concerning the need for greater co-ordination and for 'more Europe' rather than 'less Europe'. But the increasing pressure on NCA autonomy with respect to operational supervision, in combination with the central steering already in place with respect to rule-making, may place significant pressure on this consensus and so on ESMA's ability to operate effectively—whether as a direct supervisor, or with respect to supporting co-ordination and supervisory convergence.

The dynamics between ESMA and its constituent NCAs with respect to supervision are complex. There is a strong co-operative dimension to the ESMA/NCA relationship. ESMA has been careful to highlight the dominant role of NCAs in local supervision.[330] In developing supervisory policy, ESMA relies heavily on its Standing Committees and Task Forces, which are staffed in large part by the NCAs. NCAs may be able to argue for more resources or powers under the cover of ESMA demands. ESMA may also inject a

---

[329] In its 2014 Resolution on the ESFS, the Parliament claimed that the ruling 'indicated a potentially enhanced scope for activities...in comparison to the prevailing interpretation of the judgment [in *Meroni*]' and called on the Commission to assess its potential implications: European Parliament, Resolution on the European System of Financial Supervision, 11 March 2014 (P7_TA-PROV(2014)020) (2014 European Parliament ESFS Resolution) para AM.

[330] eg ESMA Chairman Maijoor, n 244.

greater degree of realism into the wider political and policy debate with respect to the limitations of supervision in preventing failure.

On the other hand, there is a coercive and hierarchical dynamic to the ESMA/NCA relationship. ESMA can, for example, supplant NCAs under ESMA Regulation Articles 17–19, demand justifications of action where 'comply or explain' applies, and shape supervisory practices, including through peer review. From the NCA perspective, the potential loss of power is real. It is also the case that operational supervision is now the only mechanism through which NCAs can exercise autonomy over national markets. The more ESMA takes direct operational decisions, the greater the possibility for conflict and tension within ESMA, and for related threats to its effectiveness.

Thus far, ESMA appears to be managing the NCA relationship well. For example, potentially sensitive intervention decisions have been taken with respect to IFRS compliance, a series of consensus opinions on equity market transparency waivers have been adopted, and the new rating agency operational model has been put in place and inspections carried out without, based on public evidence at least, significant tensions. The framework for 2010 ESMA Regulation Article 17 action has also been carefully designed (section 5.3.1).

In particular, the peer review power is being deployed sensitively, mitigating the significant potential which ESMA's peer review powers have to destabilize ESMA/NCA relations. Local factors such as institutional organization, national supervisory mandates, resources, supervisory styles, and national market features all impact on how an NCA engages in supervision; identification of the outcomes to be assessed and the best practices to be followed accordingly requires sensitivity to local contexts. Thus far, while ESMA associates peer review with the identification of a 'common supervisory approach', its approach appears flexible. The 2013 Money Market Fund Guidelines Peer Review, for example, does not identify detailed best practices or particular operational models (accommodating compliance and risk-based models, for example) but focuses on the NCA being able to justify the particular processes, approaches, and resources deployed.[331] The possibility for tension is, however, real, particularly as ESMA's powers increase, and given the stresses which undue 'harmonization' of supervision may generate.

XI.5.9 ESMA and the Removal of NCA Discretion

XI.5.9.1 Squeezing NCA Discretion?

While ESMA has a critical role to fulfil in supporting supervisory consistency and in raising standards, the extent to which ESMA should shape supervision at national level is not clear. Effectiveness risks may follow if local supervisory discretion is placed under undue pressure.

As outlined in section 2.1, flexible and nuanced supervision is regarded as central to the achievement of outcomes under the crisis-era rulebook. This is particularly the case with respect to the proactive, risk-based model being promoted under the Basel III/CRD IV

---

[331] n 277, 29–31.

prudential regime,[332] but it is also the case for financial market regulation more generally. NCAs can also be expected to resist incursions into supervisory discretion, particularly as supervision is now the only significant lever which NCAs may pull to protect their markets.[333] In the immediate wake of the crisis, the EU's largest supervisors focused closely on supervision. The French AMF's 2008 policy on Better Regulation, for example, highlighted the AMF's new focus on risk evaluation methodologies, new surveillance tools, more specialized personnel, and an internal management reorganization.[334] Similarly, the 2008 Annual Report by the Italian CONSOB highlighted its launching of a strategic planning process to define supervisory policies.[335] The Dutch AFM's efforts included a heightened focus on audits and a 2010 report which called for a fundamental change to how audits were conducted.[336] In the UK, the (then) Financial Services Authority (FSA) focused sharply on operational matters in the immediate wake of the crisis. It initially followed a 'Supervisory Enhancement Programme' over 2008–9, which led to a new 'Intensive Supervision' model being pursued by the new Financial Conduct Authority and Prudential Regulation Authority.

XI.5.9.2 Mitigating Factors: the Fiscal Check and the Institutional Environment

There are, however, mitigating factors which are likely to constrain the extent to which ESMA acquires additional supervisory powers and to which NCA discretion risks being unduly limited. As discussed in section 5.8, the Treaty restricts the extent to which supervisory powers can be conferred on ESMA.

Another major restraining factor is the asymmetry between supervisory power and fiscal responsibility which characterizes ESMA's engagement in operational supervision. The imperative to shield national tax-payers from the fiscal responsibility for supervisory decisions taken by ESMA (and the other ESAs) was a red-line issue in the Council over the ESA negotiations and has had a decisive influence on ESMA's supervisory powers. The clearest expression of the fiscal constraint is in the Article 38 fiscal check procedure which applies to 2010 ESMA Regulation Article 18 (emergency) and 19 (binding mediation) decisions.

In the case of Article 19,[337] where a Member State considers that an Article 19 binding mediation decision 'impinges on its fiscal responsibilities', the decision is suspended on notification (within two weeks of ESMA's notification of the Article 19 decision to the NCA) by the Member State of ESMA and the Commission that the decision will not be implemented by the NCA; the Member State must clearly and specifically explain why and how the decision impinges on its fiscal responsibilities. ESMA must, within one month of the Member State notification, inform the Member State as to whether it maintains its decision or whether it amends or revokes it; where the decision is maintained or amended,

---

[332] Everson, M, A Technology of Expertise: EU Financial Services Agencies (2012), LEQS WP No 49/2012.

[333] Then FSA Chief Executive Sants warned of potential pressure to harmonize how supervision is carried out, and of the risk that supervisory discretion would be removed: Sants, H, Speech on 'Update on the Regulatory Reform Programme & European Issues', Cityweek Conference, 7 February 2012.

[334] AMF, Better Regulation: Initial Assessment and 2008/2009 Work Agenda (2008) 16.

[335] CONSOB, Annual Report (2008) 15–16.

[336] AFM, Report on General Findings Regarding Audit Quality and Quality Control Monitoring (2010).

[337] Which is governed by the Art 38(2) procedure.

ESMA must state that fiscal responsibilities are not affected. Where ESMA maintains the decision, the Council may, by a simple rather than the more usual qualified majority, and within two months of ESMA's review of the decision, decide whether the ESMA decision is to be maintained and may terminate it. A similar regime, albeit with calibrations reflecting the sensitivity of the Article 18 procedure, applies to Article 18 'emergency' decisions (Article 38(3) and (4)).[338]

The availability of this get-out clause was contested over the ESA negotiations and the ESMA Regulation underlines its exceptional nature.[339] Nonetheless, its availability underscores the political restrictions on ESMA's exercise of supervisory power without fiscal responsibility.

The fiscal constraint has also shaped ESMA's other operational powers. While the conferral on ESMA of direct operational supervisory powers over rating agencies represents a radical change to the organization of EU supervision, it poses only limited direct fiscal risks to the Member States, given that a failure of a rating agency would not represent a material threat to systemic stability, and thus supervisory decisions (and related failures) by ESMA are unlikely to lead to fiscal consequences in the Member States.[340] By contrast, ESMA's more contested powers of intervention under the 2012 Short Selling Regulation do not apply to sovereign debt or sovereign CDS transactions, given the potential liquidity implications for sovereign debt and prejudicial effects on Member States' ability to raise funding. Similarly, under the 2012 EMIR, while the cross-border impact of a potential CCP failure is reflected in the central role given to the CCP college of supervisors, the NCA of the Member State of authorization can only be vetoed in highly exceptional circumstances, reflecting the location of fiscal responsibility at national level. The location of CCP authorization and supervision at national level and the location of trade repository authorization and supervision at ESMA level also underline the relative difference in the fiscal risks posed in each case.

More generally, the complex institutional and political environment within which ESMA operates acts as a restraining factor. In some respects, the direction of travel is striking. The 2011 CRA Regulation II operational template for direct supervision was deployed with respect to trade repositories under the 2012 EMIR. ESMA's intervention powers under the 2012 Short Selling Regulation have been followed by product intervention and position

---

[338] Member State notification of the Commission and ESMA must take place within three working days and where the Council decides to retain the decision, a further route opens to remove the decision. The Member State may notify the Commission and ESMA and request the Council to re-examine the decision (and must clearly set out the reasons for its disagreement). The Council must either confirm its original decision or take a new decision within four weeks (which may be extended by an additional four weeks where the particular circumstances of the case so require): Art 18(3) and (4).

[339] Any abuse of Art 38, in particular in relation to a decision which does not have a significant or material fiscal impact, is to be prohibited as incompatible with the internal market (Art 38(5)). Similarly, rec 50 states that Art 38 should not be used where the contested decision leads to a reduction of income, following the temporary prohibition of products or activities for consumer protection purposes. From the outset, the Commission was concerned that the check might be abused: 2009 ESA Proposals Impact Assessment, n 47, 29.

[340] Fiscal checks are, however, imposed, in that where ESMA decides to suspend a rating, the rating can be used for ten days after the ESMA decision; where another rating is not available, a three-month use period applies and this period may be extended by three months in exceptional circumstances related to the potential for market disruption or financial instability.

management powers under the 2014 MiFID II/MiFIR. Nonetheless, ESMA's acquisition of supervisory powers is likely to continue to be incremental and to reflect the particular institutional, political, and market interests at stake in each case. Notably, despite early reports suggesting that ESMA would be the supervisor, the September 2013 Proposal on Benchmarks[341] allocated supervisory control in this new area to NCAs, with ESMA playing a co-ordinating role.

The Commission is the location of executive power in the EU and has incentives to limit ESMA's reach in this regard, particularly as increasing supervisory influence may strengthen ESMA's capacity more generally, including with respect to quasi-rule-making. New powers are likely to be the outcome of compromises between a sceptical Commission, a pro-centralization European Parliament (which—in part emboldened by the 2014 *Short Selling* ruling—called, over the ESFS Review, for the ESAs to be conferred with direct supervisory powers over 'highly-integrated pan European entities or activities'),[342] and a generally wary Council. The UK was the only Member State to challenge the vires of the 2012 Short Selling Regulation,[343] however, suggesting a supportive consensus in the Council concerning ESMA's acquisition of operational supervisory powers. The Treaty restrictions remain significant, however, notwithstanding the facilitative 2014 *Short Selling* ruling.

XI.5.10 The ESFS Review and ESMA

As required under the 2010 ESA Regulations, an early review of the ESFS, including a review of the ESAs, was launched in 2013 with the Commission's ESFS Review Consultation.[344]

ESMA's supervisory (rather than quasi-rule-making) powers proved to be the major concern of stakeholders, with widespread support expressed for ESMA to focus more closely on its supervisory activities (particularly with respect to the support of supervisory convergence under the now massive rulebook and the development of a 'Single Supervisory Handbook', including related peer review) and for ESMA's supervisory activities to assume the same relative importance as ESMA's rulebook activities.[345] Stakeholders did not, for the most part, raise concerns in relation to the contested 2010 ESMA Regulation Article 17–19 intervention powers and ESMA's other direct supervisory powers,[346] although the Review underlined strong support for day-to-day supervision to remain at NCA level.[347] Support

---

[341] COM (2013) 641.

[342] 2014 European Parliament ESFS Resolution, n 329, Annex.

[343] The UK's action was described as demonstrating 'how hopelessly outside the process Britain is': Shaikh, F and Jones, H, 'Britain Files Suit Against EU over Short Selling Rules', 1 June 2012, Reuters, available at <http://uk.reuters.com>.

[344] Commission, Consultation on the Review of the ESFS (2013) and Background Document (2013). The extensive responses to the Commission Consultation are available at <http://ec.europa.eu/internal_market/consultations/2013/esfs/index_en.htm>.

On the review, see further Ch X sect 5.10.

[345] eg responses by trade associations AFME (Association for Financial Markets in Europe), EFAMA (European Fund and Asset Management Association), and ABI (Associations of British Insurers), and by Finance Watch and Deutsche Bank. The regulatory community was also supportive of this development: eg, response by Dutch Ministry of Finance.

[346] Although concerns were expressed as to the potential prejudicial impact on market liquidity of its short selling powers: 2013 IMF ESMA Report, n 267.

[347] eg response by ABI and Barclays.

for the conferral of additional direct powers on ESMA was limited (although not absent); some support was expressed for ESMA to acquire powers in relation to prospectuses and market abuse surveillance.[348] The Review saw some support for radical reform in the shape of institutional reorganization of the ESFS, notably in the form of some enthusiasm for a specialized EU consumer protection agency,[349] but this was generally a minority view. The 2013 Mazars Report reflected stakeholder opinion generally by reporting that ESMA's supervisory consistency work had had less impact than its regulatory activities; the Report highlighted in particular limited or no use of ESMA's peer review, mediation, and breach of EU law powers.[350]

Similarly, while the European Parliament found that the ESFS generally had enhanced the quality and consistency of supervision, it called for a number of enhancements. These included a strengthening of peer review, a clarification of the scope of binding mediation and confirmation of its application to the exercise of supervisory discretion, the development of ESA 'Single Supervisory Handbooks' (EBA is in the vanguard of this development—see section 7) and, overall, the establishment of a distinct and EU-facing 'ESA approach' and the taking of ESA action in the interests of the EU as a whole (including by means of a recasting of ESA Management Boards to include three independent members, appointed by the European Parliament, to serve the EU interest and with voting rights on the Board of Supervisors).[351]

In parallel with the ESFS Review, the IMF engaged in a close assessment of ESMA which focused primarily on supervision, in relation to which its assessment was mixed.[352] While the IMF hailed ESMA's achievements with respect to rating agency supervision, it called for a strengthening of its peer review activities (underlining the limitations of the exceptional Articles 17 and 19 breach of EU law and binding mediation powers) and of its ability to engage in risk identification and crisis management (particularly with respect to compelling data from NCAs).[353] In a related recommendation, the IMF also called for governance changes to the Board of Supervisors which, by injecting a stronger element of independence into the Board, would make it easier for ESMA to support supervisory convergence, including through 'strong follow up' of peer review.[354]

ESMA's self-assessment reflected the major themes of the Review. It acknowledged, for example, the (necessary) priority it had given to its rulebook activities and the need for ESMA to intensify its supervisory convergence activities. But it also noted the difficulties which its current governance model poses where it becomes necessary to judge the supervisory practices of a Board of Supervisors member, and suggested that its organization and governance be reviewed with respect to its effectiveness in relation to supervisory

---

[348] eg response by trade association Assonime (Italian listed companies). There was also support for such a conferral of power from the public and regulatory sector: eg response by Dutch Ministry of Finance.

[349] eg responses by Assonime, BEUC (the leading EU consumer advocate), and the Finnish Ministry of Finance.

[350] 2013 Mazars ESA Review, n 199, 89, although the Report related this to a 'structural inhibition' and not 'excessive caution'.

[351] 2014 European Parliament ESFS Resolution, n 329 (based on ECON Committee, Giegold Report with Recommendations to the Commission on the ESFS Review, February 2014 (A7-0133/2014)).

[352] 2013 IMF ESMA Report, n 267.

[353] 2013 IMF ESMA Report, n 267, 4 and 23–6.

[354] 2013 IMF ESMA Report, n 267, 10.

convergence.[355] Its formal recommendations, however, were limited to ESMA being provided with a stronger legislative mandate and adequate resources to strengthen its ability to collect and exchange data from and with NCAs.[356]

It remains to be seen whether major changes will be made to ESMA's supervisory powers. ESMA has not shown any public enthusiasm for becoming more closely involved in the direct execution of day-to-day supervisory tasks, and the related risks to its capacity could be significant, not least given resource, reputational, and political risks. The extent of stakeholder support for an intensification in supervisory convergence activities, combined with the limited political, institutional, and Treaty risks of these activities, makes it most likely that any reforms will be directed to reinforcing ESMA's 'supervisor of supervisors' role, as well as its ability to drive best practices and to implement a robust peer review process.

XI.6 The ESFS: the ESRB

XI.6.1 The ESRB

In order to reflect the interconnection between micro and macroprudential risk, the ESFS combines micro and macroprudential oversight elements. Although the ESAs are conferred with supervisory powers with respect to systemic risk, the ESRB[357] is the primary EU location for macroprudential oversight of the EU financial system,[358] albeit in co-operation with the ESAs and NCAs. Although responsible for the macroprudential oversight of the EU financial system generally, it is primarily associated with the banking sector and with the identification of related systemic risks which may threaten financial stability. But the cross-sectoral nature of financial system risk makes the ESRB a key element of the supervisory structure for financial markets.

The strengthening of institutional capacity with respect to oversight of overall financial stability through macroprudential oversight was an early theme of the crisis-era reform programme internationally,[359] and was reflected in the strengthening of the FSB and in the early US and UK proposals for what would become the Financial Stability Oversight Board and the Financial Stability Committee, respectively. In the EU, a lack of capacity with respect to overall system oversight and macroprudential review was identified as a major weakness at an early stage of the crisis reform programme.[360] The establishment of

---

[355] ESMA Chairman Maijoor, Public Hearing on Financial Supervision in the EU, 24 May 2013 (ESMA/2013/603).

[356] ESMA, Review of the European System on European Financial Supervision, Letter from Chairman Maijoor to Commissioner Barnier, 31 October 2013 (ESMA/2013/1561).

[357] Regulation (EU) No 1092/2010 [2010] OJ L331/1 (Commission Proposal COM (2009) 499; Impact Assessment SEC (2009) 1234). Council Regulation (EU) No 1096/2010 [2010] OJ L331/162 empowers the ECB to provide support to the ESRB, primarily through the ESRB Secretariat. This section discusses the ESRB in outline only. See further Alexander and Ferran, n 69, and Recine and Teixeira, n 68.

[358] It describes itself as the macroprudential pillar of the ESFS, and the NCAs and the ESAs as the microprudential pillar: ESRB, Annual Report (2012) 43.

[359] eg Pan, n 28 and Ferrarini and Chiodini, n 104, on the different approaches being taken to systemic risk regulation.

[360] The Commission's 2009 European Financial Supervision Communication highlighted that macroprudential analysis was fragmented, executed by different authorities at different levels, and without mechanisms for

a permanent institutional capacity with respect to macroprudential risk was a key element of the 2009 DLG Report's institutional reform prescription.[361] Although other institutional formats were available, notably the ECB,[362] agreement on the need for macroprudential oversight through a new institution held over the ESRB negotiations, which took place in tandem with the ESA negotiations. Most controversy attended the governance of the ESRB. While the ESRB was designed to operate impartially and to draw its legitimacy, as a non-binding body, from its expert capacity, the sensitivity of its warnings and recommendations led to close focus on its composition and, in particular, on the influence exerted by the ECB.[363]

The ESRB, which forms part of the ESFS (2010 ESRB Regulation Article 1), is responsible for the macroprudential oversight of the financial system within the EU,[364] in order to contribute to the prevention or mitigation of systemic risks to the financial stability of the EU that arise from developments within the financial system, and taking into account macroeconomic developments, so as to avoid periods of widespread financial distress; the ESRB is also to contribute to the smooth functioning of the internal market and thereby to ensure a sustainable contribution of the financial sector to economic growth (Article 1(1)). The pivotal systemic risk concept is defined as a risk of disruption in the financial system with the potential to have serious negative consequences for the internal market and the real economy; all types of financial intermediaries, markets, and infrastructure are deemed to be potentially systemically important to some degree (Article 2(c)).

In support of its objectives, the ESRB is charged with a series of tasks related to identifying, monitoring, and providing warnings and recommendations with respect to systemic risk (Article 3(2)). The ESRB is to determine and/or collect and analyse all relevant and necessary information; identify and prioritize systemic risks; issue warnings where systemic risks are deemed to be significant and, where appropriate, make them public; issue recommendations for remedial action and, where appropriate, make them public; issue confidential warnings to the Council where it deems an 'emergency situation' may arise under ESMA (ESA) Regulation Article 18; monitor the follow-up to its warnings and recommendations; co-operate closely with all other ESFS entities and develop, in collaboration with the ESAs, a 'risk dashboard', based on common qualitative and quantitative indicators, to identify and measure systemic risk; participate where appropriate in the ESA

---

translating warnings into pan-EU action. The establishment of the ESRB was necessary 'to address one of the fundamental weaknesses highlighted by the crisis': n 115, 3 and 4.

[361] 2009 DLG Report, n 104, 44–6.

[362] On the conflict of interest (between its stability and monetary functions) which the conferral of macroprudential oversight powers on the ECB, otherwise the primary location of financial stability expertise in the EU, could have generated, see Bin Smaghi, L, Going Forward: Regulation and Supervision after the Financial Turmoil, Paolo Baffi Centre Research Paper No 2009-47 (2009), available at <http://ssrn.com/abstract=1424345>. See also n 363.

[363] The scale of the ECB's influence over the ESRB, in particular, was contested. The 2009 DLG Report (n 104, 44) and Germany (Benoit, B and Tait, N, 'Berlin to Back EU Financial Regulation Plan', *Financial Times*, 4 June 2009, 9) supported the location of the ESRB within the ECB. The ECB also claimed the macroprudential oversight role as being related to its financial stability mandate (Tait, N and Hughes, J, 'Trichet Calls for Supervision of All Institutions', *Financial Times*, 24 February 2009). But political sensitivities, as well as legal complexities related to the independence of the ECB, led to a more arm's-length model being adopted.

[364] Defined as all financial institutions, markets, products, and market infrastructures: Art 2(b).

Joint Committee; co-ordinate its actions with other international financial institutions, in particular the IMF and FSB, on matters related to macroprudential oversight; and carry out other tasks as specified in EU legislation.

The ESRB is an advisory body and does not engage in ESMA's (and the other ESAs') array of supervisory and quasi-rule-making activities. Nonetheless, the ESRB is designed to have real influence and to shape fiscal, regulatory, and supervisory decision-making. Accordingly, its governance structure reflects not only the need to ensure sufficient expert intelligence, but also the representation and accountability concerns which have shaped ESMA's and the other ESAs' governance.

The ESRB is formed of a number of entities: a General Board; a Steering Committee; a Secretariat; an Advisory Scientific Committee; and an Advisory Technical Committee (Article 4). The unwieldy General Board is the decision-making body (Article 4(2));[365] it fuses intergovernmental and supranational elements, but also reflects the need to draw on NCAs and central banks. It is composed of 65 members, 37 of which have voting rights:[366] the President and Vice President of the ECB; the Governors of the national central banks;[367] a Commission member;[368] the Chairpersons of the ESAs; and the Chair and vice Chairs of the Advisory Scientific and Technical Committees (Article 6(1)). One 'high-level representative for each Member State of the competent national authorities'[369] and the President of the EFC[370] also sit on the ESRB, but as non-voting members (Article 6(2)),[371] creating an institutional bias in favour of central banks, although this bias is counterbalanced somewhat (although not at the decision-making level) by the supervisory representation on the ESRB's Advisory Technical Committee. While the General Board is an unwieldy actor, the wide reach of the ESRB's remit and the sensitivity of its mandate made it always unlikely that a smaller and less representative body would have been deployed.[372] The General Board operates on a 'one member one vote' principle and by simple majority (the ESRB Chair exercises the casting vote), reflecting the concern to promote impartial decision-making, not shaped by national or bloc interests;[373] a two-thirds majority of votes cast is required to adopt an ESRB recommendation or to make a recommendation public

---

[365] It must meet at least four times a year. Extraordinary meetings may be convened at the initiative of the ESRB Chair or at the request of one third of General Board members with voting rights: Art 9(1). Proceedings are confidential (Art 9(6)).

[366] ESRB, Annual Report (2011) 14.

[367] Reflecting the key role of central banks in the maintenance of monetary and financial stability and their lender of last resort functions: 2009 European Financial Supervision Communication, n 115, 6.

[368] In order to establish a link with the macroeconomic and financial surveillance of the EU: 2010 ESRB Regulation rec 25.

[369] The representatives in question rotate depending on the item under discussion, unless the authorities agree on a common representative: Art 6(3).

[370] EFC representation was adopted in preference to direct political representation (given independence risks) and in order to ensure there was sufficient discussion of the potential of budgetary or taxation policies to generate systemic risks: 2009 European Financial Supervision Communication, n 115 and 2010 ESRB Regulation rec 25.

[371] High-level representatives from international financial organizations carrying out activities directly related to the tasks of the ESRB may be invited to attend meetings: Art 6(4). More generally, the ESRB's work may be open to high-level representatives of third countries (in particular of EEA members), although strictly limited to issues of particular relevance to those countries: Art 6(5).

[372] Alexander and Ferran have compared the Board's composition with that of the similarly large FSB, and drawn positive conclusions as to its likely effectiveness: n 69.

[373] 2010 ESRB Regulation rec 26.

(Article 10).[374] The General Board (and the Steering Committee) is chaired by the ESRB Chair, who also represents the ESRB externally (Article 5). The position of ESRB Chair proved highly contentious, given concerns as to the potential dominance of the ECB;[375] the compromise adopted was based on the ECB President acting as Chair for the first five years, with the 2013 review of the ESRB to reconsider the appointment process (Article 5(1)). The ESRB also has two Vice Chairs, who deputize for the Chair: the First Vice Chair is elected by and from the ECB General Council (for five years), with regard to the need for a balanced representation of Member States overall and between euro-area and non-euro-area Member States; the Second Vice Chair is the Chair of the ESA Joint Committee (Article 5(2) and (3)).[376]

The General Board is supported by a Steering Committee which is tasked with assisting the decision-making process of the ESRB;[377] in practice, given the size of the General Board, the Committee is the location of significant influence within the ESRB[378] and is better equipped to act nimbly in crisis conditions. It is composed of the ESRB Chair and First Vice Chair; the ECB Vice President; four members of the ESRB General Board who are also members of the ECB General Council,[379] with regard to the need for a balanced representation between euro-area and non-euro-area Member States;[380] a Commission member; the ESA Chairpersons; the EFC President; and the Chairs of the Advisory Technical and Scientific Committees (Article 11).

The ESRB's administrative capacity is provided by the ESRB Secretariat (Article 4(4)); in practice, the Secretariat is drawn from the ECB, although procedural devices are deployed to ensure this does not threaten the ECB's Treaty-based independence guarantee. Expert technical advice and market/supervisory intelligence is provided by the Advisory Technical Committee, which is primarily composed of representatives of supervisory authorities (Article 11),[381] and by the Advisory Scientific Committee,[382] which is primarily composed of appointed experts (Article 12).[383]

---

[374] A quorum of two thirds of members with voting rights is required: Art 10(4).

[375] The 2009 DLG Report and the 2009 ESRB Proposal proposed that the ECB President permanently chair the ESRB *ex officio*, leading to concern as to non-euro area representation, particularly in the UK: Myners, P, 'Brussels' Plan for Financial Reform Needs Work', *Financial Times*, 9 June 2009, 17.

[376] Currently the ESMA Chair.

[377] By preparing General Board meetings, reviewing the documents to be discussed, and monitoring the progress of the ESRB's ongoing work. The Steering Committee meets at least quarterly, before each meeting of the General Board (Arts 4(4) and 11(2)).

[378] As has been acknowledged by the ESRB: ESRB, Annual Report (2012) 44.

[379] The ECB General Council is composed of the central bank governors of the EU Member States and the ECB President and Vice-Presidents.

[380] These members are elected by and from among the members of the General Board, who are also members of the ECB General Council, for a period of three years.

[381] The Committee is composed of: a representative of each national central bank and of the ECB; one representative per Member State of the competent national supervisory authority (which rotates depending on the issues discussed, unless the authorities agree on a common representative); a representative of the ESAs; two Commission representatives; an EFC representative; and a representative of the Advisory Scientific Committee. The Chair is appointed by the General Board.

[382] The Scientific Committee may also organize consultations with stakeholders: Art 12(5).

[383] The Committee is composed of 15 experts, 'representing a wide range of skills and experience'. The experts are proposed by the Steering Committee and appointed by the General Board for a four-year (renewable) mandate. Nominees must not be members of the ESAs and must be appointed on the basis of their general competence and diverse experience in academic fields or other sectors, in particular in SMEs or

Unlike the ESAs, the ESRB is not formally independent. Impartiality requirements apply, however. The members of the ESRB are subject to an impartiality requirement and must perform their duties impartially and solely in the interests of the EU as a whole, and must not seek or take instructions from the Member States, the EU institutions, or any public or private body.[384] Additionally, no member of the General Board (whether voting or non-voting) can have a function in the financial industry (Article 7(2)). The ESRB's formal accountability framework requires it to report annually to the European Parliament and to the Council, and for the ESRB Chair to be invited, at least annually, to a hearing of the European Parliament (Article 19(1)); the Parliament may also request the ESRB Chair to attend hearings of the competent Parliament committees and confidential discussions are provided for between the ESRB Chair and the Chair and Vice Chairs of the Parliament's ECON committee (Article 19(4) and (5)).

XI.6.2 ESRB Functions, Warnings, and Recommendations

The ESRB has two main tasks: it is charged with collecting and analysing information (2010 ESRB Regulation Article 15) and with providing warnings and recommendations (Articles 16–18).

A series of information collection and exchange obligations apply to buttress the ESRB's effectiveness. The ESRB must provide the ESAs with the information on risks necessary to achieve their tasks, while the ESAs, the ESCB, the Commission, national supervisory authorities, and national statistical authorities must co-operate closely with the ESRB and provide it with all information necessary for it to fulfil its tasks. The ESRB is expressly empowered to request (as a non-binding body, it cannot compel) information from the ESAs[385] and to request information from other entities[386] where its requests are not met. The 2010 ESMA Regulation[387] bolsters this information exchange regime, imposing a legally binding obligation that ESMA co-operate closely and on a regular basis with the ESRB and provide it with the information necessary for the achievement of its tasks (ESMA Regulation Article 36(1) and (2)).

Central to the ESRB's effectiveness as monitor of macroprudential risk is its power to issue warnings and recommendations (Articles 16–19) to the Member States, national supervisors, and EU bodies; the power does not apply in relation to individual financial institutions as it is directed towards regulatory and supervisory intervention.[388] Where

---

trade unions, or as providers or consumers of financial services. The Chair and two Vice Chairs of the Committee are appointed by the General Board following a proposal from the ESRB Chair.

[384] Art 7(1). Conversely, neither the Member States, the EU institutions, nor any other public or private body should seek to influence ESRB members in the performance of their tasks: Art 7(3).

[385] As a rule in summary or aggregate form, such that individual financial institutions cannot be identified. The ESRB must also consult with the relevant ESA to ensure that the request is justified and proportionate. Where the ESA does not consider the request so justified or proportionate, it must ask for additional information from the ESRB, following which the information must be provided, as long as the ESA has legal access to the information.

[386] The ESCB, national supervisory authorities, national statistical authorities, or, failing which, the Member States concerned.

[387] The same regime applies to the other ESAs under their founding Regulations.

[388] 2009 ESRB Proposal Impact Assessment, n 357, 42.

significant risks to the achievement of its objectives are identified, the ESRB must provide warnings and, where appropriate, issue recommendations for remedial action which include, where appropriate, recommendations for legislative initiatives (Article 16(1)). Warnings and recommendations (which must include a specified timeline for the policy response) may be of a general or specific nature, and must be addressed to: the EU as a whole or to one or more of its Member States; to one or more of the ESAs; or to one of more of the national supervisory authorities (Article 16(2)).[389] Recommendations may also be addressed to the Commission in respect to the relevant EU legislation (Article 16(2)). Warnings and recommendations to any addressee must be also transmitted to the Council and Commission and, where the addressee is a national supervisory authority, to the ESAs. Warnings and recommendations are colour-coded in accordance with the 'risk dashboard' which the ESRB, in collaboration with the ESAs, was required to develop (Article 16(3)).

ESRB warnings and recommendations are soft law and not enforceable. But they are the subject of mechanisms designed to 'harden' their impact. Time limits apply to the relevant policy response (Article 16(2)). A 'comply or explain' mechanism applies in that where the addressee is the Commission, one or more Member States, or one or more of the ESAs, the addressee must communicate to the ESRB and to the Council the actions undertaken in response, and adequate justification for any inaction (Article 17(1)). Where the ESRB decides that a recommendation has not been followed, or that inadequate justification has been provided, it must inform the addressees and, in order to increase the 'moral pressure' on the addressee,[390] inform the Council and, where relevant, the ESAs (Article 17(2)). This regime is bolstered by the 2010 ESMA Regulation which provides generally that ESMA is to respond to ESRB warnings and recommendations and to 'ensure a proper follow up' to ESRB warnings and recommendations (ESMA Regulation Article 22(1) and Article 36(3)). ESMA is also required to assess the implications of any warning or recommendation addressed to it, to decide on the action to be taken, and to inform the ESRB and Council of its reasons where it decides not to act (2010 ESMA Regulation Article 36(4)). Where the warning or recommendation is addressed to an NCA, ESMA must use its powers to 'ensure a timely follow-up'; where the NCA does not intend to follow the recommendation, it must inform the Board of Supervisors and discuss with it its reasons for not acting, and take the Board's views into account when reporting to the ESRB (ESMA Regulation Article 36(5)). The ESRB is also empowered to make its warnings and recommendations public (on a case-by-case basis), having informed the Council sufficiently in advance so that it can react; addressees must also be informed in advance (Article 18(1) and (2)). In addition, where a warning or recommendation is made public, and the addressee does not act or gives an inadequate reason for its inaction, the European Parliament may invite the ESRB Chair to present the decision and the addressees may request to participate in an exchange of views (Article 17(4)).[391]

---

[389] In the latter case, the Member State must also be informed.
[390] 2009 ESRB Proposal, n 357, 6.
[391] The ESRB has described the quasi-monitoring role of the Parliament as an important one in strengthening its warnings and recommendations: ESRB, Annual Report (2011) 12.

XI.6.3 Financial Markets, ESMA, and the ESRB

By contrast with the ESAs, the ESRB is a soft law body and does not have separate legal personality.[392] The Treaty difficulties associated with conferring binding decision-making powers on the ESAs similarly prevented the ESRB from being conferred with binding powers. Additional difficulties were generated by the ECB's independence guarantee and associated problems, particularly were it to be required to provide services to another actor (the ESRB) with separate legal personality;[393] the ECB was also reportedly hostile to the establishment of a separate legal entity whose powers would overlap with its financial stability functions.[394] Above all, the political sensitivities associated with the management of systemic risk, particularly given the fiscal and economic consequences (were the ESRB to pronounce on, for example, the credit supply or excessive deficits),[395] and the inevitably uncertain quality of *ex-ante* warnings and recommendations, militated against the ESRB having separate legal personality and binding powers.[396]

The capacity of the ESRB is designed to flow from its reputation and credibility.[397] It is designed as a 'reputational body' which influences policymakers and supervisors through its 'moral authority', given the quality and range of its constituent members.[398] A number of devices have been employed to bolster its credibility, including the 'comply or explain' mechanism and related obligations;[399] the range and depth of the expertise represented on the ESRB; the efforts to ensure its independence from political and market actors; the transparency of much of its work; and the possibility for its warnings and recommendations to be made public.[400]

The ESRB's mission is, accordingly, a challenging one.[401] It must deliver *ex-ante* warnings, often in conditions of considerable uncertainty, which may be institutionally and politically unpalatable, and avoid triggering subsequent adverse financial market reaction. It must ensure that its warnings and recommendations are effective, but must rely heavily on its credibility to do so;[402] as a new body, its credibility had to be constructed *ab initio* and

---

[392] The 2010 ESRB Regulation simply states that the ESRB is established (Art 1(1)). The ESRB describes itself in more robust terms as an 'independent EU body': ESRB, Annual Report (2011) 10.

[393] Alexander and Ferran, n 69.

[394] Lannoo, K, The Road Ahead after de Larosière, CEPS Policy Brief No 197/7 (2009).

[395] The 2009 DLG Report highlighted excessive credit expansion and fiscal difficulties, such as excessive deficits or the accumulation of debt, as risks which the new body would be expected to highlight: n 104, 45.

[396] The 2009 ESRB Proposal argued that 'given the wide scope and sensitivity of its mission' the new body should not be conferred with legal personality or binding powers: n 357, 4.

[397] The Commission argued that the ESRB was designed 'as a body drawing its legitimacy from its reputation for independent judgments, high quality analysis, and sharpness in its conclusions': n 357, 4.

[398] 2009 ESRB Proposal, n 357, 5.

[399] Which the ESRB has described as supporting flexibility and proportionality: ESRB, Annual Report (2012) 47–8.

[400] The Commission warned that the ESRB could not be 'entirely silent' as its image among market participants and the general public could be undermined: 2009 ESRB Proposal Impact Assessment, n 357, 39.

[401] An early IMF Report on its operation underlined the difficulties and warned against the ESRB being overly cautious: n 155, 15–16.

[402] For a sceptical view of the ESRB's likely effectiveness as a soft law body see Hertig, G, Lee, R, and McCahery, J, 'Empowering the ECB to Supervise Banks: A Choice-Based Approach' (2010) 7 *ECFR* 171, and, for a more positive assessment, based on the experience of the international financial law system with soft law measures, Alexander and Ferran, n 69.

without triggering unhelpful institutional tensions across the ESFS, with the ECB, and with the Member States. The nature of macroprudential risk and the optimal tools for its measurement was, certainly as the ESRB commenced its activities, still somewhat elusive,[403] although the broad definition which underpins the ESRB's objectives allowed it the freedom and flexibility to range widely. Governance difficulties existed from the outset, given the size of the General Board and its difficulties in acting nimbly.[404] There was also a risk that the ESRB would initially over-react in an attempt to build its reputational capital; alternatively, the risks to its capacity were it to be ignored might have led it to take an overly timid approach.

In practice, the ESRB appears to have steered a careful course. Its initial activities focused on institution-building and developing the Risk Dashboard;[405] with respect to systemic risk oversight, it for the most part focused on the resilience of the banking system and of the EU financial system generally in light of strains in the sovereign debt market.[406] By the end of the first quarter of 2014, the ESRB had issued six public recommendations, all but one of which focused primarily on the banking system and on macroprudential oversight generally.[407] The addressees were primarily the national supervisory authorities, although EBA, the Commission, and the Member States were recommended to take specified actions. The first set of public recommendations suggested a strong institutional commitment from the ESRB to promoting compliance. All recommendations were accompanied by detailed timelines and the arrangements for reporting and monitoring, but the initial set of recommendations were also more concerned with improving monitoring and reporting than with interventionist action.

---

[403] eg Schwarcz, S, 'Systemic Risk' (2008) 97 *Georgetown LJ* 193 and Bin Smaghi, n 362. For an early assessment see IMF, BIS and FSB, Guidance to Assess the Systemic Importance of Financial Institutions, Markets and Instruments: Initial Considerations—Background Paper. Report to the G20 Finance Ministers and Central Bank Governors (2009).

[404] The IMF raised concerns at an early stage as to the cumbersome institutional structure and the related risk that ESRB activity could be overly cautious and slow: n 155, 15–16.

[405] The Risk Dashboard sets out a series of over 50 indicators used to assess systemic risk and with respect to macro risk, credit risk, funding and liquidity, market risk, and profitability and solvency. The Dashboard also includes a number of composite measures of systemic risk, based on, eg, the likelihood of two major banking groups defaulting simultaneously, sovereign CDS spreads, degree of cross-border banking activity, and the average contribution of individual institutions to overall systemic risk.

[406] ESRB, Annual Report (2011) 19–22.

[407] The first recommendation (ESRB/2011/1) addressed lending in foreign currencies following increases in levels of this form of lending; it was addressed to national supervisory authorities and contained a series of recommendations, including with respect to improving the risk awareness of borrowers, monitoring credit growth linked to foreign currency lending, the adoption of risk management guidelines, the appropriate application of capital requirements, and monitoring of liquidity and funding risks. ESRB/2011/3 called for the Member States to establish bodies responsible for macroprudential oversight and addressed the design and governance of these bodies. ESRB/2011/12 addressed US dollar-denominated funding of credit institutions, and recommended that national supervisors monitor the related funding and liquidity risks and ensure contingency funding was in place. ESRB/2012/2 was addressed to EBA and the national supervisory authorities; it concerned the funding position of credit institutions generally and recommended a series of measures related to the assessment and monitoring of funding and of asset encumbrance. ESRB/2013/1 addressed the intermediate objectives and instruments of macroprudential risk and recommended a related 'toolkit', and was addressed to the macroprudential authorities, the Member State, and the Commission.

The financial markets are an integral element of the ESRB's oversight remit.[408] But it has been less active in the financial markets sphere, where its initial activities were more focused on general agenda-setting. Only one public recommendation was directly concerned with financial markets. The ESRB's 2012 recommendation on money-market funds (MMFs) was directed to the Commission, and called for legislative action with respect to the sector. While significantly more intrusive than CESR's earlier 2010 Guidance on Money Market Funds, it did, however, broadly reflect the institutional direction of travel on MMF regulation, in the EU and internationally.[409] More generally with respect to financial markets, the ESRB has largely focused on shaping the related legislative agenda where financial stability risks are engaged,[410] on responding to ESMA consultations where it sees a macroprudential dimension,[411] and on general reviews of stability risks in the financial markets.[412]

While these activities suggest a strengthening institutional capacity in relation to macroprudential oversight of the EU financial market, the ESRB's horizontal scope of activity may lead to difficulties. ESMA and the ESRB have a symbiotic relationship. While ESMA has operational powers and has a specific mandate with respect to systemic risk,[413] it depends on the ESRB for macroprudential intelligence and must follow ESRB warnings and recommendations or provide adequate reasons for inaction. Conversely, the ESRB can direct ESMA to take particular actions through a recommendation, but is dependent on a co-operative relationship with ESMA to embed the impact of its recommendations (including those made to NCAs). It is also dependent on ESMA for market and supervisory intelligence;[414] ESMA's burgeoning systemic risk surveillance activities underline its growing capacity with respect to data collection. A number of co-operation obligations, including the obligation to collaborate on the development of systemic risk measurement tools,[415] consultation

---

[408] Its Risk Dashboard contains a number of indicators of systemic risk related to financial markets, including in relation to sovereign CDS spreads, equity indices, equity price/earnings ratios, exchange rate volatilities, and risk aversion. The ESRB's 2012 Annual Report, eg, identified risks from CCPs, MMFs, and shadow banking-related securities lending and repurchasing activities as structural vulnerabilities within the EU financial system: at 15.

[409] In particular, the ESRB recommended that all MMFs take the form of less risky variable NAV funds; CESR's Guidance (which has been subject to peer review by ESMA) was more facilitative. See further Ch III sect 3.14.1.

[410] Notably with respect to the 2012 EMIR and the treatment of CCPs: ESRB, Annual Report (2011) 26.

[411] eg over 2011–2012, the ESRB engaged with the ESMA consultations on high frequency trading, exchange traded funds, and the EMIR BTS regime.

[412] In particular through its Macro-prudential Commentaries. While these are primarily focused on the credit markets, in 2012 the ESRB reviewed the potential systemic risk arising from the retailization of complex products to retail investors in 2012, and concluded that there was no immediate systemic risk from retailization but that it would be kept under review: ESRB, Macro-prudential Commentaries, Issue No 3, July 2012, Systemic Risk due to Retailization? (Burkart, O and Bouveret, A). The ESRB also uses its Occasional Papers, which do not represent ESRB policy but which are designed to map the risks and potential policy responses in question, to review systemic risk. eg, ESRB Occasional Paper No 2/2013, Towards a Monitoring Framework for Securities Financing Transactions (Bouveret, A, Jardelot, J, Kellor, J, Molitor, P, Theal, J, and Vital, M); and ESRB Occasional Paper No 1/2012, Money Market Funds in European Financial Stability (Ansidei, J, Bengtsson, E, Frison, D and Ward, G).

[413] 2010 ESMA Regulation Arts 22-24. See sect 5.5.3.

[414] In addition to the general Art 15 information exchange obligation which supports the ESRB, the ESRB secretariat can draw on the ESAs for technical advice: Art 4(4).

[415] 2010 ESMA Regulation Art 22(2) and 23.

requirements,[416] and the 'comply or explain' mechanism tie ESMA and the ESRB together,[417] however, as does the cross-membership of ESMA and the ESRB on their respective governance bodies.[418]

Initial indications suggest a co-operative ESRB relationship with ESMA and with the ESAs generally. Joint projects have taken place[419] and information-exchange protocols have been established, and aggregate, as well as the more sensitive firm-specific, information has been transmitted to the ESRB on request.[420] But while ESMA and the ESRB are designed to work in tandem, there is potential for conflict given the institutional territory at stake. Financial stability is new territory for financial market supervisors, and ESMA has shown itself keen to develop this mandate, as is clear from its quasi-rulebook activities with respect to, for example, shadow banking and exchange-traded funds,[421] as well as its extensive market surveillance activities. The financial stability mandate also has the potential to allow ESMA to widen its field of operation, with respect to market surveillance but also with respect to its quasi-rulebook activities.[422] Their different mandates, institutional bases, and operating environments may also lead to a divergence of opinion between ESMA and the ESRB. In particular, ESMA's and the ESRB's risk appetites appear to be somewhat different. Consultations on ESMA's proposed BTSs under the 2012 EMIR regime, for example, saw ESMA on occasion reject the ESRB's position and take a more flexible approach,[423] and ESRB adopt a robust approach in response.[424] Similarly, the ESRB has adopted a more interventionist approach to MMFs, as previously noted. Some degree of institutional tension can, however, be expected and is healthy, particularly given the different institutional mandates of both bodies, as long as it does not lead to entrenched positions. Thus far, however, the relationship appears stable.

---

[416] eg ESMA's obligation to consult with the ESRB before it takes interventionist action with respect to short selling: 2012 Short Selling Regulation Art 28(4).

[417] 2010 ESMA Regulation rec 47 underlines that close co-operation between ESMA and the ESRB is essential to give full effectiveness to the ESRB.

[418] The ESRB is a non-voting member of ESMA's Board of Supervisors. As noted, the ESA Chairs sit on the ESRB General Board and Steering Committee, and ESA representatives sit on the Advisory Technical Committee.

[419] Over 2012, ESMA and the ESRB carried out an in-depth study of the CDS market to understand the extent of interconnectedness and likely contagion channels, reflecting in particular concerns as to the impact of a credit event on Greek sovereign debt: ESRB, Annual Report (2012) 30 and 32–3.

[420] ESRB, Annual Report (2011) 11.

[421] On ESMA and the shadow banking agenda see Ch III sect 3.14.

[422] eg Speech by ESMA Chairman Maijoor on 'Regulation of Systemically Important Financial Institutions and of the Shadow Banking System', 11 March 2013 (ESMA/2013/279), highlighting ESMA's activities with respect to shadow banking. Similarly, in its Written Answers to the 19 September 2012 ECON Hearing of the ESA Chairs, ESMA argued that stricter monitoring of the shadow banking system was needed and that it was well placed to facilitate the transmission and disclosure of information: JC/2012/090, 10.

[423] The ESRB took a stricter approach, eg, to the determination of the thresholds under which non-financial counterparties are exempt from the 2012 EMIR clearing obligation than did ESMA (which was concerned to protect SMEs from excessive cost): ESMA, Final Report. Draft Technical Standards under EMIR (ESMA/2012/600) 17.

[424] It warned, eg, that ESMA's decision not to include derivatives used for commercial and treasury purposes within the clearing threshold for bringing non-financial counterparties within the 2012 EMIR clearing obligation was 'conceptually wrong': ESRB, Annual Report (2012) 39. It also recorded its unhappiness at its advice being rejected: Board of Supervisors Meeting, 24 September 2012 (ESMA/2012/BS/125).

The 2013 ESFS Review evidenced support for the ESRB's role, albeit also some concern that its independence and the nimbleness of its decision-making should be enhanced.[425] The prospects for the ESRB are, however, weakened in light of the ECB's acquisition of direct supervisory powers over euro-area credit institutions under the SSM, and the ECB's related enhanced role in financial stability oversight. The ECB's new supervisory powers, combined with its pre-eminent position with respect to financial stability, may significantly undermine the soft law-based and somewhat cumbersome ESRB, unless the ESRB's unique position with respect to the internal market is protected.

XI.7 Banking Union and Financial Market Supervision

The Banking Union agenda, and the related construction of the SSM, which is based on supervision of euro-area (deposit-taking) credit institutions by the ECB (from November 2014),[426] has seismic implications for the governance of the banking sector.[427] The SSM addresses deposit-taking banks only.[428] All other financial institutions and the shadow banking sector—whatever the implications they pose for the stability of the euro-area financial system—are excluded.[429] In addition, the SSM does not address market-related activities or conduct-related supervision.[430] The spillover effects for financial market supervision may, however, be significant.

---

[425] eg Review of the New European System of Financial Supervision Part 2: The Work of the ESRB. Study for the ECON Committee (2013) (IP/A/ECON/ST 2012-23) (2013) and 2014 European Parliament ESFS Resolution, n 329. The European Parliament supported the ESRB, but made a number of recommendations to enhance its position, streamline its decision-making, and protect its position within the SSM and with respect to the ECB.

[426] See n 2 on the two foundation legislative instruments, the 2013 ECB/SSM Regulation and the 2013 EBA Regulation. Operational supervision is shared between the ECB and banking NCAs, according to the allocation process for banks set out in the 2013 ECB/SSM Regulation, but the ECB remains responsible for the SSM as a whole.

[427] For early discussions see, eg, Ferran, E and Babis, V, 'The European Single Supervisory Mechanism' (2013) 13 *JCLS* 255; Ferrarini, G and Chiarella, L, Common Banking Supervision in the Eurozone: Strengths and Weaknesses, ECGI Law WP No 223/2013, available at <http://ssrn.com/abstract=2309897>; Howarth, D and Quaglia, L, 'Banking Union as Holy Grail: Rebuilding the Single Market in Financial Services, Stabilizing Europe's Banks, and "Completing" Economic and Monetary Union' (2013) 51 *JCMS* 103; Wymeersch, E, The European Banking Union: A First Analysis (2012), Financial Law Institute WP 2012-07, available at <http://ssrn.com/abstract=2171785>; Deutsche Bank, EU Monitor, EU Banking Union. Do it Right, Not Hastily? 23 July 2012; Carmassi, J, di Noia, C, and Micossi, S, Banking Union: A Federal Model for the European Union with Prompt Corrective Action, CEPS Policy Brief No 282, September 2012; Mayer Brown, Towards a European Banking Union—the European Commission Announces a New Legal Framework for Banking Supervision, Legal Update September 2012; and ICFR, European Commission Fires First Salvo in EU Bank Union Battle, ICFR Research, September 2012.

[428] It applies only to euro-area 'credit institutions' as defined under the 2013 CRR (in effect, deposit-taking institutions): 2013 ECB/SSM Regulation Arts 1 and 2(3).

[429] This reflects Art 127(6) TFEU which limits any empowerment of the ECB with respect to prudential supervision to credit institutions (and insurance companies), as well as the prevailing political climate and the overwhelming imperative to break the link between sovereigns and banks which the sovereign debt crisis exposed.

[430] Within a framework which allocates particular banks to the ECB and to NCAs depending, in essence, on the size and risk profile of the bank in question the SSM is responsible for the prudential supervision of euro-area credit institutions and with respect to identified tasks which include: authorization ECB, (for all banks); approval of qualifying holdings ECB, (for all banks); ensuring compliance with prudential requirements relating to own funds, securitization, large exposures, liquidity, leverage, and related reporting

The temptation to compare ESMA with the SSM and to predict a similar trajectory is considerable, in particular given ESMA's distinctive position among the other ESAs as the only ESA empowered to exercise direct supervisory powers, and given the strong momentum which has characterized institutional reforms to EU financial market governance. But, as noted in section 1, the drivers for institutional reform and supervisory organization are distinct in the banking field; there is not a natural progression to an ESMA-based SSM within a 'Financial Market Union'.

There may, however, be some spillover effects—although, in the short term at least, these are unlikely to relate directly to the conferral of additional supervisory powers on ESMA. While ESMA may acquire new supervisory powers, their acquisition is likely to be slow and incremental given the complex institutional and political context and the significant Treaty restraints. In particular, the fiscal constraint is real; while some supervisory activities generate less fiscal risks than others, as is reflected in ESMA's suite of powers, it is unlikely that any significant conferral of powers on ESMA will be politically acceptable. In addition, the ESFS Review has not revealed any significant stakeholder enthusiasm for additional powers to be conferred on ESMA, although there is some support for ESMA to be conferred with additional powers in areas with limited fiscal risks (including with respect to prospectuses and the supervision of the market abuse regime),[431] and the European Parliament's ambitions remain considerable (section 5.9.2). ESMA's relatively insecure funding position, and limited institutional and political support for increasing its resources, further limits its capacity to take on additional supervisory tasks. Intensifying ESMA's direct supervisory powers also increases the likelihood of role conflict. ESMA is currently configured as something of a 'supervisor of supervisors', but the more ESMA engages in direct supervision, the more it faces a conflict between its role as a supervisor of market actors and its role as a 'supervisor of supervisors'. While there is at present a tension between ESMA's direct supervisory powers and its oversight function, this tension is currently sustainable, given the limited reach of ESMA's direct supervisory powers. But it may become unsustainable.

The new supervisory environment for euro-area banks may, however, embolden ESMA to deploy its existing powers more assertively. A powerful ECB euro-area supervisor may well create incentives for ESMA to exert its authority more forcefully, whether through its direct intervention powers or through its 'softer' supervisory convergence powers.

A further consequence may be the reshaping of institutional dynamics within the ESFS in ESMA's favour. The 2013 ECB/SSM Regulation confers operational supervisory powers on the ECB/SSM with respect to credit institutions only, and with respect to identified areas of prudential supervision. The ECB/SSM Regulation takes some care to exclude investment firms and, with respect to their market conduct, financial institutions covered

---

requirements; ensuring compliance with governance-related prudential requirements (including management 'fit and proper' requirements, risk management processes, internal control mechanisms, remuneration requirements, and capital assessment processes); supervisory reviews, including stress testing; and supervisory tasks related to recovery and early intervention (2013 ECB/SSM Regulation Art 4(1)).

The 2013 ECB/SSM Regulation provides, however, for the ECB, where necessary, to enter into MoUs with NCAs 'responsible for markets in financial instruments' (2013 ECB/SSM Regulation Art 3(1)).

[431] eg 2013 IMF ESMA Report, n 267, 30.

within the prudential supervision of a banking group;[432] the current allocation of powers to NCAs over SSM-scope credit institutions in relation to markets in financial instruments does not change under the ECB/SSM Regulation (recital 28). But it is an axiom of the crisis era that risks must be addressed in a cross-sectoral manner, as evidenced by institutional reforms such as the establishment of the Joint Committee of the ESAs and of the ESRB. Careful co-ordination will be needed between NCAs concerned with market conduct and the ECB/SSM with respect to the supervision of multifunction banking groups with significant market operations, whether carried out by group credit institutions or group investment firms.[433] The need for careful co-ordination is all the greater as the borderline between conduct (located with NCAs) and prudential supervision (located with the ECB/SSM) is not always clearly marked.[434] In the investment services field, for example, the 2004 MiFID I generated confusion as to when particular supervisory activities came within the 'conduct' field and so within the competence of the investment firm branch host NCA (under MiFID I Article 32(7)). The need for co-ordination is acknowledged in Article 3(1) of the 2013 ECB/SSM Regulation, which provides for the ECB to enter into MoUs with NCAs 'responsible for markets in financial instruments';[435] notably, the co-ordination obligation does not extend to relations with ESMA. The ECB is, however, under a general obligation to co-operate with the ESAs and the ESRB (Article 3(3)).[436] In this complex environment, it is not unlikely that ESMA's position, particularly as it is a single market rather than a euro-area actor, will be strengthened. ESMA is the natural conduit for co-ordinating NCAs' positions in ECB discussions with respect to the sensitive prudential/conduct interface and for co-ordinating other related dealings with the ECB/SSM. The role required of ESMA may, however, be a very delicate one, given the significant sensitivities at stake in relation to how the prudential/conduct borderline is delineated. But while there are risks to ESMA's position, the need for co-ordination may allow ESMA to strengthen its position in EU financial market governance, and to operate as a counterweight to the ECB institutionally.[437]

In addition, and given the concerns widely voiced over the SSM negotiations as to the implications of the creation of a powerful ECB supervisor, ESMA may come to represent an attractive EU-level counterbalance to the ECB. The institutional difficulties which the ECB supervision model has generated—notably with respect to the challenges its independence model poses with respect to SSM appeals and review processes[438]—may also have

---

[432] See nn 428 and 430. By contrast, earlier drafts of the ECB/SSM Regulation brought within its scope investment firms and financial institutions covered by the consolidated supervision of the parent undertaking (where the parent undertaking fell within the scope of the Regulation).

[433] As ESMA (n 157, para 4.2) and the IMF (n 267, 29) have noted.

[434] In the UK, co-operation between the Financial Conduct Authority (FCA) and the Prudential Regulation Authority (PRA) is governed by a detailed and complex set of legislative and operational requirements, although the PRA ultimately can deploy a veto power over FCA activities in particular circumstances.

[435] Similarly, rec 33 to the 2013 ECB/SSM Regulation calls for MoUs between the ECB and NCAs for markets in financial instruments which describe how these actors will co-operate in their performance of supervisory tasks (these MoUs are to be made available to the European Parliament, the Council, and NCAs).

[436] Rec 31 to the 2013 ECB/SSM Regulation notes the need for co-operation to ensure the proper supervision of credit institutions operating in the securities sector and for close co-operation between the ECB/SSM and ESMA.

[437] The European Parliament, eg, has been concerned to shore up the powers of the ESAs within the SSM and in relation to the ECB: 2014 European Parliament ESFS Resolution, n 329.

[438] Highlighted in Mayer Brown, n 427.

the spillover effect of focusing attention on the merits of ESMA's institutional technology and its potential as a counterweight to the ECB.

ESMA's role in risk identification may also be strengthened, if its NCAs become concerned to develop a counterweight to the ECB. While ESMA is developing risk identification mechanisms (including the 'Risk Dashboard' and the regular Trends, Risks, and Vulnerabilities Report), the IMF has called for ESMA's role in risk identification to be strengthened.[439] The evidence suggests that ESMA has found it a challenge to extend its operations in risk identification, given blockages to data collection; there is some evidence, for example, that NCAs are reluctant to provide ESMA with data relating to the stress testing of trading venues.[440] The need to build a robust risk assessment capacity which can be compared to that of the ECB may serve as an incentive to overcome NCA resistance to sharing sensitive data.

The complex dynamics relating to the uneasy relationship between EBA and the ECB, and to the need to protect the single market perspective in banking supervision given the fragmentation risks posed by the SSM/euro area and single market mismatch, may also strengthen ESMA. EBA's remit extends to the single banking market as a whole and to support of the banking single rulebook and of supervisory convergence across the single market. The dominance of the ECB as the supervisor of euro-area banks[441] poses a significant threat to the position of EBA,[442] however, and generates the risk that the single market interest in banking regulation and supervision is undermined.[443] One of the responses to the potential euro-area/single market conflict has been to protect and reinforce EBA's role,[444] primarily through governance reforms.[445] The single market interest is also being supported by the commitment to the EBA-developed 'Single Supervisory Handbook'[446] which 'sets out supervisory best practices for methodologies and processes'

---

[439] 2013 IMF ESMA Report, n 267, 20.

[440] 2013 IMF ESMA Report, n 267, 19.

[441] The 2013 ECB/SSM Regulation also provides for participation by non-euro-area Member States on a voluntary basis; formally, the distinction therefore is between 'participating' and 'non-participating' Member States.

[442] Well reflected in the November 2013 plea by EBA Chairman Enria that EBA's governance be changed to allow it to respond more nimbly, and warning that nationalist tendencies in the EBA Board of Supervisors could prejudice the sensitive 2013/2014 bank stress tests: Jenkins, P and Fleming, S, 'EU Bank Watchdog in Governance Plea', *Financial Times*, 18 November 2013, 1.

[443] EBA Chairman Enria has warned of the risk that 'repair of the Single Market will proceed with different speeds and will be driven by different priorities within and outside the SSM jurisdiction', that there is a 'possibility that a rift opens up in the Single Market' between SSM and non-SSM Member States, and that an 'attentive focus' to the single rulebook and common supervisory practices (including with respect to resolution) is required to 'contain the risk of a split two-tier system': n 442.

[444] eg President of the European Council, Towards a Genuine Economic and Monetary Union. Interim Report, 12 October 2012, 2.

[445] The 2013 EBA/SSM Regulation governs the modalities of SSM participating NCAs/non-participating NCAs voting within EBA, and applies new voting procedures designed to protect non-participating NCAs from being outvoted by a participating NCA majority. The procedures are based on a double-majority voting system (separate majorities within the participating and non-participating blocs), special governance arrangements for highly sensitive EBA decisions (breach of EU law and binding mediation actions), and an obligation on the Board of Supervisors to strive for consensus.

[446] At an early stage of the SSM negotiations, EBA Chairman Enria called for EBA, within the SSM, to develop a 'Single Supervisory Handbook', which would address methodologies for identifying and measuring banks' risks and criteria for defining corrective action, provide a framework within which supervisors would exercise judgment, and ensure consistency of outcomes, checked through effective peer review: Chairman

(2010 EBA Regulation Article 8).[447] Institutional and political dynamics aside, the logic of a Single Supervisory Handbook for the EU single market in banking is compelling, given the need to ensure strong and consistent supervision and to avoid competitive distortions, particularly given the dense rulebook which applies under the 2013 CRD IV/CRR. But while the operating environment within which EBA will develop this Supervisory Handbook is distinct, ESMA can be expected to follow suit—if only to shore up its institutional position, and given likely political and institutional support for strong single market actors in the ESFS, as became clear over the ESFS Review (section 5.10).

More radical change seems, for the moment, unlikely. The 2013 ESFS Review has, for example, led to some discussion of whether EU financial system governance should evolve towards a 'twin peaks' model, with the ECB/SSM (prudential) and ESMA (conduct) providing the basic building blocks of a more institutionally-sophisticated twin peaks structure.[448] As discussed in Chapter IX section 10, the retail market interest is at risk of being overlooked as the ESFS adjusts to the ECB/SSM. The major battle for territory between NCAs, ESMA, and the ECB is likely to concern risk-related issues and the interface between market conduct supervision and prudential supervision—the retail interest may become sidelined and institutional reform might be helpful accordingly. But while some refinements to support the retail interest (for example, a strengthening of the ESA Joint Committee) are possible and desirable, more radical institutional change, such as a twin peaks institutional model, is unlikely given current political, institutional, and constitutional realities.

Enria, Initial Statement, ECON Committee Public Hearing on Banking Supervision and Resolution, Next Steps, 10 October 2012. EBA also underlined that it would take a 'proactive attitude' as the 'guardian of the single rule book', and highlighted the importance of a 'Single Supervisory Handbook': n 157, para 4.2.

[447] As revised by the 2013 EBA/SSM Regulation.

[448] The Commission's ESFS Review Consultation sought views on whether the current sectoral organization of the ESAs should be re-cast.

INDEX